Dictionary of Sects, Heresies, Ecclesiastical Parties, and Schools of Religious Thought

DICTIONARY

OF

SECTS, HERESIES, ECCLESIASTICAL PARTIES,

AND SCHOOLS OF RELIGIOUS THOUGHT

RIVINGTONS

London — *Waterloo Place*

Oxford — *High Street*

Cambridge — *Trinity Street*

DICTIONARY

OF

SECTS, HERESIES, ECCLESIASTICAL PARTI

AND SCHOOLS OF RELIGIOUS THOUGHT

EDITED BY THE REV

JOHN HENRY BLUNT, M A, F.S A

EDITOR OF THE "DICTIONARY OF DOCTRINAL AND HISTORICAL THEOLOGY," AND THE "ANNOTATED BOOK OF COMMON PRAYER," ETC ETC.

"*Let both grow together until the Harvest*

[MATTH xiii 30]

"*I is eorum fides nostra est*"

[HILAR *de Trinit* i 26]

RIVINGTONS

London, Oxford, and Cambridge

1874

A CLASSIFIED TABLE OF THE PRINCIPAL CONTENTS

CONTINENTAL SECTS

OF REFORMATION AND LATER DATE

ENGLISH SECTS

[Long Extinct]

[Chief existing Sects]

[See also p viii]

[All the English sects named below are very insignificant in numbers, and some of them are nearly extinct]

SCOTTISH SECTS

[See also p 609]

AMERICAN SECTS

[Most of the Sects which are to be found in Europe are also to be found in America The following list contains some among those which are of native growth]

RUSSIAN SECTS

[Rascholniks, or Kerjaki]

CHURCH PARTIES

ARE ILLUSTRATED BY THE FOLLOWING ARTICLES

SCHOOLS OF THOUGHT

ARE ILLUSTRATED BY THE FOLLOWING ARTICLES

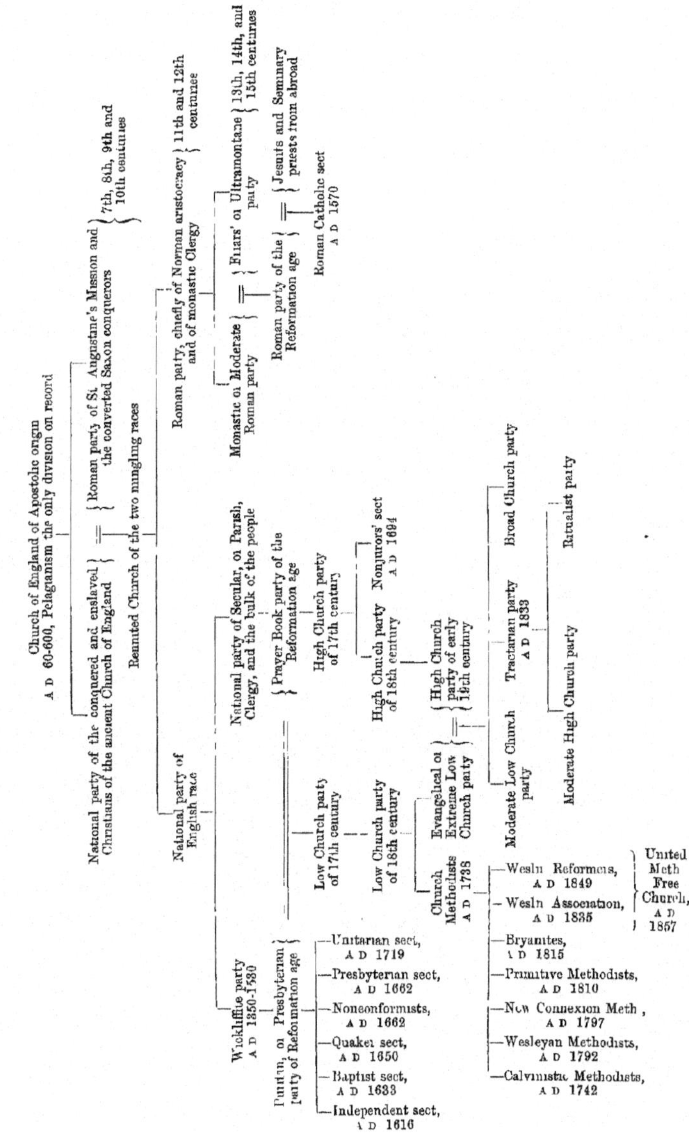
GENEALOGY OF ENGLISH CHURCH PARTIES, AND OF THE CHIEF ENGLISH SECTS
Church of England of Apostolic origin A D 60-600, Pelagianism the only division on record
National party of the conquered and enslaved Christians of the ancient Church of England
Roman party of St Augustine's Mission and the converted Saxon conquerors
7th, 8th, 9th and 10th centuries
Reunited Church of the two mingling races
National party of English race
Roman party, chiefly of Norman aristocracy and of monastic Clergy
11th and 12th centuries
Wickliffite party A D 1350-1530
National party of Secular, or Parish, Clergy, and the bulk of the people
Monastic or Moderate Roman party
Friars' or Ultramontane party
13th, 14th, and 15th centuries
Puritan, or Presbyterian party of Reformation age
Prayer Book party of the Reformation age
Roman party of the Reformation age
Jesuits and Seminary priests from abroad
Roman Catholic sect A D 1570
Unitarian sect, A D 1719
Presbyterian sect, A D 1662
Nonconformists, A D 1662
Quaker sect, A D 1650
Baptist sect, A D 1633
Independent sect, A D 1616
Low Church party of 17th century
High Church party of 17th century
Low Church party of 18th century
High Church party of 18th century
Nonjurors' sect A D 1694
Church Methodists A D 1738
Evangelical or Extreme Low Church party
High Church party of early 19th century
Wesleyan Reformers, A D 1849
Wesleyan Association, A D 1835
United Meth Free Church, A D 1857
Bryanites, A D 1815
Primitive Methodists, A D 1810
New Connexion Meth, A D 1797
Wesleyan Methodists, A D 1792
Calvinistic Methodists, A D 1742
Moderate Low Church party
Tractarian party A D 1833
Broad Church party
Moderate High Church party
Ritualist party

A

ABECEDARIANS A name given to the ZWICKAU PROPHETS [A D 1520], a section of the German Anabaptists, who claimed to have direct inspiration from God, and maintained that this inspiration was obstructed by human learning They carried this theory to such a length as to declare that it was desirable never even to learn A B C, since all human learning is founded on the alphabet, and the knowledge of it thus opens the door to that which is an obstacle to Divine illumination Nicholas Stork, a weaver of Zwickau, was the first to proclaim this principle, but it was afterwards supported by Carlstadt, once an ally of Luther, who, yielding to Stork's invectives against learning, shut up his books, resigned his degree of Doctor of Divinity, forsook all study of Holy Scripture, and looked for Divine truth at the mouths of those who, by all ordinary men, were accounted the most ignorant of mankind The Abecedarian theory, in a more moderate form, has had much influence on some modern sects, especially the more ignorant sects of Methodists.

ABELARD [SCHOOLMEN NOMINALISTS]

ABELIANS [ABELONITES]

ABELITES [ABELONITES]

ABELOITES [ABELONITES]

ABELONITES An obscure African sect, deriving its name from Abel, the son of Adam. The exact date of its origin is unknown, but it became extinct during the reign of Theodosius the Younger [A.D 408-450], for at the time when St. Augustine composed his book on Heresies [cap. 87], he alludes to it as having lingered on as late as his time in a village near Hippo, of which he was bishop [A D 395-430] The members of this sect adopted the eccentric practice of marrying wives without procreating children, in supposed imitation of Abel, who was stated to have had a wife, but not to have known her, and in lieu of the consummation of marriage, and at the same time to enable them to perpetuate their sect, the husband and wife adopted two children of different sexes, who in their turn were to abstain from all intercourse, and on the death of their foster-parents to resort to the same plan of adoption It is said that young persons were easily procured for that purpose from the superfluous families of the poor population in the neighbourhood The conduct of the Abelonites was a mistaken attempt to carry out literally such texts as, "It remaineth that both they that have wives be as though they had none" [1 Cor vii 29] But there does not seem any historical evidence for connecting them with the Gnostics generally, as Mosheim does, or with the Manichæans in particular, as does Herzog. [Aug *de Hæres* cap 87, *Prædestinati liber*, cap 87. Walch, *Hist Ketzereien*, i 607]

ABENONITÆ [ABELONITES]

ABLAVIUS The historian Nicephorus mentions a heretic of this name as having been Novatian, bishop of Nicæa about A D 430 He had been a pupil of the sophist Troilus, and became celebrated as one of the foremost orators of his day. He seems to have taught the Novatian heresy in its most extreme form, maintaining that Baptism is the only means by which remission of sins can be obtained, and that, consequently, penitence and mortification of the flesh are utterly useless [Niceph *Hist. Eccl* xiv 15. Socrat. *Hist. Eccl* vii 12]

ABRAHAMITES A branch of the PAULICIANS, so called from their founder Abraham, or Ibrahim, a native of Antioch, who lived in the end of the eighth and the beginning of the ninth century They do not appear to have held any distinctive tenets, but were simply Antiochean Paulicians and the heresy was soon suppressed in that city by the vigorous opposition of the patriarch Cyriacus

ABRAHAMITES A Bohemian sect of no importance, existing at the end of the last century in the town of Pardubitz and its neighbourhood They professed to follow the religion of Abraham before he was circumcised, rejected all distinctively Christian doctrine, and only acknowledged the Decalogue and the Lord's Prayer as Holy Scriptures

ABSTINENTES A sect which arose in Gaul and Spain, at the close of the third century, during the reigns of Diocletian and Maximian, and in the pontificate of Marcellinus. Like the Eastern ENCRATITES, they held Gnostic views on the subject of marriage, which they denounced not as absolutely wrong, but as a thing to be avoided by those who sought sanctity This was their deduction from such texts in Holy Scripture as "There be eunuchs which have made themselves eunuchs for the kingdom of Heaven's sake. He that is able to receive it, let

A

him receive it" [Matt xix 12], and "Without holiness no man shall see the Lord" [Heb xii 14], and their argument ran thus Christ must have preached some new virtue, or have performed some praiseworthy action not commanded in the Old Testament Did He come to teach the fear of God? This is contained in the Law Was it to condemn envy, covetousness, and the like? This was done in the Old Testament He could not, therefore, have any other view but to preach continence to the world, practising Himself that chastity without which everlasting life could not be attained [Epiphan *adv Hæres* lib ii tom 2, p 710] They also condemned the use of meat, as having been created by the devil and not by God [Philaster, cap 84] to which later writers add that, while admitting the Godhead of the Father and the Son, they held the Holy Ghost to be merely a created Being Led perhaps by the similarity of some of their views, Philaster connects the Abstinentes with the Gnostics and Manichæans, and Baronius [in *Annal ad ann* 288] identifies them with the HIERACITES

ACACIANS Three broad lines can be drawn among the various subdivisions into which Arianism branched about the middle of the fourth century [1] Semi-Arians, of whom Basil of Ancyra and George of Laodicæa were the leaders [2] The Anomœans (ἀνόμοιοι), or Ultra-Arians, followers of Aetius and his pupil Eunomius, Bishop of Cyzicum [3] Between these two extremes rose the Acacians, a third party, who would neither allow any approximation to the orthodox doctrine of the Homoousion, nor yet admit that the Second Person in the Trinity was a mere creature, on the level of all other created beings They derived their name from Acacius, who succeeded Eusebius as Bishop of Cæsarea in Palestine [A D 338], a person possessed of many of the qualifications necessary for the leadership of a party He was strong and active, a fluent speaker, and evinced his regard for learning by taking great pains to increase his predecessor's library [Tillemont, *Mém* vol xv 458, edit Brux 1707] At the same time he was extremely unscrupulous and fickle · at first a furious Arian under Constantius, who sheltered him from the decree of deposition passed by a majority of the Semi-Arian Council held at Sardica [A D 347], he became a Catholic under Jovian, and veered round to Arianism once more under Valens. He was prominently concerned in the banishment of Liberius and the substitution of the antipope Felix [A D 355-358], after whose expulsion a sentence of deposition was passed against him at Seleucia [A.D 359], and repeated at the Council of Lampsacus [A D 365], which he only survived for about a twelvemonth

The Acacians as a body partook of the chameleon character of their teacher, and the shifts were various by which they attempted to sustain their indeterminate position between the Semi- and the Ultra-Arians Their end would be obtained at one time by an intellectual subterfuge, at another time by the abolition of the terms of technical theology

In A D 363, on the ascent of the orthodox Jovian to the throne, they attended a synod held at Antioch under Meletius, and agreed to sign the Nicene Creed, with a mental reservation to the effect that the expression "consubstantial" or "co-essential" meant no more than begotten of the Father's essence, and therefore like Him in essence Four years previously, at Seleucia in Isauria [A.D 359], they had attempted to banish the term οὐσία altogether, with its compounds ὁμοούσιον and ὁμοιούσιον, and asked to be allowed to adopt a formula of belief in God's only Son, without any further qualification as to His nature, rejecting "consubstantial" as not found in Holy Scripture, and the phrase ἀνόμοιον τῷ Πατρί, as equally defenceless On being further pressed, they allowed the Son to be like the Father, but seemed to prefer the absence of closer definition But if the Son was like the Father, in what, asked the orthodox party, did the resemblance consist? Was it merely a resemblance in respect of will? or was it a resemblance of a still more unreal character, like that of a statue to the original, which involves no inherent element of identity? The answer of the Acacians to these questions must be discovered from the creed which was promulgated on that occasion, the precise terms of which have been preserved

"We confess and believe in one God the Father Almighty, Maker of Heaven and earth, and of things visible and invisible.

"We believe also in our Lord Jesus Christ, the Son of God, begotten of Him without any passion (ἀπαθῶς), before all ages, the God Word, God of God, Only-begotten, Light, Life, Truth, Wisdom, Virtue, by Whom all things were made which are in Heaven and earth, whether visible or invisible. We believe Him to have assumed flesh of the Blessed Virgin at the end of the world to put away sin, and that He was made man, that He suffered also for our sins, rose again, and having ascended into Heaven, is seated at the right hand of the Father, and shall come again with glory to judge the quick and dead

"We believe also in one Holy Spirit, Whom our Saviour and Lord Jesus Christ called the Paraclete, and promised that He would send the same on His Apostles after His departure, Whom He both truly sent, and by Him doth sanctify the faithful in the Church, who are baptized in the Name of the Father, and of the Son, and of the Holy Spirit. But whosoever preach anything beyond what is contained in this Creed the Catholic Church considers them as aliens" [Epiphan *Hæres* lxxiii.]

The following forty-three bishops subscribed to the above Creed .—Acacius, Bishop of Cæsarea, Basil of Ancyra, Mark of Arethusa, George of Alexandria, Pancratius, Hypatian, Uranius of Tyre, Eutychius of Eleutheropolis, Zoilus of Larissa in Syria, Seras of Parætonium in Libya, Paul of Emessa, Eustathius of Epiphania, Irenæus of Tripolis in Phœnicia, Eusebius of Seleucia in Syria, Eutychian of Patara in Lycia, Eustathius of Pinara and Didyma, Basil of Caurica in Lydia, Peter of Hippus in Palestine, Stephen of Ptolemais in Libya, Eudoxius, Apollonius of Oxyrinchus, Theoctistus of Ostracine, Leontius of Lydia, Theodosius of Philadelphia, Phœbus of Polychalanda in Lydia, Magnus of Themisi in Phrygia, Evagrius of Mytilene, Cyrion of Doliche, Augustus of Euphratesia, Pollux of the second province of Libya, Pancratius of Pelusium, Philicadus of Augustada in Phrygia, Serapion of Antipyrgum in Libya, Eusebius of Sebaste in Palestine, Heliodorus of Sezusa in Pentapolis, Ptolemy of Thmuis Augustonicæ, Angarus of Cyrus Euphrasia, Exeresius of Gerasa, Arabion of Adrai, Charisius of Azotus, Elissæus of Diocletianopolis, Germanus of Petræ, and Barochius of Arabia [Mosheim, *Eccles Hist* i 306 Tillemont, *Mémoires*, tom vi. 304, Paris edit. Nicephorus, *Eccles Hist* lib. ix Epiphanius, *Hæres* lxxiii]

ACCAOPHORI A sect of heretics which used water instead of wine for the Holy Eucharist has this name given to it by Timotheus Presbyter, and he traces their origin to the followers of Tatian, or the Encratites But he adds that they were also called Hydroparastatæ, and hence "Accaophori" is supposed to be merely a misreading for Saccaophori [Timoth Presb *in ed Combefisian Auct nov bibl Patr Græco-Latin* ii. 451 Coteler *Mon eccl Græc* i 776 Ittig, *De Heresiarch* II xii 13]

ACEPHALI [ἀ—κεφαλή] I *The Monophysite Acephali* In the year A D 482, while the Monophysite and Monothelite controversies were raging, the Emperor Zeno issued his famous letter of attempted reconciliation entitled the Henoticon Peter Mongus, who had been the bitter opponent of, and had been excommunicated by Proterius, a former bishop of Alexandria [A D 457], was informed that he might be elevated to that see, then vacant by the expulsion of John Talaia, on the two conditions of admitting the Proterians to communion and subscribing the Henoticon On Peter's assent to these conditions, most of the Catholics submitted to his jurisdiction, but the Ultra-Eutychians still clinging to their denial of the two natures in Christ, and still bitterly hostile to the Council of Chalcedon, withdrew themselves, and formed a sect which, either from having no one conspicuous leader, or from the absence of bishops to head the movement, was called the sect of the Acephali

These Acephali broke up into the three sects of Anthropomorphites, Barsanuphists, and Esaianists, but all remained separate from the body of the Monophysites for about three hundred years, though still retaining the distinctive name of the original sect. The Acephali were, however, gradually absorbed by the Jacobites (as the Monophysites were called in later times), and ceased to exist as a separate sect at the beginning of the ninth century

II *The Nestorian Acephali.* The title of Acephali was also applied to those who would not adhere to John, Patriarch of Antioch, and Cyril, Patriarch of Alexandria, in the condemnation of Nestorius at the General Council of Ephesus [A.D 431]

III. *The followers of Severus the Monophysite*, Bishop of Antioch, who added to the Trisagion the words "Who was crucified for us," and who was deprived of his see and retired to Alexandria [A D 518]

IV. All priests refusing allegiance to their diocesans, or suffragan bishops rebelling against their metropolitans.

[For further information about the Alexandrian Acephali, consult Pseudo-Jerome, *de Hæres* 43, Isidore, 67, Honorius, 82, Leontius, *Lib. de Sectis*, art. v, Gibbon's *Rom Empire*, vi 32 There is also a lengthy refutation of their doctrines by Rusticus Diaconus, *contra Acephalos præfatio, incerto interprete*]

ACŒMITÆ [ἀ—κοιμάομαι] The name of "the Sleepless," or "Watchers," was given to an Eastern monastic order founded by Alexander, himself a Syrian monk, under the auspices of Gennadius, Patriarch of Constantinople [A D 428-430] Baronius puts the date rather later, and ascribes their foundation to a person named Marcellus in the middle of the fifth century [Bar *Ann* 459, *ex actis Marcelli apud Surium*], but the earlier date is more generally received The Acœmitæ did not, as their name would imply, literally abstain from all sleep, but divided themselves into three "watches," each carrying on their devotions for eight hours, so that an uninterrupted round of worship rose perpetually from their monastery. They became famous both for their special sanctity and, notwithstanding that a suspicion of heresy attached to their founder Alexander, for their rigid orthodoxy In A D 484, when Acacius, Patriarch of Constantinople, was condemned by Felix in synod for holding communion with Peter Mongus, Bishop of Alexandria, the Acœmitæ sided with the Pope against their own bishop. This order afterwards obtained the name of Studites, from Studius, a rich Roman noble of consular dignity, who went to Constantinople during the episcopate of Gennadius, and erected a cloister especially for them [Niceph *Hist Eccl* xv 23] In later days the Acœmitæ were believed to have inclined to Nestorianism

ACTISTETES A section of the Julianists, who took their name from the Greek word by which a being is defined as uncreated [ἄκτιστος], in opposition to the Ctistolatræ. The Actistetes maintained that after the Incarnation Christ ought not to be spoken of as a created Being, even in respect of His human nature, thereby contradicting the words of the Nicene Creed, "καὶ ἐνανθρωπήσαντα," "et Homo factus est," "and was made Man." This dogma was, in reality, a form of the elder heresy of the Docetæ, for since a Being wholly uncreated must be wholly God, hence the reality of our Lord's human nature was a doctrine as incompatible with the belief of one sect as it was with that of the other. [Dorner's *Person of Christ*, II. i. 131, Clark's transl]

ACUANITES. The Manichees were so called in the time of Epiphanius, from their leader in it is uncertain whether this expression means that no two of them ever ate in common, or whether they only declined to break bread with those who did not belong to their own sect St Augustine informs us, that while holding the divinity of the First and Second Persons of the Trinity, they rejected that of the Holy Spirit [Aug *de Hæres* 71], on which, and other points, they engaged in a controversy with the bishops of Ephesus

ADELPHIANS One of the numerous names given to the different branches of the MESSALIANS or EUCHITES, which sprang up in the East during the fourth century, and all of which, in various ways, laid great stress on the necessity of incessant prayer to banish evil, and unite the soul to God. The Adelphians are so-called from their leader, Adelphius, a Galatian by birth, who is mentioned as being excluded from a synod held at Syda [c A D 368] against the Messalians They were eventually banished from Syria into Pamphylia, where they succeeded in making a limited number of converts They [1] rejected the Eucharist and other ordinances, and [2] objecting to manual labour, indulged in long sleeps and visions, whence they shared with the Euchites the title of "Enthusiastæ," [3] like the Lampetians, Marcianists, Choreutæ, and other branches of the Euchites, they treated Sunday as a fast-day, a practice condemned by many writers, and finally forbidden by the fifty-fifth canon of the council of Trullo [A.D 692]. In a conference which took place between Flavianus, Bishop of Antioch, and Adelphius [A D. 381], the latter allowed that he rejected baptism, and asserted that grace could only be obtained, and that demons could only be expelled, by incessant prayer The scriptural authority for this was the text, "Men ought always to pray and not to faint" [Luke xviii. 1] But according to the Adelphian theory, the efficacy of prayer depended solely on its length or intensity, not on the Being to Whom it was addressed, and the devotions of the Jew, the heretic, the infidel, and the sinner, were of equal avail. It was supposed that each man at his birth inherited, along with the human nature derived from Adam, the servitude of evil demons, and that after they had been driven out by incessant prayer, the Holy Spirit would come, signifying its presence in a visible and sensible fashion, freeing the body from all fear of illness, and the mind from all inclination to sin, so that there was no longer any need of fasting to keep the body in subjection, or of any doctrine to strengthen, or, as the Adelphians would say, to fetter the soul A man once fully possessed by this Divine influence, not only imagined himself free from all ill, but could foresee future events, and obtain a clear vision of the Trinity.

ADESSENARIANS A controversial designation (adopted by Prateolus, in his *Elenchus Hæreticorum*) for the Lutherans of the sixteenth century, who maintained that Christ is really and truly present (adesse) in the Holy Eucharist, but denied that His presence involved the transubstantiation of the elements in the sense of Roman theologians The term was intended to include all who hold the Real Presence of Christ's Body and Blood, "in," "with," or "under the form of," the bread and the wine, but to exclude all who hold that the presence of Christ in the Eucharist is merely His figurative presence "in the heart" (or devotional thoughts) of the faithful receiver [IMPANATORS] But it is a mistake to suppose that there was ever an organized sect bearing the name of Adessenarians

ADIAPHORISTS A name given to Melanchthon and his party, on account of their maintaining that many customs and doctrines for and against which the stricter Lutherans contended were not worth contending about, being things that were in themselves indifferent (ἀδιάφορα)

The "Adiaphoristic controversy" originated in the year 1548, when Maurice, the Elector of Saxony, began his rule by calling an assembly of Lutheran divines together at Leipsic, to consider whether or not they should adopt the INTERIM which the Emperor Charles V had imposed upon his subjects Luther had now been dead for nearly two years, and Melanchthon had become the leading theologian of the Lutheran party in Germany His great desire was for peace and the cessation of controversy, and thus, on the one hand, he wished to hold out a hand to the Calvinists by toning down Luther's dogmatism as regarded the doctrine of the Eucharist, while, on the other, he desired to draw nearer to the Church by treating as indifferent some doctrinal points which Luther had considered essential, and by a return to its ancient customs At the Leipsic conference, it was decided that "in rebus medii generis, seu Adiaphoris" the Emperor might be obeyed and his "Interim" accepted and the decision at which Melanchthon and his friends arrived is thus called "The Leipsic Interim" Among the Adiaphora they included the Eucharistic vestments, the elevation of the host and its accompanying ceremonies, the use of choral services and of intonation by the officiating clergyman, the use of Latin in Divine service, the observance of Saints' days, the use of Extreme Unction, the *Primacy* (as distinguished from the *Supremacy*) of the Pope, and lastly the doctrine of salvation by faith alone without good works. The Leipsic Interim of Melanchthon was thus only a modified form of that proposed by the Emperor at Augsburg, and the platform which it offered for reunion with the Church was hateful to the stricter Lutherans

The "Anti-Adiaphorists" were led by Flacius Illyricus, a man who inherited no small portion of Luther's controversial fire and energy, and they thus acquired the name of "Flacians," as the Adiaphorists did that of "Philippists" from Melanchthon Endless discussions were raised [1] as to the essential or non-essential character of the customs and doctrines above enumerated, and [2] as to the lawfulness of giving up or of adopting even any that were allowed to be non-essential for the sake of concession to the enemies of "the truth," that is of Lutheranism These controversies lasted long after the Interim itself had fallen to the ground, to give rise to others not less bitter. [AMSDORFIANS SYNERGISTS]

ADIMANTHUS is referred to by Nicephorus, the ecclesiastical historian, as one of the three principal followers of Manes He lived about A D 270, and wrote a book to prove that the doctrines taught in the Gospels and Epistles were opposed to those of the ancient law and of the prophets, which was confuted by St. Augustine in his treatise *Contra Adimantum, Manichæi discipulum.* [Aug *Opp* ix 153, ed Bened]

ADMONITIONISTS. A party of the Puritans was so called on account of an "Admonition to the Parliament," in twenty-three chapters, which was printed in the year 1572 This "Admonition" called for a reconstruction of the Church of England on the most extreme Puritan platform, and is characterized even by so moderate a writer as Soames as a "mass of encroaching intolerance, captiousness, inaccuracy, envy, and scurrility" It was composed principally by two London clergymen named Field and Wilcox, who were imprisoned for it as a libel Whitgift wrote a reply to it, which was answered by Cartwright The Admonitionists established a secret conventicle at Wandsworth, which was the first Presbyterian community set up in England [Neale's *Hist Puritans*, i 285, ed 1732 Soames' *Elizabethan Hist* 163 Hooker's *Eccl Pol* III vii 4 Brook's *Memoir of Cartwright*, ch iii Strype's *Life of Whitgift*]

ADOPTIONISTS This is the name of a sect which arose in Western Christendom towards the close of the eighth century, their distinctive theological tenet being that Jesus Christ, as far as His Manhood is concerned, was the Son of God the Father by adoption Their doctrine has been very generally supposed to have been a revival in the West of the ancient error of the Bonosians, condemned at the Council of Capua [A D 389], or of Nestorianism condemned at the third Œcumenical Council of Ephesus [A D 431] Such was the opinion of Pope Adrian, who described Elipandus as the successor of Nestorius in his circular letter to the orthodox bishops of Spain [A D 785], and the following passages from the Fathers have been quoted as containing an anticipatory condemnation of Adoptionism St Cyril of Jerusalem [A D 348-386] said that "Christ is the Son of God by nature, begotten of the Father, and not by adoption" [*Catech lect* xi] St Ambrose [A.D 374-396], that "we do not speak of an adopted son as a son by nature, but we do say that a son by nature is a true son" [*de Incarnat* viii] St. Augustine [A D. 395-430], that "we to whom God has given power to become His sons are not begotten of His nature and substance, as 'His Only-Begotten,' but are adopted by His love; the Apostle often using the word for no other purpose than to distinguish the Only-Begotten from the sons by adoption" [Aug *de Consens Evang* ii 3] St Hilary of Arles [A D 429-449], that "the Son of God is not a false God, or God by adoption, or God by metaphor (nec adoptivus nec connuncupatus), but true God" [Hilar *de Trin* v 5], and the eleventh Council of Toledo [A D 675] clearly laid down the same doctrine "This Son of God is His Son by nature, not by adoption" It is plain from these quotations that the idea of adoption underlay many errors on the subject of Christ's Person, from the earlier times up to the seventh century, and yet it has been the tendency of modern criticism to disconnect Adoptionism from them The reason for this will be seen if we first consider in what sense the earlier heretics held adoption, and then contrast their teaching with the fully systematized dogma of the Adoptionists themselves The Gnostics were in a certain sense Adoptionists They universally held the Manhood of Christ to have been of transient and unessential significance, but invented different theories about the reason why the Æon Christ deigned to adopt it as His habitation. The Cerinthians imagined that, by reason of His wisdom, virtue and purity, the Man Jesus became worthy of such adoption and of the title Son of God The Basilidians taught that, though not free from our common sinful nature, Jesus was arbitrarily selected by the eternal and divine decree to receive Christ, and that Christ coming into Him at the time of His baptism, purified Him and rendered Him a perfect organ for the purposes of the Divine revelation The Valentinians went further, and argued that the pre-eminent degree of wisdom and virtue possessed by the Man Jesus presupposed a previous and God-bestowed endowment, and that therefore, by a supernatural birth, He was fitted for adoption as the receptacle of the Divine element in Christ Bonosus of Sardica [A D 390] regarded Christ as a mere adopted man Migetius, reviving Sabellianism in Spain in the eighth century, taught that the Divine Wisdom or Logos adopted the Person of Jesus for an incarnate manifestation, just as God the Father had assumed the form of David, and the Holy Ghost that of St. Paul Nestorius denied the identity or unity of the Person of Christ, in Whom the two natures, the Divine and human, were united He denied the truth that the Eternal Son of God was conceived and born Mary was the mother of Christ, not the mother of God (Χριστοτόκος not Θεοτόκος), the two natures were to be distinctly separated, and he admitted only a junction by indwelling of the Deity, not a perfect union in one Person It seemed to him that the real duality of the wills and natures could only be established at the price of a duality of personalities, a human subject being required for the human, as a Divine subject was for the Divine nature He forgot that Divine mysteries are not to be explained or rejected on the ordinary principles of human reasoning And whether or not the premisses of two essentially different natures and wills render the conclusion of the existence of two persons in one Christ logically unavoidable, at least such a conclusion was inconsistent with Holy Scripture, and would be necessarily rejected by the orthodox Church, whether presented to mankind in the form of Nestorianism in the fifth, or of Adoptionism in the eighth century. We are now brought to

Adoptionists

the difficult question as to whether there was any connection doctrinally or historically between the latter and any of the former, and, if so, in what that relationship consists.

Four views of the relation of Adoptionism to preceding heresy have been held by various theologians [a] By contemporaries Adoptionism was regarded as identical with, and therefore merely a revival of, Nestorianism [b] Others have regarded it as an unvanquished remainder, or as a lineal descendant, slightly altered and disfigured, of the ancient Eastern heresies [c] More modern writers (*e.g.*, Walchius in the last century) would regard it as differing rather verbally than essentially from the Catholic doctrine, or [d] as the first proof of awakening intellectual energy in a barbarian nation, by which the logical inconsistency of the orthodox teaching on the subject of the two natures in Christ was discovered, and by which an attempt was made to avoid it None of these aspects are entirely just. The intellectual activity of Spain during preceding centuries, especially on theological questions, had been far too great to allow us to regard Adoptionism as the undisciplined exercise of a newly awakened interest in questions of Christian controversy The labours of Adrian I., Charlemagne, Alcuin, and others, to suppress it, equally preclude us from believing that it was merely a superficial deviation from the truth, and that the whole contest which raged in Christian Europe at the close of the eighth and beginning of the ninth centuries, might have been solved by explanation of the grammatical terms employed Again, an examination of the doctrines of Elipandus and Felix will present to us points which intrinsically disconnect them from those of Nestorius, and a glance at the preceding ecclesiastical contentions in Spain will shew us the gulf that historically separates the two, while they also negatively prepare the way for the distinctive features of Adoptionism

In the first place, the contact of the Spanish Church with the Arianism of the Goths and the amalgamation which took place between the Spanish population and the Germanic tribes would naturally pave the way for disputes about the Manhood and Divinity of Christ Secondly, the protracted contest with Priscillianism, with Sabellianism, with the Monophysites (condemned at the eleventh and fourteenth councils of Toledo), and with the Monothelites (condemned at the sixth General Council at Constantinople), would all equally tend to give prominence to the distinction of the two natures in the one Person of Christ. One of the primary objects of the Adoptionists was, legitimately enough, to insist on the real Humanity of our Lord, but their anxiety on this point led them to make use of arguments which implied a human person equally with a human nature, and so assimilated their doctrine to Nestorianism Although, therefore, there was a sufficient superficial resemblance between these two to account for the Pope branding the Spanish bishops with the imputation of the older heresy, (especially if we make allowance for the difficulty of obtaining correct information, and for the acrimony which too often accompanies polemical theology,) we must accurately distinguish them, and on the following points —

[a] The Adoptionists had no objection to the term Θεοτόκος as applied to the Blessed Virgin, which epithet had been expressly rejected by the Nestorians

[b] While the Nestorians laid special stress on there being two Persons in Christ, the former protested against the doctrine of the duality of Persons, as was even allowed by their opponents [Paulinus, i 48], and in their memorial to Charlemagne they acknowledged the unity of Persons in plain terms but they seem to have meant by this the juxtaposition of two distinct personal Beings, in such a way that the Son of God should be recognised as the vehicle of all predicates, but not in so close a manner as to amount to the absorption or almost transubstantiation of the human personality into the Divine Person, as was taught by the orthodox party [1]

[c] They taught that Christ assumed humanity, while the Nestorians spoke of Christ owing His exaltation to His virtue

The real error of the Adoptionists lay in dwelling too strongly on certain aspects of the truth They appealed to the repeated decisions of the Church against Monophysitism and Monothelitism, and maintained that the principle of duality, which had already been recognised in the assertion of two natures and two wills in Christ, ought to be carried into the sphere of the personality But here the Church stopped she had hitherto been gradually unfolding the dualistic view, but the German councils unanimously refused to allow the principle to be pushed into a region where it would apparently lead them back to the long vanquished error of Nestorius. If the Adoptionists were right, in what sense was Jesus the Son of God? Felix answered that the Father, Who was a Spirit, could not produce the Humanity of Christ from Himself [lib iii cap 7], that Christ could not be the natural Son of God in the same sense in which He was the natural Son of David [lib i. 12], and that to press the unity of Persons (which he still claimed to believe in), so far as to call Him, both in His divine and human nature, strictly Son of God, was to confound the Creator and the creature, the Word and the flesh, Him Who assumed and that which is assumed, and that therefore Christ in His human nature is only "Nuncupative Deus" [lib iii 17] In support of this argument, he appealed to such passages as "the Head of Christ is God" [1 Cor xi 3], to Christ's own admission that He Himself did not know the hour of judgment [Mark xiii 32], that none was good save God only [Mark x 18].

[1] The Council of Frankfort [iii 2] appealed to the following words of Paschasius —"In Christo gemina substantia sed non gemina persona est quia persona personam consumere potest, substantia vero substantiam non potest, siquidem persona res juris est, substantia res, naturæ" Alcuin wrote, "In adsumptione carnis a Deo persona perit hominis, non natura" [c Felic. ii 12].

How, he asked, if the man assumed by the Son of God was really the Son of God, could such expressions have any meaning at all? This question is met by the rejoinder that difficult passages of Scripture must not be thus isolated, but interpreted by reference to the general teaching of the Bible The texts alleged by Felix must receive an interpretation not inconsistent with other passages where Christ is plainly called the Son of God "For God so loved the world, that He gave His only-begotten Son" [John iii 16], "God sending His own Son in the likeness of sinful flesh, and for sin, condemned sin in the flesh" [Rom viii 3], "He that spared not His own Son, but delivered Him up for us all" [viii 32], "When the fulness of the time was come, God sent forth His Son, made of a woman, made under the law" [Gal. iv. 4], "God sent His only-begotten Son into the world, that we might live through Him" [1 John iv 9]

Those writers on Adoptionism who would reduce the point at issue to a mere question of words, have asked whether adoption and assumption may not mean the same thing, for it has always been considered orthodox to say that Christ assumed our human nature The answer to which is, that Felix spoke not of an assumed human nature, but of an assumed man, and secondly, that he spoke of two births in our Lord's life—the assumption of the man at the moment of conception by the Blessed Virgin Mary, the adoption of that man at the time of His baptism, thus distinguishing between the two "He Who is the second Adam received these two generations, for in so far as He is man, our Redeemer embraced and contains within Himself the first, which is according to the flesh, and the second, which is spiritual, and takes place by adoption, the first, which He took upon Himself, by being born of a virgin, the second, which he began at His baptism and continued by His resurrection from the dead"[1] The opponents of Adoptionism urged that this teaching involved two Persons in Christ, also, that if Christ, as to His humanity, was not the proper Son of God, His mediatorial position was endangered, and the distance between Him and Christians was increased To refuse therefore to attribute a separate personality to the Son of Man was no more than an act of justice to the Son of God, and no interference with the reality of the humanity To all of which Felix rejoined that the duality of Persons was no more or less involved in his teaching than it was, logically speaking, implied in the previous decisions in favour of the two natures and the two wills, and that to designate Christ, as to His humanity, the proper Son of God, was to destroy the condescension of the Incarnation, and to rob it of its chief attractiveness for Christians His view, however, involved two distinct lines, that of the Son of Man and Son of God, running in a harmonious parallel together, and either each possessing a separate personality (which the Adoptionists denied) or else reducing the personality to a meaningless and unsubstantial abstraction, a mere formal link between two essentially uncoalescing natures Such a unity of Person is very different from that taught in the older creeds, and defended on the analogy of the union of soul and body "For as the reasonable soul and flesh is one man, so God and man is one Christ" Alcuin works out this analogy with great force He asks, "If every man is the proper son of his father—if so, we are reminded that men are not sons of their fathers as to the soul, but only as to the flesh, and therefore, if it is not allowable to designate the entire Christ as the proper Son of God, by parity of reasoning, no man can be called the son of his father" Again, he asks, "Does a man adopt his own son, or a stranger?" The answer is obviously, "a stranger" At what time then was Christ in that position with reference to God? and when did God, out of affection or necessity, condescend to the act of adoption? The whole question, whether, notwithstanding the reality of His human nature, the Son of Man can be strictly called the proper Son of God, depends on the further question, whether that which properly pertains to a substance must always be of the same substance as that to which it pertains This Alcuin answers in the negative, maintaining that something which is of a different substance from another thing may possess as its property this other thing, in such a manner that, for the sake of this real and substantial relationship between the two, the latter may become a predicate of the former, and that therefore the Son of Man may be properly called the Son of God, and the Son of God identified as to Person with the Son of Man[2]

Having thus described the doctrines of the Adoptionists, and the principal arguments by which they were supported and refuted, we proceed to give some account of the history of the sect

History of the Adoptionists—The originators of the theory of adoption, and the leaders of the Adoptionist movement, were Elipandus, Archbishop of Toledo, and Felix, Bishop of Urgel, in Catalonia who both flourished towards the close of the eighth century In the year 783, the Archbishop wrote to Felix to ask his opinion about the Sonship of Christ, and the latter in his answer said, that as to His divinity, Christ was by nature and truly the Son of God, but that as man He was the Son of God in name and by adoption. Unfortunately neither letters are extant, so that we have no power to refute on intrinsic evidence the conjecture made by some historians, that their object was, by lowering the human character of Christ, to pave the way for a union between Christians and Mohammedans[3]

[1] "Qui est secundus Adam accepit has geminas generationes, primam videlicet quæ secundum carnem est, secundam vero spiritalem quæ per adoptionem fit, idem redemptor noster secundum hominem complexus in semel ipso continet primam videlicet quam suscepit ex virgine nascendo, secundam vero quam initiavit in lavacro a mortuis resurgendo" [Felix, lib ii 16]

[2] Alcuin, *Opp* i p 921

[3] Johannes Marianna, *Histor Hisp* lib vii cap 8, Baronius, *Annal. Eccles ann* DCCXLIV tom xiii. p 260

The new theory was vigorously propagated While Felix disseminated it in Septimania, Elipandus was advocating it in letters to his diocese, and tried to win over, among others, Adosinda, widow of Silo, king of Galitia, who, after her husband's death, had taken the veil She however remained firm in the Catholic faith, and induced the learned theologians of the day to remonstrate with him, among whom were Etherius, Bishop of Osma, and Beatus, Abbot of the monastery of Vallisoava, both Asturians, the latter of whom was charged by Elipandus with gross immorality The confutation of Adoptionism was continued by Paulinus of Aquileia, Benedictus of Anien, Agobard, Archbishop of Lyons, and Alcuin, friend and preceptor of Charlemagne, who both personally confuted Felix, and also composed seven books against him, four books against Elipandus, and various letters on the subject addressed to Charlemagne, Elipandus, the monks of Gothia (ad monachos Gothiæ), and the brothers of Lyons (ad fratres Lugdunenses) Pope Adrian I also [A D 785] wrote a letter to the orthodox bishops in Spain, warning them against the new doctrines, which the following passage proves him to have considered akin to Nestorianism —

"The melancholy news has reached us from your land, that certain bishops resident there, namely, Elipandus and Ascarius, with other confederates, do not hesitate to call the Son of God an adopted Son, a blasphemy which no previous heretics have dared to enounce, unless it be that perfidious Nestorius, who confessed the Son of God to be a mere man Wherefore by no means let such deadly poison insinuate itself into your neighbourhoods, or defile your love" [1]

Still the doctrine went on spreading, until it became necessary to make it the subject of conciliar condemnation This was first done at the small Council of Narbonne [A D 788 or 791], again at the Synod of Ratisbon in Germany [A D 792], where Charlemagne presided in person, and before whom Felix first defended, then abjured and anathematized his own error, [2] but being still suspected, he was sent to Rome under the charge of a certain Angilbertus, and there imprisoned, until he consented to swear before the Eucharist on St Peter's tomb that he renounced his former opinions as heretical Upon this assurance he was allowed to return to his diocese in Spain, but before he had been there long, he retracted his recantation and disseminated his former errors, until in A D 794 Charlemagne desired Alcuin to undertake a formal refutation of the Adoptionists Alcuin requested that the book of Felix and the whole subject might be submitted to the Pope, Paulinus of Aquileia, and other eminent bishops This appears to have been done at the Council of Frankfort in the same year Felix was once more condemned, and the orthodox doctrine was solemnly reasserted in these words, "That holy thing which shall be born of thee shall be called the Son of God, not an adopted and strange Son, but a true and proper" (non adoptivus sed verus, non alienus sed proprius)

This condemnation was repeated at Friuli [A D 796], at Rome under Pope Leo III [A D 799], at Aix-la-Chapelle [A D 799] At the latter council Felix argued for six days with Alcuin, was convinced, and once more retracted his heresy But he was not again trusted to return to Urgel, but placed under the charge firstly of Leodrad, then of his successor Agobard, Archbishop of Lyons, where he died A D 818 Elipandus could have no rule of faith imposed upon him, because he lived under the Saracens in Spain, and he was suffered to remain till his death in undisturbed possession of his see

History of Adoptionism after the death of Felix. —The tenets of the Adoptionists did not, however, become extinct on the death of Felix, for Œcumenius, in the following century, plainly ascribed adoption to Christ

In the eleventh century this view was not supported by any name of note In the twelfth century it has been ascribed to Euthymius Zigabenus, mainly in consequence of certain loose expressions discovered in his writings to Tolmarus, abbot of a monastery in Franconia, as appears from his controversy with Adamus and Gerhohus, dean and superior of the monastery of Reichsberg

During this and the following centuries the subject was constantly debated by the Schoolmen, and chiefly by the following —Peter Lombard, Thomas Aquinas, Duns Scotus, Durandus a S Portiano, Johannes Major, Johannes de Barsolis, Richard Fitz-Ralph, Petrus Areolus, Jacobus Almainus, &c They unanimously rejected the theory of adoption as taught by Felix and Elipandus, but some of them allowed the use of the term with certain modifications and explanations, which virtually reduced the whole discussion to a logomachy.[3]

In the seventeenth century, Georgius Calixtus, a theologian of the Academy of Helmstadt, brought out a book in which he attempted to prove that

[1] Epist xcvii p 818, edit Duchesne

[2] The proceedings at Ratisbon are thus described by Saxo, a poet of the period —

"Atque suum scriptis defendere dogma libellis
Omni quo potuit studio curavit et arte
Hinc ad catholici deductus principis aulam,
Idem regno nam tum hiemavit in urbe,
A multis ibi præsulibus synodoque frequenti
Est auditus et errorem docuisse nefandum
Convictus"

[Bouquetus, *Rerum Gallicarum et Francicarum Scriptor* tom v p 156]

[3] For example, Duns Scotus said,—"Sancti negarunt Christum esse filium adoptivum propter hæreticos qui solum dixerunt eum filium adoptivum et non naturalem, de virtute tamen vocis potest Christus dici filius adoptivus Dei, sicut unus alius homo quia prius natura habuit naturam, quam ordinatur ad hæreditatem et sic fuit sufficienter extraneus" Durandus a S P said,—"Christum dici posse adoptivum, cum additamento, in quantum homo est filium adoptivum Spiritus Sancti" Johannes Major rejected the proposition, "Christus secundum quod homo est est filius Dei adoptivus" as heretical, but held the following to be orthodox —"Christus secundum humanitatem habet adoptionem" [Forbesius, *Instruct Theol* lib vi cap 7, sec 7 See also Thom Aquin iii quæs 23, art. 4]

Pope Hadrian and the Council of Frankfort were wrong in their condemnation of the Adoptionists, whose view he defended on these among other grounds —"That it ought to be allowed Divine adoption was more excellent than human adoption, and might be free from those conditions which human infirmity might render necessary in the latter, hence, that God by virtue of His infinite power might unite more closely to Himself than man could the Son Whom He wished to adopt."

He was opposed by Dorscheus, a theologian of Strasburg [A D 1649], Conradus Dannhaverus, and Adamus Quenstedius A controversy on the same point, and about the same time, was carried on between Dannhaverus and Johannes Reinbothius, president of Schlesvig-Holstein, and the Adoptionist theory found its last advocate in Johannes Tobias Major, a theologian of the University of Jena [A.D 1656]

The Socinian heresy, that Jesus Christ is mere man according to His substance, and that he began to exist no otherwise than by the birth he received of the Virgin Mary, together with the various modifications of this doctrine held by modern sects, are the descendants of Arianism and other early heresies, and must be in no way confused with Adoptionism.

[For a fuller treatment of this subject, see Walchius, *Historia Adoptianorum*, Gottingen, 1755, 8vo, Domin Colonia, *Histoire Littér de la ville de Lyon*, ii 79, Schroeckh, *Kirchengesch* xx p 459, *Commentar in Thomam*, by Gabriel Vasquez, p 96, Ingolst 1606, fol]

ADRIANISTÆ. A sect is thus named by Theodoret as one of those which sprung from "the bitter root" of the Simonian heresy. But nothing further is known of their history and both Valesius and Ittigius consider that "Adrianistæ" is a misreading for "Menandrianistæ" [Theod *Hær fab* i 1]

ADRIANISTS An obscure sect of Dutch Anabaptists, so named after Adrian Hamsted Among other Anabaptist heresies they denied the miraculous conception of our Lord by the Virgin Mary Hamsted was minister of the Dutch sectaries in London, and was deposed by Grindal, Bishop of London, in the beginning of the year 1561 A form of recantation, stating his heretical tenets, is printed in Strype's *Annals of the Reformation*, but it was not signed by Hamsted, who was excommunicated by Grindal, and went abroad [Strype's *Ann Ref* i 176, Grindal's *Works*, 243] He seems to have organized a small community in Holland, which was called after his name

ADRUMETIANS The monks of Adrumetum, in the North African province of Byzacene, misinterpreted St Augustine's anti-Pelagian doctrine, especially that contained in his 194th Epistle, into Antinomian conclusions respecting grace and predestination, and are thus sometimes considered as the first PREDESTINARIANS

ÆLURUS The surname, or rather "nickname," of a schismatical patriarch of Alexandria, Timotheus Ælurus, who for many years was the leader of the Monophysite party there and at Constantinople in the middle of the fifth century [TIMOTHEANS]

ÆSCHINES [CATÆSCHINIANS]

ÆTERNALES This name was given by Danæus, in his edition of Augustine's treatise *de Hæresibus*, to a sect which is numbered as the sixty-seventh in that work, and as the eightieth in Philaster It was their distinctive tenet that the world will remain for ever in its present condition, even after the second coming of our Lord St Augustine remarks that Philaster gives neither the name of the sect nor of its originator The author of *Prædestinatus* mentions the same tenet as that of a sect which he names Satanniani, from one Satannius, but this name was sometimes given to the EUCHITES [*Prædest Hæres* lxvii]

AERIANS An Arian and Presbyterian sect of the fourth century, formed about A D 360-370, by Aerius of Pontus, or Armenia Minor. Aerius and Eustathius were Arian monks and fellow-students. Both becoming candidates for the bishopric of Sebaste in Armenia Minor, Eustathius was preferred, and he ordained Aerius priest, placing him over the hospital of Pontus But Aerius, dissatisfied, gave up his preferment, and set himself to traduce Eustathius, charging him with avarice and hoarding He then affirmed himself to be Eustathius' equal, and asserted that there was no difference, by the Word of God, betwixt a priest and a bishop He left the Church, and allured a great number of followers, who retreated into the wild fastnesses of the country and formed a sect Aerius was alive when Epiphanius wrote, A D 374-6, but his sect does not appear to have spread wide or lasted long The utmost which can be said from Augustine's notice of it is, that "we may be apt to think that he knew of some such people at the time of writing his book of Heresies in the year 428" [Lardner, *Works*, iv 181, Epiph *Hær* lxxv, Aug *Hær* liii] Philaster, however, states that there were many of them in Pamphylia

Of the distinctive tenets of the Aerians, the foremost, the denial of the episcopal order, is heretical Hooker writes [*Eccl Pol* VII ix 2], "Surely if heresy be an error falsely fathered upon Scriptures, but indeed repugnant to the truth of the Word of God, and by the consent of the universal church, in the councils, or in her contrary uniform practice throughout the whole world, declared to be such, and the opinion of Aerius in this point be a plain error of that nature, there is no remedy, but Aerius, so schismatically and stiffly maintaining it, must ever stand where Epiphanius and Augustine have placed him" [PRESBYTERIANISM] As the forerunner of the Presbyterians, the case of Aerius is frequently quoted in modern times

The Aerians also objected to pray for the dead, but we have not sufficient data to form a correct judgment as to the true character of Aerius' teaching on this point Prayer for the dead may be refused from principles clearly heretical, as, *e g*, from a denial of the communion of saints, or the refusal may proceed from a sense of an

 Aetians

undue extension of the range and purpose of such prayer, from a sense of abuses connected with the practice, and of dangers thought to accompany it It may be thus a measure of prudence, with or without sufficient grounds, but not involving heresy [DICT *of* THEOL] From Epiphanius' statements, Aerius appears to have been influenced by the thought that men might be tempted to neglect repentance and good works, in reliance on the prayers of the Church for them after their death, and to have been driven to the extreme of denying altogether the efficacy of such prayer, instead of ascertaining its true limits and purpose.

The third error of the Aerians was a schismatical breach of the discipline of the Church. It was pretended that set fasts were Jewish, and brought men under a yoke of servitude Fasting was not rejected altogether, but Christian liberty was not to be abridged by the appointment of times "They gloried," Epiphanius says, "in fasting on the Lord's Day," and it is probable that the Christian liberty they claimed shewed itself, as it usually does, in wilful opposition to established order Lardner's comment on this point is worth notice "Not but that they would sometimes fast on the fourth day of the week as others do, however, they said, they did it not as bound thereto, but only of their free will, which last particular is sufficient to shew, that what Epiphanius says of their choosing to fast on the Lord's Day is a calumny, and an unrighteous aggravation of their principle" [*Works*, iv p. 180] It is difficult to see how this conclusion flows from the premisses

Philaster [cap 72] states the Aerians to have been Encratites Augustine remarks that Epiphanius does not attribute to them any such abstinence Epiphanius indeed states the direct contrary But he states that Aerius advocated the renunciation of property [ἀποταξίαν κηρύσσει, *Indic* III vi], and as the Apotactites were in general Encratites, Philaster was not unnaturally led into the error

AETIANS A name of the ANOMŒAN sect of Arians which was given to them from Aetius, the first promulgator of their distinctive tenets

Aetius was the son of a military officer settled at Antioch in Cœlo-Syria, who died while Aetius was still a youth, leaving his widow and her son in extreme poverty After some time spent in servitude to the wife of a vine-dresser, Aetius learned to work in metals, rising from the position of a travelling tinker to that of a goldsmith Forsaking the latter trade, he learned some rudiments of medical practice under a quack doctor, and studied afterwards, in a more legitimate way, in the schools of medicine at Antioch, where he soon set up as a physician About A D 331, the death of his mother set him free to follow an inclination for theological studies, to which he seems to have been attracted by some success in disputation in the medical schools, where his talents led to his being engaged as the paid advocate of certain theories not generally received by the profession He was taken in hand by Paulinus, the second bishop of Antioch of that name, who was a follower of Arius, but the pupil outran the master so rapidly, that on the death of the bishop he was driven from Antioch, and had to resume his old trade as a goldsmith at Anazarbus. Here his powers of disputation attracted the notice, first of a professor of grammar, whose pupil he became, and afterwards of the Arian bishop of Anazarbus, whose name was Athanasius From thence the restless Aetius went to Tarsus, continuing his studies under a priest named Antonius, and when the latter was made bishop, the former returned to his native city, to carry them further under another priest named Leontius For a short time he studied at Alexandria, but Leontius being made Bishop of Antioch, he returned thither, and was ordained deacon by him in the year 350 This ordination was not intended, however, to qualify Aetius for the ordinary ministrations of the Church, but simply to place him in a better position for propagating his views, and the remonstrances of the laity of Antioch were so strong, that Leontius was compelled to retract what he had done, by deposing Aetius from the diaconate, when the latter was again driven from Antioch

In the year 358, Eudoxius became Bishop of Antioch, and Aetius once more returned there, having meanwhile declined to accede to a proposition made to him at Alexandria, that he himself should be raised to the episcopal office He had now a number of followers, and had acquired sufficient importance to lead the older Arians to oppose him before the Arian Emperor Constantius, who eventually banished him to Amblada in Pisidia The apostate Julian, who was a personal friend of Aetius, recalled him from exile, and he was made a bishop at Constantinople about A D 363 For the following four years he was driven from one place to another, being hated by the Arians for the logical precision with which he developed their heresy into its consequences, but his death, in the year 367, seems to have taken place at Constantinople.

The sect of Arians founded by Aetius were more commonly known by the name of Eunomians, from his disciple Eunomius But the principles of the heresy were very distinctly stated by Aetius himself, in a treatise which has been preserved by Epiphanius [Epiph *Hæres* lxxvi c 11] This work consists of a short preface and forty-seven theses or propositions, the general purport of which is, that the Second and Third Persons of the Holy Trinity are entirely different in substance and will (ἀνόμοιον) from the First Person, Who alone (he alleges) is possessed of the true quality of Deity, ἀγεννησία, or "ingenerateness" Eunomius endeavoured to formalize a system of Christian theology and morals on this distinctive principle, but the theories of Aetius acquired for him the name of "the Godless" ['Ἄθεος], and his Antinomianism in theory and practice were too notorious to be contradicted Several special misbeliefs are traced up to Aetius and his immediate followers, but the truth is that he repudiated all mystery in religion, and made theology a mere matter of intellectual reasoning, without any real dependence on revelation Such principles would naturally lead to the rejection of nearly every Christian doctrine as soon as it came under consideration [Socrat. *Hist Eccl* ii 35 Sozom *Hist Eccl* iii 15, iv 12 Theodor *Hist Eccl* ii 24 Philostorg *Hist. Eccl* iii Epiph *Hæres* lxxvi]

AGAPEMONITES [PRINCEITES]

AGAPETÆ, OR DILECTÆ I A sect which rose in Spain towards the close of the fourth century, during the reign of Theodosius, deriving its name from a certain Agapo, who with her husband Elpidius were its reputed founders They rejected the institution of marriage, and as a substitute allowed the most unrestrained intercourse and familiarity between both sexes, who, on the principle that "to the pure all things are pure" [Tit i. 15], were allowed to share the same room and even the same couch They also rejected the ordinance of fasting, indulging in festive and uproarious living, asking why they should "abstain from meats which God hath created to be received with thanksgiving of them which believe and know the truth" [1 Tim iv 3]

St Jerome thus indignantly alludes to them in a letter addressed to Eustochium [*Lib de Custod Virg*] "It is a shame even to allude to the true facts Whence did the pest of the Agapetæ creep into the Church? Whence is this new title of wives without marriage rites? Whence this new class of concubines? I will infer more Whence these harlots cleaving to one man? They occupy the same house, a single chamber, often a single bed, and call us suspicious if we think anything of it. The brother deserts his virgin sister, the virgin despises her unmarried brother, and seeks a stranger, and since they pretend to be aiming at the same object, they ask for the spiritual consolation of each other, that they may enjoy the pleasures of the flesh"

In another place [*Ad Ctesiphontem*], S Jerome, after enumerating Nicolas of Antioch led astray by the prostitute Helena, Marcion by a woman unnamed, Apelles by Philomena, Montanus by Prisca and Maximilla, mentions Agape as drawing Elpidius into heresy, and being by him the spiritual progenitor of Priscillian (successoremque suum Priscillianum habuit)

II The title of Agapetæ is also applied more generally to those monks or clergy who, under pretence of pure love, cohabited with the virgins or widows of the Church This custom, frequently condemned in the patristic writings, became a very common one It was defended by the text, "Have we not power to lead about a sister?" &c [1 Cor ix 5], which St Jerome explains [*Contra Jovin* lib. i cap 14] of sacred women who ministered to the Apostles of their substance One of the charges laid against Paul of Samosata at his deposition by the Council of Antioch [A D 270], was that of adopting himself and allowing his clergy to adopt too great and scandalous intimacy with women who were not relations, and who were hence called *συνείσακτοι* or "subintroductæ" The custom, however, appears to have been a persistent one, for it survived the condemnation of many councils, such as the first and second Councils of Carthage [A D 348-397, canons 3, 25], the second Council of Arles [A D 451, can 3], Essone [A D 517, can 20], and was only finally abolished by the fourth Lateran Council under Innocent III [A.D 1215]

AGINENSES [AGIONITES]

AGIONITES An obscure sect of ENCRATITES, condemned with the Eustathians and others of a similar character at the Council of Gangra, which was held at some time between A D 360 and A D 380 Perhaps the name was assumed by the Eustathians in some form based on the word ἅγιος, *q d* "Puritans"

AGNOETÆ. A sect of the fourth century was sometimes called by this name on account of a peculiar opinion which they maintained respecting the Omniscience of God They were a branch of the Eunomians, which struck off under the leadership of Theophronius [EUNOMIO-THEOPHRONIANS]

AGNOETÆ [ἀγνοέω] A school of Alexandrian Monophysites, who, confusing the two Natures of our Lord, attributed to Him the human defect of imperfect knowledge This opinion was developed by the Severianist and Julianist controversy which divided the Monophysites, about A D 520 Timothy having succeeded Dioscorus as Patriarch of Alexandria, endeavoured to effect a compromise between the Julianist Aphthartodocetæ and the Severianist Phthartolatræ or Corrupticolæ, privately leaning, however, to the latter as regarded his own opinions An answer given by the Patriarch Timothy to a deacon named Themistius, led the latter to maintain the conclusion, that if the body of Christ was corruptible (subject, that is, not to the corruption of the grave, which the Severianists did not believe, but to the decay arising from the wear and tear of life), then He must also have been so far subject to the defects of human nature that His very knowledge of the present and the future was imperfect, and there were, therefore, some things of which He was ignorant The Scriptural proof of this doctrine was rested on our Lord's question respecting the body of Lazarus, "Where have ye laid him?" [John xi. 34], and on His saying respecting the day of judgment, "Of that day and that hour knoweth no man, no not the angels which are in heaven, neither the Son, but the Father" [Mark xiii 32] The patriarch himself repudiated this conclusion, but a school of theorists grew up under the leadership of Themistius, and from the adoption of this conclusion as their distinctive tenet became known as Agnoetæ, or assertors of ignorance

The heresy of this opinion lies in the fact that, starting in Eutychianism, it thus attributes ignorance to the Omniscient Word. Some of the Fathers used language which attributed growth of knowledge, and therefore a preceding defect of knowledge, to the human soul of Christ, but they did so while holding most emphatically the distinction between His Human and His Divine Natures [DICT of THEOL, IGNORANCE OF CHRIST], such a distinction being as emphatically repudiated by the Agnoetes

The heresy was opposed by Eulogius of Alexandria in a treatise "Of the two Natures of Jesus Christ" [Bibl Patr Galland xii 300], and he went so far as to say that the Fathers had allowed the doctrine of a growth in Christ's knowledge by way of œconomy in dealing with the Arians Afterwards the opponents of the Agnoetians extended this idea of œconomy even to our Lord's own words, saying that He appeared not to know for the sake of His disciples

The Agnoetian heresy obtained a permanent footing as an opinion, but it does not appear that it led to the formation of any sect distinct from the general body of the Monophysites

AGONICLITES [ἀ, γόνυ, κλίνω] A fanatical sect of the seventh and eighth centuries, whose distinctive tenet was the condemnation of kneeling as the attitude of prayer They are said also to have used dancing as a devotional custom They were condemned by a synod of Jerusalem, A D 726

AGONISTICI The distinctive name of "Contenders" was given by the Donatists to the violent bands which roamed about Africa under the pretence of winning converts to that schism, but in reality gratifying their own desires for rapine, cruelty, and lust They are said to have appeared first in A D 317 [Tillemont, vi 96], and are more familiarly known by their other titles of Catrophites, Circuiti, Circumcellions, Corophites, and (at Rome) Montenses [CIRCUMCELLIONS]

AGYNIANS [ἀ, γυνή] One of the many later offshoots of Manichæism, assigned to the latter part of the seventh century [A D 694] Its adherents, as their name implies, held no intercourse with women, pretending that God was not the author of, and did not sanction, marriage

AITKENITES A party in the Church of England which owes its origin to Robert Aitken, who had been a Wesleyan preacher previous to his ordination, and subsequently to it became a High Churchman being Vicar of Pendeen in Cornwall from 1849 until his death in July 1873 The distinctive feature of Aitkenism is indicated by these two circumstances, it being a combination of Methodist peculiarities with the ritual and the sacramental theology of the High Church school The doctrines of sensible conversion and assurance of salvation are strongly maintained by the Aitkenites, and their belief in these doctrines leads them to supplement the services of the Church with prayer-meetings of an excited character, similar to those which were held by Wesley in the early days of his movement The object of Mr Aitken and his followers seems to have been the development of Wesley's original principles in the High Church direction which they were disposed to take in the first year or two of his preaching There is, consequently, no likelihood of their following Wesley's example in originating a sect, and Aitkenism will probably find its place and level in the Church of England as a home mission movement, in the same way that a similar movement has done in France

ALASCANS A name given to the foreign Protestants in London during the reign of Edward VI It was derived from John Laski, or à Lasco, a Polish refugee of noble birth, who had adopted the negative theology of Zwingli during a residence at Zurich For some years à Lasco was minister of a congregation at Embden in Friesland, but being invited to London by Cranmer, he lived with the Archbishop at Lambeth for six months, and was then made superintendent of the "foreign churches" (German, Belgian, French, and Italian) in London, the principal one being the church of the Austin Friars in Broad Street A Lasco was a forward partizan of Puritanism, opposing the use of the surplice, kneeling at Communion, &c, and it is believed that he influenced the later opinions of Cranmer in the same direction as regards the doctrine of the Holy Eucharist The German congregations were dispersed at the accession of Queen Mary, and some portions of them settled at Embden, under à Lasco, who, however, soon forsook them, and after a sojourn at Frankfort, returned to Poland, where he died in 1560. A full account of the Alascan liturgy will be found in the *British Magazine*, vol xv 614, and xvi 127 It is distinctly Zwinglian

ALBANENSES. A small mediæval sect of the Cathari, which took its name from the city and diocese of Albi in Piedmont, then forming part of the archbishopric of Arles They were a portion of that influx of heresy by which the mountainous districts of Italy, Switzerland, and France, were overrun in the twelfth century, the Manichæan character of which indicates an Eastern origin The Albanenses maintained a phase of Manichæan dualism evidently derived from the Persian system, alleging that there are two coeternal First Causes, the one being the God of light, God the Father of the orthodox creed, and the other the Prince of darkness, who was the maker of all material things They held a theory that no living thing created by God was made to perish, a doctrine which led them to Antinomianism, and which also made it a sin in their eyes to take the life of any animal The sect was subdivided into the adherents of Balazinansa, Bishop of Verona, and those of John de Lugio, Bishop of Bergamo It seems to have been confined to Venetian Lombardy, the district in which it originated, but was also associated with the Albigenses The two sects are often confounded with each other, and very probably they were actually amalgamated under the common name of ALBIGENSES Reiner numbers them at about five hundred only [Raynerus Sachonus, *Summa de Catharis et Leonistis*, in Martene's *Thes Anecd.* v 1761-8, and Gretser's Summary, entitled Reinerus *contr Waldens in Bibl Max. Lugd.* xxv 267, 269]

ALBATI [WHITE BRETHREN]

ALBIGENSES. Under this name are comprised the numerous varieties of Manichæan heretics who are found in Southern France and

Northern Italy in the twelfth and thirteenth centuries The name does not seem to be contemporaneous with the appearance of the heresy in Europe, not being found in the earlier synodical decrees against it, but these heretics are certainly so called in a work of Stephanus de Borbone written about A D 1225 It seems to have become the popular designation, about that date, of many differing sects whom the theologians of the age generically termed Manichæans, and it was probably derived, as will be shewn more at length presently, from one of the districts of Languedoc of which the city of Albi, anciently called Albiga, where a council was held against them in A D 1176, was the principal town [Gretser *Pref in* Luc Tudens *adv* Albig *error*, *Bibl. Max Lugd* XXV 190, A] The Albigenses were also called Gazari (a corruption from the name Cathari), Bulgarians, Publicians, and by an almost infinite number of other local names

Like all the Manichæan bodies, the Albigenses are distinguished by a more or less complete dualistic creed, and by the identification of the persons of the Duality with spirit or good, and matter or evil, like most of those bodies, they condemned the Old Testament as the work of the evil being, denied the lawfulness of marriage, and divided all their members into two classes of superior and inferior holiness Manichæan ideas had indeed found their way into Europe as early as the beginning of the eleventh century, but the sects had been weak in the number of adherents, doubtful and disunited in their creed and practices They had been frequently, and still remained to a great extent, confounded with various sects of pure anti-sacerdotalists, like the followers of Waldo of Lyons [WALDENSES], and of mad communists like the worshippers of Eon. [EONIANS] From Bulgaria, where Paulician Manichæism [PAULICIANS] had been established since the seventh century, the heretical ideas slowly permeated Europe So general was this infiltration in the eleventh century, that there is hardly a western or northern country in which we do not find a disturbance traceable to this source But the cold and phlegmatic temper of these regions was fatal to the oriental mysticism of Mani, upon which the new heresy was originally founded, while feudal and oligarchical institutions were ill-suited to the democratic spirit of the Paulicianism from which it was immediately derived In England, Northern France, and Germany, the Manichæan revolt was easily subdued, but in Southern France, Provence, and Italy, the case was different In these last named countries, Manichæism in its earlier stage seems, in a great measure, from different causes, to have escaped notice In Southern France and Provence this was probably due to the more urgent character of the anti-sacerdotal revolt, in Italy, to the absorbing interest of the struggle between the Papal and the Imperial powers Italy, too, was favourably situated for the dissemination of the heresy, in consequence of its proximity to Bosnia and the other provinces which bounded the home of Paulician Manichæism, and the increasing intercourse brought about by the Crusades materially assisted this dissemination Here the last of the three great waves of Manichæan opinion, which in the third, the seventh, and the eleventh centuries respectively, threatened to desolate Christianity, beaten back from the rest of Europe, for the most part was poured Here the heresy, elsewhere overpowered, was consolidated and developed, until, in the middle of the twelfth century, it burst out in that form to which the famous title of the "Albigensian" has been attached

There were many circumstances—traditions, situation, climate—predisposing the South of France to admit the influence of a heresy like Manichæism Septimania, which included Languedoc and Provence, and therefore the greater part of the Tolosan suzerainty, had, during four centuries of its early history, submitted without reluctance to the domination of Arian Goths or infidel Saracens During the centuries immediately preceding the Manichæan revolt, the inhabitants had been accustomed to the demoralizing spectacle exhibited by the flourishing courts of the infidel princes of Spain Sufficiently near to find polite intercourse with the Mohammedans agreeable, while they were too far removed to dread Mohammedan hostility, they had learnt to be tolerant when the rest of Europe was bigoted Italy, and in particular Lombardy, was next to Toulouse in its forbearing temper The Paulician Manichæism which had broken out first in Northern Europe in the neighbourhood of the emporia of the Eastern trade, at a very short interval had appeared in Italy, that province of the Western Empire nearest to the Bulgarian frontier. The outbreak, though, as has been mentioned, for the time successfully crushed in the North, in the South had the effect, not only of exciting many new leaders of heretical opinion, but of awaking the dormant Manichæism of central Italy The connection between Italy and Provence was of long standing, and Languedoc, united, for a time at least, under the same lordship, was further connected by a community of participation in the Romanesque institutions and language It was in the the independent cities of Italy that the dying institutions of Paganism had lingered longest, it was in such towns that Manichæism was earliest revived, and that this revival was a genuine rehabilitation of a dead heresy, is evidenced by the fact, that the old tenets which had been discarded by the Paulician heretics from the seventh to the tenth centuries, are found flourishing in Provence and Italy in the twelfth But if Italy was foremost in the revival of Manichæism, it is with the suzerainty of Toulouse that its connexion was most famous and fatal. That suzerainty, which comprised almost the whole of the ancient province of Narbonnensis, with the south-eastern parts of Aquitania Prima, had been, at the commencement of the eleventh century, the scene of St. Bernard's most famous triumph over the anti-sacerdotalists, and the ground so broken received the seed of the new heresy with wonderful rapidity. Nor was the Church in these provinces capable of any considerable resistance, for the influence of their clergy was then at the lowest point that it has anywhere reached in the history of Christianity A luxurious country, civilized beyond its age, almost wholly independent of the French king at Paris, (in the preceding century it had absolutely ignored his existence), Languedoc enjoyed an almost licentious freedom, at a time when the rest of Europe was held in the strongest grasp of an almost universal military despotism

It was in this country, so predisposed by circumstance to receive the poison, that the streams of heretical opinion were appointed to meet Southwards, from Trèves, Cologne, Besançon—westwards, from below the Pennine Alps—northwards, from Tuscany and the States of the Church—the flow of heretical opinion converged upon Toulouse The most fruitful and important district of the Tolosan Count was the Albigeois, or that surrounding Albi, a town on a tributary of the Garonne, and the modern capital of the department of the Tarn, and it is from this territory that the name Albigensian, now so famous, has by a somewhat obscure process been derived.

The first mention of these Manichæan, or (as they are frequently called) Arian heretics of this district, is found in the records of the Council of Tours, which took place A D 1163 The fourth canon of that Council is entitled, "ut cuncti consortium Albigensium hæreticorum fugiant" The canon itself then describes them, calling them however Cathari and Paterini, the names under which, until the middle of the next century, they are invariably known It is worthy of remark, that the name "Albigensian" occurs only in one other record of the twelfth century, a letter, nominally, to his clergy, from Bishop Odo of Paris, dated A D 1190, but conceived in terms which smack of modern authorship In A D 1165, a council was held at Lombères, near Albi, where the heretical opinions were condemned, but the name not unnaturally does not there occur It is from this council that many learned authors, including Mosheim, are inclined to derive the distinctive title of Albigenses. A more probable hypothesis derives the name from the fact that the Albigeois was the chief seat of the heresy, a fact however which rests on insufficient evidence The word Albigensian is certainly absent from the series of condemnations which extend from the middle of the twelfth to the middle of the thirteenth century These, commencing with the Council of Tours in A D 1163, carry the chain of anathema through the councils presided over by Alexander III, Lucius II., and Innocent III, but they contain no use of this word in other than a geographical sense The third Lateran of Alexander III is thus precise in its terms —"Quia in Gasconia Albigesia et partibus Tolosanis et aliis locis ita hæreticorum quos alii Catharos alii Paterinos alii Publicanos appellant invaluit damnata perversitas" Of the names applied to the Albigensian sectaries, Publicani is a manifest corruption of Pauliciani, and had been in common use for a century Of the other terms, "Cathari" or "Puritans," was, in default of more differential nomenclature, employed to express all the anti-sacerdotal bodies, whether Manichæan or otherwise, who claimed peculiar sanctity, and "Paterini" (variously spelt Patareni and Patrini), sponsors or fatherlings, originally a term of reproach flung by the secular at the regular clergy, was well adapted to the Manichæan despisers of marriage. The details of the process, during which the name Albigeois acquired the sense in which it is subsequently, and has now for so many centuries, been applied, to the heretics of Languedoc and Provence, are not discoverable with certainty The name was probably given to the war by the lay invaders, not to the heresy by the priestly invaders of Toulouse It is a significant fact, that the first crusade against this development of modern Manichæism was directed against the inhabitants of Albi, whose feudal lord defended his vassals against the attack. Besides, when, a quarter of a century later, the great crusade of Innocent commenced, the large fertile district contiguous to the frontier of Guienne, within or adjacent to which lay Toulouse and the principal towns of the invaded district, would be likely to attract much attention from crusaders, mostly from Northern and Eastern France, aliens in blood, speech, and usage. Such men might readily borrow for the title of their crusade the name of one of the principal scenes of their operations with which they were familiar, and so in succeeding years it might come to pass, that the name thus given to the crusade might be transferred to the heresy which was its cause This theory derives much support from the fact, that the earliest use of the word in the broader meaning refers it to the Albigensian crusade, and *not* to the Albigensian heresy The word first began to be applied to the heresy (but not commonly) in the latter half of the thirteenth century, about which time a second council was held at Albi, under the patronage of the Dominican inquisition

In the edict of the Council of Alexander III (the third Lateran, A D 1179) is preserved the first authentic statement, though by an enemy, of this heresy From it we learn, that the heretics (hereafter to be called Albigensians), besides their assertion of the dualistic principle, rejected the Lord's Supper, disowned the Old Testament, its law and its God, denied the resurrection of the body, salvation by faith, the efficacy of infant baptism (chiefly on Pelagian grounds), declared capital punishment, oaths, and marriage unlawful, forbade the use of churches, ritual, and the payment of tithes to the clergy, and taught that no female soul in a future state retained femininity In the year prior to this council Raymond V, the reigning Count of Toulouse, had appealed to Alexander for pontifical assistance. A commission of five of the most distinguished prelates, with the sanction of the Kings of France and England, proceeded to the assistance of the count. In their report they describe the whole land as in the possession of the heretics But the condemnation of papal and provincial councils was of little efficacy in Toulouse, nor was the persecution which Raymond set on foot more efficacious. A crusade, undertaken by Henry of Clairvaux against the Albigeois, was rendered wholly nugatory by the protection which the Viscount of Bezières and his great vassal the Count of Albi afforded to the heretics In vain did Raymond, through the last twenty years of his reign, burn the bodies and confiscate the goods of the heretics, in vain were ecclesiastical censures poured out against these Cathari in successive and continuous imprecation Florence, Brescia, Bergamo, Milan, in Italy, Montpellier, Carcassonne, Albi, Toulouse, in France; each continued to hold flourishing communities professing Albigensian opinions Toulouse, with its great subordinate fiefs, including besides those that have been mentioned, Bezières, Foix, Queray, and Narbonne, was wholly given to the heretics So completely had the country come into their possession, so fearless were they in the enjoyment of their freedom, that they possessed their own burial-grounds, and subsidized their own clergy

They divided the sect into classes, under the title of Consolati, or Perfect, and Fœderati, or Auditors. The voluptuous Tolosan nobles (and most of the Tolosan nobles were voluptuous) had probably little religion of any kind, but the discipline of the federate or auditor, which sufficed the ambitious youth of Augustine, was not a severe or ascetic rule. The devout, on the other hand, found their account in the religious excitement of the new and daring opinions, and in an asceticism which surpassed the utmost severity of which the degraded priesthood of the country was capable, while the consolation in death administered by the "perfect," whose title to confidence lay only in his holy life, seemed to them to have more than all the value of priestly absolution The vast increase in the numbers of the sect induced a more widely extended organization Bishops, with two coadjutors, the one holding the title of eldest, the other of youngest son, administered to the accumulating need of the congregations They are alleged to have possessed a complete system of churches, sixteen in number, representing the communities of France, Italy, and Bulgaria, and there is reason for believing that their ministers received ordination, or, at any rate, first appointment, from the more important stations in the Italian cities The old Zoroastrian controversy of the first causes, which had divided Persia in the hour of the birth of Manichæism, again appeared, in this the hour of its dissolution, and the Bagnolensian and the Albanensian camps respectively sustained the cause of the single and double origin of existence Albi itself, and the heretical Church of Provence, supported the theory of the single origin

How deeply imbued with the heretical opinion was the whole country may be gathered from the fact, that in one assembly, held in the year 1204, four of the most noble Provençales, numbering among them Esclarmonde, the sister of the great Count of Foix, were publicly received into the heretical community On their admission into the ranks of the Perfect, these ladies made solemn promise to touch no meat, eggs, or cheese, but to eat only vegetables and fish, neither to swear nor to lie, to abstain from all carnal intercourse, and to keep troth to their sect unto the death Even Innocent admits their virtue, but, like Leo and Cyril, he held their practice of virtue but a wile of the devil to betray the orthodox Within a few months of his accession, Innocent commenced proceedings. He wrote first to the Archbishop of Auch, then to all the great prelates and nobles of the country, urging them to exterminate the heresy, offering them for the use of their swords the blessings of the Church and the possessions of the heretics This first appeal was wholly ineffectual the nobles would not act against their vassals, and the clergy were powerless. The Pope sent legates, chosen from the monastic orders, first Reiner and Guy, subsequently Peter of Castelnau, Raoul, and Arnold of Citeaux, these last the most bigoted Churchmen of that age of bigots Eight years passed of ineffectual preaching, in the exaction of vain promises and idle protestations The cities promised, and the nobles, but neither cities nor nobles would act against inoffensive citizens, against faithful vassals The Pope called on the count himself to interfere Raymond VI, who, heretic as he is alleged to have been, was certainly no Manichæan, (he had three wives alive at the commencement of the crusade), dallied with the papal mandate, the legates were exacting, and after a short struggle the inevitable end arrived, and he was excommunicated The pretext was the murder of Peter of Castelnau, a crime of which the count was entirely innocent. The legates, who had by this time obtained some influence owing to the austerities which, by the advice of Dominic, they had sedulously practised, and thus gained the reputation of sanctity, obtained through the death of Peter the prestige of a martyrdom

The Pope issued to the king and great nobles of Northern France a public call to vengeance, while his emissaries privately urged Raymond's vassals to revolt, the death of Peter becoming the signal for a general crusade It is said that half a million of men were gathered for the enterprise In vain the count performed the most abject penance, and surrendered seven of his principal castles into the hands of the Pope, in vain he offered to join, and in fact did join, the crusade against his faithful Albigensians. The invaders had for leaders four archbishops, twelve bishops of great sees, and countless abbots, and other dignitaries The Duke of Burgundy, the Counts of Nevers and St. Pol, Simon Montfort, the Lord of Amaury in France and Leicester in England, supported the Churchmen The crusaders' advance was irresistible Bezières and Carcassonne were at once stormed, and the inhabitants indiscriminately massacred. In the first quarter of a year five hundred towns and fortresses fell or capitulated, and amongst them Albi. In their more merciful moments, the order was given by the crusading chiefs that those who recanted should be spared, and those who refused should be burned Few availed themselves of the former alternative, most boldly confessed their faith, and accepted martyrdom with cheerfulness The crusaders soon grew tired of leniency At the great papal Council of Arles, Raymond was offered terms, so contrived as to make acceptance impossible The strife was continued, marked with atrocities remarkable even for a religious war "Slay all, God will know His own," was the saying of the legate Arnold before Bezières At Lavaur, the lady paramount was thrown into a well and stones rolled upon her, eight hundred nobles were hanged on trees or hewn in pieces, four hundred of the "perfect" were burned in one pile, the rest, men, women and children, were massacred The career of Simon de Montfort, the only crusading noble base enough to accept the price of blood, was one of unchequered success In three campaigns he became a sovereign prince The arms of Montfort were everywhere irresistible Even the King of Arragon, the victor of Navas de Tolosa, was defeated and killed The nobles of Toulouse were now struggling for existence Raymond and his vassals were too weak to protect their subjects; they were fortunate if they survived themselves The fourth Lateran of Innocent III declared the formal spoliation of Raymond It is alleged that the Pope was overborne by the cardinals and priests of Montfort's party, by the men who boasted themselves more papal than the Pope himself at any rate it would seem that the Pope partially repented of his harshness, and offered the Venaissin to the young Raymond as a compensation for Toulouse Meanwhile, Montfort was occupied with the consolidation of his dominion, and with the extirpation of the Albigenses But a general insurrection of the whole people in favour of their old rulers compelled him again to take the field The two counts landed, and were enthusiastically received Shortly, the old count threw himself into Toulouse, which defied every effort of Montfort's arms, and before its gates the great crusader at length perished

Innocent had died in A D 1216, and though the new crusade preached by his successor, Honorius III., was headed by Louis of France, it accomplished nothing more than one massacre of Albigenses, that at Marmande In A.D 1222, the Count Raymond VI died, and four years later another crusading army descended into Languedoc But it was no longer a war directed against heretics, enemies of the Christian Church, but against inhabitants who refused to own the suzerainty of the French king The year A D 1229 saw, in the Council of Toulouse and the Treaty of Paris, the destruction both of political independence and of religious liberty. By the council the laity were prohibited from possessing the Scriptures By the treaty, Raymond VII promised fealty to the king He swore besides to render fealty to the Pope, to execute justice on all heretics, and to pay at first two, subsequently one mark for each heretic discovered in his dominions At the Council of Toulouse a complete code of persecution was developed In every village one clerical and three lay inquisitors were to be appointed, the property of those on whose lands heretics were found was to be forfeited, the harbourers of heretics were to be reduced to personal slavery, heretics who recanted were to be removed to Catholic cities, to wear two crosses of different colour on their dress, to abjure Albigensian tenets, and to make public confession of faith The suspect were incapable of holding office, of practising medicine, or of nursing the sick But even these decrees were considered of dangerous mildness, and were amplified and made more stringent by subsequent councils, which were levelled as well against the true Albigenses or Manichæans, as against the Leonistæ or Waldenses, many of whom had shared the sufferings of the crusade

The punishments invented for suppressing the Albigensian heresy, and universally adopted by the Inquisition, are historically instructive. For those who recanted, penance and deprivation of all honourable means of life for those whom they could not convict, perpetual imprisonment · for the guilty, death at the stake Nor were the inquisitors backward in enforcing these penalties, as the holocaust of one hundred and eighty-three persons at Vertus, and numerous other massacres, abundantly testify To Innocent and Honorius belong the credit of establishing, to Gregory is due the glory of having perpetuated, this Inquisition By him it was handed over to the Dominican Friars, from whom, as possessing a corporate succession, the heritage could not pass away Their cruelties in Toulouse at length provoked an insurrection, it was appeased by a temporary removal of the Inquisition, but with its return after four years the same cruelties returned, and the same revolt

In this their last struggle the Albigensians fought with fury They captured the castle of Avignonet, and hewed in pieces William Arnaud, the great inquisitor, with the four Dominicans and two Franciscans who formed the inquisitorial tribunal at that place. But these successes were of no long duration Raymond was forced to submit to Saint Louis, and abandonment of the Albigensians was stipulated for in the act of submission. Within two years of that submission, that is A D 1244, Mont Segur, the last refuge of the Albigensians, a strong castle perched on the edge of a ravine in the Pyrenees, to which most of the perfect, with their bishop, had fled, was forced to surrender to the Archbishop of Narbonne, the Bishop of Albi, and the Seneschal of Carcassonne All the heretics, with their bishop, and the noble Lady Esclarmonde, were burnt alive in a vast enclosure of stakes and straw In the same year, the Emperor Frederick II, himself a freethinker, published an imperial decree for the punishment of the Albigensian heretics of the empire, under the style of "Cathari," "Paterini," "Albanenses," and "Bagnolenses" The persecution was devised with such political shrewdness and so well executed that the heresy was actually stamped out in Southern Europe In fifteen years, at the beginning of the fourteenth century, the Tolosan Inquisition, at their various "sermones," or sessions, handed over to death by the civil power twenty-nine of the Albigenses, and punished, with various severity of imprisonment, nearly five hundred others This activity, it must be borne in mind, was displayed between the years A D 1307-1323, sixty years after the heresy had been forcibly suppressed, and a whole century later than the death of Montfort. Slowly and in secret the last remnant of the Albigensian heresy was strangled by the strong hand of the Inquisition A few escaped and joined themselves to the Waldenses, attracted more by the comparative security of their Piedmontese homes than from any community of religious opinion Others, it is said, escaped to Bosnia and the provinces of the Danube, where, favoured more by their obscurity than by any intentional toleration of either eastern or western Rome, they preserved a harmless and precarious existence, until they were reconciled to the Church in the fifteenth century by the eloquence of the Cardinal Carvalho

The story of the Albigensians (gross heretics as they undoubtedly were) is the shortest, brightest, and bloodiest in the annals of heresy Their precocious refinement and civilization, their high moral tone (which their enemies scarcely deny), the unchristian heresy which they themselves are bold to admit, the bloody crusade which commenced and the bloodier persecution which consummated their ruin, present features of romantic interest absolutely without parallel. Nor was this course of events less swift than the events themselves are surprising In the middle of the twelfth century, the Albigensian history commences, in A D 1244 the community had ceased to exist By that date little that was Albigensian survived, unless it was a hatred of Roman bigotry which even the Inquisition failed to extirpate It is noteworthy that the country of the Albigenses was also the country of the Camisards

Literature—The original records of the Albigensian heresy are unfortunately the work entirely of orthodox writers, and almost entirely of orthodox ecclesiastics The most important of these contemporaneous authorities are collected in the *Recueil des Historiens des Gaules et de la France* [Bouquet, &c, Paris] They consist of the history of *Petrus Sarnensis*, Peter of Vaux Cernay, who, in attendance on his uncle, the abbot of that place, was an approving eye-witness of the horrors of the crusade [Bouquet, tom XIX]; that of *Gulielmus de Podio Laurentii*, William of Puy Laurens [Bouquet, tom. XIX XX], that of *Reinerius*, himself a Catharist or Albigensian, but who, being converted to orthodoxy, became an inquisitor [Bouquet, tom XVIII], and that of the anonymous author of the history of the *Guerre des Albigeois* [Bouquet, tom XVIII] To these are to be added the controversial treatises *Adversus Catharos et Waldenses*, by Alanus de Insulis [Masson, Lyons], and by *Moneta Cremonensis* [Richinius, Rome], and the poem written by a troubadour, under the *nom de plume* of William of Tudela, edited by M. Fauriel, *Documents Historiques inédits* [Paris], and entitled *La Guerre des Albigeois* This author, whose orthodoxy is unimpeachable, gives the history of the war from A.D 1209 to 1219. At first he is furious against the heretics, but, as the work progresses, the cruelties practised by the crusaders have the effect of changing him from a staunch partizan into a bitter enemy of their opponents Besides these more important works, the papal letters of Innocent III. and Acts of Councils are to be read passim The *Codex Tolosanæ inquisitionis*, a record of the work of the Inquisition of Toulouse, from A D 1307-1323 [Limborch, Amsterdam], contains an authentic list of sentences of that tribunal during those fifteen years Of modern works on this subject, the *Histoire de Languedoc*, by MM Vich et Vaissette [Paris], and Sismondi's *History of the Crusade against the Albigenses* [London], are the most important Much information is contained in the ecclesiastical histories of Fleury, Mosheim, and Gieseler, though the two former are sometimes exceedingly partial in their views, as also in Milman's *Latin Christianity* It is necessary to observe, that the account of the Albigenses given in Milner's *Church History* is wholly untrustworthy The most valuable learning applied to the many difficulties with which their history abounds is to be found in the *Histoire de la Poesie Provençale*, by M Fauriel [Paris], and in Maitland's *Facts and Documents connected with the History of the Albigenses and Waldenses*

ALEXANDER In both of St. Paul's Epistles to Timothy an Alexander is named as one of the worst opponents of his ministry In the first he speaks of him in association with Hymenæus, as having made shipwreck of the faith, and as having put away the faith and a good conscience [1 Tim i 19, 20] In the second he says "Alexander the coppersmith did me much evil" [2 Tim. iv 14, cf Acts xix 33] There is no reason to believe that two Alexanders are here named, and as the second Epistle to Timothy was written some years after the first, we are led to the conclusion that the opposition to St Paul, and the "shipwreck" of "the faith," were of a persistent character What was the nature of Alexander's heresy is not stated, but the combination of immorality and misbelief—the putting away of both faith and conscience—points to some form of Gnosticism. That it was heresy of a very antichristian kind is shewn by St Paul's language in both places [HYMENÆUS]

ALEXANDRIAN SCHOOL The present article will be limited to the Catechetical School

I When our Lord bade His disciples baptize in His name, He also commanded that instruction should precede the initiatory rite Excepting in such abnormal instances as the first converts on the day of Pentecost, and the Ethiopian eunuch, and the gaoler at Philippi, regular instruction was conveyed from the first before the administration of baptism In the case of Jews bare admission that Jesus was the Christ might be sufficient, but heathen idolaters needed a longer and more elaborate course of instruction, and a

Alexandrian School

necessity thus arose for a distinct order of catechists At first, perhaps, the ordained and authorized teacher of each church discharged the duty in person, then, as its boundaries became extended, delegates, whether clerical or lay, were told off for the office, and even females were not considered ineligible to convey to converts of their own sex the first principles of the Christian faith In remote districts, catechetical arrangements would be simple in the extreme, but the large centres of civilization demanded more care and method St Paul himself was the first catechist of the Corinthian Church [1 Cor ix 19-23, iii 5, 6, 2 Cor x. 16], to be succeeded in due course by others [1 Cor xv 11] He instructed widely, but baptized few Athens and Rome, doubtless, had their systematic exposition of the rule of faith before that rule was confessed in baptism, but the only Church with respect to such appointments to which we can speak with certainty is the Alexandrian

II St Jerome refers the origin of this noted school to St. Mark "Pantænus Stoicæ sectæ philosophus juxta quandam veterem in Alexandria consuetudinem, ubi a Marco Evangelista semper ecclesiastici fuere doctores, tantæ prudentiæ et eruditionis tam in Scripturis divinis, quam in seculari litteratura fuit" [*Catal* 36] This same Pantænus is named by Eusebius, who speaks of the school as of old standing *ἐξ ἀρχαίου ἔθους διδασκαλείου τῶν ἱερῶν λόγων παρ' αὐτοῖς συνεστῶτος, ὃ καὶ εἰς ἡμᾶς παρατείνεται* [*H E* v 10], the origin of the Alexandrian Church being also referred by him to St Mark [*H E* ii 16]

The Evangelist would naturally provide for the succession of pure teaching in the Church of his foundation, and instruction for neophytes, at first simple in the extreme, deepened into those more severe lines of comparative scholarship, Christian and Pagan, which local peculiarities fostered, thus, milk for babes was gradually replaced by the strong meat for men The earliest name connected with this school is that of Athenagoras, in the middle of the second century, mentioned by Philippus of Sidet in Pamphylia,[1] in a fragment published by Dodwell [*Diss in Iren* 490-514], as the first of a succession of learned teachers But the writer's authority does not stand high for accuracy, and Eusebius fails to confirm the statement, although the way in which the historian mentions Pantænus at the close of the second century by no means implies that he had no predecessor in his office Both Athenagoras and Pantænus were converts from the ranks of philosophy, and certainly no more useful class of instructors could be found in such a locality than learned converts for no other men could have so complete a grasp of the various problems that have exercised the human intellect, or so demonstrate the weak points of every philosophical system, while they exhibited the spiritual simplicity of the Gospel of Christ as the power of God and the wisdom of God [1 Cor. i. 24] to every soul that believeth.

Respecting the position of Pantænus there can be no doubt, and from him the following succession may be traced down to the close of the fourth century, doubtful links in the succession being printed in italics.—

Date.	Name of Teacher	Coadjutor	Authorities
A D 160-181	*Athenagorus*		Philippus Sidetes
,, 181 190	Pantænus		Euseb *H E* v 10, Hieron *Catal* 36; Nicephorus, *H E* iv 35, v 18
,, 190 203	Pantænus	Clement	
,, 203 ,, 203-206	Pantænus, Clement, Origen		Euseb *H E* v 11, vi 6, 13, 14, Hieron *Catal* 18; Nicephorus, *H E* iv 33; Photii *Bibl* 118.
,, 206-211	Pantænus, Clement	Origen	Eus *H E* vi. 6, Photii *Bibl* 118
,, 211-213	Clement	Origen	
,, 213	Origen		Eus *H E* vi 3, Hieron *Catal* 54; Phot *B.* 118, Nicephorus, *H E* iv 33
,, 213 232	Origen	Heraclas	Eus *H E* vi 16, Hieron *Catal* 54
,, 232	Heraclas		Eus *H E* vi 26
,, 233-265	Dionysius	.	Eus *H E* vi 29, Hieron *Catal* 69; Phil Sidet, Niceph v 18
,, 265-280	Pierius		Phil Sidet, Photius, *B* 118; Eus vii 32, Hieron *Catal.* 76, Nic vi 35
,, 280-282	Pierius	*Achillas*	Eus *H E* vii 32, Nic *H E* vi 35
,, 282-290	Theognostus	*Achillas*	
,, 290	Theognostus		Phil Sidet
,, 290-295	Serapio		Phil Sidet, Epiphan *Hær* lxix 2
,, 295-312	Peter Martyr		Phil Sidet, Eus *H E* viii 13
,, 313 320	Arius	.	Theodoret, *H E* i. 1
,, 320 330	(Vacancy)		
,, 330-340	*Macarius*		Phil Sidet, Sozom, *H E* iii 14
,, 340 390	Didymus		Phil Sidet, Socr *H E* iv 23; Sozom *H E* iii 15, Ruff *H E* ii 7.
,, 390-395	Didymus	Rhodon	
,, 395	Rhodon		Teacher of Philip Sidetes

[1] Τοῦ διδασκαλείου τοῦ ἐν Ἀλεξανδρείᾳ Ἀθηναγόρας πρῶτος ἡγήσατο [Dodw p 488]

The head of this school had occasionally a coadjutor or assistant in the work of teaching, the various instances of which are tabulated above The appointment of the principal teacher was vested in the bishop, as seen in the appointment of Origen by Demetrius [Eus *H E* vi 3, Hieron *Catal.* 54], and his subsequent deposition [Eus *H E* vi 26, Hieron *Ep ad Paul.* 29], of Arius, who was appointed and also removed from the office by Achillas [A D 313] Ἀχιλλᾶς . Ἄρειον . τοῦ ἐν Ἀλεξανδρείᾳ διδασκαλείου προΐστησιν [Ararsius Papp *Synodic* i. 1494; Theodoret, *H E* i 2]; and of Didymus, who received his appointment from Athanasius [Ruffin *H E* ii 7]. There appears to have been no endowment of any kind, but the teacher received an honorarium from those who were able to pay for their instruction, while poorer students were admitted gratis In some instances, the teacher having private means, did his work for the pure love of souls, as was the case with Origen [Eus *H. E* vi 3], possibly also with Pierius, who "appetitor voluntariæ paupertatis fuit" [Hieron *Catal* 76] Since the teachers of the Museum received a state stipend, it is quite possible that the catechetical school was placed on a similar footing after the conversion of Constantine [Cassiodorus, *Præf Inst div. Scr*] The place of instruction appears to have been no public building, but some apartment in the private dwelling of the teacher, or hired for the purpose. The school gradually decayed after the removal of Rhodon, the instructor of Philip, to Sida in Pamphylia, from whence the pupil took his name of Sidetes or Sidensis.

III The spirit of the Museum determined the bearings of the Christian school at Alexandria, but it was chiefly by way of contrast The Christian teacher could shew a definite creed, his religion, as a heaven-descended system, was capable of formal proof, its followers showed a love for it that was strong as death, and they died in numbers of every age and of both sexes, rather than forswear that love The heathen teacher, on the other hand, had none of these advantages He had no creed; his philosophy was an intellectual system without warmth or definite colour, its highest excellence was the sense of duty that it inculcated Its teachers may have felt some degree of enthusiasm for systems that they helped to create, but their hearers were bound together by no catholic bond of unity, and were ready at any time to modify the teaching of the schools, and eliminate or enlarge, as suited the particular syncretistic taste of the individual. Hence arose a continual clash of jealousy between the Christian and heathen schools of Alexandria. There was sufficient similarity in certain broad features of either system to enhance the bitterness of difference The one could scarcely be understood without the other, but they eventually misunderstood each other The Eclecticism of Philo gave a substratum of mystic thought to both of these schools [MYSTICS PLOTINUS NEO-PLATONISM.] A Platonic realism was common to both that has run as a thread of gold through the speculative efforts of the human race from earliest ages. It is seen to pervade the Hindu system, it gave to Moses the "pattern," or heavenly counterpart of earthly things, in the Mount, and was received traditionally by Plato, rather than evolved by him from the germ Human thought seems so completely tinged and instinct with the realistic idea, as to suggest its descent by an unbroken tradition, the perpetual voice of living witnesses, from the very cradle of the human race Each of the two schools of Alexandria, Christian and heathen, taught it as an essential aspect of the truth, nor has the teaching ever died out again The schools of the middle ages, and the philosophy of the Reformation period, were eminently based on Platonic realism, which has supplied also the proper elements from whence Kant and Fichte and Hegel have distilled over the more subtle spirit of their later philosophic creeds. At Alexandria both the heathen and the Christian teacher maintained that the attainment of truth should unite man in spirit and intellect with God, but their respective methods were in an inverse order Philosophers held that it was for man to seek after God, *εἰ ἄρα γε ψηλαφήσειαν αὐτόν* [Acts xvii. 27], the Christian teacher announced from the revealed Word that God sought man out, and drew him with cords of love to Himself, and to a sense of his high birthright which had been lost to him in Adam, but found again in Christ The truth declared that the Good Shepherd sought His erring sheep in the wilderness, it was heathen perversion to say that the animal instinct of the wanderer led it back to its owner. Man, said the Neo-Platonist, must ascend up to the Divine, but there must first be a descent of the Divine, argued the Christian teacher, before the human principle can be in any sense assimilated to it, flame touches flame, and is united into one body of glory, but it must first find a nature with which it can coalesce and harmonize. There were principles then in the old philosophy that were not wholly repugnant to Christianity, and *in tanto* they offered an important means of approach to the heathen mind, of which the Christian teacher at Alexandria diligently availed himself Clement professedly aimed at embodying all the learning of the day in his Christian teaching, and the substance of his lectures was termed by him Στρωμάτεις—Miscellanies "Quicquid *habent* homines nostri est farrago libelli"

IV The methodical practice of class teaching based upon Scripture caused a wide induction of Scriptural fact, and nearly every book of Scripture is cited in the remains of teachers of this school that have come down to us, Clement of Alexandria and Origen being the principal sources. We may describe the Alexandrian canon from these fragmentary sources, as exactly as from the venerable Codex A. Origen supplies us with quotations and lengthened extracts from every book of the present canon, and he cites the Apocrypha as being of almost equal authority, the Book of Baruch, however, being assigned by him, as by Clement, to Jeremiah Dionysius and Didymus make a similar use of the deutero-canonical writings, more especially of Ecclesiasticus and Wisdom, while Clement cites also the fourth book of Esdras Gnostic contempt for the Old Testament perhaps caused the catechist to raise even doubtful books to the canonical level, where there was no antecedent objection to their contents The canon of the New Testament is similarly confirmed Of the four Gospels Origen declares that St. Matthew's first existed in a Hebrew form, and that a copy of it was found by Pantænus in India, both Origen and Clement term that of St John the "Spiritual Gospel," and they establish the authenticity of the Acts of the Apostles and Pauline Epistles, from whence Athenagoras also quotes The Epistle to the Hebrews is assigned to St. Paul by Pantænus, Origen, Dionysius, and Didymus, while Clement adds that it was written by him in Hebrew and translated by St Luke The authenticity of the Catholic Epistles, 1 John, 1 Peter and Jude, is affirmed, without however denying the authority of the rest · Didymus alone declaring in one place that the second Epistle of St Peter is interpolated and of no authority, while he makes use of it, as canonical, in his treatise *de Trinitate.* With respect to the Apocalypse, Dionysius was induced, by internal evidence, as he considered, to refer it to some other author than St John, with whom his predecessors, including Clement and Origen, had always associated it The labours of Origen on the Sacred Text, as shewn in his Hexapla, would have been in the highest degree valuable, if they had been guided by a sound critical judgment As it is, the true text of the LXX has only become worse confounded by the very means that were intended to secure it from error

V The hermeneutical principles of a catechetical school must always determine its value Unfortunately for the Alexandrian School, its principal exponent Clement had learned from Athenagoras and Pantænus to consider the allegorical method of Philo to be the true key for unlocking the hidden sense of Scripture But he was by no means a type of the rest Origen, with whom he was associated, followed more closely the plain grammatical method of the ANTIOCHEAN SCHOOL, and limited the application of allegory by certain rules. Pierius followed in his steps, and Dionysius sought throughout the moral sense of Scripture. Peter and Didymus also were almost entirely free from the allegorizing tendency of Clement. The truer exegesis of the Antiochean School superseded the allegorizing interpretation copied from Philo

There was nothing peculiar in the dogmatic or positive theology of this school, and space need not be occupied in describing that which was in truth the doctrine of the Church Catholic The various heads are examined by Guerike in his valuable exercise on the Alexandrian Catechetical School, to which work the reader is referred [Guerike, *de Schola quæ Alexandriæ floruit*, II. iii DICT *of* THEOL s v]

ALEXIANS [LOLLARDS]

ALMARIC [AMALRICIANS]

ALOGI This name was given by Epiphanius to those who denied St John's doctrine concerning the Logos, and who consequently rejected St John's writings

The term was not intended to imply that there was a distinct organized sect so called, but was adopted to describe a heresy common to not a few sects, and important enough to bring all who held it into one class, theologically considered, although they were formed into several bodies This is to be noticed because, while some writers of high authority, as Westcott [*Introduction to Gospels*, p 240], speak of a sect called Alogi, Lardner [*History of Heretics*, chap xxiii] says that there was never any such heresy, that there was no sect or number of Christians who rejected St John's Gospel and the Revelation, and ascribed both to Cerinthus, while they received the other books of the New Testament The former writer did not intend to assert that all the Alogi were united into one separate body; the latter cannot be thought to assert that there did not exist the heresy of denying St John's doctrine. Allowing then that there was, strictly speaking, no separate sect of Alogi, it remains for inquiry whether Lardner, who deals with the Alogi in a somewhat offhand manner, was justified in saying that there was no number of Christians who rejected St John's Gospel. Philaster [*Hær* lx] describes the heresy without using the name Augustine [*Hær* xxx] speaks of the name as in use "Alogi sic vocantur quia Deum Verbum recipere noluerunt, Johannis Evangelium respuentes" Similarly the author of *Prædestinatus* and Isidore of Seville

The two great facts which the Catholic Christian holds in this matter are the Divinity of the personal Word, and the Incarnation of that Word "The Word was with God, and was God" "The Word was made flesh, and dwelt among us" The rejection of the former brings us to the Monarchians, who affirmed that there was no real distinction between the Father and the Son, the rejection of the second to those who separated the Word from the Christ Thus Theodotus, who comes next in Epiphanius' catalogue, denied the Incarnation of the Word, asserting Jesus to have been a mere man who received Christ by the descent of the Holy Spirit upon Him in Jordan Theodotus is said by Epiphanius to have been an offshoot from the Alogi But the Arians, though they did not hold St John's doctrine, yet would not be classed among the Alogi For they did not altogether deny the Logos they wished to establish that the Son was only the λόγος προφορικὸς, by which they assigned to Him a beginning; inasmuch as the thought must precede the sound which gives it utterance Epiphanius appears to have confined his new term to those who altogether denied the Logos, and with this view to have made the rejection of St John's Gospel the test of Alogian doctrine The Arians did not reject the fourth Gospel, they tried to explain away the force of its words

Fabricius states that the Ebionites, Cerinthians, Cerdonians, Theodotians, and Marcionites, rejected St. John's Gospel. Lardner remarks, "How groundless that supposition is must clearly appear from our accounts of Theodotus, Praxeas, and others of that principle" Now the Ebionites used St. Matthew's Gospel only [Iren i 26, iii 11, 7, Euseb *H E* iii 27, Epiph *Hær* xxx sec 3], the Cerinthians only St. Matthew [Epiph *Hær* xxviii 5 and xxx 3, 14; Philast *Hær* xxxvi]; the Cerdonians only St Luke, and that mutilated [Pseudo-Tert xvi], the Theodotians rejected St. John's Gospel, if Epiphanius is to be credited, for be affiliates them to the Alogi, having defined the Alogi by that very rejection [*Hær* liv], the Marcionites used only St Luke [Iren iii 11, 6, Tert *Adv Marc* iv 5] These authorities strengthen each other, particularly with regard to Cerdo and Marcion In reply to them Lardner urges, with regard to the Ebionites, that St John is quoted in the Clementine Homilies To which we answer, that the practice of the writer of the Homilies cannot set aside the evidence of the tenets of the Ebionites in general It follows only that in this respect the writer did not faithfully represent the school to which he belonged [Lardner, *Credib* xxix 5] With regard to the Cerinthians it is said [*Hist. of Her* iv 6] that Philaster's evidence is not supported by others and needs not to be much minded, and that Epiphanius argues against Cerinthus from St John's Gospel, which implies that Cerinthus respected it Philaster is supported by Epiphanius, and Epiphanius, writing not in immediate controversy with Cerinthus, but for the benefit of the Church at large, quotes that which the Church received That Marcion rejected St John could not of course be denied Lardner thinks that in this respect he went beyond Cerdo [*Hist of Her* ix 4] But the close resemblance of the doctrines of Cerdo and Marcion, with the teaching of Cerdo, that the God proclaimed by the law and the prophets was not the Father of our Lord Jesus Christ, makes it far more probable that the evidence of Pseudo-Tertullian is correct [Iren i 27, Hippol *Ref* vii 25, x. 15] And if the appendix to the *De Præscr Hæret* is a translation of Hippolytus' early work, its authority is high It being thus proved that there were certain sects which rejected St John's Gospel, there is no reason to doubt Epiphanius' statement that Theodotus followed them in this as he did in the main feature of their doctrine His argument from a passage in St John was only an "argumentum ad hominem," drawn from a book which his opponents believed

Epiphanius goes on to state that the Alogi attributed not only the Apocalypse, but St John's writings generally, to Cerinthus If this statement be accepted, it can only be said, that "some theory was necessary to account for the origin of the Gospel, and as one of the Apostle's writings had already been assigned to Cerinthus, this was placed in the same category, in spite of its doctrinal character" [Westcott, *on the Canon*, p. 308] But it is far more likely that with Philaster we should limit the statement to the Apocalypse.

In the case of these sects, from the Cerinthians downwards, which rejected St John's Gospel, that rejection was an almost necessary consequence of their doctrine, and was not much considered in and for itself But when the rejection of the Gospel was used in opposition to other doctrines or practices, it became in itself more noticeable It came forward into the front of controversy. This was the case when, in opposition to the pretensions of the Montanists, it was urged that the fourth Gospel was spurious It was the consideration of this controversy that led Epiphanius to give a distinctive name to those who rejected the Gospel After describing the Montanists and allied sects, he proceeds to the new heresy of the Alogi That the Montanists were met by an assertion of the spuriousness of the fourth Gospel, is noticed by Irenæus [iii 11, 9]. The passage has been variously interpreted, and is as follows. "Alii vero ut donum Spiritus frustrentur, quod in novissimis temporibus secundum placitum Patris effusum est in humanum genus, illam speciem non admittunt, quæ est secundum Johannis Evangelium, in qua Paracletum se missurum Dominus promisit, sed simul et Evangelium, et propheticum repellunt Spiritum. Infelices vere, qui pseudo-prophetæ quidem esse volunt, propheticæ vero gratiam repellunt ab Ecclesia similia patientes his, qui propter eos qui in hypocrisi veniunt, etiam a fratrum communicatione se abstinent" Here the comparison made with those who abstain from true communion in order to avoid hypocritical communicants, shews that they who refused the grace of prophecy did so to avoid false prophets Consequently we must adopt Gieseler's correction [*Compend* i p 150], and read "qui pseudoprophetas quidem esse volunt" They declare their opponents to be false prophets, and thrust away from the Church the grace of prophecy The passage written when Irenæus was favourable, as Neander remarks, to the pretensions of Montanus, is to be referred to those afterwards called Alogi

To interpret the passage of the Montanists has three difficulties It accuses them of a purpose of frustrating the gifts of the Spirit, when they were claiming the fulness of those gifts, it makes them say that they wish to be false prophets (if the words are taken ironically, irony requires that we should say, "they wish forsooth to be true prophets"), and it entirely mars the pertinency of the closing comparison That at the time Irenæus wrote [about A D 185] he should have regarded the Montanist pretensions favourably is nothing wonderful. Many did so, and at a later time the Bishop of Rome, probably Victor, was on the point of admitting the Montanists to his communion. [MONTANISTS]

Turning to Epiphanius, we find a passage on the same subject [*Hær* li cap 33] He is speaking of those who rejected the Apocalypse, and who objected that there existed no church at Thyatira, and he meets them by arguing that the state of Thyatira is a fulfilment of St John's prophecy "Ἐνοικησάντων γὰρ τούτων ἐκεῖσε καὶ τῶν κατὰ Φρύγας [οἱ μὲν], δίκην λύκων ἁρπαξάντων τὰς διανοίας τῶν ἀκεραίων πιστῶν, μετήνεγκαν τὴν πᾶσαν πόλιν εἰς τὴν αὐτῶν αἵρεσιν, οἵ τε [οἱ δὲ] ἀρνούμενοι τὴν Ἀποκάλυψιν τοῦ λόγου τούτου εἰς ἀνατροπὴν κατ' ἐκείνου καιροῦ ἐστρατεύοντο" The words in brackets are corrections adopted by Giesler If we follow the uncorrected text, as it stands in Oehler's edition, it must be concluded that at Thyatira the Alogi and the Montanists joined forces Nor is there any difficulty in supposing this, for Hippolytus, writing from thirty-five to forty years later than Irenæus, tells us that a branch of the Montanists adopted Noetian tenets [*Refut* viii 12] As Noetians it would be natural to them to reject the fourth Gospel, and as Montanists, who claimed the Paraclete exclusively to themselves, it would suit them to reject the Gospel which expressly promises the Paraclete to the Apostles The corrections adopted by Gieseler shew the parties, as before, in opposition According to the text which the reader chooses, will probably be his conclusion, whether the Montanists of Thyatira were of the Noetian branch or of the elder stock.

The use of the word ἄλογος in controversy with the Arians should be noticed [See Athan *De Decret Nic Syn* sec 16, *Orat* i *Cont Arian* sec. 19 and 24] Upon the first of these passages Newman remarks, "This is a frequent argument in the controversy, viz that to deprive the Father of His Son or substantial Word (λόγος) is as great a sacrilege as to deny His reason (λόγος), from which the Son receives His name" Thus [*Orat* i sec 14] Athanasius says, "Imputing to God's Nature an absence of His Word (ἀλογίαν, or irrationality), they are most irreligious" [*vid* sec 19, fin 24 *Select Treatises*, i p 25]

AMALRICIANS A school of mediæval Pantheists, who followed the opinions of Amalric of Bena, or Amaury of Bené (so called from his native town in the diocese of Chartres), a theologian and dialectician of Paris, in the end of the twelfth and the beginning of the thirteenth century Amalric attracted many to his lectures, in which he taught simple Pantheism, that 'all things are one, that is God, that all matter proceeded originally from God, and will return to Him" From this platform he advanced to the denial of many doctrines of the Church, and among other strange opinions taught that the Father was incarnate in Abraham, the Son in the Blessed Virgin, and the Holy Ghost in ourselves [Martene, *Thes Anecd* iv 163]. The opinions of Amalric were condemned by the University of Paris in the year 1204, and he was expelled from office He appealed personally to Pope Innocent III, but in 1207 the sentence of the University was confirmed, and Amalric returned to Paris by order of the Pope, to recant his heresies In 1209 Amalric died of grief, ten of his followers were burned as heretics by order of another council of Paris, and their leader's own remains were exhumed, burned, and the ashes scattered to the winds The fourth Lateran Council [A D 1215] confirmed the sentence passed against his heresies [PANTHEISM DAVID OF DINANT]

AMBROSIANS The followers of a French Anabaptist named Ambrose, who about 1559 professed to have special Divine revelations far transcending Holy Scripture in value. They called themselves "Pneumatiques," or Spirituals

AMMONIANS This name has sometimes been used to designate the school of Ammonius Saccas, the founder of Neo-Platonism in the second century [NEO-PLATONISTS MYSTICS]

AMSDORFIANS The party of Nicolas Amsdorf in the "Majoristic controversy" [A D 1552-4], a bitter dispute between George Major, a Lutheran divine of Wittenberg, and Amsdorf, who was Lutheran bishop of Naumburg, respecting the efficacy of good works to salvation Amsdorf was a strong supporter of Luther, and he is accused of going so far in adopting his leader's Solifidianism, as to have maintained that good works are a hindrance to salvation The controversy was brought to a close by the "Formula of Concord" drawn up between the two parties at Bergen, A D 1577

AMYRALDISTS A school of Calvinists who followed the opinions of Moses Amyraut, a distinguished French Protestant Professor of Divinity at Saumur, from A D 1633 to A D 1664 Amyraut was a man of much learning, and full of an anxious desire to promote union among the Calvinists, and between the Calvinists and the Church After the failure of an attempt made by order of Cardinal Richelieu to promote the latter, Amyraut turned his studies towards a reconciliation of the endless disputes about predestination and grace in his own sect. He maintained that God wishes the salvation of all men, that none are excluded from salvation by any Divine decree, that none can be saved except through belief in Christ, but that God gives all power to believe, and it is only through men's own default that they are not saved Those who adopted these opinions were called "Hypothetical Universalists," and they spread very widely among the French and Swiss Protestants in, perhaps, a more developed form of Universalism than that actually taught by Amyraut [Mosheim, *Eccl. Hist* iii 358, Stubbs' ed]

ANABAPTISTS [ἀνὰ—βαπτίζειν] This name was given at the Reformation to a body of extreme anti-sacerdotalists which came to the surface in the north-west of Germany, in Holland, and in Switzerland, contemporaneously with the movement headed by Luther in Germany, and by Zwingli in Switzerland Some of them also emigrated from Holland to England about A D 1525, and formed the nucleus of a sect which gave the government of the country great trouble for many years afterwards

It is not at all clear how re-baptism (an ancient heretical custom of the Novatians, the Donatists, and the Eunomians) came to be regarded as so distinctive a characteristic of these anti-sacerdotalists, that they should be called Anabaptists, or Re baptizers, for they very commonly (if not universally) repudiated the doctrine of our Lord's Incarnation, and held other equally conspicuous heresies But it is probable that their custom of re-baptism was enforced upon their adherents in a very strict and ostentatious manner, and that it thus formed the most notorious part of their system They were, in reality, the Reformation descendants of those many mediæval anti-sacerdotalists who went by the names of ALBIGENSES, BOGOMILES, HENRICIANS, PETROBRUSIANS, &c , and among all such sects there was a more or less developed antipathy to infant baptism [Hagenbach, *Hist of Doct* ii 85, Clark's transl], which was likely to lead eventually to Anabaptism In the later part of the sixteenth century, in Germany, and in the following century in England, the more sober sects of the MENNONITES and the BAPTISTS originated among the Anabaptists of the two countries, and gradually superseded them

The earliest historical notice of the Anabaptists as a sect is in association with certain religious and civil disturbances, originating with the ' prophets of Zwickau," which began in the year 1521, and culminated in a fierce civil war [ZWICKAU PROPHETS] The leader of these "prophets" was Thomas Munzer, the Lutheran pastor of Zwickau, who had read the works of the mystic Tauler so exclusively, that the dreamy mysticism of the master had turned the disciple into a wild fanatic Munzer was deposed from his post at Zwickau, and after a vain attempt to win support in Bohemia, betook himself to Altstadt in Thuringia, where he propagated his tenets for two years Those tenets were [1] that the true Word of God is not Holy Scripture, but an internal inspiration, [2] that the baptism of infants is unlawful, [3] that there must be a visible kingdom of Christ upon earth, and [4] that in the kingdom of Christ all must be equal, and must enjoy a community of goods At Altstadt, Munzer established a league for the formation of this new theocracy, and summoning the nobles to co-operate with him, he threatened them with civil war if they refused to do so He was not, at present, however, strong enough to carry out his threats, and being compelled to withdraw from Altstadt in 1524, he ventured upon a new settlement at Waldshut on the borders of Switzerland, Zwingli, Grebel, Stumpf, Hubmeyer, Hottinger, and others of the Zurich reformers, being already in correspondence with him From Waldshut the principles of Munzer quickly spread through some of the Swiss cantons, especially those of Zurich and St Gall, the fanaticism of his followers beginning to grow very extreme, one of them, named Thomas Schugger, for example, cutting off the head of his brother Leonard under the pretence that he was inspired to do so Zwingli endeavoured to stem the tide of fanaticism by a work against Anabaptism, and Bullinger was equally zealous against the fanatics, but Hubmeyer, Grebel, and others of the early Swiss "Reformers" cast in their lot with them entirely, while the Unitarians, Hetzer and Denck, found natural allies among those who denied (as they seem to have done from the first) the Incarnation of our Lord

At this crisis the long impending rebellion of the peasantry against the nobility broke out in Southern Germany, and in a short time spread through Swabia, Franconia, and Alsace This rebellion, commonly known as "The Peasants' War," was provoked by the tyrannical and extortionate habits of the feudal nobility, and was so far mixed up with religion, that of twelve articles in which the peasants stated their grievances, the first was a claim to appoint and depose their own pastors, while the second was a demand for more equitable collection of tithes by the lay-appropriators who had taken possession of them The peasants appealed to Luther, who partly recognised the justice of their complaints, but at the same time severely condemned their rebellion. To the opponents of the peasantry he wrote that the latter had incurred the guilt of dreadful sin of three kinds against God and man, for which they deserved death in body and soul many times over, for they had broken their allegiance, had plundered religious houses and castles, and had cloaked their doings with the Gospel "Therefore, dear masters," he continues, "come hither to deliver, hither to the rescue; have pity on the poor folk, stab, smite, throttle, who can, and if you perish in the work it will be a blessed death, a better than which you will never accomplish" [Luther's *Works*, xvi 91, Walch's ed 1737-53].

But if the communism of these ill-used serfs had no charms for Luther, it soon found a supporter, and they a leader, in Munzer Early in the year 1525 he returned to Thuringia, and re-established his parody of a theocracy in a more formidable shape than ever at Muhlhausen, a town which had been warned against him by Luther in a letter written so long previously as August 1524 Here he headed a fierce rebellion in the character of a prophet, signing himself "Munzer, with the sword of Gideon" His exhortations to the labouring classes were as savage as that of Luther to the nobles "Let not your sword cool in blood," he wrote to the miners of Mansfeld, "On! on! on! while ye have the day, God goes before you" [Luther's *Works*, Walch's ed. xvi 150] In his subsequent confession under torture [*ibid* 157], he said that "he had stirred up this rebellion in order to bring Christendom to an equality, and that the nobles and gentry who would not stand by the Gospel, and join his league when invited to do so in a brotherly manner, should be punished and put to death The first principle of the league was to have all things common, and whatsoever duke, count, or lord would not consent to this, should be beheaded or hung" The rebellion was crushed at the battle of Frankenhausen, on May 15, 1525, by an army under the command of the Elector of Saxony, the Landgrave of Hesse, and the Duke of Brunswick, Munzer and his subordinate leaders, Pfeifer and others, being taken and afterwards executed, vast numbers of the people also being slain

For a time the Anabaptists were suppressed as

an organized body, though a vast number of persons still held the opinions of Munzer, and were ready even to die for the maintenance of them when persecuted by their Lutheran opponents The sect, however, gradually regained its strength, until the new theocracy was once more established at Munster in Westphalia nine years after the death of Munzer This final struggle of Anabaptist communism was headed by a tailor of Leyden named John Bockhold Munster had become a stronghold of the sect under its Lutheran minister, Bernard Rothmann, and two of the burghers named Krechting and Knipperdolling. These had become allies of John Matthei, originally a baker, but established at Haarlem as a bishop by Melchior Hoffmann, who had in some degree filled the place of Munzer as leader of the sect Bockhold, Matthei, and Gerard Kippenbroeck, a bookbinder of Amsterdam, organized an insurrection at Munster for the same purpose as that which Munzer had in view, the formation of a theocratic kingdom They soon gained possession of the city, and proposed to carry their plans still further by the destruction of Leyden But before this could be effected Munster was besieged by the Count of Waldeck, its temporal lord and also its bishop. in a sortie against whose forces Matthei was slain After the death of Matthei, the tailor Bockhold was crowned king of the "New Jerusalem," under the title of John of Leyden, the churches were destroyed, and for twelve months the city was a scene of fanatic lawlessness and revolting profligacy, carried on under the name of religion Munster was taken on June 24th, 1535, and in the following January the dissolution of the new "Kingdom" was completed by the cruel torture and execution of its "King," whose body was for many years afterwards hung in chains as a warning to the citizens from the steeple of St Lambert's Church

Meanwhile, however, this primary idea of the Anabaptists had travelled to Amsterdam, Deventer, and Wesel, three towns which John of Leyden claimed as given him by God, and to which he had sent some of his fanatic partizans as apostles of sedition The leader of these at Amsterdam was Van Geelen, who formed a conspiracy among his converts to take the city out of the hands of the magistrates, and establish the new kingdom there also The insurrection which he raised was quickly suppressed, and its leaders put to death A similar result followed in other parts of Holland, where like attempts were made, and thenceforth the continental Anabaptists ceased from their endeavours to establish their principles by violence and rebellion In the year 1537, Menno became their leader and head and they subsided into a peaceable, though still a fanatical sect [MENNONITES DAVIDISTS], whose distinctive tenet was that of adult baptism [Luther's *Works*, Walch's ed vol xvii Zwingli's *Elenchus contra Catabaptistas*, 1527 Bullinger's *Von dem unverschampten, &c Leeren der selbsgesandten Widertouffern*, 1531 Strobel's *Leben Schriften und Lehren T Munzers*, 1795 Schlusselberg's *Catalog Hæreticorum*, lib xii Seideman's *Munzer*, 1842 Brandt's *Hist of Reformation*, i. 2.]

In England the Anabaptists are not distinctly traceable before the year 1534, although much similarity is to be observed between their principles and those of sectarians spoken of by the bishops in 1529 as "certain apostates, friars, monks, lewd priests, bankrupt merchants, vagabonds, and lewd idle fellows of corrupt intent," who "have embraced the abominable and erroneous opinions lately sprung in Germany" [Froude's *Hist of Eng* i 211] In A D 1534, however, a royal proclamation was issued, in which it is said that many strangers are come into this realm, who, although they were baptized in their infancy, yet have, in contempt of the Holy Sacrament of Baptism, rebaptized themselves They are ordered to depart out of the realm in twelve days, under pain of death [Wilkins' *Concil* iii 779] But they were probably refugees from the Netherlands, and the prospect of death at home was even more imminent than it was in England Certain it is that Cromwell has left a memorandum in his pocketbook, "First, touching the Anabaptists, and what the king will do with them" [Ellis' *Orig Lett* II ii 120], and that nineteen men and six women (all immigrants from Holland), who were examined in St. Paul's on May 25th, 1535, and subsequently burned as heretics, two in Smithfield and the rest in several country towns, appear to be those referred to by him [Stow's *Chron* p 571]

Fresh immigrations of the sect must have taken place after this, for on October 1st, 1538, Archbishop Cranmer and others received a commission from the Crown to take stringent measures for their suppression [Wilkins' *Concil* iii 836] The result was that a set of Injunctions were issued in the year 1539, restraining the importation of books and condemning the opinions of the Anabaptists [*ibid* 847] A few months afterwards, also an Act of Parliament was passed [32 Hen VIII cap 49], granting a general pardon to all the King's subjects, except those who said "that infants ought not to be baptized, and if they were baptized that they ought to be re-baptized when they came to lawful age" and some who hold other opinions, including those who say "that Christ took no bodily substance of our Blessed Lady" Some of the unfortunate people recanted, and bore faggots in token of their recantation; but others were burned like their predecessors [Stow's *Chron* p 579, Latimer's *Sermons*, i 144, ed 1824] They seem, however, to have gone on increasing in numbers On June 25th, 1549, Hooper writes from London to Bullinger "The Anabaptists flock to the place, and give me much trouble with their opinions respecting the Incarnation of the Lord for they deny altogether that Christ was born of the Virgin Mary according to the flesh" [Parker Soc *Orig Lett* 65] At a later date, June 29th, 1550, the same writer says that Kent and Essex are "troubled with the frenzy of the Anabaptists more than any other part of the kingdom" [*ibid* 87] A year later Martin Micronius writes from London to Bullinger, that the same heretics "are now beginning to shake our churches with greater violence than ever, as they deny the Conception of Christ by the Virgin" [*ibid* 574] and, meanwhile, the Act of 1540 had been re-enacted against them by the Parliament of Edward VI in 1549 [3 & 4 Edw VI ch 24]

The Anabaptists are said by Bishop Jewel, in a letter to Peter Martyr, dated Nov 6th, 1560, to have 'sprung up like mushrooms in the darkness and unhappy night of the Marian times" [Jewel's *Works*, iv 1240, Park Soc ed] In the same year Bishop Grindal received an anonymous letter, which he supposed to be written by Adrian Hamsted [ADRIANISTS], asking that they might have the free exercise of their religion, but their petition was not granted, and instead the Queen issued a proclamation, ordering all to depart the realm within twenty-one days. In April 1573, a letter was addressed to "the Dutch Church" in London by the Privy Council, rebuking them for sowing discord among English people, when they replied that they had only four English persons in their congregation, and that all four had come from abroad [Strype's *Ann Ref* iv 520] But on Easter Day 1575, a private conventicle of them was discovered near Aldersgate Bar, and twenty-seven were apprehended. "Of these, four recanted the following errors [1] That Christ took not flesh of the substance of the Virgin, [2] that infants born of faithful parents ought to be re-baptized, [3] that no Christian man ought to be a magistrate; [4] that it is not lawful for a Christian man to take an oath But others refusing to abjure, eleven of them (all Dutchmen) were condemned in the Consistory of St Paul's to be burnt, nine of whom were banished, and two suffered the extremity of the fire in Smithfield, July 22nd, 1575, viz John Wielmacker and Hendrick Ter Woort" [Neale's *Hist of Purit* i 340, ed 1732, Strype's *Ann Ref* iii 564, ed 1824] These were the last Anabaptists who were executed for their heresy in England, one named Edward Wightman (who was condemned for Anabaptism among other errors shortly after Bartholomew Legate had been burned for Arianism in 1611) being imprisoned for life in Newgate as a more humane mode of punishment.

It seems almost certain that the Anabaptists, who were thus so severely dealt with in England, were part of the very dangerous German sect which had been founded by Munzer and Bockhold and that, in the originally understood sense of the name, there were never many English Anabaptists Their opposition to infant baptism, their practice of re-baptizing adults, were inherited by the Baptist sects, who have not unfrequently been called Anabaptists. But there is no essential historical connection between the earlier and the later sects, and though the designation "Baptists" is less distinctive than that of "Anabaptists," historical clearness favours its use [BAPTISTS]

ANDRONICIANS A temporary name given to the ANGELITÆ, from Andronicus, bishop of the sect about A D 614

ANGELIC BROTHERS A Dutch community of theosophic Pietists founded by George Gichtel, who died at Amsterdam in the year 1710 They assumed their name from a belief that they had already attained the purity of that state in which the angels of God are, neither marrying nor giving in marriage. Gichtel left behind him a work entitled *Theosophia Practica*, which was published at Leyden in six volumes in 1722

ANGELICI A sect of this name is mentioned by Epiphanius, but he states that he knows nothing about them except the name, and can only conjecture that they were so called either because they believed the world to have been created by angels (as the Gnostics believed), or because they claimed to be so pure as to be already as the angels of God, or that they took their name from a country called Angelina which lay beyond Mesopotamia [Epiph *Hær* lx] St. Augustine names the sect on the authority of Epiphanius, adding, that they were worshippers of angels [Aug *Hær* xxxix] If there ever was a sect bearing this name it was probably obscure and local, or Epiphanius would have been able to say something more respecting it. But as Angelolatry was known even in the time of the Apostles [Col ii 18], and when forbidden by the 35th canon of the Council of Laodicæa is spoken of as being carried on in private conventicles, there is much probability that the worshippers of angels were called Angelici

ANGELICS An Anabaptist sect in Silesia and Bohemia assumed this name about A D 1596 [Sianda, *Lexic Polem*]

ANGELITÆ. A name assumed by the Alexandrian Jacobites from the first church of their sect, erected A.D 540, and called the Angelium The ecclesiastical historian Nicephorus accuses them of holding tritheistic opinions [Niceph *Hist Eccl* xviii 49], but it is probable that the name Angelitæ was given to other sects of the Monophysites including the TRITHEITES

ANGLICANS This designation has been given of late years to that section of the High Church school in the Church of England whose theology and ritual customs are principally formed on those of the seventeenth century divines The school may be called that of Andrewes and Laud, and inherits some of that narrowness and want of sympathy by which the seventeenth century divines were characterized in their dealings with foreign churches and with dissenters at home

ANGLO-CALVINISTS A controversial designation applied to the Church of England in ignorance of its true principles by Romanist theologians Thus Sianda writes "Anglo-Calviniani a Puritanis, cæterisque Reformatis differunt, tum in disciplina, tum in dogmatibus, Episcopalem enim ordinem admittunt . Christi trophæum, Crucem scilicet, non solum honorant, sed ejus signum Sacramentis, et in primis baptismo adhibent. . . Anglo-Calviniani Episcopi suos habent Cancellarios, Archidiaconos, Decanos, Cathedrales Ecclesias, in quibus sunt Canonici, seu Præbendarii, qui Matutinas ac Vespertinas preces celebrant, ignota et hæc omnia cæteris Calvinistis Liturgiam etiam suo ritu celebrant diebus sacris, et in eadem Litanias diebus Mercurii et Veneris recitant . et in functionibus suis obeundis superpelliceo utuntur." &c [Sianda, *Lexicon Polemicum*, *s v* PURITANI] The association of Calvin's name, authority, and doctrine, with the Church of England is wholly unjustifiable by the facts of history or by the formularies of the Church, but the "Low Church" school have done much to earn for themselves the name wrongly given to the Church of England by foreign writers

ANGLO-CATHOLICS. A name sometimes assumed by members of the Church of England as a protection against their common classification with sectarians under the word "Protestant." It is intended as a designation that shall express the claim of English Churchmen to be regarded as members of the Catholic Church at large (whether in the Eastern or the Western world) subject to those distinctive marks which characterize them as an ecclesiastical tribe or family

ANGLO-ROMANISTS A modern appellation given to the English sect of ROMAN CATHOLICS

"ANIMALES" A name of reproach used towards those who believed in the Resurrection of the Body by an early sect who had perverted the doctrine of Origen into a belief in a mere spiritual resuscitation There was never any sect of the name

ANNIHILATIONISTS Those who believe that the wicked will, sooner or later after death, cease to exist altogether

ANOMIANS [ANTINOMIANS]

ANOMŒANS The principal sect of the Arians, which took its name from its distinctive dogma, that the Second Person in the Holy Trinity is essentially or substantially different [ἀνόμοιος] from the First Person This sect of heretics originated at Antioch about A D. 350, forming a party headed first by Aetius and subsequently by Eunomius his secretary, and being designated also after the names of these two leaders [AETIANS EUNOMIANS.] They were not, however, in reality, a new sect so much as strict Arians of the old school who were developing the principle of their first leader in its logical form, in opposition to the SEMI-ARIANS, who dared not face the full argumentative consequences of the Arian dogma Hence they were also called EXUCONTIANS, with reference to the original statement of Arius himself that there was a time when the Son of God had no existence, while the Father was acknowledged to have existed eternally

After the Nicene Council [A D 325] the party of strict Arians rapidly contracted in numbers, and the Semi-Arians became the life of the movement which Arius had started They were also the Court party, and upon the death of the Emperor Constantine in A D 337 were openly supported against the Catholics by his son and successor Constantius They endeavoured, like all Court parties, to hush up all differences between the Arians and the Church by a middle course in which the extreme statements of their founder should be suppressed, and a broader line taken which might be hoped to comprehend large numbers of the orthodox as well as themselves The Anomœan movement under Aetius and Eunomius was an intellectual recoil against this theological compromise, but although it gave some trouble to the Semi-Arian leaders, it never attracted large numbers, the majority of the Arian sect still preferring the less definite, and so apparently more safe, line which had been struck out by Eusebius and his friends The Anomœans were also a purely intellectual party, rejecting all mystery, feeling, and moral discipline, from religion, and professing to rest it solely on dogmatic reason—that is, on a kind of mechanical logic, a system which was not likely to secure followers among the multitude Thus Eunomius denied that there was anything in Divine things which was beyond human understanding "If," he wrote, "some men's minds are so obtuse that it is beyond their power to comprehend anything, either of that which lies before their feet, or of that which is above their heads, yet it would not follow from this that the knowledge of true Being is unattainable by all the rest of mankind The minds of those who believe on the Lord should . not stop even with the generation of the Son of God They soar above this, in striving, out of an earnest desire for eternal life, to attain to the Highest" [Gregor Nyssen *Orat* x *adv Eunom*] On this principle the Anomœan leaders professed to understand the exact nature of the Divine Essence, and the exact manner in which the Son of God originally came into existence

This logical revival of normal Arianism was supported by the influence of Eudoxius, who was Bishop of Antioch when it first took shape in the hands of Aetius, and afterwards of Constantinople Its principal opponent in the first instance was Basil of Ancyra in Galatia, a Semi-Arian bishop, but it was afterwards met by a more efficient antagonist, St Gregory of Nyssa The Semi-Arian party at Court endeavoured to suppress it on their usual policy of comprehension, and set forth at their partizan Synod of Sirmium [A D 357] a creed, or statement of faith, which the Eunomian party found no difficulty in subscribing Basil of Ancyra, considering this as a preliminary to the triumph of the Anomœans, obtained a very distinct exposition and condemnation of their tenets at the Synod of Ancyra [A D 358], and this having brought them prominently to the notice of the Emperor Constantius, he determined to convene a General Council for the purpose of setting all differences at rest By the influence of the Court party under the leadership of Ursacius, bishop of Singidunum in Mœsia, and Valens, bishop of Mursa in Pannonia, the projected council was broken up into two parts, the one composed of Eastern bishops and meeting at Seleucia in Syria, the other of Western bishops and meeting at Ariminum in Italy [A D 359] At both these councils the Anomœans were ultimately overpowered and condemned by the Semi-Arian bishops To the verdict of the Seleucian Council the Anomœans opposed that of a synod held by their ally Acacius at Antioch [A D. 363], but their principles received a final and decisive blow at the second Œcumenical Council held at Constantinople [A D 381], when they were condemned in the first canon, and by the seventh canon forbidden to be received into the Church except by orthodox Baptism [AETIANS ARIANS EUDOXIANS EUNOMIANS. Epiphan. *Hæres* lxxvi Gregor Nyss *adv. Eunom*]

ANSELM, ST [SCHOOLMEN.]

ANTHROPOMORPHITES Those who hold that the Almighty has a material body of human shape.

This error must be carefully distinguished from an error held by some Fathers of the early Church, who, in order to maintain the true Being and Personality of God, thought themselves obliged to assert the existence of a Divine σῶμα or Corpus They shrunk from a clear statement of the incorporeity of God, and therefore could not deny that the μορφὴ Θεοῦ [Phil. ii. 6] implies a shape or figure [see Cyril Alex *adv Anthrop*] Tertullian translates it by "effigies," but they abstained from describing its parts and shape, and struggled, in the use of contradictory terms, to declare the spirituality of the body, of the σῶμα ἀσώματον, without which they thought that the Deity would be reduced to an impersonal power

The error of these Fathers must be noticed in the first place, for evidently it might be easily developed into the grosser error of Anthropomorphism, and there are indications that it did lead to this result

Melito of Sardis, Tertullian, and Phœbadius have been charged with holding that God is not incorporeal Of Tertullian's opinions we have full statements He laid down the general axiom, "Omne quod est corpus est sui generis Nihil est incorporale nisi quod non est" [Tertull *De Carne Chr* 11] And accordingly he asked, "Quis enim negabit Deum corpus esse, etsi Deus spiritus est? Spiritus enim corpus sui generis in sua effigie?" [Tertull *adv Prax* 7] In the paragraph which contains this passage "corpus" is opposed to "vacua et inanis res," and "effigies" is the translation of μορφή in Phil ii 6 Again we read, "Et materia enim Deus, secundum formam divinitatis, innata scilicet, et infecta, et æterna" [Tertull *adv Marc.* i 15], where the words "secundum formam divinitatis" qualify the word "materia," and refer it to the very οὐσία of the Deity, declared in the former passage to be "spiritus" The extent of this qualification is shewn by the words, "Deum immutabilem et informabilem credi necesse est, ut æternum" [Tertull *adv Prax.* 27] Accordingly Tertullian expressly rejects Anthropomorphism [Tertull *adv Marc* ii. 5].

Augustine therefore [Aug *de Hær.* lxxxvi.] declares that Tertullian was not held to be heretical for this opinion, and explains his meaning "Potuit propterea putari corpus Deum dicere, quia non est nihil, non est inanitas, non est corporis vel animæ qualitas, sed ubique totus, et per locorum spatia nulla partitus, in sua tamen natura atque substantia immutabiliter permanet"

Gennadius classes Melito with Tertullian, and distinguishes the error he imputes to them from that of Anthropomorphism He says that we are to hold in the Deity "nihil corporeum, ut Melito et Tertullianus nihil corporaliter effigiatum, ut Anthropomorphus et Vadianus" [Gennad *de Eccl Dogm* iv] Melito's book, Περὶ ἐνσωμάτου Θεοῦ, is stated by Origen to have been on this subject. Origen's words shew, as Routh observes, that those who held with Melito defended his opinion by the language of Scripture, which attributes bodily members to God, and speaks of God appearing in human form. In the absence of fuller information, the inference from these premisses appears to be, that Melito advanced the same opinion as Tertullian, that his followers were passing into Anthropomorphism, and that Origen, seeing the evil, opposed the original tenet and asserted the entire immateriality of the Divine nature Phœbadius repeats Tertullian's words [Phœbad *cont Arian* c xx in Gallandi *Bibl.* v 255]

These Fathers then are by no means to be charged with Anthropomorphism, but it seems to be impossible to assert, however they extenuated their doctrine, that they held the substance or οὐσία of the Deity to be entirely "void of corporeal bulk and concretion" Whence then came this notion? It appears to have resulted from opposition to the Gnostic conception of the Supreme Being, to the notion of Bythus, one dwelling apart in the tranquillity of an unfathomable depth, the world being made and governed by inferior powers This, whether avowedly or not, represented an impersonal power In opposition to this the doctrine of a Personal God ruling the world was to be maintained Now all the words which language can supply to denote the substance of God must be metaphorical, as *spirit*, which is *aerial matter*, or negative, as *incorporeal*, *immaterial* The negative terms lent themselves more ready to the conception which was to be opposed, and the metaphorical terms were insisted on, and interpreted literally [1] In the Clementine Homilies St Peter (the ideal of orthodoxy according to the Essene-Ebionite school) is accused by Simon Magus (the impersonation of heresy), of maddening the mind by the terrible image of the shape of God Simon Magus argues, if God has a form (μορφή) He must have a shape (σχῆμα) St Peter accepts the inference, but adds, His members are for beauty's sake, not for use There is here in argument the very misapprehension of the term μορφή which appears in Tertullian's rendering it by "effigies," and which appears again, without Tertullian's contradiction of the conclusion drawn from it, in Gennadius' description of Anthropomorphism, "corporaliter

[1] See Bentley's *Remarks on Freethinking*, i cap. 10.

effigiatum" Melito's followers already named drew the same conclusion [1] The more common source, however, of Anthropomorphism is, not the depravation of the doctrine of learned and thoughtful men, but the grosser and material notions of the illiterate The difficulty of forming the conception of a purely spiritual personality, the strong metaphorical language of the Hebrew Scriptures, the carrying on that language into Christianity, the reproduction of that language to the eye by pictures and images, inevitably occasion an Anthropomorphism in popular Christianity It is better, doubtless, to have this conception of a personal God than to lose the sense of His Personality, but from time to time the conception, generally indistinct, is defined into a settled dogma Such was the case with the followers of the Syrian monk Audæus [AUDIANS] Of Audæus himself little is known, but his followers, adopting a monastic life, fell into Anthropomorphism, and Epiphanius [*Hær* lxx] and Theodoret [*Hist Eccl* iv 10] state that he was the first to interpret of outward form the image of God in which man is made Recluses, brooding over Scripture imagery, their minds often in an unhealthy state, are peculiarly liable to such an error [2] The author of *Prædestinatus* names Zenon, a Syrian bishop, as a chief opponent of the Audians Other monks besides the Audian fell from the same cause into the like error The recluses of Egypt were for the most part Anthropomorphites [Socr *H E* vi 7] Socrates notices this under the reign of Arcadius and Honorius, when the Anthropomorphite controversy was mixed up with the Origenist controversy, and the discreditable proceedings of Theophilus of Alexandria afforded more matter for history Origen was a warm defender of the incorporeity of the Divine Nature, and those who opposed him in matters more doubtful were led by the mere spirit of contradiction to oppose him in this point too, while Anti-Origenists were often accused without cause of Anthropomorphism Such a charge was brought against Epiphanius by John of Jerusalem. In the year 399, Theophilus in a paschal epistle denounced Anthropomorphism The monks who held that opinion rose against him, he pacified them, not without dissimulation, condemned Origen, and used the fanaticism of the monks and their hatred of Origen to further his own designs. Socrates states that the controversy might have been put to rest if Theophilus had not encouraged it, to revenge himself upon four monks known as the Long Brothers of Nitria. About the year 433 Cyril of Alexandria wrote against this heresy, still prevailing among the monks of Egypt.

After the fifth century, Anthropomorphism appears only among the ruder and more ignorant sections of the Church The teaching of Origen and other Fathers of the Church destroyed the fundamental misconception by which Tertullian and Melito had given some occasion for the growth of the heresy among the more educated. Among the untaught, the use of pictures representing the Father Himself in human form has, no doubt, caused an undercurrent of Anthropomorphic opinion in the Church, which has from time to time come to the surface, or has been detected by the vigilance of bishops The most prominent instance of this was in the tenth century, at Vicenza Ratherius, bishop of Verona, A D 939, found his diocese in such ignorance that many of his priests could not say the creed, and many priests and people believed the pictures they were accustomed to see on the walls were true representations of the court of heaven, of the forms of angels, and of the Most High Himself Ratherius was a reforming bishop, and there can be little doubt that what he discovered and combated at Vicenza passed unnoticed in many other dioceses [Ratherius' *Sermons* in D'Achery's *Spicileg* ii 294-98, ed 1657] Anthropomorphism is not professed in any part of Christendom, although probably popular Christianity is much tinged with it It has taken refuge among the Mormons

By the rulers of the Church Anthropomorphism, as a popular error, has been left to the correction of the clergy It is a misinterpretation of the first article of the creed to be dealt with by instruction, and not requiring the anathemas of councils It is impossible to form a true conception of spiritual substance, to hold the possibility of its existence is beyond many an untrained mind, faith, love, and obedience are compatible with an indistinct notion that God has an ethereal or luciform body, and there is danger of driving men into atheism if their error on this point be rudely handled

In a more technically theological manner, Anthropomorphism is denied in the decision that the nature of God is simple For they who attribute any materiality to God (and materiality is implied in the notion of figure and shape), must hold either that the very essence of Deity is material, or that the nature of God is compounded —that He is Mind residing in a corporeal vehicle The former is the worst and most extended form of materialism, and its consequences most impious The decision that the nature of God is simple denies the latter, and with it the possibility of Anthropomorphism Accordingly Chrysostom sums up the argument in three pregnant words, ὁ γὰρ Θεὸς ἁπλοῦς καὶ ἀσύνθετος καὶ ἀσχημάτιστος [*De Incomp D Nat*, *Hom* iv] The fourth Lateran Council determined that in God there is "Una essentia, substantia, seu natura simplex omnino." Whatever be the authority of the fourth Lateran Council, this is undoubtedly a Catholic conclusion The form (μορφή) of God is His necessary attributes, which are logically distinguishable but not separable from His being, the image of God is His Word, the image of the Word is the true man,[3] the mind which is in man, assimilated

[1] See Routh's *Reliq Sac* i 143, Liebermann, *Instit Theol* ii p 30, Pearson's *Minor Theol Works*, i 47, Prof Lightfoot, *Comment on Philipp* note, p 125

[2] Cyril's Treatise was occasioned by the reports brought him of the monks of Mount Calamon

[3] Clemens Alex *Protrept* cap x p 82, ed Klotz Compare cap xii p 101, εἰκόνα τοῦ Θεοῦ μεθ' ὁμοιώσεως. And for the perversion of the meaning given to the truth, see Cyril, *adv Anthrop* cap vi

to the Divine Word in the affections of the soul

ANTI-ADIAPHORISTS The rigid Lutherans, as distinguished from the Melanchthon or Interim party [ADIAPHORISTS]

ANTIBURGHERS The title assumed by a body which separated from the Associate Synod, or Secession Kirk, in Scotland, in the year 1746, and which derived its name from its members objecting to the oath imposed upon burgesses in some corporate towns. The statement of their views, and of the cause of the separation, will be found under the head BURGHERS, which was the title by which the other portion of the dissociated Associates was henceforward distinguished Their number, at the time of the schism, consisted of twenty-three ministers and elders, as opposed to thirty-two on the other part As if the ground of difference involved an article of the Christian faith, they immediately excluded from Church fellowship and communion all who would not at once adopt their view, and deposed and excommunicated all the "Burgher" ministers The leader in their movement, Mr Thomas Mair, minister at Orwell, however, a few years after, repented of the part he had taken, and was himself then ejected by his Antiburgher brethren "as an erroneous person, for maintaining that Christ, *in some sense*, died for all mankind" [Brown's *Rise and Progress of the Secession*] At the time of the separation, the teachers of philosophy and divinity in the Associate Synod happened to espouse the Antiburgher view, and in consequence most of the students went along with them, which for a time gave a preponderance in number of ministers to their party At the close of the last century, the influence of new political principles, derived from the revolutionary spirit of France, gave rise to a discussion on the power assigned to the civil magistrate, as to matters of religion, in the Presbyterian standards of doctrine, the old Covenanting views were regarded as too strict and intolerant, and as requiring modification to meet the spirit of the times, while the sanction given by them to the principle of Establishments was impugned by advocates of new Voluntaryism After much discussion, a new "Testimony," or Declaration of Principles, was adopted in 1804, which relaxed the statements of the old "Testimony" on these points But this change gave rise to a new separation. Dr Thomas M'Crie (the well-known author of the *Life of Knox*, &c, who had at his own ordination claimed to sign the Standards with reservations, but had afterwards abandoned his youthful views), in company with three other ministers (Professor Archibald Bruce, author of *Free Thoughts on the Toleration of Popery*, James Aitken and James Hog), established in August 1806 the "Constitutional Associate Presbytery," so named as claiming to adhere "to the true constitution of the Reformed Church of Scotland" This body was also popularly called the "Old Light Antiburghers" It is remarkable that this obscure party of Scottish Dissenters were strenuous advocates for National Establishments, and a pamphlet written by Dr. M'Crie in vindication of their proceedings, is described as being still a very valuable argument on the Voluntary controversy [1] On May 18th, 1827, they were united with a body which, with the wonderful power of infinite multiplication possessed by sects, had been formed in 1820 by persons dissatisfied with the union which then took place between the Burgher and New Light Antiburgher Synods [BURGHERS], and which was called the "Associate Synod of Protesters," the joint societies took the name of "Associate Synod of Original Seceders" They still number twenty-eight congregations, of which two are in Ireland, in 1838 they had thirty-six congregations. [J Brown of Haddington, *Historical Account of the Secession*, 8th edit 1802. J M'Kerrow, *Hist of the Secession*. Thomas M'Crie, *Life of Dr M'Crie*, 1840 BURGHERS SECESSION]

ANTI-CALVINISTS [ARMINIANS]

ANTIDICOMARIANITES The name given to some heretics who appeared in Arabia, Rome, and elsewhere, in the latter part of the fourth century. By St Augustine they are called Antidicomaritæ, and they are spoken of also as Antimarites and Antimarians The principle of the heresy is embodied in the word, "Opposers of Mary" They denied the perpetual virginity of the Blessed Virgin Mary, maintaining that she was the natural mother of those who are in the Gospels called the brethren of the Lord The name was revived for a short period in the 15th century, in regard to the controversy of the Immaculate Conception of the Virgin "Aliam præterea Antimaritæ nostri (quos eo nomine nuncupamus, quod syncerissimæ puritati Beatæ Mariæ sint contrarii et oblectantes) rationem adducunt," &c [*Concilium Basiliense*, A D. 1431 Bail's *Summa Conciliorum Omnium*, Paris, 1675, i 512]

These views were developed from the teaching of Apollinaris, but he can hardly be said to have originated the sect Epiphanius says that the heretics in question claimed Apollinaris as their founder, or at least one of his immediate followers [APOLLINARIANS], and he in part admits the claim, for this seems the meaning of the last word in the following passage Φασὶ δὲ, ὡς ἄνω μοι εἴρηται, ὅτι ἀπ' αὐτοῦ τοῦ πρεσβύτου 'Απολλιναρίου ἐξήχηται ὁ λόγος, ἤ ἀπό τινων τῶν αὐτῷ μεμαθητευμένων· καὶ ἀμφιβάλλω [Epiph. *Hær* lxxviii 1] The chief names that have come down to us as favouring the views of the Antidicomarianites, are Jovinian, Photinus, Bonosus, Helvidius The different opponents of the heresy have in turn assigned different names for

[1] With a somewhat singular scrupulosity, the Old Light party, while advocating the union of Church and State, but strongly resisting the very slightest appearance of State interference with spiritual things, objected on the latter ground to the appointment or observance, by civil authority, of national fasts or thanksgivings, while, on the other hand, the New Lights, who repudiated State connection, inconsistently complied with injunctions of that kind. Among the *Burghers*, the divided parties were more consistent, and among charges brought against the Old Light minister of that body in Aberdeen in 1800 one was, that he refused to observe days appointed by Government

the originator of it, whence we see that it sprang up rather as a natural expansion of previous heresies than as a new one Thus, in the above passage, Epiphanius, writing against the sect, κατὰ Ἀντιδικομαριανιτῶν, names Apollinaris as the founder St. Augustine attributes the error, in the first instance, to Jovinian St. Jerome, who refutes the error in his book against Helvidius, not only does not mention Jovinian, but in his works against Jovinian himself he does not allude to this heresy St Ambrose speaks of the error as unworthy of serious refutation, until it had found a patron among the order of bishops "Fuerunt qui eam [Mariam] negarent virginem perseverasse Hoc tantum sacrilegium silere jamdudum maluimus sed quia causa vocavit in medium, ita ut ejus prolapsionis etiam Episcopus argueretur, indemnatum non putamus relinquendum" [*De Institutione Virginis*, v 35] The reference here is to Bonosus, a bishop of some important place in Macedonia [Bonosians], but it is clear that St Augustine did not connect this bishop with the heresy, for in speaking of Jovinian's views, he says that no bishop has anywhere been found to favour them. The Antidicomarianites may thus be said to be traceable from the antichristian Cerinthians, who asserted that Jesus Christ was the natural son of Joseph and Mary, through the intermediate heresy of Apollinaris, who denied that the Christ was born of the Virgin Mary, or had a reasonable soul Dr Mill says of Helvidius, Bonosus, and their followers, that they "had no precursors in their sentiment respecting the Virgin, but those much worse and thorough heretics who asserted Jesus to be the son of Joseph and Mary" [*The Accounts of our Lord's Brethren in the New Testament vindicated against some recent Mythical Interpreters* The Christian Advocate's publication for 1843].

The earliest appearance of the sect in any definite shape seems to have been in Arabia, it was against this that Epiphanius wrote [c A D 367] At Rome, a few years afterwards, Helvidius advanced these views in a book which was answered, after some hesitation, by St. Jerome Still later was the case of Bonosus He was accused of maintaining that the Blessed Virgin bore several children A Council at Capua was held [A D 389] to condemn him This council gave no decision, but referred the matter to the bishops of his own province, who assembled the next year at Thessalonica, under the presidency of Anysius, bishop of that see, and formally condemned him. They at the same time recognised the priests he had ordained. The third Council of Milan, held the same year [A D. 390], under St. Ambrose, gave a similar decision against Jovinian "Joviniani errores de Maria Deipara, eam scilicet post partum Virginem esse desiisse . . aliaque dogmata damnantur" The followers of Bonosus and Photinus were condemned by Pope Gelasius [A D 492-496] Audentius, a Spanish bishop of the same period, wrote against them The term, ἀειπαρθένος, ever-Virgin, was authoritatively applied to the Blessed Virgin Mary at the General Council of Chalcedon [A D 451] The Lollards, in the fourteenth century, are said to have revived the opinion that the brethren of the Lord were sons of His mother, but there is no allusion to this tenet in the articles charged against Wickliffe at Blackfriars

In the controversies of the sixteenth century, the English reformers were often called upon to defend their belief in the doctrine of the ἀειπαρθενία. Their opponents argued thus "It is necessary to believe that Mary continued a virgin always But this is not certain from Scriptures therefore, some necessary things are known from some other source besides the Scripture" [Whitaker's *Disputation*, ed Parker Soc 539] Of the divines who had occasion to answer these objections, Whitaker appears to be the only one who went so far as to treat it as an open question [*ib*] Bishop Latimer writes very strongly in favour of the doctrine [*Sermon at Grimsthorpe*, i 105] And Cranmer says that the minor of his opponents' syllogism, that the ἀειπαρθενία is not written in Scripture, is false, and quotes Cyprian and Chrysostom, besides the other Fathers named above as writing in its favour, as saying the doctrine is to be believed of necessity [Cranmer's *Works*, ii 60, Parker Soc] The most exhaustive modern treatise on the question is that of Dr Mill cited above He gives [pp 309-311] extracts from the principal divines of the English Church. He speaks, too, of the conciliar condemnation of the opponents of the doctrine as being mild, not severe, shewing the difference of importance between a necessary belief in the virginity of our Lord's mother at His birth and a pious belief in her virginity after, which, he says, is in exact agreement with the sentiments of our own divines He refutes a chain of development of the doctrine which Strauss had conceived, and which was thus stated [1] Opinion of contemporaries and authors of genealogies, Joseph and Mary married, Jesus Christ their offspring [2] Writers of succeeding narratives held Joseph and Mary affianced, Joseph not the father of Christ, and, till His birth, without conjugal relations to Mary [3] Later writers suppose that Joseph, ever afterwards, abstained from assumption of conjugal rights [4] Epiphanius and others proceed to imagine Joseph a decrepit old man, more a guardian than a husband, his children those of a former marriage. [5] Virginity of our Lord's mother never destroyed, as held by Chrysostom and others [6] View of Jerome, Mary and Joseph always virgin, our Lord's brethren his cousins Dr Mill demonstrates the inaccuracy of all this Not one of these, except perhaps [4], which is apocryphal, and of no weight in the argument, was gradually evolved from the preceding [1] was never held by Christians, save by one denounced heretical party [2], [3], and [5] always existed in the minds of the more thoughtful from the first, and [6], was not an addition, but rather a condition by which the last two were held.

The main arguments brought forward by the Antidicomarianites, and the passages of Scripture on which they relied, together with the best received answers, are given in the Theological Dictionary [Helvidians Jovinians Bonosians Theol. Dict art Perpetual Virginity]

ANTINOMIANS Those who profess to be Christians, but reject the moral law on some ground of perverted Christian principle. The opposition to the law implied in the term Antinomian is not the opposition of the simple transgressor of the law, but the opposition which justifies itself by alleging a supposed liberty or privilege

Some of the warnings against Antinomianism in the New Testament speak of the evil as already existing, and that in no slight measure St Paul tells the Philippians [iii. 18] of those in other churches who professed apostolic doctrine, but would not follow apostolic example, whose god was their belly, whose glory was in their shame, who minded earthly things To bring these within the definition of Antinomians, as distinguished from the simply disobedient, it is requisite to shew that they acted upon some ground of perverted Christian principle And when we observe that St Paul begins with a warning against Judaizers [iii 1-3], proceeds to state that a Judaic trust in the law is carnalism, that he has renounced all that Judaism had to offer for the sake of the righteousness of faith, and then presses his own example of the mode in which such righteousness is to be attained, while many, he points out, are acting otherwise, it cannot be doubted that these were strictly Antinomians who perverted liberty from the law of Moses into immunity from the law of God There were false teachers among the people, with high-sounding doctrine, promising liberty [2 Pet ii 1, 18, 19], deceiving them with vain words, as if God's wrath would not come upon them [Eph v 6] Again, there were those who, with some variation in the form of their tenets, held the same error, and perverted St Paul's doctrine by arguing that man may do evil that good may come, and sin that grace may abound [Rom iii 8, vi 1] The existence of Antinomian parties in the Church in apostolic times is thus clear The Church was passing from the bondage of the law through the intermediate stage of Judaic Christianity into the liberty of Christ, and the wickedness of man would not allow even the wisdom of St Paul to conduct the change without this accompanying evil

But it appears that Antinomianism, pure and simple, can hardly be adopted as the basis of a sect Its preachers would be too evidently preachers of unrighteousness to be tolerated The perversion of Christian principle on which it rests is expressed, or rather perhaps veiled, in great swelling words of vanity, and in these is placed the ostensible foundation of a schism

In the first place, the Antinomian principle connected itself, in the case of the Nicolaitanes, with that which was then familiar to the popular mind, the introduction of immorality into religious rites, and with the fanaticism which treated unhallowed works of the flesh as exponents of spiritual love [Nicolaitanes] But this party (it can hardly perhaps be properly called a sect) lasted but a short time, and was lost among the Gnostics

Several sects of the latter were clearly Antinomian Irenæus states that the Gnostics imagined three divisions of men, the material, the animal, and the spiritual Of the material they took no notice they considered the Christians to be the animal, and they themselves, who had perfect knowledge of God, were the spiritual "Hence they pronounce that good moral conduct is necessary for *us*, because without it we cannot be saved but they affirm, that they themselves will be unquestionably saved, not from moral conduct, but because they are by nature spiritual. For as the material is incapable of partaking of salvation, so, on the other hand, they think that the spiritual is incapable of receiving corruption, whatever moral conduct they may practise for as gold, when deposited in mud, does not lose its beauty, but preserves its own nature, the mud not being able to injure the gold, so also they say of themselves, whatever may be the character of their material morality, that they cannot be injured by it, nor lose their spiritual substance Hence the most perfect among them perform all forbidden things without any scruple" [Iren *adv Hær* I vi. 2, 3 See Burton, *Bampton Lect* note 62, p. 443; and Articles in this Dict on Gnostic Sects] The thirty-second of the heresies named by St. Isidore is also that of the "Anomiani qui Latine sine lege dicuntur" [Isid Hisp. *de Hær* xxxii]

Within the Church the Antinomian principle is traceable in the custom, which gave so much trouble, and caused so many conciliar decrees, that of entertaining spiritual sisters The utmost which can be said for this custom is that there may have been cases in which there was no blame beyond that of unseemliness and giving offence Few will doubt that in the vast majority of cases the intercourse was criminal And those who indulged themselves in that intercourse, under a pretence of purity, must have sought to justify themselves in their own sight by some form of Antinomian delusion The same custom passed into some sects in the Middle Ages, as into the Apostolici of the twelfth and of the thirteenth centuries [Apostolicals]

The Circumcellions of the Donatist sect, although they broke every law of God and man with the cry, "For the honour of God," cannot properly be called Antinomians They were fanatics (with a large admixture, however, of mere ruffians) who had persuaded themselves that God's cause was to be upheld by brutal violence With these may be compared the lower sections of the English Puritans, whose brutality failed to equal the brutality of the Circumcellions, not from a difference of principle, but because they were not so much separated from the better men of the same party as the Circumcellions were from the better men of the Donatists, and because they were in some measure restrained by the rules of modern warfare [Dict *of* Theol , Puritanism] But the Independents (or at least not a few of them) professed Antinomian principles, as will be mentioned presently.

The Anabaptists of Munster were fanatical Antinomians, Antinomians, inasmuch as they perverted to earthly and carnal pleasure the glories and privileges of the millennial kingdom, fanatics, in that they sought to establish that kingdom presently by force [ANABAPTISTS]

Among the Lutherans a preacher of Antinomianism appeared in John Agricola In the year 1527, he maintained, in opposition to Melanchthon's Formulary of Ecclesiastical Visitation, that the law of God was not to be used to bring men to repentance, and that the preaching of the law was no work for a gospel minister In 1588 he declared, in opposition to George Major of Wittenburg, who taught the necessity of good works, that such teaching was no better than a doctrine of devils which deprived men altogether of Christ's gospel During the intermediate time his teaching did not vary In 1538, he took occasion from Luther's doctrine to "declaim against the law, maintaining that it was neither fit to be proposed to the people as a rule of manners, nor to be used in the Church as a means of instruction, and that the gospel alone was to be inculcated and explained both in the churches and in the schools of learning" Mosheim, his apologist, whose words we have used, confesses that the recantation he made when pressed by Luther was not sincere, and considers Agricola to be chargeable with vanity, presumption, and artifice Luther's influence was sufficient to suppress the sect during his lifetime after his death Agricola gained some proselytes [1]

The foreign Anabaptists who tried to settle in England were of the milder type, and free from Antinomianism Thus no mention of this error occurs in the Recantation [A D 1575] of the Dutch Anabaptists discovered in London [Collier, *Ecc Hist* vi. p 543, ed 1852] But the Independents fell into Antinomianism They learnt it from John Cotton, who in New England had added this to his other errors, and taught it to Goodwin, Nye, and other leaders of the sect Among their tenets were the following That no sin must trouble any child of God, because trouble of conscience demonstrates a man subject to the covenant of works, but a stranger to the covenant of grace that no Christian is bound to look upon the law as a rule of his conversation that no Christian is to be pressed to any duty of holiness [2] [INDEPENDENTS] Besides these a party of Antinomians appears to have been formed in the reign of Charles I by John Eaton, curate of St Catherine-Coleman, London, and, after secession from the Church, minister of Wickham-Market, Suffolk He wrote *The Discovery of a most dangerous Dead Faith*, 1641; and *The Honeycomb of Free Justification by Christ alone*, 1642, and was imprisoned for his error The object of this latter book was to shew that God does not, will not, nor cannot see any sin in any of His justified children; and his followers avowed the same tenets of Antinomianism as those received by the Independents They were probably derived from the same source [3]

For the theological connection of this heresy, with perversions of preceding doctrine, see the DICTIONARY *of* THEOLOGY, articles JUSTIFICATION, SOLIFIDIANISM

ANTIOCH, SCHOOL OF In the first centuries of the Christian era, schools of philosophy established themselves at Rome, Alexandria, and Antioch, the Macedonians having imported into the two latter cities the philosophy with the language of Greece In Antioch closer contact with the East caused the Peripatetic philosophy to prevail, which the oriental mind assimilated with greater ease, as at a later date the Moors of Spain gave to Europe its first readings in Aristotle [4] Neo-Platonism ruled paramount in the schools of Alexandria Hence the theology of these two cities had each its distinctive cast, while the Alexandrian writers allegorized, the school of Antioch occupied itself upon the plain meaning of the text, and took a judicious course between a mystical interpretation on the one hand, and a servile adherence to the mere letter of Scripture on the other The Syriac language also, with which this school stood in close contact for all the ordinary purposes of life, favoured a plain grammatical line of hermeneutics and Syriac versions older than the Latin Vulgate gave a fresh raciness to the expositions of the Antioch school, that we look for in vain from the Alexandrian divines Notwithstanding their diversity, a good understanding was always maintained between the two schools, until Alexandrian heterodoxy in the Nestorian and Monophysite period made it no longer possible But the character of Antiochian philosophy was essentially sophistical, its principle was scepticism In an evil hour the discussions of the philosophical schools were copied in the catechetical The most sacred subjects were argued *pro* and *con*, and a tone of indifferentism was fostered that could scarcely fail to affect prejudicially positive theology The two most grievous here-

[1] See M Johann Agricola's *Schriften möglichst vollständig verzeichnet*, Altona, 1817 At p 269 is Agricola's recantation Agricola is not to be charged with carrying into Antinomian practice the principles which appear to many to lead logically to an allowance of sin He considered that in the gospel men were brought under a new moral œconomy with which the law had no possible connection

[2] See the curious tract "A Short Story of the Rise, Reign, and Ruin of the Antinomians, Familists and Libertines that infected the churches of New England," London, 1692 By T Welde. Baxter writes of this party "The Vanists (for I know not by what other name to make them known who were Sir Henry Vane's disciples) first sprung up under him in New England when he was governor there But their notions were then raw and undigested [Reference is made to Welde's Tract and to the thirty monsters which Mrs Hutchinson the Antinomian teacher brought forth at one birth] Mr Cotton was too favourable to them Sir Henry Vane being governor, and found to be the secret fautor and life of their cause, was fain to steal away by night and take shipping for England" [*Life*, by Sylvester, i 74]

[3] Neale, *History of Puritans*, admits that Eaton committed some mistakes regarding the doctrines of grace [See Wood's *Athen Oxon* t ii]

[4] Munk, *Mélanges de Phil Juive et Arabe*, 314

sies that have devastated the Church may be traced back to the first germs of virus developed at Antioch Gnosticism, there first brought to life by Simon Magus [Just M. *Apol* i 26], was continued by his disciple Saturninus, and the many allusions to Gnostic tenets found scattered through the epistles of Ignatius shew how certainly the tares had taken root Origen, upon the martyrdom of his father, was as a youth exposed to sore trial from unavoidable association with a Gnostic teacher from Antioch Arianism also may be traced through Alexandria back to the same quarter Afterwards of sporadic growth, it arose endemically at Antioch from the pernicious habit of discussing the deepest mysteries of faith as an intellectual discipline Paul of Samosata, the Judaizing bishop of Antioch, was the precursor of Arius [Alex *Ep ad Const*, Theod *H E* i]. Arianism was here the early offset of dialectical theology [Socr *H E* i 5], and Epiphanius for this reason has styled Aristotle Bishop of the Arians Arius impugned the doctrine of the Eternal Filiation of the Word as Sabellian, and as the natural consequence of his error argued himself over to the opposite extreme Both Arius and his predecessor Paul popularized their error, which otherwise might have died away in the echo of the schools, by setting it forth in hymns and songs for the many

But there is a brighter side to this distinguished school of historical, grammatical, and critical exegesis, in which it always held a highly distinguished position [Conybeare, *Bampton Lectures*, iv] Theophilus, bishop of Antioch [A D. 168], in his three books *ad Autolycum* shews the well-read Platonist, and according to St Jerome [*de Vir ill*] he led the way as an expositor of Scripture in a Commentary on the Gospels Serapion, bishop of the same see [A D. 189], wrote against the Montanist heresy [Eus *H E* v 19] as the mouthpiece of a provincial council, and shewed his critical tact in rejecting the gospel falsely ascribed to St Peter [Eus *H E.* vi 12] Julius Africanus of Nicopolis [i e Emmaus, A D 232], the friend of Origen, was the first Christian annalist, χρονογραφιῶν πέντε σπουδάσματα συνέγραψε Eusebius also has preserved [*H E* i 7] part of his epistle to Aristides on the genealogies of our Lord given by St Matthew and St. Luke Fragments from the same venerable writer are found in Routh's *Reliquiæ Sacræ* [ii 105, 114], and later oriental writers have ascribed to him commentaries on the Gospels [Assoman, *Bibl Or* I29, 158], which statement may possibly be confirmed by the Nitrian MSS of the National Collection Dorotheus, who was a presbyter of Antioch [A D 290, Eus *H E* vii 32], and Lucian, who suffered martyrdom in Nicomedia [A D 312], in the persecution under Diocletian [Eus *H E* viii. 13, ix 6], were zealous promoters of a rational system of Scripture interpretation The recension of the LXX translation by Lucian went by his name, and was extensively used in the Eastern churches from Antioch to Constantinople[1] Hesychius prepared a similar recension for Alexandria, and a third was extracted from the Hexapla by Eusebius and Pamphilus Hence the corruption of the LXX by the confusion of these three recensions has become hopeless Even Jerome did not fail to note it "Totusque orbis hac inter se trifaria varietate compugnat" [*adv Ruff* ii. 27] Alexander, bishop of Alexandria, makes Lucian to have been a follower of Paul of Samosata, and to have adopted his heretical notions [Theod *H E* i 3, 4], but allowance must be made for the statement of a polemical writer, and some indulgence must also be shewn to the pupil who does not at once confirm the adverse opinion of a censorious world against the master These two elements, perhaps, are principal factors in the heresy imputed to Lucian If it had been a well-founded charge, Lucian would scarcely have been honoured as a martyr even by Eusebius, and certainly not by Athanasius, Jerome and Chrysostom, whose panegyric of Lucian is still extant Meletius, the instructor of Chrysostom, Flavian, Diodorus of Tarsus, Cyril of Jerusalem, and Theodore of Mopsuestia, were all of this school Chrysostom here delivered his homilies *De Statuis*, and through his commentaries the sound principle of Antiochian exegesis has become the property of the Church Gieseler has enlarged the area represented by the school of Antioch so as to include Eusebius of Emesa, Apollinaris of Laodicæa, and Ephraem of Edessa. They all felt the same kindly influences [Newman's *Arians* Neander, *K Gesch* iii v 3, end Gieseler, *K Gesch* DICTIONARY *of* THEOLOGY, *s v*]

ANTITACTICS The name given by Clement of Alexandria to those who first broached the dualism which characterized the Gnostic heresies. Thus Clement says, "We call them 'Antitactics' or 'Opponents,' who say that God is indeed our Father, and the Father of all things, and that He made all things good, but that one of those beings whom He Himself had made sowing tares among the wheat originated evil, of which we being made partakers ourselves become adversaries of God" [Clem Alex *Strom* iii 4]. This error of the Antitactics is confuted by St. Augustine in his *City of God* [Aug *De Civ. Dei*, xii 7], but he does not mention them by name The Antitactics were probably a branch of the CARPOCRATIANS, and, like them, were accused of gross immoralities [Theod *Hær Fab* i 16]

ANTI-PÆDOBAPTISTS The opponents of infant baptism [BAPTISTS]

ANTITRINITARIANS This term is limited to those who deny the doctrine of the Holy Trinity by opposing to it the tenet of a God without distinction of Persons Thus if a man, changing the distinction of the three inseparable Persons into a separation, were led to assert that there are three Gods, he would not be classed as an Antitrinitarian, although he does deny the

[1] Lucianus vir disertissimus, Antiochenæ ecclesiæ presbyter, tantum in Scripturarum studio laboravit, ut usque nunc quædam exemplaria Scripturarum Lucianea nuncupentur Feruntur ejus de fide libelli, et breves ad nonnullos epistolæ [Hieron *Catal* 77] Constantinopolis usque ad Antiochiam Luciani Martyris exemplaria probat [*adv Ruff* ii].

doctrine of the Trinity. The correlative term is Unitarian, an incorrect term, since there can be unity only where there is plurality, and the Unity of God requires the distinction of Persons in the Godhead

The Antitrinitarian principle in early times expended itself in producing the Sabellian and Arian heresies with their several derived heresies [MONARCHIANS] Between the time of the disappearance of the Monarchian sects and the beginning of the sixteenth century there were several heresies regarding the Nature of the Godhead and the Three Divine Persons But the former class, such as the heresies of Gilbert de la Porrée, and Joachim, abbot of Flora, which were met in the fourth Lateran Council [A D 1215], by the decision that the Nature of God is simple, do not touch the present subject Again, the controversy in the ninth century between Hincmar and Gotteschalc, regarding the words "Trina Deitas" appears to be accidental, and unconnected with the progress of thought in the Church at large It is quite otherwise with the heresies attributed to Roscellin and Abelard The scholastic controversies between the Nominalists and Realists appear to be the chief origin of the later Antitrinitarian sects Roscellin was the first great Nominalist, the authoritative interpreter if not the author of the system He was pressed by Anselm with the argument that his principles led inevitably to Tritheism or Monarchianism "If the three Persons are one thing, and not three things, as distinct as three angels or three souls, though one in will and power, the Father and the Holy Ghost must have been incarnate with the Son" This heretical conclusion from the Nominalist philosophy was attributed to Roscellin by John the monk in a letter to Anselm, and used by Anselm (though he admits all the words may not be Roscellin's own) as the statement against which he wrote his "De Fide Trinitatis" [Gieseler, *Compend* iii p 281] The conclusion appeared to follow from Roscellin's premisses "When Nominalism became theology, the Three Persons of the Trinity (this was the perpetual touchstone of all systems), if they were more than three words, were individuals, and Tritheism inevitable" [Milman, *Lat Christ* iv 367, ed 1867] It appears that Roscellin was not able to convict Anselm of a fallacy in this argument, for he accepted the former alternative of the dilemma, and averred that the existence of three Gods might be asserted with truth, however harsh the mode of expression might be Again, in the controversy between St Bernard and the great leader of the Nominalists, Abelard, the popular outcry against Abelard was that he introduced three Gods For Tritheism, it is often said, he was condemned Yet he was distinctly accused of holding the old Monarchian principle, "that the names of Father, Son, and Holy Ghost are improperly attributed to God, and that they only describe the plenitude of the Supreme Good." The Council of Soissons [A D. 1121], puzzled perhaps by his dialectics, and unable to determine which of the two heresies resulting (as it was believed) from Nominalism he really held, took the safe course of condemning him for publishing his book without the Pope's authority, and instead of enjoining him to recant any one specified heresy, compelled him to make a profession, and to utter the comprehensive anathemas of the Athanasian Creed [Fleury, tom. xiv lib lxviii art 61, Natal. Alexand. *sæc* xii diss v art vii]

The authority of Anselm, for a while, silenced the dispute among the Schoolmen, but it was again agitated with renewed vigour in the fourteenth century, and from that time ostensibly divided the schools into the two great parties of Nominalists and Realists The Nominalists were the Rationalists of the pre-Reformation Church, and "scattered here and there the seeds of scepticism, of disbelief, and of speculative license" And if Nominalism was allowed by its professors (whether rightly or wrongly) to lead to the dilemma of Tritheism or Monarchianism, we have, in those who rejected the former, a party ready to deny the divinity of the Saviour as soon as the pressure of the papal yoke was abated "Multitudes of freethinkers, who had hitherto been yielding a hollow and occasional compliance with the ritual institutions of the Church, began to ventilate their theories more publicly, and even went so far as to establish independent organizations with the hope of leavening the whole of Western Christendom" [Hardwick, *Hist. of Reform* p 271]

Antitrinitarianism then appears to be, not the genuine product of the Reformation, but the offspring of a school which had existed in the Church for centuries before the Reformation was dreamt of And the process we may fairly conclude from Anselm's argument to have been a repetition of the process which formed Arianism out of Monarchianism Adopting the Monarchian principle the rationalists were driven, through their horror of Patripassianism, to deny the divinity of the Saviour

Zanchius, himself an Italian, complained to Bullinger, when writing from Chiavenna, in which place he was minister, of the heterodoxy of his countrymen on these subjects, and used to say, "Hispania (the birthplace of Servetus) gallinas peperit, Italia fovet ova, nos jam pipientes pullos audimus" [Hardwick, *Hist of Reform* p 284] It may be noticed too that Zanchius, in a letter to Jewel, speaks of his being opposed at Chiavenna by the enemies of discipline, with whom the followers of Servetus united their forces [*Zurich Letters*, ser ii p 185] This may give the true composition of the Antitrinitarian party in the sixteenth century, Italian rationalists and malcontents of the Reformation.

A preparation such as has been described appears to be sufficient to account for the simultaneous appearance in different parts of the Church of teachers of Antitrinitarianism, and for the rapid spread of their opinions Of these teachers, acting independently, John Denk was one of the earliest He was a rationalistic Anabaptist He held the simple manhood of our

Lord, denying altogether the Atonement, and proposing Jesus Christ simply as a pattern of holy life in which the effects of divine love were exhibited. His doctrines spread in two or three years in the Rhine district, Switzerland, Franconia, Suabia, and as far as Moravia. Servetus (through Calvin's interposition) is better known. He was a Spaniard, born A.D. 1509, of Villaneuva in Arragon. From Toulouse, where he was studying civil law, he went to Basle and Strasburg, and put himself in communication with the Reformers. In 1531 his book *De Erroribus Trinitatis* was printed, and in the next year also, at Hagenau, *Dialogorum de Trinitate Libri Duo*. These books raised a great tumult among the German divines, and, circulating in Italy, were much approved by many who had thoughts of leaving the Church of Rome. In 1553 (the year of his execution) he published at Vienne another book of Antitrinitarianism, *Christianismi Restitutio*. The circulation of Servetus' books in Italy leads us to the Italian movement regarding the point in question.

At the same moment that the spread of Protestantism agitated Germany, literary societies assuming a religious colour arose in Italy [see Ranke's *History of the Popes*, by S. Austin, i. 135]. Such a society met at Vicenza, in the government of Venice, in the year 1546, to discuss not only the discipline but the doctrine of the Church, and particularly the doctrine of the Holy Trinity. The Inquisition interfered. Three members of the society were seized, the rest fled. At Geneva they found already formed a congregation of Italian refugees, into which they introduced their heretical speculations. John Valentinus Gentilis, George Blandrata, John Paul Alciatus, Lælius Socinus, Matthew Gribaud, were the chief advocates of the Antitrinitarian doctrines.[1] Upon the spread of these doctrines the Italian Consistory drew up, in 1558, a statement of the orthodox doctrine of the Holy Trinity for subscription by their members. Authorities differ as to the number of those who subscribed, and afterwards broke their promise not to do anything directly or indirectly in opposition to the Formula. The event undoubtedly was that the heretical party was broken up. Gentilis,[2] after wandering in Dauphiné and Savoy and Moravia, was taken at Berne, and put to death, in 1566, for opposing the doctrine of the Trinity in violation of his oath. Lælius Socinus visited Poland, but would not remain there. He died in Zurich in 1562. Gribaud fled to Fargiæ, in the Canton of Berne, and died in prison. Blandrata and Alciatus retreated to Poland, where the history of Socinianism centres itself.

Into Poland Antitrinitarianism had already been introduced by Spiritus of Holland in the year 1546. Lælius Socinus had, at an earlier visit than that named above, converted to his opinions Francis Lismain, the chaplain of the Queen of Sigismund I., and at a synod held at Sicemnia in 1556, the doctrine of the Trinity was, for the first time, publicly opposed by Peter Gonezius. This party was much strengthened by the arrival, in 1558, of Blandrata and Alciatus. They were honourably received by the Protestants. Blandrata gained great influence, which Calvin's letters of warning could not overcome. There was a difference of opinion, however, even at this time (it widened afterwards), some of the party allowing the miraculous conception of our Lord, and that worship is due to Him, others denying both these points. This difference in some measure checked the spread of the heresy, nevertheless the dissensions between the orthodox and the heretics increased so much, that, in 1565, Gregory Paul, the minister of a Protestant Church in Cracow, petitioned the States assembled in council, to cause a conference to be held for full discussion of the subject. The result of the conference was, that the parties which had up to that time met together in synod separated, and the Antitrinitarians formed a separate society. Toleration was granted them by the States and the Emperor. Racow was built for them by Siemienius, Prince of Podolia, and became their chief settlement; but they had conventicles in all the towns and villages of the kingdom, particularly in Cracow, Pinczow, and Lublin. Among them there were not a few shades of opinion, but they gradually formed themselves into three parties, the followers of Lælius Socinus, and the factions of Budnæus and Farnovius. The Socinians held a miraculous conception of our Lord, in virtue of which, although His Divinity was denied, He is the Son of God, and worship is proportionally due to Him. These points were denied by Budnæus. His principles appeared impious to the main body of the Socinians, and in 1584 he was deposed from his ministerial functions, and publicly excommunicated with all his disciples. Farnovius was nearer to the Arian tenets, holding that Christ had been created by the Father before the world.

[1] Socinian authors sometimes write as if this society held and propagated definite Socinian principles. This is an error. See Mosheim, *History*, cent. xvi. sect. iii. part ii. iv. 7. They only agreed in a general Antitrinitarianism, and their speculations terminated very differently. See the *History of Gentilis* (named in the next note), p. 23, *et seq.*

[2] The specific charge against Gentilis was this, "That after eight years' preparation to attack the doctrine of the Trinity he did begin openly to teach, that there were in the Trinity three distinct Spirits, differing from each other in numerical essence: amongst which (three Spirits) he acknowledges the Father only to be that infinite God which we ought to worship, which is plain blasphemy against the Son." Gentilis was accused, as Abelard was, of holding inconsistent propositions, one Monarchian, one Tritheistic. It was said that he affirmed, that the Father alone is that one only God set forth to us in the Holy Scriptures; and that there are in the Trinity Three Eternal Spirits, each of which is by Himself God. The Council of Soissons was not well qualified to judge Abelard's doctrine: the divines of Berne were little qualified to judge Gentilis. If the history of Benedictus Aretius is to be trusted, they held that the Son is αὐτόθεος, and mistook the subordination of the Son for inferiority of nature [*A Short History of Valentinus Gentilis the Tritheist*, translated, London 1696, pp. 131, 40-47. The translation of this history professes to have been made for the benefit of Dr. Sherlock.]

But this history belongs to the article SOCINIANS, which takes up the subject from the time of Faustus Socinus joining the Antitrinitarian body.

In the year 1563 Blandrata was invited to Transylvania by Prince John Sigismund. Supported by the favour of the prince, and of his prime minister Petrovitz, and after Sigismund's death by the favour of the Bathori, princes of Transylvania, he boldly and successfully propagated his heresy. In this he was assisted by Francis David, superintendent of the Reformed in Transylvania, whom he converted from Calvinism. But about the year 1574, David adopted the principles of Budnæus, and separated from Blandrata. In 1578 Blandrata invited Faustus Socinus to help him in opposing David. David, not yielding to argument, was summoned before the Diet, and condemned for blasphemy. He died a few months afterwards. In 1579 Socinus went into Poland, and united the Antitrinitarians.

In no other countries of the Continent was Antitrinitarianism established. The attempts made to form settlements in Hungary and Austria were defeated by the opposition both of Catholics and Protestants.

The subsequent History of the Continental Socinians and the history of the English sect are given in articles SOCINIANS, UNITARIANS.

ANTOSIANDRIANS. The opponents of Osiander's party. [OSIANDRIANS. STANCARISTS.]

ANTRIM, PRESBYTERY OF. A section of the Irish Presbyterians who separated from the main body in the year 1750, from a disinclination to subscribe to the Westminster Confession of Faith. They adopted the Arian or "New Light" principles, and, as far as the complex nomenclature and singular divergencies of the Presbyterians can be explained without Presbyterian verbosity, may be identified with the Scotch section known as the NEW LIGHT BURGHERS.

APELLEIANS. [APELLIANISTS.]

APELLIANISTS. A Gnostic sect which arose about the middle of the second century in the reign of Antoninus Pius, or Marcus Aurelius Antoninus, deriving its name from its founder Apelles. This heretic was originally a disciple of Marcion, but was expelled by the latter from the number of his followers, because he exchanged the rigid continence inculcated by his teaching for licentious indulgence, living with a mistress named Philumena, whose utterances he supposed to be dictated by a familiar spirit, and whom he regarded as an inspired prophetess. After his expulsion, he became the founder of a distinct sect, which, as might be expected from the laxity of conduct permitted, met with considerable success, and which was distinguished from its parent stock by the addition of the following new doctrines:—

1. He rejected his master's belief in two coeternal Gods, or active principles of good and evil, and substituted for it, as some assert, the doctrine of the eternity of matter; or, as is more probable, its creation by an inferior and hostile deity, who having been himself called into existence by God, was by Him permitted to create the world, and to be the author of all its evils [Aug. *de Hær.* c. 23].

2. He seems to have believed in the existence, sufferings, and death of Christ as the Son of God, only this Christ was not incarnate by the Holy Ghost in the womb of the Blessed Virgin as the Gospel teaches, nor was He a mere phantom, as Marcion taught, but He was supposed to have descended from heaven in a mysterious manner, and to have contracted a body composed of the four elements—earth, air, fire, and water, which were again dispersed abroad before the soul of Jesus ascended to heaven.

3. A necessary corollary from the last doctrine was a denial of the resurrection of the body, in which he coincided with Marcion and other Gnostic teachers.

4. He accused the prophets of the Old Dispensation of inconsistency, and as that could not be the result of Divine inspiration, he attributed it to the same spirit of evil which had created the world; he also wrote much against the Mosaic law,[1] spending a great deal of labour in its refutation, and ridiculing it along with the rest of the Bible in a conversation with a certain Rhodon, an Asiatic, which has been preserved by Nicephorus [*Hist. Eccles.* lib. iv. cap. 28, 29].

5. Lastly, and with the greatest inconsistency, Apelles taught that every one would be saved by remaining firm in the belief which they had once embraced.

The Apelleians are mentioned by St. Cyprian [*Ep.* lxxiii. 4] along with the Marcionites and other sects as among those whose baptism was not to be considered valid. [Aug. *de Hæres.* xxiii. Niceph. *Hist. Eccl.* iv. 28. Philaster, xlvii. Euseb. *Hist. Eccl.* v. 12. Tertull. *adv. Marc.* iv. 17; *Præscr. Hær.* xxx.]

APELLITES. [APELLIANISTS.]

APHTHARTODOCETÆ. One of the two families into which the Monophysites were divided. From the names of their leaders they were called, in Armenia and its neighbourhood, JULIANISTS; in Egypt, GAIANITÆ: the general name Aphthartodocetæ being descriptive of their doctrine.

As a consequence of the Monophysite tenet that from the union of the two natures in our Lord there resulted only one nature, the Aphthartodocetæ attributed to our Lord's Body as pertaining to that one nature ἀφθαρσία, incorruptibility—including in their term φθορά, not only sinful appetites, and the corruption which ordinarily follows death, but also all innocent physical needs and weaknesses and sufferings, πάθη ἀδιάβλητα. The human nature they considered to have been so essentially united with the Divine nature of the Logos as to have become merged or absorbed in it, and therefore to have become possessed of the inherent and indestructible life of the Logos.

It was held, however, that the actions and

[1] Ὁ γέτοι Ἀπελλῆς οὗτος μυρία κατὰ τοῦ Μωυσέως ἠσέβησε νόμον [Euseb. *Eccles. Hist.* v. 13].

sufferings of our Lord, as told in the Gospels, were real, and not merely in appearance The seeming contradiction between this and the foregoing statements was obviated by the distinction that those sufferings were voluntarily undergone by our Lord, in the way of an œconomy or dispensation of grace, for the salvation of man, and did not properly belong to the nature of that Body upon which they were inflicted

The term Docetæ, which implies that our Lord's Body was only a phantasm, is not rightly used of the Aphthartodocetæ. They doubtless held that our Lord possessed a real and substantial body, made of a woman, although the attributes of humanity had been abolished by the union of the two natures Yet it was truly said that they held our Lord's Body to be other than it appeared It appeared to be a human body, but a body impassible and immutable in itself, neither acting nor feeling as men act and feel, is not a proper human body.

The difference of opinion between the Julianists and their opponents the Severians had long existed among the Monophysites, but did not break out into controversy until the deprived Monophysite bishops met at Alexandria about A D 520 The heresy of the Aphthartodocetæ then spread rapidly Mention of its outbreak in the Homeritis in the year 549 is made in Assemani, *Bibl Orient Clementino-Vatic* tom iii pars ii p 455, where is also a reference to a strange story of the Julianists thinking to continue a succession of bishops by mortmain "De Sacerdotio quod a Julianistis in urbe Epheso per mortui manum illegitime traditum fuit anno Christi 549"

Justinian, who had been an eager defender of the Council of Chalcedon, and a persecutor of Monophysitism, in his old age issued an edict [A D 563] in favour of Aphthartodocetism. But the doctrine failed to gain the approval of the Monophysite body In the eighth or the ninth century they seem to have utterly disappeared from Syria, and in general from Asia, with the exception of Armenia, as also from Egypt A portion of them, however, pushed their way into Ethiopia and Nubia, where they had a patriarch of their own The Aphthartodocetæ were themselves divided into two parties, one party maintaining that after the Incarnation Christ ought not to be spoken of as a created being as regards His humanity, but that even as man He should be designated God and Creator, and must therefore have been a proper object of worship from the very beginning These were called ακτιστηταί, their opponents κτιστολάτραι. [ACTISTETES CTISTOLATRÆ Leontius, *De Sectis*, in Gallandii *Bibl Patr.* tom xii Anathema of Julian (directed against the errors which his opponents charged him with) in Assemani in Syriac, and in Latin in Gieseler's *Commentatio qua Monophysitarum variæ . . . opiniones . . illustrantur*, 1838, Gottingæ Gieseler's *Commentatio* Natal Alexander, sæc. vi. dissert vi Dorner *On the Person of Christ*, Clark's transl div. ii vol i p. 128, *et seq*]

APOCARITES One of the many sects which grew out of the Manichæan heresy The Apocarites appeared for the first time in the reign of Tacitus and the pontificate of Eutychian [c A D 275] They adopted the greater portion of the Gnostic and Manichæan doctrines, especially holding as their distinctive tenet a belief that man's soul was eternal and uncreated, and of the same substance as God Himself, the only authority for which was the passage in Genesis "And the Lord God formed man of the dust of the ground, and breathed into his nostrils the breath of life, and man became a living soul" [Gen ii 7]

APOCRYPHANS There were three classes of writings recognised in the early Church [1] Canonical, such as having received the imprimatur of authority, were included in the Canon of Holy Scripture, and were bound to be accepted and believed. [2] Ecclesiastical, such writings as the Apology of Tertullian, or the History of Eusebius, which, having been composed by trustworthy persons, were generally considered deserving of credit, though not accepted as *de fide* [3] Apocryphal, spurious additions to the gospels and epistles, and lives of saints, which were utterly devoid of authority, and either contained false and ridiculous accounts of miracles, or were written to bolster up some new-fangled doctrine, and attributed for that purpose to names which would ensure acceptance.

The title "Apocryphans" did not denote any one sect in particular, but was applied to any such bodies as the Manichæans, Gnostics, Nicolaitanes, or Valentinians, who based their doctrines on apocryphal writings in their private possession The Manichæans, for example, are said to have possessed a spurious life of St. Andrew the apostle, and Acts of St John the evangelist, St Peter, St Paul, &c were composed, which were replete with marvels, such as accounts of their conversation with various animals, and other trifles [Philast *De Hæres* lxxxviii]

APOLLINARIANS There are three distinct heresies connected with the name of Apollinaris They all relate to the Incarnation of our Lord, and may all be referred to one motive or principle, of which Apollinaris appears to have been the chief assertor They are therefore often spoken of as several branches of the Apollinarist heresy But when we distinguish them one from the other, that for which Apollinaris was condemned must specifically bear his name At the same time, it is not to be denied, that in his later years he added to that specific heresy one of the other heresies.

The three heresies are these the *first* holds that the Son of God acquired a body, called human, because it is in the form of man, by conversion of the substance of the Godhead into the substance of flesh, the *second* holds that in the Incarnation the two substances are confounded or blended, the *third* that our Lord assumed a human body of the Virgin, but did not assume a human soul, the Divine Nature supplying the place of the soul This last is in two stages In the earlier stage it was contended that nothing of the human soul was assumed by the Son of God, in the latter stage, that with the body He assumed the sensitive soul (ψυχή), but not the rational soul (νοῦς), and that the Logos took the place only of the rational soul.[1]

All these agree in denying to our Lord a perfect humanity In each case there is something of the human nature lacking. And the common motive and principle to which the three are referrible, is evident from Athanasius' *Epist ad Epictetum*, and the two books, *Contra Apollinarium* Those who advanced these tenets thought themselves obliged, in order to maintain the perfect sinlessness of our Lord, to deny His assumption of that which they regarded as the primal seat of sin in man By some the body, by some the body and its sensitive soul, by some the mind or rational soul, was thought the seat of sin, and its assumption therefore denied The ἐνανθρώπησις of our Lord was thought to be maintained by His assumption of the remainder of the human nature In general, accordingly, the third heresy was not combined with the first, for that would deny the ἐνανθρώπησις altogether There is evidence however which cannot be resisted that Apollinaris in the latter part of his life did so By the Apollinarist heresy, however, is understood the third Heretics of the second class have their accredited name, SYNUSIASTÆ, and they are ranked by Theodoret as an offshoot of the Apollinarists under the title "Polemians"

The third class is named by Philaster TROPITÆ In the Apollinarist heresy, thus limited by the exclusion of those two sects, the sensitive soul, or part of the soul, is considered to be not merely distinguishable in our conceptions, but really independent of and separable from the rational soul The ψυχή, that is, is thought to be both distinct and divisible from the νοῦς And it is asserted that our Lord, becoming man, assumed of the nature of man only the former, the Divine Logos supplying, in the God-Man, the place of the latter [Theodoret, *Dial Inconfusus*]. From this division of the sensitive from the rational soul, these heretics are called Dimœritæ, as holding a διμοιρία, or two-thirds of the human nature in the Person of our Lord, under which name Epiphanius describes them [*Hær* lxxvii]

Apollinaris, of the Syrian Laodicæa, son of a presbyter of the same name, a pupil of a Sophist Epiphanius, reader in the Church of Laodicæa, was made bishop of Laodicæa about A D 362 He had distinguished himself in controversy with the Arians, was a friend of Athanasius, and was known for his many theological works [see a list of them in Lardner, *Credib* xcv] Sozomen tells that the occasion of Apollinaris' falling into heresy was resentment against Georgius, bishop of Laodicæa Georgius separated him from communion on account of his intimacy with Athanasius, and brought up against him an earlier fault, his presence namely at some Bacchic rites, for which he had been dealt with by Theodotus, Georgius' predecessor [Sozom *Hist Eccl* vi 25] But (not to speak of chronological difficulties) this deliberate adoption of heresy out of pique or revenge, in no case very probable, is, in the present case, improbable from the character of the man, and negatived by the fact that Apollinaris began by adopting a portion of the Arian creed The heresy is to be attributed to the workings of a mind which had lost its way amidst the mazes of controversy, and was in some measure misled by erroneous metaphysical theories Apollinaris held the Catholic doctrine of the Holy Trinity, and in his maintenance against the Arians of the divinity of the Son of God, and his desire to maintain the impeccability of Christ, he thought himself obliged to admit the Arian[2] tenet, that the Logos supplied in Christ the place of the human soul To take the very nature of man was (it appeared to him) to take a body and soul of fallen humanity[3] This is worked out in Athanasius' argument. The Apollinarists are represented as stating that where there is a true and very man, there is sin, that Christ could not therefore be the complete man, that He used the organized body as an instrument, that the Word was in that body as a celestial soul in place of the inner man [Athan *Cont Apoll* i 2, 17, ii 6, 8, 17]

It will be observed that Athanasius expressly attributes this doctrine to the Arians He says that the Arians affirm the Saviour to have taken only the flesh of man, and impiously refer the sense of passion to the impassible Deity [*ib* i 15] Augustine speaks as unhesitatingly "Apollinaristæ dicentes sicut Ariani Deum Christum carnem sine anima accepisse" [*Hær*

[1] Leo describes three heresies of the Apollinarist sects, omitting that which is above called the second, and counting as two the two stages of the third "Nec (Deum) ita hominem (dicimus), ut aliquid ei desit, quod ad humanam certum est pertinere naturam, sive animam, sive mentem rationalem, sive carnem quæ non de femina sumpta est, sed facta de Verbo in carnem converso atque mutato quæ tria falsa et vana Apollinistarum hæreticorum tres partes variæ protulerant *Ad clerum Constant Urbis*, A D 451" [Harduin, *Conc* ii. 33]

[2] On this Arian tenet see Pearson *On the Creed*, p 160, note †, ed 1741 That this tenet was held by the Arians is little noticed, nor was it insisted on in the time of the original controversy In heretics who accounted the Word no other than a superior created Spirit, the error was but little taken into consideration by the Church [ARIANS]

[3] The misconception lies in the supposition that original sin is of the very substance of fallen man, whereas it is, on the other hand, not an essential property but a defect The substantiality of evil in human nature, as now constituted, was held by Marcion and other Gnostics Those who hold that human flesh, as such, is sinful, must, in order to avoid the impiety that our Lord assumed a sinful body, assert with the Docetæ the unreality of His body, or with the Synusiastæ, that His body was of His eternal substance prepared in Heaven, and coming down from Heaven a tenet adopted, it will be remembered, by Irving, who maintained that God prepared a body of fallen humanity for His Son Those who hold that original sin is an essential property of the human soul, to avoid a corresponding impiety, must deny the assumption of the human soul, and make the Word itself take the place of that soul. This the Apollinarists did. See Mill, *Sermons on the Temptation*, notes I and K

lv] In this first stage of Apollinarist heresy the human soul of Christ was altogether denied, and with this stage Athanasius deals. He speaks of the Apollinarists as σάρκα μόνην προσομολογοῦντες [ii 17], as holding that the ψυχή, or νοερὰ φύσις is so essentially the seat of sin [ii 8], that the Son cannot have assumed it, of the νοῦς ἐπουράνιος ἐν Χριστῷ being ἀντὶ τοῦ ἔσωθεν ἀνθρώπου τοῦ ἐν ἡμῖν [i 17] From this extreme position they were driven, and then adopted the Platonic distinction of νοῦς and ψυχή [Socr *Hist Eccl* ii 46], allowing that Christ assumed the latter but not the former "Mentem, quæ rationalis est anima hominis, defuisse animæ Christi, sed pro hac ipsum Verbum in eo fuisse dixerunt" [Augustine] To this second stage belongs the narrative of Epiphanius regarding himself, Paulinus and Vitalis Paulinus was the Bishop of Antioch, consecrated by Lucifer, Vitalis was a presbyter of Meletius, who joined Apollinaris, and was afterwards made bishop in the sect, from whom the Apollinarists were called Vitalians by the Antiochenes [Sozom *H E* vi 25] Epiphanius relates that in a conference with these two bishops, Paulinus produced a creed drawn up by Athanasius, which he had himself signed, that Vitalis, after much cavilling and many questions, avowed his belief that in Christ was the human ψυχή, not the human νοῦς, that Christ was perfect man, consisting of a human body and sensitive soul, and the divine nature—that divine nature being in the place of the rational soul [Epiph *Hær.* lxxvii. 21-25] Nemesius writes in his opening paragraph that the metaphysical tenet was borrowed from Plotinus, and the heretical doctrine raised on its foundation [1] Regarding the metaphysical tenet, it is sufficient to say that it has been rejected by the Church as inconsistent with Christian psychology Its connection with heresy is evident in other cases as well as the present case Gregory of Nyssa [*Antirrheticus*, sect viii] remarks what handles it affords to heresy

The heresy, both in its earlier and later form, denies to the Mediator a complete manhood Christ is no longer God and man, but God and imperfect man, if man at all The soul is the man, not the outward shape "Mens cujusque is est quisque" It is the living soul inbreathed from God, in virtue of which the creature, made of the dust of the earth, becomes man In the first form of the Apollinarist heresy, it is necessary to assert that the Son of God, inhabiting a soulless body, becomes man In which case, it follows directly, that all the sufferings of the Mediator were borne by the Son Himself as such, that the very nature of the Godhead suffered. In the second form, that which is confessedly the highest part of man is denied to the humanity of the Mediator, and all the sufferings of the Mediator which belong to that highest part are, in like manner as before, attributed to the Godhead In neither case can it be said that the Son of God was made in all things like unto His brethren In neither case can the highest part of man have fellowship with the sufferings of Christ, and consequently it is left incapable of salvation [2]

Gregory of Nazianzum, in his letter to Nectarius, written about the year 387, states from Apollinaris' own writings, that Apollinaris taught that the Flesh of Christ was not assumed from without, but had appertained to the Son from the beginning In the first Epistle to Cledonius, A D 382, he mentions the opinion that the Flesh of Christ had come down from heaven [sect vi], and the necessary deduction that the Body of Christ passed through His mother "tanquam per canalem" [sect. iv] This latter statement is repeated by other authorities, as by Pope Martin at the Lateran Council, A D 649 [act. iii] [3] This evidence cannot be set aside (as Basnage would do) by the assertion that Gregory must have been mistaken in the authorship of the writings he quotes, and we are constrained to believe that Apollinaris, after his condemnation by the Council, sank deeper than before into heresy, and advanced tenets which altogether destroy the Incarnation of our Lord

Again, Gregory Nazianzen [*Ep* i *ad Cledon*] states that Apollinaris introduced a scale (as it were) of divinity, asserting the Holy Spirit to be great, the Son greater, the Father greatest Theodoret repeats the statement, but says, also, that in some writings Apollinaris is orthodox. Considering which, and the testimonies there are to Apollinaris' orthodoxy concerning the Holy Trinity,[4] it is reasonable to infer that the charge

[1] It may be right to observe that the true human triad is found in the regenerate man, body, soul and spirit, the spirit being a divine principle superadded to the rational soul, the "soul" being both the "anima" and the "mens" See Irenæus' description of the saved man as a complete man, as well as a spiritual man [*adv Hær* v 6, 1] See also Justin Mart *On the Resurrection*, chap 10 Gieseler writes that Apollinaris was perhaps misled by his aversion to Origen, but does not state the grounds of the aversion A clear contrariety is found in the two concerning the fundamental proposition of Apollinaris, since Origen makes the νοῦς and the ψυχή to be essentially the same, and describes the latter as the former in a state of degeneracy [*De Princip* II viii. 3] On this subject see DICT *of* THEOL , SPIRIT

[2] This, which is a legitimate deduction from the premisses of Apollinaris, is stated by Theodoret [*H E* v 3] to have been a part of his teaching It is simply incredible that he admitted and taught it

[3] Gregory of Nyssa begins his *Antirrheticus* with the statement that Apollinaris assigned to the Son a certain incarnation, not a proper manifestation in the flesh, in words so doubtful as to leave it uncertain whether he intends to maintain the conversion of the Godhead into flesh, or the existence of a compound substance, lying between the two, neither God nor man, but partaking of the natures of both With this statement may be compared the words of Apollinaris, quoted at the Lateran Council, A D 649 "Ὄργανον καὶ τὸ κινοῦν, μίαν πέφυκεν ἀποτελεῖν τὴν ἐνέργειαν ὧν δὲ μία ἡ ἐνέργεια, μία καὶ οὐσία, μία ἄρα οὐσία γέγονε τοῦ λόγου καὶ τῆς σαρκός [Harduin, *Concil* ii 892]

[4] Vincent Lirin *Common* cap 17, Leontius, *De Sectis*, act iv These are quoted by Lardner, who refers also to Philostorgius, Suidas, *v.* Apollinarius Athanasius assumes that Apollinaris retained the Nicene faith regarding the Trinity See Socrates, *H E* ii 46

is founded only on statements relating to a subordination of office.

The charge of Sabellianism[1] is sufficiently explained by the direct conclusion from the leading Apollinarist tenet, that the *θεότης* of the Son suffered, from which it follows that the Godhead Itself, the *θεότης* of the Father, is passible

The Synod of Alexandria, held A D 362, by Athanasius and other bishops, returning from banishment after the death of Constantius, declared *ὅτι οὐ σῶμα ἄψυχον, οὐδ' ἀναίσθητον, οὐδ' ἀνόητον εἶχεν ὁ Σωτὴρ* This was before Apollinaris avowed his heresy, probably before he had adopted it Epictetus' letter to Athanasius, and Athanasius' reply, mark the outbreak of Apollinarist heresy, and these were in A D 370 The heretical tenet condemned was held by the Arians and perhaps we are justified in considering that its special condemnation, after so little notice had been taken of it during the Arian troubles, is an example of Athanasius' prescience He may have foreseen that heresy would take that course

Apollinaris was condemned in a Roman synod, A D 373[2] There is in Theodoret [*H E* v 10] an Epistle of Damasus to the Oriental bishops concerning this condemnation Baronius considers it to have been written at the time of the council, Valesius some time after, but both agree as to the condemnation in the year 373 The epistle speaks in general terms of all who deny the perfect humanity of our Lord It states that Apollinaris, as well as a follower of his, Timotheus, had been deposed

Another synodical letter of Damasus [Theod *H E* v 11] belongs probably to the Roman synod, A D 382 It anathematizes what has been defined as the proper Apollinarist heresy

The Council of Constantinople, in its synodical epistle, refers also to a condemnation of the heresy at Antioch in A D 378 or 379 But the decrees of these inferior synods need not be dwelt upon in the presence of the decisions of an Œcumenical council At Constantinople, A D 381-2, a synodical epistle declared that the Fathers held the doctrine of an entire and perfect Incarnation not the œconomy of an incarnation in which the body lacks either soul or mind Canon I anathematizes the Apollinarists, Canon VII prescribes the mode of their reception on returning to the Church, namely, by the seal of unction, their baptism being allowed Lastly, the Definition of Faith made at Chalcedon sets forth, *ἕνα καὶ τὸν αὐτὸν Χριστὸν, Υἱὸν, Κύριον, μονογενῆ, ἐν δύο φύσεσιν ἀσυγχύτως, ἀτρέπτως, ἀδιαιρέτως, ἀχωρίστως γνωριζόμενον*

It is sufficient to state that the Apollinarists were subjected to the full penalties of Theodosius' edicts against heresy A summary of these edicts is in Gibbon's *Decline and Fall*, chap xxvii A letter of Ambrose and other Italian bishops to Theodosius, A D. 381, mentions the Apollinarist heresy as proper to be added to those regarding which the Emperor had written to them [Harduin, *Concil* i 844]

It is stated by Epiphanius [*Hær* lxxviii] that the sect of Antidicomarianites sprung from Apollinaris or one of his school The latter is the more probable opinion "Epiphanius and Photius are not without reason suspected of mistake in charging, severally on the Apollinarists and Eunomians, a denial of St Mary's perpetual virginity We find St. Basil using this point as a mutually confessed one, while contending with the latter heretics for the consubstantiality of the Word; for to their allegation of the Apostle's words, *πρωτότοκος πάσης κτίσεως*, in Col i 15, as if they implied merely a precedence of primogeniture among angelic creatures, he opposes the term, *πρωτότοκος*, used of Christ's human generation in Matt i 25—though no other children certainly followed—as an illustration of a corresponding use of the word respecting the Divine and ineffable generation of the only-begotten Son" [Basil, lib iv *adv Eunom* tom. i p 414, ed Par 1839 Mill, *On the Brethren of the Lord*, p 301. Regarding the Chiliasm of Apollinaris, Basil, *Ep* cclxv MILLENARIANS]

APOSTLES, FALSE. [FALSE APOSTLES]

APOSTOLICALS This name was assumed in the twelfth century by a sect which formed itself in the neighbourhood of Cologne Our information regarding them is from a letter of Evervinus, provost of the Præmonstratensian monastery of Steinfeld, near Cologne, printed in Mabillon, *Veter Analect* iii 152, and St. Bernard, *Serm* lxv lxvi, *in Cantica* Evervinus asked Bernard to reply to their errors in his commentary on the words, "Take us the foxes" The sect was one of the reforming sects of the middle ages, in which the desire of reformation was so largely mingled with fanaticism and error Their rules of discipline were correct, except that they had the plague-mark of allowing spiritual sisters to those who professed celibacy Celibacy they preferred to marriage, even if they did not condemn marriage Infant baptism, invocation of the saints, prayers for the dead, they condemned The intermediate state they denied along with the mediæval purgatory To the private Christian they thought every meal was a Eucharist They abstained from all flesh, St Bernard says,

[1] The charge is made by Basil [*Ep* cclxv] Basil expresses a doubt whether the writings on which it is founded were genuine Neither does he appear to have been well informed regarding Apollinaris he states that he had read but few of his writings [*Ep* ccxliv] He mentions Apollinaris frequently in consequence of the report spread by Eustathius that he was a follower of Apollinaris

[2] The council condemned generally the errors which are more or less connected with the name of Apollinaris, viz of those who say [1] that Mary is not *θεοτόκος*, [2] that the Body of Christ passed through His mother as through a channel, [3] that the Manhood was first formed and then the Divine Nature superimposed, [4] that there are two sons one of God, one of Mary, [5] that the Divinity worked in Christ, as in a prophet, by grace, [6] that the Crucified is not to be adored, [7] that Christ was advanced to the Godhead as a reward of His virtue, or that He was God by adoption, [8] that Christ on His resurrection laid aside His Body, [9] that the Flesh of Christ descended from heaven, [10] that hope is to be placed in a Christ who is man without a human soul [See Mansi, under the year 377, to which he assigns the council]

upon Manichæan principles Evervinus tells of two of the sect, in a popular tumult raised against them, going joyfully to the stake It seems to be probable that they were merged in the sect of Waldenses, the principles of which were diffused even in the Rhenish provinces [Nat Alex *Hist Ecc* vii 83]

APOSTOLICALS Another mediæval sect which took its name from the profession of its members to revive the apostolic life. It was founded by Gerard Sagarelli of Parma towards the end of the thirteenth century, and was chiefly confined to Lombardy and some districts of the Tyrol Sagarelli required his followers to clothe themselves in white, after the manner of the Franciscans, to go bareheaded and unshorn, and to live in the strictest poverty, depending entirely on alms His mendicant teachers were not permitted to marry, but were attended by women whom they called sisters, according to a well-known saying of St Paul The Apostolicals were determined foes to the Papacy in private, and predicted its immediate downfall, looking also for a fulfilment of the prophecies uttered by Joachim, abbot of Flora, respecting the rise of a new and pure Church from the ruins of that which had become so corrupt Joachim's prophecies did, indeed, stimulate many to threaten the Papacy with a reformation by the sword, and thus those who trusted in them were, from the Papal point of view, a really dangerous class of fanatics In addition to this danger the Apostolicals, like all the class of mediæval sects to which they belonged, were fanatic communists, of the type of the later Anabaptists, and were thus waging war, in no small degree, on society at large They were thus opposed by the civil power as well as by the Church, and the latter made use of the Inquisition for their suppression Sagarelli was burned to death at Parma, A D 1300, but a new leader of the sect sprung up in the person of Dolcino This man (from whom the sect also acquired the name of "Dolcinists") was a native of Novara, a man of great energy and courage, and apparently of some military ability He preached vehemently against the reigning pope, Boniface VIII, and predicted that both he and all his wicked allies would shortly be slain by Frederic of Arragon, who was to enter Rome as emperor, in which he seems to have been taking up one of the prophecies of Joachim Dolcino gathered large forces together, and under his leadership the Apostolicals carried on a fierce war against the Papal troops for two years The importance of the rebellious war thus carried on by them is shewn by a passage in the contemporary poem of Dante, where Mahomet bids the poet, on his return to the light,

"Now say to Fra Dolcino, then, to arm him,
Thou, who perhaps wilt shortly see the sun,
If soon he wish not here to follow me,
So with provisions, that no stress of snow
May give the victory to the Novarese,
Which otherwise to gain would not be easy"
[Dante's *Inferno*, xxviii 55]

After several battles Dolcino was, however, taken prisoner, and was executed with cruel tortures at Vercelli in the year 1307 With him was also executed his female companion Margaret The sect still survived, but in a scattered form, some of its members being found both in Germany and in the south of France so late as the year 1402. One of them, named William, was also in that year burned to death at Lubeck The Albati, or WHITE BRETHREN, were probably a portion of them revived under a fanatic leader in Italy, and there suppressed by Pope Boniface IX The BEGHARDS were also allied with them [Mosheim's *Gesch des Apostel-ordens*, Helmstadt, 1748 Mariotti's *Fra Dolcino and his Times*, London, 1853 Natal Alex *Hist Eccl* viii. 87 Muratori's *Script rer Ital* ix 450 Eccard's *Corpus Hist Med Ævi* ii 906. Milman's *Latin Chr* vii 355]

APOSTOLICI [APOTACTICS]

APOSTOOLIANS A division of the Mennonite WATERLANDERS, taking its name from Samuel Apostool, a Baptist preacher of Amsterdam in the year 1664 The Apostoolians arose in opposition to the GALENISTS, endeavouring to maintain strict communion, and opposing the Socinian tendencies of the latter They are also enthusiastic Millenarians These two divisions of the Waterlanders still exist in Holland

APOTACTICS Those who renounced all private property The main body of the Apotactics were Encratites, who, in addition to the usual ascetic tenets of their sect, held that a renunciation of property is necessary to salvation But there were some, as the Aerians, who advocated this renunciation without practising abstinence

Epiphanius makes the Apotactics the same as the Apostolici, and calls them an ἀπόσπασμα τῶν Τατιανοῦ δογμάτων [Epiph *Hær.* xli or lxi] Augustine also identifies them with the Apostolici, and mentions their likeness to the Encratites [Aug *Hær* xl] He charges them with heresy, as separating from the Church, and denying the salvation of those who did not follow their rule, but he adds that they were also said to hold certain other heresies. Epiphanius comments at length upon the permission in the Church of voluntary poverty and celibacy, and argues that the main error of the Apotactics lay in the attempt to enforce these as of necessity Whether then they adopted the Gnosticism of the Tatianist or of the Severian Encratites, or whether they were merely in error in advocating an excessive and fanatical asceticism, is not certainly known. But, most probably, some out of all these classes held it to be a duty to renounce private property, and, from the mode of life which resulted, were formed into fraternities, in which the differences of opinion in matters of doctrine were waived They called themselves Apostolici, holding their rule to have been the Apostles' rule It may be that the Encratite Apotactics called themselves Angelici, because angels neither marry nor are given in marriage. In which case the party would be Angelici *quoad* marriage, Apostolici *quoad* property Epiphanius confesses his ignorance of the leading tenet of the Angelici [*Hær* xl or lx], and adds [*Synopsis*, lib ii] that there were none left in his day [ENCRATITES]

AQUÆI [HYDROTHEITÆ]

AQUARIANS [HYDROPARASTATÆ]

AQUILINUS A Gnostic leader mentioned by Porphyry in his Life of Plotinus, ch xvi, but of whom nothing is known

AQUINAS [SCHOOLMEN]

ARABICI, OR ARABES An obscure sect, whose founder is unknown, and which therefore some authors name from the country where it first saw light, and others by the designation "Thnetopsychitæ" It arose in Arabia early in the third century, during the reign of Severus and the pontificate of Zephyrinus, and terminated its existence, after a career of some forty years, about the middle of the same century, when a council of bishops was held [c A D 250], at which Origen, who had returned to Arabia on purpose to be present, discoursed so learnedly, that the Arabici in a body confessed their error, and returned to the bosom of the Catholic Church The error in question was a belief that the soul died with the body, though both would be recalled to life and reunited at the last day It was thought that the uninterrupted life of the soul was inconsistent with the words applied to God by St Paul, "Who only hath immortality" [1 Tim vi 16], an imaginary inconsistency caused by oblivion of the distinction between the essential immortality possessed by God alone *per se*, and the imparted immortality possessed by the soul of man as a gift from Him [Niceph *Hist Eccles* v 23. Euseb *Hist Eccles* vi 37 Aug *De Hæres* lxxxiii *Prædest Hær* lxxxiii]

ARCHONTICS A sect of heretics which arose in the second century, during the latter part of the reign of Antoninus Pius [A D 138-161], deriving their name either from those arch-spirits (ἄρχοντες) who figured in their peculiar cosmogony [Aug *De Hæres* cap 20], or from an anchorite Archon, otherwise unknown, but said to have been their founder Palestine was the original seat of this heresy, and to that country it was mainly confined, its principal opponent being Dioscorus, bishop of Crete, but some years later, in the reign of Constantius, it spread into Greater Armenia, and was conveyed thence to Lesser Armenia by Eutactus, for whom Epiphanius wittily suggests that Atactus would have been a more appropriate name Eutactus had derived his views from a certain anchorite named Peter, an inhabitant of Cabarbaricha near Hebron, who had been convicted of heresy and banished to Arabia, but had managed to return, and to continue to preach and win over converts to his strange doctrines

The Archontics agreed in many points with Simon Magus, Menander, Saturninus, and other Gnostic teachers They are charged, like other sects, with indulging in gross and open immorality, and have the singular and unexplained custom attributed to them of washing the bodies of their dead in oil and water. Among the most prominent doctrines characteristic of this sect are the following [1] In their cosmogonal works, entitled *Symphonia Major and Minor*, they asserted that there were seven worlds, each presided over by a subordinate angel or archon, who was the begetter and director of numerous ranks of spirits, and an eighth and a higher world governed by a brilliant parent power The world in which we live was under the rule of an archon called Sabaoth, not the supreme power, but identified with the God of the Jews, and said to be the father of the devil [2] They denied the inspiration of Holy Scripture, especially ridiculing the Old Testament, with the exception of a few texts which they could quote in favour of their own views, in opposition, for example, to the Biblical theory of the origin of woman, they held that she was the handiwork of the devil, and that all who married fulfilled the works of the devil [3] They denied the resurrection of the body, according to Epiphanius [Epiph *Hær* xl 8, and Aug *De Hæres* cap 20], though this fact is doubted by Tertullian [4] They rejected Baptism and the Holy Eucharist, asserting that the Sacraments were ordained by and administered in the name of the inferior archon Sabaoth, and not of the Supreme Creator [5] Redemption was supposed to consist in a knowledge of the mysteries contained in their apocryphal books, the titles of some of which have been preserved, as *Symphonia Major and Minor*, *Alienigenæ*, *Anabaticum Isaiæ* [A lengthy refutation of these points may be found in Epiphanius, *adv Hæres* lib i tom iii *Hær* 40, see also Aug *De Hæres* cap 20, Theodoret, *Hæret Fab* i c 11, Bingham, *Antiq* 478, 761, 1199]

ARCVURDIS [THONDRACIANS]

ARIANS The name given to the followers of a great and widespread heresy which began to make itself heard in the Church about the beginning of the fourth century The heresy takes its name from Arius, its first open promulgator, who was a priest of the diocese of Alexandria

I *The place of Arianism in the history of heresies* The first open irruption of Arianism into the Church is so startling a feature in the history of the time that the attention is drawn away from what preceded it, and, in part, gave rise to it It had a distinct and well-marked place in the scale of heretical development The Athanasian Creed guards against two opposite but consecutive forms of heresy in the words, "neither confounding the Persons nor dividing the substance" The first of these is Sabellianism Throughout the second century the Church was engaged in expressing definitely and defending the doctrine of the Holy Trinity against a series of attacks from heresies, the effect of which was to "confound the Persons" The last and most important of these was Sabellianism, which taught that there was but one Divine Person, and that the Word and the Holy Spirit were only emanations or functions of the Deity, the one assumed for a brief time to work out the mystery of redemption, the other to infuse life into the Church [SABELLIANS] In arguing against this, and maintaining the distinction of the Divine Persons, there was a danger of falling into an opposite error, viz that of using language which would imply Tritheism Here, then, Arianism crept in To avoid, as it seemed, the two opposite dangers of Sabellianism and Tritheism, it "divided the Substance," and so practically attacked the doctrine of the Trinity from the opposite side But the battlefield of both these heresies was the same, namely, the central truth of Christianity, the Incarnation If Sabellianism were true, the Incarnation became a mere accident of time If Arianism were true, Jesus Christ was not God Such was the conclusion to the avowal of which Arianism was driven in its later days by the necessities of argument, and thus its historical position is clear In its earliest, least impure, and most subtle form, it sprang, so far as it was sincere, from a dread of Sabellianism, while its inevitable tendency was to a definite heresy, the open denial of the Divinity of our Lord

II *The birth-place and causes of Arianism* — Though Arius was a priest of the Church of Alexandria, and there began openly to publish his opinions, yet the origin and method of his heresy may be clearly traced to Antioch The Divinity of our Lord had already been attacked at Antioch by Paul of Samosata, who was deposed from the see about A D 270 [SAMOSATENIANS] Connected with Paul, and to some extent involved in his condemnation, was Lucian, a presbyter, who afterwards suffered martyrdom, however, for the faith Lucian was a learned and able teacher of philosophy and theology, and among his pupils were several who afterwards became Arian leaders, including, it is generally thought, Arius himself Moreover, the arguments used in support of the heresy of Paul, and the general cast of arguments current in the schools of theology at Antioch, were of a rhetorical and dialectical kind They were accordingly a fit preparation for one peculiar characteristic of Arian controversy, the arguing from things earthly to things heavenly, from the things of man to the things of God One further element in the heresy may also be traced to Antioch Arianism soon began to appeal to the immorality of the time, as may be seen from the use made by Arius of a metre associated with licentious poetry in the songs composed by him to spread his opinions among the multitude Now Antioch was remarkable for a low tone of Christian life Paul was himself accused of open offences against Christian morality, and, owing to the presence of a large colony of Jews, the Christian citizens caught the tone of their luxurious habits, and were therefore, so far, ready to fall into doubts as to that part of their creed which enforced the necessity of personal self-restraint, and at the same time was most hated by all followers of Judaism And thus a number of causes combined to give scope and start to the heresy [1] A dread of Sabellianism, [2] the secret influence of Judaism, [3] a low tone of Christian life, [4] a rhetorical and dialectical habit of mind, which tried to evade mystery and reduce it to the level of argument from merely human knowledge and experience These were most prominent at Antioch, where the Divinity of our Lord had already been openly assailed, though they were to be found in other parts of the Church, and they were aided in their development by the influence of a large body of nominal Christians in all parts, who had become such not because they were attracted and subdued by its life-giving doctrines, but because the decay of heathenism had left them without a religion.

III. *Arianism in the fourth century* —The early facts about Arius and his first open declaration of heresy are somewhat involved, but it seems clear that, having been ordained deacon by Peter of Alexandria, he was connected with the MELETIAN SCHISM, and on that account was excommunicated Afterwards he regained his position, and we find him, under Achillas, in charge of one of the great city churches, Baucalis or Boucalis, and continuing to work in this position under the successor of Achillas, Alexander, for the first six years of his episcopate He had a great reputation as a logician and a preacher, as well as for strictness of life Theodoret says that he was greatly disappointed that Alexander, instead of himself, was appointed to succeed Achillas in the see of Alexandria, and that his heretical opinions took easy root in a mind which had long been prepared by discontent and envy [Theod *Hist Eccl* i 2] But his name is first distinctly connected with heretical opinions about A D 319 Rumours came to the bishop that he was privately disturbing men's faith as to the Uncreate and Eternal Being of Jesus Christ The first step taken was a private remonstrance, but nothing resulted from this Arius gained more and more support, and openly attacked the Deity of our Lord His line was to speak of Him as the Eldest and Highest of creatures, to call Him God in a certain sense, but with limitations The grounds of this view were in the main three [1] Argument from the idea of human sonship, [2] repugnance to Sabellianism, [3] a dread of dividing the Simple Essence by deriving the Son from the Father's very Being Practically, the whole view can be put in two leading propositions [1] Once the Son was not, and [2] the Son differs from other creatures in degree, not in kind.

Finding private remonstrance with Arius to be useless, Alexander was obliged to take more public and decided measures First, he assembled a public conference of the clergy, in which he himself spoke at length on the mystery of the Holy Trinity Arius was allowed full liberty of reply, and he attacked the doctrine laid down by Alexander as involving Sabellianism Finding, by the end of A.D 319, that all hopes of a peaceable arrangement were at an end, the bishop then prevailed on the majority of his presbyters and deacons to join with him in subscribing a pastoral letter, in which he exhorted the followers of Arius to renounce his heresy and submit to the Church But the heresy circulated widely and quickly, and it became necessary to bring a proportionally larger extent of influence to bear upon it. "It had spread," writes Alexander, "through all Egypt, Libya, and the upper Thebais Then we, being assembled with the bishops of Egypt and Libya, nearly one hundred in number, anathematized both them and their followers" [Athanas *Hist Tr* § 3] At this provincial council the Arian opinions, having been openly avowed and sifted, were condemned Arius and his adherents, among whom were two bishops, Secundus and Theonas, six priests, and six deacons, were excommunicated and anathematized [Socr *Hist Eccl* i 6]

Arius and his friends then withdrew to Palestine, and the next five years were occupied in arguments and remonstrances on both sides Arius found shelter, first with Paulinus of Tyre and Eusebius of Cæsarea, then with Eusebius of Nicomedia. He wrote to Alexander in a calmer and more respectful tone, withdrawing some of his extreme statements On the other hand, he sought to spread his views by poems written in a metre connected with immoral associations, and disseminated these among "sailors, millers, and travellers" [Athan *contr Arian* i 10, 22]. Several prelates espoused his cause, among them Theodotus of Laodicæa and Patrophilus of Scythopolis, and he was recognised by a synod of Bithynian bishops, which put forth a letter urging other prelates to take the same line The amount of sympathy shown by Eusebius the historian is not certain, but he wrote a letter in which he said that Christ was "not very God" [Athan *De Syn.* 5, 17], and he joined with two other bishops, Paulinus and Patrophilus, in allowing Arius to hold services for his adherents, on condition that he should seek to be reconciled to Alexander [Sozom *Hist Eccl* i 15] The whole aim of Arius, at this period of the heresy, was to treat the differences as unimportant, only made of moment by the harsh rigour of Alexander and the orthodox, but at the same time to spread the heretical opinions in every possible way

Meanwhile the principles of the new heresy began to be a matter of fierce controversy at Alexandria, and the whole city became a battlefield for the opposing parties The sacred subjects in dispute became the common talk, and were even taken up by the jesters in society and in public places of resort, while the bishop and faithful clergy became the mark for shameful accusations before the civil tribunals Alexander, however, with the aid of Athanasius, at that time a deacon, worked on steadily against the heresy He wrote letter after letter to various bishops One of these, the Encyclic, has been preserved by Socrates, and was directed against the efforts made by Eusebius of Nicomedia to procure for Arius the favour of various bishops. In it Alexander argues against and denounces the heresy as unheard of and as contrary to Holy Scripture, enumerates those who had been deposed and anathematized for holding it, and exhorts his fellow-bishops not to receive the excommunicated persons, "for it befits us as Christians to keep aloof from those who think or speak against Christ" [Socr *Hist Eccl* i. 6]. About the same time he drew up a "Tome" or doctrinal formulary, which was signed by the bishops of Egypt, including Thebais, and by those of Libya, Pentapolis, Cappadocia, Lycia, Pamphylia, Proconsular Asia, and some of those in Syria. After this he wrote to his namesake Alexander of Byzantium [Theod *Hist. Eccl* i. 3] a most important letter, in which, after complaining of the intrigues on behalf of the Arians, he went at length into their heresy and argued against it, tracing its substantial origin to those who in former times had sought to lower the dignity of the Son of God This was probably written A D 323 About the end of the same year Constantine interposed He had just triumphed over Licinius, and had become master of the East, and, finding the whole Church distracted by the controversy, he addressed a letter to Alexander and Arius In this he treated the question at issue as trivial and unimportant, and exhorted both sides to peace and unity [Euseb *De vitâ Const* ii 63-71] Hosius, bishop of Cordova, was sent with this letter to Alexandria, and there, about the end of the year A D 324 held a council, the only result of which, as regards Arianism, was to prove that the discussion caused by it could not be allayed by ordinary means Hosius, accordingly, advised the Emperor to summon a general assembly of bishops from all parts of his Empire, and, in compliance with this advice, Constantine summoned a general council of the whole Church to be held at Nicæa in Bithynia in June of the year 325

A few details as to this great council will make its important effect on the Arian heresy better understood The number of bishops present is not exactly known, but there were certainly more than three hundred, and they were attended by a multitude of other ecclesiastics "They," writes Eusebius, "who not in soul only, but in body, and country and place and nation, were far removed from one another, were brought together, and one city received all, as it were a great chaplet of priests, variegated with beauteous flowers From all the churches, which filled all Europe, Africa and Asia, there were collected together the first-fruits of the ministers of God And one house of prayer as it were enlarged by God contained within it at once Syrians and Cilicians, Phœnicians and Arabians, and those of Palestine, those moreover of Egypt, Thebais, Libya, and those who came from Mesopotamia. A Persian bishop too was present at the synod, nor was a Scythian (Goth) wanting to the choir. Pontus also, and Galatia and Pamphylia, Cappadocia and Asia and Phrygia, sent their representatives, the Thracians and Macedonians, Achæans and Epirots, and those who dwelt yet more exceedingly further, and from Spain itself the very celebrated (Hosius) one, sitting with many And of the royal city (Rome) the Bishop was absent for age, but his presbyters being present filled his place" [Euseb *De vitâ Const* iii 6. 7] The number of Arianizing prelates has also been variously stated, but probably about twenty were more or less favourable to the heresy. Its president was either Hosius of Cordova, the bearer of the Emperor's letter to the Church of Alexandria, or Eustathius of Antioch, probably the former and the place of meeting was first the great church of the city, and afterwards the palace Two other minor particulars are worth noting, viz that laymen skilled in dialectic were allowed to attend and take part in the discussions, and that Greek philosophers were also present to question [Sozom *Hist Eccl* i 18] The different elements of the Council may be stated as follows [1] The Athanasians, [2] the determined Arians, [3] the Arianizers or Eusebians; [4] a party composed of those who, on the whole, sympathized with the supporters of Alexander and Athanasius, but were not so much alive to the bearing of the points at issue A detailed history of the method pursued in the council would belong rather to a history of councils than to one of heresies, and it may suffice here to give a brief summary

The earlier discussions of the Council were private Arius had an opportunity of declaring his belief and of disputing with Athanasius, who also engaged with the other chief Arian bishops, Eusebius of Nicomedia, Maris, and Theognis But the subsequent and conclusive work of the council was to frame a creed which should state in express terms the Catholic doctrine, and guard most carefully against Arian versions The Arians offered a formula, drawn up by Eusebius of Cæsarea, in which terms of honour were given to the Son of God, but which was so contrived as to obscure and evade the point at issue. As it has been said, "The plain question at issue was whether our Lord was God in as full a sense as the Father, though not to be viewed as separable from Him, or whether, as the sole alternative, He was a creature, i e whether He was literally of and in the One Indivisible Essence which we adore as God, ὁμοούσιος Θεῷ, or of a substance which had a beginning The Arians said that He was a creature, the Catholics that He was very God; and all the subtleties of the most fertile ingenuity could not alter and could not hide this fundamental difference" [Newman's *Arians*, pp 272, 273] The Catholics, therefore, framed their creed, and the crucial point of it was the use of this word "Homoousion" To the creed were added anathemas against the Arians, and it was offered to the bishops individually for subscription By the mass of bishops it was received in its integrity Eusebius of Cæsarea accepted it after hesitating as to the "Homoousion" [Socr *Hist Eccl.* i 9]. Eusebius of Nicomedia and Theognis signed it without the anathemas Other Arian prelates gave way for fear of penalties, and in the end only Secundus and Theonas stood out They were condemned and excommunicated with Arius.

For a brief space after the Nicene Council the Church was comparatively at rest The creed was received with joy by the orthodox, and Arius, with his followers, was under the weight of the Emperor's displeasure. In this interval of rest Alexander of Alexandria died, and Athanasius was chosen in his place Towards the close of A D 328 troubles began again, and we enter upon a long and weary history of intrigues, persecutions, and violence, all intended to attack the faith which had been declared at Nicæa, and to commit the whole Church to one form or another of the heresy The first step in this direction was to gain the favour of the Emperor Arius and some of his companions, by means of court influence, some say through Constantia, the Emperor's sister, were allowed to present a fresh declaration of their belief. It was couched in moderate phraseology so as to avoid exciting suspicion. It called the Son of God, "God the Word, begotten of the Father before all ages," and was in fact intended to supplant the Nicene Creed by a politic omission which might seem to promote comprehension and peace rather than by opposition Arius was recalled A D 330 [Socr *Hist. Eccl* i 14, 16, Sozom *Hist Eccl* ii 26, 27] The next effort on the part of his adherents was to remove out of the way some of the more eminent of the orthodox bishops Eustathius of Antioch was accused of heresy and other crimes, and, notwithstanding the worthlessness of the evidence (the falsity of which was afterwards confessed by the principal witness) was deposed by an Arian synod, and banished by Constantine [Theod *Hist Eccl* i. 21, Eus *De vitâ Const* iii 60] Athanasius was made the object of a series of charges, which in the end led to his banishment After having refused to attend the Eusebian Council of Cæsarea in A D 334 [Theod *Hist Eccl* i 28], he was arraigned before another Eusebian Council at Tyre in the following year But all the accusations were refuted Afterwards, a hostile body of inquirers was sent to gather evidence against him, and on their return he was condemned in his absence, he having in the meantime gone to Constantinople to intercede with the Emperor At first the Emperor was induced to take his part and to condemn the violence of the so-called council, but his enemies then accused him of stopping the allowance of public corn made to the clergy, widows and virgins at Constantinople [Sozom *Hist Eccl* ii 28], and the Emperor banished him to Treves A D 336. In the same year Marcellus of Ancyra was accused of Sabellianism, and deposed by a synod at Constantinople; and Arius, having made another profession of faith before the Emperor, was ordered to be restored to communion in the same city His sudden death the very evening before the day appointed is one of the most awful facts of the history.

The death of Constantine [A D 337] divided the power of the Empire between his three sons, Constantine, Constantius, and Constans This change again gave the Church an interval of rest, and Athanasius was restored to his see in A D 338 [Socr *Hist Eccl* ii 3, Sozom *Hist Eccl* iii. 2] But again accusations were brought against him He was accused of having resumed his see without the sanction of a council, and an excommunicated Arian, named Pistus, was set up as a rival bishop. Charges having been laid against him before Julius of Rome, his innocence was solemnly asserted by a letter from a council of the orthodox prelates of Egypt [Athan *Apol* 3-19] But in A D 341 the Eusebians held a council at the time of the dedication of Constantine's church at Antioch, in which a canon was first passed, enacting that no bishop who should officiate after a canonical deposition should ever be restored or even heard, and this canon was made the ground for the condemnation of Athanasius At the same council three creeds were framed, all of which came as near as was politic to the truth, but avoided the test word "Homoousion" [Athan *De Synod* 22-24] Gregory of Cappadocia was made Bishop of Alexandria, and great outrages were inflicted both on the persons and churches of the orthodox at his installation Athanasius, meanwhile, withdrew to Rome Here he was favourably received, and defended by the bishop, Julius His second exile lasted until the year 349, when he was recalled by Constantius In this interval, the Council of Milan [A D 345] refused to accept a Semi-Arian Creed called the Macrostich [Socr *Hist Eccl* ii 19, 20, Sozom *Hist Eccl* iii 10], and the Council of Sardica [A D 347] once more affirmed the truth of Nicæa, while the Arian and Semi-Arian prelates, who had been summoned to meet Athanasius at Sardica, withdrew to Philippopolis, where they again condemned Athanasius, along with the Bishops of Rome, Cordova, Treves, and Sardica This was succeeded by two years of open persecution and secret intrigue, but the restoration of Athanasius in A D 349 gave a triumph to the orthodox, and in that year a large number of bishops were in communion with him The murder of Constans [A D 350] brought the West under the rule of Constantius, and a storm of trouble again fell upon the Church

Arianism, at this date, had split up into many factions, one of which had pushed the heresy to its logical conclusion, and asserted that the Son was *essentially unlike the Father* [ANOMŒANS], while another had changed the old Eusebian or Semi-Arian formula "Homoiousion," "like in essence," to "Homoion," by which they professed to avoid the term "essence" altogether, and confine themselves to asserting the "likeness" of the Son to the Father These are generally known as ACACIANS, from Acacius of Cæsarea, the pupil of Eusebius For party purposes both acted against the adherents of the Nicene faith, and for several years were able, with the aid of the imperial power, to inflict on them the gravest outrages The dispute hitherto, had been chiefly an Eastern one, but attempts were now made to Arianize the entire West The Councils of Arles [A D 353] and of Milan [A D 355], the two Conferences of Sirmium [A D 356, 357] followed one another in rapid succession Hilary of Poictiers was banished to Phrygia, Liberius the Pope to Thrace, and Hosius the aged bishop was imprisoned, while Alexandria became the scene of the greatest brutality and violence, Athanasius being compelled to find refuge from Arian fury among the monastic cells of Egypt Here he lived for five or six years, often having to fly from one place to another, and running great risks of capture, but finding time to compose epistles and orations against the Arians, and to watch with fatherly interest the trials of the Church [Athan *Hist Arian*, and *Apol de Fugâ*]. Two events must be noted in this period The first Conference of Sirmium produced an Homœan Creed, and Hosius, after having suffered a year's imprisonment as well as bodily punishment, was induced to sign it He was then allowed to return to Spain, but two years after, on his deathbed, he retracted [Athan *Hist Arian* xlv, Socr *Hist Eccl.* ii 31] Liberius having endured two years' banishment, gave up Athanasius, and signed a Semi-Arian creed, though which creed is doubtful [Athan *Hist Arian* xli, Hilar *Fragm* vi 6]. Thus by the year 357 Arianism seemed to be triumphant in the West

About this time, in the East, St Cyril of Jerusalem was deposed and exiled, while, at Antioch, the heretic Aetius was patronized and put forward by the Bishop Eudoxius [AETIANS] On the other hand the Council of Ancyra [A D 358] condemned the "Homoion" and "Homoousion" alike, and insisted on the "Homoiousion" Eudoxius and Aetius were both compelled to retire, and thus division broke up the Arian ranks About the same time Hilary of Poictiers attempted to bring about an understanding with the triumphant SEMI-ARIANS of the East, urging them to accept the "Homoousion," and explaining its true sense From this date to the death of Constantius [A D 361] there follow a succession of councils, and a succession of creeds, Semi-Arian, Homœan, or Anomœan in character The most noteworthy of these is the Western Council of Ariminum [Athan *De Synod*, Sozom *Hist. Eccl* iv], with which may be joined the Eastern Council of Seleucia [Socr *Hist Eccl* ii 39, 40] held at the same time [A D 359] Of the former it has been said, that it had "a good beginning and a foul conclusion" What is known as the "Dated Creed," drawn up under the sanction of the Emperor, and Homœan in character, was rejected, and the faith of Nicæa was affirmed but when the Council of Seleucia had held a fruitless discussion, and the delegates on both sides from Ariminum had met before the Emperor, the same Creed was sent back to the council by the Emperor, and, in the end, the bishops were persuaded to accept it, guarding it, as they thought, by anathemas against Arian opinions It is to this time that St Jerome refers in his well-known exclamation, "The whole world groaned and marvelled to find itself Arian" [Hieron *adv Lucif* vii]

The reign of Julian gave two years of comparative rest. The attempt of the Emperor to restore heathenism was combined at first with a cynical indifference for all those whom he termed "Galilæans" Accordingly, Athanasius was able to return to Alexandria, where a council was held in A D 362 This council, by its orthodoxy and moderation, did much for the Church.

It explained differences of phraseology which had arisen among the orthodox, especially as to the word Hypostasis, it anticipated the possibility of new heresies as to our Lord's Incarnation (notably that of Apollinaris), and it adhered firmly, though with moderation, to the Nicene faith The results of its wisdom were immediately felt, especially in the West Italy, Illyricum, and Gaul all made profession of the old faith, many of the bishops who had been persuaded to sign the Creed of Ariminum now repudiating it [Hieron *adv Lucif* xix] At a later date Athanasius was again compelled to fly for safety from the hatred of Julian. The short reign of Jovian for one year was the signal for his return, and brought general favour to the orthodox, but the rule of Valentinian and his brother Valens changed the aspect of the Church once more

Under Valentinian the orthodoxy of the West gained strength. The Semi-Arians indeed were allowed to reassert their formula at Lampsacus in A.D 365, but fifty-nine of their bishops conformed to the faith before Liberius in the following year, and two successive Western councils under Damasus, the successor of Liberius, denounced Arian opinions On the other hand, Valens espoused the Arian side, and gave free scope to its extreme supporters

The Epistles of St Basil describe the sufferings of the Catholics in the East, when the edict of Valens [A D 367] had again let loose the tide of persecution Athanasius was once more banished, but was shortly afterwards recalled [Sozom *Hist Eccl* vi 12, Socr *Hist Eccl* iv 13] He died in the year 373, having devoted his whole life to the maintenance of the faith of Nicæa, and again Alexandria became the scene of shameless outrages

From this date to that of the Council of Constantinople the controversy was less vehement The heresy of Apollinaris, which began with a jealousy for our Lord's Divinity and ended practically in the denial of the true humanity [APOLLINARIANS], began to absorb attention, and was a source of constant anxiety to St. Basil In A D 378, Valens put an end to Arian ascendancy and recalled the orthodox exiles His death in the same year gave the whole empire to Gratian, who had succeeded his father in the empire of the West [A D 375], and an edict was put forth giving toleration, which included all the sects connected with the Arian dispute except the Anomœans The mission of St Gregory of Nazianzum to Constantinople, where, by his gentle perseverance, he won back to the faith, to a very large extent, the city which for forty years had been the stronghold of the heresy, and the open patronage of Theodosius and Gratian, bring us to the rapid fall of Arianism

During the sixty years of its course, its success had been due in the main to two causes [1] court influence and violence, [2] the negative character of its tenets The former had now failed, and the latter had naturally resulted in divisions in its own ranks No less than twenty creeds or formulas had been put forward by councils or by individuals, while, on the other side, the one Creed of Nicæa had been stedfastly maintained This was now reaffirmed at the Council of Constantinople [A D 381], and the Church as a whole was once more free to teach the faith in its integrity. The heresy was proscribed by imperial edicts, and though, through the influence of Justina, the mother of Gratian, it gave trouble to St. Ambrose at Milan, yet newer heresies gradually took its place and absorbed the attention of the Church

IV. *Arianism among the Goths and barbarians*—The conversion of the Goths and other barbarians to Christianity, towards the end of the fourth century, was the work of Arian teachers, and introduced Arianism to a new field, of which it held possession for several centuries Ulfilas, bishop of the Goths, had subscribed the Creed of Ariminum, and was therefore, to some extent, committed to Arianism, though possibly, like others who signed the same creed, he had done so without meaning to abandon the Catholic faith [Sozom *Hist Eccl* vi 37] But at a later period, in the reign of Valens, he was sent to ask for help against the heathen Goths, and he took back to his people the Emperor's Arianism [Theod *Hist Eccl* iv 37] Through these and other barbarian tribes, Ostrogoths, Visigoths and Vandals, Arianism once more came into contact with the faith in the various countries overspread by them, viz. parts of Gaul, Spain and Africa St Chrysostom, during his episcopate at Constantinople [A D 398-407], had to deal with it among the Goths who were in that city, and tried to win over its adherents by having services in their language, and by ordaining clergy from among their own people The Burgundians, who had become Christians about A D 413, received the heresy about the middle of the same century [Socr *Hist Eccl* vii 30], and the Suevi in Spain, at the time of their conquest by the Visigoths, a few years later The end of the same century was the season of a fierce persecution of the Catholics of Africa, under the first two kings of the Vandals, Genseric and his son Hunneric But by the downfall of the Vandals in Africa and of the Ostrogoths in Italy in the sixth century, Arianism was driven from both those countries, while the conquests of the Franks served to bring back some of the other nations to the Catholic faith Thus the Burgundians became Catholic about A D 517, and Spain was also restored towards the end of the same century, after a brief outburst of persecution under the Gothic king Leovigild The heresy lived amongst the Lombards for some forty years longer, but by the middle of the seventh century it was practically extinct

V *Revival of Arianism at the time of the Reformation*—Among the many sects and heresies which accompanied the Reformation movement in the sixteenth century, a revived Arianism found a place

Michael Servetus, a native of Spain, published a work in 1531, entitled *De Trinitatis Erroribus*, in which he openly attacked the doctrine of our

Lord's Divinity He had before this been at Basle with the Reformer Œcolampadius, who had tried to make him retract For twenty years he continued teaching his heresy, travelling in various parts of Italy and France He was at last brought before the municipal council of Geneva, and was burnt alive by its order in 1553. Other individual Reformers of less note revived the heresy in one form or another, among them Lewis Hetzer, an Anabaptist, beheaded at Constance in 1529, John Campanus at Wittenberg, and Valentine Gentilis of Naples, executed at Berne in 1566 The fear of persecution in Switzerland drove some of the heretical teachers into Poland, where the doctrine of the Holy Trinity was attacked in a literary club, presided over by an Italian named Lismanini [Hardwick's *Ref* p 286, *sqq*] This, with the other partial revivals of Arianism, or as would perhaps be more accurate, of Antitrinitarianism, at last found its logical result in the more lasting and widely-spread heresy of the SOCINIANS.

VI *Arianism in England in the eighteenth century*—From A D 1690 to A D 1730 was a period of much controversy among certain divines of the English Church on the doctrine of the Holy Trinity The works of Bishop Bull were called forth, in part, by those of a number of writers, Socinian or Arian in their opinions, whose names are almost forgotten. A few years later Dr Sherlock, Dean of St. Paul's, and Dr South, Canon of Christchurch, were involved in a controversy, in which each tried to explain the doctrine of the Holy Trinity in such a way as to satisfy human reason, and each in turn incurred the charge of heresy, Dr Sherlock being accused of Tritheism and Dr South of Sabellianism Their method of disputation was essentially speculative and metaphysical They professed to deal with the question as one of pure reasoning, and neglected almost entirely the arguments from Holy Scripture and the Fathers Their language was not always reverent, and to some extent revived the recollection of Arian profanity The consequence of this dispute among those who professed to maintain the Creed was the revival of Arian opposition to it, and Arian tracts were republished and largely disseminated Many eminent persons took part in the controversy, among others Cudworth and Stillingfleet, and it is worth noticing that the former was accused of favouring the Arian view in his *Intellectual System* But the most remarkable and the closest following of Arianism was that of Dr Samuel Clarke and his friend Mr William Whiston The case of the latter was brought before Convocation in 1710, that of the former in 1714 Clarke had published, in 1712, a work entitled *The Scripture Doctrine of the Holy Trinity* In this he disclaimed the notion of being an Antitrinitarian, and professed to prove his views directly from Holy Scripture, maintaining that "whenever the terms *one* and *only* God were used in Holy Scripture they invariably meant God the Father, to the exclusion of the *other* Persons of the Godhead." From this and other arguments, especially the use of the terms "self-existent" and "unoriginated," he drew inferences derogating from the Divinity of our Lord, and maintained His *subordination in nature*. In this way he repeated the old attempt of the fourth century, to find a mean between the Catholic faith, that Jesus Christ is *essentially God*, and the extreme form of heresy which holds Him to be a *creature* Many eminent writers opposed and answered Dr Clarke's works, and some supported him. The fullest answers are those of Dr Daniel Waterland, Master of Magdalene College, Cambridge It is important to observe that this revival of Arianism was one which, for the most part, only had interest for the learned, and did not as in earlier times gain a hold over any large mass of the people.

[Eusebius, *Vit Const* Socrates, *Hist. Eccl* Sozomen, *Hist Eccl* Theodoret, *Hist Eccl* Athanasius, *Hist Arian*, *Historical Tracts*, *Contr Arian*, *De Synodis*, *Apol de Fuga* Epiphanius, *Hæres* lxix Philostorgius, *Hist Eccl* Gibbon (Milman's ed) Newman, *The Arians of the Fourth Century* Waterland's *Works* (Van Mildert's ed) vol i Neale's *Hist Eastern Church*, *Patriarchate of Alexandria* DICT *of* THEOL, ARIANISM]

ARIOMANITÆ. [ARIANS]

ARMASITES The followers of an Egyptian named Harmasius in the seventh century They were among the last offshoots of the Monothelites. [Joann Damasc *Opp* i 528]

ARMENIANS Until the Council of Chalcedon [A D 451] the Armenian Church appears to have been remarkably free from error, and in the immediately preceding period it had firmly withstood the progress of the Nestorian heresy No bishops from Armenia were, however, able to attend the Council of Chalcedon, and when the report of that council was carried to Armenia, misrepresentations and ambiguity of expression prevented its rulers from understanding the truth as to Eutyches and his heresy. In the Armenian language there is only one word to express both *Nature* and *Person*, and hence the impression was conveyed, that in recognising two Natures in our Lord, the council had proclaimed two Persons The Armenians, therefore, rejected the Council of Chalcedon, and were predisposed to favour Eutychianism. Being thus divided from the Eastern Church, the Armenians remained in an isolated position very unfavourable to the maintenance of orthodoxy, and they have always been infected with Monophysite error They have a Confession of great antiquity, which they attribute to St Gregory the Illuminator (their Apostle of the third century), in which occurs a clause respecting God the Word, "that He had one Person, one Form, and was united in one Nature," this clause—strangely enough—concluding a statement that He was incarnate of the Blessed Virgin Mary, and is undoubtedly, as far as its words go, a statement embracing the Monophysite heresy Neale, however, in his "Dissertation on the Claims of the Armenian Church to Orthodoxy" [Neale's *Hist East Ch* ii 1078], expresses his belief that the theologians of the Armenian Church completely reconcile the sense in which the clause is understood with that of the Eastern Church at large, and that the accusation of Monophysitism brought against the Armenian Church on account of their peculiar "Confession" is not really more true than the accusation of Calvinism which has often been brought against the Church of England on account of expressions contained in the Thirty-nine Articles of Religion. But all attempts to reunite the Armenians with the Eastern Church have hitherto failed

ARMINIANS. An Anti-Calvinist school of Protestants which derives its name from James Harmensen (Latinized into "Arminius"), a Calvinist minister at Amsterdam

Arminius was a cutler's son, born at Oudewater in Holland in the year 1560 He studied at Leyden from A D 1575 to 1582, and afterwards for some time at Geneva under Beza. While he was still a very young man, he was obliged to leave Geneva through fear of persecution for his bold speculations in theology, and from thence he went to become a pupil of Grynæus at Basle In 1588 he was appointed to a congregation at Amsterdam, where he was shortly put forward as champion of the SUPRALAPSARIANS in one of their endless controversies with the SUBLAPSARIANS about Predestination, Election, and Grace His championship, however, resulted in his conversion to the opinions which he had been set to oppose, and abandoning the common Calvinistic belief in predestination and the Divine decrees, he came round to the side of those who believe that Christ died for all men, and not only for an elect few He avowed this change of opinion in 1591, but still continued in his post until he was appointed Professor of Divinity at Leyden, which was in the year 1603 His lectures on the Epistle to the Romans soon raised a fierce and wide controversy so fierce that the government of the State was obliged to interfere. A synodal conference was proposed between Arminius and his followers on the one side, and the strict Calvinists, led by Francis Gomar, the professorial colleague of Arminius, on the other But the controversy preyed upon the health of Arminius, and before any steps were taken towards the convocation of the proposed synod he died, on October 19th, 1609

After the death of Arminius, the two parties became even more virulently opposed to each other than they were before, and the theological question was also mixed up with a political one, the Arminians wishing for peace with Spain, and the Calvinists urging the Prince of Orange and the States-General to undertake a war Prince Maurice was at first in favour of the Arminian party, while they had supporters at court in Barneveldt, Grotius, Hoogerbetz, and others, but the Stadtholder soon changed his mind, and became their most bitter opponent and persecutor

When the Conference met at the Hague in the year 1610, the Arminian party presented a statement of their doctrine in the form of a "Remonstrance" in five articles, which are, in substance, as follows

I. That God, before the foundation of the world, or from eternity, decreed to bestow eternal salvation on those whom He foresaw would keep their faith in Christ Jesus inviolate until death; and, on the other hand, to consign over to eternal punishments the unbelieving who resist the invitations of God to the end of their lives

II That Jesus Christ, by His death, made expiation for the sins of all and every one of mankind yet that none but believers can become partakers of this Divine benefit.

III That no one can, of himself, or by the powers of his free will, produce or generate faith in his own mind, but that it is necessary a man, who is by nature evil and incompetent (*ineptus*) both to think and to do good, should be born again, and renewed by God, for Christ's sake, through the Holy Spirit

IV That this Divine grace or energy, which heals the soul of man, commences, advances, and perfects all that can be called truly good in man and therefore all good works are ascribable to no one except to God only, and to His grace yet that this grace compels no man against his will, though it may be repelled by his perverse will.

V That those who are united to Christ by faith, are furnished with strength abundantly to overcome the snares of the devil and the allurements of sin, but whether they can fall from this state of grace, and lose their faith or not, does not yet sufficiently appear, and must be ascertained by a careful examination of the Holy Scriptures

These five articles of the "Remonstrance" became the watchword of the Arminian party, who were hence called "Remonstrants," the Calvinist or Gomarist party being "Counter-Remonstrants" The articles became known as "The Five Points," and the dispute between the two parties was dignified with the name of "The Quinquarticular Controversy"

The Hague Conference of 1610 failed to bring about any reconciliation of the two parties, as did also another held at Delft in the year 1613 Equally powerless was a conciliatory decree promulgated by the States-General in 1614, in which (under the influence of Grotius and Barneveldt) toleration was declared towards both parties, and further controversy forbidden The Calvinists grew more and more confirmed in their bitterness towards the Arminian party, refused to obey this edict, in their usual persecuting spirit called for their suppression "by blood" if it could not be effected otherwise, and became so violent that the Arminian party raised a militia in self-defence The Prince of Orange and the States-General at last determined to summon another and larger assembly of Protestant divines, the decision of which would be final.

The Synod of Dort, thus convened, met at Dort or Dordrecht on November 13, 1618, and continued to sit until the end of April 1619 It was composed entirely of Calvinist divines, comprising, besides those of Holland and Germany, some from the Presbyterians of Scotland, from Switzerland, and from England the latter being Carlton, Bishop of Llandaff, Hall, afterwards Bishop of Norwich; Davenant, afterwards Bishop of Salisbury, and Ward, his successor in the Margaret Professorship of Theology The English divines were sent by James I from a politic desire to promote some sort of union, if possible, between the Continental Protestants and the Church of England, but it is hardly necessary to say that the decisions of the Synod of Dort never had any authority whatever in the Church of England James I was, indeed, responsible in some degree for the subsequent persecution of the Arminians, having written a tract against Vorstius, one of their leaders, in which he had declared that the latter ought to be burned as a heretic

The Arminians appeared before the Synod of Dort, under the leadership of Simon Episcopius, one of the Leyden Professors of Theology, who began the proceedings by an attempt to confute the opinions of the Calvinists [DORT, SYNOD OF] The nature of the assembly was at once shewn by its refusal to hear Episcopius and his friends in any other way than as accused persons who were on their defence, and the Arminians, finding that their controversial opponents were assembled, not to confer with them, but to be their judges, declined to have anything further to do with the synod They were, of course, condemned in their absence, the opinions of the Counter-Remonstrants being adopted and enforced in ninety-three canons It was also decided that the Arminian ministers, who numbered about three hundred, should be expelled from their offices and excommunicated Some refused to submit to the decree of the synod, but fine, imprisonment, and exile were imposed upon all who resisted The aged senator, Barneveldt, who had been their protector, was put to death, Grotius and Hoogerbetz were sentenced to imprisonment for life while the bulk of the party escaped to France and England After two years' imprisonment, Grotius succeeded in escaping by concealing himself in a linen chest, but he was an object of bitter hatred to the Dutch Calvinists all his life, and when, in 1631, he ventured to return for a few months to his native country, he was once more obliged to fly through danger of fresh persecution

In the year 1634, however, an edict of toleration towards the Arminians was once more passed, and Episcopius returned to open a Remonstrant College in Amsterdam Episcopius formalized the theories of Arminius, and extended them in the direction of Socinianism and Universalism From that time the Arminians shewed a marked tendency towards Rationalism, and one after another of the doctrines held by orthodox theologians being eliminated from their system, their sect in the end has recognized Christianity as little more than a system of morality, in which every person may regulate his belief by his own conceptions of Holy Scripture They have been growing fewer in Holland during the present century, and are not now to be found in any number except in Rotterdam

ENGLISH ARMINIANS have never become a distinct sect In the reign of Charles I it was the fashion to brand with the name all who were opposed to the cruel and false dogma of the Calvinists respecting divine decrees to perdition, and the High Church party were thus called Arminians After the Restoration, the name passed away from the High Church to the Latitudinarians, the Arminianism of England thus running parallel at this time to that of Holland, but never going further in the direction of Rationalism than the half-developed Universalism of the Tillotson school When Wesley and Whitfield struck out divergent lines of theology, the original form of the dispute between Arminius and the Calvinists was revived, Wesley taking the Arminian side, and Whitfield becoming the founder of the Calvinistic Methodists In still more recent times, the dreadful dogma of Calvinism respecting Predestination and Election has been held by comparatively few persons, at least in the Church of England, and the doctrine of Universal Redemption, for which Arminius chiefly contended, is not disputed by any theologians of importance. [Heylin's *Quinquarticular History* Mosheim's *Eccl Hist* II ii 4 Nichol's *Life and Works of Arminius*, 1825 Brandt's *Hist Reform* transl 1720 (Brandt was a Remonstrant Professor of Divinity at Amsterdam) Wesley's *Works*, vol x ed 1829. DICT *of* THEOL art ARMINIANISM]

ARNOLDISTS. The supporters of a movement against the temporal power of the Papacy which was led by Arnold of Brescia, and which placed it in a position of much danger for about twenty years in the middle of the twelfth century [A D 1135-1155]

Arnold was a monk of Brescia or Brixia in the north of Italy, and a pupil of the the vain and restless Abelard About the year 1135 he began to indoctrinate the people of Lombardy with the always popular notion that it is wrong for the clergy to possess any property This teaching coincided with a movement which the Lombard towns were making to establish themselves in a position of independence as free cities, and thus the people were excited to look upon the bishops and clergy as political enemies, whose wealth was a hindrance to the development of republican institutions Arnold was condemned (in company with the PETROBUSIANS) at the second Lateran Council, under Pope Innocent II [A D. 1139], and although not excommunicated, was banished from Italy He retired to France, seeking safety with his friend Abelard, but encountering the opposition of St Bernard, and being in danger of imprisonment as an enemy of the Church, he fled to Zurich, where he lived for about five years His principles had spread so widely that the Romans raised an insurrection in the year 1143 for the purpose of establishing a republic on the ancient model, and Arnold was summoned from Zurich to become the leader of the movement Pope Lucius II was killed on

February 15th, 1145, while endeavouring to recover possession of the Capitol, and the rebellion was carried on by Arnold and his adherents through the reigns of the two succeeding Popes, Eugenius III and Anastasius IV The Englishman Hadrian IV succeeded to the Papal throne at the end of the year 1154, and he at once brought the Romans to submit to his authority by placing the city under an interdict, the first which they had ever experienced After ten years of violence and disorder the Arnoldist party was thus broken up, Arnold himself taking refuge in Campania A few months afterwards the Emperor Frederic I, having suppressed the rebellious movement in Lombardy, caused Arnold to be delivered into the hands of the Pope, when he was immediately hanged as a traitor, his dead body being burned, and the ashes of it thrown into the Tiber [A D 1155] Arnold was in close alliance with the anti-sacramental heretics of his day, and he himself was accused of unsoundness in respect to Infant Baptism and the Sacrament of the Altar "Præter hæc, de sacramento altaris et baptismo parvulorum non sane dicitur sensisse" The opposition of St Bernard points in the same direction, as do the terms in which he speaks of Arnold in his 195th Epistle, written A D 1140 There can be little doubt that he had originally imbibed a free-thinking tone of mind from Abelard, and that his republican notions made him sympathize at least with the Paulician heretics who at that time existed in considerable numbers in France and Italy After his death the party of the Arnoldists was little heard of, but they regarded their leader as a saint and a martyr [Luc Tudens in *Bibl Max Lugd* xxv 247, Otto Fris *de rebus gestis Frid* ii 20, in Murator xxi]

ARRHABONARII The name given by some Roman theologians to a small school of Polish Anti-Sacramentalists, who maintained that the Holy Eucharist conveys no present gift of grace, but the pledge or earnest (*ἀῤῥαβὼν*) of a gift to be bestowed in Heaven The opinion was first broached in the year 1543 by Stancarus, professor of Hebrew at Cracow [STANCARISTS]

ARSENIAN SCHISM This name is given to the disturbance of communion between the Churches of Alexandria and Constantinople, which occurred through the deposition of the Constantinoplitan Patriarch Arsenius [A D 1265]

On the death of the Emperor Theodore Lascaris [A D 1258], Arsenius and Michael Palæologus became guardians of his son John Lascaris, then only eight years of age Palæologus was shortly afterwards made successively despot and emperor by the army, and Arsenius consented to crown him on condition of his taking an oath to resign the empire to John Lascaris when the latter attained his majority The new emperor, however, gradually shewed that he was determined not to redeem his pledge, and the patriarch, hopeless of persuading him to do so, ceased to fulfil the duties of his office, but would not give any formal acknowledgment that he had vacated it Nicephorus, metropolitan of Ephesus, was then made patriarch, but died after holding office for a year Shortly after his death Arsenius was restored by Palæologus, whom the patriarch crowned a second time on the occasion of the re-capture of Constantinople from the hands of the Romans [A D 1261] At this second coronation the patriarch required no promise of abdication in favour of the young John Lascaris, who was soon after imprisoned and cruelly blinded by Palæologus Upon hearing, however, of this cruelty Arsenius excommunicated Palæologus, and the latter determined to displace him from the patriarchal throne A council of compliant bishops was called, who listened to the emperor's complaints and accusations, declared the deposition of Arsenius, and made Germanus of Adrianople patriarch of Constantinople in his place

The Patriarch Nicolas of Alexandria regarded this as a schismatical act, and would hold no communion with Germanus, and although he died within a year of the deposition of Arsenius the Churches ceased to hold intercourse with each other during the reign of Michael Palæologus On his death in A D 1283 a temporary reconciliation was effected, but fresh disputes arose out of the question of union between the Roman and Eastern Churches, and the two patriarchates were only reunited when the general persecution of Eastern Christians by the Mahometans in the beginning of the fourteenth century merged minor troubles in the greater one of an antichristian tyranny [Neale's *History of Church of Alexandria*, ii 311-321]

ARTEMONITES. A sect holding Monarchian views on the subject of the Trinity, and called after its founder Artemon or Artemas, who began to broach his errors in the earlier part of the third century, during the reign of Septimius Severus Exactly similar doctrines had been taught a few years previously by Theodotus, a currier of Byzantium, excommunicated by Victor [A D 192-201], with whom, in spite of the absence of any historical proof to that effect, Artemon is popularly classed [THEODOTIANS] The new sect met with considerable success, both as regards the number and distinction of those who joined it Among them was a distinguished confessor named Natalius, who consented for a time to become their bishop, but on being warned of his error by a severe flagellation (attributed to angelic hands) during his sleep, withdrew, and was readmitted to the Church by Zephyrinus [Euseb *Hist Eccl* v 28] Monarchian views however lingered on for more than a century in the Christian Church, being revived by Paul, bishop of Samosata [A D. 260-270], and afterwards by Photinus, condemned in a synod held A D 351

Artemon, the inventor of this heresy, attempted to solve the mystery of the Trinity and Unity not by supposing, with Praxeas, that Father, Son, and Holy Ghost were three phases of one Divine Monad, but by denying the Divinity of the Second and Third Persons, and accounting for the superior character of Christ by asserting that after His birth, as mere man, a certain portion of the Divine Nature was imparted to him. [BERON] He also asserted that this view was identical with that of the Roman Christians from the first foundation of their Church till the time of Zephyrinus, yet not only are there no facts on record which support such an assertion, but there are several, such as the excommunication of Theodotus by Victor [*vide supra*], which are directly incompatible with it The Artemonites appealed largely to sources external to Christianity, to philosophy and geometry, in support of their peculiar tenets, and their method of proceeding is thus summed up by Eusebius —

"They presume to alter the Holy Scriptures, to abandon the ancient rule of faith, and to form their opinions according to the subtile precepts of logic The science of the Church is neglected for the study of geometry, and they lose sight of heaven while they are employed in measuring the earth. Euclid is perpetually in their hands Aristotle and Theophrastus are the objects of their admiration, and they express an unusual reverence for the works of Galen Their errors are derived from the abuse of the arts and sciences of the infidels, and they corrupt the simplicity of the Gospel by the refinements of human reason" [Euseb *Hist Eccl* v 28]

More than a thousand years afterwards, John Crell, a German Unitarian divine [A D 1590-1633], the author of *L M Artemonii Initium Evangelii Johannis*, assumed the title of Artemonite to distinguish himself from the Socinians [Euseb *Hist Eccl* v 28 August *Hæres* xliv Pseudo-Jerome, *de Hæres* xliv Stemmler, *Diatribe de sect Artemonii* Schaffhausen, *Hist Artem et Artemonii*]

ARTOTYRITÆ A party of the later Phrygian Montanists which used cheese (τυρός) as well as bread (ἄρτος) in the celebration of the Holy Eucharist [Epiph *Hær* xlix, August *Hær* xxviii] The primitive offerings, they argued, were of the fruit of the flock as well as of the fruit of the ground, and cheese was their symbol of the former It might be thought that this fruit of the flock was only presented at the altar, a practice forbidden in *Apost Canon* ii, but Epiphanius' words can be interpreted only to mean that it was actually introduced into the greater oblation

Ittigius [*de Hæres* p 257] finds a reference to this custom in the acts of Perpetua and Felicitas Perpetua is said to have related that she saw in vision an old shepherd milking his flock He welcomed her, and gave her a morsel of cheese, which she received with joined hands, and ate, while all the bystanders said, Amen From this she inferred that she was to suffer martyrdom The inference was drawn, according to Ittigius, from the custom of giving the Viaticum to martyrs, and from the use of cheese by the Artotyritæ It is supposed therefore that Perpetua was of that sect But there is a difficulty in the words "de caseo quod mulgebat" Augustine's report of the vision is that a "buccella lactis," a mouthful of milk, was given to Perpetua, and one is unwilling to think that Perpetua was of the fanatical sect of the Artotyritæ. Above all, the history of Montanism makes it unlikely that the Artotyritæ existed at Carthage so early as A D 202 For which reasons it appears to be more probable that the compiler of the Acts, who was certainly a Montanist, altered the vision to suit the practice of his own party [See the Acts, with the notes of Holstein and Possinus, in Galland *Bibl* ii pp 175, 185]

ASCITÆ A fanatical offshoot of the Montanists towards the close of the second century, so called from their holding periodical religious revels, during which they danced on skin or leather bottles [ἀσκοί] and imagined themselves to be fulfilling the words of Holy Scripture, "Neither do men put new wine into old bottles, else the bottles break, and the wine runneth out, and the bottles perish but they put new wine into new bottles, and both are preserved" [Matt ix 17] They are with great probability identified with the ASCODRUGITÆ

ASCLEPIODOTIANS So named from Asclepiodotus, a follower of Theodotus the leather-seller of Byzantium, who, like his master, taught that Christ was a mere man, and who, with his disciples, was excommunicated, c A D. 224, by Pope Urban [THEODOTIANS]

ASCODROGITÆ [ASCODRUGITÆ]

ASCODRUGITÆ These fanatics appeared first in Galatia towards the close of the second century, in the reign of Commodus [A D 180-193]. They have been considered by some to be the same as the ASCITÆ, and by others to be identical with the PASSALORYNCHITES All agree in connecting them with the followers of Montanus, whom they regarded as the Paraclete, and with whose spirit they imagined themselves to be filled when they danced around a richly-vested inflated wine-skin [ἀσκός] placed on an altar in their fanatical revels They denied altogether the validity of the Sacraments, saying that grace could not be conferred through material means, and they made justification and sanctification equivalent terms for a knowledge of mysteries which they had borrowed from the Valentinians and Marcosians. The Constitution of Theodosius and Valentinian III [A D 428], for suppressing heresy, names this sect [*Cod Theod* XVI v 65] The tenth constitution of the same title names Tascodrogitæ, a confusion between the name of the present sect and that of the TASCODRUNGITÆ

ASCODRUPITÆ [ASCODRUTI]

ASCODRUTI, OR ASCODRUPITÆ. This name might be thought a corruption of the Montanist Ascodrogitæ, but Theodoret reckons the party so called among the Marcosian Gnostics, and describes their practice as the reverse of the Montanist practice They rejected all outward signs in religion, and consequently renounced even the Sacraments Perfect spiritual knowledge was their redemption [Theod *Hær fab* i 10] Origen [Περὶ Εὐχῆς] mentions such as these, men who take away all that can be perceived by the senses, and use neither baptism nor Eucharist.

ASCOPHITES A section of the ARCHONTICS, who are spoken of by Theodoret as having arisen about A D 173 They are alleged to have rejected the Old Testament Scriptures, to have denied the use of good works, and to have destroyed the sacred vessels in churches through hatred of the Holy Eucharist [Theod *Hær fab* i 10]

ASSOCIATE SYNOD. [BURGHERS SECESSION]

ASSOCIATE PRESBYTERY, CONSTITUTIONAL [ANTIBURGHERS]

ASSURITANS One of the many small and obscure sects of Donatists They rose in the reign of Constantius II while Liberius was Pope [c A D 358], and are mentioned by St Augustine as having been condemned by the Council of Bagai or Vaga in Numidia [A D 394], which was attended by three hundred and ten Donatist bishops [*contr Epist Parmen* lib. iii sec 29]

ASTATHIANS [ἀ—ἵστημι, called in Latin "Instabiles"] This was a name given to the followers of a certain Sergius, who rose in Phrygia, beyond whose limits the sect never extended, in the earlier part of the ninth century, and who received the greater part of the Manichæan errors. They met with some encouragement from the Emperor Nicephorus [A.D 802-811], but were suppressed by his successor Michael Rhangabes [A.D 811 813] They have been at various times identified with the Antiganians, mentioned by Theophanes, and by some French writers [Père Goar, &c], with the wandering bodies of "Bohemians" and "Egyptians" which appeared in France during the Middle Ages

ASTROLOGERS [MATHEMATICI]

ATHEISTS Those who deny the existence of God [ἀ Θεός] Such denial is rarely, however, formulated into a statement of belief in the absolute non-existence of Deity, and Atheism in its strict sense can hardly be said to have existed except in the gross Materialism of some benighted savages The dualism of spirit and matter is elsewhere universally acknowledged, and in that spirit there is always something more or less divine Believers in a divine principle will sometimes apply the term to those who do not symbolize with the same religious idea as their own Thus those who accept the teaching of revelation often look upon all without the pale of the Church as Atheists, whereas there is no Atheism in such a system as that which Plato taught, and thereby, directly or indirectly, leavened heathenism before and after the day of Christ. The heathen on the other hand denounced the Christian brotherhood as Atheists because they refused to burn incense on the altars of paganism When heresy openly attacked the Church, its most virulent exponent, the Arian, was emphatically termed "Atheist," as denying the true divinity of Christ, also as being delivered over to Satan under the excommunication of the Church, and therefore cut off from the people of God Similarly, the various forms of philosophic thought that substitute the deductions of human reason, with respect to the spiritual principle that is supreme, for the more plain and intelligible teaching of the Bible, are often classed under one wide category of Atheism If we except Materialism, an outflow from the hylozoic principle of Epicurus, which may be traced back to Moschus [Cudworth, *Int Syst*], according to Strabo contemporary with the Trojan war, if we except also the wild ravings of Comte and his deification of Humanity as "le Grand Etre," which certainly reject all notion of a God, all else have believed in a spiritual principle greater and mightier than matter, often, however, antecedently coeternal with matter, and which, like matter, would never have an end

I That which was formally called "Atheism" is now seen to be "Pantheism," a term which in Cudworth may generally be substituted for the former. Yet Pantheism is virtually Atheism, for the notion of Personality gives a broad mark of distinction between Theism and Pantheistic Atheism. A divine principle that is impersonal clearly can have no sympathy with man in his trials and sorrows, and therefore can be no object of love and adoration The life of man under such a system could in no sense be redeemed from Atheism That Being alone is to be termed God who can hear prayer, and bind his creatures by wise laws, and reward or punish according to their obedience or rebellion Pantheism therefore, practically, is nothing else than Atheism, it has no belief in a personal deity overruling the affairs of the world, as divine Providence, and therefore it is atheistic Thus in modern days the great contest without the Church, though often aided on the side of Rationalism from within it, has not been between various forms of Atheism, but between Theism on the one side and Pantheism on the other Theism believes in a spirit superior to matter, and so does Pantheism, but the spirit of Theism is self conscious, and therefore personal and of individual existence, a nature *per se*, and upholding all things by an active control, while Pantheism believes in spirit that is of a higher nature than brute matter, but is a mere unconscious principle of life, impersonal, irrational as the brute matter that it quickens, receiving the law of its existence from necessity, and wholly bound by it, its highest manifestation being the intellect of an aggregate manhood. Between these two, but nearer to Pantheistic Atheism, lies Deism, which adopts the Stoic notion of a passive Deity, eternally removed from all concern about the lower world of its creation, and therefore in no respect an object for man's adoring regard The Deism of Hobbes was essentially atheistic, as regards any moral control of the creature

II Atheism thus understood has its objective and its subjective sides, objectively it is engendered from without by theoretical and subtle reasonings, having for their object the uprooting of faith from every heart, and the setting up of the abomination of desolation in the temple of every soul Such were those numerous publications that made their appearance in Paris about the middle of the last century, and gave expression to Atheism as the latent principle of Materialism [Buckle, *H of Civil in Engl*] Baron Holbach, about that time, a wealthy native of Heidesheim in the Palatinate [b A D 1723, d A D 1789], having established himself in a noble mansion at Paris, formed the nucleus of a clique of free-thinkers afterwards famous as the Encyclopédistes They embodied the active principle of all the Materialism and Atheism which preceded, and in no slight degree prepared the way for, the old French Revolution of 1790 Such were Diderot, Duclos, Helvetius, Marmontel, Grimm, Laharpe, Condorcet, Raynal, and for a time at least Rousseau, d'Alembert, and Buffon Numerous atheistical pamphlets and papers, with translations of English Deistical treatises, were issued by this fraternity, printed chiefly at the Baron's expense, and generally anonymously. He himself, however, was the author, as it was said, of nearly fifty pieces, for which services he was duly honoured with their honorary diploma by the Universities of Mannheim, Berlin, and St Petersburg The famous *Système de la Nature, ou des lois du monde physique et moral*, appeared [A D 1770] as a posthumous work of Mirabeau, Secretary of the Academy, but was composed in reality by Holbach, La Grange, or Grimm, or by a staff of writers, which was more probably the case [DICT *of* DOCT *and* HIST THEOLOGY, ATHEISM] Its tone is that of a materialistic Atheism There is nothing in existence, it declares, save matter and motion, existing as attraction and repulsion, physical and moral. The laws of motion are eternal and invariable Man is altogether material Thought and will are mere modifications of cerebral matter Belief in God and of the soul's existence are fallacies arising from a mistaken distinction of matter and spirit. Man is no more free than he is immortal Self-interest lies at the bottom of every human action, and of all laws and morals. Failing to account for the origin of matter and motion, there is a *petitio principii* throughout the book. Other atheistical productions were professedly written by Holbach—*Le Christianisme dévoilé* [1758], and his *Histoire Critique de Jesus-Christ*, which appeared soon after the *Système de la Nature* He died in the first year of the Revolution [A D 1789]

The era of infidelity had now set in, and the march of Atheism became rapid and uninterrupted Everything suggestive of religion in public and civil life was roughly torn away and replaced by the utterances of Atheism The wayside crosses were demolished, the emblem of private devotion, the rosary, was interdicted, and under the new republican calendar the Lord's Day was abrogated, and the decades of each month were the only holidays In the end religion, stripped of every accessory of honour, of every attribute of life, was formally proscribed as the foe of equality and liberty, and Atheism was openly proclaimed in the National Assembly The Cathedral of Notre-Dame was desecrated by a solemn renunciation of the Christian religion, and by its re-dedication as the Temple of Reason [Nov 10th, A D 1793] A woman, the lowest of the low, was borne along the streets in a triumphal car, impersonating the Goddess of Reason, and enthroned upon the high altar of the cathedral, where hymns were sung and incense burned in her honour. As the crowning act of all this horrible wickedness, the Bible was burnt in public by the hangman Thenceforth it was accepted as the creed of France, that there is no God and no Providence, and as a public avowal of the persuasion that there is no future life, an inscription was placed over the entrance of each cemetery, more dreadful than the "Lasciate ogni speranza" of Dante—"Death is an eternal sleep" "The reign of Atheism," let it never be forgotten, was the "reign of Terror" But the abyss of wretchedness was too horrible even for the red republic of 1793 Atheism could not be endured long by the human spirit, and on May 7th, A D 1794, Robespierre, dripping with the blood of his victims, constituted himself the priest of Deism, and induced the National Assembly to pass a resolution to the effect that for the future the existence of a Supreme Being should be asserted; that belief in the immortality of the soul should be re-established as an article of Gallican faith; and that a solemn festival in honour of the Supreme God should be holden The reaction of society, even in this miserable degree, was a type of the reaction that has always given to the dying atheist the fearful anticipation of the worm that dieth not, the first scathing foretaste of the fire that never can be quenched The cowardice of Shelley in the storm at sea, and his horror of conscience, only more dreadful in his last moments when actually struggling for the dear life: the dying bed of Voltaire, so dreadful that his nurse would never after tend a dying infidel, the curses before which his atheistic friends took flight, the shrieks of terror that his doctor could only compare with the agony of Orestes, "furiis agitatus" also the close of the infidel Paine's life, in alternate prayer to the God whom he had defied, and in its reaction of blasphemy, his utter desertion by God and man—these are the encouragements Atheism holds out to its disciples, and which may convince any reasonable intellect that it is the fool and the fool only who can "say in his heart there is no God"

III Atheism, in its subjective phase, is seen in the historian of Atheism—Maréchal, who, from some misfortune perhaps of early association, accepted his no-creed as a Turk or a Jew accepts the religion under which he is born An account of his *Dictionnaire des Athées* is given in the DICTIONARY *of* DOCTRINAL *and* HISTORICAL THEOLOGY, ATHEISM

But there is a subjective Atheism lurking among all imperfectly instructed masses; an Atheism that crops up while men sleep, and occupies the soul by an approach so stealthy as to be imperceptible It is of such that Job says, "They meet with darkness in the day-time, and grope in the noon-day as in the night" [Job v 14], who living under the clear light of the Sun of Righteousness, deny the existence of God, because in their lives they have never known Him For there is a moral as well as an intellectual Atheism, an obliquity of judgment in those who, without troubling themselves with speculative subtleties

Atheists

and sophistical arguments, are possessed with the evil heart of unbelief, and, without talking themselves into Atheism, act it. Faith and a good conscience are inseparable, the carnal heart is always more or less dark with unbelief It may not be the prey of any active form of infidelity, which implies some exercise of the judgment and of reasoning, however wrong, but it is the blank Atheism of a heart living without God in the world It results principally from negative conditions of the soul and conscience, commencing in early life with the neglect of positive discipline in the ways of religion and moral training, fostered by a spirit rendered gross by self-indulgence or by the continuous pursuit of gain, the cowardice of shrinking from self-sacrifices that are painful to flesh and blood, and lazily sinking without an effort in the "thick clay" of worldly vice and folly, such sluggishness has its natural issue in practical Atheism The moral coward and the unbelieving, δειλοὶ καὶ ἄπιστοι, are in the same category of condemnation Akin to these negative qualities, that effectually blind the soul to all consciousness of God's presence, is a disregard of truth, the natural growth of the self-corrupting heart, the strong delusion that, as God's judgment upon sin, compels it to believe a lie [2 Thess ii 11], and act the lie it believes

But practical Atheism is not only of this negative character, its growth is also forced on by the plastic energy of evil, that is of the very essence of man's fallen nature The will of Christ was wholly one with the will of the Father, that will is our high exemplar The standard of right, which humanity at large by its sense, whatever may be its practice, shews to be true, is the manifestation of God's will to the collective soul of that humanity, the perverse will that starts aside from this general sense of humanity is altogether opposed to God's will, and as it is only by being brought under subjection to the will of God that man's will recovers its spontaneous action, so there is an irresistible logic in the life, and obedience to the divine will is a virtual acknowledgment, while disobedience is the denial, of God's being The active tendency of the unregenerate will is atheistic It is a perverse will, ἄπιστος καὶ διεστραμμένη [Matt xvii. 17] are its coupled attributes Whatever suits not its prejudices and presentiments it rejects, the sight of the eye and the hearing of the ear have a reality in them that overrules the inner teaching of the hidden sense of faith. The presence of God does not come home to the senses, and that presence is in practice denied It is a proud, imperious will Pride is the very essence of Satanic being; the heady height (ὕψωμα) "that exalteth itself against the knowledge of God" [2 Cor x 5] Pride too is vile before man as being the outcropping of untruthfulness, of which it is only a phase It fills a man with self-conceit, and is as a false varnish concealing internal defects with a specious assumption of superior wisdom It is the soul of every atheistic paradox, and treats with scorn the homely teaching of an everyday faith. Pride knows no retreading of any path of error, but to whatever conclusion it may be led it is prepared to justify its issues. Where pride is the active principle of a man's unbelief, "there is more hope of a fool than of him," more hope of him who has learned the parrot-talk of Atheism than of the heart which is darkened by a pride that can never confess its erring "Ye say ye see, therefore your sin remaineth"

But there is no school of Atheism so sure of doing its work as a vicious life flowing from the various germs of evil above noticed, in works denying the existence of a moral Governor of the universe. "Infidelity," says Barrow, "hath a larger territory than we suppose, many infidels do lurk under the mask of a Christian profession It is not the name of a Christian, nor the badges of our religion that make a Christian, more than a cowl doth make a monk, or the beard a philosopher There may be a creed in the mouth where there is no faith in the heart, and a cross impressed on the forehead of an infidel
Is he not an infidel who denieth God? such a renegado is every one that liveth profanely, as St Paul teacheth us [Tit i 16] And have we not many such renegadoes? If not, what meaneth that monstrous dissoluteness of life, that horrid profaneness of discourse, that strange neglect of God's service, or desolation of God's law? Where such luxury, such lewdness, such avarice, such uncharitableness, such universal carnality doth reign, can faith be there? Can a man believe there is a God and so affront Him? can he believe that Christ reigneth in heaven and so despise His laws? Can a man believe a judgment to come and so little regard his life? a heaven and so little seek it? a hell and so little shun it? Faith, therefore, is not so rife, infidelity is more common than we take it to be, every sin hath a spice of it, some sins smell rankly of it" [*Serm* i *on the Creed*] It may reasonably be asked, were these words only suitable to cavalier consciences, and have they no *vis viva* at the present day? Such practical Atheism is a far more active agent in the dissemination of infidelity than the productions of all the infidel presses in the world [1]

IV The present is scarcely the occasion for exhibiting the antidote of Atheism. This must chiefly be administered in the way of prevention by taking care that the young are led to a knowledge of God and of His ways, by the training of a religious education, and by the force of religious example in the Christian home. If Atheism is precipitated in the social cauldron from the presence of incompatible elements with no affinity for each other, by the heartlessness of the rich, hatred and envy on the part of the poor, and selfishness everywhere; these elements must be subdued and eliminated, if the practical Atheism that they engender is to be killed down in the

[1] Atheism and immorality go hand in hand Dr Johnson noted the fact in his own way when he told Boswell to go home and count his spoons after an infidel had been his guest

rising generation Where there is no faith in humanity, there can be little faith in the Disposer of the various estates and conditions of men If sin is the reproach of any nation, Atheism is pre-eminently so, for it is caused not merely by the viciousness of the individual intellect, but by the general tone of society that surrounds it, and has set in motion those discordant vibrations that in the end become the habitual jarring of the evil heart of unbelief. All have their work to do in the reparative process Atheism must be rooted out from the great population-beds, "by pureness, by knowledge, by long-suffering, by kindness, by the Holy Ghost, by love unfeigned, by the word of truth, by the power of God, by the armour of righteousness on the right hand and on the left" [2 Cor vi 6, 7]

ATHINGANI [ἀ—θιγγάνω] A title bestowed in the eighth century upon a sect of Paulicians which rose in Asia Minor in the reign of Constantine Pogonatus [A D 668-685] They began to be so called in the days of the Empress Irene [A D 797-802], when they acquired the name of Attingians or "Separates," because they rejected image-worship, with the veneration of the cross and of relics, and cut themselves off from all connection with the hierarchy of the dominant party They were also called Paulo Johannites. Their distinctive practice, apart from other Paulician heretics, appears to have been that of baptizing with the words "I am the living water," instead of the Catholic formula

ATHOCIANS Heretics of the thirteenth century who rejected the doctrine of the immortality of the soul [*Cent Magd*, *cent.* xv 5]

ATTINGIANS [ATHINGANI]

AUDÆANS [AUDIANS]

AUDIANS About the time of the Council of Nicæa, Audius (or Audæus) formed his sect[1] He was a Syrian of Mesopotamia, an upright and zealous man, led into schism through the workings of intemperate zeal, and the assertion of self-will He took upon himself the office of censor of Church morality, reproving to their face bishops and clergy whom he considered to be living covetously or luxuriously. He was beaten, and suffered other indignities Unable to bear them he separated himself from the Church, and was irregularly consecrated bishop by a bishop who had joined his schism. His adherents adopted a monastic life both in town and country In order to have specific points of difference from the Church they had left, they advanced in opposition to Church doctrine the heretical tenet of Anthropomorphitism, and in opposition to Church practice, as established by the Council of Nicæa, the custom of Quartodecimanism. [ANTHROPOMORPHITES QUARTODECIMANS]

In addition to these, Theodoret charges the Audians with adopting from Manichæism the tenet that the Creator was not the Former of fire and darkness [*Hist Eccl* iv 10; comp Isa xlv. 7] But this doctrine was not avowed by them

In his old age Audius was banished by Constantius to Scythia, where he converted many of the Goths, and established monasteries of strict and admirable rule Here he remained till his death, the time of which is not known

Many bishops carried on the sect in Mesopotamia, Uranius being their chief There were also bishops of the sect among the Goths A local persecution drove them from the country of the Goths, and in very much diminished numbers they collected in Chalcis in Syria and by the Euphrates The sect disappeared by the end of the fifth century [Epiph *Hær.* lxx Theod *Hist Eccl* iv 10 August *Hær* l., who calls them Vadiani, and states that some assert them to have been in Egypt in communion with the Catholic Church, *Prædest* 1, where Zenon, a Syrian bishop, is named as their chief opponent]

AUGSBURG, CONFESSION OF [PROTESTANT CONFESSIONS.]

AUGUSTINIANS The name by which the Jansenists were accustomed to designate themselves in the early days of their history. [JANSENISTS]

AZYMITES A designation used by controversialists of the Eastern Church for those who consecrate unleavened bread for the Holy Eucharist.

[1] So Epiphanius expressly states Theodoret refers it to the reign of Valens, i e later than A D 264 [*H E* iv 10] The history of the sect requires the earlier date

B

BAANITES. A name given to some local sect of the Paulicians in Armenia, from a leader named Baanes, a disciple and successor of Josephus Epaphroditus, about the year 810 [Petrus Sicul *Hist Manich* Baronius, *ad Ann* 810]

BACON, ROGER He was born at Ilchester, A D 1214, and became a Franciscan monk at Oxford, studying, probably, at Brasenose Hall He afterwards went to Paris, the Athens of the age, where he graduated as doctor, and had Robert Gros-tête as fellow-student and friend He is the connecting-link between the scholasticism of the Middle Ages and the philosophy of Europe in modern times He endeavoured to recall the learned from their blind idolatry of Aristotle, then only known in faulty Latin translations of a corrupt text. If he had his own way, he said, he would burn every copy "Si haberem potestatem super libros Aristotelis, ego facerem omnes cremari, quia tantum est temporis amissio studere in illis, et causa erroris multiplicati" [comp *Theol* i 2] But this refers only to those parts that subserved the dialectics of the Schools For Aristotle, as Peripatetic philosopher, he had a profound veneration Wherever he suspected the taint of error his hand was against every man, "nullum ordinem excludo," and, in consequence, every man's hand was against him Even the "angelic" Thomas was "vir erroneus et famosus" The work that he prepared by command of Clement IV. and transmitted to him, was intended to suggest to his patron the necessity of reform, that the onward progress of Antichrist might be stayed

Bacon was thoroughly convinced of the importance of geographical and ethnological science, and of an accurate knowledge of learned languages and grammar, while, with a knowledge of living languages, missionaries, he said, might be sent forth, who could declare to savages the marvellous works of God in their own tongue; the Greek Church might become one with the Roman through the fraternity of a common speech, and all mankind might be made one family by commerce and the amity of familiar intercourse Even comparative philology was dimly present to his mind These were notions that had never yet been heard in the Schools, where the language of the Vulgate and the mass was deemed to be all-sufficient. Philosophy as yet had grown only upon three stocks of the human family—the Hebrew, the Greek, and the Arab Bacon declared it should now be opened out to all, and in the first instance these three languages were as the keys of all knowledge [*Opus Tertium*, 10]

Mathematics he held to be the principal science, which had precedence of the rest, inasmuch as the spiritual and eternal is only to be learned by the bodily and finite In this there is a touch of the sensualism of Locke and of the method of Comte. Ethics, he said, had never yet been taught in the Schools as it had been of old The ethics of Aristotle, the treatises of Seneca, the noble and exalted moral teaching of Cicero, might well put to shame the far inferior wisdom of contemporary guides. Pagan men, without the light of grace and faith, had attained a height by the mere force of reason, that had as yet been inaccessible to Christian doctors If the *vitium originis* of the Schools was a love for disputation and endless wrangling, it was to be cured by diverting the attention of the learned to sounder studies in the way of experimental philosophy This was the queen of sciences, that investigates the truth for itself, and is not indebted to antecedent systems Bacon lays down rules for the prosecution of such studies that can scarcely fail to have helped forward the "Advancement of learning" after four more centuries had passed away Experience is the true handmaid of knowledge Authority is valueless unless it gives its reasons, "non sapit nisi detur ejus ratio" Reasoning can only amount to demonstration when its results are verified by experience and practice We see in such statements the same independence of spirit, and demand for clear intelligible reasoning, the same love of order and simplicity, which raised the name of Descartes to the highest rank, and enabled Lord Bacon to lay the foundation of modern philosophy If Roger seems, however, to depreciate authority, he means not the authority which God has committed to his Church, or that which results from merit and worth, but that which is the assumption of blind prejudice, ambition, and ignorance Of the authority due to the Fathers he says that they not only permit to us the correction of whatever is spoiled by human ignorance, but they themselves advance statements which afterwards they with humility retract If they had lived to time present they would have improved and altered many things that are still allowed to exist.

Bacon boldly laid to the charge of Schoolmen a profound ignorance of sacred and profane antiquity, which prevented them from detecting the various fallacies of the day, and he accused them of moving in a vicious circle of abstractions, which made them utterly incapable of appreciating the real and the natural, hence that the spirit of the Schools troubling itself so little about the works of nature and of God, was cramped and illiberal, captious and artificial, disputatious and pedantic If Bacon did no good in his generation, and much harm to himself by these invectives, he at least prepared the minds of succeeding generations for the emancipation of the human spirit from scholastic trammels Bacon seems scarcely to have troubled himself to ascertain the difference between realism and nominalism, but of the two he favoured the latter class of opinion, though without the precision of Roscellin or the greater subtlety of Abelard, but he was no partisan In fact he was too correctly orthodox in his theology, too ardent a maintainer of the sovereign authority of the Pope, and too earnest an advocate of the supremacy of canon over civil law, to run in the same groove with the early advocates of nominalism Like all his predecessors of the Schools he classed philosophy and theology together, they both formed one truth, and were both equally derived from the reasonable Word that was made flesh and dwelt among us He ascribed the highest authority, over the Church and everything else, to the teaching of Holy Writ, and would have the laity also study it in the original languages All wisdom, he said, is contained substantially in Scripture Its development is canon law and philosophy Nearly all the evil that abounds in the world arises from our ignorance of Scripture His strictures upon the unsatisfactory condition of the Vulgate text caused Hugh de St Caro to apply himself to its purification If ever the holy men of old, or the wiser spirits among the heathen, by their teaching anticipated revealed truth, it was because the traditions of paradise had never quite died out the torch transmitted from hand to hand had never been wholly obscured by the smoke of this world's folly

Bacon's reform of the calendar, proposed by him in earnest terms to Pope Clement IV, was only realized three centuries later, A D 1582, under Gregory XIII. His knowledge of astronomy enabled him to detect the error of the Julian year, which was longer than the astronomical year by about eleven minutes, in 128 years this would amount to an entire day, which must then be subtracted Similarly the equinoxes were observed to fall earlier by a day in every 124 years The error had its use in chronology, for it gave the exact date for calculating the lapse of time since Ptolemy, who, A D 140, declared March 22nd to be the equinoctial day, but it was a reproach to astronomy, and a constant cause of error The lunations were no less faulty, in 306 years the error of the calendar amounted to an entire day, and in 4266 years, the moon entering on her first quarter, would be marked in the calendar as at the full Infidel philosophers, he said, Arabs and Jews, regard with amazement the stupidity of Christian astronomers, and the carelessness of Christian prelates, who order the Church feasts by so fluctuating a scale of error In other respects also, Bacon showed the faultiness of the Ptolemean theory, and threw out hints that were turned to account by Copernicus

In optics, Bacon was the precursor of Newton, he himself profiting by the discoveries of Arab philosophers. Yet he first made known the delicate mechanism of the eye, and indicated the possible use of the retina He showed that Aristotle was in error when he deemed the action of light to be instantaneous, the movement of which, however inconceivable might be its rapidity, is still appreciable [*Opus Maj* 298, 300].

The light of the stars, he said, was not derived, but they shine by their own brilliancy His theory of shooting stars and meteors made a near approach to modern notions, when he said that they were no true stars, but comparatively of small bulk, "corpora parvæ quantitatis," that they traverse the earth's atmosphere and ignite by the rapidity of their movement. The principles of perspective were not unknown to Bacon The invention of telescopic and microscopic lenses is attributed to him, and when he presented his *Opus Majus* to Clement IV by John of Paris, he sent at the same time a lens, with instructions for its use "Johannes portavit crystallum sphericum ad experiendum, et instruxi eum in demonstratione et figuratione hujus rei occultæ" [*Opus Tertium*, c 31]

He first indicated the refractive power of the air, and the rationale of the rainbow It was in strict keeping with the spirit of his age, that his vast erudition and sagacious power of observation should be compromised by a belief in judicial astrology, and in the transmutation of metals by alchemy The composition of gunpowder was among the secrets of his laboratory

Bacon more than once launches startling anticipations of the possible discoveries of science Mechanism, he says, will be invented, when nature shall have been compelled to reveal her secret laws, whereby the largest vessels will be propelled without rowers, and more rapidly under the guidance of a single man than with a full crew Carriages will roll along with an inconceivable swiftness without a team Machines will fly through the air, and in the midst the guide will sit who, by touching a spring, will cause huge wings to unfold themselves and generate a bird-like movement A small implement, a few inches long and wide, will suffice to raise and lower enormous weights, and enable a man to lift himself and others from the lowest depths to the clouds, and to descend again at his will Another implement will have such tractile force as to enable a single operator to draw a thousand persons along One apparatus will be devised for walking at the bottom of the sea, another for swimming and floating on its surface without risk of sinking Bridges will be thrown across rivers without piers or arches, and to such marvels of science there will be no apparent limit [*De Mirab* and *Tr. de Mathemat.* See also Saisset, *Prec et Disc de Descartes*, 38]

Bacon had the credit with his contemporaries of having invented a burning mirror that could consume an entire army, and a brazen head which gave responses to his questionings upon the deep secrets of nature and futurity How may a rampart be thrown round England? was a question propounded by Bacon and one of his experts The oracle was silent, and they returned to their alembics Presently it spoke, but attention was absorbed in their work, and the utterance was for ever lost Saisset observes sarcastically, "Plus d'un bon Anglais de nos jours se prendra a regretter que la tête d'airain de frère Bacon n'ait pas été conservée, et qu'elle ne puisse pas dire son secret a l'oreille attentive de Lord Palmerston Que d'alarmes et d'argent épargnés a l'amirauté Anglaise! Que de soucis de moins pour M Gladstone!"

Bacon's depreciation of the scholastic system drew down upon him a bitter and life-long persecution He was accused of dealing with familiar spirits in his observatory tower at Oxford [1] He only studied his Moorish philosophers, it was said, and his followers of Mahomet, for the purposes of necromancy, he could be no true Christian who meddled with black arts, his astrology alone condemned him The rulers of his convent at length sent him for trial to Paris, "propter quasdam novitates suspectas," where he was placed under rigid surveillance and harsh discipline that continued for ten years [A D 1257-67] He gives a touching description of these trials in the introduction to his *Opus Tertium*, a work recently recovered by M Cousin from an ancient MS at Douai His books and mathematical instruments were taken from him, and he was forbidden to write and, worse than all, to teach, for, like Seneca, his only ambition was "discere ut doceam" The mildest discipline, if he resented such treatment, was solitary confinement on a bread and water diet Hope revived within him when Guy Foulques, who, as Papal legate in England, had heard of his fame, was made Pope, with the title of Clement IV. Bacon having been detected in writing to him was at first treated with greater severity; but afterwards released, when he returned to England. Unfortunately for him Clement died the next year, and was succeeded by Nicolas III, who owed his elevation to the influence of Jerome of Ascoli, general of the Franciscan order, a narrow-minded, inflexible bigot. Bacon's long imprisonment then followed, from A D 1278 to 1292 He died in A D 1294, having, in the last years of his life, composed a Summary of Theology

Such was Roger Bacon, termed by his contemporaries "Doctor mirabilis," all persecution of the object of their wonder notwithstanding And truly he was a wonderful character, whether we consider the extent of his varied knowledge, or his proud spirit of independence and heroic energy He first indicated in its dawn the brilliant future that awaited scientific induction, daring nobly, and at the cost of personal safety, to stem the tide of prejudice that opposed the onward progress of the human spirit He was content to be the victim of contemporary ignorance, if only he might be an associate of the wise in every age [Baconi *Opus Majus*, ed Jebb, Lond A D 1733 Cousin, *Baconi Opus Tertium*, from the Douai MS Saisset, *Prec et Disc de Descartes* Ritter, *Gesch d Chr Phil* IV Usher, *Hist Dogm de Sci* Neander, *K. Gesch* X]

[1] It was said that Dr Cyril Jackson always avoided walking under this tower, because tradition declared that it would fall when a greater man than Bacon passed beneath

BACULARII A sect of the Anabaptists who considered it sinful to carry any other arms than a staff, alleging that the Scriptures altogether forbid the use of the sword to Christians

BAGNOLENSES A sect of mediæval Cathari of the thirteenth century, corresponding with the ALBANENSES in most particulars, but not holding precisely the same Dualist or Manichæan theory as to the cause of evil, and believing in One only First Cause They derived their name from Bagnolo, or Baiolo, a town of Provence, and are considered by Mosheim and some other ecclesiastical historians to have been the original Albigenses Although not accepting the Manichæan theory as to the origin of evil in its customary form, they still maintained that matter being created by God it was moulded into the four elements—earth, air, fire, and water—by a rebel spirit, and that from these the world was formed. They also revived the heresy of the Docetæ respecting the human Nature of our Lord. The Bagnolians were also known by the names of Concordenses, Concorrenses, Concoretii, and Concorezenses

BAIOLENSES [BAGNOLENSES]

BAIUS, or BAJUS The Latinized name of a theologian of Louvain named Michael de Bay, whose theories respecting grace and predestination were the foundation of Jansenism

Baius was born at Melin in the territory of Aeth in the year 1513, and having been educated at Louvain, became Professor of Theology there, A D 1551. He adopted an independent line of teaching instead of that ordinarily received from the Schoolmen, founding it especially on the Pauline Epistles as interpreted by St. Augustine The pronounced Augustinianism of Baius excited opposition from the Franciscans, who brought his lectures to the notice of the Sorbonne Eighteen propositions taken from them were condemned by that body in A D 1560, and were declared heretical, but Baius still continued in his office at Louvain. In 1563 he was sent as delegate to the Council of Trent, where he took a prominent part in the discussions which took place, and where he raised up fresh opponents, who, shortly after his return to Louvain, placed seventy-six propositions taken from his works before the Pope Pius V These propositions were condemned by the Pope in the year 1567, but in the Bull of condemnation "Ex omnibus afflictionibus," the name of Baius was not mentioned. He therefore continued in his office of Divinity Professor, and even became Dean of St Peter's at Louvain, and Chancellor of the University But much opposition was raised against him by the Jesuits, and at the instigation of one of them, Francis Tolet, the Bull of Pius V was confirmed in the year 1580 by Gregory XIII Baius submitted to this condemnation, retracted his opinions that he might obtain absolution from Cardinal Granvella the Legate, and took no prominent part in theological controversy for the rest of his life, which lasted until A D 1589 He thus justified the character given of him even by his opponents, that of a humble-minded man who sought truth and the good of the Church rather than the spread of his own opinions "Michaele Baio," said Tolet, "nihil doctius, nihil humilius"

The condemned propositions of Baius maintained the theory that man might have merited eternal life if he had continued in a state of innocence, continuing in that state even without the assistance of Divine Grace, that after the Fall all his works which are not done under the influence of Divine Grace are sinful works, that all works whatever are sinful unless done from pure love of God, that all men being born in sin it is impossible that penance by itself can offer satisfaction for sin, though it may do so when united with the satisfaction offered by our Lord Some of these opinions were revived by Jansen and by the Quietists, and they were still taught at Louvain and Douai even after Baius had recanted [JANSENISTS]

BANGORIAN CONTROVERSY In the year 1717 there met in literary contest the three great parties into which England was divided, the party which had transferred the allegiance of the nation to the foreign Prince William of Orange, and had attempted to reduce the Church of England to the platform of foreign Protestantism, the members of the Church who had submitted to William, but had defeated the attempt to alter the constitution of the Church, and the Nonjurors who had set up a rival episcopate.

Hoadly, Bishop of Bangor (from whom the controversy takes its name), Nathanael Marshall, William Law, all three well known in English Church history, may be named as representatives of the three disputing parties The controversy was long and very voluminous Deeply important as its topics were, and that for all times, so much of merely personal and temporary interest entered into their handling, that the writings of the disputants are now in general unreadable Some tracts are still read by students, such as Kennett's on lay deprivations, and Law's on the priesthood and its powers, but it may be safely assumed that few living men have read, or would or could read, a connected series of the tracts Fortunately there was published in 1719, and continued in 1720, a systematic *Account of all the Considerable Pamphlets,* and without adopting the criticisms and judgments of the writer, we may by the list he gives form a sufficient notion of the course the controversy took Beginning with the main ecclesiastical point of the Nonjuring question, the validity or invalidity of lay deprivations of bishops, it widened to the general consideration of the nature of the Church of Christ, and of the constitution of the Church of Christ as established in this country, branching off on the one hand into the topics of the sacraments, Church ordinances, Church communion, and the priesthood, and on the other hand into the topics of religious sincerity, the sacramental test, the Test and Corporation Acts, and ecclesiastical authority, with episodes some purely personal, some of the rights and powers of Convocation, some of appeals to foreign Protestants

The dispute began when the Government at the time of the Scotch rebellion seized many copies of Hickes' *Collection of Papers*, 1716, in which was claimed obedience to the deprived bishops, and consequently the Church of England under Tenison and Wake was charged with schism The first stage then regarded the Nonjurors' pretensions Bennett[1] attacked them His answer was not thought satisfactory, and was therefore commented on, and a reply on other grounds made to the Nonjurors by Pierce[2] and others Hoadly wrote anonymously But the pamphlets most deserving attention are Bennett's *Letters to the Bishop of Carlisle* on the nomination and deprivation of English prelates Sykes[3] also took part. Then appeared Hoadly's *Preservative against the Principles and Practices of the Nonjurors.* Marshall,[4] from the status of a conforming Churchman, disputed some of Hoadly's arguments, and answered the Nonjurors' charge of schism Sykes appeared for Hoadly Then came Hoadly's sermon, *The Nature of the Kingdom of Christ* Before Convocation could act Snape[5] replied, and amidst a cloud of anonymous pamphlets Hoadly rejoined. This second stage, "On the nature of Christ's kingdom," was carried on by Burnet and Whitby, Trapp[6] defending Snape An episode occurred upon Bennett's being charged with having advised Hoadly regarding his sermon [see *Life of Bennett*, p 214], and a second concerning the character of De la Pillonnière, a converted Jesuit living with Hoadly Convocation moved, and a Committee of the Lower House represented that the tendency of the doctrines and positions contained in the Sermon and the Preservative was,—first, to subvert all government and discipline in the Church of Christ, and to reduce His kingdom to a state of anarchy and confusion, secondly, to impugn

[1] Thomas Bennett of Cambridge, then of Colchester, then of London, author of *History of Forms of Prayer, Rights of the Clergy, Essay on the Articles,* &c

[2] James Pierce, Dissenting preacher of Exeter

[3] Arthur Ashley Sykes of Salisbury, and then of Winchester He wrote in all the controversies of the day *Memoirs of Life* by Disney, 1785

[4] Translator of Cyprian, author of *The Penitential Discipline of the Church of England.*

[5] Head Master of Eton, then Provost of King's College, Cambridge His first letter to Hoadly passed through seventeen editions in one year, and he lost his chaplaincy to the King

[6] Joseph Trapp, Oxford Professor of Poetry, and friend of Sacheverell

and impeach the regal supremacy in causes ecclesiastical and the authority of the legislature to enforce obedience in matters of religion by civil sanctions. Sherlock, Master of the Temple, having signed this report, was accused of inconsistency, and a side-quarrel ensued between him and Sykes. Moss[1] defended the report, Hoadly replied to the report, and the controversy raged in attack and defence of the Committee, the Prolocutor, Dean Stanhope, Cannon,[2] and Dawson[3] being for the defence.

Meanwhile Law had answered Hoadly's fresh reply to Snape, the special point to which he addressed himself being Hoadly's assertion, "When you are secure of your integrity before God, this will lead you not to be afraid of the terrors of men, or the vain words of regular and uninterrupted successions, authoritative benediction, excommunications, nullity or validity of God's ordinances to the people, upon account of niceties and trifles, or any other the like dreams." Burnet defended Hoadly. Law's *Three Letters* are the most valuable of all the tracts. They were reprinted in 1812 in *The Scholar Armed*.

Sherlock turned the controversy in the Convocation branch to the particular point of the Test and Corporation Acts, the repeal of which Hoadly had urged. Sykes and Pierce stood up for Hoadly. This brought up the question of occasional conformity, and of course included the question of a sacramental test.

Some sharp skirmishing took place concerning a letter to a Zurich professor containing bitter invectives against Hoadly. It was said to have been written by Wake. Gordon, the author of the *Independent Whig*, is said to have written one of the seven pamphlets against the archbishop.

The foregoing is but a very brief statement of the heads of the controversy. It is sufficient, however, to shew its character and importance. The Nonjuring questions and the questions of the Test Acts are now only of historical interest. Of permanent interest is the main subject, the doctrine which, putting forward an alleged sincerity of good intention as all in all, would dissolve the Church as a society, and reduce all its ordinances to mere human inventions. It has so happened, said the Committee of Convocation, that this Right Reverend Bishop, in his extreme opposition to certain unwarrantable pretensions to extravagant degrees of Church power, . . . has not only condemned the abuse, but even denied the use and destroyed the being of those powers, without which the Church as a society cannot subsist, and by which our national constitution next under Christ is chiefly supported. The powers denied and destroyed were, it is notorious, not only powers of government, but also of the valid administration of the sacraments. [Herne's *Account of all the Considerable Pamphlets*, &c. 1720. Hoadly's *Works*, 1783.]

[1] Dean of Ely. His Sermons were edited by Snape, afterwards by Zachary Grey, with a Life.

[2] Robert Cannon, Archdeacon of Norfolk. In 1712 he tried in vain to procure a synodical condemnation of Brett's *Sermon on Remission of Sins*.

[3] Proctor for Sarum diocese.

BAPTISTS. A sect whose distinctive principle is that of administering baptism only to adult persons, baptizing them not to make them children of God, but as a sign that they have become so.

Infant baptism was repudiated by most of the mediæval Anti-Sacerdotalists and by the ANABAPTISTS of the Reformation age, from whom have sprung the MENNONITES or German Baptists of a later time. But the sect commonly known by the name of Baptists among English-speaking people is an offshoot of the BROWNISTS or early Independents, and was formed into a distinct community only in the reign of Charles I. Among the Brownists there were always some persons who objected to Infant Baptism, and looked upon it as invalid. These being generally identified with the foreign Anabaptists, were called by the same name, and it is probable that they were converts of the Dutch Anabaptists who emigrated to England in the time of Henry VIII and in that of Queen Elizabeth. Those Brownist Anabaptists, or "Enthusiasts" as they were often called [ENTHUSIASTS], endeavoured at a later date to ally themselves with the Mennonites of Holland, and parties of them emigrated to Amsterdam in the years 1606 and 1608. But for some reason which is not known, the attempt failed, the emigrants formed a separate community at Amsterdam, and not being able to obtain baptism from the Dutch, their leader, John Smith, first baptized himself [SE-BAPTISTS] and then his followers. But there is no historical connection between this English community at Amsterdam, and the later sect of Baptists, beyond the fact that both bodies rejected Infant Baptism, and were both composed of English Puritans.

The true origin of the English Baptists is narrated by one of their founders, William Kiffin, his account being thus printed by Crosby. "There was a congregation of Protestant Dissenters of the Independent persuasion in London, gathered in the year 1616, whereof Mr Henry Jacob was the first pastor, and after him Mr John Lathorp, who was their minister at this time. In this society several persons finding that the congregation kept not their first principles of separation, and being also convinced that Baptism was not to be administered to infants, but such only as professed faith in Christ, desired that they might be dismissed from that community, and allowed to form a distinct congregation in such order as was most agreeable to their own sentiments. The Church, considering that they were now grown very numerous, and so more than could in these times of persecution conveniently meet together, and believing also that these persons acted from a principle of conscience and not obstinacy, agreed to allow them the liberty they desired, and that they should be constituted a distinct church, which was performed the 12th of September 1633. And as they believed that baptism was not rightly administered to infants, so they looked upon the baptism they had received in that age as invalid · whereupon most or all of them received a new baptism Their minister was Mr John Spilsbury What number they were is uncertain, because in the mentioning of the names of about twenty men and women it is added 'with divers others' In the year 1638, Mr William Kiffin" (the writer of this narrative), "Mr Thomas Wilson, and others being of the same judgment, were, upon their request, dismissed to the said Mr Spilsbury's congregation In the year 1639, another congregation of Baptists was formed whose place of meeting was in Crutched Friars, the chief promoters of which were Mr Green, Mr Paul Hobson, and Captain Spencer" [Crosby's *Hist of Eng Baptists*, i 148] The same writer also records that the "new baptism" of those early Baptists was effected by communication with the Dutch Mennonites One of their number, Mr Richard Blunt, being acquainted with the Dutch language, was sent over to Holland, where he was baptized by John Batte, and on his return he baptized Mr Samuel Blacklock, the two then baptizing others to the number of fifty-three [*ibid* i. 101]

From this time the sect spread with some rapidity, but there is no evidence to shew whether all the congregations of Baptists which are soon after found existing originated from that of which the preceding account is given, or whether they were sporadic offshoots from the fermenting bodies of Puritans which had now become so numerous, and which even in the height of their prosperous times were in a constant state of disintegration Baxter writes, in an early page of his Autobiography, that he made acquaintance with the "Anabaptists" first at Gloucester, where about a dozen young men having conceived opinions against Infant Baptism had been rebaptized [Baxter's *Life and Times*, pt i p 41] He was afterwards involved in a controversy with a congregation of the sect which had been formed in a similar manner at Bewdley, within a short distance of the town of Kidderminster, of which he was vicar during the time of the Puritan ascendancy In 1646, there were said to be forty-six of their congregations in and about London About the same time also the sect was being developed in the North American colonies by an emigrant priest of the Church of England, named Roger Williams, whose political importance has given him a chapter in American history somewhat similar to that occupied by William Penn [Bancroft's *Hist Unit States*, i 277-321, ed 1852]

In 1643, the various congregations of the sect had become sufficiently organized into one body to enable them to hold a representative assembly in London, and at this a "Confession of Faith" was drawn up which was reprinted in 1644 and 1646, and lasted the sect as its standard of doctrine for seventeen years Large numbers of them enlisted in the Parliamentary army, and the help thus given to the revolutionary party won for the sect a declaration of the Lords and Commons in their favour This was promulgated in March 1647, in which it was said that "the name of Anabaptism hath indeed contracted much odium by reason of the extravagant principles and practices of some of that name in Germany, tending to the disturbance of the government and peace of all states, which opinions and practice we abhor and detest, but for their opinion against the baptism of infants, it is only a difference about a circumstance of time in the administration of an ordinance wherein, in former ages as well as this, learned men have differed both in opinion and practice. And though we could wish that all men would satisfy themselves and join with us in our judgment and practice in this point, yet herein we hold it fit that men should be convinced by the Word of God, with great gentleness and reason, and not beaten out of it with force and violence" Shortly after this edict of Parliamentary toleration, however, another was issued of a totally different character under Presbyterian influence This was an ordinance of the Lords and Commons passed on May 2nd, 1648, which declared. "Whosoever shall say that the baptism of infants is unlawful, or that such baptism is void, and that such persons ought to be baptized again, and in pursuance thereof shall baptize any person formerly baptized, or shall say the Church government of Presbytery is antichristian or unlawful, shall, upon conviction by the oath of two witnesses, or by his own confession, be ordered to renounce his said error in the public congregation of the parish where the offence was committed, and in case of refusal, he shall be committed to prison till he find sureties that he shall not publish or maintain the said error any more" [Neale's *Hist of Purit* iii 375] They shared, however, in the general moderation with which all religions except the Church were treated by Cromwell, and many of his supporters belonging to the sect, it attained considerable political influence during the time of the Great Rebellion There were also not a few of them licensed to officiate in the churches from which the clergy had been ejected, and 35 of these were among the 800 (commonly spoken of as 2000) who refused to conform to the customs of the Church at its Restoration, and were hence obliged to give place to the old clergy whom they had ousted, or to others ordained according to the custom of the Church [Stoughton's *Eccl Hist* ii 242, n NONCONFORMISTS]

Shortly before the Restoration, a division of the sect had taken place into the General and the Particular Baptists, and this division has been maintained ever since

GENERAL BAPTISTS, or "Arminian Baptists," are so called because they hold the Arminian doctrine of redemption, instead of the Calvinistic, believing that Christ died to save all men, and not only an elect few They published a "Confession of Faith," composed of twenty-five articles, in the year 1660, which was reprinted with many more subscriptions in 1691 This marks the time of their separation from the body of the sect, the third and fourth articles setting forth the doctrine of general redemption, the eighth and ninth that of election [Murray's *Hist of Relig* iv 214, 216, ed. 1764]. At the Restoration, the General Baptists claimed to be 20,000 in number, but shortly afterwards a large body of them are said to have become followers of BIDDLE the Unitarian In the following century this portion of the Baptist sect became so largely imbued with Unitarian principles, that they gradually split up into two bodies, those who seceded in 1770 taking the name of the "New Connection of General Baptists," and adopting as their standpoint the original Arminian tenets of the body from which they seceded The elder fragment of that body, still known as "General Baptists," is now wholly Unitarian The "New Connection" is believed to number about 200 congregations, and the Unitarian Baptists about 100, but some of these are composed of very few members, lingering on chiefly through the circumstance that their chapels are endowed

PARTICULAR BAPTISTS represent the original Baptist sect as it first seceded from that of the Brownist or Independents in 1633 They continue to hold the Calvinistic doctrine of "particular redemption," and hence since the secession of the Arminian portion of the sect have distinguished themselves from them by the prefix indicating that dogma They are again subdivided into two sections on the question of free or strict communion, the "free communionists" admitting to the Lord's Supper those who have been baptized only in infancy, as well as those who have been baptized as adults, while the "strict" or "close communionists" only admit those who have been baptized as adults These two classes do not, however, form separate sects, congregations of both being admitted into the "Baptist union" (a society for co-operation founded in 1812), as indeed also are those of the New Connection General Baptists. The Particular Baptists are mostly intended when Baptists without any other designation are named

The Baptists are one of "the three denominations" to which a sort of constitutional recognition has been accorded in the right to present corporate addresses to the Crown (the other two being the Independents and the Presbyterians), and are a numerous and rather influential body among English dissenters In the whole of Great Britain and Ireland they number about 2,600 places of worship, each having on an average 90 members, 100 Sunday scholars, and being also attended by persons not actually members of the sect but allied with it The whole number of actual members of the sect amounted in 1871 to 233,675, being fewer by 4000 than in 1870 [*Bapt Handbook*, 1872, p 25] In the English Colonies there are about 60,000 members, the majority of whom are negroes in the West Indies In the United States they number 1,400,000

Within the last fifty years the Baptists have made some vigorous endeavours to provide a more respectable education for their ministers than is common among dissenters. They have as many as ten colleges in England, Wales, and Scotland; and in these about 240 young men receive an elementary education in the learned languages, and a more elaborate training in Calvinistic theology They have also two Missionary Societies, which together expend about £40,000 annually in India, China, and the West Indies [Crosby's *Hist Eng Bapt* Ivimey's *Hist Eng Bapt* Evans' *Hist Early Eng Bapt.* Wayland's *Principles and Practice of Baptist Churches*, London, ed. 1861. *Baptist Handbook* (annual) FREE-WILL BAPTISTS OLD SCHOOL BAPTISTS SIX-PRINCIPLE BAPTISTS SEVENTH-DAY BAPTISTS. SE-BAPTISTS. SCOTTISH BAPTISTS TUNKERS CAMPBELLITES HARD-SHELL BAPTISTS]

BARBELIOTES Among the multitude of Gnostics, says Irenæus, who had sprung up "like mushrooms growing out of the ground," there was a sect in Iberia which called themselves after the name of Barbelos, an Æon of the Gnostic mythology, who was the special object of their veneration [Iren *adv. Hæres.* xxix]. This Barbelos, or Barbelo, is mentioned in connection with the Nicolaitanes by Philaster [*Hær* xxxiii], Augustine [*Hær* vi], and Epiphanius [*Hær* xxv 2], and it is supposed that the name is made up of two Hebrew words, בר בעלה [Bar Belah], "the son of the Lady," or else from בר בעל [Bar Bel], "the son of the Lord" Thus Barbelo they affirmed to be the offspring of the Father, and of a Mother whom some named Jaldabaoth, and others Sabaoth From Barbelo sprang Light, and Light being anointed by the Father became Christ Immortality, Truth, Grace, Will, Understanding, and Prudence, were all personified, as also Lust, Envy, Emulation, and other vices; the personality of Christ and of the Holy Spirit being thus practically allegorized away. Their system was mixed up with obscure ideas which shew that licentious practices were familiar to them, and that they were probably adopted in their mysteries, as seems to have been the case with the Nicolaitanes Hence they acquired the name of Borborians, from *βόρβορος*, filth or mud Theodoret expressly giving this play upon their original name as the application of it, Βαρβηλῶται ἤγουν Βορβοριανοί [Theodor *de Hæret fab* i. 13], and a similar explanation being given by Nicetas Choniatus [Nicet. *Thesaur orthod fid.* iv 2] Philaster states that the Borbeliotes, in common with other licentious heretics of their class, denied that there was any future judgment.

The names Borbelitæ and Borboriani are given to the Gnostics in general by some writers, as by Epiphanius

BARDESANIANS A sect founded by Bardesanes, a Syrian of Edessa in Mesopotamia, a man of great learning He flourished in the latter part of the second century, being born, according to the Edessan Chronicle [a work of the sixth century Lardner, ed Oxf ii 319], in the year 154. He was by some supposed to be the tutor of Clemens Alexandrinus, but this is not established. From a noble answer of his to Apollonius, a friend of one of the Emperors Antoninus, that he was ready to encounter death or any suffering the prince might inflict, rather than deny his faith, to which he was being urged, he has been reckoned a confessor [Epiphan *Hæres* lvi] He is said by Eusebius to have been an excellent Syriac scholar, and most keen in disputation [Euseb *Hist Eccles* iv 30] Attracted to the oriental philosophy, he relapsed, as Epiphanius says, like a goodly ship, laden with costly bales, shipwrecked in sight of harbour The great problem of the day, the existence of evil in the world, he endeavoured to solve by supposing two co-equal supreme principles, one good, one evil He adopted, more or less, the fanciful ideas of some of the Eastern Gnostics, and partly held with their opinion of the successive generation of æons [BASILIDIANS] No doubt, also, he denied the resurrection of the body, and believed that the body with which the Saviour was clothed was a celestial and unsubstantial one only Hence he would not admit that Jesus Christ was born of the Virgin Mary, but said the flesh with which He seemed to be endued was from Heaven direct The original man, created by God, had a refined body adapted to his unfallen nature After the Fall, God united his soul to a grosser and more material body There is no question that his moral system was unimpeachable. Towards the end of his life he renounced, but, as it seems, not wholly, these errors Porphyry speaks of a Bardesanes of Babylon as alive in A D 218, he is said then to have been held in high respect. Lardner has given many reasons for identifying him with Bardesanes of Edessa, which, though perhaps not conclusive, are certainly most reasonable While still sound in the faith (so Eusebius and Jerome but Epiphanius makes him a Valentinian from the first) he wrote numerous works, many of which he produced [Euseb *loc cit*] against Marcion and others These were translated by his disciples into Greek, being originally written in Syriac Epiphanius seems therefore in error when he makes Bardesanes skilled in Greek as well as Syriac His chief work was *De Fato*, written against an astrologer Abidas This was dedicated to Antoninus, not, it seems most likely, the emperor, but one of the more conspicuous among his own adherents Eusebius has preserved a very considerable fragment of this [Euseb *Præp Evang* vi 10] He wrote also a great number of hymns, as did his son Harmonius They were used in churches, and doubtless their continued use in Syria helped to retain a belief in some of his distinctive opinions, which would account for the existence of a sect of Bardesanians for nearly two centuries after his death His followers, however, were never numerous, nor actively opposed to Catholic teaching The use of his hymns was discontinued in the fourth century, and after that time we hear no more of the Bardesanians The fragment above mentioned as given by Eusebius, is also found, word for word, in the Clementine Recognitions [*Clem Recog.* ix 19, &c] From this Cave infers that Bardesanes was the author of these Recognitions, but does not affirm it as an established fact. Assuming also the identity of the Babylonian and Syrian Bardesanes, we have two other fragments preserved by Porphyry and cited by Cave [Tillemont, *Mém* ii 316 Fabric. *Biblioth Gr* ii 599 Mosheim, *de reb ante Const II* 60]

BARLAAMITES The adherents of Barlaam, abbot of St Saviour's at Constantinople, in his controversy with the HESYCHASTS or Quietist mystics of the East Barlaam was a man of much learning, belonging to the order of St Basil, and in his early life a strong controversialist on the side of the Eastern Church against the Latins In A D 1337 he brought a complaint against the Hesychast monks of Mount Athos, whom he had been directed to visit and inspect, and whose strange practice he regarded as mere fanaticism The charges brought by him were tried before a council in A D 1341, when the monks, with Palamas (afterwards archbishop of Thessalonica) for their advocate, were acquitted. Barlaam was at the same time condemned by the influence of the Quietists, and immediately leaving Constantinople he joined the Latin Church, in which he eventually became Bishop of Gieræce in Calabria, his native country

The dogma which had become the subject of controversy—viz that God dwells in an eternal light, distinct from His Being, and this was the light seen in the Mount of Transfiguration—was again opposed by ACINDYNUS, a friend of Barlaam Several other councils were held on the subject, and the Barlaamites, as the opponents of the Quietists were now called, were finally silenced by one held at Constantinople in A D 1351, in which they were severely censured [Fabricius, *Biblioth Græc* v 247, 454]

BARSANIANS One of the small and obscure sects into which the Acephali broke up in the latter half of the fifth century. St John of Damascus says that they derived their name from Barsanius, a propagator of the Theodosian and Gaianite heresy [Damasc *de Hæres.* iii] They are identical with the SEMIDALITES

BARSANUPHITES A sect of the Acephali, like the preceding, and having for their leader a pretender of the name of Barsanuphius, who falsely claimed to have received consecration as a bishop They separated off from the Acephali at the end of the fifth century, and were reunited to the Jacobite communion at the end of the ninth century [Neale's *Patriarch. of Alexandria*, ii 22, 137] Barsanuphius is not to be confounded with the monk of that name mentioned in the ecclesiastical history of Evagrius, iv 33

BARSUMAS The chief founder and leader of the Nestorians in Chaldæa, Persia, Assyria, and the adjoining countries He was ejected from the school of Edessa, but became bishop of Nisibis [A D 435—437] He persuaded the Persian sovereign Pherozes to expel the orthodox from their sees and churches, and to substitute Nestorians in their place He also founded the school of Nisibis, from which Nestorian missionaries carried the heresy in the following century to Egypt, Syria, Arabia India, Tartary, and China

BARSUMAS. A Syrian archimandrite who

took the side of Eutyches at the Latrocinium or so-called second Council of Ephesus. He and his monks so kicked and otherwise maltreated Flavian that he died within a few days from the effects of their violence. When the acts of the false council were annulled by the Council of Chalcedon Barsumas was driven from it by the general voice of those assembled as being the murderer of the holy Flavian, and afterwards convicted of heresy as a follower of Eutyches. He died about A D 460. [Fleury, *Hist Eccl* xxvii. 41, xxviii. 18]

BARULI. A sect of the Albanenses belonging to the twelfth century Their distinguishing errors are said to have been, That Christ did not become truly incarnate, but assumed a celestial kind of body; that souls were all created before the creation of the world, and all fell into sin together after the creation [Sianda, *Lexic Polem s v*]

BASILIDIANS So called from their founder Basilides He was of Alexandria, and the earliest of the Egyptian Gnostics; flourishing early in the second century Cave places him A D 112, some make him later, and he was certainly alive in the reign of the Emperor Hadrian [A D 117-138] If not actually a contemporary of the Apostles he lived at the same time as their disciples, for between the death of the Apostle John and the beginning of Hadrian's reign twenty years only elapsed It is likely that the more fantastic forms of heresy, which developed rapidly after St John's death, were in process of formation much earlier, but kept back during his lifetime Basilides had dwelt some time in Syria before settling in Egypt. Jerome [*de Vir. illustr* xxi] says that he abode, *moratus est*, in Alexandria at the time [A D 135] that Cochebas persecuted the Christians Some read *mortuus est* in this passage, but Clemens Alexandrinus, who knew Basilides personally, and on whom it seems we may certainly rely for this point, says that he lived into the reign of the elder Antoninus His death may therefore be approximately assigned to A D 139.

He was a disciple of Menander at the same period as Saturninus He claimed to derive his doctrine from St Matthias, and from one Glaucias whom he made the intimate disciple (interpres) of St. Peter This Glaucias is unknown to history, except as claimed by Basilides, and Waterland [v 123, Oxf ed] seems to suggest that he is altogether imaginary The chief features in his system, which was a compound of the Pythagorean philosophy, oriental tradition, and Christian revelation, were these First, he held there was a great First Cause, one Supreme God, to whom he gave the name Abraxas This name he associated with the number 365, which was made up (according to the Greek system of numeration) by adding together the numbers represented by the letters of which it is composed The correspondence of this number with that made by the word Mithras, the sun-god of the Persians, is some evidence that Basilides had been in Persia as well as Egypt, as is stated in the dispute between Archelaus and Manes [Routh's *Reliq. Sacr* iv 275] This correspondence is thus shewn

α	1	α	1	μ	40	μ	40
β	2	β	2	ι	10	ε	5
ρ	100	ρ	100	θ	8	ι	10
α	1	α	1	ρ	100	θ	9
ξ	60	σ	200	α	7	ρ	100
α	1	α	1	ς	200	α	1
ς	200	ξ	60			ς	200
	365		365		365		365

This name is evidently of Coptic origin, and means the Sacred Word, or perhaps more strictly "Hallowed be The Name" [King's *Gnostics*, 36] Mr King has pointed out an instance where the Egyptian word "Abrak," for kneeling down to worship, is actually retained in the Hebrew text of the Scriptures at Gen xli 43 From Abraxas, the First Cause, Basilides taught that Understanding (νοῦς, mens) was created, from the Understanding came the Word (λόγος, verbum), and so on by successive generations were produced Providence, Power, Wisdom, Righteousness, Peace From these in turn proceeded the higher order of angels, principalities, and powers, from these came again the lower order of angels The different orders of angels each made a separate heaven, 365 in all Over them all Abraxas presided By the lowest order of angels the world was created, of this order was the God of the Jews, the God of the law and the prophets, whom Basilides thus made an angel only Other angels of this order protected and took charge of other nations, and thus the interests of the angels became conflicting, and all in time became corrupt, and the God Supreme sent down from heaven His Son (νοῦς), Who joined Himself to the man Jesus, and taught corrupt man the heavenly knowledge they had allowed themselves to lose. The God of the Jews had no power against the Christ, but He had against Jesus, and His people by His instigation put Jesus to death [Massuet's *Dissertationes in Irenæum* Clemens Alex. *Strom.* vi Tertull *De Præscrip* xlvi Hippol *Refut. Hær* vii 8-15 Aug *Hær* iv Epiph *Hær.* xxiv]

The main problem which the philosophers of the second century set themselves to solve was the existence of evil in the world. Since many of them maintained the essential evil of matter, it followed that they frequently denied the Christian doctrine of the resurrection of the body. This was the case with the Basilidians Basilides denied that salvation was promised to the bodies of men His followers in the next century much exaggerated his original teaching, if we may judge from the much stronger terms used against them by Tertullian than had been used by Clemens Alexandrinus, who was not only a contemporary but an inhabitant of the same city as Basilides They recognised, says Tertullian, a half-resurrection "Being ashamed perhaps to confess Christ crucified," says Waterland [v. 190, Oxf ed], the ancient visionaries, among whom he reckons the Basilidians, "contrived any wild supposition imaginable to evade it." Their refusal to accept

 Basilidians

the doctrine of the Resurrection obliged them to explain away the Resurrection of Christ They accordingly said that Christ did not suffer on the cross, that He was a phantom or appearance only without substance of our flesh, that Simon of Cyrene was crucified in His stead, and that therefore no Christian ought to profess faith in the crucified One, lest he should be found adoring Simon This fantastic theory was an aftergrowth, and formed no part of the teaching of the founder of the sect, who certainly held the reality of the body of the man Christ Jesus This belief in an apparent suffering Christ satisfied the impugners of the Resurrection doctrine, amongst whom no doubt was Basilides himself. And this belief of utter destruction of the body at death led him to another position strongly antagonistic to the prevailing feelings of Christians, for he vigorously depreciated the glories of martyrdom. The mere denial of a resurrection of the flesh would tend to do this The hope of rising again into a perfect man supported many martyrs through their sufferings But Basilides went further than this, and endeavoured to frame a scheme to account for these sufferings He adopted in the first place a metempsychosis, or transmigration theory, saying that the faithful disciples were afflicted with torments because of sins committed in some previous stage of their existence One of his arguments was from the known sufferings of infants, believing in the destruction of the body at death, he could not explain this except by saying that they had sinned elsewhere He held consequently that the sufferings of confessors and martyrs were kinds of punishment, and inflicted necessarily "metum et laborem in martyre esse necessaria, atque hominem ad agendum semper impelli" Suffering and fear came on men like rust on iron He relied for this part of the argument on the Scripture, "The fear of the Lord is the beginning of wisdom" Clemens Alexandrinus, in his answer, maintains that the argument about punitive sufferings is worthless from the simple consideration that it was always in the power of Christians to suffer or not A compliance with the orders of the heathen always exempted them from suffering In a fragment of Basilides, preserved by Origen in his commentary on Rom vii 9 [lib v *Comment* sec v], this passage is cited as an authority for his belief in the metempsychosis, or, as Origen calls it *μετενσωμάτωσις*, "Dixit enim Apostolus, quia ego vivebam sine lege aliquando hoc est, antequam in istud corpus venirem, in eam speciem corporis vixi, quæ sub lege non esset, pecudis scilicet, vel avis" He even said men had two souls, "belluina," "rationalis," one which we share with the brute creation, and one which is our excellence above it

His opinions upon faith and the knowledge of God are involved in much obscurity, and, in the absence of any extant work of his, can only be conjectured But he seems to have held that faith and knowledge were co-ordinate, that faith should be greater or less in any man according to his natural powers, *πίστιν ἅμα καὶ ἐκλογὴν οἰκείαν εἶναι καθ' ἕκαστον διάστημα* [Clem Alex *Strom* ii 3]. In this he would differ from other forms of Gnosticism, in which they were usually made antagonistic Faith, according to him, was an assent of the soul to some proposition not apprehended by the senses, because not present; and was peculiar to some men by nature, he held that it was inborn in them, and was not the result of instruction, or conviction, or any exercise of judgment, and that such men became like God by nature The elect were therefore strangers in the world, sojourners, supra-mundane by nature All sins would not be forgiven, but those only committed in ignorance, and therefore the doctrine of the atonement had no place in his system All sins must be expiated in the sinner's own person, and in process of this expiation the soul passed through various bodies

The theory he held on the baptism of Christ was not peculiar to his system, but was common to many The descent of the Holy Spirit was the indwelling of an æon, or heavenly power, which left Him before His death His disciples retained a great veneration for this event, though they, as in many other things, greatly obscured the original teaching They were very particular in the celebration of the anniversary, spending the whole night previous in religious exercises The impurity of morals attributed by the later writers to Basilides is another instance of the corruption of his followers being laid to his charge There is little doubt that he taught and practised purity of life, but yet there were many features in his moral system which would seem to encourage the unprincipled among his followers to continue in sin The opinion for instance on election would be perverted by some into a license, let us "continue in sin that grace may abound" And even Clemens, at the earliest period of the heresy, tells us that some did use this argument, and looked forward to salvation, although deliberately sinning, as being elect by the dignity of their nature Epiphanius is much more severe in his charge of impurity [Epiph *Hær* xxiv. 3]

Irenæus mentions magic in connection with Basilides, "Utuntur autem et hi magia, et imaginibus, et incantationibus, et invocationibus, et reliqua universa periergia" [*Contra Hær* i 24] Epiphanius makes the same charge, *οὐ μὴν δὲ ἀλλὰ καὶ μαγγανικαῖς μηχανίαις προσανέχων οὐκ ἐπαύσατο, καὶ περιεργίαις ὁ ἀπατέων* Beausobre, and after him Lardner, who lose no opportunity of trying to exculpate heretics, altogether deny that there is any evidence of this profession of magic They say it is only the ignorant charge of men who understood no science against learned students of mathematics and physics. The question of the gems known as the Abraxas gems is slightly discussed by Mosheim [i 197, where references are given], and more fully examined by Lardner, who pronounces them purely heathen and destitute of all Christian character [viii 371, &c] But this question has been investigated anew by Mr King [*The Gnostics and their Remains*, 1864], whose authority on such a point will be admitted by all He considers it satisfactorily established that the form engraved on these gems was the invention of Basilides himself and intended to be used as a talisman, it was the reduction of his system to a visible representation Several passages are quoted [p. 81] which seem explicable only on the supposition that the "Pantheus upon our gems was actually intended to symbolize the deity styled Abraxas" Jerome mentions several other sacred names used by Basilides [*Ep* 75], Armagil, Leusiboras, Barbelon, Balsamus, "ceteraque magis portenta quam nomina" The first two of these names appear not to occur elsewhere, the last two, meaning respectively Son of God and Lord of Heaven, were names under which the Deity was worshipped by the Iberians [BARBELIOTES]

In the prologue to Jerome's Commentary on St Matthew mention is made of some spurious gospels, and amongst them one by Basilides. This is probably the same with the twenty-four books of commentaries mentioned by Eusebius [*Hist Eccl* iv 7] A fragment from the thirteenth book of these commentaries is quoted by Irenæus, and another by Clemens from the twenty-third book. The one cited by Origen has been given above [All may be seen in Migne's *Patrolog Ser Græca* viii 1263] A reply to this was written by Agrippa Castor, but this also has perished [Hieron *de Viris illustr* 21] Clemens speaks of a well-known book of Basilides called *Prophetia Chami* Barcobas and Barcoph were also names of prophets to whom Basilides appealed He rejected the authority of the Old Testament, and certain portions of the New Testament, as the Epistles to the Hebrews, Titus and Timothy, which he said were not St Paul's

The heresy did not survive very long, and there is but scanty allusion to it in later writers The most important authors against it are referred to above Jerome [*Ep* 75, written c A.D 400] mentions them as having recently shewn considerable activity throughout Spain, "spurcissima per Hispanias Basilidis hæresi sæviente, et instar pestis et morbi, totas infra Pyrenæum et Oceanum vastante provincias"

The fullest and most exhaustive of the replies extant is to be found in Clemens Alexandrinus, *Strom* iv 12

BASLE, CONFESSION OF. [PROTESTANT CONFESSIONS]

BASMOTHEANS. This name is found in the Apostolic Constitutions [vi 6] "Even the Jewish nation had wicked heresies for there were . the Basmotheans, who deny Providence, and say that the world is made by spontaneous motion, and take away the immortality of the soul" There can be little doubt that "Basmotheans" is a corruption of "Masbotheans." [MASBOTHEANS]

BASSUS In some MSS of Philaster a heretic appears whose name is written C Bassus, but as the COLORBASIANS are not elsewhere named by him, and Bassus is not named by any other heresiologist, no doubt C Bassus is a corrupt reading for Colorbasus [Philast *De Hær* xliii]

BEGHARDS The German name for a very widely spread sect of mediæval heretics who were closely allied in their origin with the Italian FRATICELLI and the BRETHREN OF THE FREE SPIRIT

The name "Beghard" was originally an honourable designation for those who devoted themselves to a life of prayer, and thus as "Beguines" were "praying women," Beghards were "praying men" Both are derived from the old German word "beggen" or "beggeren," which signifies to beg earnestly or heartily, and were thus analogous to such designations as "Pietists," "Evangelicals," &c But from being associated with prayer the name was corrupted by the subsequent habits of the sect into a mere association with mendicancy, and the Beghards were popularly so called because they were pertinacious "beggars" in the common English sense of the word

Female societies of Beguines appear to have been formed in many towns in the Netherlands towards the end of the twelfth century, and it is supposed that they arose out of the disproportion between the sexes caused by the number of men slain in the Crusades In the following century many of these communities of Beguines were formed in Germany and France, and Matthew Paris says that the number of Beguines at Cologne in the year 1250 was one thousand, while elsewhere in Germany an "innumerable multitude" of them had sprung up [Matth Par. p 805]. Similar communities of men, associating together for prayer and labour, began to be formed early in the same century, the first on record being one at Louvain, which was founded A D 1220 About the same time they are found also in France under the name of Boni Pueri (Bons Garçons) or Boni Valeti (Bons Valets) [Gramaye, *Antiq Brabant* pp 31, 36, 175] In this early development of the Beghard communities they were mostly affiliated to the Dominicans or Franciscans as brethren of the third or Lay Order, or Tertiaries, and this devotional stage of their history is still represented on the feminine side by the Beguines of Belgium

But the Beghards had adopted vagrant habits, and giving up all labour they professed to keep the strict Franciscan vow of poverty by living on the labour of others Thus they wandered about through towns and villages with the constant cry "Brot durch Gott" ("Bread for the sake of God"), and as their numbers increased the importunity and "professional" character of their begging increased also They obtained all their converts from among the ignorant labouring classes, many of them being also of that never-failing character which leads to the ready acceptance of any excuse for idleness and wandering Thus mechanics and field labourers left their work to become Beghards, and religion became a thin cloak for mendicancy

An alliance very quickly sprung up between the Beghards and the FRATICELLI, and it was not long before the incorporation of many of the BRETHREN AND SISTERS OF THE FREE SPIRIT with their body infected them with heresy The Council of Mayence [A D 1259] directed the clergy to read admonitions to them on three successive Sundays or festivals, and to forbid their assembling in caverns and other secret places for preaching [Mansi, *Concil* xxiii 998] From the absence of any notice of heresy in this canon it may be doubted whether it had as yet developed itself among them. But charges of licentiousness were brought against them very early, and from the number of women among them the Germans called them "Sisterers" (schwestriones) with an evident ironical meaning

The headquarters of the sect were at Cologne, but they spread along the banks of the Rhine and overran both France and the Netherlands as well In the year 1306 a decree against them was issued by a council held at Cologne, another in 1310 by a council held at Trèves, a third at Strasburg A D. 1317, and a few years later Pope John XXII published a Bull against them [A D 1330], in which they are declared to be persons who have wandered away from the Catholic faith, despising the sacraments and sowing other errors abundantly Meanwhile the Inquisition had been let loose upon them, and many were burned as heretics One of the first to suffer was a leader named Walter, who was executed in 1322, three were burned at Constance in 1339, another leader named Berthold at Speyer in 1356, and several at Strasburg in 1366 Under these persecutions the Beghards decreased in number, but traces of them are found in the fifteenth century, and down to the time of Luther

There can be no doubt that the Beghards were largely infected with the Antinomianism and licentiousness of the Brethren of the Free Spirit "Their professed object," says Ullmann, "was to restore the pure primeval state, the divine life of freedom, innocence, and nature The idea they formed of that state was that man being in and of himself one with God, requires only to act in the consciousness of this unity, and to follow unrestrained the divinely implanted impulses and inclinations of his nature in order to be good and godly, that prior to the fall he possessed such a consciousness to the full, but that it had been disturbed by that event, that the law had introduced differences among mankind, who originally stood upon a level, but that these ought now to be done away, and the Paradise state of unity and equality restored To bring this about in defiance of the imposing power of the Church, the only way open to them was by secret societies and clandestine meetings Accordingly they constructed for themselves remote and often subterraneous habitations, which they called Paradises, and where by night, and especially on the nights of festivals, persons of both sexes used to assemble On such occasions one of their "apostles" came forward, and taking off his clothes, and exemplifying in his own person the state of innocence, delivered a discourse upon the free intercourse of the sexes, which the law of marriage, contrary to nature, had supplanted The sequel, if we may credit the reports, was of a kind which forbids description"[1] [Ullmann's *Reformers before the Reformation*] These reports were those of eye-witnesses, and Mosheim considers that there is no reason to doubt their truth [Mosheim, *de Beghardis et Beguinabus*]

BEGUINE The French form of the name BEGHARD

BEGUINII One of the names given to the FRATICELLI in the Bull of Pope John XXII [A D. 1317] ordering their suppression

BEGUTTE The Dutch form of the name BEGHARD

BEHMEN, BÖEHME, or more properly BOHM, JACOB, a German mystic who gained many followers on the Continent and in England, was born, in 1575, in Allseidenberg, a village near Gorlitz in Upper Lusatia In his childhood he tended cattle, and remained to his tenth year without instruction At twelve years he was apprenticed to a shoemaker in Gorlitz It happened one day, when he was left alone in the shop, that a stranger in mean apparel, but of grave and reverend countenance, entered and bought a pair of shoes, then going out of the shop a little way, stood still, and called with a loud voice, "Jacob, Jacob, come forth!" The boy obeyed, and the stranger, taking him by the hand, and fixing his bright and piercing eyes on him, said, "Jacob, thou art little, but shalt be great, and become another man, such an one as the world shall wonder at, therefore be pious, fear God, and reverence His word Read diligently the Scriptures, wherein thou hast comfort and instruction, for thou must endure much poverty and suffer persecution, but be courageous, and persevere, for God loves and is gracious unto thee" After this mysterious visit the boy grew more and more serious and visionary, and at one time "was for seven days surrounded with a divine light, and stood in the highest contemplation, and in the kingdom of joys" At nineteen he married, and in 1604 became a master shoemaker in Gorlitz

Years passed, four sons were born to Behmen, and he was still only known as a pious and harmless mechanic Meantime his visionary faculty grew greater On one occasion he fell into a trance while gazing on the dazzling light of the sun's rays broken upon a tin vessel. Afterwards, walking in the fields, he had a new faculty opened in him to discern the virtues of plants. He began to write, but only for his private satisfaction, with no design of publishing his visions to the world A book called *Aurora*, thus written by him, was lent to a friend, who made a copy of it, and this fell into the hands of Richter the primate of Gorlitz, by whom the author was denounced from the pulpit, and summoned to

[1] The principles of a sect which appears to be a remnant of the Beghards were investigated by order of the Austrian Government in the year 1848 It was found that they still practised the custom of stripping themselves naked at their religious assemblies, and that their religion—such as it is—may be defined as an admixture of Stoical Quietism and Communism Their peculiar custom made it impossible of course that they should escape the charge of immorality.

appear before the senate He was ordered to write no more, and obeyed the order for seven years But in 1616, at the age of forty-two, he ventured to publish *Aurora, or the Morning Redness*, and during the remaining seven years of his life poured forth about thirty other publications One of the most important of his works is, *Description of the Three Principles of the Divine Being* From writing in his native language at a time when Latin was generally used, he got the name of the Teutonic philosopher He wrote at a steady rate, without haste and without correction. All that he produced was welcomed by a constantly growing circle of admirers and disciples Richter now again bestirred himself against him, and the magistrates recommended him to leave the city for the sake of peace, which he did Thereafter he was summoned before the Elector of Saxony, who appointed six Doctors of Divinity to examine him His gentle demeanour and answers won the good opinion both of the Elector and the examiners, and he was charitably dismissed. He returned to Gorlitz, where he died in 1624 On his deathbed, he asked his son Tobias whether he did not hear sweet music, and when his son answered that he heard nothing, bade him open the door, that the sound might enter He foretold the moment of his departure three hours before it came, and when it was at hand, bade his son turn him, and expired

Behmen was a small thin man, with a low forehead, but with full temples and bright blue eyes His voice was weak and sweet, his character gentle and retiring His writings utter in their own way the deepest philosophical conceptions, and are the work of an entirely spiritual mind Their phraseology is drawn from the Scriptures, with a large admixture of the terms of the mystical chemistry then in use They consist of speculations on the Deity and the origin of things, delivered in the form of Divine revelations The Deity is to be contemplated first in His own existence as "the eternal one, the silent nothing, the *temperamentum*" The Divine Unity is itself a Trinity Nature, or creature, proceeds therefrom, and is called "contrariety" But the proceeding of creature from God is at the same time the ingoing of God into creature, "the silent nothing becomes something by entering into duality" The power of seeing duality in things is spiritual-mindedness

The life of Behmen was written by his admirer Abraham von Frankenberg, who died in 1652 The first collection of his writings was made in Holland by Betke in 1673, a more complete one in 1682 by Gichtel [10 vols Amsterdam], from whom the followers of Behmen have received the name of Gichtelians, a sect valued for their virtuous, silent, and benevolent life Another edition appeared in Amsterdam in 1730, under the title *Theosophia revelata*, in two volumes, more complete in six volumes. The latest edition is by Schiebler, Leipsic, 1831-40 Besides Germany and Holland, Behmen was acknowledged in France by Pierre Poiret as a man of deep spiritual insight, and in England he gained a devoted adherent in the divine and physician John Pordage, who wrote a commentary on his works, and declared himself convinced by a special revelation of the truth of his doctrines Jane Lead, a female enthusiast, founded a sect called the PHILADELPHIANS, for the study of his writings in 1697, in which she was joined by Pordage and his celebrated disciple Thomas Bromley An English translation of Behmen was published in 1764 by William Law, the author of the *Serious Call* On the authority of Law, we learn that Sir Isaac Newton was a diligent student of Behmen, a large number of extracts from whose works was found in the handwriting of Newton amongst his papers [Brewster's *Newton*, ii p 371]

The interest in Behmen was revived by the great speculative movement in Germany about the beginning of this century The end of the philosophy of Fichte, of Schelling, of Hegel, was the cognition of the absolute, or unconditioned, terms which denote the same principle which was the root of the mystical contemplations of Behmen This identity was acknowledged by Hegel, who saw in the "silent nothing," or principle of negativity which was the origin of things of Behmen, a forecast of his own celebrated division of philosophy into the science of the idea existing in and for itself, of the idea representing itself in nature, and of the idea returning into itself Hence Hegel placed Behmen at the head of modern philosophy [For a favourable early account of Behmen and his doctrines see Arnoldi *Hist Ecclesiastica de Hæretica*. For a modern German account see *Die Lehre des Deutschen Philosophen Jacob Bohm*, Wuller, Stuttgard, 1836, and Tennemann's *Manual of Phil* A life by an unknown author was also published at Dresden, 1802 Walton's *Introduction to Theosophy*]

BERENGARIANS [BERENGARIUS]

BERENGARIUS The leader of a too small school of divines belonging to the eleventh century who opposed the ultra-Roman definition of the Real Presence, which had originated with PASCHASIUS RADBERTUS [A D 831-865], and was formally promulgated as the doctrine of the Western Church by the Fourth Council of Lateran [A D 1215]

In the earlier part of his life, Berengarius, or Bérenger, was at the head of the school attached to the cathedral of Tours, of which he was also canon But when he was about forty-two years of age [A D. 1040] he became Archdeacon of Angers, shortly after which time he first comes into notice in connection with the Eucharistic controversy As a schoolmaster he had shewn an independence and originality of mind which had brought upon him some degree of censure as being fond of novelties, especially of a novel pronunciation of Latin which he wished to introduce But his intellectual boldness was shewn soon after he went to Angers by his opposition to the Eucharistic theories of Radbertus, which had now become received as authoritative by many theologians. Berengarius had studied the work of RATRAMNUS, written against this view of the Eucharist, but was said to go much further from the received opinion, and to maintain that the consecrated elements are only symbols—"figuram quandam et similitudinem"—of the Body and Blood of Christ A remonstrance against this teaching was written to him [A.D. 1045] by an old friend and schoolfellow, Adelmann, then Archdeacon of Liège, and afterwards [A.D. 1048] Bishop of Brescia This warning was repeated two years afterwards with affectionate earnestness, the second letter being still extant [Adelmann, *De Veritate Corp et Sang Dom*, Brunswick, 1770] Berengarius having by this time got into public controversy with Hugo, bishop of Langres, on the subject, wrote a letter to Lanfranc (then Abbot of Bec, and afterwards Archbishop of Canterbury), stating his views and endeavouring to secure Lanfranc's support for them The abbot being then at Rome, the letter of Berengarius did not reach him until its contents were known to others, and the consequence was that it was laid before a council which was sitting at the time [A D 1050] as containing heresy The council convicted its author, without waiting to know whether he had any explanation or defence to offer, and the sentence was confirmed at Vercelli in the September following At this latter council Berengarius wished to be present that he might make his defence, but being then in the Abbey of Tours he was prevented from attending by Henry I, King of France, who considered that he would run into danger by carrying out his wish [Mansi, *Concil.* xix 757, 773]

Four years after this condemnation a Legatine council was held at Tours, when Hildebrand was present as the Papal representative [A D 1054] At this council Berengarius declared his belief that "Panis atque vinum altaris post consecrationem sunt Christi Corpus et Sanguis," and Hildebrand being satisfied with this declaration, did not permit him to carry the explanation of his opinions into detail, but released him from the sentence of heresy which had been passed upon him

Subsequently Berengarius was summoned to Rome, where he appeared in the year 1059 There was a popular clamour against him as a heretic, and a demand that he should suffer death as such. Either in fear of death, or for some other unknown reason, he was then persuaded by Cardinal Humbert to sign a form of recantation, in which he acknowledged Transubstantiation in its most extreme form His words, as given by Lanfranc, declare, "Panem et vinum . . . Verum Corpus et Sanguinem Domini nostri Jesu Christi esse, et sensualiter non solum sacramento, sed in veritate, manibus sacerdotum tractari, frangi, et fidelium dentibus atteri" [Lanfr. *Opp* p 232]

On his return to France Berengarius took up his former line, notwithstanding this recantation, and engaged in a controversy with Lanfranc which lasted for many years, and during the course of which the former was occasionally in danger from the populace, who by this time had become blindly violent in defence of the doctrine of Transubstantiation Hildebrand became Pope as Gregory VII in the year 1073, but although he had protected Berengarius hitherto, he was not able to withstand the demand of the Cardinals that he should again be called to account Once more, therefore, the mover of this controversy was summoned to Rome, and once more, in a council which was held in February 1079, he signed a recantation, in which the doctrine which he had so long opposed was stated in as extreme a form as before [Mansi, *Concil* xx 543].

Berengarius left Rome on this occasion with a Papal certificate of his orthodoxy, and all who should presume to call him a heretic were by this document anathematized [D'Achery, *Spicileg* iii. 413] But he was also commanded to abstain from all controversy on the subject of the Eucharist, or from teaching any one except as a means of reclaiming those whom he had led into error He lived for several years longer, much mortified and humiliated by his recantation, and not really altering the opinions which he had so long held. His death took place A D 1088 in the island of St. Cosmas near Tours, where he had latterly lived in great retirement under the protection of the Bishop of Tours Berengarius never formed a sect, but many afterwards perverted his opinions into a denial of the Real Presence, and these were named Berengarians [Lanfranc, *De Eucharist* Berengar *de Sacr Cœna.* Ebrard's *Doctr and Hist of the Lord's Supper*, Frankfort, 1845]

BERON A Valentinian heretic mentioned by Hippolytus, and not otherwise known. Hippolytus writes respecting him that he and some others had forsaken the delusion of Valentinus only to fall into deeper errors The special heresy of Beron appears to have been that against which the clause of the Athanasian Hymn, "One, not by conversion of the Godhead into flesh, but by taking of the manhood into God," was levelled He held that at the Incarnation the Divine Nature of the Second Person in the Blessed Trinity became circumscribed or limited so as to be compatible with the Human Nature to which it was united, God the Son thus becoming self-emptied, acquiring an ἰδία περιγραφή, and ceasing to be "Immensus Filius" A fragment of Hippolytus remains in which he controverts this error of Beron, and some others founded upon it, saying, "What the Divine Nature was before the Incarnation that it was afterwards in Its Essence infinite, incomprehensible, impassible, incomparable, unchangeable, inconvertible, abiding in its own natural essence, and working according to its own nature" [Hippol *contra Beronem et Helicem*, *in* Fabric. *Bibl Græc* i 225 ARTEMONITES]

BERNARD, ST [SCHOOLMEN]

BERTRAM [RATRAMNUS.]

BERYLLUS was bishop of Bostra in Arabia about A D 230 He was a man of learning and piety, but falling into heresy, a synod was held at Bostra to judge his case Origen, who attended the synod, held private conferences with Beryllus, which were followed by a public disputation The result was that Beryllus was convinced of his error and returned to the

Catholic faith. This synod is frequently assigned to the year 247 or 249. From the order of events in Eusebius it appears to have been before the death of Gordian, A.D. 244, and is dated by Cave A.D. 243.

Beryllus asserted that our Lord, before His Incarnation, did not exist in the distinction of His own Person; and that He was Divine because there dwelt in Him not the proper Divinity of the Son, but the Divinity of the Father.[1] The first proposition needs no comment. The second has been somewhat variously interpreted. Mosheim [*Eccl. Hist.* cent. III. cap. v. sec. 14] says that the opinion, when considered with attention, amounts to this: that Christ did not exist before Mary, but that a *Spirit* issuing from God Himself, and therefore superior to all human souls, as being a portion of the Divine nature, was united to Him at the time of His birth. This appears to be an explaining away the "Paternal Divinity" which was asserted to have dwelt in Christ, and to suppose that Beryllus held, perhaps by anticipation, the later Sabellian doctrine. The words of Eusebius can be satisfied only by the earlier Sabellian or Patripassian doctrine, and accordingly Bishop Bull [*Jud. Eccl. Cathol.* iii. 4, *Def. Fid. Nic.* iv. 3, 17] classes Beryllus with Praxeas, Noetus, and Sabellius.[2] Against this it may be said that Origen, in the passage quoted by all commentators [*Frag. ex Comm. in Ep. ad Titum*], has distinguished between the doctrine of Beryllus and of the Patripassians. The passage is as follows: "Sed et eos, qui hominem dicunt Dominum Jesum præcognitum et prædestinatum, qui ante adventum carnalem substantialiter et proprie non extiterit, sed quod homo natus Patris solam in se habuerit deitatem, ne illos quidem sine periculo est ecclesiæ numero sociari: sicut et illos, qui superstitiose magis quam religiose, uti ne videantur duos deos dicere, neque rursum negare Salvatoris deitatem, unam eandemque subsistentiam Patris ac Filii asseverant, i.e. duo quidem nomina secundum diversitatem causarum recipientem, unam tamen ὑπόστασιν subsistere, i.e. unam personam duobus nominibus subjacentem, qui latine Patripassiani appellantur." The only difference between the two classes, the former of them being that to which Beryllus belonged, was that the Patripassians retained the names of Father and Son to be used as the varying action of the One and same Person required. Beryllus seemed to have disdained this affectation of retaining the names while all distinction of Person was denied.

Socrates [*Hist. Eccl.* iii. 7], in error, makes Beryllus to have been bishop of Philadelphia. He says, in a somewhat marked manner, that the synod of Bostra, in its letter to Beryllus, asserted that Christ, when made flesh, assumed not only the flesh but also the soul of man. But we are not entitled to infer from this that Beryllus combined Patripassian and Apollinarian doctrine. The acts of the synod of Bostra, the disputation of Origen and Beryllus, and Beryllus' letters to Origen thanking him for saving him from heresy, are unhappily lost.

BESOCHI. [BIZOCHI.]

BEZPOPOFTSCHINS. That division of Russian dissenters which does not retain the office of "pope" or priest, except in such a form as that of the Presbyterian or Independent ministry. The Bezpopoftschins have been divided into fifteen or twenty sects, the principal of which are the DUCHOBORTZI, the PHILIPOFTSCHINS, and the POMERANE; but all the smaller and fanatical sects have sprung from them.

BEZSLOVESTNI. A name signifying "the dumb," given to a not very numerous Russian sect of the eighteenth century, whose members after conversion became perpetually speechless. Very little is known of their tenets. In order to extract some information, a governor general of Siberia, named Pestal, in the reign of Catharine II. [A.D. 1762-1796], employed the cruellest forms of torture, pouring hot sealing-wax on their flesh, and tickling the soles of their feet with feathers, but without avail.

BIANCHI. [ALBATI.]

BIBLE CHRISTIANS. [BRYANITES.]

BIBLE COMMUNISTS. [PERFECTIONISTS.]

BICHINI. [BIZOCHI.]

BICORNI. A term colloquially signifying "idiots" among the Italians, and used contemptuously as a name for the BEGHARDS by some mediæval writers.

BIZOCHI. A name for the FRATICELLI, found in the Bull of Pope John XXII. condemning that community [A.D. 1317]. By some it is derived from "Bizzoco," or in French "Besace," on account of the wallet which they carried to hold the provisions which they begged from door to door; by others from "bigio," which indicated the grey colour of their garments.

BLASTUS. A Quartodeciman of this name is mentioned by the author of the book against heresies which formerly went by the name of Tertullian; and on the ground of his teaching that the Christian passover should be kept on the day fixed by the Jewish Law, he is declared to have been desirous of introducing Judaism [Pseudo-Tertull. xxii.]. He is doubtless the same person as the Roman Blastus named by Eusebius as being nearly involved in the fall of Florinus, who became a Valentinian [Euseb. *Hist. Eccl.* v. 15]. There is no evidence that Blastus ever actually became a Gnostic; but Eusebius records that an Epistle on Schism was written to him by Irenæus, as well as one on the Monarchy of God to Florinus [*ibid.* v. 20]. For the particulars of his association with the QUARTODECIMANS, the reader is referred to the article under that title. [Theod. *Hær. fab.* i. 23.]

[1] Τὸν Σωτῆρα καὶ Κύριον ἡμῶν λέγειν τολμῶν μὴ προυφεστάναι κατ' ἰδίαν οὐσίας περιγραφὴν πρὸ τῆς εἰς ἀνθρώπους ἐπιδημίας, μηδὲ μὴν θεότητα ἰδίαν ἔχειν, ἀλλ' ἐμπολιτευομένην αὐτῷ μόνην τὴν πατρικήν [Euseb. *Hist. Eccl.* vi. 33]. Regarding the interpretation of these words, see Valesius' note, and Mosheim, *De rebus Christ.* sæc. iii. sect. 34.

[2] Gennadius [cap. iii.] mentions Beryllus together with Artemon and Marcellus. Pseudo Hieronymus [cap. 36] mentions the denial of the pre existence of Christ as common to Beryllus and Photinus.

BOCASOTI [BIZOCHI]

BOGOMILES, or (as it is corruptly written) BOGARMITÆ, was the name assumed by a sect of heretics, who appeared in the twelfth century in the Bulgarian city of Philippopolis They appear to have separated off from the Paulicians, the Manichæan heretics who were predominant in the Danubian provinces from the ninth to the thirteenth century

The founder of the Bogomiles was an heretical monk named Basil, who directed his followers to use and glory in the dissonant name of Bogomile, an appellation compounded of two Sclavic roots, "Bog" signifying God, and "mil" His mercy They were better known to the orthodox Greek world under the title of "Phundaites," or "wearers of the girdle," from the habit which poverty or the commands of Basil forced them to adopt We also meet with them in contemporary literature under the name of Massilians; it is presumable, from some fancied resemblance in doctrine to the earlier Semi-Pelagian heretics of that name

This sect was drawn from the dregs of the population, and made poverty and ignorance chief and necessary tenets By this rule, all learned persons were excluded from their body, yet they took upon themselves the revision of the Scripture Canon Their Bible consisted of seven books the Psalms, the Prophets, each of the four Gospels, the Acts, with the Epistles and the Apocalypse Like other Paulicians, they adopted an allegorical interpretation of Scripture, taught the innate evilness of matter, and its eternal hostility to spirit Pursuing the same line of reasoning, they denied all mysterious efficacy to the sacraments, and rejected altogether the baptism of water They supported their belief in a Docetic or fantastic Christ, by a reference to the distinctive quality of His baptism, as opposed to that administered by John The creation of the world they conceived to be due to a wicked Demiurge, and attributed the murder of Abel to the jealousy of Cain, whose birth they referred to a union between Eve and Satanael (the eldest son of Jehovah) while they assigned to Adam the paternity of Abel

These rude and ignorant heretics, who seem to have equally misconceived both Christianity and Manichæism, might have remained unmolested in their obscurity, but for the missionary zeal of Alexius Comnenus That emperor, whose piety or policy induced him to undertake the conversion of the Paulicians, was made acquainted, during his mission work, with the existence of the unhappy Bogomiles Diblatius, one of their chiefs or apostles (for, like Mani himself, Basil emulated the organization of primitive Christianity) disclosed the name of their leader to the emperor Impelled by a desire to effect the more complete extermination of the heresy, Alexius invited the leader of it, Basil, to a banquet, at which, in the guise of a disciple, he extracted from him a full confession of his guilt At the close of the entertainment, Basil was seized by the officers of the emperor, and by his orders kept in close confinement until the return of the court to Constantinople There the contumacious heresiarch was publicly burned the scene of his execution being the open space before the gates of St Sophia By command of the emperor, as we are informed by his daughter Anna Comnena, a monk of the Eastern Church, Euthymius Zygabenus by name, composed a full account and refutation of the Bogomilian errors, which is still to be read in his work, entitled the Δογματικὴ Πανοπλία The total dispersion of the sect ensued upon the death of their founder.

In A D 1140, a Constantinopolitan council formally anathematized the heresy of the followers of Basil, but three years later, two bishops of Cappadocia, Clement and Leontinus, were condemned for holding these opinions It may, however, be reasonably supposed, that these perverts, whose dioceses were situated in the original seat from which Paulician Manichæism (the parent of the Bogomilian heresy) had emigrated into Europe, were only primitive Paulicians, whose tenets, being discovered to resemble (though with material differences) those of their Bulgarian brothers, were fitted, in default of a more exact nomenclature, with the title of Bogomiles The last mention of the heresy is the condemnation of a monk named Niphorion about the middle of the twelfth century

[All that is known about this obscure and illiterate body has been collected in the work by Joh. Christ Wolf, *Historia Bogomilorum*, Dissert iii, Wittenberg, 1712]

BOHEMIA, CONFESSION OF [PROTESTANT CONFESSIONS]

BOHEMIAN BRETHREN This name was given to a semi-religious, semi-political party which sprung up in Bohemia, early in the fifteenth century They directed their efforts to preserve the religious independence of their country from the exorbitant claims of the Pope, and their constitutional freedom against the pretensions of the princes of the house of Austria

The Bohemians were a branch of the Sclavonic race They were originally called Czechs, and occupied the country of the Teutonic Boii, in the middle of the sixth century, having subdued the original inhabitants They were converted to Christianity by the labours of Methodius, a Greek priest of Thessalonica, towards the end of the ninth century. The Eastern Church, therefore, may justly claim them as her own sons, and for a long time they knew no other form of Christianity But Latin tendencies gradually prevailed in spite of strong opposition In 968 they were brought under the Papal supremacy, and in the following century Latin was made the language of their Liturgy in direct opposition to the Sclavonic vernacular Shortly afterwards the celibacy of the clergy was forced upon them, and the cup was withdrawn from the laity But these changes, brought about by *external* power, excited a strong feeling of discontent, which received further increase in consequence of the close connection of the country with England, arising from the marriage between our own Richard II and Anne, sister of King

Wenceslaus of Bohemia Through this Wickliffe's writings were diffused in the latter country. These causes, coupled with the Papal schism that was then raging, gave rise to a party, of which the celebrated Huss was the chief ornament, Catholic so far as doctrine was concerned, yet national and therefore anti-papal in spirit For a time, under the mild but somewhat weak rule of Wenceslaus, the public peace was maintained, notwithstanding the execution of Huss, which excited and alarmed the whole country, and gave strength to the extreme men, who now began to appear as the Taborites, or Hussites proper But the death of the king kindled the flame of a religious war, of all such wars the most bloodily waged on both sides. The natural successor of Wenceslaus was his brother Sigismund, the emperor who had weakly given up Huss to death at Constance, and although the crown was elective, he at once took measures to assert what he considered his just rights For a time the nation was united against him as one man, and the war which followed, first under the leadership of John Ziska, and afterwards under that of Procopius, was one of the most remarkable, as a national uprising against a powerful foreign foe, that history has recorded [HUSSITES]

But what the whole power of the Empire and of the Papacy combined could not effect was soon brought about by internal dissension There were two chief parties among the Bohemians The larger, which comprised almost all the clergy and the greater part of the nobles, was Catholic, but anti-papal Not a single heresy could be laid to their charge. They were of the old national party, and had never willingly submitted to the claims of the Pope, which they now openly abjured as antichristian They also claimed the restoration of the cup to the laity, and the subjection of the spirituality to the temporal power in all things temporal They were usually styled Calixtines or Utraquists, and had but little in common with the Taborite followers of Ziska, who had departed as much from the principles of Huss as the modern Wesleyans have from those of Wesley

When Sigismund found that he could not subdue the Bohemians by force of arms, he made use of this distinction to divide his opponents, and subdue them in detail. He invited them to send deputies to the Council of Basle, where they might state their grievances, and if possible effect an accommodation This proposal was scornfully rejected by the Taborites, and eagerly accepted by the Catholic or Calixtine party These latter made the following four demands of the Council [1] That the Communion should be in both kinds, [2] that the secular power should have dominion over the persons of criminous clerks, [3] that there should be perfect liberty of preaching to all ecclesiastics, [4] that the clergy should not be allowed to hold civil offices After fierce discussion the first of these was granted, and for a time a hollow truce existed between the national Bohemian party and Rome Sigismund had gained his object, and shortly afterwards the more extreme Taborites were utterly crushed as a political party, Sigismund was acknowledged as king, peace was restored to the country, and the Bohemians were allowed to continue members of a national, Catholic, and yet anti-papal Church. This was in 1435

But the Papal court could not rest permanently content with anything short of absolute submission, and this well known fact, coupled with small annoyances and petty persecutions, kept alive the suspicions and jealousies of the Bohemians, so that in 1450 they sent an embassy to the Patriarch of Constantinople, desiring to be readmitted into communion, on the ground that they had originally derived their Christianity from the East. But though the embassy was well received, the advance of the Turks and other changes prevented anything from coming out of it Political troubles followed in Bohemia, which led to the loss of the ancient constitutional rights of the people against their sovereigns The differences between the Romanizing and the national parties became the more marked, so that as the former were favoured by the rulers, the latter found some difficulty in preserving the succession At one time, in 1482, an Italian wandering bishop, Augustine Lucian, appeared most opportunely for them, when the archbishopric of Prague was purposely kept vacant by the authorities who favoured Rome. Shortly after they sought for and received ordination from the Armenians The consequence was that the country was kept in a state of religious ferment by the contests between the two parties, until King Ladislaus, in a Diet held at Kuttenberg in 1485, caused a religious truce for thirty-three years to be concluded Each party agreed to refrain from annoying the other, freedom of preaching was allowed, and the compacts of Basle were reaffirmed against the Papal opposition

The following century saw a great change in the Bohemians The Lutherans of Germany crowded into their country, and joined the national party of the Bohemians, obtaining shelter and toleration under their name, and infecting the Bohemian Church with their peculiarities So matters continued until 1556, when the Jesuits were introduced The public education was placed in their hands, and they were commissioned to use all efforts of influence and persuasion to bring the people back into unity with the See of Rome, but at the same time, to quiet apprehension, the privileges of the national party were confirmed In 1609, Rudolph, after various efforts to enforce uniformity, was compelled to grant the Bohemian charter, allowing complete toleration to the three parties, the Romans, the Bohemians, and the Protestants (Lutherans and Calvinists), and exhorting them all to live in peace with each other To each of them was allowed full liberty to build churches, to found schools, and to hold their own ecclesiastical courts But the peace did not continue for long Lutheranism began to infect the national party more and more, owing to the influx from Germany, while on the other hand Rudolph's successor, Ferdinand, in his own hereditary dominions of Styria (the crown of Bohemia was elective), had distinguished himself by a zealous persecution of the Protestants Suspicion united the old Bohemians and the later foreign bodies against him, and a civil war followed, stained by the usual atrocities on both sides It proved the commencement of the Thirty Years' War The insurgents elected Frederick Count Palatine to be their king, but he was a rigid Calvinist, and commenced his reign with the destruction of altars, crucifixes, and monumental tombs in Prague, whereby he alienated the old Bohemian party, which had never (at least as a body) abandoned either Catholic ritual or Catholic doctrine Moreover, he was not fitted by firmness of character to be the leader in any great movement, and his first defeat on the White Mountains near Prague, in November 1620, destroying his hopes, he fled from the kingdom, taking with him the crown jewels, but leaving his unfortunate Bohemian followers a prey to the vengeance of the merciless Ferdinand

This was the last effort of the Bohemians to maintain their religious liberties by force of arms. Henceforth they submitted to the power of the house of Austria, to which they have ever since been attached The Jesuits whom Frederick had banished were restored, Roman Catholicism was made the established religion of the country, and every effort was made to bring back the natives to the communion of Rome To the legitimate means of conversion used by the Jesuits were added others of a more questionable character The government put forth all its strength to crush those who were regarded as political opponents Persecutions, the quartering of soldiers upon the disaffected, and the uprooting of families, did their work Moreover, Protestantism pure and simple had never found great favour in the eyes of the people, and with the political decay of the national party, the peculiar religious fire of the nation was quenched An immense majority of the people is now Roman Catholic There are a few Lutherans and Calvinists among them, chiefly of German extraction, a remnant also of the Hussites still lingers on under the name of Bohemian Brethren [HUSSITES], but the national, Catholic, and antipapal party has long been extinct [Palacky, *Hist Bohemia*]

BOLINGBROKE A sceptical nobleman of the last century [A D 1672-1751] who promoted among the higher classes that flippant infidelity for which they were so conspicuous during the reigns of Queen Anne and the first two Hanoverian Kings, and which he himself had learned in Paris Bolingbroke may be said to have originated in England that supercilious and superficial style of infidelity which looks upon religion as an useful institution for women, children, and the lower classes, and which is worth the support of a government as a means of preserving order and the rights of property [SCEPTICS DICT *of* THEOL, art DEISM]

BONI HOMINES. [PERFECTI]

BONI PUERI [BEGHARDS]

BONI VALETI [BEGHARDS]

BONOSIANS [BONOSIANI or BONOSIACI] A sect formed in Macedonia at the end of the fourth century by Bonosus, Bishop of Sardica Bonosus held that Jesus Christ is the Son of God by adoption only [Pseud -Hier xlii, Isid Hisp liii] This identifies his doctrine with that of Photinus, an identification made by the second Council of Arles, can xvi and xvii Gennadius also states, that Audentius, a Spanish bishop, wrote against the Photinians, "who are now called Bonosiaci" [*de Vir Ill* cap 14, quoted by Lardner, *Cred* cap lxxxix. *q v*] How soon Bonosus and his followers reached this stage of complete Photinianism is not known There appears to have been an intermediate stage, during which the party was gradually drifting into the open denial of the pre-existence of Christ For in no other way can we reconcile the high authorities of the Council of Arles and Gregory the Great, which are seemingly in direct contradiction The council [II Arel can xvii] says it is manifest that the Bonosians baptize in the name of the Trinity, and orders, therefore, converts from them to be received with chrism and imposition of hands Gregory says as unhesitatingly that they do not baptize in that name [*Decret Collect* pars iii dist iv can *Hi vero hæretici*] It is easy to conclude (and it agrees with the natural course of heresy) that the council refers to the early practice of the sect, and Gregory to the later practice In the year 389 or 390, Bonosus was condemned by Theophilus, Bishop of Alexandria, and Anysius, Bishop of Thessalonica, and others, as delegates of the Synod of Capua, for teaching that the Blessed Virgin, after our Lord's birth, bore children to Joseph The two bishops wrote to Ambrose inquiring his opinion Ambrose replied that the case was referred to them by the synod, and that it was not his place to give a judicial opinion,—"Vicem enim Synodi recepistis," "Vos enim totius Synodi vice decernitis, nos quasi ex Synodi auctoritate judicare non convenit" But privately he approves their sentence. He names no other charge against Bonosus than that relating to the Blessed Virgin [Ambrose *Epist* i v ed 1616] It seems then that after his condemnation on this point Bonosus fell by degrees into Photinianism [ANTIDICOMARIANITES] The sentence was of suspension from his episcopal functions, but Bonosus continued to ordain those who applied to him

The Decretal Epistles of Innocent I make mention of Bonosus more than once The larger number of the epistles are no doubt forgeries, it is doubtful whether any are genuine Still they were early forgeries, for Dionysius Exiguus accepted them, and they may be taken as evidence of facts where the object of the forger did not call for misrepresentation In the present case his object would be not to misrepresent the facts, but to ascribe the conduct held towards Bonosus to the principle of obedience to the See of Rome The letter to Laurentius, Bishop of

Senia in Dalmatia, directs that the Defensors of the Church drive away the Bonosians, who deny Christ to have been born of the Substance of the Father before the world That to Martianus, bishop of Naissus in Dacia, directs that they who were ordained by Bonosus before his condemnation be continued in the clergy That to the bishops and deacons of Macedonia warns that the reception of some ordained by Bonosus which has been already allowed is not to be made a precedent, and states that many who despaired of obtaining orders in the Church procured ordination from Bonosus with the view of returning to the Church, and the hope of being received as of the clergy [Johnson, *Vade Mecum,* ii 301] How long the sect existed is not known.

BONS HOMMES [PERFECTI]

BORBELITES [BARBELIOTES]

BORBORIANS [BARBELIOTES]

BORRELISTS A sect of the Mennonites or Dutch Baptists which originated with Adam Borrel, a man of good station and learning, in the latter half of the seventeenth century Their distinction from the Mennonite body at large was that they professed an austere life and rejected all external ordinances of Divine worship, being thus analogous to the English Quakers. [Stoupp, *Traité de la Religion des Hollandais*]

BOUGRES [BULGARIANS]

BOURIGNONISTS A sect of French Quietists of the seventeenth century, followers of Antoinette Bourignon de la Porte, a lady of Flanders, who was born at Lisle in the year 1616, and died at Franeker in Friesland in the year 1680 Madame Bourignon imagined that she had received a direct inspiration from God to restore the Christian religion, which she alleged to have been lost in the midst of the controversies which it had raised Setting her face against all churches and sects, she devoted herself to the task of forming a new community of which she should be the living instructress, her qualification for that office being based on a claim that the true spiritual meaning of Holy Scripture had been specially revealed to her Full of enthusiasm, she also possessed great conversational powers, and these qualities gained her many converts even among persons of high education She was also a most industrious author, her collected writings filling nineteen volumes, but these, and probably her conversation also, were largely borrowed from the mystical theology of an earlier date. The leading point of her system was that common to the Pietistic mystics, that religion consists in emotion and conscious feeling, not in knowledge and practice.

The most distinguished of the Bourignonists were a Jansenist priest of the Oratory of Mechlin, named Bartholomew de Cordt, and Peter Poiret, a Calvinistic minister of considerable learning The latter was an energetic coadjutor of Madame Bourignon, and after her death became the leader of her sect, his exposition of its principles being printed in 1713, in six volumes, entitled *The Divine Œconomy, or an universal system of the works and purposes of God,* written originally in French.

The Bourignonists spread from Holland to Germany, France, Switzerland and England, and at the end of the seventeenth and the beginning of the eighteenth century held a position not unlike to that of the Swedenborgians in later times Some still kept up their connection with the churches or sects to which they had previously belonged, others separated themselves from all Christian societies and followed a life of private contemplation, studying the works of the Quietists and Pietists in general, but looking to those of their founder as the great source of spiritual knowledge

BOURNEANS This name has been given to the disciples of a Birmingham preacher named Bourne, who maintained the most extreme form of the doctrine of annihilation, which places the final punishment of impenitent sinners not in suffering but in the total extinction of their existence

BRACHITÆ A sect of the Manichæans, which Prateolus assigns to the end of the third century, but of which nothing is known [Prateol *Hæres* xxxiii]

BRAHMINS The religion of Brahminism is professed by about 150,000,000 people in the peninsula of India. It derives its name from the title of the chief caste of its votaries, from which alone the priests are taken, but it is also known as Hindooism, or the Hindoo religion Brahminism is the oldest of the religions that have sprung from the Aryan family of mankind The religion of Zoroaster, or Magianism, is an offshoot from it Buddhism was a schism and an antagonism It is derived from and professes to be based on sacred writings in the Sanscrit language, the oldest of which are of extreme antiquity. In its present form it differs widely from the primitive religion, owing to successive corruptions, arising partly from the development of religious thought, partly, as it appears, from unknown foreign accretions, partly from impositions devised for the purpose of maintaining and extending the power of the Brahmins or priestly caste.

I *The primitive form* of the Hindoo religion is known to us only from the sacred books, or Vedas, written in the Sanscrit language These are four in number—the Rig-Veda, the Yagur-Veda, the Sama-Veda, and the Atharva-Veda Collectively, they are known as the Veda, from the same root as οἶδα, meaning originally knowledge Of these the Rig-Veda, or Veda of Praise, is by far the most ancient and important, and alone deserves the name of Veda, being the basis of the other three, which are liturgical books for the use of the different orders of priests and ministers who take part in the sacrifices Each Veda consists of two portions, the Sanhita or Mantras, which are hymns to the gods, and the Brahmanas and Sutras, commentaries in prose There is a further class of works called Aranakas and Upanishads, which may be regarded as an appendix to the Brahmanas. These commentaries are all of much later date than the hymns, the Brahmanas with their appendix preceding the Sutras, as is evident from their style and contents. The Rig-Veda Sanhita—which is alone the true record of the primitive faith—consists of ten books, containing 1028 (or excluding 11 generally held to be spurious 1017) hymns by many different authors, addressed to various deities The latest of these hymns date from at least B C 1200, the earliest are placed by some authorities as high as B C 2000, by others at about B C 1500 Though all our MSS are modern, yet the evidence, internal and external, for an extremely early date is incontrovertible [For a brief summary see Max-Muller's *Chips from a German Workshop*, i 10-17, also the same writer's *History of Ancient Sanscrit Literature*] The Veda is held to be absolutely the work of the Deity, no mortal having composed a single line of it, and to have been revealed to mankind through the agency of "Rishis"—persons raised above the level of ordinary humanity, who were therefore preserved from error in the reception and tradition of truth The Rishis, who were in fact the authors, are said by the Brahmins to have "seen" the respective portions they transmitted. There is nothing, however, in the Veda itself to countenance this theory, which is found in some other religions [MAHOMETANISM], and may be regarded simply as an expression of dependence on the Divine Being.

The religion of the Rig-Veda is apparently a gross polytheism—derived from the deification so natural to the childhood of the human race—of the powers and aspects of nature Some of the deities mentioned are plainly of this character Agni, the fire, Surya, the sun, the Maruts, storms • Others appear as proper names, having so far lost the natural aspect which was once theirs Varuna [Οὐρανός], the heavens, Mitra, the sun-light, Indra, the firmament. The most prominent deities are Indra and Agni, to whom nearly half the hymns are addressed. There is no recognition of the Hindoo Triad of later times—Brahma, Vishnu, Siva,—and no mention at all is made of other deities which are now most popular But this polytheism is of a very peculiar character There is an entire absence of any consciousness of that limitation of the powers of the respective gods which seems the necessary consequence of a plurality of deities By the worshipper for the time being each god is looked on as absolute and supreme, while the others, for the moment, pass out of sight To almost all in different hymns are these attributes assigned, no one god being ever regarded as superior or inferior to any other In a few passages the different gods are regarded as but different names and powers of one supreme deity While the hymns contain much that is literally childish—the product of the infancy of religion,—mean, tedious, commonplace, there is little that is positively bad Degrading passions and acts are ascribed to the gods, the conception of them is in many respects low and unworthy A low level is also assigned on the whole to human nature, the wants expressed are mostly of an earthly, material nature But there is also much that is true and sublime The gods are generally spoken of as immortal, and of expressions that seem to imply the contrary, as in speaking of the birth of certain gods, it may be seen that a physical phenomenon is the foundation,—the rising of the sun, the beginning of the day or year The gods, as a rule, dwell in heaven, but some of them at times are present with men, draw near to the sacrifices, and listen to the praises of their worshippers It is often said that the heavens and earth were created by certain gods, but occasionally ignorance is confessed of the beginning of the universe A consciousness, somewhat vague indeed, of sin and moral evil is expressed, and there are frequent prayers for forgiveness The gods are represented as rewarding good and punishing evil, and yet as forgiving, as just yet merciful But their anger is chiefly represented as excited by some failure of service or offering to themselves, rather than by moral evil. There is no sign of a belief in metempsychosis, but in its place a belief in actual personal immortality, with, seemingly, rewards and punishments for the good and evil There is no mention of either idols or temples, but there is in the later hymns a manifest tendency to the worship of symbols, even of the objects of sacrifice, as the horse, the symbol of and offering to the sun, the soma plant, of the moon, and the post to which the sacrificial victim was tied. There is no trace of the existence of caste, nor of suttee or widow-burning, which was a later introduction supported by corrupting a text of the Rig-Veda The worship was offered only in each man's house, in a chamber set apart for the purpose It was of a very simple character, consisting of prayers, chiefly for material benefits, riches, prosperity, good crops, success over enemies and in the chase, and great spoils, and the like; of praises, and of offerings In the earlier hymns these consist only of clarified butter poured on the fire, of cakes, parched grain, and other simple viands, and of the intoxicating juice of the soma plant In the later period we read of animal sacrifices, especially of the horse [See for further details, Max-Muller, *History of Ancient Sanscrit Literature*, and *Chips from a German Workshop*, vol i, Mrs Manning, *Ancient and Mediæval India*, Elphinstone, *Hist of India*, 5th ed., edited by E B Cowell, bk i chap iv and app i and vii, J T Wheeler, *Hist of India*, vol. i pt i; H. H Wilson *Essays and Lectures*, Colebrooke, *Miscellaneous Essays*]

II *The transitional form* of Brahminism from this simple elemental religion to the later system is especially seen in the works called Brahmanas and Upanishads The former are a development on the ceremonial side. They contain legends and allegories which have their germ in the Veda, derived in many cases from divine epithets personified, sometimes from absolute misunderstanding of expressions On these legends is based a most complex and artificial ceremonial. The Upanishads, on the other hand, contain a development from the philosophical and theosophical side, explaining the nature of the Supreme Being, his relation to the human soul, the process of creation, &c The Upanishads are the basis of the enlightened and philosophical faith, and of the different systems of Hindoo philosophy, and are the only portions of the sacred literature that are much read and studied at the present day. This transition period is often called the epic period, its chief illustration being derived from the great Sanscrit epics,—the Maha Bharata and the Ramayana. The ritual and ceremonial is systematized in the so-called *Institutes of Manu*, still the great text-book of Brahminism, and held to be of supreme authority, though not a revelation in the same sense as the Veda. This work contains materials of various dates, but was compiled at latest three or four centuries B C While professing to be based on the Veda, it contains elements entirely alien to that religion, which have been plausibly supposed to come from a foreign source [see Wheeler, *History of India*, vol. ii.]

The religion taught in the Institutes of Manu is mainly the worship of Brahmà, an emanation from and the creative energy of Brahma, the supreme spirit of the universe Other inferior deities are mentioned, mostly identical with those of the Veda The germs of the doctrine of the Triad are found, and their development may be seen in the epic poems But the main point is the ritual and ceremonial, which are of the most complicated, precise, and burdensome character, embracing almost every act and moment of life The caste system is found in all its rigour The danger of offending the gods by imperfect service is set forth very vividly, and hence the necessity of constantly consulting the Brahmins, who were alone held to be acquainted with the details The doctrine of metempsychosis is also set forth in its most developed form

III *Modern Brahminism* Against this system of priestly domination Buddhism was an uprising, and for a time it obtained the supremacy. But a reaction came in favour of Brahminism, which succeeded in expelling Buddhism from India altogether, and entered upon a fresh development, especially in regard to the objects of worship. This forms the third and last period of Brahminism The sources of this development are the works called Puranas and, in a less degree, the Tantras The Puranas are eighteen in number, of various dates, from the eighth to the sixteenth century A D, but incorporating older materials They all begin with a cosmogony, and contain also theogonies, philosophical speculations, instructions in ritual, fragments of history, and countless legends Their religion may be described as sectarian in character, supporting the doctrines of various sects, and so they do not form a consistent whole, though they are all accepted as incontrovertible authority Hence arise various inconsistencies, anomalies, and contradictions

The existence of a supreme being is indeed still set forth, from whom all other beings—the deities, men, the world—derive their existence, from whose substance they are, and whom, in fact, they in some sense constitute But this monotheism or pantheism is practically obscured by the direction of devotion to a multitude of deities, said to be 330,000,000 in number. This number, however, includes spirits and demons of various kinds The gods universally acknowledged are seventeen in number, the great Triad (Trimurti) Brahma, Vishnu, and Siva, the creating, preserving, and destroying principles, with the corresponding female divinities, being the most important. The other deities are mostly powers of nature, including many of those mentioned in the Veda,—Indra, Varuna, Agni, &c Besides these, veneration is paid to the planets, to many sacred rivers, to a host of local gods. Of the three great gods, Brahma, though once supreme, is but little worshipped now, having only one temple in all India Vishnu and Siva have attracted almost all the veneration Vishnu is mainly worshipped under the form of avatars, or incarnations—manifestations on earth in various forms, animal and human—ten in number, of which one is yet to come The most reverenced of these are Krishna and Rama Siva, the principle of destruction, is also looked on as the principle of renewal, and hence is worshipped under the form of the lingam, identical with the ancient phallus [see Herod. ii 48, 49]. In his honour frequent and bloody sacrifices are offered, and his votaries inflict horrible and protracted tortures on themselves His consort Devi is also much worshipped, especially with great sacrifices It is said that 100 goats per month, besides other animals, are offered at her temple near Calcutta Most of the other deities have no separate temples, but have their especial images, votaries, and festivals Each god is regarded as having a separate heaven, to which its most assiduous worshippers are borne after death, where they are attended by good spirits, and also a separate hell for the wicked. Besides the deities whose worship is spread more or less over the country, each village has its own local gods, which are sometimes the spirits of men who have in any way distinguished themselves while living, sometimes incarnations or avatars of the more famous gods There is a universal belief in the existence of good and evil spirits pervading the universe, with power to bless or to harm The legends respecting the gods are of the most extravagant character The three gods of the Triad are supposed to be equal in power, and yet quarrel and fight, and wound each other There is no regular system of subordination of the gods, either to these three or to one another The images have in most cases a monstrous character, with many heads, arms, or bodies In the legends extraordinary power is ascribed to asceticism, even the deities are sometimes represented as subdued by it, and thus although the ascetic may be a wicked man The popular religion extols the efficacy of faith, *i e.* reliance and entire dependence on and submission to some one deity While morality and purity of life are inculcated, it is taught that neither they nor any religious forms avail without this faith, which also compensates for all deficiencies in them

The religious sects which devote themselves exclusively to the cultus of one deity are exceedingly numerous. They may be divided into three chief classes—Vaishnavas, worshippers of Vishnu,

Saivas, of Siva, Saktas, of one of the female associates of the gods of the Triad. Each of these classes contains numerous subordinate sects There are also small sects worshipping some one of the inferior gods The members of the different sects are distinguished by painted marks on their foreheads Many of them have monastic orders attached to them, both for males and females, in which distinctions of caste are comparatively disregarded The sects also have appointed heads, who have very great influence and power; and there are mystic ceremonies of admission, differing in each case

Such is the form which Brahminism assumes at this day among the masses. But such vulgar polytheism could not commend itself to the keen intellect and philosophizing spirit of the educated Hindoos With them religion is based upon philosophy, a monotheism derived from pantheism The learned Brahmins earnestly disclaim polytheism—such as that, for instance, of the ancient Greeks or Romans They teach that there is but one God, manifesting himself primarily in his several functions as creator, preserver, and destroyer, under the several forms of Brahma, Vishnu, and Siva, they profess also that they look on images simply as aids to the mind in meditation on and prayer to the one supreme deity. The system of religious philosophy that is regarded as most orthodox teaches that the only truly existing being is the deity, all other forms are, as to their material properties, mere illusions as to their spiritual attributes, transient sparks, scintillations, emanations of his glory The deity, existing in unapproachable, solitary supremacy, longed for offspring, from this desire has sprung every existing thing, by a series of emanations—first Brahmà the creator, and from him gods, men, demons, beasts, the earth All these comprising the whole universe, in so far as they have true existence, are consubstantial with the deity, who is the basis underlying all the forms which they assume In fact, the deity is the world undeveloped, the world is the deity in his development The supreme deity, also called Brahma, is yet a pure abstraction, self-centred, and absorbed in self-contemplation, the end and cause of all things Beings and matter owe their existence simply to the impulse of his will The various forms that matter assumes are all pure illusions, possessing but a semblance of reality. This semblance of reality is due to Máyá, which, originally a personification of the longing for offspring felt by the deity, became a synonym for delusion and unreality The world and all that is in it passes through three stages, growth, perfection, and decay this latter was deified as Siva, who is opposed to Brahmà, the creative power of the supreme Brahma, while Vishnu is the power that, by preserving all things, limits the dominion of Siva A remarkable feature of Brahminism is that of "cycles of existence," a feature which is almost peculiar to it It is held that at the end of a cycle of prodigious length, the universe ceases to exist, the Triad and all the inferior gods pass out of being, and the First Cause alone exists in his primeval singleness But, after a long course of ages, he again puts forth his power, through which the whole creation, divine and human, comes into existence again This process is being continually repeated. The soul of man is regarded as part of the divine spirit, taken out of his substance and of his nature, but, whereas he is unlimited, the soul is limited. This limitation was one result of the wish of the supreme for offspring Souls were originally possessed of freedom and happiness, but through envy and ambition they fell, and thereby separated themselves still further from the divine essence. Then this world came into being as a place of trial, and souls were attached to bodies Souls may animate all species of organic life, from the highest to the lowest, and rise by a succession of births through different bodies up to the human Then their trial begins, which is to determine their future existence. Almost all acts are regarded as either merits or demerits, and the individual soul is rewarded or punished according to the balance of them The rewards consist either of a superior lot in future existences, or of a removal to one of the heavens of bliss belonging to one or other of the deities, where the soul remains till it has been sufficiently rewarded The punishments consist either of misery or degradation in future existences, or of suffering in one of the hells of the deities, till the balance of evil is expiated In each case, after ages of enjoyment or misery, the stages of existence begin anew Even the worst of men, after a purification by intense sufferings, may rise through the scale of being again and attain to bliss The supreme point of bliss is to escape from the evil of a limited and separate existence by being absorbed or incorporated into the essence of the deity, or supreme soul from which the soul sprung, and of which it is a part This is to be obtained either by works, by faith, or by knowledge. Works consist of devotion to the deities, sacrifices and offerings, prayers and praises, and a careful performance of the prescribed ceremonial of life and action Knowledge is attained through one of the various systems of philosophy. The ceremonial is that prescribed in the laws of Manu, being most precise and exact. Five "sacraments" are prescribed for the daily use of the "twice-born man"—the superior castes [1] The reading of the Vedas, [2] the offering of cakes to departed ancestors, [3] the pouring of clarified butter on the fire as a sacrifice to the fire, or to the powers of nature generally, [4] the offering of rice to the spirits, [5] the exercise of hospitality All these, especially the first, are surrounded by many complicated ceremonies There are also other observances, such as the three suppressions of the breath in honour of Brahma, the use of the mystic word "aum," and of the Gayatri, a text of the Veda used as a prayer Besides these distinctly religious acts, the law prescribes how to eat, drink, clothe one's self, bathe, cut hair and nails, and even how to relieve nature, and assigns special rights and duties to each caste, and each subdivision of a caste. But in practice these injunctions are very generally disregarded, and either by abbreviation, or by the doctrine of faith mentioned above for instance, the devotions of the Brahmins, which, if performed fully, would take four hours, are contracted into half an hour, while the men of the lower castes simply repeat the name of their patron god as they bathe The pursuit of philosophy again is regarded as of equal excellence with the life of religion, and as equally capable of leading to unity with the supreme spirit There are six different systems of philosophy, all more or less pantheistic, identifying the deity and the universe, the universal supreme spirit and the individual soul; and all with the same end, to escape further existence in the world of sin and evil through absorption into the deity. But the systems differ in the means prescribed, in some simply knowledge, in others meditation, accompanied and purified by asceticism For the most part the gods of the Hindoo pantheon are ignored, especially in the Sankhya system of Kapila, supposed by some to be the source of Buddhism

It remains to sketch briefly the system of caste, through which Brahminism has obtained such power The original division was simply into four—the Brahmins or priests, the Kshatryas or warriors (including kings), the Vaisyas or merchants, tradesman, &c , and the Sudras The three former are called twice-born, and were regarded as being on a very different level from the fourth There is no trace of such a division in the Rig-Veda, but indications are found of a class below the people for whom the Veda was given. These afterwards became the Sudras, and were probably the earlier population whom the Aryan race conquered. In the Brahmanas the beginnings of the system are seen, while in the Institutes of Manu it exists in full force The means by which the distinction was established seem to have been nearly as follows The Kshatryas, who originally offered the sacrifices and performed the religious ceremonies for themselves, devolved these duties upon the Brahmins, who, by making them more difficult by additions and the like, gradually monopolized them, and began to attempt a general control of life and habits Then came a struggle for supremacy between the Brahmins and Kshatryas, in which the latter were vanquished, and, according to legend, ultimately destroyed The Rajpoots, however, and some others, contend that the Kshatryas still exist with them From the struggle arose the distinction between the Brahmins, the Kshatryas, and the great bulk of the people —the trading, working, and mercantile class The Institutes of Manu contain an attempt to map out the adult life of every man of the three twice-born castes to his burial, into four distinct phases, so as to bring every part of life under the intimate control of religion—that is to say, of the Brahmin caste, the authorized expounders and teachers of it. The first period is that of the student of the sacred books. During this time, which was begun at various ages—earlier for the Brahmins than for the other castes—the student, under the guidance of some distinguished Brahmin, to whom he was bound to pay almost servile devotion, learned all the religious observances, and the means of subduing and quenching all desires for material things The second period was that of the married man and householder, performing his various duties to the gods, the state and his fellows. The third period was that of the hermit, during which the twice-born man learned to mortify his passions and desires altogether, and by means of ascetic practices to obtain the power of abstracting his thoughts from all material things, and fixing them only on the deity The fourth period, that of the devotee, followed when this latter power was obtained, by the entire subjugation and eradication of the passions, and was spent simply in contemplation This system is still followed among the Brahmins, who declare that both the other castes of the twice-born have died out, themselves alone remaining Below the Brahmins now exist a great number of subdivisions, embracing different trades and occupations These have apparently arisen from trade guilds, which, established to preserve the respectability and privileges of their respective trades, have gradually been transmuted into hereditary societies The attribution of a sacred character to the castes is a mere imposition of the Brahmins to support their power, and the exclusiveness of the system—through contact with the English—seems to be dying out

The weakness of Brahminism consists [1] In the horrible theory of transmigration, which leads men to embrace other religions to be free from it, [2] in the exclusiveness of the caste system, and the isolation it produces among individuals who are thus led to apostatize, [3] in the contending claims of religion and philosophy, of faith, works, and knowledge, from which arises a low standard of morality, and of religious obligations [Hardwick, *Christ and other Masters*, pt. 2 , Baring-Gould, *Origin and Development of Religious Belief*, vol 1 , Maurice, *Lectures on the Religions of the World*, Ballantyne, *Christianity contrasted with Hindoo Philosophy*, Rowland Williams, *Christianity and Hindooism*, Muir, *Original Sanscrit Texts*, Bunsen, *God in History*. The *Works* of Colebrooke and Professor H H Wilson]

BRAHMOO SOMAJ, or BRAHMO SAMAJ A Hindoo sect of Monotheists originated in recent times by the contact of Brahminism with anti-sacerdotal forms of Christianity The name is derived from the Sanscrit words *Brahmá*, the Creator, or Supreme Cause of the Universe, and *Samája*, an assembly; and thus signifies "the Church of the One God"

The religion of India appears at the present day to be in a state of transition, and those who know the country expect the occurrence of some important change Three such changes have been considered possible [1] either the restoration of a decaying Brahminism, with its 330,000,000 gods, and superstitions of such an extravagant character as those of the Yogi devotees, and the orgies of such sects as the Maharajahs, or [2] the conversion of the whole population to Christianity, or [3] the rise of an indigenous and more enlightened faith on the ruins of the dead Hindooism Such a faith is believed by its supporters to be provided by the Brahmoo Somaj, which is therefore sometimes called "the Reformed National Church of India"

Its founder was Ramohun Roy (Rama Mohuna Raya), who was born of Brahmin parents in the district of Bordouan [c A.D 1774] His object was not to found a new religion, but to revive the pure monotheism of the primitive Hindoo faith, as prescribed in the Vedas, and as opposed to the idolatrous teaching of the later Hindoo books, an object which eventually caused a schism in the Brahmoo Somaj, and was abandoned by the more advanced school, who discovered that the Vedas, on which they professed to base their faith, taught, amid much that was true, such doctrines as nature-worship, transmigration of souls, with many grotesque rites and ceremonies Ramohun Roy received a good education, acquiring while still young a knowledge of Arabic, Persian, and Sanscrit, to which he afterwards added Hebrew, Greek, and English He showed early signs of dislike for the gross forms of religion by which he was surrounded, and during a visit to Thibet in his fifteenth year excited the animosity of its inhabitants by ridiculing the worship of the Llama The early death of his father [A D 1804] and of his two brothers left him in the possession of a large property, and free to express those sentiments which regard for paternal authority prevented his previously publishing to the world His first book was written in Persian with an Arabic preface, and was entitled *Against the Idolatry of all Religions* The public hostility which it provoked, and the numerous enemies arising in his own caste and kinsfolk, led him to move to Calcutta [A D 1814], where, four years later, he first gathered a few intelligent Hindoos around him in regular monotheistic worship [A D 1818], from which time may be dated the commencement of the Brahmoo Somaj as an organized community His next important works were *An Essay on the Vedas, with a collection of extracts of pure, simple, and moral passages, and an abridged translation of the Vedant,*[1] and *The Precepts of Jesus, a Guide to peace and happiness,* in Sanscrit and Bengalee [A D 1820] The latter work showed a careful acquaintance with Christianity, and involved him for many years in controversy with members of various Christian bodies, as well as with his Hindoo antagonists. In A D 1831 he came to England, with the title of Rajah, to negotiate an increase of the East India Company's allowance to the King of Delhi. After landing at Liverpool he proceeded to London, where he was courteously received, being assigned a place among the ambassadors at the coronation of William IV, and finding a welcome among several dissenting bodies, more especially the Unitarians About this time he successfully opposed an appeal made by the Hindoos to the King in Council against an enactment of the East India Council abolishing the suttee In September [A D 1833] he went to Stapleton Lodge near Bristol, at which house he died rather suddenly of fever

The small community which Ramohun Roy had established at Calcutta continued to exist for about a quarter of a century after his death, without much life or propagandist energy, supported by his bequests, and those of Dwarkanauth Tagore, which enabled them to retain a place of worship called the Brahmoo Somaj of Jorsauko, and to chronicle their proceedings in a monthly magazine entitled the Tattwabodhini Putrika. The next aggressive step was the opening of a Sunday school at Calcutta [A D 1859] under Debendro Nath Tagore, at that time president of the Brahmoo Somaj, for the purpose of giving young men a regular course of instruction in Brahmic theology and ethics In the next year [A D 1860] they made a convert of Keshub (Kesava) Chunder Sen, grandson of Ram Kamal Sen, a man of distinction of the Vaida or physician caste He was at this time twenty-three years of age, and being left an orphan had been educated in an English school, and had graduated in the college at Calcutta Enthusiastic in the cause of the reform of religion he issued (with the assistance of Hurro Lall Roy, a talented Brahmin) various tracts, and, at the cost of an open breach with the older members of the sect [c A D 1864], rejected the doctrine of the infallibility of the Vedas, which had been taught by its founder, and which seemed the connecting link between his teaching and that of the old Hindoo religion

Chunder Sen visited England [A D 1870], and was welcomed at a soiree in Hanover Square Rooms on April 12th, by a miscellaneous collection of ministers and laity of ten various denominations, several persons of distinction being also present, including Lord Lawrence, the Dean of Westminster, Louis Blanc, &c During the five months which he spent in this country he preached in different dissenting chapels, chiefly Unitarian, Congregational, or Baptist, and spoke at public meetings in London, and in most of the large provincial towns, including Bath, Birmingham, Bristol, Edinburgh, Glasgow, Leeds, Leicester, Liverpool, Manchester, and Nottingham The Queen granted him a personal interview at Osborne, August 13th He preached a farewell sermon in the Unitarian chapel at Islington, September 4th, was again entertained at a soiree at the Hanover Square Rooms, September 12th, by invitation of the Committee of the British and Foreign Unitarian Association, and sailed for India from Southampton, September 17th, 1870

General character of the Brahmoo Somaj The religion of this new sect, which its founders hope will develope into the national Church of India, may be described as a pure or "pectoral" theism,

[1] The Vedant is a digest of the still older Vedas drawn up by Vyas two thousand years ago For a complete list of the works of Ramohun Roy which have been published in England, see Miss Carpenter's *Last Days in England of Ramohun Roy*, Appendix A, p 247.

entirely evolved out of man's own consciousness, and not based on any external support of revelation or tradition Hence the importance attached to the study of mental philosophy and psychology, which have not only a subjective utility, as the best means of affording intellectual and moral exercise to the mind, but also an objective value as the means of attaining the truths of theology and ethics [*Lectures and Tracts*, p 197] *Faith* is defined as a direct vision, it is no dogma of books nor tradition of venerable antiquity, it relies upon no evidence, and will have no mediation, it neither borrows an idea of God from metaphysics, nor a narrative of God from history, it bows its neck to no logical or historical deity [p 256] Prayer is not a matter which can be argued out by any appeal to books or to deductions of logic [p 236] Of the three component elements of worship—adoration, gratitude, and prayer—the latter is by far the most important, provided that its nature is rightly understood, and that instead of being debased into petitions for rain, and for pleasant breezes, and for outward prosperity, it is confined to its proper objects, spiritual knowledge, spiritual power, and spiritual holiness [p 241, *English Visit*, p 75] "Prayer makes the weak powerful, the timid heroic, the corrupt righteous, and the ignorant wise Prayer lifts the soul above all that is earthly, shadowy, and mean, and ushers it into the very presence of the All-Holy" [*Fraser's Mag* August 1866] Thus purified and spiritualized the Brahmoo Somaj is to form a golden mean between mysticism and scepticism, between the superstition of Brahmins and the materialism of Buddhists, it is to be an eclectic religion, rejecting the dross while extracting what is good out of the profound devotion of Hindooism, and the heroic enthusiasm of Mahometanism and the moral precepts of Christianity It will uphold the absolute infinity and unity of the Divine Creator, and will suffer no created thing to usurp His sovereignty It will worship Him alone, and thoroughly set its face against every form of creature-worship But while admitting the unity of the divinity, the future Church will recognize a trinity of divine manifestations God manifests Himself to us through external nature, through the inner spirit, and through moral greatness impersonated in man Here, therefore, the idolater, the pantheist, and the prophet worshipper will find what they severally want Their delusions, errors, and aims will certainly be destroyed, but the genuine aspirations of their nature, all their normal cravings for spiritual aids, will be duly satisfied, and, instead of a hundred hostile churches, there will be upreared in the fulness of time one vast cathedral, where all mankind will worship with one heart the Supreme Creator [*Lectures*, pp 145, 147] This homage will be extremely simple, for there will be no teacher, no priest, no rites or ceremonies, and no books, if we except a very small manual of occasional prayers drawn up by Chunder Sen In short, this new religion will resemble the theistic society recently established by Mr. Voysey in London, or the "Société de la Conscience Libre, et du Theisme Progressif" in France

Its attitude towards Christianity. This is not so much one of hostility as of patronizing condescension "Every Christian sect," says Chunder Sen, "has tried to realize the kingdom of God, but has failed, and has succeeded, after all, in representing one side only of Christianity . . I should be a traitor to the universal Church of Theism to which I belong, if my heart and soul were not capacious enough to take in the whole length and breadth of the Christian Church Come unto me, brothers and sisters of England and France, Germany and Switzerland, and Italy and all Europe, come unto me, brothers and sisters of America," &c [*Eng Visit*, pp 253, 254]. In the earlier days of the Brahmoo Somaj, many persons imagined that its members would not accept the name of Christians, or undergo the rite of baptism, simply because of the social persecution which such a step would involve at the hands of their relations and the members of their caste This charge may have had some foundation in those days, but the present leader of the sect makes the unambiguous declaration, "I never put myself forward as a Christian, and I never will" [p. 322] Though the Brahmoo Somaj is thus not to be described by the epithet "Christian," it is decidedly Unitarian in form and tendency "I tell you candidly," said Chunder Sen, addressing a Unitarian audience, "that I have felt quite at home in all Unitarian assemblies private and public" [p 309] Many years before, A D 1824, Ramohun Roy, writing to Dr Ware, had made a similar assertion "To the enlightened members of Hindostan the ideas of a Triune God, of a Man-God, of the appearance of God in the bodily shape of a dove, or of the blood of God shed for the payment of a debt, seem entirely heathenish and absurd, and consequently their sincere conversion to Trinitarian Christianity must be morally impossible But they would not scruple to embrace, or at least to encourage, the Unitarian system of Christianity, were it inculcated on them in an intelligible manner" [*Correspondence with Rev H Ware*, London, C Fox, 1825, p 135] There are plentiful acknowledgments in various places of Jesus Christ, as (if not the greatest and truest, yet) a great and true benefactor of mankind, and worthy of being classed with Vyasa in the honour and esteem demanded at the hands of humanity There seems to be much fascination for the Indian mind in the idea of His Asiatic descent, and His birth on the boundary line between Europe and Asia but when He is honoured above others, as the Incarnation of Deity, we are to understand the superiority accorded to be one of degree only The Christian Scriptures, like the Hindoo Vedas, contain a superstitious element along with much that is admirable "Had not experience too clearly proved that some of the metaphorical expressions, when taken singly, and without attention to their contexts, may be made the foundation of doctrines quite at variance with (what I conceive to be) the tenor of the rest of the Scriptures, I should have had no hesitation in submitting indiscriminately the whole of the doctrines of the New Testament to my countrymen, as I should have felt no apprehension that even the most ignorant of them, if left to the guidance of their own unprejudiced views of the matter, could misconceive the clear and distinct assertions they everywhere contain of the unity of God and subordinate nature of His messenger Jesus Christ" [*Ramohun Roy's second appeal to the Christian public in defence of the Precepts of Jesus*, p 167]

Special reforms aimed at by the Brahmoo Somaj However far this new Indian sect is thus seen to differ on fundamental points of doctrine from the teaching of the Catholic Church, it is nevertheless engaged in a crusade against abuses, and in a promotion of practical reforms, which win the sympathy of every civilized man. But they do not involve, as they appear to do on first sight, any approximation to Christianity, so much as a return to the purer system and teaching of the older Hindoo religion and sacred writings

First, it aims at the abolition of idolatry and restoration of a pure monotheism "Not only," says Chunder Sen, in one of his appeals to young India, "must you not worship idols yourselves, but you must discountenance it in others, and hunt it out of the country; for the sake of your souls, and of the souls of millions of your countrymen, you must acknowledge only one Supreme and true God, our Maker, Preserver, and Moral Governor" This is in accordance with the teaching of the older Hindoo writings, as will be evident from the following passage in the Vedas "They called him Indra, Mitra, Varuna, and Agni That which is one the wise call by divers names," and from the later books of the Upanishads, "Let us endeavour to know the Ruler of the universe, who is God of gods, Deity of deities, Lord of lords, above all, who manifests Himself and is worthy of all reverence" [*English Visit*, p 492]

Secondly, it seeks the abolition of caste, as the bulwark of Hindoo idolatry, the safeguard of the Brahminical priesthood, and, on wider grounds, as an audacious and sacrilegious violation of God's law of human brotherhood, and of the doctrine of the equality of all souls in His sight For the future, a Kshatriya is not to look down on a Vaisya, and even a high class Brahmin, if so inclined, is to accept as wife a low class Sudra Caste, which was originally a system of social distinctions, or a division of society into trades and professions, became in later times fortified by religious sanctions, which were unknown to the earlier Hindoo writings [*English Visit*, p 494].

Thirdly, it desires the reform of the zenana, or amelioration of the condition of the women of India, by the promotion of female education, the establishment of girls' schools, and the alteration of the rule by which woman is treated as a menial in the household, a cipher in society, and a victim to a life-long seclusion, by the alteration of the custom of early marriage, which has been proved to be physically, intellectually, and morally pernicious, by the abolition of the law of compulsory widowhood, a burden more intolerable on account of the practice of polygamy. A man not unfrequently dies, leaving fifty women doomed to perpetual widowhood, and ready in their social solitude to become victims to all the mortifications which the Brahminical priesthood has invented for persons in their condition

Its present strength as to numbers and position As there is no initiatory rite or formal admission into the Brahmoo Somaj it is not easy to obtain precise information on this head The following report of its position was furnished to its representative council some years ago

There are fifty-four Brahmoo Somajes in India, of which fifty are in Bengal, two in the North-western provinces, one in the Punjaub, and one in Madras, the latter bearing the name of the Veda Somajum. Five of the Somajes are in Calcutta, the oldest of them being in its thirty-sixth year. Twenty-five new ones have been added in the last ten years Eight of these churches have established religious schools for instruction in the tenets of Brahminism For secular education, there is the Calcutta College, established and instituted by the leading members of the Calcutta Somaj There are also boys' and girls' schools in connection with ten provincial Somajes All these are under the direct management of the members of the local Somajes, and are mostly assisted by Government grants. There are seven periodicals regularly maintained by the body; the monthly "Tattwabodhini Putrika" at Calcutta, and two others of the same name published in Urdoo and Telegu, at Bareilly and Madras, four other magazines in native tongues, two newspapers in English, the *Mirror* and the *National Paper*, and two more native newspapers in Dacca [*Indian Mirror*, Jan 1, 1866]

In the course of lectures delivered in Scotland [A D 1870], Chunder Sen estimated its number of adherents at about six thousand, almost exclusively men, and the number of places of worship at about sixty

Its future prospects The more sanguine adherents of the Brahmoo Somaj, buoyed up by its past development, and seeing the scant success which has attended the attempts to introduce Christianity among the natives of India, predict for it the position of the Hindoo Church of the future, looking forward to the time when a grand national organization shall have been effected among the one hundred and eighty millions of the population, and when, all distinctions of religion and caste being destroyed, "the Church of the one supreme Lord" will be established throughout the length and breadth of the country [*English Visit*, p 123].

[*Lectures and Tracts by Keshub Chunder Sen*, edited by S D. Collet, London, 1870. *Keshub Chunder Sen's English Visit, ibid* *Fraser's Magazine*, Aug. 1866 *Hours of Work and Play*, F P Cobbe, 1867 *Last Days in England of Ramohun Roy*, by M Carpenter, London and Calcutta, 1866 Gregoire, *Histoire des Sectes Religieuses*, tom iv cap. 26]

BRETHREN. [TUNKERS]

BRETHREN, CHRISTIAN [CHRISTIAN BRETHREN]

BRETHREN OF THE COMMON LIFE [FRIENDS OF GOD]

BRETHREN OF THE FREE SPIRIT A later name for the sect of the ORTLIBENSES and AMALRICIANS The name was assumed from the words of St Paul, "For the law of the Spirit of life in Christ Jesus hath made me free from the law of sin and death . For as many as are led by the Spirit of God they are the sons of God" [Rom viii 2, 14] The liberty thus claimed was, *first*, freedom from outward ordinances, and, *secondly*, freedom from the guilt of sin They were simply Antinomians of the most extreme form.

The teachers of the sect wandered about from place to place in imitation of the Apostles, and that sacred name was given to them by their followers They brought over to their opinions many of the Waldenses and most of the Beghards, and their fanatical lawlessness led to the revival of the Inquisition in Germany in the fourteenth century After the end of the thirteenth century they seem to have been identified with the BEGHARDS, and in later times were represented by the FAMILISTS

BRETHREN, PLYMOUTH. [PLYMOUTH BRETHREN]

BROAD CHURCHMEN A modern school of Latitudinarians, composed of those clergy and laity of the Church of England who dissent from the principles developed during the revival of exact theological learning The designation "Broad" has been assumed as expressive of the comprehensiveness which the theology of this school offers to men of various opinions, but it is scarcely a fitting designation, as well defined opinions of a positive kind are not included The most distinctive characteristic of the Broad Church School is, in reality, its rejection of traditional beliefs, and the substitution in their place of what has been aptly called a "Negative Theology," in which much is doubted and rejected, and very little believed

This school of thought is generally traced back to Dr Arnold, Master of Rugby School from 1828 until his death in 1842 But he was only one of a band of intellectual men who floated on the stream of reaction from the High Church movement, and he did no more to originate the reaction than was done by Hare, Whately, or Maurice Its real origin is to be traced to the instinctive opposition raised in the minds of forcible thinkers whose occupations had led them in other directions than that of theological study, to the positive conclusions at which other forcible thinkers were arriving, who made theological study the special object of their lives. Whately and Arnold were obviously representative men of the one class, Newman and Pusey of the other

The sporadic elements of this school were aggregated into a party by the "Hampden Controversy." When Hampden was appointed Regius Professor of Divinity at Oxford, on the nomination of Lord Melbourne in 1836, the searching critical power of Newman, then Fellow of Oriel, was brought to bear upon the Bampton Lectures on the scholastic theology which the new Professor had delivered four years previously Newman's pamphlet, "Elucidations of the Bampton Lectures," stimulated a growing discontent with the appointment, and the Convocation of the University passed a vote of censure upon their author, a vote in which Dr Hampden was, perhaps, condemned by some as a nominee of the Whig party In 1848 he was appointed to the Bishopric of Hereford The controversy was revived with great bitterness, and an unsuccessful attempt was made to prevent his consecration. From that time Dr Hampden was never again heard of in the theological world, and it is difficult to understand how it was that his lectures—which have long been relegated to the usual Bampton Lecture shelf at the top of the library, and contained nothing remarkably unorthodox —should ever have raised so great a storm of controversy as they did

A work much more expressive of Broad Church principles was published in the year 1853, namely, a volume of *Theological Essays*, by Mr Maurice, Professor of Theology in King's College, London, a man of much higher intellectual mark than Dr Hampden In these the doctrines of the Holy Trinity, the Incarnation, the Atonement, Inspiration, and Eternal Punishment, among others, were dealt with in language remarkable for its beauty, and for its inconsistency with the opinions of orthodox Churchmen They were at once accepted by Broad Churchmen as a statement of their opinions, and have continued ever since to influence them The Council of King's College, on October 28th, 1853, declared the opinions expressed, the doubts indicated in the Essays, with the subsequent correspondence respecting future punishments and the final issue of the day of judgment, to be of dangerous tendency, and likely to unsettle the minds of the theological students, and further decided that Mr Maurice's continuance as Professor would be seriously detrimental to the interests of the College. Notwithstanding this dismissal, Mr Maurice afterwards held office as a Professor at Cambridge, and subsequently became a London incumbent, and no writer did more to mould the opinions of the Broad Church School

The greatest literary success of the school was however a composite work of third-rate merit, —but now historical,—entitled *Essays and Reviews*, which was published in February 1860. It was an octavo volume of 434 pages, containing seven articles on theological questions of the day by as many writers (who were said to have written quite independently of each other), and edited by Professor Jowett The book was not at all remarkable for originality, but was strikingly so for the boldness with which it revived old sceptical theories, and the skill with which they were clothed in decent language, such as would alone secure their reception in the present day Although far below Maurice's Essays in talent, the *Essays and Reviews* volume

Broad Churchmen

obtained an enormous circulation, and affected the opinions of so many superficial thinkers that it will be proper to state shortly what is the nature of its contents

The first Essay is by Dr Temple, at that time Master of Rugby School, but subsequently Bishop of Exeter It is entitled "The Education of the World," and is substantially a plagiarism of Lessing's Essay on the same subject The object of it may be stated to be to prove that the world has gone through several stages of religious education, and has now reached a higher development of religious knowledge than it has reached before A parallel is drawn between the history of the individual man and that of the world, there being in each the three stages of childhood, youth and manhood The Old Testament ages were the time of the world's childhood, when it was subject to positive laws and restrictions upon its freedom The New Testament age was the world's youth, when external discipline was supplanted by example in the Person of Christ This has been followed by the world's manhood, in which conscience is supreme, and the only limitation of freedom is that which it imposes.

The second Essay is by Dr Rowland Williams, Vice-Principal of Lampeter, a Welsh College in which young men are educated for Holy Orders He tries to prove that the ordinary ways of understanding the Bible are a mistake, and that now we have arrived at such a highly educated stage of the world's history, we ought not to be content with the interpretations to which our forefathers bowed down. The prophets did not *predict* events, but wrote down past or current history It was not an angel or supernatural being that slew the first-born, but the "Bedouin host" The fifty-third chapter of Isaiah describes the sufferings of Jeremiah, not those of the Messiah, &c &c

The third Essay had for its author Mr Baden Powell, Savilian Professor of Geometry at Oxford, and is written to prove the unreasonableness of believing that God ever worked miracles, or that He created the world The world made itself somehow or other in the course of millions of years, and miracles are "nature" improperly described by ignorant people Such being the case, what greater mistake could there be than to suppose that creation is an evidence that there is a Divine Being, or that miracles are evidence of the Divine Being having commissioned those who work them, as, *e g*, Moses before Pharaoh, or St Peter and St John at Jerusalem?

The fourth Essay is by the Rev H B. Wilson, Vicar of Great Staughton, and is an evidence of the way in which people sometimes argue against an opponent so vehemently that they end by converting themselves to that opponent's side. The author of this Essay was one of the leaders in a very intemperate attack on the writers in the Tracts for the Times for a supposed claim made by them to interpret the Thirty-nine Articles in a "non-natural sense" Mr Wilson afterwards came to think that this inestimable privilege is the birthright of every enlightened Churchman, and that it is the height of intellectual subtlety to make anything out of anything, according to opinions and circumstances, at least in the interpretation of the Holy Bible or the Prayer Book His own examples of this kind of interpretation are among the most dreadful things in the book He considers many of the "traits in the Scriptural Person of Jesus" to belong to an ideal rather than an historical person, *e g*, the Temptation did not really happen, but is an imaginary scene put into the Gospels to complete the picture The Annunciation "may be of ideal origin" also, the writer says, and much more to the same purpose

The fifth Essay was written by Mr C Goodwin, a layman This author deals with what is called Scripture cosmogony, and the manner in which he does so is sufficiently explained by saying that he considers the Book of Genesis to have been written by some Hebrew man of science, who invented a theoretical account of creation, but living in a time when he had no geological discoveries to guide him, simply wrote down what proves to be full of mistakes

The sixth is by the Rev Mark Pattison, at the time of writing Fellow, and afterwards Rector, of Lincoln College, Oxford It is on "the Tendencies of Religious Thought in England from 1688 to 1750" Although a very dry and uninteresting history of the subject, it is not nearly so much opposed to Christian interests and Christian principles as the others, and while many would have differed from the author's views, few would have attached much significance to his Essay if it had not appeared in such objectionable company.

The last Essay is on the "Interpretation of Scripture," by Mr Jowett, then Regius Professor of Greek at Oxford, and subsequently Master of Balliol College It is a sort of adaptation of the Bible to the theories contained in the previous Essays; and its chief object appears to be to lower the authority of Holy Scripture by showing that very little of it was inspired in any ordinary sense of inspiration

The agitation raised by the publication of *Essays and Reviews* was greater than any that had taken place during the progress of the theological revival High Churchmen and Low Churchmen combined in censuring the work the bishops were all opposed to its teaching 9,000 of the clergy signed a protest against it and the Convocations of Canterbury and York passed a synodical condemnation upon "the pernicious doctrines and heretical tendencies of the book" in July 1864 This synodical judgment was suspended for some time on account of ecclesiastical suits which were being prosecuted against Dr Williams by Bishop Hamilton of Salisbury, and against Mr Wilson by Mr Fendall These two writers were both condemned by the Court of Arches, each being suspended from his benefice for a year by the sentence of Dr Lushington on December 15th, 1862 This judgment was reversed on appeal to the Queen in Council, on February 8th, 1864, the Judicial Committee fencing their judgment by adding to it this paragraph "We desire to repeat that the meagre and disjointed extracts which have been allowed to remain in the reformed Articles" of the suit "are alone the subject of our judgment. On the design and general tendency of the book called *Essays and Reviews*, and on the effect or aim of the whole Essay of Dr. Williams, or the whole Essay of Mr Wilson, we neither can nor do pronounce any opinion. On the short extracts before us, our judgment is that the charges are not proved" [Brodrick and Fremantle, *Eccl. Cases*, p 289] This significant intimation that the book was placed before the court in a way which made its thorough judicial criticism impossible did not, however, damp the satisfaction of the Broad Church party, the judgment being considered as a triumphant vindication of the theological laxness which its members advocate and practise

It was probably under the encouragement of this supposed victory that Dr Colenso, Bishop of Natal in South-eastern Africa, published his speculations on the Pentateuch, by means of which he endeavoured to make the high-road of Biblical interpretation so very broad that the most arrogant sceptic would find no difficulty in walking along it The purpose of this work was to minimize to the utmost the authority of the Pentateuch, and with it of all Holy Scripture, the first principle of the author being indicated by the words, "There is not the slightest reason to suppose that the first writer of the story in the Pentateuch ever professed to be recording *infallible truth*, or even *actual historical truth* He wrote certainly a narrative But what indications are there that he published it at large, even to the people of his own time, as a record of *matter of fact*, *veracious history?*" On the appearance of this volume—which looked very learned to unlearned people—Colenso was at once elevated to the post of choragus by the bulk of the Broad Churchmen On the other hand, all the bishops of England, except Thirlwall, Bishop of St David's, and all those of Ireland, except the less distinguished Fitzgerald of Killaloe, and Griffin of Limerick, wrote an united letter to the Bishop of Natal requesting him to resign his see On his positive refusal, he was tried before a provincial synod at Cape Town, on charges of denying the Atonement, of believing in the justification of those who have no knowledge of the Saviour, of denying the inspiration of Holy Scripture, the Divinity of our Lord, and everlasting punishments, and of depraving and impugning the Book of Common Prayer. Having been found guilty of these charges, he was formally deposed from the see of Natal on November 27th, 1863 This deposition was subsequently declared null and void by the Queen in Council on the ground that the Metropolitan of Cape Town had not authority over the Bishop of Natal But on January 7th, 1866, a solemn sentence of excommunication was published against him by the Bishop of Cape Town in the Cathedral of Pieter-Maritzburg, and subsequently a new Bishop was consecrated to take charge of the Colony. From that time Bishop Colenso was little heard of as a leader of the Broad Church party, but his works are said to be extensively used by the Buddhists as a controversial authority against Christianity.

The opinions of a better informed posterity respecting the theological productions of the Broad Church school will probably be in accordance with that expressed by the learned Hengstenberg "The authors of the Essays," he wrote, "have been trained in a German school It is only the echo of German infidelity which we hear from the midst of the English Church They appear to us as parrots, with only this distinction, common among parrots, that they imitate more or less perfectly The treatise of Temple is in its scientific value about equal to an essay written by the pupils of the middle classes of our colleges . The Essay of Goodwin on the Mosaic cosmogony displays the naive assurance of one who receives the modern critical science from the second or tenth hand The editor" (Hengstenberg) "asked the now deceased Andreas Wagner, a distinguished professor of natural sciences at the University of Munich, to subject this treatise to an examination from the standpoint of natural science. The offer was accepted, and the book given to him But after some time it was returned with the remark, that he must take back his promise, as the book was beneath all criticism. All these Essays tend toward atheism Their subordinate value is seen in the inability of their authors to recognise their goal clearly, and in their want of courage to declare this knowledge Only Baden Powell forms in this respect an exception. He uses several expressions, in which the grinning spectre makes his appearance almost undisguisedly He speaks not only sneeringly of the idea of a positive external revelation, which has hitherto formed the basis of all systems of the Christian faith; he even raises himself against the 'Architect of the world,' whom the old English freethinkers and freemasons had not dared to attack" [*Evangelische Kirchenzeitung, Vorwort*, 1862]

The theological tendency of the Broad Church school in general is to drift through the channel of Unitarianism into Theism Its Christology is restricted almost entirely to the human aspect of Christ's earthly life and ministrations; and so little of its Divine aspect, of Christ's Pre-existence, or of His present work, is recognised, that belief in His Deity has no real place in the personal creed of many Broad Churchmen, and all they have to say about our Lord is "Ecce Homo" The practical religion of the school is based on philosophical views of morals, in which self-control, rather than grace, is considered as the power by which holy living is to be accomplished, "manliness" rather than "godliness" being set up as the true ideal of Christian life

But successive controversies have developed out of the original Broad Church party an extreme school, whose theology is of a much more positive character This school is of a distinctly rationalist type, carrying Broad Church views about inspiration to the length of practical disbelief in Scripture, Broad Church views about our Lord to the length of Unitarianism, Broad Church views about everlasting punishment to Universalism, and Broad Church views about the priesthood and the Sacraments to an utter denial of their reality Such is the natural terminus of the original school, and such must be the logical outcome of its opinions when they are taken up by men who are not satisfied to rest in negations and generalities

BROWNISTS [INDEPENDENTS]

BRUGGLENIANS A small sect of fanatics so called from the Swiss canton of Brugglen In a village within that canton two brothers named Christian and Jerome Rohler blasphemously pretended [A D 1746] to be the two witnesses of the Book of Revelation, and the former of the two promised his followers that on a certain day he would ascend to Heaven and carry them with him The Rohlers were both of them executed in the year 1753, and the fanaticism soon afterwards died out among their followers

BRYANITES [METHODISTS, BRYANITE]

BUCHANITES An insignificant sect which existed in Scotland for a few years at the close of the last century, and which bore, in its later development, some correspondence to the subsequent sect of Southcotians in England. Its foundress was Mrs Buchan, the wife of a workman in a delf manufactory at Glasgow, and previously a domestic servant She was originally an Episcopalian, but on her marriage about 1760 joined the sect to which her husband belonged, that of the Burgher Secession About 1780 she began, probably under the influence of some religious excitement which deranged her mind, to teach that the millennium was close at hand, that no one of those who became her followers would die, but would be caught up to meet the Lord, and that while all the wicked would be at once struck dead for a thousand years, the believers in this immediate coming would, with their Lord, possess the earth for that period She soon numbered among her followers a Relief Minister named Hugh Whyte of Irvine, a writer to the signet, a merchant, and various other persons These forthwith, regarding the world as close to its end, forsook their worldly occupations, renounced marriage and attention to the duties of married life, and lived together in a society numbering forty-six members, with a common stock and purse, and occupied in the sole work of watching for the Great Appearing Being assaulted by a mob at Irvine in April 1784, they moved to a farmhouse near Thornhill in Dumfriesshire Here, in December of the same year, they were again attacked by a mob, for which thirteen of the assailants were fined in the Sheriff-court at Dumfries In 1786 a number of Mrs Buchan's followers returned to their homes at Irvine, relating the tricks and impositions which she had practised, and which were supposed to have for their aim the exhausting the patience and fidelity of her disciples so as to secure for herself the undivided possession of the goods which they contributed to the common stock One of her latest pretended revelations was, that in order to be fit to ascend to Christ a previous fast of forty days and nights was requisite This was immediately attempted by some, who would soon have died had they not been surreptitiously supported with spirits and water She died in June 1791, and on her deathbed communicated to the few who remained with her (among whom was still Mr Whyte) that she was none other than the Blessed Virgin, and the Woman spoken of in the Revelation as clothed with the sun, that she had been on the earth ever since the days of our Lord, that she should not now die, but only sleep for a while, and then awake and lead them to the New Jerusalem Her infatuated followers in consequence would not bury her, but when compelled by the process of decay to place her body in a coffin, fixed it in a corner of a barn, until the neighbours procured an order from a justice of the peace for her interment It is said that Mr Whyte then went to America [*Scots Magazine*, 1784, pp 589, 590, 1785, p 148, 1786, pp 461, 462 *Ann Reg* 1791, Chron pp 26, 27 Train's *Buchanites from first to last*, Edinb 1846]

BUDDHISTS The believers in a faith originated in India about 2500 years ago by Siddhartha, better known as Sakya-mouni, or by the title of Buddha (the enlightened) which he afterwards assumed, and from which his religion is named Buddhism, though it has now disappeared from India, is professed by 455,000,000, being 31 2 per cent of the human race, in Cashmere, Nepaul, Thibet, Tartary, Mongolia, China, Japan, Siam, Burmah, and Ceylon [Max-Muller, *Chips from a German Workshop*, i 214, J B Saint-Hilaire, *Le Bouddha et sa Religion*, introd ii]

Buddhism was on one side the result of a protest against the religious and social despotism of Brahminism, which had wound itself round every act and moment of life On another side it was an attempt to escape from the terrible theories involved in the doctrine of metempsychosis Though many of the metaphysical doctrines of Buddhism may be found among the philosophers of Brahminism, yet, in practical bearing and social relations, the two religions are entirely at variance with each other

The founder of Buddhism was born at Kapilavastu, the capital of a kingdom of the same name in Central India, at the foot of the mountains of Nepaul, to the north of the present Oude The date of his birth is variously given by M Saint-Hilaire and other writers at B C 622 [*Le Bouddha*, introd ii.], and by Professor Max-Muller about seventy years later [*Chips*, i 205] His father, the king of the country, was of the family of the Sakyas and the clan of the Gautamas, hence the son was called afterwards Sakya-mouni—the solitary of the Sakyas. He is also known as Gautama, from the name of his clan, but his original name seems to have been Siddhartha [Saint-Hilaire, 3], though it is doubtful whether this name, like that of Buddha, was not adopted by him in later life [*Chips*, i.

218] He was, as the son of a king, of the Kshatrya or warrior caste From boyhood he was noted for his talents and beauty, and also for his melancholy temper and love of solitary meditation on the problems of life and death amid the shadows of the forests He married early, in compliance with his father's wishes, who vainly desired thus to drive away his melancholy The sight, on various occasions, of a man overwhelmed by the miseries and infirmities of age, of one dying of fever and overcome by the fear of death, of a funeral attended by the lamenting relatives of the deceased, set him on thinking how to escape from the miseries and the fear of old age, disease and death An encounter with a mendicant or devotee—one who, renouncing all pleasures and desires, lived a life of austerity, without passion or envy, supported only by alms, and seeking only to obtain self-conquest—determined Buddha to retire from the world He left his father's palace by night in secret, and became the pupil, first of one, then of a second, of the most famous of the Brahmin teachers, but from them he learned no means of deliverance for man He then, with five companions, retired for six years into solitude, subjecting himself to the most frightful penances At the end of this time he became convinced that the austerities availed no more than the doctrines of Brahminism in producing peace of mind, and deliverance from the fears with which he was troubled He gave up his exercises and set himself to elaborate his own system After long meditations and ecstatic visions, he imagined that he had at last arrived at the true knowledge which discloses the cause, and so removes the fear, of all the changes inherent in life From this time he adopted the title of Buddha (the enlightened) For a while he hesitated whether he should communicate his knowledge to the world, but compassion for the sufferings of man prevailed He went to Benares, the sacred city of the Brahmins, where he preached and lectured with great success He afterwards travelled over many parts of India, making converts wherever he went. Several of the kings, including his father, and all his relations, embraced his doctrines, but he was vehemently opposed and persecuted by the Brahmins, over whom however he was victorious in every discussion At last, having reached the age of seventy, or, according to some accounts, of eighty years, he died while sitting under a tree in a forest near the city of Kusinagara, B C 543 [Saint-Hilaire], or 477 [Max Muller] His funeral rites were celebrated with great solemnity, amid thousands of his followers After his body was burned, his remains were divided into eight portions, to be preserved as relics in different parts of the country

The story of the life of Buddha was handed down by tradition, and, as we now possess it, was committed to writing about the first century B C. A vast mass of childish legend and fiction had grown up around his history [For some account of these, see Saint-Hilaire, *Le Bouddha*, pt i chap ii pp 48-78, Spence Hardy, *A Manual of Buddhism*, sec 7] Though many of the details are doubtful, the general outline of his life may be accepted He left no writings, but his discourses were collected by his disciples from tradition, and now form a portion of the Buddhist sacred writings

It is necessary to notice a theory concerning Buddha propounded by the late Professor Wilson, in his Essay on Buddha and Buddhism, and adopted in part by Mr Maurice [*Lectures on the Religions of the World*] Professor Wilson, gathering up the different dates assigned to him, the mythical character attaching to several parts of the story, the mass of miraculous legend that had grown up about him, and various geographical difficulties, considers it doubtful whether such a person as Buddha ever existed But many of the difficulties of the history have now been solved, and this theory is not accepted by the most recent students of Buddhism [For a refutation of it, see Max Muller, *Chips*, i 217, 218]

The most striking feature in the history of Buddhism is its spirit of proselytism, in which it has been surpassed by no religion except Christianity. This spirit arose from the feeling of sympathy and brotherhood between all men, from the prince to the outcast, which it taught. The only means adopted for its propagation was persuasion It speedily made way in India, and about the end of the fourth century B C was established in that country by King Asoka or Piyadasi, many of whose edicts are preserved in rock inscriptions In this king's reign missionaries were first sent to some of the countries beyond India, and, at one of the great councils of Buddhism, about B C. 246, a regular plan of missions was developed by teaching, preaching, and publishing translations of the sacred books. Cashmere was the first country converted, the Himalayan countries and Thibet soon followed; while in the south Ceylon became almost wholly Buddhist. From Ceylon it spread to Siam and Burmah The first mention of a Buddhist mission in China is about B C 217, where Buddhism flourished greatly, and in A D 65 was admitted as a state religion by the Emperor Ming ti It was alternately persecuted and favoured, but a great impulse was given to its extension about the fifth century A D Streams of pilgrims came into India from China, and carried back with them sacred pictures, books, and relics, and at the same time it spread largely in other countries, Mongolia, and Central Asia especially In the next century, however, it received a formidable blow from the great uprising of Brahminist feeling in India, by which it was utterly expelled from that country, and never recovered the slightest footing there For this loss it gained compensation by extensive conversions in China and Central and Eastern Asia, and has never had since that time to lament any serious permanent losses, unless indeed it has suffered in any way by the rise of the curious creed of the Chinese rebels.

The tenets of Buddhism are contained in the canonical sacred writings, which were originally composed in Sanscrit, but have been translated into the languages of Thibet, Ceylon, China, Mongolia, Japan, and Burmah These were entirely unknown to Europeans until 1824, when they were discovered in Nepaul, in the original Sanscrit, by Mr B H Hodgson, Political Resident in that state They comprised sixty volumes Shortly after, Alexander Csoma, of Koros in Transylvania, having acquired, in spite of great difficulties, a knowledge of Thibetan, gave himself up to the study of the Buddhist literature in that language, which consists of about 330 folio volumes, mostly translations from the Sanscrit works discovered by Mr Hodgson M Csoma published an analysis of this immense bible in the *Asiatic Researches*, vol xx About the same period the existence of a Mongolian version, made from the Thibetan, of the Buddhist canon was made known by M J L Schmidt of St Petersburg, who published some extracts in 1829 A further great discovery was made in Ceylon by the Hon G Turnour of a version of the Buddhist canon, and also some historical works in Pali, the ancient sacred language of Ceylon China, Japan, Burmah, and Siam also possess Buddhist literatures, the two former derived from the Sanscrit, the two latter, of which little is known, from the Pali

The Buddhist canon was settled at three great councils, held in different parts of India, the last in B C 308 It is called the Tripitaki, or three baskets, being divided into three parts, the Sutras or discourses of Buddha, the Vinaya, containing all that has reference to morality, and the Abhidharma, which treats of metaphysical questions The first two contain each five separate works, the last seven

Buddhism is not a religion as Judaism, Christianity, Mahometanism are religions It contains not a trace of the idea of God from first to last; it acknowledges man as the only being in the universe Neither is it simply a philosophy, in the ordinary sense of the term, a theory of knowing and being But it contains elements of both Obstinately refusing to recognise aught else but man, it confounds man with nature, in the midst of which he lives, while it still preaches earnestly the laws of virtue It is the practical element that has had such a great force with the multitudes To the people at large Buddhism was a moral and religious reform Its metaphysical speculations could have been followed by very few among its votaries, but the sight of a prince throwing away all his splendour, living as a beggar a life of the utmost privation, and withal of the utmost purity and virtue, proclaiming a deliverance from the religious and social despotism of the Brahmins, opening the way of happiness, not to one class or caste but to the veriest outcasts, this it was that caused its rapid spread Hence it is that the social and moral code of Buddhism is far more important than its metaphysical theories, though in the Buddhist system they are closely connected with each other That moral code is, taken by itself, one of the purest in the world It forbids even such vices as pride, uncharitableness, hypocrisy, and enjoins such virtues as forgiveness of injuries, contentment, humility, patience

The basis of the morals of Buddha is the Four Great Verities [1] Pain and sorrow exist, [2] the cause of these is our affections and passions and our sins, [3] pain and sorrow can cease by Nirvana, [4] points out the way to Nirvana, the means of deliverance This way to Nirvana consists of eight parts [1] Right faith, or orthodoxy, [2] right judgment, dispersing all uncertainty and doubt; [3] right language, or the study of perfect and unswerving truthfulness, [4] right purpose, or the choice of an upright purpose in all words and deeds, [5] right practice, or the pursuit of a religious life, [6] right obedience, or the following all the precepts of the Buddhist law, [7] right memory, [8] right meditation

These Four Verities alone comprise the earliest teaching of Buddha, he taught them indeed to the last, but with important additions in his latter years The Four Verities are followed by a body of moral precepts The first are the Five Great Commandments binding upon all, namely, not to kill, not to steal, not to commit adultery, not to lie, not to get drunk Next come five precepts, of less importance, binding on professed disciples, namely, to abstain from unseasonable meals, from public spectacles (music, dancing, singing), from expensive dresses and personal ornaments and perfumes, from having a large or soft bed, and from receiving gold or silver. For those who embrace a religious life, twelve observances of the severest character are prescribed [1] To wear only clothes made of rags cast away by others, [2] to wear only three garments, made by their own hands from these rags, [3] to wear over these rags only a yellow cloak, [4] to live only on the alms they have collected, [5] to eat only one meal daily, [6] to take no food after noon, [7] to live in forests and solitary places, entering towns only to obtain alms, [8] the only shelter is to be the shadow of trees, [9] to rest only sitting at the foot of a tree, [10] to sleep there, without lying down, but resting against the tree, [11] when once settled not to move the sitting-carpet about, [12] to meditate at night among the tombs in the cemeteries on the vanity of all things The title given to those who follow these last precepts is Sramana, "victors over self." On ordinary persons, who could not attain such a height of virtue, were enjoined the Six Ordinary Virtues, alms-giving or charity, purity, patience, courage, contemplation, and knowledge These virtues are inculcated in their very fullest extent An instance of Buddha's charity is given for imitation He saw one day a tigress starved and unable to feed her cubs, whereon he offered his body to be devoured by them Among a number of minor precepts are included the government of the tongue, in its widest sense, humility, modesty, love for and dutifulness to parents and relations. One of the most remarkable of Buddha's institutions is that of public confession, before the whole congregation, of faults and sins.

What then is the end to be obtained by a life of such self-sacrificing charity and humility? That stated in the third and fourth of the Four Verities, namely, Nirvana To ascertain what Nirvana is, we must go on to consider the metaphysical side of Buddhism

The idea of God is utterly banished from Buddhism. Not even is there the notion of a Universal Spirit common to so many Eastern religions. The universe is a mere fleeting illusion without any reality The only being that can lay claim to any real existence is the thinking subject, or man, for and to whom the universe seems to exist Even his own ideas are thus but illusions, the effect of ignorance Existence then is for man but sorrow, misery and trouble But existence is not confined to human life nor closed by death Before this human life man has gone through a multitude of states of existence of all kinds, and he may pass through a countless number hereafter, not merely animate, but also inanimate, and in fact through all forms of every kind The transformations are regulated by the conduct of beings in their different states, virtue is rewarded, vice punished There is no means whatever of escaping the consequences of deeds as long as existence continues, man is ever reappearing, under some form or other, in this scene of misery, sorrow, and illusion The great end of man then is to escape from existence by extirpating its cause This cause of existence is "attachment"—an inclination towards something, which arises from desire Desire must be preceded by perception, perception by contact, and this contact implies the existence of the senses As the senses can only perceive what has form and name, that is, what is distinct, distinction is the real cause of all the effects which end in existence, birth and pain. This distinction is itself the result of conceptions or ideas, these ideas are mere illusions, the effects of ignorance Ignorance therefore is the primary cause of all seeming existence To know that ignorance as the root of all evil is identical with destroying it, and with it all the effects which flow from it. This can be done only by attaining to Nirvana, or extinction, that is in fact utter annihilation. As it is misery to be, not to be must be felicity True wisdom consists in the desire for Nirvana Nirvana is the reward and the end of the life of painful virtue described above The means of entering into that state is by contemplation or ecstasy This contemplation has four stages In the first there is no desire but for Nirvana, there is a sense of freedom from sin, a knowledge of the nature of things But the devotee still has a sense of pleasure in his own condition, the subject can reason, can distinguish, and choose between what conduces to the final state and what draws from it In the second stage the use of these powers ceases, and nothing remains but the desire for Nirvana, and the satisfaction arising from the consciousness of growing perfection In the third stage that satisfaction is extinguished, pure indifference succeeds, but there remains still some self-consciousness, and some amount of physical pleasure. In the fourth stage these last remnants vanish, memory is gone, all pleasure and pain have departed, nothing remains but absolute apathy This is incomplete Nirvana, as near to that state as this life can attain, and a pledge of the future and perfect Nirvana. In attaining this state the votary acquires also omniscience and magic power. But there is a yet higher state to be attained by passing through the four regions of the formless world—the infinity of space, the infinity of intelligence, the region of nothing, and lastly, a region where not even the idea of nothing is left, not even the idea of the absence of ideas, where there is complete rest, undisturbed by nothing, or what is not nothing This alone is perfect Nirvana He who had attained the incomplete Nirvana, the only one possible in this life, was called a Buddha, and was greatly reverenced, especially after his death, that is when he had attained to perfect Nirvana He who was striving after this state, but had not yet attained it, was a Bodhisatva, and was also reverenced, but in a less degree [1]

In consequence of the atheistic character of Buddhism, it admits of no idea of sacrifice, mediation, satisfaction, or propitiation The worship is very simple, consisting simply of prayers and the offering of flowers, perfumes, &c, before the images and relics of Buddha. Reverence also is paid to his footmarks, and other traces of his presence, and especially to any spot where it is recorded that any remarkable occurrence happened to him The statues of Buddha are very numerous, and generally of great size, to some of them miraculous powers of motion have been ascribed Reverence is also paid to the statues of distinguished Buddhists, the Buddhas and Bodhisatvas. Different sects and individuals select certain of these to whom they pay special regard The ministers, called Bonzes, are simply confraternities of mendicants, who act as patterns of the sternest self-renunciation, or else simply as teachers and preachers They usually live in communities often containing thousands of persons, under rules strikingly resembling those of some of the mediæval monastic bodies Many of them employ themselves in study of the sacred books, and in making translations of them, others in teaching young men and boys, the novices of the convents In some countries there are also convents of women

Such a system would naturally, in its pure atheistic philosophy, have but little hold upon the mass of unintelligent men In the dreary blank of Nirvana it held out no hope worth striving for It gave no comfort from the protection of higher and more mighty beings Hence it suffered corruptions and changes in nearly every country where it was adopted, and in consequence became divided into numerous sects In Nepaul it lost its

[1] There is reason to believe that the conception of Nirvana as annihilation is the work of later philosophers and theologians, and does not proceed from Buddha, who appears to have regarded Nirvana as the absorption of the soul in itself, involving rest, freedom from pain and desire, and from the circle of existences [Muller, *Buddhist Nihilism*, 12 14]

atheistic character entirely Buddhism there has adopted the belief in one supreme, self-existent intelligence, Adi-Buddha, who projects from his own essence five Buddhas, intelligences of the first order, who in turn produce five of the second order, called Bodhisatvas These inferior divinities are regarded as agents in the hands of the Supreme Deity, and as links which unite him with the lower orders of beings Probably these features are connected with the previous religion of the country, which was superseded by Buddhism for it is one peculiarity of this religion, and apparently also a cause of its rapid progress, that it easily allied itself with and adopted parts of those religions with which it came in contact. Thus even in India, its birthplace, it became in some points assimilated with Brahminism [1] In China it allows the worship of ancestors, and of good and evil spirits In Thibet, the poorer classes, with the sanction of the Lamas, make offerings to the genii of the rivers, woods, hills, &c

In China, the only genuine Buddhists are the monks and mendicants These alone have a common confession of faith, submit to initiatory rites, and form a separate corporation The great mass of the worshippers of Fo, the Chinese corruption of Buddha, are rather tolerated than approved by the authorities of the sect They are only expected to acknowledge the general superiority of their religion, to abstain from gross vice, to reverence the sacred writings, relics, statues, &c, and the various Buddhas and Bodhisatvas, and to contribute to the support of the monks, ascetics, devotees, &c Those who fulfil only these conditions attain a higher sphere of being in the next life, but do not become enlightened The only worship is paid to the Buddhas, who are popularly regarded as deified, and hence is really man-worship Temples are very numerous, and filled with images, among which are always three of colossal size, representing Buddhas, to whom different spheres are allotted—one, ruling the world of intellect, a second, the author of joy and happiness in the family circle, who is also deputed to govern the whole earth, and the third and most important, the source of grace, mercy and deliverance Under the charge of this last is a paradise, of which the most glowing descriptions are given, but totally free from the grossness of those in the Koran Admission to this paradise is obtained solely by faith and trust in the third of this triad of Buddhas.

The remarkable features of the Buddhism of Thibet are the hierarchy of Lamas, the doctrine of the incarnations of Buddha, the severity of its discipline, the fervour of its moral tone, and the remarkable correspondence of its ritual and life with that of the mediæval Christian Church The Lamas are very numerous, one at least of each family being devoted to the priesthood There are also many large communities of nuns, and, owing to the numbers of those who adopt the religious life, they are allowed to work The supreme, temporal, and spiritual, head of the country is the Grand Lama, who, by a gradual development, has come to be looked on as an incarnation of Buddha, who is ever being born again into the world for the guidance and help of man [2] It has been suggested that, as this system was not elaborated till the thirteenth century A D, the ritual correspondences, which are certainly very striking, are due to the influence of Christian missions [See Hardwick, *Christ and other Masters*, ii app ii pp 214-219]

It remains briefly to state the strength and weakness of Buddhism as a religion One of its most important points is its practical character Its end is the salvation of mankind, or rather of the universe As a means of attaining this, it preaches the most exalted virtue, and holds up for imitation ideals—the founder and his chief followers—of the loftiest character It propagates itself only by persuasion, it exhibits the most unbounded charity and toleration On the other hand, the atheistic and nihilistic character of Buddhism takes from it all the power it might have gained for man's good There is no hope of future life, no means of expiation for sin, no sanction to its precepts to inspire awe, no beneficent Creator to love, all is dark and drear and gloomy Hence the many corruptions it has undergone, such as the elevation of Buddha to a god, and the lowering Nirvana into a paradise of pleasures. Hence also the weak hold it has over so many of its professors, so that even the professed religious are often utterly selfish, immoral and contemptible

[Maurice, *Lect on the Religions of the World* Bunsen, *God in History*, iii 8 *n* *K. L M* Hardwick, *Christ and other Masters*, ii iii Max Muller, *Chips from a German Workshop*, i; *Lect on Buddhist Nihilism* Baring-Gould, *Origin and Development of Religious Beliefs*, i R Spence Hardy, *A Manual of Buddhism*, *Legends and Theories of the Buddhists.* J B Saint-Hilaire, *Le Bouddha et sa Religion* Von Koeppen, *Die Religion des Buddha und ihre Entstehung*]

BUDNÆANS One of the parties into which the Antitrinitarians of Poland and Transylvania were divided shortly after their separation from the Reformed Churches in the year 1565, until Faustus Socinus succeeded in uniting them in one heresy The Budnæans denied the miraculous conception of our Lord, and consequently refused that degree of worship which the Socinians held to be due to Him Simon Budnæus, their leader, was deposed in 1584 from the ministry, and excommunicated with all his followers. It is said that he afterwards recanted, and was re-admitted into the sect, which had then become Socinian

[1] Buddha himself looks on the old gods of India as superhuman beings, though not as divine [Muller, *Buddhist Nihilism*, 6]

[2] Besides the Grand Lama, numerous other persons are regarded as incarnations of Buddha, or "living Buddhas"—these are recognised by certain signs, and are treated with great reverence, but are obliged to submit to rigid rules of life and conduct. [Huc, *Travels in Tartary*, Schlagintweit, *Buddhism in Thibet*]

BULGARIANS A name given to the mediæval Catharists, or Albigenses It is found in the *Chronicon Autissiodorense*, written in the year 1211, and also in Matthew Paris, and is elsewhere found in the form "Bulgri," "Bogri," and in the French forms "Boulgares," "Boulgres," and "Bougres" The name suggests a migration from Bulgaria, the chief seat of the Bogomiles, and a great home of the Paulicians

BURGHERS In the year 1746 a discussion arose in the Associate Secession Synod in Scotland respecting the lawfulness of the religious clause of the oath administered to the burgesses of Edinburgh, Perth, Stirling, and Glasgow The clause was as follows —"I profess and allow with all my heart the true religion presently professed within this realm, and authorized by the laws thereof, I shall abide at and defend the same to my life's end, renouncing the Roman religion called Papistry" It was maintained by some that for seceders from the Established Kirk to make this declaration was to place themselves at once in a false position, that the oath must be taken in the sense of its imposers, that having forsaken the Kirk on account of the abuses of patronage and the license given to teaching held to be contrary to the Westminster Confession and the other Presbyterian standards, they could not then call the form of religion which was authorized by the laws the *true* religion, nor declare that they would defend it. It was answered on the other hand by some, amongst whom were the Erskines, that the oath itself spoke only of the true religion professed in Scotland, and not of the faulty human manner of professing and settling it, that it spoke indeed of the religion authorized by the laws, but not of that *as* authorized, which would have carried a different meaning, that in their various testimonies they had solemnly approved the doctrine, worship, discipline, and government of the Church of Scotland, and had declared their adherence to their former ordination vows, which pledged them to their maintenance, that their quarrel had been only with the corruptions in Church and State, and not with the true religion professed and authorized in the realm The defenders of the clause offered for the sake of peace to consent to an act of synod declaring it *inexpedient* for Seceders to swear the oath in the present circumstances, viz the circumstances of controversy as to its precise meaning Their opponents however would consent to nothing which did not declare the oath to be sinful and inconsistent with their testimony and engagement, and in a meeting of synod on April 9th, 1746, they carried a decision accordingly Agreement with this decision was then made by the victorious party—now called ANTIBURGHERS —a term of communion They rejected, deposed and excommunicated their *Burgher* brethren (as the maintainers of the oath were now called), and in the following year two distinct bodies were constituted.

When Brown of Haddington wrote his *Historical Account of the Secession*, the congregations belonging to the two bodies numbered about 200, they both professed entire agreement with the Presbyterian standards, and were at one on all the articles of faith, but the Antiburghers still professed that their own religion was different from that of the Establishment, because they regarded the constitution of the latter, as authorized by the laws of the realm since the Revolution, as Erastian and founded on the will of the civil magistrate, and consequently still retained their hostility to the Burghers. In both bodies the rise of "free thought" tended to modify the earlier views Among the Burghers the "rights of conscience," the "right of private judgment and private opinion," began to be put forward, and the power assigned in the standard documents to the civil magistrate for the maintenance of true religion was disputed as incompatible with these rights and with the duty of toleration The principle of establishments (hitherto warmly maintained) was impugned, and a change was made which limited the assent given at ordination to the old *Act and Testimony* of the Seceders, to an approval only of its "scope and design," while subsequently, in 1797, a preamble to the *Confession of Faith* was adopted which disclaimed approbation of any principle therein supposed to favour compulsory measures in religion, and left the nature and kind of the obligation imposed by the Covenants an entirely open question On September 5th, 1799, an attempt to remove the Preamble was defeated in synod by 91 to 28, and thereupon the Burgher body immediately split into two parties, called respectively (as in the case at the same time of the divided Antiburghers) the Old-Light and the New-Light On October 2nd the Old-Light minority constituted themselves into a separate Presbytery, and as their number of ministers in settled charges gradually increased to fifteen, they established a Synod in September 1805, under the old name of The Associate Synod In 1820 the New-Light Burghers united with the New-Light Antiburghers, and took the name of the United Secession, a body which is now represented, since its further union in 1847 with the RELIEF SECESSION, by the United Presbyterian Synod The Old-Light Burghers retained their separate existence until 1839, when, in consequence of an act which passed the General Assembly on May 25th, by which their ministers and congregations were admitted to full and equal fellowship, they returned to the Established Kirk

[*Vindication of Adherence to the Principles and Constitution of the Church of Scotland, by the Associate Synod*, Perth, 1809 J Brown, *Hist Account of the Secession*, 8th ed 1802. *Information by A Campbell for the Managers of the Burgher Seceding Meeting-House in Aberdeen against Rev Will Brunton, designing himself the Minister*, Edinb 1800. ANTIBURGHERS. SECESSION]

C

CACANGELICI The word κακαγγελία as opposed to εὐαγγέλιον, in association with the idea that "the children of the wicked one" [Matt. xiii 38], and the "angels" of the devil [Matt xxv 41, Rev xii 9], are heretical and apostate men [Iren *adv Hær* iv 41], appears to have suggested this name as that of heretics in general The designation is not used by Epiphanius or Augustine, as might have been expected, as a play upon the sect of the ANGELICI, and was probably never used of any particular sect, but merely as a polemical term Thus it is applied to the Lutherans and Calvinists by Hosius, Prateolus, and in Sianda's *Lexicon Polemicum*

CADOLAITÆ A name given to the adherents of the Anti-Pope Honorius III [A D 1061], his name being Cadolaus [Baronius, *Annal ad ann* 1061]

CAIANITES [GAIANITÆ]

CAINITES A strange sect of heretics mentioned by Irenæus and all later heresiologists of the patristic ages Irenæus speaks of them rather as a school among the followers of Valentinus than as a distinct sect, but Tertullian incidentally mentions a distinct "Cainite heresy" in his treatise on Baptism [Tertull *de Bapt* i], and is usually supposed to refer to them when he writes "Sunt et nunc alii Nicolaitæ, Caiana hæresis dicitur," in the authentic work on heresies which bears his name [Tertull *de Præscript Hær.* xxxiii], though the reading is disputed. [GAIANA] Later writers always class them as a separate sect

The account of the Cainites given by Irenæus is very brief He says they "declare that Cain derived his being from the Superior Power" of the Valentinian theory, "together with Esau, Korah, and the Sodomites All such persons they acknowledge as being of their kindred For this reason, they add, that they have been assailed by the Demiurge, yet none of them had suffered injury, for Sophia always carried off from them to herself that which was hers They say that Judas the traitor had diligently studied the truth, and that it was because his knowledge of it was in advance of that possessed by all others that he brought about the mystery of the betrayal" He also states that the Cainites possessed an apocryphal gospel which they called the "Gospel of Judas" [Iren *adv Hær* xxxi] Tertullian speaks of "a viper of the Cainite heresy" who had led away a great number of persons in the locality where he was writing, and who had made it her chief aim to oppose the ministration of baptism For this reason he wrote his treatise on that sacrament [Tertull *de Bapt* i], but he gives no further indication of the doctrines professed by the Cainites

The account given of them by Epiphanius does not appear to be founded on any further acquaintance with the heresy than that which might be derived from Irenæus [Epiph *Hær* xxxviii], and Origen declares that the Cainites were not Christians at all, and that Celsus had classed them as such in ignorance [Orig *contr. Cels* iii 13], though it is evident that he himself knew little or nothing about them But the account of them given by Epiphanius shews that whether they were still existing or not as a separate sect in his time, he believed them to have held some form of those dualistic theories of good and evil which characterized all the Gnostic sects For, according to him, Cain was regarded by the Cainites as the offspring of Eve by a superior power, and Abel as her offspring by an inferior power Thus, it is probable, that the philosophy, such as it was, of the sect, set forth the struggle of good and evil under a rationalistic version of the murder of Abel, the two brothers being represented in exactly the opposite light to that in which they are shewn in Holy Scripture [Pseudo-Tertull *adv. Hær* iii]

It is observable that both St John and St Jude bring the name of Cain into their epistles in a way that is consistent with the idea that they were protesting against some misbelief associated with it St John declares that Cain was a murderer as being of "that wicked one," not a spiritual seed of the holy Eve [1 John iii 12], while St Jude expressly pronounces a "woe" against some who had gone in "the way of Cain," associating their error with that of Balaam, with the gainsaying of Korah, and with the wickedness of Sodom and Gomorrah [Jude 11-19] The epistle of St Jude is expressly written against certain persons "who separate themselves," and there is an unmistakeable likeness between his denunciation of them and the description given of the Cainites by Irenæus

Probably these heretics were one of those many early sects of Asia Minor which were so adulterated, first with the dualism, and secondly with the licentious theories and practices of Oriental heathenism, that what Christian elements of belief had been originally current among them became all but obliterated in the course of a few years Such were the SETHITES, the OPHITES, and the NICOLAITANES, with all three of which sects the Cainites are vaguely associated by ancient writers Their relationship to the Gnostic family of heresies in general is shown by the statement of Epiphanius respecting their apocryphal book the "Ascension of St Paul" (Ἀναβατικὸν Παύλου) "They find their pretext for this in what the Apostle says of his having ascended to the third heaven, and heard unspeakable words, which it is not lawful for a man to utter [2 Cor xii 2, 4] These, as they say, are the unspeakable words" Like the Gnostic sects in general they evidently professed to have some special revelation respecting their religion which had not been communicated to other Christians, and their practical antichristianism is very evident

CAJANISTS [GAIANITÆ]

CALIXTINES A section of the Hussites who resisted the withdrawal of the cup from the laity of Bohemia in the fifteenth century, and received their name from the "calix," the Latin word for the Eucharistic chalice They were called also "Utraquists," from the words *sub utraque specie*

Huss himself had been willing to conform to the custom of administering the Blessed Sacrament in the form of the bread only, as he held the theory of "concomitance," which makes the virtue of the Presence of Christ to be contained in its integrity in either element. But his follower Jacobellus de Misa refused to administer it except in both kinds, and so general had the opposite custom become, that he is spoken of by the Moravian *Apology* of 1538 as "Primus omnium communionem utriusque speciei in Bohemia practicare cœpit" [*Apolog veræ Doctrin.* in *Lydii Waldensia*, ii 292, Dort, 1617] The revival of the ancient practice formed one element in the most bitter and violent contest between the ruling powers in Church and State and the Hussites after the Council of Constance [A D 1415] and the execution of Huss and Jerome of Prague The University of Prague pronounced in favour of the Communion in both kinds, and the Hussites immediately banded together under Nicolas of Hussinecz and John Zisca for armed defence of their practice Among their number there was a large party of fanatics, who were chiefly the adherents of Zisca, and these acted with great violence and committed inexcusable cruelties in their attack upon Prague [A D 1419] This violence led to a separation of the more moderate Calixtines from the party of Zisca, the former retaining the original name, and the latter being called TABORITES, from Mount Tabor in Bohemia, where they had first gathered their forces together to a Communion in which the cup was administered to a vast multitude

From this time the Calixtines began to draw towards the dominant party in the Church In the year 1421 they made, at Prague, a statement of their wishes which is contained in four articles, as follows —[1] that the Word of God should be preached freely and without impediment throughout the kingdom of Bohemia [2] That the Sacrament of the Divine Eucharist should be freely administered in both kinds, that is, under the species of bread and of wine, to all Christians not disqualified by mortal sin, according to the command and institution of the Saviour [3] That any clergyman engaged in the pursuit of secular power, or of wealth and temporal goods, contrary to the precept of Christ, to the prejudice of his office, and to the injury of the State, should be forbidden such pursuits and made to live according to the Evangelical rule and Apostolic life which Christ lived with His Apostles [4] That all mortal sins, and particularly public ones, should be properly punished by those to whom the duty of suppressing them belong, and by reason of the law of God The war still went on for some years with the Taborites, but when the Council of Basle met [A D 1433] these four "Articles of Prague" were made the basis of a compact, which was ratified at Iglau The principal article, that respecting administration of the Holy Sacrament in both kinds, was so far modified and restricted that the priests in Bohemia and Moravia were to be permitted to administer it in that manner, but to those only who, being come to years of discretion, devoutly and reverently desired it, and who heartily acknowledged that either species was by itself "integer et totus Christus"

This compact was assailed over and over again by the Romanizing party, and their attempts were in some degree justified by the violence of the Taborites, with whom the Calixtines had once been so closely allied Before the time of the Reformation arrived, a large number of them had been gradually reconciled to the Roman usage, while others had coalesced with the Taborites, and become the ancestors of the Moravian Brethren, or "Unitas Fratrum" [BOHEMIANS HUSSITES MORAVIANS Brzezyna or Byzynius, *Diarium belli Hussit* in Ludwig's *Reliq MSS* vi 175 Æneas Sylvius, *Hist Bohem*]

CALIXTUS [SYNCRETISTS]

CALLISTIANS This name is given to the partizans of Callixtus, bishop of Rome [A D 218-223], by Hippolytus, who accuses him of compounding a new heresy from the heresies of Noetus and Theodotus The substance of the opinions attributed to him is that which was afterwards called Patripassianism But the account given of Callixtus by Hippolytus (who was bishop of a suburban see, and resided in Rome) is so mingled with personal invective and bitterness, that there can be little doubt it is exaggerated [Hippol *Refut Hær* ix 2-7] Callixtus has always been reckoned among the martyrs of the early Roman Church, and the abuse heaped on his memory by his contemporary has the air of being suggested by rivalry and disappointment.

CALVINISTIC METHODISTS [METHODISTS]

CALVINISTS. That large body of Protestants in various sects who profess to follow the opinions of Calvin, especially as regards the ministry, the sacraments, and divine grace During the reign of Queen Elizabeth these opinions were also widely diffused in the Church of England, and when, at a later time, large numbers of the Puritans became dissenters, there still remained many Calvinists among the Low Church party, down even to the present day

The founder of this school of Protestants, John Cauvin, Chauvin, or in a Latinized form, Calvinus, was the son of a notary at Noyon in Picardy [A D 1509-1564], and being intended for holy orders received the tonsure at seven years of age from the bishop to whom his father was secretary. Such were the abuses of the times that he was nominated to a chaplaincy in the cathedral of his native town when he was only twelve years of age, to the benefice of Marteville when he was eighteen, and a little later to that of Pont l'Eveque, the last of which he sold in 1534, when his connection with the Huguenots made it impossible for him to hold the sinecure much longer While Calvin held these benefices he was receiving his education successively at the High School of Paris, and the Universities of Orleans and Bourges, and became distinguished at each for his industry and learning At Orleans he studied civil law with such success that he was occasionally appointed to supply the place of absent professors, and on leaving Orleans for Bourges the honorary degree of Doctor of Civil Law was conferred upon him At Bourges Calvin continued his studies under Alciati, the first lawyer of the age, but he also turned his attention to theology under the tuition of Melchior Wolmar, one of the reforming party, Professor of Greek and the tutor of Beza On the death of his father he returned to Paris, where he shortly published a Commentary on Seneca's *de Clementia*, being then twenty-three years of age At this time Calvin became known as one of the Huguenot party, and he escaped danger only through the protection of the Queen of Navarre, sister to Francis I But in 1534 he left his native country altogether, settling first at Basle, and afterwards, when he was twenty-eight years of age [A D 1536], at Geneva Before leaving France he printed a treatise entitled *Psychopannychia*, against the heresy of the soul's unconsciousness between death and the resurrection. But within a few months afterwards [A D 1534-5] he published, first in French and then in Latin, a far more important work, his *Institutes of the Christian Religion*, which he expanded into a much larger form in a subsequent edition [A D 1559], as the exponent of his theological system

At the time when Calvin first came into notice, Geneva was a hotbed of immorality, and the profligacy of the laity having extended to the bishop and some of the clergy [Ruchat, *Hist. de la Reform. de Suisse*, ii 277], the Church had lost all influence. Opposition between clergy and laity was the necessary consequence, and this was stimulated by the visit of an impetuous French Huguenot and doctrinnaire named Farel, whose agitation led to tumult and bloodshed which ended in the withdrawal of the bishop from Geneva to Gex in Savoy [A D 1534], in the see being then declared vacant by the municipal council, and in the usurpation of the bishop's authority by Farel. It was during the time of Farel's supremacy that Calvin visited Geneva on his way from Italy to Germany, where he was about to take up his residence Being introduced by a friend to the then chief man of the city the two proved to be such kindred spirits that Calvin was earnestly entreated to support Farel in his project of reformation, and threatened with the vengeance of God if he refused to do so These persuasions and threats prevailed with Calvin, and he settled down at Geneva as a coadjutor of Farel, and as one of the chief "pastors" of the city [A D 1536]. The newly-fledged republicans were at first highly delighted with a divine whose principles were decidedly opposed to Episcopacy, and therefore to the authority which they had recently rejected. But when Calvin attempted a crusade against the wickedness by which he was surrounded they at once revolted, banishing both him and Farel from the city [A D 1538]

For three years afterwards Calvin acted as Professor of Theology at Strasburg, and was also pastor to the French congregation But a fresh turn of affairs at Geneva led to his recall, and he returned there on September 13th, 1541 Thenceforward until his death, twenty-three years later, he was the ruler of Geneva in as absolute a sense as its former bishops had been, and often exercised his authority in the most tyrannical manner At the same time he never slackened in literary industry, and by this means acquired an influence which extended far beyond Geneva even in his lifetime, and which made him only second, if second, to Luther, as a leader of thought among Protestants after his death

It was as a leader of thought that Calvin became the founder of a great party, his politico-religious rule at Geneva being dependent chiefly on his personal influence, and, although copied by his followers in Scotland, for a short time (during the supremacy of the Presbyterians) in England, and in New England, never being definitely associated with his name [PRESBYTERIANS] Some of his works had become known in England as early as 1542, when there appear in a list of prohibited books, *The Lytell Tretyse in Frensche of ye Soper of the Lorde made by Callwyn*, and *The Works every one of Callwyn* [*Brit. Mag.* xxxvi 395, Burnet's *Hist Reform* iv 519, Pocock's ed] A few years later Cranmer projected a general union of foreign Protestants with the Church of England, and Calvin among others was invited to a conference at Lambeth [Jenkyns' *Cranmer's Remains*, i 330, 346] He did not accept the invitation, but wrote many letters to the Protector Somerset, to Edward VI. (by Cranmer's advice),[1] and to Cranmer himself, con-

[1] Calvin wrote to Farel on June 15th, 1551, "Canter-

demning the Reformation of the Church of England as incomplete, and urging them to carry it further towards the Presbyterian pattern of Geneva [*State Pap* v 9, Edward VI], and it appears to have been in some degree through his influence over Somerset, Bucer, Peter Martyr, and John A'Lasco, that the alterations of 1551 were made in the Book of Common Prayer On the accession of Queen Elizabeth he sent her his Commentary on Isaiah, but the Queen declined to accept the volume in such Tudor language as brought from its author a remonstrance addressed to Sir William Cecil [*Zurich Letters*, II 34]

Calvin's influence in England and Scotland was, however, greatly extended by the return of those who had fled from the Marian persecution, and had lived during the greater part of Mary's reign at Frankfort, Zurich and Geneva John Knox (who had lived in London as Chaplain to Edward VI from 1549 to 1554) was pastor of a congregation in Geneva from 1556 until 1559, and returned thoroughly impregnated with the spirit and principles of the Genevese leader Goodman, Bishop Pilkington, Dean Whittingham, Whitaker, and some others, accompanied Knox, and were thus brought under the direct influence of Calvin; while many others, such as Fox the Martyrologist, Bishop Jewel, and Bishop Parkhurst, though not in personal intercourse with him, had their opinions very decidedly moulded by his during their residence abroad The extraordinary extension of Calvin's influence before the end of the sixteenth century is thus mentioned by Hooker in 1594. "Of what account the Master of the Sentences was in the Church of Rome, the same and more amongst the preachers of Reformed Churches Calvin had purchased, so that the perfectest divines were judged they which were skilfullest in Calvin's writings His books were almost the very canon to judge both doctrine and discipline by French churches, both under others abroad and at home in their own country, all cast according to that mould which Calvin made The Church of Scotland, in erecting the fabric of their Reformation, took the selfsame pattern" [Hooker's *Eccl Polit* pref. ii 8] "Do we not daily see," he elsewhere says, "that men are accused of heresy for holding that which the Fathers held, and that they never are clear if they find not somewhat in Calvin to justify themselves?" Archbishop Whitgift himself was strongly imbued with this deference to the Genevan Reformer's authority, and in the original draft of the Lambeth Articles (approved by him but repudiated by the Church) certain expressions were said to be "ad mentem Calvini," though the words were eventually altered to "ad mentem Augustini" [Hardw on *XXXIX Art* app] In the following century Bishop Sanderson wrote "When I began to set myself to the study of Divinity as my proper business, Calvin's Institutions were recommended to me, as they were generally to all young scholars in those times, as the best and perfectest system of Divinity, and the fittest to be laid as the groundwork in the study of this profession"

The earlier followers of Calvin were principally bent on the substitution of his Presbyterian system for that of Episcopacy, but in the beginning of the seventeenth century Arminius brought into special prominence certain features of Calvinist theology which he opposed as inconsistent with the love of God and the free-will of man. [ARMINIANS.] The condemnation of Arminius by the Synod of Dort gave additional authority to the doctrines which he had controverted [DORT, SYNOD OF], and since that time the Calvinists have maintained the doctrines of election, predestination, and irresistible grace as the distinguishing points of their system, many of them being as tenacious for Episcopacy as others are for Presbyterianism According to these doctrines God has decreed from eternity the salvation of some men, who are called the "elect," and the everlasting perdition of others Both the elect and non-elect come into the world in a state of total depravity and alienation from God, and can, of themselves, do nothing but sin His grace, however, seizes hold of the elect, and, by an irresistible power works out their salvation, bringing them into such a condition that their final perseverance in holiness is certain, and they cannot finally fall or be lost. Thus the elect are saved without any will or work of their own. On the other hand, the non-elect or reprobate can by no means whatever attain to salvation, and must be eternally lost, not because they have made themselves worthy of perdition by their sins, but because God has so decreed in excluding them from the number of the elect. "We assert," says Calvin, "that by an eternal and unchangeable decree God hath determined whom He shall one day permit to have a share in eternal felicity, and whom He shall doom to destruction In respect of the elect the decree is founded in His unmerited mercy, without any regard to human worthiness, but those whom He delivers up to damnation are, by a just and irreprehensible judgment, excluded from all access to eternal life" [Calvin, *Inst* III ii. 11] From the doctrine of "Election" follows that of "Particular Redemption," i e. that Christ died only for the elect and not for all men A full statement of these dreadful opinions may be found in the Confession of Faith set forth by the Westminster Assembly of Divines [A D. 1643], which is still the authoritative Confession of the Kirk of Scotland, and is recognised as more or less authoritative by all Calvinistic sects Great controversies have arisen among Calvinists respecting the Divine decrees, and they are divided into two parties, the one holding that those imagined decrees were positively issued, and thus "absolute;" the other that they were only God's foresight of the Fall Whitfield also separated from Wesley on account of the determined opposition which the latter offered to the Calvinism of the former In the present day the number

bury has assured me that I can do nothing more useful than to write frequently to the King, this affords me much greater delight than if I had received a present of a large sum of money" [Gorham's *Reform Gleanings*, 267]

He says, in a somewhat marked manner, that the synod of Bostra, in its letter to Beryllus, asserted that Christ, when made flesh, assumed not only the flesh but also the soul of man But we are not entitled to infer from this that Beryllus combined Patripassian and Apollinarian doctrine The acts of the synod of Bostra, the disputation of Origen and Beryllus, and Beryllus' letters to Origen thanking him for saving him from heresy, are unhappily lost

BEZPOPOFTSCHINS. That division of Russian dissenters which does not retain the office of "pope" or priest, except in such a form as that of the Presbyterian or Independent ministry. The Bezpopoftschins have been divided into fifteen or twenty sects, the principal of which are the DUCHOBORTZI, the PHILIPOFTSCHINS, and the POMERANE, but all the smaller and fanatical sects have sprung from them

BEZSLOVESTNI A name signifying "the dumb," given to a not very numerous Russian sect of the eighteenth century, whose members after conversion became perpetually speechless Very little is known of their tenets. In order to extract some information, a governor general of Siberia, named Pestal, in the reign of Catharine II [A D 1762-1796], employed the cruellest forms of torture, pouring hot sealing-wax on their flesh, and tickling the soles of their feet with feathers, but without avail.

BIBLE CHRISTIANS. [BRYANITES]

BIBLE COMMUNISTS [PERFECTIONISTS]

BICORNI. A term colloquially signifying "idiots" among the Italians, and used contemptuously as a name for the BEGHARDS by some mediæval writers.

BIZOCHI A name for the FRATICELLI, found in the Bull of Pope John XXII condemning that community [A D 1317] By some it is derived from "Bizzoco," or in French "Besace," on account of the wallet which they carried to hold the provisions which they begged from door to door. by others from "bigio," which indicated the grey colour of their garments

BLASTUS A Quartodeciman of this name is mentioned by the author of the book against heresies which formerly went by the name of Tertullian and on the ground of his teaching that the Christian passover should be kept on the day fixed by the Jewish Law, he is declared to have been desirous of introducing Judaism [Pseudo-Tertull xxii.] He is doubtless the same person as the Roman Blastus named by Eusebius as being nearly involved in the fall of Florinus, who became a Valentinian [Euseb *Hist Eccl* v 15] There is no evidence that Blastus ever actually became a Gnostic, but Eusebius records that an Epistle on Schism was written to him by Irenæus, as well as one on the Monarchy of God to Florinus [*ibid* v 20] For the particulars of his association with the QUARTODECIMANS, the reader is referred to the article under that title [Theod. *Hæret fab* i 23]

The earlier followers of Calvin were principally bent on the substitution of his Presbyterian system for that of Episcopacy, but in the beginning of the seventeenth century Arminius brought into special prominence certain features of Calvinist theology which he opposed as inconsistent with the love of God and the free-will of man [ARMINIANS] The condemnation of Arminius by the Synod of Dort gave additional authority to the doctrines which he had controverted [DORT, SYNOD OF], and since that time the Calvinists have maintained the doctrines of election, predestination, and irresistible grace as the distinguishing points of their system, many of them being as tenacious for Episcopacy as others are for Presbyterianism According to these doctrines God has decreed from eternity the salvation of some men, who are called the "elect," and the everlasting perdition of others Both the elect and non-elect come into the world in a state of total depravity and alienation from God, and can, of themselves, do nothing but sin His grace, however, seizes hold of the elect, and, by an irresistible power works out their salvation, bringing them into such a condition that their final perseverance in holiness is certain, and they cannot finally fall or be lost Thus the elect are saved without any will or work of their own On the other hand, the non-elect or reprobate can by no means whatever attain to salvation, and must be eternally lost, not because they have made themselves worthy of perdition by their sins, but because God has so decreed in excluding them from the number of the elect. "We assert," says Calvin, "that by an eternal and unchangeable decree God hath determined whom He shall one day permit to have a share in eternal felicity, and whom He shall doom to destruction In respect of the elect the decree is founded in His unmerited mercy, without any regard to human worthiness, but those whom He delivers up to damnation are, by a just and irreprehensible judgment, excluded from all access to eternal life" [Calvin, *Inst* III ii 11] From the doctrine of "Election" follows that of "Particular Redemption," *i e.* that Christ died only for the elect and not for all men A full statement of these dreadful opinions may be found in the Confession of Faith set forth by the Westminster Assembly of Divines [A D. 1643], which is still the authoritative Confession of the Kirk of Scotland, and is recognised as more or less authoritative by all Calvinistic sects Great controversies have arisen among Calvinists respecting the Divine decrees, and they are divided into two parties, the one holding that those imagined decrees were positively issued, and thus "absolute," the other that they were only God's foresight of the Fall Whitfield also separated from Wesley on account of the determined opposition which the latter offered to the Calvinism of the former In the present day the number

of Calvinists in the Church of England is not large [SUBLAPSARIANS SUPRALAPSARIANS CALVINISTIC METHODISTS WESTMINSTER ASSEMBLY Dyer's *Life of Calvin* DICT *of* THEOL art CALVINISM LAMBETH ARTICLES]

CALVINO-PAPISTÆ. A name given by the Puritans to those Churchmen whose admiration of Calvin prompted them to consider the Church of England and its formularies as Calvinistic [Stapleton, *Promptuar Cathol* i 285, iii 116 Sianda, *Lexic Polem* iii 627, *s v* "Puritani."]

CAMERONIANS, or SOCIETY PEOPLE Names given to a party formed among the Scotch Covenanters in the reign of Charles II Upon the publication of the Indulgences in 1669 and 1672, which permitted Nonconforming ministers to return to their parishes upon certain easy conditions, specially that they should not publicly speak against the royal supremacy, a division of opinion ensued amongst those to whom those Indulgences were offered Some accepted the proffered toleration, others rejected it as involving a sinful compliance with Erastianism and Prelacy After the battle of Bothwell Bridge the latter formed, under the leadership of Richard Cameron and Donald Cargill, a distinct party, which claimed to represent, with the most uncompromising rigour and intolerant bitterness, the true principles and spirit of the original framers of the Covenant In a statement of principles (called the "Queensferry Paper" from the place of its discovery), which was intended as the outline of a Declaration, they disowned monarchy, and avowed their intention to set up some other government in accordance with the Word of God, and in a declaration publicly read at Sanquhar on 22nd June 1680, they openly declared war against the King and all who acknowledged his authority Cameron was killed in a skirmish at Airdsmoss on the 22nd of the following month, and Cargill, after solemnly excommunicating the King, was apprehended and executed at Edinburgh on July 27th, 1681 They were succeeded in the leadership of the party, first by James Renwick, who was executed at Edinburgh, February 17th, 1688, for, in his own words, "disowning the usurpation and tyranny of James, Duke of York," and maintaining the lawfulness of defending their meetings by force of arms, &c, and afterwards by Alexander Shields Upon the Revolution[1] the three ministers who had adhered to the Cameronians, Shields, Thomas Linning, and William Boyd, were admitted as ministers of the Established Kirk, but because the General Assembly did not at that time expressly renew the Solemn League and Covenant, their people refused to follow them, and remained for some years without a minister

At length Mr John Macmillan, who was expelled from the Kirk in 1703, for refusing to take, and preaching against, the oath of allegiance, and for intruding himself into the parishes of others, became their leader With him a few others became associated, particularly Mr John Hepburn, who had been at first suspended for similar practices, restored in 1699, and finally deposed in 1705[2] The union of the two kingdoms was particularly offensive to the Cameronians from the absence in the Act of any recognition of the Covenant (which absence they regarded as invalidating the authority of the civil magistrates), and also because by it Episcopacy was allowed and perpetuated as the established form of Church government in England, for the religion of which country the rigid Presbyterians wished to legislate as well as for their own. To such an extreme of indignation did the fanaticism of the Cameronians lead them, that, through the agency of Ker of Kersland, they entered into negotiations with the exiled Chevalier, were hardly restrained from at once taking arms, and, had the abortive expedition from France in 1708 actually landed in Scotland, would have been found united heartily for the time with Episcopalian and Roman Catholic Jacobites[3] In 1743, Macmillan, together with only one other minister, Mr Thomas Nairn (who had been expelled from the Secession body for maintaining that none but a covenanted Presbyterian could be the lawful sovereign of these realms), established the *Reformed Presbytery*, and organized a distinct body, to which small accessions from time to time accrued

Under the name of *Reformed Presbyterians* the society still exists, claiming to be the representative of the old Covenanters in maintaining the Solemn League and Covenant as one of the standards, and still deploring the constitution of Church and State as established in both kingdoms at the Revolution of 1688 and at the Union In accordance with these views it is, by the formal Act of Testimony, forbidden to the members to take the oath of allegiance or to exercise the franchise in elections for Parliament, because the persons so elected have themselves to take that oath This prohibition had of late been frequently disregarded, though while some kirk-sessions had at times suspended or cut off offenders, the presbytery or synod had never upon appeal confirmed the sentence, but upon the rise of the Volunteer movement in 1860 the question of the oath assumed fresh prominence Some sessions attempted to prevent their kirk members from becoming volunteers, the case was thereupon referred to the synod in 1862, which in 1863 enacted by a large majority, in accordance with previous practice, that, "while

[1] The strength of the party was shewn at this time by their raising in one day the regiment known by the name of Cameronians for the purpose of opposing Viscount Dundee

[2] Among the articles presented against him in the General Assembly, and which he admitted, it was objected that for sixteen years he had neither administered nor received the Holy Communion lest he should be a fellow partaker with unworthy recipients! A story is told by Boston, whose parish Macmillan visited, that one of the followers of the latter understood by the Solemn League and Covenant no other than the "Covenant sealed with Christ's blood" [Boston's *Memoirs*, Edinb 1776, p 226]

[3] They offered to raise 5000 men from amongst themselves, and promised that Ker should raise 8000 more amongst the other Presbyterians See *Hooke's Correspondence* (Roxburghe Club, 1871), ii 308-313.

recommending the members of the Church to abstain from the use of the franchise and from taking the oath of allegiance, discipline to the effect of suspension and expulsion from the Church shall cease" Three ministers and eight elders, however, immediately protested against this formal abandonment, as they regarded it, of fundamental principles, withdrew from the synod, and formed another body under the same name, which has since then somewhat increased in numbers There are therefore at the present time two distinct bodies in Scotland bearing the same name of "Reformed Presbyterians" The larger body numbers forty-five congregations and maintains six missionaries in the New Hebrides, the smaller (being the secession of 1863) has eleven congregations At the census in 1851 the united body had thirty-nine places of worship Branches of the Reformed Presbytery are found in Ireland and in America, and in both of these branches divisions took place earlier than in Scotland, on the same general grounds of modification of administrative rules and the application of fundamental principles to the varying circumstances of the times Consequently the two Scottish bodies find themselves supported alike in their later controversy by distinct Irish and American synods The larger body in Ireland has at present about thirty-three congregations, with a branch presbytery in New Brunswick and Nova Scotia, and the smaller has seven congregations [*Acts of the General Assembly. Hist. of the Church of Scotland*, by John Brown of Haddington, Glasgow, 1784. Howie's *Scots Worthies* Hetherington's *Hist of the Church of Scotland*, Edinburgh, 1843 *Note on the Reformed Presbyterian Secession*, by M S T, 1863, &c]

CAMERONITES A school of French Protestants taking their name from John Cameron, a native of Glasgow, who emigrated to France in the beginning of the seventeenth century He was a man of learning, and became a Professor of Theology among the Protestants at Sedan, Saumur, and Montauban At Saumur he originated opinions afterwards taken up by Moses Amyraut [AMYRALDISTS], and which had for their object the reconciliation of the Calvinist and the Arminian doctrines respecting the Divine decrees The substance of these opinions was that God wills the salvation of all men, and not of the elect only, that none are excluded from the possibility of salvation, and that those are saved who co-operate with God by using the power of judging between good and evil which He infuses into their understanding for the choice of good. This mitigated form of Calvinism was condemned by the Ultra-Calvinist Synod of Dort [A D 1518], and Cameron returned to Scotland to become for one year Professor of Theology in the University of Glasgow. He afterwards returned to Montauban, where he died, at the age of forty-five, in 1625. His *Theological Lectures* were published immediately after his death, and his collected works in a folio Latin volume, printed at Geneva in 1658

CAMISARDS A name given to the French Calvinists of the Cevennes who rose to resist the tyranny of Louis XIV after the revocation of the Edict of Nantes The name is said to have been given them because of the camisole or blouse which they commonly wore, others say that it arose from their wearing a white shirt, or camise, to disguise themselves in their night attacks; and others derive the word from "camis," a road-runner The fanatics to whom it was applied never called themselves by any other name than the Children of God (les Enfants de Dieu).

From the revocation of the Edict of Nantes in 1685, a cruel and systematic persecution had raged against the Protestants of the South of France Monks and priests, supported by large bodies of troops, were sent into the suspected districts, to convert by force all who were not "of the king's religion" The secret meetings for worship, which were held by night in woods, caves, and the hollows of the mountains, were attacked and dispersed with much barbarity Hundreds of Protestants went to the scaffold in Montpelier and Nismes The rack, the wheel, and the stake were unsparingly used to put an end to those "Assemblies of the Desert," as they were called, in which the peasantry strove to maintain their religious freedom The Intendant Lamvignon de Baville held the country with forty thousand troops and militia, and opened the mountains by above a hundred new roads. His soldiers surprised the assemblies of Anduze and Vigan, and put nearly all who were present to the sword By the express command of Luvois, the Minister of War, it was attempted to get rid of the whole Protestant population of Languedoc and Dauphiné, amounting to near half a million, by extermination or deportation These severities are known by the name of the Dragonnades After the peace of Ryswick, in 1697, they were redoubled, and seemed on the point of succeeding, when the fanatic and cruel vengeance which the Camisards perpetrated against the Abbé du Cheylu, one of the bitterest of the persecutors, gave the signal for a general insurrection Du Cheylu was inspector of the mission for the conversion of the Huguenots, and the supposed instigator of the cruelties of De Baville. He had imprisoned in his house at Pont de Montvert a band of fugitives whom he had caught making their way to Geneva. It was resolved at a meeting in the Desert to rescue these prisoners The house was surrounded in the night by the armed peasants under their leader Pierre Ségnier, a notorious seditious preacher and one of their pretended prophets It was set on fire, and Du Cheylu was put to death with great violence and barbarity From that night for three years, 1702 to 1705, the mountainous district of the Cevennes was the theatre of a revolt which baffled the efforts of the generals of Louis, maintained itself against overwhelming numbers and the most bloody rigour, and was at last subdued more by policy than by arms

After this first success Ségnier descended from the mountains, in the words of the Cevenol historians, "like the storm out of the cloud," and executed on the Catholics of the plain of Nismes a wild vengeance, which he called the judgment of God He was however soon defeated, taken, and burnt alive at Pont de Montvert, the scene of his first triumph. Laporte, a veteran soldier, succeeded him as leader, styling himself "Colonel of the Children of God" Around him was gathered a number of chiefs of various character, and often of the lowest origin, who afterwards became famous in the annals of the Cevennes Among these may be named Castinat, Catinat, Salomon, Cavalier, Rastelet, and Ravenal. An indecisive battle was fought at Champ Domergue, between the Camisards and the royalist troops under Captain Paul Shortly afterwards Laporte was surprised and slain. His nephew Roland was unanimously raised to the chief command, and soon shewed himself the most capable leader who had yet appeared. Under him the insurrection took the shape of an organized revolt, the country was divided into military districts, each under a subordinate chief, and magazines of arms were laid up in the caves of the mountains Roland took the title of "General of the Troops of the French Protestants assembled in the Cevennes" He was a man of politic and far-reaching mind, superior to the rest of the Cevenol leaders in intelligence, while he was their equal in religious enthusiasm. His chief associate was the young and brilliant Cavalier, originally a baker, who by his military talents nearly ensured the triumph of the revolt, and by his desertion caused its ruin Innumerable skirmishes only added to the strength and boldness of the insurgents, and in 1703 Marshal Montrevel was sent with a powerful army to the seat of war He defeated the Camisards in two pitched battles at Vagnas and Pompignan, but without subduing them At the head of sixty thousand men he swept the country, committing the most horrible cruelties Thirty-two parishes were entirely desolated, and nearly five hundred villages destroyed On one occasion, three hundred people were burnt alive in a mill where they had assembled for worship The reprisals of the Camisards doubled these atrocities, and the country was reduced to a desert

Next year the Camisards opened the campaign by gaining their two greatest victories, that of Martinarques under Cavalier, and of the Bridge of Salindres under Roland But these successes were instantly counterbalanced by the severe defeat of Cavalier at Nages, and of Roland at Brenoux; and the victors of an hour before suddenly saw themselves reduced to extremities Meanwhile Montrevel had been succeeded by Marshal Villars, who adopted a more humane and conciliatory policy, offering a free pardon to all who would lay down their arms, and professing the warmest admiration of the Cevenol leaders, especially Cavalier Twenty thousand men had fallen in the last year of the war, and the country was completely exhausted Nevertheless the indomitable Roland was preparing to renew the struggle, and refused to listen to any overtures. But Cavalier was won over by his courtly antagonist, and declared himself anxious for peace, provided that his religion were respected Conferences and negotiations followed between him and the royalist captains, and the result was that the terms offered were rejected by the other Cevenol leaders, who would be satisfied with nothing short of absolute religious liberty; but Cavalier was detached from the cause, and the greater part of the country was reclaimed by the generous policy of Villars After this further resistance was hopeless Roland died in battle, refusing all compromise to the last, and the insurrection did not long survive him The bands were dispersed, and the leaders banished In the summer of 1705 Villars returned in triumph to Versailles One or two attempts were made to renew the struggle by Castinat, Catinat, Salomon, Ravenal, and other chieftains, who stole back from exile, but they were put down with terrible severity Castinat and Salomon were broken alive on the wheel at Montpelier, Catinat and Ravenal were burnt alive at Nismes Cavalier entered the English service, fought with desperate valour at Almanza, became Governor of Jersey, and died in 1740

The cause of the revolt of the Cevennes was barbarous tyranny But its animating spirit from first to last was not rational resistance, but the wildest superstition, and in this it stands apart from all the popular movements in favour of religious freedom which took place in the same age. The "Children of God" believed themselves to be under the direct influence of the Spirit of prophecy They chose their leaders for their spiritual gifts, not for their warlike skill, and marched forth to conquer or die "for the eternal" At their nocturnal meetings sights and sounds were never wanting, which their excited fancy proclaimed to be supernatural They had a complete system of spiritual gifts and grades, innumerable prophets arose among them, ecstasies and trances were frequent, and the wildest utterances that could be prompted by misery, distress, and privation, were regarded as the teachings of the Spirit Something of the mystic was displayed in the character of the most politic of their chiefs Ségnier was moved by a vision to that attack on Du Cheylu which was the outbreak of the insurrection. Roland professed the gift of supreme inspiration Cavalier was accompanied in the field by a prophetess of gigantic stature

The supernatural gifts to which these fanatics laid claim in England (where, as in Holland and Germany, they were known as the "French Prophets"), are indicated by the following letter — "Dear Sir,—I spake with Sr R Bulkeley yesterday, who solemnly affirms that there is a gift of languages among them, and that specimens will be printed, and that they shall speedily have the gift of healing. I would desire you to refrain printing anything against them for a while, for if these (truly miraculous) are manifest, they will demand an awful Regard. I called at your House yesterday to have spoken with you, who am, Sir, yr affectionate Bro'r, J W. July 11, 1717. To the Reverend Dr Kennett, This" [*Lansd MS* 938, f 39]. They desired to join the Moravian Brethren, but were repelled, chiefly on account of the hideous circumstances which attended their pretended inspirations. In England they sought in vain to join the Methodists; Wesley pronounced them to be a set of enthusiasts, whose imaginary inspirations "contradicted the law and the testimony"

[*Hist of the Camisards*, 1709 *Mémoires M de Bavile*. *Œuvres de Louis XIV*. *Mémoires Historiques*, i p 84 Cavalier's *Memoirs of the Wars of the Cevennes*, Lond 1726 *Histoire des Troubles des Cevennes, ou de la Guerre des Camisards*, Villefranche, 1760 Schulz's *Geschichte der Camisarden*, Weimar, 1790 Smiles' *Country of the Camisards*, 1870 Mrs Bray's *Revolt of the Protestants in the Cevennes*, 1870 Southey's *Wesley*, ch. 8 *Life of Calamy*, ii 71, 94, ed 1629. Burnet, *Hist. of his own Times*, iv. 15]

CAMPBELLITES, or ROWITES. In the year 1830, the Rev John M'Leod Campbell, Minister of Row, Dumbartonshire, was condemned by the Presbytery of Dumbarton for teaching [1] the universality of the Atonement, *i e* that Christ died for all men, and not for the elect only, [2] that God so far has pardoned all men as to make past sin no longer any barrier to the returning to God's love and favour, [3] that personal assurance is of the essence of faith, in the sense that in believing the Gospel there is necessarily present in the mind of the believer the certainty that he is (according to the views stated in the preceding articles) the object of God's love, that he has the remission of sins, the gift of the Spirit, and all things pertaining to life and godliness, bestowed by the free grace of God On an appeal to the Synod of Glasgow and Ayr, the question was remitted by them to the General Assembly, by sentence of which body Mr Campbell was deposed on May 24th, 1831, from the ministry of the Established Church of Scotland The judgment could hardly have been other than it was, for the opinions of Mr Campbell were plainly contradictory, in some respects to the Calvinistic standards of the Kirk, however agreeable to Holy Scripture. Mr (afterwards Dr) Campbell subsequently established a congregation in Glasgow, and (without on his own part ever formally seceding from the Kirk of Scotland) officiated as its minister from 1833 until 1859 In the census report of 1851, eleven persons were returned as having attended the place of worship of the "Campbellites" on the morning of the census Sunday, and fourteen in the afternoon Dr Campbell's views have lately attracted considerable notice in consequence of his work on the *Nature of the Atonement* [1856, 3rd ed 1869], in which the Incarnation being regarded as the principal means of man's redemption and restoration, the humanity and life of our Lord are represented as themselves the Atonement, in which we share by fellowship with Christ. The death of Christ is considered as an offering to the Father in Christ's character of man's representative, of a confession of human sin and of sorrow for sin; while exhibiting at the same time a perfect sinless obedience and faith, the obedience "even unto death" Dr Campbell's work is written in a style far from clear or attractive, and is very diffuse, but its general aim is to represent the At-one-ment as wrought out in the love exhibited by the whole of our blessed Lord's life, and not in any sense as consisting in a vicarious satisfaction of justice by His death Dr. Campbell died at Roseneath, Argyllshire, February 27th, 1872

[*The Proceedings before the Presbytery of Dumbarton and Synod of Glasgow in the case of J M Campbell*, Greenock, 1831. *Proceedings of the General Assembly* Story's *Life of R. Story of Roseneath*, 1862]

CAMPBELLITES, AMERICAN. A sect of American Baptists known also as "Reformed Baptists," and "Reformers." They originated with an Irish preacher of the Presbyterian Seceders named Thomas Campbell, who emigrated to America from the North of Ireland, and settled in Washington county, Pennsylvania, at the beginning of the present century. Campbell, and his son Alexander Campbell, who had been educated at Glasgow, originated a movement for the promotion of unity on the plan of ignoring all creeds, confessions of faith, and formularies, and admitting persons to a communion in which the only test should be a satisfactory reply to the question "What is the meritorious cause of the sinner's acceptance with God?" The first place of worship built for this new communion was at Brush Run, and was opened on September 7th, 1810, with the two Campbells for its joint pastors. This pattern of dogmatic simplicity and primitive unity was, however, immediately divided into Pædobaptists and Anti-Pædobaptists, and the former separating off in the year 1812 the Campbells and their adherents were all re-baptized by immersion, and were received into the local Baptist community as members of that body. Still continuing their endeavours to promote union, the Campbells aroused the jealousy of the Baptists, and the younger of the two, Alexander, with about thirty of their adherents, departed from Brush Run in 1828 to form a new community at Wellsburg in Virginia, where they called themselves the "Mahoning Association," and established the separate congregations of which it was formed on the original footing of "unsectarianism" The Baptists again opposed Campbell, and he finally separated from them, re-forming his congregations on Independent or Congregational principles, and calling his followers "The Disciples" or "Disciples of Christ" On assuming this independent position the Campbellite sect began to extend itself largely, and they now number many congregations in Kentucky, Ohio, Indiana, Illinois, Missouri, and Virginia A few are to be found in British North America and in England Their present sectarian position is that of the Independents, *plus* baptism by immersion as an essential requirement for admission to their body

CAMPITÆ A name given to the small Donatist congregation at Rome, in allusion to their being driven to the plains outside the city for the purpose of carrying out unmolested their religious rites and ceremonies

CANISTÆ A sect of heretics of this name is mentioned by Theodoret [*Hær fab* i 1], and by Clement of Alexandria [*Strom.* vii 549] Danæus, in his introduction to St. Augustine's work on heresies, suggests that they were so named "a caninis et turpissimis moribus," but Ittigius considers that "Canistæ" is only a misreading for "Cainistæ," and that the CAINITES are the heretics referred to It may, however, be remarked that St Augustine speaks of the Cynics as "illi canini philosophi" [Aug *de Civit Dei*, xiv 20 *Cf* Hippol *Refut* iv 48]

CAPHARNAITES A controversial designation sometimes applied to those who—from John vi 52, 59—hold the doctrine of Transubstantiation in a gross and material form.

CAPUTIATI A fanatic sect of the twelfth century which caused much excitement in Burgundy and Auxerre, and was suppressed by troops led by the bishop of the latter diocese They began, about A D 1182, to proclaim universal liberty and equality They derived their name from caps in which they wore as a badge a leaden image of the Blessed Virgin, under whose patronage they professed to be acting [Schroeckh's *Kirchengesch* xxix 636 Le Bœuf, *Mémoires sur l'Histoire d'Auxerre*, i 317]

CARAITES [KARAITES]

CARLSTADT [ABECEDARIANS]

CARPOCRATIANS A branch of Gnostics who derived their doctrine from Carpocrates of Alexandria, one of the very earliest teachers of heresy His name appears thus in Irenæus, Eusebius, and the majority of writers, but by Epiphanius and Philaster he is called Carpocras This form is adopted by Baronius, who writes "Carpocras, fæx omnium hæreticorum, fax totius continentiæ" His followers are called Carpocrasii by Epiphanius, Carpocratenı by Nicetas, Carpocratiani by Augustine and most others. The date assigned to the birth of Carpocrates has not been given, and writers are divided as to the exact time when his sect took definite form, but all agree in placing it in the former half of the second century, some as early as the year 120 Eusebius says he was a contemporary of Basilides in the time of Adrian Some details of his life have been preserved His wife was Alexandria of Cephallenia, and his son Epiphanes, who died young, but not before he had written a book entitled *De Justitiâ*, a few fragments of which are extant in Clemens Alexandrinus [*Strom* iii 430, and elsewhere]

These sectarians called themselves Gnostics In most respects the teaching of their founder coincides with that of Basilides [BASILIDIANS] He held there was one principal Virtue from whom proceeded all other virtues and angels, who founded this world, that Jesus Christ was not born of a Virgin, but a man truly born of the seed of Joseph, though better than other men in integrity of life He was endued with a more robust soul, virtue was given Him by the Great First Cause, whereby He retained the recollection of things seen in a former state of existence, and being thus strengthened with the memory of things divine, He could escape the control of the angels, the founders of the world, and through the agency of this inherent virtue or power discharged the debt of nature, and so went to the Father Metempsychosis and the pre-existence of the soul was an integral part of the system In a former state, he maintained, the soul could not attain the height of perfection, except it overthrew the yoke of the angels, and so became eligible for the liberty of heaven Thus bad deeds as well as good were necessarily wrought in pursuance of this idea An extraordinary interpretation of our Lord's parable in Matthew v. 25, 26 was advanced to support this position. The adversary there (whom he named Abolus) is one of the angels who made the world and has the special charge of taking souls to judgment, being there convicted of not having done everything, ἐλεγχομένας μὴ ποιησάσας πᾶσαν ἐργασίαν, they are delivered to a minister, and put again into another body to work out their admission to heaven "Prison" is the body, the "last farthing" is the migration of the soul, which must go through every experience, so that no kind of deed is left undone. It is remarkable how exactly this corresponds to the Platonic view The office of leading souls to judgment is given by Pythagoras to Mercury [see also Hor *Carm* i 10] Faith and charity alone were necessary virtues · all others were useless There is nothing evil in nature except as men think it, and this life becomes consummated to no one until all those blemishes which are held to disfigure it have been fully displayed in its conduct. [Epiphanius, *adv Hæres* i 2, 27 Irenæus, *contra Hæres* i 25, and Massuet's *Dissertationes Prœviæ* Augustine, *de Hæresibus*, vii. Tertullian, *De Præscr* 48, *de Anima*, 23, 35]

It is manifest that, without some corrective, this system appears to encourage sin [Mosheim, i 199] and hence the earlier writers do not hesitate to speak of the heresy in the bitterest terms Carpocrates, "docebat omnem turpem operationem, omnemque adinventionem peccati," says Augustine Lardner denies that the founders countenanced any of the grosser impurities which are specifically charged upon their followers, but that their principles led to them is clear, and the whole body of Christians suffered from the bad name acquired by the Carpocratians

The resurrection of the body was of course rejected by them. It does not appear that they formally renounced any of the New Testament They are however named by Jerome [*adv. Luciferianos*, 22] among the heretics who mutilated the Gospels, "qui Evangelia laniaverunt" The idea of a special grant of power, as it were, induced the belief that the career of Jesus might be achieved by any man who had strength to despise the angels, and by the excellences of knowledge, as well as accumulation of work, arrive at the unknown Father Hence too they boasted themselves not only equal to the Apostles, but qualified to rival, if not to excel, the Saviour Himself Irenæus charges them with magical superstitions, "incantationes, philtra quoque et charitesia, et paredros, et oniropompos, et reliquas malignationes" They are said also to have branded their followers with a hot iron "in posterioribus partibus exstantiæ dextræ auris"

The spread of the heresy in the East was more rapid than in the West It is said to have been first brought to Rome [A D 160] by Marcellina From the importance attached to Epiphanes, although dying at the age of seventeen, it is thought that Carpocrates must have died before him for a temple is even said to have been erected to him at Cephallene and worship paid to him [Clem Alex *Strom* 3] Marcellina adored indiscriminately images of Christ, Paul, and Pythagoras Many sects known by different names are allied to the Carpocratians, and distinguished from them only in some one tenet. Some of these are named by Baronius [anno 120, xli] References to modern writers are given by Lardner and Mosheim Great weight was attached by this sect, as countenancing a migration of the soul, to the example of Elias [Matt xvii 12], suppressing the obvious answer that John Baptist came not in the person but in the spirit and power of Elias The second Epistle of St Peter, and that of St Jude, are thought to have been directed against the first appearance of the unsound views which developed into this heresy Philaster [*de Hæres* 57] speaks of Floriani, a variety of this sect, composed mainly of military men The notes of Fabricius and Galeardus on this author, given by Migne [*Patrolog* xii. 1151, 1171], contain many references to other sources The sect survived, but without great influence, until the sixth century

CARTESIANS [DESCARTES]

CATABAPTISTS. [ANABAPTISTS]

CATÆSCHINETANS [οἱ κατ' Αἰσχύνην] A sect of Montanists who were followers of Æschines, an empiric of Athens in the second century The writer who supplemented Tertullian *De Præscriptione hæreticorum* with the work *Adversus omnes Hæreticos* says, that the particular point in which they differed from the common blasphemy of the Cataphrygians was that they affirmed Christ to be Himself Son and Father in one [Tertull *adv. omn Hæres* vii] Ittigius also says that they distinguished between the Holy Spirit and the Paraclete, identifying the former with the Person who inspired the Apostles, and the latter with Montanus [Ittig. *de Hæres* 243]

CATANI [CAINITES]

CATAPHRYGIANS [MONTANISTS]

CATAPROCLIANISTS [PROCLIANISTS]

CATHARI [NOVATIANS]

CATHARI This name was that by which the ALBIGENSES were chiefly known in their earlier days They are also frequently so called by later ecclesiastical historians

CATHARISTÆ A local name for the Manichees [Aug *Hær* xlvi]

CATHOLIC AND APOSTOLIC CHURCH. [IRVINGITES]

CATROPITES [CIRCUMCELLIONS]

CAUCAUBARDITES A branch of the Eutychian heretics belonging to the sixth century, who took their name from the place where they held their first assemblies They followed the party of Severus of Antioch and the Acephali, rejecting the decrees of the Council of Chalcedon [Nicephor *Hist Eccl* xviii 49 Baron *Annal ad ann* 335]

CELESTIAL PROPHETS A name given to or assumed by the early Anabaptists, or ZWICKAU PROPHETS [Hosius, *de Orig Hær nostri temp*, 1559]

CELESTIANS An alternative name frequently met with for the Pelagians [Aug *de Hæres* lxxxviii., Prædest. lxxxviii], more commonly used in the East than the West. Cælestius was studying at Rome when Pelagius arrived there from Britain early in the fifth century, and accompanied him to Africa [A D 410-11] after the sack of Rome by the Goths. It is not known whether he was an Italian by birth or an Irishman, the latter view is based on an expression of St Jerome [*in Jerem* iv.] which the context permits to be referred to either Pelagius or Cælestius His contemporary Marius Mercator further adds, that he was of noble birth, and of some weight at the bar, where he was employed in pleading the causes of cities or communities before the higher tribunals [nobilis natu, auditorialis scholasticus, naturæ vitio eunuchus *Common ad Lect* p 30, ed Garnier] Much later fables trace his descent from a Gaelic chieftain in the wilds of Erin, or assert that his father was a certain Solomon, duke of Cornwall [Walch. *Hist Ketz.* vol iv p 506] One more fact relating to his early life is preserved by Gennadius While still a youth, before he had embraced the doctrines of Pelagius, he wrote three epistles, *De Monasterio*, to his parents, of the size of little books, possibly explanatory of his change from secular to monastic life, which contained no symptoms of the errors afterwards disclosed, but everything which could excite to virtue [*de Viris Illustribus*, cap 44] On reaching Africa [A D 411] he applied for priest's orders, but was publicly challenged by Paulinus, a deacon of Milan, and the biographer of St. Ambrose, with having taught various false doctrines, especially the four subjoined · [1] that Adam was created mortal, and that whether he sinned or not he would have died, [2] that the sin of Adam hurt himself only and not mankind, [3] that infants new born are in the same state that Adam was before his fall, [4] that a man may be without sin and keep the commandments easily if he will Cælestius returned an evasive answer to these accusations, and was condemned by a council at Carthage [A D 412], presided over by Aurelius, bishop of that city, the first of twenty-four councils in connection with the Pelagian controversy [A D 412-431] He then left Africa, saying that he would appeal to Rome, but it is doubtful whether he ever carried out his intention, because he is next found in Sicily, where he is said to have broached some very strange views,[1] and a little later on at Ephesus, where he succeeded in being ordained priest. A few years later [A D 416] he went to Constantinople, where Atticus its bishop would receive neither him nor his doctrine, so that after a very short stay he travelled to Rome [A D 417], and there at first met with a favourable reception from Zosimus, who had just succeeded Innocent I, and who, in spite of a warning letter from Paulinus, was pleased by the deference shewn by Cælestius to the papal see When he asked him whether "he would renounce all those tenets objected to him formerly by the deacon Paulinus, and could give his assent to the letters of the apostolic see, which had been written by his predecessor of holy memory, he refused to renounce the articles objected by the deacon, but he did not dare to oppose the letters of the holy Pope Innocent, and he promised to renounce all things which that see did renounce" But the letters which hereupon Zosimus wrote in his favour, and the summons to all accusers to substantiate their accusations, were ignored by the various African synods, and when their indignant replies reached Rome, Cælestius was formally cited to appear again before the Pope, when, probably foreseeing that his cause was hopeless, instead of responding to the citation he disappeared from Rome, and a sentence of excommunication presently followed from the ecclesiastical, and a sentence of banishment from the civil court His subsequent history is obscure, he wandered about in the East without being able anywhere to establish his views, which were condemned at synods in all parts of Europe, at St Alban's [A D 429], at Rome [A D 430], at the General Council of Ephesus [A D 431] After this he is said to have retired to the monastery at Lerins, thence to Sicily, where his death occurred within a few years, although the exact date is unknown [PELAGIANISM]

CELLITES [LOLLARDS]

CERDONIANS A sect that derived its name from Cerdon, or Cerdo, a Syrian Gnostic, who slightly varied the ordinary teaching of Simon Magus and Saturninus His first appearance at Rome is assigned to the year 141, but he is mentioned by some as early as 125, and by others as late as 155 He was teacher of Marcion, and associated with him at Rome in the publication of his special views. We are told by Irenæus, in a passage where a fragment of the original Greek is extant, that Cerdon confessed his errors, but again relapsed into open heresy, or secret teaching of it, and that this happened more than once, so that at last he separated himself from the communion of the faithful [Iren *contra Hær* iii 4] The word used by Irenæus, ἀφιστάμενος, does not necessarily convey that he was ejected from the Church, as some have rendered it, but rather that he anticipated such an expulsion, as Valesius interprets it, by a voluntary secession Epiphanius considers him a successor in heresy to Heracleon Of his death there is no record

He appears in the main to have adopted the principles of Simon Magus and Saturninus, but to have detached himself from them on the great question of the day, the existence of evil. He held that there were two first causes, one good, one evil, that one was not subject or inferior to the other He maintained a distinct duality in the Supreme Being, which Bardesanes, whose difficulties were similar to those of Cerdon, had hesitated to affirm [BARDESANIANS] The moral code of the Jews proceeded from the malevolent spirit, that of the Christians from the beneficent one The evil principle was known to men as the Creator of the world, revealed by the law and the prophets, the good principle was the unknown Father of Jesus Christ. The later followers of this heresy, Marcionites and others, separated the Creator of the world from the Supreme Being, and assigned Him an intermediate place between the good and bad first cause Cerdon denied also the Incarnation, maintained that the Saviour was clothed with the appearance of flesh, that His sufferings were not real, since he was unable to account for such a passion on the supposition that it was allowed by a being infinitely good Tertullian [*adv Marcionem*, 2] compares Cerdon and his followers, in their inability to see one God clearly, to the blear-eyed, to whom one lamp appears manifold Cerdon thus varied from those branches of the Gnostic heresy which held that the Saviour descended in the flesh from Heaven He denied, of course, the resurrection of the body.

He rejected the whole of the Old Testament, of the Gospels, accepted only that of St Luke, and that in part only, he acknowledged parts of some of St Paul's Epistles, but altogether rejected the Acts of the Apostles, and the Apocalypse Origen [*contra Hær* x 19] accuses Cerdon of holding three first causes, ἀγαθὸν, δίκαιον, ὕλην and says his disciples added a fourth, πονηρόν His position that the world was created by an evil principle necessitated a rejection of pleasure, virginity therefore in his system was highly commended, and matrimony despised. No writings have been attributed to him

The name Cerdonians, as a distinct sect, did not long survive, and, except the treatise of Epiphanius against them, their tenets are only disproved in writings against the Marcionites

CERINTHIANS The Cerinthians were the earliest Gnostics of the Judæo-Christian Church Their Judaism was that which refused obedience to the Jerusalem decree regarding circumcision, their Gnosticism included the essential principles of that system, though it was not yet drawn out into a long detail of emanations Thus they held the doctrine of an inferior Demiurge, and of a Christ or Power of God descending upon a man Jesus to form Jesus Christ. Cerinthus stands at the head of those who, being within the Church, adopted Gnosticism, as Simon Magus

[1] To be found at the close of the article on PELAGIANISM [Ussher, *Brit Eccles Antiq* cap ix.]

stands at the head of those who, being without the Church, added to their Gnosticism more or less of Christianity

The undeveloped Gnosticism of Cerinthus points to an early date Cabbalistic Gnosticism was completed by Basilides and Valentinus Basilides probably flourished about A D 120, and Valentinus came to Rome in the pontificate of Hyginus, A D 137-141 [Euseb *Hist Eccl* iv 11], and was then probably aged, for he had heard Theodas, a disciple of St Paul [Clem Alex *Strom* VII xvii 106] But there is stronger evidence for an early date The story of St John meeting Cerinthus in the bath is too well attested to be lightly thrown aside Epiphanius, it is true, names Ebion instead of Cerinthus Mosheim remarks (and he is not credulous of legends) that if the disagreement between Irenæus and Epiphanius is to make us reject this story, the greatest part of ancient history must be laid aside and accused of falsehood Further, Irenæus [*Hær* iii. 11] says expressly that John sought by the proclamation of his gospel to remove Cerinthian errors. Jerome asserts the same [*Proœm. ad Matth*] The Cerinthian heresy was probably, therefore, formed before A.D. 75-85 Again, Cerinthus' connection with the Ebionites leads us to infer that it must have been some time before For it is not doubted that the Ebionites learnt their denial of our Lord's divinity and their partial Gnosticism from Cerinthus, and probably through Ebion [EBIONITES] But the doctrine of celestial emanations, as opposed to the Catholic doctrine of angels, must have been considerably advanced at the time of St Paul's writing to the Colossians, that is, A D 58-63 Ittigius allows that St Paul in that Epistle may refer to Cerinthianism [*Dis* sect. i cap v] We cannot choose but think that at that time Cerinthus had begun to propagate his opinions If so, there is no difficulty in believing that there may be some foundation of truth in Epiphanius' statement that Cerinthus in person opposed St Peter [Acts xi 3], and led the opposition to Gentile liberty at Antioch He may at least have acted then with the Anti-Pauline party, and have afterwards adopted and propagated his Gnosticism These reasons lead to the date A D 60 (the date assigned by Waterland) for this heresy Irenæus is in favour of an early date, for he first describes the Gnostics generally, then [*Hær* i 23] he begins his account of the separate sects with Simon Magus, deriving from him the succession of Menander, Saturninus with Basilides, and Carpocrates Then follow [cap 26] Cerinthus, the Ebionites, the Nicolaitanes It is quite clear that Irenæus described the schools that sprung from Simon Magus, and then recurred to an earlier period for the beginning of the schools which sprung from Cerinthus For to suppose a chronological order throughout would be inconsistent with Irenæus' own statement regarding the design of St John's Gospel. Epiphanius, it seems, misunderstood Irenæus, and forgetting his own statement that Cerinthus opposed St Peter at Jerusalem, makes Cerinthus succeed Carpocrates, as Carpocrates[1] had succeeded Basilides and Valentinus Against this conclusion appears to be Eusebius' authority He refers Menander, the Ebionites, Cerinthus, and the Nicolaitanes to the reign of Trajan, A D. 98-117 But there is good reason to believe that Eusebius is speaking of the outburst of heresies which had for some time been burrowing under ground [Hegesippus in Euseb *H E* iii 32] Menander, a disciple of Simon Magus [Justin M. *First Apology*, ch. 26], requires to be dated earlier The Nicolaitanes also must be dated earlier, for the internal evidence that the Apocalypse is a work of the Judæo-Christian Church is so strong that only the most direct contemporary evidence could set it aside. In the same way Cerinthus may be dated earlier, and Eusebius be understood to speak of a more bold publication of the heresy, or a more definite formation of a sect at the time of Thebuthis Upon the whole therefore we may adopt A D. 60[2] as the date of Cerinthus' heretical teaching. [See Danæus, note on Augustine, *de Hæres* ch viii]

The Judaism of the Cerinthians is not related by the older writers, but it is rendered probable, if not implied, in the classification of them with the Ebionites and Nicolaitanes By Jerome [Ep. *ad August* lxxxix tom ii p 265, ed 1616], Epiphanius [*Hær* xxviii], and Augustine [cap viii], it is told in the usual terms, that circumcision and the observance of the other rites of the law were held to be necessary to salvation "Sic nova confessi sunt," writes Jerome, "ut vetera non amitterent" Cerinthus was circumcised, and appears to have been of Jewish extraction He studied a long time in Egypt, and then removed to Asia, where he formed his sect The Gnostic principles which he taught are given by Irenæus According to this heresy the world was not made by the primary God, but by a certain power far separated from Him, and at a distance from that Principality who is supreme over the universe, and ignorant of Him Who is above all He represented Jesus as not having been born of a virgin, but as being the son of Joseph and Mary according to the ordinary course of human generation, while He was yet nevertheless more righteous, prudent, and wise than other men Moreover, that, after His baptism, Christ descended upon Him in the form of a dove from the Supreme Ruler, and then He proclaimed the unknown Father and performed miracles But that at last Christ departed from Jesus, and then Jesus suffered and rose again, while Christ remained impassable, inasmuch as He was a spiritual being [Iren *adv Hær* i 26] Again, the Cerinthians allege that the Creator was one, but the Father of the Lord another, and that the Son of the carpenter[3] was one, but the Christ from above another, who also con-

[1] But for the earlier date which some assign to Carpocrates, see Burton, *Bampton Lect* note 75, p 481

[2] Waterland gives the date A D 60, v p 184, ed. 1823

[3] "Fabricatoris," usually translated "Creator," but the translation "carpenter" is necessary, for Jesus was said to be the Son of Joseph and Mary, not an Æon from

tinued impassible, descending upon Jesus the Son of the carpenter, and flying back again into His Pleroma, that the beginning was Monogenes, but that Logos was the true son of the Only Begotten, and that the creation of our world was not effected by the Supreme God, but by some power lying far below Him and shut off from communion with the things invisible and ineffable [*ibid* iii 11]

We have here the Supreme Being existing in the Pleroma, not named Bythus, but clearly the same idea, Monogenes, from whom Logos, and an inferior Demiurge There is no mention of other Æons Epiphanius names "angels" as givers of the law and prophets as well as formers of the world [*Hær* xxviii] Theodoret [*Hær fab* ii 3] names "separate powers," and [v 4] ascribes to Cerinthus the holding the same doctrine of angels as Basilides, of which angels Ialdabaoth is the chief These statements may very well be true of the later sect, Irenæus reporting Cerinthus' own tenets It will be remarked that nothing is said of an assertion of the eternity of matter, but this tenet was so closely connected with the notion of an inferior demiurge that perhaps we should not err in ascribing it to Cerinthus

Epiphanius relates that the Cerinthians used the Gospel of St Matthew (mutilated indeed) on account of its genealogy, which proves (they said) that Jesus was born of Joseph and Mary [xxviii 5, and xxx 14] [EBIONITES]

Those who denied the doctrine of a millennium sought to discredit the doctrine by insisting that it had been held by Cerinthus There is little doubt that he did hold the doctrine, which was generally received by the Jews and passed into the Judæo-Christian Church, but that he held it in the sensual form ascribed to him by some is not likely Controversial misrepresentation is probably at the bottom of the charge [Regarding the statements of Caius and Dionysius quoted by Eusebius, *H E* iii 28 see Lardner *Credib* ii 400, art *Caius*, and p 705, art. *Dionysius;* and Routh, *Reliq Sac* ii p 138. See also DICT *of* THEOLOGY, MILLENNIUM] Lardner acquits Cerinthus of immorality [viii 414].

The sect did not last very long, being merged in other Gnostic sects, but the time of its disappearance as a distinct body is not known

CHARURGITÆ [THNEPTOPSYCHITÆ]

CHAZINZARIANS An Armenian sect mentioned by Nicephorus Their name is derived from "Chaza," the Armenian word for the Cross The members of the sect are described as worshippers of the cross, and hence are also called Staurolatræ [Niceph *Hist Eccl* xviii 54]. Demetrius of Cizycus, writing in the seventh century, speaks of the sect as still existing, and says that its adherents were Nestorians in principle, maintaining a dual Personality in Christ instead of two Natures in one Person He also records that they used fermented bread, and wine unmixed with water, in celebrating the Holy Eucharist. [Demetr Cizycens *de Jacobit Hær ac Chatzitzariorum,* in *Bibl Max. Lugd* xii 814]

CHILIASTS [MILLENARIANS]

CHILIONETITÆ. [MILLENARIANS]

CHOREUTÆ [EUCHITES]

CHRISTADELPHIANS A small but arrogant sect of recent origin which owes its rise to a Baptist preacher named Watts, and which claims "to be 'the sect everywhere spoken against,' in the first century, *newly revived*" They adopt the name of Christadelphians, or "Christ's brethren," to distinguish themselves from Christians, whom they consider as apostates from the original religion of Christ "They style their congregations *ecclesias* to distinguish them from the *churches* of the apostasy" Their tenets are much the same as those of the Unitarian or GENERAL BAPTISTS, except that they have in addition a partial acquaintance with and belief in the theory well-known to theologians, that the soul becomes immortal by supernatural regeneration, and is not so by natural birth They profess to believe in "One God, the Eternal Father, dwelling in heaven, in light of glory inconceivable, one universal irradiant Spirit, by which the Father fills all and knows all, and, when He wills, performs all, one Lord Jesus Christ, Son of God, and begotten by the Spirit of the Virgin Mary, put to death for sin, raised from the dead for righteousness, and exalted to the heavens as a Mediator between God and man; man a creature of the ground, under sentence of death because of sin, which is his great enemy—the devil; deliverance from death by resurrection, and bodily glorification at the coming of Christ, and inheritance of the kingdom of God, offered to all men on condition, [1] of believing the glad tidings of Christ's accomplishment at His first appearing, and of His coming manifestation in the earth as King of Israel and Ruler of the whole earth, at the setting up of the kingdom of God, [2] of being immersed in water for His name, and [3] of continuing in well-doing to the end of this probationary career"

The Christadelphians have places of meeting in London, Edinburgh, Birmingham, Swansea, and Oystermouth They have also a growing literature, including several periodicals The following is a copy of the notice-board on one of their meeting-houses, and is given as an illustration of the manner in which they invite persons to join their community —"Christadelphian Synagogue The Christadelphians meet within on Sunday mornings at eleven o'clock for worship and breaking of bread On Sunday evenings at six o'clock for proclaiming the Truth as it is set forth in the writings of Moses and the Prophets, Christ and His Apostles, in contradiction to the writings and teachings of the Clergy of the Church of Rome and her Harlot Daughters the Church of England and Protestant Dissenters On Tuesday and Thursday evenings

the Demiurge Burton translates the word "Creator," but adds a note that Mosheim "thinks this may rather be taken for Joseph the carpenter" [Burton's *Bampton Lect.* 477] at half-past seven for reading and consideration of Scriptural subjects To all of which the Public are respectfully invited All seats free and no collections 'To the Law and to the Testimony If they (the Clergy) speak not according to this Word, it is because they have no light in them' [Isa viii 20]" It is believed that the Christadelphians are an increasing sect. [Thomas' *Who are the Christadelphians?* 1869 *Declaration of the first principles of the Oracles of the Deity, &c. The Christadelphian* Ritchie's *Rel Life of London*, 291]

CHRISTIAN ASSOCIATION When a "religious census" of England and Wales was taken in the year 1851, there were eight congregations which returned themselves under this designation, their aggregate number being given by them at 800 Nothing is known of their principles, and the name does not now appear on the Registrar-General's list of places registered for public worship

CHRISTIAN BRETHREN Some Unitarian Societies in Lancashire and Yorkshire are accustomed to call themselves by this title, but they are not distinguishable from the sect ordinarily known as Unitarians [*Relig of the World*, p 339, ed 1870]

CHRISTIAN CONNEXION. A sect which originated in the beginning of this century in the United States by the union of seceders from other sects—chiefly the Baptists, Methodists, and Presbyterians—who professed to have no earthly leaders and no inspired creed, but to be guided entirely by individual interpretation of Holy Scripture They are exactly analogous to the CHRISTO SACRUM in theory, but are practically undistinguishable from the great body of INDEPENDENTS or "Congregationalists"

CHRISTIAN DISCIPLES An insignificant sect of recent origin, having for its leader an uneducated herb doctor at Wakefield of the name of Hodgson It claims to be part of the American sect of CAMPBELLITES The sect has one place of meeting only, which is called the "Christian Church," in Queen Street, Wakefield

CHRISTIAN ELIASITES [HICKESITES]

CHRISTIAN ISRAELITES A sect founded a few years ago at Wakefield by a follower of Joanna Southcote named John Wroe, who died while on a visit to Australia in the year 1863 At the time of the religious census of 1851 they had three places of meeting in England, and professed to number about 1000 members, but 160 only is the number given as attending the chapels on the enumeration Sunday Wroe pretended to be possessed of a prophetic gift, and taught that the Second Advent was immediately at hand, when God's promises of restoration to Israel would be fulfilled. To this end it was necessary that there should be a great ingathering of Israel, that is of the lost tribes, which was to take place under the leadership of the Christian Israelites, Divinely inspired for the work The sect has a larger body of adherents in Australia than in England, and members of it there pretend to perform miracles Wroe's successors in Australia are, however, charged with imposture and profligacy of no ordinary character, and the sect, such as it is, has assumed a very antichristian character

CHRISTIANS A number of obscure local sects in England and Wales distinguish themselves by the special name of "Christians," as if Christianity was peculiar to them In the census of 1851 there were returned 96 places of worship belonging to sectarians so designated Others to the number of 26 were appropriated to Free-Gospel Christians, Freethinking Christians, New Christians, Original Christians, Primitive Christians, Protestant Christians, and United Christians. Some of these sects still appear on the Registrar-General's list of licensed chapels

CHRISTIANS OF ST JOHN [SABIANS]

CHRISTOLYTÆ [Χριστός λύω] Heretics of this name are mentioned by St. John of Damascus and by Nicetas Choniates, as belonging to the sixth century Their name is derived from their distinguishing tenet that the Divine Nature of Christ was separated from His Human Nature when the latter descended into hell, and that only his Divine Nature ascended into heaven [Nicetas, *Thesaur orthod fid* iv 41]

CHRISTO SACRUM A society for the union of all Christians who professed belief in the Divine Nature of our Lord, and in the redemption of the world by His Passion, which was founded by Jacob Hendrick, a burgomaster of Delft in Holland [A.D. 1797-1801] They met every Sunday for adoration of the greatness of God as manifested in His works of creation, and every Friday to study the principles of revealed religion It numbered at one time two or three thousand members, but soon became extinct.

CHRISTS, FALSE [FALSE CHRISTS]

CHUBB One of the leading sceptics of the last century [A D 1679-1747] He was a self-educated man, and followed the trade of a tallow-chandler, but was a most voluminous writer of Deistical pamphlets, and carried considerable weight with the infidels of his own and the succeeding generation. He denied the Divinity of our Lord, the truth of Scripture miracles, the doctrine of vicarious suffering and intercession, the inspiration of Scripture, the future judgment and everlasting punishment He was a great promoter of infidelity among the middle classes [SCEPTICS DICT. *of* THEOL , DEISM]

CIRCUITORES [CIRCUMCELLIONS]

CIRCUMCELLIONS, CIRCELLIONS, or CIRCUITORES An extremely fanatical section of the Donatists, whose rise has sometimes been placed as early as A D 317, but more generally about twenty-five years later [Tillemont, *Mém* vi p 96] They consisted mainly of the poorer inhabitants of North Africa, who gained their livelihood, as well as their name from their predatory and vagrant habits ("circum cellas"), living from hand to mouth, obtaining food by begging, or, if that failed, by violence, from the various hamlets or houses which lay in their way In later times, as the controversy between the Catholics and the Donatists assumed more and more the character of a civil war, they formed the soldiery, or rather the volunteer or militia bands of the latter, and under the sanction of a religious cause committed every form of outrage, so that they became notorious for their lawlessness Sallying forth under two leaders named Faser and Axid (or Faserus and Maxidus), and assuming as their watchword the motto "Deo Laudes" [St. Aug *contra litteras Petiliani*, ii 146], they everywhere took the part of debtors against their creditors, and of slaves against their masters Their cruel habits are shewn by the fact that every member of these lawless bands was armed with a club, which was called an "Israel," in allusion to the staffs which the Jews held in their hands when they ate the Paschal lamb, and that, besides this habitual use of the club, other modes of injuring their opponents were by degrees resorted to, it being a common practice with them in later days [c A D 405] to put out the eyes of their prisoners with lime and water Their fanaticism was of the most extreme type, for the forms of violent death which they imposed on others were courted by many of the Circumcellions themselves They sought an imaginary martyrdom by suicide, rushing into the fire, hurling themselves headlong from precipices, compelling those whom they met to kill them, or to expect their own death as the penalty for refusing to comply with the strange request Their character is thus summed up by St Augustine, their contemporary as Bishop of Hippo "They are a class of persons idly abstaining from all useful employments, most cruel in putting others to death, and yet with a fanatical contempt of their own lives, ranging up and down the country, and, for the sake of food, surrounding the houses (cellas) of the villagers, whence they have obtained the name of Circumcellions" [Aug *contr Gaudent Donatist Episc* I i. 32] A history of the suppression and final extinction of the Circumcellions would be merely a repetition of the account of the Donatist schism, of which they formed so important a feature. The change from the mild policy of Constantine the Great [A D 324-337] to the harsh measures of Honorius [A D 395-425] was undoubtedly caused by their excesses. When they demolished a church which the first named emperor had erected at Constantina, he contented himself with ordering it to be rebuilt at his own expense, without exacting any penalty from the perpetrators of the mischief Under his successor Constans, commissioners were sent to Africa, Ursacius and Leontius [A D 340], Count Gregory [A D 347], Macarius, and Paulus [A D 348], who attempted a reconciliation by a distribution of alms and presents before resorting to harsher measures It was not till the fifth century, after a decision adverse to Donatism had been pronounced by the imperial legate Marcellinus at the Conference at Carthage [A D 411], that the severe laws of banishment, confiscation, and fine, were permitted to be put in force with their full severity by Honorius The Circumcellions did not become totally extinct till the close of the same century, and in A D. 429 they were sufficiently numerous to be of considerable assistance to Genseric, king of the Vandals, in his desolating expeditions through Africa. [Tillemont's *Mémoires*, vi 147-165. Aug *Opera*, Paris ed 1694, vol ix *passim*. DONATISTS]

The name of Circumcellions is also given to a religious body which existed in Germany in the thirteenth century. Politically they were adherents of Frederick II [A D 1210-1250], and were condemned by Pope Innocent IV at Lyons [A D 1244], at the same time that this emperor was excommunicated But their religious views alone were sufficiently eccentric to have merited the sentence They taught [1] that the Pope was a heretic, [2] that all bishops were guilty of simony, [3] that no priest in mortal sin could validly administer the sacraments, and [4] amid a general abuse of all church teachers and officers, asserted that Frederick II and Conrad ought to be commemorated instead of the Pope.

CIRCUMCISI [PASAGIANS]

CLANCULARS An obscure sect of the Anabaptists in the sixteenth century, who also called themselves "Fratres hortenses" because they were accustomed to meet in gardens Their principles were similar to those of the Quakers, consisting chiefly in the repudiation of outward means of grace, and in the asseveration of an inward spirit which superseded them

CLAUDIANISTS A sect of Donatists whom Primian, the successor of Parmenian in the see of Carthage, received into communion [c A D 391] They are mentioned in Tillemont's *Mémoires*, vi. art 61

CLAUDIUS A heretic of this name is mentioned by Epiphanius Speaking of those who denied the Divine Nature and the Miraculous Conception of our Lord, he says, "Hence Cerinthus and Ebion held Him to be a mere man, as did Merinthus, and Cleobius, or Cleobulus, and Claudius, and Demas, and Hermogenes" [Epiph *Hær* li 6] No other notice of Claudius appears in ecclesiastical writers

CLEMENS SCOTUS was an Irish bishop accused of heresy by St Boniface Winfred, at the second Roman Council, in A D 745, along with the more celebrated Adalbert He was no doubt one of those dioceseless bishops of the ancient Church of Ireland who passed over in numbers to the Continent. These were always regarded with dislike by Rome, which everywhere established diocesan Episcopacy We know nothing of the career of Clemens, except from the letter of Boniface to Pope Zacharias, which contains his accusation According to this, he was entirely free from the fanatical self-exaltation imputed to Adalbert, and far less likely to attract the eyes of the multitude. He was accused of denying the authority of the canons of councils, and of the writings of St Jerome, Augustine, and Gregory, the Fathers who were regarded with the greatest reverence in the Western Church It was also laid to his charge that though he had two sons "in adulterio natos," he asserted that he might still continue in the state of a Christian bishop This can hardly mean anything but that in the eyes of Boniface the marriage of Clemens was an adulterous connection, as that of any bishop would have been It is well known that there was no rule of clerical celibacy in the Irish Church Boniface accuses him still further of bringing in Judaism, by maintaining that it was lawful for a Christian man to marry his brother's widow. As however the Mosaic law only allowed this in case of a man dying without children, it follows either that Clemens went far beyond the Mosaic law, or else that the accusation against him was very loose and general The last thing alleged against him was that he said that Christ in the descent into hell set free all, believers and unbelievers alike, and that he uttered "many other horrible" opinions concerning Divine predestination

For these heresies Boniface, who had already in the Synod of Soissons, in the year 744, caused Clemens to be condemned and silenced, now demanded from the Pope and Council of Rome that he should be imprisoned for life Indeed he seems to have already put him in prison, and at this time to have simply demanded the Pope's sanction of what he had done A severer sentence was passed by the Council upon Clemens than upon his fellow-sufferer Adalbert He was stripped of his sacerdotal office, and laid under an anathema (ab omni sacerdotali officio sit nudatus et anathematis vinculo obligatus) This sentence cannot be termed a just one, since no evidence was given against the accused, as there was in the case of Adalbert, nor was he heard in his own defence. But it was a milder one than Boniface had demanded, and gave no warrant for the imprisonment of Clemens He remained in prison nevertheless, and in the year 747 the mild and just Pope Zacharias vainly interfered to procure a more equitable examination of his case, and that of Adalbert Of the ultimate fate of Clemens we know nothing [ADALBERTINES]

CLEMENTINES. A name given to the adherents or followers of CLEMENS SCOTUS

CLEOBIANS A very early sect of this name is mentioned by Hegesippus, who says they were one of the seven Jewish sects, the Simonians, the Cleobians, the Dositheans, &c. [Euseb. *Hist Eccl.* iv 22] Theodoret names them in a similar connection [Theodor *Hær fab* i 1] Both these authors also assigned their origin to Cleobius, a contemporary of Simon Magus and Menander With their testimony agrees that of the longer Ignatian Epistle to the Trallians, in which we read, "Avoid the branches which spring from the Devil, Simon his first begotten son, and Menander and Basilides; . . . avoid the impure Nicolaitanes, . . avoid also the children of the Evil One, Theodotus and Cleobulus" [Ignat *ad Trall* 11] The Apostolical Constitutions go a little more into detail, making the Apostles say, "But when we went forth among the Gentiles to preach the word of life, then the Devil wrought in the people to send after us false apostles to the corrupting of the word, and they sent forth Cleobius, and joined him with Simon, and these became disciples to one Dositheus, whom despising, they deposed from the chief place" [*Constit Apost.* vi 8] Archbishop Ussher further mentions, in his commentary on the Epistles of Ignatius, an apocryphal letter of the Corinthian Church to St Paul, in which they tell him that Simon and Cleobius had been spreading their dangerous doctrines at Corinth, teaching that the prophets were not to be read, that God was not omnipotent, and denying the resurrection of the dead Beyond these vague notices nothing authentic is known of the Cleobians, who probably retained the name of their founder only for a short time, and then became lost in one of the larger Gnostic family of heresies

CLEOMENES. [NOETIANS]

CLERICI ACEPHALI A term used to designate those clergy who were ordained without cure of souls, by "absolute ordinations" as they were called, and who generally obtained their orders by paying for them, that is by simony. In the year 853 the Council of Pavia passed its 18th and 23rd Canons against them, from which it appears that they were mostly chaplains to noblemen, that they produced much scandal in the Church, and that they disseminated many errors [Harduin, *Concil* v 98]

COCCEIANS A school of theologians which arose in the University of Leyden in the seventeenth century, under the leadership of John Koch, or Cocceius, Professor of Theology there Cocceius was strongly opposed to the mode of interpreting the Scriptures which was adopted by Calvin and Grotius, viewing with special dislike the rationalistic tone of the latter, which regarded the Old Testament as a mere collection of national history and poetry Cocceius maintained that there is a strict unity between the Old and the New Testament, that a proper interpretation of the former makes it full of evangelical revelations, and that the fulness of the Divine Word is such that its language must bear many meanings, suited to many times and persons It became a common saying that Cocceius saw Christ everywhere in the Old Testament, but that Grotius saw him nowhere; a saying which shows how largely the former must have influenced the recoil from that dry literalness of mere scholarship which characterized so many of the Lutheran and Calvinist writers of the seventeenth century The commentaries of Cocceius on Holy Scripture were printed at Amsterdam in A D 1701 in ten folio volumes.

CODDIANI. A local name of the Gnostics Epiphanius thinks that they were so called from the Syriac word Codda, which signifies a dainty side-dish [παροψίς], and that it refers to the Gnostic peculiarities respecting food, especially their habit of feeding apart from others lest they should be polluted with "unclean" meats [Epiph *Hær* xxvi 3]

CŒLICOLÆ. A satirical name bestowed upon the Jews by the Romans in the later days of the Empire. Tacitus mentions with astonishment the fact that they had no images in their cities, and not even inside their temples.

[*Hist* v 5] Juvenal describes them as persons who

"Nil præter nubes et cœli numen adorant"

[*Sat* xiv 97] According to another satirist the Jew is one who

"Et cœli summas advocat auriculas"

[Petronius, *Fr* p 683, li] These taunts may have reference to the pure monotheistic worship of the Jews, and to the narrative of the cloud in the wilderness and on Mount Sinai [Exod xiv xix], but they may also be justified by a relapse of the Jews into those idolatrous habits which led them in old times to make molten images and a grove, and to worship all the host of heaven, and to serve Baal [2 Kings xvii 16] Some such tendency is supposed to be condemned by St Paul in his reference to "the worshipping of angels" [Jerome, in *Col.* ii. 18]

[2] The name is applied to certain heretics who, early in the fifth century, partially relapsed into Judaism, practising circumcision as well as baptism, rejecting the Christian doctrine of the Trinity, and, according to the monotheistic principles of the Jews, worshipping only the God of heaven This is probably the true meaning of their designation of "Cœlicolæ," Sianda's idea that they rendered idolatrous homage to the moon and the stars, or to a certain image supposed to have fallen from heaven and erected at Carthage, being founded on a misinterpretation They are specified for condemnation in three distinct laws in the Theodosian Code [lib xvi tit 5, *de Hæret* leg 43, 44, and tit 8, leg 19], in which they are ranked with the Donatists, Manichæans, and other sectarians, are ordered to return to the Church within a year under pain of having their conventicles forfeited, and all the laws against heretics put in force against them. They are described as a new and audacious sect of Jews, whose doctrines are an unheard of superstition, and who dare like the Donatists to rebaptize all converts from without, a fact which is corroborated by St Augustine [*Ep* 163, *ad Eleusium*, p 284 Bingham, *Antiq* p 950 Baron *Annal ad ann* 60, vol i p 605]

COGLERS. A sect of teetotallers having their origin at Kirdford in Sussex, and also known as "Coplers" A man named Sirgood was the first teacher of the sect, the chief characteristic of which is Antinomianism, its members considering themselves (but not being so considered by their neighbours) to be incapable of committing sin They are said to have a "Book of Cople," in imitation probably of the Mormonites

COLENSO CONTROVERSY [BROAD CHURCHMEN]

COLLEGIANTS. A Dutch sect of an eclectic character founded in A D 1619 by three brothers named John James, Hadrian, and Gisbert van der Kodde, as a refuge from the bitterness of the Calvinist and Arminian controversies of the day. The name is derived from the custom which they had of calling their communities "Colleges," in which they were followed by Spener and the Pietists of Germany

The Collegiants' first place of meeting was at the village of Warmand, the residence of one of the brothers, but they shortly established their headquarters at Rheinberg, near Leyden, and were hence called also "Rheinbergers" They rapidly increased in numbers, and at the present time they still form a considerable body in Holland and Hanover

Their principle from the beginning has been to admit all persons to their society who are willing to acknowledge their belief in the Bible as inspired Scripture, and to take it as the guide for Christian life, but no confession of faith is used, and the widest diversity of opinion is permitted Their form of worship consists of prayer meetings held on Sundays and Wednesdays, at which any men of the community may pray and expound the Scriptures, but there is no regular organization of a ministry among them They recognise the necessity of baptism, which they administer by immersion, and twice a year they have sacramental meetings extending over several days, similar to those of the Scotch Presbyterians

At the end of the seventeenth century the opinions of Spinoza had obtained a strong hold upon the Collegiants, and caused a temporary division of their members into two parties, with separate places of meeting The leader of the Spinozist party was John Bredenburg, a merchant of Rotterdam, and he was opposed by a bookseller of Amsterdam, named Francis Couper, who attained some eminence by a work which he wrote against Bredenburg under the title *Arcana Atheismi detecta* He was also the publisher of the *Bibliotheca Fratrum Polonorum seu Unitariorum.* The two parties were reunited on the death of these two controversialists, and attracted many to their society from other sects during the last century [Picart's *Rel Cerem* vi ed 1737]

COLLUCIANISTS This name was assumed by Arius and by Eusebius of Nicomedia [Theod *Hist Eccl* i 5] to signify that they were in doctrinal agreement with the martyred Lucian, bishop of Antioch There is, however, no evidence that St Lucian really countenanced Arian misbelief [LUCIANISTS]

COLLYRIDIANS An obscure sect of female heretics who lived towards the close of the fourth century They idolized the Blessed Virgin Mary as a goddess, offering little cakes in her honour, and their name is derived from this feature in their worship The Greek κολλύρα, or κολλυρίς, appears to have been a round cake The word does not occur in classical Greek, but it is used in the Septuagint, κολλυρίδα ἄρτου, "to every one a cake of bread" [2 Sam vi. 19]. the Vulgate having, in this passage, "collyridam panis unam." The Greek σεμίδαλις, at Lev vii 12, and ἄρτος, Lev viii 26, are also rendered by "collyrida" in the Vulgate The ordinary shape is said to have resembled the boss of a shield, and the name became applied to a fashion of dressing the hair by Roman ladies, "cujus formæ cum essent scutorum umbilici, et suggestus comarum, matronis Romanis in usu, hic quoque nomen id adeptus est" [Hoffman's *Lexicon, s v Collyra*]

Almost our whole information on the subject of this heresy is derived from a notice in Epiphanius [*Hær* 78, *adv Antidicomarianitas*], and a treatise by him against them [*Hær* 79] In the former passage he speaks of the dishonour cast upon the Blessed Virgin by the Antidicomarianites naturally producing a reaction, which took the form of honour in excess. Some women in Arabia, having gone thither from Thrace, introduced this new fashion (*τοῦτό γε τὸ κενοφώνημα ἐνηνόχασιν, ὡς εἰς ὄνομα τῆς ἀειπαρθένου κολλυρίδα τινὰ ἐπιτελεῖν*), and Epiphanius cites in illustration of such a practice two cases in which women had divine rights paid to them instead of honourable commemoration At Sicimi, afterwards Neapolis, there were some ceremonies in honour of a maiden (*εἰς ὄνομα τῆς Κόρης*), derived from the memory of Jephthah's daughter, of whom it is said in the sacred narrative that a memorial celebration of her death was instituted by the daughters of Israel [Judg xi 40] The Egyptians also paid an unfit honour (*ὑπὲρ τὸ δέον τιμήσαντες Αἰγύπτιοι ἀντὶ Θεοῦ*) to Thermutis, the daughter of Pharaoh who brought up Moses In his book directed specially against the Collyridians, Epiphanius repeats what was said before about this heresy being a sort of reaction It is an instance, he says, of extremes meeting, *μακρότητες ἰσότητες* For the heresies in defect and in excess are equally noxious (*ἴση γὰρ ἐπ' ἀμφοτέραις ταύταις ταῖς αἱρέσεσιν ἡ βλάβη τῶν μὲν κατευτελιζόντων τὴν ἁγίαν Παρθένον, τῶν δὲ πάλιν ὑπὲρ τὸ δέον δοξαζόντων*)

The Collyridians existed, as has been said, chiefly in Arabia The main feature in their rites is thus described Some women used to decorate a four-cornered chariot board (*δίφρον τετράγωνον*), and spread a linen cloth thereupon, and on this they placed bread previously prepared, and offered it in the name of the Virgin They all in the end partook of the bread thus offered These ceremonies took place once only in the year It is conjectured with great probability that the women who practised these rites were simple persons, with considerable heathenism among them, that they had been attached to some such form of worship which was customary among pagans; and that on embracing Christianity they had adapted the old ritual into the new worship The heathen, it is known, offered cakes of some sort to the goddess Venus and to Astarte. [Mosheim, ed Murdock and Soames, i 410, note, where the annotator suggests th[illegible] Mosheim was thinking of that very remarkable passage in Jer. vii 18 References are also made to Walch, *Historie der Ketzereien*, iii 577, &c , and Tillemont, *Mémoires*, xii 83]

The confutation in Epiphanius is directed against two errors of the heresy. [1] The offering to the Blessed Virgin Mary worship which is due only to God She should be honoured, but God alone worshipped (*'Εν τιμῇ ἔστω Μαρία ὁ δὲ Πατὴρ, καὶ Υἱὸς, καὶ ἅγιον Πνεῦμα προσκυνείσθω τὴν Μαρίαν μηδεὶς προσκυνείτω*) [*Hær* 79, 7], and [2] the irregularity of women taking upon themselves the office of the priesthood From abundant instances in the Old Testament it is proved that men alone discharged this duty It is shown that there were indeed orders of deaconesses for certain church work, assisting in the baptism of females and the like, and that these were called *πρεσβύτιδες*, and never *πρεσβυτερίδες*, that women were not even allowed to speak in the Church, much less to discharge any sacrificial function. The entire absence of reference to this heresy after Epiphanius proves that it was very short-lived

It is worthy of notice that the Reformers of the sixteenth century argued from this treatise against the Collyridians that image-worship was abhorrent to the mind of the early Church [Jewel, iii 576, *Park. Soc ed* Bp Forbes' *Instruct Historico-Theologic* iv 8, sec 4 ANTIDICOMARIANITES]

COLORBASIANS, COLARBASIANS, COLOBRASIANS, or COLOBROSIANS These derive their named from Colorbasus, a Gnostic teacher of the second century, condemned by Theodotus, bishop of Pergamus Little is known of his personal history beyond the fact that he was the successor of Menander, Marcus, and Valentinus, with one of whose pupils named Bassus he is identified by Philaster [*Hær* 43] but not by other writers [Theodoret, *Hæi fab* lib 1]. He associated much with Marcus, but surpassed him in the strangeness of some of his doctrines, which were the following: [1] that the scheme of salvation was contained in some mystical way in the Greek alphabet, whence Christ was called Alpha and Omega, [2] that life was to be sought in the seven stars, that is, the seven churches mentioned in the Book of Revelation, [3] that Christ was not a true man, and that there would be no true resurrection of the flesh, [4] that there were two contrary supreme principles of good and evil at work, [5] that baptism should be administered in his own name and not in that of the Trinity [Hippol *Refut omn Hær.* iv 13, vi 50, Philaster, 43, Epiphanius, 251-261, Theodor *Hæi et fab* i. 12]

COLUTHIANS. The followers of Coluthus, or as he is called by Gregory of Nyssa, Acoluthus [Greg Nyss *contr Eunom.* xi] He was one of the Alexandrian clergy at the time when Arius was first coming into prominence, and seceded from the communion of the Patriarch Alexander, about A D 319 through discontent at the moderation which that noble champion of the truth shewed in the first instance towards the rising heresy Thus impatiently rushing into schism, Coluthus began to ordain priests as if he were himself a bishop [Theod *Hist Eccl.* i 4], and then went on to develope a new heresy in the opinion that God is not the author of those just punishments which providentially afflict men [Aug *Hæres* lxv] When Hosius of Cordova was commissioned by Constantine to inquire into the Arian controversy in a council at Alexandria [A D. 324], he was also directed to inquire into the Meletian and Coluthian schisms Coluthus and his adherents were summoned before the council, and on the recantation of their leader most of them followed his example and were with him received back into the communion of the Church The sect was thus very short-lived and was never large in numbers Coluthus died A D 340, having resumed his place as a parish priest in one of the districts of Alexandria He is not to be confused with a Coluthus who subscribed the synodal condemnation of Arius at Alexandria in A D 320 [Epiph *Hæres* lxix. Tillemont, *Mém* vi 219 Neale's *Eastern Ch. Patriarch. Alex* i 116]

COMARISTÆ [NEW PELAGIANS]

COMMUNISTS [BIBLE COMMUNISTS]

COMTISTS [POSITIVISTS.]

CONCORDENSES [CONCOREZENSES]

CONCORENSES [CONCOREZENSES]

CONCORETII [CONCOREZENSES]

CONCOREZENSES The name by which the mediæval Catharists, afterwards more generally called Albigenses, were known in Lombardy in the thirteenth century. Reiner, in his treatise against the Waldenses, says that the Concorezenses spread over the whole of Lombardy, and were more than 500,000 in number [Reiner, *contr Waldens* in *Bible Max.* xxv 269, G]

CONFERENTIE PARTY A section of the Dutch Calvinists or "Dutch Reformed Church" in America, who wished to make their community in the Western Continent entirely dependent on that in Holland. An opposite section, who wished to establish the independence of the American Dutch Calvinists, was called the "Cœtus Party" A bitter dispute on this subject raged among these sectarians from 1737 to 1772, which Dr Brownlee, their historian, speaks of as "a war that waged for fifteen years with unmitigated fury," and during which there were "scenes of animosity, divisions, and actual violence, . tumults and disgraceful scenes, frequently occurring on the holy Sabbath, ministers occasionally assaulted in the pulpits," &c &c

CONFESSIONS [PROTESTANT CONFESSIONS]

CONFORMISTS A name temporarily given to those Puritan clergy who accepted the conditions required by the Act of Uniformity of A D 1661, by conforming to the customs of the Church of England as set forth in the Book of Common Prayer

CONGREGATIONALISTS This name has been recently used by the sect of Independents to express their principle of making each congregation autocephalous [INDEPENDENTS]

CONONITES A section of the sixth century Tritheists, so called after their leader Conon, bishop of Tarsus They differed from the rest of the Tritheists, who were called PHILOPONISTS, on the question of the resurrection of the body, Conon maintaining that the matter only and not the form of bodies is corruptible, and that hence their matter will be revived in the resurrection without being limited by their present form [Niceph *Hist Eccl.* xviii 49 Walch, *Hist. Ketz* viii. 762.]

CONSOLATI. A name assumed by the stricter Catharists of the twelfth and thirteenth centuries [PERFECTI] But it was probably given only to those Catharists who were received among the "Perfects" when in danger of death by means of some rite which was called the "consolamentum," and which appears to have been a form of clinic baptism and imposition of hands [Reiner, *contr Waldens* in *Bibl Max. Lugd* xxv 268 A, 269 F] By this "consolamentum" the recipients were supposed to escape purgatory and pass at once into paradise.

CONSTITUTIONAL ASSOCIATE PRESBYTERY [ANTIBURGHERS]

CONTOREZENSES [CONCOREZENSES]

CONVULSIONARIES The fanatics who obtained this name appeared in France in the second quarter of the eighteenth century and vanished before the commencement of the nineteenth They were a remote product of the posthumous strife which Jansenism [JANSENISTS] had bequeathed to the Roman Catholic world, an immediate effect of the religious ardour which was awakened by the banishment of Quesnel and the suppression of the PORT-ROYALISTS

It was only in an atmosphere which had been highly charged with elements of political and religious discord that the appearance of such a body as the Convulsionaries was a possible phenomenon, but in the France of the Regent Orleans such an atmosphere was found Already, in 1699, the war between Jesuit and Jansenist, which had been appeased by the wisdom of Clement IX and the liberality of Innocent XI, had been rekindled by the publication of Quesnel's *Reflexions Morales.* Louis XIV, in advancing years the willing tool of persecution, at the instigation of Le Tellier, the unworthy successor of Père la Chaise, had both exiled the innocent Quesnel, and expelled from their homes, with revolting accompaniments of cruelty and indecency, the harmless solitaries of Port-Royal The detested opinions, however, far from being extirpated by those harsh measures, continued to give increased trouble to the Church, as the numerous briefs which they elicited from the Holy See abundantly testify At length Clement XI, desirous if possible to quell the scandalous controversy, issued the famous bull "Unigenitus," in which one hundred and one propositions of Quesnel were formally condemned It was fondly hoped that an end would thus have been put to the dispute, but instead of producing the hoped for effect, the publication of the Papal bull was the signal for the rise of a new and hostile Jansenistic sect, which claimed on Quesnel's behalf to appeal from the Pope to a general council The opponents of Rome had always possessed some popularity in France, and the adherents of the appeal were soon a numerous and powerful minority of the Gallican Church They counted among their numbers one cardinal (De Noailles), and at least three bishops, besides other high dignitaries and learned doctors At this juncture Louis XIV, the main support of the Jesuitical party, died Neither the Regent

Orleans nor his favourite Dubois cared to intermeddle with the contending factions. The Appellants had besides a certain popular political value, which the Government was unwilling to discredit, and some interest at the Regent's Court. Under these singularly favourable circumstances the faction just contrived to hold its own against the Roman party. But the Pope's friends were not inactive. They intrigued with the government of the Regent, they permitted the installation of Dubois, though a laic and of infamous character, on the throne of the Archbishop of Cambray, and subsequently procured for him a cardinal's hat on condition of the enforcement of the acceptance of the "Unigenitus" by the French episcopacy. Dubois died, however, soon after the last bribe was received, and after his death the French Government either could not or would not assist them. That these intrigues were unsuccessful must in part have been due to the watchfulness and anxiety of the Appellant party, who were painfully conscious of their own weakness.

Such being the state of affairs in 1727, there died in that year at Paris, in the parish of St Médard (a dependency of Saint Geneviève), on the southern side of the Seine, a popular preacher of the Appellants named Pâris. He was the son of a man of ample means who was a Parisian, and a member of the Parlement of the City. In an access of devotion he had abandoned his possessions to his younger brother, had taken deacon's orders, and had become celebrated for his charities and piety. On May the 1st, 1727, the deacon Pâris died, having only just previous to his decease published an eloquent protest against the injustice of the "Unigenitus." On the 3rd of May he was buried in the cemetery of Saint Médard. His well-known character for piety and eloquence attracted a large number of admiring mourners to the funeral. The cemetery was thronged, both on the day of the interment and during the week which followed. Suddenly a rumour arose that a miraculous convulsion had taken place in the body of a sick and deformed person (it was said to have been followed by a miraculous cure of the disease) at the deacon's grave. Persons subject to epileptic or other seizures crowded to the cemetery. The grave of the eloquent Appellant was thronged by a crowd of excited sympathizers. Again some persons were seized with convulsions. Gradually the fame of the new shrine was established; it was thought to be the grave of a saint, whose bones, like Elisha's, had miraculous life-giving powers. The Cardinal Noailles, desirous that the Appellant cause should benefit by the enthusiasm excited, was eager to take advantage of the accident. He wisely directed all cures to be registered, thus at once increasing the credibility and the fame of the new miracles. This specious appearance of fairness did not fail of effect; more and more surprising phenomena recurring daily. The miracles, which had at first been simply involuntary convulsions, were soon produced at will, and the powers by which the crippled and paralytic had been restored were now vested in persons who joined to them the gifts of prophecy and of universal healing. It is worth noting that the famous Convulsionaries in whose persons miracles were worked were nearly all women. "La petite Lepère," a child of seven years of age, "Marguerite Thibaut," "Marie Couroneau," "Louise Coizin," "Louise Hardouin," "Françoise Duchesne," and "Marie Sonnet," are the most celebrated names. It is to be noted, also, that most of them were poor, all of them ignorant. Bishops, great lords, judges, and advocates visited the tomb with veneration or worship, but among the lower classes only do we find the personal arrogation of miraculous powers.

By 1730 the delusion had risen to such a pitch as to attract the attention and remonstrance of the Government, but it was not until nearly two years later, after a delay which is simply unaccountable, that the executive interfered. The cemetery was closed, and a royal guard stationed at the gates. A few days after this was done an inscription was found upon the doors to the following effect:—

> "De par le roi défense a Dieu
> De faire miracle en ce lieu."

Expelled from the cemetery, the Convulsionaries found shelter in the great houses of the adherents of the Appeal, and, in the privacy of their new life, they developed all the latent powers of human self-delusion. They prophesied, they worked cures, they inflicted the most frightful tortures upon themselves, and they obtained a singular facility in producing or simulating the symptoms of catalepsy, hysteria and convulsion. As their numbers increased they began to divide themselves into groups, named after their respective functions in the performance of miracles or the infliction or endurance of torture. Such are the titles "Vaillantistes," "Secouristes," "Discernans," "Figuristes, "Melangistes," &c, which they adopted. Their principal performances were divided into two parts, "Les grands Secours," and "Les petits Secours," the great and the little aids to the work of God. "Les grands Secours" consisted of the torture or exercise of the "chenet" or burning andiron, "the buche" or beam, the "caillou" or flint rock, the "broche" or spit, while the scourge seems to have served for the principal instrument in "Les petits." In these hideous exercises a woman named Marie Sonnet, surnamed "La Sœur de feu," was the most accomplished performer. She was in the habit first of undergoing with cheerfulness the scorching infliction of the "chenet," afterwards, upon rising from this bed of torture, she used to cry to the brother Convulsionaries who assisted at these horrid mysteries "Sucre d'orge, sucre d'orge." When she uttered these cries a pointed beam was brought to her, and placed upright on the ground. On this the wretched woman would fling herself, and, resting the middle part of her spine on the sharp end of the pole, she would remain with her feet and head hanging downwards for a considerable period. As soon as this "pose" was accomplished, her cries for a new and more appalling torture recommenced, which she besought the assistants to give her under the designation of "biscuit."

Upon this further demand, an enormous stone weighing fifty pounds was dropped from the ceiling of the room upon the convulsed form of the woman, inflicting a frightful blow upon her chest The stone was then withdrawn by means of a cord and pulley, and the blow repeated at short intervals, until the physical fatigue of the assistants or the weariness of the spectators compelled the cessation of the torture

Despite the incredible nature of these practices, their authenticity is beyond all question, and attested by the evidence of friends and foes alike, nor indeed were the tortures that have been detailed by any means the most cruel or objectionable of these Colyttian rites The scandal caused by their performance (doubtless exaggerated by admiration and hatred) at length became intolerable The wiser Appellants saw the danger of these exhibitions, and seceded from the Convulsionary faction The Jesuits exerted the whole force of their powerful organization to suppress these hated relics of Jansenism The philosophers ridiculed their supernatural pretensions The Society of Jesus and the author of *La Religieuse* are for once to be found fighting on the same side Yet the hold which the Convulsionary delusion had on the popular mind was considerable, for when D'Alembert, consulted as to the best means of discrediting these miracles, advised a performance of the simpler of them at the theatres, the Government, represented by D'Argenson, fearful of an émeute, at once declined the suggestion, preferring the safer means offered by a strict law of prohibition By a rigorous infliction of penalties and an unsparing use of "lettres de cachet," all the more important personages who had lent their names to strengthen the Convulsionary cause were quietly removed The less devoted Convulsionaries meanwhile gradually deserted the failing party, savants at the same time described the material character of the phenomenon to the educated world, while the necessity of complete secresy from the police made proselytism impossible, and rendered the losses of the community almost irreparable. Gradually the lower classes, thus left alone, tired of their folly By the middle of the eighteenth century the sect was discredited, before the era of the Revolution it had disappeared, and in that gigantic cataclysm all traces of its existence, if any then remained, were swept away In 1772, however, the year of the publication of the *Encyclopédie*, the continued existence of these fanatics still calls forth the scorn and indignation of Diderot The utmost period of the life of the Convulsionary sect is sixty years

Literature of the Convulsionaries —The most remarkable original book on this subject is the work of one Carré de Montgeron, who aspired to be the St Paul of the Convulsionaries A man of the world, a Conseiller de Parlement, a sceptic and a debauchee, he was suddenly converted by the spectacle of a miraculous cure, and became a bigoted Convulsionary His book, which is copiously illustrated in the manner of the century, is entitled *La vérité des miracles opérés à l'intercession de M de Paris et autres Appellans demontrée contre M l'Archevêque de Sens* He presented a copy to Louis XV, but this homage did not avail him, for he was imprisoned for complicity with the sect, and died in confinement A most interesting account of a Convulsionary crucifixion by an eyewitness and a disbeliever is to be found in Baron H C Von Gleichen's *Denkwurdigkeiten* Friedrich Bulau's *Geheime Geschichten und Rathselhaften Menschen*, Lanfrey's *L'Eglise et les Philosophes du 18me siècle*, and the Abbé Duvernel's work entitled *l'Histoire de la Sorbonne dans laquelle on voit l'influence de la Theologie sur l'ordre social* may also be consulted

COPLERS [COGLERS]

COPTS The Jacobite natives of Egypt, who have almost entirely supplanted the orthodox and once flourishing Church of St Mark They have thirteen Bishops and a Patriarch, the latter being nominally the Patriarch of Alexandria, but residing at Cairo They have also twenty-six monasteries in Upper and Lower Egypt The Coptic Church at Alexandria is said to cover the site of St Mark's martyrdom, and his head is supposed to be preserved there. An intimate communion is kept up between the Coptic Jacobites and the Church of Abyssinia, the Patriarch of the former nominating the Abuna or Patriarch of the latter on every vacancy Their Liturgy is a Jacobite version of that of St Basil, and is thus a representative of the primitive Liturgy of St Mark It is still used in the ancient Coptic language, which is now understood neither by the people nor the clergy, but the Scripture lections which are said in the services are afterwards translated to the people in Arabic. The number of Coptic Christians is supposed to be about 150,000 [JACOBITES. Neale's *Eastern Ch Introd* i. 117]

CORACION [NEPOS]

CORNARISTS A Dutch sect of the followers of Theodore Coornhart, or Cornarus, secretary to the States of Holland at the end of the sixteenth century Cornarus wrote against the Calvinistic doctrine of absolute decrees, and Arminius, who was set to refute his writings, became one of his converts The Cornarists were afterwards absorbed into the sect of ARMINIANS.

COROPITÆ [CIRCUMCELLIONS]

CORPIANI A local name for the Gnostics Probably it is a corruption of "Scorpiani," which is said to have been found in some MSS by Casaubon [Ittig *de Hæresiarch*, II. ix 11] In his notes on Tertullian, Pamelius suggests that his treatise "Scorpiacus" was so called because it was written as an antidote to the poison of a heretic named Scorpianus Epiphanius compares the many sects of the Gnostics to the articulations of the scorpion [Epiphan *Hær* xxxi 38]

CORRUPTICOLÆ. [PHTHARTOLATRÆ]

COTILIANI [COLUTHIANS]

COTOPITES, or COTHOPITHÆ An African name for the Circumcellions It is probably equivalent to the Latin "Agrestes," rustics or vagrants [Isidore, *Orig* viii 5, 53 Honorius. Aug *de Hæres* 69]

COUNTER REMONSTRANTS. [GOMARISTS.]

COVENANTERS. Those who bound themselves by "a Solemn League and Covenant" to substitute the Presbyterian sect for the Church in the reign of Charles I.

The document originally used for the purpose of subscription by those who were seeking this object was one which had been concocted in Scotland as "a Confession of Faith" in the year 1580, and revived under the name of "The National Covenant" in 1638 It was first set forth by the Scottish Privy Council and the General Assembly, and general subscription was enforced in the years 1581, 1590, 1638 and 1640 In the latter year it was ratified by an Act of Parliament, and it was subscribed by Charles II at Spey on June 23rd, 1650, and at Scone on January 1st, 1651 The "National Covenant" in this original form was intended only for Scotland It begins with a wordy protest against "Papistry," "the Roman Antichrist," "his five bastard Sacraments," "his absolute necessity of baptism," "his blasphemous opinion of transubstantiation or real presence of Christ's body in the elements," "his profane sacrifice for sins of the dead and the quick," "his blasphemous litany," "his three solemn vows with shavellings of sundry sorts, his erroneous and bloody decrees made at Trent, with all the subscribers or approvers of that cruel and bloody band, conjured against the Kirk of God" It then goes on to recite and enforce a number of Acts of the Scottish Parliament, which "ordain all Papists and priests to be punished with manifold civil and ecclesiastical pains, as adversaries to God's true religion," together with the "spreaders and makers of books or libels, or letters or writs of that nature," and "all sayers, wilful hearers, and concealers of the mass, the maintainers and resetters of the priests, Jesuits, trafficking Papists," who are "to be punished without any exception or restriction," and if they "go to crosses" or observe "the festival days of saints," are "to be punished for the second fault as 'idolaters'" It then goes on to order that "none shall be reputed as loyal and faithful subjects to our sovereign Lord, or his authority, but be punishable as rebellers and gainstanders of the same, who shall not give their confession and make their profession of the said true religion."

The "National Covenant" then closes with a very long oath, taken "before God, His angels, and the world"—called in the Act of Assembly of August 30th, 1639, sess 23, "our great oath" —covenanting to perform all that is required by the document so sworn to and subscribed

The "Solemn League and Covenant" was aimed at the Church of England, under the general name of "prelacy," as well as at "the Roman Antichrist" It also was of Scottish origin, and the terms of it are even more outrageously intolerant than those of the previous one Its history is as follows When the Civil War began, the Scottish Presbyterians endeavoured to extend their own "National Covenant" of 1580 and 1638 to the English people, the General Assembly writing to the English Parliament on August 3rd, 1643, to urge what they called a thorough reformation, with one Confession of Faith, one Directory of Worship, one public Catechism, and one form of Church government This application proving ineffectual at the time, a petition in similar terms was sent by the Assembly to the King on January 4th, 1642-3, and this was now accompanied by propositions embodying the same requests, which were presented to Charles I by the Commissioners of the Parliament as he was walking in the Broad Walk of Christ Church, Oxford. The King and his Council refused to grant what was desired, and sent a reply, in which the following sentence is to be found, shewing (as subsequent events have proved) how much better the Royalists had felt the pulse of the English people than had the Puritans "Nor are you a little mistaken if either you believe the generality of this nation to desire a change of Church government, or that most of those who desire it, desire by it to introduce that which you only esteem a reformation, but are as unwilling to what you call the yoke of Christ, and obedience to the Gospel, as those whom you call profane and worldly men, and so equally averse both to Episcopacy and Presbytery" In the following summer the WESTMINSTER ASSEMBLY of Divines was convened by the Parliament, but without any authority from the Crown It met on July 1st, 1643, and was a packed assembly of Presbyterians, the few Episcopalians and Independents who had been summoned being utterly powerless on a division

The Westminster Assembly immediately wrote to the General Assembly of Scotland, requesting their assistance to "strengthen them in standing up against Antichrist," their letter accompanying the request for armed assistance which was sent by the Parliament The Scottish Government and Divines immediately proposed that the English nation should adopt the Scottish "National Covenant" The English Commissioners objected to this, and proposed a civil "League" or treaty between the two nations. In the end a nominal compromise was effected, in which the astute Scotch easily got the better of the unstatesmanlike English rulers of the day, a new Covenant being framed and approved by the General Assembly on August 17th, 1643, to which the double name was given of "a Solemn League and Covenant," but which related entirely to the abolition of the English system of Church government and the establishment of Scottish Presbyterianism in its place This Covenant was presented to the Westminster Assembly on September 1st, 1643 It consisted of a preamble, six articles, and the enacting or covenanting clause, and was adopted by the Assembly and the House of Commons—with an explanatory parenthesis added after the word "prelacy"—on September 25th, 1643, in St Margaret's Church, under the shadow of Westminster Abbey All those present lifted up their hands to signify their assent to it, and then going up in turn to the chancel, affixed their names to the parchment on which it was written.

The force of the "Solemn League and Covenant" was contained in the first, second, and fourth articles, which are as follows —

"I That we shall sincerely, really, and constantly, through the grace of God, endeavour, in our several places and callings, the preservation of the reformed religion in the Church of Scotland, in doctrine, worship, discipline, and government, against our common enemies, the reformation of religion in the kingdoms of England and Ireland, in doctrine, worship, discipline, and government, according to the Word of God, and the example of the best reformed Churches, and shall endeavour to bring the Churches of God in the three kingdoms to the nearest conjunction and uniformity in religion, confession of faith, form of church government, directory for worship and catechizing, that we and our posterity after us may as brethren live in faith and love, and the Lord may delight to dwell in the midst of us

"II That we shall in like manner, without respect of persons, endeavour the extirpation of Popery, Prelacy (that is, Church government by Archbishops, Bishops, their Chancellors and Commissaries, Deans, Deans and Chapters, Archdeacons, and all other ecclesiastical officers depending on that hierarchy), superstition, heresy, schism, profaneness, and whatever shall be found to be contrary to sound doctrine and the power of godliness, lest we partake in other men's sins, and thereby be in danger to receive of their plagues, and that the Lord may be one, and His Name one, in the three kingdoms

"IV We shall also, with all faithfulness, endeavour the discovery of all such as have been or shall be incendiaries, malignants, or evil instruments, by hindering the reformation of religion, dividing the King from his people, or one of the kingdoms from another, or making any faction or parties amongst the people, contrary to this League and Covenant, that they may be brought to public trial, and receive condign punishment, as the degree of their offences shall require or deserve, or the supreme judicatories of both kingdoms respectively, or others having power from them for that effect, shall judge convenient"

This new Covenant was ratified by an Act of the Scottish Parliament on July 15th, 1644, and again in 1649 It was sent to the justices of the peace and other influential persons in every parish in England, and during the reign of terror which followed multitudes were forced to subscribe to it Copies of it are still to be found here and there in the parish registers—*e g* at Houghton-le-Spring, near Durham, and at Over, near Cambridge —to which the names and marks of the parishioners are affixed, and which are a standing witness to the industrious energy of the Presbyterians when endeavouring to carry their Scottish innovations into every corner of England Charles II signed it in Scotland, and as King of Scotland, at the same time that he signed the "National Covenant," in 1650 and 1651.

At the Restoration in 1661, the Solemn League and Covenant, which had long been an object of contempt, was altogether set aside in England, but it continues to this day (as well as the National Covenant) to be one of the authoritative formularies of the Kirk of Scotland, being as regularly set forth by the "Publishers of Bibles, Testaments, Prayer and Psalms Books, Confessions of Faith, Catechisms, &c, by Royal Authority" as the Thirty nine Articles of the Church of England, and bound in one volume with the "Confession of Faith" and the "Larger" and "Shorter Catechism" It has never, however, been formally renewed by the General Assembly, and may be supposed to be in abeyance. The refusal of the Assembly to renew it at the time of the Revolution Settlement of A D 1688 caused the secession of the CAMERONIANS, or Reformed Presbyterians, among whom it is still a received dogma that only a "covenanted" sovereign has any right to the throne of the United Kingdoms of England and Scotland

No more intolerant body of religionists ever existed than the Covenanters The school of historical romancists has given a turn to their later history in Scotland which has invested them with a false colouring, and has thus won for them great sympathy among superficial readers, but in reality the spirit of the Covenanters was that of most bitter and unscrupulous persecutors, they were deadly foes to the religious liberty of any but those of their own faction, and it was only the want of power which (happily for England) made this Scottish aggression comparatively harmless [Rushworth's *Hist. Collect* Clarendon's *Hist Rebell. Confessions of Faith*, &c, Glasgow, 1844]

COZARENSES [CONCOREZENSES]

CREATICOLÆ [CTISTOLATRÆ]

CREATIONISTS A controversial name for that school of Divines which maintains the theory that each soul is a separate creation of God infused into the unborn child This theory is opposed to that of Traducianism, which is that the soul is derived, like the body, from the parents. St Jerome, St Leo, St Anselm, Peter Lombard. and Thomas Aquinas, were of the Creationist school, and although there are many great names among the supporters of the opposite theory, the Creationist view is now generally regarded as orthodox [DICT *of* THEOL, CREATIONISM]

CREDENTES A name assumed by the Catharists of the twelfth and thirteenth centuries Reinerius speaks of it as if, like some modern religionists, they generally called themselves by the name of "Believers" [Reiner *contr Waldens* in *Bibl. Max. Lugd* xxv 269, G]

CRISPITES. This name was used at the end of the seventeenth and in the eighteenth century, to designate those dissenters of various sects who adopted the extreme Antinomian opinions of Dr Tobias Crisp He was a clergyman of good family, educated at Eton and Balliol College, Oxford, and Rector of Brinkworth in Wiltshire from 1627 until his death at the early age of forty-two in the year 1642 Having attracted some attention by his Antinomian preaching, he was afterwards (when driven to London by the outbreak of the civil war) involved in controversy with Baxter, Howe, Flavel, and other Puritan Divines, but in the midst of this controversy he died After his decease three volumes of sermons were published from his notes, but they did not at the time obtain much notice, although the Westminster Assembly of Divines proposed to have them publicly burnt. But after the Revolution in 1690, the sermons were republished in a quarto volume by the son of Dr. Crisp, at a time when the Socinian controversy was being actively carried on, the names of twelve Independent ministers being prefixed as approving and recommending the book "By the means of this book," says Nelson, "thus recommended and authorized, the poison of Antinomianism soon spread, not only in the country, but infected this great city to that degree that the more sober of the Presbyterian ministers were scarce able to preach a sermon wherein either hope was arrested by conditional promises, or the fear of sin was pressed by Divine threatenings, but they were immediately censured and condemned as enemies of Christ and of free grace, and especially were cried out against by many of the Anabaptists and Independents" The sermons were answered by Dr Daniel Williams, the founder of the Dissenters' Library in Redcross Street, in a volume entitled *Gospel Truth Stated and Vindicated*, and published in 1692 Further controversy arose between the supporters of Dr Williams and the Antinomian party, and an appeal was made to Bishop Bull, whose *Harmonia Apostolica* contains a full refutation of Antinomianism The sermons of Crisp were again republished by Dr. Gill in 1745, and are still a great authority among the Antinomian school of Dissenters [Nelson's *Life of Bishop Bull*, ch xlviii]

CRYPTO-CALVINISTS A name applied to the followers of Melanchthon by the Lutherans, on account of their supposed secret sympathy with the doctrines of Calvin, especially with his theory of the Holy Eucharist [PHILIPPISTS]

CTISTOLATRÆ A name compounded of a Greek word which was used in an ecclesiastical sense to designate a nature or being that is created (κτιστός), and of a word signifying Divine worship (λατρεία) Such "creature-worshippers" the APHTHARTODOCETÆ declared the opponents of their heresy were, and it was only by them that the designation was used [SEVERIANISTS]

CUBRICUS A name by which Manes, the founder of the Manichee heresy, was also known [Epiph *Hær* lxvi 4.]

CULDEES. An ancient religious order in Ireland and North Britain Much research has been spent upon the derivation of the name, some supposing it to have come from the Gaelic *Kill*, a cell, and *Dee*, a house, and to mean the dwellers in the cell-house There is nothing however known of the habits of the Culdees which should entitle them to such an appellation, their tendency having been to secularize religious offices and endowments rather than to keep up regular strictness of life The true origin of the name is no doubt that which is pointed out by Braun [*De Culdeis*, 1840], and by Dr Reeves, who derive it from the Celtic *Cele-dé*, Servus Dei, an appellation not uncommon among the regular orders, and which was afterwards corrected in the Pope's style into *Servus Servorum Dei* [see Burton's *Hist of Scotland*, vol ii p 7] In Latin originals they are called Keledei, and in old Scotch Kyldees The forms Culdei and Colidei, worshippers of God, first occur in later writers, such as Giraldus Cambrensis (in the twelfth century), and seem to have arisen from the desire to suggest a Latin derivation for a word, the true origin of which was forgotten

The history of the Culdees has acquired a factitious importance through the controversy in the seventeenth century between the Presbyterians and Episcopalians, the former party asserting them to have been of extreme antiquity, and addicted to the Presbyterian form of Church government, the latter denying both these positions It may be confidently affirmed that there is no extant evidence of the extreme antiquity of the Culdees as a wide-spread and influential religious organization There is no warrant for connecting them with St Columba and his mission at Iona, nor are they named by Adamnan in his life of that saint, though it is true that when in the ninth century the ecclesiastical supremacy of Iona was transferred to Dunkeld, the latter establishment is mentioned at a still later period as belonging to Culdees If they had been numerous in the eighth or ninth centuries, they could hardly have escaped the notice of Bede or of Nennius, by neither of whom they are mentioned, nor indeed by any historian for some hundreds of years after Nor, whenever they occur in Scotland, are they found in any of the old west-lying settlements of the Scots, who came from Ireland, but always in the country of the Picts, the east of Scotland; and generally in some connection with the great see of St. Andrews A leaf in the Register of St Andrews, written about 1130, records that the son of the last king of the Picts gave an island in Lochleven to the Culdee hermits serving God there. These Culdees were under an abbot, and about the year 1090 they gave up their island to the bishop of St Andrews, and a few years later were suppressed and replaced by canons regular [Chalmers' *Encyclop* s v]. The Culdees of St Andrews itself were probably as ancient as, and more important than, those of Lochleven, but we have no distinct notice of them until long after the time when St. Andrews had become a diocesan see, which began to be about A D 850 A hundred years after that, in A D 943, Constantine III, King of the Scots, is said to have voluntarily abdicated, and to have become abbot of the Culdees of St Andrews In the twelfth century, under the influence of the royal Saint Margaret and her sons Edgar and Alexander, the various establishments of the Culdees in Scotland, after a vain struggle to preserve their peculiar rights, were absorbed into the system of diocesan Episcopacy which was extended by Rome over every part of Europe It was their extinction which procured them what notice they have in the scanty records of that age, and their antiquity can only be conjecturally estimated from the firmness with which they resisted change The account of their long struggle at headquarters in St Andrews is the chief memorial that we have of them.

It is related in the Durham Chronicle [Twysden's *Decem Scriptores*] that in the year 1108, Turgot, prior of Durham, was made bishop of St Andrews, and that in his time all the right of the Culdees throughout the kingdom of Scotland passed from them to the bishopric of St Andrews "totum jus Keledeorum per totum regnum Scotiæ transivit in Episcopatum St. Andreæ" [Ussher, *de Prim* p. 1032] What this right might be has been the subject of much controversy, but there can scarcely be any doubt that it was the right of confirming the election of all the bishops in Scotland, which they possessed as dean and chapter of the metropolitan see of St. Andrews Of this right, the first attempt to deprive them was made at the election of Turgot At that time there were two parties in St Andrews the old foundation of the Culdees, consisting of a prior and twelve brethren, who performed divine service as clerical vicars and the bishop and new representatives of offices which under the Culdees had passed into the hands of laymen, such as that of abbot It was the object of the kings under papal influence to displace the former party and fill their room by canons regular So tenacious however were the Culdees, that notwithstanding a succession of royal ordinances and papal decrees, they kept their ground, and exerted their peculiar elective right, to the middle of the fourteenth century Thus, in 1297, they opposed the election of Lamberton to St. Andrews, who had been chosen by the canons, and their provost vainly appealed to Rome [Ussher, *de Prim* p 659] On that occasion it is asserted in the Scotichronicon [lib vi] that "omne jus deinceps Keldeis abrogatum," but they were not finally excluded from taking part in the election of bishops before 1332, from which time their name never occurs in records, their ancient corporation being changed into a provostry under the title of "præpositum ecclesiæ beatæ Mariæ civitatis Sancti Andreæ," which after the Reformation was vested in the Crown [Reeves' *Culdees*, 38, Burton's *Scotland*, ii p 31]

In this way the Culdees throughout Scotland appear to have been absorbed or transformed during the great Catholic revival of the twelfth century Some of their establishments were important enough to be turned into bishoprics, as St. Andrews and Dunkeld, with chapters of secular canons, others were replanted with Augustinian canons regular, others again were gradually resolved into parishes Far from manifesting sectarian rigour and purity, they present the aspect of a decayed and corrupt corporation, clinging to its temporalities, and settling into a secularization which was arrested by the spiritual strength of papal Catholicism. [A list of the establishments of the Culdees in Scotland, in which the struggle at St Andrews was uniformly repeated, may be found in Chalmers' *Encyclopædia*, *s v*]

Authentic records of the Culdees of Ireland are singularly scanty An abbot and bishop in the North of Ireland, who wrote a metrical calendar of Irish saints about the year 800, bears in ancient chronicles the name of Ængus the Ceile-De And in Irish annals of undoubted authority it is recorded that in 919 "a Ceile-De came across the sea westward to establish laws in Ireland" The annals of Ulster record that, in 920, Armagh was plundered by Godfrey, son of Ivor the Dane, but that he spared the oratories with the Culdees and the sick. These Culdees of Armagh, like those of St Andrews, seem to have been the dean and chapter of the Church, and were compelled to give place to canons of later institution, but yet were allowed to continue in the inferior capacity of vicars choral Ussher mentions that the vicars choral of Armagh, and those of the collegiate Church of Cluanynish [Clones], were called Colidei in his day, and the chief of them, who was called their prior, served as precentor [*de Primord* p. 657] Ussher also produces a sentence of an archbishop of Armagh in the year 1445, to the effect that the office of prior or of an inferior Culdee not being accounted a cure of souls, may be held with any other benefice, provided that the holder keep his due residence in the Church of Armagh, and this sentence is expressly said to be founded on the chronologies of the holy Fathers and the Year Books of former archbishops (Sanctorum Patrum antiquis chronicis et prædecessorum Libris Annalibus perscrutatis) [*de Primor* p 637] A papal brief of the year 1447 declared, to the same effect, that the priorate of the college of secular priests called Colidei was not a benefice but a simple office without cure [*ibid*] There were about seven other establishments of Culdees in Ireland besides these; but no writer mentions any of them before Giraldus Cambrensis, who speaks of the Cœlicolæ or Colidei of an island called Insula Viventium, of Tipperary, who devoutly served a chapel there [Girald C, Ussher, *de Primord* p 637] The same writer affords the solitary notice which remains of Culdees in Wales He speaks of the little island of Bardsey in North Wales as inhabited in his own time by a set of very religious monks named Cœlibes or Colidei [*ibid*].

In England there is no trace of them, except that the canons of St Peter's at York were called Culdees in the reign of Æthelstan in the first half of the tenth century, and that a suspected charter of Æthelred, in the year 1005, speaks of the canons of English cathedrals generally as "cultores clerici," a term of doubtful import.

It will be seen from the scantiness of these records how little can be concluded concerning the manners and institutions of the Culdees As monks they were under the government of abbots, not of bishops, and in this were nothing different from other monastic orders. But some of their abbots may have borne the title of bishops, and have thus been bishops without dioceses, contrary to the law of the Church There is no proof of this, though it is possible enough, since the Culdees may be held to have belonged to the ancient British or Scots' Church, in which no doubt dioceseless bishops abounded This is a slender foundation for the theory of the Presbyterian controversialists, that the Culdees were the upholders of the primitive simplicity of Church government, by monks and priests, rejecting diocesan Episcopacy, clerical celibacy, and all later abuses, until they were finally overpowered by the frauds of Rome Enquiry has completely upset this view, and it now finds no support among archæologists Yet, as it occasioned a violent controversy in the seventeenth century, it may be worth while to mention the authorities from which it arose

John of Fordoun, a monk of the fourteenth century, author of the *Scotichronicon* of obsolete authority, was the first to assert that the Scots were originally governed by monks and priests alone, and that in this they followed the usage of the primitive Church [*Scotichron* iii 8] He was followed by John Major the Sorbonnist [*Hist Scot* ii 2], who, like the monk of Fordoun himself, fell into the error of confounding Scotland, the ancient name of Ireland, with the present Scotland In a similar way Hector Boetius [*Scot Hist* i 6, quoted by Ussher, *de Prim* p 636] had improved his account by making these monks and priests Culdees, and giving that account of their organization which has been the foundation of the Presbyterian theory He says that they were called for their piety "cultores Dei," under which title they were recognised by all the people, that they came in the third century; that they elected among themselves a chief priest, who had power in things belonging to God, and that he was for many years after known as Episcopus Scotorum, or bishop of the Scots He alleges for this the authority of ancient annals, but in his preface he owns that the most ancient annalist that he had seen was Veremundus, who wrote in the last half of the eleventh century To say no more, the whole story of the Scots Church being governed by monks and priests in the third century is disproved by the fact that there were no monks at all in the Western Church at that time, a difficulty which Dempster the Jesuit tries to get over by supposing that the Culdees of Boetius were canons regular [Ussher, *de Prim* 637] Selden was the first who brought the Culdees into the Presbyterian controversy, by his celebrated preface to Twysden's *Historiæ Anglicanæ Decem Scriptores*, London, 1652

The best account of the Scots Culdees is in Grub's *Ecclesiastical Hist of Scotland*, of the Irish Culdees, in Dr. Reeve's *Dissertation* in the *Proceedings of the Royal Irish Academy*, 1860

CUMBERLAND PRESBYTERIANS An American sect which originated in some "revivals" that took place among the Presbyterians of Cumberland County in Kentucky about the year 1800, and which constituted itself a separate community by formal separation from the general body of the American Presbyterians on February 4th, 1810 The cause of separation was the refusal of the governing body of the Presbyterians to recognise as ministers certain persons who had been admitted to their office without the usual education and preparation, and who also repudiated the doctrines of election and reprobation The "Cumberland Presbytery" soon extended itself beyond its original locality, and the sect taking its name from this origin is said to number 900 ministers, 1250 places of worship, and 100,000 members having also established Cumberland College, Princeton, Kentucky, and several other colleges for the education of its ministers It is strictly Presbyterian in its character, with the exception that its "Confession of Faith," founded on the Westminster Confession, rejects the Calvinistic dogmas of election and reprobation, and maintains the doctrine of universal redemption

CUTZUPITÆ This name is used for the CIRCUMCELLIONS by St Augustine in his 163rd Epistle, and is probably another form of Gotispitæ

CYRTIANI. [PSATHYRIANS]

D

DALEITES A sect in Glasgow at the end of the last century, which differed little from the Independents. The founder, David Dale (born 6th January 1739) was a wealthy cotton-manufacturer, and the original proprietor (in conjunction with Sir R. Arkwright) of the Lanark Mills, who had risen from the rank of a journeyman weaver, but was more distinguished by his munificent charities and the benevolence of his character At an early period he adopted in general the views of Robert Glas, the founder of Scottish Independency, but differing from him in some few points, established a distinct congregation in Glasgow, to which he ministered up to the period of his death, which occurred on 17th March 1805 In order to qualify himself in point of learning for his self-imposed office, he is said to have studied the languages of both the Old and New Testaments with some considerable degree of success The points of separation between his followers and the Glassites consisted partly in doctrine, the former laying more stress upon practical holiness than the latter, but chiefly in matters of discipline The Daleites did not keep aloof from other Christian bodies with the exclusiveness (so distinctive of petty sects) with which the Glassites regarded them, and they entertained somewhat different views respecting the office of elders, particularly holding that the apostolic description of an office-bearer, as being "the husband of one wife," forbade only the having more than one wife at the same time, while the Glassites generally held that an elder was disqualified for office by re-marriage after a first wife's death

At the time of Mr Dale's death small congregations in connection with his Glasgow followers existed at Edinburgh, Perth, Kirkcaldy, and several other places Probably they have now all become merged either among the few remaining Glassites, or among the Congregationalists Dale's son-in-law was the notorious Robert Owen, the originator of the English socialist theories. [*New Theological Dictionary*, Edinb (for Jas. Morison, Perth), 1807 *Scots Magazine*, 1806, pp 239, 653]

DAMIANISTS. A section of the Alexandrian Monophysites which took its name from Damian, the Monophysite patriarch [A D 570] In opposing the TRITHEISTS, Damian fell into the opposite error of Sabellianism, for he denied that each of the Divine Persons of the Trinity is in Himself God, and maintained that the Three have One Divine Personality only The theory of the Damianists was, in fact, practically identical with that of Sabellius, namely, that God is One Person distinguished into three hypotheses by characteristic differences of His operations But by maintaining these characteristic differences in the way they were maintained by the Damianists, their theory really led to the conclusion that there are four Gods, the three separate and subordinate Hypostases and the one superior Αὐτόθεος, hence they were also named Tetratheites [Niceph *Hist Eccl* xiii 49 Walch, *Hist Ketz* viii 753]

DANCERS These were a sect of weak-brained fanatics, who appeared in the last quarter of the fourteenth century, and disappeared at the commencement of the fifteenth The scene of their performances was the western part of the ancient province of Belgica, comprising Rhenish Prussia, Holland and Hainault. The origin of the outbreak is difficult to be accurately deciphered, but the famous black death or pestilence of Froissart was doubtless the remote or predisposing cause. This fearful visitation, which had more than decimated Northern Europe, produced and left behind it a vast amount of intellectual debility in the populations attacked by it, as is attested by the numerous fanatical enterprises which followed its disappearance Though each of these, as it appeared, was invariably suppressed to the utmost of the sacerdotal and governmental ability of the time and place of its occurrence, similar new forms of mental disease were continually bursting forth, the sufferers being distinguished by this one abiding feature in creed or ritual, namely, the substitution of corporeal exertion for spiritual or intellectual worship It was thus that in the month of July A D 1374, the dancing form of fanaticism appeared in the old capital of Charlemagne The brotherhood, a crowd of all ages and of both sexes, began their celebrations with a kind of dervish dance in the public squares of that town Emboldened by impunity they proceeded to the churches, and there, half naked and crowned with garlands, they supported the most laborious dances until they fell fainting into the arms of the bystanders They alleged that they were enabled to endure these incredible fatigues by the special grace of the Virgin and the Saints, whose aid during their performances they incessantly invoked The orthodox, however, referred their vigour to Satanic rather than heavenly interposition. From the city of Aix-la-Chapelle they spread rapidly through Hainault, making some stir, and perhaps acquiring some proselytes, both at Utrecht and Liège. Without definitely objectionable tenets, the people appeared to tolerate their folly, and they supported their precarious lives, like various recognised religious orders, by professional mendicancy. Fortunately their poverty, coupled with their numerical and intellectual weakness, preserved them from the persecution which might have given to even such fanatics a factitious importance in the eyes of the world. Saner and more merciful counsels prevailed than are sometimes met with in the history of the Church, and, as these sectaries were too ignorant or imbecile to confess themselves heretics, the orthodox were content to treat them, not as the accomplices, but as the victims of diabolical agency We gather that, when the fainting performers were taken possession of by the clergy, and the evil spirit duly exorcised, they were at least in some cases entirely restored It is stated that St Weit, or Vitus, was on such occasions successfully appealed to With the generation that had suffered from the debilitating effects of the Great Pestilence, or was born of parents who had so suffered, this form of frenzy died away, and its easy, rapid and complete extinction is a striking and satirical commentary on the prolonged existence of the greater portion of the other mediæval fanaticisms In the fifteenth century there is hardly any trace of the Dancers to be discovered Their modern homologues are to be found in the Convulsionary prophets of the eighteenth century [CONVULSIONARIES] and the Jumpers of the present day

[The best account of these sectaries is from the pen of the monk Radulph de Rive, to be found in a work by Chapeauville, entitled *Qui gesta Pontificum Tongrensium Trajectensium et Leodensium scripserunt auctores præcipui*," &c See also the *Chronicon Belgicum, sub anno* 1374, and Mosheim's *Ecclesiastical History*, cent. xiv]

DANISH PROTESTANTS The Reformation first obtained a formal recognition in Denmark A D 1526 In that year King Frederick I openly proclaimed his favour towards the Reformed doctrines, and issued orders for convoking a diet at Odensee [A D 1527], at which full liberty of conscience was allowed for both reforming and non-reforming parties, the marriage of the clergy and religious orders was legalized, and the bishops were forbidden any longer to receive the pallium from Rome For some years previously the Reformed doctrines had been spreading, especially owing to the labours of John Tausen, who, after attending the lectures of Melanchthon at Wittenberg, returned home to teach them in his native town of Viborg in Jutland [A D 1521] Two years later Christian II. was succeeded on the throne by Frederick I, Duke of Schleswig-Holstein [A D 1523] His own personal feeling in favour of Lutheran tenets led him immediately to proclaim liberty of worship in his own duchy, though he was prevented by the antipathy of the bishops from extending the same principle to his new kingdom till A D 1527. A Danish confession was subsequently drawn up and published at a diet held at Copenhagen [A D 1530] It consists of forty-three articles, and resembles in many points the Confession of Augsburg, being partly based on the Schwaback and Torgau Articles [A D 1529], which also form the groundwork of the latter work After a reign of ten years Frederick I was succeeded by his son Christian III [A D. 1533], who, while travelling in Germany before assuming the crown, had been present at the Diet of Worms, and who at once showed his intention of standing fast by his father's policy in religious matters by being crowned by the Lutheran Pomeranian John Bugenhagen, whom he caused to be summoned from Wittenberg for that purpose. In taking this significant step the new king was actuated by a political as well as a religious antipathy The Catholic clergy, especially the hierarchy, had supported the pretensions of his younger brother John, who, along with his exiled predecessor Christian II, were competitors for the vacant throne. They were forthwith banished from their sees, a new class of "superintendents" was substituted for the ancient order of bishops, the University of Copenhagen was remodelled on a Protestant basis, and the triumph of Lutheranism in Denmark proper may be considered complete.

It soon extended into Norway, which was finally incorporated into Denmark proper A D. 1537 Here the Catholic bishops, after some opposition, were either deposed or conformed, and at the present date Lutheranism is the predominant and almost the exclusive form of religion in Norway

The history of Iceland is similar The Reformed doctrines were first propagated by Gisser Einarsen, who, at the age of twenty-five, was elected under Protestant influence to the bishopric of Skalholt in that island [A D 1540] Supported by royal favour, his teaching spread so rapidly, that in the course of eleven years the whole island had changed its religious complexion, and has remained exclusively Lutheran up to the present day

DAVID-GEORGIANS [FAMILISTS]

DAVID OF DINANT [DAVIDISTS]

DAVIDIANS [DAVID-GEORGIANS]

DAVIDISTS A sect of the thirteenth century, the followers of David of Dinant.

Of the personal history of this heretic little or nothing is known beyond the fact that he was a disciple of Amalric of Bena, and was, like his master, trained in the pantheistic philosophy of Erigena He however went beyond his teacher in heresy, for whereas Amalric had taught that the Deity is the *principium formale* of all things, David de Dinanto asserted that He is the *materia prima* of all things [Thom Aq *Summa* I *qu.* iii *art* 8] The pantheism of the latter went, therefore, to the length of asserting that the Deity alone has any real existence, and that all other beings and things are part of Him This principle the sect applied to Christianity in such a manner as to explain it away Thus, instead of our Lord becoming the One Incarnation of God, each human being was represented as a separate and individual incarnation of Deity In a similar manner the received doctrine of a Divine Presence in the Blessed Sacrament was admitted, but was also explained away by the statement that the species of it was already part of the Deity before it was consecrated, and that the act of consecration was merely such an annunciation of the fact as brought it home to the consciousness of those who heard and saw the priest at the altar To this pantheism they added many other anticipations of later unbelief, such as that God had revealed Himself by the words of heathen poets like Ovid, as much as by Christian Fathers like Augustine, that heaven and hell are simply the present consequences of sin, that religion does not consist in what a man does, but in love alone, independently of good life and works

The principles of the sect were at first propagated with great secresy among the French laity by means of books written in the vernacular But William of Aria, a goldsmith, making them known by public preaching, they were brought before a synod at Paris in A D 1209, and condemned as profoundly heretical Its author was degraded from the priesthood, but had fled from Paris, while several of his clerical and lay adherents were apprehended, and refusing to recant were burnt as heretics [A D 1210] A priest named Bernard shewed the full force of the principles he had learned by declaring that the fire could have no power to destroy his being, because it was part of the Divine existence, and so far as he had any being he was God himself

The chief work of Dinanto was one entitled *Quatermarii* On the condemnation of his heresy it and all his vernacular writings were destroyed, and so great was the odium into which they had brought the use of the vernacular for theological teaching, that all other theological works in the French language were also ordered to be burned, including the *Metaphysics* of Aristotle, which had been especially used in support of the heresy, having been lately recovered from oblivion through the prevalence of Moorish literature in Europe [Martene, *Thes Anecdot* iv. 163 Natal Alex *Hist Eccl* viii 73, ed. 1762 Neander's *Ch Hist* viii 129, ed. 1852]

DAVIDISTS [DAVID-GEORGIANS]

DAVISTS [DAVID-GEORGIANS.]

DEISTS A general name applied in the seventeenth and eighteenth centuries to those who professed a belief in the existence of God (as distinguished from Atheists), but went little or not at all further towards belief in the truths of Christianity In more recent times Deism has been regarded as a tenet of many schools of sceptics rather than as the distinguishing tenet of one The reader is therefore referred to the article SCEPTICS in this volume, and to that of DEISM in the DICTIONARY *of* THEOLOGY, for historical and philosophical information on the subject

DEMAS The "fellow-labourer" of St Paul [Philem 24, Col iv 14]—of whom he says towards the close of his ministry, "Demas hath forsaken me, having loved this present world, and is departed unto Thessalonica" [2 Tim iv 10]—is classed by Epiphanius with Cerinthus, Ebion, and others, as one who denied the Divine Nature and miraculous Conception of our Lord [Epiphan *Hæres* li 6] Another writer, in a work entitled *Synopsis de vita et morte Prophetarum, Apostolorum et Discipulorum Domini*, alleges that Demas became a priest in a heathen temple at Thessalonica, but this work is probably of later date than Epiphanius, though attributed to Dorotheus, who flourished A D 303 The expression used by St Paul is consistent with the opinion of Baronius, Hammond, and others, that Demas did not forsake the faith when he forsook St. Paul, and even with that of Grotius that he is the same as the Demetrius of whom St John many years afterwards wrote that he had "good report of all men, and of the truth itself," and that he himself bore record to the same effect [3 John 12] On the other hand, Epiphanius and the other writer named may have had authentic sources of information from which they drew their statements, but which are now lost to us

DESCARTES René Descartes is the father of modern philosophy He was born A D 1596 in La Haye of the Tourdane, of an old French family, and educated from his fourteenth to his eighteenth year in the Jesuit College at La Flèche, which he left well grounded in the mathematics of the day, and with a smattering of so many branches of learning as to have earned for himself the name of "Le petit philosophe" He took service under Tilly in the Bavarian army, and was present at the Battle of Prague, but quitted the army again, A D 1621, and, after travelling for some years in Europe, settled down in Holland [A D 1629-1649] for the purpose of working out the philosophical problems that had engaged his attention by flood and field His system was branded as Atheism His astronomical heresies were a serious gravamen, and read curiously at the present day "Quod terram stellis annumerat, solem qui hactenus inter planetas fuit stellis fixis accenset, terram vero stellis erraticis; lunam in terram quandam convertit, dum ei montes, valles tribuit, denique motum, qui per tot mille annos solis fuit, in terram transfert" [Maestricht, *Novitatum Cartesianarum Gangræna*, 1675] He was proscribed by the University of Utrecht, but opposition only attracted to him a greater following, and having accepted an invitation from Christine, Queen of Sweden, to become her preceptor in philosophy, he accepted it, but died the same year at Stockholm [A D 1650], in his fifty-fifth year. Descartes established a powerful school, in which the first principles of modern rationalism were developed To accept a creed because it was ancient, not because it was true, was to give up the prerogative of thought rather than to think Evidence must lie at the bottom of truth, but first the character of evidence must be determined. All, therefore, must be discussed, all must be sifted, weighed, and tested, and, after an elimination of every false or doubtful element, that alone must be retained which shews the raciness of truth It was the death-knell of Scholasticism Everything for the future was to be determined by reason, not by prescription Bacon had shewed that a wide induction of facts must precede all attempt at scientific generalization, Descartes taught that those very facts in the first instance should be subjected to the "experimentum crucis" of doubt, hence termed "methodical doubt" [*Med* i]. There was so much in all antecedent systems of philosophy that was self-contradictory and positively wrong, that he assumed this as the surest basis of operations in building up a newer philosophy "De omnibus dubitandum" was the negative germ of his system From doubting he proceeded to deny every fact and every conceivable opinion, even in mathematical demonstration there might be elements of doubt Doubt was the certainty of uncertainty, the only sure truth in the intellectual world, itself the only doubt in which there is no doubt. Thought is only self-certain in its doubt. Uncertainty is the negative certainty of doubt, and this negative certainty is as the positive self-certainty of thought. Everything but thought is open to doubt, we may imagine that there is neither God nor matter, that we have no real bodily substance, but we can never imagine, while thought is thus occupied, that we do not think Thought, therefore, is true existence, and the self-consciousness of thought is the self-consciousness of being, hence the famous Cartesian maxim "Cogito ergo sum" The negative certainty of doubt is the positive certainty of existence, the first is the negative origin of philosophic reasoning, the latter is its positive source "Hæc cognitio, Ego cogito ergo sum, est omnium prima et certissima quæ cuilibet ordine philosophanti occurrat" [Cartesius, *Princ* i]. Being and thought are reciprocal terms, the one is the predicate of the other, either may be taken as subject "Cogito ergo sum unica est propositio, quæ huic, Ego sum cogitans æquivalet" [*Med* ii] It is a subjective inconsequential certainty founded, not upon reasoning, but on self-intuition. The phrase is not a syllogism but an equation Thought = existence. Thought, therefore, in its external relations is doubt; esoterically it is self-evidence of its own real existence Doubt with respect to all that is external to my own being is the certitude of that being, and giving power of abstraction from all external phenomena, it leaves a residuum of pure thought which is the certitude of my being Spirit is the antagonism of bodily nature, which is and ought to be a subject of doubt; "de rebus omnibus præsertim corporeis dubitandum" It needs no other being for its existence, it is self-existent But that being which needs nothing else for its existence is substance, the essential property without which substance cannot become the object of thought is attribute Thus thought is the attribute of spirit, and spirit is thinking substance. The antagonism of spirit is corporeal existence or matter As its abstract antagonism, matter has no relation with spirit, it has its own independent being, and is equally substance The attribute of matter is abstractedly opposed to the attribute of spirit, which is involutional thought, the attribute of matter is evolutional extension. Matter is extended substance Hence the axiom "Cogito ergo sum" involves the two definitions, that spirit is "thinking substance," and that matter is "extended substance" The one is "res cogitans," the other is "res extensa" It is the foundation of the Cartesian philosophy. Its physics are based upon the latter definition, its metaphysics on the former. Thought, it should be observed, in Cartesian terminology means "consciousness" "Cogitationis nomine intelligo alia omnia, quæ nobis consciis in nobis fiunt, quatenus in nobis eorum conscientia est" Thought assures me of my own existence even though the objects of thought be illusory, I see an object, it may or not be, but the very act of thought assures me of my own individual being Descartes could not deny the sensation caused by external objects, it was the proof to him of his being All truth he said must be sure, but the only sure thing is that I exist.

Descartes manifestly speaks of substance in a double sense, and this at once gives inconsistency to an important part of his scheme Infinite Substance means that which is self-existent and requires no other substance to bring it into being. It is its own cause Finite substance is wholly dependent and must be referred back to the infinite, hence it is not substance according to the preceding definition Therefore with reference to the Divine Substance, finite substance is not substance but create being; but with reference to its various individual forms it is substance, because these forms reciprocally exclude each other, they are antagonistic and exist in mutual independence of being "Hæc enim est natura substantiarum quod sese mutuo excludant"

Ordinary consciousness has faith in the reality of its objects. Philosophical consciousness replaces faith with doubt; it does not believe, it thinks Certainty only extends so far as thought reaches, subjective existence is co-ordinate with thought, and is surrounded with an atmosphere of light Objective existence in the external world is wrapt in darkness and doubt. They are as the two hemispheres, the one light and the other dark, only there is no penumbra at their point of contact In the former reigns the lorn and lonely "I," which is mated with no "Thou." The next step opens out the solution of this unpromising problem

To know the objective is to resolve the antagonism between subject and object, for knowledge of the objective is only then possible when the two interpenetrate each other Some "tertium quid" is required, a synthetic principle that is wholly independent of either, and may serve as a connecting link between the two, thinking and extended substance, subject and object These two substances are mutually exclusive of each other, and for this cause they are limited, the "tertium quid" or synthetic principle must have no limit, or it would be implicated in one or other of these two substances, and be neutralized Infinite Substance is the synthetic principle that alone can solve the antithesis of self-certainty on the one hand, absolute doubt on the other, that can throw the light of knowledge upon the world lying in the shades of doubt, and add abstract self-certainty to objective certainty. It is by this infinite Substance that from the axiom "Cogito ergo sum" doubt is raised into objective knowledge This axiom is absolute certainty, and it is certainty because my perception of it is clear and distinct and everything is to us truth of which we have a clear and distinct perception "Illud omne est verum, quod clare et distincte percipio" [*Medit* iii]

Everything must have its cause. Cause and effect are connected as truly as thought and existence Cause must always be at least co-extensive with effect, often it is of far wider range The artist's idea is the cause of his work of art, but it also reaches far beyond it. In the first case the effect is contained formally in the cause, in the latter transcendentally (eminenter) "Cogito ergo sum" is not clearer as an axiom than this relation of cause and effect Ideas present themselves to the mind, whether imaginative or intellectual, and as modes of mental existence they are real These ideas may represent substance, or the accidents of substance. They are the "objective reality" of Descartes, the objective reality of substance exceeding that of its accidents But every effect must have its cause, and an idea is the effect of an occult cause, also if the idea be an objective reality, so also will its cause be an objective reality, and be comprised in its effect either formally or transcendentally This objective real cause is the "archetype," and every real idea has its archetype in or without ourselves "Neque etiam in nobis idea sive imago ullius rei esse potest, cujus non alicubi sive in nobis, sive extra nos archetypus aliquis, omnes ejus perfectiones re ipsa continens, existat" [*Princ* i]. But the objective reality of an idea in its full dimensions may transcend the individual mind which conceives it, the mind then cannot be its origin, the cause must be external to it. The perfect cannot have its rise in the imperfect, or the greater in the less "Hinc necessario sequitur me non solum esse in mundo, sed aliquam aliam rem, quæ istius ideæ est causa, etiam existere" [*Med* iii]. The ideal accident of substance may be conceived in my mind transcendentally, for I am substance The idea of substance can be conceived "formally" for the same reason, but the idea of an infinite substance is beyond my grasp, for I am only finite substance This idea, therefore, is the only one that convinces me that there is an existence above and beyond my own, the only one that cannot possibly be devoid of cause without me, and which for this reason is an immediate representation to me of objective existence as a reality. As truly, therefore, as I exist, there is an existent being without me I am no solitary existence There is a "Thou" and an "It" in addition to the "I" of individual being, an objective as well as a subjective reality Light is dawning on the darker hemisphere, and the mind has learned to acknowledge everything to be as really existent as itself, the idea of which presents itself as a clear and manifest entity The idea of "objective reality" is gained The sun of infinite substance has risen and cleared away the darkness By the light of this sun every following school of philosophy has pursued its course, though some, as Spinoza, have confounded the light with the illumined substance, the subjective with the objective

The infinite substance of philosophy is the God of theology But it is not by the above process that the human mind has reasoned out for itself the idea of God God Himself has implanted it indelibly in the soul, it is the artist's symbol engraved upon his work, "Tamquam nota Artificis operi suo impressa" [*Med* iii] The Absolute or Infinite, therefore, is a third substance, external to and independent of thinking and extended substance, both of which are finite, and are reciprocally antagonistic, in infinite substance there is no antagonism. This notion of the immanence of the Deity in the mind occupies a very subordinate part in the Cartesian system It is as a mere mathematical point, but it extended itself concentrically on every side, and in Spinoza's scheme it comprised the universe

The idea of an external infinite substance thus impressed upon the soul as an innate idea, is the existence of God within the soul. The same axiom here also applies, by the same certitude that I exist because I am a thinking being I am sure that God exists in the universe because He exists in my thought, "Deus cogitatur ergo est" It is a certitude gained by immediate intuition, and not by dialectical reasoning The idea of God is at once the proof of His existence, for it is the proof of that very existence. Every other idea presented to the mind suggests the possibility of existence, the idea of God involves the necessity of His being I may form the idea of a griffin in my mind, but the idea does not give reality to such a being The idea of the infinite is exactly co-ordinate with infinite existence, the mind could form no idea of such perfection if it did not really exist. Anselm professed to demonstrate the subjective Being of God, Descartes argues that the innate idea of the Deity shows His immanence in the soul The propositions are of a cognate character, they are not identical According to Descartes, in infinite substance the essential idea and real existence are co-ordinate terms (essentia et existentia), and the idea of Perfect Being comprehends within itself that of necessary existence To have by intuition an idea of God is to have an intuitive knowledge of His Being The idea of God and the Being of God are one It is from this point that Spinoza took up the reasoning, and carried out the Cartesian theory in a thoroughgoing Pantheistic sense The Schools had always kept philosophy in subordination to theology, both however being treated as parts of an entire unity Descartes disjoined them, and applied to philosophy a new ontological nomenclature Spinoza advanced further, and devised a system with which theology could have nothing further to do . it was practical atheism , its god was necessity

The "primum movens" that sets all in movement is the Deity , but the idea included in the Deity is not a Divine Being that works everything according to His own good pleasure and with a benevolent design, but a principle of mere causation irrespective of any moral quality , a mechanical Deity that is only so far supranatural as that Infinite Substance must always stand in antagonism with the finite A very easy step led Spinoza to discard the *supra*, and to find in nature its own immanent causation "Deus supra naturam" then became "Deus sive natura" God, who is the cause of objective knowledge in the mind, is as the phenomenon of movement in inert and passive matter We are on the threshold of pure naturalism All nature is a huge unvarying machine The Divine Principle created indeed, but exercises no further control over the work of his hands "Semel jussit semper paret" [Remusat, *Essais*, art *Descartes* Saisset, *Manuel de la Phil , Précurseurs et Disc. de Descartes , Philosophie religieuse , Ænesidème*, 261, 275 Ritter, *Gesch d Phil* Fischer, *Gesch d n Phil* Dorner, *Gesch d Wissensch in Deutschland*]

DEVIL WORSHIPPERS [Yezeedees]

DIACONOFTSCHINS A Russian sect of Dissenters which separated from the Popoftschins in the year 1706, under the leadership of Alexander the Deacon, at Veska, from whom it takes its name

DIACRINOMENI [Hæsitantes]

DILECTÆ. [Agapetæ]

DIMŒRITÆ [Tropitæ]

DIOTREPHES. The Venerable Bede, in his Commentary on St John, speaks of Diotrephes, who in some unexplained way withstood the authority of the Apostle [3 John 9, 10]—as "a proud and insolent heresiarch" Other writers have also included him among the early heretics, and Hammond inclines to the opinion that he became a Gnostic [*Dissert de Antichristo,* xiii p 43] There is however no early evidence whatever on the subject of his heresy, and the words of St John point to his having assumed a schismatical rather than an heretical position at the time when his name is mentioned He is not noticed by Epiphanius, nor by any of the other early heresiologists

DISCIPLES OF CHRIST [Campbellites, American]

DISCIPLES OF ST JOHN [Sabæans]

DISCIPLINARIANS The Ultra-Calvinists of the Elizabethan age, whose object was to substitute the Presbyterian system established by Calvin at Geneva under the name of "the Discipline" for the Episcopal system of the Church of England It was against this party, and especially in answer to the writings of their leader Thomas Cartwright, that Hooker wrote his work on *Ecclesiastical Polity.* The Disciplinarian "platform," as they were accustomed to call it, comprised the abolition of bishops, archdeacons, deans, canons, and all other ecclesiastical officers except "presbyters" It would also have abolished all existing courts as tyrannical and oppressive, substituting in their place the far more tyrannical system of "consistories," such as Calvin originated at Geneva, or that of "presbyteries" and "kirk-sessions" which has been established in Scotland It also aimed at great strictness in repelling persons from the Holy Communion At one time the Disciplinarians had so much expectation of carrying out their plans as openly to express their conviction that Parker would be the last Archbishop of Canterbury [Admonitionists]

DISSENTERS A general name used in England and Wales for those who belong to any sect, to distinguish them from members of the Church of England The term came into use soon after the Revolution of A D 1688, and its origin is indicated by words used in the title and body of an Act passed in that year, in which those formerly called "Nonconformists" are styled "Their Majesties' Protestant subjects dissenting from the Church of England" [1 Will & Mar cap. 18] Their present numbers in England and Wales are estimated as follows —

Sects	Members	Children under 15	Total	Percentage to Pop.
Methodists .	655,800	515,272	1,171,072	5 2
Independents	296,300	232,807	529,107	2 2
Baptists	233,088	183,140	416,228	1 8
Roman Catholics				
English .	100,240	78,760	179,000	7
Irish .	469,260	263,300	732,560	3 2
Miscellaneous	118,518	93,121	211,639	9
Total	1,873,206	1,366,400	3,239,606	14

Deducting the Irish Roman Catholics the Dissenting population of England and Wales thus numbers 2½ millions, or 11 per cent in a population of 22,704,108 [Nonconformists Puritans]

DISSIDENTS The inclusive name for Polish Protestants, as Dissenters is for the Protestants of England It was first used at the time of the Reformation, appearing in the Acts of the Warsaw Confederation of A D 1573 [Polish Protestants Krasinski's *Reform in Poland*, ii. 11.]

DOCETÆ. Heretics of very early date who held our Lord's Body to have been only the appearance (δόκησις) of a body, not a material or real one.

This heresy rests upon the notion of the inherent evil of matter For with a material body inherently evil the Divine Nature cannot be thought to have united Itself, neither in the systems of the Gnostics, who tried, by a succession of Æons, to bridge over the space between the Deity and Matter, could it be thought that the Æon, derived from the Divine Nature, whose office was to correct the work of the evil Demiurge, united himself with the handiwork of that Demiurge In this difficulty, some were led to deny the reality of the body, some the truth of the union The former were the Docetæ Of them, some held that the Body of our Lord was merely simulated, that it was an immaterial phantasm. some allowed that it was a substantial body, but of a celestial substance.

Hippolytus ascribes this heresy to Simon Magus "And so it was," he writes, "that Jesus appeared as man, when in reality He was not a man He suffered, not as actually undergoing suffering, but appearing to the Jews to do so" [*Refut* vi 14] Docetism thus appeared along with Gnosticism But, again, Hippolytus [viii 1-8] treats the Docetæ as a separate sect, and describes the system of Æons which they held Of this system it is sufficient to say that it is much more developed than the system of Simon, and very nearly identical with the system of Valentinus It appears, therefore, that this point of Gnostic teaching was brought more prominently forward, so as to give to a division of Gnostics a distinctive name By this, consequently, is to be interpreted the statement of Clement of Alexandria, that Julius Cassianus was the author of the sect of Docetæ [*Strom* iii 13] The tenet had been held before,[1] but Cassianus insisted more upon it. Cassianus was a disciple of Valentinus He brought Docetism into notice in connection with Encratite austerity His book, quoted by Clement, was *On Continence*, and Clement states that in this matter he agreed with Tatian, with whom he was contemporary. Of this Encratite phase of Docetism Jerome speaks, making Tatian the author of the heresy as Clement made Cassian "Tatianus qui putativam Christi carnem introducens, omnem conjunctionem masculi ad feminam immundam arbitrabatur" [*Comm in cap* vi *Epist ad Galat*] It appears strange that Clement and Jerome should speak of the heresy as introduced by Cassian and Tatian, for there is no doubt that it existed in apostolic times, and was generally held by the Gnostics

Serapion, consecrated Bishop of Antioch in A D 190 or 191, found the error in the Gospel of Peter, which he obtained from the successors of some heretics called Docetæ [Euseb *H E* vi 12] Grabe and Beausobre suppose, with much probability, that this Gospel was forged by Leucius, who is placed by Lardner A D 135-150 [*Hist of Heretics, Leucius*] From this Gospel Serapion says he learnt what the heresy of Marcianus was Lardner assumes that Marcianus was Marcion, but it is very improbable that Serapion was not before acquainted with the tenets of so notorious a heretic If, however, Leucius were the author of the Gospel of Peter, we have a connection with Marcion, Leucius being his disciple Marcion undoubtedly was a Docetic [Tertull *adv Marc.* iii 8, 9] So were Cerdo, Bardesanes, Saturninus [Epiph *Hær* xli lvi xxiii][2] In short, the tenets of Gnosticism include the Docetic heresy, unless, as an alternative, one of two opinions be adopted, either that upon Jesus, born of human parents, the Æon Christ descended, or that the body assumed by Christ was of celestial substance, which passed through the person of the Virgin as water through a tube This last was the opinion of Valentinus[3] [Epiph *Panar Indic* tom II xi] These three, it is evident, alike deny that the Word was made Flesh See Irenæus, *adv Hær* III xi 3, and xvi 1, V 1, 2. The first, or Docetic opinion, was held both earlier and more widely than the other opinions It was opposed by Ignatius, εἰ δὲ λέγουσιν τὸ δοκεῖν πεπονθέναι αὐτὸν [*ad Trall* x, *ad Symrn* ii], by Hermas, as to that form of it which separates the Son of God from the body in death, and so gives up the body itself [*Past* III v 6 see Dorner, *On the Person of Christ*, A i 132], and Hippolytus' ascription of it to Simon Magus is supported by the general voice of antiquity Jerome said that the Lord's body was declared to be a phantom while the Apostles were still in the world and the blood of Christ still fresh in Judæa [*adv Lucif* xxiii] There can be little doubt, then, that the words of St. John [1 Ep iv 3] were directed against a sect of Docetæ then existing

Thus in the early Church there were two principal heresies, each of several branches, the Gnostic and the Jewish The Gnostics were in general Docetæ Erring with regard to the nature of God, they allowed, with more or less departure from Catholic truth, a divine nature, more or less clearly defined, in our Lord, but they denied His humanity The Jewish sects avoided the error of an inferior creator, but asserted that our Lord was no more than man All the Docetæ denied the resurrection of the body This is a necessary consequence of their denial of the reality of Christ's body, and it is perhaps correct to infer that those of whom St Paul speaks [1 Cor xv 12] were Docetæ whose existence somewhat later is proved by St John's words

We return then to Cassian and Tatian, who gave a new impulse to Docetism They are placed by Cave in A D 173-4 Of the former nothing more is known than has been mentioned, except that his exegetical works are referred to by Clement of Alexandria [*Strom.* i 21], where Tatian's works are also referred to Tatian was an Assyrian, founder of a sect of Encratite Gnostics, which lasted till after the fourth century The congruity of Docetic and Hyperas-

[1] See Ittigius, *Dis de Hær* ii x 193 Ittigius shews that Cassianus did not originate, but renewed the heresy

[2] Basilides held the proper manhood of Jesus, and that the Divine Intelligence united itself with Him at His baptism [Neander and Ritter] The later followers of Basilides received into their system the views of the Docetæ. [Basilidians]

[3] Of Valentinus' opinion Irenæus says, "I have proved already that it is the same thing to say that He appeared merely to outward seeming, and to affirm that He received nothing from Mary" [*adv Hær* v 1, 2] To the minor subdivisions of the Valentinian School Docetism is attributed, as to the Secundians, by Philaster expressly [*Hær.* xl.], and by Epiphanius [*Hær* xxxii], in the general assertion that, regarding Christ, they agreed with the Valentinians and to the Marcosians by Prædestinatus [cap xiv] But of these minor sects, testimony is hardly required. Vincent of Lerins writes, "Valentinus, Eutyches, Saturninus, Marcion, Basilides (but see foregoing note), Cerdo et Manichæus phantasiæ prædicatores, aiunt filium Dei Deum, et personam hominis non substantive extitisse, sed actu putativo quodam et conversatione simulasse" [*cont. Hær* cxx]

cetic notions is too manifest to be dwelt upon, and the expression of their union is fitly the practice of using water alone in the Holy Eucharist. [HYDROPARASTATÆ][1]

Lastly, with a theosophy differing from Tatian's, Manichæus held the fundamental principle of the inherent evil of matter, and followed it to its conclusion of the necessity of mortifying, not the flesh with its affections and lusts in the scriptural sense, but the body as a body His Docetism consequently was identical with that of Tatian Prudentius names Manichæus as the representative of the Docetæ [*Apoth* 961].

DONATISTS A sect which separated itself from the Church in Africa early in the fourth century It grew out of the misguided zeal, passing into fanaticism, which had adopted or produced Montanism and Novatianism This spirit working in the Church was sure to find or to make an occasion of schism, and it now laid hold of the tenderness shewn to the "Traditores" who had given up the sacred books to escape martyrdom in the Diocletian persecution Irregular and schismatical proceedings had taken place before the year 311, such as the sending envoys to Carthage by Secundus, senior bishop, and therefore, according to the custom of the province, primate of Numidia, who through these envoys appointed a visitor of the Church of Carthage [August *Serm* xlvi cap xv] Such also was the rebaptizing of Catholics, and the uncanonical treatment of bishops who had fallen in persecution, by Donatus of Casæ Nigræ [Optat I xxiv and Dupin's note] But the immediate occasion of the Donatist schism was the disputing the election of Cæcilian to the bishopric of Carthage, and the schism was formed by the irregular consecration of Majorinus as his rival, Donatus of Casæ Nigræ being the chief consecrator Heresy was superadded, principally under another Donatus, successor to Majorinus in the schismatical episcopate, in the astounding assertion that the whole Church, with the exception of the Donatist section, had failed through the contamination of communion with Cæcilian In this assertion was reduced to a dogma that which is in fact virtually assumed in every schism, namely, the purity of the separating body, and the apostasy of the body which is deserted The Novatians had made a similar assertion but upon different grounds Donatism is also a separate schism, inasmuch as there was a second departure from the Church and a second line of irregular consecrations The character of the younger party is moreover distinguished from the elder by greater fanaticism

In the beginning of the fourth century Mensurius, bishop of Carthage, was cited to appear before Maxentius, on the charge of concealing in his house the author of a libel on the Emperor He died, in his return home, in the year 311 Two presbyters, Botrus and Celestius, aspired to the bishopric. They belonged to a fanatical party,[2] which Mensurius and his Archdeacon Cæcilian had opposed, the party which courted martyrdom not unfrequently from unhallowed motives. Optatus states that Botrus and Celestius, in order to further their own purposes, contrived to bring on the election and consecration without summoning the bishops of Numidia[3] [Opt I xviii, Dupin's ed p 15] This certainly implies that the Numidian bishops had customarily been summoned, whether of right or by courtesy, to assist at such elections Cæcilian however was elected in their absence, and was consecrated by Felix of Aptunga, a suffragan of the proconsular province of which Carthage was the metropolis

The disappointed presbyters organized an opposition to the new bishop Donatus of Casæ Nigræ was put at its head, and it was strengthened by the wealth and influence of Lucilla, a Spanish lady residing in Carthage The party comprised also those to whom Mensurius, on leaving Carthage, had entrusted the church property, which (to their disappointment it is said) they were obliged to refund to Cæcilian At the invitation of this party seventy Numidian bishops, under Secundus of Tigisis, the Nu-

[1] A difficulty with regard to Artemon, about twenty-five years later than Tatian, ought not to be passed over Artemon was a Psilanthropist, but Methodius is generally thought to attribute to him the directly contrary heresy of Docetism Methodius' words are given in Clark's translation They "have gone astray with regard to one of the three Persons of the Trinity As when they say, like Sabellius, that the Almighty Person of the Father Himself suffered, or as when they say, like Artemas, that the Person of the Son was born and manifested only in appearance,' &c [*Banquet Disc.* viii cap x] But Methodius, we venture to say, is misinterpreted He is speaking of errors regarding the Divine Persons Regarding the First Person, he notes the error of Patripassianism; regarding the second, the error that the Son was not really incarnate The δόκησις which he names is not the unreality of the body in which the Divine nature appeared, but the simulation of an incarnation presented by the mere man Jesus when the Divine nature descended upon Him without a personal union

[2] There were those who, courting persecution, boasted unasked that they possessed copies of the Scriptures which they would not surrender This Mensurius did not approve He opposed also the visiting the martyrs in prison "incaute et glomeratim" [Compare Cyprian, *Epist* v Oxf ed]

[3] Optatus' words are "Botrus et Celestius, ut dicitur, apud Carthaginem ordinari cupientes, operam dederunt, ut absentibus Numidis soli vicini episcopi peterentur qui ordinationem apud Carthaginem celebrarent Tunc suffragio totius populi Cæcilianus eligitur et manus imponente Felice Autumnitano episcopus ordinatur" Dupin explains the words by the statement of Augustine, which will be quoted above, and refers the supposed right of the Numidian bishops simply to the consecration But Optatus relates the election of Cæcilian so pointedly, after the statement of the absence of these bishops, that one cannot but infer his meaning to be that Botrus and Celestius (mistaking perhaps the propensities of the several parties) manœuvred to prevent the Numidians taking part in the *election* Augustine relates the objection as made at the Conference of Carthage [A D 410], when doubtless the objection was put in the form which appeared most tenable Dupin states "Secundus et Episcopi Numidiæ vocati Carthaginem ad ordinationem Episcopi invenerunt Cæcilianum jam ordinatum" [*Hist Donatist* p viii] Optatus plainly states that the Numidian bishops were sent for after the ordination "Ab his tribus personis contra Cæcilianum causæ confictæ sunt, ut vitiosa ejus ordinatio diceretur. Ad Secundum Tigisitanum missum est, ut Carthaginem veniretur" [p 16]

midian primate, met at Carthage, and cited Cæcilian to appear at their synod They alleged that an election and consecration in their absence was irregular, that Cæcilian's consecration was null, because his chief consecrator Felix was a Traditor, and they charged Cæcilian with cruelty to the confessors in prison Cæcilian refused to obey their summons They excommunicated him, and consecrated a rival, Majorinus, a member of Lucilla's household [1]

The first of these allegations against Cæcilian refers directly to the schism, the second to the incipient heresy of the Donatists, the third is a personal charge brought by way of aggravation

It seems plain that Optatus has stated the first as resting on a supposed right of the Numidian bishops to take part in the election At the Conference at Carthage it was stated differently, and made to rest on the claim of the Numidian primate to be the consecrator of the Carthaginian primate The two claims are really inconsistent, for the latter supposes Numidia to be a distinct province with its own metropolitan, the former (unless the presence of the Numidian prelates was merely by invitation of courtesy, in which case no charge of irregularity could be founded on their absence) supposes the Numidian bishops to have seats in the provincial synod of Carthage. Nevertheless, it is possible that both claims were made, for the province was only of recent formation, and the primate may have claimed what he thought his new rights, and the bishops not forgotten their old customs Neither are factious men very careful to be consistent At the Conference of Carthage the Donatists objected that Cæcilian's consecration was uncanonical, because he had not sent for the primate of Numidia to come and ordain him, "ut princeps a principe ordinaretur" Augustine answered, "that Cæcilian had no need of this, since the custom of the Catholic Church was otherwise," which was, not to have the Numidian bishops to ordain the Bishop of Carthage, but the neighbouring bishops of the province of Carthage, as it was not the custom at Rome to send for a metropolitan out of another province to ordain the Bishop of Rome, but he was always ordained by the Bishop of Ostia, a neighbouring bishop of the same province [August *Brevic Collat Tert Die* 29] The former claim, viz. to take part in the election, supposes the Numidian bishops to be of the proconsular province But they had certainly acted as a separate province six years previously, when their synod met at Cirta, the civil metropolis, under the presidency of Secundus of Tigisis, to elect a bishop for Cirta This independent action shows that the Numidian bishops were not an integral part of the provincial synod of Africa Proconsularis, and that their presence at the election of a bishop of Carthage was therefore unnecessary In Cyprian's time Numidia and Mauritania were attached to the proconsular province [Cypr *Ep* xlviii Oxf ed], and probably continued so nearly to the time of Constantine The claim to take part in the Carthaginian election, if really made, was, it seems, an attempt to retain their old privileges under their new status

The second allegation against Cæcilian was that he had been consecrated by Traditors, Felix of Aptunga, the chief consecrator, being charged with this crime In this allegation, besides the question of the fact, there is also the question of the character of the fact The crime of Tradition was a new one It was a peculiarity of the Diocletian persecution to endeavour to destroy all copies of the Scriptures Was the surrender of the Scriptures to be considered equivalent to a denial of Christ? Those who put forward the objection as a justification of their separation from Cæcilian must have asserted this equivalence, and rested on the rule of the Church that they who lapsed in time of persecution were not to be ordained. [See Origen, *cont Cel* iii p 143, Spenser's ed Cyprian, *Ep* lxvii Oxf ed *Conc Nic Canon* x, which refers to *Apost Can* liv or lxi Bruns' *Canons*, p 17] Cæcilian's adherents however did not argue the question of the canonical capacity or incapacity of Traditors for receiving and conveying the grace of ordination. They met their opponents on the question of fact, and the several courts to which, as we shall see, the case was submitted, acquitted Felix The charge was retorted on the objectors with terrible distinctness and certainty The Numidian bishops under Secundus had at Cirta waived the inquiries which were inculpating the larger number of the members of the synod, and had elected to the see of Cirta a Traditor, Sylvanus [August. *cont Crescen* iii 30, Optat. I xiv] The third allegation, which charged Cæcilian with cruelty, was also disproved.

The schism being thus formed by the consecration of Majorinus, and Cæcilian standing firm, the Donatists set the first example of referring spiritual affairs to the decision of the civil ruler They prayed the Emperor to appoint a commission of ecclesiastical judges, specifying the bishops of Gaul as men from whom impartiality might be expected Perhaps it may be considered to afford some show of excuse for this appeal, that the Emperor had limited to the adherents of Cæcilian the distribution of a large sum of money, sent by him for the relief of the African Christians Constantine[2] issued a commission to Miltiades of Rome, with whom he joined the bishops of Cologne, Autun, and Arles, but the commission was afterwards extended, and in virtue of it twenty bishops met at the Lateran in Rome [A D. 313] to try the case.

[1] Lucilla bribed these bishops The price of Majorinus' consecration was 400 Folles [*Monum Vet* in Dupin, p 263] Every Follis contained 125 pieces of silver, and the whole sum may be computed at about £2400 [Gibbon, *Decl and Fall.* ch. xvii note, 127].

[2] Constantine's commission is directed to Miltiades, Bishop of Rome, and to Marcus [Euseb *H E* x 5] Valesius thinks that Marcus was a presbyter of Rome, who became Pope in the year A D 336 Baronius tries to get rid of Marcus by a correction which no one can accept (says Valesius) who knows Greek The bishops clearly sat as imperial commissioners.

The decision was in Cæcilian's favour So also was the decision of the Council of Arles [A.D. 314], and the judgment of the Emperor himself [A.D. 316], which were successively taken upon the prayer of the Donatists for a further hearing By the two last courts Felix was acquitted as well as Cæcilian

Majorinus was succeeded by Donatus, called the Great, to distinguish him from Donatus of Casæ Nigræ Under him the schismatic principles of the sect ossified themselves into a formal heresy, and its fanaticism was largely increased The factious conduct of the sect provoked Constantine to take severe measures with them; they were deprived of their churches, their bishops banished. A fanatical banditti sprung from the exasperated body, and these ruffians grew so strong, and spread so much alarm, that the Emperor, in fear of civil war, recalled his edicts, and tried to appease the Donatists by a toleration But the Circumcellions were not to be so checked, nor the general body to be so appeased Constans was obliged to have recourse to arms, but he used them in such a manner that punishment became persecution Julian favoured the sect, and in no long time it spread over the larger part of the province of Africa, while in Numidia it had an uncontested superiority. It is said to have numbered four hundred bishops Gratian and Valentinian prohibited the assemblies of the Donatists, and commanded that their churches should be closed or restored to the Catholics. But these attempts to stop the schism were in vain, and a law of Honorius in the year 405, occasioned by the renewed violences of the Circumcellions, commanded these men under the severest penalties to reunite themselves to the Catholic Church Augustine had now brought his power to bear on the controversy In the year 411 a conference, at which were present two hundred and eighty-six Catholic, and two hundred and seventy-nine Donatist bishops, was held at Carthage, at the command of the Emperor, and under the superintendence of the prætor Marcellinus The Catholic bishops pledged themselves, in the event of reunion, to receive the Donatist bishops with all their ecclesiastical dignities, an act of self-denial which was met with pride and contempt "The sons of martyrs can have nothing to do with the race of Traditors" After evasive delays St Augustine was enabled to refute the dogmatical proposition which his adversaries finally advanced, he proved that the Church, by the unavoidable tolerance of wicked men, had not forfeited its character of sanctity, truth, and Catholicity [Dollinger's *Ch Hist* Cox's *transl* ii p 101]

Marcellinus, the Emperor's deputy, who presided in the assembly, decided in favour of the Catholics, and ordered them to take possession of the churches which the Donatist bishops had unjustly become possessed of

Another and a more decisive law of the year 413 produced the effect, that many of the Donatist communities, together with their bishops, passed over to the Church The prudence of the Catholic bishops, and the moderation of the canons of the Council of Carthage [A.D. 418-419], which will be detailed hereafter, restored many to the unity of the Church But the sect was not quite extinct until the seventh century.

This outline, however brief, will be sufficient to introduce the consideration of the essential points and leading character of the Donatist schism Montanism, which arose in Phrygia, grew in Africa as in a congenial soil Novatianism, which sprung from Africa, returned from Rome to be received in its birth-place with enthusiasm Donatism is to be attributed to the working of the same schismatic spirit, springing from a perversion of the fervency and zeal of African Christianity The disputed election of Cæcilian was but an opportune occasion for this spirit to shew itself, the simony of Lucilla was but an accident in its development Montanism, in setting up its claim to be the Church, had sheltered itself under the pretence of a new prophecy, by which the constitution and discipline of the Church was to be perfected. Novatianism had cast off this disguise, and proclaimed itself the Church of the pure, simply from the discipline which it enforced. It was to be the true Church, because of the character of its members. The Donatists rejected these principles of the Novatians[1] as heretical, boasted that they deviated in nothing from Catholic doctrine and practice, but maintained that they alone possessed an uncorrupted priesthood, that the ministry of the Church Catholic was invalidated by guilt Donatism was to be the true Church[2] in regard of the validity of its apostolical succession. The sectarians of Africa thus bade the Church stand by, in the first case because it was incomplete, in the second case because it was impure, in the third case because it was priestless Consequently, while both Novatians and Donatists[3] rebaptized the Catholics who joined them, there were these differences in their practice. The Donatists retained the use of chrism, and admitted the lapsed to penance, and did not condemn second marriages They were very strong Episcopalians, however irregular in their mode of working out their principles, while Novatian appears to have rather yielded to Episcopacy from necessity than to have adopted it from principle. [NOVATIANS]

[1] Cresconius, whose words are quoted by Augustine, names the Novatians along with the Manichæans, Arians, and other heretics, and proceeds, "Inter nos, quibus idem Christus natus, mortuus et resurgens, una religio, eadem Sacramenta, nihil in Christiana observatione diversum, schisma factum, non hæresis dicitur" Nor does Augustine in reply fix upon Cresconius any of these special heresies, but argues from the fact of the Donatist rebaptism [*cont Cresc* ii 4 6]

[2] "Inter nos et Donatistas quæstio est, ubi sit hoc corpus (sc Christi), id est, ubi sit Ecclesia" [Aug *De Unit Eccl* 2]

[3] The Donatists were not unanimous in rebaptizing Tichonius, a Donatist quoted by Augustine, tells of a synod at Carthage of two hundred and seventy bishops of the sect which passed a decree against the practice This must have been about the year 330 The authority of this synod did not prevail [August *Epist ad Vincent.* 93, n. 43. See Dupin's *Hist.* p. xxiv].

Fanaticism, which was increasing in the African Church, thus gained a special object, the Catholic priesthood, against which it could concentrate itself; and it burst forth in profanation of Church, altar, and Eucharist, in everything which could mark contempt for the body it counted profane Outrage and cruelty followed, culminating in the ruffianism and rebellion of the Circumcellions These excesses were disapproved and checked by the governing body of the Donatists to the best of their power, but those who have themselves rebelled against authority are seldom able to enforce order among their followers

The history of the Synod of Cirta appears to guide us to the cause of this rigorous fanaticism Inquiry being then made into the number of Traditors, so many of the bishops appeared to be implicated in that guilt that the assembly dared not proceed with the inquiry, and closed the matter by referring all to the judgment of God It is commonly observed that men who have been guilty of a crime are most severe upon that crime; and it seems that the Numidian bishops, conscience-stricken at the extent of guilt, instead of endeavouring to possess their souls in patience in future trials, instead of revenging their disobedience upon themselves in repentance, revenged themselves upon others, charging Cæcilian (wrongfully however) with the guilt from which they were not themselves free, and drawing conclusions from that guilt which they had not drawn in their own case The history of the Church presents many an example of such inconsistency They were compelled by the necessity of self-justification to extend those conclusions to the whole body of the Church.

It has been already observed that the Donatists set the first example of referring spiritual affairs to the decision of the civil ruler In the consideration of this point it must be borne in mind that the established constitutional doctrine of Rome was that the Republic (now the Emperor) was the religious as well as the civil head of the State.[1] Accordingly when Christianity was established (at the very time we are speaking of), and when Constantine professed Christianity, the Emperor, by constitutional rule, accepted the chief government of all estates of his realm, whether ecclesiastical or civil But it remained to define the true limits of the peculiar and special jurisprudence which had grown up in the action of courts Christian, to define the limits and rights of the internal legislation of the Church It is nothing wonderful that at the very first establishment of Christianity men had no correct notions of the nature and extent of the imperial supremacy; nor is it any special blame to the Donatists, for they share it with all Christendom, that zeal made them think it right to call in the secular power to advance what was believed to be the truth Catholics and schismatics alike upheld the imperial supremacy when it was on their side But there must be bounds to these concessions and allowances; and surely the nature of the crime with which Felix was charged, and the effect of the fact, if proved, upon Cæcilian's consecration, was a matter, if any could be, for determination by Church authority. Again the appeal from the Council of Arles to the Emperor cannot be extenuated by any uncertainty as to the limits of the imperial supremacy It was at the petition of the Donatists that the Emperor, whether or not exceeding his legitimate powers, had appointed ecclesiastical commissioners to try the case; and when they complained of the insufficiency of the tribunal he summoned a synod so large that writers of good repute have asserted it to be a plenary council To appeal from this to the Emperor in person was to surrender the liberties of the Church by denying the power of her synods The Emperor himself felt that their conduct was not that of Churchmen "Sicut in causis gentilium fieri solet, appellationem interposuerunt" [Optat i 25, and Dupin's note] Vexed at their successive defeats, and urged by the haughty temper of Donatus of Carthage, the party now asserted their independence of the civil power as insolently as they had before submissively courted its aid "Quid Christianis cum regibus, aut quid Episcopis cum palatio?" "Quid est Imperatori cum Ecclesia?" [Optat i 22, and iii 3.] Nor did their opponents fail to remind them of the inconsistency One suit appears to have been heard in a civil court at the request of the Catholics It was one step in the controversy, a part of the case, the whole of which had been referred to the Emperor Silvanus had been elected bishop of Cirta or Constantina A deacon, Naudinarius, was excommunicated by him, and in revenge betrayed the secrets of the party He made known that Silvanus was a Traditor, and he revealed the simony of Lucilla An inquiry into this was conducted by Zenophilus, Proconsul of Numidia, and ended in the banishment of Silvanus [Aug *cont. Cres* iii. 30 *Gesta apud Zenoph in Monum*, Dupin, p 261] Ursacius, a Comes in the province, then beginning to restrain the Donatists by force, they reckoned him their first persecutor

From the time of their condemnation by Constans in A D 348, the Donatists remained in exile until the reign of Julian Their demeanour towards this Emperor is a remarkable instance of the deterioration of mind and conscience produced by schism The simple fact that they sought and obtained Julian's permission to return from exile is surely no blame to them, while at the same time the character of the man who favoured them, and the degree of favour shewed them, are not unimportant in forming an estimate of the party favoured But there is sufficient evidence of unseemly flattery and unworthy compliances having been used to obtain the favour Augustine quotes and comments upon their petition "Vobis enim, qui sic nos arguitis (the subject being the friendship between the Catholics and Christian kings) quid fuit cum rege pagano, et quod est gravius, apostata et Christiani nominis hoste Juliano, a quo vobis basilicas quasi vestras reddi deprecantes, hoc in ejus laude posuistis, 'quod apud eum sola justitia locum

[1] See Milman, *Latin Christianity*, III v.

haberet?' Quibus verbis (credo enim vos latine intelligere) et idololatria Juliani, et apostasia justitia est appellata Tenetur petitio, quam vestri majores dederunt, constitutio, quam impetraverunt, gesta, ubi allegaverunt. Evigilate et attendite, inimico Christi, apostatæ, adversario Christianorum, servo dæmoniorum, talibus verbis ille, ille, vester ille Pontius supplicavit Ite nunc, et nobis dicite, 'Quid vobis est cum regibus sæculi'?" [*cont Lit Petil* ii 203 See also *cont Ep Parmen* i 12] A stronger proof of the character of the petition is the law of Arcadius and Honorius [A D 400], ordering the petition and Julian's Rescript to be posted up, "quo omnibus innotescat et Catholicæ confidentiæ stabilita constantia et Donatistarum desperatio fucata perfidia" [*Cod. Theod* XVI v 37]

Socrates tells us that the way to Julian's favour was to vilify the memory of Constantius, an accusation of Constantius ensued the granting a request without it Julian indulged his hatred of all Christians [iii 9] It is not unreasonable to conclude that in this way the Donatists gained Julian's ear, and laid themselves open to the bitter taunt of Optatus, "Eadem voce vobis libertas est reddita, qua voce idolorum patefieri jussa sunt templa" [ii 16]

We must now turn to the action of the Church with regard to this sect, and to the status of the sect as determined by canon The assembly at Rome under Miltiades was clearly not a proper synod, but a meeting of imperial commissioners Its authority seems to be derived in part from the imperial supremacy, in part to be that of arbitrators But as its decision was appealed against, and the appeal allowed, a discussion of its authority would be superfluous It is all important, however, to ascertain, if possible, the character of the assembly of Arles That it was summoned by the Emperor will be no difficulty to an English Churchman, and we may pass over that point as concerning those of the Romish obedience, with a reference to the Dissertation of Natalis Alexander, and the animadversions of his editors [*Diss* v vol vii p 372, ed Bingii ad Rhen 1787]

Constantine, in his letter to Chrestus, says that he has summoned πλείστους ἐκ διαφόρων καὶ ἀμυθήτων τόπων ἐπισκόπους" [Euseb *H E* x 5] Two hundred bishops met[1] They were principally from Italy, Spain, and Gaul [Aug *cont Parmen* i 5], but the subscriptions shew also bishops from Apuleia, Dalmatia, Britannia, Sardinia, Sicilia, Africa They held themselves to be a formal synod, and proceeded accordingly Without accepting then the estimate which some have formed of this council, that it was plenary, we can hardly reduce it to the rank of a provincial council of Gaul It reckons as a great council of the Western Church, and such Dollinger calls it Besides the special consideration of Cæcilian's case, the council enacted twenty-two Canons [DICT *of* THEOL., COUNCILS] Of these Canon viii lays down the principle by which the baptism of heretics is to be judged, and by consequence allows the baptism of the Donatists, and condemns their practice of rebaptizing Heretics are to be received with imposition of hands Canon xiii deals with the case of Traditors Traditors of the clergy are to be degraded if the crime is proved by public process; ordinations by Traditor bishops are valid if no other crime is charged to the ordained Some manuscripts add six more canons, of which one is that a convert, "de Donatistis vel de Montensibus," is to be received with imposition of hands, as their baptism is irregular But these probably belong to some other council [see Mansi *in loc*]

The status of the sect was determined by the great Council of Carthage which framed the celebrated African code.[2] By this code those who were baptized in infancy by the Donatists may be ordained if they renounce their heresy, and have been received into the Church by imposition of hands [Can lvii, see also Can xlvii a re-enactment of *Conc Carthag* III xlviii] the Donatist clergy may be received, retaining the same honour, if the bishop of the place thinks fit [Can lxviii This canon mentions a canon of a transmarine council to the contrary, which it does not pretend to annul, leaving each Church to its liberty] Donatist dioceses on conversion may retain their bishops without consulting the synod, on the death of such bishops, the diocese may be united to another diocese if the people wish it, bishops who converted people before the decree of unity shall retain that people, but since that decree all churches with their dioceses, and all the utensils of the Church, shall be challenged by the Catholic bishops, whether the people be converted or not [Can xcix] the Donatists are to be treated with lenity and temper, their leaders to be called to conferences [Can lxvi xci and xcii]

The attempts of the Donatists to establish themselves elsewhere than in Africa were unsuccessful The sect early tried to obtain a footing in Rome, and sent thither Victor, Bishop of Garbis in Numidia, one of the Synod of Cirta, to attach the African residents to the party Victor could not obtain one of the forty basilicas of Rome, and was forced to wattle in a hill cavern for a conventicle, whence his few adherents were called Montenses He was, Optatus writes, "Pastor sine grege, episcopus sine populo."

[1] See Nat Alex vii p 35, and *Diss* iv *Quæst* ii p 370 Sismondi and Launoi hold the council plenary Dupin, resting on the number of subscriptions, will not allow that two hundred bishops were present 'Αμυθήτων in Constantine's letter is to be translated "unspeakably numerous"

[2] In the year 418 419 all canons formerly made in sixteen councils held at Carthage, one at Milevis, one at Hippo, that were approved of, were read, and received a new sanction from a great number of bishops then met in Synod at Carthage This collection is the code of the African Church, which was always in greatest repute in all churches next after the code of the Universal Church This code was of very great authority in the old English Churches, for many of the excerpts of Egbert were transcribed from it And though the code of the Universal Church ends with the Canons of Chalcedon, yet these African Canons are inserted into the ancient code both of the Eastern and Western Churches. [Johnson's *Vade Mecum*, ii 171]

Yet there was a succession of schismatical bishops down to Optatus' time [Opt ii 4] The attempt to gain a footing in Spain failed also completely A bishop was settled there on one private estate, the estate of a woman whom the Benedictine editors of Augustine not unnaturally suppose to have been Lucilla The absurdity of the Donatists' claim to be the Catholic Church was convincingly shewn Augustine applied to the Church the Psalmist's words, "A finibus terræ ad te clamavi," and remarked, "Non est ergo in sola Africa, vel solis Afris, episcopum Romam paucis Montensibus,[1] et in Hispaniam domui unius mulieris ex Africa mittentibus" [*cont Petil* ii 247, see also *De Unit Eccl* 6] Not less instructive is the internal history of the sect This presents two things for consideration —the connection of the Circumcellions with the Donatist body, and the breaking up of the Donatist body into minor schisms

Gibbon, who calls the Circumcellions the strength and the scandal of the Donatists, states that they were peasants of Numidia and Mauritania who had been imperfectly reduced under the authority of the Roman law, who were imperfectly converted to the Christian faith, but who were actuated by a blind and furious enthusiasm in the cause of their Donatist teachers They pretended also to restore the primitive equality of mankind, and to reform the abuses of civil society, and opened a secure asylum for the slaves and debtors who flocked in crowds to their holy standard [*Decline and Fall*, ch xxi] Mere motives of polity, however, whether of ecclesiastical or civil polity, will not account for the fanaticism of the Circumcellions It was not simple enthusiasm for their teachers that inspired them, but enthusiasm for their teachers because they believed themselves to be, in connection with those teachers, the chosen of God To engender religious fanaticism there must be a belief of some more special and closer relationship to Almighty God than is possessed by those from whom the fanatic is separated, with the belief, in which lies the original spring of the fanaticism, that the relationship to God is not mediate through a body which God has chosen, but immediate and direct. Herein lies the difference and total opposition of the genuine enthusiasm of the Jew as one of a holy nation, of the Christian as a member of a holy body, and of the spurious enthusiasm, leading to fanaticism, of the self-sufficient Jew and the self-sufficient and sectarian Christian. In the former is the abnegation, in the latter the predominance of self In the former the individual is holy because he is a member of a holy body, in the latter the body is holy because it has the aggregate holiness of all its members Now this predominance of self may be either personal, by a perversion of the doctrine of election, which sets aside the general body of the Church as non-elect, or sectarian, by a perversion of the doctrine of the ministry, which sets aside the general body of the Church as destitute of the grace of God The English Puritans were fanatics of the first kind, the Donatists were fanatics of the second kind Both agreed in the self-righteousness by which they alike held themselves to be the only pure and holy of men And from this sprung the attachment of the Puritan to his Gospel preacher and of the Donatist to his immaculate priesthood. The Circumcellions, therefore, we must consider to be a body which was inevitably formed from the inculcation of the fanatical principles of the Donatist body upon a ferocious and half-civilized population It was on this account that the opposition to them from the moderate part of the body was in reality so weak Excesses might be disavowed and condemned, but the original principle of the fanaticism could not be controverted Gibbon remarks that habits of idleness and rapine were consecrated by the name of religion and faintly condemned by the doctors of the sect [CIRCUMCELLIONS]

It was not long before the sect suffered the usual fate of sects, and was subdivided Donatus was succeeded in the bishopric of Carthage by Parmenian Primian followed, A D 391; but presently Maximian was consecrated in opposition to him by no inconsiderable minority Opposing councils were held, one by fifty-three Maximian bishops in the neighbourhood of Carthage, A D 394, in which Primian was condemned on the score of many irregularities and crimes The synodal Epistle of this council is given by Augustine, *Enarr in Ps.* xxxvi Primian was again condemned by a council of one hundred bishops, which met at Cabarsassis in the province of Byzacena [Aug *cont Crescon* iv 6] But the Primian party prevailed Three hundred and ten bishops of his side met at Bagai (in Numidia [Dupin], incerta sedes [Fell]), and condemned Maximian and his twelve ordainers Maximian's adherents were allowed to return to the main body without penance if they returned within a limited period [*cont Crescon* iii 56, 60] The Primianists now claimed the title of Catholic, and prayed the proconsuls to eject the Maximianists from their churches by virtue of laws made against the Donatists in favour of the Catholics There seems to have been hesitation regarding the validity of the Maximian baptism, but after a while both the baptism and the orders of the

[1] If the name Montenses was confined to the Roman Donatists, and these were so insignificant as Optatus and Augustine represent them, it is not easy to understand how the Montenses, as a distinct sect, occur in the Canon which has been quoted regarding converts, "De Donatistis vel de Montensibus" The Canon, though wrongly attributed to the Council of Arles, appears to have been a canon of an early Council, and probably of a Council of Gaul The Montenses are named also in the Decretal Epistle to Victricius ascribed to Innocent, which is an early forgery It seems unlikely that one small congregation of Donatist hill-folk should be so noticed Epiphanius and Theodoret class the Donatists with the Novatians, and the latter says that the Novatians were called Montenses at Rome [Epiph *Hær* lix, Theodor *Hær fab* iii 5] May it not be that Theodoret was right, that the Novatians of Rome imported the name Montenses from Carthage [see Fell's note on *Cyprian, Ep* xli, "Cum Felicissimus comminatus sit non communicaturos in monte secum"], and that a small party of them becoming Donatists were still called Montenses

smaller party were allowed. By this conduct the Primianists, or larger party, afforded the Catholics strong arguments against themselves. The taint of the many crimes for which Maximian had been condemned did not unchurch those who had been in communion with him: how could the taint of Cæcilian's crimes unchurch the whole of Christendom? The baptism of the Maximianists was valid: why not the baptism of the Catholics? [August. *de Hær* lxix, *cont Crescon* iii 1, 7, 14, *Brev Collat* iii 8, *cont Gaud* i 39] The same argument is urged in the 69th canon of the African Code, which is, "That legates be sent to preach peace to the Donatists, both bishops and laity; and to shew them that they departed from the Church as causelessly as the Maximianists have from them, and that they receive converts from the Maximianists as the Church does from the Donatists, viz allowing their ordination and baptism" [Johnson's abridged translation in *Vade mecum*, p 196] Augustine relates that there were many other divisions, little known, among the Donatists Next in importance to the division of Maximian appears that of Rogatus, but the cause of division is uncertain. The party of Rogatists inclined to moderation, and rejected the aid of the Circumcellions

DORMITANTES [NYCTAGES.]

DORRELLITES The followers of a fanatic named Dorrell, who appeared at Leyden in Massachusetts at the end of the last century, and proclaimed himself as a prophet sent to supersede Christianity He denied the Resurrection of our Lord, and of Christians, declaring that the only resurrection known to the Scriptures was the change from sin to righteousness. But the Scriptures are only a type of true revelation, which is an inward light given to the soul, those who possess the latter being incapable of sinning The outcome of his heterogeneous heresy was simply Antinomian Deism, as he denied also the Omniscience of God

DORT, SYNOD OF. A Calvinist Assembly of the United Provinces of Holland, joined by Royal Commissioners from England, and by Deputies from Hesse, Bremen, Switzerland, and the Palatinate, held at Dordrecht, or Dort, in the years A D 1618-1619, regarding the Five Points in controversy between Arminians and Calvinists

This Synod is of considerable interest both in ecclesiastical and civil history: in ecclesiastical history, not from any weight which its canons have in the Catholic Church, but as an exhibition of Calvinistic theology, and as the turning-point at which Calvinism, seemingly triumphant, began to decline, while Arminianism rapidly degenerated into a dangerous Latitudinarianism, in civil history, from its close connection with the contest carried on between the ambitious Maurice and the republicans who were headed by Barneveldt and Grotius.

Political and religious motives united to bring about the Synod. Maurice and his partisans in the States knew that a synodical condemnation of the Arminians would further their purposes, and they fostered and made use of the "odium theologicum" to hasten the ends of the "odium politicum" The States accordingly ordered the Council to be assembled on the 1st of November 1618 In each provincial synod six representatives were to be chosen, four or three clerics, two or three laics. In these synods gravamina and instructions to the representatives were to be prepared In the provinces of Holland and Utrecht, where a formal separation had taken place between the Calvinists and Arminians, the number of representatives was to be divided between the two. Delegates were appointed by the States to open the Synod and to act as moderators It is to be noticed that in A D. 1618 the controversy between the two parties was limited to the well-known Five Articles, the other subjects of contention were of later date The substance of the Five Articles is given in the article ARMINIANS, and need not be repeated at length It is enough to remind the reader, that [1] is De Electione et Reprobatione, [2] De Universalitate Mortis Christi, [3] De Libero Arbitrio, [4] De Operatione Gratiæ Dei, [5] De Perseverantia vere Fidelium

The Synod met at the time appointed, and after several sessions spent in preliminaries, at the fifth session there was passed a citation to the leaders of the Remonstrants to appear in fourteen days, "Ut in eadem (synodo) dictos Articulos libero proponant, explicent, et defendant quantum possunt et necessarium judicabunt" Until the real business could begin, on the appearance of the Remonstrants, the Synod occupied itself in debates concerning catechisms, the translation of the Bible, and the baptism of heathens adopted into Christian families[1] On the 6th of December the Remonstrants appeared Episcopius was their leader and chief spokesman. As business was now about to begin, a difficulty occurred with regard to the Arminians (particularly those of Utrecht) who had been returned as members of the Synod, and it was agreed that they should be allowed to act as members of the Synod on condition of not consulting with and assisting the Citati. They determined, however, to join their brethren The Remonstrants now made objections to the Synod It was, they urged, only a dominant party sitting to judge those to whom it was notoriously opposed It contained many schismatics, for with that dominant party rested the guilt of the schism in several provinces between the Arminians and Calvinists The Synod, backed by the power of the moderators, commanded the Remonstrants to plead their cause They did not refuse to do so, but difficulties arose as to the mode of doing it. The Remonstrants insisted on beginning with the point of Reprobation, which the Synod determined to defer till cognate points had been discussed; they objected to the system of interrogatories, not choosing to be catechized as by

[1] Regarding infants it was determined, that till they came to years of discretion they should by no means be baptized "A strange decision," Hales wrote, "and such as, if my memory and reading fail me not, no Church, either ancient or modern, ever gave"

pædagogues, they insisted on full freedom of disputation The Synod insisted on prescribing the course and manner of the discussion, and ordered each man, as cited separately, to answer separately for himself The Remonstrants would not yield, and were dismissed, the prolocutor telling them that they came with a lie and went away with a lie, that their actions had all been full of fraud, equivocation and deceit The Synod then proceeded to gather the opinions of the Remonstrants out of their published books. They obtained in writing the judgments of the deputies of the provinces, province by province, and of the deputies of the foreign churches, church by church, from which they framed their canons, on the first point 18 articles and 9 rejections of errors, on the second, 9 and 7, on the third and fourth, 17 and 9, on the fifth, 15 and 9 "All I can say is," wrote Walter Balcanqual, "me thinketh it is very hard that every man should be deposed from his ministry who will not hold every particular canon, never did any church of old, nor any reformed church, propose so many articles to be held *sub pœna excommunicationis*' He had before warned Sir Dudley Carleton of the course things were taking "We are like to make the Synod a thing to be laughed at in after ages The president and his provincials would have their canons so full charged with catechetical speculations, as they will be ready to burst, and I perceive it plainly that there is never a Contra-Remonstrant minister in the Synod that hath delivered any doctrine which hath been excepted against by the Remonstrants, but they would have it in by head and shoulders in some canon, that so they might have something to shew for that which they have said" [Balcanqual's[1] *Letters* in Hales' *Remains*, pp 146, 141] These canons may be read in the Oxford *Sylloge Confess* 1827 To describe them we will borrow the words of a writer in the *Encyclopædia Metropolitana*, who speaks of the Synod of Dort as an "assembly which by its absurd definitions shewed that it had yet to learn the mere elements of scholastic theology, yet which had the impudence to boast that its miraculous labours had caused hell itself to tremble" [xiii p 621]

The English commissioners to the Synod were Carleton, Bishop of Llandaff, Joseph Hall, Dean of Worcester, John Davenant, Margaret Professor, Cambridge, and Samuel Ward, Master of Sidney College, Cambridge These were joined after a while by Walter Balcanqual, a Scottish divine These were only King's commissioners, and the Church of England is no way compromised by any act of theirs James' instruction to them may be seen in *Collier*, vii p 409, ed 1852.

[1] Balcanqual, opposed as he was to the Arminians, quite saw the character of the other party "They are so eager to kill the Remonstrants, that they would make their words have that sense which no grammar can find in them" [p 144] The president "makes canons and passes them by placet or non placet, and then he hath so many of the provincials at command to pass what he will" [p 140] Both he and Hales complain of the treatment the foreigners met with [pp 73, 78]

They appear to have followed their instructions, and to have held a moderate course In the 145th session, upon the introduction of the Belgic Confession, Bishop Carleton made a protestation on behalf of Episcopacy His declaration to this effect, published upon his return to England, is in Collier This is mentioned also in Balcanqual's notes of that session [Hales' *Remains*, p 161] but in the published Acts of the Synod no notice whatever is taken of the protestation [*Acta*, p 148]

The tenets of Arminius were thus condemned by the Synod, and the Remonstrants were required to subscribe the condemnation Upon their refusal about seven hundred families were banished by an order of the States General Aided by the religious fanaticism which he had fostered, Maurice summoned a council of his own creatures, and condemned Barneveldt to death, Hoogarbetz and Grotius to perpetual imprisonment

[*Acta Synodi Nationalis, Dordrechti hab* Dordrechti, 1620 *Golden Remains of J Hales*, 1673 (*Letters of Hales, Balcanqual, and of the British Divines, with some documents*) Collier *Ecc Hist* vol vii]

DOSITHEANS. There were two sects of this name, neither of them Christian, one, which might perhaps be more properly called Dosthenes,[2] an ancient Samaritan sect, the other, the followers of Dositheus, a Samaritan, who after our Lord's death (but at what exact time is not known) claimed to be the Messiah

I According to Jewish tradition the name of the priest sent to teach the settlers in Samaria [2 Kings xvii 27] was Dosthai Fabricius pointed out that this Dosthai was frequently confounded even by ancient writers with the later impostor Thus the author of the *Recognitions*, knowing of the later Dositheus, and believing that the Sadducees were connected with the Dositheans (that is, with the early sect, as is stated by Epiphanius) has brought down the rise of Sadduceism to the late date, to the time of John the Baptist [i 54] This confusion will account for several inconsistencies in the notices of Dositheus It explains, *e g*, why many of the Fathers, as Gieseler remarked, attribute to Dositheus, as if peculiar to him, what was common to all the Samaritans Fabricius further identifies with Dosthai the Dositheus of Epiphanius [note on *Philast* cap iv in Oehler's *Corp Hæres* i p 8] No doubt Epiphanius, as also Pseudo-Tertullian, speaks of an early Samaritan sect for he derives from it the ancient sect of the Sadducees [Epiph *Hær* xiii xiv, Ps-Tertull cap i] But it is not explained how the original Dosthai, a teacher of the whole population, became founder of a sect of Samaritans, nor does the character of that sect at all suit the early times of Sennacherib The sect is manifestly the product of a later time, though still early with regard to the time of Christ Whether

[2] Eulogius called Dositheus Dosthes, and his followers Dostheni, apparently a nearer form of the original name Dosthai [Phot *Bibl Cod* 230]

it was founded by a second Dosthai or Dositheus, or took the name of the original teacher of the Samaritans, imports little These Dositheans believed in the Resurrection; lived an ascetic life, some in celibacy, some avoiding second marriages,[1] practised circumcision, and kept the Sabbath as the other Samaritans did. [See Drusius, *de Tribus Sectis*, III iv vi]

II. That about the time of our Saviour there was a Dositheus, a Samaritan, who claimed to be the Messiah, is certain Origen states that Dositheus, the Samaritan, endeavoured to persuade his countrymen that he was the Christ foretold by Moses, that this was after the time of Christ, that he appears to have gained some disciples, but that the sect did not flourish, and was extinct at the time of Origen's writing [*cont. Celsum*, pp 44, 382, ed Spencer] Jerome says that he preceded the coming of Christ [*adv Lucif* 23]. Origen's statement is more probably correct, not only because he is the earlier authority, but because the false Christs were in general after Christ's death, and because Dositheus' connection with Simon Magus, and the Gnosticism he appears to have held, require the later date. With Simon, Dositheus is connected, but some make him the master, some the disciple The author of the *Recognitions* makes him the master, influenced probably by the confusion with Dosthai. Theodoret reckons the Dositheans a branch of the Simonians [*Hær fab* i 1] In the Clementine Homilies, Simon and Dositheus appear as followers of John Hemero-Baptist, and contending after his death for the leadership of the party [ii 24] Starting from the theology and practice of the Samaritan ascetics, Dositheus took so much of the system of Simon as would facilitate his pretension to be the prophet like Moses Thus Origen tells of his over scrupulous observance of the Sabbath [*de Princ* IV i 17], and couples him with Simon, the latter pretending to be the great power of God, the former to be the Son of God Himself [*cont Cels* vi] Origen has been quoted as saying that the sect was extinct In another place [*in Joan* tom xiv] he speaks of Dositheans then existing, who asserted their master to be alive As late as A D 588 the Dositheans and Samaritans had a controversy in Egypt about Deut xviii 18, Eulogius the Patriarch of Alexandria interfering in the dispute, and publishing an oration entitled *Decretum in Samaritanos* Some of the Samaritans asserted that Joshua was the prophet like Moses, others that the prophet was Dositheus, the contemporary of Simon Magus [Eulogius in Photius, *Bibl Cod* 230, *s f*]

DOULEIANS [PSATHYRIANS]

DRABICIANS. A temporary sect of MORAVIAN BRETHREN, followers of a fanatic named Nicolas Drabik or Drabicius, who appeared in Hungary about A.D. 1630. Drabik was a pedlar who had been compelled to leave Moravia, his native country, when the Protestants were driven thence by persecution in the previous year. A few years later he professed to have seen heavenly visions announcing the approach of great armies from the North and the East, which were about to overthrow the house of Austria These visions he printed in the form of a prophetic book, prefaced by the formula, "The word of the Lord came to me," and entitled *Light out of Darkness* They spoke of the reigning dynasty as being the house of Ahab, which, like it, was doomed to be utterly destroyed, and pronounced a sentence of equally rapid destruction upon Rome This book was written in his native tongue, but was translated into Latin (then spoken as much as the Magyar in Hungary) by one of Drabik's followers, and printed at Amsterdam in the year 1665 Its fanatical contents, and the number of followers which such teaching attracted, caused Drabik to be apprehended and tried for treason and heresy, and upon his execution in 1671 his followers are lost sight of in the ten years' severity which followed this and several other rebellious movements among the Protestants of Hungary [Debiezenus, *Hist Eccl Reform in Hungar*, *Hist of Prot Ch. in Hungary*]

DUALISTS Early Christianity was so much brought into contact with Oriental philosophy, that many speculative thinkers were led to seek for some means of reconciling its fundamental theories with Christian revelation. Hence the Oriental theories of two Deities, one the author of good, the other the author of evil, were introduced into every early heresy that pretended to view Christianity in its philosophical aspect, and the opinion so floating down along the stream of Eastern heresy, found a broader means of diffusion in the Manichæan system, which infected not only the waning East, but mediæval Europe Some account of the dualism of particular sects will be found under their respective names, but for a general view of the origin and course of the theory the reader is referred to the article DUALISM in the DICTIONARY *of* THEOLOGY

DUCES SANCTORUM A complimentary title given to the CIRCUMCELLIONS by Donatus as the military "champions or leaders of the Saints"

DUCHOBORTZI A name signifying "combatants in the spirit," which was given to a Russian sect of BEZPOPOFTSCHINS, whose existence dates from the reign of the Empress Anne in the middle of the eighteenth century [A D 1730-40] From the opposition of the sect to the use of devotional pictures or "icons" it is also sometimes called Ikonobortzi

The Duchobortzi were persecuted under Catharine II. and Paul I [A D 1762-1801] for refusing to serve in the army, but they were tolerated under Alexander I [A D. 1801-1825], who allowed them to settle in some numbers on the banks of the river Molochna They believed themselves to be descended in a mystical manner from Shadrach, Meshach and Abednego, and were sufficiently conservative in their views to reject the emendations of the Patriarch Nicon and to use the old Sclavonic liturgies in public worship. They

[1] This point is doubtful See the note in Oehler on Epiph *Hær* xiii

combined in a remarkable degree a metaphysical belief, full of abstract ideas, and much resembling Gnosticism, with gross practical superstitions One of their most famous leaders, named Kapustin, who resided at Terpenie, introduced the community of goods He was imprisoned [A D. 1814] for proselytizing, and died [A D. 1820] in a cave in which he had spent the last few years of his life The following are some of the chief points of their creed, as presented to Kochowski, governor of Jekatrinoslaf, during their persecution by Catharine II :—

"God is only one, but He is one in the Trinity. This holy Trinity is an inscrutable Being The Father is the light, the Son is the life, the Holy Ghost is the peace In man the Father is manifested as the memory, the Son as the reason, the Holy Ghost as the will The human soul is the image of God, but this image in us is nothing else than the memory, the reason and the will The soul had existed before the creation of the visible world. The soul fell before the creation of the world, together with many spirits who fell in the spiritual world alone, therefore the fall of Adam and Eve, which is described in the Scripture, must not be taken in its usual sense; but this part of the Scripture is an image, wherein is represented, firstly, the fall of the human soul from a state of exalted purity in a spiritual sphere, before it came into this world; secondly, the fall, which was repeated by Adam in the beginning of the days of this world, and which is adapted to our understanding; thirdly, the fall, which since Adam is spiritually and carnally repeated by all of us men, and which will be repeated till the end of the world. Originally the fall of the soul was brought about by its contemplating itself, and beginning to love only itself, so that it turned away from the contemplation and love of God, and by a voluntary pride When the soul was for its punishment enclosed in the prison of the body, it fell for the second time in the person of Adam, through the guilt of the seductive serpent; that is to say, through the evil-corrupted will of the flesh At present the fall of all of us is caused by the seduction of the same serpent, which has entered into us through Adam, through the use of the forbidden fruit, that is to say, through the pride and vaingloriousness of the spirit, and the lasciviousness of the flesh"

With regard to miracles the Duchobortzi said, "We believe that Christ has performed them We were ourselves through our sins dead, blind, and deaf, and He has animated us again But we do not know of any outward bodily miracles"

This last view did not imply the rejection of Holy Writ as either false or as uninspired by God, but they maintained that everything recorded there had a mysterious and symbolical meaning which was exclusively revealed to themselves. The history of Cain was an allegory of the wicked sons of Adam, who persecute the invisible church typified by Abel The confusion of tongues at Babel was the separation of churches The drowning of Pharaoh and the Egyptians was a symbol of the defeat of Satan, who, with all his adherents, will perish in a Red Sea of fire, through which the elect, i.e the Duchobortzi, will pass unscathed The same principle of interpretation was applied to all the facts of the New Testament, which were not considered to have literally taken place, but to be an allegorical mode of conveying spiritual truths

This metaphysical creed did not preserve the members of this sect from gross practical superstitions and the exercise of intolerable cruelties. A judicial inquiry ordered by the government [A D 1834-9] established the fact that they gave asylum to military deserters, concealed the crimes of their brethren, and were in the habit of carrying off all whom they suspected of defection from their sect and from the regulations laid down for its welfare by Kapustin, their convert and leader in the earlier part of the present century, to an island of the Molochna, ironically termed by them Ray i Muka, i e "paradise and torment," and putting them to death in various ways They were sentenced by the Emperor Nicholas I to transportation to the Trans-Caucasian provinces, where they were so divided from each other that they could not meet for consultation or for any form of public worship.

DULCINISTÆ [APOSTOLICALS]

DUNKERS [TUNKERS]

DUNS SCOTUS. [SCHOOLMEN]

DUTCH PROTESTANTS The Reformation spread in the Netherlands in spite of State opposition, rather than in consequence of royal favour. The writings of Erasmus on the abuses of religion, quite early in the sixteenth century, and those of Luther some years afterwards, first began to rouse general attention to the subject, the latter works having become so popular that Charles V, two years after his accession to the Empire of Germany [A D 1521], placed them under a ban throughout Holland. From this time to the end of his reign [A D 1556] the Emperor pursued a policy of extermination which effectually checked for the time the progress of Protestantism. It is calculated that at least fifty thousand persons were put to death for their religious opinions during this period, including a vast number of the Anabaptists, whose outrages cast discredit on the reformed doctrines generally, and whose political principles went far to justify the imperial severity. In consequence of the continued spread of the obnoxious doctrines the Inquisition was introduced from Spain [A D 1550], and was mercilessly worked under Philip II, who succeeded his father A D. 1556, and by the Romish prelates (increased by him from five to seventeen in number), under the leadership of Granvella, Cardinal bishop of Arras. The Dutch Confession of Faith, "Confessio Belgica," consisting of thirty-seven articles [PROTESTANT CONFESSIONS], was publicly put forward in 1562, probably with a view of mitigating, if not the cruelty of the Inquisition, at least the antipathy of the authorities, by proving the political harmlessness of the doctrines of the Reforming party. This manifesto was disregarded, as also was a protest signed [A D. 1566] by a hundred thousand Protestants Under a feeling of exasperation many of the latter now began to retaliate, by attacking the churches of the opposite party and breaking their ornaments, and the title of "Gueux," or beggars, has been contemptuously bestowed upon the ringleaders of these iconoclastic tumults The Duke of Alva, with Spanish and Italian soldiers, was sent to chastise them [A D 1567], but the national spirit was now fairly roused, and nobles and people alike combined to throw off the oppression of a foreign yoke William of Orange, who had openly espoused the Protestant cause, was placed at the head of the revolt against Philip II, and after several years of varying success was elected Stadtholder [A D 1573] Six years later he had been so far successful that the seven northern provinces were rent from the Spanish rule [A D 1579] The Roman Catholic religion was formally interdicted, and a Protestant university was founded at Leyden, from which time [A D 1581] Holland has remained as staunchly Protestant as the Lower Provinces, constituting the modern kingdom of Belgium, have continued devotedly Catholic The Protestantism of Holland assumed a strong Calvinistic complexion, the Dutch Confession having been avowedly based on that of the French Protestants, while, at the first provincial synod held at Dort [A D 1574], the Heidelberg Catechism was recognised and ordered to be publicly taught. There is contemporary evidence of this fact in a letter which has been preserved, written by Viglius Van Zuichem, dated Brussels, May 23rd, 1567, and in which the following sentence occurs — "Very few of them abide by the Confession of Augsburg, but Calvinism has possession of nearly every one, for the door being opened by the Lutherans to further errors nearly all of them proceed beyond" [Gieseler's *Eccl Hist.* iii 1, 559] In recent times Holland has been a hotbed of Rationalism [ANABAPTISTS DORT, SYNOD OF. MENNONITES. RATIONALISTS]

E

EBIONITES A sect of heretics developed from among the Judaizing Christians of Apostolic times late in the first or early in the second century They accepted Christianity only as a reformed Judaism, and believed in our Blessed Lord only as a mere natural man spiritually perfected by exact observance of the Mosaic law

It is disputed whether these heretics were so designated from a leader named Ebion, or whether they were called Ebionites because the Hebrew word Ebion (אביון) expressed the "poor" substance of their creed, which was that return to "the weak and beggarly elements" (τὰ ἀσθενῆ καὶ πτωχὰ στοιχεῖα) of an effete law so strongly condemned by St Paul [Gal iv 9] If the longer recension of his Epistles is genuine, St Ignatius writes in such a manner as partly to support the latter opinion, saying of the Judaizer, "such a man is poor in understanding, even as he is by name an Ebionite" [Ignat *ad Philadelph.* vi] The same may be also said respecting a statement of Origen that "the Ebionites, who savour of earthly things, derive their appellation of 'poor' from their very name, for 'Ebion' means 'poor' in Hebrew" [Orig *de Princip* iv 22] On the other hand, Tertullian, who wrote earlier than Origen, distinctly speaks of "the heresy of Ebion" as being confuted by St Paul's Epistle to the Galatians and the Gospel of St John [Tertull *de Præsc Hæret* xxxiii , *de Carn Chr* xxiv], says that certain opinions are "very suitable for Ebion" [Tertull *de Carn Chr* xiv], and that Ebion believed Christ to be a mere man [*ibid* xviii] These passages shew that Tertullian had no doubt as to the existence of an individual heretic so named, later writers all speak of him as a real person, and no writer whatever of early times expresses any actual doubt as to his existence There is, in fact, no better historical ground for supposing that there was no such person as Ebion than the play upon the name, which seems to have been suggested by St Paul's apposite language respecting the poverty of a Judaizing creed, and it would be much the same to suppose that there was no such person as Heber because a similar play upon the name was observable in the case of his descendant "Abram the Hebrew" or "crosser over" The non-existence of Ebion is however maintained by Vitringa [*Obs Sacr* ii 127], Le Clerc [*Hist Eccl* 476], Priestley [*Hist early Opin* 177], and Matter [*Hist du Gnost* ii. 320] His existence is supported by Fabricius [*Annot. ad Philast* 81], Ittigius [*de Hæresiarch* 59, and *App* 17], and Bishop Bull [*Judic Eccl Cath* ii 17] Other writers of less importance are also referred to in Burton's *Inquiries into the Heresies of the Apostolic Age* [Burton's *Bampt Lect* 496]

It is easy to trace up the Ebionite heresy to the Judaizing Christians of whom St Paul so frequently wrote, and whom he so vigorously condemned When Jews first became Christians they all agreed in observing the Mosaic law, as did the Apostles themselves, at least during their residence in Judæa But Hebrew Christians soon began to differ among themselves as to the necessity of such observance Certain "men from Judæa" criticized and objected to the free manner in which Jewish customs were set aside by the Christians of Antioch, and the consequent dispute had to be referred to the Apostles at Jerusalem Before that final tribunal the objectors were supported by "certain of the sect of the Pharisees who believed," and a distinct Judaizing party seems at once to have been formed [Acts xv 1-31] The fanaticism of this party resisted even the authority of the Apostles They would not recognise St Paul's mission to the Gentiles or his office as an Apostle, and his life was, hence, a continual struggle with them In Galatia the Judaism which opposed him was "of the sharp Pharisaic type, unclouded or unrelieved by any haze of Essene mysticism, such as prevailed a few years later in the neighbouring Colossian Church The necessity of circumcision was strongly insisted upon. Great stress was laid on the observance of days and months, and seasons and years In short, nothing less than submission to the whole ceremonial law seems to have been contemplated by the innovators At all events this was the logical consequence of the adoption of the initiatory rite" [Prof. Lightfoot, *Comm on Galatians*, p. 26, *et sqq*] At Philippi the opposition was of the same character [Phil. iii 3-14] At Corinth [2 Cor xi 4, 22], as most probably in Galatia, emissaries from the headquarters of Judaism, coming with commendatory letters [2 Cor iii 1], headed the opposition Their ministration was of the letter of the Old Testament, which, although glorious in its proper period, was even then, and much more therefore since Christ's coming, a ministration of death. These false apostles, transforming themselves into apostles of Christ, were really ministers of Satan in the guise of ministers of the righteousness of the New Testament [compare 2 Cor iii 1-9 and xi 13-15] Although, then, circumcision and the rites of the law are not specified, this general description, and the pretence of the leaders that they were Hebrews of the Hebrews, sufficiently mark the character of the false teaching At Colossæ, St. Paul's opponents are of a different character They appear to be Jews of the Essene school, with elements of theosophy which belong to Gnosticism Thus, Col i 16, ii 18, 19, are statements of the true doctrine of angels, and of the dependence of the whole Church on Christ, in opposition to the celestial powers of Gnostic theories, to the vanities of a deceitful philosophy [ii 8], to fables and endless genealogies [1 Tim i 4], to profane and vain babblings and oppositions of science falsely so called [1 Tim vi 20] The rudiments of the world [Col ii 8, 20] denoting Judaism [see Gal iv 3, 9], exhibit themselves not only in meats and drinks, holy days, new moons, and sabbaths of Pharisaism, but also in the "Touch not taste not, handle not" of Essene asceticism [ESSENES]

The connection of the Ebionites with Cerinthus appears to rest upon sufficient testimony It is shewn in the myth or the historical fact, whichever it be, that the Eponymus of the sect was the successor, perhaps the pupil, of Cerinthus. Whether there was a man Ebion, from whom the sect was called, is a matter comparatively unimportant That which is shewn alike by the fact or the myth, the transmission of doctrine, is the really important point, and it is in itself most probable The appendix to Tertullian's *De Præscr* states it thus, "Hujus (Cerinthi) successor Ebion fuit, Cerintho non in omni parte consentiens "[1] Philastrius also declares Ebion to have been a scholar of Cerinthus Cerinthus was himself of Jewish extraction , he insisted on the observance of the law , his esoteric teaching was mainly founded on the Cabbala—all which points would recommend him to the Essene Christians and on the other hand, their desire to identify Judaism and Christianity could not but tend to depreciate the character of our Lord, to rank Him with Moses, and therefore to predispose them to learn from Cerinthus to deny His divinity It is easy to imagine, and appears to be the natural result of such a combination, that the Jews, who had originally derived their Christianity from the Apostles, surrendered to Cerinthus their belief in our Lord's proper divinity, but retained their belief in His miraculous birth, and thus formed the higher of the two classes named by Origen , while those who joined the party later, after Cerinthianism had established itself among them, accepted only so much of Christianity as Cerinthus had to give, and formed the lower of the two classes.

The doctrines of the Ebionites may be shortly stated as follows, on the authority of Irenæus, Hippolytus, Tertullian, Eusebius, and Theodoret They believed in the creation of the world by Almighty God, therein differing from Cerinthus , their opinions (*i e* of one party) with respect to our Lord were similar to those of Cerinthus and Carpocrates, for they considered Him a mere common man, raised above other men only by His exalted virtue , holding His birth to have been by ordinary generation, yet that He was more glorious than the prophets, inasmuch as God's angel dwelt within him

A second party did not deny Christ's birth of a Virgin by the Holy Ghost, yet did not acknowledge His pre-existence They practised circumcision, and persevered in the observance of all customs enjoined by the law, of the sabbath, and other similar rites of the Jews, saying that otherwise the servant would be above his lord and they held this observance to be necessary to justification They were so Judaic in their style of life as even to adore Jerusalem as the house of God On the other hand, they also celebrated the Lord's day in commemoration of Christ's Resurrection In the Holy Eucharist they rejected the commixture of the "heavenly wine" [HYDROPARASTATÆ], and wished it to be "water of the world only," not receiving God so as to have union with Him They used the Gospel according to Matthew or, that is, the Gospel of the Hebrews , those who held our Lord's human birth the Gospel of the Hebrews, those who held His miraculous birth the Gospel of St Matthew [Theod], they rejected all the Epistles of St Paul, whom they branded as an apostate from the law.

These notices belong to the earlier Ebionites. In Epiphanius we have a description of the later or Essene school He states in general [*Hær* xxx] that the Ebionites, in imitation of the Samaritans, go beyond the Jews It will be remembered that Epiphanius considered the Essenes to be a Samaritan sect This Essene element appears in voluntary poverty, in ceremonial washings, as, *e g* , after the touch of a person of another religion, in abstinence from flesh and wine But Essene practice was forsaken in refusing the honour once paid to virginity, in denying the duty of continence, in allowing divorces and remarriage without limit

The Dualism which Epiphanius attributes to the Ebionites appears to have been held by them before Elchasai joined them [ELCHASAITES] Epiphanius describes it while speaking of Cerinthus and Ebion [xvi compare with xiv and xv] Two, it is said, were appointed by God, Christ and the Devil , to the former was assigned the world to come, to the latter the present world, by the ordinance of the Almighty, at the request of each [DICT *of* THEOL , DUALISM, p 223, *d*] This delegation of the kingdoms to two opposing powers involves the conception of the Supreme Being not ruling His creation by His providence and grace, but existing apart , the conception of Bythus and Sige And, further, when we connect it with the emanations of the

[1] On the authority of this appendix see a note in article ELCHASAITES

Cabbala, from which the world was evolved, we are led to the Zoroastrian tenet that the First Principle and Cause of all, existing in solitude, contained within itself the germ of antagonizing principles, light and darkness It may be concluded, therefore, that Essene Ebionites held those parts of Gnosticism which were contributed to Gnosticism by the Cabbala, and were at least ready to adopt its other elements They held a partial or undeveloped Gnosticism

Jerome states that the Ebionites held millenarian doctrine [*Comm ad Esa* lxvi] Optatus Milevitanus states that they were Patripassians [lib iv *de Schism. Donat*]. His authority is not given, and the statement is not in itself probable [Ittigius, *de Hæresiarch.* I vi. 8]

Epiphanius relates that Cerinthus and Carpocrates used the same Gospel as the Ebionites, and wished to prove from the genealogy at the beginning of Matthew's Gospel that Christ (Jesus) was born of Joseph and Mary but that the Ebionites had a different notion, for they cut away the genealogies in Matthew and began with the words, "In those days," iii 1 [*Hær* xxx 14] The Ebionites felt that the Cerinthian argument from the genealogy was inconclusive, and took the surer course of rejecting the genealogy

[Irenæus, *Hær* i. 26, v 3, comp also iii 15. Hippolytus, *Ref* vii 22, x. 18 Eusebius, *Hist Eccl.* iii. 27 Tertullian, *de Carne Christi*, p. 370, ed 1641; *De Præscr* p 243; *App to De Præscr* p 252 Origen, *contr Cels* v p 272, ed Spencer, 1677 Theodoret, *Hær fab* ii 1]

ECEBOLIANS This was a favourite controversial nickname in the sixteenth and seventeenth centuries for those who changed their opinions So Bullinger, in A D 1566, classes together "Ecebolians, Lutherans, and semi-Papists" [*Zurich Letters*, i 169], and so Antonio de Dominis was called "Alter Ecebolius" after his return to Rome in A.D 1622 The original Ecebolius was a sophist of Constantinople, who professed to be a Christian under Constantius, turned his coat to the colour of heathenism during the reign of Julian the Apostate, and returned to Christianity again in that of his successor [Socr *Hist Eccl* iii 1, 13]

ECHETÆ [ἠχεῖν] Some monks are mentioned under this name by Nicetas Choniates, who held it to be a religious duty for monks and nuns to follow the example of Moses and Miriam by celebrating Divine service with dancing and exuberant displays of joy In all other respects they were, he says, orthodox [Nicetas, *Thesaur Orthod fid* iv 38]

ECKHART [FRIENDS OF GOD]

ECLECTICS. A school of philosophers which arose at Alexandria in the third century, and took its name from the principle on which it was founded, that of selecting truths out of every system in which they were to be discovered (πᾶν τὸ ἐκλεκτικόν), and combining them into one common theology

Although the eclectic principle is to be traced in the writings of Clement of Alexandria, the definite formation of a school of thought upon it is traceable to Ammonius Saccas [A.D. 193-242], his contemporary and survivor, who carried on the humble occupation of sack porter to the cornships, but was only next to St Clement in his intellectual influence at Alexandria

The original idea of the Eclectics was to reconcile portions of the philosophical systems of Pythagoras, Plato, and Aristotle with Christianity, and it found material expression in the domestic Pantheon of the heathen Emperor Alexander Severus, who placed on one level the statues of Orpheus, Pythagoras, and our Lord. As far as Christianity was concerned the Eclectics were willing to water it down to a similar level with the ancient philosophies, denying inspiration, explaining away miracles, and allegorizing facts, and the reconciliation of Christianity and philosophy came practically to a compromise, in which the former was made to give up everything that was of vital importance The Neo-Platonism which developed out of Eclecticism, partly in the hands of Ammonius himself but still more in those of Plotinus and Porphyry, gradually assumed a more definite position of hostility to Christianity, and neither have much right to be associated with it, though claiming to be Christian But the Eclectics and Neo-Platonists represent a transitional influence by which many philosophers who had hitherto looked on Christianity with such contempt that they would not even listen to its history and reasoning—as Tertullian so often complains—were led to investigate its claims to respect They were beginning to see that it could not be passed by, and their earlier acquaintance with it led them to give it a place in what seemed to them to be the new universal religion and philosophy which thoughtful minds among the heathen were craving after when Polytheism had become dead to them. Over such minds Christianity would often, in the end, assume its proper supremacy [NEO-PLATONISTS]

ECTHESIS An heretical edict promulgated by the Emperor Heraclius [A D. 638] for the purpose of reconciling the Monophysites to the Church. This Exposition of the Faith (Ἔκθεσις τῆς πίστεως) was drawn up by Sergius, the patriarch of Constantinople "After an orthodox statement of faith, so far as respects the Holy Trinity, the Incarnation, the one Person and the two Natures of our Blessed Lord, it proceeded to forbid the teaching of either one or two operations, the former as appearing to destroy the doctrine of the two Natures, the latter as an expression entirely new to theology, appearing to imply two contrary wills, and leading to results more dangerous than even the tenets of Nestorius At the same time it was clearly and positively stated that the Catholic Faith required the acknowledgment of only one will" in our Lord [Neale's *Hist East Ch*, *Alexand* ii 70] The text of this document is given in Harduin's *Concilia*, iii 791. It was rejected as heretical by a council held at Rome [A D 639] under John IV, and by a great number of bishops, and was superseded nine years later by an edict of the Emperor Constans, entitled the TYPE, which enjoined silence respecting the doctrine of one or two wills in Christ In the following year both the Type and the Ecthesis were condemned by the first Lateran Council [A D 649], a condemnation which led to the deposition and exile of the Pope, Martin I, by the Emperor. [MONOTHELITES]

EDGEITES A sect quite recently established at Rangoon, combining the principles and practices of the Baptists and the Plymouth Brethren

EFFRONTES An obscure sect of heretical fanatics who appeared in Transylvania about the year 1534 They professed to be Christians, but rejected the use of Baptism, and substituted for it a strange custom of shaving the forehead until blood flowed, and then anointing the scarified surface with oil They blasphemously declared the worship of the Third Person in the Blessed Trinity to be idolatry, and maintained that His Name only represented a divine operation on the soul of man [Pluquet, *Dict des Hérés s v.*]

ELCHASAITES A sect, dating, so far as is known of them in history, from the pontificate of Callistus [A D 219-224], which proclaimed a second baptism of remission of sins, over and above Christian baptism, to all believers in the revelations of a book named Elchasai. The leading tenet of the book was, that the Son of God had many times manifested Himself in the world in the persons of righteous men, that Jesus Christ was such a manifestation, Jesus being the Son, naturally, of Joseph and Mary. To this was added, as the rule of life, the observance of the law of Moses, with the exception of sacrifice, the practice of astrology and magic, the use of incantations and charms. The revelation was said to have been made in the third year of Trajan [A D 100] to some one of the tribe of the Seres, described as a Parthian tribe

"These Seres hold the same place in the fictions of Essene Ebionitism as the Hyperboreans in Greek legend, they are a mythical race, perfectly pure, and therefore perfectly happy, long-lived and free from pain, scrupulous in the performance of all ceremonial rites, and thus exempt from the penalties attaching to their neglect" [See *Recogn* viii 48, ix 19 Prof. Lightfoot, "*St. Paul and the Three*" *Comm on Galat* p 304]

Eusebius states that the sect was almost stifled in its birth [Euseb. *Hist Eccl* vi 38] Its leading tenets were however adopted by other sects, particularly by the Ossenes and the Ebionites [Epiph *Hær* xix xxx], and in this way its author exercised great influence

Hippolytus states that upon Callistus sanctioning a practice of rebaptizing, which was noised abroad throughout the entire world, one Alcibiades, of Apamea in Syria, took occasion to repair to Rome, carrying with him a book which a certain just man, Elchasai, had received from the Seres, a Parthian tribe, and had given to one named Sobiai There is little doubt that Elchasai is originally the name of the book—Epiphanius rightly interprets it δύναμις κεκαλυμμένη, and that Sobiai means the sworn member, who might be initiated into the revelation. But it is quite likely that the founder of the sect, or that Alcibiades, whether he was an emissary or an adventurer, took the name Elchasai In Hippolytus [chap viii] Elchasai is used as synonymous with Alcibiades Theodoret states that the sect takes its name from one Elchasai, the founder of the heresy, and ends his chapter by saying that Alcibiades (συνεκρότησε) hammered it out. Although it may appear unlikely that the heresy should have existed from the time of Trajan to the time of Callistus without any record or trace of its existence, still a passage quoted from the book—"Take care not to commence your works the third day from a Sabbath, since when three years of the reign of the Emperor Trajan are completed from the time that he subjected the Parthians to his sway, war rages between the impious angels of the northern constellations" [Hippol ix 11]—looks very much like one of those supposed prophecies which are made soon after the events A few years later this supposed prophecy would have been scarcely understood Upon the whole, the notices we have lead to the conclusion that the book Elchasai was written in Trajan's time in Parthia, and brought to Rome by Alcibiades, that Alcibiades took the name of Elchasai, and was the Elchasai who, according to Epiphanius, joined the Ossenes and the Ebionites, of whose family the sisters Marthus and Marthana were said to be [Epiph *Hær* xix 2]

The book was delivered by an angel ninety-six miles high, who was accompanied by a female form of like stature, the former being the Son of God, the latter the Holy Spirit According to Hippolytus this vision was stated to have been simply for the delivery of the book It must not be extended, as it is by Epiphanius, into a dogma of the Elchasaite creed, as if they taught such to be the proper forms of the Son and the Holy Spirit Neither are these forms to be identified with any pair of male and female Æons of Gnosticism They are rather the expression of a belief borrowed from the Egyptian mysteries through the Alexandrian school, the belief in a male and female principle as pervading the Deity [DICT *of* THEOL, CABBALISM *Christ Rememb* xliii 352], for Elchasai's system did not involve a series of world-creating angels He acknowledged that the principles of the universe were originated by the Deity [Hippol x 25] "Concerning the beginning of all things they agree with us They hold that there is one Unbegotten, and Him they call the creator of all things" [Theod *Hær fab* ii 7]

The leading doctrine of the Elchasaites is that which regards Jesus and Christ. They held the Pythagorean tenet of the transmigration of souls, and accordingly believed that the soul of Jesus had inhabited many human bodies When Jesus became the Son of Mary, as the last of the transmigrations, some held that His birth was as the birth of other men, some that it was miraculous, Mary being a virgin But in this latter case the birth was a miracle merely of God's creating power, not such a birth as the Church understands it to be from Luke i 35 These successive births of Jesus had also been manifestations of Christ "Christ" appears to have been a term equivalent to Power of God, including both the Son of God and the Spirit of God "Thus Christ appeared and existed among men from time to time, undergoing alterations of birth and having his soul" (the soul of Jesus) ' transferred from body to body"

Elchasai taught that believers ought to be circumcised and live according to the Law [Hippol ix 9], but condemned sacrifice and priestly ministrations, as foreign from God's nature, and denied that they were offered to God according to the Law and the Fathers [Epiph *Hær* xix 3]

His theory of baptism is thus given in a quotation from his book "Whoso is desirous of obtaining remission of sins, from the moment that he hearkens to this book, let him be baptized a second time in the Name of the Great and Most High God, and in the Name of His Son the Mighty King Thus let him be purified and cleansed, and let him adjure for himself those seven witnesses that have been described in this book—Heaven, Water, Holy Spirits, Angels of Prayer, Oil, Salt, Earth" [Hippol. ix. 10] This baptism [ἐπὶ τῇ τῶν στοιχείων ὁμολογίᾳ, Theod *Hær fab*] is connected with the Cabbalistic magic, which commands the aid of good angels, and brings evil ones into subjection, which controls the forces of nature, and makes the elements of the world subservient And it was a second baptism, not as denying the former and Christian baptism, but as in addition to it, with a second remission of sins, and that a plenary remission

The invocation of the powers of nature was not confined to this baptism Men were taught to swear by Salt, Water, Earth, Bread, Sky, Air, Winds, and these powers or principles, Epiphanius tells us, were marked out for adoration Water was the emblem or principle of good, fire of deception [Epiph. *Hær* xix 3] Astrology and magic were deeply studied the latter with its train of incantations and charms, the former with its pretence of predictions

The Elchasaites held it to be indifferent to deny Christ, and urged that a prudent man will so deny with his lips, not in his heart [Origen in Euseb *Hist Eccl* vi 38] They despised virginity, and compelled to marry They set aside certain parts of the collective Scriptures, and made use of passages from the Old Testament, and from the Gospels, rejecting the Apostles altogether

Epiphanius states that among the Ossenes, in Nabathæa and Peræa, two sisters, Marthus and Marthana, were in his time reverenced as deities, on account of their being of the family of Elchasai One was still alive when he wrote, the other had not long been dead It appears that the Roman Ebionites adopted much of the system of Elchasai, but there is no evidence that they idolized him May it not then be that, failing to secure in Rome the position he aimed at, he retired to Peræa, was more successful there, and that his rank remained with his family?

The system of the Clementine Homilies is in many features identical with that of Elchasai It is summed up thus by Gieseler —"God, a pure, simple being of light, has allowed the world to be formed in contrasts, and so also the history of the world and of men runs off in contrasts (συζυγίαι), corresponding by way of pairs, in which the lower constantly precedes the higher. From the beginning onward, God has revealed Himself to man, while His Holy Spirit (Σοφία, Υἱὸς Θεοῦ, Θεῖον Πνεῦμα, Πνεῦμα Ἅγιον) from time to time in the form of individual men (Adam, Enoch, Abraham, Isaac, Jacob, Moses, Jesus), as the True Prophet (ὁ προφήτης τῆς ἀληθείας), constantly announced the very same truth, and in Jesus caused it also to be communicated to the heathen According to the law of syzygies, false prophets also are always produced in addition to the true [γεννητοὶ γυναικῶν, Matt xi 11], who corrupt the truth Thus, the original doctrines of Mosaism are perfectly identical with Christianity, though they have not been preserved in their purity in the Pentateuch, which was not composed until long after Moses, and in the present form of Judaism have been utterly perverted In general, the truth has been constantly maintained in its purity only by a few, by means of secret tradition Man is free, and must expect after death a spiritual continuation of life, with rewards and punishments The conditions of happiness are love to God and man, and struggling against the demons, which draw away to evil through sensuality. For this purpose these sectaries prescribed abstinence from animal food, frequent fastings and washings, recommended early marriage and voluntary poverty, but rejected all sacrifice" [Gieseler's *Compend* i 209]

This system would be produced by adopting into Ebionitism Elchasai's doctrine of the early manifestations of Christ, but without his second baptism, and the magic with which it was connected Whether the Ebionites had received from Cerinthus the doctrine of world-forming angels, and renounced it through the influence of Elchasaitism, or whether they never accepted that doctrine, is uncertain But the testimony of the appendix to Tertullian's *de Præscr* is strong in favour of the latter alternative "Hujus successor Hebion fuit, Cerintho non in omni parte consentiens, quod a Deo dicat mundum, non ab angelis factum" The authority of this appendix is high, if (as is supposed) it is an early work of Hippolytus translated by Victorinus, and the early date will account for the omission of all mention of Elchasai Hippolytus' early work would date before the appearance of Alcibiades in Rome The Ebionites then had the following points in common with Elchasai the ascribing creation to the Supreme Being, the denial of the divinity of Jesus, the observance of the Law, the importance of lustrations, the rejection of St Paul They were at least prepared to reject the prophets, for the earlier Ebionites had adopted a singular mode of expounding them, and the Samaritans who joined the party accepted only the Pentateuch The acceptance of the doctrine, that certain holy men were manifestations of Christ or the True Prophet, would suit their controversial position, which aimed at identifying Judaism and Christianity Seeing this, and assuming that the Clementine Homilies proceeded from Rome about the time of the appearance there of Alcibiades the prophet of Elchasaitism, the inference is, that these Homilies represent the Elchasaitism of the Ebionites, while, as already suggested, the reverence paid to the descendants of Elchasai in Nabathæa and Peræa shews that among the Essenes an unmitigated Elchasaitism established itself Elchasaitism, as Gieseler has remarked, is opposed to that theosophy which is in historical possession of the name Gnosis [Gieseler's *Compend* i p 101, n], and its influence (whether or not its leading doctrine was accepted by all the Ebionites) probably prevented the Ebionites from fully adopting and developing the system of Cerinthus

With this doctrine there could be no other feeling towards St Paul, than that of strong antagonism, and this antagonism, which underlies the conception of the whole narrative on which the Homilies are based, manifests itself, though for the most part indirectly, with much bitterness [See Schliemann, *Die Clementinen*, pp 96 and 534] The other Apostles who acknowledged St Paul's commission (although St Peter is made in the Homilies the exponent of true doctrine) were yet really subordinated to the authority of the Ebionite Gospel Epiphanius states, that the Ebionites only pretended to admit the names of the Apostles, attributing to them fictitious writings [Epiph *Hær* xxx 23], and Eusebius states that they esteemed the Gospels as of little value in comparison with the Gospel according to the Hebrews.

The doctrine of the True Prophet appears in a less objectionable, though still heretical, form in the Recognitions of Clement, in the form, namely, that from the beginning Christ Himself was the True Prophet, assuming humanity (though not a human body) by uniting Himself with a pre-existent human soul, and appearing from time to time to the Fathers, but not being properly incarnate until born of the Virgin Mary This phase of the doctrine is farther exhibited in the article on JUDAISM The desire to identify Judaism and Christianity, and at the same time to avoid Ebionite psilanthropism, appears to have occasioned its adoption in the more orthodox portion of the anti-Pauline school

There was much uncertainty regarding the heresy of the Elchasaites before the publication in 1851 of the "Refutation of all Heresies" of Hippolytus, and how little was known may be seen by what Lardner has brought together [Lardner's *Hist of Heretics*, ii 22] The authorities now available for their history are Hippolytus, *Philosophum* ix 8-12, x 25, Origen, quoted in Eusebius, *Hist Eccl* vi 38, Epiphanius, *Hær* xix *the Ossenes*, and xxx *the Ebionites;* Theodoret, *Hær fab.* ii 7, who used other writings than the revelation itself; and may be taken as an independent authority Augustine merely quotes Epiphanius, from whom, too, Damascenus' notices are borrowed Of modern commentators, Ritschl, *Die Entstehung der Altkatholischen Kirche*, 1857, may be especially named.

'ENANTIOΔOKH'TAI A controversial term used by Leontius of Constantinople to express the opposition between the heresies of Nestorius and Eutyches, one heresy making the Divine Nature and the other the Human Nature of our Lord an unreality [Leont. Byzant. *contr Nestor et Eutych* in *Bibl Max Lugd* ix 675, F]

ENCRATITES [Ἐγκρατεῖς, Iren, Ἐγκρατηταί, Clem Alex and Theod, Ἐγκρατῖται, Epiph.] This name was taken, in the second century, by those who renounced marriage and abstained from flesh and wine, not from an excess of Christian asceticism, but from the heretical principle of the inherent evil of matter The principle that matter is inherently evil, and its consequence, that creation is the work of an inferior and evil agent, was common to all Gnostics From this principle some inferred the necessity of mortifying the body, and, consistently with their erroneous assumption, carried, or professed to carry, that mortification to the extent of asserting that the propagation of men and animals is only a ministering to the evil work of an evil creator (inconsistently, however, stopping short of the point of self-starvation) others, holding that knowledge is all in all, disregarded the rules of chastity and temperance, as pertaining only to the work of the inferior demiurge [Clem Alex *Strom* iii 5, 6, 7] Out of the former class those who laid especial stress on this practical deduction from their principles called themselves Encratites, "the continent," "the self-controllers,"

St. Paul names such precepts as "forbidding to marry, and commanding to abstain from meats," as proceeding from those who give heed to seducing spirits and doctrines of devils [1 Tim iv 1-5] There can be little doubt that although he spoke in the main prophetically, the Gnostic doctrine of asceticism had been already started, and the principles of that doctrine had certainly been laid But the doctrine is not attributed to any known teacher of Gnosticism before Saturninus in the beginning of the second century After him Cerdon, Marcion, and Apelles held it, and the followers of all those heretics must be considered as Encratites, though they may not have assumed the name Irenæus states that the Encratites sprang from Saturninus and Marcion [Iren *Hær* i 28], and passes on to connect them with Tatian, Theodoret also calling Tatian the leader of the Encratites and Hydroparastatæ [Theod *Hær. fab* i 20] It appears from this that the Encratites who had existed previously as dispersed among several sects, or as schismatical congregations, gathered themselves into a separate and heretical sect under Tatian

Epiphanius relates that in his time they existed in great numbers in Pisidia, Phrygia, Galatia, and in the whole of Asia Minor [Epiph *Hær.* xlvii]

The fundamental tenet of the Encratites doubtless of itself constitutes a heresy [Hippol *Philosophum* viii 20], and might of itself be the cause of schism But it was not held, and indeed cannot be held, independently of other heresies The notion of the inherent evil of matter affects not only the doctrines regarding God the Creator, but the doctrine of the Incarnation and Human Nature of our Lord, and it penetrates therefore to the doctrine of the Sacraments The reader is referred therefore to the notices of the sects whose doctrines involve this tenet, particularly SATURNINIANS, MARCIONITES, TATIANISTS, SEVERIANS, HYDROPARASTATÆ.

Encratite practice is rightly described by Epiphanius "Most of these heresies forbid to marry, and order men to abstain from meats, not giving such precepts for the regulation of life, nor for the sake of superior virtue and its rewards and crowns, but because they think those things abominable which were instituted by the Lord" [Epiph *Hær* xlviii 8] So too by Theodoret "They abstain from flesh and wine, abhorring them as evil Lawful wedlock they call the work of the devil" [Theod *Hær fab* i 20] Against this practice and its principle the 51st and 53rd (or 43rd and 45th) Apostolic Canons are directed The 51st is, "If any bishop, priest, deacon, or any of the sacerdotal catalogue, do abstain from marriage, and flesh, and wine, not for mortification but out of abhorrence, as having forgotten that all things are very good, and that God made man male and female, and blasphemously reproaching the workmanship of God, let him amend, or else be deposed and cast out of the Church, and so also shall a layman" The 14th Ancyran Canon [A D 314] decrees "That those of the clergy, priests and deacons, who abstain from flesh, shall taste it, and then abstain if they think fit, but if they will not, nor even eat of the herbs which are mingled with the flesh, nor obey the canon, then they cease from their function" The tasting was a declaration that they did not hold there was uncleanness in the meat itself. The Council of Gangra anathematized those who declared marriage to be incompatible with a state of salvation, but Eustathius, whose errors occasioned the council, probably advanced not Gnostic tenets, but a fanatical standard of sanctity

The baptism of the Encratites is mentioned, among other baptisms, some heretical, some schismatical, in St. Basil's first and second canonical Epistles, canons i and xlvii The first of these canons was much discussed in the controversy between Bingham and Lawrence regarding the validity of lay-baptism; and the controversy shews that the interpretation of St Basil's words is not without difficulty For Johnson renders one sentence thus "The Encratites have *altered* their baptism to make themselves incapable of being received by the Church" [Johnson's *Vade mecum*, ii 226] Lawrence thus "They gave it with precipitation on purpose to hinder the receiving of it from the Church" [Lawrence, *Lay Bapt Invalid*, p 15] St Basil's words are, Τὸ δὲ τῶν Ἐγκρατιτῶν κακούργημα νοῆσαι ἡμᾶς δεῖ, ὅτι, ἵν' αὐτοὺς ἀπροσδέκτους ποιήσωσι τῇ Ἐκκλησίᾳ, ἐπεχείρησαν λοιπὸν ἰδίῳ προκαταλαμβάνειν βαπτίσματι The only point we are now concerned with is, whether in these words is necessarily implied an alteration of the Catholic form of baptism They would doubtless carry such an interpretation if history and the context required it, but they do not necessarily demand it; and canon xlvii is against such an interpretation Canon xlvii. introduces the Encratites saying that they are baptized in the Catholic form, and warns them not to rest on this, because they do not hold a right faith in the God in whose Name they are baptized [see the note of the Benedictine editor on canon i] The κακούργημα, then, of the Encratites appears to be the undue haste of administration in opposition to Catholic practice, and perhaps the addition of uncatholic ceremonies

Epiphanius writes regarding the Encratites, Tatianists, and Cathari, παρήλλακται δὲ παρ' αὐτοῖς καὶ τὰ μυστήρια [*Hær.* xli or lxi] These words are sufficiently verified in the Encratite rejection of wine from the Eucharist, and the addition of novel ceremonies in Baptism, without pressing them so far as to imply from them a change of the form of baptism Further, St Basil [canon xlvii] classes together the Encratites, Saccophori, and Apotactics, and (as his text stands) subjects them all to the same rule as the Novatians, namely that they are to be baptized for admission to the Church The Benedictine editor wishes to insert a negative, and does so in his translation Johnson accepts the present text It is clear that the baptisms of the three are of one rank, and there can be little doubt that St Basil disallowed them as of no more efficacy than lay baptisms The 7th canon of Constantinople [A D 381], which determined against St. Basil in favour of the baptism of the Novatians, does not specify these sects

The Gospel according to the Egyptians, the fragments of which were collected by Grabe [*Spicileg* i. pp 31-37], was probably composed in the second century by an Encratite

ENCYCLOPEDISTS. The term ἐγκύκλιος παιδεία was used of old to designate the entire curriculum of instruction which qualified the student for public office Encyclopédiste is a term applied to certain French savans who, in the middle of the eighteenth century [A D 1751], put forth an Encyclopédie by joint-stock contribution, under the general editorship of Diderot, and of D'Alembert for the mathematical articles English Deism paved the way for it, but the Encyclopédie has had a more permanent effect upon the French national character than Deism on the English The other colleagues were the Abbé Mallet, Regius Professor of Theology in the University of Paris, who was author of most of the articles on theology and history, with others on poetry and general literature. the Abbé Bergier also supplied theological articles, and the Abbé Yvon was author of metaphysical and philosophical papers, to which section the Abbé Pestré and the Abbé de Prades also contributed the political metaphysics that were termed by Coleridge "Metapolitics" Rousseau helped out the musical section, but withstood the materialistic tone of his colleagues; Daubenton represented the department of natural history. Toussaint took charge of the juridical subjects; Le Mounier and Malouin of the physical and chemical, Blondel wrote the architectural papers The Baron d'Argenville, privy councillor, and the Comte d'Heronville de Claye, high in military command, supplied articles respectively on diplomatic and strategical subjects Voltaire, Marie François Arouet, also, may be named as having had a definite object in floating the scheme. Five or six men of head, he said, might easily overthrow a religion set up by a dozen illiterate fishermen and peasants The names may be added of Marmontel, Condorcet, La Lande, Adanson, Turpin, Montigny, and De Sacy Among the learned of foreign lands, Bernouilli contributed to the astronomical sections, Haller to the anatomical and physiological, Engel to the geographical, and Sulzer to the theory of the fine arts Many of the writers enumerated contributed highly valuable articles but the capacity of the Encyclopédie for mischief wholly counteracted the good Papers written by Baillet, the apostle of infidelity, were incorporated in the work, as were others by the atheist Nicolas Freret La Mettrie the materialist was another writer, whose works, saturated with the grossest immorality, were publicly burnt at Paris and Leyden, yet he failed not to receive the distinguished patronage of Frederick, and ended his days at Berlin as protégé of the "Grand Monarque" Charles de St. Denys, Baron de St. Egremont, was equally corrupt, whose work on the "Morality of Epicurus" was dedicated to Ninon de l'Enclos It was in her house that Rousseau learned his first lessons of evil Even dignitaries of the Church were not the last in the race of vice and irreligion The Abbé Chaulieu was known as the "Anacreon of the Temple" Pierre Camus was the "Lucian of the Episcopate," a sneering, scoffing spirit, and Berni, afterwards cardinal, was the composer of Pompadour erotics Even the purer Montesquieu was carried away by the evil spirit of the day, and supplied articles in the tone of his "Lettres Persanes," rather than of his "Esprit des lois," though he afterwards expressed regret for the way in which he had spoken of sacred matters

The first two volumes appeared A D 1751, and in the first instance the continuation of the work was prohibited, but, unfortunately, it was to the taste of the public, and obtained the suicidal patronage of the Court and noblesse The preliminary discourse of the editors at once excited attention It avowed Locke's principle of sensualism, deriving from sensation the origin of all our ideas, but they fused into one the external and internal sense of the English philosopher,—our mental experience being summed, not by the combined factors of sense and reflection, but by the impact of sense alone. In their introduction D'Alembert takes a rapid view of the various subjects on which the work treats, and indicates the relation in which they stand to each other All direct knowledge, he says, reduces itself to that which we gain from sensation That our senses may originate knowledge, leads him to assume that they do so in all cases, and he argues from the particular to the universal To the objection that the perception of sensation is something subjective, and that there is no relation between sensation and the object that causes it, or to which we refer it, and therefore that there is no substantial connection between the two, he answers, that a kind of instinct, more mighty than reason, bridges over the intermediate gulf, and gives to the object as real a subjective existence in our sensation as it already has an objectivity in the great world without us He leaves it for metaphysicians to determine how the soul distracted from without by a vast mass of objects suggestive of sensation, and thereby liable to perpetual dissipation of its power of centralization, or again, cramped and limited by its own confined sphere, should step forth, as it were, from itself, and gain its first elements of knowledge from things external, acting upon its inner being For example, a mathematical proposition is true, and we are conscious of the train of reasoning that issues in the necessary demonstration, but what is the connecting-link between the mathematical truth and the inner consciousness? There is a void between them that has always been a mystery, and the sensualist theory least of all has been able to throw any light into it

Further, D'Alembert's theory of morality is thoroughly abject and unsatisfying The idea of justice, he says, originates as an antagonism from fear of the oppression that the strong will always inflict upon the weak, and of virtue, from the evil that the vices of others cause to us Our comfort we find to be concerned in the development of these necessary notions Hence the readiness with which the world rewards the just and virtuous, and punishes the deceitful and vicious · and the general axiom being true, its principle is good for the whole extent to which it can reach

He rises in the following way to the idea of God What is the active principle, the determining and perceptive being in us that exercises judgment and will? It is not the body, for matter has no properties in common with will and thought But there is a double self in the individual "Ego" of two very different natures, so intimately interwoven, that there is a perfect unity between the affections of the one and the movements of the other, a spontaneity that leaves nothing to be distinguished between the two, or to mark the point where volition ends and action begins This co-ordination of which we are conscious, together with the speculations into which our thoughts for ever glide, with reference to our twofold nature and its manifold imperfections, raises us to the contemplation of a

Supreme Intelligence, to whom we owe our existence, and ought to render an unswerving loyalty Consequently, proof of the Divine existence arises from our own inner perception it is D'Alembert's ontological proof It is demonstrable in the same way that our ideas of virtue and vice, the principle and necessity of laws, every art and every science, the spirituality of the soul, as well as our knowledge of the Being of God, of our duty to Him, and of every other needful truth, are only the results of our reflective powers, exercising themselves under the sway of material sensation This train of reasoning at once took possession of the popular mind, and is still found fossilized in the various strata of French society.

It will be seen, therefore, that the Encyclopédistes are not fairly chargeable with blank atheism With all their sensualism, they acknowledged the necessity for a Divine revelation, and that the written Word contains it But its truths, they say, lie within certain limits Only so much is revealed as it concerns us to know. There is a Divine and a human element in the Word A few necessary matters of faith, and some practical precepts, comprise its truths, yet even these have thrown more light on human life, present and future, than all the schools of an enlightened philosophy. The learned Abbés engaged upon the work have even given to it a certain tone of anti-Protestant Church principle, which raises it above the mere Theism of the articles on "God" and "Providence" Under "Deists," it notes that natural religion is insufficient to teach men how to worship God—a point upon which Deists have always been supremely indifferent—or to guide them to the highest happiness of which human nature is capable "Christianity" is declared to be the sole form of revealed religion, and its title-deeds are shewn to be contained in the Old and New Testaments, while further confirmation of the same fact is given under "Bible," "Prophecy," "Revelation," "Testament," &c The doctrine of the Holy Trinity also is maintained against the assault of Jews, Heathens and Socinians, as well as of more modern Deists and Atheists, still, these articles scarcely rise above the old deistical axiom, that Christianity is a mere republication of the law of Nature The general tone of the work induces the belief that its religion was suggested by a temporizing prudence rather than by genuine conviction The Goddess of Reason had not yet been publicly enshrined

The spirit of the Encyclopédie gives to it a highly dangerous character Faith is the handmaid of Reason, taking up the work only where Reason fails. Under Morality, it exalts the subject treated above faith, because, forsooth, it is easier to be good and to benefit our fellow creatures by moral excellence without faith, than by faith without morality,—as though faith worthy of the name were really separable from morality. Christian faith is, in fact, morality Our sinnings are a want of faith "Natural religion" is made to convey so clear a knowledge of the Deity, as almost to supersede the necessity for revealed religion, while "Theism" is shewn to be more excellent than Atheism, only because belief in the existence of God and Providence is more serviceable to the state and society than unbelief. "Monasticism" is to be discouraged, because it withdraws so many from taking their proper share in the active duties of life Its philosopher, like Spinoza or Horace, "Epicuri de grege porcus," is not to imagine that because he upholds truth and morality, he may not lawfully enjoy the good things of life, it is no part of a wise man's duty to be content with bare necessaries, like Cynics and Stoics and such pseudo-philosophers. True wisdom consists in the enjoyment of the good things of life, and in promoting the greatest happiness of the greatest number. there is nothing in him of the ascetic "Il vaut mieux être gastronome qu'astronome," would seem to have been the ultimate idea of the literary associates at the Holbach banquetings

This worldliness marks the character of the work throughout—sensualist in its philosophy and sensualist in its morals, it is answerable for much of the miserable irreligion into which France sunk in the next generation. The idealism of the Bible and of the Church of all ages is not openly attacked, but it is entirely overlaid by the materialism of Epicurus and the sensualism of Locke, the step from whence to infidelity is easy and natural Articles that give scope for the exhibition of the dominant influence of soul and spirit are slurred over, or altogether omitted. High art, as Marmontel states it, is only admirable for the pleasure that it can confer, and owes its origin to the satisfaction felt by man in his social condition when his wants are supplied a sense of the beautiful issues forth from this material comfort To talk of the high ideal of art is, with the Encyclopedist, to utter words without meaning, and ends as it began in the perceptions of sense The liberal only differ from mechanical arts in this, that the latter minister to our wants, the former to our pleasures Of any connection between the fine arts and religion no single trace is seen. Architecture, Religion's most faithful ally, can neither symbolize deep truths nor raise the soul to high and worthy thoughts of its relations and destiny its whole mission is accomplished when use and pleasure are combined in its results

Important articles are treated superficially, to give room for lengthy articles on Theatre, Dance, various "objets d'agrément," trades and manufactures, and Pantheism is passed over to make place for trifling talk on Pantomime and Pantoufles The after effects of the Encyclopédie shew how easily sensualism gravitates through materialism into the dregs of atheism, and for that reason the lesson that it holds out is a memorable one

It is an observation of Buckle, that until the Encyclopédie had made its appearance, there was scarcely an atheistical book or tract in existence [*Civilization*, i. c 14, DICT *of* DOCT *and* HIST. THEOLOGY, ATHEISM] After the horrors of the French Revolution, there came the inevitable reaction The weak points of sensualism were detected and brought to the light Its narrow scope and extraordinary assumption of results, "per saltum," were exposed The spiritual once more gained the ascendancy over the material, and from four several quarters an overwhelming tide set in The religious argument was brought to bear upon it by Joseph de Maître and De Bonald, legitimatist and literary sentiments were developed once more by Chateaubriand and Mme. de Stael; Laromiguière and Main de Biran opened fire upon it from the metaphysical side, and Royer-Collard from the moral Materialism was held to be one with atheism, and the way was opened out for the philosophical idea of Scotch and German universities The reign of the Encyclopédistes was over; unhappily the evil that they have done could not so easily be stamped out. It seems to demand a periodical baptism of blood [Barante, *Lit Fr du* 18*me siècle* Schutz, *Staatsveranderung in Frankreich* Berthier, *Journal de Trévoux.*]

ENERGICI. This name was given to those foreign Reformers in the sixteenth century, pupils of Zuingli and Calvin, who taught that the bread and wine in the Holy Eucharist were merely efficacious signs of the Body and Blood of Christ Thus the original words of Institution, "This is My Body," were explained away to mean, "This is an efficacious sign of My Body," not the Body but the virtues of the Body at the most being believed to be present

ENTHUSIASTÆ [EUCHITES]

ENTHUSIASTS Writers of Elizabethan days not unfrequently refer to sectarians called by this name Thus Thomas Rogers, Archbishop Bancroft's chaplain, in his treatise on the Thirty-Nine Articles of Religion, says, "This truth is gainsaid by the Phrygians, Montanists, and Messalians, also by the Enthusiasts, Anabaptists, and Family of Love" [Rogers *on XXXIX Art* 158, Parker Soc. ed] They are noticed by Hooper, Jewel, and other writers of that age, and also by Enoch Clapham in his curious little volume *Errour on the right hand through preposterous Zeal* In this there is a satirical dialogue between two voyagers on board a "fly-boat" or "hoy" between London Bridge and Gravesend, the one of whom is called "Flyer," and the other "Anabaptist" At the end of this dialogue Anabaptist, having converted Flyer, says, "Stay, holy Proselyte, thou must first be baptized, and have some divine vision from above, and so, being made a perfect Enthusiast, thou shalt be able to turn back the floods of Jordan" Rogers also speaks of their "depending wholly upon visions and revelations" [Rogers *on XXXIX Art* 196, Parker Soc ed] There is no reason to think that there was ever any organized sect of the name, and probably the persons referred to are simply that fanatical section of the Puritans, from which sprung the Fifth Monarchy Men and the Quakers in the days of Vavasour Powell, and Fox When writing about the Familists, the quaint Fuller says, "In a word, as in the small-pox (pardon my plain and homely but true and proper comparison), when at first they kindly come forth, every one of them may severally and distinctly be discerned, but when once they run and matter they break into one another, and can no longer be dividedly discovered. So though at first there was a real difference betwixt Familists, Enthusiasts, Antinomians (not to add high-flown Anabaptists) in their opinions, yet (process of time plucking up the pales betwixt them) afterwards, they did so interfuse amongst themselves, that it is almost impossible to bank and bound their several absurdities" [Fuller's *Ch Hist* ix 3, § 38] Henry More uses the name in many parts of his works, and almost always with reference to the Family of Love.

ENTYCHITES [EUTYCHITES]

EONIANS A sect of Breton fanatics, followers of Eon d'Etoile, in the middle of the twelfth century He was a wealthy nobleman, either very ignorant or very mad, who imagined himself to be the Messiah, his profane fancy being founded on the similarity between his own name Eon and the word "Eum" in the formula of exorcism, "Per Eum Qui venturus est judicare vivos et mortuos" He drew together so large a number of followers as to become a dangerous political fanatic of the Communist kind, and was therefore imprisoned by the civil authorities. While in prison Eon died [A D 1148], but his followers maintained that he would appear again as the judge of quick and dead Some were burned as heretics, and the heresy was condemned by the Council of Rheims [Labbe and Cossart, *Concil.* x 1107] This fanatical movement is mentioned by Matthew Paris and William of Newbury [*Hist rerum Anglic.* i 50]

EPEFANOFTSCHINS A sect of Russian Dissenters which separated from the POPOFTSCHINS about the year 1724 under the leadership of a monk from whom it takes its name He assumed the office of bishop, and was in consequence placed in prison, where he died, but his death was considered as a martyrdom by his followers, and they made pilgrimages to his tomb at Kief.

EPIGONUS [NOETIANS.]

EPIPHANES. A son of Carpocrates is mentioned by this name in the *Stromata* of St Clement of Alexandria as having been the real founder of the heresy of the CARPOCRATIANS Epiphanes is described by St Clement as being the son of Carpocrates' wife Alexandria, a woman of Cephallenia, and as living only to the age of seventeen His father is said to have instructed him in all ordinary learning, and especially in the philosophy of Plato, and, young as he was Epiphanes is said to have been the author of the Monadic γνῶσις, out of which arose the heresy going by his father's name He accuses him also of originating the profligate practice which accompanied that heresy, the community of women The works of Epiphanes were extant in the time of St Clement, who quotes a passage from a treatise on Justice, the object of which is to shew that the institution of marriage is opposed to the justice of God, who intended all things to be common to all as the light of the sun is common to all. St Clement adds that, after the death of Epiphanes, he was worshipped by the Cephallenians, who erected a temple at Sama in his honour, with altars, a grove, and a museum, and celebrated his apotheosis on every new moon with hymns, libations, and sacrificial feasts Epiphanius gives a similar account [Clem Alex. *Strom.* iii 2, Epiph *Hæres* xxxii 3]

ERASTIANS A conventional name for those who lean more or less to the opinion that the Church is only a department of the State The extreme form of this opinion was maintained by a physician of Heidelberg named Lieber, who lived in the Reformation age [A D 1524-1583], and wrote "Theses" under the classic form of his name "Erastus" These were levelled against the Calvinists, whose outrageous tyranny wherever they gained the upper hand was as extreme a form of Ecclesiasticism as that of Ultramontanists Recoil from this drove Erastus to maintain a theory which goes to the opposite extreme, namely, that the spiritual part of religion is entirely a matter of individual conscience, and that the external organization of it, such as the nomination and commission of ministers, is entirely a matter of civil government. English Erastians have found their most conspicuous advocate in Hobbes, who maintained that the Church has no authority whatever except such as is conferred upon it by Act of Parliament or an equivalent authority [Hobbes' *Leviathan*, iii 42]

ERIGENA [SCHOOLMEN]

ESAIANITES One of the sects into which the Alexandrian ACEPHALI split up at the end of the fifth century They were the followers of Esaias, a deacon of Palestine, who claimed to have been consecrated to the episcopal office by the Bishop Eusebius His opponents averred that after the bishop's death his hands had been laid upon the head of Esaias by some of his friends [Neale's *Patriarchate of Alexandria*, ii. 22] This consecration by mortmain was also charged against the APHTHARTODOCETÆ half a century later

ESSAYS AND REVIEWS CONTROVERSY. [BROAD CHURCHMEN]

ESSENES An ancient Jewish sect which renounced the Temple worship and the Levitical priesthood, and embodied in itself the ascetic and mystical elements of the Jewish religion, with an admixture of tenets and practices derived from the Oriental philosophy

This sect is described at length by Josephus [*De Bell Jud* II viii , *Antiq Jud* XVIII i 5, and XIII v 9], more briefly by Philo [*Quod omn prob Liber* ii p 457, and *Fragment*, ii p 632, Mangey's ed , *De Vita Contempl* ii. 471], and is mentioned by Pliny [*Hist Nat* v 17] From these three writers the accounts of all later writers appear to be derived Philo distinguishes between the Practical Essenes, those of Judæa and Syria, and the Contemplative Essenes, those of Egypt, the Therapeutæ.[1] Regarding the Essenes of Judæa the authority of Josephus stands highest, because he was some time conversant among them and under their discipline. As regards the Essenes of Egypt Philo's authority is good

I The doctrines of this sect are but briefly described They believed in God the Governor of all things, and were strict predestinarians They believed in the immortality of the soul, but denied the resurrection of the body They described the states of future reward and punishment as the Greeks described them, that is, as regions of delight and warmth, or regions of gloom and cold

II To the Temple, Josephus writes, they sent gifts, but offered no sacrifices there on account of the superiority of their own purifications (διαφορότητι ἁγνειῶν ἃς νομίζοιεν) Wherefore, being excluded from the Temple, they perform their own sacrifices apart [Joseph *Ant* XVIII i 5] These sacrifices were in fact the ordinary meals of their societies, taken with such solemnity as to turn the meal into a religious service There was a ceremonial washing, a linen garment, the refectory was considered as a temple, prayer was made before and after meat [Joseph *Bell Jud* II viii. 5] Again, Philo says of them, "that they do not sacrifice to God any living creature, but rather choose to form their minds to be holy, thereby to make them a fit offering to Him" [Philo, *Omn prob Lib*] From these premisses Ritschl concludes that the principle of Essenism was to recover from the Levites the prerogative of the priesthood, according to God's original design that the nation should be a kingdom of priests, and to form themselves into a priestly society, which should carry out the prophetical idea of self-sacrifice, along with the sacrifice of prayer and praise [Ritschl, *Die Entstehung der Altk Kirche*, p 179, *et seq*] Hence the lustrations [Exod xl 30-32], the linen garment [Lev vi 10], the disuse of wine [Lev x 9], because as priests they were always on service, the rejection of oil as the sign of consecration to a separate priesthood, the priest, not of Levi, but one of themselves Thus instead of the Temple-ritual was established the ritual of a solemn public table, "Sind alle ihre Mahlzeiten Opfermahlzeiten."

III To introduce and carry out this principle of a common priesthood requires separate societies under a strict rule The principle was probably suggested to men already forming themselves into distinct bodies for the sake of leading a stricter and more devout life These bodies it would define more sharply as well as consolidate, while at the same time it would strengthen their

[1] This distinction cannot be pressed very far The Essenes had their own theosophy as will be shewn And Philo himself says, that they employed themselves with a φιλοσόφία διὰ σύμβολων, a philosophy which was supported by an allegorical interpretation of Scripture, for this kind of allegorizing interpretaion was usually the accompaniment of a certain speculative system [Neander, i 40, Rose's transl] The chief difference in the practice of the Essenes and the Therapeutæ appears to be that the former, living in societies, had their fixed hours of labour, the latter, living apart, so long as they could procure food, might contemplate or dream at their pleasure. [THERAPEUTÆ]

purpose of attaining to a higher degree of holiness Accordingly, in almost every respect, the Essenes became the monastic orders of the Jews. Their rules of morality were severe They were bound by vow to despise pleasure, to live in continence, to despise riches, to keep fidelity, truth, and justice, to be reverent to the aged, sparing in speech, grave in demeanour, peaceful, laborious For this end they were distributed into sodalities, and had in every place one or more sodalities according to their number, in which they lived according to the rules of each particular order In these societies there was an absolute community of goods, no employment but agriculture and study of their sacred books, the religious common table, set hours of labour and sleep [1]

IV So far the fairer side has been shewn But neither the principles of a common priesthood, nor the genuine mysticism and asceticism of the Jewish religion, are sufficient to explain some further parts of the system or the general tone and character of the whole The forbidding to marry, and commanding to abstain from meats, are of the kind which St. Paul denounced, not of the kind which he practised Milman has observed that the main principles of Essene tenets are evidently grounded on that widespread oriental philosophy, which, supposing matter either the creation of the Evil Being, or itself the Evil Being, considered all the appetites and propensities of the material body in themselves evil, and therefore esteemed the most severe mortification the perfection of virtue [Milman's *Hist of Jews*, ii 151] It is alleged that the forbidding to marry cannot have arisen from an application of the principles of Dualism, because it was not universal, in some societies marriage being allowed In these, however, no other conjugal intercourse was allowed than that necessary for the procreation of children, it was allowed as of inevitable necessity, not as being consistent with the highest state that man ought to aim at

"The reverence for the names of the angels," says Milman, "points to the same source" It will be remembered that the latest revelation concerning the office of angels was made to the Jews during the Captivity, as if, by possessing them with the full truth, to guard them against the corruptions of the truth which prevailed in the East [Rawlinson, *Five Monarchies*, iii p 98, iv. p 329] By Josephus the "names of the angels" are so closely connected with the "sacred books" of the Essenes as to leave little doubt that Prideaux is right in translating the passage thus "The books containing the doctrines of their sect, and the names of the messengers (angels) by whose hand they were written and conveyed to them" [Prideaux, *Connect* iii 489] Men who professed to receive the books of the Old Testament, and yet rejected the national priesthood, certainly needed for their justification a new revelation A like pretension occurs in later times among the Ossenes, who were the Essenes of the east side of the Dead Sea The book Elchasai was said to have been brought from heaven by an angel. Again, the Essenes appear to have added to their worship of God a worship of the sun, as the image or representative of God. The meaning of Josephus' words has been much disputed. They are, Πρός γε μὴν τὸ Θεῖον ἰδίως εὐσεβεῖς πρὶν γὰρ ἀνασχεῖν τὸν ἥλιον, οὐδὲν φθέγγονται τῶν βεβήλων, πατρίους δέ τινας εἰς αὐτὸν εὐχάς, ὥσπερ ἱκετεύοντες ἀνατεῖλαι [Joseph *Bell Jud.* VIII. i 5] The natural interpretation is that the prayers were made to the sun Also the regulation for preserving cleanliness in the wilderness camp [Deut xxiii. 12, 13], which was adopted most strictly by the Essenes, was said to be that they might not offend τὰς αὐγὰς τοῦ Θεοῦ.[2]

In general, also, the readiness with which Essenism lent itself to early Gnosticism to form Ebionitism is a strong indication that there were Oriental elements already existing in Essenism It may be stated therefore, with little chance of error, that the asceticism and mysticism of the Essenes was not a pure product of Jewish religion, but was largely mingled with the principles of Eastern philosophy The self-righteous pride of the four classes of ascetics, by which the touch of one of a lower class was pollution to the upper class, might be Pharisaic, the refusal of marriage is not Judaic And the ground on which, according to Josephus, that refusal was adopted, namely, that, "being aware of the lasciviousness of women, they are persuaded that none of them can keep true faith to one man," appears to be morally absurd One is little inclined to believe in a continence of men which is grounded on the lasciviousness of women

The growth of the sect of Essenes is not recorded, but we have in the Assideans a party "voluntarily devoted unto the law" [1 Macc ii 42], bound by vow to its stricter observance. They would naturally fall into two classes, as the ceremonial or the moral law was put foremost, and form the parties of Pharisees and Essenes In the latter a mystic asceticism was gradually developed When the rejection of the Temple service and Levitical priesthood took place we have no information From that time, whenever it was, the formation of the sect must be dated It seems to be no improbable supposition that the treacherous slaughter of Assideans by Alcimus [1 Macc. vii 16] alienated them from the "priests of the seed of Aaron," that they then added to their ascetic principles the principle of a common

[1] One regulation does not appear to have been explained—in company the Essenes were not to expectorate except on the left hand.

[2] So strongly was this regulation insisted on, that by a connection of it with the sabbatical prohibition of labour, the ordinary relief of nature on the seventh day became unlawful The little pickaxe which was carried about for the purpose became, as it were, a masonic badge It was presented with a white dress to the novices. There must have been some mystical meaning given to it Was it a mark that the Essenes thought themselves to be in the same state as Israel in the early days of the wilderness before the separation of the Levites? or was it rather only a badge in general of agricultural employment to the exclusion of commerce?

priesthood, and being separated from the Church of the nation, and under the disadvantages of schism, were open to the temptations of Eastern philosophy The earliest Essene mentioned, about fifty years later, is Judas, an Essene prophet, who foretold the death of Antigonus, brother of Aristobulus, which took place in B C 107 [Joseph *Bell Jud* I iii 5] This notice shews that the sect must have existed a considerable time

The Essenes were cruelly persecuted by the Romans, who probably entered their country after the capture of Jericho Josephus records their perfect patience under torture Herod favoured the sect, one of their prophets having foretold to him when a boy that he should be King of Judæa [Joseph *Antiq* XV x 5] Philo computed the number of the Essenes to be four thousand, and Josephus states that there were above four thousand of the stricter sort who forbad marriage [*ibid* XVIII i 5] One of the gates of Jerusalem was called the Essene gate [Joseph *Bell Jud* V iv 2]

ETHNOPHRONIANS. A name given by some early heresiologists to those who mixed up heathen customs and superstitions with Christianity Those who practised astrology, fortune-telling, divination, sortilege, or auguries, were all reprobated under this title [Nicetas, *Thesaur. orthod fid* iv 42]

EUCHITES [Εὐχῖται] A sect which arose in the fourth century, and which reappeared, with slight variations in their tenets, and under other names, at various subsequent times Their original designation of Euchites, or "praying people," refers to a special feature in their system, that of regarding prayer as the one means of grace, to the exclusion of all others The Latin name, Precatores, and the Syrian form, Massalians or Messalians, both allude to the same characteristic They themselves seem to have preferred the appellation of Spirituales or Enthusiastæ Some extravagances in their public worship gave rise to the latter name, which they however accepted, the same reason may be alleged for the names Choreutæ Psaliens, and others Some early imitators of their eccentricities called themselves Euphemites

Baronius speaks of them first under the year A D. 361, by which time they had probably begun to attract attention Epiphanius, who died A D 403, makes them the latest in his treatise of Heresies They were sufficiently numerous and important, A D 383, to occasion synodical action in Pamphylia No founder of the sect appears to have been assigned by contemporary writers, but Pagius [Notes to Baronius, *sub anno* 1118, xxxiii] names as such Petrus or Lycopetrus It seems more reasonable to suppose them to have taken definite shape in consequence of a systematic attempt to combine the older forms of religion with Christianity, and Gieseler [ed. Cunningham, i 182] considers them to have held a sort of fashionable mean between the old and the new religions Their first recognised appearance as a sect was in Mesopotamia, from whence their views spread to Syria At Antioch there was a considerable congregation.

The original heretics maintained that prayer only was necessary to salvation They understood the injunctions of our Lord [Luke xviii 1] and St Paul [1 Thess v 17] to prescribe an *unceasing* practice of prayer, and rejected any such interpretations as a habit of prayer, a daily certain time assigned for prayer, and the like. They therefore gave themselves wholly to an ascetic life, detached from the world. As they lived in community, and are said to have held that monks ought to do nothing whatever towards the support of life, they were joined in large numbers by some whose only aim was to live without work. The principle of almsgiving to the worldly poor they denounced, saying that they, the poor in spirit, were the true mendicants, and the only proper recipients of alms Baptism, holy orders, marriage, were all rejected as useless They had little oratories, προσευχαί, in public places

Epiphanius makes the description above given apply to a second kind of Euchites The more ancient, and far less numerous kind, were neither Jews nor Christians, but pagans, who admitted many gods, but worshipped one only as the Supreme, or Most High. These are nearly identical with Hypsistarians They too had places of prayer, which were built in imitation of Christian churches

The name Enthusiasts was given in allusion to the perfection they professed to have attained in the religious life Every man at his birth, they said, became the abode of a demon ever enticing to ill, which was not driven forth by baptism (hence the uselessness of that sacrament), but by prayer only After this demon had been wholly expelled by ceaseless prayer, *then* the Holy Spirit descended upon the soul, and gave sensible indications of His presence, by illumination, the gift of prophecy, by the privilege of beholding the Divinity (which they said could be done with the bodily eyes), and by revelations of the future. In this state they considered themselves as wholly perfect, and assumed the names of the old prophets, of the angels, and even of the Redeemer They had become entirely free from all movements of the passions and every inclination to ill, they had then no need of fasts, mortification, or any religious exercise, no need of labour or of good deeds, the soul had become like to God, and absolutely sinless [Theodor *Eccl Hist* iv 11]

"Their principles," says Mosheim, "did not necessarily lead to vicious conduct, yet they might afford occasion for practising vice." And, accordingly, it is but seldom that any impugners of their practices do more than accuse them of excessive frivolity in their services, bordering upon impiety They did not openly separate from the Church, as they professed indifference In some places they became the subjects of persecution, and many were even put to death by some magistrates One of the earliest persecutors was Lupicianus, and from this persecution arose another phase of error, and another name, Martyriani, as they claimed the glory of martyrdom The theory of an indwelling demon became expanded into one of a power co-ordinate with the Almighty, if not superior, from this they were called Satanians Why, they argued, should we not fly to Satan and worship him, so that, conciliated by our devotion, he may cease to afflict us? There are full replies to all the earlier tenets of the sect in Epiphanius [Epiph *Hær* lxxx]

The first public action taken against them was at the Synod of Syda, in Pamphylia [A D 383] Amphilochius, Bishop of Iconium, presided, and twenty-five other bishops are said to have been present. Letters were sent to Flavianus, Bishop of Antioch, and by him another synod was convened At this one of their leaders, Adelphius, though he professed penitence, was not admitted Baronius says the sect broke out in Africa, A D 398 They were many times condemned in various dioceses, and the bishops at last, wearied out with repeated lapses, decreed that the lapsed should not be readmitted An important condemnation was issued at a council at Constantinople, A D 427, held under the presidency of Sisinnius In the following year they are mentioned in a general law of Theodosius and Valentinianus against heretics, "Massaliani, Euchitæ, sive Enthusiastæ," being forbidden to have places of prayer. Proceedings were also taken against them at Alexandria, and these, as well as the condemnation by Sisinnius, were confirmed at the Council of Ephesus, A D 431, where Valerian, a Pamphylian bishop, and Amphilochius, who had presided at Syda, were the principal opponents of the sect The former produced a book called Asceticon, by one of the body, and it was condemned This book, and some writings, said to have been brought out by Johannes Cassianus, who founded two monasteries for the Euchites, and died A D 448, are the only literary efforts which are mentioned Atticus, Bishop of Constantinople, wrote against them, and so did Euthymius Zigabenus, the title of whose work, "Damnatio et triumphus de impia et multiplici execrabilium Massalianorum secta, qui et Phundaitæ et Bogomili, nec non Euchitæ, Enthusiastæ, Encratitæ, et Marcionitæ appellantur," shews how many sects had adopted the chief characteristics of the Euchites [Cave, *Hist Liter* i 410, ii. 199]

In the tenth century a resuscitation of the sect took place, which seems to have embraced some of the views of Manicheism. They admitted two gods, born of one Supreme Being, who were continually at war, though ultimately to be reconciled [Le Clerc, *Bibl Univ.* xv 119]. Again in the twelfth century some heretics appeared, calling themselves Euchites and Massalians, who are said to have been precursors of the Bogomiles· but it is hard to discover their points of identity with the older forms of the heresy· and in A D 1347 the names of both these sects were given to the Hesychasts [BOGOMILES Natal Alex *Hist Eccl.* iv. 270 Nicet. Choniat. *Thesaur orthod.* iv 36]

EUDOXIANS This sect derives its name from Eudoxius, one of the most prominent figures in the Arian controversy in the fourth century There is some uncertainty attaching to the dates of the earlier events in his life. He was the son of Cæsarius, a martyr of Arabissus in Lesser Armenia, and as a boy was a pupil of St Lucian the Martyr, whose firmness cannot have been very deeply imbibed by one who, while still young, is taunted with having sacrificed to idols in the Diocletian persecution [c A D 303], and who, when older, passed through successively the phases of Arianism, Semi-Arianism, and Aetianism His good education enabled him to support these views at various times with much success, although none of his numerous works are extant, with the exception of some fragments of one of them entitled "De Incarnatione Dei Verbi" At some period between A D 330-340 he was made Bishop of Germanicia in Syria, which he held till his translation to Antioch [A D. 357] The mode in which he obtained that see is given at length by Nicephorus [*Hist. Eccles* ix 36], and affords us some insight into the scheming character of the new bishop He was in attendance on the Emperor in the West when the news of the death of Leontius of Antioch was brought to the court Directly that the intelligence reached him he obtained leave from the Emperor on false pretences to return home, and by extremely rapid stages went straight to Antioch, where he declared himself to have been the imperial nominee for the bishopric, and obtained consecration before there was time to prove the falsehood of his statement Four years later [A D 461], on the deposition of Macedonius, against whom he himself, in conjunction with Acacius, had laid various charges and stirred up the popular enmity, Eudoxius was translated to Constantinople, and his occupation of this see lasted, with the exception of a brief banishment by Constantius, till his death [A D 370], when he was succeeded by the Arian Demophilus.

During the latter part of his life Eudoxius not only held himself, but laboured among his flock for the propagation of, Arianism of the most advanced type His Aetian or Eunomian views on the complete inferiority of the Son to the Father, and his denial of the Trinity, brought down upon him the condemnation of the Semi-Arian Council of Seleucia [A D 359] as well as that of Lampsacus [A.D. 365] While at Antioch he laboured to restore his friend Aetius to the Church, and held a synod for his readmission to the diaconate When he officiated at the baptism of Valens, before that Emperor started on his Gothic expedition [A D 367], he extracted an oath from him to persecute the Catholics, a fact which, taken in connection with the way in which he obtained promotion to the sees of both Antioch and Constantinople, is extremely inconsistent with the character of mildness and timidity bestowed upon him by the historian Gibbon [Nicephorus, *Eccles Hist* ix 36, 45, xi 15 Tillemont's *Mémoires*, vi art lxx p 422, *et passim* Gibbon's *Decl and Fall*, iii. 25, p 250, note]

EUNOMIANS A name given to the ANOMŒAN sect of Arians as followers of Eunomius,

Bishop of Cyzicus The sect originated with Aetius, whose name was at first associated with it, but his friend and disciple Eunomius was a man of more popular influence and authority, who had not acquired the reputation for immorality which brought disgrace upon the former, and thereby made his name one that none would willingly assume, however much they might agree with his speculations in theology

Eunomius was a native of Dacora in Cappadocia, but became secretary to Aetius at Antioch, where he was ordained deacon He was afterwards taken up by Eudoxius, the Acacian Patriarch of Constantinople, and through his influence was sent to succeed Eleusius the Macedonian, Bishop of Cyzicus, in the year 360 In the very same year, however, he was deposed from his see by order of the Arian Emperor Constantius, and was never permitted to return From that time until the reign of Theodosius the Great he lived at Constantinople and Chalcedon, but Theodosius sent him into exile, where he was driven from one country to another by the Arians, with whom he continued an unceasing controversy. He was allowed to return from exile a short time before his death, which took place at his native village about A.D. 394, more than a quarter of a century after that of Aetius.

The literary reputation of Eunomius was considerable, and the influence which he gained for the Anomœan opinions by means of his works was so great that imperial edicts were several times issued for the destruction of them [*Cod. Theod* xvi 34]. They consisted of a commentary on St Paul's Epistle to the Romans, an apology for Anomœan doctrines, forty Epistles, and an Ecthesis or exposition of faith The latter alone of these is extant, and may be found in Greek in the annotations of Valesius to the Ecclesiastical History of Socrates, or in an English translation in Whiston's *Eunomianismus Redivivus*, printed in the year 1711. Although adopting many Scriptural expressions respecting our Lord, it distinctly denies that He partakes in the Divine Glory of the Father, and acknowledges His Preexistence before the Incarnation only as a Being possessing the nature of an angel His statements respecting the Third Person in the Holy Trinity are inconsistent with the real existence of that Person, verbally denying His Divine Nature, and inferentially His Personality This Ecthesis was presented to the Emperor Theodosius by Eunomius at a synod held by the latter at Constantinople [A D 383], he having been summoned to the council as the representative of the Anomœan party

Eunomius was the first to discontinue the practice of trine immersion in baptism, and he further corrupted the rite by administering it with a form which set aside the Name of the Holy Trinity and substituted words which made it a baptism in the Name of the Creator and into the death of Christ. This change in the formula of baptism being a very glaring deviation from the words of our Lord's command, was considered to invalidate the baptism of the Eunomians, and while that of the Arians in general was recognised by the Church, and converts from their sects admitted to communion by imposition of hands only, Eunomian converts were ordered to be baptized in the orthodox manner by the General Council of Constantinople [can vii], which also anathematized the heresy in its first canon [Socr *Hist Eccl* ii 35, iv 7, 13 Sozom *Hist Eccl* iv 26, vi 26 Philostorg *Hist Eccl* vi-x]

EUNOMIO-EUPSYCHIANS [EUNOMIO-EUTYCHIANS]

EUNOMIO-EUTYCHIANS A sect of Eunomian heretics, followers of Eutychius of Constantinople They are spoken of by Socrates the ecclesiastical historian in association with the sect noticed in the next article, and what he says of them seems to be said also of these [Socr *Hist Eccl* v 24]

EUNOMIO-THEOPHRONIANS A sect of Eunomian heretics, followers of Theophronius of Cappadocia, in the end of the fourth century. Socrates the ecclesiastical historian speaks of him as being trained up under Eunomius in the subtleties of logic and of Aristotle's philosophy, and as being himself the author of a book on metaphysics, of which the title only, "Concerning the exercise of the intellect," has come down to us Being reckoned an apostate by the Anomœans, he formed a sect of his own, adding to the Eunomian heresy that of baptizing in the Name of Christ alone instead of in that of the Blessed Trinity [Socr *Hist Eccl* v 24]

EUPHEMITES A synonym for the ENTHUSIASTÆ or EUCHITES [August *de Hæres* cap 57] But, according to Epiphanius, the Euphemites were heathens, who, in the reign of Constantine, rejected polytheistic worship, and, without attaching themselves to Christianity, met in temples day by day for the worship of one Almighty God, resembling the Enthusiastæ in other respects, but differing from them in not being formally members of the Christian Church [Epiphan. *Hær* lxxx]

EUPHRATAS There is a common statement in ecclesiastical histories that an heretical bishop of Cologne of this name was condemned by a Council of Cologne in the year 346 for denying the Divinity of our Lord It is, however, established on good evidence that there was no such council nor any such bishop of Cologne, though it has not been discovered out of what circumstances the mistake originally arose. [Mansi, *Concil* i 173 Natal Alex *Hist. Eccl* iv 276 Dupin, *Biblioth* ii 326]

EUPHRATES According to Origen, the founder of the OPHITES [Origen, *contr Cels* vi 28]

EUPHRATES According to Hippolytus, the founder of the PERATÆ [Hippol *Philosoph* v 8]

EUPHRONOMIANS [EUNOMIO-THEOPHRONIANS]

EUSEBIANS. A name given first to the Arians from the violent partizanship shewn by Eusebius, Bishop of Nicomedia, at the Council of Nicæa, and afterwards more generally to the

Semi-Arians of Palestine, from the leadership of Eusebius the historian, Bishop of Cæsarea [ARIANS SEMI-ARIANS]

EUSTATHIANS A local name given to the Euchites from Eustathius, Bishop of Sebaste in Armenia, who was deposed by the Council of Gangra [A D 380], and his principles condemned in twenty-one canons of that council [Socr *Hist Eccl* ii. 33]

EUSTATHIANS During the time of Arian ascendancy at Antioch [A D 358] the Catholics were called by the name of Eustathius, the last presiding orthodox bishop of that see [MELETIANS OF ANTIOCH Sozom *Hist Eccl.* iii 20 Theod *Hist Eccl.* ii. 12]

EUTICHISTÆ [EUTYCHETÆ]

EUTYCHITES [EUTYCHETÆ.]

EUTYCHETÆ. A sect of heretics of this name is mentioned by Theodoret, who writes, "From this most bitter root" of Simonianism "sprang the Cleobians, Dositheæans, Gorthæans, Masbothæans, Adrianists, Eutychetæ, and Canistæ," adding that they lasted but a short time, and were then consigned to perpetual oblivion [Theod *Hær. fab* i 1] In the edition of Cotelerius the sect is supposed to be identical with the Euchites, Theodoret in one place naming together Carpocrates, Epiphanes, Prodicus, the Cainites, the Antitactics, and the Euchites [Coteler in Theod *Hær fab* v 9] Ittigius, however, considers that they are the same as the Entychites mentioned by Clement of Alexandria as being named from their iniquitous practices [*Stromat* vii. 17, *ad fin*], and that they probably made their profligacies (ἐντυχίαι), as did the Nicolaitanes, part of their religion

EUTYCHIANS Eutyches and his followers were the early Monophysites They asserted that from the union of the two Natures in our Lord there resulted only one Nature. In virtue of this assertion they were Monophysites when that term is taken in its wider and proper signification But they went on to assert that the one resulting Nature is the Divine Nature, the Nature of the Incarnate Word This the later Monophysites, led by Xenaias and Fullo, denied, and the term Monophysites is often used in a limited sense, as the name of those who defined in a different manner from the Eutychians the character of the one resulting Nature

Eutyches, a presbyter and archimandrite of Constantinople, had exerted himself to the uttermost in opposing the Nestorian heresy, and had distinguished himself in this manner at the Council of Ephesus [A D 431] But the genuine development of Christian doctrine is seldom, if ever, carried on in a direct course It has aberrations to the right and then to the left, between which the truth nevertheless makes its way So Eutyches, in combating Nestorianism, fell into the opposite error In the enunciation of his error he used language which had been used in a Catholic sense both by earlier and contemporary theologians Dogmatic terms were not then accurately defined. The language of theology was still in a state of change This was the case with the word φύσις, which had been not infrequently used to signify "Persona" Photius noticed this in the writings of Pierius of Alexandria [c A.D. 283, *Cod* 119] In this way Bull explains the passage of Clement of Alexandria [*Strom* vii 2, p 831, Pott's ed] ἡ υἱοῦ φύσις ἡ τῷ μόνῳ παντοκράτορι προσεχεστάτη, of which Petavius said, "Ariani dogmatis indolem sapit" [Bull's *Defens Fid Nic* II vi 6] Bull afterwards says, "Atque eodem sensu vocabulum (φύσις) accipi a Gregorio Nysseno, ab Epiphanio, adeoque ab ipso Athanasio ostendit Petavius de Trinit iv. 1, n 2, 3" [*ibid* II ix. 11] This uncertainty of theological terms, though of considerable importance, is however by no means sufficient for an explanation of the origin of the errors of Eutyches

There was a real difference between the theology of Alexandria and that of Antioch, and consequently an antagonism between the schools Each held adequately a portion of the truth concerning the person of Christ, but failed to set forth adequately the complement of that portion, and was therefore liable each to its distinctive heresy "The school of Antioch, by way of preventing an Apollinarian identification of the divine and the human in the νοῦς of Christ, distinguished between the two aspects as two natures, the school of Alexandria started with laying emphasis on the unity (ἕνωσις φυσική), and then proceeded to consider what could be said concerning the duality. Both held that the divine nature, the Logos, had a substantial existence, an hypostasis, but whilst the Alexandrians attached the humanity of Christ, including the soul and its powers, to the divine hypostasis as little more than a receptive passive material, the Antiochenes, for the reasons previously mentioned, strove to prove that the human factor also had a relative independence, but shewed themselves not infrequently inclined to the use of expressions which attributed to the human aspect an independent hypostasis or personality" [Dorner's *Person of Christ*, II i 56, Clark's tr] Cyril of Alexandria, whose side Eutyches warmly took, and by whose words he afterwards defended himself, was thus, by the character of the theological school to which he belonged, inclined to use that language which set forth most strongly the union of the two natures, and his fault, Dorner remarks, was principally that of too tenaciously clinging to the vagueness of expression and thought which prevailed at an earlier period, without its defectiveness being felt,—treating it as though it were perfect and satisfactory, and setting himself in opposition to those who demanded that the unity should be more accurately defined, and the *rationale* thereof be more distinctly exhibited Eutyches, with a theological acumen far inferior to Cyril's, imperfectly understood his leader, exaggerated his forms of expression, and drew inferences from them which Cyril would not have allowed About A D 448, he taught that in Christ there was but one nature, that of the Incarnate Word Cyril had expressed himself in this manner, and had appealed to the authority of Athanasius, and had protested that he had used the word "nature" according to the ancient usage to signify "person," and that he professed in Christ two substances, the divine and the human. Eutyches put forward this Athanasian formula *μίαν φύσιν τοῦ Θεοῦ λόγου σεσαρκωμένην*, and pushed it to an extent which seemed to annihilate the Humanity of Christ. Petavius remarks that there may be three senses of this expression, and that Eutyches had not the penetration to discriminate between the sound and the unsound senses [Petavius, *de Incarn.* I xiv. 6 8, IV vi 8].

It appears that a representation on the subject of Eutyches' errors was first made by Domnus, Bishop of Antioch, to Flavian of Constantinople, but was little attended to. In A.D 448, Eusebius, Bishop of Dorylæum, in Phrygia, at a synod at Constantinople, accused Eutyches of heresy, stating that private remonstrance had failed. At a second synod Eusebius presented his articles of accusation, and Eutyches was summoned. After repeated citations he appeared. [1] He professed his belief that in Christ is the union of two natures. This is not to be understood as an assertion of the pre-existence of Christ's Humanity, but only as of our conception of the existence of Christ. [2] He professed the Nicene faith. [3] He confessed that up to that time he had not spoken of Christ's Human Nature as consubstantial with ours. [4] At the bidding of the synod he admitted this consubstantiality, though with hesitation and reluctance[1]. But [5] he refused to acknowledge the two natures in Christ, and to anathematize the contrary opinion. Upon this he was sentenced to be deposed from the priesthood and deprived of his abbey. He afterwards asserted that he had appealed to Rome, Alexandria, and Jerusalem, but it does not appear that a formal appeal was made.

Eutyches then sought the advocacy of Peter Chrysologus, Bishop of Ravenna, with Pope Leo, which Chrysologus refused, advising him to submit himself to Leo's judgment. Both Eutyches and Flavian appealed by letter to Rome, and the former, through the favour of the eunuch Chrysaphius, induced the Emperor Theodosius to recommend his cause to Leo, and to procure the convocation of another council, at which the acts of the former council were examined, and the question of Eutyches' alleged appeal considered. The result of this was that Dioscorus of Alexandria, a personal enemy of Flavian, and Chrysaphius, who favoured Eutyches, persuaded the Emperor to convene a general council, as if to free the Church from Nestorianism. Leo thought the proposed council unnecessary, and if it met at all, it ought to meet in Italy. But he at length consented, and appointed his legates for the council, and wrote his celebrated letter to Flavian, declaring the doctrine of the Church on the mystery of the Incarnation. The council met at Ephesus in August, A D 449. It had been unfairly packed, and its proceedings were conducted with such violent outrage that it came to be called the "Robber-synod" of Ephesus. The Emperor had assigned to Dioscorus the presidency of the synod. Its whole power was in his hands, and he extorted from the bishops the condemnation and deposition of Flavian and Eusebius. Flavian lodged his appeal to Rome in the hands of Leo's legates. He died shortly afterwards, in consequence of the violence he had suffered in the synod.

In the same year a synod at Rome under Leo declared the acts of the Latrocinium invalid, and two other synods consulted upon the assembling a general council. In the next year [A D 451] a synod was also held at Milan against the Ephesine assembly. Leo expressed his wish that a general council should meet in Italy, and Valentinian III. joined in the request. But Theodosius, who had confirmed the Ephesine acts, adhered to them till his death. In the year 450, Marcian ascended the throne, and a synod was held at Constantinople by Anatolius, although he had been created patriarch through the influence of Dioscorus, in which Leo's letter to Flavian was subscribed, and both Nestorius and Eutyches were condemned. Leo now thought a general council unnecessary, but Marcian had already summoned it. It met at Chalcedon in October, A D 451, and determined the Catholic faith, and fixed the most suitable terms for its enunciation. The profession of faith it is unnecessary to give at length. It describes Christ, True God and True Man, consubstantial with the Father according to the Divinity, with us according to the Humanity, One and the Same Christ, Son, Lord, and Only-begotten *ἐν δύο φύσεσιν ἀσυγχύτως, ἀτρέπτως, ἀδιαιρέτως, ἀχωρίστως γνωριζόμενον*. The Greek text in the common editions of the councils has the preposition in this quotation, *ἐκ*. At first it was so proposed. The influence of Leo's legates prevailed, and *ἐν* was inserted, as Evagrius gives it [Evagr *Hist Eccl* ii 4]. Routh has accordingly admitted *ἐν* in his text [Routh's *Opusc* ii. 426, 475, n].

Eutyches, who had been already banished by the Emperor, was condemned. Dioscorus was condemned, deposed, and banished. Of the last days of Eutyches nothing is known.

The salutary effects of a council are to be looked for in the whole course of subsequent Church history. the council is not to be judged by disturbances which may immediately follow its decisions. The direction given to the stream is to be regarded, not the eddying of the waters at the time of building the breakwater. And they who regard the definition of Chalcedon as the great guide in the doctrine of the Incarnation need not be disconcerted at the tumults which followed, much as they are to be lamented. Upon the death of Marcian, Proterius, the successor of Dioscorus in the see of Alexandria, was murdered in a rising of the people. Timotheus Ælurus, a Eutychian, was placed in his room

[1] Evagrius states that he denied this fourth point [*H E* i 9]

After his death there was a formal schism, Peter Mongus being chosen by the Eutychians in opposition to Timotheus Mongus was banished by the Emperor Zeno, but restored to the see, and Talaia, the successor of Timotheus, displaced Meanwhile in Syria, Barsumas, an abbot who had assisted Dioscorus at the Latrocinium, spread widely the doctrines of Eutyches But his followers, about A D 460, received from Xenaias, Bishop of Hierapolis, and Peter Fullo, a modification of the Monophysite tenet

Eutyches taught that the one Nature of our Lord, which is ἐκ δύο φύσεων, is the nature of the Incarnate Word From this it appears to follow of necessity that the Human Nature is absorbed in the Divine, and in this way the doctrine of Eutyches is commonly stated But Eutyches expressly repudiated the notion of a transmutation of the human element, as also the doctrine of its absorption, which Theodoret tried to fasten on him How he explained the transition from duality to unity it is not easy to discover "His idea must have been," Dorner writes, "that the effect of the Unio was not merely an exaltation or glorification, but an ennobling transmutation of humanity [Dorner's *Person of Christ,* II i pp 81, 82] Xenaias and Fullo rejected both the definition of Chalcedon and the doctrine of Eutyches They asserted the oneness of Christ's Nature, but held at the same time that this one nature was twofold Eutychianism, as distinguished from Monophysitism, thus soon disappeared, and in the latter doctrine is seen something of a less departure from the faith regarding the verity of our Lord's Human Nature [MONOPHYSITES]

EVANGELICAL ASSOCIATION An American sect founded in the beginning of the present century by a German Lutheran of Pennsylvania, named Jacob Albrecht, and hence also going by the name of the Albrecht Brethren They were organized into a kind of Episcopal form by him in the year 1803, Albrecht going through a form of ordination at the hands of the other preachers of the sect, by which he was made the presiding elder, an officer intended to be analogous to the primitive bishop For many years the sect was confined exclusively to German immigrants, and their services were all carried on in the German language, but recently they have begun to use English in a large proportion of their places of worship The principles of the sect are those of the Methodists, except that they more or less deny the doctrine of original sin Their so-called bishops are elected every four years, and they have under them the ordinary organization of Methodist communities In 1871 the sect was said to number 60,241 members

EVANGELICAL LUTHERANS [UNITED EVANGELICAL CHURCH]

EVANGELICAL UNION [MORISONIANS]

EVANGELICALS A name assumed by the modern "Low Church" party in the Church of England in the early part of the nineteenth century It is equivalent to that of GOSPELLERS, which was assumed by their predecessors at the time of the Reformation, and is much to be deprecated for the arrogance of the assumption which it expresses, that they are the only faithful preachers of the Gospel in the Church of England. [LOW CHURCHMEN]

EXCALCEATI A superstitious sect is mentioned under this name by the ancient heresiologists, who thought it a duty of religion to walk barefoot, pleading in support of their notion the command given to Moses and Joshua and the example of Isaiah [Philast. *de Hær* lxxxi , Aug *de Hær* lxviii] They are called Gymnopodæ by the author of *Prædestinatus* [*Præd* lxviii]

EXOTIANS A name given to the Arians of Constantinople when they were deprived of their churches by Theodosius the Great, and compelled to carry on their services—ἔξω τῆς πόλεως—beyond the walls of the city [Socr *Hist Eccl* v 7] The name occurs in the chronicle of Alexandria, and in a decree of Justinian by which he gives all the churches of the heretics to the orthodox except those of the Exotians The name was probably limited to the EUNOMIANS

EXUCONTII A name given to the Arians at Antioch to express their distinctive tenet that the Son of God, although entitled to divine rank, was a created Being, brought forth from non-existence—ἐξ οὐκ ὄντων, and not eternally existing [Socr *Hist Eccl.* ii 45]

F

FALSE APOSTLES By this term we are no doubt referred in the first place, and most properly, to apostolic times But inasmuch as the reception of apostolic doctrine enters into all Church communion, and as apostolic powers for the ordinary government of the Church are vested in the episcopate, there is a proper sense, although it may be a lower sense, in which the term belongs to all ages

In the first place, then, regarding apostolic times, St Paul denounces as false apostles the leaders of the party which tried to supplant him in the Church of Corinth [2 Cor xi 13] It was evidently the Judaizing party which there, as in other churches, opposed him If not actually subdivided, this party was yet at variance within itself as to the name its members should adopt One said "I am of Apollos," another "I of Cephas," and the extreme section wished to take the name of Christian as if by an exclusive title [comp 1 Cor. i 12 and 2 Cor x 7] This gives emphasis and full meaning to the term ψευδαπόστολοι, and to the ironical designation οἱ ὑπερλίαν ἀπόστολοι The absence of allusions to false doctrine, and the description of the way in which these men lorded it over God's heritage [2 Cor xi 20], lead to the conclusion that they were men who sought their own interests in fomenting the differences between the Jewish and the Gentile Christians So Tertullian remarks, "Conversationis non prædicationis adulteratæ reos taxat adeo de disciplina non de divinitate dissidebatur" [Tertull *adv Marc* v 12] These false apostles put forward some special claim to be apostles of Christ [from 1 Cor ix 1 it may perhaps be inferred that they had seen, and so pretended to be witnesses of, Christ], they commended themselves, they were intruders into another man's line, of things made ready to their hands They assumed an office to which they had no mission

In another case the teaching of antichristian doctrine is insisted on, while we are left to form from history our judgment as to the assumption of apostolic powers "Many false prophets," writes St John, "are gone out into the world" [1 John iv 1] Those of them who set up altar against altar, and claimed the obedience of their followers, would be raised thereby above the general rank of false teachers into the grade of false apostles The false doctrine appears to be that of the DOCETÆ, which was common to the Gnostic sects It was not denied that Jesus Christ was come, but that He was come in the flesh Where the Gnostics formed sects, their leaders were false apostles

A different class of heretics is referred to in 1 John ii 22, those namely who separate Jesus from the Christ. Its teachers are called antichrists, a designation given also to the heretics named in the former passage

Diotrephes is clearly a false apostle, comparable to those of Corinth, loving to have the pre-eminence, resisting St John, excommunicating by his own authority Hymenæus resembles the false prophets named by St John, the denial of the resurrection following from Docetic doctrine, but whether he was in any degree a usurper of apostolic power is not known

No true Episcopalian will deny that we may rightly pass from the powers of the apostles to the powers of their successors, and that in what degree the episcopate is the successor of the apostolate in the same degree those who form separate communions in opposition to rightful bishops are false apostles In the leaders of schisms then we have a line of successors of the ὑπερλίαν ἀπόστολοι, and the characteristics of pretending exclusively to be Christ's, of self-commendation, as well as the essential, the usurpation of authority, are seen in them but too clearly

If then we take into consideration the other terms connected with the present subject, namely false Christs and false prophets, we have *outside* of the Church false Messiahs and their attending prophets, such as Barcochab and his prophet Akiba, within the Church prophets or teachers of Christ, but of Christ wrongly set forth, such as the teachers of Docetism, of whom those that assume apostolic authority, and make themselves rulers in the Church, are false apostles All these, it is evident, have their representatives in later times

Our Lord's prophecy, delivered on the Mount of Olives, includes all these, and is not only a prophecy of the times immediately before the destruction of Jerusalem and the Coming of the Son of Man, but a prophecy regarding the whole period of Christianity, the latter days, the final dispensation of religion [FALSE CHRISTS] Between the destruction of Jerusalem and the Second Advent the fulfilment of the prophecy is found in the teachers who misrepresent the Person and Office of Christ And the part which is of universal application is the verse [Matt xxiv 26], "Wherefore, if they say unto you, He is in the desert," &c. For as the errors named by St John are sufficient examples (so comprehensive indeed as to be almost exhaustive) of the false doctrines regarding our Lord's nature which have rent the Church, so these words of Christ's prophecy point to the two great errors regarding our Lord's relation to the Church which tend to disunion Both errors are a forsaking the general society of the faithful, one to seek Christ in the solitudes of ascetic seclusion, the other to seek Him in the secret chambers of self-constituted conventicles The Church is warned on the one hand against a perverted and exaggerated monasticism, on the other hand against the false pretences of Catharism or Puritanism

To this latter head may be referred also the schisms of those who pretend to special and new revelations and dispensations of the Spirit. The error in these cases seems at first sight to be solely regarding the Third Person of the Blessed Trinity But it is remarkable how in these cases error regarding the Second Person is brought to light, as if it were really the fundamental or original error Theology gathers itself around the doctrine of the Incarnation, and heresy is found sooner or later to refer itself to the belief and estimate of the Son of God. So that, if we include erroneous representations of Christ in the term False Christs, it is hardly too much to say that all heresies and schisms are referrible to the false apostles of false Christs [Heretics]

FALSE CHRISTS Ψευδόχριστοι are named in our Lord's prophecy, Matt xxiv and Mark xiii They are manifestly those who deny the Son of Mary to be the Christ, and themselves assume and counterfeit the very Person of Christ With them are named false prophets, and guided by this connection the term false prophets may be limited to those who proclaim a false Messiah, either said to be already come or yet to come In 1 John iv 1-3, the term is used more widely It is applied to those who did not deny that the Word of God had come into the world, but who denied that He had come in the flesh These false prophets are to be classed with the false apostles of 2 Cor xi 13. [False Apostles]

Our Lord's prophecy, delivered on the Mount of Olives, is eminently one of those prophecies "which are not fulfilled punctually at once, but have springing and germinant accomplishment throughout many ages, though the height or fulness of them may refer to some one age" It is possible, indeed, with a certain degree of verisimilitude, to distribute this prophecy between the last great event to which its fulness refers, and the most signal anticipation of that fulfilment,—to say that in Matt. xxiv verses 4-14 are general, pertaining to the subject at large, that verses 15-22 belong specifically to the destruction of Jerusalem, and verses 23-31 to the second coming of Christ.[1] But, regarding the middle portion of these three, although it is expressed, for the guidance of the disciples, in terms belonging to the destruction of Jerusalem, yet the assertion [ver 21] of the extremity of tribulation can only refer to the tribulation of the last days, and leads to the conclusion that before Christ's Second Coming there will be an abomination of desolation standing where it ought not, which will constrain the faithful to flee from the Holy City to the mountains[2] There seems, again, to be no good reason why the second capture of Jerusalem, and the false Messiah Barcochab should not be accepted as another partial accomplishment of the prophecy, nor why the many Antichrists [1 John ii 18] who, though they may not have assumed and counterfeited the very person of Christ, yet challenged and pretended His authority and pre-eminence, should not also be included in its scope It is better to consider our Lord's prophecy as one and entire, without attempting to refer one portion to one time and another portion to another time, to say that it is a prophecy of the last days, with earlier and therefore partial accomplishments The disciples who inquired "What shall be the sign of Thy coming, and of the end of the world?" and connected these last things with the destruction of the Holy City, approached in their ignorance to the knowledge of God, with whom there is no time [Williams' *Holy Week*, p 245, ed 1870] In this view of the prophecy are also to be admitted, for the perpetual instruction of the Church, the pregnant lessons to be drawn from the 26th verse There have been few ages of the Church in which false prophets and false apostles have not bade men leave the true society of God's House to seek Christ either in the deserts of ascetic seclusion or in the secret chambers of self-righteous conventicles We shall thus be relieved also from the necessity which many commentators have felt themselves to lie under, the necessity of finding false Christs, in the strictest sense of the term, at the time of the destruction of Jerusalem for we shall have to seek only a partial accomplishment of the prophecy. A false Christ, to that generation, could be only one who threw himself upon the Messianic hope of his nation, and pretended to meet it In later times, and in the Christian Church, a false Christ might be one who based his pretensions on Gnostic theories, as is recognised by Hegesippus [Euseb *Hist Eccl* iv. 22], but such men were not Jews speaking to Jews Simon Magus little answers to our conception of a false Christ appealing to the national hope of a Messiah Dositheus, it may be, made some attempt to enlist that hope on his side, still, the foundation of

[1] Chrysostom makes the word εὐθέως of ver 29 connect the subject of that verse immediately with the preceding subject, so that the tribulation spoken of is the tribulation of the time of Antichrist named in ver 24, and the word τότε of ver 23 an indefinite term, = at some later time [*Hom. in Matt* lxxvi vol ii. p 388 of Field's ed]

[2] Is this to be interpreted, from that which ought to be the centre of unity, but which Christ has forsaken (μεταβαίνωμεν ἐντεῦθεν), to what appears to be the outskirts, but where Christ really is?

his claim was the same as that of Simon's Nor does any false Messiah appear in history before Barcochab False prophets there were who promised a miraculous interference of God on behalf of the Jews, and it is probable they based this promise on the promise of the Messiah Many were mere impostors, suborned, Josephus says, by the tyrannical leaders to prevent the people from deserting to the Romans [Joseph *Bell Jud* VI v 2], others appear to have been genuine fanatics, and to have added the elements of fanaticism to the party of insurgent Galilæans formed by Theudas [Joseph *Antiq* XX v 1, *cf Bell Jud* VII xi 1, *Antiq* XX vii 6]

Barcochab is known in history as the first false Messiah He appeared when Hadrian's edict forbidding circumcision [JUDAISM] had threatened to exterminate Judaism, and the additional insult of intending to settle a Roman colony at Jerusalem, and to build a heathen temple on the site of the Holy of Holies, had driven the Jews to a mad despair His name (whether real or assumed is not certainly known) was held to identify him with the star of Balaam's prophecy He professed to exhibit signs and wonders The most celebrated Rabbi of the time, Akiba, was his adherent and standard-bearer The advantages he gained over the Romans, and the time he is said to have held Jerusalem, shew the extent to which his imposture prevailed After him, a long list of false Messiahs and false prophets might be produced The chief in the list are—*Moses*, in Crete, in the fifth century [Soci. *Hist Eccl* vii 38], the failure of whose pretensions led to the conversion of many Jews to Christianity, *Julian*, in Palestine, about A D 530, whose followers were dispersed, and he himself taken by the troops of Justinian [Basnage, *Hist of Jews*, VI xxi 9], *Serenus*, in Spain, about A D 714, who professed that he would lead the Jews to Palestine [Marca, *Hist de Bearn* ii 2, Finn, *Sephardim*, p 139]; in the twelfth century, no fewer than seven or eight in France, Spain, and Persia [Basnage, *Hist* vii 9], *Sabbatai Levi*, a native of Aleppo or Smyrna, about the year 1666, who was proclaimed in Jerusalem [Milman, *Hist of Jews*, xxvii]

But these instances, interesting as they are to a historian of the Jews, scarcely belong to our present subject For our Lord's prophecy, which is our guide, considers the false Christs as connected with and bearing on the Christian Church In the case of Barcochab that connection and bearing is most close He appeared when the last barrier of Judaism was about to be thrown down, and the line of bishops of the circumcision about to cease His insurrection led to the capture of the city and to its rebuilding under its new name, which determined the Church of Jerusalem to embrace Catholicity It was meet that the faith of the Jewish Christians at such a time should be tried, but the conduct of the later impostors can have no such bearing on Christianity [1]

[1] The opinions of modern Jews regarding the coming of the Messiah may be seen in *Allan's Modern Judaism*, chap xv

To return, then, to the early Christian Church It has been already noticed, that Hegesippus finds a fulfilment of our Lord's prophecy in the various teachers who "divided the unity of the Church by the introduction of corrupt doctrines against God and against His Christ" Hegesippus specifies several Gnostic sects The Gnostic heresies, however, did not follow the example of Dositheus, and set up false Christs in the strict sense of the term, *i e* men denying altogether that Jesus is the Christ, and themselves assuming the person of Christ, they were antichristian, as denying, in one form or another, the true nature of Christ They were, for example, in general Docetæ, not denying that Christ was come in some way or other, but denying that He was truly come in the flesh [1 John iv 2] According to the distinction drawn between false prophets and false apostles, these Gnostic heresies, and all heretical teaching regarding the person of Christ, must be considered as the work of false apostles There have appeared, indeed, in the Church from time to time, impostors, fanatics, or madmen (and these three classes blend together in a wonderful manner), who have proclaimed themselves "the Christ," but they have been for the most part obscure adventurers, and certainly have not founded sects of note, or left any mark upon the Church. The trial of false doctrine, which has sifted and winnowed the faith of the Church, has been heresy regarding the Person of our Lord, and then the claim of a new and special dispensation of the Spirit

Still, the pretensions to be the Christ are interesting, as illustrating the state of that part of the Church in which they occur Every lunatic asylum has an inmate calling himself Christ, and not a few of these have cunning enough to play the part, and gather followers, if there be fanaticism enough in the Church Thus, in the year 591, at Gabalum, in Aquitania Prima (now Javols), "an immense multitude of people was seduced" by such an impostor, and those "not only rustics, but also priests of the Church" [Gregor Turon *Hist* x 25; ix 6] In 1663 Simon Morinus was burnt alive at Paris, for taking the title of the Son of God [Bayle's *Dict* art *Morinus*]

These are only very partial outbursts of fanaticism, and it may be concluded that not until the near approach of the Second Coming of our Lord will there appear a false Christ who shall deceive many, so as to seduce, if it were possible, even the elect [DICT *of* THEOLOGY, ANTICHRIST]

FAMILISTS A section of the Anabaptists, which was known also by the name of "The Family of Love" Some of them emigrating to England, won over many disciples from among the Puritans, and thus a separate sect was organized, which attracted much attention during the reigns of Queen Elizabeth and James I, but was assimilated to other sects during the time of the Great Rebellion.

The Familists are traced up in the first instance to a Dutch Anabaptist named David Joris, or

George, who was born at Delft in the year 1501, and died at Basle, under the assumed name of John Von Brugge, in 1556 He was a man of no education, but had travelled in France and England, and having obstructed a procession in the former country, was punished by flogging, imprisonment, and the boring of his tongue About the year 1535, he separated from the Anabaptists, and formed a sect of his own, professing to have visions and revelations by which he was guided, and some of which he printed in his "Wonder Book" in 1542 But after having seen his own mother beheaded at Delft in 1537 for her opinions as one of his followers, together with the persecution, sometimes to a similar end, of others among his adherents, he finally settled down into the safe *rôle* of a rich citizen of Basle, where he lived under his assumed name, and with the appearance of being a respectable Calvinist during the last twelve years of his life After his death he was accused of heresy by his son-in-law (to whom he had not left his property), and his body having been tried and condemned by the Calvinist senate of Basle, was publicly burned by the hangman The accuser afterwards added to this indignity that of publishing his father-in-law's life [Blesdyck, *Hist Davidis Georgii*, *Displaying of an Horrible Sect, &c* by J R 1579]

The leadership which had been dropped by Joris, was taken up by Henry Nicolas (generally called "H N"), an Anabaptist who had been mixed up with the Munzer insurrection in his native city of Amsterdam [ANABAPTISTS], and had fled thence to Emden in the year 1533 During the time of Joris' wandering life, he and Nicolas had become acquainted, and thus the fanaticism of the latter became more fanatical He set himself to oppose all existing forms of religion, and to establish an entirely new one As the contemporary writer just referred to says, "Henry gave himself to writing of books, which he put in print, especially one among the rest which was the chief, called 'The Glass of Righteousness' the less (for he compiled two books of that title), wherein he certifieth his Family of Love, that they must pass four most terrible castles, full of cumbersome enemies, before they come to the house of love. The first is John Calvin, the second the Papists, the third Martin Luther, the fourth the Anabaptists, and passing these dangers, they may be of the Family, else not" [*Displaying, &c*]

Fuller says that Nicolas came to England "in the latter end of the reign of Edward VI, and joined himself to the Dutch congregation in London, where he seduced a number of artificers and silly women, amongst whom two daughters of one Warwick, to whom he dedicated an epistle, were his principal perverts" [Fuller's *Church Hist* ix 3, § 38] The statement is confirmed by a letter of Micronius to Bullinger, dated May 20th, 1550, in which he expresses satisfaction at the arrival of John à Lasco in England, because it is a matter of the first importance that the Word of God should be preached in London in the German language, "to guard against the heresies which are introduced by our countrymen, there being Arians, Marcionists, Libertines, Davists, and the like monstrosities, in great numbers" [*Orig Lett* Park Soc ii 560] Davidians are also numbered among the "damnable sects" which were then troubling the reign of Edward VI, by Becon [*Works*, ii. 379, Park Soc ed], and on the accession of Queen Elizabeth, Archbishop Parker writes that "the realm is full of Anabaptists, Arians, Libertines, Free-will Men," &c [Parker's *Corresp.* 61]

The Familists maintained that there was no true knowledge of Christ or of the Scriptures out of their community that as Moses had taught law, and Christ had taught faith, so their mission, superior to both, was to teach love. They professed to have attained a kind of deification by direct communion with God, and spoke of others as "ungodded" and "unilluminated" men [Henry More's *Theol. Works*, 171, Sir F Knollys to Lord Burghley, Wright's *Q Eliz. and her Times*, ii 153] Every principal doctrine of Christianity was interpreted allegorically, so that they denied the reality of our Lord's Incarnation, and of His future Advent, explained away the resurrection of the body and the general judgment, and taught that the "Last Day" was the time of the new dispensation established by themselves, in which "the Service of Love" had become the climax of all dispensations, and the entrance into the Holy of Holies This habit of explaining away the truths of Christianity is spoken of by Hooker, who writes, "When they of the Family of Love have it once in their heads that Christ doth not signify any one person, but a quality whereof many are partakers—that to be raised is nothing else but to be regenerated, or endued with the said quality, and that when separation of them which have it from them which have it not is here made, this is judgment; how plainly do they imagine that the Scripture ever speaketh in the favour of that sect" [Hooker's *Eccl Polit* pref iii 9] Bishop Bancroft also writes of Nicolas, "He turneth the whole doctrine of our salvation into a vain mystery, and an allegorical conceit of his own, leaving the Church no mediator at all beside himself He hath framed a platform or new kingdom and gospel of his own invention, bearing this title, 'Evangelium regni Dei' Into this kingdom as vicegerents he hath brought for our ministers his Seniores sanctæ intelligentiæ, Patres familiæ Christi,' and for our archbishops and bishops his 'primates,' his 'seniores parentes,' and I know not how many illuminated and deified governors" [Bancroft, *Survey, &c* p 2]

It is evident from all accounts of the Familists that they were extreme Antinomians Indeed Strype mentions two sections of them, the "Family of the Mount," and the "Family of the Essentialists," who denied that there was such a thing as sin [Strype's *Ann.* II i 563, ed 1824] Immorality was, therefore, very common among them. William Penn says of them, that "divers fell into gross and enormous practices, pretending, in excuse thereof, that they could, without evil, commit the same act which was sin in another to do" [Penn's *Journal of Fox*, pref i 7, ed 1852] Baxter speaks of them as infidels [Baxter's *Life and Times*, i 91], and his severe condemnation is fully justified by the facts stated by one of themselves, that many among them questioned whether there were any heaven or hell beyond the pleasures and pains of the present life It was thus that they acquired the name of Epicureans with some writers, as if their distinctive tenet had been the lawless saying, "Let us eat and drink, for to-morrow we die"

It was to be expected that such principles as these would attract the attention of the Government, for in those days they would be considered dangerous to civil order as well as to morality and religion We find, accordingly, that in 1574 Robert Sharp, rector of Strethal in Essex, was apprehended on the charge of having formed a congregation of these lawless fanatics at Balsham in Cambridgeshire [*ibid* 556], and that in 1576 David Thickpenny, vicar of Brighton, was brought before the Privy Council on a similar charge [Grindal's *Remains*, 359, Parker Soc] In both cases they denied the accusation, although events proved, at least in the latter case, that the denial involved shameless falsehood This agrees with what is stated respecting their principles by Archbishop Sandys, who charged them with teaching "that it is good Christendom to lie, swear and forswear, to say and unsay, to any saving such as be of the same Family, with whom they must only use all plainness, and keep their mysteries secret from all others to themselves" [Sandys' *Serm* 130, Parker Soc] A vigorous attempt was made to suppress them by a proclamation issued 'against the Sectaries of the Family of Love" on October 3rd, 1580, and this was followed by a form of abjuration issued by the Privy Council, in which the members of the sect were required to abjure their most conspicuous heresies [Wilkins' *Concil* iv 296, 297] These measures seem to have broken up the sect, although some persons were found for half a century afterwards who still owned to the name They were, however, gradually absorbed into the ranks of the Puritans, and Strype writes, "I remember a gentleman, a great admirer of that sect, within less than twenty years ago, told me, that there was then but one of the Family of Love alive, and he an old man," which shews that they must have ceased to exist as a body about the middle of the seventeenth century Latterly, Fuller says, they were known by the name of "Ranters"

FAMILY OF LOVE [FAMILISTS]

FARNOVIANS The Antitrinitarians of Poland and Transylvania, who separated from the Reformed Churches in the year 1565, were divided into several parties, until Faustus Socinus brought them together into one sect Of these parties the Farnovians held Arian opinions Being able therefore to render a certain degree of worship to our Lord, a point on which the Socinians laid much stress, they were treated much more leniently than the Budnæans, who were Psilanthropists, and gradually passed into Socinianism Their leader Farnovius died in the year 1615 [SOCINIANS]

FATALISTS [NECESSITARIANS]

FELIX OF URGEL [ADOPTIONISTS]

FEODOSIANS [POMORANE]

FERI [ADELOPHAGI.]

FIFTH MONARCHY MEN A section of Puritans whose Millenarian opinions were so heated by the temporary overthrow of the Monarchy and the Church during the Great Rebellion that they expected it to be followed by the personal reign on earth of Christ and His Saints

This fanatical form of Millenarianism first began to make itself conspicuous about the year 1653, when a majority of the members in what is called the "Little Parliament" set themselves (under the leadership of the regicide Harrison) to carry out a great number of reforms by way of preparing for the Divine reign These preparations, however, which were to go the length of destroying cathedrals, dissolving the universities, confiscating church tithes, and superseding all other laws by the law of Moses, were interrupted by Cromwell's dissolution of the Parliament But the preachers of the party kept up its excitement and expectation long after its political hopes had been thus summarily extinguished, the chief of them being Feake and Vavasour Powell The substance of their teaching was "that Christ was setting up a fifth monarchy in the world, that a spirit of prophecy had been communicated to the saints, whereby they were enabled to describe future events, and that the design of Christ was to destroy all antichristian "forms," including established churches, together with their clergy," and Powell is said once to have broken out while preaching into the ejaculation, "Let us go home and pray and say, 'Lord, wilt Thou have Oliver Cromwell to reign over us, or Jesus Christ to reign over us'" These visionaries were also strong supporters of the Dutch War, believing that God had given Holland to the English as a "landing-place of the saints, whence they should proceed to pluck the whore of Babylon from her chair, and to establish the kingdom of Christ on the Continent' [Stoughton's *Eccl Hist* ii 65, 72] But the strong hand of Cromwell prevented any attempt to bring about the fulfilment of their hopes, and after the arrest of Feake and Powell the "Monarchy Men" continued their agitations in a more private manner

The disbanding of the army after the settlement of Charles II on his throne stimulated the sect, however, to a frantic effort at obtaining possession of London A wine-cooper, named Venner, had persuaded a number of them to accept him for their leader, promising them that they would be able to bear down all opponents, as Jonathan and his armour-bearer had borne down the Philistine garrison, and that the Lord would fight for them Full of these ideas they issued forth from their meeting-house in Blackfriars at midnight on Sunday, January 6th, 1661, carrying a banner inscribed with the words ' The

Lord God and Gideon," and marching through the City with the cry "Long live King Jesus!" Their sudden attack overpowered for the moment the City guard, but they did not remain in the City, Venner marching off his followers to Caen Wood at Highgate. There they were attacked by a regiment of Guards on the following day, and after a desperate resistance, in which many were killed, Venner and those who remained were taken prisoners, covered with wounds Venner and ten others were executed for high treason on January 19th and 21st, and thus the projected Fifth Monarchy came to an end [*Secret Hist of Charles II's Court*, 343, 1792. Pepys' *Diary*, i 167 *State Trials*, vi 105 Pagitt's *Heresiography*, pp 269-295, ed 1662, contains a contemporary account]

FLACIANS [ADIAPHORISTS]

FLAGELLANTS The ascetic devotees whose astounding practices won them this appellation appeared in Italy in the middle of the thirteenth century, and thenceforth, at intervals, their fitful outbreaks continued to vex Europe for above a hundred and fifty years The tenets of these sectaries were indeed simple, their creed being the scourge, their ritual flagellation In its first presentation, this singular fanaticism seems simply to have been a paroxysm of devotional hysteria, undirected by any rational hope or fear, without aim, method, or formula, and one which a unique combination of time and circumstance alone made possible Though public collective penance was known perhaps fifty years before, the date of this movement is not earlier than A D 1260, which year, marking as it does, nearly the central point of the thirteenth century, was perhaps that moment of all others when the profligacy which made penance desirable had reached its flood Never had the wars of Guelph and Ghibelline produced such monsters of selfishness, treachery, and brutish ferocity as at this time The intellectual despotism of the Church of the great Innocent was degraded into the mere selfish tyranny of a self-seeking pontiff The imperial throne was vacant There was no longer a common cause of civic freedom to fight for under the Church's blessing, no longer even any loyalty to the Cæsar In every city and state, each fought for his own hand, each sought only his personal aggrandizement With the exception perhaps of France, whose throne was still filled by the saintly Louis IX, continental Europe presented at this epoch one monotonous scene of bloodshed, desolation, and more than Indian savagery In Italy of all countries was this degradation most entire, and there of all countries would it be most keenly felt, and thus it was natural that an Italian city should be the first to quiver with this strange spasm of remorse or repentance

The desire for expiation, once awakened, ran naturally into the channels which the labours of the great ascetics Peter Damiani and Dominic "Loricatus" had made for it These leaders and popularizers of penance had preached largely on the merits of flagellation, and had gone so far as to teach, without the disapproval of other churchmen, that years of ordinary mortification might be condensed into the less troublesome, if more painful, infliction of the scourge. It is to be noted, however, that this movement was in no sense a Church movement, nor was this self-inflicted punishment in any way to be connected with that penance received from the hands of the priest (though flagellation itself had thus obtained a certain spurious dignity), which was recognized as the last mark of subjection to the sacerdotal power Furthermore, it was not the effect of the eloquence of some fiery preacher, eager for the fame and influence attaching to the founder of a new sect of ascetics, for the first leader of a Flagellant pilgrimage, Rainer, a monk of Perugia, though his eloquence excited the actual outburst of the fanaticism, does not seem to have been responsible either for its continuance or its rapid spread throughout the rest of Italy In A D 1260 it appeared in Perugia, in a few months or weeks it was heard of in every town of Italy, but, although its passage of the Alps was not slow, it is not until the next century that the Flagellant devotees succeeded in making a permanent impression on the Teutonic peoples By that time the first wave of the fanaticism had passed clear over Italy, and that country, no longer the prey of two contending powers only, was forgetting her unrivalled miseries in an almost equally unrivalled material prosperity

The subsequent outbursts in Italy appear rather to have been the ineffectual work of a small body of sentimental revivalists, than the spontaneous outcome of a profound popular agitation. Of this most interesting and unique phenomenon, the first appearance of the Flagellants, two writers, one an Italian monk of Padua, the other the Abbot of Nieder Altaisch, have left us a history The account given by the former of these, in all respects corroborated by his German brother, is to this effect "When all Italy was stained with crimes of every kind, this superstition, hitherto unknown to the world, suddenly appeared It first seized the inhabitants of Perugia, then those of Rome, and afterwards almost all the inhabitants of Italy To such a degree were they affected by the fear of God, that both noble as well as ignoble persons, young and old, even children of five years of age, went naked about the streets without any sense of shame, walking in public, two and two, in solemn procession Every one of them held in his hand a scourge, made of leather thongs, and with tears and groans they lashed themselves on their backs till the blood ran from the infliction. All the while they continued weeping and giving tokens of a sorrow as bitter as if they had been actually witnessing the Passion of our Saviour, imploring the forgiveness of God and His Mother, and praying that He Who had been appeased by the repentance of so many sinners, would not disdain theirs Nor was this done in the daytime only, but during the night, and in the depths of winter, hundreds, thousands, and tens of thousands of these penitents, with lighted tapers in their hands, and preceded by priests who carried crosses and banners, filled the streets and the churches, humbly prostrating themselves before the altars. The same scenes were enacted in the small towns and country villages, so that both hill and valley resounded with the voice of men crying unto God. All musical instruments were silenced, all songs of love were hushed. The only music that prevailed (both in town and country) was that of the mournful voice of the penitent, whose dolorous accents might have moved hearts of flint. The most obdurate sinners were melted to tears. Nor were women exempt from the general spirit of devotion, and not only was it the common people who did this, but girls and matrons of noble family underwent the same mortifications in the retirement of their own chambers." The monk's account of the effect of these proceedings is equally marvellous. "Enemies," he says, "became friends, usurers and robbers hastened to restore their ill-gotten gains, criminals of all sorts confessed their offences, the gaols were opened, prisoners set at liberty (doubtless without ransom) by their captors, the exiles were permitted to return to their homes." So many and so great were the good works thus performed that the writer can only account for it by the hypothesis that "a universal apprehension had fallen on mankind that the Divine Power was preparing to consume them with fire, or destroy them by earthquake, or by some other of those agencies within the ken of Divine justice for taking vengeance upon crime."

When the mania had spread throughout all Italy, it passed beyond the Alps as far as Hungary. Outbursts similar to that of Perugia, are, though less authentically, reported in Alsace, Bavaria, Poland, and Bohemia—countries, it is to be observed, in which numerous free spiritual organizations already practised a rigorous and kindred asceticism. In Italy, however, this access of devotion was as ephemeral as from its purely emotional character might be expected. The wealthier classes tired of these scenes of equality with the poor, the magistrates looked with suspicion on these tumultuous assemblages, the priests looked coldly on a movement in which the laity took so leading a part, and, as if by the consent of the community, the sect, bound by no ties except that of a common penance, melted into the surrounding population. For half a century and more no further outbreaks disturbed the peace of Italy, while in Germany the fanaticism slumbered. North of the Alps the Flagellants doubtless found shelter among the schismatic associations, of whom the Beghards were the most audacious and enduring in their hostility to the Church, while in Italy and Piedmont, where the cities swarmed with heretics flying from the Albigensian massacres, they were not likely to find a too austere hospitality. Partly, doubtless, through absorption by the more rational sects, partly through the decay of their enthusiasm, the Flagellants are scarcely to be heard of again until the time of the Great Plague.

That awful visitation known as the Black Death swept over Europe in A.D. 1348, and never had pestilence been so fatal in its nature, or so unsparing in its ravages. No country was exempt, no precaution or remedy availed. Death, sudden, cruel, of the most loathsome kind, knocked at every door. The feelings of men passed suddenly from an everyday confidence in existence to the extremity of despair. No expiation seemed too great for a penance, no suffering too heavy, compared with the appalling misery which the penance or suffering it was hoped might allay. To Europe in such a mood came the Flagellants again, offering to the distraught and despairing souls penances the rigour of which diverted the mind, and an enthusiasm which raised it, at least temporarily, above the agony of material grief and terror. But the Flagellants, as they issued from their retirement in Hungary and the German States, were very different from the early emotionalists of Italy. They brought with them a genuine dislike to the Church, a creed very distinctly heretical, and a comparatively complete though simple organization. They were led by a general of devotion and two lieutenants, and governed according to a very stringent code. They affirmed that they derived their authority from St Peter, who had placed a letter of authorization on the altar of his church at Jerusalem. Sabbath-breaking, blasphemy, usury, adultery, and non-observance of fasts, were the sins they especially reprobated. Those who joined them had to be capable of self-support, for they would accept no gifts except banners for their processions. They marched through the cities in long processions, clad in mourning garments, with red crosses on back and breast, their eyes fixed on the ground. Lighted candles, banners of velvet, of purple, and cloth of gold, preceded them. Gradually, as their influence increased (as with the decrease of the pestilence it was certain to do), they were welcomed with the ringing of bells, with the admiration of the crowd that came to listen to their psalms, and to see the penance that would avert the plague.

That penance was indeed, at least when it was fully organized, a bizarre spectacle. Twice a day they went forth to the place of flagellation. There, amid penitential hymns, they stripped themselves naked to the waist, or retained only a thin linen tunic to protect their flesh from the blows of the scourge. They then lay down in different positions, the adulterer with his face to the ground, the perjurer holding up three fingers, their attitudes being adjusted to the nature of their several crimes. The master commenced the ceremony by administering punishment to each in turn, then bade them rise and scourge themselves; at other times, after administering one blow to each, the master himself lay down at the head of the procession, and one by one, each as he became the hindmost of the brethren, rose in turn, scourged his fellows, and again lay down. For thirty-three days and a half, the number of years of Christ's sojourn upon earth, did they ply their triple scourges, iron-knotted, in each town where they made halt.

Joined by large numbers, the brotherhood passed through Hungary, Austria, Germany, and threatening France, they entered Spain. At Bergamo in Italy was a notorious flagellation, but there and there only did the papal mandate silence the ineffectual revival Venturini, the leader of the movement, was banished to the mountains and his band dispersed But in other countries Flagellants were more successful, in some they took possession of the churches The Emperor Charles IV applied to the Pope for aid in his German dominions, the Sorbonne asked advice for France The Pope Clement VI fulminated his anathema upon them, but the papal bull was ineffectual in hushing the sounds with which all ears were grown familiar, the lash, the cry of pain, the droning psalm or "Geisslerlied" Interdicted though their processions were, and excluded from France by Philip VI, a colony of one hundred and twenty succeeded in reaching London The citizens gazed and wondered at this baptism of blood, but they went no further, nor did a single English proselyte recompense the fanatics for the dangers of their voyage Though excluded from France, unwelcomed in England, having made but little impression on the fickle Italians, yet so sincere and audacious were these voluntaries of the scourge (they attempted to carry on their proselytizing in Avignon itself), that the Inquisition was directed to turn its attention to their heresy In proportion, however, as the Flagellants are tracked into more distant regions by the Church, they are found to have developed the constitution of their unorthodoxy, and in Thuringia, under the leadership of Conrad Schmidt, they were successful in giving to their dislike of the established religion and their passion for the scourge the form of a connected system of heretical doctrine In the year 1414 the Dominican Henry Schonefeld, a most able inquisitor, conducted a judicial inquiry of unexampled rigour and success at Sangerhausen Above one hundred and twenty Flagellants were convicted and given to the flames in that district alone, and it was mainly owing to the activity of the Inquisition that the Council of Constance was enabled to distinguish and condemn fifty errors of the Flagellant sect Of these the chief were, that the sect was miraculously instituted by St Peter; that God had decreed the abolition of the special power of the priesthood that the baptism of water was abolished, and that of blood substituted, that Transubstantiation was untrue, that the sale of masses was a selling of Christ, worse than that of Judas, that by the institution of flagellation the seven sacraments were abolished, that a Beghard burnt at Erfurt in A D 1366 was Elias, that Conrad himself was Enoch, that Enoch and Elias had thus returned, and that the Pope was Antichrist

It is not difficult to discern Lollard proclivities in these tenets, nor to recognise their undisguised hostility to the papal pretensions. The Inquisition triumphed again as it had done in Toulouse, and was about to do in Spain The Flagellants disappeared in Germany, but the evil fashion, which in the last years of the fourteenth century had been again coquetted with in Italy where it produced the Bianchi of the Peninsula, found under the orthodox leadership of another Dominican Vincent Ferreri, new victims in Spain It required the influence of the great Gerson himself to induce the Flagellant leader to forego his foolish enterprise Persecution, while it did not destroy the practice of flagellation, was entirely successful in destroying the corporate or sectarian existence of the Flagellants; and although in the sixteenth and even seventeenth centuries numerous devotees of the scourge appear under the name of white, black, grey, blue, and other penitents, subsisting under the protection of popes, and by the encouragement of the Jesuits, yet these are orthodox bodies, and the heretical Flagellant has disappeared The fifteenth century saw the complete destruction of the sect, the total suppression of the heresy, so far at any rate as any public manifestation is concerned, though there is reason for believing that under the title of Beghards a remnant continued to exist until the date of the Reformation

[For the first period of the history of the Flagellants the authorities are Justinus, *Monachus Patavinensis*, in Muratori, Hermannus Altahensis, in Bohmer's *Fontes rerum Germanicarum* and the *Brit Mus Chronicle* For the second period, that which followed the Great Pestilence Closener's *Strasburg Chronicle*, and the other authorities cited in Gieseler's *Eccl History* The modern authors to be consulted are Boileau's *Historia Flagellantium*, Hecker's *Epidemics of the Middle Ages*, and in particular the work entitled, *Die Christlichen Geissler-gesellschaften*, by Dr E G Förstemann, which last leaves little to be desired]

FLANDRIANS [FLEMINGS]

FLEMINGS The stricter sect of the Mennonites, whose members profess to maintain the more rigid principles and practices of their founder, and hence are called the "Fine," or rigid Mennonites ("die Feinen"), as distinguished from the lax or "Gross" Mennonites ("die Groben"), who are also known as WATERLANDERS The Flemings were so called, because a majority of the sect lived in Flanders, the Waterlanders, because they were principally people of Waterland, in the north of Holland The question on which they separated was that of discipline, and social custom—not of doctrine, the Flemings maintaining the manners of the rigid Puritans, and excommunicating members of their sect for "worldliness," as well as for immorality But the Flemings also maintain tenaciously the original heresy of Menno respecting the Incarnation, namely, that the Son of God became Man by a special act of creation in the womb of the Blessed Virgin, and not by natural growth "of the substance of His mother" They practise the ancient rite of washing each other's feet as a Divine law, and are hence called also Podoniptæ, or "feet-washers" [Mosheim's *Eccl Hist* iii 153, Stubbs' ed]

FLORINIANS A sect of Valentinians, who followed Florinus, a Roman priest, contemporary with Blastus, the founder of the Quartodeciman schism Florinus had been a disciple of Polycarp, and Irenæus wrote to him, "While I was yet a boy, I saw thee in Lower Asia with Polycarp, distinguishing thyself in the royal court, and endeavouring to gain his approbation" In his later years he embraced the heretical opinion, that God was the author of evil, and being deposed from the priesthood by Eleutherus [Euseb *Hist Eccl* v 15], he afterward became a Valentinian, seducing many others to that heresy [*ibid* 20] Irenæus wrote to him before his fall an epistle, which formed a work entitled "De Ogdoade," and of which a most interesting fragment is preserved by Eusebius [*ibid*] He also addressed to Florinus another treatise, Περὶ μοναρχίας, but this is entirely lost

What the opinions of Florinus were is indicated by the words of Irenæus, "These doctrines, Florinus to say the least, are not sound doctrines They are not in agreement with the Church, and they are calculated to involve those that maintain them in the greatest impiety Not even the heretics outside the pale of the Church ever ventured to assert such doctrines, and they were never delivered to thee by the presbyters who were before us" Then, speaking of his intimacy with Polycarp, and of the distinctness with which he remembered what he used to say about St John, and others who had seen the Lord, Irenæus goes on to say, "I can bear witness before God, that if that blessed and apostolic Father had heard any such thing, he would have cried out and stopped his ears, and would have exclaimed, according to his custom, 'O, good God, unto what times hast Thou reserved me, that I should endure such things?' He would have fled, too, from the place in which he had been sitting or standing when he heard such words" [Euseb *Hist Eccl* v 20]

St Augustine gives as the characteristic feature of the Florinian heresy the tenet, that God is the author of evil [Aug *de Hæres* lxvi] But if the "Floriani" named by Philaster are the same sect, they also denied the resurrection and future judgment, together with the Divine Nature and miraculous conception of our Lord [Philast *de Hæres* lvii] Philaster identifies them, indeed, with the CARPOCRATIANS, and says that they were also called Milites "quia de militaribus fuerunt," this expression agreeing with what Epiphanius says of the Egyptian Gnostics, Οἱ αὐτοὶ δὲ ἐν Αἰγύπτῳ Στρατιωτικοὶ καλοῦνται [Epiph. *Hæres* xxvi 3]. The Florinians, like the Quartodecimans, are associated with Judaizing tendencies by the ancient heresiologists [Theod *Hæret fab* i 23]

FRATERCULI [FRATICELLI]

FRATICELLI Italian fanatics of the fourteenth century, who also called themselves "Fratres de paupere vitâ," and were closely allied to the BEGHARDS and the BRETHREN OF THE FREE SPIRIT

The Fraticelli were, in the first instance, a body of Franciscan friars or Minorites [PAULO-JOANNITES], who were permitted to form themselves into a separate community, under a friar named Liberatus, for the more rigorous observance of their rule, especially as to poverty, and who received the pet name of "Little Brethren" from the populace, of whom they begged their daily bread These "Cœlestine Hermits" were established by a bull of Pope Cœlestine V [A D 1294], but the bull was said to have been obtained by misrepresentation, and the order was dissolved by Boniface VIII [A D 1302] before it had been in existence eight years, on the ground that heresy had become prevalent among its members The Fraticelli openly resisted this decree of the Pope, and fled to Sicily Clement V endeavoured to suppress them by conciliating the original party, and inviting them to reunite with the Franciscans, for which purpose he heard their complaints in person, and published a new interpretation of the rule of the order [A D 1310], in the hope of winning them over A few years later [A D 1317] they were the subject of a bull of condemnation issued by Pope John XXII, in which they were threatened with excommunication. The next year another bull was published, ordering the bishops of Sicily to imprison the pseudo-Minorites, and to hand them over to the Franciscans for punishment He also wrote to the sovereigns into whose territories they were now beginning to spread, to assist in their suppression, and charged the Inquisition with the duty of effecting it.

From this time the Fraticelli began to lose their original character, the Franciscans who had formed the original body dying off, and its new members consisting principally of workmen and labourers, for whom a new fanaticism, a wandering life, and subsistence on alms after the manner of the mendicant orders, proved a combination of attractions strong enough to draw them from their homes, and take up with a professedly religious life Thus cast loose from the Church, resisting authority, and having no religious teachers except those who set themselves up as such from the midst of themselves, the later Fraticelli became simply one of those fanatical sects of the Middle Ages among whom antagonism to the Church took the place of religion Many of them fell into the hands of the Inquisition, and were accounted as martyrs by the sect. Eventually they were most of them absorbed into the Beghard community, but some still existed under the original name in Central Italy, as late as the middle of the fifteenth century, when a missionary named John de Capistran was sent to them in the Marshes of Ancona, to bring about their conversion Their principles appear to have become developed into the same Antinomian form which characterized the Beghards, the Apostolicals, and other continental sects of mediæval times Wadding, *Ann Min Fratr* Natal Alex *Hist Eccl* vii 85 Mosheim, *Eccl Hist* ii. 202, Stubbs' ed]

FRATRICELLI [FRATICELLI]

FRATRES POLONI [SOCINIANS]

FREE CHURCH OF ENGLAND This title is assumed by a few sporadic bodies of seceders from the Church of England, some of whom are of that extreme Low Church type, which was originally represented by Lady Huntingdon's connection, and others of the extreme Broad Church type developed in the direction of Unitarianism There is at present no coherent body of any extent calling itself the "Free Church of England," and the separate communities which use that name would more logically describe themselves if they were to assume instead the names of the respective sects with which they are, in fact, allied in their principles and customs They generally consist, however, of clergymen and laymen who are dissatisfied with some features in the doctrine or discipline of the Church of England, but yet retain some affection for its general principles, and are unwilling to dissociate themselves altogether from its name Modified forms of the Prayer-Book are used by them, the changes following the anti-sacerdotal or the Unitarian line, according to the views of the seceders

FREE CONGREGATIONS This name was assumed by a section of the German Rationalists in the days preceding the Revolution of the year 1848 The first "free congregation" was established by Pastor Rupp in Konigsberg in 1845, after he had been turned out of the Lutheran ministry for his attacks upon the Athanasian Creed Others quickly followed in other parts of Germany, but their principles soon attracted the notice of the civil authorities the police broke up their meetings, and as many as forty such congregations were suppressed in Prussia alone

The "Free Congregations" professed to admit the witness of Scripture so far as it teaches the Unity of God, but rejected its authority They also rejected the Creeds and the Sacraments In the place of Baptism, they invented a rite in which they used the form—"I baptize thee after the manner of the old apostolic baptism, that Jesus is the Christ, I anoint thy head with water as a sign that thy soul remains pure, pure as the water that runs down the mountain side and as the water rises to heaven and then returns to the earth, so may you be continually mindful of your heavenly home" This substitution of sentiment for reality is characteristic of sects which reject the old traditions of Christianity, and yet cling to its imaginative influences [Hurst's *Hist of Rationalism*, 228, ed 1867]

FREE KIRK OF SCOTLAND A large body of Presbyterians which separated from the Scottish Presbyterian Establishment in the year 1843 The movement towards this secession began in 1834, and hence it is often called "The Ten Years' Conflict." But it might equally well be called The Hundred-and-Ten Years' Conflict, for it was the last fight in a war between opposing elements in the Scottish Establishment which had been going on for fully that period

The question of *Patronage* had ever since the time of Queen Anne been the great question in the Kirk Lay patronage had been abolished in 1690, and the heritors and elders of each parish were authorized, upon the occurrence of vacancies, to propose the name of some eligible minister to the congregation, who approved or disapproved, their reasons in the latter case being given in to the Presbytery, whose judgment was final But in 1712 an Act of Parliament (conceived, as its opponents supposed, in the interest of the Jacobites and Episcopalians) restored to the Crown and all other patrons their lost rights, expressly providing, however, that the persons presented by them should be received and admitted by the respective presbyteries in the same manner as persons presented before the passing of the Act ought to have been admitted, a provision which appeared to reserve to the Church Courts the right of final judgment which they previously possessed For some years the Act worked quietly, patrons judiciously deferring to the wishes of congregations, and the presbyteries and higher courts in several disputed cases maintaining their old position But by degrees the rights of presenters and presentees were more and more pressed, and when presbyteries refused to induct ministers whose "call" was not sustained by the majority of the congregation, the General Assembly, anxious to preserve peace and to avoid involving the recusants in legal proceedings, sent out deputies (who were popularly called "Riding Committees") from their own body to act in the room of the presbyteries Parties rapidly developed, and in 1733 Ralph and Ebenezer Erskine headed the "Secession" which then took place, solely on the ground of the growing interference with the people's alleged rights—rights which the Erskines pushed to extravagant extremes, and maintained with intemperate violence In 1752 the General Assembly had become so far composed of "Moderates" (the name given to those who in general subserviency to the civil power, lack of evangelical teaching, and worldliness of tone, corresponded to the "High and Dry" clergy in the Church of England during the same period of spiritual deadness[1]), as to dispense with the formality of "Riding Committees," and to compel unwilling presbyteries themselves to institute unacceptable presentees. From this came the next great secession, the "Relief" body of dissenters thereupon originating with Mr Gillespie of Carnock, who had been deposed for disobedience The new method of procedure was adopted at the instance of Dr Robertson, who thenceforward, down to the year 1780, was the ruling spirit in the Kirk, and under whose management "Moderatism" became dominant and the right of presentation to livings became as purely in practice a matter of external patronage as it is at present in the Church of England The form of a "call" by the congregation was still maintained, and objectors were invited to appear before the presbytery on the day appointed for ordination and admission of the presentee, and if objections were found relevant, proceedings could be stopped,[2] but the form had

[1] A complete picture of the life of a "Moderate" minister, as given of himself, by an able and distinguished representative, is to be found in the Autobiography of Dr Alex Carlyle, published in 1860.

[2] Sir H Moncreiff-Wellwood's *Life of Dr. J Erskine*, 1818, Appendix, p 537

degenerated into a mere matter of course, and objectors never appeared After Robertson's retirement, the abolition even of the form of a call was proposed by his successor, Dr Hill, but his motion was rejected by the Assembly In 1784, however, he procured the omission of a clause which, from the year 1712, had been inserted in the Instructions annually given to the Commission of the Assembly, directing application to be made to the Crown and Parliament for redress from the grievances of patronage But the question began again to be agitated, and a reforming party arose, headed by Dr Andrew Thomson, a leading minister in Edinburgh, who founded in 1825 an "Anti-Patronage Society"

In 1833 the new contest was formally initiated under the guidance of the great leader who conducted it to its close, Dr Thomas Chalmers He proposed in the General Assembly of that year the adoption of the Veto Act, which provided that the dissent of a majority of resident male heads of families, being communicants, *with or without reasons*, should set aside a presentation The proposal was rejected by a majority of twelve (149 *v* 137), but an equivalent proposition brought forward in the following year by Lord Moncreiff (one of the Judges of the Court of Session) was carried by 184 to 138 It was at once acted upon as the law of the Church, and regarded as in no way contrary to the law of the land In October, however, of the same year, the famous parish of Auchterarder began to make itself known The Earl of Kinnoull having presented one Mr Robert Young as minister, whose call was only approved by two persons, but rejected by 287 out of 330 who were qualified, the presbytery refused to institute The case was carried from one court to another, in slow succession, until at length the final decision was given in the House of Lords by Lords Brougham and Cottenham, on 2nd May 1839, which altogether denied the legality of the veto, and pronounced that the only valid objections which could be made to a call were such as distinctly related to doctrine, literature, and life, and that therefore reasons must be alleged, and must involve heresy, ignorance, or immorality Mere questions of acceptableness in manners, in preaching, and the like, could, consequently, afford no legal ground for objection Simultaneously with the litigation in this case, two others were carried into the Courts, in the first, that of Lethendy, the presbytery were condemned in heavy costs and damages for refusing to institute, in the other, that of Marnoch seven ministers who formed the presbytery of Strathbogie were first suspended, and at last formally deposed by the Assembly on 29th May 1841, for obeying the decrees of the civil court and instituting a presentee whose call was signed by only one out of 300 communicants A bill was introduced by the Earl of Aberdeen in the House of Lords with a view to a settlement, which allowed the right of presbyteries to reject presentees upon approval of reasons of dissent, but because it did not allow rejection irrespective of reasons, it was condemned in the General Assembly by a majority of 221 to 134, and at last withdrawn. Thereupon a bill, approved by the Assembly, was brought forward by the Duke of Argyll, which allowed the veto, unless it should be proved that the opposition proceeded from factious and causeless prejudice Being dropped however, in the House of Lords, it was introduced in the House of Commons, but there, in June 1843, its progress was stopped, on the technical ground that the Royal assent to its introduction had not been obtained, as is requisite in the case of bills affecting (as this did with reference to patronage) the rights of the Crown

A second adverse judgment by the House of Lords now accelerated the course of events, a Petition of Right, embodying the claims of the Non-Intrusionists, was sent from the Assembly to Parliament, but a motion for inquiry, founded upon it was rejected by the House of Commons on 8th March 1843, by 211 to 76 It was the final blow, it was seen that no concessions sufficient to satisfy the claims preferred were now to be hoped for from Government or Parliament, and the secession was resolved upon, which was to deprive the Establishment of some of its best blood and of the majority of its members The General Assembly met on 18th May 1843, but as soon as it was constituted, the Moderator, Dr Welsh, rose to read a solemn protest, signed by 203 members, against the alleged civil aggressions and the action of Parliament, and then quitting his place, headed, with Dr Chalmers, a long procession which in silence quitted the hall of meeting, and passed out at once from all the endowments and privileges of the Establishment Out of 1203 ministers 451 seceded, leaving only 752 in the Establishment [1]

The Free Kirk at once sprang into vigorous life, it had all the enthusiasm of self-sacrifice, all the zeal of earnest conscientiousness, all the inspiriting influences of old Covenanting traditions, all the confidence of numbers, and carried with it most of the real religious feeling of the country Extravagant as the claim cannot but be regarded which would submit the question of every minister's pastoral fitness to the irresponsible judgment, given without reasons, of the mere majority of the male communicant members (the communicants, it is to be remembered, including in Scotland every person who is not notoriously immoral, or a total abstainer from church services) of every congregation in town and country, unreasonable as was the opposition which refused the compromise of leaving the decision in the hands of each presbytery, and wild and even profane as was the declamation which represented this submission of ministerial qualification absolutely, to the judgment of the ignorant and prejudiced,[2] as well

[1] In the same year an Act of Parliament was passed [6 & 7 Vict c 61] fully meeting the grievance, by providing that objections, stated in detail, may be laid before the presbytery of the district, and adjudicated on by them

[2] In Story's life an anecdote is told of the veto being

as the instructed and impartial, as being simply a vindication of the Supreme Headship of our Lord over His Church, and the opposite course as being a dethroning of Him and denial of His Sovereignty, it is nevertheless impossible to contemplate the final action of the Seceders without the highest admiration of their unshrinking consistency, and their noble testimony to the power of conscientious principle Well might even the worldly-minded Lord Jeffrey, the lawyer and the essayist, exclaim when he heard of it, "I am proud of my country!"

The appeal made by the Seceders to their countrymen was enthusiastically responded to, the collection of nearly £3000 on the following Sunday in but one place of meeting gave an earnest of what would follow Every parish ere long, in spite of obstacles, had its Free Kirk and Manse planted within it, while a "Sustentation Fund" was raised for endowments, which at present provides a minimum dividend of £150 for 775 ministers, irrespective of the separate congregational collections The total amount of the sums raised for all purposes was, in 1844-5, £334,484, and in the twenty-six years from 1843 to 1869 the sum amounted to £8,487,774 The number of congregations is now about 920, with 597 schools There are large bodies in England and Ireland and Canada which are in connection, as well as congregations in many of the Colonies The total number in Canada and the Colonies is about 1000 congregations, with 800 ministers Missions are maintained in India and South Africa, and amongst the Jews

The principles of the Free Kirk are on all points identical with those of the Established Kirk, except as regards patronage, and the right of the State to interfere in ecclesiastical causes The Free Kirk is *Voluntary* not by choice, but by necessity, it maintains (like its great leader Dr Chalmers) the rightfulness and national advantage of Establishments, and therefore disagrees with the other dissenting Presbyterian bodies which are Voluntary in principle. But the standing outside the Establishment for a quarter of a century has much weakened the adherence in this respect to the original views maintained at the Disruption, and a movement is consequently making rapid progress for an incorporating union between the Free Kirk, the Reformed Presbyterians, and the United Presbyterians, on "the basis of the Westminster Standards, as at present accepted by the said Churches" The union will probably take place at an early date, for a motion strongly in favour of the measure was carried in the General Assembly, on 25th May 1871, by 435 votes to 165, against a motion which proposed that the pending negotiations should cease [Buchanan's *Ten Years' Conflict*, Hanna's *Life of Chalmers* On the side of the Establishment, see Bryce's *Ten Years of the Church of Scotland*, 1833-43, 2 vols 1850, Alex Turner's *The Scottish Secession of* 1843, Edinb 1859. The Bodleian Library possesses a very large collection of the pamphlets and ephemeral papers issued during the Non-Intrusion Controversy, in 33 volumes, which was formed by a minister of the Kirk, who has added the names of the writers to some of the tracts which appeared anonymously]

exercised against an excellent minister on the ground, "Div ye think that we're gaun to hae a minister that wears a sark collar like thon?" [Story's *Life of Story*, 261]

FREE LOVERS [PERFECTIONISTS]

FREETHINKERS A school of English Deists which arose in the beginning of the seventeenth century among those unbelieving members of the "polite society" of the day, for whom Spinoza was too learned, the materialism of Hobbes too unfashionable, and the obscene atheism of the Caroline roués too vulgar

The leading principle of the Freethinkers was that of liberating thought from the tyranny of creed and dogma, and relying on the understanding alone as the means of arriving at truth. "By Freethinking," says the leader of the school, "I mean the use of the understanding in endeavouring to find out the meaning of any proposition whatsoever, in considering the nature of the evidence for or against, and in judging of it according to the seeming force or weakness of the evidence" [Collins' *Discourse of Freethinking*, p 2] This proposition was applied to Christianity in such a manner as to place it on a level with other religions, and then to shew that all are false together "The priests throughout the world differ about Scriptures and the authority of Scriptures. The Bramins have a book of Scripture call'd the Shaster The Persees have their Zundavastaw The Bonzes of China have books written by the disciples of Fo-he, whom they call the God and Saviour of the world, who was born to teach the way of salvation, and to give satisfaction for all men's sins The Talapoins of Siam have a book of Scripture written by Sommonocodom, who, the Siamese say, was born of a Virgin, and was the God expected by the universe. The Dervizes have their Alchoran" [*ibid* p 52] But all these books, and the Christian Scriptures, are equally the productions of ancient writers who invented the Jewish, the Christian, and other religions, and then persuaded the world to believe in their impostures It was assumed, with a freedom of thought which was quite above weighing their respective authority, that the evidences for Christianity are of no more worth than those for Brahminism, of which next to nothing was known by those who thus flippantly wrote about them

This school of Deists maintained, in respect to morality, that Christianity, whether true or false, is wholly unnecessary for the good of individual persons or of society at large, but dwelt much upon the excellence and beauty of virtue in the abstract. They also gave great prominence to the necessary benevolence of the Deity, but in such a manner as practically to set aside His justice, and thus to undermine the foundation of moral responsibility

The original leaders of this school may be said to have been Lord Shaftesbury and Anthony Collins, although the former really belonged to the earlier school of Deists Collins was a man of fortune and good taste, and gave a "respectable" tone to infidelity which it had not previously possessed He printed his "Discourse of Freethinking, occasioned by the rise and growth of a sect called Freethinkers," in the year 1713, and his "Discourse on the grounds and reasons of the Christian religion" in 1724 The former was answered by Dr Bentley, in "Remarks on a late Discourse of Freethinking by Phileleutherus Lipsiensis," who opposed the shallowness of its apparent learning, and by Hoadley, afterwards Bishop of Winchester, in "Queries addressed to the author of a late Discourse of Freethinking," in which Hoadley exposed many irrational errors and dishonest statements that had been made by Collins But the principles of the Freethinkers proved very attractive to superficial thinkers, and have been perpetuated to our own time. [RATIONALISTS]

FREE-WILL BAPTISTS An American sect answering to the General Baptists of England, which struck off from the body of the Baptist sect in the year 1780

The founder of this sect was Benjamin Randall [A D 1749-1808] He had been one of George Whitfield's converts at twenty-two years of age, but five years afterwards joined the Baptists and became a preacher, when he very shortly gave up the Calvinistic dogma of election, and began to teach that the Atonement of our Lord was made for all men, that salvation is possible for all, that the will of every man is free to choose or to refuse salvation, and that there is no eternal decree of any to perdition such as makes their salvation impossible These "free-will" doctrines constituted the only difference between the followers of Randall and the ordinary Baptists, but they were considered incompatible with continued union between the two bodies, and a separate sect was therefore established at New Durham on June 30th, 1780, under the name of "Free-Will Baptists," and under the ministry of Randall They are now a large body numbering about 70,000, being represented in British North America as well as in the United States In the latter they have shewn themselves strongly opposed to slavery Some of them copy the FLEMINGS of Holland in using as a necessary Divine ordinance the ceremony of washing each other's feet

FREE-WILLERS [FAMILISTS]

FRENCH PROPHETS [CAMISARDS]

FRENCH PROTESTANTS The earliest class of persons meriting this title are the ALBIGENSES and WALDENSES at the close of the twelfth and commencement of the thirteenth centuries But the term must, with historic propriety, be confined to those who, early in the sixteenth century, were affected by the tide of feeling then passing over the religious mind of Europe In A D 1523, the doctors of the Sorbonne at Paris first took active steps alarmed by the proceedings of Jacques Lefevre, a native of Picardy, and Briçonnet, Bishop of Meaux, whose opinions found a still more powerful advocate in Margaret d'Angoulême, sister of Francis I and wife of Henry d'Albert, King of Navarre, whose territory afforded shelter to those suspected of heresy The persecution which followed nearly extinguished the hopes, if it did not exterminate the persons, of the Protestants Calvin fled from Paris to Switzerland [A D 1534] In Provence alone [A D 1545] two towns, Merindol and Cabrières, and twenty-eight villages were destroyed, and four thousand persons put to the sword The feeling of hostility rather increased than decreased under Henry II [A D 1547], who married Catharine de Medici, niece of Pope Clement VII Yet in spite of this opposition the French Protestants found themselves sufficiently numerous, and with such leaders as Anthony of Bourbon, King of Navarre, Louis Prince de Condé, the Admiral de Coligny, and his brother the Seigneur d'Andelot, sufficiently influential to organize themselves into a body [A D 1555] and formally to accept the Genevan discipline and doctrine Four years later [A D 1559] the Gallican Confession of Faith, consisting of forty articles, first drawn up in Latin, and then translated into French, was publicly adopted Their increasing numbers compelled the regent queen mother to assume a conciliatory tone, both during the short reign of Francis II and the earlier years of Charles IX. In the hopes of accommodating matters, a conference was held between the Romanists and Protestants at Poissy [A D 1561], the latter being championed by Beza and Peter Martyr, when, though an edict was passed removing the penalties of nonconformity, no lasting reconciliation was achieved In the very next year a Protestant congregation, while engaged in worship at Vassy, was massacred in cold blood [A D 1562] Their friends flew to arms, but were defeated at the battle of Dreux The assassination of the Duke of Guise followed, by the Huguenot Poltrot de Merey, in revenge for his supposed instigation of the massacre of Vassy Ten years of civil discord succeeded, hardly broken by the pacification of Amboise [A D 1563], until the deeds of atrocity perpetrated on both sides culminated in the massacre of St Bartholomew, planned by Catharine de Medici, and executed on August 24th, 1572 Though nearly annihilated at the moment, the Protestants revived again, to meet with more favourable terms under Henry IV, who, although a convert to Catholicism, accorded them full liberty of worship by the Edict of Nantes [A D 1598] a concession which was afterwards revoked by Louis XIV [A D 1685] According to recent calculations the Protestants in France now number about a twentieth part of the population, and Rationalist views of the very broadest type prevail among them [Merle d'Aubigné's *History of the Reformation* De Felice, *History of the Protestants of France*, Lond. 1853]

FRIENDS [QUAKERS]

FRIENDS OF GOD A designation by which the mystics of Germany were commonly known among themselves during the fourteenth century, and which was taken from our Lord's words, "Henceforth I call you not servants, for the servant knoweth not what his lord doeth but I have called you friends" [John xv 15] It may be doubted whether they ever formed a separate community, yet there is a succession of names associated with the title which distinguishes the "Friends of God" as in some degree a school of themselves, and they mark clearly a period of transition from the mere speculative mystics of the Middle Ages to the practical pietists of post-Reformation times

The first of these names is that of the Dominican Henry Eckhart [A D 1304-1328], generally known as Master Eckhart He became the first provincial of the Dominicans in Saxony when that country was made into a separate province of the Order in the year 1304, and was the teacher of Tauler, whose influence has extended even to our own times In 1324, while he was presiding over the Dominican monastery at Frankfort-on-Maine, he was brought to trial for his opinions by the General of the Order, and afterwards, in 1327, by the Bishop of Cologne The accusations brought against him were framed on twenty-six propositions taken from his sermons, which were alleged to be pantheistic in their teaching These were formally condemned, and the condemnation was afterwards confirmed (but with conspicuous tenderness towards Eckhart's memory) by a Bull of John XXII, issued in A D 1329, after Eckhart's death Although the tendency of his teaching was dangerously suggestive of Pantheism, his object was to set forth the closeness of the union with God into which the soul may be brought by holy living Thus he maintained that we should be united with God essentially, individually, and entirely, by means of contemplation, and that just in proportion as man is united with God he is more God than creature "Wherefore," he asks, "is God become man? that I may be born the same God God died for this reason that I may die to all the world and all created things" [Giesler's *Compend Eccl Hist* iv. 176, Clark's transl] These principles were corrupted into Antinomianism by the BRETHREN OF THE FREE SPIRIT, and a similar result followed their revival in the case of the Methodists

Nicolas of Basle [A D 1330-1383] took up the principles of Eckhart on their practical side, and endeavoured so to purify his life by ascetic devotion that he might effect a complete separation of his soul from the world, and perfect its union with God After a long course of such devotion he believed himself to be favoured with Divine revelations and visions and ecstasies Though a layman he became spiritual director to multitudes, and seems to have been associated in this capacity with some of the early and purer Beghards When he was very old he was arrested as a Beghard by the Inquisition, while he was travelling through France, and was burnt to death at Vienne about the year 1383, in company with one of his disciples

John Tauler [A D 1290-1361] was a Dominican at Strasburg, and had been brought under the influence of Nicolas of Basle about the year 1340, having previously been a disciple of Eckhart Nicolas had won followers as a layman by the private influence of his character, but Tauler was one of the great Dominican preachers, and was listened to by crowds in the cities and villages on the banks of the Rhine, as Wesley and Whitfield were in England in later days While Germany was under an interdict by which the Pope forbad all ministrations of the clergy, Tauler boldly continued his work, and when the dreadful "Black Death" desolated every house and drove away the few surviving clergy, he and a few other Dominicans went fearlessly from house to house in Strasburg, comforting the dying, giving courage to the living, and winning the hearts of all This noble friar was the practical expositor of Eckhart's intellectual speculations, and the one aim of his life was that of persuading men to give up worldliness and sin, and to become "friends of God" by deepening and widening their spiritual communion with Him His *Theologia Germanica* and his sermons were widely circulated after his death, and had great influence upon the mind of John Wesley four centuries later The former was translated into French by Castalion, who was closely associated with the 'Family of Love," and it is extremely likely that its fervid teaching of what has been called the deification of man's nature was perverted to the support of the Antinomian principles for which those enthusiasts became notorious

Henry Suso [A D 1300-1365] was of the same school of Dominicans as Tauler, but belonged to Suabia His influence among the "Friends of God" was exerted chiefly by his writings, which were in the dialogue and catechetical form, and being written in the vernacular circulated widely among those who were able to read Neander speaks of him as conspicuously setting forth the mediation of our Lord as the channel by which communion with God is to be attained, and as thus counteracting the pantheistic tendency of the mysticism which spoke constantly and strongly about union with the Divine Essence, but omitted to shew that this was the result of a mediatorial, not a direct, intercourse with God

The "Brethren of the Common Life" were a Dutch section of the "Friends of God," and owed their origin to Gerard Groot of Deventer [A D. 1340-84], a Canon of Utrecht and Aix, who gave up his preferments to become a missionary preacher throughout the diocese of Utrecht. Preaching at Utrecht, Deventer, Amsterdam, Haarlem, and many other places, he became so popular, that people left their business and their meals to hear his sermons, so that the churches could not hold the crowds that flocked wherever he came [Thom à Kemp *Vita M Gerardi magni* xv] When his preaching was prohibited, Groot established in his house a theological college for those who were preparing to take Holy Orders, and this was developed two years after his death into a house of regular canons at Windesheim in Zwolle, with a cell at Deventer At Windesheim the clergy continued to prepare candidates for Holy Orders, and they were joined by many laymen, who lived together in a community of goods and labour, but without any monastic vow, as "Fratres vitæ Communis," "Fratres bonæ voluntatis," or "Fratres Collationarii" It was at Deventer that Thomas à Kempis was trained, at Windesheim that he spent the greater portion of his days, and through him another link of connection was established between the Friends of God and devotional Christians of subsequent ages. Within fifty years of Groot's death the Brothers of the Common Life numbered seventeen collegiate churches in the Netherlands, and contributed much to the mystical theology of the Church The Order was extinguished by the flood of the Dutch Reformation [Schmidt's *Johannes Tauler von Strasburg*, 1841 Ullmann's *Reformers before the Reformation*, Clark's transl Neale's *Hist of Jansenist Ch of Holl* ch ii]

FRIENDS OF LIGHT. A sect of Lutheran Rationalists which originated in Prussian Saxony about the year 1841 Their founder was pastor Uhlich, who, in company with sixteen friends, held the first meeting at Gnaden in July of that year A second convention met at Halle, and was numerously attended by clergymen, professors, and laymen of every class of society A session held at Kothen in 1844, was a great popular assembly, and attention being drawn to the new sect, and to its new leader, Pastor Wislicenus, by Guericke the ecclesiastical historian, an order in council was issued by the Prussian Government in August 1845, prohibiting them from holding further meetings

The Friends of Light professed to develope the principles of the Reformation by a recurrence to the spirit of the Reformers as distinguished from the actual shape into which their reforms were forced by the circumstances of the times in which they lived This spirit they interpreted as that of perfect intellectual freedom in religion, with individual judgment for the sole guide Such a fundamental principle as this was calculated to embrace every school of Rationalists, and does in fact represent the common ground on which all rationalizing systems take their stand Although therefore they were not allowed to organize themselves into a community, the "Friends of Light" have found many converts both in Germany and England. [Hurst's *Hist Rationalism*, 228, ed 1867]

FRIESLANDERS A section of the Mennonites who separated from the FLEMINGS, and maintained a separate position for some time on the questions of discipline which had caused division among the Mennonites They eventually coalesced with the WATERLANDERS [Mosheim's *Eccl Hist* iii. 149, Stubbs' ed]

G

GAIANA. In a passage of Tertullian, which is according to ordinary texts read "Sunt et nunc alii Nicolaitæ, Caiana hæresis dicitur" [Tertull *de Prescrip Hær* xxxiii], Oehler reads Gaiana instead of Caiana Nothing is known of any early sect of Gaianites, and it is commonly supposed that the CAINITES are the sect referred to

GAIANITÆ The Alexandrian section of the APHTHARTODOCETÆ, so called from their leader Gaianus, a contemporary and theological colleague of Julian of Halicarnassus Gaianus was Archdeacon of Alexandria, and on the death of the Patriarch Timotheus III [A D 536] was tumultuously placed on the patriarchal throne by the monks and people in opposition to Theodosius, who had been nominated by the Emperor and consecrated to the see. After three months, Gaianus was however deposed and exiled, first to Carthage and then to Sardinia, after which his name appears only in association with the sect to which it was given.

GALENISTS The Arminian division of the Mennonite WATERLANDERS, who owe their origin to Galen Abraham de Haan, a physician and Baptist preacher at Amsterdam in the year 1664 Galen advocated open communion, and taught Socinian doctrine

GALLICAN CONFESSION. [PROTESTANT CONFESSIONS]

GALLICANS A name given to an historical party in the Church of France which has constantly protested against, and, when it was able to do so, opposed, the invasion of its liberties by the See of Rome Without developing any special school of thought, and without in any important particulars deviating from Roman doctrine, the Gallicans maintain much the same theory as to the independence of national churches that is maintained by learned writers in the Church of England. but circumstances have never compelled the Church of France to seek so entire a repudiation of the papal claims to authority as has taken place in the Church of England The principal efforts of the Gallican party, as opposed to the Ultramontane party, in recent times, have been directed towards the revival of the native Liturgy, a local form of the great Ephesine Liturgy of Asia Minor, variations of which continued in use in several dioceses of France down to our own time But these efforts have been effectually counteracted by Ultramontane influences, and no breviaries or missals except the Roman are now permitted to be used in French churches. [DICT *of* THEOLOGY, PRAGMATIC SANCTION]

GAZARES. [GAZZARI]

GAZZARI The Italian name for the mediæval Catharists or Albigenses [Steph. de Borbone in d'Argentre, i 90]

GENERAL ASSOCIATE SYNOD. [ANTI-BURGHERS]

GENERAL BAPTISTS, NEW CONNEXION [BAPTISTS]

GENERAL BAPTISTS, UNITARIAN [BAPTISTS]

GENERAL PROVISIONERS A nickname of the FREE-WILL BAPTISTS

GENISTÆ A Jewish sect named by Justin Martyr [*Dial. c. Tryph* c. lxxx] It is probably to be identified with the Nazaræans of Epiphanius [*Hær* xviii] The name, which would be better written Genitæ, implies that its bearers were of the original stock of the Jews, and preserved the ancient patriarchal faith [JEWISH SECTS]

GEORGIANS [DAVID-GEORGIANS]

GERMAN CATHOLICS Two movements of German Catholics have occurred during the last quarter of a century, having a promise of the more important results still to flow from them

I The question of mixed marriages between Catholics and Protestants had become an aggravated difficulty in the kingdom of Prussia, where both forms of religion exist side by side Benedict XIV [A D 1741], in the case of the Netherlands, declared mixed marriages to be abominable, wretched, and accursed proceedings, and such as never could be allowed by the Roman See Still such marriages were not wholly interdicted, and papal dispensation was never refused to rich suitors But the clergy were forbidden to solemnize such marriages, they were a mere civil contract, the priest acting only as witness by "passive assistance" The same Pope [A D 1748] by a formal constitution, decreed that mixed marriages could only take place under a pledge that the children should be brought up as Catholics, and that the Catholic party in the contract should not be molested in the exercise of Catholic duties, for that there was always a hope of reclaiming the uncatholic element to the faith of the Church Accordingly, such marriages were celebrated in Prussia, either unconditionally, or with the sole engagement that, according to sex, children should be brought up in the faith of the parent A D 1825, engagements of this kind were abrogated by order of the State, but by papal edict of Pius VIII, March 1830, they were still to be enforced as a necessary condition for obtaining dispensation The civil and ecclesiastical powers were in open antagonism But the State, wise in its generation, prevailed Count Spiegel, Archbishop of Cologne, was persuaded to circulate the edict among his suffragans, with a pastoral brief, and accompanied with secret instructions to obey the Cabinet order of 1825, "passive assistance" also might be rendered even where no engagement was made with respect to the education of the children, such marriages only being forbidden under the unlikely contingency of the woman certainly knowing that all her children would be brought up as Protestants In 1835, Baron Droste-Vischering succeeded to the see of Cologne, having engaged to carry out the Cabinet regulation with respect to mixed marriages, the papal edict, however, was enforced by him, and the Government removed him to Minden, the effect of which was that all restriction upon mixed marriages was rescinded throughout Rhenish Westphalia

In the eastern State of Posen, the Church authorities took vigorous action against all Catholics who contracted such marriages, the provost shewing much fiery zeal in the matter A strong bond of sympathy existed between Czerski, the provost's vicar, and his flock, for while they demanded toleration in their alliances, he himself was secretly married to a Polish lady Both priest and people soon proceeded to question the scriptural grounds on which the ecclesiastical decrees rested; and they came to the conclusion that the Church view with respect to matrimony was one thing and the law of Christ something widely different Czerski was suspended March 1844, and in the August following he separated himself altogether from the Roman communion Twenty-four members of his congregation, threatened with excommunication, declared themselves at the same time an extra Roman community, under the name of Apostolical Catholic Christians They next set up a place of worship of their own where Czerski officiated as priest, now publicly married by a Protestant pastor The whole party were of course excommunicated, but neither Czerski nor his flock considered themselves to be anything but Catholic Christians, and still preserved a broadly marked distinction from the Protestant body by their retention of the seven sacraments They also drew up a brief formula of faith [October 19th] to mark their total separation from the Roman communion, in which nine fundamental errors of the Roman Church were condemned communion in one kind, canonization of saints, worship of saints, absolution that involved auricular confession, indulgence, prescriptive fasts, public service in a foreign language, celibacy of clergy, prohibition of mixed marriages, and the temporal power of the Pope. Their Confession of Faith commenced with the Nicene Creed, Holy Scripture is declared to be the only sure ground of faith, and private judgment is a sufficient guide to its meaning, the seven sacraments are means of grace ordained by Christ, the sacrifice of the mass is a memorial of the death of Christ, and is of efficacy for the living and the dead, the Body and Blood of Christ are truly present in the sacrifice of the altar, confession and absolution are no prerequisites for communicating The reality of a purgatorial fire is affirmed, but not in the material sense of the Romish dogma Marriage of the clergy is not only allowed, but encouraged, as being conducive to the edification of the flock through the influence of domestic example The kingdom of God must be realized in the believer's life upon earth The new community applied for State recognition as a security against persecution, but obtained no answer The seceders at the commencement, A D 1844, numbered eighty-five of burgher rank, who were known as the Schneidemuhl section of German Catholics, and kept more closely to the faith of the Church Catholic than the second or Breslau-Dresden section of seceders under Ronge

II For the Czerski movement was eclipsed by the contemporaneous defection of Ronge in the more southern province of Silesia His pen had got him into disgrace, and he was suspended from all clerical duty, when the exhibition of the seamless coat of Christ[1] at Treves [A D 1844] drew from him a vigorous protest[2] His attack aroused attention in the highest degree, and procured for him the further publicity of excommunication He at once became a martyr, addresses and rich presents poured in upon him The circle widened, and Dr Regenbrecht, Professor of Canon Law at Breslau, ostentatiously quitted the Church of Rome, German Catholic communities sprung up in all the principal towns of Northern Germany [A D 1844-45], and hopes were entertained of the formation of a German Reformed National Church, maintaining the doctrine but denying the authority and regimen of Rome All such hope was soon dispelled, for at a meeting held at Leipsic [March 23rd, 1845], at which thirty delegates from thirteen German Catholic congregations were present, the following formula was drawn up, shorn of nearly every distinctive attribute of the faith, and toned down to suit the coldest rationalism "I believe in God the Father, who, by His

[1] "E mal trovato" For a thousand years nothing was known of the relic The Virgin is stated to have woven this coat for her infant Son, it grew with His increase of stature, and for it the Roman soldiers cast lots Helena, the mother of Constantine, was said to have brought it from Palestine, and sent it by St Agricius to Treves, as recorded in the "Gesta Trevirorum," A D 1106 1124 In the year 1186, the cathedral being under repair, the coat was placed in a chest under the high altar, and there it remained till the Emperor Maximilian caused search to be made for it, A D 1512, when it was brought to light, and A D 1514, a Bull of Leo X directed that it should be exposed to the view of the faithful every seven years Three such solemnities are on record A D 1585, on the restoration of the Catholic religion in the district of Treves, A D 1655, after the Thirty Years' War, and A D 1810, on its return from Augsburg, whither it had been conveyed during the French Revolution

[2] *Das Urtheil eines Katholischen Priesters über d h. Rock in Trier*, October 1844

Almighty Word, created the world, and governs it in wisdom, righteousness, and love. I believe in Jesus Christ our Saviour. I believe in the Holy Ghost, one holy universal Christian Church, the forgiveness of sins, and life eternal." Only two sacraments were retained, and the Bible interpreted by private judgment was declared to be sufficient for salvation. Czerski's endeavour to procure the recognition of Christ's Divinity was ineffectual. The Ronge or Breslau party became known as German Catholics, and were thoroughly rationalistic; the Posen Separatists retained the denomination of Apostolical Catholics, but silently acquiesced in the exposition of faith put forth by the Breslau party, which became the dominant type of German Catholicism.

These new notions rapidly spread through Northern Germany, wherever an exclusively Romanist population and a determined Romanist government could not withstand the tide. But the original taint of dissension clung to the movement. Neither was Ronge exactly the character to inspire confidence. He had nothing solid or dignified to recommend him. Vain of the noise that he had made in the world, and self-conceited, he hoped by thrusting himself for ever before the public in meetings and ovational gatherings, to open a new page in the history of the world. But his most serious drawback was, that there was no depth of religion in him, without which it is impossible for the reformer to make any permanent impression upon old established modes of religious thought. Already, in May 1845, Czerski declared, by letters to the several congregations, his dissatisfaction with the Leipsic Declaration, which he had also refused to sign, because it ignored the Lord's Divinity. Ronge in reply objected, that to stop short at that point would be to re-enact the Reformation of Luther; that the march of opinion demanded a radical reform in matters of faith; the time had come for the Church to cast aside old traditional forms, such as the Apostles' Creed, and to generalize in the direction of the rational conviction of the age. Christ was no longer to be worshipped as God over all, but to be hailed as a brother. By such notions he hoped to recover that grasp upon Germany which the Protestant movement had missed. The two rival leaders met and fraternized at the Conference in Rawitz, February 3rd, 1846; but their difference of opinion, as in the case of Luther and Zwingli, was too decided for a thorough reconciliation, and each continued to propagate his own particular form of German Catholicism.

The political relations of the community presented considerable difficulty. What claim had they on the toleration of the Catholic States which only recognised the Church of Rome and the Evangelical party as bound by the Augsburg Confession? And who were the German Catholics? In Bavaria they were looked upon, not as a religious community, but as political radicals and communists. In Austria the very name of German Catholic was proscribed. Internal distraction weakened their hold upon public respect, and a soulless liberalism was the only idea in which the entire party could agree. Ronge's views having been taken up by members of the Chamber on the side of the opposition, they assumed some public importance; but the political changes of 1848 brought about a coalition between his party, and the Pantheistic Hegelian following, the FRIENDS OF LIGHT, whereby German Catholicism ranks now among the various denominations of rationalizing Protestantism, rather than with any section of the Church Catholic. A more formal alliance was made between German Catholicism and the Protestant party at Leipsic, A.D. 1850, under the name of the "Religious Association" (Religions-Gesellschaft). The principles of communism, in a religious direction, are not disowned by this sect; and it has always had the strongest sympathies with political democracy. It exhibits an altogether humanitarian form of religion as compared with the spiritual faith of the Church Catholic. [Gervinus, *Die Mission d. Deutschkath.*; *Die Prot. Geistlichk. u. d. Deutschkath.* Kampe, *Gesch. d. Relig. Beweg. d. n. Zeit*; *Das Wesen d. Deutschkath.* OLD CATHOLICS.]

GERMAN PROTESTANTS. The history of the rise of German Protestantism is so closely allied with that of LUTHERANISM that it will be sufficient here to present a summary of the important events which took place between A.D. 1517, when Luther, at that time philosophical lecturer at Wittenberg, was roused into action by Tetzel's sales of indulgences at the neighbouring town of Juterboch, and when the religious peace was extorted from the Emperor Charles V. at Augsburg in 1555. The first overt act of hostility was a bull of excommunication launched against Luther by Leo X. [A.D. 1520], and publicly burnt by him at Wittenberg. In the following year he was declared a heretic, and his writings were proscribed at the Diet of Worms, on January 28th. Great commotions followed. The Anabaptists at Zwickau in Misnia, and the ultra-Reformers under Carlstadt at Wittenberg, flew to arms, and hence "The Peasants' War" [A.D. 1524], in which the excesses of the Protestant party, which Luther was unable to influence or control, gained them an unenviable notoriety, and helped to detach Erasmus from the cause of the Reformation. In A.D. 1526, the league of Torgau was formed, John Elector of Saxony, and Philip Landgrave of Hesse, with others, demanding reforms, which were discussed at the first Diet of Spires, but instead of being adopted, were recommended to be referred to a future General Council. Any delay was favourable to the reforming cause, and the opposition of Charles V. was at the same time mitigated by his quarrel with the Pope, which led to the storming of Rome and the surrender of Clement VII., and by the claim of Archduke Ferdinand to the crowns of Hungary and Bohemia. A second diet was summoned at Spires, A.D. 1529, at which the name of Protestants was first assigned to those who differed from the Church of Rome, in consequence of a document or protestation submitted to the Emperor, signed by John Elector of Saxony, George Elector of

Brandenberg, Ernest Duke of Lunenberg, Philip Landgrave of Hesse, and by fourteen imperial cities, Strasburg, Ulm, Nuremberg, Constance, Reutlingen, Windesheim, Memmingen, Nordlingen, Lindan, Isny, Kempten, Heilbron, Wissenburg and St Gall A conference of the leaders of the Reformation also took place at Marburg, at which fifteen articles were drawn up, revised and augmented to seventeen at the convent of Schabach [Oct 17th], and embodied in the Confession of Augsburg [A D 1530] In the next year, alarmed by an imperial decree in favour of Catholicism, nine Protestant princes and eleven cities formed the Smalkaldic League, by which they bound themselves for six years to maintain the tenets of Augsburg On seeing their determined attitude, and now in his turn alarmed by the Ottoman invasion of Hungary, and by the opposition of the German princes to the election of his brother Ferdinand as King of the Romans, Charles made peace with the Reformers at Nuremberg [A D 1532], and agreed to a compromise until the session of a General Council Various proposals were made during the next few years to summon it at Mantua, Piacenza, or Bologna, but a formal protest against a German question being settled on Italian soil, and a re-vindication of Protestant principles, was published under the title of the Smalkaldic Articles [A D 1537] About the same time, on the Catholic side, a union called the Holy League was formed between Charles V, Ferdinand Elector of Mayence, the Archbishop of Salzburg, and the Dukes of Bavaria, Saxony, and Brunswick Both sides were too strong to think of yielding unconditionally, and once more a reconciliation was attempted, and nearly but not quite achieved at a conference at Ratisbon [A D 1541], Melanchthon and others acting as the Protestant advocates against Eck and his coadjutors on the Catholic side So matters stood till Charles V., having made peace with the King of France at Cressy [A D 1544], and the Romish party, elated by the prospect of the General Council summoned to meet in the following year at Trent, found themselves in a position to recommence hostilities on the German Protestants Death spared Luther from witnessing the horrors of the Smalkaldic War which followed [A D 1546], with disastrous results to the Protestants, who were completely routed at the battle of Muhlberg [A D 1547], and saw their champion, John Frederick, fall into the Emperor's hands They were saved, however, from utter annihilation by a coolness which sprang up between Charles V and Paul III, who, to the Emperor's dissatisfaction, ordered the removal of the council from Trent to Bologna Soon afterwards, at a Diet held at Augsburg [A D 1548], a provisional formula was put forth with Charles' permission, known as the Interim Augustanum, to last till the final settlement of disputed points by the General Council It was disliked by many Protestants for its decided leaning to Roman views, but was accepted by others called "the Adiaphoristic party," who were willing to treat a great many points as open questions The Tridentine Council resumed its sittings under Julius III [A D 1551], and renewed activity was simultaneously displayed by the Protestants The Confession of Saxony was drawn up by Melanchthon The Confession of Wurtemberg was composed by Brentius, and submitted at Trent The German princes again resorted to arms, attacked the Emperor unexpectedly at Innspruck, and extorted from his fears, by the Treaty of Passau [A D 1552], full liberty of opinion, which was extended and ratified at the Diet of Augsburg [A D 1555] in the following terms, viz "That those who followed the Confession of Augsburg should be for the future considered as entirely free from the jurisdiction of the Roman Pontiff, and from the authority and superintendence of the bishops, that they should possess perfect liberty to enact laws for themselves relating to their religious sentiments, discipline and worship, that all the inhabitants of the German Empire should be allowed to join the church whose doctrine and worship they thought the purest and most consonant to the spirit of true Christianity, and that all those who should injure or persecute any persons, under religious pretences, and on account of their opinions, should be declared and proceeded against as public enemies of the Empire, invaders of its liberty and disturbers of its peace" This principle of toleration was acted upon throughout the reigns of Ferdinand [A D 1558-1564], Maximilian II [A D 1564-1576], and Rudolph II. [A D 1576-1612], until the smothered jealousy between Catholics and Protestants broke out into the Thirty Years' War [A D 1618-1648]

The smaller states in and round Germany embraced the Reformation at the following dates. Silesia [A D 1523], Hesse [A D 1526], Linden [A D 1527], Electoral Saxony [A.D. 1527], East Friesland [A D 1527], Franconian Brandenberg [A D 1528], Wirtemberg [A D. 1535], Ducal Saxony [A.D 1539], Electoral Brandenberg [A D 1539], the Palatinate [A D 1546] [LUTHERANISM]

GERMAN TEMPLE [JERUSALEM FRIENDS]

GEULINCX Arnold Geulincx [born at Antwerp A D 1625, d A D 1669] followed generally the Cartesian system, but developed from it a more thoroughgoing Rationalism His fundamental axiom was that no intelligent agent can produce any effect of the means of which it is ignorant, or, in the converse way, any agent can only effect that of which it knows the operative cause Hence, since we know nothing of our own springs of action, it is not we who act, but some power external to us He accounted for the apparent action and reaction of mind and matter by affirming that Mind is a mode of Infinite Substance, and that bodily action is the result, not of individual will, nor of any inherent power of the body, for this is merely passive, but of the Divine Energy, which is causative of every movement of the human machine Mind (i e Divine Substance)[1] and Body are as two watches that

[1] "Sumus igitur modi Mentis, si auferas modum remanet Deus" [*Met* 116] "Nota Deum esse Mentem simpliciter, proprie et vere Mentes creatæ seu mentes

keep exact time with each other, but are of entirely independent action; to the Divine Artificer alone they owe their exact correspondence "Obstupesce ergo, cum hæc sic animadvertis, cum vides a Deo hæc ita moveri, et corporis ejusque membrorum motum ad arbitrium voluntatis nostræ dirigi, idque ita ab ejus providentia temperatum esse" [*de Humil* 328] "Qui motum indidit materiæ et leges ei dixit, is idem voluntatem meam formavit, itaque has res diversissimas inter se devinxit, ut cum voluntas mea vellet motus talis adesset, et contra cum motus adesset, voluntas eum vellet, sine ulla alterius in alterum causalitate vel influxu; sicut duobus horologiis rite inter se et ad solis diurnum cursum quadratis, propter meram dependentiam, qua utrumque ab eadem arte et simili industria constitutum est" [*Eth* 124] Leibnitz made use of the same illustration in explaining his very similar notion of a "Pre-established Harmony." The following are the main principles developed by Geulincx [1] I can effect nothing externally to myself, [2] all that I can effect is esoterically within myself, [3] by Divine energy my sphere of action extends at times beyond myself, [4] but the act is not my own, it is of God, [5] and that according to Divine laws ordained arbitrarily, but with perfect freedom of the Divine will when I utter the word "earth," it is as great a marvel that my tongue should vibrate as it would be if the earth itself should quake, [6] I can only contemplate the world, [7] the world cannot offer itself to my vision, [8] God alone causes that I should behold the world in an incomprehensible manner; and I myself, among the innumerable wonders of the world that I am allowed to witness, am of all the greatest and most continuous wonder It was thus that Geulincx accounted for the phenomenon of apparently spontaneous action, by referring it to the will and energy of the Divine Being, perpetually directing the mechanism of the world as its motive power In every movement God alone works The whole universe is a series of the perpetually recurring marvels of Divine Providence

This notion of Occasionalism, or of bodily action harmonizing with mental impulse by Divine regulation, had already been broached by Louis De la Forge, a French physician, and a devoted follower of Descartes [Brucker, Buhle, Walch, but denied by Tennemann] It was termed "Occasionalism," because, on the occasion of any impulse of human will, the Divine Being moved the body, and on the occasion of any bodily affection the same cause produced sensation in the mind The causality in either case being in God, the system was one of absolute fatalism,[1] so far as any moral agency in man is concerned, and philosophically considered, it was only a modification of Pantheism, towards which scientific opinion was now verging Thus the secondary causes, acting on mind and matter which Descartes harmonized by the intervention of Infinite Substance, Geulincx treated as occasional phenomena, coming and going, as the Divine principle supplemented the action of one or other substance by corresponding impulse in its correlative. Malebranche, as will be seen, affirmed that these secondary causes have a reality and harmony only in the Deity; and Spinoza brought the pantheistic notion to a culminating point in the assertion, that these reciprocal impulses of mind and matter only represent to us the one action of that one Divine Energy which quickens the universe in all its parts As regards Occasionalism, however, Geulincx is its principal exponent, and stands as a true mean between Descartes and Leibnitz [Tennemann, *Gesch d Phil* x Fischer, *Gesch d Neuern Phil.* i 195 Ritter, *Gesch d Phil* xi 2]

GIBBITES. [SWEET SINGERS]

GICHTELIANS [ANGELIC BROTHERS]

GLASSITES This Scottish sect derives its name from John Glas or Glass [born 1695, died 1773], minister of Tealing in Forfarshire He at a very early period of his ministry began to teach that all national establishments of religion are contrary to the teaching of the New Testament, and that the Church and State may in no way be connected, and he consequently opposed the principles inculcated in the Solemn League and Covenant, and denied some of the articles of the Westminster Confession of Faith He maintained that congregations may appoint their own teachers, and was the first in Scotland to admit uneducated persons and persons engaged in trade to the office of preachers He also taught that all members of Christian congregations should have a share in Church government, and that civil magistrates ought not in any way to interfere in religious matters, either for the encouragement of true religion or for the restraint of heresy He was thus the original promulgator in Scotland of the distinctive views of the English Independents which he put forth to the world in 1728, in a book entitled *The Testimony of the King of Martyrs* He was thereupon suspended by the Synod of Angus and Mearns "for holding tenets inconsistent with the established government of this Church, and declining to come under engagements to forbear venting them " He appealed against this sentence to the General Assembly, but was deposed from the ministry by

particulares et limitatæ non sunt Mens, sed Mens eo usque, sed cum certo limite" [*ib* 235] "Ratione in mundo non sumus, sed supra mundum et apud Deum" [*Phys* 147] And with respect to the moving power he says, "Si corpus movendum est, movendum est a mente Non potest enim a se moveri " "Extra corpus nihil est præter mentem, igitur si motus ponendus est, ponendus est a mente" [*Met.* 85] "Nos corpora nostra non movere, si moveremus, sciremus utique quomodo moveremus, at hoc profundissime nescimus" [*Phys.* 110] "Ad arbitrium voluntatis meæ quædam subinde partes in corpore meo moventur, non quidem a me sed a Motore" [*Met* 34].

[1] Even death was no manumission from a servile subjection, "corporis exuviis solutus liber non es censendus, manet Dei potestas et jus, quo te possidet, non tu manumissus es aut jure aliquo gaudes, Dei adhuc et semper manes" [*de Humil* p 327] "Inspiciendo ergo nos ipsos invenimus servos nos esse, nec id simpliciter vel ad tempus aliquod, sed essentialiter et semper" [*ib* 325]

the Commission of the Assembly on 12th March 1730 Mr Francis Archibald, minister of Guthrie, Forfarshire, his first supporter among the ministers of the Kirk, shared in his sentence of suspension He was, however, restored to the ministry by the General Assembly on 22nd May 1739, the Assembly "declaring, notwithstanding, that he is not to be esteemed a minister of the Established Church of Scotland, or capable to be called and settled therein, until he shall renounce the principles embraced by him that are inconsistent with the constitution of this Church" Glas established congregations in Dundee, Perth, and other places, but the distinctive teaching of the sect was before long largely affected by the views of one of its elders, Robert Sandeman, on the nature of justifying faith Sandeman maintained in some controversial letters addressed to Hervey on his *Theron and Aspasio*, that faith is simply an assent to the Divine testimony concerning Christ, and his notion being generally adopted by the Glassites, the sect gradually became better known by the name of Sandemanians, under which title a few congregations were established in England A notice of the subsequent history of the sect, with further particulars of their distinctive peculiarities, will be found under the article SANDEMANIANS [*Acts of the General Assembly* Morison's *Theological Dict* Perth, 1807 J Brown's *Hist of the Ch of Scotland*]

GNOSIMACHI [RHETORIANS]

GNOSTICS An appellation which was probably assumed by the heretics of apostolic times, and which was afterwards extended in its application until it became the generic name of about twenty-five sects that arose in various parts of the Church during the first two centuries of its existence

The earliest form of Gnosticism is indicated by the word γνῶσις, from which the name is derived, and which had acquired the ecclesiastical meaning of "theological" knowledge, as distinguished from the knowledge arising out of the mere reception of truth [1] Such γνῶσις is often spoken of in the New Testament as a thing to be desired, but when so spoken of it is clear that purely intellectual knowledge of Christianity is not intended, but such an intellectual knowledge as runs parallel with a development of holiness, a comprehension of the breadth and length, and depth and height of Divine Truth which leads up to the knowledge of the love of Christ [Eph iii 18, 19] In one of St Paul's last epistles [1 Tim vi 20], he speaks of a γνῶσις which was evidently dissociated from this progressive holiness and associated with subtle speculations about the oppositions (ἀντιθέσεις) of good and evil, and this he declares to be "science," or theological knowledge "falsely so called" (ψευδώνυμος γνῶσις) The cultivation of the true γνῶσις had therefore passed, in some cases, into that of a speculative, unspiritual γνῶσις even in the lifetime of St. Paul, and the latter had already begun to deal with those questions respecting the origin of evil, moral light and moral darkness, which were an invariable feature of Gnostic speculations

Whether those who cultivated the true γνῶσις were ever called Gnostics is uncertain That they may have been so seems likely from St Paul's use of the name when he speaks of Herod Agrippa as an expert (γνώστης) in all Jewish "customs and questions:" and, as is well known, Clement of Alexandria uses the name in this good sense throughout his *Stromata*, which work was probably written in the latter part of the second century But in the common sense of the name as used in later ages of γνωστικοί are first so designated by Irenæus, late in the second, and Hippolytus early in the third century [Iren *adv Hær* iii 4, Hippol *Philosoph* v *ad init*] The epistles of St Ignatius however, and especially his Epistle to the Church of Smyrna, contain such numerous references to the principles of the Gnostics as to shew that they had become widely diffused in the beginning of the second century, whether the name was or was not in use at so early a period as distinctive of the heretics who taught them

The Gnostics have been commonly traced up to particular founders, such as Simon Magus, but it seems more in accordance with historical evidence to consider them as the natural outcome of Jewish and Gentile intellect when exercised in a speculative manner upon the philosophical phase of Christianity and of other religions of the world The first principle of the Gnostics was that "the beginning of perfection is the science (γνῶσις) of man, and the science of God is absolute perfection" [Hippol *Philosoph.* v 1, 3] This principle was worked out in its details by intellectual Christians who lived in the midst of religious systems which were much older than Christianity The Jew had his Rabbinical traditions, the Oriental his Zoroastrian system of philosophical light-worship, the Greek or Roman his classical philosophy and mythology Though the force of Christianity could not be resisted, yet the old national faiths had their charms both for the mind and the heart, at least where the convert was only subdued by the intellectual and not by the spiritual force of the new faith At the same time an uninquiring reception of truth by mere faith had no attraction for such minds, and they were accustomed to sneer, Irenæus tells us, at the simple Christianity which sufficed for "Catholics and Ecclesiastics" [Iren *adv Hær* iii 15]

Two elements thus combined towards the development of the Gnostic, *first*, a desire to form a philosophy of Christianity, and *secondly*, the craving after a philosophy of religion to which Christianity and the old faiths of the world should each contribute their share of truth and theory Hence arose three principal types of intellectual speculation, the Judaizing, the Oriental, and the Greek All three had the common feature of

[1] "As we assert," says Clement of Alexandria, "that a man may be a believer without learning, so also we assert that it is impossible for a man without learning to comprehend the things which are declared in the faith" [Clem Alex *Strom* i 6]

eclecticism, but the eclecticism of each was influenced by local colouring, and hence the general speculative tendency which produced Gnosticism produced a Cabbalistic, a Zoroastrian, or a mythological Gnostic, according to his antecedent habits of thought and the intellectual atmosphere in which he lived All experience teaches that the first outbreak of such a speculative tendency at various centres, and into each particular type of Gnosticism, would be sporadic, and that those who became leaders of its various systems would not be the originators of them, but the condensers and moulders of materials which they found already in existence They laid hold of the spirit of inquiry which pervaded the intellectual part of the Christian world, and offered to satisfy it by means of a knowledge which had not been given to the Christian world at large, but only to a select few of whom they were the representatives [Iren *adv Hær* i 25, iii 2] Hence the Gnostic claimed to be not only the philosophical Christian, who evolved truth out of thought, but also the depositary of a secret tradition on which his system was mainly grounded as that of the ordinary Christian was grounded on the less recondite foundation of a revelation whose statements were open to all The chief of such leaders of Gnostic thought were Simon Magus, Basilides, Valentinus, and Marcion, each of whose systems, as well as those of less conspicuous founders of Gnostic sects, are explained in separate articles [SIMONIANS, VALENTINIANS, &c]

The development of these various systems of Gnosticism led to a most involved and complicated theosophy and anthropology, a large portion of which seems to the modern student, as it seemed to the ancient Father, neither more nor less than nonsense, though it is just barely possible that there is a key to it unknown to contemporaries as it is to moderns, which might shew that it was a kind of verbal hieroglyphics. But amidst this maze of incoherent absurdity there are to be found certain definite theories respecting God and man which may be taken as representing the generic character of Gnostic thought These may be shortly stated in a summary form

1 One Infinite and Self-Existent Being alone has existed from all eternity, and is the original source of all being

2 At some epoch or epochs of eternity, there emanated from Him other Beings called Æons, in whom He limited His own Infinity by manifesting in each of them one of His Divine attributes

3 These inferior Divine Beings made the creation of still inferior beings possible, for they themselves were a transition from the Infinite towards the Finite

4 Further processes of emanation ensued by which the circles of beings evolved from the first emanation became more and more distant from the Infinite, making a nearer and nearer approach to the Finite, yet not becoming material.

5 The material world, on the contrary, is a kingdom of creation opposed to the kingdom of emanation, the only explanation of whose original existence is that it was the work of a rebellious Divine Being who constituted himself a "Demiurge," *i e* first, a Creator of matter, and secondly a Disposer of matter into form

6 Thus arose a dualism in which there was on the one hand a Kingdom of Spirit, Light, and Good, and on the other hand a Kingdom of Matter, Darkness, and Evil

7 Human nature became a mixture of spirit and matter, and therefore of good and evil

8 To eliminate the matter from human nature, and make it consist of spirit alone, is the great work of man's moral discipline, reaching its climax in final reception into the higher world of Spirit and Light

9 But this work is hindered by the power of the Demiurge, who being the ruler of the material world opposes this process of spiritualization as one that removes man from his kingdom

10 To counteract the evil work of the Demiurge, therefore, to assist man in working out his moral probation, and to secure his final removal from the bondage of matter and the Demiurge, one of the Æons (from the innermost circle in some Gnostic systems, from a more outward one in others) came into the world to be man's Saviour

11 This Divine and Heavenly Spirit or Æon united Himself to the material and earthly body of the Man Jesus whom John the Baptist baptized in Jordan, and thus constituted Him Jesus the Christ, heavenly as to His Spirit, earthly as to His Body. But some sects of Gnostics, as the Docetæ, imagined that the Body of Christ was only a phantom or ideal Body and not one of real flesh and blood

12. The death of Christ was the work of the evil Demiurge, but was thwarted by the return of the heavenly Æon to the place from whence He had descended, the crucified Body, or apparent Body, having no further part in the work of man's redemption

As regards the influence of Christ on the moral probation and the ultimate salvation of mankind, all the Gnostic systems were extremely indefinite There was one general idea that He was a Divine Teacher who secretly communicated to His apostles the γνῶσις, which was soon treated as a mysterious tradition rather than intellectual theology, and this γνῶσις was held to be the means by which human nature was purified But there was, in reality, no place for Christ in the Gnostic systems The purification of human nature was effected by each individual man's own efforts of self discipline and progressive acquisition of the secret science, neither sacramental nor other grace being required In early times this principle led the Gnostics to practise severe mortifications for the purpose of bringing the body into subjection to the spirit and they also made the contemplative life a means towards the same end But their theory of the Demiurge was soon extended from the sphere of physical creation to that of moral law, and then the moral law shared with the material world in condemnation as his evil work Thus a theoretical antinomianism sprung up which soon developed into practical license and profligacy, marriage especially being despised, first, as inconsistent with a life of mortification, and afterwards as being part of the bondage of a law which spiritual persons were called on to despise and renounce Thus, more and more, the historical Moral Teacher of the Gospels, and the mystical Giver of grace of the Church system, would have to be explained away, for He was always a disturbing element in the consistency of the Gnostic systems, the New Creation of the Gospel being as alien to their theories as the Old Creation of Genesis This congeries of heresies thus essentially represented antichristianism, and they who moulded them into form and disseminated them in the world were often looked upon as representatives of the personal Antichrist

The Gnostics are little heard of after the second century, but many of their principles survived among the Manichæans, and there is so much analogy between those of the Oriental Gnostics and the Buddhists as to suggest some connection between them [DICT *of* THEOL, GNOSTICISM Burton's *Inquiry into the Heresies of the Apostolic Age* Dorner's *Person of Christ*]

GOMARISTS The Supralapsarian Calvinist party opposed to Arminius and his followers, and taking this name from its leader, Francis Gomar, who was (like Arminius himself) a Professor of Theology in the University of Leyden [ARMINIANS SUPRALAPSARIANS]

GORTHÆANS These are mentioned as a sect founded by Gorthæus, a follower of Simon Magus [Euseb *Hist Eccl* iv 22] They are also mentioned in the same way by Theodoret [*Hær fab* i 12] Epiphanius names them as the third sect of the Samaritans, the Essenes and the Sebuæ being the first and second [Epiph *Hær* xii], and the Dositheans the fourth

GOSPELLERS A name assumed in spiritual conceit by the early Puritans, as that of "Evangelicals" was by the Low Church party of recent times, to signify that they were exceptional representatives of the life and truth taught in the New Testament It became a general popular term among the party opposed to the Puritans, for those factious religionists who made an ostentatious profession of piety but had a keen eye to worldly interests Thus Latimer quaintly describes the man who appealed to our Lord to make his brother divide the inheritance with him [Luke xii 13] as "a thorny brother, a gospeller, a carnal gospeller (as many be nowadays for a piece of an abbey or for a portion of chantry-lands), to get somewhat by it, and serve his commodity He was a gospeller, one of the new brethren, somewhat worse than a rank papist" In another place he speaks of the "carnal gospellers, which commonly begin well at the first, but now having rest and tranquillity, and all things going with them, they leave the Gospel, and set their minds upon this naughty world" [Latimer's *Sermons*, i 233, ii 36, ed 1824] Archbishop Cranmer describes them with some minuteness "It is reported that there be many among these unlawful assemblers that pretend knowledge of the Gospel, and will needs be called Gospellers, as though the Gospel were the cause of disobedience, sedition, and carnal liberality, and the destruction of those policies, kingdoms, and commonweals where it is received" Elsewhere they are spoken of as men "whose wit and virtue is in their tongues, hot disputers, busy talkers, taunters, and fault-finders with others, rather than menders of themselves" [Cranmer's Works, ii 260, iv 161] Such was the estimate of the "Gospellers" formed by those of their contemporaries who stood in the forefront of the Reformation struggle Later writers have been accustomed to characterize them simply by their own idea of what the name ought to have indicated, as when Bishop Burnet writes of them, "so were all those called who were given to the reading of the Scriptures." [Burnet's *Hist Reform* ii 182, Pocock's ed]

GOTISPITÆ One of the numerous names by which the CIRCUMCELLIONS were known [CUTZUPITÆ Pseudo-Hieron *de Hær* xxxii]

GRINDLETONIANS A sect of Familists in the North of England, who are described as repudiating the use of Prayer, the observance of the Lord's Day except as a "Lecture Day," and of the Holy Scriptures as maintaining that "their spirit is not to be tried by the Scripture, but the Scripture by their spirit," and "that when God comes to dwell in a man, he so fills the soul that there is no more lusting" [Knewstub's *Familists*, 1575 Denison's *White Wolf, a Paul's Cross Sermon of* 1627, p 39]

GRONINGEN SCHOOL An eclectic section of Dutch theologians, arising out of a recoil from Calvinism on the one hand and Rationalism on the other, uniting some of the features of both, but chiefly characterized by a Socinian form of Theism Its immediate origin was an attempt of Professor Van Heusde to modernize Platonism and adapt it to modern modes of thought and action, but its principal literary expositor has been Professor Hofstede de Groot, in *Die Groninger Theologen*, published at Gotha in the year 1863

This school teaches with Plato that there is a kind of Divine spirit or element [τι θεῖον πνεῦμα, Plato, *Opp* III iii 514] in human nature by which the moral life is actuated, and the development of which carries man on to the highest perfection of which he is capable This development is a state of progress towards perfect conformity to God which was attained in its degree by good heathens such as Zoroaster, Plato, and Confucius, and in its highest degree by the Son of Man Their view of our Lord is that he was a holy man who became the Theanthropos by this process of development, and not by what is ordinarily understood as the Incarnation of Deity Hence He is not a person possessing two natures, but having only one, the human developed to such an extent that it has become in a manner deified His death was the great manifestation of His love, but it did not constitute Him a Redeemer, nor was His resurrection anything more to mankind than an earnest of that to which all men universally will at last attain

This negative theology is scarcely to be distinguished from positive Rationalism, and such probably is the terminus which it reaches in the minds of most of its disciples

GRONINGENISTS. [Flemings, Old]

GUEBERS [Parsees]

GUEUX This name, meaning "Beggars," was given to the confederate nobles and other malcontents of the Netherlands in the time of Philip II In 1566, the last year of the administration of the Regent Margaret, Duchess of Parma, Philip re-established the Inquisition in the Netherlands, thereby precipitating the open revolt which previous misgovernment had prepared It was computed that before this fatal measure fifty thousand persons had been put to death for religion and thirty thousand driven from the country These severities had been mainly instigated by Granvella, Margaret's minister, and when he was recalled in 1564 a mitigation was hoped for Catholics no less than Reformers held the Inquisition in horror, and felt that the government was ruining the country Count Egmont, a devout Catholic, as the rest of the nobles were, was sent in 1565 on an embassy to Madrid to lay the state of affairs before the King The reply of Philip was to send nine Inquisitors to put in force the decrees of the Council of Trent Hereupon a number of nobles bound themselves by a compact, known as the Compromise, to resist the Inquisition, though still professing that they meant nothing against the King's dominion The principal members of this league were the heroic Louis of Nassau, the illustrious Sainte Aldegonde, Broderode, and De Hammes The more cautious Orange held aloof from it A deputation of three hundred of the confederates entered Brussels in procession, and presented to the Regent Margaret their celebrated Request, in which, amidst abundant expressions of loyalty, they declared plainly that the recent resolutions of the King were likely to produce a general rebellion. This declaration was received with contempt The Princess happening to shew some embarrassment during the audience, it is said that Berlaymont, president of finance, exclaimed that she should not have any fear of such a mob of beggars (tas de gueux) This sarcasm, which he is said to have repeated elsewhere the same day, was communicated by Broderode to the rest of the confederates at an evening banquet They immediately resolved to call themselves by that name, and drank to the health of "the beggars" with loud shouts A wallet and bowl were hung up in the hall, and each of the company in turn threw some salt into his goblet, and standing beneath those symbols of the order of mendicity, repeated the following distich —

"Par le sel, par le pain, et par le besache,
Les gueulx ne changeront pas, quoy qu'on se fache"

"By the salt, by the bread, and by the wallet,
The beggars shall change not, let whoso will fret."

They adopted the costume of beggars, appearing in doublet, hose, and short cloak of ashen grey, with common felt hats, and pouches and bowls at their sides They also caused medals of lead and copper to be struck, bearing on one side the head of Philip, on the other two hands meeting in a wallet, with the motto, "Faithful to the King, even to wearing the beggars' sack" Such was the origin of this famous name, destined to be carried far and wide by the exploits of the "wild beggars," the "wood beggars," the "beggars of the sea," in the war which soon broke out [De Thou, *Hist Univ* v lib xx 218 Bentivoglio, *Guerra di Flandra*, lib ii p 27, Monmouth's transl (1654) Motley's *Rise of the Dutch Repub* pt ii ch vi]

In origin the Beggars were a confederacy of nobles to resist the merciless dominion of foreigners, and it was they who offered the first armed opposition to Alva, on his arrival from Spain at the head of a powerful army to succeed the Duchess Margaret in 1568 Louis of Nassau gained the victory of Heiliger See the same year, but the army of the Beggars was immediately afterwards annihilated at Jenningen by Alva himself Then Orange, who had refused to join the Beggars, took the field with an army raised by himself, and in a long campaign was completely baffled by Alva, driven without a battle over the French frontier, and compelled to disband at Strasburg About the same time Orange began the navy of Holland by giving commissions to seafaring persons to cruise against Spanish commerce These privateers called themselves "Beggars of the Sea," they were under strict regulations and discipline, and each ship was ordered to have on board a minister to preach and keep piety [Grotii *Annal* ii 49] By a fleet of these marine outlaws, under their most famous leader De la Marck, was effected the memorable seizure of the port of Brill in 1572, which was the first real success of the Dutch patriots, and laid the foundation of the republic

The Beggars were not at first a religious sect, but Bentivoglio seems always to use the word "heretics" as an equivalent designation No doubt, as the great struggle with Spain proceeded they better deserved to be so called by a Roman cardinal They belonged to the Calvinists, not the Lutherans; for the Reformation reached the Netherlands not from Germany but France The Gueux of the Walloon or Western Provinces were in constant intercourse with the French Huguenots, and were often called Huguenots The Prince of Orange stated that in 1566, at the beginning of the war, there were only two Lutheran churches in all the Netherlands, and that of the others half were Calvinist [Motley's *Rise*, &c. pt ii ch vi]

GUERINETS [Illuminati]

GYMNOPODÆ [Excalceati]

H

HÆMATITES A sect of heretics named by Clement of Alexandria as one of those which, like the Docetæ, took their names from peculiar dogmas [Clem Alex *Stromat* vii 17] What the dogma was in the case of the Hæmatites he does not state, merely leaving us to draw the inference that it was in some way associated with blood [αἷμα] Spencer, in his treatise on Jewish laws, supposes that the sect was so called because those who belonged to it ate either animals which had been strangled without blood-shedding, or animals offered to idols [Spencer, *De leg Hebr Diss in loc* Act xv 20] Others have supposed that they offered sacrifices of human blood, but nothing is really known of them but what is indicated by the name

HÆSITANTES The name by which those who refused to acknowledge the authority of the Council of Chalcedon were originally called The ACEPHALI were eventually developed from among them, and the earlier name seems to have been used only for a short time [Leontius Byzant *de Sectis*, vi-ix in *Bibl Max Lugd* ix]

HAGARENES Apostates from Christianity to Mahometanism were so called in the early days of the latter

HALDANITES The followers of Robert and James Haldane, two Scotch gentlemen, of Airthrie, near Stirling, who established Independent meeting-houses with their property in Edinburgh, Glasgow, Dundee, and many other places in Scotland, at the beginning of the nineteenth century The principles of the sect were identical with those of the Daleites, but the members of it were, within a few years, absorbed into other denominations

HAMSTEDIANS [ADRIANISTS]

HARD-SHELL BAPTISTS A small sect of Baptists in the Southern States of America, known only by name

HARDTHOFITES [JERUSALEM FRIENDS]

HARMONIUS The son of Bardesanes, who is said to have promoted the heresy of his father by writing hymns by which the people at large learned his doctrine The hymns of Ephraem Syrus were composed on the orthodox side to counteract the evil wrought by those of Harmonius [Theod *Hist Eccl* iv 29, *Hæret fab* i BARDESANIANS]

HARMONY SOCIETY A community formed in 1805 by an emigrant seceder from the Lutherans of Wurtemburg, named George Rapp, on the principle of having all things common, according to the example of the first Christians It still exists in Pennsylvania, where about 4000 of the community occupy the town of Economy in Beaver county They do not maintain communion with the general body of the Lutherans, but their religious principles and practices do not differ from those of the sect from which they separated

HATTEMISTS A Dutch sect, taking its name from Pontianus von Hattem of Philipsland in Zealand He was a great admirer of Spinoza, and although wishing still to be considered as a Lutheran, was deposed from his office as pastor on account of his heretical views Mosheim says that both the Hattemists and the Verschorists deduced a doctrine of necessity from that of the absolute decrees of Calvinism, denied the doctrine of original sin, and maintained that Christianity does not impose a law of good actions but only a law of suffering, God punishing men not for their sins but by them Hattem denied the expiatory virtue of Christ's death, and considered the latter to signify that there is nothing in us which can offend God It seems impossible that such teaching should not lead to Antinomianism The sects are said still to exist, but to have discarded the names of their founders. [Mosh *Eccl Hist* iii 390, Stubbs' ed]

HEGELIANS A school of philosophy founded by George William Frederick Hegel in the early part of the nineteenth century, the leading point of which is "Absolute Idealism," *i e* that all "being" is represented by "idea," and that thus absolute thought and absolute existence are identical The law of this is defined as that of the "identity of contraries"

Hegel was born at Stuttgart on August 27th, 1770, and educated in the University of Tubingen After being occupied for some years as a private tutor he went to the University of Jena with the object of becoming lecturer, and in the year 1806 he was made professor of philosophy there In 1808 he was appointed rector of the Academy of Nuremburg, in 1816 he was made professor of philosophy at Heidelberg, and from 1818 until his death by cholera in 1831 he was professor of philosophy at Berlin His literary work during this comparatively short life was of so industrious a character that his collected writings on philosophy fill eighteen octavo volumes.

The Hegelian system has been called a *process* rather than a principle. The Absolute of Spinoza was found in an universal substance, that of Fichte, the predecessor of Hegel at Berlin, in an universal "ego," that of Schelling, his contemporary, in an universal mind Hegel took up the theory of his friend Schelling, and attempted to give it more scientific exactness by shewing that "absolute thought" is the highest stage of a process of which the two lower stages are sensational intuition and intelligent perception Following up this line of logical abstraction, Hegel denied the existence of Object and Subject, and averred that nothing exists except Relation, which he further explains by saying that Thoughts are not only Thoughts but also the realities of things, that Being and non-Being are identical All nature thus becomes only a manifestation of Thought, and a Pantheism of Idea is substituted for a Pantheism of Substance, by the conclusion that Absolute Thought is God "It appears," says Hegel, "that the World-spirit (Weltgeist) has at last succeeded in freeing Himself from all encumbrances, and is able to conceive Himself as Absolute Intelligence . For He is this only in as far as He knows Himself to be Absolute Intelligence, and this He knows only in Science, and this knowledge alone constitutes His true existence" [*Gesch der Philos* iii 689]

This singularly shadowy principle being once developed, and accepted as having a tangible meaning, its application to Christianity was easy *First*, the Personality of God vanishes from the Hegelian view of Christianity, absolute thought and absolute existence finding their highest development in human intelligence *Secondly*, but although human nature seems thus to be deified it loses in reality the quality by which it is made in the image of the Divine, ceasing to possess free will, and becoming merely a portion of the Universal Intelligence, the continual evolution of which, under the operation of the law of the "identity of contraries," is the history of mankind Thus human personality, and with it moral responsibility, vanishes in the personality of God, as the Divine personality vanishes in the personality of man

Particular doctrines of Christianity might have seemed unworthy the attention of a philosopher who had attained so sublime a height as this, but it was a peculiarity of Hegel's mind that he clung to the terminology of Holy Scripture and to the practice of Christianity, wishing only to find the theoretical explanation of them in his own philosophy Thus the doctrine of the Trinity became a threefold movement of Absolute Thought developed by the action of the law of contraries, the Fall of Man became a departure of the Absolute Idea into a state of objectivity or externality, redemption became the restoration of unity between opposites, and the practical forces of Christianity, such as means of grace, both signify and accomplish this restoration

After the death of Hegel his followers immediately began to wrangle with great bitterness over his system, the difficulty of finding out what that system really meant in its application to religion and politics being the real cause of division But while the metaphysicians of the school were arguing, a race of practical Hegelians arose, who were content to take up the philosopher's principles where he laid them down, and to carry them on to their natural consequences, Republicanism of the wildest type in politics, and Rationalism of an equally extreme form in religion The exponent of the latter was Strauss, whose "Life of Jesus" idealized the Gospel history into a congeries of myths

Hegelianism, however, like many other speculations of a similar kind, loses much of its force when it is translated into plain language and divested of that abstruse verbiage which has so great a charm for some minds "The mountain looming through a fog," says Lewes, "turns out to be a miserable hut as soon as the fog is scattered, and so the boasted system of Absolute Idealism turns out to be only a play upon words as soon as it is dragged from out the misty terminology in which it is enshrouded" [Lewes' *Biog Hist Philosophy*, 613, ed 1857]

HEIDELBERG CONFESSION. [PROTESTANT CONFESSIONS]

HELIX There is a fragment of a treatise of Hippolytus entitled *Κατὰ Βήρωνος καὶ Ἥλικος*, against Beron and Helix But Fabricius considers that the second proper name is a misreading, and that the true title of the treatise was *Κατὰ Βήρωνος καὶ ἡλικωτῶν αἱρετικῶν*, against Beron and his fellow heretics No heretic of the name of Helix is elsewhere mentioned [BERON]

HELLENIANS A Jewish sect named by Justin Martyr [*Dial c Tryph* clxxx]. They are not mentioned elsewhere By a comparison with other lists of Jewish sects it appears most probable that they are to be identified with the Herodians, and to be considered a political rather than a religious body [JEWISH SECTS]

HELMSTADIAN CONTROVERSY [SYNCRETISTS]

HELVETIC REFORMED CHURCH [SWISS PROTESTANTS]

HELVIDIANS A sect of heretics who denied the perpetual virginity of the Blessed Virgin Mary They took their name from Helvidius, who lived at Rome in the latter part of the fourth century, and was the first who, at that place, had advanced this view. Earlier heretics, who had said that Jesus Christ was the natural son of Joseph and Mary, had of course denied the virginity of our Lord's mother, but until Helvidius no one at Rome who believed our Lord was born of a virgin, had denied that she remained a virgin for the rest of her life Helvidius wrote a book in support of his views, and this was at last answered by St Jerome This refutation, *De perpetua Virginitate Beatæ Mariæ, adversus Helvidium* is assigned from internal evidence to the year 383 Helvidius is said to have been an ignorant and obscure man, "vix primis imbutus litteris," and for a long time St Jerome refused to reply to an adversary so unworthy At length he did so, "ut discat aliquando reticere, qui nunquam didicit loqui" St Jerome speaks very strongly of his illiterate production, and of his obscurity says, "Ego ipse qui contra te scribo, cum in eadem tecum urbe consisto, albus, ut aiunt, aterve sis nescio" Helvidius quoted two Fathers of the Church, Tertullian and Victorinus Petaviensis. It is suggested [Migne, *Patrologiæ Cursus*] that the passages he may have cited from Tertullian as supporting his doctrine were possibly *De velandis Virginibus*, c 6 n 48, or else *De Carne Christi*, c 23, n 164 His other authority was probably martyred in the fourth century very few fragments of his works being extant, and certainly none that could have served Helvidius in this connection Cave calls Helvidius a disciple of Auxentius, and the precursor of Jovinian, and supposes him to have been of the dignity of a presbyter But this last seems unlikely, or St Jerome would hardly have spoken in so marked a manner of his obscurity [Cave's *Hist Lit* 1720, i 278] Gennadius also says that he followed the teaching of Auxentius, an Arian who had intruded himself into the see of Milan, at which place Helvidius was at one time residing, and an imitator of Symmachus, who wrote in defence of idolatry But these points are not mentioned in St. Jerome's book, and are therefore doubtful The book written against the virginity of the Blessed Virgin is not now extant, nor any other writings of Helvidius, except the few passages quoted by St. Jerome for the purpose of refutation

No proceedings of councils seem to have been taken against Helvidius personally, nor is his name mentioned in contemporary conciliar acts. His tenets were condemned at Milan and Thessalonica [ANTIDICOMARIANITES, where see the different places at which the heresy obtained a footing, and references for the theological question]. In the seventh century Hildefonsus, Archbishop of Toledo [died A D 669], wrote a book (which is rather invective than argument) against certain people in Spain who attempted to revive the Helvidian heresy It is entitled *De Virginitate perpetua Sanctæ Mariæ*, and is directed "adversus tres infideles" Hugo de Sancto Victore [died A D 1140] wrote a lengthy work on the same subject, but not, as it seems, with reference to any special reappearance of the heresy in his own time Alfonsus a Castro [A D 1665] compares Helvidius to Ishmael "Oportet ergo ut manus omnium catholicorum contra Elvidium leventur, quia ille manus contra omnes levare tentavit" [*adv Hær* lib x]

Of Helvidius himself we know nothing more than we can gather from St Jerome's treatise His followers were at no time numerous or important, and although at various periods the Antidicomarianite heresy has broken out afresh, it has not since the fourth century had any supporters of sufficient weight to be remembered by name

The following curious verses, relating to the subject of the Blessed Virgin's relatives, have lately been discovered written on the vellum binding of a book in the Cathedral Library at Peterborough —

"Nupserat Anna viris tribus, hoc si forte requiris
Hic manifestatur quo nomine quisque vocatur
Quod Joachim scimus, hanc duxit in ordine primus.
Hanc Cleophas duxit, Salomeque postea nupsit
Nostis nempe piam Joachim genuisse Mariam
Post Joachim sacre Cleophas conjungitur Anne
Filia tunc alia fuit illi dicta Maria
Post Cleopham tandem Salomas sibi junxit eandem
De quo mox aliam concepit ex Anna Mariam
Filia prima datur Joseph, quo virgo regatur
In qua Salvator fit homo, mundique creator
Alphieus medie sociatur nempe Marie
Unde fuit natus, Jacobus minor vocitatus
Tercia Judeo, desponsatur Zebedeo
Hii Jacobum vere, fratremque suum genuere
Johannem justum, viciusque scimus inustum"

HEMERO-BAPTISTS A sect of the Jews, so called from their daily ceremonial ablution, which was used by them as a daily means of spiritual cleansing from sin. They appear to have been a sect of the Pharisees, but are said to have agreed with the Sadducees in denying the Resurrection [Epiphan *Hæres* xvii] This is all the information we possess about the sect, but it is mentioned by Hegesippus [Euseb *Hist Eccl* iv 22], and by Justin Martyr [Justin M *Dial cum Tryph*] In the second of the Clementine Homilies St John the Baptist is spoken of under the name of a Hemero-Baptist [*Hom. Clem* ii 23]; and some modern writers believe that the MENDÆANS, or Christians of St John, are the descendants of this Jewish sect [Mosh *Comment de Reb Chr* 43 Paciandius, *De cultu S Johann Bapt.* dissert ii. cap 7, Rome, 1755]

HENOTICON An edict promulgated by the Emperor Zeno [A D 482], as a formulary for the promotion of unity ['Ενοτης] between the Monophysites and the Church This document is given at length by Evagrius [Evagr *Hist Eccl* iii 14] It was suggested and composed by Acacius, Patriarch of Constantinople, and addressed to the bishops and faithful in Alexandria, Libya, Egypt, and Pentapolis It commanded the reception of the decrees of the first three councils, and the rejection of those of the Council of Chalcedon Although it contains no directly heretical statement, but on the contrary anathematizes the Nestorians and the Eutychians, and all who taught doctrines dividing or confounding the two Natures of Christ, the implied condemnation of a general council by an individual person was in itself on the very boundary of heresy, to say the least, and hence the Henoticon was far from promoting the unity which it professed to desire [MONOPHYSITES]

HENRICIANS[1] This sect of anti sacerdotalists was founded by Henry the Deacon, known otherwise as Henry of Lausanne, at the

[1] In reading the ecclesiastical authors of the eleventh and twelfth centuries the use of the word "Henricians" is to be noted, as being a title not unfrequently given to those who held the opinion of the Emperor Henry IV to the effect that bishops were bound to receive investiture at the hands of the temporal power, an opinion which was declared heretical and excommunicate by more than one pontiff

close of the first quarter of the twelfth century. Henry, who was of Swiss or Italian extraction, had been one of the regular clergy and attached to the renowned Abbey of Clugny About the year A D 1116 he came from Switzerland, and commenced a course of preaching at Le Mans, the capital of Maine Central and Southern France was at this moment in a mood most favourable to receive his teaching, agitated as the country was with the deep discontent inspired by the arrogance of the regular, the godlessness of the secular, clergy At first he did not profess, or at least laid no stress on, the peculiarities of his own dogmatic system, but his preaching wrought marvels on the morality of the almost barbarous populace He was of imposing stature, wore a cropped beard and flowing hair, went barefooted in winter, with a frame so robust as to endure with ease the utmost rigours of the climate, and a voice so powerful that his adversaries compared it to the roar of legions of devils His rude eloquence, coupled with the ascetic life he led, and the manifest sincerity of his enthusiasm, appears to have favourably impressed even Hildebert, the Bishop of Le Mans On Henry's arrival he was received with respect by this prelate, who on his departure to Rome accorded to Henry the free use of the pulpits of his diocese The whole country yielded to his eloquence, and gave themselves up to his direction

Henry dwelt much on two points Although a monk by education, and by profession and practice a rigid ascetic, he was emphatically the apostle of marriage and the uncompromising foe of the clergy He especially undertook the reclamation of the courtezans These unfortunate women flocked to his preaching, and readily obeyed his singular rule He bade them cast into the flames all their adornments, their costly robes, their jewels, and even their long hair Young men of noble families wedded at his bidding these reclaimed harlots, dressed in the vilest rags, purchased, the chroniclers state, at the meanest price (quatuor solidorum), in the face of the day So universal was his influence, that, when in the insolence of popularity he proceeded to arraign the vices of the ecclesiastics not only did the populace desert the churches, but even threatened the persons of the clergy On the return of Hildebert to his see, his flock, instead of meeting him, and advancing to receive his episcopal blessing with rejoicing, met him with the greeting — "We have a father, a bishop, an advocate, far above thee in worship, wisdom, and sanctity" The wise and gentle bishop bore the indignity in silence, but forcing Henry to a public interview, he asked him to recite the Morning Hymn Through ignorance or insolence Henry could not or would not repeat it The populace, though by no means filled with indignation at this spectacle, could not but be gravely affected by it, for, attached as they were to Henry's person, they took no steps to protect him from further discomfiture The bishop declared him a poor and ignorant man, and to mark the contempt with which he inspired him, he took no harsher measure than that of expulsion from his diocese Henry therefore retired into the South of France, and became a disciple of, and fellow-worker with, a heretic who held similar opinions, named Peter de Brueys [PETROBRUSIANS] This is denied on the grounds of the hostility of that heretic for the emblem of the cross, which it was Henry's custom in early times to carry, but the evidence of Peter the Venerable is conclusive to the effect that Henry, whom he terms a "pseudapostolus," was also the "hæres nequitiæ," the inheritor of the wickedness of De Brueys Adopting the heretical tenets of the latter (they were already at one in their morality), he recommenced his heretical ministrations in South-eastern France about the year 1119, and continued to preach there until the death of his coadjutor, which took place about A D 1126

Henry escaped the fate of De Brueys, and retired into Gascony, but, some years afterwards, venturing to enter the diocese of Arles, he was captured by the archbishop and sent a prisoner to Innocent II The Pope, who was opposed to violent measures, himself an exile at Pisa, contented himself with placing him in the care and custody of St Bernard His confinement did not last many years he escaped and returned to Languedoc, where he was protected by Ildefons, Count of St Filler and Toulouse A short period sufficed for the re-establishment of all his ancient influence again the churches grew deserted, and indignities were heaped upon the clergy. He continued unmolested during some years, for the times were busy, and the advocacy of the Second Crusade employed all the resources of the Roman Pontiff At length, Eugenius III despatched Alberic, Cardinal of Ostia, to restore order in heretical Languedoc He implored the assistance of Bernard, in a letter which is the best testimony to the ability and character of the heresiarch "Heresy," says he, "is an antagonist that can only be overthrown by the conquerors of Abelard and Arnold" The indefatigable Bernard acceded to the request, and it is thus that he epitomizes the condition of the country "I have found," he writes, "the churches without people, the people without priests, the priests without respect, the Christians without Christ, God's holy places denied to be holy, the sacraments no longer honoured, the holy days without solemnities" As ever, Bernard was victorious, and shortly afterwards Henry was taken prisoner by the Archbishop of Toulouse, and sent to Rheims, where Eugenius was engaged in presiding at a general council At the intercession of the archbishop his life was spared, but he was cast into prison, where he shortly afterwards died his career thus closing about the year 1149 The sources of information in respect of this sect that have been preserved to us are *Acta Episcoporum Cenomanensium*, in Mabillon's *Analect. Vet* cap 35-6, De Hildebert's Episc S Bernardi's *Epistol.* 241, and Pet. Venerabilis' *Epistola adv Petrobrusianos*

HERACLEONITES. A sect of Gnostics belonging to the second century, and followers of

Heracleon, whom Clement speaks of as "the most distinguished of the school of the Valentinians" [Clem Alex *Strom* iv 9] He seems to have been contemporary with Valentinus, and the date assigned to him by Cave is A D 126 He is mentioned by Irenæus, who speaks of the "Æons of Ptolemy and Heracleon" [Iren *adv Hær* ii 4], by Tertullian [*adv. Valentin* iv], and by Origen in his Commentary on St John's Gospel The treatise "against all heresies" going under the name of Tertullian speaks of him as a heretic of the same class with Ptolemy and Secundus, whose opinions agreed with those of Valentinus but who introduced an original terminology, speaking of a Monad as the original source of all things, of two beings who sprung from that Monad, and of Æons as emanating from those, after which he introduced the whole system of Valentinus [Pseudo-Tertull. *adv. omn Hæres* iv] The few words of Philaster [*Hær* xli] and Augustine [*Hær* xvi] respecting the Heracleonites agree with this statement. Epiphanius identifies his teaching with that of the Marcosians, mentioning especially his theory of Ogdoads [Epiphan *Hæres* xxxvi]

The followers of Heracleon are little spoken of, and were probably identified with the Valentinian stock from which they grew Heracleon himself seems to have exercised much influence upon Christian philosophy by a Commentary on St John's Gospel; some fragments of which are preserved by Origen in his own [Grabe, *Spiceleg.* 85-117] In this he appears to have worked out a Christian trichotomy, and to have adopted a highly mystical system of interpretation. Both Clement of Alexandria and Origen speak of him with considerable respect, the former preserving also, in the passage previously quoted, what seems to be a fragment of a commentary on St Luke But they and all other early heresiologists associate him and his followers with the Valentinian school of Gnostics Prædestinatus speaks of him as teaching his heresy in Sicily, and as flying thence on board ship in the middle of the night when refuted by the Bishop Alexander [Prædest xvi] The story seems doubtful, not being mentioned by any earlier writer

HERESIOLOGISTS Writers on heresies and sects are of three classes. *first*, those, especially among the early Fathers of the Church, who had to oppose the originators and supporters of heresies, or who endeavoured by their writings to convert such as had been misled by them, *secondly*, those who necessarily wrote respecting them when writing general ecclesiastical history, and *thirdly*, those who dealt with the history and principles of particular heresies and sects, or of all which came within their knowledge. All three classes of these writers must be consulted for obtaining a complete acquaintance with heresiology, but for the reader's convenience a catalogue is here given of the principal writers of the third class, to whom the designation at the head of this article more properly belongs

JUSTIN MARTYR [A D 89-163] In his *First Apology* Justin Martyr tells Antoninus Pius, "There is a book against all heresies and sects which we ourselves have written, and which we will give you if you wish to read it" [Just Mart. *Apol* ii p 54, ed 1593] This work is referred to by Eusebius and Theodoret, and Irenæus quotes a work of Justin Martyr against Marcion [Iren *adv Hæres.* iv 14, v 26], which seems to be referred to by Eusebius as if it had been distinct from that on "all heresies" [Euseb *Hist Eccl* iv 2] But neither of these have come down to us

The heretics named by Justin Martyr are as follows —

Simon Magus.	Valentinians
Menander	Basilidians
Marcionites	Saturnilians
Marcians	

IRENÆUS [A D 130-202] The important work of Irenæus, the Apostolic Bishop of Lyons, "against all heresies," is supposed to have been written about the year 185 It is extant only in a Latin version (which is however of very early date) under the title *Adversus Hæreses libri quinque,* but its original Greek title was, "A Refutation and Subversion of Knowledge falsely so called" [Euseb *Hist. Eccl.*], from which it appears to have been written against the Gnostics The Valentinians are, in fact, the heretics against whom Irenæus chiefly argues throughout the work, but he also gives short notices of all the following heretics, in addition to those named by Justin Martyr —

Colorbasians.	Tatianites.
Carpocrates	Encratites
Cerinthians.	Barbeliotes
Ebionites.	Ophites
Nicolaitanes.	Sethians
Cerdonians	Cainites

CLEMENT OF ALEXANDRIA [A D 150-216] notices many heresies in his eight books of *Miscellanies* [Στρωματεῖς], the object of which was to shew what are the principles of the true Gnostic as opposed to the false This work was probably written before the close of the second century, and its accounts of heretics are very valuable, coming as they do from a man of the highest learning among the learned men of Alexandria The following are the heretics named by him —

Simon Magus	Heracleonites
Nicolaitanes	Hermogenes.
Marcion	Encratites
Valentinus	Peratici
Basilides	Hæmatitæ
Carpocrates	Entychites
Epiphanes	Hydroparastatæ.
Prodicus	Julius Cassianus
Ophites	Montanists
Caianistæ	

TERTULLIAN [A D 150-220] wrote voluminous treatises against Marcion, Praxeas, and the Valentinians, and also a refutation from Scripture and tradition of all other heresies which had arisen during the century and a half of Christianity preceding his time, under the title *De Præscriptione Hæreticorum,* which was written about the year 207. There is also a shorter work entitled *Catalogus Hæreticorum,* which has often been attributed to Tertullian, but is probably of rather later date [Oehler's *Corpus Heresiol*, i 271-279] Tertullian names the following heretics in addition to those named by Justin Martyr, but does not mention the Marcians —

Cerdo	Cainites
Lucian	Nicolaitanes
Apelles	Praxeas
Tatian	Hermogenes
Carpocrates	

To these the catalogue of later date going under his name adds—

Ophites.	Cataphrygians
Sethites.	Cataproclians
Ptolemy	Catæschinetans
Secundus	Blastus
Heracleon	Theodotus the Currier
Marcians.	Theodotus the Banker
Colorbasus	Victorinus

HIPPOLYTUS [A D 160-236] was a disciple of Irenæus, and Bishop of Portus or Ostia near Rome A work of his, entitled *Refutatio omnium Hæresium*, was formerly known in a fragmentary form under the name of *Philosophumena*, and attributed to Origen, but it has recently been discovered entire and shewn to be the work of Hippolytus It is largely indebted to the works of Irenæus and St Clement of Alexandria, but also contains much that is original and of great value Hippolytus treats of the following heresies —

Pharisees	Apelles
Sadducees.	Hermogenes
Essenes	Cleomenes
Docetæ	Quartodecimans
Theodotus	Montanists
Melchisedicheans	Noetians
Elchasaites	Callistians
Monoimus	

EPIPHANIUS [A D 303-403] This most voluminous of early heresiologists was the first of the Post-Nicene He was Bishop of Constantia, or Salamis, in the island of Cyprus, from A.D. 367 to A D 403, when he died at not less than one hundred years of age, having written a work against eighty heresies, entitled the *Panarium* or *Arcula*, which was commenced in the year 373, and afterwards added to it an epitome or *Anacephalæosis* In the *Panarium*, which is generally referred to as *Epiphanius adversus Hæreses*, he deals with all heresies known to him at great length, the work occupying 1100 pages in the folio edition Although Epiphanius is a valuable writer, because he goes into details at such length as apparently to exhaust his subject, he must be read with judgment, having evidently been of a credulous disposition, and inclined to exaggeration [Oehler's *Corpus Hæresiol* i. ii. iii]

PHILASTER [circ A D 380] was Bishop of Brescia, and wrote a work, *De Hæresibus*, which was probably quite independent of that of Epiphanius, but which goes very much less into detail respecting them He enumerates 28 before Christ and 128 after Christ [Galland *Bibl Vet Patr* vii. 480 Oehler, *Corpus Hæresiol* i. 2-185]

JEROME [A D 329-420] St Augustine, at the end of his own book on heresies, says that he had heard of a work *De Hæresibus* written by St. Jerome, but that it was not in their library at Hippo This was supposed by Menard to be the *Indiculus de Hæresibus* which he published in 1617, but the latter is not now considered to be the work of St Jerome, and the one referred to by St Augustine is not known to be extant [Oehler, *Corpus Hæresiol* i 283-300]

AUGUSTINE [A D 354 430] A concise account of eighty-eight heresies was written by St. Augustine under the title *Catalogus Hæreseon*, generally referred to as *Augustin adv Hær* It was written at the close of his life for a deacon named Quodvultdeus, and was professedly taken chiefly from the great work of Epiphanius It also bears much resemblance to the work of Philaster, of which however St Augustine speaks slightingly, saying that Philaster was a man of much less learning than Epiphanius. [Oehler, *Corpus Hæresiol* i 189-225]

THEODORET [A.D 393-457] The historian Theodoret, Bishop of Cyrus in Syria, wrote a work against all heresies, known generally by its Latin title *Hæreticarum fabularum Compendium*, about the year 452 It is the most detailed of all early works of the kind next to that of Epiphanius, and is of higher historical value than the latter [Theodoret, *Opp* iv 187, ed. 1642]

PRÆDESTINATUS [circ A D 461] A work under this name, or that of *Prædestinatorum Hæresis*, is extant, the author of which is unknown, but which is supposed to have been written by an African bishop named Primasius It consists of a treatise on ninety heresies, the first eighty-nine occupying less than one-half of the treatise, and the remaining portion being taken up with a refutation of the Predestinarians [Galland *Bibl Vet Patr* x 363. Oehler, *Corpus Hæresiol* i. 229-268]

ANASTASIUS SINAITA [circ A D 561], a Patriarch of Antioch, left a short account or catalogue of heresies in the fourth chapter of his work entitled *Hodegus* [Fabricius, *Bibl Græc.* viii 350, ed 1802]

LEONTIUS OF BYZANTIUM [circ A D 610] wrote a small treatise entitled *De Sectis*, which is very valuable on account of the personal knowledge he possessed respecting sects which were at that period striking off from the Eastern Churches He also wrote separate treatises against the Eutychians and Nestorians [Galland. *Bibl. Vet Patr* xii 623]

TIMOTHEUS PRESBYTER [circ A D 620] of Constantinople, wrote a tract on the manner in which heretics and schismatics are to be received into the Church It contains the names and a very short account of early heretics, and of several Constantinopolitan sects otherwise unknown [Timoth Presb in Combefis *Hist Monothelit* 650]

SOPHRONIUS [circ A D 629], a Patriarch of Jerusalem, compiled a catalogue of heresies in an epistle to Sergius, Patriarch of Constantinople [Fabricius, *Bibl Græc* viii 353, ed 1802]

ISIDORUS HISPALENSIS [A D 570-636] In the

eighth book of St Isidore's *Origines* there are three chapters, the third, fourth, and fifth, in which he gives a succinct catalogue of the heresies down to his own time [Isidor Hispal *Opp* p 64, ed 1617 Oehler, *Corpus Hæresiol* i 303-310]

JOHANNES DAMASCENUS [A D 730], or St John of Damascus, left a catalogue of eighty heresies among his works, but it is compiled from Epiphanius, and contains nothing original except a short notice of the Nestorians and Eutychians

RABANUS MAURUS [A D 847] gives a catalogue of fifty-eight heresies in his work *De Clericorum Institutione*, but it has no original feature about it, and is probably copied from that of St. Isidore [Raban Maur *Opp* vi 32, ed 1626]

EUTHYMIUS ZIGABENUS [circ A D 1118], a monk of Constantinople, wrote a work against all heresies entitled *A Dogmatic Panoply of the Orthodox Faith*, in which there is much valuable matter respecting the early, and early mediæval, Eastern sects The original Greek work still remains in manuscript only in the Bodleian and other great libraries, but it has been several times printed in a Latin version It is also in *Bibl Patr Lugd.* xix 1

ZONARAS [circ A D 1120], in early life commander of the Emperor's body-guard, and afterwards a monk of Mount Athos, refuted several heresies in a tract entitled *Canon in Sanctissimam Deiparam*, which is printed in Cotelerius' *Monumenta Ecclesiæ Græcæ*, iii 465 , and in a less complete form in *Bibl Patr. Lugd* xxiii. 633

HONORIUS [circ. A.D. 1130], a priest of Autun in Burgundy, wrote a *Catalogue of Heresies from the beginning of the world*, which was printed at Basle in the year 1544. [Oehler's *Corpus Hæresiol* i 325-332]

CONSTANTINUS HARMENOPULUS [circ A D 1150] was author of a work entitled *Liber de Sectis Hæreticis*, which was printed at Basle in 1578

NICETAS CHONIATES [A D 1205], historian of the Byzantine Emperors, wrote also a work entitled *Thesaurus Orthodoxæ Fidei sive Panoplia Dogmatica*, of which the fourth book contains an account of forty-four heresies of the first three centuries, and the fifth is against the Arians and Eunomians Only the first five books of the work have ever been printed, and that in a Latin version, but the whole remain in Greek in the Bodleian Library [*Bibl Patr Lugd* xxv 108-180]

LUCAS TUDENSIS [circ A D 1230], wrote a work of much value as regards mediæval sects under the title *Adversus Albigensium Errores* [*Ibid* 188-262]

REINERUS [circ A D 1230] About the same time Reinerus de Saccho, a preaching Friar, wrote a tract of great historical value against the Waldenses, he himself having been formerly one of their number [*Ibid* 262-277]

PILICHDORFF, PETER [circ A D 1250], wrote a somewhat larger work in the same age, *Contra Waldenses*, which also contains a valuable chapter upon the Beghards [*Ibid* 277-310.]

BLASTARES, MATTHEW [circ A D 1330] deals with some of the early heresies in the second chapter of his *Alphabeticum Canonum Syntagma*, which was the basis of Bishop Beveridge's *Synodicon*

PERPINIANO, GUIDO DE [circ A D 1330], was the author of a work entitled *Summa de Hæresibus omnibus, et earum confutationibus*, which was printed at Paris in 1528, and at Cologne in 1631 This is the largest work on heresies that had then been written since the time of Epiphanius, consisting of 228 folio pages, and no other of any importance appeared until the epoch of the Reformation

LUTZENBURGUS, BERNHARDUS [A D 1522] was the first to write a Dictionary of Sects and Heresies in an alphabetical order His work is a small volume of about 270 pages, entitled *Catalogus Hæreticorum*, the latter thirty of which are *de Lutero et Luteranis* in the fourth edition, printed at Cologne in 1529

A'CASTRO, ALPHONSUS [A D. 1534], a Spanish Friar Observant, wrote a folio work of fourteen books, *Adversus omnes Hæreses*, in which he dealt with them under doctrinal headings and not under those of the sects or heretics themselves An edition of 1556 is dedicated to Philip, King of Spain, England, France, and Ireland, and appears from this dedication to have been prepared by A'Castro, as the King's chaplain and director, for his information when dealing with the English "heretics"

HOSIUS, STANISLAUS [A D 1559], Cardinal, and Bishop of Wormia in Poland, published a small work entitled *De origine Hæresium nostri temporis*, in which he dealt chiefly with the Calvinistic, Lutheran, and Unitarian sects of various kinds that had sprung up since the beginning of the Reformation

PRATEOLUS, GABRIEL [A D 1567] The *Elenchus Hæreticorum Omnium* of this writer consists of 519 closely printed quarto pages containing notices of 600 heresies and heretics alphabetically arranged, and preceded by 100 pages of chronological apparatus, and a full index It is a valuable work which gives the cream of all its predecessors, but it is also rather uncritical and very Ultramontane, and thus tends towards exaggeration

SCHLUSSELBURG'S [A D 1597-9] *Hæreticorum Catalogus*, in twelve small but thick volumes, is a bitter and most prolix Lutheran confutation of Anabaptist and Calvinist sects

GRAVINA [A D 1619], a Neapolitan professor of theology, printed two folio volumes entitled *Catholicæ Præscriptiones adversus omnes veteres et nostri temporis Hæreticos* A valuable comparison of the principles of ancient and modern heresies is to be found in vol i pp 606-687

ROSS, ALEXANDER [A D 1658], printed a small volume entitled *Πανσεβεία or a View of all Religions also a discovery of all known heresies in all ages and places*, which has gone through several editions

MALVASIA BONAVENTURA [A.D. 1661] printed a *Catalogus omnium Hæresium et Conciliorum* of no value

ARNOLD'S *Kirchen- und Ketzer-Historie, from New Testament times to the year* 1688, was published in two folio volumes in the year 1699 The accounts of heresies and sects are not so full as in Walch, but those of the mediæval and Reformation periods are very valuable

ITTIGIUS, THOMAS [A D 1690] was the author of a very learned and authoritative dissertation *De Hæresiarchis ævi Apostolici et Apostolico proximi, seu primi et secundi à Christo nato seculi* It was by far the most critical history of the early heretics that had as yet appeared, and has not been entirely superseded by more recent works

DEFOE [A D 1704] is said to have been the compiler of the small work entitled *Dictionarium Sacrum, seu Religiosum* It is of no value.

NEAL [A D 1720], a learned dissenting preacher, wrote a *History of the Puritans or Protestant Nonconformists from the Reformation in* 1517 *to the Revolution in* 1688, in three octavo volumes It is a laborious book, generally accurate, but written with strong prejudices against the Church

PICART [A D 1723], a French engraver, published seven folio volumes entitled *Cerémonies et Coutumes religieuses de tous les peuples du monde* The letterpress was written by J F Bernard and Bruzen de la Martinière It was translated into English, and published with the same magnificent array of copperplates in the years 1731-39 The text is of little value

SIANDA'S [A D 1733] *Lexicon Polemicon,* in two folio, or in three small, volumes, is chiefly occupied with an alphabetical list of heretics, whose history is generally borrowed from Prateolus, and an original refutation added, probably from second-hand resources

PINCHINNAT, BARTHOLOMEW [A D 1736] published a *Dictionnaire des Sectes, Hérésies, Schismes, &c*, in a quarto volume.

BROUGHTON, THOMAS [A D 1737], a Prebendary of Salisbury, was the author or compiler of a work of no modern value in two folio volumes, entitled *Bibliotheca Historica Sacra* Later editions bear the title *An Historical Dictionary of all Religions*

PLUQUET [A D. 1762] A distinguished French Abbé of this name was the author of a very valuable *Dictionnaire des Hérésies, des Erreurs, et des Schismes, &c*, in two volumes, which has been frequently republished, and which was again printed, with additions by L'Abbé Claris, in L'Abbé Migne's *Encyclopédie Théologique*, in the year 1863 The work is largely indebted to Prateolus, but it is the most valuable of all works of the kind that have been published for ordinary readers It is supplemented by a very full account of all Jansenist writers, and by the *Index Expurgatorius*, but is of a Gallican rather than an Ultramontane tone The work is deficient in references

WALCH, CHRISTIAN WILHELM FRANZ [A D 1762] This learned writer produced an invaluable History of Sects and Heresies in eleven octavo volumes under the title *Entwurf einen Vollständigen Historie der Kezereien, Spaltungen und Religionsstreitigkeiten, bis auf die Zeiten der Reformation* It is a great treasury of information, and also of references to original sources of history on the subject

MURRAY [A D 1764], a dissenting preacher at Newcastle, was the author of a *History of Religion* in four octavo volumes He was the writer of the well known *Sermons to Asses and Doctors of Divinity*, and the former work is often, as may be supposed, eccentric and superficial, though written in some parts after careful research

LARDNER [A D 1780] A posthumous work of Dr Lardner's was printed sometime after his death, entitled *The History of the Heretics of the first two centuries after Christ* Having been left in a very unfinished state by Lardner, it was completed with large additions by John Hogg The historical account is supplemented with many quotations in the original, but the disposition of the writer to apologize for all heretics, and to explain away all heresies makes the history itself of little value

ADAMS, HANNAH [A D 1805], compiled (chiefly from Mosheim) an American *View of religions* in one octavo volume

BOGUE and BENNETT'S [A D 1808] *History of Dissenters from the Revolution in* 1688 *to the year* 1808, in four octavo volumes, is the standard history of Dissenters from an extreme dissenting standpoint, and contains much valuable information

ADAM'S [A D 1809] *Religious World Displayed*, in three octavo volumes, contains much useful information respecting the state of English sects early in the nineteenth century Mr Adam was a Scotch Episcopalian clergyman

GREGOIRE [A D 1810], Bishop of Blois, wrote a *Histoire des Sectes Religieuses depuis le commencement du Siècle dernier jusqu'à l'epoque actuelle* A new edition of this, in six octavo volumes, was printed with large additions in 1845 It contains a very full account of all the schools of French Deists, and may be called a religious history of the Revolution

EVANS' [A D 1827] *Sketch of the various Denominations of the Christian World* is a small volume compiled from authorities of no value It is a work of the most flimsy character, yet perhaps the most popular book of its kind The edition of 1841 is the least worthless

BURTON [A D 1829], Regius Professor of Divinity at Oxford, printed his Bampton Lectures for that year under the title of *An Inquiry into the Heresies of the Apostolic Age* This work is of the highest authority, dealing with the history and principles of the Gnostic sects More than 350 out of 600 octavo pages are occupied with elaborate notes, abounding in references to original authorities

CONDER'S [A D 1838], *Analytical and Comparative view of all Religions now Extant*, was written by a popular dissenting minister of some learning

GUYOT'S [A D 1847] *Dictionnaire Universelle des Hérésies*, &c, was printed in a single volume at Lyons, a second edition appearing in 1855

A CYCLOPÆDIA OF ALL DENOMINATIONS [A D 1851], republished in 1870 as *the Religions of the World*, gives an account, from the "Low Church" point of view, of the Jews, the Roman Catholics, the Greek Church, the Church of England, the Presbyterians, Independents, Baptists, &c The book was compiled for the Evangelical Alliance, and in a polemical and homiletic style (by writers of the sects described) rather than with any historical research

MARSDEN'S [A D 1856] *History of Churches and Sects*, republished as a *Dictionary of Churches and Sects*, deals with a few only of the principal ancient and modern sects, and is of rather more authority than the last named work

GARDNER'S *Faiths of the World, a Dictionary of all Religions and Religious Sects*, is an undated work extending to three large and thick volumes, and published about 1865 at Glasgow and in America. It is compiled from Neander's *Church History* and Pluquet's *Dictionnaire des Hérésies*, &c, and is carefully written, though with too great diffuseness, and with a total absence of reference to authorities

SKEAT'S [A D 1869] *History of the Free Churches of England from* 1688 *to* 1851, the second edition of which was printed in 1869, contains many valuable particulars respecting English Dissenters during the last two centuries, and is an useful supplement to Neal's *History of the Puritans*

CURTEIS [A D 1871] The Bampton Lectures for that year, by G H Curteis, Principal of the Lichfield Theological College, are entitled *Dissent in its relation to the Church of England* They comprise an admirable and very trustworthy account of the Independents, the Romanists, the Baptists, the Quakers, the Unitarians, and the Wesleyans

HERETICS The "one faith" [Eph iv 5] was given "once for all" [ἅπαξ, Jude 3] by the Apostles from the momentary Voice of God the Father [Luke iii 22, ix 35], the long continued instruction by word and act of God the Son [John xiv. 25, xvi 33, xx 31], and the abiding inspiration of God the Holy Ghost [John xiv 26, xvi 13, Acts ii 3, 4] The faith thus delivered by the Apostles as the messengers of God was gradually formulated into a few principal propositions (as particular doctrines were successively called in question), by the collected representatives of the Church, until a Standard of Faith was completed in the Nicene Creed, comprising those truths which all hang together in such an unity that one link of the chain cannot be taken away without injury to the whole chain

Heretics are, therefore, those who break the "one faith" by making a selection [αἵρεσις] of some parts of it for acceptance and belief and of others for rejection and disbelief

That heresies would arise in the Church was predicted by our Lord in the parable of the tares which were sown among the wheat, and from His use of the word "enemy" [Matt xiii. 25] He seems to direct us to consider them as originating with that Sower of division who originally separated man from God, and broke up the first human family by the suggestion of crime But Christianity was almost necessarily reacted upon by Judaism, and by the Greek and Oriental philosophy with which it came into contact, and such reaction may be considered as the first sowing of the tares The early forms of opposition to Christianity, therefore, the denial of the facts which lay at the foundation of its principles, soon passed into a perversion of those facts, and this again into misleading interpretations of the principles themselves

All heresy, moreover, may be described as an answer more or less false to the question, "What think ye of Christ, whose Son is He?" for as the germ of the whole faith was contained in its first Divine proclamation from heaven, "Thou art My Beloved Son," so the correlation of all parts of the Creed is such that every form of heresy may be traced to some misbelief respecting the Incarnate Person of the Blessed Trinity The earliest heretics, consequently, after those who actually denied the Incarnation or the Resurrection, were those who endeavoured to depreciate the glory of Christ, by setting themselves up as rival claimants to a Divine mission.

In SIMON MAGUS, MENANDER, and DOSITHEUS, we thus see a type of the earliest heretics as distinguished from the open antagonists of Christianity. Simon Magus, born a Samaritan (as were the other two also), but educated in Egypt, probably in Alexandria, where he became imbued with Oriental philosophy, represented that he was "the great power of God," not denying the Divine Nature of Christ, but claiming for himself a still nearer place to the Godhead, the Father to Samaritans, the Son to Jews, the Holy Ghost to Gentiles, come as the true redeemer of the human race Menander and Dositheus appear in a similar manner to have assumed the character of redeemers, although very little else is known about them Such were, therefore, the very type of the "false Christs" predicted by our Lord, who tried to suppress the religion of the true One by presenting themselves in some similar relation to Christ as that which the Egyptian magicians assumed towards Moses

The next development of heresy is represented by CERINTHUS and the DOCETÆ, who methodized into a pseudo-philosophical system that which in Simon Magus was nothing but a crude, though supernatural, imposture Cerinthus maintained that the Incarnate Son of God was at first a mere human child, brought into being as other children, that when he grew up to manhood, Christ came in the form of a dove and settled on Jesus, to be united to His natural person until the Crucifixion, when the Christ departed and Jesus alone, as a mere natural man, suffered and died To this impious theory the Docetæ added that the body which was crucified was the mere δόκησις, or appearance of a body, a phantom which seemed to suffer and seemed to die, but which had no substantial existence Against this attempt to rationalize a mystery, St. John opposed arguments of more truly reasonable a character, drawn from practical knowledge and experience, "That which was from the beginning, which we have seen with our eyes, which we have looked upon, and our hands have handled . . That which we have seen and heard declare we unto you" [1 John i 1, 3]

The more subtle reaction of Oriental philosophy on Christianity began with the GNOSTICS, of whom Cerinthus was indeed the precursor They began to speculate on the moral phase of religion, and passed on from thence to its doctrine The world is not all good as God is how did evil come there? The explanation of this, and the consequences following from that explanation were their γνῶσις, a knowledge of things Divine which they alone possessed, and which constituted them the true "knowers" of truth, or "Gnostics" But this γνῶσις was a mere adaptation of Christianity to old Persian speculations (little better than the poetical mythology of the Greeks), in which Ormuzd figured as the First Cause of a Kingdom of Light and Good, while Ahriman was the First Cause of a kingdom of Darkness and Evil There was no history in these speculations, but mere imagination, and the Christianity whose history was so recent as almost to belong to that generation was treated as if it had little or no connection with facts, and almost as if it, like the Persian dualism, was an ideal system evolved out of some philosopher's brain Thus the dualistic philosophy and the Christian history were fused into a clumsy amalgam, of which these were the component parts [1] God was never manifested to the world until Christ came [2] Everything material belonging to the kingdom of evil, the material world cannot be a creation of the good God [3] But all created things came into being by a process of emanation from God, those emanations proceeding more directly from Him being nearest to Him in spirituality and goodness, and those emanating indirectly through previous emanations gradually deteriorating until material and evil things came into existence at a vast distance from the "Pleroma," or Fulness of the Divine Nature [4] That Christ was one of the inferior beings, sent into the world to give the true γνῶσις or knowledge of things Divine [5] That He descended on the man Jesus at His baptism, as held by the Docetæ [6] That after death, the soul is absorbed into God, and the body, being material and evil, has no future existence

All these blasphemous theories are plainly part of the chain which Cerinthus and his predecessors began to forge and in the third century they culminated in the heresy of the MANICHÆANS Manes, the originator of this heresy, who claimed to be the Comforter promised by Christ, took up the dualistic notions of his predecessors, and carried to its extremest length their heretical principle that everything material is essentially evil He represented this world as the battlefield of the two opposite kingdoms, and each particular man as an epitome of the world itself, in whom matter and spirit are continually struggling for supremacy On these principles was founded a severe austerity, the object of which was to emancipate the spirit of man from the power of his material body, but which became the root of fanaticism and Antinomianism in subsequent times For there was a singular vitality in Manicheeism, and though apparently suppressed in the fourth century, it crops up in every direction, even in the middle ages, among those numerous anti-sacerdotal sects which sprung from the Paulicians, and which, under cover of professed superiority to Church ordinances, veiled profligacies that made them hateful to Church and State alike

These flagrant and broad lines of heresy were followed by a more subtle class, in which the two natures of Christ as God on the one hand, or as Man on the other, were made the subject of assault, doubt, and misbelief These all grafted themselves on the original fundamental denial that He was anything more than man, a denial that underlay the systems of preceding heresies, and originated with the unbelieving Jews

The SABELLIANS, the earliest of these heretics, built their heresy upon the opinion of PRAXEAS, that "Father, Son, and Holy Ghost" were but three names for one Person, Sabellius originating the more subtle notion that these names indicate three properties or capacities of one Person This rejection of the doctrine of the Trinity was, in reality, the form in which the Divine Nature of our Lord was repudiated, the Word of God being considered to be not a distinct Person in the Godhead, but only one of its properties

The Sabellian heresy failed to account for the historical wonder of Christ's life The SAMOSATANIANS, therefore, followers of Paul, Bishop of Samosata, while still accepting the doctrine of the Trinity only in the Sabellian sense, admitted a certain supernatural connection between God and Christ, maintaining that Jesus was a man only, though miraculously conceived, but that being supernaturally favoured he grew up to a sinless manhood, and then received that property of the Divine Nature called the Word and Wisdom of God in such a manner as to be clothed with it though not being it Thus Christ was represented as a deified man, and as such received a certain amount of worship, but He was not adored as God

Out of such opinions arose those of the ARIANS Their founder, Arius, followed in the track of former heretics, and kept up the succession which is to be traced through Paul of Samosata, Sabellius, Praxeas, the Gnostics, the Docetæ, and Cerinthus, back to the Apostolic age itself But as the last general persecution of Christians was the most severe trial which the Church had to undergo from brute force, so the heresy of Arius was its most severe intellectual trial in those early ages. The substance of the Arian heresy stated in a few words is That the Second Person in the Holy Trinity is not God in the same sense as the First, or in any true sense, for the Second Person is not eternal, and there was, therefore a time when God the Father existed, but the Son of God did not exist. Like all preceding heresies it was thus a consistent part of the enduring opposition which from the first had been made to the Incarnation, that is to the union of *Perfect* God with Perfect man

Subsequent heresies that have arisen in the Church have, to a very large extent, been developed out of Arianism Thus the MACEDONIANS found it a natural consequence of that heresy to deny the Godhead of the Third Person in the Holy Trinity, the NESTORIANS to deny that the Mother of Jesus was the Mother of One who was God as well as man from the time when He began to be incarnate by taking of her substance, the EUTYCHIANS to deny the Incarnation altogether, maintaining that Christ was God alone In a similar manner the Unitarianism and Socinianism of the Reformation period embodied the misbelief of the Arianism of a thousand years' earlier date, and modern Rationalism, as represented by Strauss' or Rénan's *Life of Jesus*, continue the attack upon the great central dogma of Christianity

But our Lord Himself predicted that the tares should grow with the wheat until the harvest, and the race of heretics cannot be expected to become extinct, though the capacity for inventing quite novel heresies seems long since to have been exhausted The truths that were proved and the errors that were confuted twelve or fourteen hundred years ago, have to be proved and refuted over and over again through the ignorance and perverseness of those who are seduced by the pleasures of controversy, and the pages of the present volume bear witness to the multitudinous variety of forms in which a few main lines of heresy can be moulded By providing materials for *comparative heresiology* it will also contribute towards an exhibition of the intellectual weakness which in reality pervades heresy in general, for, in the words of St Jerome, "Hæreses suam ad originem revocasse, refutasse est"

HERMIANS [HERMIONITES]

HERMIONITES [SELEUCIANS]

HERMOGENES In the last of St Paul's writings he records that "all they which are in Asia" had turned away from him, and he particularly specifies Phygellus and Hermogenes [2 Tim i 15] His words do not necessarily convict them of heresy, but Tertullian speaks of them as among those who denied the resurrection of the body [Tertull *de Resurr Carn* xxiv], and Epiphanius classes them with Cerinthus, Ebion, and others, as heretics who denied our Lord's Divine Nature and His miraculous conception [Epiphan *Hæres* li 6] This is all that is known respecting Hermogenes, unless a legend under the name of Abdias is taken into account, which states that he had been a magician, and was converted by St James the Greater [Fabricius, *Cod Apocr* IV i p 517]

HERMOGENIANS A school of very early Christian Materialists who took their name and their tenets from Hermogenes about A D 170

This heretic is known to us almost entirely from a chapter of Hippolytus [*Refut* viii 10], and from Tertullian's tract, *Adversus Hermogenem* Philaster and Augustine name him in their respective articles on Sabellius Irenæus and Epiphanius do not notice him at all Theodoret's summary is probably second-hand [*Hær fab* i 19], but it mentions one particular not given by Hippolytus or Tertullian

Hermogenes asserted in the first place the eternity of a subject-matter out of which the world was made Lardner remarks, "I do not see that Hermogenes argued so much from the impossibility of God's making the world out of nothing, as from the unfitness of it If the world has been made out of nothing, he feared that the evil therein must be ascribed to the will of God, which would have been a reflection on His goodness But matter, out of which the world was made, being inherently evil, he supposed that he thereby vindicated the Divine goodness" [Lardner's *Works*, viii 583, ed 1861] This remark is based upon Tertullian's second chapter, in which Hermogenes is represented as arguing thus The Lord made all things either out of Himself, or out of nothing, or out of something; not out of Himself, for then He would be dissoluble into parts, not out of nothing, for then all things would have been made good, as good as the Maker Himself is good; therefore out of something, coeval with Himself, but in itself faulty This argument proceeds, not on the supposition of a physical impossibility of an act of creation, but on the supposition of an inherency of evil in all matter On which supposition "unfitness" and "impossibility," when used with regard to Almighty God, become synonymous terms

Hippolytus and Theodoret state that Hermogenes held simply the impossibility of a creation out of nothing Tertullian says that the doctrine of an eternal subject-matter was learnt from the Stoics He represents Hermogenes as deserting Christianity for the old philosophy Hippolytus says that Hermogenes unconsciously followed the Platonists

Hermogenes' second argument was this There never was a time when the title of "Dominus" did not belong to God, but that title is relative, it implies the existence of something over which God was Lord, that something was matter. Tertullian denies the major of the syllogism

To the main argument brought against Hermogenes, that by attributing eternity to matter he invested it with the attributes of Deity, and thereby introduced two Gods, he is represented as replying that in his system the prerogative of the Almighty, as the Author of all things, is preserved Tertullian's rejoinder is an attempt to shew that according to Hermogenes' principles matter must be also the author of all things (auctrix omnium) It is not told in what manner and in what terms the distinction between the eternity of matter and the eternity of God was made The course of Tertullian's remarks leads us to think that Hermogenes considered the existence of matter to be a necessary result of the eternal self-existence of God, and matter therefore to be eternal, not in itself as if it were self-existing, but by consequence [1] Such a notion it is true involves greater difficulties than those the theory is intended to remove, but it usually happens that a heresy adopted to remove difficulties only plunges its author into greater difficulties

I This eternal matter was said to be partly corporeal, and partly incorporeal, and we are told that by the incorporeal part was meant its unregulated motion (inconditus motus) [*adv Herm* ch xxxvi] One cannot think that Hermogenes made the absurd assertion that motion *is* a substance, however incorporeal, it may be supposed that he asserted some active principle, styled an incorporeal substance, some principle of nascent life, combined with matter, causing and manifesting itself in motion His homely illustration, mentioned both by Hippolytus and Tertullian, is that of a seething-pot According to Hippolytus, he described the formation of the world as follows —"When matter was continually moving in a rude and disorderly manner, God reduced it into order by the following expedient As He gazed upon matter in a seething condition, like the contents of a pot when a fire is burning underneath, He effected a partial separation And taking one portion from the whole He subdued it, but another portion He allowed to be whirled about in a disorderly manner What was thus subdued is the world, but that other portion remains wild, and is denominated chaotic matter" [Hippol *Refut* viii 10, Clark's *tr*]

Hermogenes' arguments, as has been already noticed, proceed on the assumption that matter is inherently evil, but on this point Tertullian charges him with ambiguity In chapters xii xiii, Tertullian argues on the assumption of that inherent evil, in chapter xxxvii he says that matter is alleged to be neither good nor evil Still, in this case, it was considered to retain "a certain blind force, a degree of inflexibility, owing to which it could not be entirely bent and conformed to the will of the Deity Hence the evils and disorders that afflict the world" [Prof. Jeremie, in *Enc Met* xi 159] The tenet of the inherent evil of matter was doubtless the origin of the wild notion that our Lord in the course of His Ascension deposited His Body in the sun [2] This notion is mentioned by Hippolytus and Theodoret, and is named in a fragment of Clemens Alexandrinus [iv. 49, ed Klotz] The same belief was held by Hermias and Seleucus of Galatia, who were probably disciples of Hermogenes [Philast. lv, August lix SELEUCIANS] The words "in the sun hath He placed his tabernacle" [Ps xix 4, Sept vers] were, Theodoret says, alleged in support of this notion, to which was added that the devil and all demons are to be related into matter

II From this primæval matter Hermogenes maintained that not the body only but also the soul of man was formed "Ex materiæ suggestu" are the words employed to describe this second materialistic tenet [Tert *de Anima*, i] Tertullian here refers to another tract on this special point, *De censu Animæ*, which is not extant, and does not dwell at length upon it in the existing tract *Adversus Hermogenem* We are not told therefore precisely what Hermogenes meant by "anima" Probably he meant only the principle of animal life, derived from the incorporeal substance of his supposed original matter [3] Certainly there is no reason to say that he meant "soul and spirit," as his tenet has been represented In ch xxi. of the treatise *De Anima* Hermogenes is charged with denying the freedom of the will

Both Hippolytus and Tertullian acknowledge the orthodoxy of Hermogenes in other respects The former writes, "He acknowledges, however, that Christ is the Son of God, who created all things, and he confesses that He was born of a virgin and of the Spirit, according to the voice of the gospels " the latter writes, "He does not appear to acknowledge any other Christ as Lord," but goes on to argue that holding Him in a different way, he really makes Him another being

The work of Theophilus of Antioch against "the heresy of Hermogenes" [Euseb *Hist Eccl* iv 24] is lost. Neither is there any record of a special synodical condemnation of Hermogenes [SABELLIANS]

HERNNHUTTERS. [MORAVIANS]

HESYCHASTS [ἡσυχία, *stillness*] A school of Greek Quietists which sprung up among the monks of Mount Athos in the middle of the fourteenth century They were also called Ὀμφαλόψυχοι, or "Umbilicanimi," from the strange mystical opinion which they held that the illumination of his soul was made visible to the monk who practised perfect stillness, by fixing his intent gaze upon the umbilical region of his person The names of the Euchites and the Massalians were also revived as appellations of the Hesychasts by their opponents, and they were called "Palamites," from Palamis their leader

The mysticism of these Greek monks appears to have been founded on that of Dionysius, the author of the "Celestial Hierarchy" and "Mystical Theology," whose works were extensively

[1] Certainly, although Hermogenes considered matter as coeval with the Deity, he nevertheless maintained that the Deity had from all eternity ruled over it [See Mosheim, *de Rebus Christ* ii p 368, Vidal's tr]

[2] From the silence of Tertullian as to this singular opinion Mosheim argues, notwithstanding Theodoret's authority, that the Hermogenes referred to by Clement is not the Hermogenes of Tertullian Hippolytus' testimony settles the point against Mosheim The passage in Clement is from the *Eclogæ ex Prophetis* [See Routh, *Rel Sac* i 378]

[3] Many of the Gnostic sects held man's soul to be twofold, a sensitive and concupiscent soul derived from the soul of the world, and an intelligent and rational soul added by the goodness of the Creator [See Mosheim, *de Rebus Chr ante Const* Vidal's tr ii p 233]

read during the middle ages, and from being uncritically assigned to Dionysius the Areopagite, were considered to possess an almost apostolical authority. The well-known Light theory of Dionysius was adopted by the Hesychasts in the form of these three propositions [1] That God dwells in an eternal Light, and that although His Person is never seen, this Divine Light sometimes becomes visible to His saints on earth, as at the Transfiguration [2] That this Divine Light is the *activity* of God, as distinguished from His Person [3] That it operates in men by illuminating the soul from within, in the case of those who practise intense abstraction and self-renunciation (ἀπάθεια), and that it may become visible to those who possess it. Dionysius had written in his third chapter that prayer "is a chain of light let down from the height of heaven and reaching to earth, and, as we grasp it, first with the one hand and then with the other, we seem to draw it to us, while really we are raised by it to the loftier splendour of the light," and the Hesychast notion seems to have been a perversion of Dionysius' spiritual perception into a sensuous perception

In the year 1337, the Hesychasts were brought into controversy with Barlaam, Abbot of the Basilian monastery of St Saviour's at Constantinople He was a native of Calabria, and to his Western mind the Eastern mysticism was a fanatical heresy He carried on the controversy for four years, his opponent being Gregory Palamas, the intellectual leader of the Hesychasts, who was afterwards Archbishop of Thessalonica A Constantinopolitan Council of 1341 deciding in favour of the Hesychasts, Barlaam returned to the Latin Church and became Bishop of Gieræce in his native country The controversy was afterwards revived by Acindynus, a monk also of Constantinople, who wrote a treatise *De Essentia et Operatione Dei* The principal writer on the opposite side was Nicolas Cabasilas, the then Bishop of Thessalonica, in his *Life of Christ,* in which he put in the background the Light theory and Umbilicanimism of the Hesychasts, and maintained from an intellectual standpoint the principle that there is an incommunicable essence in the Divine Nature, and also a communicable property of that Nature, the latter being the operating power of Christian perfection This theory was applied especially by Cabasilas to the operation of the Sacraments, associating the spiritual life of the Christian with the life-giving Light proceeding from the Person of Christ In doing so he seems to have lost sight of the very questionable, if not heretical, proposition of the Hesychasts respecting the Nature of God, and to have passed onward to such a development of Sacramental theology as that founded on Hooker's well-known statement that Sacraments are an extension of the Incarnation

The Hesychast controversy was but of a few years' duration, closing with the work of Cabasilas, the mystics of Mount Athos being dispersed in the troubles of the waning Empire [Natal Alex. *Hist Eccl* viii 90, ed 1762 Dorner's *Person of Christ*, II i 236, Clark's transl]

HETEROUSIANS A name given to the extreme Arians, who maintained in its broadest form the heresy that the essence of the Second Person of the Blessed Trinity was different from that of the First Person (ἑτερούσιος) The more commonly used name was that of ANOMŒANS.

HETHERINGTONIANS A sect of London Familists, whose distinctive tenet was (like that of the Grindletonians in the North of England) a repudiation of the observance of the Lord's Day Hetherington did penance at Paul's Cross on February 11th, 1627, when Dr Stephen Denison, Rector of St Catharine Cree, preached a sermon, afterwards published under the title of *The White Wolf,* and containing some interesting notices of contemporary Puritanism

HICKSITES The principal section of the American Quakers They are so called from Elias Hicks of Philadelphia, who endeavoured, in the year 1827, to revive what he considered to be the original tenets and practices of George Fox and the earlier members of his sect. This revival, however, is on the Rationalist side rather than the Quietist side of Quakerism For the Hicksites repudiate altogether the doctrines of the Trinity and the Atonement, and their view of the "light within" reduces it to mere natural conscience, by following the dictates of which alone they consider that men will gain salvation The Hicksites are not recognised by the English Quakers, and the older section of the American Quakers consider them to have openly denied the fundamental principles of Christianity. They are, however, by far the most numerous section of the Quakers in America

HIEL Under this name, which means "salvation," some mystical books were published in the latter half of the sixteenth century, by a fanatical Dutch writer whose real name was Hendrik Jansen Translations into German were printed as late as between 1680 and 1690, and English translations of several of them, made in that century, exist in MS in the Bodleian Library, and probably elsewhere Some account of Jansen's writings is given in vol iii of Arnold's *Kirchen- und Ketzer-Historie* He is erroneously identified by Adelung, in his Supplement to Jocher's *Allg Gelehrten-Lexicon,* with Fred Breckling, a voluminous German writer of similar books of mystical fanaticism, who died in 1711 Of the latter a very full account is given in Möller's *Cimbria Literata*

HIERACITES Hierax, the leader of this school, was of Leontium in Egypt, and flourished in the beginning of the fourth century He was confessedly a man of great ability and learning, and of unblameable life His followers were chiefly gathered from the Egyptian monks, who were attracted by his ascetic teaching, but he himself was neither monk nor priest

Hierax is placed by Epiphanius [*Hær.* lxvii] immediately after Manichæus, and some have therefore inferred that he was of the Manichæan school But Epiphanius attributes to him none of the peculiar tenets of that school There is late authority indeed, that of Photius and Peter of Sicily in the ninth century, for calling Hierax a Manichee[1]. This evidence however cannot outweigh the statement of doctrines made by Epiphanius In two particulars, Epiphanius refers the doctrine he names to Origen and Hierax' "allegorical interpretation, his rejection of the resurrection of the body, and of sensual notions of a future life, as also his disapprobation of marriage, and of the use of flesh and wine, point rather to a maintenance of Origenist principles carried out to extremes, than to a Manichæan origin" [Gieseler, *Comp* i p 246] But with regard to the doctrine of the Holy Trinity, Epiphanius expressly states that Hierax did not hold with Origen, that he rather held that the Son is truly begotten of the Father, and that the Holy Ghost proceeds from the Father. Against this testimony to Hierax' orthodoxy in the first article of our faith is the charge of Arius, who, in his letter to Alexander, declaring his own belief in a true generation of the Son, denies several heresies, and among them ὡς Ἱέρακας λύχνον ἀπὸ λύχνου, ἢ ὡς λαμπάδα εἰς δύο [Epiph *Hær* lxix cap 7] The former illustration of fire kindled from fire, however weak, may be used, and was used by Catholic Fathers The illustration of a lamp with two wicks, fed with the same oil, points rather, if it be pressed, to a much later heresy, condemned at the fourth Lateran Council, the heresy which taught that there is a distinct substance or common essence from which the Three Persons of the Trinity derived their being, so that in reality the Trinity became a Quaternity. It cannot be thought, in opposition to Epiphanius' testimony, that Hierax held this tenet The illustration may have been unadvisedly used, or it may have been misrepresented The errors ascribed by Epiphanius to Hierax, stated also by Augustine [*Hær* xlvii] and in Prædestinatus [xlvii] are—

I The denial of the resurrection of the body This, it is said, seems to be borrowed from Origen, and it may be doubted whether it arises from anything more than an assertion of the spiritual body [1 Cor. xv 44]

II The denial of a visible Paradise This also is said to be an error of Origen's Few will now dispute Augustine's dictum, that the argument concerning the place to which God translated Enoch and Elias does not touch Christian faith[2] [*de Peccato Orig.* ii 23]

III The assertion that Melchizedech was the Third Person of the Holy Trinity This is doubtless heretical [MELCHIZEDECHIANS] Hierax supported this notion by appealing to an apocryphal book called *Anabaticon, the Ascension of Isaiah.*

IV The assertion that infants cannot inherit the kingdom of God This was grounded on an argument from the words, that a man is not crowned except he strive lawfully, in which by a fallacy, the state of those who do not strive lawfully is attributed to those whom God has not called to strive at all The error is connected with the hyperascetic errors which follow

V On the ground that Christ requires a higher righteousness than Moses, and that there is no other way in which such higher righteousness can be exhibited than in mortification of the body, Hierax taught that marriage, and the use of meats and wine, were inconsistent with Gospel perfection He wished to admit to Church communion only monks, nuns, and the unmarried The author of Prædestinatus tells that a controversy with Hierax was undertaken by Aphrodisius, Bishop of the Hellespont, of whom nothing is known Hierax lived to the age it is said of ninety years, and strictly observed his own rule His followers do not appear to have formed themselves into a separate sect.

HIERARCHITÆ [HIERACITES]

HIGH CHURCHMEN Those lay and clerical members of the Church of England who exalt the authority of the Church, as being derived from Christ and His Apostles, and give prominence to the sacerdotal aspect of the ministerial office

The name first came into use in the early years of the eighteenth century, a writer of 1705 speaking of it as being then quite novel "By whom," he writes, "this distinction has been set up my narrow sphere of intelligence will not reach to inform me" [*The Distinction of High Church and Low Church, &c*] but the term had been freely used in pamphlets of the preceding year It was at first applied to that party in the Church which, on the accession of Queen Anne, supported the

[1] Fabricius and Beausobre reckon Hierax among Manichees Mosheim, Lardner and Gieseler deny that he was so [See Lardner, *Credib* chap lxiii sec 7]

[2] That the denial of a visible paradise is mentioned as a grave error in Hierax, as it is mentioned also in the case of the Seleucians, shews that much stress was laid on the point in the early Church Irenæus writes [*adv Hær* v 2] "Where, then, was the first man placed? In Paradise, certainly Wherefore, also, the elders who were disciples of the Apostles tell us that those who were translated were transferred to that place (for Paradise has been prepared for righteous men, such as have the Spirit, in which place also Paul the Apostle, when he was caught up, heard words which are unspeakable as regards us in our present condition), and that there shall they who have been translated remain until the consummation, as a prelude to immortality" [Tr in *Ante-Nic Lib*] Here paradise is the paradise of the intermediate state But in the end of the same book, Paradise appears as the earth during the period of the Millennium At the first resurrection of the just, some are admitted to Heaven, some enjoy the delights of Paradise, some possess the beauty of the city [chap xxxvi sect 2, compared with sect 3] The two descriptions harmonize The paradise of the intermediate state was thought to be the original paradise of Adam, still existing on earth, and to be extended over the whole earth at the first resurrection The denial of a visible paradise is thus connected with the rejection of the Millennium, Origen, from whom Hierax learnt that denial, having been the first to reject the Millennium It must be observed that a belief in the Millennium by no means presupposes or requires a belief in a visible earthly paradise now existing, or rather that the true doctrine of the Millennium is only encumbered by the unfounded notion It may well be that the early Fathers were led to their belief in a visible paradise from opposition to the Rabbinical conceits on the subject adopted by the Gnostics [See Harvey's note on *Iren.* v 5, 1, and i 30, 8, vol i p 235, ii p 331 See also Routh, *Reliq Sac* iv p 66]

High Churchmen

direct succession of the Stuarts as of divine right and opposed the settlement of the crown on the Hanoverian dynasty During the Sacheverell disturbances [A D 1709-1713] it acquired a still narrower political sense, and at the end of the last century it had come to be a half political half ecclesiastical nickname for those orthodox clergy (of a rather chilly school of orthodoxy) who discountenanced alike Whiggery, Methodism, and Calvinism Since the revival of theological principles and ritual practices, the term has been generally used to designate those who adopt them, the political meaning of it having entirely passed out of use

It is customary, for the rough-and-ready purposes of popular literature, to fix upon some particular names as the founders of the High Church party, according to the phase of controversy which happens to be uppermost in the popular view, and the particular person of that party who happens to be most prominently associated with it But, in reality, the Christian Church has always had parties within its walls, from the days when orthodox Christians who held a common faith said, "I am of Paul, and I of Apollos, and I of Cephas, and I of Christ" [1 Cor i 12], to the days when they began to be divided into "High" Churchmen and "Low" Churchmen There have always, in fact, been a Petrine and a Pauline school of Christianity, the one magnifying the sacrificial work of the Church under the traditional shadow of the Apostle who especially pointed out Christ's pastoral relation to His people [1 Pet. ii 25], the other magnifying the pastoral work of the Church under the patronage of the Apostle who especially taught its sacerdotal relation to Christ [Heb v —x] These are, however, but the golden and the silver sides of the same "shield of faith," and it is only impatience, intellectual intolerance, and deficiency of love, which have divided into parties those who gazed on different aspects of one truth as if they had looked on two doctrines which were opposed to each other in their essential character, and could not both be truths. It may also be added that it is only the comprehensive bond of true faith which can so hold together even intolerant, impatient, and unloving men, that such parties within an orthodox Church do not wander beyond its periphery and become sects outside of it

The lineage of the two great parties is distinctly traceable in the Church of England during the last three centuries, as may be seen by placing some few of the more conspicuous names at various periods opposite to each other

	High Church	*Low Church*
Reformation Period	Bp Ridley and the Prayer Book Divines, Abp Parker, Abp Bancroft, Hooker	Bp Hooper, Abp Grindal, Bp Jewel, Cartwright, Travers, and the Puritans
Seventeenth Century	Bp Andrewes, Herbert, Abp Laud, Bp Cosin, Abp Sancroft and the Nonjurors, Thorndike, Heylin, Bp Beveridge, Bp Bull, Bp Pearson	Abp Abbot, Abp Williams, Bp Hall, Chillingworth and the Latitudinarians, Abp Tillotson, Bp Burnet
Eighteenth Century	Nelson, South, Dean Stanhope, Bp Butler, Bp Gibson, Bp Wilson Abp Wake, Dr Johnson, Wilkins, Wheatley	Bp Hoadley Abp Secker, H Venn, Romaine, Berridge, Toplady, Lady Huntingdon, J Milner, Cowper, Bp Porteus
Nineteenth Century	Alex Knox, Bp Jebb, Coleridge, Routh, Bp Van Mildert, Joshua Watson, Abp Howley, Bp Phillpotts, Newman, Pusey	Js Milner, Scott, Wilberforce, Simeon, D Wilson, Abp Magee, Abp Sumner, Dean Goode, Lord Shaftesbury

The continuity of these two leading schools in the Church of England having been thus exhibited, the history of the High Church school may be best shewn by a sketch of its course through each of the four periods indicated, from the Reformation epoch, which began in the earlier half of the sixteenth century, to that development of the theological and ritual phases of High Churchmanship which has been so conspicuous in the middle of the nineteenth

I *High Churchmen of the Reformation period* The controversies which reached their climax during the reigns of the Tudors divided Englishmen into three parties, the Mediævalists, who took the authority of Rome as the key of their position, the Puritans, who desired to supplant the ancient theology and ritual of the Church of England by a Calvinistic system of Presbyterianism, and the Reformers, in the exact sense of the word, who endeavoured so to re-form the Church of England as to clear it from mere mediæval and foreign accretions, so to preserve its Catholic position, that it should still remain the true Church of England, and so to adapt its customs to the altered condition of society, that it should continue to be the Church of the people The third of these parties were the High Churchmen of the Reformation, allied with the Roman party, on the one hand, in their anxiety to preserve the Episcopal system, and with the Puritan party, on the other hand, in their determination to get rid of Ultramontanism from our theological and devotional standards

The abiding monuments of this party are the Book of Common Prayer and the Thirty-nine Articles of Religion Both of these were, indeed, modified to a considerable extent through the influence of the Puritans, but even after these changes they continued to represent, in the main, the principles of the High Church Reformers, and attempts to impose an opposite sense upon them have never been permanently successful Another admirable monument of the school is the "Ecclesiastical Polity" of one of its most obscure members, the great Hooker

II *High Churchmen of the seventeenth century.* The controversies of the Reformation period were handed down to the next century, but the Roman party had left the Church of England and formed a sect outside of its borders in the year 1570 [Roman Catholics], while the extreme Puritans were also gradually forming sects of Baptists, Independents, and Presbyterians There still remained, however, a very distinct division of High Churchmen and Low Churchmen, the latter being the parents of the Nonconformists, who were expelled from their benefices because their anti-sacerdotal principles would not allow them to receive holy orders in 1662. [NONCONFORMISTS.]

In the earlier part of the seventeenth century the devotional spirit was very strongly developed among High Churchmen being carried on also, in a remarkable degree, into the next century. This development gave rise to the production of several books of private prayers, in which the theological framework of practical devotion was much more accurately articulated than in the loose and verbose rhetoric which went for prayer among the Puritans. Such were the private devotions of Bishop Andrewes, Archbishop Laud, and Bishop Cosin. From the same cause a ritual movement arose among High Churchmen, who endeavoured, by restoring the Lord's Table to the east end of the chancel, and placing it "altar-wise" instead of "table-wise," to bring about a more reverent recognition of Divine Service as an act of worship towards God, and not a mere act of preaching, and of precatory forms said before the congregation. To the same time may be traced the education of a school of independent theologians such as Bishop Pearson, Bishop Bull, Archbishop Bramhall, Bishop Beveridge, Dean Jackson, Bishop Sanderson, Bishop Barrow, Thorndike, and Hammond.

In this century High Churchmen had to defend the principles of the Reformation against the Puritans and the Roman Catholics at the cost of great sufferings. The life of Archbishop Laud was sacrificed to the Puritans, and a generation later seven bishops were sent to prison for making a stand against those encroachments of Popery which the Nonconformists were abetting under James II. During the Great Rebellion few escaped loss of property, and many were persecuted even to the loss of their lives. It was the same school of Churchmen which furnished the ranks of the Nonjurors—eight bishops, including the Primate and several of those who had been foremost in the defence of the Church during the late reign, with about four hundred of the clergy [Hallam's *Const Hist* iii 148]—among whom were such holy men as Archbishop Sancroft, Bishop Ken, and Kettlewell. [NONJURORS.]

For the restoration of the Prayer Book in 1661, and its preservation from Presbyterian adulteration in 1689, later generations are also indebted to the High Churchmen of the seventeenth century. The Prayer Book Annotations and Commentaries of Andrewes, Cosin, L'Estrange, Sparrow, and Comber, shew how faithful the divines of this century were to the traditions of the Reformation, while Bishop Pearson's Commentary on the Apostles' Creed—a work of the highest theological rank—contributed greatly to the maintenance of orthodoxy when the dangerous errors of Arianism were being revived.

Two great monuments of the practical work originated by the High Church laity and clergy at the end of the seventeenth century still remain in the Societies for Promoting Christian Knowledge at home and for the Propagation of the Gospel abroad.

III. *High Churchmen of the eighteenth century.* The Revolution of 1688, and the following expulsion of the Nonjuring bishops and clergy, placed the most influential positions of the Church of England in the hands of the Latitudinarians, and tended greatly to suppress the school of orthodox theology and earnest devotion which had arisen under the guidance of the divines referred to in the preceding section. A similar result was produced by the cold shade of philosophical scepticism which pervaded society, and by the demoralized condition of the latter under the first two Hanoverian sovereigns. High Churchmanship too generally assumed a political aspect, and always lay under the cloud of disloyalty to the *de facto* sovereigns and of a desire to see them supplanted by the exiled Stuarts, so that "High Churchman" and "Jacobite" became synonymous to the popular mind [Matthew Tindall's *Jacobitism, Perjury, and Popery of High Church Priests*, 1710]. There were, however, many literary men of the party who were never, like Dean Swift and Bishop Sprat, swallowed up in the political whirlpool, and whose works are among the greatest treasures of an ecclesiastical library. Bishop Butler's *Analogy* provided the Church with a keen and nearly irresistible philosophical weapon against the unbelief of the age, while almost equally good service was done for logical minds by Paley's work on the Evidences of Christianity.

Vast accumulations of material for Church history were made in the works of the great canonists, Johnson, Bishop Gibson, and Wilkins, in a work which has commanded as much respect among foreign as among English theologians, the *Origines Ecclesiasticæ* of Bingham, in the *Fasti Ecclesiæ Anglicanæ* of Le Neve, and in the most laborious works of Strype on Reformation History. Among the more distinctly theological works of the party during the eighteenth century are Hickes' *Treatises on the Christian Priesthood and the Episcopal Order*, Wall's great *History of Infant Baptism*, and Waterland's controversial treatises against the Arians of his day. Many valuable works on Holy Scripture were the production of the same school in this century, such as Dean Prideaux's *Connection of the Old and New Testament*, with Shuckford's Continuation, Bishop Lowth's Commentary on Isaiah, and Bishop Horne's Commentary on the Psalms. The Prayer Book was also well illustrated by Wheatley, in a volume which continued to be the standard work on the subject for more than a century.

IV. *High Churchmen of the nineteenth century.* The literary phase of the High Churchmanship of the eighteenth century left its legacy to the nineteenth in the shape of a scholarly class of divines, who held ignorance and ignorant enthusiasm in great abhorrence, and who were very often designated—though often most unjustly as to the latter of the two epithets—"high and dry." They were mostly unobtrusive men, of refined culture, strongly opposed to changes in the Church, and better adapted for filling quiet positions as dignitaries than for keeping pace with the world's progress in good or evil, as leaders in the one or combatants of the other A strong intellectual influence was, however, ripening in the midst of this quiet school, the type of which may be traced in such men as Alexander Knox, Bishop Jebb, Wordsworth, Dr Routh, Bishop Van Mildert, and John Miller [1] It was by such an influence that this "old school" of High Churchmen (best represented perhaps by Dr Routh, President of Magdalen College, who died, when more than ninety-nine years of age, in the year 1854) were training up another generation whose practical work made the name of "High Churchmen" more conspicuous than it had ever been before

THE TRACTARIANS The development of this new school of High Churchmen was, however, the ecclesiastical result of political circumstances in the first instance, rather than of any design founded in ecclesiastical learning

At the time of the Reform Bill agitation, the Reform politicians exhibited great indignation against the clergy on account of the conservative principles which were manifested by their leaders, and especially by the twenty-one bishops whose votes were supposed to have thrown out the Bill in 1831 The course taken is indicated by the well-known admonition of the dictatorial Lord Grey to the bishops "to set their house in order," by frequent appeals of the *Times* newspaper, such as "Will no question occur to the people of England touching my lords the bishops? Will nobody ask what business have they in Parliament at all?" [*Times*, October 10th, 1831], and by the motions which were made in the House of Commons at the time for the expulsion of the bishops from Parliament At the same time, the Dissenters began to organize their discordant sects into a united opposition to the Church. "The whole machinery of popular agitation was put in motion, and it appeared that English Dissent was at last organized for the overthrow of the Church Establishment" [Skeats' *Hist of the Free Churches of Eng* 589] First one, and then (on its failure) another, society was formed to carry on this work of opposition, and no means were left untried for the accomplishment of the unchristian object in view [2] By the assistance of O'Connell and the Roman Catholics, these efforts were so far successful, that in the year 1833 ten of the Irish bishoprics were abolished, and it was in contemplation to suppress others also This course of events created general alarm among the members of the Church of England, and, in the absence of any special organization for its defence, there seemed little prospect of averting further assaults

It was as the religious result of this crisis that the Tractarian party originated The real founder of the party was a distinguished High Church divine, who had long been labouring with his pen towards the accomplishment of that revival which his failing health and early death threw into the hands of others This was Hugh James Rose, editor of the *British Magazine*, and subsequently Professor of Theology at Durham, Principal of King's College, London, and Chaplain to the Archbishop of Canterbury He was consulted in July 1833 by Arthur Perceval, Hurrel Froude of Oriel, and William Palmer of Worcester College, with reference to a movement projected by them for stemming the tide of destruction which seemed to be flowing over the Church, and after a week's conference of this small party at Hadleigh, it was agreed that an united effort should be attempted among High Churchmen in behalf of two points, the maintenance of the doctrine of Apostolical Succession, and the preservation of the Prayer Book from Socinian adulterations When the subsequent intellectual leader of the party, John Henry Newman, returned from his long vacation tour on the Continent, he also took part in the Oriel conferences, and they were occasionally joined in by Keble, whose *Christian Year* had already made him famous as a reviver of devotional Churchmanship The first measure taken in consequence of these consultations was an attempt to form an "Association of Friends of the Church," of which the objects were to be these "[1] To maintain pure and inviolate the doctrines, the services, and the discipline of the Church, that is, to withstand all change which involves the denial and suppression of doctrine, a departure from primitive practice in religious offices, or innovation upon the apostolic prerogatives, order, and commission of bishops, priests, and deacons [2] To afford Churchmen an opportunity of exchanging their sentiments, and co-operating together on a large scale" This plan, however, failed through discouragement by the bishops, and only a few country associations were formed on the principles proposed.

But although no such general agitation was permitted as had been contemplated, the feelings of Churchmen had been thoroughly aroused by the course taken in Parliament and elsewhere, and both clergy and laity spoke out in a manner that shewed how great was then latent strength In February 1834, an address was presented to the Archbishop of Canterbury signed by 7000 clergy, in which anything like reckless change was deprecated, but a promise given of "cheerful co-operation and dutiful support" in any measure that would "tend to revive the discipline of ancient times, to strengthen the connection be-

[1] It is curious to find a correspondence between Dr Doyle, John O'Driscol, Alexander Knox, and Thomas Newenham, published at Dublin in the year 1824, on "A Reunion of the Churches of England and Rome" The last named layman was sanguine on the subject, but Knox considered that there was no ground for expecting that obstacles to reunion would be removed [See also Knox's *Remains*, iii 814, ed 1837]

[2] These Anti-Church Associations were [1] The Protestant Society, [2] The Ecclesiastical Knowledge Society, [3] The Voluntary Church Association, [4] The Religious Freedom Society, [5] The Evangelical Voluntary Church Association, [6] The Anti-Church Association, [7] The Society for the Liberation of Religion from State Patronage and Control None of these seven societies were co existent

tween the bishops, clergy, and people, and to promote the purity, the efficiency, and the unity of the Church" A similar address was signed by 230,000 lay heads of families, declaring their determination to uphold the Church with all their power In May of the same year, King William IV made a birthday speech to the bishops, in which he also declared his firm determination to uphold the Church, and added with emphasis, "I have spoken more strongly than usual, because of unhappy circumstances that have forced themselves upon the observation of all The threats of those who are enemies of the Church make it the more necessary for those who feel their duty to that Church to *speak out* The words which you hear are indeed spoken by my mouth, but they flow from my heart" [Perceval's *Collection of Papers*, 1842, Palmer's *Narrative of Events*, 1843] There was then a general arousing of Churchmen Meetings were held throughout the country to organize for defence of the Church in opposition to those who were seeking its destruction, and when the real strength of Churchmen began to be exhibited in Parliament by the constitutional method of presenting petitions, it was found expedient to delay for the present the contemplated attacks that were to have been made

The plan ultimately adopted by the "Friends of the Church" at Oxford, was that of endeavouring to influence public opinion by the publication of that series of pamphlets on Church History and Doctrine which, soon after its commencement, took the general title of *Tracts for the Times* The first of these was published in 1833, the last, the famous "No 90," in 1841 The writers of them were chiefly Newman, Froude, Pusey, and Isaac Williams The first sixty-six of these publications consisted of extracts from Cosin, Beveridge, Wilson, and Bull, with "Records of the Church," consisting of fragments from the Ante-Nicene Fathers, and a few original tracts on the Church, the Liturgy, and similar subjects The succeeding twenty-four tracts comprised several on a much larger scale, and of a more theological character, including Dr Pusey's large work on Baptism, printed in 1834-5, a catena of authorities on the Apostolic Succession, a similar catena on the Eucharistic Sacrifice, with compact treatises by Keble on Tradition, by Isaac Williams on "Reserve in communicating Religious Knowledge," and by Newman on the Thirty-nine Articles of Religion Several of them have been republished as separate works

The last of these tracts was the most important of all Its object was to shew that the Articles, "the offspring of an uncatholic age are, through God's Providence, to say the least, not uncatholic, and may be subscribed by those who aim at being Catholic in heart and doctrine" This view was in reality (as Dr Pusey shewed when reprinting this tract a quarter of a century afterwards) a necessary result of the theological knowledge which the writers of the tracts and many others of the clergy were now acquiring, and no sober-minded and well-informed person would now dream of contradicting the main point of this assertion, or the line taken in Tract 90 itself But some of the leading tutors at Oxford were not then either sober-minded or well-informed, and four of them, Messrs T T Churton, H B Wilson [1] (one of the writers of *Essays and Reviews*), John Griffiths, afterwards Warden of Wadham, and A C Tait, afterwards Archbishop of Canterbury, having represented in a letter, dated March 8th, 1841, that a mode of interpreting the Articles which was consistent with Catholic belief had a "tendency" to mitigate the differences between Roman and Anglican doctrine, the Tract was condemned by a decree of the Hebdomadal Board, signed by Dr Wynter, the Vice-Chancellor, on March 18th, 1841 This was done in the face of an explanation printed by Newman two days before in a letter to Dr Jelf, and without waiting for a fuller explanation which was then in the press, in which Newman stated that he did consider that "the Thirty-nine Articles *do* contain a condemnation of authoritative teaching of the Church of Rome, upon the very subjects upon which the 'Four Tutors' had alleged that he suggested that they do *not*" The heads of houses refused to grant the respite of twelve hours which Newman had asked for the publication of this explanation, knowing that it would have been impossible for them then to condemn the Tract in the terms in which they did so, "for the ground of the censure was cut away No one can tell how much of the subsequent history of the Church of England might not have been altered had that respite of twelve hours been granted" Dr Pusey adds, "It appears from the letter of John Keble . that the Heads of Houses knew that they were condemning the author of *The Christian Year* as well as Newman" [Pusey's *Pref to Tract* xc ed 1865] The names of these local officials can doubtless be exhumed from old Oxford Calendars, but the names of those whom they condemned are written in the world-wide records of ecclesiastical history, and of a nation's devotional habits

These events ultimately led to the secession of Newman, and some of his more intimate friends and followers, from the Church of England, though he himself did not take that step until the year 1845 In that year a Fellow of Balliol College, named Ward, was censured by a vote of the University for publishing a fanciful volume called *The Ideal of a Christian Church*, an ideal which he and other theorizing members of the party found in their optimist view of the Church of Rome The clique which had censured Newman now endeavoured to include him in the

[1] Mr Wilson, who in this letter censured Newman for explaining Article XXII as not denying all doctrines of Purgatory, was condemned in the Court of Arches for denying Eternal Punishments. The condemnation was reversed by a majority of the Committee of Privy Council, which included another of the Four Tutors, then Bishop of London, but the judge, Dr Lushington, had declared that Wilson "suggested modes by which the Articles subscribed may be evaded"

censure of Ward, but the Proctors prevented this by exercising their right of veto upon the proposition, and were thanked by 554 Members of Convocation for taking this most unusual course[1] The patience of the great High Church leader had, however, been overstretched, his leadership of the party came to a close, and he transferred his acute intellect into the ranks of the Roman Catholic sect, where he was soon—happily, perhaps, for the Church of England—as completely extinguished by authority (though by a different process) as in the University of Oxford

Meanwhile the same party which had driven Newman out of Oxford was lying in wait for Pusey also, and in the year 1843 the Vice-Chancellor, Wynter, suspended him from his office of University Preacher for a sermon on the Holy Eucharist This step did not drive Pusey from Oxford, or from the Church of England, and for more than thirty years afterwards he was conspicuous in both as the most learned English theologian of the age But it considerably accelerated the fashion of "secession" which had set in, and during the next few years some hundreds of recruits were added to the ranks of the Roman Catholic dissenters, the "seceders" consisting chiefly of impressible undergraduates, young ladies, and young ladies' curates This secession acquired a factitious importance in after years, when it was joined by Archdeacon Wilberforce, a very able theologian, Maskell, a Ritual scholar, and Archdeacon Manning (afterwards the schismatical "Archbishop of Westminster"), one of the most gifted preachers of the day Wilberforce died shortly after his secession, and, with the exception of Newman, none of the other seceders were persons of any great theological weight either as a loss to the Church which they left or a gain to the sect which they joined

It might have been expected that the defection of so great a leader as Newman would have broken up the High Church party and stopped the movement which it had begun Instead of this it went on rapidly increasing in numbers and influence, and, in spite of most vigorous opposition from Low Churchmen, statesmen, newspapers, and the thoughtless multitude, it became in a very few years the dominant party in the Church of England This result was owing, in a large degree, to the controversies which were raised on the subject of Baptism and the Holy Eucharist For these controversies a most effective preparation had been made by the "Library of the Fathers" (commenced in the year 1838), which had attracted the attention of the clergy to Patristic Theology, and by Isaac Wilberforce's admirable work on the Incarnation (published in the year 1848), which formulated the ideas of the clergy on the subject of the Sacraments to an extent that can hardly be appreciated by a generation which has received such ideas by inheritance in their already formulated condition

[1] A similar veto was exercised in the case of Bishop Hampden

The *Baptismal Controversy* was brought to a crisis in 1848 by the refusal of Bishop Phillpotts to institute a clergyman named Gorham to a benefice in the diocese of Exeter, to which he had been presented by the Lord Chancellor The litigation which followed turned substantially upon the following three questions, which were placed before Gorham in an examination to which the Bishop of Exeter thought it necessary to subject him before deciding whether or not to admit him for Institution —"*Q* V Does our Church hold, and do you hold, that every infant baptized by a lawful minister, with water, in the Name of the Father, and of the Son, and of the Holy Ghost, is made by God in such Baptism a member of Christ, the child of God, and an inheritor of the Kingdom of Heaven? *Q.* VI Does our Church hold, and do you hold, that such children, by the laver of regeneration in Baptism, are received into the number of the children of God, and heirs of everlasting life? *Q* VII Does our Church hold, and do you hold, that all infants so baptized are born again of water and of the Holy Ghost?" It is only necessary to say respecting the answers made to these questions by the candidate for Institution, that it was to the effect that the benefits of Baptism are suspended until baptized persons shew themselves worthy to receive them, and that the Committee of Privy Council considering that it was not unlawful for a clergyman to hold such an opinion, Gorham was instituted by Archbishop Sumner in the year 1850 It is of more importance to add that the storm of controversy raised by the "Gorham case" so cleared the atmosphere of the clouds by which the subject of Baptismal Regeneration had been obscured, as practically to put an end to all discussion about it, and a later generation wonders how such a discussion could ever have arisen when the language of Holy Scripture and of the Prayer Book is now seen to be so singularly plain and dogmatic

The *Eucharistic Controversy*, raised by the sharply definite teaching of the Tractarians respecting the Real Presence, was of longer duration It was brought before the Courts in the "Denison case," in which the Archdeacon of Taunton was deprived by Archbishop Sumner (sitting at Bath as President of a pro-Diocesan Court) on October 22nd, 1856, for having preached three sermons in Wells Cathedral, in the years 1853 and 1854, in which it was alleged that the Body and Blood of Christ are given to all, without exception, who receive the consecrated Bread and Wine administered in the Holy Communion This was practically a statement that the sacred Substance of the Blessed Sacrament is present in the consecrated elements before they are received by the communicant, and cannot be dissociated from them even by unworthy reception The sentence of deprivation was reversed by the Court of Arches on preliminary technical grounds, and the accuser having appealed against the decision of the Court to the Judicial Committee of the Privy Council, the decision of the Arches Court was confirmed on February 6th, 1858

The question of doctrine did not come before either of the Courts above, and no opinion was expressed upon it by either of them

Ten years later, issue was again joined in behalf of opposite schools of thought respecting the Holy Eucharist by the prosecution of Bennett, Vicar of Frome, by one of his parishioners named Sheppard In this case the clergyman was accused of using language respecting the Blessed Sacrament which expressed the same doctrine of the Real Presence in the Elements as distinguished from the Presence of Christ in the faithful receiver of them, and which also embraced the question of the Eucharistic Sacrifice Sir Robert Phillimore gave judgment in this case on July 23rd, 1870, the substance of his decision on the real point at issue being contained in the following words —"Upon the whole it will appear, I think, from an examination of the Formularies, and from the language of the authorities which I am about to cite, that they were intended to set forth, and do set forth, the doctrine of a real Spiritual Presence in the Holy Eucharist It may be said with truth that on some formularies this doctrine is more doubtfully, or more faintly, expressed than on others, but the result which I have stated is not only the legal inference from the construction of all the formularies, but also especially from those which are in their nature the most important and, as a matter of history, the latest in date Though, indeed, that there is a change in the Holy Elements after consecration, and that they then convey in a divine ineffable way the Body and Blood of Christ, seem necessary inferences from the language of the Communion Service alone

I say that the Objective, Actual, and Real Presence, or the Spiritual Real Presence, a Presence external to the act of the communicant, appears to me to be the doctrine which the Formularies of our Church, duly considered and construed, so as to be harmonious, are intended to maintain" [Phillimore's *Rep of Judgm* 117] This judgment was appealed against, and (although some of the expressions used by the Judge were censured as extra-judicial) it was not altered by the Committee of Privy Council when they gave their more than usually careful decision in 1872 Thus the High Church view of Eucharistic doctrine was declared finally to be that of the Church of England it may be said that the conclusion of the Eucharistic controversy completed the justification of the Tractarian movement, establishing the fact that the main principles on which that movement was founded, those of "the Sacramental system," are as truly Anglican as they are truly Catholic.

THE RITUALISTS The revival of ecclesiastical learning, which was so conspicuous a feature of the Tractarian movement, necessarily made the clergy better acquainted with the Primitive Liturgies and with the ancient Service Books of the Church of England Palmer's *Origines Liturgicæ*, Maskell's *Ancient Liturgy of the Church of England*, and *Monumenta Ritualia Ecclesiæ Anglicanæ*, with Neale's *Tetralogia Liturgica*, laid the foundation for many smaller works on liturgical subjects, and thus spread among the laity, as well as the clergy, a larger amount of information respecting the principles and practice of Divine Service than had been possessed by any modern generation of English Churchmen Contemporary with this revival of liturgical knowledge, there sprung up also a widely diffused taste for ecclesiastical design in the fabric and furniture of churches, a taste which was greatly promoted by the works of Augustus Welby Pugin, and by the formation of the "Cambridge Camden Society" in the year 1839 This study of "Ecclesiology," as the science came to be named, was soon brought to bear upon the restoration of old churches and the construction of new ones, and as men of taste could no longer be contented with such churches as were built in the eighteenth century, so the educated clergy and laity were beginning to revolt against a type of Divine Service in which it was represented almost entirely as intended for the edification of those who took part in it Theological knowledge and an intelligent spirit of devotion were combining to raise a general feeling that there should be more recognition of the fact that Prayer, Praise, and the Holy Eucharist are offered to God, as well as used for the spiritual advantage of man It was out of such circumstances, and under such influences, that what was afterwards called "Ritualism" took its rise

The earliest form in which it was manifested was that of introducing into parish churches customs which recent generations had known only in connection with cathedrals, minsters, and college chapels Instead of the old "parson and clerk duet," carried on with occasional interludes of "Brady and Tate," or even "Sternhold and Hopkins," performed by a few singers in a distant gallery, choral services were established, choirs, analogous to those of cathedrals, being formed, clad in surplices, and placed beside the officiating clergy

The second stage of the Ritualist movement consisted of attempts to follow out with exactness the rubrics of the Prayer Book, when the ritual customs of the existing book were soon found to be supplemented to a large extent by those of the "First Book of Edward VI," the Prayer Book of 1549, to which reference was supposed to be made in the "Ornaments Rubric" prefixed to Morning Prayer This development of ritual was promoted by a work entitled "*Hierurgia Anglicana*, or documents and extracts illustrative of the ritual of the Church in England after the Reformation," which was published in 1848 In the preface to this the editors said, "We take our stand on the ground held by Andrewes, Bancroft, Laud, Wren, Montague, and their fellow confessors, and we claim, with them, for the English Church, the revival of all the vestments and ornaments to which it can be proved she is justly entitled" This principle was fully developed at several churches in London, Oxford, Leeds, and elsewhere, during the next few years, the development of it at St Paul's Church,

Knightsbridge, and the more recent Church of St Barnabas, Pimlico (which had been opened in 1850 for the purpose of carrying it out completely and honestly), leading to litigation which ultimately brought the advocates and the opponents of ritual to issue before the Privy Council in the year 1857 Some portions of the furniture of those churches were considered, by those members of the Privy Council who constituted the tribunal, to be unsanctioned by the existing law, but the principle then contended for by the Ritualists was affirmed by their interpretation of the "Ornaments Rubric," respecting the varying forms of which they decided that "they all obviously mean the same thing, that the same dresses and the same utensils, or articles, which were used under the First Prayer Book of Edward VI may still be used" [Brodrick and Fremantle's *Eccl Rep* 131]

The third stage of the Ritualist movement began to develope itself soon after the "St Barnabas case" had been decided, and was originated by a younger school of clergy and laity on the principle that the ritual standard of "the Ornaments Rubric of the Prayer Book" is the practice of the Church of England in the second year of Edward VI, which is interpreted to be that of pre-Reformation times adapted to the English Prayer Book, and including a much larger amount of ceremonial than that which is actually ordered in the rubric of that book The practical use of such a standard was set forth in a volume entitled "*Directorium Anglicanum*, being a manual of directions for the right celebration of the Holy Communion, for the saying of Matins and Evensong, and for the performance of other rites and ceremonies of the Church, according to ancient uses of the Church of England," edited by the Rev John Purchas and published in the year 1858 A full development of ritual usages on the principle thus indicated was established at St Alban's Church, Holborn, built about 1861, and at a later date at a Brighton Chapel, of which Mr Purchas became incumbent, while at many other churches the ceremonial of Divine Service was raised to a much higher standard than had been contemplated by the elder school of Ritualists There was much, indeed, to provoke opposition in the ritual adopted by this younger school of Ritualists—very inferior in learning to their predecessors—for it was chiefly copied from modern Continental customs, and was mixed up with a sentimentalism about candles and flowers, as well as with an excessive minuteness in regard to postures and gestures, which made it easy to charge the school with trifling and want of manliness Prejudices thus excited, led to the prosecution of Mackonochie, the Vicar of St Alban's, and Purchas, the Incumbent of St James's Chapel, Brighton, and their cases were eventually carried, on appeal, before the Privy Council A surprising want of knowledge respecting ecclesiastical history and ritual on the part of the Privy Councillors, enabled them to condemn such ancient and Catholic customs as the use of the mixed Cup and of Eucharistic lights But the general tendency of the judicial decisions which were given, was—notwithstanding Mackonochie, the Vicar of St. Alban's, and Purchas, the Incumbent of St James's Chapel, Brighton, were both prosecuted, and some of their practices were condemned—to raise the limit to which the ritual of the Prayer Book may lawfully be carried far higher than it was before placed and there was consequently a corresponding movement throughout the country in the direction which the Ritualists had taken, even Bishops resuming that use of copes which had been dropped in the middle of the eighteenth century Thus the danger of a narrow reaction which had been provoked passed away, and a revival of ritual such as kept pace with the revival of devotion and taste received the sanction of authority

In the year 1867, the Visitatorial authority of the Crown was exercised for the appointment of a Royal Commission "to inquire into and report upon differences of practice which had arisen, and varying interpretations which were put upon the rubrics, orders, and directions for regulating the course and conduct of public worship, the administration of the Sacraments, and the other services contained in the Book of Common Prayer." This Commission was also directed to reconstruct the Tables of Lessons used at Morning and Evening Prayer Several reports were made by it, and its reconstructed Lectionary was authorized for use by Parliament and Convocation in the year 1871, but no further action was taken at that time on the subject which it was appointed to investigate

One great work of the High Church party from the Reformation downwards has been that of preserving the substantial catholicity of the Church of England, during the forty years' revival between 1833 and 1873, it was also that of renewing its life and vigour The High Churchmen of the Reformation age saved the Church from becoming Lutheranized or Calvinized, and carefully preserved its continuity with the English Church of preceding ages Those of the seventeenth century restored health to the Church of England when it was being fatally cankered by the blood-poison of Presbyterianism, those of the eighteenth century withstood the dangers in which it was placed by the scepticism that in the end overturned the Church of France, those of the nineteenth century have revived ecclesiastical learning and the devotional spirit, and have carried the influence of the Church home to the hearts of rich and poor in face of difficulties arising from very novel conditions of social, religious, and intellectual life

HINDOOS [BRAHMINS.]

HISTOPEDES A name given to the Eunomians with reference to a strange custom which they are said to have practised, of baptizing persons with the head and breast in the water and the feet upright [ἱστός] in the air [Epiph *Hær* lxxvi *ad fin* Theod. *Hæret fab.* iv 30]

HOADLY There were two branches of the English Latitudinarian School; the one headed by Cudworth, More, and Smith, the other by Wilkins and Tillotson The former was distinguished by its Platonism, which imparted a depth and fervour, not without a strain of mysticism, to a theology which otherwise would have been both shallow and cold, the latter lacking this adjunct, and little addicted to patristic study, found no better guide, in the revulsion from Puritanism, than the foreign Arminian divines Thus, Birch refers the formation of Tillotson's mind first to Chillingworth on the desertion of Puritanism, and then to Episcopius The writings of Episcopius,[1] he says, contributed very much to the forming of some of the greatest divines of our country in the last age, and in particular Archbishop Tillotson himself [*Life of Tillotson*, pp 5, 219]

The leaders of the Platonists for the most part lived and died in colleges The latter school furnished the Latitudinarian political bishops by whom the Church was afflicted in the eighteenth century Of these Hoadly is the most thorough specimen Tillotson was kept at a higher level by some knowledge of the Fathers, and by his intimacy with Barrow and Nelson Hoadly followed out his principles to their legitimate results, and produced what Secker called a Christianity "secundum usum Winton"

Benjamin Hoadly, born 1676, Fellow of Catherine Hall, Cambridge, then Rector of St Peter-le-Poer, London, brought himself into general notice by becoming (as the Nonconformist Calamy writes) a strenuous assertor of our civil and religious rights In a sermon before the Lord Mayor, he represented the public good as the end of the magistrate's office, and asserted the warrantableness of resistance when that end is destroyed Objection[2] being made to his doctrine, he defended himself in *Measures of Obedience to the Civil Magistrate*, which was answered by Atterbury in *Concio ad Clerum*, Lond 1709 That passive obedience has its limits few will now doubt, and it is the hardest problem that can be presented to the mind and conscience of a statesman to fix those limits [DICT *of* THEOL, NONJURORS] Hoadly's error appears to be not of principle but in the application of the principle

The House of Commons thanked him for his zeal and recommended him for promotion Queen Anne did not attend to the recommendation George I made him Bishop of Bangor (he never visited this see), and he was translated afterwards to Hereford, Salisbury, and Winchester in quick succession The last bishopric he held twenty six years [BANGORIAN CONTROVERSY]

Hoadly's doctrine proved to be that which vacates the office of the Church, undermines its constitution, denies the power of its ministry and the efficacy of its sacraments The Church he defined to be "the number of men, whether small or great, dispersed or united, who truly and sincerely are subjects to Jesus Christ alone, as their Lawgiver and Judge, in matters relating to the favour of God and their eternal salvation" [*Sermon on Nature of the Church*] There is not a word of the bands which knit men together in one communion and fellowship, but each man, in isolation, stands in immediate reference (it is not said to his Saviour, but) to his Lawgiver and Judge In this relation of the individual to his Judge it is said that a man's "title to God's favour cannot depend upon his actual being or continuing in any particular method, but upon his real sincerity in the conduct of his conscience" that "the favour of God follows sincerity, considered as such, and consequently equally follows every equal degree of sincerity" [*Preservative against Principles of Nonjurors*] That is, Saul the persecutor, who verily thought he ought to do many things contrary to the Name of Jesus, had an equal title to God's favour with Paul the Apostle

Further, Hoadly argued that, inasmuch as "the Church of Christ is the kingdom of Christ, He Himself is King," that "in this it is implied that He is Himself the sole Lawgiver to His subjects, and Himself the sole Judge of their behaviour, in the affairs of conscience and eternal salvation And in this sense, therefore, His kingdom is not of this world, that He hath left behind Him no visible human authority, no vicegerents, who can be said properly to supply His place, no interpreters upon whom His subjects are absolutely to depend, no judges over the consciences or religion of His people" This passage seems to deny (the Committee of the Lower House of Convocation observed) all authority to the Church, and under pretence of exalting the kingdom of Christ, to leave it without any visible human authority to judge, censure, or punish offenders, in the affairs of conscience and eternal salvation

Hoadly of course denied the existence of a line of rightful bishops "As far as we can judge of things, God's Providence never yet in fact kept up a regular uninterrupted succession of rightful bishops" "It hath not pleased God in His Providence to keep up any proof of the least probability, or moral possibility, of a regular uninterrupted succession" He holds up to scorn and contempt "all trifles and niceties of authoritative benedictions, absolutions, excommunications" "human benedictions, human absolutions, human excommunications have nothing to do with the favour of God" [*Preservative*, fol edit pp 588, 592, 593, 595] In these trifles and niceties are included all exercise of the power of the keys, all ministries of the Word and Sacraments

Let it be sufficient to notice how the Holy Eucharist is dealt with "The phrase of eating

[1] Burnet says of the Cambridge school that "they read Episcopius much" [*Own Times*, i p 188, ed 1724] This was clearly true, writes A Knox, of such as Wilkins and Tillotson, for no writer, I imagine, is more un-Platonic than Episcopius, nor probably did any more contribute to spoil English theology [*Correspondence*, i p 259]

[2] Compton complained of it in the House of Lords, and was told by Burnet that he ought to have been the last man to complain, for if the doctrine were not good he could not be defended for appearing in arms at Northampton [*Life of Calamy*, ii p 40]

Christ's Flesh and drinking His Blood, signifies the duty of believing and digesting His doctrine, and not any benefits accruing from that eating and drinking" "I now give you this Bread, and call it My Body, in order to shew you that you are to take and eat bread in this manner after My death, and to introduce My command to you to do this, to break and eat bread in remembrance of Me and of My Body broken, after it shall be broken, and after I shall be removed from you" "The Bread and Wine are outward and visible signs or marks, ordained by Christ to call to our minds, and to point out to us, the greatest inward and spiritual grace (*i e* favour or mercy) bestowed on man by Almighty God. They call to mind the death of Christ," &c [*Plain Account*]

While Hoadly thus rejected on the one hand all that flows to man through the society of the Church, through her ministers and sacraments, he rejected no less on the other hand those parts of Christian truth which he might have learnt from Leighton, which were soon to form the strength of the Evangelical School [DICT *of* THEOL, EVANGELICALS] Regarding Prayer, the Atonement, Grace, Justification, and kindred topics, his opinions are scarcely discernible from those of modern Unitarians [1] Destitute of the excellencies of the schools and leading men with whom he was connected, which preserved them from the full effects of their Latitudinarian principles, he has shewn to what those principles really lead, to a system, namely, of prayer without fervour, sacraments without grace, clergy without a calling, and a church without cohesion

Such is the natural issue of the rationalizing Christianity introduced by Hales and Chillingworth, aided presently by the Dutch Remonstrants The deterioration of the Arminian divines after the Synod of Dort was rapid Episcopius drew perilously near to Socinianism His form of Arminianism, as embraced by the English Latitudinarians, never possessed the Church's sacramental element, and it had rejected or at least neglected the doctrine of the Atonement which had given an evangelical tone to the teaching of Arminius It set forth Christ as an example rather than as a Saviour In Hoadly, therefore, Arminian Latitudinarianism became a kind of Protestantism within the Church of England, protesting not only against the doctrinal system of Calvin (for which it might be excused), but against all the vital powers and agencies of Apostolical Christianity An alleged sincerity of purpose took the place of faith, revelation was to be brought down to human comprehension, all mysteries were to be excluded All who said that they loved Jesus Christ in sincerity, whatever their creed, whatever their worship, were Christian brethren and (as a necessary consequence of Chillingworth's original dictum) all who held the Scriptures to be the rule of belief and morals were alike members of the Church Many in the Church of England fell into this state of indifferentism. They were not Arminians in a true sense of the word, they were such only because they were not Calvinists When a revival of religion came there was, besides a recurrence to primitive doctrine through the leading of the English Church, a reappearance also of the distinctive tenets of Arminius and Calvin Wesley reinvigorated Arminianism, while a fervent and more spiritual Latitudinarianism (of which Leighton remained the unsurpassable type) joined with distinct Calvinistic tenets, revived in Evangelicalism But the Evangelical School has borne marks of Hoadly throughout its whole course Its doctrine of the Sacraments, particularly of the Holy Eucharist, fell below Calvin's, and is only distinguishable from Hoadly's by greater devotion Hoadly's tenet that a man's title to God's favour cannot depend upon his actual being or continuing in any particular method, which, if it mean anything, means first that there is no Church to which God joins those whom He will save, and then that all sects whatever (the Catholic Church being a sect) are equal, remained theoretically in Evangelicalism, with the practical distinction however that dissenters from the Church of England were commonly looked upon as the more godly

[1] Hoadly defined prayer thus "A calm and undisturbed address to God"

HOBBES Few philosophical writers who have not written directly against Christianity have had a wider influence in promoting scepticism than Thomas Hobbes and yet his philosophy is rather one of politics than of religion

He was the son of a clergyman, was born at Malmesbury on April 5th, 1588, took his degree at Oxford, was private tutor, first to Lord Cavendish, and afterwards to his surviving brother, the Earl of Devonshire, and through his pupils became intimate with Bacon and Lord Herbert of Cherbury During his absence from England under the Long Parliament he also became acquainted at Paris with Descartes In the year 1651 he published his principal work, *The Leviathan*, and shortly afterwards returned to England Having been for a short time mathematical tutor to Charles II (though he had not learned the first rudiments till after his fortieth year) he received a pension of £100 a year at the Restoration, and lived to the great age of ninety-two, dying on December 4th, 1679

Religion received little attention from Hobbes except as a part of government, a matter of police, by means of which the absolute sovereign may be assisted in maintaining order in his kingdom But the whole of his philosophy is pervaded by Materialism, the foundation of which he thus lays in the first chapter of his *Leviathan* "Concerning the thoughts of man I will consider them first singly, and afterwards in a train or dependence upon one another Singly they are every one a representation or appearance of some quality or other accident of a body without us, which is commonly called an object—which object worketh on the eyes, ears, and other parts of a man's body, and by diversity of working, produceth diversity of appearances The original of them all is that which we call 'Sense,' for there is no conception in a man's mind which hath not at first, totally or by parts, been begotten upon the organs of sense The rest are derived from that original" Elsewhere he says, "All the qualities called 'sensible' are, in the object that causeth them, but so many several motions of the matter by which it presseth on our organs diversely Neither in us that are pressed are they anything else but divers motions, for motion produceth nothing but motion" "Conception is a motion in some internal substance of the head"

The Materialism of Hobbes did not develope into Atheism, for he acknowledged the existence of God, and looked upon Pantheism as absurd But he denied the possibility of knowing anything about God beyond the fact of His existence, and as regards the duty owing to Him by man he expressly defines religion as "the fear of an invisible power feigned by the mind or imagined from tales publicly allowed" When such fear is associated with "tales," not "publicly allowed" by the civil authority, he defines it as "superstition."

The principal opponents of Hobbes were Archbishop Bramhall, who printed *The Catching of the Leviathan* in 1658, with the object of shewing that no man who is thoroughly a Hobbeist can be a good Christian, or a good Commonwealth's man, or reconcile himself to himself Lord Clarendon, who wrote *A Brief View of the Dangerous and Pernicious Views to Church and State in Mr Hobbes' book entitled Leviathan*, and Archbishop Tenison, the author of the *Creed of Mr Hobbes Examined* The *Leviathan* has been little read since the age in which it was published, but a new edition of Hobbes' works was edited by Sir William Molesworth in the year 1845. [DICT *of* THEOL, DEISM]

HOFFMANITES [JERUSALEM FRIENDS]

HOMINICOLÆ This is not the name of a sect, but a controversial term of reproach used by the Apollinarians and other heretics towards the orthodox as worshippers of "the Man Christ Jesus"

HOMMES D'INTELLIGENCE. [MEN OF UNDERSTANDING]

HOMOIOUSIANS A name given to the SEMI-ARIANS, who refused to accept the statement of the Nicene Creed that the Son is of one substance with the Father, and maintained instead that He was of a like or similar substance

HOMOOUSIANS The orthodox believers in the doctrine stated in the Nicene Creed, that the Son is "of one substance with the Father."

HOMUNCIONITÆ This name is given by the author of Prædestinatus to those who maintained the opinion that the image of God was to be found in the body and not in the soul of man [Prædest *Hær* lxxvi] St Augustine just mentions the opinion, writing "alia dicit corpus hominis non animam, esse imaginem Dei," but gives no name to those who held it [Aug *Hær* lxxvi]

Philaster confutes at some length an opinion that the body was created before the soul, and that it, and not the soul, was created in the image of God, but neither does he give any name to those who maintained it [Philast *de Hær* xcvii] Epiphanius attributes the same opinion to the Audians [Epiphan *Hær* 1], as does also Theodoret [*Hist Eccl.* iv 10] It has also been attributed to Melito of Sardis and his followers, whose belief respecting the corporeity of God approached Anthropomorphism [ANTHROPOMORPHITES], but there seems no foundation for this beyond the presence of the word "Melitonii" against the opinion in the *Indiculus* which precedes St Augustine's work on heresies, but which is of very doubtful authenticity

It is singular that Prudentius, who wrote his *Apotheosis* about the end of the fourth century, entitles a portion of it "contra Homuncionitas," without saying a word about the opinion referred to in the preceding paragraphs The opinion condemned by him is stated in the lines—

> "Hoc tantum quod verus homo est, at cœlitus illum
> Affirmant non esse Deum, pietate fatentur
> Majestate negant morum pro laude sacratum
> Concelebrant adimunt naturæ summa supernæ"
> [Prudent *Apoth.* 553]

This so plainly refers to the Arians that the title "contra Homusionitas" has sometimes been substituted

HOPKINSIANS A party among the Independents of America, who slightly differ from their sect in general as to their view of Calvinism, but who have never formed themselves into a separate body Their name is taken from Samuel Hopkins, an Independent minister at Newport in Rhode Island, whose *System of Divinity* was published in the year 1803, shortly after his death The principal point in which they differ from ordinary Supralapsarian Calvinists is in denying the imputation of Adam's guilt or of Christ's righteousness They also make a great point of maintaining that holiness consists in disinterested benevolence, and sin in interested selfishness [H Adams' *Dict of Sects*]

HOREBITES A party of the Hussites who took their name from a mountain in Bohemia, to which they gave the Scriptural name of Horeb, and on which they encamped when commencing the war with Germany [BOHEMIANS HUSSITES] A similar party called themselves Taborites, and they were accustomed to name the adjacent German provinces Edom, Moab, Amalek, &c, after the nations who were opposed to the Israelites

HUME The historian Hume [A D 1711 1776] became also known as the founder of a sceptical school of thought which carries into the province of religion the great principle of the Baconian philosophy, that the only way of certainly arriving at truth is by experience This had led Hobbes, the friend of Bacon, to Materialism, and was in no small degree the teaching of Locke, but it was reserved for David Hume to formulate the opinion in such a manner as to bring it to bear directly on Christianity, the key of his position having two fronts, the denial of a First Cause and the denial of miracles Both forms of denial Hume based upon the principle that only that can be received as true which can be proved on the evidence of experience

Hume's theory respecting God may be condensed into two statements [1] That when we argue from the course of nature, and infer a particular intelligent Cause which at first bestowed, and still preserves, order in the universe, we embrace a principle which is both uncertain and useless, because the subject lies entirely beyond the reach of human experience [2] That the idea of God as an infinitely intelligent, wise, and good Being, arises from reflecting on the operations of our own minds, and augmenting those qualities of goodness and wisdom without bound or limit, so that, whatever we esteem good in human nature, we elevate into an attribute of Deity by adding to it an arbitrary idea of infinity

His theory respecting miracles was [1] That there can, by no possibility, be sufficient ground for believing in them Experience, he alleged, is our only guide in reasoning on matters of fact, and even experience is not an infallible guide Thus, when any testimony is presented to us respecting alleged miracles, we must balance it against opposite circumstances which may create doubt, and thus the value of the evidence on one side may be destroyed by that on the other, or by the very nature of the facts alleged when interpreted by evidence so balanced The experience of mankind, he maintained is against the truth of miracles, and we do not know the attributes of God sufficiently to know whether He can or cannot work them, and thus no evidence in proof of their occurrence is possible [2] But he further maintained that no miracle had ever been recorded on historical testimony that was sufficiently good to establish it as a matter of belief The witnesses of a miracle ought, he said, to be of such unquestionable good sense, education, and learning, as to secure us against any mistake on their part. They should also be of such integrity as to raise their evidence beyond suspicions of interestedness or of untruthfulness And, lastly, miracles should be performed so publicly, and under such circumstances of publicity, that imposture should be evidently impossible Of course Hume's conclusion was that the Gospel miracles will not stand the test required by the *à posteriori* argument; but it is the *à priori* argument alone which has any force, as the general opinion of thinkers altogether favours the soundness of the Gospel history

Hume's reasonings had much influence on the scepticism of his time, and have affected later literature to an extent far greater than might be supposed from the obscurity into which his Philosophical Essays have fallen Perhaps this may have arisen from the great perspicuity of his writings, in which he presents a conspicuous contrast to German philosophers [SCEPTICS]

HUMANITARIANS This is a term occasionally used to designate those who believe only in the humanity or human nature of our Lord, rejecting the doctrine of His Divine Nature

HUMANITY, RELIGION OF. [POSITIVISTS]

HUNGARIAN PROTESTANTS An anti-papal party existed in Hungary very long before the Reformation It has been calculated that it contained as many as eighty thousand Waldenses in the earlier part of the fourteenth century The Hussites in the succeeding century were equally numerous, so that it causes no surprise to learn that Lutheran teaching speedily found its way into Hungary. As early as A D 1521, George Szakmary, Archbishop of Gran, ordered a condemnation of Luther's books to be read from the pulpits of all the principal churches, episcopal edicts to the same effect followed [A D 1523-1525] accompanied by a persecution so relentless that the Protestant party was nearly destroyed Political events, however, caused a respite. On the death of Louis II [A D 1526] John Zapolski and Ferdinand I endeavoured to enlist sympathy for their rival claims to the crown by denouncing the Reformers, who continued to grow in numbers and importance, and even ventured to retaliate on the inmates of the religious houses, while the minds of the community were distracted by the civil war Some years later a printing-office was established at Cronstadt by John Honter [A D 1533], for the purpose of disseminating Protestant opinions through the press as well as through the pulpit, and Matthew Devay, "the Luther of Hungary," published a Magyar translation of St. Paul's Epistles, followed in three years' time by the Gospels, and afterwards by the whole New Testament both in Magyar and in the Croatian dialect [A D 1563]. Originally Devay was a Lutheran in his opinions, and as such had signed the Augsburg Confession, but he subsequently changed, and adopted Zwinglian views, especially on the Holy Eucharist This led to a division in the Reformers' camp Five leading cities drew up a protest against the Swiss doctrines known as the "Confessio Pentapolitana" [A D 1549] The common Confession of Faith of the Reformed Hungarians, "Confessio Czengerina," was published at Czenger [A D 1557], containing strong Calvinistic teaching, and based on the Helvetic Confession, which had been printed at Torgau in Prussian Saxony in the previous year The issue of these confessions proves by itself the sway by this time obtained by Protestantism in Hungary Leave to conform to it was demanded and obtained by five free cities in North Hungary, twelve market towns in the county of Zips, a few towns in Lower Hungary, and by the heads of several noble houses [A D 1555] The final abandonment of Lutheranism and open union with the Swiss Calvinists took place A D 1566

In Transylvania, which became an independent kingdom A D 1540, the widow of John Zapolski granted full religious liberty to the Lutherans A D 1557, and to the Calvinistic Protestants a few years later Her successor, John Sigismund, extended this toleration to the Socinians, who, on being driven out of Hungary, settled in great numbers in Transylvania.

HUNTINGDON CONNEXION A sect of Calvinistic Methodists which derives its name from Selina, widow of the ninth Earl of Huntingdon. Its history dates from the year 1748, and is closely connected with that of the "Evangelical" party in the Church of England [LOW CHURCHMEN]

Lady Huntingdon was brought into an early association with the Methodists through the marriage of her husband's sister, Lady Margaret Hastings, to Mr Ingham, one of the Oxford "Religious Society" out of which Methodism took its origin, and one of Wesley's companions on his voyage to Georgia [INGHAMITES] On the separation of Wesley and Whitefield, Lady Huntingdon attached herself closely to the latter, and in 1748 appointed him one of her chaplains, that she might have a claim on his services to preach to her friends at her residence, afterwards Cremorne House, Chelsea, and the next mansion to that of Count Zinzendorf, the founder of the Moravians. Here, and at her house in Park Street, large assemblies of the nobility, including even such men as Lord Bolingbroke, Lord Chesterfield, and Horace Walpole, used to gather to listen to the famous preacher, and under his influence fashionable ladies invited parties for prayer at each others' houses as they had been accustomed to invite parties for cards

The next step taken by Lady Huntingdon was to build chapels in fashionable towns, such as Bath, Clifton, Tunbridge Wells, Brighton, &c, which she kept entirely in her own hands, and provided with clergymen, whom she called her chaplains. This she did on the ground that as a peeress she had a right to employ as many chaplains as she pleased, and that she was entitled to employ them where she pleased To secure a succession of such chaplains of her own way of thinking, she then set up a theological college in an old mansion named Trevecca House, at Talgarth, near Brecon This was opened by herself and George Whitfield on August 24th, 1768, the first principal being Sir Richard Hill's well-known French chaplain, Fletcher, or Jean Guillaume de la Flechère, afterwards Vicar of Madeley Lady Huntingdon required the bishops to ordain as her chaplains, and for her chapels, such candidates for orders as should be sent to them from this college, but this they declined to do, the number of chaplains to an earl, and therefore to a countess, being limited to five by the Act of Parliament 21 Henry VIII c 13, and the kind of duty for which they are intended being ministrations within the domestic chapels of mansions, and not in public chapels like those erected by Lady Huntingdon It was not to be expected, however, that a lady whose ecclesiastical habits had acquired for her the name of Pope Joan would be easily brought to submit to any other discipline than her own, and she therefore continued to tempt clergymen into her chapels by the bribe of a "scarf," the badge of a nobleman's chaplain, which was at that time considered a mark of dignity and social position Thus many "Free Churches," as they would now be called, were set up throughout the country, in which Calvinistic clergymen officiated according to the customs of the Church of England, but entirely without any ecclesiastical authority They were appointed and removed entirely at the pleasure of their patroness, and nothing could be more abject than the submission with which they bowed to "her ladyship's condescension" on every occasion

The extravagant claims of Lady Huntingdon were brought to the test of law in the year 1776 Shortly before that time a large chapel in Spa Fields called the "Pantheon"—intended for the worship of all denominations—had been taken by a company for the purpose of being used as a chapel on the same plan as Lady Huntingdon's, and two clergymen named Jones and Taylor were engaged to officiate in it The Vicar of the parish of St James, Clerkenwell, in which "Northampton Chapel" was situated, at once took proceedings against these two clergymen, and they were prohibited from further ministration, neither they nor the chapel being licensed by the Bishop Lady Huntingdon then bought the chapel, placing there as her "chaplains" Dr. Haweis and Mr Glascott. Proceedings were taken against them with the same result, when it was determined to license the place as a dissenting meeting-house, and two clergymen named Wills and Taylor qualified themselves, under the Toleration Act, as dissenters, for the purpose of taking charge of it From this time many of Lady Huntingdon's chaplains, including Romaine, De Courcy, Venn and Toplady, withdrew from her service, and became distinguished as early members of the Low Church school in the Church of England But the discovery of her sectarian position had not the same effect upon Lady Huntingdon, for when she found that the law of England requires every place of worship to be licensed either for the use of the Church or for the use of dissenters, she gave up all connection with the former, and chose that her chapels should become avowedly those of dissenters rather than yield her authority over them Thus, in the year 1783, a sect was formally established by her, and to provide ministers for some of the vacated chapels six of the young men from Trevecca were "ordained" by the seceding priests at Spa Fields

At Lady Huntingdon's death in 1791, at the age of eighty-four, her chapels were, by her will, bequeathed to Dr Haweis, Mrs Haweis, Lady Ann Erskine, and Mr Lloyd, who formed a trust for the administration of them and of Trevecca College The latter, however, was removed to Cheshunt in Hertfordshire, in the following year, where it was eventually reformed for the education of young men "who are left entirely free in their choice of the denomination of Christians among whom they may prefer to exercise their ministry" The result has been that the college has become a nursery for ministers of the "Congregationalist" or Independent sect, though its numbers have always been very small

The position taken up by Lady Huntingdon's Connexion was that of a "Free Church," in which the Calvinistic aspect that some Divines have discovered in the Church of England should be strongly wrought out in association with the use of the Prayer Book During her lifetime it attained enough popularity to win the jealousy of Wesley, who hated Calvinism, and did not much love a successful rival who could be as imperious a pope as himself Four years after her death, Dr Haweis estimated that her preachers had Sunday congregations amounting in the aggregate to 100,000 people But when the Religious Census was taken in 1851, the Connexion only returned 19,159 members with 101 chapels A large number of its members were absorbed into the Low Church section of the Church of England during the first half of the nineteenth century, and the sect is now very small [Lady Huntingdon's *Life and Times* Gledstane's *Life of Whitfield* Middleton's *Eccl Mem of the First Four Decades of George III*]

HUNTINGTONIANS The followers of an Antinomian preacher known as William Huntington, the "preaching coalheaver," who collected a congregation around him first in a chapel in Margaret Street, Cavendish Square, and then at Providence Chapel in Gray's Inn Lane, London, at the end of the last and the beginning of the present century He made some stir among the Dissenters in London, but did not leave any formally constituted sect behind him

Huntington was the son of a man of some social position named Russel, by the wife of a Kentish labourer named Hunt He was born near Cranbrook in the year 1743, and was brought up as one of his large family by the labourer, whose name he bore for the first thirty or thirty-five years of his life He professed to have changed his name from Hunt to Huntington at his "conversion," writing "with this name I was born again," &c, but he also gives as his reason that being unable or unwilling to pay the parish officers for the maintenance of a bastard son, he made the addition of the two latter syllables to the one by which he was known, on the ground that "if I let my present name stand, I may by that be traced by means of the newspapers" When he became a preacher he always wrote his name "William Huntington, S S," the initials representing his spiritual degree of "Sinner Saved"[1] He worked as a labourer until he found preaching more profitable, but died a wealthy man, having drawn largely upon the pockets of his admirers, and having (after the death of his wife and six infants) married Lady Saunderson, the widow of a Lord Mayor He had been accustomed to rail at the bishops for "rolling their fat carcases about in chariots," but having now a chariot of his own he justified the change to himself and his followers by quoting Acts xxi 15, "And after those days we took up our carriages, and went up to Jerusalem."

This popular preacher of his day seems to have acquired considerable influence by preaching in an exaggerated form the two doctrines of Faith and Indefectible Grace which were made so prominent by the Methodists and the Calvinistic clergy, and by spicing his sermons with coarse humour, such as attracted so many to Spurgeon in a later generation He was strongly, though justly denounced by Rowland Hill, who is said to have shewn his detestation of the man and his works by taking up one of Huntington's volumes with a pair of tongs, and giving it thus to his servant for lighting the kitchen fire But the humour and invective of the gentleman were no match for those of the coalheaver

Huntington contrived to leave twenty volumes in print, but his own portion of them is filled with cant and vulgar wit and they also include whole volumes of letters written to him by his obsequious dupes [Huntington's Works. *Quart Rev* xxiv 462]

HUGUENOTS The origin of this name, which was given in contempt to the Calvinists of France, is uncertain. It is generally thought to be a corruption of the German word *Eidgenossen*, confederates, but it is difficult to see how a German name ever came to be applied to the French Calvinists, who took their beginning from Geneva, not from Augsburg Davila says that they were called Huguenots because their first conventicles in the city of Tours, where their doctrines first gained strength, were in certain cellars near the gate of Count Hugo, which seems a more plausible derivation [Dav *Hist des Guerres Civ* t 1] In public documents they were called Religionaires, or "Ceux de la Religion pretendue Reformée" They were not called Protestants before the seventeenth century

The doctrines of the Reformers, especially as formulated by Calvin, spread widely in France during the reign of Francis I [1515-47] That Prince, while he lent support to the German Protestants, as a means of annoying his rival Charles V, persecuted the Calvinists in his own country It was during his reign that Calvin, having been driven from France published his *Institutio Christianæ Religionis*, expressly as the confession of faith of those who were persecuted in France [Basle, 1553], a work which he republished almost every year with additions and amendments In 1538 he formed a French community in Strasburg, the number of refugees even at that early date being great enough to require organization The persecution grew more severe toward the end of Francis' reign, it was made criminal to aid the new doctrines in any way whatever, and an inquisition was set up, which had the power of hunting out heretics and delivering them over to the ecclesiastical and criminal courts

Under Henry II, the feeble successor of Francis [1547-9], the same double policy was continued The war of the Protestant party, headed by Maurice of Saxony, against the Emperor, broke

[1] It is not unlikely that Huntington borrowed these letters from the "S S" with which Sowers of Sedition were formally branded Leighton was ordered to be so branded in 1630, the "S S" being mentioned in his sentence

out in 1552 Henry agreed to join the Protestants; and the war was made memorable by the French conquest of Metz, which was retained to the kingdom mainly by the skill of the Duke of Guise This was perhaps the greatest public service rendered by the great house of Guise, which at this time became eminent for the talents of its members and for its bitter hostility to the Reformed religion The house of Guise, of French Lorraine, was a branch of the old sovereign house of Lorraine, and in this century became united with the Bourbon branch of the royal family of France The defender of Metz had married a granddaughter of Louis XII His brother, the Cardinal of Lorraine, was not inferior to him in ambition or ability The chief rival of the Guises was the Constable Montmorency, a soldier who had shared the wars of Francis I, but whose harsh and unpopular character little fitted him to dispute the ascendancy of the Guises The religionists were at this time held in contempt as a misguided rabble an accident revealed to the Guises that many men of high rank were among their adherents Some followers of the new faith met together in Paris, where they were attacked by the mob A riot followed, and the whole of them being taken in custody, they were found to have among them a number of the highest rank, including the celebrated Admiral Coligny, the nephew of Montmorency Several of them were condemned and burned under the existing edicts by the alarmed court, and greater powers for the suppression of heresy were demanded from the Parliament of Paris. The King held a bed of justice in 1559, and with apparent candour requested the members of the Parliament to give utterance to their opinions of the new doctrines Two of them incautiously spoke in favour of the Reformers, and were put to death for that reason

Under Francis II [1559-60] these dissensions first began to threaten the peace of the kingdom The power of the Guises was increased by their relation to Mary of Scotland, the new Queen of France, who was their niece On the other hand the Bourbons openly avowed the new doctrines These princes of the blood—the King of Navarre and his brother Louis, Prince of Condé—were however unable to resist the Guises at court The latter had gained a powerful auxiliary in the Queen mother, Catharine of Medici, who had no other motive than to increase her own power by joining the prevailing faction The Guises continued the persecution of the heretics with fanatical fury In every parliament there was established a chamber called the burning chamber (chambre ardente), for the purpose of examining and punishing heretics The estates of those who fled were sold and their children reduced to beggary But notwithstanding this persecution the Reformers would not have thought of rebellion unless they had been countenanced by a prince of the blood They inquired of lawyers and theologians whether they could with a good conscience make war against the Guises and the divines of Germany answered that with the aid of a prince of the blood it would be lawful to do so In 1560 was formed the conspiracy of Amboise for seizing the person of the young king The brave Prince Louis of Condé was chosen to be leader of the enterprise, but his name was kept secret, and a gentleman of Perigord, Jean du Barry, Sieur of Renaudie, was appointed his deputy The plot was betrayed, and about 1200 persons paid with their lives the penalty of being concerned in it. The Guises now desired to establish the Inquisition, but the good Chancellor De l'Hôpital, to avoid the greater evil, obtained the amendment that all cases of heresy should be put into the hands of the bishops, the parliament ceasing to have any jurisdiction therein. This was ordered by the edict of Romorantin [A D 1560], and the civil power was thus superseded

About the same time an assembly of notables was held at Fontainebleau, where Coligny presented a petition for liberty of conscience, which, he said, would ere long be signed by ten thousand persons holding the same faith with himself "And I," replied the Duke of Guise, "will present another, which a hundred thousand men under my orders will sign with their blood" The States-General met at Orleans at the end of the year, and both parties regarded the meeting as a battlefield for the superiority Before the day arrived however the two Bourbon princes were arrested and thrown into prison by the contrivance of the Guises, Condé was condemned to death, and, in order to strike terror into the Religionaires, his execution was fixed for the first day of the meeting, and the scaffold was to be raised in the hall where the sittings were to be held The sudden death of the king saved the life of Condé

On the accession of Charles IX [A D 1560-74] the power of the house of Lorraine seemed to be on the wane They lost the hold on the court which they had through the young Queen Mary, their niece. A long minority ensued, the King being only ten years old, and though the Queen mother got herself appointed regent, yet the King of Navarre was named lieutenant-general of the kingdom The Constable Montmorency, on the other hand, joined himself more closely with the five Guises An edict, known as the Edict of July 1561, freed the Huguenots from the penalty of death, but remitted no other severity, and ordered their ministers to be expelled the kingdom [Davila, t 11] Shortly afterwards a meeting was held, which is known as the Conference of Poissy, at which the two parties entered into theological controversy in a spirit of conciliation, which was only prevented by the Sorbonne from ending in pacification The following year the edict of January granted the Huguenots freedom of worship But their enemies continued to disturb their assemblies Bloody scenes frequently ensued, and the massacre of Vassy in 1562 was the immediate cause of the *First Civil War* The Huguenots made Orleans their headquarters, where a considerable army was gathered The war was marked by petty conflicts, in which both sides behaved with perfidy and cruelty. At the outset the King of Navarre deserted the Huguenots, and formed a union with Guise and Montmorency, which the Huguenots called the Triumvirate Condé advanced on Paris with a small army, but was compelled to retreat, then came the bloody battle of Dreux in Normandy, in which Condé was taken prisoner on one side and Montmorency on the other The Huguenots were defeated, and Guise advanced on Orleans, before the walls of which he was assassinated by a pretended deserter named Poltrot His death inclined both sides to come to terms, and the first religious war was concluded by the peace of Amboise, by which certain cities were assigned in every province for the religious assemblies of the Huguenots This peace was made upon the fatal principle of treating the Huguenots not as part of the general population, to be dealt with under a uniform law, but as a separate community of pacified rebels They had been declared rebels, and it must be admitted that they had behaved as such in calling in the English, to whom they had surrendered several fortified towns

The terms granted by the peace of Amboise were gradually infringed, and in 1567 the Huguenots again had recourse to arms Montmorency was slain at the beginning of the struggle in the indecisive action of St Denis Cruelty and treachery marked this second religious war, which ended in a peace as hollow as the former

The third war was memorable for the death of the great Huguenot leader Condé, who fell in the battle of Jarnac in 1569. Coligny was now the only great leader left on either side of those who had seen the beginning of the troubles, so rapidly fatal were the religious wars to the leaders on both sides But the place of Condé was filled by the illustrious Henry IV, then Prince of Béarn, who joined the Huguenots with three thousand men His presence compensated for the defeat of Coligny at Moncontour, and an advantageous peace was concluded in 1570

Meanwhile the young King of France, as he advanced towards manhood, manifested a disposition singularly cruel, bigoted, and treacherous The Queen mother fostered these qualities, which she shared to the full, and along with him began that system of deceitful blandishments, lavished upon Coligny and the other Huguenot leaders, which were to be the prelude of St Bartholomew Coligny appeared at court, and was loaded with favours A marriage was proposed between Henry of Béarn, now King of Navarre, and the king's sister Margaret For two years the mask was worn The royal marriage was celebrated on the 17th August 1572, and Paris was filled with the principal Huguenot gentry On the evening of the 24th August the festival of St Bartholomew, that crime was enacted, which in magnitude, malice, and success stands unrivalled even in the blood-stained streets of Paris There, and throughout France, vast numbers, calculated by historians at from 30,000 to 100 000, were slaughtered in cold blood, and the aged Coligny was among the number of the victims. The slaughter had been planned with the knowledge and advice of the Pope Clement VIII, and when the news of it arrived, "a Solemn Procession" was "made by the Sovereign Pontiff" to the Church of St Louis, "for the most happy news of the destruction of the Huguenot sect," as is shewn by the official document, of which a copy exists in the Bodleian Library Silver and copper medals were also struck by the Pope, with his head on one side, and a representation of the slaughter on the other, above the latter being the inscription "VGONOTTORVM STRAGES 1572" Medals of a similar kind were also struck at Paris and the national fratricide was treated as if it had been a victory over foreign enemies Yet the blow eventually improved the position of the Huguenots who, shutting themselves up in Rochelle and Montauban, defeated with great slaughter the armies sent against them Another hasty peace was made, and in two years the wretched king ceased to pollute the throne of France

He was succeeded by his brother Henry III [A D 1574-89], in whose reign the relations between the contending factions became still more intricate A body called the Politiques had formed itself, consisting of moderate Catholics, who condemned the excesses of civil war On the other hand, the dependants of the Ultramontane party were formed by Guise into one well united body, which obtained the name of the League This body had its centre in the fanatical populace of Paris, by whom Guise was idolized, and it became evident that they intended to raise him to the throne. Yet the feeble king, after a vain attempt to abide by more moderate counsels, was compelled to become the head of the League, and to lend a sanction to the violent war which was waged by it against Henry of Navarre, the next heir to the throne Guise was all powerful, his army overran the Huguenot part of the country, town after town was taken, and at last resistance was confined to the small but unconquerable kingdom of Navarre Four distinct wars, divided from one another by short, scarcely observed treaties, are enumerated by the historians between St Bartholomew's Day and the accession of Henry IV In 1587 Henry while still King of Navarre, defeated the army of the League at Contros, near Bordeaux The assassination of Guise by the King in 1588 was followed by the assassination of the King by the Duchess of Montpensier, Guise's sister, in the following year, and Henry IV was left heir to a vacant throne

A rival candidate was set up by Mayence, brother of Guise, who now headed the League, in the person of the Cardinal of Bourbon, the only Catholic member of the Bourbon family. Henry now entered on that war for the maintenance of his rights, which was made memorable by the victories of Arques and Tory, and the siege of Paris The capital was reduced to the utmost extremities of famine, and must have yielded but for the generosity of Henry, who allowed convoys of provisions to enter, and women and children to leave the place This enabled the League to hold out until a Spanish force under the great Parma entered the field against Henry, whose cause was then reduced to desperation It was not until, by the advice of Sully, he had embraced the Roman Catholic religion, that he obtained possession of his kingdom in 1593 Five years afterwards he secured to the Huguenots their civil rights by the *Edict of Nantes* which confirmed to them the free exercise of their religion, and gave them equal claims with the Catholics to all offices and dignities. But, according to the old system, this edict, by leaving to them as a security the towns and fortresses which had been ceded to them, afforded them the means of forming a kind of republic within the kingdom, and such a powerful body, established on terms of mistrust towards the government, could not fail to become sooner or later a source of danger to the state

It was the work of Richelieu, in the succeeding reign of Louis XIII, to destroy this territorial independence of the Huguenots The religious war broke out afresh in 1621; and the Huguenots lost the greater part of their strongholds through the treachery or cowardice of the governors Some of them however were still remaining, and among them the important fortified city of Rochelle, when, weary of the war and disunited among themselves, they concluded a peace But while Rochelle remained, the great cardinal saw that his work was imperfect That stronghold, situated on the sea, enabled them to keep open their communications with England, and gave them a meeting-place for their independent representative assemblies The siege of Rochelle was formed, and prosecuted with the utmost vigour by Richelieu in person, the cardinal shewing a genius for war worthy of his political renown. After enduring every extremity, after seeing the English fleet retire without being able to relieve it, Rochelle fell in 1629 The Huguenots were compelled to surrender all their other strongholds, and lay at the mercy of their enemies But the opposition of Richelieu was political, not fanatical. Having broken down their autonomy, which was becoming dangerous to the consolidation of France under the monarchy, the object of his policy, he left the Huguenots undisturbed in their religious freedom, and thus a final settlement seemed to be made of the great struggle which had convulsed France for more than half a century

This settlement was not disturbed by Mazarin, and might have remained for ever, but for the orthodoxy of Louis XIV Not to be "of the King's religion" was an offence in the eyes of that monarch, of his confessors, and of his mistresses, an offence for which civic harmlessness could not atone Louis began to persecute the Huguenots, and in 1681 he deprived them of most of their civil rights. After the death of the moderate Colbert, he was urged still further in the path of persecution by Louvois, Le Jellin, and his confessor, La Chaise the Jesuit. Bodies of dragoons were sent into the South, where the Protestants most abounded, to compel them to abjure their religion The frontiers were strictly guarded to prevent emigration Yet more than half a million of Huguenots made their escape to Holland, Germany, Switzerland, and England Many who remained were forced to renounce their faith Lists of convicts, real or pretended, were sent to the King, who was led to believe that he had nearly extirpated false opinions in France Under this impression he took the fatal step of the *Revocation of the Edict of Nantes*, the great charter of religious liberty, in 1685 But he had still half a million of Protestant subjects, and this unjust and senseless policy deprived the kingdom of a great number of rich and useful subjects, whose wealth and skill found a welcome in foreign countries In the provinces between the Rhone and the Garonne the Protestants continued numerous in spite of emigration, and the mountains of the Cevennes afforded them shelter There the CAMISARDS maintained a resistance for twenty years, and in 1706 compelled the government to come to terms with them

Under Louis XV the rigour of the persecution was relaxed and in 1746 the Protestants began to shew themselves publicly in Languedoc and Dauphiné The court was as fanatical as ever, but public opinion was now set strongly against persecution, and though severe edicts were issued, they could no longer be carried out The horrible fate of John Calas put an end to all active persecution. This unhappy man, on a false accusation of murdering his son for turning Catholic, was condemned in 1762 by the Parliament of Toulouse to be tortured and then broken on the wheel, and this sentence was carried out Voltaire brought the case before the bar of public opinion in his Essay on Toleration, in which he drew attention to the defective state of the criminal law The family of Calas solicited a revision of the trial. Fifty judges re-examined the evidence, and pronounced Calas to have been entirely innocent From that time the Protestants were no longer molested, they were restored to equal rights, but still remained ineligible for public offices

The Revolution gave them back all their rights, and they frequently laid out their concealed treasures in the purchase of public domains Their equality with the Catholics was confirmed by the *Code Napoleon* At the Restoration they manifested a strong attachment to the former government, and though they did not offer any opposition to the new order of things, yet troubles, attended with bloodshed, took place at Nismes and the vicinity, which were however suppressed by the judicious measures of the government After the Revolution of 1830, universal freedom of religion was proclaimed by the Reformed Charter of France, and this principle has prevailed ever since The Protestant Church, in which are included both the Reformed and the Lutheran, is under the control of the State, from which its pastors receive their salaries

The doctrines held by the Huguenots were those of Calvin, their worship was extremely simple, preaching being the principal feature in it The Confession of France was first presented in French in the year 1559, to Francis II at Amboise, "in the behalf of all the godly of the kingdom," again in 1561 at Poissy to Charles IX, and at length was published in Latin in 1566 by the pastors of the French Churches, with a preface to all other evangelical pastors It may be seen in the *Harmonia Confessionum Reformatarum Ecclesiarum*, which was published at Geneva in 1581 [English transl Lond 1842, Hall's ed]

[Davila, *Hist des Guerres Civiles* De Thou, *Historia sui Temporis* Puaux, *Hist de la Reformation Française*, *Memoire de Condé*, *Mem. de Sully* Browning, *Hist of the Huguenots*, 1829 Aignan, *De l'Etat de Protestans en France* Burn, *Hist of the Protestant Refugees* Michelet, *Louis XIV et la Revocation de l'Edit de Nantes* Benoit, *Hist de l'Edit de Nantes* Rulhière, *Sur les Causes de la Revocation de l'Edit de Nantes* Smiles, *The Huguenots in England*]

HUSSITES The Hussites were a party among the Bohemians, who, after the execution of Huss, professed to be his immediate followers, and received from their opponents a name derived from his, although they differed from him in many important points both of doctrine and ritual. As soon as the execution of Huss was known, the nobles of Bohemia met together in the chapel of the Bethlehem, and issued an address, denouncing the deed of the Council of Constance In this Wenceslaus, the king, joined, but the storm of public indignation soon passed beyond his control A large body of Hussites, consisting of more than 30,000 men, met together on the White Mountain, afterwards called Tabor, near Prague, to celebrate the Eucharist in both kinds, under the guidance of two noblemen, Nicholas of Hussinetz, and Ziska The first of these died shortly afterwards, and the latter assumed the command in the war that followed This John of Trocznow, surnamed Ziska, was a nobleman of small means, who had won distinction, and lost an eye in a war between the Prussians and Lithuanians in A D 1410 He was afterwards appointed chamberlain to Wenceslaus, with whom he became a great favourite After the meeting on the White Mountain he led his followers to Prague, where a street tumult kindled the flame of the war which agitated Bohemia for many years During a procession to the Church of St Stephen one of the Hussite priests was struck by a stone thrown from the senate-house, Ziska and his followers broke into the house, and murdered the city judge, and seven of the senators, by *defenestration*, that is, throwing them out of the window, according to the old Bohemian mode of putting criminals to death This act threw Wenceslaus into a fit of passion, of which he died A D 1419

An important distinction now became observable between the Bohemians in general and the Hussites, or followers of Ziska. The latter set on foot a system of iconoclasm, they defaced the altars, seriously injured the churches, overthrew the monuments, and utterly destroyed a Carthusian convent near Prague Bohemia at that time prided herself on her beautiful churches, and the havoc caused by the religious war which followed may be estimated by the fact that she has now only one of earlier date than the introduction of the Jesuits. During this civil warfare, a foreign war was also in progress with the Emperor Sigismund, who laid claim to the crown The national Bohemians or Calixtines, and the Taborite followers of Ziska, united to oppose him, but they held very different opinions The Bohemians, though Catholic, were antipapal, and while they opposed the Emperor, had yet no objection to monarchy in the abstract, much less to their own old constitutional monarchy, the party of Ziska, on the other hand, anticipated the Protestants of the following century, and the seeds of Socialism had been sown among them They appealed to no authority in religious matters except the Scriptures, as interpreted by every man's individual judgment In 1420 they published fourteen articles, of which the following are the most important —

I No other writings of learned men are to be received by the faithful, except those that are contained in the Canon All the rest should be destroyed as the work of Antichrist

II Every student in polite literature, and every graduate therein, is vain and a Gentile, and sins against the gospel of Christ.

III No decrees of the Fathers, no ancient rite or tradition of men, is to be retained, save those which Christ and His apostles have declared in the New Testament, all others are to be abolished as the traditions of Antichrist.

IV Whence it follows that the holy oil, and the consecration of the water in Baptism, and, in fact, the whole ritual of the Church is rejected

V Infants ought not to be baptized with exorcisms, and the use of sponsors is to be discontinued

VI All the office books, vestments, monstrances, chalices, &c, are to be destroyed.

VII. Auricular confession is not to be retained

VIII The stated fasts of the Church, as Lent, Ember-tide, and the vigils, and in like manner the festivals, except the Lord's Day, are not to be considered of obligatory observance.

IX The clergy are not to be allowed, as such, to hold property

To these follow protests against Elevation, Reservation of the Sacrament, Purgatory, Prayers for the Dead, the Invocation of Saints, the erection of images for any purpose whatever

They did not, however, go to the fullest length in their opposition to the received doctrines Some of them, indeed, maintained that the bread and wine in the Eucharist are mere signs, but these were expelled from the community A strange sect, the Adamites, Men of the Free Spirit, who held that, like Adam, they were the sons of God, and went so far as to discard the use of any clothing, alleging his example, were ruthlessly exterminated by Ziska

Upon the death of Wenceslaus, his widow, Sophia, assumed the regency, and occupied the citadel of Prague with those who had espoused the cause of Sigismund Ziska failed to reduce the citadel, and at length a suspension of arms was concluded, during which an appeal might be made to the Emperor Ziska retired to Pilsen, which he fortified, and there proceeded to discipline his forces, in preparation for the conflict he saw was at hand

The commissioners sent to Sigismund could effect no accommodation The national excitement increased, and when the Pope (Martin V) published a crusade against the Bohemians, and the Emperor denounced the ban of the empire against them, they retaliated by a solemn league at Pilsen, in which they rejected him as their king

The war that followed, glorious as it was for the Bohemians, who, though single-handed, and often divided among themselves, more than held their own against all the power of the papacy and the empire combined, exceeded all former wars in horror, and in the disasters that it brought upon all persons concerned in it On the one side, it was held that no faith should be kept with heretics, and on the other that it was a sacred duty to destroy the enemies of God's people In Kuttenberg, a German and Catholic city, no less than 1600 prisoners of war were burned, beheaded, or hanged as heretics, and Ziska retaliated upon priests and monks wherever he could take them His soldiers were for the most part infantry, but he trained some of them to fight from war chariots, the fiery onset of which was a terror to the Germans, while, when the fight was over, they served to strengthen the fortifications of the camp He was soon forced by a movement of the royal troops to evacuate Pilsen, whence he betook himself to a mountain in the district of Bechin, which his followers named Tabor, and from it derived their distinctive name of Taborites It was a hill almost encircled by a river and a torrent. On the exposed side he formed an artificial trench, and within a triple line of fortifications.

In the first campaign [A D 1420] Sigismund advanced as far as Prague, and went through the ceremony of his coronation in the castle, granting at the same time general liberty of conscience, but the constant assaults of Ziska forced him to beat a retreat, which soon became a flight, and was followed by a signal defeat in the battle of Wyschebrad It was in this campaign that Ziska lost his remaining eye by an arrow-shot, but his total blindness did not break off his career of victory. It was his custom to take his stand in the centre of his army on some elevated position, surrounded by his officers, they reported to him the state of affairs, and he issued his orders to them accordingly In the next campaign another invasion was made, the Germans penetrated as far as Saaz, but the approach of Ziska threw them into a panic, and in the flight that followed they suffered terrible slaughter.

Nor did they fare the better in the following year, A.D 1422 Sigismund advanced into Moravia with a Hungarian force, but was utterly routed in the battle of Deutchbrod

A ray of hope was afforded to the Emperor by a quarrel between Ziska and the people of Prague, headed by the nobles, to whom his exactions and sacrilegious excesses had given great dissatisfaction Ziska fled some distance to the mountains, in which his pursuers became entangled, and were routed with the loss of 3000 men. He fired Cuthna, with the fugitives that were in it, and laid siege to Prague, but a reconciliation was effected by the friendly intervention of John Rochezana, afterwards archbishop. Sigismund now tried to gain over Ziska. He offered him the government of Bohemia, the command of the armies, and a yearly tribute, if he would acknowledge the Emperor as king of Bohemia But these negotiations were broken off by the death of Ziska from the plague, before the town of Prebislana, which he was besieging After his death his followers were divided. Many submitted to the leadership of his favourite officer, Procopius, a priest, surnamed the elder to distinguish him from another of the same name, but many refused to acknowledge any successor to their great captain, and, in their sorrow for his loss, styled themselves "orphans" These, however, although governed in the main by councils of war, were always ready to march with the followers of Procopius against their common enemies, and consequently the Taborites continued as formidable as ever.

A new campaign was commenced by a plundering foray into Moravia and Silesia, and another crusade was preached by the Pope against these irreclaimable Bohemians, who had become as great an object of terror as the Turks themselves to the Empire. Three large armies invaded Bohemia, composed of Saxons, Franconians, and Rhinelanders—200,000 in all. But the mere rumour of the enemy's approach served to put them to a shameful flight, with the abandonment of all their treasures and munitions of war in 1427 The Bohemians now determined to retaliate They assembled together at the White Mountain, whence they broke into the enemy's country on every side, plundering and destroying, and their conduct may be estimated by the fact that they took for their rule of warfare the invasion of Canaan by the Israelites

Again Sigismund attempted to conciliate his opponents, and at least to detach the national Bohemians or Calixtines from the Taborites. Each party was invited to send commissioners to the Council of Basle, where their grievances might be discussed In the debate upon their demands Procopius distinguished himself by his eloquence and by the firmness with which he maintained his views, but the Council would concede nothing A reconciliation was afterwards effected with the Calixtines, chiefly by the labours of Æneas Sylvius, who obtained the concession that the cup should be allowed to the laity. But the requirements of Procopius and his Taborites were far more extensive, and they refused to be bound by this arrangement Another invasion of the country proved as unsuccessful as the former, and the victory of Taas was the most complete one gained during the war Meanwhile the national Bohemians, who had been won over by Æneas Sylvius, determined to put an end to this exhausting strife, and turned against the Taborites The nobles and burghers met in Diet, and chose Alexius of Wzestiof as chief of the state, an office that was meant to be annual, and a civil war followed Procopius, the elder, was besieging Pilsen, when he heard of the failure of his younger namesake to maintain himself at Prague against the new governor Upon this he raised the siege and marched to Prague. He was met at Bochmischgrod, in the neighbourhood of the city, and after an obstinate engagement was himself slain, whilst his followers were exterminated Tabor itself surrendered, and shortly afterwards the authority of Sigismund was acknowledged throughout the kingdom

As a political party and military power the Hussites had now ceased to exist, but as a religious body they may be said to have been represented to later ages by the BOHEMIAN BRETHREN

HUTCHINSONIANS A school of divines which sprung up in the early part of the eighteenth century, whose leading principle was that the key to all scientific and philosophical truth is to be found in the Holy Scriptures

John Hutchinson, the founder of this school, was a self-educated Yorkshireman, born at Spennythorn in 1674, and for about twenty years, between the age of twenty and forty, steward in the households of Mr Bathurst, Lord Scarborough, and the Duke of Somerset The latter obtained him a sinecure office as purveyor of the royal stables, worth about £200 a year, and this he retained until his death in the year 1737. Hutchinson was an ingenious mechanic, attained some knowledge of Hebrew, and had an empirical acquaintance with natural science After he obtained his sinecure, he became a voluminous writer, and his collected works, republished in 1748 and 1749, fill twelve octavo volumes, the whole of them having been printed during the last thirteen years of his life

The philosophy of Hutchinson is chiefly contained in his *Moses' Principia*, *Power Essential and Mechanical, Glory or Gravity*, and *Glory Mechanical, or the Agent of Nature, and Manner of their Agency explained* He supposes the air to exist in three conditions, fire, light, and spirit, pure fire forming the life and motion-imparting body of the sun, pure light its surrounding medium, and a commixture of light and spirit constituting the atmosphere in which the earth is placed Beyond the earth, onward to the periphery of the solar system, he imagined the atmosphere to become more and more dense, and as it recedes in distance from the sun, to be less and less capable of that motion which the heat of the sun imparts until at the verge of the solar system, he found the "outer darkness" and "blackness of darkness" of the Scriptures In his *Moses' Sine Principio*, and elsewhere, he suggests that Fire, Light, and Spirit, the three principal agents in nature, are three conditions of one substance, in which he seems to have had a dim foresight of the modern scientific dogma of the "correlation of forces" But the philosophy of Hutchinson oscillated dangerously towards the heresies of Sabellius and the Tritheists when he made these three conditions of one substance explanatory of the doctrine of the Holy Trinity Jones of Nayland expresses this opinion in the words "Nature shews us these three agents in the world, on which all natural life and motion depend, and these three are used in the Scripture to signify to us the three supreme *powers* of the Godhead in the administration of the spiritual world" [Jones' *Life of Bp Horne*, p 29, ed 1801]

Some other characteristics of the Hutchinsonian system are also stated by the last writer, who was one of Hutchinson's greatest admirers "Few writers for natural religion," he writes, "have shewn any regard to the types and figures of the Scripture, or known much about them But the Hutchinsonians, with the old Christian Fathers, and the Divines of the Reformation, are very attentive to them, and take great delight in them They differ in their nature from all the learning of the world, and so much of the wisdom of revelation is contained in them, that no Christian should neglect the knowledge of them All infidels abominate them Lord Bolingbroke calls St Paul a cabbalist for arguing from them, but the Hutchinsonians are ambitious of being such cabbalists as St. Paul was In natural philosophy they have great regard to the name of Newton as the most wonderful genius of his kind But they are sure his method of proving a vacuum is not agreeable to nature." Hutchinson, in fact, spent a large part of his time in endeavouring to overthrow the Newtonian theory of gravitation, denying that inert matter could be capable of active qualities, and maintaining that motion was the result of an universal force, exercised by the fluid medium which he divided into Fire, Light, and Spirit.

Among many other interpretations which the Hutchinsonians gave to the Old Testament Scriptures, they believed the cherubim of Eden, of the Tabernacle, and of Ezekiel's vision, to be mystical figures of deep signification, especially as typifying the Divine attributes, and it was part of their theory that all heathen idolatry originated in corrupt notions respecting these mystical figures Laborious and interminable essays on the cherubim are extant in the writings of Hutchinson's disciples, as well as in his own, and this mysticism also occupies a large place in the sermons of the clergy belonging to the school Almost equally prolix were their speculations on the Names of God, on the garden of Eden, and on the symbolism of sacrificial ceremonies These speculations are not without a certain value, but they are too often of a one-sided character, based almost entirely on peculiar and untrustworthy notions respecting the Hebrew language, and undertaken with far too little knowledge of, or regard for, the received theology of Christendom

The most distinguished divines of the Hutchinsonian school were Bishop Horne, Jones of Nayland, Parkhurst and Romaine, and most of the more learned clergy among the early Evangelicals belonged to the school Many of the Scotch Episcopal clergy also adopted Hutchinsonian tenets, and among others, Macfarlane, Bishop of Moray and Ross in 1787, who carried out Hutchinson's view of the doctrine of the Trinity in such a manner as to lay himself open to the charge of Sabellianism

There were, indeed, few of the school who did not fall into error respecting the eternal generation of the Second Person in the Blessed Trinity, and Neale remarks that even a few passages of Jones of Nayland require to be received with all possible charity, while some of Bishop Horne's assertions cannot be defended at all [Neale's *Life of Bishop Torry*, 29]

Hutchinsonianism died out during the first quarter of the nineteenth century The later Evangelical clergy had not the same taste for speculative study that had made it attractive to their predecessors, and were more engaged in writing hortatory sermons than in working out labyrinthine problems respecting the cherubim Hutchinson's opposition to the Newtonian system failed, moreover, to hold its place against the faith of modern science, which will not permit that system even to be called in question. While, lastly, his philological views respecting Hebrew have been exploded by the more thorough knowledge of the Semitic languages

HUTITES A religious fraternity formed in the sixteenth century by an Anabaptist, named John Hut, Huta, or Hutter, at Marhern, in Moravia A writer in the time of the Commonwealth describes them as living "at this day in great number at Marhern in palaces and convents, upon their accidental contributions, and where they get their livelihood with their hands, and apply themselves to any handicraft whereof they are the masters and governors, who by the commodities gained by them increase the common stock They have at home with them their cooks, their scullions, their errand boys, and their butlers, who have a care, and dispose of all things as they do in monasteries and hospitals They study to maintain mutual peace and concord, being all equal These, even to this day, are commonly known by the name of the Hutsian Fraternity" [Pagitt's *Heresiology*, app] This settlement of Hut at Marhern appears likely to have been the original from which the Herrnhut settlement of the Moravians under Count Zindendorff, in the eighteenth century, was copied [MORAVIANS]

HYDROPARASTATÆ Water-offerers that is, those who offered water instead of wine in the Holy Eucharist. This heretical practice was not confined to one sect, but was common to several Gieseler says to "many" parties, but he does not enumerate the parties Clement of Alexandria, giving a mystical interpretation of the "bread and water" of Prov ix 17, and using the additional verses which are found in the Septuagint, says that the Scripture manifestly applies the terms "bread and water" to those heresies which use bread and water in the Eucharist, not according to the rule of the Church "For there are some who celebrate the Eucharist with water only" [Clem Alex. *Strom.* I xix] St Chrysostom speaks of the evil heresy of those who used water only in the mysteries He cites our Lord's words, "I will not henceforth drink," &c [Matt xxvi 29], and urges that, to pluck up this heresy by the roots, the cup of our Lord's ordinary resurrection-table was a cup of wine [Chrysost *Hom in Matt* lxxxii Field's ed ii. p 462-3]. St. Cyprian's Epistle to Cæcilius is on this practice; on the practice, however, not as proceeding from an heretical principle, but from a desire to avoid notice in time of persecution Cyprian shews that wine is necessary for the legitimate consecration of the sacrifice, and expressing his hope that the omission may have been pardonable in the case he is dealing with, as arising from ignorance or misapprehension, he warns Cæcilius of the guilt that will be incurred by continuing the practice after admonition [Cypr *Ep* lxiii. DICT *of* THEOL, CONCOMITANCE]

Leaving this case, and confining ourselves to the practice as proceeding from heresy, it will be seen at once that the practice indicates heresy regarding our Lord's Person, and the sacrifice of His death If the Holy Eucharist were instituted merely on the principle of a *memoria technica*, merely a reminder to us, it would be otherwise But when the Body broken and Blood shed are to be re-presented to God, and are to be our necessary spiritual food and sustenance, the Mysteries must needs correspond to the Passion, and the outward signs to the thing signified A departure from the sign shews a previous departure from the faith Whence Irenæus writes of the Ebionites, "They are vain, not receiving by faith into their soul the union of God and man . . . Therefore do these men reject the commixture of the heavenly wine, and wish it to be water of the world only, not receiving God so as to have union with Him" [Iren *Hær* v. 1].

The followers of Tatian, again, used the same custom; the asceticism of the ENCRATITES springing from the belief that matter is the source of evil. Hence they endeavoured by excessive rigour to mortify the flesh Consistently, they denied the reality of Christ's Body. From this came their rejection of the element of wine As Docetæ, they held that Christ did not die, and consequently that we are not redeemed by His blood. And if there be no real bloodshedding, why should wine, the symbol of blood, be used? The unreal, shadowy blood, cannot have a real, substantial symbol

The practice of the Hydroparastatæ incidentally draws out the opinions of some of the Fathers respecting the mixture of water with wine (an almost universal custom of the Church) in the Eucharist Irenæus and Cyprian take the same view respecting it, Irenæus stating its symbolism as it looks to the Divine Nature of Christ Himself, Cyprian as it looks to those who are made members of Christ. In the former view, the union of God and man is typified in the commixture, the two natures of Christ being set forth in the latter, from the foundation of the general principle that in Scripture water symbolizes peoples, the water of the mixed cup is taken to represent the faithful who are joined unto Christ The two views coalesce "When, therefore, the mingled cup and the manufactured bread receive the Word of God, and the Eucharist becomes the Body of Christ, from which the substance of our flesh is increased and supported, how can it be affirmed that the flesh is incapable of receiving the gift of God, which is life eternal, which flesh is nourished from the Body and Blood of the Lord, and is a member of Him? Even as the blessed Paul declares, 'We are members of His Body, of His Flesh, and of His Bones'" [Iren v 2]

Cyprian, although his primary object was to shew the necessity of the wine in the mixed cup, speaks very strongly on the necessity of the element of water "Water cannot be offered alone, as neither can the wine be offered alone for if the wine be offered by itself, the blood of Christ begins to be without us, and if the water be alone, the people begin to be without Christ" [*Ep ad Cæcil* p 154, Fell]

The Canons relating to this subject are. [I] St Basil, Canon i [A D 370], in which the Hydroparastatæ are named after the Encratites, as if their custom had not been adopted by all the Encratites The chief point named in the Canon is the alteration of the form of baptism by the Encratites [II.] The third Council of Braga, Canon I. [A.D 675], which condemns sundry errors in the celebration of the Holy Eucharist, and quotes St. Cyprian, as given above [III] The Quinisextine Council, Canon xxxii. [A D 692], which condemns both the Hydroparastatæ and the Armenians, who offered wine alone This Canon quotes St Chrysostom (as referred to above), and, secondly, produces the authorities of the Liturgies of SS Basil and James, and the fortieth Canon of the Council of Carthage [A D 408]

HYDROTHEITÆ A sect of heretics are mentioned by several of the early heresiologists as holding the opinion that all created things had emanated by a process of spontaneous evolution from the element of water, which they alleged to be co-eternal with God Nothing is known of their history, or of the locality to which this heresy belonged Probably it was nothing more than the speculation of some early materialists [HERMOGENIANS], never formulated into the dogma of a sect The name is found only in Prædestinatus, but Danæus assigns that of "Aquæi" to them in his edition of St Augustine [Philast. *Hær* xcvi Aug *Hær* lxxv Prædest *Hær* lxxv]

HYMENÆUS One of the two heretics mentioned by St Paul, as having "erred concerning the truth, saying that the resurrection is past already," and who had not only been guilty of holding such errors themselves, but had spread their false doctrine among others, and "overthrown the faith of some" [2 Tim ii 18] He was probably the same person who is elsewhere named with Alexander as having put away a good conscience, and made shipwreck concerning the faith [1 Tim i 19] The heresy of Hymenæus and Alexander was of so serious a description, that St Paul had passed on them the extreme sentence of excommunication, which he expresses in the words, "Whom I have delivered unto Satan, that they may learn not to blaspheme" [1 Tim. i 20] The Apostle also characterizes the heresy of Hymenæus and Philetus as "profane and vain babblings" of which he predicts that "they will increase to more ungodliness," and that their doctrine "will eat as doth a cancer" or gangrene [2 Tim ii 16-18] From these few indications, it would seem that the heresy of Hymenæus was an early form of that which afterwards became known by the name of Valentinus, the dogma that "the resurrection is past already" being one which Tertullian specially attributes to the Valentinians [Tertull. *De Præscr Hæret* xxxiii], and the "profane and vain babblings" being singularly characteristic of the Gnostic theories, which did indeed eat into the Eastern Churches like a deadly cancer

The Gnostics in general interpreted the resurrection allegorically, maintaining that to "rise again" was to receive the γνῶσις, or secret knowledge of God, which they possessed and handed on to the initiated Hence "the resurrection" was "passed already" when a man received this knowledge Such, probably, was the heresy of Hymenæus and Philetus The wide extent to which such a heresy reached in the very first age of the Church is shewn by St. Paul's words to the Corinthians, "How say some among you, that there is no resurrection of the dead?" [1 Cor xv 12], and by those of Polycarp to the Philippians, "Whosoever perverts the oracles of the Lord to his own lusts, and says that there is neither resurrection nor judgment, he is the first-born of Satan" [Polyc. *ad Philipp* vii] The immoral tendency of a heresy which virtually repudiates the expectation of a future life is obvious, and when St Paul says that Hymenæus and Alexander had put away a good conscience, he indicates that this tendency was already manifested

HYPOTHETICAL UNIVERSALISTS [AMYRALDISTS]

HYPSISTARIANS A sect of heretics which existed in Cappadocia in the fourth century, the leading principle of whose belief was the recognition of God only as "the Most High" [Ὕψιστος] They rejected sacrifices and circumcision, but observed the Jewish Sabbath and Jewish distinctions of clean and unclean food They also held the Jewish objection to pictures and images, but used fire and lights as representative symbols of the Deity, apparently using them in the same manner in which they were used by the Magians

These heretics are only noticed under the name of ὑψιστάριοι by St Gregory of Nyssa [*adv Eunom.* ii] and St Gregory of Nazianzum [*Orat* xviii 5], but they appear to be the Cappadocian representatives of a widely-spread eclectic heresy in which an attempt was made to combine such portions of Judaism, Magianism, and Christianity as were not utterly irreconcilable They seem to be closely allied to the EUPHEMITES or Massalian Syrians and Phœnicians [Epiphan *Hær* lxviii], who professed to be neither heathens nor Christians, yet originated in heathenism

I

ICONOCLASTS. The name of a party in the Church which maintained a long controversy on the subject of the devotional use of pictures and statues, a controversy that raged with great violence in the East for more than a century, *i e* from the tenth year of the reign of Leo III [A D 726] to the second year of the regency of the Empress Theodora [A D 843]

To understand its bearings we must recollect that a great change had swept over the whole Christian Church on the question of the use of external aids to devotion Not only had an elaborate ritual arisen, but the arts of painting and sculpture had been pressed into the service of the sanctuary, and by the eighth century almost every church possessed its pictures or images or relics, in which some special virtue was believed to reside, and which were the objects of attachment and veneration to the whole congregation Some indeed enjoyed a far wider reputation. At Edessa there was a famous statue made after a likeness of our Saviour, which Christ Himself had sent to King Abgarus [Euseb *Eccl Hist* i 13, ii 1], and which was said to have saved that city from the arms of the Persian monarch, Chosroes Mishirvan [A D 611] This miraculous image was often appealed to during the controversy, by Gregory II in an epistle to Leo the Isaurian [*Isaur Concil* tom viii 656], by John of Damascus [*Opera,* tom i. p 281, edit. Lequien], and by the second Nicene Council [Act v p 1030] At Rome there was the famous "veronica" handkerchief In Diospolis in Phrygia there was a church on one of whose marble pillars the face of the Blessed Virgin had been supernaturally outlined All this was a great contrast to the belief and habits of the first centuries of the Christian era Churches then possessed neither images nor pictures On the contrary there was an actual dislike of both, which is quite accounted for by the opposition raised by the early Christians to the idolatry that surrounded them.

There are however frequent protests made by early writers which seem to betoken a change of sentiment on this subject Tertullian [A D 160-240] insisted that God forbade the making equally with the worship of an image [Tertull *de Idolatria,* c 3]. In another tract he appears to disapprove of a Christian pursuing the trade of either a painter or a statuary [Tertull *contr Hermog* c 3]. Origen [A D 185-255] said that the use of images was of the Ophites [Orig *contr Cels* vii. 4] The thirty-sixth canon of the Council of Illiberis [c A D 305] forbids pictures in churches, "lest that which is worshipped and adored be painted on the walls," an enactment evidently levelled against a recent and growing practice Eusebius of Cæsarea, writing to Constantia, sister of Constantine the Great, says that no one ought to attempt to represent the personages of Scripture, that the glory of the Saviour cannot be represented, and that the true image of the saints is a holy life [Hardu. *Concil.* iv. 405] St Augustine [A D 354-430] wrote· "Do not follow the crowds of ignorant persons, who even under the shelter of the true religion itself become so superstitious or surrender themselves so far to their lustful imaginations (libidinibus) that they forget what they have promised to God. I know that many are adorers of sepulchres and pictures," &c [Aug *de Mor Eccl Cath* xxxiv]

Epiphanius, Bishop of Constantia in Cyprus [A D 394], tore with his own hands a curtain in a church of Palestine, declaring that the painting of a figure of the Saviour or of a saint upon it was contrary to Scripture [Hieron *Ep* li 9] About two hundred years later Serenus, Bishop of Marseilles, removed or demolished the pictures in the churches of that town, because of the misuse the common people made of them. This involved him in a correspondence with Gregory the Great, whose verdict on his conduct ran thus "We altogether commend you for having forbidden the worship of images, but we blame you for having broken them" [Greg *Ep* ix. 91] This moderate judgment found much favour in the Western Church, and Charlemagne closes the four Caroline Books with an allusion to it, although the ardent Roman apologist Baronius [A D 1538-1607] has endeavoured to evacuate it of its real meaning, by interpreting Gregory's prohibition as against the worship of the material colours used in making the image or picture

The above quoted passages amount to an occasional protest against what at the same time they prove the existence of, a gradual reaction against the primitive simplicity of worship, and a widespreading sentiment in favour of the use of images, a sentiment which became firmly established by the close of the sixth century, and had run into such extremes by the commencement of the eighth century that many writers have considered them to justify as well as explain the iconoclastic mania People knelt before images, burned incense and lighted candles before them

Some of the clergy scraped off the paint from them, and mingling it with the eucharistic elements, administered the mixture to the communicants [Mich *ap Baron* 824, 16] The rich used to send their bread to the church, to have it held up to an image before eating it Some people even employed images as sponsors for their children, a course defended by Theodore, nephew of the Abbot Plato, when introduced by the Patriarch Nicephorus to argue with Leo the Armenian [A D 814]

But in the earlier part of the eighth century a reaction sprung up in the East of Europe A party of "image-breakers" arose, which was even more fanatical and extreme in its opposition to images, and in the means employed to abolish them The rise of the "Iconoclastic Controversy" which followed is by some writers thrown as far back as A D 712 In that year the Emperor Philippicus Bardanes ordered the removal of a picture of the sixth General Council from the Church of St Sophia in Constantinople, and sent an order of a similar character to Rome Pope Constantine made a vigorous protest, and caused the Emperor to be condemned as an apostate for what looks like a repudiation of the council rather than of the picture, and he also followed up this protest by directing that pictures of the six General Councils should be suspended in the porch of St Peter's But Leo III "the Isaurian," who came to the throne A D 717, was undoubtedly an iconoclastic emperor At the time of his elevation from the army to the imperial dignity, the Mahometans were pressing hard on the Byzantine empire, and the first eight or ten years of his reign were occupied in defending his kingdom and his capital itself against the Saracen foe under Moslemah During this time there were no symptoms of his future hostility to images, it was only as external troubles disappeared that his secret antipathy began to manifest itself. As a first step he wanted the Pope to consent to a General Council being summoned to consider the whole question, but Gregory demurred to the proposal He then desired that the images and paintings on the walls of the churches should be raised higher so as to be out of the reach of the embraces and kisses of the devout multitude. Then discovering that his object was by no means attained, he issued an edict forbidding the worship of all statues, paintings, or mosaics The chronology of this period is obscure, but the date of the last step is generally placed at A D 724-726 There is much obscurity also attending the investigation of the causes which led both Leo and his successors into this line of action The edicts and letters which might have thrown light on the reasons assigned are not extant, but conjecture would certainly suggest that in the case of the once humble Isaurian, it must have been a barbarian dislike of the fine arts, rather than the championship of a more spiritual religion, which actuated him in the course that he pursued Others have supposed it to be the action of a general who found men relying for safety on their tutelar images instead of their own military exertions, or part of the scheme of an ambitious monarch wishing to establish an ecclesiastical as well as a civil autocracy Legend also has attempted to supply the motive A thick smoke was said to have been seen rising from the sea between the islands of Thera and Terasia, and this was interpreted to Leo as a token of the displeasure of Heaven against the permission of image-worship It was rumoured that Leo, while still an obscure youth on his native hills, had been met by two Jews, who promised him the sovereignty on a condition which they afterwards called on him to fulfil, that condition being the extirpation of image-worship throughout his dominions Another report said that he was under the influence of a certain Bezer, formerly in the service of the Caliph, and an apostate from the Christian faith. But whether the emperor acted *proprio motu* or at the suggestion of others, it is certain that this first edict was shortly followed by a second of a far more sweeping and severe character, ordering a general destruction of images throughout the Western empire. Its precise date is unknown, but it must be placed before the death of Gregory II in A D 731, as that Pontiff was among its most strenuous opponents No words can exaggerate the dismay which it occasioned, or the tumult and agitation which followed its promulgation, unlike the decision of some abstruse question in a court of law, or the authoritative solution of some metaphysical subtlety which would only agitate the narrow intellectual circle capable of understanding its bearings, this was a question affecting the religious life of multitudes Every church had its picture or its image, before which rich and poor had been accustomed to offer their devotions, almost every household had its representation of some patron saints, which they had been wont to regard with feelings of the utmost affection It has been suggested that the effect would be similar if an order were issued to destroy the images of the Blessed Virgin which deck the thoroughfares of a modern Roman Catholic town, but even this would not effect such a total revulsion of both domestic and public feeling as the first iconoclastic edict of Leo the Isaurian. It was the signal for sedition at home and revolt abroad In Constantinople the soldiers who were charged with the execution of the order were insulted and maltreated The man who dared to plant his ladder against the palace gate, and to demolish the time-honoured image of Christ with which it was adorned, was hurled to the ground and killed by the indignant mob Abroad an insurrection was organized in the Cyclades, under a leader named Stephanus In Greece the usurper Cosmas was proclaimed by the rebels In Italy the provinces subject to the Greek empire threw off their allegiance At an appeal from Gregory II, Ravenna, whose exarch lost his life, Venice, the cities of the exarchate, and Pentapolis, declared against Leo, and refused the usual tribute, and what caused more anxiety, the fleet despatched against them to the Adriatic Sea was repulsed off Ravenna.

But Leo was not without his supporters The army was devoted to him, and there was a small section of the ecclesiastical body which declined to oppose him, of which Theodosius, metropolitan of Ephesus, Constantine, Bishop of Nacolia in Phrygia, John, Bishop of Synnada, Thomas, Bishop of Claudiopolis in Paphlagonia, are mentioned as leaders But it had far more formidable opponents, both in position and ability First of all there was Germanus, the Patriarch of Constantinople, who had reached the venerable age of ninety-six, and whom, when unable to win him over, Leo did not hesitate to depose, and to supersede by his own secretary Anastasius Then there was the famous controversialist, John of Damascus, who delivered three orations advocating the proper use of images, which from their learning and eloquence have won for their author the title of Doctor of Christian art. Pope Gregory II [A D 715-731] likewise wrote in favour of images He is the author of two extant letters to Leo, in which he upbraids him with fickleness and impiety, refuses the request for a General Council, defies him to attempt to carry his edicts into execution, and finally predicts the most disastrous consequences if he does so His successor, Gregory III, pursued the same policy, and summoning a synod of ninety-three bishops at Rome, openly pronounced sentence of condemnation on iconoclasm and its imperial author

The Emperor Leo was succeeded, A D 741, by his son Constantine Copronymus During the first year of his reign, while he was absent on an expedition against the Saracens, the hopes of the image-worshippers revived, and a report being spread of the Emperor's death, they attempted to place Artavasdus, his brother-in-law, and a favourer of images, on the throne in his stead This resolution was supported by the Patriarch, who, having been an iconoclast under Leo, changed sides under Artavasdus, and veered round once more to his original party under Constantine

Ten years of comparative quiet followed the suppression of this rebellion, lasting until Constantine summoned the bishops to meet at the capital in a council known as the third Council of Constantinople [A D 754], and which also aspired to the grander title (one never acknowledged in the West) of the seventh Œcumenical Council It consisted of three hundred and forty-eight bishops, who unanimously condemned image-worship Unfortunately the Acts of the Council have perished, but from the passages which are quoted for condemnation by the Fathers assembled at Nice [A D 787] we learn that it ordered the destruction of all images and paintings both public and private, persons found with images in their possession, if ecclesiastics, were to be degraded, if laymen, excommunicated, to make an image of Christ was said to involve either Nestorianism in separating the persons of Christ, or Eutychianism in confounding the two substances, and the chief champions of image-worship, the Patriarch Germanus, John of Damascus, and George of Cyprus, were anathematized by name The great flaw in the constitution of this Council was that none of the patriarchates were represented in it The Bishop of Rome was not present either in person or by deputy The see of Constantinople was vacant, Anastasius having died just before the first sitting, and his successor, an iconoclastic monk named Constantine, Bishop of Sylæum, not being nominated till its close, lest it should be said that its deliberations had been presided over by a nominee of the Emperor The other three patriarchs, those of Antioch, Alexandria, and Jerusalem, were under Mahometan dominion, and could not have obtained leave to be present In their absence the council was presided over by Theodosius, Bishop of Ephesus and exarch of Asia, and Pastillus, Bishop of Perga and Metropolitan of Pamphylia

The attempt to carry out the decisions of the Council was met by universal opposition on the part of the monks, and then followed a general persecution of the monks by the Emperor, who attempted to exterminate the whole order Among the most famous victims were a certain Andrew, who for having ventured contumeliously to remonstrate with the Emperor, was publicly scourged and afterwards strangled, another zealous monk named Stephen was thrown into prison and there assassinated The patriarch himself having incurred the suspicions of the Emperor's party, was deposed, insulted, scourged, led round the city on an ass, and having been compelled to assent to the consecration of Nicetas, a Sclavonian eunuch in his place, finally beheaded These cruelties, of which the above instances are only samples, were effectual for the time Iconoclasm was triumphant for the rest of the reign of Constantine Copronymus, who died during an expedition against the Bulgarians [A D 775] He was succeeded by his son and heir Leo IV, surnamed the Chazar, a man of feeble health and mild disposition, who continued his father's opposition to the monkish party, but in a much less severe form This was partly owing to the influence of his wife Irene, a lady sprung from an Athenian family well known for their attachment to image-worship, and who figures very prominently during the next twenty years of the controversy Emboldened by a knowledge of Irene's sympathy and Leo's mildness of character some officers ventured stealthily to introduce images into the palace itself They were detected and severely punished, and for the rest of his short reign of four years and a half Leo's persecuting character was more strongly developed

Constantine VI, who succeeded his father on the throne [A D 780], was a boy only ten years of age, and his mother Irene acted as regent during his minority Her opposition to the iconoclastic policy of the last three Emperors began now more plainly to manifest itself As a first step permission was publicly granted to every one to employ images in domestic acts of worship Then Paul, a Cypriot by birth, who had been elevated by Leo IV from the office of

Iconoclasts

reader to that of patriarch, was induced, probably by Irene's solicitations, to retire from his dignity into a monastery This left the Empress free to elect a successor who would carry out her views She selected a layman, Tarasius, one of her privy counsellors, who was known to be favourable to images, and his appointment was followed by the summoning of a general council to be held at Constantinople To this course Pope Hadrian gave his consent, allowing himself to be represented by two legates, Peter, chief presbyter of St Peter's, and another Peter, abbot of St Sabes The Eastern patriarchs were also indirectly represented by two monks, John, the late syncellus of the patriarch of Antioch, and Thomas, who had been Abbot of St Arsenius in Egypt, and became afterwards Archbishop of Thessalonica The Council held its first session at Constantinople, but in consequence of the disturbances raised by the troops, who were still devotedly attached to the memory of Leo III and Constantine Copronymus, no business could be transacted, and the session was adjourned. It met again [A D 787] at the quieter town of Nice. Here between three hundred and thirty and three hundred and eighty-seven prelates assembled and proclaimed the legality of image-worship with as much vehemence and unanimity as the Council of Constantinople [A D 754] had condemned it. They were at the same time careful to distinguish between the reverence (τιμητικὴ προσκύνησις) due to images and the worship (λατρεία) to be paid to God alone It has also been asserted that they referred to pictures only, a limitation to which the Greek Church adheres to this day Much exception has been taken to the arguments employed and the apocryphal miracles quoted in defence of images on this occasion, but over and beyond this reason the English Church has refused to recognise the claim of this second Council of Nice to the title of Seventh General Council on these grounds [1] Because no subsequent recognition of its œcumenicity has been given by the universal Church, [2] because the Eastern Church was only informally represented so far as concerned the patriarchs of Alexandria, Antioch, and Jerusalem, [3] because the representation of the Western Church was more nominal still, and neither Gaul nor Germany acquiesced in its decisions This is proved by the Caroline Books, which, composed by Alcuin and the French bishops, but published in the name of Charlemagne [A D 788], reject this second Council of Nicæa equally with the third of Constantinople, and also by the Council of Frankfort [A D 794], whose second canon is to the same effect

Constantine VI came of age A D 791, and the remaining six years were occupied in a desperate struggle between him and his mother for the reins of government. At last Irene gained the upper hand, and after blinding her son, a deed of cruelty which Cardinal Baronius and other Roman advocates have vainly attempted to palliate [Baron *Annal sub ann* 796], she enjoyed five years of sole rule [A D 797-802], until, in the latter year, she was dethroned and banished to the island of Lesbos, where she died in the year following Her secretary, Nicephorus, who had headed the rebellion, then ascended the throne During his reign [A D 802-811] and that of his successor's, Stauracius, who only reigned a few months, and of Michael I, surnamed Rhangabes [A D 811-813], the controversy was allowed to slumber But when in the latter year Michael, feeling his own incapacity for the sovereignty, retired into a monastery in favour of Leo V, surnamed the Armenian [A D 813 820], it broke out again This Emperor, nicknamed the Chameleon, from his vacillating policy at his consecration, when he declined to make any personal declaration of faith, seems to have allowed several synods to be held, the first under Nicephorus [A D 814], which pronounced in favour of images, the second [A D 815], which consented to the deposition of that patriarch as a heretic, in consequence of which he was banished and lingered fourteen years in a monastery, the third [A D 816], under the presidency of Theodotus Cassiteras, a layman of noble birth but of iconoclastic family, being a collateral descendant of Constantine Copronymus, and whom Leo had raised to the vacant throne, this synod openly annulled the decisions of the second Nicene Council [A D 787] and re-affirmed those of the third Council of Constantinople [A D 754] It was accompanied by an imperial edict forbidding image-worship, to which the Emperor is said to have been urged by the prophecies of some obscure monk, who foretold a glorious reign if he would tread in the steps of his famous predecessor Leo the Isaurian John the Grammarian and Antony, Bishop of Sylæum in Pamphylia, were among the few men of eminence who supported this policy, which was unrelentingly opposed by the monks, especially by Theodore the Studite, who, like many others, endured scourging and imprisonment rather than acknowledge Cassiteras or consent to give up the use of images In A D 820 Leo V was assassinated by conspirators in the midst of the sacred rites early on Christmas morning, and one of his generals named Michael was taken from prison and chains for elevation to the imperial throne Michael II, surnamed the Stammerer, being an ignorant man, and generally indifferent to all ecclesiastical questions, tolerated both parties with a contemptuous impartiality. Antony of Sylæum, the Iconoclast, was raised to the patriarchate A D 821, but the banished monks were at the same time allowed to return, not excepting Theodore the Studite, who however was found intractable, and being again banished died in exile [A D 826]

In A D 829 Michael was succeeded by Theophilus, his son by his first wife Thecla, and the most bitter and cruel of all the iconoclast emperors He had been the pupil of John the Grammarian, whom he raised to the patriarchate on the death of Antony in A D 832, and who probably presided at the local synod which in that year repeated the condemnation of image-worship Thereupon Theophilus announced his determination no longer to copy his predecessors' indifference, but to root out the whole race of monks from the face of the earth The cruelties of preceding reigns were repeated in an exaggerated form One entire confraternity, the Abrahamites, are said to have suffered martyrdom on an island in the Euxine Sea. Others were scourged and imprisoned A celebrated painter Lazarus had his hands burnt with hot-iron plates to prevent his pursuing his hated art. Two brothers, Theophanes the singer and Theodore the illuminator, were branded in the face with some iambics which had been composed by the Emperor, who in consequence of these and similar cruelties has been called by his opponents a second Belshazzar, but has been described by his apologists as "a most virtuous prince, equal to the greatest emperors, a most rigid exacter of justice, and the severe punisher of all impiety, a *Tydides melior patre*" [Spanheim, *Hist Imag* p 584] But the failure of these violent efforts to extirpate the popular affection for images might be traced to his own roof. His wife Theodora and her mother Theoctista, had always cherished a fondness for them, and though the secret was discovered by the impertinent curiosity of a dwarf and revealed to the husband, he would not resort to harsh measures against his nearest relations He died in A D 842, and the history of A D 780 repeated itself There was another minor, Michael III, afterwards known as "The Drunkard," entrusted to the guardianship of two image-worshipping uncles, Manuel and Theoctistus, and another empress mother left as regent, whose sentiments corresponded to those of Irene At first indeed Theodora was restrained by affection for her late husband and unwillingness to compromise his memory, but when these scruples had been overcome she gladly gave vent to her own prepossessions The monks were recalled from banishment, a synod was summoned which restored the Nicene decrees. John the Grammarian, who had been made patriarch by Theophilus, being found unwilling to recant his iconoclasm, was deposed, and Methodius, a monk and confessor in the late reign, substituted in his place

On the 19th of February, the first Sunday in Lent [A D 842], a solemn perambulation of St Sophia took place, headed by the archbishop and clergy, the Empress and her infant son, and that day has ever since been observed by the Eastern Church as the Feast of Orthodoxy, or thanksgiving for the final overthrow of that iconoclastic heresy which for more than a century had disturbed the peace of the Church

There is little to record of that party after this date beyond the fact, supported by two later allusions to it, that it dwindled gradually away When the patriarch Photius appealed to Pope Nicolas against his rival Ignatius [A D 860], the application was *nominally* made for aid to extinguish a remnant of the iconoclastic party Nine years later, at the eighth General Council at Constantinople [A D 869], Theodore, surnamed Κρίθινος, Nicetas, an ecclesiastic, and two laymen, Theophanes a jurist, and Theophilus, were accused of iconoclasm. The three latter, overawed by the unanimity of the Council, confessed their error, the first named, along with all who then did or should hereafter share his opinions, were pronounced to be under an anathema

Papal share in the Iconoclastic controversy The Roman Church was largely and not always indirectly affected by the controversy that raged at Constantinople Its members, like those of the Greek Church, were devotedly attached to images and pictures, and used them habitually as aids to devotion and as decorations of their churches Pope John VII [A D 705-708] dedicated a chapel in St. Peter's to the Blessed Virgin, whose walls were inlaid with representations of the saints of former days, and his successors, still in theory subjects of the Eastern empire, were only the representatives of the popular feeling in the various steps by which they resented the impious decrees of the Byzantine emperors It may be useful to subjoin a summary of the different occasions on which collisions occurred, although most of them have been alluded to in the foregoing columns

In A D 712, when Philippicus Bardanes sent an order to Rome for the removal of a picture of the sixth General Council, Pope Constantine not only declined to obey it but had several additional pictures suspended, and in a synod summoned at the same time caused the Emperor to be condemned as an apostate His successor Gregory II [A D 715-731] was the author of two letters of remonstrance to Leo the Isaurian, which have been preserved, without date, in the Acts of the Nicene Council [Isaur Conc viii 651-674] In them he declares Leo unworthy of the name of a Christian, to which Theophanes and other Byzantine historians add that it was at his suggestion that the Italian provinces refused to pay the usual tribute, though they continued nominally under the Eastern rule till the coronation of Charlemagne [A D 800], but for whose succour and that of his father Pepin they must have become the subjects of the Lombards under their successive monarchs, Liutprand, Astolphus, and Desiderius Pope Gregory III [A D 731-741], a Syrian by birth, pursued the same policy In the second year of his pontificate ninety-three bishops met at Rome and condemned iconoclasm and all its abettors, a step for which Leo took revenge by confiscating Sicily, Calabria, and other parts of his dominions, and transferring Greece and Illyricum from the Roman to the Byzantine patriarchate His successor Zacharias was the first pope who did not obtain the imperial sanction to his election through the exarch of Ravenna From the Iconoclast Council of Constantinople [A D 754] Stephen II held entirely aloof, but when twenty-one years later it was proposed by Tarasius to summon a council for the purpose of restoring image-worship, Pope Adrian not only expressed his approbation but consented to be represented at Nice [A D 787] by two legates In his answer to the Eastern patriarch he fortifies the orthodox party by repeating how, when on one occasion St Paul and St Peter appeared to Constantine the Great in a dream, the latter recognised his heavenly visitors by their resemblance to pictures of them in the possession of Pope Sylvester Later on Pascal [A D 817] refused to admit the envoys of Leo the Armenian, but sent his own legates to the Emperor to intercede for image-worship, and built a monastery for the reception of Greek refugees, and assigned a church for the performance of the liturgy in their own language In a similar way he dismissed the legates of Michael the Stammerer, who arrived [A D 824] with costly presents for St Peter's, to justify that Emperor's attitude by quoting the extremes to which image-worship sometimes ventured He also censured a work against the use of images in divine worship which appeared about this time from the pen of Claudius, Bishop of Turin Once afterwards [A D 860] Photius thought that the surest way to secure papal sympathy for his side would be by representing to Nicolas that his appeal against his rival Ignatius was really an appeal for aid in suppressing the then dormant, if not quite extinct, spirit of iconoclasm

Western share in the Iconoclastic controversy The Western Church, by which we mean the Churches of Germany, Gaul, and England, pursued a middle course between both the extreme parties in this controversy. Just as the Eastern Christians seem to have cherished images for the sake of contrast with the Mahometans, so the Franks were restrained from any ultra reverence for images, to oppose the idolatry of the unconverted Germans Still it was impossible that the atmosphere of Western Christendom should remain entirely unaffected by the storm which raged at Constantinople, and the question is said to have been discussed at a mixed assembly held at Gentilly, under Pepin [A D 767], in consequence of an embassy from Constantine Copronymus to that king The result is uncertain Paul I expressed his satisfaction with it, probably out of gratitude to Pepin for his refusal to restore to the Greek Emperor the territory which had been seized from the Lombards and given to the Roman See In A D 790, Charlemagne, influenced possibly by irritation with Irene for breaking off the match between her son and the Princess Rothrud, issued four books on the subject of images, known as the *Caroline Books*[1] They were probably only in part the Emperor's own composition, and mainly the work of the English Alcuin and other ecclesiastics In them the independent and medium view of the Western Church is clearly mapped out The Council of Constantinople [A D 754] is condemned for its destruction of images, and the Council of Nice [A D 787] for allowing their worship, its edicts being combated and all its views examined at great length, and its claim to œcumenicity denied Four years later the Council of Frankfort was summoned by Charlemagne [A D 794] It was attended by three hundred bishops, who were unanimous in allowing the use of images while forbidding their worship, the conclusions of the Council of Nice were openly rejected [canon ii], the *Caroline Books* confirmed, and Pope Adrian's answer to them [A D 792] condemned It should be added that their rejection of the decrees of the second Nicene Council was based upon a mistake. The passage most objected to was, "that those should be anathematized who should not bestow service or adoration on the images of the saints even as on the Divine Trinity"—a resolution which could not possibly have been passed by a council which carefully distinguished between the reverence due to images and the worship to be reserved for God alone

Charlemagne was succeeded [A D 814] by Louis the Meek When the Emperor Michael despatched an embassy to him [A D 824] for the purpose of renewing bonds of confederation, and with the view of winning him openly over to iconoclastic principles, Louis assembled a council at Paris [A D 825], which refused to depart in any way from the resolutions of the preceding council at Frankfort, and repeated its censure of the Council of Nice, and its condemnation of the papal views, as expressed in Adrian's answer to the *Caroline Books* Michael was apparently too indifferent, and the Pope too much indebted to the Western Emperor, to make any further remonstrance, and the Franks became shortly afterwards engaged in domestic troubles, which prevented their taking further active interest in the controversy

Two tracts, strongly tinged with iconoclasm, were written about this time by Western authors The first by Agobard, Archbishop of Lyons [died A D 840], the second, and the more violent, by Claudius, a pupil of Felix of Urgel, raised by Louis to the see of Turin [A D 814] The latter work was censured not only by Pope Pascal, but by the general voice of the West, as represented by the Abbot Theodemir, Dungal, a Scot, Jonas, of Orleans; and Walafrid Strabo

The iconoclastic movement was never a popular one. Throughout its course the monks, who were a very numerous body, and the great majority of the population, especially of the poorer classes, were devotedly attached to the use of images Iconoclasm emanated from the Emperors only, and was the attempt of despots to force their views on their subjects. No religious movement has ever been successful under these conditions; and, therefore, in spite of the spiritual tendency of which its admirers regard it as a manifestation, it ultimately failed

Nor was the movement grounded on any principle of abstract theology The questions which had hitherto agitated the Church had been mainly abstract and metaphysical in their character Nestorianism, Eutychianism, and other previous heresies, referred to notional distinctions, and disturbed the small and intellectual circles rather than the mass of men. Iconoclasm, although the philosopher might detect in it a phase of the contest between spiritualism and material-

[1] They are still extant, and were printed by Heumann at Hanover A D 1731

ism, was in the eyes of the many merely an unprovoked attack on their sensible, outward, and familiar aids to devotion, and would therefore occupy their thoughts, and create a resentment unparalleled in the history of previous religious controversies

It was also an inherent element of weakness in iconoclasm, that it was negative rather than positive, it pulled down without being able to build up, it destroyed the popular objects of veneration and accessories of worship, but had nothing wherewith to supply the minds of those worshippers whose walls it had denuded of their pictures and statues Unlike the Reformation it did not attempt to concentrate men's minds on some overpowering conviction, such as personal illumination or justification by faith, and unlike the Reformation it failed

The view in which the advocates of iconoclasm have always delighted to regard it, is as a protest against a transformed paganism. It was the view of the Emperor Theophilus and his tutor, John the Grammarian [Neander, *Church Hist* vi 368] It is endorsed by the Deist historian, who says, "By a slow though inevitable progression the honours of the original were transferred to the copy The devout Christian prayed before the image of a saint, and the pagan rites of genuflexion, luminaries, and incense again stole into the Catholic Church" [Gibbon's *Rom Emp* chap xlix.] Again, "So long as the ancient mythology had any separate establishment in the empire, the spiritual worship which our religion demands, and so essentially implies, as only fitting for it, was presented in its purity by means of the salutary contrast, but as soon as the Church became completely triumphant and exclusive, and the parallel of pagan idolatry totally removed, then the old constitutional appetite revived in all its force, and after a short but famous struggle with the iconoclasts, an image-worship was established and consecrated by bulls and canons, which, in whatever light it is regarded, differed in no respects but the names of its objects from that which had existed for so many years as the chief characteristic of the religion and faith of the Gentiles" [H Nelson Coleridge] It will be observed that the last quotation ignores entirely the distinction laid down carefully by the second Nicene Council between προσκύνησις and λατρεία —a distinction which had never been insisted on in paganism.

The defenders of image-worship during the time of the controversy, and its apologists in later days, have always identified the opposition to it with the iconoclastic religion of Mahomet, which was making such rapid progress at the expense of Christianity during the seventh and eighth centuries There is much in favour of this view It explains the intense opposition raised by the monks of the West It is suggested by the resemblance of the edicts of such Emperors as Leo and Constantine to those of the Mahometan princes, as when the Caliph Yezid, the ninth of the race of the Ommiadæ, caused all the images in Syria to be destroyed [A D 719]. It is also supported by the fact of the friendship which existed between Theophilus, the cruellest of all the iconoclastic emperors, and the Caliph of Bagdad, to whom he sent a magnificent embassy under the charge of John the Grammarian Others have regarded it as a retrogression towards Judaism, or, with John of Damascus, as a result of the Manichæan theory of the essential evil of matter

The consequences of the iconoclast movement were very disastrous

[1] Such eminent soldiers as Leo the Isaurian and Constantine spent their lives amid the turmoil of civil disturbances, instead of being able to devote all their energies, and to concentrate the Empire's forces, against the inroads of Mahometanism

[2] Iconoclasm was never acceptable in Italy, whose inhabitants opposed it consistently, and from the very first, and the schism between the Eastern and Western Churches, which commenced by the refusal of the Italian provinces to pay tribute [A D 729], continued to grow in intensity until it was completed territorially by the coronation of Charlemagne [A D. 800], ecclesiastically by the excommunication of Eastern Christendom [A D 1053] by Leo IX.

[3] While the power of the Patriarchs of Constantinople sensibly waned, from the character of some of those whom successive emperors raised to that dignity, and from the ignominious treatment which they repeatedly received at their hands, the influence of the popes continued steadily to increase, not only from the high character of such men as Gregory II and III, but from the unshaken fidelity with which both they and their successors supported the orthodox, and in Italy the universally popular, cause

[This subject has been treated from the Catholic point of view by Baronius, *Annales Eccles.*, Natalis Alexander, *Hist Eccles sæc* viii ix, Maimbourg, *Hist. des Iconoclastes* and from the Protestant side by Fred Spanheim, *Hist Imag*, James Basnage, *Hist des Eglises Reform* ii See also Schlosser's *Hist of the Iconocl Emp*, Schroek's *Kirchengeschichte*, vols xx. xxiii; Walch's *Hist der Ketzer* x. xi, and Neale's *Hist East Ch*]

IDEALISTS [DESCARTES MALEBRANCHE SPINOZA. KANT]

IKONOBORTZI. A name signifying the same as "Iconoclasts," and used as a designation of the Russian sect of Dissenters more generally known as DUCHOBORTZI

ILLUMINATI [HESYCHASTS]

ILLUMINATI. A Spanish sect, known by the vernacular name of "Alombrados," which originated about the year 1575 in the teaching of a Carmelite named Catherine de Jesus, and a native of Teneriffe, named John of Willelpando. They were almost identical with the Familists, rejecting the use of sacraments, holding that by mental prayer they could attain such a state of perfection as to make it unnecessary for them to do good works, and that they might commit any kind of crime without sin. Many of them were burned as heretics at Cordova, and others, abjuring their heresy, the sect was for the time suppressed in the usual high-handed manner of the Spanish Inquisition, but it again revived, again to be suppressed in a similar manner in the year 1623 [Spondanus, *Annal Eccl ad ann* 1623, n 7]

ILLUMINATI An obscure sect of French Familists arose under this name in Picardy, in the year 1634, which united with the Guérinists, disciples of Peter Guérin, and afterwards spread into Flanders They claimed to have a special revelation as to the mode of attaining Christian perfection, which had been first made to one of their number named Anthony Bocquet This "perfection" resulted in that which the Familists called "deification," and, as with that sect, this principle led them into Antinomianism, for they held that no act could be sinful to those who were so deified The sect was soon exterminated by Louis XIII [Spondanus, *Annal Eccl. ad ann* 1623]

ILLUMINATI A society of Atheists was founded under the name of "Illuminaten" in the year 1777, by a Professor of Canon Law in the University of Ingoldstadt, named Adam Weishaupt The professed objects of the Society were those of diffusing light, union, charity, and tolerance, of abolishing wrongs, of spreading education, and ameliorating, in general, the condition of society But they were, in reality, an association for the abolition of Christianity, and the introduction of Freethinking Republicanism The "Illuminaten" adopted a curious secret system which was made up of a pseudo-classicism and freemasonry, each member of the association assuming a Greek or Roman name, similar names being given to cities and countries, a new calendar being formed, with the year 630 for its era, and new names being given to the months When the organization of the Freemasons was combined with this new paganism it became politically dangerous, and the "Illuminaten" were suppressed in 1785 on the accession of Frederick William II to the throne of Prussia But the flood of infidelity flowed on notwithstanding, and the principles of the "Illuminaten" of Prussia are sufficiently evident in those of the leaders of the French Revolution

ILLUMINATI. A name given to the French infidels elsewhere noticed as ENCYCLOPEDISTS

IMPANATORES There has never been any sect of this name, but it is given by some Roman controversialists to those who maintain the co-existence of the natural Bread and the Body of Christ in the consecrated element used in the Holy Eucharist The term "Impanation" has been used both by Lutheran and by English divines, and is a very unsatisfactory one, since analogy with the Incarnation requires us to believe that the lower nature is taken into the higher, not the higher into the lower But it only expresses a sporadic and rather rare form of opinion on the subject of the Eucharist, and neither Lutheran nor Anglican divines can truly be called "Impanators," as if they were generically distinguished by the name The most conspicuous English divine who has held the theory of Impanation, was Johnson, the author of *The Unbloody Sacrifice*, who accounted for the Real Presence by the theory that a special Eucharistic Body of Christ exists which is associated with the elements used by consecration [ADESSENARIANS]

IMPECCABLES A name assumed by the Antinomian BRETHREN OF THE FREE SPIRIT.

INCORRUPTICOLÆ [APHTHARTODOCETÆ]

INDEPENDENT METHODISTS A name assumed by the very few remaining congregations of the Calvinistic Methodist followers of Whitfield [METHODISTS, CALVINISTIC]

INDEPENDENT CHRISTIAN UNIVERSALISTS [RELLYANISTS]

INDEPENDENTS or CONGREGATIONALISTS A sect so called from its fundamental principle that every particular congregation of Christians is an independent body, which has within itself the right of electing and deposing its pastors, of settling its faith, and of exercising discipline over its members, and that there ought to be no such organized unity among congregations as may in any way interfere with their perfect independence of each other.

All congregations of Puritans which separated from the Church of England before the reign of Elizabeth were necessarily of this independent character in practice, and until the Presbyterians began to establish their system, which was about the year 1572, they were so to some extent in theory Thus such congregations as Foxe speaks of as being surprised in a house in Bow Churchyard, on New Year's Day 1555-6, and sent to prison, or at the Saracen's Head in Islington in December 1557, held themselves independent of the Church of England and of every one except themselves so far as religious discipline was concerned, and thus fairly represented the principle Of a similar kind was that congregation under Richard Fitz, which was sent to the Bridewell on May 20th 1567 [PURITANS], and which is often spoken of as the first Independent community in England But the principle of Independency was not their reason for thus separating, and was not probably in their minds. They would have been quite content with the system which Calvin had originated at Geneva, and yet this was as far removed from Independency as that of the Church itself, and their object in holding assemblies apart from the Church was to escape from the liturgical and doctrinal system of the latter, and to have such preaching and praying as suited their tastes

The first person, in fact, to formulate the Independent or Congregational principle was no doubt the Robert Browne on whom tradition has fastened it for three centuries, and from whom the sect was known by the name of "Brownists" down to about the year 1642

Fuller (who in his youth had seen him) says that Browne belonged to "an ancient and worshipful" family settled at Tolethorp in Rutlandshire, that he was educated at Corpus Christi College, Cambridge, and that he was chaplain to the Duke of Norfolk. For two years he was also Master of the Free School of St Olave's, in the borough of Southwark, at which time he used to preach in a gravel pit in Islington In June 1571 he was cited before the High Commission Court, with other Puritan preachers, for refusing to subscribe the Thirty-nine Articles, but was screened by the Duke of Norfolk, and seems to have left London at this time for Norwich This was at that time, and long afterwards, the principal manufacturing town of England, and contained a large Dutch population of Calvinists with whom Browne at first associated himself. But he afterwards formed separate congregations in several parts of the Diocese of Norwich, until he was apprehended by the Ecclesiastical Commissioners in April 1581, "upon complaint made by many godly preachers for delivering unto the people corrupt and contentious doctrine" In reporting this apprehension to Lord Burleigh the Bishop of Norwich speaks of Browne's "arrogant spirit of reproving being such as is to be marvelled at, the man being also to be feared, lest if he were at liberty he would seduce the vulgar sort of the people who greatly depend on him, assembling themselves to the number of a hundred at a time in private houses and conventicles to hear him, not without danger to some thereabout" [*Lansd MS* 33] Burleigh replied to this communication immediately, on April 21st, 1581 "Forasmuch as he is my kinsman, if he be son to him whom I take him to be, and that his error seemeth to proceed of zeal rather than of malice, I do therefore wish he were charitably conferred with and reformed, which course I pray your lordship may be taken with him either by your lordship or such as your lordship shall assign for that purpose; and in case there shall not follow thereof such success as may be to your liking, that then you would be content to permit him to repair hither to London, to be further dealt with as I shall take order for upon his coming, for which purpose I have written a letter to the sheriff, if your lordship shall like thereof" [Fuller's *Ch Hist* iii 62] Shortly after this Browne was released, and in company with fifty or sixty other persons, and a Puritan preacher named Harrison, left England and settled at Middleburgh in Zealand. Here he became teacher of the little colony in conjunction with Harrison, and from thence he sent forth "A book which sheweth the life and manners of all true Christians, and how unlike they are to Turks and Papists and Heathen folk. Also, the points and parts of all Divinity, that is of the revealed will and word of God, are declared by their several definitions and divisions" In this work he stated those principles of congregational self-government which have since been made the distinctive characteristic of the Independent sect.

The "arrogant spirit" of Browne was, however, so intolerable to his independent community that he was driven from them within three months, and recrossed the North Sea to land in Scotland But even there "he was so great a malcontent that he was committed to ward and detained a night or two in prison" From Scotland he returned to his own neighbourhood, but his arrogant spirit again broke out to such an extent in Northampton that he was solemnly excommunicated by Lindsell, Bishop of Peterborough This brought to a close his association with the sect which he had founded On July 17th, 1584, Lord Burleigh wrote to Archbishop Whitgift, "I am content that your grace and my lord of London, where I hear Browne is, should use him as your wisdoms think meet I have cause to pity the poor man" By Burleigh's permission Browne retired for a time to his father's house, and on June 20th, 1589, the great minister wrote to the Bishop of Peterborough, saying, that "he hath now a good time" forsaken his opinions and "submitted himself to the order and government of the Church," and asking the Bishop "to receive him again into the ministry, and to give him your best means and help for some ecclesiastical preferment" [*Lansd MSS* 103, 60] The founder of the Independent sect then became Rector of Thorpe-Achurch in Northamptonshire, where he died after a forty years' incumbency, in the year 1630, just as the shadow of those national troubles which his sect helped so much to originate was beginning to fall upon the country

The principles of Church government which Browne invented fell in with the inclination of large numbers of the Puritans, and the sect increased very rapidly In a speech made in the House of Commons by Sir Walter Raleigh in April 1580, he says, "In my conceit the Brownists are worthy to be rooted out of the Commonwealth, but what danger may grow to ourselves if this law pass it were fit to be considered. If two or three thousand Brownists meet at the sea, at whose charge shall they be transported, or whither will you send them? I am sorry for it, I am afraid there are near 20,000 of them in England, and when they be gone, who shall maintain their wives and children?" [D'Ewes' *Journ.* 517]

After Browne's personal influence had been withdrawn from the growing sect, his place was filled by a barrister of Gray's Inn, named Henry Barrow, a Cambridge graduate, and from him the early Independents were called "Barrowists," as well as Brownists In November 1586, Barrow was summoned before the Court of High Commission, and his own account of his examination shews that he held principles similar in many respects to those of the Quakers of the next century, objecting to the whole system of ecclesiastical government, refusing to take an oath, and having a fanatical antipathy to set prayers Lord Bacon says of him that "he made a leap from a vain and libertine youth to a preciseness in the highest degree, the strangeness of which alteration made him much spoken of" [Bacon's *Works*, i 383, Child's ed] The tone of his Independency may be illustrated by two quotations from this examination When he was asked, "Whether the Church of England, as it standeth now established, be the true established Church of Christ, and whether the people therein be the true and faithful people of God or no?" his answer was, "I think that these parish assemblies, as they stand generally in England, are not the true established Churches of England" Respecting the Prayer Book he said, "I think that this Book of Common Prayer, publicly enjoined and received in the assemblies of this land, is well-nigh altogether idolatrous, superstitious, and Popish" When, again, he was asked, whether it was lawful to use the Lord's Prayer "publicly in Church, or privately, as a prayer, or no?" he replied thus "It is to be used to that end for which it was given by our Saviour Christ to His disciples, as a summary groundwork or foundation of all faithful prayers, whereby to instruct and assure their consciences that their petitions are according to the will and glory of God, but that these prescript words are enjoined, or that Christ or His apostles ever used them as or in their prayer, I find not in the Scripture Moreover I see not how it can be used as a prayer, seeing that our particular wants, and present occasions and necessities, are not therein expressed, and, therefore, I think it not to be used as a prayer" [*Harleian Misc.* iv. 347. Egerton, *Pap Camd Soc.* 167]

Barrow's chief assistant in spreading these principles was a young clergyman, named John Greenwood, who had been his associate as an undergraduate at Cambridge He, too, was brought before the High Commission Court in November 1586, and was interrogated respecting his office and opinions When asked if he was a minister in orders, and if so, who had degraded him, he answered, "I was one according to your orders, and I degraded myself, through God's mercy by repentance" He too condemned the Church in similar language to that of Barrow In an appeal which they and others of their sect made to the Privy Council, these opinionative young men also declared their conviction that the English hierarchy was dissonant from Christ's institution, and derived from Antichrist, and that they had therefore joined in a new community, and had chosen to themselves a ministry of pastor, teacher, elders, and deacons as Christ had appointed, which new order they were ready to prove by the word of God, and by the same evidence to disprove the Church system [Neale's *Puritans,* i 365]. After several years' imprisonment Barrow and Greenwood were brought to trial at the Old Bailey "for writing and publishing sundry seditious books and pamphlets, tending to the slander of the Queen and government," and were executed at Tyburn on April 6th, 1593

At the end of the following May, another of the sect, John Penry ("Martin-Marprelate"), also a clergyman, educated at Cambridge, and afterwards of St Alban's Hall, Oxford, was executed in Southwark These three were the only Brownists executed in London, although a great number had been arrested, but two others named Thacker and Copping had been executed at Bury St. Edmunds in 1583 They were executed for conscientious principles, which impelled them to say that the Queen was perjured, that she was an enemy to religion and her people, and when Penry writes to her while free, that his purpose, and that of his friends, "is to take the penalty of the transgressions against your laws," he doubtless expressed the feeling of all, that they meant to have their own way, or to suffer the penalty of not getting it A law of conscience which bade young fanatics write and talk treason wholesale came into conflict with the law of the land, which required that talkers of treason should be sent to Tyburn. If these three could have been spared like the rest, it is just possible that the one would have found his level and his work in his practice as a barrister, and the other two theirs as country clergymen, by the time they had respectively reached the more sober age of five-and-thirty or forty But they had greedily sought the distinction so captivating to half matured minds, that of being martyrs for their cause, and they suffered for the "insane fanaticism which led them to urge the overthrow of the ecclesiastical constitution of the country in language so violent and inflammatory, that no court of justice, in such dangerous times as those were, could possibly forbear to put the Act of Parliament into execution" [Curteis' *Bampton Lect* 78]

The next leader of the Brownists was a clergyman named Francis Johnson, Fellow of Christ's College, Cambridge, who had been expelled from the university for a seditious sermon preached at St Mary's in January 1589. He was one of those who had been set at liberty when Barrow and his companions were executed, and leaving England, with a company of other liberated prisoners, established a Brownist community at Amsterdam Here at Rotterdam, the Hague, Leyden,[1] and Utrecht, a number of the sect expatriated themselves, but they were looked upon with suspicion by the Dutch authorities, being characterized as ' a discontented, factious, and conceited people who could not be tolerated in their own land" At Amsterdam Johnson and a coadjutor named Ainsworth published *The Confession of Faith of certain English people, living in the Low Countries exiled,* of which successive editions were printed in 1596, 1598, and 1602, and which was also translated into Latin by Ainsworth, and sent forth to the learned of various European countries in his own name In the 23rd article of this confession the Independent principle is thus stated "As every Christian congregation hath power and commandment to elect and ordain their own ministry, according to the rules in God's Word prescribed, and, whilst they shall faithfully execute their office, to have them in superabundant love for their works' sake, to provide for them, to honour them, and reverence them, according to the dignity of

[1] That at Leyden was presided over by John Robinson, a [A D 1570-1624] Cambridge man, and once beneficed near Yarmouth He died of ague while preparing to take charge of the "Pilgrim Fathers" emigrants in New England Some writers call him "The father of the modern Independents," probably on account of the influence produced by his writings.

the office they execute. so have they also power and commandment when any such defaulters, either in their life, doctrine, or administration, breaketh out as by the rule of the Word debarreth them from, or depriveth them of, their ministry, by one order to depose them from the ministry they exercised, yea, if the case so require, and they remain obstinate and impenitent, orderly to cut them off by excommunication" This is followed by the statement in the 24th article, that "Christ hath given this power to receive in or cut off any member, to the whole body together of every Christian congregation, and not to any one member apart, or to more members sequestered from the whole, or to any other congregation, to do it for them"

The principles thus set forth were combated by Henry Jacob, a Kentish clergyman, in a work printed at Middleburgh in 1599, and entitled *A Defence of the Churches and Ministry of England Written in two Treatises against the Reasons and Obligations of Mr Francis Johnson and others of the Separation called Brownists* This was answered by Johnson in the following year, in *An Answer to Master H Jacob His Defence, &c*, and Master H Jacob was so convinced by the reply, that he left the Church, and joined the sect against whose principles he had written

Anthony Wood says that Jacob's son used to say his father was the first Independent in England In the beginning of James the First's reign he is found as the leader and spokesman of the sect, and in the year 1616 he established a community at Blackfriars in London, which is usually called "The first Independent or Congregational Church in England" It was Jacob also who began to substitute the more modern name for that of Brownists or Separatists, by defining each congregation as "an entire and independent body-politic, endued with power immediately under, and from, Christ, as every proper Church is and ought to be"[1] [Jacob's *Declaration and Plainer Opening of Certain Points, &c*, p 13, 1611]. Jacob emigrated to New England after a few years, and died there in 1624, his place being taken in London by John Lathrop, also a Kentish clergyman, who got into trouble with the High Commission Court in 1632, but of whom very little else is known

In the year 1620, the Leyden Independents matured a plan which had been in view for some years, for joining in the stream of emigration which was now beginning to flow towards North America They found life in a continental city extremely distasteful to them, they could not compete in trade with their Dutch neighbours, and they were losing their hold upon the rising generation of their own families Some of the home Independents fell in with the scheme, and arrangements were made with a Plymouth emigrant company, recently incorporated, for their transport to "New England," the northern part of the colony of Virginia, formed in Queen Elizabeth's time Two ships were chartered for the purpose, one at Leyden and one at Plymouth, but eventually the Leyden party took in the few who were going from England, and the united company of one hundred and one sailed from Plymouth in the *Mayflower* on August 21st, 1620, arriving in New England on November 11th of the same year An absurd sentimentality has been connected with this emigration, and many who gaze on the very unhistorical painting of the "Pilgrim Fathers" which adorns the Royal Robing Room in the House of Lords, suppose that it was a general transfer of all the Dissenters of England, under the effect of a bitter persecution, to a foreign shore But of the fifteen or twenty families of "Pilgrim Fathers" only two or three started from England, and the whole of the party went, as many other parties of emigrants were going in that generation, to "seek their fortunes," as shrewd and bold "adventurers," for so colonists were then significantly called, in a land, the rapid development of whose resources soon justified their enterprise

The English Independents were meanwhile becoming so prosperous a sect, and so influential a political party, that they found it much more for their interest to remain at home. In a short time some of them became leaders in a revolution which overthrew for half a generation the Church and the Monarchy, and from the district which had been principally leavened with their principles by Browne, sprung one of their number whose power gave him a place among the sovereigns of his day During the time of Cromwell's rule, although he himself was an Independent, the Scottish Presbyterian system was established throughout the country, and the Presbyterians made vigorous attempts to suppress the rival sect altogether Many Independent preachers, however, were made rectors and vicars by the Government, while in not a few places, as in Exeter Cathedral, Holy Trinity, Hull, and St Nicholas, Great Yarmouth, walls were built up in the choir arch, that the two sects might share alike in the sacred buildings which they had taken from the Church

After its first triumph, however, the Presbyterian system began at once to lose ground, being always distasteful to the people of England and those who were not at heart lovers of the old Church were generally turning towards the Independent system as that which most suited their tastes Thus it came to pass that when the Church returned to its position again, and the Act of Uniformity of 1662 enacted that none should officiate in churches who were not episcopally ordained, a large proportion of those who became Nonconformists were Independents and not Presbyterians Independent congregations were established in great numbers, while of those

[1] The term is found used in a similar way in a rather later work "Cœtum quemlibet particularem (recte institutum et ordinatum) esse totam, integram, et perfectam ecclesiam ex suis partibus constantem immediate et *independenter* (quoad alias ecclesias) sub ipso Christo" [Robinson's *Apol Christianorum dictorum Brownistarum ac Barrowistarum*, p 22] But Pagitt in his *Heresiography*, which was written about 1638, says that the term was then so little in use that he had not heard it when he began to write his work

P

in which it was endeavoured to preserve the system of Presbyterianism, some soon lapsed into that of ordinary Independency; while others, though remaining Presbyterian in name, became Unitarian in doctrine and Independent in government [PRESBYTERIANS]

During the eighteenth century, the Independents, and the Presbyterians thus assimilated to them, formed the great bulk of English Dissenters (being fairly represented by the names of Dr Watts and Dr Doddridge), and continued to do so until the death of Wesley brought about the formal separation of the Methodists from the Church [METHODISTS] In May 1688, a return of the numbers of Dissenters was made to the Government, from which it appears that there were then 93,153 in the province of York, and 15,525 in the province of Canterbury Of these 108,678 Dissenters no doubt seventy or eighty thousand were Independents In the year 1716, Neal, the historian of the Puritans, stated that there were 1397 Dissenting congregations in England and Wales Of these 247 were Baptist congregations, but of the remaining 1150 no classification is given In 1812 there were 1024 Independent congregations in England and Wales, one-fourth of them being in the principality In 1838, the number had increased to 1840 congregations, and in 1851 to 3244, of which one-fifth were in Wales It is estimated that in the year 1870 the number of the sect amounted to 296,300 members, to whom are to be added 242,430 children under sixteen years of age

By the fundamental theory of Congregationalism, every particular congregation has the right to settle its own doctrine, and no person or persons external to it have any right to interfere with its belief any more than with its government But this theory is contrary to the religious instincts of Christians, which inevitably point towards some bond of unity in matters of faith, and it has never been strictly carried out With the object of establishing some kind of uniformity in the midst of Independency, there was published in 1659 *A Declaration of the Faith and Order owned and practised in the Congregational Churches in England* With the same object the "Congregational Union" was formed in 1831, and has set forth a "Declaration of the Faith, Order, and Discipline of the Congregational or Independent Dissenters" This Declaration consists of thirty-three articles, twenty of which relate to the "Principles of Religion," and the remaining thirteen to the "Principles of Church Order and Discipline"

Two of these articles may be quoted as shewing the relation of the sect to the peculiar doctrines of Calvinism "XIV They believe that all who will be saved were the objects of God's eternal and electing love, and were given by an act of Divine sovereignty to the Son of God, which in no way interferes with the system of means, nor with the grounds of human responsibility, being wholly unrevealed as to its objects, and not a rule of human duty XV They believe that the Scriptures teach the final perseverance of all true believers to a state of eternal blessedness, which they are appointed to obtain through constant faith in Christ, and uniform obedience to His commands"

In two of the articles on Church order and discipline, may also be seen the existing official utterance of the sect on the subject of its ministry and its Independency "IV They believe that the New Testament authorizes every Christian Church to elect its own officers, to manage all its own affairs, and to stand independent of, and irresponsible to, all authority saving that only of the Supreme and Divine Head of the Church, the Lord Jesus Christ X They believe that it is the duty of Christian Churches to hold communion with each other, to entertain an enlarged affection for each other as members of the same body, and to co-operate for the promotion of the Christian cause, but that no church, nor union of churches, has any right or power to interfere with the faith or discipline of any other church, further than to separate from such as, in faith or practice, depart from the Gospel of Christ"

The Independents maintain sixteen colleges in various parts of Great Britain, in which 316 students were being educated in 1870 The "London Missionary Society," with an income and expenditure of about £100,000 a-year, is also substantially one of their institutions, though founded in 1796 on a nominally undenominational plan They also principally maintain the "British and Foreign School Society," with an income and expenditure of £10,000 a-year though that also was founded for promoting the education of the labouring and manufacturing poor of every persuasion [*The Raising of the Foundations of Brownism*, 1588 White's *Discovery of Brownism*, 1605. Neal's *Hist of the Puritans* Stoughton's *Eccl Hist Congreg Year-Books*]

INFERNALES The name given by Roman Heresiologists to those who maintained the opinion that when Christ descended into Hell, He descended thither to suffer torment The invention of this opinion is attributed to Nicolas Gallus and James Smidelin It was held also by Beza, Calvin, and by some of the early Puritans Calvin's words are "Si [Christus] ad inferos descendisse dicitur, nihil mirum est, cum eam mortem pertulerit quæ sceleratis ab irato Deo infligitur Cum diros in anima cruciatus damnati ac perditi hominis pertulerit" [Calvin, *Inst* ii 16, c xvi sec 10]

INFIDELS Those who have never received the faith were formerly called by this name, especially the Mahometans, and this negative sense is that in which the word Infidel [ἄπιστος] is used by St Paul [2 Cor vi 15, 1 Tim v. 8] But the term has been applied during the last two centuries (and perhaps, in the Good Friday Collect, as early as 1548) to all classes of persons who consciously reject those articles of the Christian Faith which bear upon the Personality and Providence of Almighty God The collective and negative term is not now much in use, particular forms and developments of infidelity being generally spoken of under names assumed by their adherents as specially defining them Such for instance are Positivism, Secularism, and Deism

INFRALAPSARIANS. [SUBLAPSARIANS]

INGHAMITES A sect formed in the North of England in the middle of the eighteenth century by Benjamin Ingham, of Aberford, near York, its particular characteristics being drawn from the Moravians and the Methodists

When at Queen's College, Oxford, Ingham became a member of Wesley's original community there, and the friendship between him and the two brothers was so close that he accompanied them on their missionary voyage to Georgia The Moravian influences under which John Wesley fell during that voyage affected Ingham, and on their return from America he accompanied him also to Heinnhut When Wesley separated from the Moravians, Ingham returned to the district in Yorkshire where the property of his family was situated, and from that centre began to form societies on Wesley's plan, being, however, assisted by some Moravian friends by whom he continued to be chiefly guided These societies shortly increased to the number of eighty, extending into the adjoining counties, and finding much support from those clergy who countenanced the Methodist revival

Ingham was brought into intimate relations with Lady Huntingdon, having married Lord Huntingdon's sister, Lady Margaret Hastings, and also with Count Zinzendorf, the founder of the Moravian sect It was probably the example of Zinzendorf (fortified by the hyper-Episcopal authority exercised by Lady Huntingdon) which led Ingham to assume the position of "general overseer" or bishop Having done so he proposed an union between his own societies and those of Wesley, but the latter declined this arrangement. Wesley's record of this in the Minutes of Conference for 1749 is, "Mr Ingham seems to desire a reunion Can we unite with him? Yes, as soon as he returns to the old Methodist doctrine Meantime let us behave with all tenderness and love" [*Min. of Conf* i 43, ed 1812]

About the year 1759, Ingham was so much impressed with the writings of Glas and Sandeman that he sent two of his preachers to Scotland to investigate the principles of the sect which was there being formed These preachers returned to Yorkshire as zealous Sandemanians, and won over so many converts from among the members of Ingham's societies and caused so much dissension among the sect, that in a short time only thirteen out of the eighty remained attached to their original founder Some of these have lingered on until recent times, nine Inghamite chapels being enumerated in the Religious Census of 1851. The sect was thus of very short duration, its founder having lived to see its almost total extinction

INSABATATI [SABOTIERS]

INSTABILES [ASTATHIANS]

INTERIMISTS The party who supported the Emperor Charles V in his attempt to bring about a scheme of comprehension by which the Lutherans might be reunited to the German Church The "Interim" itself was a proclamation of the Emperor, composed by two bishops and the Lutheran John Agricola, making concessions to the reforming party with the view of keeping them in union with the Church during the time necessary for assembling a General Council [ADIAPHORISTS] The thirteenth volume of Schlusselberg's *Hæreticorum Catalogus* contains 879 pages, "De Secta Adiaphoristarum seu Interimistarum"

INTUITIONISTS A name assumed by those American Deists of whom Emerson and Theodore Parker are the leaders It indicates the repudiation of all religion dependent on an external revelation, and looks to the intuitions of the soul as the only guide of humanity Shortly described, this may be defined as a substitution of the idolatry of self for the worship of God, and hence it is often called the "Religion of Humanity"—a name more commonly recognised in connection with the Positivist followers of Comte—as if consciously opposed to the religion of Deity

INVISIBLES Those who deny the visible character, that is the external organization, of the Church, are thus named by some controversial writers

IRVINGITES A sect originated in the year 1831 by Edward Irving, a popular Presbyterian preacher in London, and Mary Campbell, a poor Scotch widow's daughter of Fernicarry, on the borders of the parishes of Rosneath and Row, a few miles from Greenock. The distinctive characteristic of the sect is the belief that a new "outpouring" of God the Holy Ghost has re-established the prophetic and apostolic offices, and also the power of speaking in unknown tongues, and of working miracles The Irvingites give themselves the name of "The Catholic and Apostolic Church," the arrogant assumption of which title they explain as signifying that they form an orthodox community with an apostolic ministry

Irving [A D 1792-1834] was a man of glowing enthusiasm, gifted with a rich eloquence which attracted large congregations to his chapel in Regent Square, London, during the reign of George IV But his eloquence was like the paintings of Turner, which surround common objects with exaggerated splendour, and however well suited his mind might be for the delivery of rhetorical "orations"—as he called his sermons—it was of a very excitable, dreamy cast, looking for wonders, and unconsciously turning common events into wonders when real marvels did not appear It thus happened that between 1826 and 1830 Irving's enthusiastic nature was much influenced by two movements in the "religious world," one being that of the formation of a brotherhood in 1827 by James Haldane Stewart organized to offer united prayers for a fresh "outpouring of the Spirit," and the other that of the meetings held at Albury Park, from 1826 to

1830, by Henry Drummond for the study of prophecy

One of the forty-three clergymen and laymen[1] who attended the Albury meetings was Robert Story, the minister of Rosneath in Dumbartonshire, and when Irving was engaged, in 1828, on a tour in Scotland preaching those glowing lectures on the Apocalypse which he published under the title of *The Last Days*, he paid a visit to Rosneath Mary Campbell was at this time in a very impressible condition, having been prostrated by the death of her lover, and being supposed to be at death's door herself from decline She partook in the excitement[2] of the whole district respecting Irving and his preaching, and easily fell into the tone of his mind, that of looking for wonders Her attention was especially directed at first to an idea of Irving's which had already attracted much notice, "viz, that bodily disease was the direct infliction of Satan, and that therefore faith and prayer, and these only, should be employed as the means of deliverance from it, and that moreover, by the due exercise of these, the power of effecting miracles of healing and other wonderful works, would be restored to the Church—a power hitherto kept in abeyance because of the Church's faithlessness" [Story's *Life of Story*, 195 Oliphant's *Life of Irving*, 275] On a mind so excited by Irving's visit to Rosneath his influence was again brought to bear not long afterwards by the return home in 1829 of his assistant preacher, a young "probationer" named Alexander Scott, whom Irving had carried up from Rosneath to London Of this visit and its results Irving himself gives the following account in *Fraser's Magazine* —

"Being called down to Scotland upon some occasion, and residing for a while at his father's house, which is in the heart of that district of Scotland upon which the light of Mr Campbell's ministry had arisen, he was led to open his mind to some of the godly people in these parts, and among others to a young woman who was at that time lying ill of a consumption, from which afterwards, when brought to the very door of death, she was raised up instantaneously by the mighty hand of God Being a woman of a very fixed and constant spirit, he was not able, with all his power of statement and argument, which is unequalled by that of any other man I have ever met with, to convince her of the distinction between regeneration and baptism with the Holy Ghost, and when he could not prevail he left her with a solemn charge to read over the Acts of the Apostles, with that distinction in her mind, and to beware how she rashly rejected what he believed to be the truth of God By this young woman it was that God, not many months after, did restore the gift of speaking with tongues and prophesying to the Church" [*Fraser's Magazine*, January 1832] The nature of this conversation is more exactly indicated by the fact that a number of people at Port-Glasgow, a neighbouring town, "had been led to pray for and to expect the restoration of 'spiritual gifts' to the Church by a sermon on the nature of the 'Charismata' of the Corinthians, preached by Mr A J Scott" [Story's *Life of Story*, 205]

The expected wonders now arrived quickly both at Port-Glasgow and Fernicarry, and in both places they came to invalid young women For at Port-Glasgow there was a counterpart of Mary Campbell, named Macdonald she also having been in bad health for eighteen months After she and her family had been praying in obedience to the teaching of Mr Irving's juvenile but self-confident curate, this young woman suddenly exclaimed, "'There will be a mighty baptism of the Spirit this day,' and then broke forth in a most marvellous setting forth of the wonderful works of God, and, as if her own weakness had been altogether lost in the strength of the Holy Ghost, continued, with little or no intermission, for two or three hours in mingled praise, prayer, and exhortation" At dinner time, "her twin brothers James and George,"—who were shipbuilders, and had recently been converted, and had become very enthusiastic young men as to their religion,—"came home as usual, whom she then addressed at great length, concluding with a solemn prayer for James that he might *at that time* be endowed with the power of the Holy Ghost Almost instantly James calmly said, 'I have got it' He walked to the window, and stood silent for a minute or two I looked at him, and almost trembled, there was such a change upon his whole countenance He then, with a step and manner of the most indescribable majesty, walked up to ——'s bedside, and addressed her in those words of the twentieth Psalm, 'Arise, and stand upright' He repeated the words, took her by the hand, and she arose, when we all quietly sat down and had our dinner After it, my brothers went to the shipbuilding yard, as usual, where James wrote over to Miss Campbell, commanding her in the name of the Lord to arise' The result may be told in Miss Campbell's own words 'I received dear brother James M'Donald's letter, giving an account of his sister's being raised up, and commanding me to rise and walk I had scarcely read the first page when I became quite overpowered, and laid it aside for a few minutes, but I had no rest in my mind until I took it up again, and began to read As I read, every word came home with power; and when I came to the command to arise, it came home with a power which no one can describe; it was felt to be indeed the voice of Christ, it was such a voice as could not be resisted A mighty power was instantaneously exerted upon me I felt as if I had been lifted from off the earth, and all my diseases taken from me at the voice of Christ I was verily made in a moment to stand upon my

[1] A list of these is given in Evans' *Sketch of Christian Denominations*, p 289, ed 1841 The only names afterwards distinguished are those of Edward Irving, Daniel Wilson, and Hugh M'Neile

[2] This was so great that at Kirkcaldy the church was overcrowded to an extent which broke down a gallery, when, and in the subsequent panic, more than thirty persons were killed

feet, leap and walk, sing and rejoice" [Norton's *Mem of James and George M'Donald*, 107-110]

Meanwhile the expected gift of working miracles had been accompanied, or just preceded, by the expected gift of tongues, for which also Mary Campbell had been prepared by Irving's writings [Story's *Life of Story*, 215] "On a Sunday evening in the month of March" [A D 1830], "Mary, in the presence of a few friends, began to utter sounds to them incomprehensible, and believed by her to be a tongue such as of old might have been spoken on the day of Pentecost, or among the Christians of Corinth This was the first manifestation of the restored 'gift,'—for such it was imagined to be She desired to ascertain what the tongue was in order that she might, if strengthened to do so, repair to the country where it was intelligible, and there begin her long contemplated labours" as a missionary "By and by she announced that she believed it to be the language of a group of islands in the South Pacific Ocean, but as nobody knew the speech of the islanders, it was impossible either to refute or corroborate her assertion, and for the present, at least, she was unable to proceed in person in quest of the remote savages whose mother tongue she held had been revealed to her" [Story's *Life of Story*, 204] Irving's Turnerosque account of the same incident is, "In the midst of their devotion the Holy Ghost came with mighty power upon the sick woman as she lay in her weakness, and constrained her to speak at great length and with superhuman strength in an unknown tongue, to the astonishment of all who heard and to her own great edification,—for 'he that speaketh in an unknown tongue edifieth himself'" [*Fraser's Mag* Jan. 1832]

The account of this occurrence would be incomplete if the reader were not provided with a specimen of the "tongue" thus spoken, as taken down with much care by a man of education who believed in its supernatural character "I now proceed," he writes, "to insert a written specimen of the gift of tongues—this specimen is a very brief vocabulary of a tongue. It was collected by me, on different occasions, in the beginning of this present year [1831], on which I heard the same individual speak in a tongue, and it was written down by me on the spot while the individual was in the act of speaking

The words of the tongue, as written down by me, are widely scattered, none in the order they were spoken, except those marked within inverted commas Hippo—Gerosto—Hippo—Booros—Senoote—'Foorime—Oorin Hoopo Tanto Noos tin'—Noorastin—Niparos—Hipanos—Bantos—Boorin—'O Pinitos'—Elelastina—Halimungitos—Dantitu—Hampootina—Farini—Aristos—Ekrampos—'Epoongos Vangami'—Beressino—Tereston—Sastinootino—Almoosis—'O Fastos Sungor O Fastos Sungor'—Denpangito—Boorinos—Hypen—Elctanteti—Eretini—Menati" [M'Kerrell's *Apology for the Gift of Tongues, &c.* Greenock, 1831].[1]

Such "utterances," made by a hysterical young girl[2] lately disappointed of marriage to a few credulous village people in the West of Scotland, are as unlike as possible to those of the twelve Apostles, who had companied with their Lord all the time that He went in and out among them from the time of His baptism until that of His Resurrection [Acts i 21, 22], and whose utterances among the devout men out of every nation under heaven confounded the multitude, because that every man heard them speak in his own language [Acts ii 4-6] Nor was it exactly consonant with an experience which if true was so astounding, that Mary Campbell immediately afterwards filled up the place of her lost lover by marrying a lawyer's clerk, named Caird, whose acquaintance she had recently made. But such critical considerations did not occur to Irving, who, after very little inquiry, was satisfied that the "gift" was a reality, and invited the young couple to his house in London, whence they went to be fêted at Brampton Park by Lady Olivia Sparrow, and at Albury Park by Lady Harriet and Mr Henry Drummond[3]

Before this visit to London took place, however, three gentlemen (one of whom was a member of Irving's congregation) went down to Scotland to make inquiries respecting the alleged "gifts" These returned in October 1830, and their report[4] was of such a nature as to lead to the organization of prayer meetings (under the guidance of Irving and several Evangelical clergymen), "to seek of God the revival of the gifts of the Holy Ghost in the Church" These prayer-meetings began towards the close of 1830, and on April 30th, 1831, the first "utterance" was heard from the lips of a lady (the wife of one of the three who had formed the deputation), who was attending such a prayer-meeting in her own house, Mary Campbell (now Mrs Caird) being then, or within a few days, a visitor in Irving's house [*Letter on certain Statements in the Old Church Porch* ed 1855, pp

[1] The FRENCH PROPHETS had long before claimed to speak in unknown tongues, and to work miracles. Calamy describes the "tongues" in their case as "syllabical, with a distinct heave and breathe between each syllable, but it required attention to distinguish the words" The SHAKERS of America, who were descended from the Camisards, professed to do the same, and Dr Dwight describes their "unknown language," as he heard it in 1783, as a succession of unmeaning sounds, frequently repeated, and half articulated" At the very time also when the "unknown tongues" began to be uttered in Scotland and England they were being uttered among the MORMONS (clearly without any communication) in America

[2] The two young men before referred to, and some others, also professed to have the gift They were never in any way connected with Mr Irving's London ministrations, and both died in 1835

[3] Although this "destitute girl" married only a lawyer's clerk, who was glad to be employed as a lay missionary by Lady Olivia Sparrow, Mr Story speaks of seeing her not long afterwards maintaining the rôle of a fine lady at Rosneath, where "one of her sisters, clad in the coarsest garb, had not long before been seen loading a dung cart in the adjoining field" [Story's *Life of Story*, 213]

[4] *A Brief Account of a Visit to some of the Brethren in the West of Scotland*, 1831

14, 15] On her arrival, the "manifestations" began among Irving's own people, but they were not permitted by Irving to be made in public until Sunday, October 16th, 1831 From the account given in the *Times*, it appears that on the morning of that day Irving preached in his chapel in Regent Square on the extraordinary gifts of the Holy Spirit, and that a Miss Hall, a governess, mindful of her pastor's fiat as to privacy, retired to the vestry, and spoke there for some time in an unknown tongue In the evening, Irving preached on the same subject, and expressed doubts whether he was doing right in forbidding the publicity of the "utterances" Upon this, the master of a "young gentlemen's academy," named Taplin, rose and gave forth the first "utterance" that had as yet proceeded from a masculine voice this effusion ending with the intelligible words, "Oh! Britain, thou anointed of the Lord! thy destruction is at hand! Fear not ye people of God" Much confusion of course ensued, and when Taplin had sunk into his pew exhausted, Irving put an end to it by concluding the service [*Times*, October 19th, 1831] Some illustrations of the unknown tongues spoken at this stage of the sect's history, are given by one who had himself been carried away by the excitement [Pilkington's *Unknown Tongues*, p 27], and they are of just the same character as those of Mary Campbell, allowing for the difference between Scotch-English and London-English Such were "gthis dil emma sumo," 'hozeghin alta stare," "holmoth holif au thau" [holy, most holy father], 'hozehamenanostra, hozehamenanostra, hozehamenanostra" [oh! send men and apostles], "casa sera hastha caro, yeo cogo nomo," which look like scraps of English broken up and spoken in an hysterical voice Nine times out of ten, the utterances of this "unknown" type were long drawn "Ohs" and "Ahs" with a fragmentary syllable interposed at rare intervals, the whole being brought to a close in a cadence which ended in a theatrical whisper

Irving now wrote to his father-in-law, Dr Martin, on October 26th, "Thanks should be returned in all the churches for the work which the Lord has done, and is doing amongst us He has raised up the order of prophets amongst us, who, being filled with the Holy Ghost, do speak with tongues and prophesy" [Oliphant's *Life of Irving*, ii 193]

Three months afterwards, on January 24th, 1832, he was able to write again respecting an old acquaintance who had joined him in London, "The Lord hath anointed Baxter of Doncaster after another kind, I think the apostolical . the prophetical being the ministration of the Word, the apostolical being the administration of the Spirit" [*ibid* 234]

Irving was now expelled from the Scotch Kirk, partly for an unsound opinion that the human nature of our Lord was capable of sin, and partly on account of the 'manifestations" made under his sanction, the sentence of expulsion being passed by the Presbytery of London on May 2nd, 1832, and by that of Annan in March 1833 For a time he preached in the streets and fields, collecting congregations such as had surrounded Whitfield nearly a century before, at Charing Cross, in Goodman's Fields, on Islington Green, and in such public localities But a temporary chapel was shortly obtained for him in Gray's Inn Lane, and a permanent one before long in Newman Street, and in these he began to resume the ministrations which had been broken in upon by his expulsion from Regent Square He was now, however, reduced to the ranks by the powers which he had been instrumental in calling into existence Having been absent from London for a short time he was about, on his return, "to resume his functions, when he was directed by a word spoken supernaturally by the apostle who had been first called," "to suspend his ministry except in preaching, and not to administer the sacraments in the congregation until he should receive a new ordination" [Davenport's *Edw Irving and the Cath Ap Ch* 2nd ed 16] Having thus been brought into a proper submission to the new authorities he was soon afterwards reinstated in office by being ordained as "angel over the Church in Newman Street," on April 5th, 1833 but he exercised his new office for a very short time, being soon afterwards prostrated by his last illness, and dying at Glasgow, in the cathedral of which city he was buried, on December 8th, 1834, when he was only forty-two years old

The "apostolical anointing of Baxter," spoken of by Irving in the letter recently quoted, indicates the development of the sect into its characteristic ministerial organization Some of the leading members of the rising sect at this time were members of the Church of England, especially Mr Henry Drummond, the financial backbone of the sect, Mr Bayford and his sons, Proctors in Doctors' Commons, and Mr Bayford's son-in-law, H J Owen, the minister of Park Chapel, Chelsea, and son of one of the principal founders of the Bible Society, who had been minister there before him, and a prominent member of the Evangelical party Mr Bayford, who was afterwards conspicuous for his utterances in the Irvingite Chapel at Chelsea, began them on a Sunday morning in 1833 at Park Chapel by shouting out, during his son in-law's sermon, "The darkness, the darkness, the darkness, covereth, covereth the earth, and gross darkness the people thereof." An unmarried daughter afflicted with epileptic hysteria, was one of the most frequent speakers of "utterances" of the "unknown tongues," which in her case were precisely such sounds as are usually made by persons in that sad condition Her case (which was known to so wide a circle of persons that it became a matter of public knowledge) is mentioned as indicating the probable origin of these alleged supernatural manifestations in natural causes It must be remembered that the "utterances" all came from young women at first · and the sympathetic contagiousness of hysteria is well known Mr Owen, son-in-law to Mr Bayford, was "ordained angel of the Church in Chelsea" in January 1834

To none of these was the Presbyterian system

acceptable, but at the same time as Churchmen they well knew that the Episcopalian system could not be adopted for a permanency without an episcopate Just at this time much prominence was also being given to the doctrine of apostolical succession by the rising school of High Churchmen, under the teaching of Bishop Lloyd, Hugh James Rose, Keble, and Isaac Williams, and the idea of an apostolate as the only true source of a ministry had become familiar to the thoughtful laity and clergy of the Church of England Thus a want was felt by them in respect to the organization of any new body in which the supernatural gifts of the Spirit should manifest themselves, a want which would not have been felt by Irving (who was quite content with the Presbyterian system), and "at the very beginning of the utterances, the cry in the Spirit came, 'Send us apostles—send us apostles' The same word was often heard, though but imperfectly" [*ibid*] This want was, as usual, met by an "utterance" While Mr Drummond was holding a prayer-meeting in his house on December 26th, 1832, "The Spirit spoke through Mr Caird"—who with his wife, Mary Campbell, was staying at Albury Park—"saying, Let the Lord do His work let Him declare all His mind let His working alone be seen in the midst of you" Lady Olivia Sparrow's rising young "lay missionary" was shortly followed by the master of the young gentlemen's academy "The Spirit broke forth in Mr Taplin with great power in a tongue, and thus said, 'The Lord commandeth you, you who have been called to be an apostle, to lay hands on the angel of this church, and ordain him to rule and feed this people—to feed them with the Body and Blood of the Lord, be faithful, be faithful, and Jesus will honour you' After a short pause, Mr Cardale advanced to Mr Drummond, who was kneeling at the desk, and after a prayer, mighty in the Spirit, beginning at Creation, and going through the manifestations of God unto the Person, sufferings, and glory of the Lord Jesus, with strong crying for faith, and that the hand of the Lord alone might be seen, put both his hands on Mr. Drummond's head, the latter seemingly deeply absorbed in communion with God, the Spirit in Mr Cardale saying, 'Be thou filled with the Holy Ghost, and with the spirit of wisdom and of knowledge, and of a sound mind, be thou of a quick understanding in the fear of the Lord, feed and rule this people, be thou faithful unto death, and thou shalt receive the crown of life which the Lord hath prepared for thee, and for all who love the Lord Jesus' Then turning to Mr Bayford, he blessed him, and spake words of encouragement, exhorting him to feed this people, and in so doing he himself should be fed Immediately after this, the Spirit burst forth in Mr Drummond in a song, 'Glory to God in the highest,' when the Spirit in Mr Caird took up the same strain in the name of the Church, singing the doxology, in which the congregation joined" After further exhortations to Mr. Drummond and Mr Bayford, "the Spirit in Mr Taplin then, after singing for a while in a tongue, declared that Jesus had been in the midst of us, that His arms were open to receive us, that we should flee into them" [*A Letter written from Albury Park, on Dec 28th*, 1832 Story's *Life of Story*, 409].

It was in this manner, by several persons of low education and station, and in needy circumstances, designating their patron the rich banker as a minister, that the manifestation of the new apostolate was made, and thus that a new apostolic fountain is alleged to have been opened for the outflow of a new stream of ministry in the Church of God According to an Irvingite writer, "the apostolate to the Gentiles, of which the beginning and pattern were seen in Paul, was restored, in order that the work of presenting the Church as a chaste Virgin to Christ at His coming, which Paul was compelled to leave unfinished, might be taken up and carried to its completion" [Andrews' *Ch History, &c of Cath and Ap Ch* 1868, p 16] By July 14th, 1835, other "apostles" to the number of twelve had been appointed, and by these the "angels" and "elders" were ordained, who are supposed to have the same ministerial standing as bishops and priests in the Church of England and other churches Having shut themselves out from that historical succession which is derived from the call and the ordination of Christ, the sect has supplied itself with another succession derived from the call of "utterances," made under the peculiar circumstances above indicated

The value of such utterances in "unknown tongues" may be estimated by the specimen given above It was necessary for practical purposes, such as the deposition of Mr Irving and the establishment of an apostolate, that the utterances should be in plain English, and there are some which are on record as spoken on the day when the Newman Street Chapel was opened In expounding the history of Hannah, Irving spoke of the Church as barren, "conceiving, but not having brought forth" An utterance—not quite catching the idea—comes in, "Oh, but she shall be fruitful, oh! oh! oh! she shall replenish the earth and subdue it—and subdue it" A little further on another, still less apposite to the subject of the discourse, breaks in as follows —"Oh! you do grieve the Spirit—you do grieve the Spirit! Oh! the Body of Jesus is to be sorrowful in spirit! You are to cry to your Father—to cry, to cry in the bitterness of your souls! Oh! it is a mourning, a mourning, a mourning before the Lord—a sighing and crying unto the Lord because of the desolations of Zion—because of the desolations of Zion—because of the desolations of Zion!" Another utterance is thus given —"Oh! grieve Him not! Oh! grieve not your Father! Rest in His love! Oh! rejoice in your Father's love! Oh! rejoice in the love of Jesus! in the love of Jesus! Oh! for it passeth knowledge! Oh! the length! Oh! the breadth! Oh! the height! Oh! the depth of the love of Jesus! Oh! it passeth knowledge! Oh! rejoice in the love of Jesus! Oh! sinner! for what, for what, what,

Oh! sinner! what can separate, separate, separate from the love of Jesus! Oh! nothing, nothing! Oh! none can pluck you out of His hands! Oh! none shall be able to pluck you out of your Father's hand." Notice is given that persons will only be admitted to the body of the church by ticket, when Mr Drummond—a forcible speaker in the House of Commons—adds the following "utterance" —"Ah! be ye warned! be ye warned! Ye have been warned! The Lord hath prepared you a table, but it is a table in the presence of your enemies Ah! look you well to it! the city shall be builded—ah! every jot, every piece of the edifice Be faithful each under his load—each under his load, but see that ye build with one hand, and with a weapon in the other Look to it! Look to it! Ye have been warned! Ah! Sanballat! Sanballat! Sanballat! The Horonite! The Moabite! The Ammonite! Ah! confederate! confederate! confederate with the Horonite! Ah! look ye to it! look ye to it!" [Oliphant's *Life of Irving*, ii 223-5] Such utterances as these were to be heard in Irvingite chapels for many years, but the better educated and less hysterical portion of the sect has been long growing ashamed of them[1] On no other ground than their validity can the sect, however, lay claim to a divinely commissioned ministry, and if they are given up then also the claims of the community to be "catholic" or "apostolic" must be given up likewise.

The ceremonial first adopted by the Irvingites was intended to be as near an approach as was practicable to that of the Primitive Church At the upper end of the chapel a "bema" or platform was erected, affording room for forty or fifty persons On the front of it seven seats were arranged, the middle one being occupied by the "angel," and the three on either side by the "elders" On a step lower down were seven other seats for the "prophets," the centre one being occupied by the senior or principal one On a still lower step seven deacons were seated in a similar manner The general direction of the service rested with the "angel," but the elders preached short sermons in order, the prophets spoke occasionally, and every now and then, with more or less frequency, the services were interrupted by utterances either of the "unknown tongue" type or of that shewn in the specimens given from those spoken by Mr Drummond As the High Church movement and literature developed in the Church many progressive changes in accordance with it took place in the Irvingite chapels, choral services, copes, and splendidly vested altars being introduced, and this ritual movement in the sect reached its climax in a magnificent chapel which was erected in Gordon Square, London, and opened on Christmas Eve in the year 1854. A very elaborate ritual is now adopted, and a Service Book has been compiled, which shews a high degree of liturgical knowledge, and great ability on the part of its compilers in applying it to the wants of the day

In the early days of the Irvingite movement it was expected that the Day of Judgment and the Millennium were close at hand, that the movement itself was the immediate preparation for Christ's Second Advent, and that hence it would spread far and wide throughout the world The "apostles," therefore, first of all prepared a "Testimony," which was delivered in 1836 to King William IV and his Privy Councillors, and in 1837 to the Pope and Prince Metternich, and, secondly, dispersed themselves among the "twelve tribes of the Gentiles" throughout Europe "Their hearts had been enlarged to embrace all the baptized, and they longed for the perfecting of that one body, of which every tribe was an essential part, and each necessary to the completion of the whole But those aspirations were not destined to be immediately realized" [*Chron of Events*, 28] In fact nothing came of this apostolic mission except a pleasant ecclesiastical tour and some instruction respecting the Christianity of European nations A tour of a similar kind was undertaken again in the year 1845, when a few converts were made in America and in Germany In England the sect has never grown beyond a few thousands, and is more important as to its principles and claims than as to its numbers [Story's *Life of Story of Rosneath* Oliphant's *Life of Irving* Norton's *Memoirs of J and G Macdonald* Baxter's *Irvingism, its Rise, Progress, and Present State*, 1836 *A Chronicle of certain Events which have taken place in the Church of Christ, principally in England, between* 1826 *and* 1852]

ISBRANIKI, or "The Company of the Elect" One of the numerous sects which were formed in Russia in the middle of the seventeenth century, during the patriarchate of Nicon [A D 1654] The cause of separation was not any difference of doctrine or ritual, but a desire to protest against the laxity and inclination to change displayed by the clergy, and to adopt a greater piety and purity of life. They were termed by the orthodox party Roscolschika, or "Seditionists" Pinkerton in his dissertation on Russian sects speaks of the Isbraniki as identical with the STAROVERTZI, or "Believers of the old faith" [Platon, *Present State of Greek Church in Russia*, Pinkerton's transl]

ISCARIOTÆ Among the strange freaks of early heretics was that of honouring Judas Iscariot, on the ground that his act of betraying our Lord into the hands of His persecutors and executioners was done with the intention of bringing about the salvation of mankind They are alleged also to have maintained that this act of Judas was the more meritorious because he knew that the "Virtutes" desired to hinder the sufferings of Christ, and therefore to obstruct the salvation of men The sect is mentioned only by Philaster, and he does not assign to it any particular locality [Philast. *de Hæres* XXXIV]. But Irenæus attributes a similar belief to the Cainites [Iren *adv Hæres* i. 31], and it has not been

[1] A quantity of ejaculatory rhapsodies of a similar kind are to be found at pages 158-167 of a book previously quoted, Norton's *Memoirs of James and George Macdonald*

without a place in the speculations of even modern writers [CAINITES]

ISCARIOTÆ. A controversial name given by some Roman Catholic writers about 1560 to those Lutherans who denied that Judas Iscariot partook of the Eucharist with the other Apostles at the time of its institution [Sianda, *Lexic Polem s v*]

ISIDORUS A disciple of Basilides, perhaps his son [Hippol *Ref Hær* vii 8]

ISTINEEYE CHRISTIANE [MALAKANES]

ITALIAN PROTESTANTS Protestantism never obtained a firm footing in Italy, where, as in Spain, and in Southern Europe generally, it was crushed out by the Inquisition Its history consists of little more than the enumeration of the names of certain distinguished individuals, who betrayed a leaning towards some of the Reformed doctrines, especially that of Justification by Faith as taught by Luther and his contemporaries Such were the Cardinal Gaspar Contarini, the exile Reginald Pole, afterwards Archbishop of Canterbury, Cardinal Morone, Archbishop of Modena, imprisoned for his opinions by Paul IV A D 1557, Brucioli, who translated the Bible into Italian, first the New Testament A D 1630, and the remainder two years afterwards, Juan de Valdez, the Spanish secretary at Naples, Aonio Paleario, the probable author of a book entitled *The Benefit of Christ's Death*, which appeared A D 1543, and of which 40,000 copies were afterwards bought up and burned by the Inquisition About this period also [A D 1530-1542] many refugees took shelter in different parts of Italy, holding Protestant opinions, which they began to disseminate with activity In this course they were aided by Bernardino Ochino, who was compelled to fly to Geneva A D 1542, and Peter Martyr Vermigli, who about the same time found refuge at Zurich These events led to a strong counter-movement, commenced under Pope Paul III and continued under his successor Julius III Commotions caused by the Reformers in Naples [A D 1546] were quelled by the united forces of Charles V and his viceroy Don Pedro de Toledo But it was the spiritual power directed by Cardinal Caraffa, afterwards Paul IV, and carrying out its purpose by the establishment of the Inquisition, which effectually quelled the tendency to Protestantism, and rendered it till recent years, under Victor Emanuel, a stranger to the soil of Italy. [M'Crie's *History of the Progress and Suppression of the Reformation in Italy.*]

J

JACOBELLUS The parish priest of St Michael's Church at Prague, with whom the CALIXTINES originated His native place was Misa in Bohemia, though he is sometimes called Jacobellus Misnensis from the mistaken impression that he belonged to Misnia Huss had not considered it essential that the laity should receive the Cup in the Holy Communion, although he stated his opinion at the Council of Constance that it was proper they should do so But about the end of the year 1414, James of Misa revived the practice of administering the Holy Communion in both elements at the instigation of Peter of Dresden, who had himself been recently driven out of Bohemia. Jacobellus defended his practice before the Council of Constance on June 15th, 1415, a few weeks before the condemnation and execution of Huss [Hardt's *Hist Conc Const* iii 591] He also wrote *Demonstratio per testimonia Scripturæ Patrum ac Doctorum, communicationem Calicis esse necessarium*, and other tracts, in support of the practice in the controversy that arose [*ibid* 805] The account of his first administration of the Cup is given from the Roman side by Æneas Sylvius, in the 35th chapter of his *History of Bohemia*, and by an eye-witness on the Calixtine side, Laurence Brzezyna, or Byzinus, Chancellor of the city of Prague, in his *Diarium belli Hussitici ab anno* 1414 *ad* 1423 in Ludwig's *Reliq MSS* vi 124

JACOBITES The name by which the adherents of the Monophysite heresy have been known since the sixth century Some Jacobite writers trace the origin of the name to James the brother of our Lord, others to Dioscorus, whose name was James before he became Patriarch of Alexandria The more probable derivation of it is from Jacobus Baradæus, a Syrian monk, who was Bishop of Edessa, about a century after the rise of the sect [A D 541-578], and who was the greatest propagator of its distinctive principles in Syria and Egypt Baradæus was also surnamed Zanzalus, and hence the Jacobites have been sometimes called Zanzalians [Neale's *Patriarch Alex.* ii 7]

The history of the heresy will be found under the title MONOPHYSITES It is sufficient here to notice that the Jacobite Churches comprise three Patriarchates, those of Alexandria, the East or Antioch, and Armenia, and that since the conquest of Alexandria by the Saracens, the Jacobite form of Christianity has been that recognised or established by the Mahometan rulers of Egypt This arose partly from the fact that the Jacobites were far more numerous than the orthodox, or MELCHITES, and partly because the latter represented the established religion under the Greek Emperors, had offered vigorous opposition to the conquerors, and were looked upon as "royalists" in the sense of still adhering to the Greek Emperors [Renaudot's *Hist Patriarch Alex.*, Neale's *Hist Patriarch Alex.* COPTS]

JAMBLICHUS [NEO PLATONISTS]

JAMNICH [BOHEMIAN BRETHREN MORAVIANS]

JANOW [MATTHIAS OF JANOW]

JANSENISTS A school of Roman Catholic theologians which derives its name from Cornelius Jansen, the great champion of Augustinianism in the sixteenth century

From the fifth century to the present time the Western Church has ever taken St. Augustine as its leading theologian, but in the scholastic age a disturbed view of his teaching had been adopted, and the severe Pelagianism of the Schools was notorious During the Reformation period, Baius, Professor of Theology at Louvain, aimed at a restoration of the true Augustinian scheme of grace, and laboured at this work from the year 1551 to 1580, when he was silenced by Pope Gregory XIII [BAIUS]

In A D 1588, Molina, a Spanish Jesuit, published a work *On the Agreement of Free-Will with Grace and Predestination* It was more Pelagian than anything that had been advanced by the Schoolmen The different theories of the doctrine of grace had been made needlessly intricate by a confused use of terms The Thomists allowed that divine grace *per se* is efficacious, and requires no co-operation on the part of man's will to give it full effect, though the will side with it, but that it does depend in some degree on external circumstances for its efficacious virtue The Augustinians agreed with the Thomists, only in lieu of this external "premotion" associated with the action of grace they imagined a moral or esoteric "premotion," the virtue of which is the same But beside this efficacious grace, or grace which cannot fail of its effect, both parties recognised grace of a lower order, which the will of man has power to thwart. The Thomists called it "sufficient," but it was a misnomer, for it was an insufficient agent upon the will of man, which may and does rebel against it, the Augustinians therefore, with more preciseness, termed it "excitant." The adoption of two terms to express a single idea was sure to cause misunderstanding. A fresh element of confusion was introduced by Molina, who, discarding the idea of efficacious grace, as already defined, retained the name. This grace was simply the "sufficient" grace of the one school, the "excitant" grace of the other; but whereas that grace might or might not be resisted by the will of the recipient, so he made a twofold distinction: "efficacious" grace which is not resisted, and "sufficient" grace which is thwarted by yielding to concupiscence. The Roman doctrine has never swerved: it has always been that of Aquinas and Augustine.

In the controversies that ensued on the publication of Molina's work the Franciscans took part with the Jesuits, now called Molinists, against the Dominicans, who were chiefly formidable as being the living soul of the Inquisition. The case was brought before that tribunal, having already been prejudged in favour of Augustinianism by the Universities of Salamanca and of Louvain and Douay in the Low Countries. Even Baronius allows that the book of Molina contained more than half a hundred Pelagian propositions. The Jesuits however were sufficiently powerful to avoid impending condemnation, for which purpose a bull, still extant, was prepared, though never put in force. The Molinist system sets forth, that all possible action of free-will is foreseen; that God wills to save where man is willing to be saved; He gives all necessary help in varying degree; predestination and reprobation are dependent upon God's foreknowledge; His grace *per se* is not efficacious, for it was not so in our first parents; God wills the salvation of all through Christ, and grace is given to all sufficient for salvation, "sufficient" meaning grace supplemented and made efficacious by the will of man. The Dominicans attacked these notions with vigour; and, with the view of composing the strife, Clement VIII [A.D. 1597] called into being the "Congregatio de auxiliis," to consider and report upon the true doctrine of Divine aid by grace. Its deliberations were continued interruptedly till A.D. 1607, when Molinist doctrine was declared to be Pelagian; though the Bull prepared for its formal condemnation was reserved till some favourable time for its promulgation: but the Jesuits were known and feared, and the "fulmen" was never launched.

Such were the controversies on grace that were going on during the younger years of Jansen, and determined the complexion of his theology, and that of the writers of Port-Royal. This convent, the headquarters of Jansenism, was situated in a romantic valley three miles from Versailles. It was originally a cell of the Cistercian order, but transferred by papal authority to the jurisdiction of the Archbishop of Paris. Pope Honorius III. [A.D. 1223] granted to it certain privileges as an asylum for lay persons who were weary of the world. La Mère Angelique, still of tender age, of the Arnauld family, became abbess of the house A.D. 1602. By the advice of her confessor, the Jesuit Binet, she removed her nuns to a house in the Rue St. Jacques, Paris [A.D. 1638], known as Port Royal de Paris, when the original establishment, designated "Port Royal des Champs," became, under the rectorship of St. Cyran, an asylum for those who wished for seclusion without taking monastic vows. Here he gathered around him Antoine le Maistre, who renounced a brilliant parliamentary position, with his brother, Simon Séricourt, and Isaac de Sacy, the translator of the New Testament; Robert and Dr. Antoine Arnauld, author of the work on *Frequent Communion*, in opposition to the scholastic theory of the "opus operatum;" Lancelot, and other distinguished men. Prayer, reading of Scripture, study, and bodily exercise, filled out the day; and the severe simplicity of Port Royal life contrasted significantly with the neighbouring frivolity and courtly vices of Paris. St. Francis of Sales and its first abbé, St. Cyran, of the Benedictine order, gave to the establishment a tone of mysticism, and at the same time its character of literary enthusiasm and educational zeal.

Cornelius Jansen was born [A.D. 1585] at Acqoi in Holland, and became Professor of Theology at Louvain, A.D. 1630. His *Mars Gallicus* obtained for him the bishopric of Ypres [A.D. 1636], and for his friend Jean Duvergier de Hauranne, better known as the Abbé St. Cyran, a seven years' imprisonment in the Château of Vincennes till the year of his death, A.D. 1643. Jansen having, to use his own expression, played long enough "the school pedant and ass," made it the great object of his life to restore the teaching of Augustine to its proper position in the Church, and to shew how much it had been perverted by the Schoolmen, and more especially by the Scotist party. In a twenty years' preparation he read over Augustine's treatises on Pelagianism thirty times, and the remainder of that Father's works ten times. His *Augustinus* was still in MS. when he died of the plague, A.D. 1637, commending the publication of it to his friends Libert-Fromond and Calenus. It was a service of difficulty and of some risk, for the Jesuits, aware that it was aimed at their Molinist notions, obtained possession of sheets as they passed through the press, and denounced the work both at Rome and to the Faculty of Theology at Louvain, as contravening the injunctions of Sixtus V. against the maintenance of controversies with respect to grace. Before any steps could be taken, the printers, by redoubled diligence and with the connivance of the university, had completed their work; the *Augustinus* was published at Louvain, in the centenary year of the Jesuit order [A.D. 1640],[1] and reprinted shortly afterwards at Paris and Rouen.

In the first volume Jansen defines the distinctive tenets of the Pelagian and Semi-Pelagian, and shews that the doctrines of Molina essentially agreed with them. The second volume assigns

[1] *Augustinus, Doctrina S. Augustini de Humanæ Naturæ sanitate, ægritudine, medicina, adversus Pelagianos et Massilienses.* T. i. *in quo hæreses et mores Pelagii ex S. Augustino recensentur et refutantur.* T. ii. *in quo genuina sententia profundissimi doctoris de auxilio gratiæ, etc. proponitur.*

the limits of human reason and adjusts the claims of authority with a particular reference to the authoritative teaching of Augustine. Reversing the scholastic principle, he affirmed that philosophy and theology were entirely unconnected with each other, the former affecting the intellectual faculty, the latter being determined by prescription and traditions flowing from the fountain-head. Augustine is the careful exponent of these traditions, raised up for that purpose by Divine Providence, inspired by God's Spirit, and predestined by His grace, to advance beyond the lines laid down by him is full of peril. The germ of evil in Adam, which led to the Fall, was his freedom of will, unfettered by the grace in which he was created, Jansen adopting the Infralapsarian view. Grace was no superadded gift, it was the dowry of Adam's being. He was at liberty to forfeit his freedom, if he cast away the love of God, which alone is perfect freedom. Original sin is not mere imputation of sin, it is a depravation of nature. Concupiscence is a taint of sin in body and soul. The penal consequences of birth-sin are ignorance and evil desires, both of which are truly sin as corresponding with nothing in the divine exemplar in which man was created. The position of concupiscence is to be noted, which the Manichee and Pelagian make the antecedent, and Augustine a consequence, of the Fall. The sinner's will is free though bound by sin, as the Divine Will is free though bound by its own law of mercy and truth. The best deeds of the natural man are no better than splendid sins, a proposition that had been condemned in Baius by Pius V, as Jansen stated, through an insufficient acquaintance with Augustine and the decisions of former popes.

The third book treats in ten sections of the Grace of Christ. This is not merely revealed truth, but inward remedial aid, a real power. The fear of God and of eternal punishment cannot remove evil from the heart, fear is the self-growth of the fallen soul, there is nothing of God in it, and occasion is taken to attack by the way the scholastic notion of attrition.[1] Grace as a divine power restores to man his freedom in will and deed. God is the Author of all grace, and He gives it according to His good pleasure, not as foreseeing in the recipient any fitness, but simply because He wills it. Yet the recipient is no mere passive agent in the hand of God, for God's work, co-ordinate with human action, obtains its adjustment through the will of the agent. God gives to many a desire for His love and for gracious deeds, but vouchsafes to few power and performance. Faith is the source of all good, and love is its fruit. God bestows the gift of faith on many, but the rare "gift of perseverance" alone can make faith effective. All things work together for good to the elect, and all things, even the gifts of faith and love, apart from perseverance, work together for the damnation of those that are rejected. God determines their destined end, both to the objects of election and of preterition, He appoints also the correlative mean, the stirrings of grace and the errings of sin. The fulfilment of duty is the happiest condition of man, and it is the pledge of his election. The reprobate by their sins are as a lurid beacon-light to the elect, to warn off from the rock of destruction, and thus even these fulfil the purpose of their being. In bestowing His grace upon the elect God bestows Himself.

The Bull of Urban VIII, "In eminenti" [A D 1642], condemned the *Augustinus* as a revival of Baian error, but its publication was deferred from a hope of stifling controversy by quiet means. In the next year Dr Antoine Arnauld, "the great Arnauld" as the Jansenists termed him, but whose name was derived by the Jesuits from ἀρνοῦμαι, "the renegade," published his treatise *De la fréquente Communion*,[2] based entirely on Jansen's view of predestination and rejection. His legal training suggested the notable distinction of "de facto" and "de jure" that afterwards acquired so much importance. The book was denounced at once by the Jesuit College at Rome, and condemned by Urban VIII, A D 1643. Arnauld yielded to the storm by retiring into private life to exercise his pen in the Jansenist cause [A D 1649]. Dr Cornet, Syndic of the Theological Faculty, laid before the Sorbonne seven propositions, subsequently reduced to five, framed from Jansen's writings, but without his name. The Doctors were divided, but the propositions were referred to the Court of Rome, where they were formally considered and condemned by Innocent X in the Bull "Cum occasione," A D 1653. The distinction of "de facto" and "de jure" now came to the rescue of the perplexed Jansenists. All of the clerical order and members of religious houses were commanded to subscribe the condemnation of the propositions as drawn from Jansen's writings. It was generally denied that the terms were "de facto" Jansen's, their heretical tendency "de jure" was another thing. The distinction was pressed home, and while infallibility was allowed to the Court of Rome in synod assembled "de jure," in matters of doctrine its complete fallibility was shewn from several historical instances, in which it was seen that the Holy See had often erred in matters of fact.[3] Thus the Jansenist party could subscribe the document in the "de jure" point of view, while they denied "de facto" that it contained any ground of personal condemnation as regarded Jansen. The impugnment of infallibility in any sense was a serious gravamen. But were the five

[1] See also Arnauld's work *De la fréquente Communion*

[2] *Où les sentiments des Peres, des Papes et des Conciles touchant l'usage des Sacramens de pénitence et d'Eucharistie sont fidèlement exposés, pour servir d'addresse aux personnes qui pensent sérieusement à se convertir à Dieu, et aux pasteurs et confesseurs zélés pour le bien des âmes*

[3] A clear instance of Papal fallibility in matters of fact occurred on the death of Steenoven, Archbishop of Utrecht, while under papal interdict. In a brief the Pope declared his death to be "a visible mark of Divine vengeance; so also was that of Doncker, who died in impenitence and damnable disobedience." Doncker, a most respectable parish priest of Amsterdam, read the brief on the next Sunday from his pulpit.

propositions really to be found in the *Augustinus*? Cornet, the originator of the movement, had made no such statement The Papal Bull had not named Jansen, though in a brief from the Pope to the Bishop of Tulle the propositions were assumed "to have been taken from the book of Cornelius Jansen"

While the subscription was being enforced another element of discord arose [A D 1655] The Duc de Liancourt was refused absolution in the Church of St Sulpice at Paris for harbouring a Jansenist abbé under his roof This drew forth the letters from Arnauld "To a Person of Quality," from which the watchful adversary extracted two points contrary to Roman authority 1 That the five propositions had never been held by Jansen 2 That the grace without which man is inoperative was wanting to St Peter, since it is impossible to say that he was without sin Arnauld, it should be noted, maintained that it is not only after deadly sin that grace deserts a man, but after sin of whatever kind, the incitement to which is not loyally resisted Upon these points Arnauld was condemned, though informally, by the Sorbonne, and degraded from the doctorate[1] Eighty others shared his disgrace rather than subscribe an unjust sentence From that time Arnauld was emphatically known by his party as "the Doctor"

It was at this juncture that Blaise Pascal, on intimate terms with the inmates of Port Royal, put forth his *Provincial Letters*[2] The injustice done to his friend by the Jesuits drove him to carry war to the knife into their camp. The rough material for his weapons of offence was prepared by Arnauld, who knew thoroughly well the whole system of equivocation called by the Jesuits casuistical divinity, but they were polished up by Pascal, pointed with an exquisite irony, and feathered with a wit that has never had its parallel The way in which he disposes of the inadequate notion of "sufficient" grace may be cited as an example "'Well now, my father,' he says to an imaginary Thomist, 'is this grace, vouchsafed to all, sufficient?' 'Certainly' 'Yet void of effect without efficacious grace?' 'Just so' 'Then all men have sufficient but not efficacious grace?' 'Yes' 'That is, all have sufficient and not sufficient grace In truth, a subtle distinction Have you then forgotten on giving up the world what the word "sufficient" means there? To use an illustration that you will comprehend If they gave you no more than a couple of ounces of bread and a glass of water for your daily meal, would you be content with your superior if he were to tell you that it was sufficient for your need? that is, with something else that he withheld from you, you would have all that was required for your support How then can you bring yourself to say that all men have sufficient grace to act, when you add that another grace which all men have not is absolutely necessary that action may be possible? If I deny sufficient grace you call me a Jansenist, if I acknowledge it with the Jesuits, and affirm that efficacious grace is not necessary, you brand me with heresy, if I confess its necessity with you, asserting that efficacious grace is also necessary, I sin against common sense, and I am a fool, as the Jesuits say What am I to believe then in this inevitable predicament of being either a Jansenist, a heretic, or a fool?'"

Elsewhere there is a grotesqueness in his description of Jesuit doctrine with respect to the love of God that sadly jars with the sacred subject on which it treats But Pascal was the vivisector rather than the anatomist If the nerve could be demonstrated quivering beneath the scalpel, why be nice about the means? "Listen to Escobar on this question," he says, "When is a man bound to feel a positive love for God? Suarez says it suffices if we love Him before the moment of death, without defining any exact time,[3] Vasquez, that it will do if we love Him at the moment of departure, others, at baptism, others, when we are bound to feel contrition, others, on fête days Father Castro Palao contests all these notions, and with reason Hurtado de Mendoza declares that we are bound to love God once in the year, and are so far treated with much consideration But Father Koninck imagines that the obligation recurs every three or four years; Henriquez, every five years, while Filiutius affirms that, correctly speaking, we are not bound to love God every five years, but leaves the matter for wiser heads to settle . Dr Thomas teaches that we must love God as soon as we attain an age of reason, that is somewhat early, Scotus, every Sunday, others, when we are grievously tempted, in case there be no other way of avoiding temptation, Soto, when we receive any blessing from God, it is a fit way of shewing thanks, others at our death, which is somewhat late Nor would it seem to be necessary at every communion, attrition with confession (where opportunity serves) is enough" He disposes of the Jesuit masters of casuistry in a similar way "'But, father, I do not see how you are to act when the Fathers of the Church are in antagonism with your casuists' 'You do not understand,' he said, 'the Fathers were good for the morality of their age, but they are too distant for ours They no longer guide the conscience, but our casuists' 'That is to say, my father, that at your appearance St Augustine, St Chrysostom, St Jerome, St Ambrose, and others vanished, so far as Christian morality is concerned, but tell me now the names of their successors who are these more recent authors?' 'They

[1] "Your opponents are backed by more monks than reasons," said Pascal, alluding to the fact that forty-one monks, whose votes were not usually admitted as of the Sorbonne, had voted against Arnauld

[2] *Les Provinciales, ou Lettres écrites par Louis de Montalt à un Provincial de ses amis, et aux R R P P Jésuites sur la Morale et la Politique de ces Pères*

[3] Again, a little further on, "he concludes that, rigorously speaking, a man is only bound to obey the other commandments without any love for God, and without giving our heart to Him, so that we do not hate Him" "See," says Suarez, "the goodness of God, we are not so much enjoined to love Him as to forbear from hating Him'

are able and celebrated men ' he said, 'Villalobos, Koninck, Llamas, Achokier, Dealkoser, Dellacruz, Veracruz Ugolin Tambourin, Fernandez, Martinez, Suarez, Henriquez, Vasquez, Lopez, Gomez, Sanchez,' &c 'But oh, my father,' said I in alarm, 'were all these Christians?'" [*lett* v] [1]

As these letters appeared all Europe enjoyed the discomfiture of the Jesuits, but Louis XIV made it a matter of conscience, as he declared to the Assembly of the Clergy [A D 1660], to extirpate Jansenism A formulary therefore was prepared containing a condemnation of the five propositions, extracted professedly from the *Augustinus*, and every ecclesiastical person, whether monk or nun, parish priest or dignitary of the Church, was compelled to sign it Recusants were thrown into prison, and De Sacy in the Bastille commenced his translation of the New Testament [*Le N Test de Mons*] Arnauld still maintained his stand on the distinction "de facto" and "de jure," but Pope Alexander VII, by a constitution of February 15th, 1665, demanded a faithful submission to the papal declaration "de facto" Four bishops, in lieu of signature, promised a "respectful silence" on the question of fact, and were marked down for penal visitation, when nineteen others made the cause their own, and discretion was seen to be the wiser course Clement IX, no friend to Molinist doctrine having succeeded to the papal throne [A D 1667], allowed the distinction to be valid, when peace having been apparently restored, a medal was struck in commemoration of the "Pacification," the specimens of which however the Jesuits have contrived to make very scarce

Port Royal was now once more filled with its recluses, who directed their energies against the writings of the Reformed communities. Thus Nicole and Arnauld defended the Catholic doctrine of the Eucharist against Claude and Blondel But the old paths of controversy were not forgotten in Arnauld's *Morals of the Jesuits* and Nicole's Latin translation of the *Provincial Letters* Tillemont, representing the party that met the papal claim to authority "de facto," with the "silence respectueux," and denying that Jansen was justly charged with the substance of the five propositions, there compiled his invaluable historical works and *Mémoires*, De Sacy completed his translation of Scripture, the Mère Angélique composed her *Reflections*, *Conferences*, and *Spiritual Letters*, to brace her nuns for the recurrence of persecution, and more important in its results than all, Quesnel wrote his *Moral Reflections on the New Testament* which quickly superseded the *Augustinus* in the acrimonious disputes that followed, and called forth the Bull "Unigenitus" This work also gave occasion to the celebrated *Problème Ecclésiastique*, by Thierry de Viaixnes, written in true "Provincial" style, for the Cardinal de Noailles having, as Bishop of Chalons, approved the *Réflexions Morales*, and recommended it to his clergy, condemned it in the next year as Archbishop of Paris, in condemning the *Exposition de la Foi de l'Eglise*, by a nephew of St Cyran, which wholly followed the *Réflexions* The problem to be solved therefore was whether the same individual as the Bishop of Chalons in 1695 or as the Archbishop of Paris in 1696 were the safer guide The Jansenist party seemed to be at the top of the tide, when sixty-five Jesuit propositions, of a lax casuistry, which Nicole and Arnauld had drawn up, were condemned by Innocent XI. [A.D 1679], but it was the last Jansenist triumph, for Louis XIV, wholly devoted to his pleasures and his ghostly counsellors the Jesuits, made Jansenism a matter of personal offence, and when Arnauld and his party took the Pope's side in the quarrel that led to the Gallican Articles [DICT *of* THEOL, GALLICANISM], Arnauld found it safer to migrate as a voluntary exile to the Spanish Netherlands, where he lived for the remainder of his days, from A D 1679-1694 Quesnel had gone thither in the preceding year, and Gerberon, the learned Benedictine, followed in A D 1682

Although the Jansenists had always repudiated the idea of any dalliance with Protestantism, many of their notions were more in unison with the Reformation idea than with the traditions of the Schools, the key of the Roman position They were the Calvinists of the Roman Communion [2] The Schools had drifted away from pure Augustinian teaching, Luther and Melanchthon insisted on recurring to it, as did Baius and Jansen Hence the two widely divergent systems that divided the Gallican Church, and the ease with which men learned to believe that "Jansenist" was only a synonym for "Protestant," notwithstanding the overt fact that Arnauld and Nicole, the master spirits of Jansenism, both wrote against the principles of the Reformation In a moral point of view the teaching of Augustine was very different from that of Mariana and Suarez, whose ethics had filled Europe with astonishment But the Jansenists taught the necessity of simple goodness and deep religious feeling, they demanded the moral and spiritual reform of monastery and manse, the dissemination of the Word of God among the people, and the encouragement of primary education, as the only means of dispelling error These principles being of a more popular cast, made the Jansenist community an object of intense aversion to the Jesuits and at the same time truly formidable Religious austerity, pietism, and a strain of mysticism, will always make a sect popular with the lower orders The laxity of court morals on the other hand found more indulgent confessors in the Jesuit body Hence the recluses of Port Royal were regarded by the lower orders with something like veneration, while the noblesse sided with the Jesuits in bringing about their suppression, and Jansenist disregard of papal authority where it was manifestly in error gave the desired opportunity to their foes

In 1700 the *Case of Conscience* reopened the whole question of the five propositions Forty doctors of the Sorbonne declared that the papal claim of infallible authority in matters of fact

[1] Neale's *Hist Jansenist Church*, &c

[2] Buckle, *Civilization in England*, I, xiv

might be received in a passive attitude, however the individual judgment might reject it, the Pacification of Clement IX permitting such a course, but Clement XI, strong in the Molinist interest, condemned their decision in the Bull "Vineam Domini Sabaoth" The complete destruction of Port Royal was determined when its inmates refused to subscribe the papal decree, and a commission was issued to the Cardinal Archbishop of Paris to suppress the convent [A D. 1709]. Ten minutes alone were allowed for the nuns to clear out from the premises The buildings were demolished, and even the cemetery was desecrated by a horrible exposure of the recently interred, to the lasting reproach of Molinism French Jansenism was from that time destroyed, but its spirit survived in Holland

When the Bull "Vineam Domini" was accepted by the clergy, Clement XI made good another step, and condemned Quesnel's *Réflexions Morales* on the New Testament [13th July 1708], which he had at first read with pleasure and profit A D 1712, a congregation of five cardinals and eleven theologians was appointed to reconsider the work After close deliberation for more than a year, the famous Bull "Unigenitus" appeared [Nov A.D 1713], in which one hundred and one propositions in Quesnel's book were declared to be heretical, the number is precise, le Père le Tellier, confessor to Louis XIV, having pledged himself to find in it more than a hundred heretical statements The Abbé Guettée in his history classes the propositions as follows —twelve heretical, twelve not worthy of censure, and eighty-seven erroneous, suspicious, or offensive to pious ears His information is drawn from original documents preserved at Rome The propositions were condemned, not *seriatim* but in bulk, that Le Tellier might save his credit as a prophet of evil Among these propositions several were taken from Scripture, others either echoed the statements of Augustine or harmonized entirely with Tridentine doctrine

A serious division now took place in the French Church on the constitutional question, whether the Bull should be acted upon or rejected as an infringement of Gallican liberties The two parties were named respectively Constitutionists and Anti-Constitutionists, Acceptants and Recusants To determine the strife an appeal was organized from the papal decree to the next general council, a step that had ample precedent in its favour The Archbishop of Paris, at the head of fifteen bishops, the Sorbonne of old historic fame, and a whole host of abbots, canons, and clergy of every grade, joined in the appeal [March 1st, A D 1717] Clement XI met them with the Bull "Pastoralis Officii," which excommunicated all who joined in the appeal, of whatever grade, from the cardinalate downwards The Parliament was throughout on the side of the appellants, and ordered a remonstrance to the Regent from Mailly, the Molinist Bishop of Rheims, to be publicly burnt by the hangman The writer was promoted to the cardinalate A D 1727 Soanen, the aged Bishop of Senez in Provence, one of the appellant bishops, having commended in a pastoral letter the *Réflexions Morales*, and added to his offence by strong expressions against Papal infallibility and the Bull "Unigenitus," was summoned before a provincial council at Embrun He was deposed and consigned to the Chaise Dieu, a keep in the high ground of the Haute Loire

At this juncture a large body of Benedictine, Carthusian, and Cistercian dissentients from the Bull "Unigenitus" settled at Utrecht, which church had also put in an appeal, powerfully drawn up by Van Erkel, in favour of Quesnel According to Ranke [*Hist of Popes*, viii. 18], Jansenists found their way at this period in considerable numbers to Vienna, Brussels, Spain, Portugal, and Italy, disseminating their doctrines and detailing their many grievances either openly or by stealth Jansenism, after originating in such men as Jansen and St Cyran Arnauld and De Sacy, thenceforth evaporated in France in a rout of fanatics, as the Rhine loses itself amid the sandbanks of the coast A D 1727 marks the year in which this decay set in A deacon named François de Paris, who had lived as a Jansenist ascetic, and refused to sign the "Unigenitus," died, and was buried in the cemetery of St Médard His grave, as Voltaire said, was the grave of Jansenism Miraculous cures were said to have been performed at his tomb [1] The place was soon thronged by devotees, whose frenzied extravagances procured for them the name of CONVULSIONARIES Fanaticism and immorality are often closely allied, and the place of sacred associations became notorious for licentious excesses that compelled the authorities to close it, when the excluded avenged themselves with the epigram —

> "De par le roi, défense à Dieu
> De faire miracles en ce lieu "

Various sects of Convulsionists still existed in the time of the Revolution, but they had nothing essentially in common with Jansenism, of which Utrecht thenceforth became the headquarters The troubles caused by the Bull "Unigenitus," and the discord that it created, dividing the inferior clergy from the upper, may be considered to have been one of the remote causes of the French Revolution

Jansenism again shewed front on the death of Louis XIV, the great patron of its rivals The Sorbonne, Molinist under his reign, became Jansenist in the regency [Duvernet, *Hist de la Sorbonne*, ii 225] By the middle of the century Jansenism was sensibly felt in the French parliament, and its principles were openly professed by men of high political position

[Jansenii *Augustinus* Lancelot, *Mém de St Cyran* Fontaine, *Mém p. servir à l'Histoire de P R* Fénélon, *Œuvres*, x-xvi *Bibliothèque U* xiv. Bayle's *Dict*, *Jansenius*, *Baius* Gerberon, *H de Jansenism* Reuchlin, *Gesch des P R*

[1] For an able critique on these so called miracles see *Leland's Deistical Writers*, lib xix

L'Abbé Guettée, *Hist* Tregelles, *Jansenists* Pascal, *Lettres Provinciales* Racine, *H d P R* Ranke, *G d P R* vii Macaulay, *H* II vi. Hallam, *Introd* 1650-1700 Baur, *K G d Neueren Zeit*, *Zweite Periode*, I. 3. Buckle *on Civilization in England*, I xiv]

JERKERS AND BARKERS. A name given to the fanatics who, at "camp-meetings" in America, indulge religious "exercises of falling down, rolling, shouting, jerking, dancing, barking," &c Like the Welsh Methodist practice of jumping, that of "jerking" is a kind of nervous epidemic which attacks those persons who are devoid of self-control, and who give way to the excitement of a crowd, under the influence of stimulating harangues from their preachers. [CONVULSIONARIES DANCERS JUMPERS SHAKERS]

JEROME OF PRAGUE A contemporary and colleague of Huss, whose full name was Jerome Faulfisch He was of a noble family in Bohemia, and is said to have studied at Oxford (where he drank in greedily the principles of Wickliffe), as well as at Paris and Heidelberg Wherever he went Jerome seems to have shewn himself an ardent defender of Wickliffe, being imprisoned at Venice and elsewhere through the extravagance of his opinions When the troubles about Huss had reached their height, Jerome left Prague to visit Cracow, but on the imprisonment of Huss, he returned to the city, and travelling thence arrived secretly at Constance on April 4th, 1415 He shortly fled from the dangers of Constance to a place of security in the neighbourhood, from whence he applied for a safe-conduct, that he might return to defend his own principles and those of Huss before the council This was not granted, and having been apprehended, Jerome was brought before the council in chains on May 23rd Huss was executed on July 6th, 1415, and two months afterwards, on September 23rd, Jerome recanted, abjuring the heresies of both Wickliffe and Huss, and acknowledging the justice of their condemnation He was still kept in prison, and having demanded a public trial, he was once more brought before the council, where he defended himself from seven in the morning until one in the afternoon on May 23rd and 26th, and retracted his recantation A few days afterwards he was condemned, and was executed on May 30th, 1416 [Æneas Sylvius' *Hist Bohem* Hardt's *Hist Conc Const*]

JERUSALEM FRIENDS Henry Nicolas and "his New Jerusalem Friends" are spoken of by Ross in the last page of his Πανσεβεία, shewing that this was a name by which the "Family of Love" was known in 1654

JERUSALEM FRIENDS [*Jerusalems-freunde*] A German sect, known also by the name of Hoffmanites [*Hoffmanianer*], Hardthofites [*Hardthofer*], and "the German Temple" [*der Deutsche Tempel*] They originated in the year 1854 at Kirchenhardthof, near Winnenden, in Wurtemburg, their founder being Christian Hoffmann, whose father had established the KORNTHALITES [A D 1819] Their distinctive idea is that of collecting together a community of faithful Christians in the Holy Land, and from thence extending a revived kingdom of Christ into other lands Their number amounts to about 3000, and they have founded colonies at Jaffa and Haifa under the superintendence of Hoffmann, who takes the title of bishop in the sect In principle the Hoffmanites are simply Pietistic Lutherans, holding extreme Millenarian opinions

JEWISH SECTS. There are two lists of Jewish sects, one given by Hegesippus and the other by Epiphanius, which must be considered as professing to be complete Each gives seven names each includes the three great sects, Pharisees, Sadducees, Essenes [Ossenes, Epiph], each has Hemerobaptists but Hegesippus gives the other three, Galilæans, Masbothæans, Samaritans, Epiphanius' other three are Scribes, Nazaræans, Herodians. In comparing these lists, and others which will be named, it will be assumed, in consequence of Josephus' mention of three great sects, that all other sects which may occur were branches of these three, and included by Josephus under the three They may be mentioned or not by other writers, according to the point of view from which those writers regarded the sects. Hegesippus evidently gives under his seven heads all the different bodies which inhabited Palestine, and takes into his consideration political divisions as well as religious differences Accordingly, he names as a sect the insurgent Galilæans, the party formed by Theudas, as well as the Samaritans and Masbothæans The Samaritan sects do not enter into our present subject, neither does the political body, the Galilæans. There remains, therefore, as a Jewish religious sect, only the Hemerobaptists From the mention of these in a politico-religious list, it is fair to infer that they were a large body.

Epiphanius rightly distinguishes the Samaritans from the Jews, and he deals only with religious bodies Such he considered the Herodians to be, for he attributes to them the notion that Herod was the Messiah Such the Scribes were, but certainly they did not constitute a sect Dismissing these, then, there remains, besides the Hemerobaptists, only the Nazaræans

Another enumeration of Jewish sects is made by Justin Martyr [*Dial c. Tryph* lxxx] He says to Trypho, "One would not admit that the Sadducees, or similar sects of Genistæ, Meristæ, Galilæans, Hellenians, Pharisee-Baptists, are Jews" Here we must read "Pharisee-Baptists," not "Pharisees, Baptists" For the typical Jew Trypho was a Pharisee,[1] and could not be called upon to grant that a Pharisee was only nominally a Jew The Pharisee-Baptists must have been the Hemerobaptists, a party who exaggerated the

[1] The present passage is sufficient to shew this Trypho cannot have belonged to any one of the sects named, and there is no pretence for calling him an Essene There is no possible way of understanding the passage except that of joining Pharisees and Baptists In ch cv Trypho is addressed, "Christ exhorted His disciples to surpass the Pharisaic way of living," with particular reference to Trypho's own belief

Pharisaic washings, and separated from the Pharisees on that account From Justin's list, therefore, there remains to be considered the Genistæ, Meristæ, and Hellenians. Of these Kaye wrote, "in the enumeration of Jewish sects, the names of the Genistæ, Meristæ, and Helleniani occur, of the former two Isidore [*Origin* viii 4, p 63], has given some though not a satisfactory account, of the Helleniani no trace, I believe, is to be found in any other writer" [*Account of Justin M* p 45] Now the list of Pseudo-Hieronymus [*Indic.* i-x] is evidently made up of the lists of Hegesippus and Justin (if it be allowed that in Justin the Pharisee-Baptists are only one sect), with the exception that the Herodians take the place of the Helleniani It is very probable then that Justin's Helleniani are only Herodians

Again, comparing Justin's list with that of Hegesippus, there appears to be no sect named by Hegesippus which can possibly be identified with, or can include the Genistæ and Meristæ But comparing it with the list of Epiphanius, the Nazaræans present themselves for consideration Now Epiphanius describes the Nazaræans (to use modern sectarian language) as primitive Jews They reverenced the Fathers down to Moses, and Moses himself, but said that the books of Moses were forgeries. They offered no sacrifices they ate no flesh Is it not probable, then, that "Genistæ" is only another name[1] of this sect, that the Nazaræans were so called from their claim, not merely to be descended from the original stock of the Jews, but to have preserved uncorrupted the faith of the patriarchs? The occurrence of the name in Justin and its omission in Epiphanius, who was diligent in accumulating his sects, are otherwise difficult to account for Isidore missed the true point aimed at in the term, and to the statement of Pseudo-Hieronymus, that the Genistæ boasted to be of the stock of Abraham, which clearly is not of itself sufficient to constitute a Jewish sect, he added his own explanation founded upon the Babylonish intermarriages It seems also as probable that "Meristæ" is another name of the same sect, or perhaps the distinguishing name of a portion of it. Pseudo-Hieronymus and Isidore, absurdly enough, derive the term from separating the Scriptures by rejecting some books This rejection of certain books cannot be attributed to any ancient Jewish sect except these Nazaræans.[2] Scaliger says, "Hoc potius pertinet ad Karraim, et non video quo applicetur nomen Meristarum" [*Elench* cap iii] It may serve to identify the Meristæ with the Nazaræans, but instead of deriving the name from such separation we may conjecture that it was given in opposition to the pretensions of the name "Genistæ" The sect pretended to be the true representative of the γένος of the nation, but to the true children they only represented those who divided the inheritance

[1] The name should rather be γενῖται [Scaliger, *Elench Trihær* cap iii.]

[2] The old notion that the Sadducees received only the Pentateuch has long been given up

From these four authorities which have been named we have then only two sects, the Hemerobaptists and the Nazaræans, to add to the three great sects Philaster's supposed Jewish sects are really not worth consideration The Hemerobaptists manifestly border on the Pharisees; they were Pharisee-Baptists The Nazaræans (whose existence[3] we thus take to be guaranteed by Justin Martyr), by their rejection of sacrifices and the Levitical law, are connected with the Essenes

The Sadducees and the Essenes, with the minor sects, disappeared in the second century [see Epiph *Hær* xx. *s f*], and the Jews justly consider themselves successors of the Pharisees [ESSENES HEMEROBAPTISTS. KARAITES. PHARISEES SADDUCEES]

JOACHIMITES The heretical followers of Joachim, Abbot of the Cistercian monastery of Floris in Calabria, who lived through a large portion of the twelfth century, A D 1130-1200

Joachim was an enthusiastic preacher and writer on the subject of Old and New Testament prophecies, and these he applied in such a manner to the existing corruption and future condition of the Church, that he himself came to be regarded by many as a prophet, and the *Prophecies of the Abbot Joachim* are well known to the reader of mediæval history He also wrote a treatise on the doctrine of the Trinity, in which he opposed the theology of Peter Lombard, and fell into an error very nearly akin to Tritheism, asserting that when Lombard maintained that there are Three Persons in One Essence he really maintained a quaternity rather than a Trinity This error was controverted at some length, and condemned, in the second canon of the fourth Council of Lateran [A D 1215], "De errore Abbatis Joachim," within a few years of his death [Hardu *Concil.* vii. 18] In the Trinitarian controversy of the seventeenth century Bishop Sherlock was accused of having maintained a similar error in his *Vindication of the Doctrine of the Trinity*, printed in 1691

The apocalyptical tone of Joachim's writings led his followers into the most extreme fanaticism One of them—probably a monk, named Gerard, belonging to the newly created Franciscan order, whose rise, with that of the Dominicans, Joachim was alleged to have predicted—collected three works of his master into one under the title of *The Everlasting Gospel*, probably interpolating it here and there with sentences of his own. This he declared to be the Gospel named in Rev xiv 6, representing that St. Francis, the founder of his order, was "the angel" who was to bear it forth to the world, and that it would supersede the New Testament in the year 1260. This wild and profane book was suppressed by order of Alexander IV. in the year 1255, but some of the principles contained in the work had already acquired a strong hold upon the ignorant, and had much influence in the production of that wild and lawless phase of Millenarianism which

[3] "Sed ejusmodi Judaici nominis hæresin haud scio an alius præter Epiphanium commemoraverit" [Petavius, note in Epiph *Hæres* xviii.].

formed so conspicuous a feature in the mediæval sects

The theory thus started into life by Joachim was that the successive periods of human history are associated with the Three Persons of the Blessed Trinity The ages before Christ were those in which God the Father was revealing Himself in the letter of the Old Testament by power, fear, and faith. Then followed the ages of the New Testament, in which God the Son was revealing Himself by the letter of the Gospel, and giving to men the fulness of humility, truth, and wisdom This dispensation of the Son was to be succeeded by the "Last Days," in which God the Holy Ghost would crown all that had gone before with perfect love, joy and freedom It is easy to see how this theory could be perverted into the notion broached in the *Evangelium Æternum*, that Christianity as it had been hitherto known was passing away, and was to be superseded by a spiritual religion of the heart, in which sacraments and all outward means of grace were to be superseded by contemplative love It is also easy to see how the "freedom" of the predicted "Last Days" could without effort be perverted into Antinomianism, as in the case of the "Brethren of the Free Spirit," the Franciscan Fraticelli, the Beghards, the Albigenses, and other mediæval sects and how the idea that the active life of Christianity was to give place to the contemplative life of the Spirit was the parent of that mendicancy which characterized them all As early as the year 1260 the Council of Arles spoke of the Joachitist error as spreading like a cancer [Hardu. *Concil* vii 511], and already it was found necessary to pass canons enjoining the clergy to teach the people that Baptism was a necessary sacrament, and that the union of man and woman, without the blessing of the Church, was not marriage.

Thus, although the Abbot Joachim never founded a sect, and can scarcely be said, at least in his lifetime, to have formed a school, his writings fell upon the excited Christianity of his age like sparks on stubble, and very soon indeed the flames of Antinomian and antisacerdotal fanaticism burst forth in every direction throughout Europe as the result of the principles which he taught Those principles however went side by side with the pantheistic spiritualism of Amalric of Bema, who originated the notion that the Holy Spirit becomes present by a kind of incarnation in every spiritual Christian and it may be that in both cases the teachers were riding on the wave of opinion rather than directing it, that they were merely expressing in forcible language opinions which had arisen from subtile and, now at least, undiscoverable causes.

The works of Joachim were printed at Venice in the years 1517-19, and his life was written by a Dominican named Gervaise in 1745 A full summary of his opinions, and those contained in *The Everlasting Gospel*, may be found in Natalis Alexander's *Ecclesiastical History*, vol viii pp 73-76.

JOANNITES Those who refused to recognise the deposition of St. John Chrysostom from the See of Constantinople by the Emperor Arcadius [A.D 404], and would not submit themselves to his successors until some time after his death. They took up a position somewhat similar to that of the English Nonjurors, but it does not appear that they ever attempted to continue a succession, although many bishops and clergy, besides those at Constantinople, belonged to the party Some of them returned to the communion of St Chrysostom's second successor, Atticus, when he introduced the confessor's name into the Diptych of the Church of Constantinople The rest conformed when Proclus persuaded the Emperor Theodosius II. to bring back the remains of St. Chrysostom, to be buried with reverence in the principal church of the city, A D 438. [Socr *Hist Eccl* vii 25, 45]

JOANNITES. [WATERLANDERS.]

JOHN, DISCIPLES OF ST [MENDÆANS.]

JORIS. [DAVID-GEORGIANS]

JOSEPHISTÆ. A mediæval sect which modified the practice of the ABELONITES respecting marriage by adopting that of the ESSENES [Reinerus, *contr Waldens* vi *ad fin*]

JOSEPPINI [JOSEPHISTÆ]

JOVINIANISTS This sect or school was named after Jovinian, a Milanese monk, who left Milan for Rome, and about the year 388 opposed the estimate then prevalent in the Church of celibacy, monasticism, fasting and martyrdom His character is accordingly represented in very different lights by different branches of the Church, and by different parties in the same Church In some histories he appears as the honest and bold reformer, in some as the sensual monk and abandoned heretic Our knowledge of him coming from his opponents, it is impossible to say exactly what allowance is to be made for personal animosity and controversial bitterness. More or less of Jerome's vituperation is believed according to the style of the reader's theology—few believe the whole

The extent to which it was right in the fourth century to carry the practice of celibacy it is difficult for us to judge correctly That it was right for many to make themselves eunuchs for the Kingdom of Heaven's sake, and that they gained the reward of chastity and self-denial, no one can doubt. In many cases, celibacy was incumbent on clergy for the service of God's ministry, and in many cases expedient for both clergy and laity on account of the distress of the times. At the same time, there can be no doubt that the same motive for enforcing the celibacy of the clergy which acted so powerfully in later ages, was then working, the desire, namely, to separate the sacerdotal order from the rest of society, and for the sake of clerical power, to raise the clergy to a seemingly higher level than men in general could attain To oppose this was the part of a wise and good man.

Jovinian, however, appears to have opposed, not so much this particular instance, as the pernicious principle which had then entered

Jovinianists

into the doctrine of celibacy itself, whether applied to clergy or laity The Manichæan tenet of the innate sinfulness of all sexual intercourse, as partaking of the inextinguishable impurity of matter, was working itself into the general feeling of religious men [see Milman, *Latin Christ* i 98, ed. 1867] It came in under the disguise that there are not merely degrees, but states of righteousness differing in kind, with the higher of which marriage is incompatible. So that celibacy was recommended, not upon the ground named by our Lord, that is, for the sake of the Church, that God's work might be better done [Matt xix. 12], not in the case named by St Paul [1 Cor vii. 26], in the time of a present distress,[1] but in and for itself, as a state in itself holier than marriage, until, by a perversion of St John's words [Rev xiv 4], defilement was attributed to the state which God has consecrated Augustine's notice of Jovinian [*Hær* lxxxii] is an instance of this false estimate Jovinian, who remained unmarried, is condemned for doing so, "Quod non propter aliquod apud Deum majus meritum in regno vitæ perpetuæ profuturum, sed propter præsentem prodesse necessitatem, hoc est, ne homo conjugales patiatur molestias, disputabat," a condemnation from which we cannot see how St Paul is excluded Into monasticism there entered, besides this false estimate of celibacy, the mischievous belief that in order to attain the higher degree of righteousness it was necessary to withdraw from the general body of the Church Christ was to be sought in deserts and secret chambers Fasting, instead of being the accompaniment and expression of penitence, the aid to penitential devotion, and the means of subduing the flesh to the spirit, became the maceration of the body meritorious in and for itself Ingenious self-torture frequently took the place of a healthy asceticism · and the principle which brought about these changes was that which influenced the heretics, whose command, "Touch not, taste not, handle not," was denounced by St Paul The ordinances were no longer founded on the will of God and on conscience, but were after the doctrines and commandments of men That the veneration of martyrs was become excessive in the fourth century is allowed on all hands It does not appear however, that there was any new and erroneous principle introduced as in the former cases. The abuses were of degree only

It was about three years after the appearance of Siricius' decretal, which peremptorily forbad the marriage of the clergy and implied the ascendancy of monastic opinions, that Jovinian, with Helvidius and Vigilantius, attempted in vain to stem the mingling tide of authority and popular sentiment.

[1] These words must be held to rule the whole chapter, otherwise we should be putting into St Paul's mouth the intolerable assertion that God's purpose, who gave woman to be a helpmeet for man, was defeated by Christianity [ver 32-34] In the present Vulgate the words are "Propter instantem necessitatem," with which compare Augustine's words which follow in the text

Jovinian taught,[2] first, that virgins, widows and married women, being baptized, and not differing in other works, have the same degree of merit Secondly, that between fasting and eating with thanksgiving there is no difference of merit It is clear that this denial of merit is made regarding celibacy and fasting when they are considered in and for themselves that no assertion is made regarding the one when adopted for the sake of God's service, or regarding the other when practised with reference to the penitence and devotion which it accompanies and assists Augustine's words before quoted are a proof of this Thus far Jovinian taught the truth, and a truth most wanted in those times In making his protest against growing error, he fell certainly into other errors, but probably by no means to the extent represented by some historians [3] For, looking to Jerome's statement as quoted below, it is at once seen that the terms of the first tenet are inconsistent with that wide interpretation of the fourth tenet, which considers it to be a denial of different degrees of bliss in heaven The words "si non discrepent cæteris operibus" expressly require an equality of works in order to an equality of merit, and surely Jovinian would have allowed that the reward will be in proportion to the merit. So far it appears therefore that the fourth tenet only denies a distinctly separate and higher state in the Kingdom of Heaven to be assigned to virgins It was thought that there are two states, each allowing different degrees, the existence of the supposed higher state is denied, not the different degrees of the one state Nor is there anything inconsistent with this explanation in the words, apparently Jovinian's, in which future punishment is referred to [4] All evil-doers are alike said to be doomed to one state, the state of Gehenna, but there is nothing that denies a difference in that one state of degrees of punishment. In like manner all who endure to the end in persecution wear the victor's crown, but one victor's crown may be brighter than another The two parables which are then quoted (the parables of the two sons and of the labourers hired at different hours) un-

[2] Jerome's statement of Jovinian's tenets is as follows "Dicit virgines, viduas et maritatas, quæ semel in Christo lotæ sunt, si non discrepent cæteris operibus, ejusdem esse meriti Nititur approbare, eos qui plena fide in baptismate renati sunt, a diabolo non posse subverti Tertium proponit inter abstinentiam ciborum et cum gratiarum actione perceptionem eorum, nullam esse distantiam Quartum, quod et extremum, esse omnium qui suum baptisma servaverint, unam in regno cœlorum remunerationem' [*adv Jovinian.* i 2]

[3] The statements of Fleury differ widely, for example, from those of Natalis Alexander and Liguori, not to mention Protestant historians.

[4] "Qui fratri dixerit fatue et raca, reus erit Geennæ · et qui homicida fuerit et adulter, mittetur similiter in Geennam In persecutione, qui inceditur, qui suffocatur, qui decollatur, qui fugerit, qui in carcere inclusus obierit, varia quidem luctæ genera, sed una corona victorum est Inter eum fratrem qui semper cum patre fuerat, et qui postea pœnitens est receptus, nulla diversitas est Operariis primæ horæ et tertiæ et sextæ et nonæ et undecimæ unus denarius æqualiter redditur et quo magis admireris, ab iis incipit præmium qui minus in vinea laborarunt" [*adv Jovin* ii 12]

doubtedly refer to the different dispensations of revelation An argument regarding the merits of celibacy and marriage founded upon these parables must have been, that as the Gentiles called at the eleventh hour were admitted to equal privileges with those called earlier, so neither of the two competing states conferred a distinctive privilege With the validity of the argument we are not concerned

Further, Jovinian is said to have taught that they who have been once truly born again in baptism cannot be subverted by Satan There does not appear to be in this particular, as there was in the last particular, any inconsistency leading us to doubt the accuracy of the statement. The evidence goes to shew that Jovinian held the error of indefectible grace. Lastly, there is no doubt that he denied the perpetual virginity of the Mother of our Lord. This he did probably through the mistake of treating the case of her who was the instrument of the Incarnation as if it were an ordinary case of the comparative merits of the two states

Jovinian made many converts at Rome, chiefly among the laity Being condemned and excommunicated by a synod at Rome under Siricius [A D 390] he returned to Milan Siricius warned Ambrose against him, and he was again condemned in the same year by a Milanese synod [*Letters of Siricius and Ambrose* Harduin, *Concil* i 852-853]. Jerome speaks of him as dead in the year 404 It is much more probable that the edict of Honorius [A D 412], ordering one Jovian or Jovinian to be severely scourged and then banished, for holding conventicles in the neighbourhood of Rome, refers to him [*Cod Theod* lib xvi tit. v legg liii], in the old editions "Jovian" stands in the text of this constitution, but Haenel [ed 1839], upon manuscript authority, admits "Jovinian" into the text Augustine states that the Jovinianist heresy was quickly extinguished

JUDAISTÆ [ISCARIOTÆ]

JUDAIZERS The term Judaizers, which in a Christian mouth cannot but be a term of disparagement, is used of those who refused to join in the several steps by which Catholic Christianity was evolved out of Mosaism through the intermediate stage of Jewish Christianity It is used also in a less definite sense of those who, being members of the Catholic Church, seek to reintroduce some of the thoughts, feelings, and observances of the earlier dispensation

The classes of men to be united into a Catholic church were Jews who believed, Gentiles who joined Judaic churches, and Gentiles neither of the churches nor under the Apostles of the Circumcision. The work to be done was to bring all alike into the freedom of the Gospel, that is, to free the first and second classes from the bondage of the Mosaic law, to prevent the imposition of that law on the third class, to raise the Gentile churches to an equality with the Church of Jerusalem, and to stop the supremacy which Jerusalem held over Judaic churches from extending itself into a supremacy over the Church Catholic

In considering the steps by which this work was accomplished, it is to be remembered that Mosaism was not only a dispensation of revealed religion, but also an established national religion Such of its ordinances as were compatible with a belief in Christ had the claim of national law on the obedience of the people, and the providence of God permitted a certain time in which there was rightfully a blending of Mosaism and Christianity It may be conceded also, that even after this time was really come to an end, so that it could no longer be required of any "to walk orderly and keep the law," it was still open to the Church of Jerusalem to retain those ordinances a while, in the hope, excusable at least though groundless, that the Jews might yet regain their place as one of the nations of the world, provided always that there was no attempt to impose this burden on others, or to represent the bearing it as necessary to salvation

The main steps in this work, the turning-points in its history, are manifestly the determination of the conditions on which Gentiles should be received into Judaic churches, the recognition of St Paul's mission to the Gentiles, involving the recognition of the entire freedom of the Gentile churches, the renunciation of Judaism by the Apostles of the Circumcision, the renunciation of Judaism by the Church of Jerusalem

It will be the object of this article to trace the action of the Judaizers in the several periods defined by these steps

On St Peter's return from Cæsarea to Jerusalem after the conversion of Cornelius, the believing Jews contended with him for eating with Gentiles Hearing his statement, they submitted but some (perhaps not a few) were only silenced for a time, and soon renewed their opposition, not, however, so far as we know, against St Peter personally, but by interfering in the churches which in Antioch, Syria, and Cilicia were receiving the Gentiles into communion, and that (in Antioch at least) upon terms of freedom Converted Pharisees from Judæa preached at Antioch the necessity of circumcision Appeal was made upon this to the Apostles at Jerusalem The Apostles were still Apostles of the Circumcision, having their headquarters at Jerusalem, and (as it seems) leaving the city only upon occasional missions The Church at Antioch was in its foundation a Judaic church, so that it appealed, as a daughter church, to the mother church St Paul and St. Barnabas appeared in the synod at Jerusalem, not as assessors with the Apostles, but as counsel for the appellants The decree which issued asserted the principle contended for, but abstinence from things strangled, from blood, and from fornication, was enjoined as necessary for Gentile not less than for Jewish Christians Being thus defeated in the Judaic churches, the Judaizers turned to the Gentile churches, and so soon as these were in process of formation endeavoured to pervert them.

The Apostles at Jerusalem fully recognised St. Paul's mission, they did not impose any terms of communion on his converts, they requested only that as Jerusalem had ministered to the Gentiles in spiritual things, the Gentiles would minister to the poor saints of Jerusalem in temporal things [Gal ii 10, Rom xv 27] Their influence however, which was sufficient to give peace to their own churches, was not able to establish St Paul's authority in the estimation of the discontented Pharisees The Judaizers felt also, not only that St Paul was the leader in the cause of liberty whose course they ought to hinder, but also that they had some plausible arguments to produce against him He had not followed Christ upon earth, therefore he was no true Apostle He flinched from claiming the rights of an Apostle [1 Cor ix. 1-6 Conybeare and Howson, ch xiii] Nor were ungenerous representations wanting [2 Cor x 10] With such arguments, and in such spirit, was the Apostle of the Gentiles constantly followed "His career was one life-long conflict with Judaizing antagonists Setting aside the Epistles to the Thessalonians, which were written too early to be affected by this struggle, all his letters addressed to churches, with but one exception, refer more or less directly to such opposition It assumed different forms in different places in Galatia it was purely Pharisaic, in Phrygia and Asia it was strongly tinged with speculative mysticism, but everywhere, and under all circumstances, zeal for the law was its ruling passion" [Prof Lightfoot, *Comment on Gal*, *St Paul and the Three*, p 292] These attacks on the Apostle did not cease at his death In the *Clementine Homilies* and *Recognitions* they are carried on with increased virulence [*Recognitions* DICT *of* THEOL] Such was the second stage of Judaizing efforts, the efforts of parties within the Judaic churches, who falsely alleged the authority of the Apostles of the Circumcision to impose on the Gentiles the yoke of the law [comp Gal ii 12, 2 Cor iii 1]

The next turning-point in the history of the Judaizers was said to be the renunciation of Judaism by the Apostles. It cannot be thought that when the Apostles left Jerusalem to preach the Gospel to the whole world they carried with them the restrictions to which they had submitted as Apostles of the Circumcision Their withdrawal from Jerusalem must have tended in no small degree to reduce the supremacy of the Church of Jerusalem and to raise the Gentile churches to their proper level. at the same time it must have given freer scope to the Judaizing faction by removing the immediate check of apostolic authority But of the time when this change took place, and of the results which we naturally attribute to it, we have no information, except in the case of St John. It appears to be most probable that the time was when Cestius [A D 66] retired from before Jerusalem, and gave the Christian Church the opportunity of retreating to Pella. St John retired to Ephesus, and entered upon the last stage of his long career, no longer an Apostle of the Circumcision, but an apostle and bishop of the Church Catholic To this time the Apocalypse may be referred [NICOLAITANES]

The Judaism of the Jerusalem Church was not destroyed even by the destruction of the city The main body which returned from Pella retained such forms of the law as the circumstances of a desolated city and destroyed temple permitted Until the rebuilding of the city as Ælia Capitolina their bishops were all of the Circumcision Nor was there in this course anything to hinder communion with Catholic churches, provided there was no attempt to rule the consciences of others In the insurrection of the Jews under Barcocheba, Jerusalem was for a time in the possession of the insurgents, and an attempt was made to rebuild the temple The Christians, persecuted by Barcocheba, were regarded favourably by Hadrian, and were allowed to settle in Ælia Capitolina The Church of Jerusalem was then collected as a Catholic Church, Marcus being the first bishop of the uncircumcision. Sulpitius Severus [*Chron* ii 31] remarks concerning the forbidding the Jews to approach Jerusalem, "Quod quidem Christianæ fidei proficiebat, quia tum pæne omnes Christum Deum sub legis observatione credebant nimirum id Domino ordinante dispositum, ut legis servitus a libertate fidei atque ecclesiæ tolleretur"

A part of the Jerusalem Church remained in Pella These persisted in retaining Judaism even after the election of Marcus at Jerusalem, and formed the sect of the NAZARENES But the activity of the Judaizing faction is now to be looked for outside the Church From the large party which so perseveringly opposed St Paul, with the addition of members of the sect of the ESSENES, and a modification of their doctrine, sprang the EBIONITES From these elements, again, but with a doctrine opposed to the Gnosticism which was developing among the Ebionites, sprang the ELCHASAITES

The catholicity of the Church was thus formally established, but for a considerable time there were remains of Judaic practices, and the spirit of Judaism, as a natural impulse of man's heart, is ever working Such Judaic practices may be in themselves perfectly innocent, and may call for the interference of the Church only when they are likely to breed contention, or when they are made to rest upon unsound doctrine Thus the custom in the Asiatic churches of celebrating Easter according to the Jewish calculation, on account of the uncharitable feelings which it called forth, required the authoritative settlement of the question, which it received at Nicæa and Antioch [QUARTODECIMANS] The apostolic decree of Jerusalem was observed for some centuries in many parts of the Church We have proof of this, not only in history (as *e g* in the martyr's answer to the charge of eating human flesh, "How could such as these devour children, who consider it unlawful even to taste the blood of irrational animals?") but also in canons which recognise the observance [Apost lxiii, Conc

Gangren ii, Conc Aurel. ii 20, Conc. Trull. lxviii] Beveridge, upon the Apostolic Canons, writes that the primitive Church, both Eastern and Western, for a long time kept this decree The observance proceeded from reverence to an apostolic decree, the temporary character of which was not clearly perceived Some modern divines of great name, as Grotius, have held its perpetual obligation, and to this day it is thought by the Greek and Æthiopic Churches to be a portion of Christian law Again, in some churches, the Sabbath has been observed as a fast, in some as a festival, the difference arising from opposition to heresies which connected themselves with one or the other side of the question [SABBATARIANS]

JULIANISTS. A name given to the APHTHARTODOCETÆ, from their leader, Julian, Bishop of Halicarnassus in Caria [A.D 510], who fled to Alexandria on the accession of the Emperor Justin [A.D. 518], and there originated the opinion that the body of our Lord was always incapable of corruption, in opposition to the Monophysites, Severus of Antioch, and Damianus of Alexandria, who maintained that until His Resurrection it was liable to the ordinary changes of human bodies, and therefore was corruptible The dogma of the sect is extinct, says Neale, except so far as its general type is preserved among the Armenians [Neale's *Patriarchate of Alexandria*, ii 9] They seem to have disappeared from Syria in the eighth or ninth century, and also from Egypt, but a portion of them penetrated into Ethiopia and Nubia, where they had a patriarch as late as A D 798 Julian wrote a commentary on Job, which is sometimes quoted by more recent writers as a not unorthodox work

JULIUS CASSIANUS [DOCETÆ]

JUMPERS This name was originally given to the Welsh Methodists on account of a peculiar frenzy which arose among them soon after the introduction of Methodism into Wales The excited ravings of their preachers produced a sympathetic excitement among some of their hearers which led them to supplement the ordinary Methodist "Amen," "Glory," and other expressions of feeling, with shouts of joy and marvellous efforts of jumping, those so excited leaping about with cries of "Gogoniant, Gogoniant!" until they fell down exhausted. The practice was grounded on the authority of such texts of Holy Scripture as "The King of Israel danced and leaped before the Lord [2 Sam vi 16], and a perverted literal interpretation of our Lord's words to His disciples, "Rejoice ye in that day, and leap for joy" [Luke vi 23] The original Methodist body discouraged from the first the revival meetings from which these hysterical phenomena developed, and the less uneducated Welsh Methodists have always been ashamed of them, but the strange custom has not altogether vanished.

From Wales the custom of jumping devotion spread to America, where all religious oddities find a ready soil for germination, and where the Shakers had already established a somewhat similar practice. It is thus described by an eye witness "Being told of this practice, I attended one of their meetings in New York in 1850. During the sermon much excitement prevailed, and loud shouts arose at intervals from all parts of the building The sermon ended, one of the usual tunes was sung, accompanied, almost universally, with stamping of the feet, keeping tolerably good time with the measure of the strain. After a prayer, which could hardly be heard amid the surrounding confusion, a short interval of silence followed Then I was somewhat startled by seeing a venerable "coloured sister" in one of the front pews jumping up and down with great rapidity for some minutes Shortly after, amid loud stamping of the feet, I distinctly saw her jump over the front of the pew, and, commencing from the pew she had left, she made a series of tremendous jumps up and down the aisle, shouting the whole time with a loud voice, and presenting a spectacle which I shall not easily forget. She was soon joined by others, and not knowing what might be the next part of the programme, I made a rapid exit feeling, when fairly outside, not a little thankful to have effected my escape I may add that it is a well known fact that at the chapel I refer to, during their revival meetings, these zealous worshippers often protract their services from eight p m to seven or eight o'clock next morning, singing, shouting, praying, jumping, &c, the whole time" [*Notes and Queries*, 2nd ser ii. 512]

There is an annual festival at Echternach, in Luxembourg, about twenty miles from Trèves, which takes place on Whitsun-Tuesday, and is called "The Jumping Dance of Echternach" It seems to be a relic of the fanaticism of the "Dancers" of the fourteenth century, and is thus described "The procession starts from the bridge, accompanied by several bands of music, the pilgrims of both sexes form in rows, and spring first four steps forward and three back, then eight steps forward and three back, and so on, continually increasing the steps forward, but making no change in those backward, until they reach the church, when they fall on their faces and begin to pray,' high mass being immediately celebrated [*Ibid* 188]. This jumping dance has been several times suppressed, but is always revived again, and it is attended by an average of 8,000 persons.

This singular mania is heard of in much earlier times than those of the mediæval Dancers, in the case of the monks and nuns who are called "Echetæ" by Nicetas Choniates It is also found in Russia, where the Khlisti mix up the practice of jumping with their horrible rites. [ECHETÆ. DANCERS KHLISTI. SHAKERS]

JUST-FAST-MEN. This name is spoken of by Foxe in connection with that of KNOWN-MEN It appears to be a later form of "æw-fæst-men," which signified "men bound by the law," and is similar to "sooth-fæst" men, which would mean "just men" or "men fast in truth" It was probably one of the many names by which the Lollards were known among themselves and their opponents.

JUSTINUS Nothing whatever is known of this heretic except from the pages of Hippolytus He appears to have been a leader of the OPHITES, and perhaps contemporary with the Apostles Hippolytus speaks of his heresy as an attempted amalgamation of Greek mythology with Scriptural history, and gives as an illustration a very curious account of the way in which the legend of Hercules was associated with the Scripture story from the Garden of Eden to the Incarnation of our Lord. This curious anticipation of eclecticism is said by Hippolytus to be contained in an apocryphal "Book of Baruch," which was in high repute with the followers of Justinus Nothing is now known of such a book [Hippol *Refut. Hær* v. 18-23, x. 11].

K

KANT, EMMANUEL [A.D. 1724-1804], was born at Konigsberg in Prussia, his father being a saddler, of a Scotch family named Cant. He was provided with a good education from his early boyhood and acquired a knowledge, not only of Latin and Greek, but also of French and English. After many years spent as tutor in private families, and in his native university, he became Professor of Metaphysics in the latter in the year 1770 and held that office until his death, never quitting his native place.

The great work by which Kant became known was his *Critic of Pure Reason* [*Kritik der reinen Vernunft*], which first appeared in 1781. It attracted no notice at first beyond the university in which its author lectured; but in 1784, Schulze, one of his disciples, printed an *Elucidation* of it, which immediately drew the eyes of philosophers to the original work. In 1786 Reinhold began to use it as the text-book of his lectures in the University of Jena, and before long it became known through the length and breadth of Germany, not only among philosophers, but as one of the fashionable books of the day, which people must talk about even though they do not understand it.

The *Critic of Pure Reason* is a critical analysis of the intellectual faculty in its purity, that is, as a faculty uninfluenced by experience. The philosophical speculations of German thinkers had been recently much influenced by Locke's work *On the Human Understanding*, which had been made known at the court of Frederick the Great through the French literati by whom he was surrounded. This had come into conflict with the philosophy of Wolf, and the struggles of the two systems had made way for a scepticism which was throwing contempt on the study of mental science. This was the opportunity which brought Kant forward as the founder of a critical school of philosophers in which loose methods of thought were to be put aside and a scientific inquiry made into the extent and limits of human reason, that should not be prejudiced, as that of Locke had been, by the *a priori* distrust of reason itself, which had been bred by the sceptical limitation of all knowledge by experience. It may be stated shortly that the result was a compromise between the idealist school of Descartes, which would accept only demonstration by intellectual ideas, and the sensationalism afterwards specially connected with the name of Hume, which would accept only that which flows from experience.

The effect of Kant's philosophy upon religion was to revive the power of natural religion, which had been undermined by the materialism of the French illuminati; but it did not go beyond. He looked down loftily upon Christianity as a not altogether valueless corroboration of the law of moral duty which is written in the natural conscience, and upon revelation in general as an image of that law. He held that it was impossible for either sense or reason to demonstrate the existence of God or of the immortality of the soul, but that an intuition of their existence forms part of our moral consciousness, and that thus they are to be accepted as morally certain. [SCEPTICS.]

KARABLIKI. [SKOPTZI.]

KARAITES. The "Karaim" or "Scripturists"[1] are a Jewish sect which adheres to the text and letter of Scripture, rejecting alike the mystical theosophy of the Cabbala and the interpretations and additions of the Talmuds.

If we compare the Karaites with the old Jewish sects, it may be said that with the Pharisees they reject the Pantheism of the Cabbala, and hold against the Sadducees the doctrines of the resurrection, angels and spirits; that with the Sadducees they reject the system of tradition upheld by the Pharisees, and that with the Essenes they insist on the knowledge of the divine law and on a closer observance of its moral precepts. The characteristic of the sect is opposition to rabbinical traditions, and the Karaites affirm that they can shew an uninterrupted catena of teachers of their principles from the time of Ezra. This is probably an exaggeration, not an entire misstatement.[2] In our Lord's time the traditions of the elders had reached the point of making the Word of God of none effect [Matt. xv. 1-9, Mark vii. 1-13]. Josephus tells that Jonathan, a Sadducee, persuaded Hyrcanus to

[1] See particularly Isa. xxix. 11-13, where in ver. 11, 12 the verb Kara is used, and in ver. 13 are the words which our Lord quoted [Matt. xv. 9] from the Sept. version regarding tradition. In the English version the latter words are "Their fear towards me is taught by the precept of men." So Aquila, Symmachus, and Theodotion [See Field, *Orig. Hexap.* tom. ii. fasc. ii. p. 484].

[2] Scaliger considers Karaim to be the correlative term to Chasidim or Assidei, those who observed the Scriptures simply in opposition to those who voluntarily imposed on themselves other rules [see Trigland, *Diatribe de Secta Kar.* cap. iii. in *Syntagma Trihæresium*].

leave the party of the Pharisees, who held by tradition many things not delivered in the law of Moses [*Antiq* xiii 10, 6]. It can hardly be that there were not those who opposed these innovations without falling into the scepticism of the Sadducees regarding the Resurrection, and such Sadducees denying a Mosaic oral law, but not denying the Resurrection, might well be claimed by the Karaites as of their sect The Pharisaic traditions were collected in the Mishna at the end of the first century The Gemarists, or commentators on the Mishna, made up the Talmud of Babylon at the beginning of the sixth century As the Sadducees declined [SADDUCEES] the remaining opposition to the Pharisaic system of tradition appears to have formed itself into the sect of Scripturists Anan, a Babylonish Jew of the race of David, and his son Saul, about the year 750 declared openly for the written Word of God alone, exclusive of tradition These are specially singled out by the Rabbinists as the leaders of their opponents, and it appears reasonable, in the absence of exact information, to date from them the formation of the sect of Karaites, allowing that a party, not forming a schism, had long before held their principles At no time has the number of Karaites been large Prideaux states, from Hottinger's *Thesaurus*, that in the middle of the seventeenth century there were of them in Poland 2,000, at Caffa in Tartaria Crimæa 1200, at Cairo 300, at Damascus 200, at Jerusalem 30, in Babylonia 100, in Persia 600 [*Connection*, iii 478] Dr Clark found a colony of them in the Crimea, in the full enjoyment and exercise of their ancient customs and peculiarities [*Travels*, part i. vol ii ch 4] Pierotti, in 1861, stated the number of Karaite Jews in Jerusalem to be only 38 He added that they were superior to all the rest in intelligence, education, cleanliness, and probity [*Jerus. Explored*, i 11]. This character is generally given to the sect Scaliger says that they are reckoned men of the best learning and the best probity of all the Jewish nation [Trigland, *Syntag* i p 176] Clarke found them to have in the Crimea the same good name. They read the Scriptures and their liturgies everywhere, both publicly and privately, in the language of the country in which they dwell, and hold it an act of piety to copy out the Scriptures once in their lives They are rigid in their fasts, strict observers of the Sabbath, and very careful in the education of their children, who are instructed publicly in the synagogues

Trigland gives from Karaite writings the ten articles of the Karaite Creed [I] All things were created [II] by an Uncreated Being, [III] Who is without form, and is in every respect One alone, [IV] Who sent Moses, [V] and by Moses His perfect law, [VI] which with its exposition, that is the Scripture and its interpretation, the faithful are bound to know, [VII] Who guided the other prophets by His Spirit, [VIII] Who will raise the dead, [IX] and judge them according to their works, [X] Who "has not rejected His people in captivity even while under His chastisements, but it is proper that even every day they should receive their salvation by Messiah the son of David" [*Syntag* ii cap. 10] The latter part of this article is paraphrased by Milman, "that they must daily strive to render themselves worthy of redemption through the Messiah" [*Hist of Jews*, iii 273] In articles IV V VI are included the points of difference between the Karaites and other Jews, the causes, in short, of the schism They assert the perfection of the written law of Moses, in opposition to the alleged authority of the oral law with its additions and alterations of the Mosaic law, and they assert the necessity of the pure interpretation of the written law, in opposition to the expositions of the Cabbala.

Between the adherents to the text of Scripture and the advocates of tradition arose a number of questions, ritual, ceremonial, and moral, regarding the celebration of the feasts, the laws of the Sabbath, and the laws of marriage It would be useless to detail these In general, the Sabbath was more rigidly observed by the Karaites, the laws of marriage were more strict, the table of prohibited degrees was larger [Trigland's *Diatribe*, cap ix] In one insignificant particular the two parties appear to have changed sides, the Textualists insisting on a figurative interpretation of the comands to wear phylacteries and use door-labels [Deut. vi 8, 9], the rabbis interpreting them literally

As regards the Karaites of modern times, the most interesting fact is their desire to exculpate themselves from the national sin of the death of Christ During the reign of the Empress Catharine a communication was made to the Russian government in which the Karaites declared that their ancestors had taken no part in the crucifixion of our Lord Dr Wolff reports that he found in the neighbourhood of Babylon the original stock of the Karaites, who asserted that they had remained ever since the Captivity on the spot where he found them The agreement of these two testimonies is remarkable [See *Colonial Church Chronicle*, Febr 1871, p 56, where is also a Karaite hymn now used in Jerusalem]

KEITHIANS An offshoot of the American Quakers, who formed a temporary secession from that sect under the leadership of a Scotchman named George Keith, at the end of the seventeenth century In the year 1700 Keith was ordained as a missionary of the Society for the Propagation of the Gospel, but returning to England some years afterwards became rector of Edburton in Sussex, where he died in 1714 On losing their leader the sect of the Keithians became almost entirely dissolved, some of its members joining the Church, Keith baptizing 200 with his own hands, others becoming Baptists, and some returning to the Quakers

KERJAKIS or KORSAKEN. A name employed in many parts of Russia to denote the Raskolnicks, or dissenters from the Established Church

KETZER This name seems to have been applied in the middle of the twelfth century in a special way to the Gazzari, some of whom came to Germany at that time from Italy [Gretser in *Bibl Max Lugd* xxv 253, B]

KILHAMITES [NEW CONNEXION METHODISTS]

KIRK OF SCOTLAND [SCOTTISH KIRK]

KHLESTOVSCHIKI [KHLISTI]

KHLISTI A name signifying "Flagellants" given to a Russian sect, usually considered as an offshoot of the SKOPTZI, and formed about 1645 by a deserter from the army named Daniel Philipitch This man went about declaring himself to be Divine, and his followers accordingly called themselves "God's people" Philipitch imposed ascetic practices upon his followers, and among others that of self-flagellation, which was inflicted with extreme rigour Far more reprehensible extravagances have also been attributed to them akin to those of the Adamites. The police are recorded to have visited one of their meeting-houses in Moscow [A D 1840], and to have discovered that their religious exercises resembled those of the American Shakers, and that they had a community of women, although in order to conceal the fact they lived in couples, and even went through the form of marriage at the hands of the clergy of the Established Church The following almost incredible account is given by a traveller of their ceremonies on Easter night, when they hold a festival service in honour of the Blessed Virgin "On this night the Khlisti all assemble for a great solemnity, the worship of the Mother of God A virgin fifteen years of age, whom they have induced to act the part by tempting promises, is bound and placed in a tub of warm water, some old women come, and first make a large incision in the left breast, then cut it off, and stanch the blood in a wonderfully short time During the operation a mystical picture of the Holy Spirit is put into the victim's hand, in order that she may be absorbed in regarding it. The breast which has been removed is laid upon a plate and cut into small pieces, which are eaten by all the members of the sect present, the girl in the tub is then raised upon an altar which stands near, and the whole congregation dance wildly round it, singing at the same time The jumping then grows madder and wilder, till the lights are suddenly extinguished and horrible orgies commence My secretary has become acquainted with several of these girls, who were always afterwards regarded as sacred, and said that at the age of nineteen or twenty they looked quite like women of fifty or sixty. They die generally before their thirtieth year, one of them however had married and had two children" [Baron von Haxthausen's *Visit to the Russian Empire*, i 254, Lond. 1856] Such an apparently authentic narrative should be remembered in association with Hepworth Dixon's favourable statements respecting these and all other Russian Dissenters [Dixon's *Free Russia*, i 259, 3rd ed]

KNIPPERDOLLINGS A section of the Munster Anabaptists, so called after their leader Bertrand Knipperdolling, a confederate of Munzer [ANABAPTISTS]

KNOWN-MEN Foxe says of the Puritans of Henry VIII's days, that "after the great abjuration aforesaid, which was under William Smith, Bishop of Lincoln, they were noted and known among themselves by the name of 'known men' or 'just-fast' men, as now they are called by the name of 'Protestants'" [Foxe's *Acts and Mon* p 820, ed 1583]

The former designation had, however, been much longer in use, having been appropriated by the Lollards, and being thus explained by Pecock, Bishop of Chichester, in the middle of the fifteenth century "The first of those texts is written 1 Cor xiv. in the end thus. 'Sotheli if eny man unknowith, he schal be unknowun' By this text they take that if any man knoweth not or put not, in what he may, his business for to learn the writing of the Bible as it lieth in the text, namely, the writing of the New Testament, he shall be unknown of God for to be any of His And for this, that they busy themselves for to learn and know the Bible, namely the New Testament, in the form as it is written word by word in the Bible, they give a name proper to themselves and call themselves 'knowun men' as though all other than them be unknown, and when one of them talketh with another of them of some other third man the hearer will ask thus: 'Is he a knowen man?' and if it [be] answered to him thus 'Yea, he is a knowen man,' all is safe, peril is not for to deal with him and if it be answered to him thus 'He is no knowen man,' then peril is casted for to much homely deal with him" [Pecock's *Repressor*, p 53, Record Off ed] Some readers will remember when the question, "Is he a converted character?" used to be asked in a precisely similar manner four centuries later

KNOX, JOHN [SCOTTISH KIRK]

KORNTHALITES or KORNTHALER. A Pietistic community of Lutherans founded near Stuttgart in Kornthal, Wurtemberg, about the year 1819, by G W Hoffmann, with the view of eventually emigrating to the Holy Land, and there establishing a fresh, unrenewed purity, the kingdom of Christ This idea was revived by Hoffmann the younger in 1854 [JERUSALEM FRIENDS], but the original body has subsided into a separate community of Evangelical Lutherans, forming a kind of Moravian settlement in their native valley.

L

LABADISTS A Quietist sect of Dutch Protestants which took its name from John Labadie, a French Jesuit priest. Labadie quitted the Jesuit College at Bordeaux in the year 1639, being then about thirty years of age, and became canon of Amiens Here he became a favourite confessor and director among women of the upper classes, but was obliged to leave the city on account of scandals These charges of intrigues hung about him at Toulouse also, and he finally lost credit altogether in the Church In the year 1650 he seceded to the Calvinists, and was pastor at Montauban until 1660, when he was banished thence for exciting sedition, and once more endeavoured to settle at Geneva. But his presence seems to have caused disturbance wherever he went, and on a similar charge of sedition being there also made against him, he removed in 1666 to Middleburg in Zealand, accompanied by a band of followers. On his way through Utrecht he won over the learned lady Anna Maria Schurmann, and, through her zealous support, the Princess Palatine Elizabeth, who gave a refuge to many of his followers at Erfurt, of which place she was titular abbess When shut out from the church by the Lutherans of Middleburg Labadie and his followers broke open its doors, and this violence again led to their expulsion by the magistrates of the city. Driven from Zealand, notwithstanding the support which their leader received, the Labadist fanatics formed a small settlement near Amsterdam, but were obliged to move thence first to Erfurt and thence to Altona, where Labadie died on February 16th, 1674. After his death his followers held together for a few years at Wiewart in North Holland, but the sect died out with the death of Labadie's original adherents. They were in many respects similar in character to the early Quakers, attaching much importance to "inward light," and professing great austerity of manners [Moller's *Cimbria Litterata* Weismann's *Hist Eccl sæcul* XVII]

LAMPETIANS. A sect probably of the fourth or fifth century, and said to be so called from a leader named Lampetius, of whom, however, nothing is known. St. John Damascene describes them as repudiating all vows, on the ground that no Christian ought to do anything unwillingly or by constraint, and as hence being led into a freedom of life which became licentious [Damascen. *de Hær* p 359, ed 1548]; and a similar notice of them occurs in the *Scholia* of St Maximus on the Ecclesiastical Hierarchies of Dionysius [Dionys *de Eccl Hier* in *Bibl Max. Lugd* I. 228, D] The latter also identifies them with the Massalians, Adelphians, and Marcianists, from which it would seem that they were a local variety of the Euchites

LAMPETER BRETHREN [PRINCEITES]

LATITUDINARIANS [LOW CHURCHMEN]

LATTER-DAY SAINTS [MORMONS]

LEIBNITZ, GOTTFRIED WILHELM, [A.D 1646-1716] was the son of a Leipsic professor, and was brought up to the profession of the law. He rose to very high position as a diplomatist, became an intimate of Sophia Charlotte, Queen of Prussia, and was made a baron in 1711 by the Emperor Charles VI. He occupied a very high position in almost every branch of learning, and from him all the subsequent speculations of German philosophy may be said to have flowed. "The mind of Leibnitz was cast in a gigantic mould, and made by nature to tower above the rest of the world around him. By virtue of this it was that, like all great minds, he cast his shadow before him, and gave more pregnant suggestions in some of his cursory writings than most other men could do in the combined and systematic labour of their whole life" [Morell's *Hist of Phil* I. 186]

When Leibnitz came upon the field of philosophical speculation the theological results of the Cartesian system had made themselves evident in the writings of Malebranche and Spinoza The influence of the former had led to the denial of all secondary causes by making all force the activity of the Supreme Being Spinoza took every existing thing to be a part of the Universal Substance The tendency of both lines of philosophy had been to destroy the idea of Causation, as coming from without the sphere of individual being, and to make all existing things simply modes of the one infinite existence Leibnitz strove to recover the idea of external causation by his system of "Monadology," in which he considered Force as a quality imposed upon Substance in its original creation and then left to work out an inevitable destiny. This original combination of Force and Substance he supposes to have been made in an infinite number of distinct and dissimilar "monads"—having something of the character of atoms—which upon their creation became self-subsistent and indestructible, each monad being a living and germinal microcosm with a fixed capacity of developing itself spontaneously

In applying this theory to the natural world Leibnitz classified his monads in such a manner as to exhibit them in a developing sequence, the monad of inorganic life possessing all the qualities of other monads, but all except one, that of motion (as in crystallization), remaining dormant The monad of the vegetable creation developes formative vitality, leaving consciousness still dormant To this succeeds the developement of sensation and memory as in animals Then follows the monad in which reason and reflection are aroused from their dormant condition and added to all preceding qualities Each of these stages of developement represents the unveiling of an infinite quality of Deity, and the primary Monad is Deity itself, the fountain from which all others have derived their origin

The theology of monadology is necessarily Deism When once the monads have been brought into existence they become self-existent and self-developing, no external power being able to change their nature, to alter their course of developement, or to destroy them They are indestructible machines, having an irresistible power of perpetual motion in a given direction Its morality was also of necessity Fatalism For according as the self-contained force of the monad was originally destined to exert itself, so must it exert itself, whether in the fully developed form of a conscious soul or in the half-developed form of unconscious matter Although, therefore, there was something more of free-will in the system of Leibnitz than in that of Spinoza, from the introduction of the element of self-development in the monad, yet it was still not such a free-will as extends to moral action, for the law of development was already laid down in the law of existence

The system of Leibnitz was embodied by him in his *Théodicée* and his *Monadologie*, the latter work being published only a short time before his death It failed to produce so much effect as might have been expected from its author's great living influence upon the mind of Europe This arose from the want of a clear, logical, and systematic way of stating it But shortly after the death of Leibnitz his disciple WOLF placed it before the world in such a manner as to win it a foremost place in the ranks of philosophical speculations [Tennemann's *Manual* Ritter's *Geschichte der Christlichen Philosophie* Morell's *History of Philosophy* *Edinb Rev* July 1846]

LEONISTS. A name given to the Waldenses from Leon, the German name of the city of Lyons where they originated, and from which they called themselves the "Poor of Lyons" Some Calvinist writers are said by Gretser to have derived the name from Leo IV, son of Constantine Copronymus! [*Bibl Max* xxv 253, B]

LESSING [RATIONALISTS]

LEYDEN, JOHN OF [ANABAPTISTS]

LIBERATORES [ADECERDITÆ]

LIBERTINES A Flemish sect of Antinomians, who also called themselves "Spirituals" They originated with Anthony Poekes, Gerhard Ruff, Quintin, and others in Flanders, and thence passed into France, where they were patronized by Margaret, Queen of Navarre and sister of Francis I Their principles were, that God being the Author of all human actions no human action could be evil, that religion consists in union with God by contemplation, and that any one who had attained to this was free to act according to their pleasure These were the principles of the BRETHREN OF THE FREE SPIRIT, from whom the Libertines were doubtless descended Calvin wrote against them, *Instructio adversus fanaticam et furiosam sectam Libertinorum, qui se Spirituales vocant*

The name was also given to the RANTERS and FAMILISTS by many English writers of the seventeenth century, from their Antinomian claims of immoral liberty

LOLLARDS. The followers of Wickliffe in the fourteenth and fifteenth centuries The name seems to be identical with that of the German LULLARDS, but it was used in England simply in the sense of heretics, and thus had a clever turn given to it as if it had been derived from "lolium," and signified tares among the wheat The name is found in a bull of Gregory XI [A D 1377], in a constitution of Archbishop Arundel [A D 1408], and in Netter of Walden's *Fasciculus Zizaniorum*, which was written early in the fifteenth century

The Lollards were partly a political party of socialists, and partly a school of anti-sacerdotalists, and represent in England that wave of disloyalty to Church and State which was sweeping over every continental country in the thirteenth and fourteenth centuries But it is also evident that they were associated by contemporaries with the influence and particular teaching of Wickliffe, and that they themselves claimed to be his disciples The truth seems to be that a party answering to the Lollards had arisen in England in the first half of the fourteenth century in the same subtle way in which a similar social and religious epidemic had broken out in Italy, Germany and France, and that circumstances which cannot now be clearly traced had given the intellectual leadership of that party into the hands of Wickliffe

This remarkable man, John de Wickliffe [A D 1324-84], was a Yorkshireman, born at Wickliffe on the Tees At the age of sixteen he was sent to Oxford, where he was entered as a commoner of Queen's College, then a recent foundation He was removed to Merton, the college of Ockham and Roger Bacon, the influence of whose example perhaps excited Wickliffe to strike out a bold line for himself He became successively probationer and fellow of Merton, where he soon distinguished himself by his skill in logic, his knowledge of the scholastic philosophy, his acquaintance with the four great Latin Fathers (he seems never to have acquired Greek), and his fierce unsparing hostility to everything that he deemed evil It is uncertain against

Lollards

what abuse his first efforts were directed. A tract is extant of the date of A.D. 1356, entitled the *Last Ages of the Church*, but its genuineness is not admitted. The only evidence of his authorship is, that it has been found in the Library of Trinity College, Dublin, bound up in a volume with works that are his [Milman, *Lat. Chris.* xiii. 6; Shirley's *Catalogue of Wickliffe's Works*, xiii.] It was written in a time of pestilence, and advocates the theory of the nearness of the Last Day, which Abbot Joachim first started. In this tract the secular clergy, and particularly those well beneficed, are denounced as simoniacs.

In A.D. 1360, Wickliffe commenced his warfare with the Mendicant Friars, who had intruded into the universities as elsewhere, and by claiming degrees on their own terms, and striving to draw into their body the most promising students at an earlier age than the statutes allowed, seemed likely to subvert academic discipline, as they had already subverted parochial discipline in the country at large. In his tract against them, Wickliffe denied their favourite position that our Lord was a vagrant and a beggar, exposed their almost blasphemous regard for their founder, and branded the richer as hypocrites, the poorer as mere vagrants, and all alike as misleaders of the people. The popularity which he thus gained in the university won for him in A.D. 1361 the appointment of Master of Balliol College, to which was attached the rectory of Fylingham in the diocese of Lincoln. Four years later he became Warden of Canterbury Hall.

This Hall had been only lately founded by Simon Islip for a warden and eleven fellows. Three out of the whole number were to be chosen from the monks of Canterbury, and eight from the secular clergy. Having become dissatisfied with the turbulent character of Wodehull, the first warden, Islip dispossessed him and the regulars, and appointed none but seculars in their room, with Wickliffe for their head. But this arrangement was reversed immediately afterwards by Simon Langham, Islip's successor in the see of Canterbury, who, having once been a monk himself, favoured the cause of the monks, and restored Wodehull and the regulars, whereupon Wickliffe, according to the ordinary custom of the day, appealed to the Pope. After the usual delay in such matters, the papal decision was given against him, perhaps owing to the fact that Wickliffe, as Royal chaplain, had been appointed to withstand in writing the papal claim to tribute and homage from the King of England which Urban had just pressed, basing it upon the surrender of the kingdom by John. Wickliffe performed his task with his usual energy and vigour, but his success did not prevent Edward from confirming the appointment of Wodehull upon the receipt of 200 marks.[1]

Wickliffe remained at Oxford, took his Doctor's degree in A.D. 1372, and being thus "Sanctæ Theologiæ Professor," he commenced lecturing in divinity. At the same time he continued to wage war with the friars, whom he accused of holding fifty errors and heresies. It was perhaps about this time that he wrote against the abuse of promoting clergy to State offices, owing to which the ecclesiastic was too often sunk in the statesman, and on the other hand statesmen were paid for their services at the expense of the Church by the possession of benefices. The question created so much excitement at the time in Parliament, that the Bishops of Winchester and Exeter were compelled to resign their offices of Chancellor and Treasurer.

Altogether Wickliffe's conduct had so far been such as to bring him into favour with the ruling powers. He was particularly patronized by John of Gaunt, through whose influence he was in A.D. 1374 placed on a commission to treat with the Papal Legate at Bruges respecting points in dispute between the King and the Pope, the chief of them being the right claimed by the latter to appoint to certain benefices in England. Against this claim sundry statutes had been passed by Parliament, but the right was still asserted and often exercised. The case was compromised, but Wickliffe, for his services on this occasion, when he seems for the first time to have spoken of the Pope as Antichrist, received the prebend of Aust in the collegiate church of Westbury, and the rectory of Lutterworth, which he held till his death.

The opposition against him was now increased, and the Pope required the Primate to deal summarily with him. This the law of the land would not permit, but he was cited by Courtenay, then Bishop of London, to appear before a synod held at St. Paul's, and to answer to nineteen articles that had been alleged against him.[2] He appeared, supported by the presence of John of Gaunt and Lord Percy, Earl Marshal, who behaved with insolence and rudeness to the synod—a duly convened and fully authorized judicial tribunal—behaviour which Courtenay met by mildness and dignity. The populace, indignant at the turbulent conduct of these noblemen, who were already deservedly disliked, behaved with such tumultuous violence that the two were forced to fly for their lives, and the synod was broken up without coming to any decision [A.D. 1377].

Early in the reign of Richard II., the Pope Gregory IX. issued three bulls against Wickliffe, addressed to the King, to Sudbury, Archbishop of Canterbury, and to the University of Oxford. The bulls to the King and to the University seem to have produced no effect; the Archbishop summoned Wickliffe to appear before him at his private chapel at Lambeth, but the proceedings there were arrested, partly by a tumultuous assembly of the Londoners, and partly by a mandate from the Princess Dowager of Wales, who headed the Regency Government. At the same time Wickliffe declared that his opinions had

[1] It has been doubted whether the Warden of Canterbury Hall was not another John Wickliffe, Vicar of Mayfield, who flourished about the same time [*Fasciculi Zizaniorum*, ed. Shirley, note], but Wodeford, a contemporary, speaks of the Reformer as Warden [*Quæstiones in Fasc. Zizan.*]

[2] For these see Walsingham, p. 204.

been formed from the Sacred Scriptures and from holy doctors and that if they were proved to be adverse to the faith he was ready and willing to recant The only result was that he was enjoined to keep silence, and the death of Gregory, with the schism that followed, greatly strengthened his position He wrote a tract comparing the rival popes who were anathematizing each other to Simon Magus

It was about this time that he commenced his most important work, the translation of the Scriptures It may be remarked in passing that it is quite a mistake to suppose that the Church of the Middle Ages was opposed to the devotional reading of the Holy Scripture Translations of the Bible had been made into the English tongue during many centuries [Blunt's *Plain Account of the Eng Bible*] The real objection was to the claim of some to form for themselves a scheme of Christian doctrine out of Scripture, interpreted according to their own individual judgment, a claim which the Church of England has never allowed Besides this, particular translations were objected to as having been made by heretics, and not without reason But though the mediæval Church never as a body opposed the devotional reading of the Holy Bible in the vulgar tongue, sufficient pains were not taken to supply the people with authorized versions This defect Wickliffe endeavoured to supply, prefacing his effort by the issue of a tract on the truth of Scripture His translation was made into good, vigorous, racy, English from the Vulgate Many copies were transcribed by the hands of loving disciples, so that it soon became widely circulated, chiefly by means of a band of followers whom he now began to organize and send forth to preach everywhere, either in the churches or in the highways, calling them his "poor" preachers. They went about in blue or russet gowns, barefoot, depending for their maintenance upon the hospitality of their hearers, and they gained many followers, particularly in the neighbourhood of Lutterworth

In A D 1379, his work was interrupted by a severe illness at Oxford, which almost carried him off, however he recovered and developed still further his opposition to the current beliefs Hitherto he had not attacked any of the doctrines of the Church, but in A D 1381 he began to express doubts concerning transubstantiation, and published his twelve conclusions on the matter [Vaughan, *Life*, ii 45] This turned against him many who had hitherto been his main supporters The University censured him, and forbade any of its members to hold and maintain such doctrines on pain of the greater excommunication and imprisonment He appealed to the King, but his appeal was rejected, and his protector, John of Gaunt, coldly admonished him to submit to his ecclesiastical superiors on such a question But Wickliffe's spirit was not one that would yield to the counsels of an Erastian statesman on questions of Church doctrine, and he continued to declare what he conceived to be the truth He was in consequence summoned before an ecclesiastical court at Oxford,[1] but obtained an acquittal on the ground that passages of doubtful import in his writings ought to be construed in *meliorem partem* An attempt was now made to identify him with those wild lawless bands which, under Wat Tyler and others, were rising against the Government Although Wickliffe had no real connection with them, his known views on the lawfulness of confiscating Church property, if mal-administered, was thought to threaten all property, and it was accordingly provided by Act of Parliament that unlicensed preachers, or Lollards, should be arrested and held in strong prisons until they should justify themselves according to law and reason of Holy Church [5 Ric II st 2, c. 5] This Act passed the Lords, and was promulgated by the King, probably at the instance of Courtenay, now Archbishop of Canterbury, but it had never been submitted to the Commons, and at their remonstrance some time afterwards it was withdrawn

In A D 1382, the Archbishop proceeded against Wickliffe, and he was cited before an assembly of eight bishops and fourteen doctors at Greyfriars in London He refused to appear, alleging the privileges of the University; but the investigation continued, and out of twenty-four articles gathered from his writings ten were condemned as heretical and fourteen as erroneous [DICT *of* THEOL, LOLLARDS Gieseler's *Eccl Hist* iv p 248, Clark's tr] This condemnation was publicly proclaimed in London, but Wickliffe appealed to the civil powers in Parliament, requiring them to relax the monastic vows, to see that tithes were applied to the maintenance of the poor, that Christ's doctrine on the Eucharist was taught, that if a bishop or curate were notoriously guilty of contempt of God his temporalities should be confiscated, that the clergy should not be allowed to hold secular offices, and that no one should be imprisoned on account of excommunication to which were added certain articles against the Pope [Vaughan, ii 97] The Commons did not accede to this petition, but protested against the Act for the imprisonment of heretics mentioned above

Wickliffe still had many adherents at Oxford, among whom was the Chancellor, who refused to expel him from the University, or cause his followers to be sought out for punishment, but Parliament happened to be transferred to Oxford, and with it went the Convocation, before which his views on the Eucharist were questioned They were condemned, but it is uncertain whether Wickliffe was actually expelled from Oxford or withdrew of his own accord He did retire to Lutterworth in A D 1382, where he was allowed to end his days without farther molestation from the Archbishop But his last moments were not undisturbed Pope Urban VI of Rome had proclaimed a crusade against his rival of Avignon, and the war-loving Bishop of Norwich headed those English who took part in it, to the

[1] The order of events at this time of his life is not quite clear

indignation of many patriotic men, who could ill bear to see so much English blood and treasure wasted upon a profitless foreign enterprise Wickliffe saw his opportunity, and sent forth a tract, in which he severely censured the wickedness of a war among Christian nations undertaken to promote the ambitious designs of two "antichristian priests," as he styled them The crusade proved a failure, but Urban's anger was roused, and he summoned Wickliffe to appear before him at Rome Wickliffe replied that his weak state of health would not allow him to undertake the fatigues of such a journey, and in fact he had been ailing for some time On Innocents' Day A D 1384 he was struck with paralysis while celebrating mass in the Church of Lutterworth, and died on the last day of the year, St Sylvester's Day He was buried in the chancel of the church, but forty years after, in obedience to a decree of the Council of Constance, his bones were exhumed, burnt to ashes, and cast into a brook But he had won the respect of those who opposed him, as being undoubtedly one of the most learned Englishmen of the day He left behind him numerous writings on the most varied subjects, more than two hundred being said to have been burnt in Bohemia. Shirley's catalogue reckons up ninety-six extant Latin, sixty-five extant English works, besides about one hundred works that have been lost Wickliffe was no Protestant. He did indeed wage war with the papal claims, and he opposed extreme materialistic views on the Eucharist, but he maintained the Real Presence His distinctive views were political and social rather than religious He withstood the monks, friars, and the dignified clergy He held peculiar views on ecclesiastical property, and the right of the State to confiscate it, which his followers developed to their logical extent, and applied to all property, and this in the unsettled state of those times was the main cause of the persecuting statutes which Parliament from time to time passed against them He himself organized no band of followers, though he had, indeed, sent forth his poor priests, but all those who in after days were influenced by his writings, and held his views, political or religious, as well as those who went beyond him, were classed together as Lollards

These Lollards included men of the most diverse character and principles, from the sincere, honest religious reformer to the wild socialist visionary, whose opinions, if allowed to prevail, would have plunged society into chaos. They comprised all orders of men, knights, merchants and peasants Even a peer, the Earl of Salisbury, has been branded by Walsingham as a favourer of Lollards all his life, as a reviler of images, a despiser of canons, and a scoffer at sacraments He was beheaded in A D 1400 for conspiring to restore Richard II [1] The Lollards arrayed against themselves all the friends of order, as well as the supporters of the existing hierarchy They judged their ecclesiastical superiors according to a standard of their own, and went about interfering in parishes in contempt of the parochial system, much as the friars had done Some of them objected to church music and organs, and quoted Scripture in support of their views, without regard to the context.

An Act has been already mentioned as passed against the Lollards in A D 1381. Thirteen years later they presented a bold remonstrance to the Parliament, complaining of the wealth and power of the clergy, and protesting against celibacy, transubstantiation, benedictions and exorcisms, the union of spiritual and secular offices in the same person, chantries for the dead, pilgrimages, the worshipping of images and relics, auricular confession, indulgences, capital punishments, and trades which minister to pride or luxury [*Fasciculus Zizaniorum*, p 300] They proved so mutinous in London that an insurrection was apprehended, and Richard was hurriedly summoned back from Ireland In his reign the sheriffs' oath required them to watch the Lollards, as being known to be turbulent and disaffected, and the practice was afterwards confirmed by Henry IV, and continued in force until the time of Charles I, when it was dropped as obsolete in consequence of an objection made by Sir Edward Coke, when Sheriff of Buckingham

The state of the kingdom in Henry's reign was alarming His adherents and those of the deposed Richard divided the realm, while the Lollards in the background were threatening ecclesiastical property, and in some cases all property Accordingly, in A D 1401, the Act "De hæretico comburendo" was passed by all the estates of the realm, providing that the bishop should arrest, imprison, and bring heretics to trial at his courts If they should refuse to recant, or should relapse after recanting, he was to hand them over to the sheriff of the county, or to the mayor or bailiff of the nearest borough, to be burnt alive on a high place before the people The Scotch passed a similar Act in A D 1425 It may be remarked that in no country except Great Britain was a special law necessary for the execution of heretics, the mere will of the government being elsewhere sufficient

The first to suffer under the new Act was William Sautree, a clergyman of Norwich diocese He had recanted before his bishop, but continuing to preach in London was condemned as a relapsed heretic, degraded and burnt [A D 1401] Another priest, William Thorpe, was arraigned before Arundel, but his fate has not been handed down to us. The only other known sufferer in Henry IV's reign was Thomas Bradby, a tailor, from the diocese of Worcester Prince Henry was present at his execution, and when he cried for mercy as the flames mounted up, ordered them to be quenched, and offered him his life and a pension on condition of his recantation, but he refused and was burnt. The fact that these were the only two executed in that reign, while the Lollards boasted that their number exceeded 100,000, shews the unwillingness of the bishops

[1] For a more particular account of his principal disciples, see Lewis' *Life of Wickliffe*.

to put the Act into force As in Queen Mary's reign, the laity of Parliament, the noble lords and knights of the shires, however covetous they may have been of the temporal power and wealth of the clergy, were the most fierce in urging them on to seek out, imprison, and burn the Lollards When, after every effort had been made in vain to persuade them to recant, the bishops, as the law required, handed them over to the secular power, the local authorities were always ready to carry out the law as it then stood, without remonstrance. It was, in fact, a brutal age, as is shewn by the savage punishment for treason frequently inflicted under Henry IV, and the power of the Commons in the State having in his reign become a reality, the whole nation was responsible for the burnings The country had, indeed, become so dissatisfied with the remissness of the bishops, that in 1412 a petition against the Lollards was presented to Parliament through Sir John Tiptoft

After the accession of Henry V the condition of the Lollards became worse, and there can be no doubt that some of their number by their seditious conduct provoked severe action on the part of the Government [Hook's *Lives of Abps Arundel and Chichele*] At the beginning of this reign occurred the case of Sir John Oldcastle, sometimes called Lord Cobham in right of his wife, and hitherto known chiefly as a tried soldier, and a man high in favour with the King He was accused before Convocation of heretical notions on the sacraments, pilgrimage, penance, and the power of the keys, and that through his influence unlicensed preachers had been sent forth in the dioceses of London, Rochester, and Hereford Henry took this case in hand himself, argued with Oldcastle, and remonstrated with him, particularly on the heretical books that he had in his possession Oldcastle replied that he had not yet read them, and so could not be answerable for what they contained He was allowed to retire to his castle of Cowling, near Rochester, where he treated with contempt the summons of the archbishop, and despised his excommunications, until a king's officer was employed in the case, when he gave way, and was committed, not to the Archbishop's house at Lambeth, but to the Tower of London He then published a confession of faith, satisfactory on many points, but defective on the question of the Eucharist Cobham at the same time offered to produce one hundred knights as his "compurgators," and expressed himself willing to submit to the wager of battle, but those ancient forms of judicial decision were already beginning to become obsolete He was arraigned again before the archbishop and other bishops, and a long contest ensued, during which, while the primate was mild and conciliatory, Oldcastle displayed an insolence of conduct which would have provoked any court even of our own day After several examinations he was solemnly condemned, and committed again to the Tower, whence he contrived to make his escape and fly to Wales, where he became the centre of the disaffected, who were then very numerous How far he may have been personally implicated is uncertain, but well grounded reports of Lollard risings began to spread. The Lollards were supposed to be preparing to march to London, with the intention of overthrowing the King's present counsellors, making Oldcastle prime minister, destroying the union between Church and State, suppressing all the religious orders, and confiscating Church property generally It must be remembered that the country was in a very distracted state, that Henry had not as yet had the opportunity of displaying the ability to rule, or the generous and noble qualities which afterwards won him popularity, that his title to the throne was disputed by numbers, who either believed that Richard was yet alive or looked up for the rightful heir, and that many of the Lollards had proclaimed doctrines destructive alike of civil rule and proprietary rights, so as to band together all parties in the State against them Henry, alarmed, issued a proclamation against the Lollards, indicting Oldcastle, Sir Roger Acton and others by name, removed from Eltham to Westminster, and called upon his friends to arm in his defence The city was suspected, as many of the inhabitants were known favourers of the Lollard party, the gates were closed, and several arrests were made, but probably owing to the promptness and boldness of the King's measures no outbreak took place The imminence of the danger so alarmed the Government, that thirty-nine persons were tried and executed for treason and heresy. but a very large number were pardoned, and a general amnesty was proclaimed, with twelve exceptions At the same time [A D 1414], an Act was passed extending that of Henry IV, and requiring all officials upon entering office to take an oath to destroy Lollards, and assure the ordinaries therein, the justices were empowered to inquire concerning offenders, and to deliver them up to the ordinaries within ten days. A relapsed heretic was to be hanged (probably in chains round the middle) for treason against the King, and burnt for heresy against God [2 Henry V stat 1 c 7] It is to be noted that this statute was the act, not of the clergy, but of the laity in Parliament, having been originated in the Commons as usual by petition, adopted by the Lords, and assented to by the King

Two years later, there appeared a constitution of the Convocation under Archbishop Chichele. It provided that heretics should be inquired after by the bishops or their officials in each rural deanery twice a year, but we do not read of any executions in consequence, nor of any close search In fact the more turbulent spirits who had brought Lollardism into disrepute as a political faction were being drafted off into the French war

Oldcastle remained in concealment in Wales for some years, although a price of 1000 marks had been set upon his head, a proof that the Government considered him really dangerous to civil order Once only he shewed himself near St Alban's, and that was during an invasion of the Scotch, with whom he was supposed to be in secret treaty At length, in 1418, he was taken by Sir E. Charlton after vigorous resistance, and brought to London He was interrogated by Parliament, but when he denied their jurisdiction over him, affirming that King Richard was still alive, they condemned him without further hearing to be hanged as a traitor and to be burnt as a heretic

We do not read of any other executions under Henry V, except that of Taylor, a priest, in the last year of his reign Several occurred in the early years of Henry VI, and numbers were committed to prison, and persuaded or compelled to recant The bishops were as a rule exceedingly unwilling to deliver them over to the secular arm, and often kept them in confinement at their own expense to preserve their lives The Wars of the Roses stayed the persecution and wrought a great change in the character of the Lollards All the turbulent and disaffected of the nation were absorbed into the contending parties, and the Lollards proper became a quiet and peaceful school, which, by spreading the Scriptures, and by persuasive measures, sought to extend their principles as far as possible, and prepared the public mind for the Reformation effected in the course of the following century An attempt has been made to claim a bishop, Pecock of Chichester, as a favourer of their cause, and in fact a confessor But as a matter of fact he was thoroughly opposed to them in two important points He advocated the union of ecclesiastical and civil offices in one person, maintaining that it was no business of the bishops to go about preaching in their dioceses, but that they were much better employed in advocating the cause of the Church at the courts of kings He was also a fervid champion of extreme papal pretensions, affirming that the Pope was the one source of all episcopal power, and that all bishops were his delegates It was this that set the English bishops against him, and caused his deprivation, but the bare fact that he was so deprived by the existing powers was enough to make Foxe and his believers turn a champion of extreme Ultramontanism into a Protestant martyr [Pecock's *Repressor*, Record Off edition]

After the accession of Henry VII the persecution broke out afresh, and several were burnt in his reign, among whom was Joan Boughton in 1494, the first woman who suffered for heresy in England Still the number of those who were put to death for heresy is remarkably small, compared with those who in the same period of time met a like fate on the Continent Foxe, who is generally so minute in his accounts, gives the names of twenty (not including Oldcastle and the thirty-nine who were executed for the Lollard rising under Henry V) as having suffered from the burning of Sautree to the accession of Henry VIII, a period of 108 years, an Italian or Spanish inquisitor would have thought the whole number barely sufficient for one single "Auto da Fé" The early days of Henry VIII were comparatively free from the stains of blood, Wolsey being no persecutor From that time the name of Lollard disappears, being succeeded by that of the PURITANS

LOMBARD, PETER [SCHOOLMEN]

LOVE, FAMILY OF [FAMILISTS]

LOW CHURCHMEN Those laymen and clergymen of the Church of England who regard the Ministry and Sacraments principally in their relation to mankind

The name was first used in the time of Queen Anne, but, as has been shewn under the title HIGH CHURCHMEN, there has always been such a school in the Church of England since the Reformation, and the existence of distinct schools of thought is not peculiar to the Church of England, but is traceable through the whole course of Christian history In the eighteenth and nineteenth centuries Low Churchmen often assumed the name of "Evangelicals" or "the Evangelical party," a name which, as an assumption of exclusiveness, carries its own condemnation, but which has become historical

I LOW CHURCHMEN OF THE REFORMATION PERIOD The warmest sympathies of Low Churchmen have generally been stimulated by influences outside of the Church of England In modern times the stimulus has come from Dissent and Scotch Presbyterianism, in earlier days it came from Geneva. Thus the Low Churchmen of the Reformation period were that strong Calvinistic party within the Church which desired to retain the Episcopal system and the Prayer Book, but to modify the former in the Presbyterian direction, and to get rid from the latter of those distinctively Catholic principles and practices which foreign Protestants like Calvin stigmatized as "bearable fooleries" This party sprung originally from Cambridge, where, before the days of Calvin, its predecessors were in possession of the University, and strong enough to send out a colony under the auspices of Wolsey to "Cardinal" College in Oxford In Edward VI's time the Calvinistic influence grew strong at Court through the encouragement received from the Duke of Somerset and Cranmer [CALVINISTS] it was consequently strong on the bench of bishops, and both the Universities were then tuned by the imposition upon them of two foreigners, Peter Martyr and Martin Bucer, as Divinity Professors The efforts of the party were directed, during Edward's reign, towards a remodelling of the Prayer Book in such a manner as to free it from the taint of Popery, which was considered to corrupt the First Prayer Book, that of 1548, the work of Henry VIII's Convocation and although their efforts were not entirely successful, they sufficed to make changes which theologians of later days have always regretted, and which introduced into the Communion Service original novelties that had been previously avoided with care

In the reign of Queen Elizabeth the Low Churchmen were led by Cartwright and Travers, and by those who had fled for safety to Zurich and Geneva during the reign of her sister, among the most notable were Jewel, Bishop of Salisbury,

Grindal, Bishop of London, and Horne, Bishop of Winchester The efforts of the party were now turned against the retention of the old Liturgical customs, such as the use of vestments (which Jewel called "relics of the Amorites"), of altar lights and altar crosses, of wafers for the Holy Communion, and of kneeling at its reception The Thirty-nine Articles were also attacked by them for the purpose of giving them a strongly Calvinistic colour, and when this endeavour failed, the Lambeth Articles were prepared, and would have been imposed upon the Church but for the resistance of Queen Elizabeth [DICT *of* THEOL, LAMBETH ARTICLES] On James I's arrival in England great hopes were entertained by the Low Church party that his Presbyterian education would make him favourable to these changes, but the Hampton Court Conference destroyed these expectations It was during his reign, however, that they succeeded in weaning the people from the sacrificial aspect of the Holy Communion by very generally removing the Lord's Table from the east end of the chancel, where it stood "altar wise," and placing it as a communicant's or "communion-table" in the middle of the chancel or in the nave The attempts made by Laud and other High Churchmen to undo the Low Church innovations of the Jacobean period had, as is well known, great influence in bringing about the Great Rebellion, and yet prevented those innovations from being imposed upon the Church in subsequent generations [PURITANS]

II THE LATITUDINARIANS A regular current of secession from the ranks of the Low Church party to those of the Presbyterians, the Independents, and the Roman Catholics, deprived it of its more zealous elements, and prepared it to assume a position which may be defined as that of an *expediency settlement*, a position which the party occupied from soon after the Restoration until the latter half of the eighteenth century They had now grown very indifferent about extreme Calvinism on the one hand, and very indifferent about the Episcopal system on the other and it thus seemed possible for them to establish a colourless theology and colourless Episcopacy that might become a platform on which moderate Calvinists, moderate Arminians, moderate Presbyterians, and moderate Independents, might all unite in one common Church This scheme of "comprehension'—and an honest and true comprehension would have been a glory to them for ever—won for Low Churchmen the new title of "Latitudinarians" Their motto for the next hundred years was that of the publication which first set forth their principles in detail, "Let your moderation be known unto all men '

The name of "Latitude-men" was first given by the Puritans to those of the clergy who conformed to Presbyterianism and Independency under the government of Cromwell They were "men of a prelatical spirit that had apostatized to the onions and garlic of Egypt, because they were generally ordained by bishops, and in opposition to that hide-bound, strait-laced spirit that did then prevail they were called 'Latitude-men,' for that was the first original of the name whatever sense hath since been put upon it This was a certain bar to their preferment, as they were sure to find if any of them came before the Committee of Tryers" [*Brief account of a new sect of Latitude-men, together with some reflections upon the new Philosophy*, by S P, Cambridge, June 1662] About 1770 the class of men described by this writer began to be called by the more lasting name of Latitudinarians, as is shewn in the following dialogue "*Philalethes* Have you not heard the cholerick gentlemen distinguish these persons by a long nickname, which they have taught their tongues to pronounce as roundly as if it were a shorter than it is by four or five syllables? *Theophilus* Yes Philalethes, oftener, I presume, than you have for though we are both countrymen, and wonted more than most to a solitary life, yet my occasions call me abroad, and into variety of companies, more frequently than yours do you where I hear, ever and anon, the word of a foot and a half long sounded out with a great grace; and that not only at fires and tables, but sometimes from pulpits too nay, and it accompanied good store of other bombasts and little witticisms in seasoning, not long since, the stately Oxonian Theatre *Phil* I am not so little skilled in the language of the Beast as to be ignorant of the derivation of that long name but I pray, Theophilus, what do those that so please themselves with it mean by it? *Theoph* That I can tell you from their own mouths for I have heard them give a description of a Latitudinarian, and it is this short one, 'He is a gentleman of a wide swallow'" [*Principles and Practices of certain moderate Divines of the Church of England (much misunderstood) truly represented and defended*, in 3 parts, 1670, p 10][1] Baxter refers to them in his usual sardonic manner as at first only "Cambridge Arminians, and some of them not so much, and were much for free and new philosophy, and especially for Cartes [Baxter's *Life and Times*, iii 20]

During this age of the school, Low Churchmen broke away from that slavery to the theology of Calvin by which they had previously been characterized, and which was revived by their successors They were extremely averse to dogmas altogether, and the rigid theories of Predestination and Election gave way to a much less unwholesome kind of teaching, which was practically that of an Universal Redemption from which no sinner is arbitrarily excluded, or excluded at all by anything except his own free will In thus emancipating the Church of England from the "horribile dictum" of Geneva they did good service to the Christianity of the

[1] A fourth part of this work was written by John Lewis of Margate, which remains in MS in Lord Spencer's Library at Althorp But the first three parts are attributed to Fowler, Bishop of Gloucester In the second edition, printed in 1671, "abusively called Latitudinarians" is substituted on the title page for "much misunderstood"

country, and prevented it from ever again running so generally in that groove which had led to the Antinomianism of the preceding times

The lax creed of the Latitudinarians tended, however, to loosen men's hold upon truth, and gave rise to an opinion somewhat similar to that of the Hegelian school of more recent days, namely, that absolute truth has no existence, and that what presents itself as truth to any sect (within reasonable bounds) is to be taken as truth relatively to them though it may not be so to others This principle is expressed by the writer previously quoted in the following words. "But I will now, in a more distinct manner, give you an account of their opinions They may be referred to matters of doctrine and discipline As to the former, they profess to dissent from none that have been held to be fundamentals of the Christian faith, either by the primitive or the best reformed modern Churches and heartily subscribe to the Thirty-nine Articles of our Church, taking that liberty in the interpretation of them that is allowed by the Church herself Though it is most reasonable to presume that she requires subscription to them as to an instrument of peace only" [*Principles*, &c p 191] This he repeats in another part of his work in the words, "nor do they require our internal assent to their Articles, but enjoin our submission to them as to an instrument of peace only" [*ibid* p 305]

This principle influenced all the opinions of the school, and its action upon the essential doctrines of the creed may be seen in the writings of men like Archbishop Tillotson [A D 1630-94], whose once popular sermons are a good illustration of that "moral" tone (as it was afterwards called) which the Christian faith assumed when thus watered down. Its particular tendency was towards Arianism, a heresy with which the Latitudinarian clergy were largely infected It may be further illustrated by the view which divines of this school took of Episcopacy, a view which gained a permanent hold upon Low Churchmen, and which was derived from Chillingworth, whom the author of the Apology for Latitudinarianism thus quotes "If we abstract from Episcopal government all accidentals, and consider only what is essential and necessary in it, we shall find no more than this, an appointment of one man of eminent sanctity and sufficiency to have the care of all the churches within a certain precinct or diocese, and furnishing him with authority (not absolute or arbitrary, but regulated and bounded by laws, and moderated by joining to him a convenient number of assistants) to the intent that all the churches under him may be provided of able and good pastors, and that both of pastors and peoples conformity to laws and performance of their duties may be required, under penalties not left to discretion but by law appointed" [*ibid* 324]

Such principles (which are exactly the same as those attributed to the party in the tract of 1662 previously quoted) led satirical writers to characterize the Low Churchmen of William III and Queen Anne's days as "No Churchmen." "Low Churchmen are so called," says one of them, "who make a shift to keep in the communion and bosom of the Church, and maintain a sort of outward conformity, but at the same time have no liking to her constitution, . these Low Churchmen are indeed No Churchmen" [*The distinction of High Church and Low Church distinctly considered and fairly stated*, 1705] "Ne'er a barrel the better herring between Low Church and No Church," is the title given to his tract by another writer in the year 1713 But these writers were attacking the Latitudinarians when they were become less respectable than they had been in their early days, when the principles of the school were bearing their natural fruit, that of being as careful not to have "overmuch righteousness" as not to have overmuch faith

III The Evangelicals In the middle of the eighteenth century a Pietistic school of Low Churchmen began to be developed, which grew into that great and influential section of the clergy and laity known as the "Evangelical party" This Pietistic school ran parallel with Methodism, and both may be traced up in a great measure to the same origin, the influence of the works of William Law [A D 1686-1761], especially of his *Serious Call to a Devout and Holy Life* The one was an educated Pietism keeping within the borders of the Church, the other an ignorant Pietism which soon wandered outside those borders

The influence of the pious Nonjurors' writings on the "Evangelical" school is well seen in the case of Henry Venn [A D 1724-97], one of its earliest members Soon after Venn had been ordained, his son records that he had heard him say it was his custom to walk almost every evening in the cloisters of Trinity College for the purpose of devotional meditation "In this frame of mind Law's *Serious Call to a Devout and Holy Life*—a book which has been the means of exciting many to a life of holiness—was particularly useful to him, he read it repeatedly with peculiar interest and advantage, and immediately began, with great sincerity, to frame his life according to the Christian model there delineated" [Venn's *Life of Venn*, 16] At a later time "his plan of life was very methodical, realizing as far as he was able that laid down by Mr Law in his *Christian Perfection*" [*ibid* 19] The influence which the works of Law had on Wesley's mind is well known, and even the journals of the period shew how widely those works were changing the character of the clergy

But at the time when Venn was leaving college life [A D 1750], after being three years in orders, for the life of a parish priest, the new school of Low Churchmen was only just coming to light, and although there were a few excellent members of it whose holy lives have kept their names in remembrance, such as James Hervey of Weston Favell [A D 1714-58], Samuel Walker of Truro [A D 1714-61], William Talbot of Reading [A D 1717-74], Thomas Adam of Wintringham [A D 1701-84], the name of Venn is the

Low Churchmen

earliest of those who attained anything like distinction [1] He was, however, only one of a large body, for during the early part of George III's reign, and the ten years' rule of the good Archbishop Secker [A D 1758-68], the numbers of the "Evangelical" clergy rapidly increased, and towards the latter years of the century they had reached to about three hundred [*Evang Mag* Nov 1795, p 449] It is impossible here to do more than mention the names of some of those who took a leading part—chiefly as preachers —among them, and indeed few of them were men of sufficient ability to leave their mark on the page of history, so that even the 'lives" of those whose lives found friendly pens to write them are mere records of personal feelings and social incidents The chief of them were William Romaine of St. Anne's, Blackfriars [A D 1714-94], John Fletcher of Madeley [A D 1729-1785], John Berridge of Everton [A D 1716-1793], William Grimshaw of Haworth [A D *-1763], Richard de Courcy of St Alkmund's, Shrewsbury, William Bromley Cadogan of Chelsea and Reading [A D 1751-1797], Joseph Milner of Hull [A D 1744-97], and his brother Isaac Milner, Dean of Carlisle [A D 1751-1820], John Newton of Olney and St Mary Woolnoth [A D 1725-1807], Beilby Porteus, Bishop of London [A D 1787-1804], Richard Cecil of St John's, Bedford Row [A D 1748-1810], and Thomas Robinson of Leicester [A D 1749-1813] To these names may be added those of a rather later generation Thomas Scott of Aston Sandford [A D 1747-1821], Legh Richmond of Turvey [A D 1772-1827], and Charles Simeon of Cambridge [A D 1759-1836] [2] But perhaps none of these clergy, except Milner, Scott, and Simeon, exercised so great an influence in the revival of religion within the Church as was exercised by the great layman William Wilberforce [A D 1759-1833], whose missionary book, entitled *A Practical View of Christianity* [A D 1797], circulated by many thousands, and whose holy example in public and private life leavened English society as it was never leavened by a single layman before, except, perhaps, by Robert Nelson

The Evangelical movement within the Church was contemporary with the Methodist movement under the Wesleys and Whitfield Some of the clergy engaged in the former held aloof from the Methodists, as did Walker of Truro, who wrote "My conduct with regard to the Methodists hath been upon the plan of Gamaliel's advice for though there appeared a zeal and boldness in them which might very justly engage my heart to them, yet I could never persuade myself their proceedings were justifiable, . nevertheless I trust they have been the means of kindling Gospel principles among us, and seem about to leave the work to more regular and capable heads than their own" [Sidney's *Life of Walker*, 281] He afterwards wrote to John Wesley, endeavouring to persuade him to give up his Methodist societies into the hands of the Evangelical clergy, in whose parishes they were formed, and received a reply from the great autocrat, which is amusingly illustrative of his love of power Others, however, among the early Evangelicals associated themselves heartily with the Methodists, leaning to Wesley or Whitfield as their own views inclined to the Arminian or the Calvinistic side Fletcher of Madeley and Hervey, the author of *Theron and Aspasio*, and of the *Meditations in a Country Churchyard* (a work in its day almost as popular as the *Christian Year* in later times), were among Wesley's earliest coadjutors, while Grimshaw, Berridge, and Romaine,[3] co-operated with Whitfield, Lady Huntingdon, and the Calvinistic Methodists in general [HUNTINGDONIANS]

A few of the earlier school were indeed on very friendly terms with Dissenters, though generally with those belonging to the parishes of other clergymen rather than with those of their own "Influenced by the hope of doing good," says the biographer of Venn, with respectful disapproval, "my father in certain instances preached in unconsecrated places" [Venn's *Life of Venn*, 177] Wesley's clerical friends often assisted him in the same way, and the practice had gone to an inconvenient length when it was stopped by the proceedings taken against Lady Huntingdon's chaplains. Venn preached at Rowland Hill's Meeting-House, Surrey Chapel, whenever he visited London, and for several Sundays in succession as late as the year 1790 [*ibid* 176, 485] But the principles of the Church weighed so lightly with men of this school when balanced against individual opinion and feeling, that when Venn left Huddersfield in 1751, and was succeeded by a vicar of whom he and his admirers did not approve, he instantly advised the latter to build a dissenting chapel for themselves, and although, very shortly after it was built, a vicar of Huddersfield arrived who was of their own way of thinking, these people were permanently alienated from the Church [*ibid* 174] The later school which followed the lead of Milner the Church historian, and Scott the Commentator, was more true to the Church and its principles, and in recent times (notwithstanding the establishment of "the Evangelical Alliance" in the year 1846) its members have generally been vigorous opponents of the Dissenters in their own parishes

The absence of any other organized party in the Church, their active preaching and their many good works, combined with the influence of Joseph Milner's unhistorical *Church History*, and Thomas Scott's more valuable *Commentary*

[1] It is a fact of some interest that the Venn family have kept up a direct line of clergy, from father to son, from the time of the Reformation to the present day

[2] The reader who wishes for a more detailed account of the early Evangelical clergy should consult Erasmus Middleton's *Biographia Evangelica*, 1816, and John White Middleton's *Ecclesiastical Memoirs of the First Four Decades of the Reign of George III*, reprinted in 1822 from the *Christian Guardian* of 1820 and 1821

[3] On the death of Romaine the pulpits of the Calvinistic meeting houses in London were hung with black [*Evang Mag* Nov 1795, p 453]

on the Bible (a work not yet [A D 1873] superseded by a better one), placed the Low Church school in the front ranks of the Church of England from about the end of the eighteenth century until the rise of the Tractarian movement, that is, for about half a century During that time a large proportion of the important and influential posts in the Church fell into their hands, and especially a great number of those town parishes which take the lead in religious movements They did not build many churches, and the restoration of churches was seldom carried by them beyond the building of pews and galleries for the use of an audience [1] But they did a great and good work in the country, and prepared the way for a movement into which large numbers of them afterwards drifted, that High Church or "Tractarian" movement which was substantially a continuation and development of their own The general result of their labours upon the religious life of the country was that [1] they taught multitudes a sense of sin, and the need of conversion from it, [2] they trained people to habits of private and family prayer, [3] they revived a spirit of faith, which had almost died out under the influence of the Latitudinarians and the Sceptics, [4] they cultivated the religious affections and kindled afresh the love of God

There was also a large amount of active benevolence among them which led them to undertake several good works of public interest and importance In the year 1799 the Church Missionary Society, intended originally for missions to Africa and India, was established by them, and out of its bosom were developed such men as Henry Martyn and Bishop Heber Again, they took a most active part, under the leadership of Wilberforce, in procuring the abolition of slavery and the slave-trade, which was finally accomplished, as far as England was concerned, in the year 1833 They co-operated likewise with the Dissenters in establishing the "British and Foreign Bible Society" in 1804, and the "Church Pastoral Aid Society" was founded by them in 1829. These good works were effected at a time when there was but little energy for organization among the "High" Church party, and when if they had not been done by Low Churchmen they would not have been done at all It may also be added that they used the press extensively for the publication of books and tracts of a religious character, though no high literary power was ever developed under the wing of the party

But the good which was done by the Evangelical school in reviving personal religion was largely counterbalanced by the recklessness with which they neglected education both among the clergy and the laity They expended all their energies on educating the heart, and treated mankind as if it was rather wrong than otherwise to educate the head They would not, in terms, have denied that reason and intellect are the gifts of God as well as faith and love, but there was always among them a latent prejudice against the exercise of the intellect, on the ground that it interfered with the work of grace in the soul Whatever educational work, therefore, the Evangelical school engaged in, it was undertaken as a concession to "the world" which needed to be apologized for on the part of those who were "true Christians." The consequence was that no sufficient measures were adopted for educating the poor, that the schools of the middle classes fell into the hands of those who were incompetent to teach anything beyond such rudimentary knowledge as would barely suffice for shopkeeping (a teaching unworthy the name of "commercial education" which was given to it), and that the higher education of the public schools and the universities became, practically, of the most secular character possible

Added to this, the Evangelical clergy entirely failed to guide the intellect of the country in their sermons Their system was built up on a few leading doctrines, and on these two or three strings they were ever harping They set an excellent object before themselves, that of converting the world, but their scheme of conversion did not comprehend the subjugation of the intellectual powers to the power of grace, it rather looked to their suppression by it Hence the "march of intellect" left such pulpits of the Church of England as were occupied by them far in the rear The Bible was made to run on Calvinistic rails, and those who declined to force all interpretation of it in this direction were looked upon as bringing "human reasoning" to bear upon the Word of God, and as treating that Word with disrespect instead of reverence by so doing In the earlier days of the Evangelical movement there was indeed a section of the clergy engaged in it who revolted against this narrow view of Holy Scripture, and endeavoured to establish that system of Biblical science which is known as "Hutchinsonianism," but this peculiar mysticism was as unintelligible to the world at large as German philosophy, it made no impression whatever on the age, and touched none of the Biblical questions which are of vital interest to mankind. [HUTCHINSONIANS.] Almost the only other direction in which the intellectual studies of the school ever turned was that of the interpretation of unfulfilled prophecy, and the mean results of their researches in this direction were uninspired predictions respecting the fall of the papacy, the advent of the millennium, and the end of the world, predictions the rashness and valuelessness of which has been shewn in most cases by the "logic of events" in their non-fulfilment The consequence of all this was that the Low Church clergy were utterly powerless against the irreligious intellect which they had permitted to develope itself unchecked, their pulpit teaching never touched the educated mind of the age, and their own mental power was so dwarfed that they were wholly unable to influence for good the won-

[1] In the year 1844 one of the leading men of the later Low Church party, Close, afterwards Dean of Carlisle, published a pamphlet against such work, entitled *The Restoration of Churches the Restoration of Popery* He happily lived to restore Carlisle Cathedral in the highest ecclesiastical taste

derfully rapid growth of literature during the last generation

The Evangelical movement may thus be characterized generally as a movement of transition, so far as national religious life is concerned It was a movement of unintellectual subjective religion, leading onwards to a movement of intellectual objective religion It taught habits of prayer as a stage on the road towards habits of adoration, so that the idea of getting good for ourselves by prayer was supplemented (under the influence of a later school) by the idea of worshipping God for His own glory It revived the spirit of faith that others might afterwards set before believers definite objects in which to believe Such a work should never be valued lightly, for when men had been brought to a sense of sin, to repentance, and to the love of God, there was but a little way further for the religious life of the nation to travel before it would reach that higher ground to which, in the next generation, it attained [HIGH CHURCHMEN]

LUCIANISTS A section of the Marcionites, followers of Lucian, as he is called by Hippolytus and Epiphanius, or Lucan, as he is called by Tertullian and Origen This heretic was originally a disciple of Marcion [Hippol *Refut Hær* vii 25], and seems to have formed a sect of his own (as his companion Apelles did) about A D 140 Beausobre, Lardner, and some others of the same school, consider that they are identical with the SELEUCIANS, who are mentioned by Augustine and Philaster, but the principal ground for this opinion is that the name of Seleucus is given as Leucius in some manuscripts of St Jerome's works [Lardner's *Hist Heret* 283]

The particular tenet by which the Lucianists were distinguished from the Marcionites in general was that, in the resurrection from the dead, neither the actual body nor the actual soul of the deceased person would arise, but that a "tertium quid," something created for the purpose, would represent his personality "We may ignore," says Tertullian, "a certain Lucan, who does not spare even this part of our nature, the soul, which he follows Aristotle in reducing to dissolution, and substitutes some other thing in lieu of it Some third nature it is which, according to him is to rise again, neither soul nor flesh, in other words, not a man, but a bear perhaps—for instance, Lucan himself" [Tertull *de Resurr carn* ii] This may have been intended by Tertullian to indicate that Lucan believed in the transmigration of human souls into animals of a lower nature than man [Mill's *N T Prolegom* 334, p 37] But this opinion was attributed to Marcion by Epiphanius, and the words of Tertullian seem to be rather a contemptuous rejection of Lucan's opinion, whatever it was, than a statement that such was the terminus of that opinion Neander considers that Lucan "thought himself compelled to believe that everything 'psychical' was perishable, but that the πνευματικον only, which participated of the Divine life, was immortal" [Neander, *Ch Hist* ii 151, Bohn's transl]

There is no evidence that the Lucianists ever occupied any important position as a sect, Epiphanius knowing scarcely anything about them in his time [Epiph *Hæres* xliii] Lucan himself, however, exercised no small influence for evil, being condemned as the author of many forged imitations of Scripture as early as the end of the fifth century by Gelasius [Gelas. *Decret* Labb *Concil* iv 1264] Many of the apocryphal writings now extant under the names of the Apostles are also traced up to him by Grabe [Spicileg *S S Patr ut et Hæret.* vol. i.], Mill [*Prolegom ad N T*], and Beausobre [*Hist Manich* vol i]

LUCIANISTS A name sometimes given to the early Arians from Lucian, who was one of the most famous heads of the school of Antioch, and among whose pupils had been the Arian bishops Eusebius of Nicomedia, Maris of Chalcedon, Theognis of Nicæa, Leontius of Antioch, Antonius of Tarsus, and others [Philostorg *Hist Eccl* ii 14] Lucian was himself a pupil of the heretical Paul of Samosata, and Alexander, Bishop of Alexandria, accuses him of having adopted his opinions [Theodor *Hist Eccl* i 4] During the persecution of Athanasius the Eusebian party brought forward a Semi-Arian creed, which they alleged to be in the handwriting of Lucian [Sozom *Hist Eccl* iii 5], but Sozomen seems to doubt whether this was a true assertion, and adds that Lucian was a most estimable man, and learned in the Holy Scriptures Epiphanius speaks of him as infected with Arian errors [Epiph *Hæres* xliii] If Lucian was in any sense the father of the errors taught by his pupils he must have renounced them himself in his later life, for he is spoken of in the highest terms by St Athanasius, St Jerome [*Catal* cap lxxvii], and St Chrysostom [*Opp* i *Hom* xlvi], and the touching account of his martyrdom at Nicomedia [A D 311], during the Diocletian persecution [Euseb *Hist Eccl* viii 13, ix 6, Philostorg *Hist Eccl* ii 13], offers no indication that he was then an Arian Epiphanius [*l c*] says that the Arians in his time had indeed claimed Lucian as one of their martyrs, but he has had a place in Catholic martyrologies from the earliest times to which they can be traced

LUCIFERIANS A schismatical party, followers of Lucifer, Bishop of Caralis (Cagliari) in Sardinia, who in the year 362 separated from the Church, on the ground that Arian bishops and clergy, on their return to the Church, ought to be admitted only to lay communion, and that the Church which receives them into the clergy is contaminated, and her communion to be avoided.

Lucifer, the fellow-labourer of Athanasius, Eusebius of Vercelli, and Hilary of Poitiers, commended by Athanasius and Jerome [*Apol de Fuga Opp* i p 703, ed 1627, *adv. Lucif Opp* i p 169, ed 1616], the undaunted opponent of the Arian Emperor at the Council of Milan [Hieron *de Vir Illustr*], fell into this schism through dissatisfaction at the lenity of the Council of Alexandria, which decided that Arian bishops and clergy, on reception into the

Church should retain their rank and office [Athan *Epist ad Antioch,* i p 374] The divisions of the Church of Antioch at the time of this council, and the part which Lucifer took are narrated elsewhere [MELETIANS, ANTIOCHENE] It is frequently said that the general disapproval of the consecration of Paulinus for the Eustathians was the first cause of Lucifer's separating himself from the communion of the Catholic bishops But Paulinus' title was recognised by the Council of Alexandria, and generally by the Western Church The disapproval of Eusebius [Sozom *Hist Eccl* v 13], and of others in private, may have led to a breach of communion with them individually, but could not have outweighed the reception of Paulinus by the council The vehemence of Lucifer's opposition to the Arians drove him into an excess of rigour in discipline, and led him to advance maxims which excommunicated the whole Church He retired to his diocese, and for the remainder of his life continued with his followers in separation from the Church Theodoret states that he added certain new dogmas to the doctrine of the Church [*H E* iii 5] But the testimonies of Ambrose, Jerome, and Augustine clear him of this charge [Amb *Orat de obitu Satyri*, Jerome, *adv Lucif*, August *Hær* lxxxi] His rule was that laymen coming over from the Arians were to be received by imposition of hands, with invocation of the Holy Spirit, that clerics could be received only to lay communion, and that the Church deciding otherwise was turned into a brothel This last was a familiar word with the Luciferians, and Lucifer's known violence of language makes it probable enough that the word was his The usual assumption of schismatics that the Church has apostatized is reproved by Jerome, "Christ did not come down solely for the Sardinian sheepskin," "Christ is too poor if he has only a church in Sardinia," and the disciplinary maxim is controverted at length in the dialogue referred to

From these expressions of Jerome Lardner inferred that the schism never spread very far This is construing Jerome's words too literally The schism found its way into Italy, Antioch, Spain, and Egypt, and a bishop of the sect was created for Rome [Marcell et Faust *in Bibl Patr Lugd* v] Hilary the Deacon, a Sardinian, who had been associated with Lucifer and Eusebius at the Council of Milan, followed Lucifer, and presently went beyond him by rebaptizing the Arians, for which Jerome calls him "Deucalion orbis" [*adv Lucif* p 170]

About A D 384 the Luciferians obtained a rescript from Theodosius, to secure them from persecution, since they made no innovations in the faith But the party came to an end rapidly Theodoret speaks of it as extinct in his time [*H E* iii 5].

The Church of Cagliari celebrated the feast of a Saint Lucifer on the 20th of May Two Archbishops of Sardinia wrote for and against the sanctity of Lucifer The Congregation of the Inquisition imposed silence on both parties, and decreed that the veneration of Lucifer should stand as it was The Bollandists defend this decree of the Congregation, Baillet, in his Life of Lucifer (and Natalis Alexander), contending that the Lucifer in question is not the author of the schism, but another Lucifer who suffered martyrdom in the persecution of the Vandals [Calmet, *Sac and Prof History*, lxv 110 Liguori, *Hist Hæres* I iv 3, 50 Nat Alex vii 117, ed 1787]

LUCIFERIANS A local name of the BEGHARDS, by which they were known in Angermundo about A D 1336 [*Chronic Magd ap.* Meibom ii 340 Mosh *de Beghard* 338]

LUCOPETRIANS A name given to the MESSALIANS from an alleged founder named Peter Euthymius Zigabenus says that he set himself up as the Messiah, and promised to appear again after his death, that three days after his death his disciples were watching for his resurrection when the devil appeared to them in the form of a wolf, and that hence they named their founder in derision Λυκόπετρος, or Wolf-Peter The principal disciple and successor of Peter is said to have been Tychicus, whom Euthymius alleges to have applied to his master all the texts in Holy Scripture which speak of the First and Third Persons of the Holy Trinity What is the true foundation of this legend it is impossible to say [Euthymius, *Triumph de Secta Messalian.*]

LULLARDS The name of some fraternities in Germany and the Netherlands, which were formed in the twelfth century for carrying to the grave the bodies of those who had died of the plague when no other persons were willing to perform this office of charity, and who were popularly so called from the soft funeral hymns which they sang ["lullen," "lollen," "lallen," *Old German*] as their mournful processions went on their way. These fraternities were known among themselves by the names of "Cellite Brothers and Sisters" or "Brothers and Sisters of St Alexius," the one from their houses claiming to be monastic cells, the other from their patron saint They were also known as "die Nollbruder," from the obsolete word "Nollen"

The Lullards appear to have been viewed with distrust at a very early date by the ecclesiastical authorities In the year 1309 they are spoken of in the neighbourhood of Liège as "quidam hypocritæ gyrovagi, qui 'Lollardi,' sive Deum laudantes, vocabantur" [*Gest Pontif Leod Script* ii 350] In 1395 the Pope Boniface IX recalls any privileges which had been granted by himself or his predecessors to persons of either sex "vulgo Beghardi, seu 'Lullardi' et 'Zuestriones,' a seipsis 'Fratricelli' seu 'Pauperes pueruli' nominati," on the ground that heresies were lurking among them A few years afterwards [A D 1408] Arundel, Archbishop of Canterbury, complains that his province is infected with "new unprofitable doctrines, and blemished with the new damnable brand of Lollardy" [Johnson's *Canons*, ii 470]

In the year 1472 the Cellites were admitted among the exempt religious orders by Sixtus IV, and had further privileges conferred upon them in 1506 by Julius III It is probable therefore that the name of Lullard had come to signify two different classes of persons, the original fraternities for the burial of the dead, and those who were associated with the general stream of heresy which began to flow so strongly in the Beghards and the Wickliffites in the fourteenth and fifteenth centuries [Mosh *Eccl Hist* ii 285, Stubbs' ed]

LUTHERANS In the beginning of the sixteenth century the urgent need of a Reformation in the Church became universally acknowledged Corruption tainted every order Bishops and abbots had become more like secular princes than spiritual fathers, or had degenerated into unscrupulous statesmen, their example naturally affecting the lower orders of the clergy and the laity also The Papacy had been polluted by the immoralities of Alexander VI, and was not raised very highly again as a religious institution by Julius II, a man in whom there was more of the soldier than the priest, or by Leo X, whose elegant tastes and refined scholarship were chequered by a scarcely disguised infidelity In fact the revival of learning had become, in Italy at least, a revival of heathenism, and the state of morals, as revealed in Boccaccio's *Decameron*, was frightful in the extreme, while the wealth of nations was drained into Italy upon religious pretexts, to support the luxuriousness of the Roman Court It was under these circumstances that Lutheranism sprang into being, and as all reform within the Church was at first refused, the Catholic Church lost a considerable part of the Teutonic and all the Scandinavian race

Martin Luther, the son of John Luther, a refiner of metals, was born at Eisleben in Saxony, on the Eve of St Martin's Day 1483 His childhood was passed at Mansfield, were his father had settled as chief magistrate The Universities, first of Eisenach and then of Magdeburg, laid in him the foundations of that learning of which he afterwards made such effectual use In 1501 he migrated to the University of Erfurt, where he took his degree He had originally intended to devote himself to the study of civil law, but the sudden death of a friend, struck by lightning, strengthened in him those religious impressions by which he had always been to a great extent influenced Accordingly, he entered in 1505 the monastery of Augustine Eremites at Erfurt, supposing that the life and discipline of a monk was the best aid to the practice of religion and study of theology His religious history at this period is interesting He used often to meditate upon the anger of God and His many judgments of sin, until at length he became possessed by an extreme dread of eternal judgment His fears urged him on to a more diligent study of the Scriptures, with which it is said that he first became acquainted in his monastery, and at the same time the sermons of an aged monk at Erfurt on the remission of sins taught him to discriminate between a general belief in the article, such as devils might have, and the particular adaptation of it to his own needs This led him to a more attentive study of St. Paul's Epistles, and from them he at length evolved his doctrine of justification by faith only His principle was, believe, or rather feel, that your sins are forgiven, and they are forgiven This *faith* would cover anything He is reported to have said, "Pecca fortiter, crede fortius" Meanwhile he studied carefully the works of St. Augustine, nor did he neglect the authors who had the best repute in his day, the Schoolman Ockham, as might have been expected, being his favourite among them

In 1508 he was summoned to the newly-founded University of Wittenberg, at the instance of John Staupitz, Provincial of the Augustinians, and Professor at Wittenberg There his fame for philosophical and theological knowledge increased In 1507 he had been ordained priest and celebrated his first mass Three years later he was sent on business connected with his order to Rome, where the profligacy, the infidelity, and the irreligion that prevailed, did not help to confirm his attachment to the existing order of things In 1512 he took his Doctor's degree, and began to give public instruction in Theology In his lectures he based his teaching upon the Scriptures and the writings of St Augustine, rather than upon the Schoolmen, against whom he wrote several theses

At this time Leo X, who wanted money partly to meet his extravagances and partly to complete St. Peter's, sought to supply the want by issuing an extraordinary number of indulgences These had originally been remissions or relaxations of canonical penance, but were now regarded as full pardons for every kind of sin, past, present, or to come, so that the fortunate possessor would be secure of an immediate entrance into Paradise after death The sale of these indulgences was conducted with scarcely less decorum than that of quack medicines at a fair, one of their most scandalous vendors being Tetzel, a Dominican friar, the sub-commissary of the Elector Archbishop of Mayence, who carried on the business as a mere matter of ordinary trade, wherein the object was to gain the largest possible return It was even said that indulgences were staked at the gaming-table The discontent which this conduct caused impelled John of Staupitz to put forward Luther to oppose him, a task which Luther was ready enough to undertake, for some of those who had confessed to him had held forth the indulgences as a plea against the penance which he had imposed whereupon he had refused them absolution, and so drew upon himself the angry threats of Tetzel

Luther, having appealed in vain to the Elector Archbishop to stop the sale, first preached a sermon against the abuse, and then in the autumn of 1517 set up on the door of the Castle Church in Wittenberg ninety-five theses against indulgences, copies of which he also sent to the neighbouring bishops [Loscher, *Acts of the Reformation*, i 4387] He maintained therein that the whole life of a Christian ought to be one continued act of penance, that the papal indulgences could not go beyond the remission of canonical penance, which could be imposed on the living only, therefore, they did not affect the dead that those who trusted in them for salvation would with their deluders perish everlastingly, that they are in fact quite distinct from the pardon of God, that contrition alone is necessary, that the truly penitent have full remission from all pains or guilt, even though they be without a written indulgence He did not however undervalue papal absolution as a declaration of remission, but he considered it most hurtful if men got to trust in it, or lost through it the fear of God if the Pope possessed the power he ought to exercise it freely for the love of God, and not for the sake of money or to build a church He also preached a sermon on indulgence and grace, in which he attacked the doctrine that satisfaction necessarily finds place in true repentance These proceedings drew out from Tetzel a reply in the shape of counter theses, in which he was seconded by other men of learning, chiefly Dominicans, to whom Luther replied with great acrimony and zeal

The Pope, though at first he did not trouble himself about the matter, was at length persuaded to interfere Instead, however, of requiring Luther's presence at Rome, which had been his first intention, he deputed his Cardinal Legate Cajetan, at Augsburg, to arrange the dispute His haughty demand of unconditional submission provoked Luther to appeal from a Pope who had been ill informed to one who should be better informed, and at length from the Pope to a General Council About this time the Emperor Maximilian died, and during the interval before the election of a successor the government was conducted by the Vicar of the Empire, Frederick, Elector of Saxony, Luther's immediate sovereign and protector Meanwhile the papal proceedings were suspended, and Luther had time to draw around him friends and followers, among whom the most celebrated was Schwartzerd, or Melanchthon, a professor of Wittenberg Leo wished to win over Frederick with a view to the imperial election, and accordingly sent his chamberlain, Charles of Miltitz, to settle affairs By his conciliating manner he persuaded Luther to promise to keep silent, if his enemies did the same, and to profess publicly obedience to Rome This Luther was the more easily persuaded to do as Miltitz had stopped the proceedings of Tetzel

But a disputation at Leipsic upon free-will between Eck and Bodenstein of Carlstadt, a follower of Luther's, opened the controversy afresh, as the primacy of the Pope was dragged into the question, and Eck stigmatized his opponents as Hussites and Lutheran heretics It was at this time that Luther began seriously to inquire into the grounds of the papal claims, and to express those doubts which afterwards led to an open rupture After the actual conference the dispute was continued in writing, so that men's attention was once more drawn to him and his opinions The Bohemian CALIXTINES wrote to him congratulating and encouraging him, and he was thus the more confirmed in his design to appear as a Church reformer Frederick of Saxony proved his firm friend, Erasmus pleaded for him with the Elector Archbishop of Mayence, and supporters began to shew themselves in various parts of Germany, whereupon he issued an appeal to the Christian nobles

A bull of excommunication was issued against Luther on July 15th, 1520 Forty-one propositions taken from his works were pronounced heretical, his writings were proscribed; he was declared excommunicate if he should not retract within sixty days, and all the princes were called upon to seize his person The bull was received in Germany with open marks of disapprobation, and met by Luther's work *De Captivitate Babylonica Ecclesiæ*, in which he entirely threw over indulgences (hitherto allowed by him in a modified form), and declared the papacy to be the Kingdom of Babylon, and the power of Nimrod the mighty hunter He requested his friends to burn his early books on each of these subjects, he maintained that there were three Sacraments, Baptism, Penance, and the Eucharist, in the last he claimed the cup for the laity, denied transubstantiation as a Thomist and papal doctrine, he declared that the elements continued true bread and true wine, but that there was in them a real Presence of Christ's true Body and true Blood, he denied the doctrine of sacrifice in the mass, and the sacrament of extreme unction As his friends encouraged him to go on in his resistance, and demanded an impartial investigation into the point at issue, Luther was emboldened to send a fierce letter to the Pope, together with his work on Christian Liberty, in which he maintained his doctrine on justification in its most offensive form, and inveighed furiously against the vices of the papal court At length, after having appealed to a General Council, on December 10th, 1520, he appeared in public at the eastern gate of Wittenberg, formally abjured the papal authority, and flung into a large fire which had been prepared the Bull, the Decretals, the Extravagants, and the Clementines, adding the words, "Because thou hast troubled the sanctuary of the Lord, therefore may the eternal fire torment thee" In consequence the Pope issued another bull of excommunication and interdict upon any place where he or his followers might reside, calling in also the aid of the secular arm, which the newly elected Emperor Charles V was glad to afford

A diet had been assembled at Worms early in 1521, to which Aleander, the papal legate, appealed, but the assembled princes were unwilling to condemn Luther at the mere instance of pope or emperor, they had also a quarrel of their own with the Pope, and drew up a list of a hundred and one grievances

As they required that the reformer should be summoned to answer for himself, a safe conduct was granted to him, and he appeared before the diet There he avowed his works and refused to recant, but his safe conduct was respected, and no violence was done to his person, notwithstanding the suggestions of the papal legates.

After his departure the ban of the empire was published against him and his adherents The safe-conduct gave him protection for twenty-one days only, after which he would be exposed to the attacks of his watchful enemies, the Elector of Saxony therefore, who had no desire to oppose directly the imperial power, devised a stratagem to secure his safety A body of masked horsemen, disguised as brigands, seized him and carried him off to the Castle of Wartburg, where he remained for three quarters of a year in honourable captivity, concealed alike from friends and foes, being unknown even to his guards During this interval he gave himself up to study, and commenced the translation of the Scriptures into German This was not however the first translation of the kind, for there were no fewer than fourteen printed editions of the Bible in High and Low German between 1462 and 1518 [Walch, *Biblioth* iv 76] He also issued various tracts against confession, masses, vows, and enforced clerical celibacy, and sent a very combative reply to Henry VIII 's treatise on the seven sacraments

The ban of the Empire fell with comparative harmlessness upon his followers The Emperor was too much engaged with the French War to put it into execution, many of the princes openly favoured the Lutherans, and others were indifferent or did not care to make themselves unpopular with their subjects It had practical force only in the personal domains of the Emperor and his brother, in Bavaria and the Duchy of Saxony, and where some of the prince bishops thought fit to enforce it Meanwhile the Church system was overthrown at Wittenberg, and a new state of things brought in under the auspices of Carlstadt The monks were encouraged to desert their monasteries, several priests contracted marriage, private masses were abolished, images were removed from the churches, auricular confession and the invocation of the saints were discontinued, and the cup was restored to the laity Those clergy who still persisted in celebrating mass and chanting the hours were exposed to mob violence Those changes alarmed Luther as being too hasty, and accordingly he wrote to the Elector to deprecate them There was the more urgent cause to do so, for fanatics like the ANABAPTISTS began to appear, teaching the doctrine of a visible kingdom of Christ upon earth, soon to be manifested, in which rights of property should be unknown, and denying Infant Baptism Luther, therefore, left his retreat without consulting the Elector (to whom he afterwards wrote an apology), and hastened back to Wittenberg, where the control of ecclesiastical affairs was placed in his hands Of the changes made by Carlstadt, he confirmed some and moderated others Private masses were abolished, the use of images and the practice of confession were restored, and the reception of the communion, under one or both kinds was left to the discretion of the people themselves He now [A D 1522] published his translation of the New Testament

Much opposition was checked by the fact that the new Pope, Hadrian VI, was an honest, sincere, and religious man, who had a real desire to remedy the evils that he saw existing round him, and openly admitted that the whole Church required a thorough reform That he was sincere is unquestionable, though he may have also hoped to lessen the influence of Luther, by taking the work into his own hands As it was, he only damped the ardour of his own supporters, and drew out from the Diet of Nuremberg a more urgent demand for the redress of grievances, and a petition for a general council But Hadrian's efforts were cut short by his death, and the accession of the most conservative of Popes, Clement VII, in 1523 Luther won over many of the Princes by his proposal to secularize the monastic and episcopal property, and about this time the Kings of Sweden and Denmark leagued together to establish Lutheranism in their own dominions The whole of the north coast of Germany was now on his side, as were many of the free towns, and he confirmed his followers everywhere in their belief by his writings But they had become so numerous that a closer organization was necessary Accordingly, he prepared a revised and translated form of the mass, and arranged for the systematic management of the revenues of his communion, according to the primitive plan, by appointing definite portions for the clergy, for the schools, for the relief of the poor, for the repair of churches At first his changes were designed for Saxony only, but they were afterwards adopted in all the countries where his doctrines prevailed The successful spread of those doctrines was very rapid It was in vain that the papal legates demanded from one diet after another the execution of the decree of Worms against him and his followers, and that the Emperor confirmed the request by his rescript They were met with demands for the redress of grievances and the convocation of a general council It was indeed proposed that a diet to be summoned at Spires should arrange matters, but meanwhile the Lutherans were left practically in peace

In 1524, Luther threw off the monastic dress which he had up to this time retained The same year witnessed his quarrel with Erasmus, who had hitherto been able to occupy a middle position and though he was strongly in favour of reform, would not renounce communion with Rome This was a position that Luther could neither endure nor understand, and the admirers of each were constantly urging on their chiefs to break with the other as a time-server or a heretic Luther's violence, and a request from Henry of England, provoked Erasmus to publish his work on Free Will, in which he opposed, though with moderation, the Augustinian opinions that Luther had adopted Luther rejoined in a treatise on the Slavery of the Will, which was in part an intemperate answer to Erasmus, and in part a personal attack upon him To this Erasmus replied in his Hyperaspistes [A D 1526], and then threw himself entirely into the arms of the party opposed to Luther

This was followed by the controversy with Zwingli on the Eucharist Luther ever held firmly to the belief in the Real Presence ("Objective" as we should now term it), although he was not always consistent with himself in his manner of explaining it Carlstadt had effected at Orlamund what he considered a more thorough reformation He disallowed the use of images entirely, and in his views on the Eucharist dissented from his old master But Luther proved too strong for him, and being obliged to retire to Basle, he was at length reduced to such narrow circumstances that he gave way and returned to Saxony Zwingli had adopted Carlstadt's theory that the Eucharist is a mere memorial rite, and defended it in several works, and as it thus began to prevail in Southern Germany as well as in Switzerland, Luther again plunged into the conflict A conference held between him and Zwingli, at Marburg, in A.D 1529, at the instance of Philip Landgrave of Hesse, ended in a final separation Luther has been censured for his conduct on this occasion, and, no doubt, he did carry on the controversy with all the violence natural to his character, but no permanent union could be expected between an earnest believer in the Real Presence and a dogmatic denier of it Another blow fell upon him through the insurrection of the Anabaptists, for although Luther had ascribed their principles to the inspiration of the Devil, and encouraged the Princes to wield the temporal sword that God had entrusted to them against the fanatics, many supposed that they were only carrying out Luther's own principles to their extreme, and thus his cause was not a little damaged.

In 1525, Luther, a professed monk, married a nun, Catherine Bora, a lady of high rank His friends greatly blamed him for this act, concerning which he himself had misgivings at times Both parties concerned were under a vow of celibacy, and whatever may be thought of the expediency of such vows, few would deny, that having been taken, a religious reformer ought to have self-command enough to keep them, and to be above suspicion in his own conduct

In spite of these drawbacks, Luther's sect rapidly extended itself Besides the Elector of Saxony, he had the Landgrave of Hesse, the Dukes of Mecklenburg, Pomerania, and Zell, among his followers, together with many free cities of the Empire The Grand Master of the Teutonic Order and Margrave of Brandenburg broke through his vows, secularized Eastern Prussia, the possession of his order, added it to Brandenburg, and so founded in sacrilege what afterwards became the Kingdom of Prussia Associations for defence were formed by the Princes of both sides, by the Catholics in the League of Ratisbon, by the Lutherans in that of Torgau

The Diet of Spires, in 1526, allowed freedom and toleration to the Lutherans until a General Council should be assembled, but the Council was delayed owing to the wars of the Emperor with France and Italy, and the intrigues of the Pope Three years later, in a second Diet at Spires, the tolerant decrees of the first Diet were virtually repealed by the following enactments —

[1] That where the Edict of Worms had been executed it should be still observed

[2] That no further innovations should be made by the Lutherans

[3] That the Mass should be re-established in all places where it had been abolished, and that the Catholic subjects of Lutheran Princes should enjoy complete toleration

[4] No new doctrines were to be preached, or any contrary to the interpretation of the Church

[5] There were to be no new hostilities under pretence of religion

[6] The Zwinglians and Anabaptists were to be proscribed

The Lutheran Princes published a protest against this Edict, and so won for themselves the name of "Protestants" In this protest they declared,—

[1] That the unanimous decision of one Diet ought not to be rescinded by a mere majority in another

[2] That their consciences would not allow them to restore the Mass among their subjects, *i e* the Catholic minority, or allow two forms of administering the Communion in one place

[3] They objected to clause 4, the question being, What is the true Church?

[4] They held to Scripture as the sole infallible rule of life, to be interpreted by itself alone, and not by tradition, they would not allow anything to be taught within their dominions except Scripture

[5] They consented to proscribe the Anabaptists, but desired to exempt from persecution the Zwinglians. [Coxe, *House of Austria*, c xxviii *sub fin*]

This protest was signed by the Elector of Saxony, the Margrave of Brandenburg Anspach, the Landgrave of Hesse, the Duke of Brunswick and his brother, the Prince of Anhalt, with the representatives of the imperial cities, Strasburg, Nuremburg, Ulm, Constance, and ten others of less note; to which shortly afterwards were added Augsburg, Frankfort, Hanover, Hamburg, and others The protest was sent to the Emperor, who received it with marks of severe displeasure, and arrested the deputies who had been appointed to convey it, but he was shortly afterwards induced to act with more moderation, and summon a Diet to meet at Augsburg Here the Protestants, who were still labouring under the stigma of a connection with the Anabaptists, put forth the Confession of Faith known as the Confession of Augsburg, which has become one of the authorized formularies of the Lutheran communion It had been drawn up by Luther, but was revised and somewhat softened down by Melanchthon It contains twenty-eight articles, of which twenty-one are affirmative and declaratory of doctrine, and seven polemical, against Roman doctrine or practice The Emperor received the Confession with coldness, and forbade its publication Fruitless discussions followed, but the divisions of the Catholics proved the safeguard of the Protestants, some advocating extreme measures, while others, headed by the Elector Archbishop of Mentz, recommended conciliation Finally a decree was passed ordering the re-establishment of all suppressed doctrines and practices, the enforcement of clerical celibacy, and the restoration of all the plundered Church property But no practical result followed, for all parties were looking forward to the meeting of a General Council, which, however, the Pope still contrived to delay. But the election in 1531 of the Emperor's brother, Ferdinand of Austria, King of Hungary and Bohemia, to be King of the Romans, alarmed the Protestant Princes, who at Smalkald formed a league for the protection of their religion and liberty The history of this League, with its first transient success and final disastrous failure, forms part of the history of the Holy Roman Empire, and not of the Lutherans A civil war followed, and the result was that the Protestants were entirely foiled on every side Hermann, the reforming Elector Archbishop of Cologne, was deposed, the Margrave of Brandenburg and the Duke of Saxony were won over by Charles to desert their party, other Princes were compelled to submit, and the two great champions of the Protestant cause, the Elector of Saxony, the son of Luther's old friend, and the Landgrave of Hesse, were made prisoners Charles was everywhere triumphant Wittenberg itself fell into his hands, but he used his victory with moderation, allowing the Protestants to continue in peace

The remainder of Luther's life was uneventful, but he was fully occupied in writing, and in superintending the communities which were called by his name, living in security at Wittenberg, where he could defy alike the thunders of the Vatican and the menaces of the Emperor Death carried him off before the triumph of Charles and the fall of Wittenberg, which probably would have been followed by more severe measures against him He died shortly after the first meeting of the Council of Trent, in 1546 at his native place, Eisleben, whither he had been summoned by the Count of Mansfeldt to settle by his local knowledge a dispute that had arisen about boundaries He was buried at Wittenberg with great pomp

Luther's extraordinary strength of character is shewn by the great Revolution which owes its origin, its course, and its final triumph to him Nothing but a strong self-will would have enabled him to withstand the powers alike of the Pope and the Emperor, but it often hurried him into too great violence in his controversies with his opponents For the Pope, as might be expected, he had no consideration, but in his disputes with Henry VIII and Duke George of Saxony, he displayed a violence of temper which only injured his cause His final breach with Zwingli was unavoidable, but the controversy with Erasmus was carried on by him with an unbecoming heat which only alienated and sent into the arms of the opposite party one who had strong yearnings after reform

The other great defect of Luther's character was his subjectiveness He had himself gone through a certain spiritual course, by which he had been brought from sorrow and despondency to find peace, and, like Wesley, he supposed that every one else must experience the same, or else forfeit his claim to be considered a child of light In a similar spirit he rejected the Epistle of St. James and the Apocalypse from the Canon, because they did not accommodate themselves to his judgment, or rather his theory, and thus he laid the foundation of that Rationalism which afterwards prevailed so extensively in Germany He claimed for himself to throw off Church authority, but it was that he might set up an authority of his own, and he would not allow to Erasmus, to Carlstadt, to Zwingli, or to the Anabaptists the right of differing from him

The history of Lutheranism after the death of Luther may be shortly told

When Charles had destroyed the power of the League he contented himself with asserting his political supremacy over the Protestant Princes, and did not interfere with their religious principles His desire was to effect a comprehension through the Council of Trent, which was then commencing its sittings Of the history of the Council it is not the place to speak, save that at the critical moment, the Pope, for his private ends, baffled the Emperor's design, by suspending its sittings Thus disappointed, Charles drew up twenty-six articles of compromise, known as the Interim, which he submitted to both parties It was to hold good only until the Council had given judgment on the disputed points, whence it derived its name For the most part it allowed matters to remain for the time as they were, and was therefore gladly accepted by the moderate Lutherans, although the more rigid, particularly those in the imperial cities, still held aloof, until they were reduced by force of arms But these victories lessened the Emperor's authority, by kindling the jealousies of Catholic and Protestant Princes alike, and Maurice, the new Elector of Saxony, by whose aid he had won most of his power, was still a zealous Protestant, although ambition had hitherto got the better of his religious principles Maurice now felt alarm for the existence of his party, and accordingly began to intrigue against the Emperor, until seizing a favourable opportunity, when the attention of the latter was drawn off to the Council of Trent, he again raised the standard of civil war His professed object was to protect the liberties of the Empire, to maintain the Protestant religion, and to liberate the Landgrave of Hesse, whom Charles had long detained in unjust captivity In the war that followed, the ascendancy of the Protestant party was once more established, and Charles himself narrowly escaped being made prisoner His ill success, the advance of the Turks into Hungary, and the mediation of his brother Ferdinand, the King of the Romans, at length induced him to consent to the treaty of Passau, 1552 The Landgrave was set at liberty, and the Lutherans were placed on an equal footing with the Catholics of the Empire until a diet could meet which should settle all religious and civil difficulties But Albert of Brandenburg refused to be bound by the treaty, and carried on a war of plunder with the Catholic Princes, until the ban of the Empire having been published against him, he was driven into exile, and his dominions were granted to his nephew, the Margrave of Anspach

The long expected diet met at Augsburg in 1555, under Ferdinand King of the Romans, who used all his influence to effect a reconciliation between the contending parties The result was an act of perpetual peace and toleration for all who adhered to the Confession of Augsburg Henceforth Lutheranism became the established religion of North Germany, and was placed on an equal footing with the Church in the imperial government The only remaining point of dispute concerned the ecclesiastical fiefs Ferdinand decreed that toleration should be granted to subjects, but that the change of religion in any prelate should *ipso facto* vacate his benefice This decision was disputed in later times, but the question was finally settled after the Thirty Years' War, when the treaty of Passau was again confirmed

To return now to the internal history of Luther's communion His place was at first filled by Melanchthon, but he was too gentle to maintain Luther's pre-eminence, and henceforth the cause won no more triumphs, but rather retrogressed, first before the reformations effected in the Church by the Council of Trent, and then before Calvinism The causes for this are easy to see The chief cause was the fearful spread of immorality among Luther's followers, arising from his doctrine of justification an evil which was acknowledged alike by friend and foe There were first the Antinomians, who appeared before Luther's death under Agricola He maintained that the Gospel only should be taught in the Churches to the exclusion of the Law, but his disciples claimed the right to sin as much as they pleased if only they held to Christ Even among the Lutherans Nicholas Amsdorf declared that good works were pernicious to salvation, and many others, without going so far, were indifferent about Christian holiness The preachers in their sermons confined themselves more and more to polemics, or to dry points of philosophical theology, to the loss of spiritual religion And though learning flourished, Erastianism swallowed up zeal and piety

The later history of the Lutherans resolves itself into two chapters, their controversies among themselves, and their efforts to bring about union with the Calvinists.

The first controversy was that of the Adiaphora, or things indifferent, arising from the Interim This decree proved distasteful to both Catholics and Protestants, and Melanchthon, when called upon to give his opinion on the matter, declared that while it could not be accepted as a whole, submission would prove the best course in things indifferent, such as concerning the exact number of the Sacraments, many rites and ceremonies, particularly chanting, unction, &c. This decision gave rise to a fierce controversy The rigid Lutherans branded the accepters of the Interim as ADIAPHORISTS, and alleged that Melanchthon was defective on the doctrine of Justification, because he maintained the necessity of good works The controversy was put an end to by the Formula of Concord, and in the interval was thrown into the background by the Synergistic dispute

The SYNERGISTS declared that man co-operates with God in the work of salvation On this point also Melanchthon sided with them in opposition to the rigid Lutherans, who were headed by Flacius of Saxe-Weimar, Professor of Divinity at Jena. His intemperate zeal threatened to cause a schism between the Lutherans of Saxony and of Saxe-Weimar, which was prevented only by the interference of the Princes Many other disputes broke out and sectarian divisions arose, and their result was seriously to impede the progress of Lutheranism At length, at the instance of the Elector of Saxony and the Duke of Saxe-Weimar, who saw and lamented the evils of division, a body of moderate men was appointed to draw up a Formula of Concord, which might be accepted by the whole Lutheran body Difficult although this undertaking was, it proved successful beyond anticipation The Form was produced at a conference at Torgau in 1576 It was examined and corrected by a large number of Lutheran Doctors, was submitted to the consideration of the Princes, was at last brought forward before a general assembly of divines that met at Magdeburg, and was adopted by them as an authoritative exponent of Lutheran doctrine against Calvinists on the one hand, and Lutheran innovators on the other

The next important controversy was that of the SYNCRETISTS, commenced by George Calixtus in the following century His aim was to induce the Lutheran and Reformed (or Calvinist) communions, to which he was quite ready to add the Catholics, not indeed to unite in one body, but to abstain from mutual enmity and to join together in the bonds of brotherly love He believed, to the scandal of many of that time, that the knowledge of the Holy Trinity is less clearly revealed in the Old Testament than in the New, that good works are necessary to salvation, and that God is accidentally (per accidens) the author of sin This dispute was ended by the rise of Pietism [See further, J G Walch's *Introduction to the Controversies in the Lutheran Church*]

PIETISM was an attempt to lessen the profligacy, want of discipline, and the general disorders which had been caused by the Thirty Years' War It originated with Spener of Frankfort, who strove to effect a reform similar to that which Wesley afterwards had in view in England He instituted prayer meetings, private classes for religious instruction, to be carried on side by side with the public services and exegetical teaching of Scripture But many of his followers degenerated into wild enthusiasts, prophecy-mongers and fanatics, so that in some places laws were enacted against them, and the magistrates were compelled to suppress their meetings, owing to the commotions to which they gave occasion

In the last century a body of men, the Herrenhutter of Lusatia, formed a distinct social and religious community under Count Zinzendorf. Many of them had originally been Lutherans, with whom they professed to agree in doctrine, though their ecclesiastical discipline was peculiar, but they actually formed a distinct sect, and as such have ever been discountenanced by the rigid Lutherans [MORAVIANS]

It only remains to glance at the relations between the Lutheran and the Calvinistic bodies An attempt had been made in the sixteenth century to effect a union, but this was rendered hopeless by the Formula of Concord It may have been in consequence of this Formula that Maurice Landgrave of Hesse-Cassel went over to the Calvinists, and displaced all the Lutheran teachers in the University of Marburg, and the ministers generally throughout his dominions This was in 1604 The dispossessed found shelter in Hesse-Darmstadt, which has continued Lutheran.

In 1610 the Elector of Brandenburg adopted a modified Calvinism He introduced the simpler form of worship, and embraced Calvin's views on the Person of Christ, and on the Eucharist, but rejected his teaching on Grace and the Divine decrees. He was content to hold these opinions himself, and put no restraint upon his subjects, but allowed, what was rare in those days, liberty of conscience to all Henceforth his successors, the Electors and Kings of Prussia, have distinguished themselves by their efforts to bring about a union from time to time, as in A.D 1631, 1662, 1736, and in 1817 The last endeavour has met with a certain amount of success The King of Prussia in that year formed out of both communions in his dominions one Evangelical Christian Church, the names alike of Protestant and Reformed being abolished In A D 1822 a new Liturgy was drawn up and accepted by 7750 out of 8950 congregations, the opposition coming partly from Berlin, where a protest was made by the magistrates and twelve ministers, and partly from Silesia The old Lutherans, as they were called, were for some time subjected to persecution, particularly in Silesia, where troops were quartered upon them to bring them into submission, and numbers of them fled to America, but they are now recognised by the law [UNITED EVANGELICAL CHURCH]

While the Lutheran and Reformed bodies exist side by side in many parts of Germany, it may be said generally that the greater part of North Germany, Hanover, Saxony, Hesse-Darmstadt, and Saxe-Coburg, and, in the south, Wurtemberg, are Lutherans, whereas in Hesse-Cassel, Baden, and Anhalt, Calvinism prevails The Scandinavian kingdoms are rigidly Lutheran, and there an Episcopal form of Church Government and some ancient Catholic customs have been retained. [SWEDISH PROTESTANTS]

Latterly, Lutheranism has spread widely in America owing to the German immigration Its adherents are, however, very much divided, especially on questions connected with ceremonial worship On the one hand are the "Old Lutherans," who used many ancient liturgical customs, such as altar crucifixes and altar lights, on the other are the "New," or "Reformed Lutherans," who discourage the use of liturgies and liturgical customs, and adopt the American fanaticism of "revivals" [Seckendorf, *Historia Lutheranismi* DICT *of* THEOL, art LUTHERANISM For a good detailed history of Lutheran theology and its relations, see Krauth's *Conservative Reformation*, Philadelphia, 1871]

LYONS, POOR OF [WALDENSES.]

M

MACARIANS The Monothelites of Antioch, so called from Macarius, who was patriarch at the time of the second Council of Constantinople [A D 680], at which he attended, and where he defended his opinions [MONOTHELITES.]

MACEDONIANS [PNEUMATOMACHI]

MACMILLANITES [CAMERONIANS]

MAGIANS [PARSEES]

MAHOMETANS The followers of Mahomet [A D 571-632], who began to propagate his new faith in Arabia, his native country, about A D 611 The name given by the founder to his religion and adopted by its professors, is "Islam," the meaning of which is said by some to be "to make peace, obtain unanimity," especially by submission—hence "to surrender," and in a religious sense, "to submit wholly to God, and acknowledge him only as Lord,"—but by others, to be "to seek righteousness with all one's strength"

I PERSONAL HISTORY OF MAHOMET Mahomet, or, as the word is more correctly written, Mohammed, Mohammad, or Muhammad ("the praised" or "the desired"), was born at Mecca, April 20th, A D 571 [1] It seems that he was named Kotham, and that he adopted the title Mohammed, about the time of the Hegira, to apply to himself some Old Testament Messianic prophecies [Hagg ii 8, Cant v 16] He was the only son of Abdallah and Amina, of the noble but impoverished family of Hashim, of the tribe of Koreish His father died two months before his birth, and his mother when he was six years old, his grandfather, and, on his death in two years, his uncle Abu-Talib, though poor and with a large family, took charge of him, and treated him kindly As a boy he earned his living as a shepherd, an occupation much despised by Arabs, but little is known with certainty of his early life In his twenty-fourth year he entered the service of Khadijah, a rich and clever widow, thirty-eight years old, whom he subsequently married, and by whom he had two sons, who died young, and four daughters We learn nothing further of him till he came before the world as a religious reformer

Arabia was at this time ripe for a moral and religious reformation Christianity had been early introduced [Gal i 17], but was only slightly diffused, chiefly in the petty kingdoms on the borders of Syria, in Irak, and in some desert oases Orthodoxy was rare, persecution had from early times driven into the Peninsula heretics of all kinds and shades Judaizing Christians—Ebionites, Nazaræans, MENDÆANS,—were most numerous. From these, especially the Mendæans, Mahomet seems to have borrowed his Christology and several ritual and devotional practices, his early converts being indeed sometimes called Sabians in the traditions Judaism was more widely extended and powerful Several Jewish communities were scattered over the country, and Jewish ideas, owing to the high intellectual culture of the Jews, were widely spread among the heathen, seeming to have tainted Arabic Christianity also Magianism [PARSEES] had a few adherents, chiefly on the borders of Persia But idolatry prevailed over the greater part of Arabia One personal God (Allah) and Creator was acknowledged, but he was too far above man to care for him, hence various deities, who usurped most of his honour, were set beside him, especially several goddesses, daughters of, and mediators with Allah Worship was paid to the host of heaven, to fetishes, symbols of higher powers, to stones and trees Each tribe had its own deity, priesthood, and temple, but the centre of worship for all was the Kaaba or holy house of Mecca, with its numerous idols, said to be 360, whither the Arabs yearly went on pilgrimage Belief in evil spirits (Jinn), by whom soothsayers and oracles were inspired, and in angels, was universal, some tribes had a vague belief in a resurrection Their moral condition was of the lowest They practised polygamy, with unlimited liberty of divorce, marriage was allowed to near relations, widespread profligacy prevailed among both sexes They were passionately fond of wine, gambling, and marauding, were very revengeful, and had a horrible custom of burying their infant daughters alive On the other hand, they were, as at the present day, brave, generous, hospitable, high-spirited and eloquent. On the borders small kingdoms had been established, the kings of which were vassals to the Byzantines, to the Persians, or to the Abyssinians, but the greater part of the Arabs, whether settled in towns or nomads, were divided into numerous tribes, each with its own chief, which were perpetually at war with each other.

[1] This date must be regarded only as conventional, being that generally accepted soon after Mahomet's death [Sprenger, i 138] Muir [i 13] and C de Perceval [i 282, 283] give Aug 20th, 570, others fix it in 569 [See Weil, 21, note 1, Sprenger (English), 75, Syed Ahmed, *On the Early Childhood*, 2, 3]

From among these profligate idolaters, just before, and during, Mahomet's youth, had arisen a number of inquirers, who, probably influenced indirectly by Jewish and Christian ideas, were seeking a higher faith These had cast off idolatry, with the superstitions and cruelties which it involved, and professed to teach the religion of Abraham, having sacred books of their own and calling themselves Hanifs, i e "Puritans" Four of them were relations of Mahomet, with one of whom, Waraka, his wife's cousin, he was very intimate He at first called himself a Hanif, adopting their teaching and often their words.

As regards the rest of the world, it will suffice to give these historical landmarks Mahomet's appearance as a prophet nearly coincided with the foundation of Westminster Abbey, Boniface IV had recently attained the Papacy, the Saxons and other tribes of Northern Germany were adopting Christianity France was slumbering under the Merovingians, the Eastern Empire was being ravaged by the Persians and Avars, but Heraclius, who had just [A D 610] ascended the throne, was preparing for his victorious campaigns [For the pre-Islamic state of Arabia, see Pocock, *Spec Hist Arab* 1-7, 33, 173, Sale, *P D* § 1, C de Perceval, *Essai*, &c vols i and ii, Weil, chap i, Sprenger (English) chap i, (German) i 13-92, 249-268; Cazenove, *Mahometanism*, 29-50, Muir, vol i, *Introduction, Quart Rev* cxxvii 314-322, Syed Ahmed, *Essays, On the Religion of the Pre-Islamic Arabs*]

When Mahomet was about forty years old, he began, under the influences above described, to doubt the truth of idolatry, to ponder in solitude, among the valleys and rocks near Mecca, on the Unity of God, immortality, judgment to come After a severe mental struggle, amounting at times almost to insanity, accompanied with epileptic fits (to which he had been subject in childhood), horrible dreams and hallucinations, he imagined, that as he slept in a cave in Mount Hira, an angel, who afterwards declared himself to be Gabriel, appeared to him, and, calling him thrice, bade him "cry" Mahomet answered, "What shall I cry?" whereon the angel delivered to him a message from God, the first revelation [*Kor* xcvi 1-5, *cf* Isaiah xxix 11, xl 6] No further revelations came for some time[1] Mahomet's mental distress returned, he thought himself possessed by devils, and was only prevented from suicide by a second appearance of the angel, followed by a violent fit, on recovery from which he received a second revelation, bidding him "arise and preach" [*Kor* lxxiv 1, *seq*] From that time to his death the revelations were constant, sometimes coming quietly, but generally accompanied by horrible fits, after which he was conscious of God's message to him Such is the traditional account of Mahomet's call, and it is important as throwing light on his belief in himself

Mahomet's mission was at once acknowledged by his own household—his wife, the confidante of his doubts, Ali, his cousin, who was however only seven years old, and Zeid, his freedman and adopted son, who had been a Christian Others soon joined him, some being persons of position, as Abu-Bekr, and Othman, afterwards caliphs, and several slaves At first he and his converts suffered only from derision, and there was a general feeling in his favour But when, after about two years, he proceeded publicly to attack idolatry, violent persecutions arose, he was compelled to teach only in private, in the house of a follower named Arkam, he himself had to endure insult and violence, his poorer followers were tortured, many of them recanted, and others fled to Abyssinia [A D 616] The fugitives however returned in a few months, on a rumour that a reconciliation had taken place between the prophet and his persecutors The truth was, that Mahomet's faith in his mission had for a time given way, and he acknowledged idols as intercessors with God But finding his converts much scandalized [*Kor* liii 34], and himself despised, he retracted his concession, declaring that the devil had misled him [*Kor* xvii 74, 75, xxii 51] Persecution therefore was renewed, but indignation at his treatment led to the conversion of his uncle, Hamza, and soon after the valiant and energetic Omar, hitherto a bitter persecutor, joined him This caused a great increase in the ranks of the Moslems, who now ventured publicly to proclaim their faith Plots were then formed against Mahomet's life, and when the family of Hashim, headed by Abu-Talib, declared that they would avenge his death, the rest of the Koreishites formed a league against them, put them under a ban, forced them to retire in a body to their own quarter of Mecca (the "Shib"), and there blockaded them [A D 617] About the same time[2] some Moslems again took refuge in Abyssinia, where the Christian King (Najashi) protected them Others afterwards joined these, and few of them rejoined Mahomet till after the Hegira The Hashimites suffered much from privation, but after two (perhaps three) years [A D 619 or 620], dissensions arose among the confederates, the league was broken up, and the ban removed Soon after this event Mahomet lost his wife, and his uncle and protector, Abu-Talib In a few weeks he married a second wife, and was betrothed to a third, thus adopting polygamy For a time, another uncle, Abu-Lahab, subsequently his bitterest foe, protected Mahomet, but withdrew this protection in disgust at his teaching that all their heathen forefathers were in hell Mahomet then attempted to gain converts at Tayif, three days' journey from Mecca, but after a short stay was driven out with insult and violence. On his road back to Mecca, he imagined that a company of Jinn were converted by hearing him recite the Koran [*Kor* xlvi 29 *sq*, lxxii 1 *sq*] By preaching at fairs, to caravans of pilgrims, and wherever numbers of people were collected, Mahomet had during some years won adherents in different parts of Arabia, especially at Yathrib, afterwards called Medina—

[1] This interval is called the Fatrah, or intermission [Rodwell, 3, note 2]

[2] Some authorities put this second emigration soon after the first [Sprenger, ii 42, *seq* 142, Muir, ii. 161, *seq*]

an abbreviation of Medinat-an-Nabi, "the city of the Prophet" At two successive pilgrimages deputies from that city had secret interviews with the Prophet in a valley near Mecca, they promised to propagate Islam by every means in their power, gentle or forcible, and to receive and protect the Prophet if he were compelled to leave Mecca On discovering this, the Koreishites resolved that Mahomet should be murdered, and he was nearly surprised, only escaping by the devotion of Ali Accompanied by Abu-Bekr, he fled from Mecca, and they took refuge from pursuit in a cave, before which, say the traditions, a spider wove its web, a pigeon laid two eggs in its nest, and a tree grew up, to testify to its solitude. After three days they reached Medina, whither Mahomet's chief followers had already betaken themselves, and the Prophet entered the city in triumphal procession This event is the Hegira or flight, it took place in A D 622, in the summer or early autumn

The Hegira marks an epoch in Mahomet's life Islam and its founder henceforth have their place in the history of the world Hitherto the Prophet had had no field for action, he had been the man of thought and speech, the persecuted preacher of a Monotheism which looked to himself as its prophet Henceforth he was the man of action Accordingly, he soon became Prince as well as Prophet, he formed the design of spreading his faith and rule first over Arabia, then over the world His revelations underwent a corresponding change Hitherto they had consisted of doctrinal and moral precepts, threats of a judgment on the wicked, promises of bliss for the good, accounts of God's dealings with the men of old Their style is earnest, poetic, full of fire, and often very striking Now they assumed a more prosaic tone · they concern passing events, contain laws, political and social, and military directions, not unlike the "general orders" of an army,[1] justifications of Mahomet's acts, public and even private, such as his dealings with his wives The morality of the Koran also deteriorates, polygamy is formally sanctioned; the liberty of divorce is extended, force takes the place of persuasion We see at the same time a very marked declension in Mahomet's character, he gradually gives himself up to the gratification of his passions and produces revelations which allow to himself that which he forbids to others, he becomes treacherous, vindictive, cruel, countenancing and ordering assassination of his enemies, wholesale massacre of his prisoners. Nevertheless such were his attractive qualities and his force of will, that he retained and increased to the last the devotion of the great body of his followers

The Prophet's first care was the organization of the believers Forms and times of worship and practical observances (fasting and alms), were definitely settled, a mosque was built, with houses adjoining for Mahomet and his wives the number of whom was constantly increasing To prevent jealousy between the two classes of his followers, the Muhajerin, or "refugees," from Mecca, and the Ansares, or "helpers," of Medina, he formed them into a brotherhood by pairs, one of each party He soon acquired such power in the city, that even those who disbelieved him were compelled to dissemble, but yet took every opportunity of thwarting him These are often mentioned in the Koran as "the hypocrites" [ii 9-19, xxxiii 12, 47, lvii 13], and gave Mahomet much trouble The Prophet tried to win over the Jews also, having already adopted many of their ceremonies and institutions He made a few converts, but the great body repelled his overtures, and became his bitter opponents Mahomet thereupon altered most of the observances intended to gain them, and, as soon as he was strong enough, attacked, and either exterminated them or expelled them from their lands with circumstances of great cruelty and treachery

The next six years of his life [A D 622-628] were passed in almost constant fighting, which began with attacks on Meccan caravans, but soon developed into regular warfare. The first pitched battle, at Badr [A D 624], was a great victory to Mahomet, which he ascribed to angelic aid [*Kor* iii 120, *seq*, viii 9, 10] But in the battle of Ohod [A D 625] the Moslems were completely defeated, and Mahomet himself was severely wounded For a time his influence was much weakened, but his undaunted spirit and self-confidence soon regained their sway At length the Koreishites and their allies, in alarm at Mahomet's growing power, with 10,000 men besieged Medina, which was fortified against them [A D. 627] The Moslems defended themselves vigorously for fifteen days, dissensions, fomented by emissaries of the Prophet, broke out in the enemy's camp, and they retired discomfited Henceforth Mahomet had little to fear from his enemies. He had adopted the policy of conquering and converting Arabia in detail, and encouraged by his successes, he marched with a great force on Mecca [A D 628], under pretext of performing pilgrimage The Koreishites opposed him in formidable numbers, and, after some negotiations a truce for ten years was concluded at Hodeibia, close to Mecca, one condition being that the Moslem pilgrimage should be postponed till the next year This caused great discontent, which Mahomet tried to appease by calling the truce a victory [*Kor* xlviii 1, *seq*]. Soon after, a Jewess, whose relations had been slain in battle with the Moslems, set some poisoned meat before the Prophet, one of his companions died, and Mahomet himself, who only tasted a morsel, felt the effect to the day of his death The next year [A D 629] he made the pilgrimage to Mecca, and many of his chief enemies in that city came over to him But his forces shortly after suffered a severe defeat at Muta in Syria, in their first encounter with the Empire, on which the Koreishites broke the truce Mahomet, with 10,000 men, marched on Mecca, which submitted with little resistance [A D 630] The Prophet entered the city, went at once to the Kaaba, and with the words, "Truth is come, let lies depart," ordered all the idols to be broken before his eyes With wise magnanimity he spared even his bitterest opponents, and, if they embraced his faith, loaded them

[1] Sprenger says, "The Koran became a sort of 'Moniteur.'" [Pref to vol iv p. 29]

with honours and wealth From Mecca he sent expeditions against the neighbouring tribes, and destroyed their idols The next year, called the year of deputations, was marked by the submission of almost all the Arabic tribes Henceforth the policy of intolerance and exclusiveness was proclaimed in all its rigour Idolaters were forbidden to set foot in the Holy City of Mecca, they were to be destroyed whenever and wherever they were found To Jews, Christians, Sabians, Magians ("The people of the Book"), was offered only the alternative, "the Koran, tribute, or the sword" [*Kor* ix 1-7, 29-35] After the conquest of Mecca, Mahomet returned to Medina, his refuge in distress and poverty, where, notwithstanding his immense power, he continued to live the same ostentatiously simple life as before, mending his own clothes, and milking his own goats In 631 he led another expedition against the empire, which, partly through the faint-heartedness of some of his followers, partly from the privations of the long march, effected only the conversion of some border tribes Mahomet was now past sixty years of age, his health was broken by fatigues, mental and bodily, by the effects of his malady, his licentiousness, and the poison which had been administered to him The last year of his life was troubled by pretenders, who, aware of his feeble health, hoped to seize his power These, however, with the exception of Moseilama of Yemama, the most formidable, were crushed before his death Mahomet, feeling his end approaching, made the pilgrimage to Mecca, which was conducted with unexampled splendour, in the spring of 632 Soon after his return to Medina he was attacked by a fever, and died after an illness of fourteen days on June 8th, 632 He was buried in the house of his wife Ayesha, and almost on the spot where he had died One daughter, Fatima, married to her cousin Ali, survived him After Khadijah's death he had sixteen wives and several concubines, but only one son was born to him, who died an infant [For his person and habits, see Gagnier's *Abulfeda*, chaps 65 and 66, Weil, 339-348; Irving, ch 29, C de Perceval, iii 332-337, Sprenger (English), 84 94, Muir, ii 28-31 iv 302, *seq*, *Quart Rev* cxxvii 301-304]

The Mahometan biographers ascribe an immense number of miracles to their Prophet, but in this they contradict many passages of the Koran [vi 32-37, 109, 124, vii 92-98, &c], from which it is plain that Mahomet, when appealed to, as he often was, for a miracle, referred his objectors to the Koran itself as a proof of his mission, and declares that even if a miracle were granted them they would not believe The only wonder hinted at in the Koran is the journey to Jerusalem and the seventh heaven in one night, which was pretended, or was dreamt, to have taken place just before the Hegira [*Kor* xvii 1 For the traditional account of this journey, see Irving, *Life of Mahomet*, chap. xii, Taylor, *Hist Mohammedanism*, 367-379]

It is difficult to decide how far Mahomet was sincere in his claim to be God's messenger, and to what extent he was a conscious deceiver The theory that he was an impostor of the type of Joseph Smith [Mormons] is in contradiction with his whole life and with the character of his system, as a real advance, religious and moral, upon Arabian heathenism On the other hand his gross immorality in his dealings with his wives, his breaches of faith, such as the making war in the holy months, and the revelations published to sanction these crimes, his publishing as divine inspirations to himself legends which he had learnt from Jews and others, the opportuneness of so many revelations to suit his own wishes and plans, make it impossible to acquit him of imposture The probable explanation is, that his earnestness and belief in his mission led him, as it has led many others, to look upon all his impulses, desires, and excuses, as coming from divine prompting [Mohler, *Ueber das Verhaltniss, &c*, i 368-370] The nature of those impulses, especially towards the end of Mahomet's life, and the character and history of his religion as the greatest foe of Christianity, make it probable also that he was a special instrument in the hands of Satan [Muir, ii 60, *seq*]

History of Mahometanism Before entering in detail into this subject, it is necessary to describe the nature of Islam as a political power. Its peculiarity is the predominance, both in idea and in fact, of the religious element The acquisition of political power is a religious principle The whole social and civil fabric rests on the divine law The State, therefore, is only the religious community in its unavoidable political relations The head of the Church is *ipso facto* head of the State, and that because he is head of the Church Hence, in theory, Islam forms only one community, under one head there is no room for national distinctions, every believer is a fellow countryman; only a Moslem can rule Moslems The head of the one community is an absolute despot, spiritual and temporal, controlled only by the divine law given to Mahomet And as Islam claims to be the universal faith of mankind, that head is the lawful lord of the world [1] The result of this theory was the establishment for a time of the mightiest empire which the world has ever seen That empire was dismembered, not by national revolts from a foreign rule, but by disputes as to the lawful successor of the Prophet Hence every rebel was a heretic also, orthodoxy and loyalty were identical theological differences produced, or were produced by, political changes [Dollinger, *Muhammad's Religion*, &c, 33-36, Freeman, *Lectures on the Saracens*, lect iii]

As the Prophet had appointed no successor, on his death there was much disputing, and some danger of a schism Finally, Abu-Bekr, whom Mahomet had seemed on several occasions to point out for the office, was generally accepted He took the title of Caliph (properly Khalif, "Successor") On the news of Mahomet's death, almost all Arabia revolted, but after a short and bloody struggle was finally subdued Abu-Bekr [A D 632 634] bequeathed his office to Omar [634-644], who

[1] The Sultan of Turkey, in his official titles, still makes this claim

named six of Mahomet's companions to appoint his successor They passing over Ali, appointed Othman [A D 644-656], under whom the primitive simplicity of his predecessors began to be exchanged for luxury and corruption He was murdered in the mosque at Medina, having provoked a rebellion by his partiality and injustice Ali [A D 656-661] succeeded him, but, encouraged by his unpopularity, Moawiyah, son of Abu-Sophian, of the family of the Ommiads, claimed the caliphate, and in a campaign against him Ali was murdered His weak and gentle son, Hassan, was in six months compelled to resign in favour of Moawiyah [A D 661-680], who removed the seat of power to Damascus, and made the caliphate hereditary On his death, many Moslems refused to acknowledge his son Yezid, advocating the claims of Ali's family hence arose the sect of the Shiites Hosein, son of Ali, grandson of the Prophet, tried to raise a rebellion, but was defeated and slain on the plain of Kerbela [A D 680] Several civil wars followed, during which the holy cities of Mecca and Medina were twice stormed, and the Kaaba was much damaged Under the Ommiads the caliphate became little more than an ordinary Eastern despotism

In A D 750, after a fierce war, the caliphate was transferred to the Abbasides, descendants of Mahomet's uncle Abbas, whereon the now vast empire began to be dismembered Abderrahman, an Ommiad, established a caliphate in Spain [A D 755-1030] Different dynasties, nominally subject to the caliph, really independent, occupied outlying provinces—the Aglabites, in Tripoli and Tunis [A D 800], the Edrisites, in the west of Barbary [A D 808], the Taherites, in Khorassan [A D 820], and others A third (the Fatimite) caliphate was established in Egypt [A D 908-1168] by Mohammad-al-Merdi, who professed to be descended from the Prophet. One of this line, Al-Hakim [A D 996-1020], claimed divine honours as an emanation of the Deity, and is still worshipped by the Druses The name of Al-Mostanser was [A D 1055], by order of the Emir-al-Omra, substituted for that of the Abbaside caliph in the prayers of the mosques in Bagdad Against Mustali, who had captured Jerusalem [A D 1096], the first crusade was directed The Fatimites were finally [A D 1168] overthrown by Saladin The rival caliphs were constantly at war, and did not scruple to use the aid of infidels against each other In 762 the Abbaside Al-Mansor removed the seat of the caliphate to Bagdad. The Abbaside caliphs were great patrons of science and literature, but by their luxury and extravagance hastened the decline of the caliphate In the middle of the ninth century, the Caliph Al-Motassem formed a bodyguard of Turkish slaves, who soon were able to dispose of the throne at will among the Abbaside family From this time the caliphs of Bagdad, though venerated in their spiritual capacity, had little temporal power beyond Bagdad and its neighbourhood. They became mere puppets in the hands of a new officer, the Emir-al-Omra, "Commander of Commanders" Finally [A D 1258], the Mongols took Bagdad and slew the last caliph, Al-Mostassem. A person claiming to be his uncle fled to Egypt, where he and his successors were recognised as spiritual powers, being found by Mahometan rulers to be useful instruments The last of them [A D 1377] ceded his claims to Selim the Terrible, Sultan of the Ottomans, whose successors have since that time been regarded by orthodox Moslems as the rightful caliphs

The detailed history of the Mahometan conquests and empire must be left to strictly historical works,[1] a brief summary will suffice The Saracens[2]—so the Arabs were known to the West,—in little more than a century [A D 650-730], in spite of two repulses from Constantinople [A D 668-675 and 717-718], and the great defeat of Tours [A D 732], conquered Syria, Persia, and Western Asia to the Oxus, Egypt, almost all Africa and Spain Between A D 750-1050, owing to the revival of the Eastern Empire, the decline of the caliphate, and internal dissensions, the Moslem arms were on the whole stationary or retrograding Crete [A D 823], however, and Sicily [A D 827-878] were conquered, and even Rome was sacked from the sea [A D 846] In Asia Mahmoud of Ghizni [A D 997-1028] won Transoxiana and Cabul, and introduced Islam into India The revival of military zeal, under the Seljukian Turks [eleventh century], who took the place of the now worn-out Saracens, was checked by the Crusades [A D 1095-1270] in the West and the Mongol ravages in the East At the end of the thirteenth century, Islam was at its lowest ebb, ruling only in Egypt, part of Syria, part of Hindostan, and Spain But in 1299 the Ottoman Empire began its great career It established itself in Europe [A D 1353], subdued Thrace [A D 1354], and the remains of the Byzantine possessions in Asia [A D 1390] The defeat and capture of Bajazet by Tamerlane [A D. 1402] scarcely checked their course Bosnia [A D 1415], Wallachia [A D 1418], were subdued, and after several attempts Constantinople was taken by Mahomet II, and the Eastern Empire destroyed [A D. 1453]. On the other hand the Saracens were finally expelled from Spain [A D 1492] Moldavia [A.D 1456], Servia, the Morea, Albania [A D 1466], the Crimea [A D 1475], Rhodes [A D. 1522], most of Hungary [A D 1550], Croatia [A D 1537], Transylvania [A.D 1552], were successively subdued Germany was twice invaded [A D 1529, 1532], Italy was ravaged [A D 1543], and several great victories were gained at sea From about A D 1550, owing to the great naval defeat at Lepanto, a wearing struggle with Persia, and internal dissensions, the Ottoman power declined, yet Cyprus [A D. 1573], Crete [A D 1669], and part of Poland [A D 1676], were added to their dominions In 1678 came the first struggle with Russia; and the utter rout of

[1] See especially Gibbon, *Decline and Fall*, chaps 51 to end, Finlay, *Byzantine Empire*, Ockley, *Hist of Saracens*; Washington Irving, *Lives of the Successors of Mahomet*, E A. Freeman, *Lectures on the Saracens*, Weil, *Geschichte der Chalifen*, J H Newman, *Lectures on the Turks*, Creasy, *Hist Ottoman Turks*, Von Hammer, *Geschichte des Osmanischen Reiches*

[2] This name, originally that of a small tribe of Arabia-Felix, is derived from Zara, Sara, "the desert," Sarrik, "a robber," or Sharkioun, "Eastern" [Smith, *Dict Anc Geogr Saracens*, ii 204, Gibbon, ed Smith, vi. 204, notes 30 and a, Pococke, *Spec.* 33 35].

the Turks before Vienna [A.D 1683], finally overthrew their military ascendancy by the end of the century the Ottoman power was completely broken The Turks have gradually been stripped of almost all their European provinces, and their wars have been almost wholly defensive

The effects of the Mahometan conquests on the religion of the conquered have been very various In Christian countries where the Moslem power has not been lasting, as in Spain, Sicily, and those parts of Eastern Europe conquered by the Turks, no trace of them is left except buildings and some popular customs and superstitions But where their dominion has endured, as in Western Asia and Northern Africa, Christianity, once supreme, has now almost perished This has been caused partly by individual conversions—for no Christian population, except perhaps that of Crete, has ever in a body apostatized—but mainly by the substitution of a Moslem for a Christian population Baptism and the teaching of Christianity were forbidden, Christian women were forced into the harems of Mahometans, Christian children were forcibly brought up as Moslems, indignities, burdensome taxes, and personal duties, were imposed on Christians, from time to time violent persecutions took place Moreover, in many countries heresy largely prevailed, which is unable to furnish any firm ground of faith Heretics frequently invited or combined with Mahometans for the sake of overthrowing their orthodox rivals [Egypt Lane, ii 276, Gibbon, vi 332, 428. Syria and North Africa Finlay, *Byzantine Empire*, i 159 Asia Minor *ib* i 198] One remarkable effect of the Mahometan spirit of conquest must be noticed As it attacked Christianity as a religion, at first defence, and subsequently reprisals on the part of the Church became a religious duty The unwarlike spirit of the early Church entirely passed away, and in its stead appeared that military Christianity which is so conspicuous in the history of the Crusades [Milman, *Lat Chr* ii 220-222, Lecky, *Hist Europ Morals*, ii 262-268] In heathen countries, the inhabitants usually embraced, after a longer or shorter time, the Moslem faith Persia since its first conquest has undergone many vicissitudes between heathenism (under the Mongols), Sonnism, and Shiism, which is now the national faith, and has become in many points assimilated to the ancient Magianism In India, during the Moslem dominion, Islam was confined to the ruling classes at the various courts, and found little acceptance with the natives The Emperor Akbar discarded Mahometan peculiarities, and was a simple Deist In many points Islam has approximated to Brahmanism Persecution has done its work here also, even in modern times, especially by Tippoo Saib of Mysore [Dollinger, 15, 16] The sword and persecution have ever been the chief means of propagating Islam, no missionary organization has at any time existed, and individual efforts for voluntary conversion have been rare and accidental Yet instances are frequent—the Turks [eleventh century], the Mongols [thirteenth century]—of whole heathen nations brought in contact with Mahometans having voluntarily accepted Islam Astonishing progress has been made by it for many years past in Central Africa, while in China and the Asiatic Islands it has made many converts [Dollinger, *Muhammad's Religion*, &c 16-20, Mohler, *Ueber das Verhaltniss*, &c i 386].

The causes of the success and rapid extension of Islam may be thus summarized —

[1] The great power over nomadic and Eastern races—as were the Saracens and Turks—of Mahomet's personal character and religion Even in his faults he nearly corresponds with their ideal, and his religion suits their habits and ways of thought

[2] Extension by the sword, as a religious principle, together with the intense and burning religious zeal of the Mahometans, fanned by hopes of immediate bliss, sensual or spiritual, to suit different temperaments, to those who died fighting for the faith

[3] Want of religious depth and earnestness among the Christians to whom Islam was opposed In early times, this was in great measure the result of widespread heresy, which weakened faith, caused indifference through weariness of controversy, and created numerous divisions and discords, in later times, of discords between the Roman and Eastern Churches, and Protestants Christendom was divided, Mahometanism was, at the time of its successes, absolute unity, spiritual and temporal

[4] The outward character presented by Mahometanism The permission in this life, and promise in the next, of sensuality influenced low and coarse minds, asceticism in the long and strict fast, regular prayers and ablutions, almsgiving, abstinence from intoxicating liquors, and other burdensome precepts, and a generally austere and scrupulous spirit, suited higher characters [See Hallam, *Middle Ages*, ii 117, ed 1872]

[5] The inward truth in the religion, namely, the intense acknowledgment of God's sole supremacy, hatred of idolatry, and of everything that trenched upon His prerogatives

[6] The military skill and wise policy of both Saracens and Turks in dealing with Christians, and the consequent strength of their government as opposed to the weakness and discords among Christian powers

The cause of Mahometan decline is mainly that Islam is especially a religion for nomad and half-nomad races, hence when they settle they lose their strength, which arises from their nomadic life, and their religion loses its purity and power They degenerate, become luxurious and inactive, internal dissensions and divisions arise; the same doctrines (*e g* fatalism) that strengthened them in their success weaken them in their depression Moreover, the opposition to progress innate in Islam tends to keep Mahometan nations stationary, while Christian powers advance in power and wealth

Authoritative Sources of Doctrine. These are the Koran and the Sonna

[1] *The Koran* consists of the revelations which Mahomet professed to receive from time

to time, either directly from God or through the Angel Gabriel. The name *Koran* (lit "that which is read" or "that which ought to be read") is applied both to the whole work and to any part of it. It has many other titles with the Mahometans Al Forkan, "Liberation," "Deliverance," hence "Illumination," "Revelation," Al Moshaf, "The Volume," Al Kitâb, "The Book," Al Dhikr, "The Admonition" It is divided into 114 Chapters ("Suras," "rows, primarily of bricks in a wall," thence "a line" of writing) Each chapter is divided into verses (Ayât, "signs," "wonders"), which vary slightly in different editions Both suras and verses are of very different lengths, the suras having from three to 286 verses, the verses being from one to nearly twenty lines Each sura has its title, taken either from some subject treated or some person mentioned in it, or from some important word, often in the middle or near the end of the sura. Some suras have two titles, some verses have also titles of their own. Next to the title comes the mention of the place where, according to tradition, the sura was revealed—Mecca, Medina, or partly at Mecca, partly at Medina To every sura but the ninth is prefixed the form of blessing, "In the name of God, the Compassionate, the Merciful" This blessing is often called "Bismillah," from the first word in the Arabic It is used at the beginning of all books and public documents, before meals and other actions, and is constantly on the lips of Mahometans.

As Mahomet thought expedient, he recited each revelation to those who happened to be present, one or more of whom usually committed it to writing, on palm leaves, leather, stones, mutton-bones, or any rude material which might be at hand After the Hegira, the Prophet had regular secretaries always in attendance on him Mahomet professed to recite each passage immediately on receiving it, in fact, most of them were carefully elaborated in private before they were published. When the passages were taken down, some few copied them, but most learnt them by heart, as Mahomet wished his words to "live in men's hearts" It is said that at the Prophet's death a few persons could repeat the whole Koran. Two years after, many of those who knew the Koran were slain in the campaign against Moseilama, whereon Abu-Bekr, fearing the loss of some of it, commissioned Zeid ibn Thabit of Medina, one of Mahomet's secretaries, to collect and arrange the fragments, he is said to have gathered the text from "date leaves and tablets of white stone, and from the breasts of men" Apparently few or no copies of this recension were made, for in A D 652; the Caliph Othman, learning that there were important variations in the existing texts and in the recital of the Koran by different persons, commissioned the same Zeid ibn Thabit, aided by three Koreishites, to make a new revision. Several copies were sent to the chief military stations, and all others were destroyed by the caliph's command This recension of Othman has come down to us almost unaltered. The greatest care has been exercised in maintaining the text pure, hence there are very few various readings, and those mostly confined to the differences in the vowel points and diacritical signs, which did not exist in Othman's time. There is good reason for believing that the first recension under Abu-Bekr contained the Koran as taken down from the Prophet's lips, with doubtless some omissions, but without important falsifications or interpolations, and that Othman's revision—that is, the present text—faithfully reproduces that recension

The Koran is composed absolutely without any arrangement or system whatsoever. It has neither beginning, middle, nor end; it is a gathering of irregular scraps indiscriminately put together Zeid ibn Thabit seems to have arranged the suras in their present order, putting the opening prayer at the beginning, and the rest like the pipes of an organ, the longest first. The division into suras is, in a great measure, due to Mahomet himself To suit his own purposes and the needs of his community, while at Medina, he seems to have arranged his revelations, by mixing up those of different dates and on different subjects all in a chaos Hence in the same sura the most discordant matters are treated, the writer passing abruptly from one to another without the slightest transition Of modern authors no two agree as to the chronological order of the different parts Numberless volumes have been written by Mahometan theologians to point out the connection and train of thought "Detailed injunctions of things allowed and forbidden, legendary stories of Jewish and Christian religion, amplifications of all kinds, boundless tautologies and repetitions, form the body of this sacred volume" [Goethe, quoted in *Quart Rev* cxxvii 348] Few of the legends are repeated less than twice, some of them eight or ten times Descriptions of the last day, judgment, hell, paradise, form nearly one-sixth of the whole Many of the repetitions are to be ascribed to the redactors, who accepted and incorporated all that proceeded from Mahomet, even although it might have been superseded by later utterances We have, more than once, several drafts of the same passage [comp. *Kor* lxxxiv. 1-5, lxxxii 1-5, lxxxi. 1-14]. In spite, therefore, of many passages of striking power and grandeur, of much vigour and beauty of description, of moral sentiments tersely and keenly expressed, in spite, too, of the deep earnestness of conviction, the real devotion and piety that pervades the Koran, it is to an English reader dreary, monotonous, tedious, and dull But no work suffers so much from a translation, however masterly, because its beauties consist mainly in its rhythm and diction There are no less than an hundred names for the last day, and as many epithets of God Moreover, it was intended not for reading, but for chanting, or recitation, hence, almost throughout runs a kind of continuous rhyme, to which the sense is frequently sacrificed, often very striking, which no translation can exactly reproduce

Three stages may be recognised in the composition of the Koran [1.] The period of early struggles, marked by a higher poetical spirit, an appreciation of the beauties of nature, more intense feeling and earnestness [2.] The period of controversy and the formation of doctrine, shewing a more prosaic and didactic style, with frequent repetitions of histories and legends [3.] Period of power, of legislation, moral and ecclesiastical, indicated by a more dogmatic and commanding tone, and comparative freedom from histories and legends Yet, even to the last, there come at times grand and wild poetic utterances, like those of the first period A certain unity of style runs through the whole A special peculiarity of the Koran is, that every word is ascribed to God speaking to Mahomet, in order to mark this, the word "say" is prefixed to the didactic portions [see *e g* *Kor* cxii 1].

The orthodox Mahometans hold that the Koran is divine and uncreated, that the first transcript has existed from everlasting beneath the throne of God, written on a tablet of vast size, called "The Preserved Tablet," which contains also the divine decrees, past and future A copy from this tablet, in a single paper volume, bound in silk and ornamented with gems, was, on the "Night of Power" [*Kor* xcvii 1], in the month Ramadhan, sent down by the hands of Gabriel to the lowest heaven, whence the Archangel revealed it to Mahomet in portions, as occasion arose, shewing the whole volume to the Prophet once a year [Pococke, *Spec Hist Arab* 222, *seq*, D'Herbelot, *B O* art *Alcoran*] The most extravagant language is used in its praise Mahomet himself appeals to its surpassing excellence in proof of his mission [*Kor* ii 21, iv 84, xi 16, xvii 90, xlvi 2-7, &c], and this has been a favourite argument with his followers A living Mahometan writer heads a subdivision of an essay, "That the perfection of the *Koran* proves its divine origin" [Syed Ahmed, *On the Holy Koran*, 35], in which we read, "We boldly and confidently assert, in the face of all our antagonists, that a like unto it has never been, and never will be produced" [*ibid* 36] To explain the various contradictions and discrepancies, they put forth the doctrine of abrogation [*Kor* ii 100, xvi 103], that God cancelled some verses and supplied them by others 225 verses of the present text are said to be abrogated

The Koran is with the Mahometans not only all that the Bible is to Christians, but also their code of law and jurisprudence, and to a great extent also their Book of Common Prayer They hold it to contain, implicitly or explicitly, all knowledge They treat it with the utmost reverence, being very careful so to hold or hang it that it may not be below the girdle; no other book is ever put on the top of it, no Moslem may touch it unless he is legally pure; it may not be printed, for fear of something unclean in the ink, paper, or printer, it may not be sold to, or even touched by, an unbeliever, they use it, the whole, or separate verses, as an amulet or charm, they consult it and divine by it on all important occasions

[2.] *The Sonna* (lit "custom") The second authoritative source of doctrine is an amplification and explanation of the Koran It consists of the sayings and doings of the Prophet, as handed down by tradition, put into writing, at the earliest at the end of the first century after the Hegira The original purpose of the collectors of traditions was to supply materials for the decision of questions of doctrine, morals, law, and even of habits and customs, when the *Koran* is silent. The Sonna, therefore, chiefly deals with matters of practice As Mahomet was an inspired prophet, all his deeds and words are regarded as prompted by God, and therefore as authoritative guides to his followers Hence it became a regular business to collect all statements about the Prophet that rested on credible authority They were at first learnt by heart, and taught in lectures, afterwards, when the number increased to an enormous extent, they were brought into one form and put into writing At first any professed traditions were accepted, at length, learned Moslems undertook to sift and criticise them Hence the formation of the Six Canonical Collections, which were composed between A D 870-930 There are also others of later date and inferior authority The traditions are all cast in the same form They are seldom more than ten lines long, each relates usually only to one fact, in the same style, and in the form of a dialogue At the head of each is put the chain of witnesses (Isnad) on whose authority the tradition rests, beginning with the writer, and going up to some companion of the Prophet This is of great importance, and is, with Mahometans, a test of the "soundness" of a tradition They are on all possible subjects A single specimen will suffice,—"Ibn Saad, from Wakidy, from Zakariya ibn Yahia ibn Yazid Saadi, from his father. The Prophet said, 'I speak purest Arabic, I am a Koreishite and speak the dialect of the Banu-Saad'" Many of these traditions are spurious, those that relate to questions of law and morals have been of great advantage in enlarging and giving breadth to the narrowness of the Koran [Muir, 1. xxviii-cv, Sprenger, i. 9-12, iii. lxvii-civ, Dollinger, 9-12]

DOCTRINES. On this subject it is important to bear in mind two points [1.] According to Islam, revealed religion has the same extent as in the law of Moses, including civil and criminal laws, and also, to some degree, social habits [2.] Islam, as professed, does not represent Mahomet's personal views at any period of his life The Koran and the genuine traditions represent all the stages of belief and action through which the Prophet passed in twenty years, whereas all therein contained is of equal and absolute authority with Mahometans Moreover, there are many accretions of later date, to supply felt deficiencies either in theology or jurisprudence, most of these accretions being derived from the same sources as the teaching of Mahomet, namely, Judaism and Christianity.

The faith of Islam is summed up in the two articles —"1 There is no God but God 2.

Mahomet is the Prophet of God" Hence all the doctrines and ordinances taught or practised by the Prophet are of divine authority Mahometan theologians divide their religion into two parts—Faith (Iman) and Practice (Din)

[A] FAITH is divided into six heads. 1 God 2 His Angels 3 His Scriptures 4. His Prophets 5. The Resurrection and Day of Judgment. 6. God's absolute decree and predestination of good and evil

1] *God* is the creator and preserver of all things in heaven and earth, without beginning or end, omnipotent, omniscient, omnipresent Beyond all other attributes is that of absolute unity. Mahometanism teaches the sternest and strictest monotheism Nothing exists but the Creator and the creation The Creator is the only power, force, and act, in the universe, all things are effected at His will and by His passive ministers Hence God is immeasurably above His creatures, who are but His tools Angels, devils, jinn (or genii), all owe their being to Him, and are liable to death or extinction at His will Thus Mahometanism is far removed on the one hand from Epicureanism, Pantheism, and idolatry, on the other, from the Christian doctrines of the Trinity and the Incarnation Christians, and even Jews, because they hold Ezra to be the Son of God [*Kor* ix. 30], are included with heathens as polytheists—those who pay divine honours to creatures

2] *Angels* are inferior to men, because they were bidden to worship Adam, and because Mahomet was a man They are God's ministers and servants, free from sin, who praise God day and night, and are never weary of serving Him. They have pure and subtle bodies, created of an ethereal kind of fire or light, they have neither distinction of sexes nor carnal appetites, but differ in form, degree and duties Some bear the throne of God, others intercede for the faithful, others guide the affairs of earth, and help and guard the faithful, others watch over heaven, others preside over hell, others bear away the soul at death, two, one on the right hand, one on the left of each living person, record his good and evil deeds respectively, two shall bear each soul to judgment The four most important angels are—Gabriel, their chief, the angel of revelations, declared to be identical with the Holy Ghost, Michael, the friend and protector of the Jews, Azrael, the angel of death, Izrafil, who shall sound the trumpet on the resurrection-day. One of the angels was called Azazil Refusing God's command to worship Adam at his creation, he was cursed, and lost his high position, hence he became Iblis [Διάβολος], or Satan, the enemy of God and man Besides angels there are also Jinn (sing Jinnee), a race inferior to angels, created before Adam, of fire The jinn are both good and evil The former accepted Islam, the latter rebelled against God, and refused to believe Islam, they are called Sheitans (Satans), Ifrits, or Merids Of these Iblis is the lord, and, according to some, the father These evil jinn, by listening at the doors of heaven, learn God's secrets, which they impart to soothsayers, the angels drive them away with stones, *i e.* shooting-stars. The jinn are of both sexes, propagate their species, sometimes with human beings, eat, drink, and are subject to death. They are generally invisible, but can assume various forms at pleasure. Many men, especially Solomon, have gained great power over the jinn. The doctrine of angels and jinn is derived mainly from Jewish tradition and Arabic belief, with a slight admixture of Christian notions [Geiger, *Was hat Mohammad aus dem Judenthume aufgenommen*, 83-85, 185, Sprenger, ii 238-251, Rodwell and Sale, notes *passim*].

3] *Scriptures*, or Divine Books These have been in all 104, sent down by God to man ten to Adam, fifty to Seth, thirty to Idris (Enoch), ten to Abraham, one to Moses (the Law or Pentateuch), one to David (the Psalms), one to Jesus (the Gospel), one to Mahomet Each of these abrogated the preceding, and confirmed that which followed All are lost but the last four, of which all but the Koran have been misinterpreted and corrupted by the Jews and Christians, but yet some passages remain confirming the Koran and prophesying Mahomet The whole Old Testament is regarded as sacred, but not so highly as the Psalms and Law The following texts are quoted as referring to Mahomet —Gen xvii 20, xxi 13, Deut. xviii 15, 18, compared with xxxiv 10, xxxiii 2, Hab iii 3 (Sinai = Judaism, Seir = Christianity, Paran = Islam) Cant v 10-16 (a description of Mahomet), Isa xxi 7 (Chariot of Camels, or, more literally (Vulg), Rider upon a camel = Mahomet, chariot of asses, or rider upon an ass = Jesus), Hagg ii 7, Luke xxiv 49, John i 20-25 (that Prophet = Mahomet), xiv 25, 26, xvi 7 (Παράκλητος, a corruption of Περικλυτὸς = Mahomet) [Syed Ahmed, *Essays, On the Prophecies respecting Mohammed*, esp pp 9, 10, Pococke, *Spec. Hist Arabum*, 17, *seq*]

4] *Prophets* These are men sent down from God to teach mankind, all believing the same creed (Islam), honoured by communications from God, workers of miracles Of these there have been, according to one tradition, 224,000, according to another, 124,000, of whom 313 have been ambassadors or apostles. Of these there are mentioned in the Koran, Adam, Abel, Seth, Idris (Enoch), Noah, Hud (identified by some with Heber), Abraham, Lot, Ishmael, Isaac, Jacob, Joseph, Moses, Aaron, Shoaib (the same as Reuel, Raguel, or Jethro, Moses' father in-law), David, Solomon, Elijah, Elisha, Jonah, Job, Ezra. Very curious and unscriptural legends are told of many of these, derived chiefly from Jewish tradition [Geiger, *Was hat Mohammad*, &c 98-196] From the New Testament, Zachariah, John the Baptist, and Jesus, are named prophets in the Koran, the accounts of these are derived from an heretical, apparently Ebionite or Judæo-Christian, source Besides these, there are mentioned also Lokman, Saleh, Arabian prophets, Dhulkifl, whose identity is disputed (Ezekiel, Obadiah [1 Kings xviii 4], or Isaiah [Rodwell, 179]), and Dhulkarnain (Alexander the Great)

5.] *Resurrection and the Day of Judgment.* Under this head it will be convenient to take the whole doctrine of the state of the soul after death. When a corpse has been laid in the tomb the soul returns to it for a short time, and the deceased is then visited by two terrible angels, Munkar and Nekir, who question him concerning his faith. The wicked they will severely torture, but the good they will leave in peace. There are many opinions about the state of the soul of ordinary believers between death and the resurrection [Sale, *P. D.*, § 4 , or Lane, *Mod. Egypt*, ii. 269]. The souls of prophets are admitted into paradise at once ; the souls of martyrs—those who die in battle against infidels—rest in the crops of green birds, which eat of the fruits and drink of the rivers of paradise. Many fearful signs will go before the resurrection, eclipses, earthquakes, wars, the coming of Antichrist (Dijjal), who will be defeated and slain by Jesus Christ. It will be preceded by three blasts of the trumpet: at the first of which the universe will be shaken, the sea dried up, the mountains levelled, and the works of man destroyed ; at the second, all living creatures, even angels and jinn, will be annihilated ; only God and the dwellers in paradise and hell will remain. Forty years after will be sounded the blast of resurrection, when all will come to life again, will appear before God and be judged ; their deeds shall be weighed in a balance, and as good or evil preponderates, so shall be the sentence. Not only men but also brutes and jinn will be thus judged. After the judgment retribution will be exacted for every wrong and injury done to others. This being finished, all men will be led over the bridge Al Sirat, which extends over the midst of hell, finer than a hair and sharper than a sword's edge, beset on both sides by briars and thorns. The good, led by Mahomet and the prophets, will pass safely over it into paradise ; the wicked will fall into hell. In hell there are seven regions: the first of these is reserved for wicked Mahometans, who will only remain till their sins are expiated, and will then be admitted into paradise ; the other six regions are assigned to those of other religions, who will be tortured for ever. The horrors of hell are very vividly described ; fear being, according to Mahometan doctors, the chief motive of morality. Between hell and paradise there is a partition (Al-Araf), or intermediate region, where those shall be placed whose good and evil deeds are equal. The descriptions of the joys of Paradise are very minute ; the reward of the blessed will consist chiefly in sensual enjoyments—most delicious meats and drinks, the society of each man's wives, and of the houries or girls of paradise. To enjoy these thoroughly they will live in perpetual youth. But these sensual delights will be little regarded by the most blessed, to whom it will be granted to see the face of God. Many Moslems hold that the descriptions of paradise are figurative: and it is worth notice that they were written when Mahomet had only one wife. Persons will be admitted to paradise, not by their own merits, but simply by the mercy of God, through faith ; but the happiness of each will be measured by his merits. To estimate these, sins are divided into those that deserve punishment in the next world and those whose penalty is inflicted during this life. Doctors differ in the assignment of particular sins to these categories [Palgrave, *Arabia*, 281-285, sm. ed.]. The doctrine of the future state is derived mainly from Jewish tradition, with an admixture of Christian and Parsee elements.

6.] *Predestination.* Every event has been absolutely predestined by God, and written from all eternity on the "Preserved Tablet." Hence each man's lot is irrevocably fixed—how, and how long, he is to live, what his end will be, and no human care can vary or ward off God's decree.

[B.] Practice. This has four branches: 1. Prayer, including Purification. 2. Almsgiving. 3. Fasting. 4. Pilgrimage.

1.] *Prayer and Purification.* Purification is a necessary preparative for prayer, which will not be accepted from an unclean person. It is of two kinds. The greater or extraordinary purification is of the whole body, to cleanse from certain ceremonial defilements. These defilements are nearly the same as those of the Jewish Law [Lev. xv.]. It is also performed on the morning of Friday and of the great festivals. The lesser or ordinary purification takes place before the ordinary prayers, and on some other occasions ; it consists in washing the face, arms, elbows, feet, hands, mouth, nostrils, ears, feet, with prayers, and reciting sura 97 of the Koran. The prayers, &c., are often omitted [Lane, *Mod. Egypt*, i. 85-89]. When water cannot be procured, sand is allowed to be used. This relaxation occurs in the Talmud [Geiger, 89]. Prayer is ordered to be made five times daily: [1] in the morning at daybreak and before sunrise ; [2] just after noon, when the sun begins to decline ; [3] in the afternoon, midway between noon and nightfall ; [4] a few minutes after sunset ; [5] at nightfall, when the evening has just shut in. Some add two other times, which are not imperative: [6] between sunrise and noon ; [7] a little after midnight. The second and third and the fourth and fifth services may be kept together, thus making three prayers daily [Syed Ahmed, *On the Religion of the Pre-Islamitic Arabs*, 17]. The times of prayer are proclaimed by muezzins from the minarets of the mosque, in a sort of chant, with very striking effect. The prayers may be performed either at home or in the mosque. The worshipper always turns towards Mecca (the Kaaba) ; he adopts various attitudes. The worship consists of repeated ejaculations of the Takbír (Allahu Akbar, God is most great), Raka, or inclinations, prayers and recitations from the Koran, especially suras iii., v. 256, cviii. cxii. cxiii. cxiv. The prayers are short forms, incessantly repeated, inelastic, inexpansive, with few ideas. The regular public service in the mosque takes place at noon on Friday, "the day of the assembly;" it is of the same nature as the private daily devotions, with the addition of a sermon Except on certain festivals women are not allowed to attend the public services, or to pray in the mosque Intercession, both for the living and the dead, forms a conspicuous part of the devotions The prayers are all addressed to God, but the intercession of Mahomet and the saints is intreated The Mahometans are very reverent and devout during their devotions, both private and public

2] *Alms* are of two kinds, those prescribed by the law, and those which are voluntary The former were in early ages collected by officers appointed by the sovereign, and applied to pious uses, their payment and application is now left to the conscience The proportion to be given varies according to the kind of property from which it is given

3] *Fasting* There is one obligatory fast in the year—the month of Ramadhan, because the *Koran* was given in that month. From the time the new moon appears to the next new moon, the Moslem is bidden to fast every day, from the time when one can distinguish plainly the white thread from the black—explained by some to mean the white and black streaks seen in the east before daybreak—until sunset. He must abstain during that time from eating, drinking, smoking, perfumes, and all sensual indulgences There are some few exemptions, but those who are hindered by any temporary cause must fast an equal number of days in another month This fast is kept with great strictness, and when Ramadhan falls in summer [1] it is most oppressive The idea was probably derived from the Christian Lent. There are also some optional fasts, the most important being the Ashura, the 10th day of Moharram (1st month) This was in imitation of the Jewish day of Atonement, it was instituted as obligatory soon after the Hegira, when Mahomet was trying to win over the Jews, and was afterwards made optional The same day is also kept in memory of the martyrdom of Hosein, the Prophet's grandson, at Kerbela

4] *Pilgrimage* Every believer is bound once in his life, either in person and by another, whose expenses he pays, to make the pilgrimage to Mecca and Mount Arafat, unless prevented by poverty or ill-health It takes place in the month Dzul-hajji The ceremonies to be performed by pilgrims are very numerous and complicated, the chief of them are the wearing of the Ihram or sacred garment, consisting of two simple pieces of cloth wrapped round the loins and over the shoulder, compassing seven times the Kaaba or holy house of Mecca, kissing or touching each time the black stone, fabled to have fallen from heaven, a journey to Mount Arafat, about ten miles from Mecca, and the offering of victims (sheep, goats, kine, or camel) [For further particulars see Burckhardt, *Travels in Arabia*, vol i, Burton, *A Pilgrimage to Mecca and El-Medinah*, Sale, *P D*, § 4] The practice of pilgrimage and most of the customs connected therewith were borrowed from the heathen Arabs, but a fresh meaning, connected with the legend that Abraham and Ishmael instituted the pilgrimage, was assigned to them Pilgrimages are also often made to the tombs of saints, to pray for their intercession Besides the above observances, all the Mahometans practise circumcision and wear beards. These customs, derived from the Arabs, are not mentioned in the Koran, their institution is ascribed to Abraham [Syed Ahmed, *Rel of Pre-Islamitic Arabs*, 8]

There are certain *things forbidden* by Islam—partly heathen practices, partly unclean meats, partly things likely to do harm These are various superstitions about cattle, burying female children alive, divining by arrows, casting lots, gambling, usury, wine, and all intoxicating liquors and drugs (some add even coffee and tobacco), eating blood swine's flesh, whatever dies of itself or is strangled, or killed by a blow or fall, or by another beast, or is slain in honour of an idol, or anything at the slaughtering of which the name of God has not been said.[2] Some Moslems add many other meats to this list, being, with some exceptions, those forbidden by the law of Moses

War against all unbelievers, if they have been the aggressors, is enjoined as a sacred duty, if not fighting for pay, those who are killed in it are regarded as martyrs Of those enemies who, refusing to capitulate or surrender, are reduced by force of arms, the men may be killed or enslaved, and the women and children enslaved Life and liberty may be granted them if they surrender and agree to pay a poll-tax, or embrace Islam If they have acted treacherously they may be exterminated It has been a great question with Mahometan theologians when "religious war" (Jihad) is allowed or commanded [Hunter's *Indian Musulmans*, chap iii]

CIVIL AND CRIMINAL LAWS The most important of these are the laws relating to marriage. A Moslem may not have at the same time more than four wives, who must all be free women and Moslems, but, in addition, he may keep any number of slave concubines [*Kor* iv. 3, Lane, i 122] An unlimited power of divorce, without giving any reason, is allowed to the husband, and is fully taken advantage of, cases are mentioned of middle-aged Mahometans who have had thirty, forty, or even fifty wives [Dollinger, 26] A wife cannot obtain a divorce except for cruelty or neglect, and then she loses her dowry A man may divorce his wife twice, and take her back without any ceremony, but if he divorce her a third time, or pronounce a triple divorce in one sentence, and then wish to marry her again, she must be first married and divorced by another husband, who must have consummated the marriage A divorced woman must wait three months, or, if pregnant, till she is delivered, before she can marry again An adulteress is punished by stoning if detected, but there must be four *eye* witnesses of the deed, and a false accusation against any woman is punished by scourging If a man have a child

[1] The Mahometan year is lunar, hence each month goes through all the seasons in about thirty two years.

[2] Hence the Moslem butchers always say the "Bismillah" on slaughtering a beast.

by a concubine, the child is free, the mother cannot afterwards be sold or given away, and on her master's death becomes free The prohibited degrees are somewhat wide, and apply both to wives and concubines Women may not shew their faces to any man but their husbands and those within the prohibited degrees Slavery is allowed, with almost absolute power to the owner For murder, manslaughter, and personal injuries, retaliation or satisfaction in money is prescribed Theft is punished by loss of limbs, lesser crimes by scourging, apostasy or blasphemy by death The laws of inheritance are very elaborate, the chief principles being the rejection of any privileges of primogeniture, and the assigning to a female half the share of the male of the same degree of relationship

RELATION TO JUDAISM AND CHRISTIANITY On this point the Koran is inconsistent In many passages [ii 3, 59, 285, iv 50, v 53, vi 92, x 38, xlvi 8-11, 29, &c] the view is put forth that the Old and New Testaments and the teaching of Mahomet are identical, that all three are books sent down from God, equally sacred and to be obeyed, and the believers in each (with, in some passages [ii 59, v 73], the Sabians also) will be saved In other later passages it is taught that Judaism, Christianity, and Islam, are successive revelations from God, confirming but superseding each other, Jesus being a greater Prophet than Moses, and Mahomet than Jesus, that the Jews were perverse and wicked in not accepting Christianity, and both Jews and Christians in not accepting Islam Whenever opportunity offered, they were to be compelled to embrace it or pay tribute [*Kor* ix 28-35] To support this view, which is that now held by Mahometans, it is constantly asserted that the Jewish and Christian Scriptures had been misinterpreted and falsified This inconsistency is explained by the change in Mahomet's views, through which from the Prophet of Arabia only he proclaimed himself the Prophet of the World [Mohler, *Ueber das Verhaltniss* &c, 361 385] From Judaism is derived all that distinguishes Islam from pure Deism Its local character—the Kaaba standing in somewhat the same relation to Islam as the Temple to Judaism—its strong religious and national unity, its conception of the nature of a divine revelation, as prescribing not only principles, but detailed laws, and even habits and customs, many theological notions, moral and ritual, civil and criminal laws, and a very large portion of the substance of the Koran, are of Jewish origin But frequent errors and confusions [see *e g* *Kor* ii 250], numerous coincidences, verbal and in matters of fact with the Talmud, prove that Mahomet's knowledge of Judaism was obtained not from the Scriptures, or any written document, but from oral tradition It is doubtful, indeed, whether he could read Christianity, known to Mahomet in a similar way, evidently in great part from an heretical source, though theoretically superior to Judaism,[1] had little real influence on his teaching The doctrine of the Trinity [supposed to consist of the Father, Jesus, and Mary, iv 169, v 76-79], and of the Sonship of Jesus, is repeatedly and vehemently attacked The Holy Ghost is identified with the angel Gabriel Yet Jesus is set forth as the Word of God, and a spirit proceeding from Him, as the greatest Prophet before Mahomet, conceived miraculously of a pure virgin,[2] Mary or Miriam, the daughter of Amram and sister of Aaron [*Kor* iii 33, xix 23] Stories are told of Him which appear also in the Apocryphal Gospels [*Kor* iii 40, 41], and finally, when the Jews wished to crucify Him, God rescued Him, and substituted another person in His place [*Kor* iii 48, iv 156] while He died a natural death But He will appear again at the last day and destroy Antichrist Baptism and the Holy Eucharist are barely alluded to [ii 132, v 112-115]

OTHER CHARACTERISTICS There are several *festivals* kept by the Moslems The first ten days of Moharram, the first month of the year, are considered as eminently blessed, and are kept with rejoicing Many are in the habit of giving alms on this day The tenth Moharram, as already mentioned, is kept by some as a fast, and by all is held sacred, as the day on which the Prophet's grandson, Hosein, was slain on the plain of Kerbela It is a great day with some orders of dervishes From the third to the twelfth of Rabia I. (the third month), the Prophet's birthday is kept with decorations and great rejoicing, and with chanting the Koran and hymns in honour of Mahomet The eve of the twenty-seventh Rajib (the seventh month), is a festival in honour of the "Miraj"—the Prophet's journey to heaven The eve of the fifteenth Shaban (the eighth month), is kept with solemn reverence as the day on which each person's fate for the year is determined A special form of prayer is used on this night, either at home or in the mosques The two chief festivals are called the two Ids, and by the Turks, the two Bairams The lesser Bairam, or Id-al-Fitr (feast of the breaking of the fast), is immediately after the fast of Ramadhan, on the first three days of Shawal (tenth month) The greater Bairam, Id-al-Kurban, or Id-al-Adha (the feast of the sacrifice), begins the tenth Dzul-Hajjeh, the last month of the year, on which day, that on which the pilgrims at Mecca offer sacrifice, animals are sacrificed, and the meat given to the poor Both feasts are kept with general rejoicing and special public prayers Moslems also visit the tombs of their relations, and have part or all of the Koran recited there There are many festivals kept in honour of the birthdays of saints or "Welis," especially of near relatives of the Prophet. Very great and superstitious reverence, unauthorized by the Koran or traditions, is paid to saints. In fact, Mahomet and the saints are put almost on an equality with God Over the graves of the most celebrated saints mosques are erected, and over all, a small building, which is

[1] For evidence that Mahomet made large and dishonest use of the sacred books of the Sabians and Hanifs, "the Rolls of Abraham and Moses," "the oldest rolls," &c, see Sprenger's *Life of Mohammad*, i 53, *seq*, for Mahomet's instructors, the same, ii 348 390

[2] The Immaculate Conception of the Blessed Virgin Mary is hinted at in *Kor* iii 31, 37

held sacred These sanctuaries are visited to pay honour to the saint, or to obtain his intercession with God for some benefit to the devotee On these occasions prayers are said, parts of the Koran are recited, and votive offerings made *Marriages* are performed in private, with prayers, pious ejaculations, and recitations of the Koran At *burials* there is a service in the mosque, and sometimes a sacrifice is offered at the grave

Islam has no priesthood, nor even a regular order of ministers The Imams who usually lead the public services and preach, generally have other occupations, any competent person may take their place, they may be dismissed from their office, and then lose their title, they have no religious authority, and no official respect The sacrifices are simply commemorative, any person may slay the victims The Ulemas of Constantinople are a corporation of men learned in theology and jurisprudence, who give decisions in cases of conscience, law and religion and public policy, their sentence (Fetwa) has great weight Muftis, or Doctors of Law and Theology, are numerous and much respected, the concurrence of the doctors makes with strict Moslems an article of faith. Orders or societies of persons uniting for devotional purposes are very numerous The members of them are called Dervishes Some of their devotional practices are very strange. Many of them give themselves up to an ascetic life, and live on alms, these are sometimes called Fakirs, and receive much reverence Both the strange devotions and asceticism are the results chiefly of widespread Pantheism (Sufism) among Mahometans, though this theory is utterly at variance with the principles of Islam [Taylor's *Hist Mohamm.* ch. 13, Dollinger, 70-79, Lane, i 304-311, ii 151-154, 168-182, 187-190].

Religious *Sects* among the Mahometans are almost countless The orthodox, or Sonnites, are divided into four sects, named, after their founders, Hanifites, Malekites, Shafeites, and Hanbalites, who differ in some unimportant points of ritual and Koranic interpretation Of the heretical sects, the most important are the Shiites, who reject the first three caliphs as usurpers, holding Ali, and the Imams, his descendants, to be the lawful successors of Mahomet. They also reject the Sonna, accepting in its place four collections of traditions of their own. Shiism is the established religion of Persia, where it has adopted some peculiarities of Zoroastrianism There are several sects of Shiites, some of whom hold the Imams to be incarnations of God The Sufies, who are mystic pantheists, have been mentioned The Babs, a recent sect in Persia, have mixed Christian and Magian doctrines with Islam. The Wahabees, founded by Abd-al-Wahb (died 1787), accept only the Koran and Sonna, and desire to purify Islam from superstitious accretions, saint-worship, &c They have founded a great power in Central Arabia, and have caused much trouble in India by preaching the duty of war against infidels They call orthodox Moslems, with Christians and idolaters, polytheists Many sects differ only in abstruse points regarding God's attributes and predestination, the eternity of the Koran, &c [See Pococke, *Spec Hist Arabum*, 26, 27, 199-327, D'Herbelot, *B O*, under the different names, Sale, *P D*, § 8, Dollinger, 80-133]

The *effects* of Mahometanism, as shewn in life and character, must be briefly noticed The minuteness of the ritual and the social rules, together with the hardness and coldness of the morality taught, produces a great amount of formalism. The name of God and pious ejaculations are constantly on the lips, even in the midst of the most indecent conversation Mahometans often say the "Bismillah" before committing a crime [Sprenger, ii 206] Hence the most scrupulous observance of outward duties is not unfrequently united with the grossest habitual immorality and crime [Dollinger, 26-29], religion and morality seem completely sundered. Another great evil results from the minuteness of the laws concerning marriage and divorce. Many volumes have been written to explain them, entering into the closest and most disgusting details, forming "a mass of corruption, poisoning the mind and morals of every Mahometan student" [Muir, iii 302], and utterly defiling the very language. Hence arises the prevalence not only of most indecent language and conduct, but also of extreme profligacy among both sexes Unnatural vice is fearfully common The pictures of the sensual joys of paradise contribute in some degree to this profligacy; these come to be the chief object of their thoughts, and are anticipated, so far as possible, on earth The doctrine of predestination, or rather fatalism, produces extreme apathy and want of energy in action, while the notion that all Mahometans are God's chosen in a special sense, though causing a deep brotherly feeling among themselves, which is fostered by the precepts on almsgiving, leads them to a bitter contempt and hatred for all other religions

It remains to sum up the good and evil sides of Mahometanism On the one hand, it is a rigid foe to idolatry, as it teaches the unity, perfection, providence and government of God, and hence submission and resignation to His will, together with the great doctrine of a judgment and eternal retribution It inculcates, moreover, brotherly love and union with fellow-believers, and many social virtues, with almsgiving, temperance, and a certain standard of morality On the other hand, it perpetuates the great evils of the East—polygamy, slavery, and absolute despotism, it opposes all political and social progress, while the semi-civilized arbitrary character of its law and justice renders property insecure Its doctrine of propagation by the sword leads to constant wars and rebellions, with an utter contempt for human life It is, in fact, a semi-barbarous religion On its religious side it fails to satisfy the natural longing for some mediation between God and man, while yet it bows before God as an irresistible Power, its morality, in itself defective, is dry, cold, hard, lifeless, without any amiable traits, and, finally, as substituting Mahomet for Christ, it is essentially antichristian While it may be an advance on heathenism, it is an advance which almost excludes the further advance of

Christianity, missionary efforts being almost without result

[Abulfeda, *de Vita et Rebus Gestis Mohammedis* (an Arabic writer of fourteenth century), ed et trans Gagnier, Oxford, 1723 Maracci, *Alcorani textus universus*, Pavia, 1698 Dr G Weil, *Mohammed der Prophet, sein Leben und seine Lehre* Id, *Einleitung in den Koran* Washington Irving, *Life of Mahomet* Caussin de Perceval, *Essai sur l'Histoire des Arabes* Sir W Muir, *Life of Mahomet* Dr A Sprenger, *Life of Mohammed* (in English), part i, Allahabad, 1851 *Das Leben und die Lehre des Mohammad*, 2d ed, Berlin, 1869 Carlyle, *Heroes and Hero Worship*. Syed Ahmed Khan Bahadoor, C S I, *A Series of Essays on the Life of Mohammed, and subjects subsidiary thereto*, vol i, London, 1870 (each Essay is paged separately) Sale, *The Koran*, translated, with notes and a Preliminary Discourse Lane, *Selections from the Kur-an* Rev J M. Rodwell, *The Koran*, translated, with a preface and notes T Noldeke, *Geschichte des Qorans* Forster, *Mahometanism Unveiled* A Geiger, *Was hat Mohammed aus dem Judenthume aufgenommen* H H Milman, *Hist Lat Christianity*, 4th ed. 1867. J M. Neale, *History of the Holy Eastern Church* A P Stanley, *Lectures on the Eastern Church*, 4th ed. W C Taylor, *History of Mohammedanism* D'Herbelot, *Bibliothèque Orientale*. Pococke, *Specimen Historiæ Arabum*, Oxford, 1806 Reland, *de Religione Mohammedicâ* J. G Cazenove, *Mahometanism*, reprinted from the *Christian Remembrancer*, Jan 1855 Mohler, *Ueber das Verhaltniss des Islams zum Evangelium*, in his *Gesammelte Schriften und Aufsatze*, i 348-402 Dollinger, *Muhammed's Religion nach ihrer inneren Entwicklung* Lane, *The Modern Egyptians*, 5th ed 1871 F B Zincke, *Egypt of the Pharaohs and of the Khedivé* W W. Hunter, *The Indian Musalmans*, 2d ed 1872 Articles in the *North British Review*, Jan 1855, Aug 1855, *Quarterly Review*, Oct 1869, vol cxxvii 293-356, *British Quarterly Review*, Jan 1872, vol lv 100-135]

MAJORINI PARS The party of Majorinus This was the name by which the Donatist party in Africa always referred to themselves, before the Catholics had invented the later title by which, in spite of their resentment, they became popularly designated Majorinus was consecrated to the see of Carthage, in opposition to Cæcilian [A D 311], and was the predecessor of Donatus in that episcopate.

MAJORISTS The followers of Major in his controversy with Amsdorf. The seventh volume of Schlusselburg's *Hæreticorum Catalogus* has 859 pages treating "De Secta Majoristorum" [AMSDORFIANS]

MALAKANES, or MOLOKANE A Russian sect, which arose first in the government of Tambof, in the middle of the eighteenth century, and which was so called from their custom of living on milk (Malako), instead of fasting altogether, upon fast-days They call themselves Istineeye Christiane, i e true Christians, and also "Gospellers" A colony of about three thousand Malakanes were settled in the earlier part of this century in the Crimea, where they were visited by Baron Haxthausen [A D 1843], who discovered that, among various erroneous points, they rejected the necessity of Baptism and the Holy Eucharist, as well as the lesser sacraments, explaining away the words which refer to material elements by a spiritualizing interpretation This sect, composed of the lowest and most illiterate peasants, was imposed upon [A D 1833] by a certain Terenti Belioreff, who, claiming to be the Elias, announced the advent of the Millennium within thirty months, the immediate cessation of all business, and the community of goods He then summoned them in large numbers to witness his ascent to heaven like Elijah, but when, upon making the attempt, he fell to the earth instead, he was seized as an impostor and a disturber of the peace, and sent to prison, where he shortly died Many of his followers, to avoid persecution, emigrated to Georgia, where they are said to be still awaiting the promised Millennium The following extracts from their Confession of Faith will shew that, unlike most Russian sects, this one was much akin to modern forms of Protestantism.

Of Baptism "Paul says, Christ did not send me to baptize but to preach we, therefore, understand by the Sacrament of Baptism, not the earthly water, but the spiritual cleansing of our souls from sin in faith, and the destruction of the old Adam within us, with all his works, that we may become clothed anew with a true and perfect life" Of the Ministry "We have a bishop and high-priest in the person of Christ alone, Who has called us all alike" [Haxthausen, *Studien uber Russland*, Hanover, 1847]

MALEBRANCHE Nicholas Malebranche [A D 1638-1715] was born at Paris, and was afflicted from his birth with deformity and disease His theological studies were pursued at the Sorbonne, where he read Eusebius and the other ecclesiastical historians,—while the celebrated father Richard Simon taught him Hebrew and Syriac But all was labour in vain, he confused his roots, applied to one century the events of another, and had a very dim appreciation of the nature of heresy In his twenty-second year he joined the Congregation of the Oratory, but happening to purchase at a bookstall the treatise of Descartes *De Homine*, it took such effect upon him as to cause him to abandon the study of theology, and to devote himself to philosophy as an earnest Cartesian, though prosecuting at the same time mathematical studies

The basis of the creed of Malebranche was the axiom, thoroughly Cartesian in its principle, that our only perception and knowledge of things is in God Knowledge is the solution of the antagonism between the thinking subject and the external object. It can only be this solution by our immanence in God Finite substance remains finite, and eternally distinct from the Absolute, the Absolute is the sole fountain and source of knowledge, which alone can harmonize the antithesis of thought and its object.

A brilliant flash of lightning in the dark night illuminates every object and reveals the distant country as in broad day, and we know the different features of the landscape, but we know it only in the light that is external to ourselves so knowledge, of whatever kind, can only be attained in the Light of the Divine Substance In ourselves we are wholly dark. In the Cartesian system Infinite Substance is a mere copula, whereby the mind acquires a perception of finite substance in its true nature—it is as a mere mathematical point of spirit innate in the mind of man but in the system of Malebranche it widens out Although there can be no interpenetration of mind and matter[1]—the two substances being mutually opposed—yet there can be a true and permanent union between the mind of man and the Absolute, both being of spiritual substance Malebranche declares that he was at times tempted to consider himself and his thoughts as a part of the Divine Nature, which Geulinex before him, and Spinoza afterwards, did not hesitate to affirm He says, for instance, "Je me suis porté à croire que ma substance est éternelle, et que je suis partie de l'être divin, et que toutes mes diverses pensées ne sont que des modifications de la raison universelle" [*Méd Chrét* ix 16] Human reason may coalesce with the Absolute reason from whence it derives its light God knows everything, and we who know God have a true perception of the ideas that God has of all that is Although the spirit, therefore, cannot penetrate material substance so as to gain an objective knowledge of it, yet it has a subjective knowledge of it in a perception of the ideas that God has of it. Such is his theory of vision in God The idea of God therefore teems with the spirits of men, and is the world of ideal existence All our knowledge of things is in the Absolute Substance of God, and since this knowledge as a mode of mind is our very selves, therefore our spirit has an immanence in God; and the subject-matter of our knowledge, that is, the idea of external things, is in God, the Absolute is peopled with spirits and with ideas Absolute Substance, from this point of view, teems with life and reality, while in the Cartesian scheme it is a vast and dreamy void

Malebranche explained our knowledge of a Divine Being as Descartes had done Spiritual and extended material substance are diametrically opposed, therefore the idea of extended matter could never originate in the human spirit. The spirit of man is divided out among the millions of individuals of which the human race consists, an aggregate of being that can never produce unity of idea Hence, any universal sense in which all men are agreed can never have had its source in this herd of spirits, it must be traced to some other source than the mind of man But belief in the existence of God is such a universal sense, for it underlies the consciousness of every human being, and it can only have been communicated by God Himself

Malebranche declared that bodily movement is under the immediate direction of God The notion that the spirit of man should move the body he thought to be a metaphysical difficulty that could not be got over God being the Supreme Cause, there can be no other cause for anything; for, if there were any co-ordinate cause, it would either act in opposition to the Absolute, which is absurd, or in co-operation, which is superfluous, therefore he came to the conclusion that all movement emanates from God I will to move, but God effects the movement, will is suggestive rather than causative of movement It was the occasionalism, again, of Geulincx, whose ideas received a considerable development in Malebranche, the difference between the two being chiefly referable to the difference of their religious belief

Descartes had remained satisfied with demonstrating, by solid reasoning, the existence of a Deity, he rather flinched from discussing the relation that subsists between God and the external creation His treatises declare that the extension of matter is indefinite His letters, in a more pronounced way, laugh at those who circumscribe the work of God within a ball; but he nowhere pushes on the notion of infinitude to duration as well as extension, only when Queen Christina questioned him with respect to the eternity of the world, he declared that the world would never perish, and that as the mind gains wider ideas of the universe, in the same proportion it has reason to praise the Creator in the infinity of His works. As regards the moral government of the world he said that everything is of God—good and evil, fair and foul, true and false From Him it comes that good is good and evil is evil, that murder and incest are crimes, as well as that the radii of a circle are equal, or that the square of the hypotenuse in a right-angled triangle is equal to the squares of perpendicular and base Here Malebranche diverges from the Cartesian theory, and engrafts upon it those Platonic views of the justice and benevolence of the Deity that he derived from Augustine God is the absolute and all-powerful Cause of all, but He is the intelligent and designing Cause, and the happiness of the creature is the final cause of creation He is the universal reason, the Light that lighteth every man that cometh into the world God exists not simply because we have an inborn idea of His power and vastness, but because we believe Him to be holy and just and true, otherwise the Deity would be infinite indeed in power, but no object for the creature's love, and differing in degree only, but not at all in kind from the brute force of nature Benevolence is the general design (volonté générale) of the Divine order of things, though there must of necessity be occasional interruption in its working Rain will fall on barren sands, and fertile tracts are rendered barren by drought. The worst evils of life will befal the good, while the evil prosper. The general

[1] Still it was a favourite speculation with him to refer memory to certain material ἴχνη, or images in the brain, which was nothing else than a feeble compromise between materialism and spiritualism.

rule is only established by such exceptions And, in an ascending scale, the world of grace is ordered by the same general design (volontés générales) as the natural and moral world All is ruled by the same purpose of deep counsel, all proceeds according to one law of general design There is no capricious choice, no blind election The God of theology, as the God of philosophy, is still the same Infinite Being of eternal justice, intelligence and wisdom God moves in simple ways, and those ways, throughout every part of His government, whether in the order of nature or of grace, are general

Are these two orders separate? or are they parts of one system? A knotty point which Malebranche solves through the revealed doctrine of God made Man That which had been always held to be a deep unfathomable mystery was to Malebranche the central sun of his system The Infinite, he said, in calling the universe into existence, could only have proposed to Himself an infinite result The finite is wholly absorbed in His infinity The worlds that teem through space, the spiritual essences which rise in ascending scale from man to God, and far transcend in their worth myriads of worlds, are all as nothing in the Presence of the Infinite But creation, to be worthy of the Creator, must also be infinite Then it was needed that the Creator should impart to it His own infinity of Being, and cause the Eternal Word to descend into it, and become part of it, that the Word should be "made flesh" The Incarnation of the Son of God is the key of the whole mystery, the centre on which everything turns, the answer of Malebranche to Anselm's question, "Cur Deus Homo?" For it raises man, and with man all nature, to the Being of God The several systems of nature, moral order and grace here blend in harmony, the one dominant idea of which is the Divine progression by ways that are at once simple and general The more we know of the laws that govern the universe, the more we perceive that they are simple and harmonious in their design and action, and that they resolve themselves more and more under the comprehensive heading of general laws Organic anatomy demonstrates unity of principle, philology is comparative by reason of the inherent harmony of its parts Extinct fossil species have their counterpart in living organisms, and dead languages, in their broad distinctive features, are one with those of to day Malebranche could only trace the same analogies and wide-spreading laws in the relation subsisting between the Creator and His universe

But such a scheme from a gentle and loving son of the Church was a novelty, and Antoine Arnaud of Port-Royal celebrity, and Bossuet denounced it at once as neoterizing, as contradictory to the Fathers, especially to Augustine, —as chimerical and as subversive of all that had ever been held to be true in theology The most mysterious doctrines, they urged, were submitted to rationalizing investigation, the doctrine of the Incarnation became only an element of the general scheme of creation, and the antagonizing systems of nature and of grace were made to blend together in reciprocating harmony of action. Prophecy, revelation, miracles, which the Church could only refer to the predestined purposes of God, were reduced by Malebranche under the head of general laws and designs Thus Butler also considered that, under the operation of general laws, "five or six thousand years may have given scope for causes, occasions, reasons, or circumstances from whence miraculous interpositions may have arisen" [*Anal* II ii, Ritter, *Gesch d Phil* XI iv 2]

MANICHÆANS Manichæism was the system of religious and philosophical eclecticism founded by an Oriental named Mani, at the commencement of the latter half of the third century A D It rose in Persia during the reign of Sapor II, prince of the dynasty of the Sassanidæ, and spread with extraordinary rapidity through the adjacent provinces of the Roman Empire Much mystery attaches to each phase of its existence, even to the name, pretensions, and death, of its founder, and an almost romantic interest has been thrown around its history by the frequent and sanguinary persecutions it has suffered, and the dark and incredible charges by which those persecutions have been justified

It professed to identify, and was in fact an attempt to harmonize, the dominant principles of Zoroastrianism and Christianity Unlike almost every other form of error, it had the fortune to possess a distinct creed, discipline, and ethical system, the salient features of which have remained constant under all variations of latitude and fortune, and it has thus gained the repute rather of a separate false religion than of the heresy of a sect Its philosophy rested on the purest Dualism of the East, and by its recognition of the complete identity of matter and evil, purported to reduce morality within the domain of physical law Its moral code arrogated the principles of the most elevated virtue, and inculcated the most rigorous asceticism The practice of few sects is entirely adequate to their professions, still it is hard to conceive, as the possible outcome of such a system, the Manichæism described by Leo the Great [Leo *Opp* i *Serm* xxxvi] as the sum of all the profane in paganism, the blind in Judaism, the sacrilegious and blasphemous in all other heresies At no time, indeed, has the purity of its professions saved it from the hatred and contempt of mankind, and yet, despite this hatred, and despite the persecutions of Cæsar and pontiff, this faith, amidst infinite discouragements, preserved, during a thousand years, a vigorous life in Europe, and still, it is alleged, survives in Asia

Mani, as the Orientals write his name—Manes and Manichæus, as the Europeans—was born about A D 240 in Persia, or at least in some district obeying the Persian rule Probably of Magian family, he was certainly educated among, if not admitted to the fellowship of, the Magi, but his native dialect appears nevertheless to have been Chaldee The Greeks (as we read in the *Acta Archelai cum Manete*, n 53, p 97, from whom most of the orthodox writers have borrowed) have a story that his real name was Cubricus or Corbicius, that he was a slave-boy in the house of a widow, to whose bounty he owed both freedom and position, that in the house of this widow died, by diabolical visitation, Terebinthus or Buddas, an arch-heretic, who bequeathed to her his books of impiety (themselves the work of Scythian, a Saracen disciple of Empedocles and an opponent of the Apostles), that Cubricus, taking possession of the heretical library, assumed the mission of the deceased Terebinthus, and thereupon exchanged the name of his servitude for the more honourable one of Manes, or "the eloquent" There are many circumstances calculated to discredit this plausible narrative which is found in the authorities who have followed the *Acta*, but in none others for it is all but impossible that Scythian could have confronted the Apostles, and there is evidence that, of the so-called predecessors who instructed Mani, one at least was a disciple and contemporary Besides, Mani indisputably was admitted to the Magian court of Sapor, where a slave-boy would not readily have found an entrance Finally, the doubtful authenticity of the *Acta* [see *literature* of Manichæism], and the manifest plagiarism of the other authors in whose writings we find this narrative, must destroy our confidence in a story not probable in itself, and altogether at variance with the unsuspected Oriental authorities It is probable that the resemblance between the Oriental "mani" and the Greek "manes," the typical slave-name of Greece, is the parent of this remarkable legend St Augustine tells us that the name of Manes was changed to Manichæus to avoid the preposterous ribaldry of opponents, to which its resemblance to the Greek μανία was found to give occasion The name of Mani, somewhat fancifully connected with the Hebrew "menahem," or "comforter," more probably belongs to the same Sanskrit family with the Greek "manes"

All accounts agree in placing Mani at the court of Sapor in the middle of the third century, and in describing him as learned in all the wisdom of the Magians,—physician, astronomer, artist, philosopher and poet. He found the religion of Zoroaster, which had languished under the Parthian rule, just restored to life and vigour by the successors of Cyrus The sword of Aristotle (so the Persians named the science of the Greeks) had been broken in the strong hands of Artaxerxes, Christianity was groaning under the persecution of Sapor, but Zoroastrianism, in the moment of its triumph over foreign and domestic rivals, was divided into two hostile factions of dogmatic opinion Of these the Magusian, to which Mani was attached, desired to restore the pure primitive faith, which made Ahura-mazda, or Ormuzd, and Angra-mainjus, or Ahriman, (themselves the eidola of the Divine ideas of the Vedas) the sole tenants of the Zoroastrian Olympus The other, or specifically Magian faction, supported the pretensions of a third and superior being, known as Zarvana-akarane, or "Time without bounds" It was a notable moment for a reformer, and Mani came forward, offering Christianity to the Persians as the pure Magusian creed, which the Christians ignorantly followed At first Sapor received his teaching in good part, but nationality and faction were soon arrayed against him, and he escaped with difficulty from the indignation of his countrymen From the court of Sapor he fled northwards into Turkestan His flight was the Hegira of Manichæism From this moment he assumed the prophet and claimed the full rights of an apostle—that apostle, he alleged, through whom was the coming of the Paraclete From the place of his exile missions were despatched to all parts of Asia, reaching, it is said, as far as China and Thibet, and here, with more or less of conscious imposture, he wrote and decorated with pictures or carvings his sacred book, the Ertenghi Mani

From the Christian sources before referred to, comes a tale to the effect that the exile of Mani was due to his want of medical skill, that, called in by Sapor to cure the sickness of his son, and proving unsuccessful, he fled from the anger of the bereaved father Some (Mosheim among the number) have supposed this to be an allegory describing the moral sickness with which the apostatizing son of Sapor was afflicted, a supposition only less improbable than the tale itself The production of the Ertenghi Mani, the same writers tell us, was accompanied by a pretended miracle of a journey to heaven, evidenced by the disappearance of the prophet in a cave, into which he had previously conveyed a large store of provisions, and whence, after the completion of his work, he came forth to the world, announcing it as a gift from the hand of the Deity It may not be unreasonable to suppose that a man persecuted for his life should have spent many months in a cavern in the mountains, nor that the credulous enthusiasm of his followers should have attributed a celestial journey to their martyred teacher, at any rate the legend rests on a very slender foundation of probability

In exile, the heresiarch certainly adapted the Scriptures to his canon, and composed besides certain theological treatises, of which the principal were known as the Mysteries, Chapters, Gospels, and Treasures Such of the rude science and astronomy of the East as was current in Persia was carefully collected by the hands of the immediate followers of Mani, and as they dwelt in exile, far from the Persian centres of learning, this scientific bent must have been given to their labours by the individual influence of their leader They proposed to explain both the origin of things and the nature of the Deity, and propounded a solution of theological doubt as well as a removal of scientific difficulty The testimony of St. Augustine is given to the alluring quality of these pretensions, and at least to the eloquence of the authors who supported them These authors anticipated, by a fortunate guess, the existence of the antipodes, and were among the many speculators respecting the existence and character of purgatory

Followers, and devoted followers, very soon collected around the prophet, and it is particularly noticeable that the preaching of Mani met with this marked success, because, in this early period, Manichæism appears as a belief addressed to the reason of a small and cultivated class rather than one calculated to rouse the enthusiasm of an ignorant multitude From his exile in Turkestan, the preaching of Mani penetrated the Roman Empire of Valerian and Gallienus, and reached the capital and palace of Sapor On the death of that prince, his son and successor, Hormisdas, embraced the heresy and recalled the heresiarch Either to secure his safety, or for convenience in superintending his missions, the prince allowed him to inhabit a strong castle near his western frontier But the reign of Hormisdas lasted less than two years, and on the accession of his successor Varanes, the same Magian jealousy which had caused the exile of Mani successfully contrived his death He was induced to accept a disputation with the Magi, and being declared defeated in the contest, his skin was flayed from his body and his carcase given to the dogs It is not quite clear whether this took place during the short reign of Varanes I or of his successor Varanes II, but the date given to the encounter and the execution is A D 277 This date is the same as that given to the supposed controversy with Archelaus, Bishop of Cascar, according to the doubtful work so entitled, that work, however, ascribes the death of Mani to Sapor, into whose kingdom Mani, although under proscription, is alleged to have withdrawn after his humiliating defeat by the Christian bishop The Orientals ascribe his death to the causes we have mentioned, and in fact to the inconsiderate zeal with which he laboured to introduce Christianity into Zoroastrianism

The death of Mani crowned the edifice of Manichæism, and the fresh Magian persecution, for which it was the signal, dispersed, without disheartening, his followers, who continued the dissemination of their opinions in the countries of their dispersion

The mythological scheme which Mani bequeathed to the world shews Ormuzd, the spirit deity or principle of good, eternally dwelling in his peculiar realm, with five ministers, light, air, fire, bright water, and gentle wind Opposite to him is Ahriman, the author of evil, in a separate dominion, also having five servants, darkness, fire, smoke, foul waters, and tempestuous winds The creatures of the kingdom of Ahriman had always pursued the congenial occupation of internecine strife, in ignorance of the existence of the kingdom of Ormuzd Accident discovered to the powers of darkness the realm of light, it was the signal for its immediate invasion For its defence a spiritual emanation, called "the first man," was produced, under whose guidance the spiritual armies suffered defeat, if not captivity, at the hands of Ahriman As a consequence of this defeat, beings made in the likeness of this Adam, but of evil nature, were in turn produced The contest was soon however renewed by the servants of Ormuzd A further emanation of light, styled "the Spirit of Life," took command of the armies of his defeated predecessor, and obtained a partial success over the creatures of darkness, and the victor was enabled to arrange the particles of evil into such a form, and so to blend the spiritual and the material Adam, that, though temporarily united in this Mezentian embrace of material evil, the light should possess the means of subsequent escape It is to these labours of the Spirit of Life that we owe the condition of the world on which man lives It follows, therefore, that no creation, in the Christian sense, can be predicated of the belief of Mani We have only here a process of mixture by means of which the two opposing elements pervade and permeate each other, so that the existing system partakes of the nature of both To the subjugation of the forces of light by the powers of darkness is attributed the loss of that free will which is the rule of human souls in the pure and spiritual condition From these conquered beings, who by the force or guile of Ahriman underwent the material bondage of the body, the tainted inheritance of the enslaved will has been transmitted In each body of a man thus descended there is a soul of darkness derived from the creations of Ahriman a soul of light from those of Ormuzd, while the body of its own nature is material and vicious Salvation is the freeing of the soul of Ormuzd Ormuzd, the first person of the Christian Trinity, (not in any case to be identified with Jehovah, a subordinate Demiurgic minister of Ahriman), produced (contemporaneously with the production or rather the arrangement of the earth by the Spirit of Life,) the Christ, a spirit of light—misnamed Mithras by the Persians, residing in the sun by His power and in the moon by His wisdom, and the third Divine Person, the Holy Spirit Christ descended upon the earth in a docetic body, to draw upwards the souls of light The sufferings which seemed to mar His divine person were the phantoms of the unpurged material eyesight, and symbolized the dishonour of the material effigy According to Mani, those who confess Christ must renounce Jehovah, the servant of Ahriman and the minister of matter, and by obedience to the law of Christ, as expounded by his prophet, seek the freedom of the immaterial heaven Leaving the vicious earth, the soul which achieves salvation will, after death, undergo a twofold purgation, the first, by water in the moon, whose phases mark the ebb and flow of arriving and departing souls, the second, by fire in the sun The soul that has lived in sin must reenter matter, and there undergo the ordeal of a new life, or if only fit for the Manichæan purgatory, be given over to the demon people of the terrestrial air When all are purified save the irrecoverable, fire will consume the matter of the earth, and Ahriman, with the existences that belong to him, relegated to the proper realm of darkness, will be eternally guarded by the remorseful watchfulness of the damned Holding this bizarre faith, the Manichæans declared themselves orthodox, as Trinitarians, as believers in a final judgment, in a resurrection of the spirit (not, of course, of the body, which they accounted evil), and in a salvation through Christ, dexterously claimed by the advent of His power, not by His sacrifice or expiation

The whole sect was divided into two classes, the elect or perfect, and the auditors or catechumens, a circumstance which gave rise to the mocking accusation, that they possessed an *ecclesia in ecclesiâ* Their hierarchy consisted of twelve magistri or apostles, with a president or successor to Mani, under whom were seventy-two bishops, with presbyters and deacons in descending series All of these were selected from the higher rank of the perfect, though that order included many of the laity, and indeed it is everywhere a note of Manichæism, that it was to the pure life and not to the sacerdotal function that the dignity of "perfection" attached No distinction of sanctity existed between the perfect the priestly office was purely ministerial, and the lay and ecclesiastical members of the order were upon a footing of absolute equality In these democratic elements, or rather in their capacity for democratic development, lies the secret of much of the vitality of Manichæism The perfect were solemnly admitted by a baptism of purification, and to them were confined the highest sacra of their religion They obeyed a rule of the most severe asceticism, were forbidden all animal food (including eggs and milk), wine, and all sensual gratifications, even marriage and the bath were proscribed To till the land, to attend to private or public business, to do anything save to pray, bless, and receive the homage of the catechumens, was to depart from virtue

It is scarcely possible to conceive a system more antagonistic to the Zoroastrian ideal, for the rule of life of the "Destour" enjoins, in the first place, activity and usefulness The saint, as Zoroaster paints him, is an industrious citizen, who begets children, plants trees in bare places, carries water to the dry land, and indeed the Zendavesta tells us, that he who sows the ground with care and diligence acquires a greater store of merit than he who repeats a thousand prayers Such antagonism explains the abhorrence of the Magi, and almost justifies the persecutions of the Sassanidæ The life of the auditor or catechumen was equally inimical to Zoroastrian theory, although rather one of profession than of practice. His rule of morality was the same as that of the perfect, but he enjoyed the license of the weaker nature and was not bound to the ascetic life. Even the elect, unless the final act of lustration had been accomplished, were permitted to retire, if strength failed them, into the humbler condition of the catechumen

The ritual of the Manichæans consisted of daily, almost hourly, prayer and fasting, and the perusal of the Scripture according to their canon, but no special temple was allowed to be devoted to the purposes of worship They used certain hymns, which were however probably recited not sung, addressed, in great part, to certain beings, whose names ὠμόφορος and στεφανόφορος, recall the attributes and functions of angels They turned in prayer to the sun by day and the moon by night, the visible signs of the deity of Ormuzd, the dwellings of the power and wisdom of Christ. Although denying the sacramental efficacy of Baptism, they continued its use as a token of the necessity of purgation, the obligation under which, as they declared, all persons lay of recovering the freedom of the will They certainly used the orthodox invocation, for their apologists appeal to it in proof of their orthodoxy, and the fact that there is no mention of the rebaptism of any converts made by the Christian Church is conclusive of the reputed efficacy of the Manichæan administration of this sacrament Similarly, while wholly denying the sacrifice of the cross, they retained a rite which they termed Eucharistic, but as the cup was filled with water, and the tenor of the service was one of thanksgiving, it cannot be said to have partaken of any sacramental or sacrificial character In addition, these heretics are charged by St. Cyril of Jerusalem and St. Augustine with polluting the Communion under circumstances of the most revolting horror They are alleged to have practised a rite called the ἰσχάς (the name means the wild fig, the symbol of lewdness), which is said to have consisted of a ceremonial pollution of the elements with the vilest products of the human organization The story is in the highest degree improbable The Manichæans at any rate called themselves Christians, and revered the name of Christ The authors best capable of knowing, like St Ephrem (himself an inhabitant of Mesopotamia), altogether ignore it From St Cyril, (who drew his historical information wholly from the *Acta Archelai*, which give no express information on the point,) down to St Augustine, a long line of silent enemies acquit the heretics of the charge Indeed, the general purity of their manners is admitted by many earlier Christians Fortunatus, a Manichæan, in his controversy with St. Augustine, appeals confidently to his opponent's experience during nine years of fellowship, and St Augustine is unable to allege that he had seen anything of a revolting character Again, it is to be noted that St Augustine, when writing to Honoratus, a pagan friend, whom the Saint, while yet a Manichæan, had induced to embrace the heresy, omits to use the obvious and cogent argument to be drawn from the repulsive character of these mysterious rites. This is alone fairly conclusive of the unfounded nature of the charge

The Manichæan Church calendar was simple, all days were by the perfect appropriated to prayer, but the Lord's Day was specially observed by both orders, and kept as a strict fast both by perfect and catechumens Easter, and perhaps Pentecost, was kept as a feast, though Christmas and Lent were seasons of no special significance The great festival was the Bema or Commemoration of the teaching of their founder, which took place near the usual time of Easter, and was so named from the empty chair placed in the room where the solemnity was enacted, symbolizing the authority of the murdered founder of the heresy The Manichæan Scripture canon rejected the Old Testament, as the work of evil inspiration, portions of the Acts of the Apostles, as containing false views of the Paraclete, and certain Epistles Many alterations, the effect of which was to justify the doctrine and discipline of Manichæism, were, under the pretext of removing corruptions, introduced into the Gospels themselves These, the Pauline Epistles, the books of Mani, and perhaps certain of the apocryphal scriptures, said to be the forgeries of Leucius, probably make up the whole of their canon

In allusion to these striking peculiarities of ritual and discipline, the Manichæans received and adopted many strange titles, such are the names σακκόφοροι and ἐγκρατῖται (the penitential and the continent), ἀποτακτικοί and ὑδροπαραστάται (the set apart and the partakers of water), names partly assumed to protect them from notice, partly affixed, in times of persecution, by the contempt of their enemies To these persecutions we owe both our knowledge and ignorance of the early history of the heresy

The troubled state of the Persian religion which marked the moment of Mani's attempt, seemed admirably suited to the rise and development of his more advanced system But success, which priestly jealousy would in any case have made doubtful, national hatred rendered impossible, and though the sword of persecution raised in Persia by Sapor drooped in the hands of his successors (at least until the reigns of Kobad and Yezdeshird), Manichæism soon became the religion of an obscure minority, and purchased by its silence and insignificance a prolonged and ineffectual existence In the empire, on the contrary, the epoch seemed unpropitious The old Gnosticism, which, like the heresy of the Manichæans, was a growth of the Dualistic dogma, had been lately overthrown by the Platonism of Plotinus and the idealism of Origen Christianity, just triumphing over her intellectual adversaries, about to enter upon the dominion of the world, seemed little likely to brook the intrusion of a new and Oriental heresy But on this ground Manichæism was successful. To its faint resemblance to honoured weapons used in the defence of orthodoxy much of this success was due Through the country of the Platonists the heresy flowed rapidly into Western Africa, of all the Churches of Christendom the most prolific both in orthodox and heretical talent—the African apostle of the heresy being one Adimantus or Addas, whose name has been preserved by the fame of his treatise on the disagreement of the Hebrew and Christian Scriptures

In Africa the success of Manichæism was almost national, and it was in Africa that Roman persecution first overtook the Manichæan sectaries A rescript of Diocletian, now generally admitted to be genuine, was the signal for that series of assaults by sovereign princes, which have their crowning victory in the establishment of the Tolosan inquisition But neither in Egypt nor Western Africa was the persecution effectual in stopping the march of the devouring heresy It is curious to observe that the first great convert of these countries, Alexander, is a citizen of Lycopolis, the birth-place and residence of Plotinus During the century succeeding the first inroad of Manichæan teaching, the sectaries appear to have evaded, by policy or obscurity, the special sufferings with which they were afterwards afflicted, or to have been confounded with some others of the innumerable herd of heretics which the orthodoxy of Constantine proscribed Alexander Lycopolitanus, the greatest name of the period, does not seem to have suffered or witnessed persecution, and in the reign of Gratian, just a century after the death of Mani, we find a Manichæan, Sebastian by name, in command of the imperial contingent in Egypt, and continued in high office under succeeding princes; but repressive legislation had then at least begun Valentinian I, with true imperial policy, had declared that all lands or tenements in which a Manichæan should be found were forfeited to the imperial fiscus His coadjutor, the tolerant Gratian, when granting an amnesty to nearly all the sectaries in his dominion, specially excepts these dangerous heretics The edicts of Theodosius decree death to the "perfect," outlawry to the "catechumen" The second Valentinian and Honorius confirm these severe enactments Nor is it from orthodox enmity alone that the Manichæans needed shelter The persecutions of the Vandal kings of Africa drove into Sicily and Italy the remnants of Manichæan vitality, where the acumen of Pope Leo and the ready subservience of Valentinian III were exhausted in the destruction or conversion of the heretics At the instigation of the Roman bishop, a special commission of inquiry was set on foot by the Emperor From such prosecutors we can scarcely expect marked fairness, nor complete justice from such a tribunal, but it is alleged that the guilt of the heretics was ascertained before the most worthy, if not the highest, Roman tribunal, "coram senatu amplissimo," and made plain by the conspicuous evidence of the accused themselves, "manifestâ confessione ipsorum patefacti" We have already quoted the verdict of Leo upon these unhappy religionists The charges made against them, if really substantiated, certainly warranted the imperial severity Not only are they accused of polluting the Eucharistic elements, but the ceremonial violation of a maiden of tender years in the presence of the "perfect" is said to have formed part of their ritual The terms of the edict which Leo obtained from the Emperor are conceived in a sufficiently repressive spirit These heretics are to be banished from the world, they are everywhere to be liable to the penalties of sacrilege, to approve their opinions is to commit a public offence, it is felony to harbour them; no penalties for delation are to attach to their accusers, they are in every case to be deprived of the "testamenti factio" Some dissoluteness of manners may well have arisen within a sect whose constitution was so peculiar as theirs, but it is reasonable to conceive that the eagerness of Christian witnesses and judges confounded some of the viler pagan mysteries with the comparatively innocent profanations of the Manichæans. The heretics bowed to the storm They conformed to certain of the Christian usages, they accepted the orthodox Eucharist, in which however they were not seldom detected by their avoidance of the cup, they changed their names, they forebore their outward observances, and probably in part forgot their meaning. Though incomplete, the work of Leo was not wholly in vain. His letters to the Bishops of Tuscany, Campania and Sicily shew how great an undertaking was the work of extermination. Thirty years after Leo's death his efforts were emulated by Gelasius, but notwithstanding that a century and a half of repression had elapsed before Gregory I ascended the chair of the Roman See, that pontiff had still to complain of the multitude of these heretics, who had in many cases the audacity to occupy the lands of the Church itself. But if the exertions of the Pontiffs and Cæsars had failed to exterminate the sectaries, they had reduced them in the West at least to a body whose exertions were confined chiefly to self-preservation, and who, though they might aspire to the dignity of martyrs, no longer could arrogate the title of apostles.

It is in the early times of these imperial persecutions that Manichæism appears in its most attractive guise. The central figure of the heresy in this period is that of Faustus, Bishop of Milevi in Africa, that "laqueus diaboli" whom St Augustine praises as the most eloquent of preachers. In him we have the type of the perfect Manichæan teacher, as St. Augustine himself is the type of the catechumen. In its progress through the land of the Platonic philosophy, the heresy, although it continued to retain the mystic Oriental mythology of its founder, slowly became adapted to the more rational requirements of Latin civilization. Faustus, African though he was, and though the African sect was reputed one of the most conservative, lays vast stress on morality, little on doctrines. He especially declares that it was by its moral results, by the piety that was the fruit of ascetic teaching, and not by the peculiar doctrine, that they would be judged. In A D 373 St. Augustine was a Manichæan, and for at least nine years afterwards remained in thraldom to the heresy in the condition of a catechumen. We have already described the singular professions of the "perfect." The life of the catechumen, as revealed by St Augustine, is scarcely other than commonplace. Some peculiar cultivation, resulting from their scientific literature, an air of refinement and luxury, not to say of licentiousness, are the distinguishing marks of this ordinary life, while the perilous distinction of less and greater virtue, was, it would seem, already betraying the more ambitious and vigorous portion of the community into a life of cultivated sensualism. But St Augustine had not the temperament which can remain perfectly satisfied with a merely material refinement, and his conversion, which gave to the side of orthodoxy the most vigorous intellect of the century, proved a fatal blow to the heretical cause. Almost the immediate result of this hostility was the deportation of the Manichæan leaders, the total destruction of their sacred books, and the proscription of the sect by the Roman power. Comparative clemency or ineffectiveness must however have on the whole marked these attacks, for the Manichæans fled unhesitatingly from the tender mercies of the Vandal to the proscription of the Roman executive. By that proscription, over which the Great Leo presided, the vigour of the early or Oriental Manichæism was destroyed.

This first period, that of the pure primitive Oriental heresy, commences with the mission of Mani in the third century, and closes with the pontificate of Gregory the Great in the early years of the seventh. After three centuries and a half of active life, we find it depressed, shorn of its special ceremonial, having lost, or in the act of losing, its mythology, its sacred books destroyed, its votaries, both "perfect" and "auditors," conforming to the manners and confounded in the mob of converted heretics. During the next four centuries, in its Italian exile it is slowly being moulded into the more available shape, receiving the more rational ideas, armed with which it was to terrify and to be destroyed by the iron power of Papal Christianity. During this middle period, while the old faith of Mani is slowly yielding up the Oriental and taking in the Western idea, the torch of heresy is successfully borne by the descendants of the Persian Manichæans, who had propagated his errors in the Eastern provinces of the Roman Empire. These heretics became first famous in Cappadocia and Armenia, the place of their rise, but are chiefly associated with Bulgaria, the seat of their exile. They were, however, very different from their African brothers. Policy or conscience had led them both to renounce the name and leadership of Mani, and to reject his more objectionable and complicated dogmas. Indeed, they anticipated and formularized much of that organic change subsequently observed in Western Europe, and present variations, at least in their Bulgarian exile, even more marked than those which are observable in the famous Manichees of the thirteenth century. Fortunately for these earlier heretics, the patriarchal influence at Constantinople was in no wise comparable with the power of the Roman Pontiff, and the doubtful orthodoxy of numerous emperors gave moments of respite from ecclesiastical oppression. Still, though in a feeble way, in its persecution by the Eastern emperors, the history of Paulicianism (for such is the title assumed by this reformed Church of the Manichæans) rehearses the great Albigensian tragedy. This, the second presentation of Manichæism, is its reformed or Eastern development, and the period of its history is from the seventh to the eleventh century. [PAULICIANS.] The third and last phase of the heresy is the Western development. This, which engages attention from the eleventh to the fourteenth century, is a far purer representation of the primitive Manichæism than that of the middle or Paulician period. It has a double origin, the one drawn from the Bulgarian innovators, the other from the primitive remnant in the Italian cities. But the northern stream flowed through an unfavourable country, and was mainly absorbed by the persuasion, or diverted by the persecution, of the Church of Rome Its attenuated bulk became wholly insufficient to preserve any distinctive congenital traits, and it was finally lost in the torrent of Southern Manichæism But before the formulation of the heresy which we afterwards meet with as the Albigensian, its presence is indicated by a series of outbreaks in which traits, more or less Manichæan, are plainly visible The earliest of these cases of reputed Manichæism is that of a peasant of Champagne, one Leutardus, an inhabitant of Virtus, near Chalons-sur-Marne. He is said to have dreamed, while engaged in the agriculture by which he lived, that he was commissioned to introduce a new practice and profession in Christianity Obedient to this vision, he came forward as a preacher, announcing that marriage was unlawful, that the Cross was to be dishonoured, and that no tithes were to be paid He appears to have been sincere, for he divorced his wife, and to have at first earned by his sincerity the contemptuous tolerance of the clergy, but as his following increased rapidly, they were soon compelled to expose his pretensions, and being a poor and ignorant creature he was readily discredited, and fell a victim to his preposterous mania The date of this occurrence is A D 1000 Glaber Radulphus, from whom the story is taken, also gives us full particulars of the more celebrated case of the canons of Orleans, who, twenty-two years later, are said "to have been infected with an Italian heresy" The allusion to Italy, the refuge of the primitive and Oriental heresy, is particularly noteworthy Although the story is variously told, the main features and approximate date can be made out About the year A D 1022, a Society was discovered in Orleans, comprising several of the canons of the Church of St. Croix, and including besides many other persons, chiefly men of noble birth and studious habits They were accused of rejecting the sacraments, and of asserting the viciousness of matter, testified by the same profligacy of ceremonial of which Leo accuses the Italian heretics, with this feature of additional horror, that the bodies of the children, the fruit of their debauchery, were at these orgies calcined, and the fragments distributed by way of Eucharist A pervert discovered their crime, and they all cheerfully suffered the extreme penalty These men are accused of profligacy, but their learning is undoubted, and the two were not generally united in the eleventh century In Lombardy, the heretics, in whom we discover something of Paulician valour, occupied and defended through many weeks the castle of Monteforte, which only yielded to the superior forces of Heribert, the Archbishop of Milan Taken prisoners, they refused to recant, and, with scarcely any exceptions, accepted the stake in preference to Christianity Manichæans they undoubtedly were, holding the peculiar doctrines which spring from the dualistic theory, but we have an express allegation that they believed in the Old Testament They are accused of Judaism and Manichæism, an accusation which must remain unintelligible At Goslar similar scenes were enacted At Arras alone was there any successful attempt at conversion There the eloquent ministration of the Bishop of Cambray subdued the obstinacy of the Manichæans of the district, and the sixteen errors which they recanted are conclusive evidence of their Manichæan origin They are found to reject Baptism and the Lord's Supper, to deny the sanctity of churches, of altars, of relics, to be strenuously opposed to the use of bells and of chanting, to deny the efficacy of ordination, of funeral rites, of penance, of confession, above all, they strictly repudiated the lawfulness of marriage Everywhere the obstinate heretics were punished with death, only one voice, that of Wazon, the Bishop of Liège, being raised on the side of clemency But in the next century Manichæism was in its zenith. Everywhere pursued by the detestation of mankind, the heretics held on their way through Germany, France, England, and Italy At Cologne the populace joined in the outbreak, and flung the heretics into the flames, but the conduct of the perfect, and even of the auditors, astonished and perplexed the judges, who did not however abate the rigour of their sentences In England, indeed, the rising was unimportant, and the heterodox opinions were easily stamped out.

From the executions at Orleans and Milan in A D 1022 and 1031, down to that of Cologne in A D 1163, the chain of persecution is completely continuous, but these persecutions, while they swept away Manichæism from the other districts of Europe, steadily drove downwards within the pale of Albigensian heresy the despairing remnants that escaped the justice of orthodoxy Like their younger and more famous brethren, the Albigenses, they are known by many names, and like all anti-sacerdotal ascetics, rejoiced in the vague appellation of Cathari But one fact of their nomenclature is noteworthy, namely, that these early isolated Manichæans are frequently called "Tisserands," or weavers This seems curiously like an illustration of the democratic tendencies of skilled labour

While the feeble exotic Manichæism of the North was thus dispersed, in the South it culminated in the great Albigensian revolt [ALBIGENSES] This was the final effort of Manichæism, which for a time defied the power of Christianity It was finally crushed, however, in the middle of the fourteenth century, and thenceforth Manichæism appears only as the doubtful parent of the strange sects of the Beghards, Schwestrians, Turlupins, Albati Fratres, and Flagellants, who, in various disguises, penetrated, at a later period, into the France of Philip le Bel, the Italy of Boniface VIII, and the England of the Plantagenets From all these countries the heretics were shortly expelled by the indignation of the people or by the hostility of the government In Bosnia, a doubtful Manichæism, assumably derived from Paulician sources, appears to have maintained itself far into the fifteenth century, but the people were illiterate and barbarous, and their doubtful conversion by Cardinal

Carvalho, which is alleged to have taken place A D 1422, anticipated only by about forty years their destruction by the Ottoman Turks In Bulgaria only a remnant is said to have survived the Turkish wars, and the merit of having brought them back to the fold of orthodox Christianity is claimed by Deodatus, Archbishop of Sophia

We have noted, then, the epoch of the three great waves of this heresy, which are seen to rise against, and be destroyed by contact with, the orthodox religion The great heresy, once the rival of Christianity in Egypt and Africa, the conqueror of the Grecian Church in Bulgaria, and the equal opponent of orthodoxy in Southern France, would seem to be now approaching absolute extinction In modern times the only trace of Manichæism in Europe is found in some savage and idolatrous tribes of the northern frontiers of Turkey (the descendants probably of the fierce Dualists whom the arts and arms of the Comneni failed to convert), but these have long since disowned, or rather have been incapable of comprehending, the tenets of their Manichæan forefathers In Asia, in the Persian highlands, a remnant of primitive heresy is said still to linger among an obscure and predatory population If, therefore, we except these few idolaters in the Bulgarian province, and the wild and treacherous hordes in the Persian mountains, nothing remains of this famous heresy which, in more than one century and in more than one region, menaced the very existence of orthodox Christianity

THE LITERATURE of the ancient MANICHÆISM, once of considerable extent, and including works as well of science as of religion, is now, at least in its original form, wholly lost to us The pitiless, if necessary, advice of St Augustine, to burn the whole of that heretical library, which numbered in Africa alone [St. Aug *contra Faustum,* lxiii 14], "tam multi, tam grandes, tam pretiosi codices," has been but too faithfully obeyed It is only therefore from the fragments selected for confutation by its orthodox opponents, and embedded in the writings of those opponents, that any idea can be gained of the temper and extent of Manichæan culture The most nearly contemporaneous and important work of this character is the piece known as the *Acta disputationis Archelai episcopi Mesopotamiensis cum Manete,* a work from which all writers, other than Orientals, who offer any account of the life and doings of Mani, have very manifestly drawn their information It is said to have been written in Syriac, and translated by an unknown hand into Greek, and thence into Latin It purports to be a relation by Archelaus, Bishop of Cascar or Carchar, of a contest between himself and Mani, as to the rival pretensions of orthodox and Manichæistic Christianity We have before pointed out the improbability, not to say impossibility, of the line of action which it attributes to Mani, its patent error as to the possessor of the Persian sceptre at the date of his execution, and its almost total variance with those Oriental accounts which are wholly free from suspicion. Further objections present themselves in the fact that, while Cascar or Carchar is very distinctly marked in this work as an episcopal town, situate just within the borders of Roman Mesopotamia, and described as a place enjoying all the luxurious civilization belonging to long-continued Roman occupation, research is unable to discover in the topographical records of the district anything at all answering to the description in the *Acta* Three Carcars or Carchars are to be found, none of which are in Mesopotamia, two Cascars, one in Syria, far from the supposed scene of the dispute, the other in the neighbourhood of Seleucia, a Persian city under Persian domination Both Karchesium and Carres have been suggested as names which might obviate these objections, but the city of Archelaus is described as wealthy and populous, and in particular, enthusiastically Christian, whereas Karchesium was a mere barren fortress perched in an angle of the Euphrates, while Carres was perhaps the most intensely pagan town in the Roman Empire Add to this, the contest is unknown to any Oriental writer, the name of Archelaus is unmentioned by Eusebius, by St Ephrem (himself an inhabitant of Mesopotamia), or by Theodoret. it also is omitted from the lists constructed by Photius in the seventh century, and by the learned Ebed-Jesu in the thirteenth century, which contain the names of the faithful who defended orthodoxy from the attacks of Mani We have certainly the express testimony of St Cyril of Jerusalem that he had seen the work, which is his sole guide to the history of the heresiarch, and a similar mention of it by St Epiphanius and St Jerome But such testimony from its nature is worth very little, and under no circumstances is it so noteworthy as the silence of a countryman like St. Ephrem. Finally, Photius distinctly states that Heraclean, Bishop of Chalcedon, whose refutations of Manichæism he praises in the highest terms, had expressly declared that Hegemonius was the author of the *Acta Archelai* [Phot *Cod* 85, 20] The date of this composition is to be found in the *Acta* themselves, where an argument of the falsity of the pretensions of Mani to be the Comforter is founded on the fact that, whereas Christ's promise was immediate, Mani's advent was not till upwards of three hundred years from the death of Christ It would thus seem that this fourth century writer for the moment forgot that Mani and himself were not contemporaries, having forgotten that he had himself fixed the date of the supposed transaction by reference to the reign of Probus [Archel *Acta,* n 27], at the commencement of the last quarter of the third century A D Without laying too much stress on errors of chronology or topographical ignorance, the circumstance that Photius gives us the very explanation which a consideration of the various difficulties would by itself suggest, leads irresistibly to the conviction of the truth of that explanation This shews the work attributed to Archelaus to be a theological essay written by some orthodox Greek, thrown into the form of contemporaneous chronicle, the idea having been no doubt suggested by the fatal Magian controversy and this work, written in the early part of the fourth century A D, and coming, in the unsettled times that followed the death of Constantine, into the hands of St. Cyril, was accepted by him as an authentic record of historical fact. As a nearly contemporaneous recital of the Greek view of Mani's life and character, containing as it does fragments of dogmatic teaching, and in particular a portion of an *Epistola ad Marcellum* attributed to him, the work of course possesses a very high value Besides these *Acta* of Archelaus, the most important original sources of our information are to be found in St. Epiphanius in a portion of a sermon *De fide* attributed to Mani (of doubtful authenticity however), and in the works of St. Augustine The thirty-three books of the latter, *contra Faustum Manichæum*, contain the text of a treatise, or at least one division of a treatise, written by the Manichæan Bishop of Milevi Portions of Manichæan statements are also found in St Augustine's two books, *De Actis cum Felice*, in his work *contra Fortunatum Manichæum*, and that *contra Epistolam fundamenti*, in which last an abstract of the work of Mani is given These, with one other fragment of an epistle contained in St Augustine's piece, *adversus Julianum Pelagianum*, exhaust the list of this heterodox literature The orthodox opinions of the Fathers and philosophers who opposed Manichæism are to be best read in St. Augustine, *de Hæresibus*, in Titus of Bostra, *contra Manichæos*, and in works of similar title and character by Didymus Alexandrinus and Alexander Lycopolitanus, and *passim* in St Epiphanius, Eusebius, Theodoret and Socrates The modern literature of Manichæism is copious but undigested The *Histoire critique de Manichée et du Manichéisme*, by Isaac de Beausobre, Amsterdam 1734, an author whose Protestantism is more decided than his Christianity, is a learned and accurate account of the early history of the heresy, with which, for the same period, may be advantageously compared the history of the Manichæans, contained in vol iv of *Mémoires pour servir à l'histoire ecclésiastique* by Le Nain de Tillemont, Paris, 1701 C W F Walch s *Entwurf einer vollständigen Historie der Ketzereien*, vol i., Nathaniel Lardner's *Credibility of Gospel History*, part ii vol iii, are the most important works on the early period of the subject, and in these the labours of predecessors in this field of inquiry will be found accurately collated and criticized The philosophical aspects of the heresy have deserved and obtained the labour of Ferdinand Christian Baur, in whose *Manichaische Religionssystem* the subject is treated in the most modern spirit, as it is also by G Flugel in in his work, *Mani, seine Lehre und seine Schriften* The Oriental authorities are Hyde, *de vetere Persarum Religione*, D'Herbelot, *Bibliothèque Orientale*, and Pococke's *Specimen Historiæ Arabum* The ecclesiastical histories of Mosheim and Gieseler offer the best general account of Manichæism the latter contains, besides, very full citations from original authors, and provides the reader with an invaluable catalogue of the ancient and modern literature, including that of the middle and later as well as that of the early Manichæism

MARATHONIANS [PNEUMATOMACHI]

MARCELLIANS Marcellus, Bishop of Ancyra in Galatia, and his followers, held a third and advanced stage of Sabellianism For this heresy Marcellus was condemned by several Arian Councils, particularly by that of Constantinople in A D 336 Socrates states that the charge against him was, that he held Christ to be a mere man [*H E* i 36], Sozomenus, no doubt correctly,[1] that he held the Son of God to have His beginning from His birth of the Virgin, and the kingdom of the Son not to be without end [*H E* ii 33] This charge was founded on Marcellus' book against Asterius, an Arian, entitled *de Subjectione Filii Dei* [Hilary, *Frag Hist* ii 22, col 1300, Bened ed] Marcellus, together with Athanasius, was acquitted of heterodoxy at Rome in A D 341, and at the Council of Sardica in 347[2] It may reasonably be thought that Marcellus' judges proceeded rather upon a sense of his opposition to Arianism,[3] and of his connection with Athanasius, than upon any clear and detailed proof of his correctness of doctrine, for from this time the charges against him were taken up by the Catholics, and Athanasius, who long declared him orthodox [*Apolog* 2, *Epist ad sol vit agentes*], was eventually obliged

[1] Thus the charge stands in the decree of the Arian opposition-synod of Sardica, "Marcellus, qui velit Christi Domini regnum perpetuum, æternum et sine tempore, disterminare, initium regnandi accepisse Dominum dicens ante quadringentos annos, finemque ei venturam simul cum mundi occasu Etiam hoc asserere cœpti temeritate conatur, quod in corporis conceptione tunc factus sit imago invisibilis Dei, tuncque et paries et janua et vita effectus" [Hilary, *Frag Hist* iii 2] The contrariety of the Sabellian and Arian heresies is much insisted on by the Catholics "Lis eorum, nostra fides est" And the Semi-Arians in particular were most bitter against the Sabellians It might gain them favour to condemn the opposite heresy

[2] The terms of the acquittal at Sardica may be seen in the Synodical Letter to the Churches in Hilary [*Frag Hist.* ii 6] It is said that Eusebius and his colleagues alleged as Marcellus' own statements what he only proposed as questions It is said also that Marcellus declared in his book that the kingdom of Christ is without beginning and without end Eusebius [*cont Mar* ii 4] allows that the contrary assertion was not made without hesitation Hilary mentions the point [*de Trin* xi 21], but does not name Marcellus After naming and denying this particular charge, the Synod refers to a previous acquittal at Antioch

On another point, the assertion of One God in the sense of denying the eternal Sonship of the Second Person, Hilary refers to Marcellus without naming him, "Impie multos ad unius Dei professionem Galatia nutrivit" [*de Trin* vii 3] To this passage Jerome doubtless refers when, writing of Marcellus, he says, "Sed et Hilarius septimo adversus Arianos libro nominis ejus quasi hæretici meminit" [*de Vir Ill* 86] But in the second book to Constantius Marcellus is named as a heretic The *de Trinitate* was written in Phrygia, the book to Constantius at Constantinople It seems fair to infer that, coming from his banishment, Hilary found the heresy of Marcellus, of which he had himself little doubt before, generally acknowledged

[3] "Maximeque ei a studiis partium innocentia accesserat" [Sulp Sever ii 36]

to suspend him from communion [Sulp Sever. ii 37] A reference to these acquittals and to the subsequent condemnation was made in the Council of Constantinople [A D 869, *Actio* vi], when Zacharias of Chalcedon, on the side of the Photian bishops, urged as an example that Marcellus had been acquitted by Pope Julius and by the Synod of Sardica, yet that he was always considered to be a heretic under anathema It was replied that Marcellus was rightfully and regularly acquitted, because he had anathematized all heresy, and especially that of which he was accused, that when he afterwards returned to his heresy he was anathematized by those who acted with Silvanus, whose decision was ratified by Liberius This was not a condemnation of the act of Julius and the council, but a subsequent proceeding upon Marcellus' change of mind Eusebius' treatises, *contra Marcellum* and *de Ecclesiastica Theologia*, were occasioned by the answer to Asterius, and give in their citations and references "the only existing document of Marcellus' opinions" These opinions are most carefully drawn out by Newman [*Select Treatises of S Athanasius*, p 503], who relates also the connection between Athanasius and Marcellus Newman's statement is as follows

Marcellus held, according to Eusebius, that [1] there was but one person (πρόσωπον) in the Divine Nature, but he differed from Sabellius in maintaining, [2] not that the Father was the Son, and the Son the Father, (which is called the doctrine of the υἱοπάτωρ), but that [3] Father and Son were mere names or titles, and [4] not expressive of essential characteristics,—names or titles given to Almighty God and [5] His eternal Word, on occasion of the Word's appearing in the flesh, in the person or subsistence (ὑπόστασις) of Jesus Christ, the Son of Mary The Word, he considered, was from all eternity in the One God, being analogous to man's reason within him, or the ἐνδιάθετος λόγος of the philosophical schools [6] This One God, or μόνας, has condescended to extend or expand Himself, πλατύνεσθαι, to effect our salvation [7 and 8] The expansion consists in the action, ἐνεργεία, of the λόγος, which then becomes the λόγος προφορικός, or voice of God, instead of the inward reason. [9] The incarnation is a special Divine expansion, viz an expansion in the flesh of Jesus, Son of Mary, [10] in order to which the Word went forth, as at the end of the dispensation He will return Consequently the λόγος is not [11] the Son, nor [12] the Image of God, nor the Christ, nor the First-begotten, nor King, but Jesus is all these, and if these titles are applied to the Word in Scripture they are applied prophetically, in anticipation of His manifestation in the flesh [13] And when He has accomplished the object of His coming, they will cease to apply to Him, for He will leave the flesh, return to God, and be merely the Word as before, and His kingdom, as being the kingdom of the flesh or manhood, will come to an end

It is sufficient to refer to Newman's note for the proofs from Eusebius that Marcellus held these tenets, and for the comparison of the tenets with the arguments of Athanasius in his fourth Oration It is rightly remarked that there is no reason to doubt the correctness of the statement, on account of the Arianizing tendencies of the reporter "Eusebius supports his charges by various extracts from Marcellus' works, and he is corroborated by the testimony of others" But we venture to differ from Newman in this, that we consider a large part of this scheme to be common to Sabellius and Marcellus, and not to belong distinctively to the latter In the article SABELLIANS it is shewn that Father and Son were considered, as regards the Deity itself, to be mere names or titles, and the "Deus protendens usque ad Virginem" to be the Son The Hermogenian notion of Christ leaving His body in the sun, whether or not the Sabellians adopted its terms, agrees in principle with the Marcellian tenet of the Son leaving the flesh, returning to God, and relinquishing the kingdom Marcellus then appears to differ from Sabellius in his modification of the πλατυσμός, by introducing into it the doctrine of the λόγος, the ἐνεργεία of which he considered to constitute the "expansion"

Gieseler [*Comp* i 220] considers very probable the opinion of Baur [*Dreieinigkeit*, i 26], that in the sense of Sabellius (rather we should say of Marcellus) the Logos, in opposition to the Monas, is the manifested God generally, and that the three πρόσωπα are to be considered as the changing forms of the Logos Newman's statement appears to be the better supported of the two. But in whichever form the conception of the Logos was introduced, it creates no essential difference between Sabellianism and Marcellianism, and the general classification of the two as one heresy is perfectly legitimate "Marcellus Sabellianæ hæresis assertor extiterat" [Sulp Sever ii. 37]. The formal condemnation of this heresy by the party of Silvanus, and its ratification by Liberius, has been named The ratification by Liberius [1] is his acceptance of the letters presented by Silvanus, Theophilus and Eustathius, after a series of synods at Lampsacus, Smyrna, and other places, his letter to the Macedonian bishops in reply, his receiving them into communion upon this proof of their adherence to the Nicene faith In the letter of the three bishops, the Marcellians are declared to have been condemned [Socr *H E* iv 12 Whether they were condemned in all the preliminary synods does not appear Silvanus was present at the Synod of Antioch A D 363. Socr *H E* iii 25, Sozom *H E* vi 4]

The Marcellians are condemned in the first Canon of Constantinople [A D 381] They are named after the Sabellians, and are followed by the Photinians They were soon merged into the sect of the Photinians The Allocution of the Council of Chalcedon [A D 451] to the Emperor Marcian [Hardum, *Concil* ii col 645] describes the Monarchianism of Photinus and Marcellus [PHOTINIANS]

[1] Liberius died in September A D 366 Socrates puts this application to him in A D 368 Baronius corrects the error and dates it A D 365

MARCELLINIANS A section of the followers of Carpocrates, who had a woman named Marcellina for their leader Epiphanius speaks of them as worshipping images of Marcellina, and his statement seems to be confirmed by Irenæus and Origen, as well as by the custom of the Carpocratians in worshipping Epiphanes, the son of their founder [Iren i 24 Origen, *conti Cels* v Epiph *Hæres* xxvii.]

MARCIANS [MARCOSIANS]

MARCIONITES, or MARCIONISTS The followers of the famous heretic Marcion of the second century Marcion was a native of Sinope, a wealthy shipmaster [nauclerus, Tertull] Rhodon, a writer of the latter part of the second century calls him the mariner Marcion [*ap* Euseb *H E* v 13] The late and prejudiced writer Epiphanius says that he was the son of a bishop of the Catholic communion, an account which seems at variance with that of Tertullian, who says that he had been a Stoic, and uses several expressions that shew that his conversion to Christianity was at an advanced period in life As little credit is due to the rest of the story of Epiphanius, that Marcion was excommunicated by his own father for seducing a young woman The venerable and orthodox father and the profligate and heretical son formed a good contrast But his great adversary, Tertullian, knows nothing of Marcion's profligacy, though the story is found in the spurious additions to his treatise *de Præsc Hær* c 57 On the contrary, Tertullian calls Marcion *most holy* (sanctissimus), and speaks of the difference between him and his incontinent follower Apelles, whom he calls "Desertor continentiæ Marcionensis" [Tertull *de Præsc Hær* 30]

Marcion left Pontus after being, according to Epiphanius, excommunicated by his father, and came to Rome The date of his coming is involved in the difficulties of the early papal chronology Epiphanius says that it was after the death of Hyginus [A D 142, Tillemont, 132, Bunsen], that is, during the vacancy of the Roman See It was certainly before the year 139, if that be accepted as the date of the Greater Apology of Justin Martyr [Pagi, Neander, Bunsen], for in that Apology he is twice spoken of as then living and teaching in Rome Epiphanius relates that on his arrival he went to the Roman presbytery and demanded the Proedria, that is, the episcopal chair, then vacant, such a demand could hardly have been made by a man of infamous character His wealth also must have been considerable, since, according to Tertullian, he gave to the Roman Church no less a sum than 200,000 sesterces (ducenta sestertia, = about £1670) Being put under examination by the Roman presbyters, he is said to have retorted on them by the question What is the meaning of that saying of our Lord, No man putteth new wine into old bottles? This anecdote, too characteristic not to be true, may explain his non-election. It was such a revelation of what was in Marcion, as could not fail to alarm the Judaizing party prevalent in the Roman Church Epiphanius goes on to say that he left the Roman presbyters with the threat that he would cause a perpetual schism among them, and immediately joined himself with the heretic Cerdo, a Syrian Gnostic then in Rome But the statement that Marcion was merely a revengeful schismatic seems confuted by Tertullian's assertion, that he remained in communion with the Roman Church until the episcopate of Eleutherius, though he was put out of communion more than once (semel atque iterum) As Eleutherius did not come to the Roman See before the year 172 [Bunsen], Marcion remained in communion more or less consistently for at least forty years, that is, during the greater part of his life Tertullian says furthermore, that after Marcion's final excommunication, the large sum of money which he had given to the Roman Church was restored to him, but that, as he expressed penitence, the peace of the Church was offered to him on condition of his bringing back his followers with him, which death prevented him from doing [*de Præsc Hær* 30] The well-known story of Marcion's meeting with Polycarp in Rome, shews the same anxiety to keep from schism When Polycarp visited Rome about the Paschal question, Marcion met him, and asked him to acknowledge him, to which Polycarp replied, I acknowledge the first-born of Satan All this is in accordance with what we know of the practical bent of Marcion, who never elaborated such a system as that of Basilides or Valentinus, a system irreconcilable with Catholic doctrine, but based his peculiar views upon one or two tenets, easily comprehended in any system, and which he strove to get admitted into the Catholic system itself Such a man would be anxious to avoid schism and excommunication above all things

The coming of Marcion to Rome makes up one of those concurrences which belong to the explanation of the historical position of Rome in the Catholic Church The first of these concurrences was the residence there together of St Paul, St Peter and Simon Magus The three great elements of Christian liberty, of liberal yet positive Judaism, and of Gnosticism, met for the first time in Rome in the persons of their original and greatest representatives So, on his arrival, Marcion found there the full-blown Gnosticism of Valentinus and Cerdo, the Alexandrian descendants of Simon Magus through Menander, and he found these teachers spreading themselves in opposition to a Church fixed upon the Judaizing compromise of Peter, while he himself became known as the representative of extreme Paulinism So far as we know, Marcion, whatever phraseology he may have taken in from Valentinus or Cerdo, was not to be regarded as a Gnostic, so far as Gnosticism involved a scholastic system, and still less so far as it revived the esoteric and aristocratically exclusive spirit of the pagan religions His purpose was to reopen the question which seemed in danger of being closed for ever, whether Christianity were reformed Judaism or something distinct from it [Comp Bunsen's *Christianity and Mankind*, v i] He is rightly regarded by Neander as the opposite pole to the Judaizing Clementine Recognitions and Homilies put forth about the middle of the second century, and therefore during his residence in Rome

In re-opening this great question, Marcion unhappily went far beyond the wisdom of St. Paul So far was he from acknowledging the harmony between the Old and New Testaments, or allowing an allegorical interpretation, as St Paul did, that he was led to reject the Old Testament altogether, because in the literal interpretation he found many things contrary to Christianity. For instance he accused the God of the Jews of cruelty in commanding them to tread on the necks of their enemies, and to hang the kings whom they invaded, nor would he allow, as Origen complains, that there could be an allegorical reference to the conquest of spiritual enemies in such a command [Origen, *in Jesu Nave, Hom* xii] Many of the other difficulties that he made bear the stamp of a rugged simplicity of intellect, rather than of the deep and subtle malice with which his orthodox enemies continually charge him

He went on to deny that the two books could have come from the same author The Old Testament was from the God who made the world, the author of evil and fosterer of wars, whom he called the Cosmocrator (Irenæus), or Demiurge, the New Testament was from the Supreme, the Bonus Deus, the Invisible, who having long borne with the works of the Demiurge, at length, in the fulness of time, sent forth His Son to destroy them Tertullian says that Marcion's supreme God, ' better because of His tranquillity, came from the Stoics" [Deus melior de tranquillitate a Stoicis venerat, *de Præsc. Her* 39], and that his whole system was patched together out of different philosophies According to Epiphanius, while Cerdon had two, Marcion had three principles, the third being the Devil, intermediate however between the Bonus Deus and the Demiurge [p 304, ed Petavii, 1622] The principles and details of his system, so far as he had one, are however chiefly interesting as they prompted his evil treatment of the records of Christianity, which seems to have caused him to be more feared and hated than any of the early heretics He regarded Christ as the Son of the invisible and incomprehensible God, and therefore as incorporeal Thus landed in Docetiscm, he was led to mutilate the New Testament as unhesitatingly as he had rejected the Old Of the Gospels, he is said by all the Fathers to have accepted only that according to St Luke, and that much garbled, of the Epistles only those of St Paul, and only ten of them, and those placed in an order of his own, thus Galatians, 1 Corinthians, 2 Corinthians, Romans, 1 Thessalonians, 2 Thessalonians, Ephesians, Colossians, Philippians, Philemon To these he added some portions of a supposed epistle to the Laodiceans He disposed them in two volumes, one of which he called the Evangelium, taking away from the title the name of St Luke, the other the Apostolicum Modern criticism has perhaps disproved that Marcion's Gospel was simply a designed mutilation and garbling of St Luke, but, on the other hand, cannot succeed in proving that it was the original version of the same [See Neander's *Antignostik*]

Of these alleged mutilations and interpolations a long list is given by Epiphanius [i 3] Most of them are referable to Docetic or to Antinomian principles, yet many are slight and trivial, and might be nothing but various readings It is impossible to tell which were due to Marcion himself, and which to his followers In fact, it is impossible to tell to what extent Marcion tampered with the text of Scripture, although it is, at the same time, quite certain that he gave his opponents good reason for charging him with falsification Tertullian goes upon the method of confuting him from what he himself admitted into his canon, and in so doing continually appeals to passages which, on the shewing of Epiphanius, he rejected or garbled Again, it is by no means clear what Epiphanius means by his list It is introduced apparently as a list of passages, corrupted or cut out by Marcion Yet presently in his Scholium of Refutations these passages come over again as if they were common ground to him and his opponent [p 322, Petavii ed Par 1622] Again, after saying with Tertullian that Marcion only received ten of St. Paul's Epistles, he enumerates them all as received by him [p 321] It may be noticed that Irenæus says nothing of the rejection of any of St Paul's Epistles, though he speaks of their mutilation

The choice of St. Luke marks Marcion as the follower of St Paul Irenæus observes that while Marcion kept to St Luke, the Valentinians as generally made use of the Gospel after John It has been argued, that if the latter Gospel had been openly published in the days of Marcion, he would have preferred it to St Luke [C de Bunsen, *Hidden Wisdom of Christ*, ch viii vol i p 477], even though St John wrote against the Docetics

The passages just mentioned in Irenæus can scarcely be held to make against the supposition that St John's Gospel was unknown to Marcion He speaks of Marcion, and then not of Valentinus, but of the Valentinians, a change which is very observable in reading the passage Irenæus may refer to the Commentary on St John by the Valentinian Heracleon in the latter part of the second century. Equally remarkable is the fact, that Marcion gave the first place in his Apostolicum to the Epistle to the Galatians, the most anti-Judaic and independent of St Paul's writings His rejection of the Epistles to Timothy (if true) may be explained perhaps from their directions about marriage and denunciation of forbidding to marry Virginity, fasting, and the Sabbath, says Epiphanius, were enjoined by Marcion ; but the Sabbath was a fast with him, because it was the rest of the Creator

Epiphanius bears witness to the wide extent of Marcion's heresy in Italy, Egypt, Palestine, Arabia, Syria, Cyprus, and Persia

Justin Martyr says that the Marcionites were not persecuted as the Christians were, which may have been because they could not be mistaken for Jews, and also because of the greater openness of their religious worship Baptism, says Epiphanius, was thrice repeated among them, because Jesus twice spoke of having a baptism to be baptized with after His baptism by John St Augustine [*de Bapt* iii 15] seems to imply that they baptized in the Name of the Father, of the Son, and of the Holy Ghost Women were allowed to baptize, to teach, to exorcise, to profess the gift of healing [Tert *de Præsc Hær* 41] The mysteries, says Epiphanius, were celebrated in the presence of the catechumens, and not only before the baptized entitled to communion [*cf* Jerome, *ad Gal* vi 6] Marcion thus appears as the combatant of hierarchical mystery and the advocate of congregational unity The dismissal of the catechumens at a certain point in the divine service he regarded as an innovation foreign to the original simplicity of the Church It was impossible, as Tertullian complains, to distinguish between catechumens and baptized in these celebrations, and if pagans entered, then that which was holy, even though not truly so, was cast to dogs They made peace with everybody, of whatever opinions, it made no difference to them, they ordained everybody They gave offices to neophytes, persons tied to the world, Christian apostates Among them one man was bishop to-day, another to-morrow, the reader to-day, to-morrow would be deacon, to-day a presbyter, to-morrow a layman, for they committed the priestly offices even to laymen [*de Præsc Hær* c 41] Such was Marcion's restoration of the primitive or Pauline simplicity, as related by his great adversary

Marcion denied the resurrection of the body, and, according to Epiphanius, believed in transmigration Of his own works the most important was the Antitheses, or Oppositions between the Old and New Testaments, which is confuted by Tertullian in his fourth book against Marcion Tertullian also mentions an epistle written by him [*de Carne Christi*, c 2] The only fragment of his writings is unfortunately a very brief one, preserved by Hippolytus [Bunsen, *Christ and Mank*, vol. v p 99] The date of his death is unknown [The numerous passages in other ancient writers, besides those who expressly wrote about him, are collected by Ittigius, *de Hæresiarchis*, sect ii c 7, Tillemont, *Mém* ii p 266, Beausobre, *Hist de Manichéisme*, liv iv ch v-viii, Lardner, *Hist of Heretics*, bk ii ch x See also Cave's *Hist Lit ad ann* 128, and Volkmar's *Evangelium Marcions*, 1852]

MARCOSIANS A sect of early Gnostics who were named after Marcus, a contemporary of Colorbasus and Heracleon, and perhaps a disciple of Valentinus Irenæus seems to speak of him, when writing his book on heresies about the year 185, as still living, but also as if he had begun to propagate his heresy many years before

This heretic is called "Marcus the Magician" by Irenæus in the beginning of the preface to his second book, and also "a perfect adept in magical impostures joining the buffooneries of Anaxilaus" [Pliny, *Hist Nat* xxxv 15] "to the craftiness of the Magi" [Iren *adv Hær* I xiii 1] He narrates also that Marcus had, among other women, seduced the wife of "a certain Asiatic, one of our deacons" [*ibid* 5], meaning apparently a deacon of the Church of Ephesus, which was the cradle of that of Lyons, where Irenæus was then writing The strange cabbalistic theory of letters attributed to Marcus appears likely also to have been derived from the system of "Ephesian letters," which formed a conspicuous part of the old Artemisian religion, and this confirms the other indications of an Ephesian origin for the Marcosian heresy Such an origin will also account for the fact, that when Irenæus wrote a considerable number of the Marcosians existed in what he calls "our own district of the Rhone," where many women had been deluded by them [*ibid* 7]

All that we know respecting the heresy of Marcus comes down to us from Irenæus, who wrote at some length about them, evidently influenced by their local association with the district of which he became bishop, and his consequent personal acquaintance with their tenets Hippolytus and Epiphanius reproduced most of what he has said about them, while in Philaster, Augustine, and Theodoret, there are only short summary notices of the sect, gathered out of his account

The first statement of Irenæus respecting Marcus is that he associated magical arts with the rites of Christianity Consecrating cups of mingled wine and water in imitation of the Christian Liturgy (which he is said to have extended to great length), he contrived to give a purple red colour to the fluid, as if Charis, whom he spoke of as one of the highest Æons, had dropped her own blood into the chalice. Again, handing a mixed cup to one of his women disciples, he bade her consecrate it in his presence, and then, producing a larger chalice, he caused the wine and water to be poured from the smaller into the larger vessel, at the same time making the latter overflow with that which was naturally not nearly sufficient to fill it The object of this apparent miracle, Irenæus says, was so to work upon the women as to draw them after him, and he suggests that it was done by the help of a familiar spirit Upon this follow charges of great and systematic licentiousness, on the part both of Marcus and his disciples their conduct being founded on the Antinomian plea, so common in later times, "that they have attained to a height above all power, and that therefore they are free in every respect to act as they please, having no one to fear in anything" For they affirm that because of the "redemption" —by which Harvey supposes they meant a second baptism, which removed them out of the power of the Demiurge—"it has come to pass that they can neither be apprehended nor seen by the judge" [*ibid* 6]

The Marcosian mystery of the alphabet was partly similar in character to the numerical system of the Basilidians and Valentinians, but it was chiefly based on the apocalyptic saying of our Lord, "I am A and Ω" The key to the system seems to be that the letters of particular sacred names were used in such a manner that the name of each letter composing those names was again subdivided into its letters, and those letters set out at length as the foundation of a mystical meaning Thus the name of our Lord being set out in this manner,—

Ἰῶτα	=	10
Ἦτα	=	8
Σίγμα	=	200
Ὄμικρόν	=	70
Ὑψιλόν	=	400
Σίγμα		
Χῖ	=	600
Ῥῶ	=	100
Ἰῶτα		
Σίγμα		
Ταῦ	=	300
Ὄμικρόν		
Σίγμα		

the letters used in the names of the letters composing it, and in the names of the letters of those names, are α γ ε η ι κ λ μ ν ο π ρ σ τ υ φ χ ψ ω, which, with a little manipulation, might be turned into one or more pronounceable though unmeaning words [1] Add to this that the numbers represented by the letters of the sacred name amount to 1688, and it is clear that the field of speculation laid open by this system is infinite, "letters," as Irenæus says, "continually generating other letters, and following one another in constant succession," and numbers arising in a still more prolific manner The Greek Title placed upon the Cross would thus be made to contain all the letters of the alphabet except ζ θ ξ So also the Greek name of the Dove resolved into numerals sums up the same amount as is represented by the two letters in question,—

π	=	80	α	=	1
ε	=	5	ω	=	800
ρ	=	100			801
ι	=	10			
σ	=	200			
τ	=	300			
ε	=	5			
ρ	=	100			
α	=	1			
		801			

and the word being exhaustively treated as before takes in all the letters of the alphabet, except ζ η θ χ It is thus very likely that some recognized title of our Lord might be found, which might by this exhaustive process be made literally to represent the A and Ω in the Marcosian sense

From this alphabetical mystery was developed a system of Tetrads, Ogdoads, Decads, and Duodecads, in which the letters were in a manner personified, representing Æons, and even the Divine Persons themselves, with their attributes And in connection with this theory of letters and numbers Marcosians provided themselves with a cosmogony, and a theory of creation, in which visible things were made to match the images of those that are invisible,—earthly Ogdoads, etc, of heavenly Ogdoads, and all of them proceeding from one supreme Monad

That the Marcosians were ever a large sect does not seem to be likely from the little notice taken of them by writers later than Irenæus. Those in the East were probably absorbed into the great body of the Valentinian Gnostics, while in the West their mysticism was of a kind which was not likely to take hold upon the European mind, and would die out with the generation that imported it

Prædestinatus says that Marcus was confuted before all the people, and afterwards excommunicated, by St Clement of Rome [Prædest *Hær* xiv] St Jerome makes him out to have been a Montanist [Hieron *Ep.* xxix. *Comm in Isaí* lxiv]. Both of these are evidently mistakes either of date or person Philaster and Augustine throw no further light upon his heresy than by saying that he denied the Resurrection.

MARDAITES [Maronites]

MARONITES The ecclesiastical, and now national name, of a Syrian tribe anciently known as the Mardaites, and inhabiting the slopes of Lebanon and Anti-Lebanon Their present name is derived from a monk who probably taught them Christianity early in the eighth century, and who from his monastery of St Maro on the river Orontes was known as John Maro or Marun The Monothelite heresy was at that time prevalent in the Patriarchate of Antioch, and Maro was consecrated bishop by some of the Monothelite bishops, with the title of Patriarch of Antioch, that he might exercise his office as a missionary among the mountain tribes The Maronites were thus Monothelites for five centuries, not becoming Mahometan (as so many Christian nations of the East became under similar circumstances) when they lost their independence by Mahometan conquest under Amurath in A D 992

The Maronites gave up the Monothelite heresy under the influence of Aymeric, their titular Patriarch of Antioch, in the year 1182, and the Latin kingdom of Jerusalem being then established, they entered into communion with the Roman Church, their number being then about 40,000 On the final destruction of that kingdom, two centuries afterwards, the Maronites ceased for some time to have any intercourse with Western Christendom, but were formally reunited to Rome at the Council of Florence [A D 1445] In the following century a Maronite college was founded at Rome [A D 1584], for the education of their clergy, and from it have proceeded several theologians of great eminence, especially the illustrious family of the Assemani, of whom Joseph Simon [A D 1687-1768] and his brother Joseph Aloysius [d A D 1782] are among the greatest of Oriental scholars and liturgical writers.

Although the Maronites are in union with Rome, it has been found expedient to leave them in a condition of unusual independence The election of their Patriarch is left entirely to themselves, and notwithstanding that a synod, held on Sept. 30th, 1736, subscribed to the decrees

[1] Such seem a number of names mentioned by Irenæus as used by the Marcosians,—Basema, Chamosse, Bace naora, Mistadia, Ruada, Kousta, Babaphor, Kalachthei, Messia, Upbareg, Namempsœman, Chaldœaner, Moso medœa, Acphranœ, Psaua, Jesus Nazaria

of the Council of Trent, they retain their own liturgical customs They have bishops at Aleppo, Tripoli, Byblus, Baalbek, Damascus, Cyprus, Berytus and Tyre, and their patriarch resides in the monastery of Karnobin In modern times they have suffered much persecution from the Druses [Le Quien, *Oriens Christ* iii 10 Asseman *Biblioth Orient Vatican* i 487 Neale's *Eastern Ch* Introd i 153]

MARROW MEN In the year 1646, Edward Fisher, a lay member of Brasenose College, Oxford, published a compilation, chiefly from foreign Reformers and Puritan writers, on the subjects of Justification and Sanctification, in the form of a dialogue, which he entitled, *The Marrow of Modern Divinity* About the year 1700, Thomas Boston having met with a copy in a farmhouse, in his then parish of Simprin, Berwickshire, was much attracted by it, and having recommended it to the notice of others, it was reprinted in 1718 at Edinburgh, with a preface by Thomas Hog, minister of Carnock in Fifeshire The book excited considerable notice, and it is said to have been esteemed by many Presbyterians as next in value to the Bible and their Shorter Catechism, but a controversy arising upon some of the points in its teaching, an unfavourable report was made to the General Assembly by a committee appointed to examine it, and on May 20th, 1720, the Assembly formally condemned various propositions which it contained, and prohibited all ministers from using or recommending it The propositions censured were to the following effect [1] That personal assurance is of the essence of faith, faith being a belief that Christ has done all for each individual [2] That Christ made a universal atonement (in sufficiency of merit) for the sins of all men, and that eternal life is offered to all in Him by the Father as by a deed of gift, although He died for the elect only, who were chosen before by an irreversible decree [3] That holiness is not necessary as a condition of salvation (although absolutely necessary as its accompaniment) [4] That fear of punishment and hope of reward ought not to be motives of a believer's obedience [5] That the believer is not under the law as a rule of life With these were condemned various extravagant Antinomian paradoxes, *e g* that the believer does not commit sin, that the Lord sees no sin in him, and is not angry with him for his sins, and that he has no cause to confess his sins or seek for pardon Hereupon, twelve ministers (including Boston and the two Erskines) drew up a *Representation*, complaining of the Act of Assembly, and vindicating the teaching of the *Marrow* from the interpretation put on it, hence they became known in Scottish polemics by the names of *Representers* and *Marrow Men* A somewhat modified or explanatory act was in consequence passed in 1722, but at the same time the prohibition against teaching the condemned propositions was strictly renewed, and the Representers, "because of the injurious reflections contained in their *Representation*," were ordered to be rebuked and admonished by the Moderator, "though their offence deserves a much higher censure" However, as is usual in such cases of ecclesiastical admonition, the Representers only protested against the new act, and forthwith proceeded to disobey it. The controversy, however, gradually died out, but the discontent engendered by it at length found vent in the Secession originated by Ralph and Ebenezer Erskine in 1734

[*Acts of the General Assembly*, *Papers on the Marrow Controversy*, by Dr M'Crie, in the *Edinb Christian Instructor* for 1834, not reprinted in his Works, *State of the Controversy concerning the Marrow, as debated in* 1720 *and* 1721, Glasg 1773, Andr Robertson, *Atonement Controversy in the Secession Church*, Edinb 1846]

MARTINISTS A school of religionists, formed originally by the Chevalier St Martin a few years before the French Revolution broke out, as a kind of Pietistic freemasonry, but afterwards swept into the general tide of Republican infidelity by which France was overwhelmed

St Martin [A D 1743-1804] had originally been brought up to the bar, but exchanged the profession of the law for that of the army Forming some opinions, however, against the lawfulness of war, he left the army and settled down as a private gentleman at Paris There he became acquainted with a Portuguese named Martinez Pasqualis, who had elaborated a peculiar mystical system of Christian philosophy, which seems to have contained a good deal of Cabbalistic Gnosticism, and who afterwards emigrated to St. Domingo, where he died in the year 1799 From the instructions of Martinez, and from his own studies, St Martin became a mystic of the class called Theosophists, and he appears to have been an ardent student of the works of Jacob Boehm and Emanuel Swedenborg His indignation was excited by a work of Boulanger, in which was revived the ancient tenet of Atheists, that all religions have had their origin in the terror of mankind at some great convulsions of nature To this work St Martin replied in 1775, in a volume, an English edition of which was published at Edinburgh, under the title *Error and Truth*, a book written in obscure and mystical language, apparently with the intention of shewing that all true religions contain common elements of Christianity In the preface to this he says, "Though the light be made for all eyes, it is still more certain that all eyes are not made to behold it in its brightness, and the small number of those who are the depositaries of the truths which I announce are bound to prudence and discretion by the strictest engagements Therefore I have allowed myself to use a great reserve in this country, and oftentimes to cover myself with a veil, through which even eyes that are not ordinary ones cannot always pierce, especially as I speak sometimes of something altogether different from that of which I seem to be treating" This reference to a secret understanding between him and his followers led to the supposition that St. Martin was engaged in a revolutionary plot, and it has been asserted that he was connected with the notorious secret society of Jacobins, formed at Avignon by Count Grabianca, a Polish refugee, and the Benedictine monk Pernetty But the secrecy really referred to a new order of freemasonry, with masonic signs, hieroglyphs, &c, of which lodges were formed in several parts of France, especially at Lyons and Montpellier, and by means of which St Martin was endeavouring to spread his theosophy Barruel says that St. Martin's book circulated more widely even than the writings of Voltaire It was especially read by ladies, whose "dressing-rooms were metamorphosed into secret schools, where the interpreting adept developed the mysteries of each page, and the novice in ecstasy applauded the mystery which was hidden from the vulgar Little by little the novice herself became an interpreter, and founded a species of school This is not a mere assertion," continues Barruel, "such schools for the explanation of the code existed at Paris and in the provinces, particularly at Avignon, the headquarters of the Martinists I was and am acquainted with several persons who were introduced to these schools" Such a circulation must have tended greatly to the promotion of infidelity, for, among all its mystical nonsense, the book contains such statements as that man is antecedent to any being in nature, existing in spirit before he existed in body, and being of the same essence as God Himself

After publishing several other works, and extending his societies into Russia, where they were more successful than in France, St Martin printed his last book in the year 1802, entitling it *Ministère de l'homme esprit, par le Philosophe inconnu* This was an attempt to shew that Christianity exists as something separate from the doctrines of the Church, and that the latter are only a means by which to attain the former, that there is in fact, as is so often asserted by Pietists, but so often disproved by the history of religion, an "undogmatic Christianity" which is the true theosophy or knowledge of God.

There is probably no truth in the bitter accusations of Jacobinism which Barruel brings against St Martin, but there can be little doubt that the charges are true as regards those who called themselves after his name [Didot's *Nouv Biogr. Univ* Gregoire's *Hist des Sectes Relig* ii 217 Barruel's *Mémoires du Jacobinisme*, Eng ed ii 339-355]

The Martinists were transplanted to Russia during the reign of Catharine II by Grabianca, already mentioned as one of the Avignon Jacobins, and the Russian Admiral Pleschkeyoff There also they attempted to promote their principles by the formation of masonic lodges and confraternities, and professed to devote themselves to the study of the writings of Swedenborg, Boehm, Ekartshausen, and other mystics A large library was established at Moscow for the purchase, and a printing-press for the publication, of moral and religious literature, to which free access was permitted to young men of talent, who were even searched out and offered pecuniary assistance for the development of their powers But the suspicion of revolutionary societies hung about them, justly or unjustly, and the Empress Catharine persecuted their leading members in various ways Norikoff was imprisoned in a fortress, the wealthy Lapoukhin, Prince Nicholas Trubetzki, and Tourgheneff were banished from Moscow to their own estates, and although under her successors the Emperors Paul I [A D 1796-1801] and Alexander I [A D 1801-1825], rather more liberty was allowed, the whole genius of the Russian nation was against them, and its ecclesiastical conservatism and social traditions have prevailed

MARTIN MARPRELATE [PURITANS]

MARTYRIANI [EUCHITES]

MASBOTHEANS An obscure sect of Jewish freethinkers who denied the Providence of God, said that the world was formed by a spontaneous motion, and denied the immortality of the soul

This statement rests on the authority of the Apostolic Constitutions, and on the assumption that the Basmotheans there named [vi 6] are no other than the Masbotheans This assumption is most probably correct, and if so, the Masbotheans were Jews who had learnt the philosophy of Epicurus. Hegesippus [in Euseb *H E* iv. 22] undoubtedly speaks of a Jewish sect of Masbotheans, but (supposing the text to be correct) his words certainly imply a Christian sect of the same name. Valesius concludes that the text is corrupted Later notices however shew, that in one particular the Masbotheans alleged the authority of our Lord's teaching, and from this may have sprung the notion of a Christian sect of this name Pseudo-Hieronymus mentions the Masbotheans thus, "Masbothei dicunt ipsum esse Christum qui docuit illos in omni re sabbatizare" [*Indic* iii] Isidore of Hispalis repeats the words In this statement there are two difficulties, first, a rigid Sabbatism is quite inconsistent with the denial of the creation of the world and of God's Providence; and secondly, it is not easy to see how our Lord's teaching, by any amount of plausible misrepresentation, could be quoted in favour of it. Instead then of giving up the identification of the Basmotheans and Masbotheans, and asserting the existence of a Judæo-Christian sect of Sabbatarians, distinguished only by the rigour of their Sabbatism from the ordinary practice of the Jewish Christians, it may be allowed us to conjecture that the Masbotheans were the very reverse of rigid Sabbatarians, that they availed themselves of Christ's teaching to proclaim that men are lords of the Sabbath [compare Clem Alexand *Strom* III iv, who says that the Gnostics claimed to be lords of the Sabbath], that their opponents retorted by asserting their Sabbath to be a sabbath of desolation, of Gentile domination, giving it a name from Lament i 7,[1] for in that passage the sabbath which the adversaries derided was the desolation of the land [see 2 Chron xxxvi 21, Lev xxvi 34] From the word signifying "cessationes" the name Masbotheans was given to the sect, and later writers, knowing the derivation of the word from "Sabbath," erroneously imagined Masbotheans to mean Sabbatarians

[1] "Her adversaries did mock at her sabbaths" [Eng vers] "Riserunt de cessationibus ejus O' ἐγέλασαν ἐπὶ κατοικεσίᾳ (alia exempl μετοικεσίᾳ, s τῇ μετοικεσίᾳ) αὐτῆς 'Α . καθέδρᾳ αὐτῆς Σ ἐγέλασαν de abolitione αὐτῆς" [Orig *Hexap in loc* Field's edit.]

MASSALIANS [EUCHITES]
MASSILIANS [BOGOMILES]

MATERIALISTS Materialism reverses the creed of all philosophical systems, which assert that spirit is at least co-eternal with matter, whereas the Materialist affirms matter to be the first and only principle, of which mind is a derived result. Its congener Naturalism endues matter with a soul of life, while Sensualism derives all intellectual and moral phenomena from matter and from the material impressions of sense. The three may be treated as modifications of one principle. Materialism dates from the school of Epicurus. Naturalism, which is only another term for Pantheism, was Spinoza's logical result from the Cartesian theory. He in fact begins where Descartes ends. While Sensualism, as developed by Locke, became the creed of the Encyclopédistes of France in the last century, Materialism may be referred back to its origin through Epicurus [B.C. 300], Leucippus, and Democritus [B.C. 500], to the far more ancient Moschus [Cudworth, *Intell. Syst.* I. i. 10]. Epicurus, however, gave roundness and consistency to the atomic theory, and may be considered virtually to have been its founder, and later Materialists have added little to the principles derived from him. The universe, he said, is atomic; it is uncreate and imperishable.

"Doctum nil posse creari
De nihilo, neque item genita ad nihilum revocari."
[*Lucret.* i. 265.]

There is an infinity of worlds such as ours, and space is boundless. The component elements of all things are indivisible and indestructible atoms. They alone are the first cause of all things. They have from all eternity a gravitating movement through empty space, of infinite swiftness. This movement is the work of blind chance, of which the whole cosmic system is the result. The soul of man is material, and is wholly dissolved by death through a redistribution of its atoms. Modern Materialism accounts for mental phenomena as the products of cerebral organism, chemically acted upon by the phosphates of the blood. Passion and reason are only the result of a congeries of atoms variously combined, and acted upon through chemical affinities. The addition or subtraction of certain elements and properties determine the action of the human machine in the direction of what moralists term respectively virtue and vice.[1] Modern Epicureanism makes bodily sense to be the only source of human knowledge. That alone is infallible and sure, the fountain-head of every mental perception. Generalization is only a memory of many antecedent relative perceptions. These, variously combined, cause the phenomena of judgment, will, determination. The reflective habit of the mind, apart from sensible impression, generates error; sensible impression alone is truth. Bodily sense, physical fact, material impulse, bear the stamp of reality; such notions as soul and spirit begin and end in fallacy. The illogical assumptions of such a system are transparent. From whence did the movement of these atomic corpuscles derive its first impulse, and how can it possibly account for the various phenomena of creation? Whence come memory and mental reflection? How are unalterable mathematical truths to be referred to the impact of bodily sense? How is the religious idea, the birthright alike of savage and of sage, a result of material combination? If this be maintained, then each religious being must have been subject to the same external accidents to be productive of the same internal perception. Whatever occupies space is capable of more or less, and is divisible; how then are these indivisible atoms the tenants of space? They are not to be appreciated by the senses; how then are they the elements of all truth, which it is assumed is only cognizable through the senses? How is life the result of myriads of atoms fortuitously thrown into juxtaposition? If some dead mechanism could possibly result from such chance arrangement, life would still be wanting to it; where, then, in such a system, is there room for the attribute of life? Whence also these teeming proofs of design with which the universe abounds, so far as it can be tested by the human intellect, if blind chance be the universal mother? Could accident be productive of so much regularity? Bodily enjoyment is the mainspring of morality in the Materialist school. Virtue and vice are only the bodily advantage or pain caused by the rewards and punishments awarded by society, with a view to its own ease and comfort.

The Epicurean system was widely prevalent when Christ appeared. Platonic and Peripatetic notions were easily capable of being reconciled with the faith of Christ. Stoic severity was asceticism in the embryo; but Materialism could never harmonize with a true theology. "Let us eat and drink, for to-morrow we die," was the universal maxim; "true," said the Apostle, "and after that the judgment." And it was that sure doctrine of a future life after this world of matter is dissolved that arrested the step of sages and easy-going men of the world, and showed to them a more excellent way than the sensual principles of Epicurus. We owe to Platonic and Pythagorean notions a debt of gratitude in the early ages of the Church, for keeping Materialism in abeyance. In the seventeenth century, Locke's purely objective and sensualistic theory revived more than one principle of the Epicurean philosophy. As in the older system, all thought and knowledge were based upon sensible perception, so also Locke traced both back to the experience of the senses. There is nothing in the intellect, he said,

[1] The banter of Pope scarcely involves greater improbability than the misty reasoning of the Materialist. "We are so much persuaded of the truth of this our hypothesis, that we have employed one of our members, a great virtuoso of Nuremberg, to make a sort of hydraulic engine, in which a chemical liquor resembling blood is driven through elastic channels resembling arteries and veins, by the force of an embolus like the heart, and wrought by a pneumatic machine of the nature of the lungs, with ropes and pulleys, like the nerves, tendons, and muscles; and we are persuaded that this, our artificial man, will not only walk and speak and perform most of the outward actions of the animal life, but, being wound up once a week, will perhaps reason as well as most of your country parsons." [Pope's *Works*, v. 57.]

that was not first in the sense, to which Leibnitz added the rider, "nothing, if you except intellect" But when Locke referred all our ideas to experience, he made a twofold distinction, there is experience of sensation, referring to the external world, and experience of reflection, which is of internal action Hence the mental phenomena of retention, involving attention, memory, reproduction, and discernment, including comparative and complex ideas, abstraction and generalization, hence also the importance of observation, and of variously combining the results of experience in habits of thought We owe to Locke those clearer psychological views that now exist, and for this reason his influence as a teacher is permanent In his essay he determines the nature and limitation of the understanding, a subject that had never yet engaged the attention of the philosopher Yet while he indicates the only safe road of knowledge, he moves along it with an uncertain step, and confines himself to a narrow and exclusive path that is wholly inconsistent with the vastness and grandeur of his general direction. [Cousin, *Ecole Sensualiste*] All idea of God, and of a moral law written on the heart, co-extensive with humanity, and therefore innate in human consciousness, as Descartes taught, is discarded A guiding and overruling Providence is ignored but there was the phenomenon of intellect to be accounted for, and brute matter could never evolve intellect, therefore the notion of Deism was supplemented, cold, unsympathizing and comfortless—a "caput mortuum" of religious belief, a "Deus ex machinâ," because no modern system could stand without it The philosophical notion of a Deity became the involucre of other moral and religious ideas, such as the freedom of human action, the probability first, and then the necessity, of a Divine revelation to help out man's need of a higher knowledge than is attainable through the senses But there was no more substantive relation between the Deism and the intellectual system of Locke than between thought and action in the pre-established harmony of Leibnitz

As Spinoza gave a development to the Cartesian idea that was never intended, so the theory of Locke led to a more open and undisguised advocacy of Materialism by French writers in the second half of the eighteenth century, such as the naturalist Bossuet, Diderot, projector of the Encyclopédie, D'Alembert, Condorcet, who poisoned himself to avoid the guillotine [A D 1794], La Mettrie, the title of whose works sufficiently declare his principles, *The Natural History of the Soul, The Man-Machine, The Man-Plant* Voltaire also was an intense admirer of Locke, and Helvetius exhibited the moral code of sensualism Condillac [born A D 1715, died 1780] presents the exceptional case of a thorough acceptance of the metaphysical principles of Locke, combined with a hearty spiritualism and a higher view of the nature of God and the duties and destiny of man He applied his method to the whole curriculum of human knowledge, and inherited, for a time at least, in the French schools the old Cartesian influence. He represents a school that, adopting his sensualistic basis, by a similar inconsistency remained faithful to every spiritual instinct, the immortality of the soul, and the moral duties of man as a religious being But after his day an undisguised return to Epicurean Materialism became perceptible Thus the Baron Holbach, who died in the first year of the French Revolution, advocated a Materialistic Atheism. The work *Le Système de la Nature, ou des lois du monde physique et moral*, published under a dead name, but written either by or under the guidance of Holbach, was a revival of Democritic Atheism Nothing exists, it says, but matter, which is eternal, and subsists as a vortical motion of infinite atoms Man is wholly material, his soul is the result of bodily organism, thought and will are mere modifications of cerebral matter. Belief in God and in the immateriality of the soul are fond notions that originate in a mistaken resolution of the one incomposite function of nature Man is no more a free agent than an heir of eternity Blind chance is his moving power, and a final resolution into constituent atoms is his ultimate destiny Self interest is the guiding principle of all, and human society is based on the antagonism of conflicting principles Holbach is the unhappy type of many other kindred spirits of the same school

In England, Priestly, as attached to the Encyclopédist school of thought, undertook to demonstrate the materiality of the soul But Locke's system met with a by no means universal acceptance at home Dr S Clarke attacked it on Newtonian principles, Cumberland and Shaftesbury recoiled from the moral conclusions that it indicated, while Berkeley's exaggerated idealism was in direct antagonism to it Hume converted it into a thoroughgoing scepticism that furnished out the more subtle reasonings of Kant The Scotch school followed the theory of Locke, but gave to it a higher tone It is represented by the honoured names, among others, of Reid, Adam Smith, and Dugald Stewart

There can be little doubt but that the tendency of physical investigation is to encourage Materialism. While the inductive mind is only led by such researches to a purer and more spiritual perception of God's ways in the world around it, the mind to which the thought of God is no thought of love sees in the operation of mutually harmonious laws no more than ultimate results, principles that are in themselves all that is divine, necessary antecedents of the inevitable consequence An all-wise benevolent Deity being denied, the spirit of man is also ignored It is only a result of material organism The many know nothing of speculative infidelity, but unfortunately its results are easily massed and assimilated Thus the Materialism of Paris in the last century is producing its fruit in our great centres of industry now To earn, to enjoy, and to die, is accepted as its whole destiny by many a deathless soul It is the mission of the Church to grapple with this gigantic evil, to apply its remedy in giving a better form to the plastic intellect of youth, and to reclaim older hearts, when experience of the unsatisfying nature of the world has prepared the way for God's ordained ministry of discipline

No nearer approach to theoretical Materialism has been made in any English system than in the sensualism of Locke, and it has sunk English thinkers to no lower deep than Deism But Materialistic teaching has pushed itself to the front in Germany An account of the works that advocate it, with their respective answers, may be seen in Fabri's article in Herzog's Encyclopædia

MATHEMATICI Astrologers, "Qui dicunt hominem nasci sub fato, id est, substella" [Ebrard, in *Bibl Max Lugd* xxiv 1575] St Augustine writes, "Those impostors whom they call 'Mathematicians' I consulted without scruple because they seemed to use no sacrifice, nor to pray to any spirit for their divinations which art, however, Christian piety consistently rejects and condemns" [Aug *Conf* iv 3, cf *Civ Dei*, v 5] Philaster mentions, as a distinct heresy, the belief that every man is born under the influence of one or other of the signs of the Zodiac, a notion, he says, derived from the Mathematicians, "illi vanissimi totiusque erroris et sceleris adsertores" [Philast *Hær* cxiii] Priests were forbidden to be Mathematicians by the 36th Canon of Laodicea [circ A D 350]

MATTHIAS OF JANOW One of those earnest preachers of a spiritual reformation who preceded Huss at Prague He was the son of a Bohemian knight, and received a high education in the University of Paris, from which fact he came to be named "Magister Parisiensis" After spending some years in travel, he returned to Prague, and came under the influence of the ascetic preacher MILITZ, upon whose death at Avignon in 1334, Matthias took up his work, though in a more sober spirit He also followed Militz in enjoining frequent communion upon his converts, and although neither of them were Utraquists, their teaching eventually led to the revival of communion in both species Matthias was obliged to retract some of his opinions on the subject before the Synod of Prague which met in the year 1388, and a canon was then enacted forbidding laymen to communicate more frequently than once a month He died in 1394, ten years after Wickliffe (on whose writings his opinions were partly formed), leaving behind him two works on *The Abomination of Desolation in the Church* and on *The Rules of the Old and New Testament* These books both contain many severe censures of the monks and clergy for the corruptions which had grown up in the Church, and are known chiefly through the voluminous summary given in Neander's *Church History*

MAXIMIANI The followers of a Donatist deacon named Maximian, who quarrelled with Primian, the schismatic bishop of Carthage, in the latter part of the fourth century, and who, on being excommunicated at the Donatist Council of Bagai [A D 398], set up a rival sect of his own The main point in which he differed from Donatus was in holding that valid baptism could be administered outside the Donatist communion [Augustine, *de Hæres* 69 *Contra Cresconium Donatist* iv 70]

MECHARISTIANS See APPENDIX

MELCHIORISTS A sect of Strasburg Anabaptists, taking its name from a leader named Melchior Hoffmann They denied the chief point of the doctrine of the Incarnation, namely, that our Lord was made Man "of the substance of His mother" They also held to the ordinary extravagances of the Anabaptists, and after Hoffmann's death, his followers alleged that he would come again before the judgment in company with the prophet Elijah [Paget's *Heresiography*, p 37, ed 1662]

MELCHISEDECHIANS Theodotus the Banker added to the tenets of the Theodotians the following opinion concerning Melchisedech He affirmed that Melchisedech was not a man but a heavenly power, unbegotten (ἀπάτωρ, ἀμήτωρ), located in a supreme but unnamed place, superior to Christ in that He is the mediator and intercessor for angels, whereas Christ is such only for men, the true priest, of whose priesthood the priesthood of Christ was only an inferior copy This tenet formed a branch of the Theodotians into a separate sect The founder of the sect being the younger Theodotus, and the sect being mentioned by Hippolytus, it must be dated about A D 210

What was really meant by an unbegotten heavenly power does not appear Hierax afterwards gave the words the only definite meaning they can bear, and plainly declared Melchisedech to be the Holy Ghost [HIERACITES] So an anonymous author is mentioned by Jerome, who began by asserting Melchisedech to be a divine power, and at last dared to identify him with the Holy Spirit [Hieron *Ep* 126, *ad Evagrium*]

Theodotus' notion is clearly connected with his heresy regarding our Lord [THEODOTIANS], and it is plainly heretical to assert a mediation and priesthood superior to that of Christ's Lardner's remark, therefore, that Epiphanius might as well have made a separate heresy of each of the opinions he has named regarding Melchisedech is unworthy even of a Unitarian Peter Cunæus and Peter du Moulin held Melchisedech to be the Son of God, Hierax, and the author of Questions on the Old and New Testaments,[1] the Holy Ghost, Origen and Didymus, it is said, a created angel, the Samaritans, Shem, Jurieu, Ham, Suidas, of the race of Canaan

The first of these opinions is admissible for trial, inasmuch as a Theophany may be catholically predicated of the Second Person of the Holy Trinity, but on trial it will be found that a Theophany such as others were before the Incarnation will not fulfil the necessary conditions To hold Melchisedech to have been the Son of God must imply a true incarnation, which it would be heretical to assert The second opinion is not even admissible for trial A Theophany of the Holy

[1] Among the spurious works of St Augustine It is often said to be by Hilary the Deacon [Cave, *Hist Liter*, art *Augustinus*]

Spirit cannot be supposed The third opinion is admissible for trial, inasmuch as the appearance of an angel is very conceivable It will be rejected on the ground that, since the Son of God became Mediator and Priest by taking man's nature, the priesthood which was to prefigure His priesthood could not have been that of an angel Opinions of the fourth class are historical speculations [Jerome, *Trad Heb in Genes*]

Timotheus Presbyter alleges that the Melchisedechians were in his time called Athingani, and attributes to them very strict practices respecting the pollution of food by the touch of those who were not of their sect [1] [Hippol *Refut* vii 24 Epiph. *Hær* 55. August. et Prædest. 34. Theod. *Hær fab* ii 6 Pseudo-Tert xxiv]

MELCHITES. A term signifying "royalists," or "followers of the King" (Melcha), and used as a designation for the orthodox Egyptians to distinguish them from the Jacobites It was used by some orthodox writers in the early part of the fifth century, and after the Council of Chalcedon [A D 451] was adopted by the Jacobites as the ordinary name for the orthodox, on the pretence that the latter had accepted the decrees of the council solely on the authority of the Emperor Marcian, by whom the council had been summoned When the Mahometan caliphs became rulers of Egypt, the title thus fastened on and accepted by the orthodox was looked upon as a sign of their adherence to the Eastern emperors, and the Melchites, who had been reduced to a comparatively small number, suffered further troubles on this account In more recent times, the few orthodox Christians of Egypt have given up their independence to so great an extent that the name Melchite has acquired a further meaning, their close connection with the Patriarch of Constantinople making them appear as foreigners, with Greek customs and ceremonial, rather than as native Christians of Egypt [Renaudot's *Hist Patriarch Alex Jacob* Neale's *Hist Patr Alex.*]

MELETIANS A schismatical party in the Church of Alexandria, formed [A D 306] by Meletius, Bishop of Lycopolis in the Thebaid Athanasius, in his Epistle to the bishops of Egypt and Libya, written A D 361, says that the schism had then lasted fifty-five years. No heresy is charged to the sect until after the Council of Nicæa, when the Meletians embraced Arianism, influenced by a common hostility against Athanasius

The schism arose from a refusal of Meletius to submit to a sentence passed on him by his metropolitan, Peter of Alexandria. In a full synod of bishops Meletius was convicted of certain crimes, and particularly of sacrificing He was therefore deposed The sentence, it must be observed, did not imply suspension from communion [see *Apost. Can* 18] Meletius neither appealed to another synod, nor took any pains to vindicate himself, but presently made a schism [Athan] Theodoret gives the same account of the origin of the schism. He writes, that Meletius being convicted of certain crimes, and deposed, would not submit to the sentence, but rebelled against the primacy of Alexandria, and filled the Thebaid and the neighbouring part of Egypt with strife and tumult [*Hist.* i 9] That at an early period he took the final step of schism, by intruding into other dioceses, and erecting altar against altar, is shewn by the letter addressed to him by certain Egyptian bishops who were then in prison. The letter was probably written by Phileas It states, "Qualem etiam commotionen et tristitiam communiter omnibus, et singillatim unicuique, præbuit a te facta ordinatio in paroeciis ad te minime pertinentibus, nec dicere etiam prævalemus"[2] Meletius paid no attention to the remonstrance, but continued his irregular ordinations Consequently, Peter, by letter to the Church of Alexandria, suspended him from communion until the case should be duly heard The result of this hearing we may conclude to be that which is told by Sozomenus [i. 15], that Peter excommunicated the adherents of Meletius, and rejected their baptism The defence set up by Meletius appears to have been, that it was necessary for him to act in Peter's absence, in order that a sufficient supply of clergy might be maintained Peter had fled to avoid persecution, and the Bishop of Lycopolis, ranked next to him, was the first of the suffragans of Alexandria. This plea is answered by the Egyptian bishops in the letter already quoted [Sozom i 24, Routh's *Reliq Sac* iv p 92] The numbers that adhered to Meletius were considerable. Athanasius mentions twenty-eight bishops of his party, but of these the larger number at least were Meletius' own consecration Socrates speaks of his many followers [Socr *H E* I iv] He did not yield therefore to this second sentence, but ordained bishops as well as priests and deacons, and even extended his sect into Palestine, where he visited Jerusalem, Eleutheropolis and Gaza

It will be observed that in these later proceedings against Meletius he is dealt with simply as a schismatic the crimes of which he had been convicted, and the subsequent deposition, are not noticed. Particularly Peter, in his letter to the Alexandrians, charges him, so far as appears, only with coveting the primacy. Whether any doubt had arisen as to the validity of the sentence of deposition, or whether some motive of prudence dictated its suppression, it is impossible to say But Meletius had passed from the simple sin of disobedience to the sentence into the wider sin of creating a schism, and that wider sin appears to have been dealt with exclusively In this light the matter was presented to the Council of

[1] "Melchisedeciani Qui nunc Athingani appellantur Hi videntur quidem servare sabbatum, cum tamen nec carnem circumcidere nec quemquam hominum ipsos tangere permittant sed si quis panem, vel aquam, aut aliud quid dederit, jubent ut is qui dat, deponat humi sicque illi venientes, tollunt ea sed et alios simili impertiunt ratione Unde appellati sunt Athingani, quod non sinant ut quis eos tetigerit" [Timoth Presb Combefis transl p 455]

[2] See the letters in Routh's *Reliq Sac* iv pp 51, 94 "Communiter" in the above quotation is the correction of Maffei, by whom the letters were first printed, for "communionem"

Nicæa, but we can only understand the language of the Council by supposing that it contains at least an allusion to the earlier proceedings The Council declared by canon [Can vi] that the bishop of Alexandria by ancient custom, the maintenance of which it enjoined, had power over the Bishops of Egypt, Libya, and Pentapolis It decreed that Meletius should remain in his own city Lycopolis, retaining the title and dignity of a bishop, but without the power of ordaining, or of promoting any one to an ecclesiastical office, that those whom he had ordained were capable of reordination, and might be so admitted to communion, and to the same grade of the ministry, provided that they always ranked after the clergy of Alexander's ordination They were not to elect to any office in the Church, nor to do any thing without the consent of the Catholic bishop They might, however, be made bishops, if the Bishop of Alexandria should confirm their election by the people [*Synodical Ep to the Church of Alex*, Theod *H E* I ix., Socr *H E* I ix] The Nicene Fathers take credit to themselves for dealing leniently with Meletius This is intelligible only on the supposition that they waived inquiry into the earlier charges Against Meletius and his party, as schismatics, the sentence was not lenient, it was just. It may be contrasted with the terms on which the Church received back the Donatists, whose ordinations were admitted "The Church did not always allow of the ordinations of schismatical or heretical bishops, but sometimes for discipline's sake, and to put a mark of infamy on their errors, made them take a new ordination" [Bingham's example in illustration of this remark in the case of the Meletians] He adds, "In pursuance of this decree, Theodore, Bishop of Oxyrinchus, reordained the Meletian presbyters upon their return to the Church, as Valesius shews out of Marcellinus' and Faustinus' petition to the Emperor Theodosius" [Orig IV vii 7, Valesius, *Not. in Theod H E.* i 9][1] Meletius lived but a few months after the Council of Nicæa During this time, in obedience to the council he remained at Lycopolis, and when Alexander returned to Egypt, restored the churches which had been unjustly taken from him But his obedience was not sincere, for shortly before his death he appointed John Archaph his successor This was contrary to the conciliar decree, and can only have been done from a desire to keep up the schism [Sozom *H E* II xx] Alexander died shortly after Meletius, and in the absence of Athanasius, who was recommended to be his successor, the Meletians consecrated Theonas But Theonas died in three months, and Athanasius was elected [Epiph *Hær* lxviii.]. The Meletians now joined the Arians at the solicitation of Eusebius of Nicomedia, and the larger number of them adopted the Arian heresy [ARIANS], but the schism continued into the fifth century, and adopted childish practices, lustrations, with clapping of hands, dancing with the tinkling of little bells [Theod *Hær fab* iv. 7]

Epiphanius gives an account of the origin of the Meletian schism altogether different from the foregoing He states as follows —In the Diocletian persecution, Peter, Meletius, and other confessors were together in prison Upon the application of certain who had fallen in the persecution to be admitted to penance, disputes arose regarding their reception Meletius, Peleas, and very many others, held, that when the persecution had ceased, they might be received after a fitting period of penance, but the clergy to lay-communion only Peter, on the other hand, thought they might be admitted immediately upon repentance The separation was caused by Peter rather than by Meletius, for Peter called for a division "Let those who think with me stand by me"—from which time they refused to communicate with one another When Peter was put to death, and Alexander succeeded him, Meletius was sent to the Phœnician mines in Arabia Petræa[2] In his journey he ordained bishops, priests, and deacons wherever he could When liberated from the mines, he lived in friendship with Alexander, to whom he reported the heretical teaching of Arius After the death of Meletius, Alexander began to persecute the Meletians, upon which, through the intervention of Eusebius of Nicomedia, they joined the Arians

Epiphanius' authority for this statement is not given Athanasius, from his friendship with Alexander, and his possession of the records of the see, had the best possible means of information It is a singular estimate of evidence which sets aside his testimony on the authority of Epiphanius' anonymous report Lardner remarks that Athanasius was prejudiced, and wrote in a passion, while he gravely adduces, on the other side, Meletius' testimony in his own favour; "Meletius always complained of injustice" [*Credib* ch lxi] But there are several things in Epiphanius' statement inconsistent with documentary evidence He reports that the schism was formed while Meletius was a prisoner The letter of the Egyptian bishops is addressed to Meletius at liberty The report of Peter's dealing with the lapsed is inconsistent with Peter's own canons [See Nat Alexander, vol vii diss viii Routh, *Rel Sacr* iv pp 105-111]

MELETIANS OF ANTIOCH One of the two communions into which the orthodox of the Church of Antioch were divided from about A D 360 to A D 393 The other communion was that of the Eustathians Theologically, they differed only in the use of the terms employed in stating the doctrine of the Holy Trinity, the Meletians following the Eastern usage, the Eustathians the Western usage This difference of usage was not the cause of the separation of the two bodies, but was superadded to the schism The schism resulted

[1] Valesius [in note *b* on Socr I ix] comments on the leniency of Meletius' sentence, but in note *g* he writes, "Porro notandum est, Melitium, utpote auctorem schismatis, durius tractatum esse quam Melitianos Omnem enim episcopalem functionem ademerunt Melitio Nicæni Patres, solum ei nomen Episcopi relinquentes."

[2] Epiphanius takes no notice of Achillas, Peter's immediate successor

from Meletius, a prelate of the Arian party, being deposed for avowing the Nicene faith, and gathering round him some of the old orthodox party The circumstances were as follows.—

In the year 329, Eustathius, a Catholic, was in rightful possession of the see of Antioch In A D 330 or 331 he was deposed, uncanonically, on calumnious charges by the prevailing Arian party, and a series of Arian prelates succeeded Besides their heresy these prelates were intruders. Many of the orthodox seceded from their communion, but some submitted, and kept alive an orthodox party in the midst of the Arian communion About A D. 360, Meletius, Bishop of Sebaste, was appointed to the see of Antioch. He had been brought up in the Arian party, and was thought to belong to it, but at his installation, or some other solemn occasion soon after his appointment, he professed publicly the Nicene faith, accurately fixing the meaning of his expressions, although avoiding the use of the word Homoousion Upon this he was banished, and a new prelate, Euzoius, was appointed [1] Eustathius had died before the appointment of Meletius Thus, at the accession of Julian, the Arian Euzoius was in possession of the see and of the churches of Antioch, the line of bishops from whom he derived his mission being originally intruders, and he himself again an intruder, Meletius having been wrongfully deposed Of the orthodox there were two parties First, the old adherents of Eustathius, now without a bishop, but keeping together under Paulinus, a presbyter ordained by Eustathius These did not wish to join the communion of Meletius, although he had disclaimed Arianism, not only because he had been brought up an Arian, but because his appointment to Antioch was by intruding bishops And, secondly, the adherents of Meletius, who could aver that they had an orthodox bishop, whose title was undoubtedly preferable to that of Euzoius, while the Eustathians had not kept up the episcopal succession An edict of Julian allowed the banished bishops to return home. Several bishops, Lucifer of Cagliari, Eusebius of Vercellæ, Hilary of Poitiers, and others [Theod. iii 4], on their return met in consultation on the state of the Church [Socr iii. 5, 6]. They agreed that Eusebius should proceed to Alexandria to join Athanasius and assist him in summoning a synod to confirm the decrees of Nicæa, and that Lucifer should go to Antioch The way of reconciliation at Antioch was open. It was in the power of the representatives of the Catholic Church to heal the breach, by recognizing Meletius, whose consecration was valid, and joining his communion [2] It was in the power of the Church, as Eustathius had no successor, to condone the original intrusion of the line of bishops from whom Meletius derived his succession But as if the original entanglement were not sufficient, Lucifer added to it Together with Cymatius and Anatolius, Bishops of Paltus and Berœa, he consecrated Paulinus for the Eustathians, thus setting up an orthodox competitor to Meletius, and consolidating by opposition the Meletian schism Meletius, on his return, found Paulinus consecrated, and as his adherents would not recognise Paulinus, he put himself again at their head The schism was thus fully formed, altar against altar Paulinus sent his legates, Maximus and Calemerus, to the Alexandrian synod It appears that the synod received them, thus recognising Paulinus' title

The synod, breaking up after consultation, left it in charge to Athanasius and a few bishops who remained at Alexandria to write to the bishops collected at Antioch, that is, to the three consecrators of Paulinus, and Eusebius and Asterius who had left Alexandria for Antioch Athanasius did so, and urged these bishops to strive to unite the dissentient parties especially to bring over, if possible, τοὺς ἐν τῇ παλαιᾷ συναγομένους, those who assembled in the old city, *i e.* the Meletians But there were now three competing bishops in the city, and the dissension, which had run its course and was dying of itself, was reanimated Eusebius retired in disgust, and the schism was left to its new career

The Arians continued in possession of all the churches of the city except one, which Paulinus had been allowed to retain The Meletians met outside the city walls [Socr iii 9] Valens, baptized by the Arian Eudoxius, pledged himself to uphold their cause, and among other orthodox bishops he banished Meletius On the accession of Gratian [A D 378] Meletius was recalled [Theod iv 13, v 2, 3, Sozom vii 3, Socr v 5], and the churches which had been held by the Arians were restored to him [Theod v 3] By this the Meletian party was put in the position of the established Church Meletius now made overtures to Paulinus, and an agreement was concluded that the schism should cease by the common recognition of the survivor of the two On Meletius' death, however, his party did not keep to the agreement, but consecrated Flavian On the death of Paulinus, Evagrius was consecrated He lived but a few years Jerome mentions him as alive in A D 392 St Chrysostom took the opportunity of his death to end the schism, by bringing the parties into communion under Flavian

In which of these two lines of bishops the right to the throne of Antioch was really vested it is difficult to determine Assuming that Eustathius was the rightful bishop, and that Meletius' claim was preferable to that of Euzoius, the question narrows itself to this, whether, after Eustathius' death, without a successor in his line, the party which had adhered to him so fully represented the Catholic Church of Antioch as to be entitled to proceed to a fresh election, and call in a metropolitan of another patriarchate (Cagliari was a metropolis in the patriarchate of Rome), to supply from a new source a new line of conse-

[1] Regarding Euzoius, see Jerome, *adv Lucifer* Opp i p 169, B ed 1616 Jerome omits Meletius, as if his episcopacy were not allowed, and makes Euzoius succeed the Arian Eudoxius

[2] It is sometimes said, particularly by Newman [*Hist of Arians*, p 387], that the Council of Alexandria recommended this course, and that their commission arriving at Antioch, found Paulinus already consecrated, the consecration having taken place without their knowledge This is inconsistent with the fact that the legates of Paulinus signed the letter of Athanasius We have followed Valesius' Notes to Socr iii 5 and 6

crations According to the order of the Church, the bishops of the province should have been applied to, and Lucifer's act must needs be judged intrusive However, Athanasius and the Egyptian Churches, the Western Church generally, and the Churches of Cyprus, upheld Paulinus' title the Orientals took part with the Meletians

There is no doubt that both Eustathians and Meletians held substantially the Catholic faith regarding the Holy Trinity, and differed only in the terms which they thought most suitable to express its doctrine The Meletians believed that they must abide by the formula of Three Hypostases, while the Eustathians would only acknowledge Three Prosopa [DICT *of* THEOL, HYPOSTASIS] Thus the usages of the East and West confronted each other, the Church of Antioch being as it were the stage upon which the two parties in dispute were represented, the Meletians siding with the orthodox of the East, and the Eustathians with those of the West The Council of Alexandria agreed that the language of the Nicene Creed was the more desirable and accurate. But the verbal controversy had been taken up and was carried on, not in an unimpassioned endeavour to ascertain correct forms of doctrine, but as furnishing watchwords for the contending parties in a schism, and it ceased only when the Eustathians were finally absorbed by the larger and more powerful body

MELITONIANS [ANTHROPOMORPHITES HOMUNCIONITÆ]

MEN, THE This title is one popularly given, in certain districts of the Scottish Highlands, to a class of lay preachers and catechists Owing to lack of pastoral superintendence, through the latter part of the last century and the beginning of this, in the more remote parts, specially in Ross, Sutherland, Caithness, Argyle, and the Isle of Skye, and to the deficiency of Gaelic Bibles, which were too costly in price for general possession, lay-helpers were appointed to hold meetings for exposition and prayer These persons themselves used the English Bible, and from it made extempore Gaelic translations, a practice which admitted of considerable and fervid "embellishment," as well as of departures from received interpretation, insomuch that it was no uncommon thing for the better educated among their hearers to maintain that the Bible then in use was quite different from that to which they had formerly been accustomed The new light thus shed upon Holy Scripture proved very attractive, the meetings were thronged, the powers of the catechists gradually developed, their office became more recognised, their ministrations more varied and more valued Doubtless in many cases these ministrations were greatly blessed in the awakening of the careless and in reaching neglected districts, but the general result was that a class of illiterate, self-appointed teachers sprang up, whose only claim to office rested upon their self-stated "experience" and the display of their "superior gifts" These gifts they had special opportunities for displaying at the funeral services, or "lykewakes," held in private houses, and at the "sacramental occasions," or preparatory services on the Friday before the periodical Communion This day is still popularly called "the Men's Day" On it perhaps twenty or thirty Men from different parishes may be present, who engross all the public services, permitting the parish minister only to sum up their exhortations at the close But sometimes The Men have (like the Wesleyan preachers in England, to whom in origin and history they bear a strong resemblance) carried on their own ministrations in direct opposition to the Kirk It is stated in a tract (published at Glasgow about 1840), containing an account of a revival of religion in the Isle of Skye in 1812-1814, which owed its origin to the labours of one of these preachers, that there followed from this awakening an "entire abandonment of ordinances." The "professors," as The Men are there called, "lifted their protest against the clergy by refusing to accept ordinances as by them administered Hence it soon ceased to be matter of reproach to live in the non-enjoyment of ordinances More than this, it came to be counted an evidence of seriousness not to apply to the clergy, or a mark of carelessness and irreligion when application was made" A curious instance of the narrow ignorance and intense presumption which were compatible with a reputation for the greatest sanctity and insight into spiritual things, is afforded by the "Dying Testimony" of a leading Man, one Alex Campbell, published in 1824, which, after generally denouncing the Kirk, the King, the Cameronians, and everybody and everything not agreeable to his judgment, ends with a sweeping and indiscriminating testimony against "Quakers, Tabernacle folk, Haldians, Independents, Anabaptists, Antiburghers, Burghers, Chapels of Ease, Relief, Roman Catholics, Socinians, Prelacy, Arminians, Deists, Atheists, Universalists, New Jerusalemites, Unitarians, Methodists, Bereans, Glassites, *and all sectarians*"

The dress of The Men is distinctive They generally wear, when engaged in religious exercises, a large blue cloak, a revival of that which St Paul left at Troas, but which is claimed by another school as the prototype of the chasuble But a peculiar head-gear is a still more usual characteristic In Skye they wear red, striped, or blue woollen night-caps, elsewhere, coloured or spotted handkerchiefs, which gradually, as higher degrees of sanctity are reached and the stains of earth are removed, give place to napkins of white

It is said that since the establishment of the Free Kirk, the influence of The Men has been greatly on the wane. [*Quart. Rev*, Sept. 1851, *Puritanism in the Highlands* Eadie's *Eccles Cyclop Brit and For Evang Rev*, July 1872, *The Religion of the Highlands*, referring to books in favour of The Men]

MEN OF UNDERSTANDING This name was assumed by a set of fanatics who appear to have been a branch of the Brethren of the Free Spirit They appeared in the Netherlands, chiefly at Brussels, about the year 1411, under the leadership of an illiterate man named Giles the Singer, and of a Carmelite monk named William of Hildesheim or Hildeinssen. Giles appears to have taken up the position of a false Christ, making the blasphemous declaration, "I am the Saviour of men, by me men shall see Christ, as by Christ they see the Father" This perhaps was the broad and ignorant form of the fanaticism Its more intelligent side seems to have been a modification of the theory of the JOACHIMITES, that the time of the Jews was that in which the Father ruled the Church, the times from Christ to their own that in which the Son ruled, and that thenceforward the Church was under the rule of the Holy Spirit, with whom they associated or identified the prophet Elijah These latter days they maintained to be a time of higher illumination than any which had preceded, an illumination which practically superseded Holy Scripture, and established a new dispensation of spiritual liberty. Among other opinions which they added on to this fundamental one, they maintained that the only resurrection of the body which would ever take place, had taken place already in that of Christ, that the spirit is not defiled by bodily sin, that the punishments of hell are not eternal, and that even the evil angels would be eventually saved [Baluze, *Miscell* ii 277]

MENANDRIANS The followers of Menander, one of the primitive heretics or false Christs of sub-apostolic times The sect was the latest of the three Samaritan sects which contributed so much to the formation of Gnosticism, coming between the schools of Simon Magus and of Saturninus and its origin dating about A D 75 Pearson held that Menander flourished under Vespasian [Pearson's *Vindic Ignat* ii 7]

The common consent of antiquity connects Menander closely with Simon Magus Justin Martyr [*First Apol* xxvi] and the appendix to Tertullian's *de Præscr* call him Simon's disciple, Irenæus [i 23] and Eusebius [*Hist Eccl* iii 26] Simon's successor He was a Samaritan of the town Capparetæa or Chabrai [Theod *Hær fab* i 2], an adept in magic, which he practised with success at Antioch He taught that the Primary Power continued unknown to all, that the world was made by Angels, whom (like Simon) he maintained to have been produced by Ennoia He professed himself to have been sent forth from the presence of the invisible beings as a saviour for the deliverance of men from the power of the demiurgic angels He promised by means of magic to give men knowledge to overcome those angels, to obtain the resurrection, and to remain in possession of undying youth For this purpose he baptized men in his own name What Simon had professed to be, Menander also in turn professed to be, or rather gave himself out to be greater than Simon [Epiph *Hær* xxii]

The Fathers, from whom these particulars have been gathered, certainly understood the immortality promised by Menander to have been in this world [see particularly, Tertull *de Anima*, p 349, edit. 1641] Walch thinks that they must have been mistaken, but even such an excess of folly or imposture is not incredible Epiphanius, in his abstract, remarks that in some points Menander differed from his master, but he does not state the differences The doctrine of evil demiurgic angels is certainly not the doctrine of Simon's "Announcement," but some reasons have been given in the article on "Simonians," for thinking that Simon may in latter years have adopted this doctrine, and deserted the Cabbala. In this doctrine is involved the principle of the inherent evil of matter, and the author of Prædestinatus states that Pope Linus condemned the Menandrians for this tenet He states also that Linus excommunicated them (a consortio conversationis nostræ ejectos æterna damnatione multavit) He therefore took them to be Christian heretics, but this is probably an error Mosheim believes the opinion that Menander was a disciple of Simon to have no other foundation than the general notion that all the various sects of Gnostics derived their origin from that magician, which notion he asserts to be entirely groundless. But the notion is not likely to be groundless with regard to the Samaritan Gnostics, and Justin Martyr's assertion is probably well founded Gieseler concludes that the three Samaritan sects continued for several centuries [Gieseler's *Eccl Hist* i 50], Mosheim, that the Menandrians existed but for a short period, and appear to have been always confined within very narrow limits [Mosheim, *de Rebus Christ* Vidal's tr i 335] Certainly the sect is little noticed by historians It was probably merged in the later Gnostic sects [SIMONIANS]

MENDÆANS An ancient Eastern sect found in the borders of Persia and Arabia, but chiefly at Bassora and the district around, who profess to be "Mendai Ijahi," or "Disciples of St. John" the Baptist. They are called "Christians of St John" by many European writers, and "Sabians" or "Tsabians" by the Mahometans

The origin of the Mendæans is involved in obscurity Some writers associate them with the idolatrous Sabæans out of whom the Mahometans sprung [MAHOMETANS] They themselves allege that they are Hebrews A Carmelite named Ignatius à Jesu, who lived near them as a missionary to the Chaldæan Nestorians for forty years [A D 1622-1662], believed them to be truly descended from some of the original disciples of St John, and compares their name with that of the Christians of St Thomas on the coast of Malabar, whose claim to be descended from some of the original converts of the Apostle St Thomas is generally allowed It seems not unlikely that some of John the Baptist's converts may never have heard of Apostolic Christianity A quarter of a century after the Day of Pentecost there were "certain disciples" at Ephesus, who, as had recently been the case with Apollos, knew "only the baptism of John" into which they had been baptized, and had not so much as heard of the great event of Pentecost [Acts xviii 25, xix 1, 5] and if this could be the case at Alexandria or Ephesus it was far more likely to be so in the deserts of Arabia, where indeed Christianity never made any great progress It is not unreasonable therefore to conclude that the modern Sabians or Mendæans are descendants of some of the ancient Arabian descendants of Abraham who had been converted from Sabæan idolatry and had been baptized by St John the Baptist, but who were never brought under the influence of Apostolic Christianity To the descendants of such men the Baptist himself would seem to be "that Christ" which he was supposed to be by some even in his lifetime, and the influence of later Christianity upon them would be analogous in its results to those which were produced upon the early Mahometans, though of a far higher character, because building on a better foundation

These half Christians are said by Ignatius à Jesu to have imitations or perversions of the Christian Sacraments They administer baptism on Sunday only, with a liturgy, and by semi-immersion in a flowing stream, water being poured thrice on the head of the child "In the name of the Lord Himself, the First and the Last, the Lord of the world, and of Paradise, of Him Who is above all and Creator of all"[1] For their Eucharist they use wafers composed of flour, wine, and oil, the other element being a kind of wine made by steeping dry grapes in water the same which is used also for making the wafers They maintain a line of bishops and priests, in which the Levitical system of lineal descent is kept up, the nearest relative being elected to succeed a deceased bishop if he left no son to take his place None can be ordained priest who does not belong to the sacerdotal family, nor any who is the son of a mother who was otherwise than a virgin when she married

The Christians of St John hold the Cross in the highest veneration, and have a curious superstition that the original Cross was placed in the sun, and that the sun and the moon derive their light from it St John Baptist is kept in memory by an annual five days' festival, when all, young and old, flock to their patriarch and are baptized in a flowing river by him, a rite which has led some writers to identify them with the HEMERO-BAPTISTS Among many singular superstitions respecting St John Baptist, one is that he commanded his disciples to crucify his dead body, which they did, and that afterwards it was preserved in a crystal sepulchre at Scuster, a city of Persia

The Christology of the Mendæans is of a very heretical character They hold that Christ is the Soul of God, as the Mahometans say that He is the Spirit of God Some of them have Docetic notions respecting the Crucifixion, believing that Christ passed through the hands of those who held Him, and that only an appearance of His body was nailed to the Cross while others maintain that His Soul only ascended to heaven, and that His Body remains on earth, not locally, but everywhere

They have four sacred books, written in the peculiar dialect of Arabic which goes by the name of Mendæan, and which seem never to have been examined with the critical learning necessary to determine what is the real value of their contents The *first* is called "The Divan," or Audience-Hall, and is alleged to have been given by God Himself to Angels It contains statements respecting the Fall of the Angels, the Creation of Man, and the future changes which are to occur in the world The *second* is the "Book of Adam," which is said to have been communicated to our first forefather by the Angel Gabriel It also contains much respecting the origin of the world and of mankind, and abounds in devotional expressions of adoration towards God as Light. The *third* is a volume of smaller size, called the "Book of John the Baptist," and contains a summary of the Sacred History The *fourth* is called "Cholasteh" or the completion, and is the book of rites used by the Mendæans Of these the book of Adam was printed in Mendæan and Latin by Norberg in the year 1815 The rest remain in manuscript in the National Library at Paris, and in the Bodleian [Ignatius à Jesu, *Narratio origin rituum et errorum Christian Scti Joan* 1652 Assemann, *Bibl Orient* III ii 10 Norberg, *De relig et ling Sabæorum* Norberg, *Codex Nasaræus, lib Adami appellat* Paciaudius, *De cultu Scti Joan. Bapt* II vii 1755]

MENNONITES A general name given to the four sects of Dutch Baptists, the Flemings, Frieslanders, Germans, and Waterlanders They were originally called "Anabaptists," but after their reformation by Menno in the middle of the sixteenth century that name, which had become very odious through the iniquities with which it was associated [ANABAPTISTS], was exchanged for the name of "Mennonites" in memory of their reformer. They are also called "Doopsgezinden" or "Dippers," and, in America, by a name of similar meaning, TUNKERS

Menno Simonis, or Symons [A D 1505-1561] was a priest, and rector of his native village, Witmarsum, near Bolswert, in Friesland He gives the somewhat improbable account of himself that, having as a priest lived a profligate life, he yet discovered by reading the New Testament that Infant Baptism is not a scriptural practice, and that on this account, at the age of thirty-one, he gave up his position and became a reformed character As he is found married after his connection with the Anabaptists, it is probable that marriage had something to do with his secession

In the following year [A D 1537] he became a teacher among the Anabaptists, the fiercest and worst part of the sect having been exterminated in the siege and capture of Munster, and in the suppression of the insurrections which followed at Amsterdam, Deventer, and elsewhere The remnant of the sect was in so depressed a condition, and so entirely without a leader, that the accession of a man of position and ability was

[1] This formula is given in the Mendæan dialect of Arabia by Ignatius à Jesu, and is translated somewhat differently The above is as given by Norberg, in his *De relig et ling Sabæorum*, p. 9.

extremely welcome, and he soon acquired so much influence and power among them as to become their new leader and head, an office which he held until his death, a quarter of a century afterwards

Under Menno's guidance the Anabaptists entirely lost their revolutionary character, so that some have found it difficult to recognise the one continuous sectarian body under two such different aspects But the notion of an immediate Millennium had been exploded by the failure and death of John of Leyden, the "King" of their "New Jerusalem," and with that notion their motives for insurrection and aggression had passed away It is also probable that those who were spared from slaughter were a milder and less political kind of Anabaptists than those who became so conspicuous under Munzer and Bockhold, and that thus the religious element of the sect alone survived, and that among a comparatively quiet and religious class of people The character of Menno would influence his followers in the same direction, for he was a gentle and peaceful man, whose ambition, if he possessed any, was the ambition of a religious leader in the sense of later times, and not in that of the fierce fanatics of the Middle Ages

Another conspicuous change which arose among the Anabaptists from the violent explosion of their millennial expectations was, that they no longer entertained the notion of a superior dispensation of the Spirit having arrived, a notion grounded entirely on that of the Millennium itself Hence they no longer claimed a direct inspiration superseding the teaching of the Scriptures such as had been claimed before [ZWICKAU PROPHETS] The Scriptures, therefore, regained their influence both as a rule of belief and a rule of life, and whatever errors the Anabaptists may be chargeable with, even under Menno's leadership, they cannot be justly accused of that frightful Antinomianism which had characterized them before their suppression as an insurrectionary sect They became, in fact, notorious for their deference to the Scriptures, and instead of claiming an inspiration superior to it, bowed down to the most literal interpretation of its precepts

Before the accession of Menno the Anabaptists cannot be said to have had any theological system Under his guidance, however, a form of Protestantism was established among them which is, in some particulars, quite independent of the systems of Luther, Calvin, or Zwingli But Menno was averse to "Confessions," such as were common among the Continental Protestants, and did not draw up any for his followers. He wrote, however, in 1556 a treatise under the title of "The True Christian Belief," in which he compared his own teaching with that of the Romanists and the Protestants in such parts as they differed, and from this basis, two Mennonite preachers named Lubbert Gerardi and Hans de Rys, constructed, in the year 1580, a "Confession of Waterland," which professes to set forth the tenets of the sect This was at first drawn up for the information of the English congregation of Brownists which had emigrated to Holland [INDEPENDENTS], and was regarded only as a private document, but it has been recognised in subsequent times as containing, substantially, a statement of Mennonite doctrine [Schyn, *Hist Mennonitarum*, vii] [1] It begins with an expression of belief in the doctrines of the Blessed Trinity and Incarnation, which is necessarily vague and incomplete, for Menno denied that our Lord became incarnate through taking the natural substance of His Mother, maintaining that His Human Body was a direct creation out of nothing in the womb of the immaculate Virgin, by the power of the Holy Ghost This opinion is still held by the Flemings or old Mennonites, but the sect in general has been strongly tainted with Arianism, perhaps by a not unnatural recoil from this tenet of Menno [2] Original sin is a doctrine almost entirely repudiated, the guilt of Adam not being considered as transmitted to his descendants, but only some germ of sinfulness such as orthodox Christians believe still to lurk in the will of the baptized This repudiation of the doctrine of original sin may be considered as the theological ground for the repudiation of Infant Baptism, though the latter is usually stated as founded on the absence of any direct notice of such a rite in the New Testament The practice of the Mennonites is to baptize children at twelve years of age, not by immersion, but by affusion, or pouring water on the head [3] The sacrifice of Christ's death is set forth as applicable to all mankind, the Mennonite doctrine thus symbolizing with Arminianism and not Calvinism [4] The Lutheran doctrine of "Justification by faith alone" is as distinctly ignored as the Calvinist doctrine of the "decrees," faith being defined as that which leads men to do works of love, co-operating with the righteous work of Christ [5] The Mennonite view of the Eucharist is, however, neither more nor less than the "memorial" theory of Zwingli [6] In the recoil from the early Anabaptist fury of the sect, the Mennonites went to the opposite extreme, considering war, and even resistance to injury, to be altogether unlawful for Christian men They also considered oaths to be unlawful, and that it was unfit for a Christian man to undertake the duties of any office of civil government

Such were the original principles of the Mennonites, as set forth in the Confession of 1580 They were in some degree modified by a subsequent Confession, drawn up in 1632, with the view of uniting the several sects into which the original one had broken up, but no substantial alteration has taken place in their belief, except that above mentioned, the development in the direction of Arianism of Menno's original belief respecting the Incarnation

While Menno was still living, his followers broke up into two divisions on the subject of discipline. Leonard Bowenson and Theodore Philippi headed a party which maintained the strictest views possible respecting the treatment of those who fell into sin, requiring that they should not only be excommunicated, but that they should never be received back into the sect again, and that they should be debarred all intercourse with their relatives, even their husbands, wives, or children. The same party also defined sin in so strict a manner as to make even innocent amusements a cause for excommunication. Menno endeavoured to unite the two parties, and in his own person set an example of compromise and conciliation, but his attempts met with no success, and his followers became henceforward divided into the "Fine" or strict Mennonites (*Die Feinen*), the party of Bowenson and Philippi, and the "Coarse" or lax Mennonites (*Die Groben*), the one being the ascetic representatives of the original sect, the other the representatives of the more ordinary Protestant phase of the sect into which it had begun to develope under Menno's own guidance. These two parties were also marked off from each other geographically, as well as theologically, and as most of the lax Mennonites were inhabitants of a region in the north of Holland named Waterland, they were called WATERLANDERS, while the strict Mennonites being chiefly in Flanders, they acquired the name of FLEMINGS. The latter were soon subdivided into "Flandrians," "Frieslanders," and "Germans," the subject of their disputes being still that of discipline and the exact standard of strictness or laxness which should be permitted. In subsequent times, however, the Flemings grew fewer and fewer, and now most of the Mennonites are Waterlanders.

The number of the Mennonites now existing in Holland is said to be small, there being only about 150 congregations of them. There are also about the same number in Germany, on the Lower Rhine. Large numbers of them emigrated to America by invitation of William Penn in the latter part of the seventeenth century; and it is calculated that the sect in the United States and in Canada now numbers about 240 ministers, 400 congregations, and about 50,000 members. [Schyn's *Hist Christ qui in Belgio fœderato Mennonitæ appellantur*, Amst 1723. Schyn's *Hist Mennonit plenior Deductio*, 1729. Menno's *Works*, Amst 1651. Brandt's *Hist Reform*.]

MERINTHIANS. [CERINTHIANS.]

MERISTÆ. A Jewish sect named, along with the Genistæ, by Justin Martyr [*Dial c Tryph* lxxx.]. The name (=Dividers) is probably the correlative name in opposition to Genistæ, which implied that its bearers represented the true γένος of the nation. The sect is probably the sect of Nazaræans described by Epiphanius in his eighteenth heresy. St Isidore says respecting them, "Meristæ appellati eo quod separant Scripturas, non credentes omnibus prophetis, dicentes aliis et aliis spiritibus illos prophetasse. Μέρος enim Græce portio dicitur" [Isidor. Hisp cap v 8.]

MESSALIANS. [EUCHITES.]

METAGENETÆ. Some heretics are mentioned by Prædestinatus, who maintained that the Second Person of the Blessed Trinity was not co-eternal with the First, and that being begotten by the Father's will, had that will been wanting He would not have existed. In the "Elenchus Hæresum" prefixed to the work of Prædestinatus these heretics are named Metagenetæ [Prædest. *Hær* lxxx.]

METANGISMONITÆ. A sect of heretics belonging to the third century, who maintained that the union between the Father and the Son in the Holy Trinity was effected by the Son entering into the Father as a lesser vessel (ἀγγεῖον) may be placed in one that is greater. It is remarkable that, when describing this heresy, Philaster [A D 380] confutes their opinion in words which contain a peculiar expression nearly identical with a clause of the Athanasian Hymn, "Et separant se a catholica ecclesia, propter illos suos pseudoprophetas insaniunt adsentientes, et non intelligentes quod *qualis immensus est Pater, talis est et Filius, talis est et Spiritus Sanctus*, æqualis in omnibus, ita ut sit immobilis Trinitas, immensa et omnipotens atque sempiterna ubique, quæ nobis nuntiatur ex sanctis scripturis apertissime, ut et sint tres Personæ viventes in perpetuum, et æquales in omni majestate et potentia, Filius tamen et Spiritus Sanctus de Patre sint proprie" [Philast *Hær* li.]. These words are not quoted by St. Augustine, although he names the heresy [Aug *Hær* lviii.], but Prædestinatus writes in analogous terms, "Quos ideo repudiat ecclesia, quia de incorporeo carnaliter sentiunt, et de *incomprehensibili* limitatis agunt, et de æqualitate divinitatis gradus statuunt" [Prædest *Hær* lviii.]. The last author says that the heresy was opposed by Diodorus, Bishop of Nicomedia.

METHODISTS. The general name given to a number of sects which are derived more or less directly from the confraternity formed in the year 1739 by John Wesley, Fellow of Lincoln College, Oxford. The parent sect is now usually distinguished as that of the "Wesleyan Methodists," or simply as "Wesleyans." The other principal sects are the "Welsh Calvinistic," "New Connexion," "Primitive," and "United Free Church" Methodists. There are also several smaller divisions of the sect both in England and in America. The following article will deal with the history, organization, principles and practices of the original body, and the offshoots of it will be noticed in succeeding articles in chronological order.

I. ORIGIN OF THE NAME. When John Wesley first founded his confraternity he called it the "United Society," after the Moravians or Unitas Fratrum, but the vulgar tongue was too strong for him, and the name of "Methodists"—given in banter to a small brotherhood of fellows of colleges and undergraduates formed by him at Oxford some years earlier—became the world-wide designation of his followers. The lineage of that name is curious and interesting. Early in the seventeenth century it came into use in France to designate a class of theologians, "Méthodistes," who endeavoured by precise and fair statements of the case on both sides to bring about the reunion of the Huguenots with the Church. Of these theological Methodists, the most distinguished representative was Bossuet.[1] [Mosheim's

[1] In classical times the same name was used for those who practised any study or profession, as oratory for example, according to rule: but its best known application

Eccl Hist. iii 242, Stubbs' ed. F. Spanheim, *Diss de Præscript in reb fid adv Novos Methodistas pontificios, Opp* III ii 1079.] It was probably of similar exact writers on the Puritan side that a preacher spoke when he satirized the "plain pikestaff Methodists" who "esteemed all flowers of rhetoric in their sermons no better than stinking weeds" [Spence's *Sermons*, 1657] and it is obvious that the name "Precisians," so commonly used for the Puritans, was analogous to that of Methodists in its later sense. The term, however, came closest to its modern signification in the "New Methodists," who held "the great point of justification" in peculiar prominence about ten years before John Wesley's birth [*War among the Angels of the Churches*, 1693], and in those who were so called because they "stood up for God," as mentioned about the same time by Calamy. It was first appropriated to Wesley and his half-dozen friends as a piece of Oxford undergraduate banter in the year 1728, and, becoming the popular name of his followers, was fully accepted by himself and them as early as the year 1744. [*Min of Conf* i 9, 10.]

II. HISTORY OF METHODISM. The original form of Methodism was that of a Society or Brotherhood for the promotion of personal piety, according to the principles and practices of the Church of England; and it was part of that wave of Pietism which passed over Germany and England in the dissolute times of the seventeenth century. Early in that century such societies had been formed in Holland by the COLLEGIANTS, a section of the Arminians; in the latter part of the century they were organized by Spener under the name of Colleges of Piety [PIETISTS], and both these had their type in the FRIENDS OF GOD, of whom Tauler, a great authority with Wesley, was one of the most famous. Societies of a similar kind were very generally established in England during the reigns of William III. and Queen Anne by the name of "Religious Societies." The Wesleys belonged to one of these latter Societies when they were at Oxford, and the early stage of their movement was simply a development of the obligations undertaken by them in association with it; they and several other young men, banding together in 1727 to study the Bible, to visit the poor, to observe Wednesday and Friday fasts, and to communicate more frequently than was then the custom in the Universities. In the year 1735 this Brotherhood consisted of fourteen or fifteen in number, including John and Charles Wesley, George Whitfield, Hervey, Ingham, Clayton, and Broughton. Some years later, on Wesley's return from his unsuccessful work in Georgia [A.D. 1735-1738] as a missionary of the Society for the Propagation of the Gospel, the movement was revived in a similar form in London. "In November 1738," writes Wesley, "two or three persons who desired to flee from the wrath to come, and then seven or eight more, came to me in London, and desired me to advise and pray with them. I said, 'If you will meet on Thursday night I will help you as well as I can.' More and more then desired to meet with them, till they increased to many hundreds. The case was afterwards the same at Bristol, Kingswood, Newcastle, and many other parts of England, Scotland, and Ireland. It may be observed the desire was on *their* part, not *mine*. My desire was to live and die in retirement. But I did not see that I could refuse them my help and be guiltless before God." [*Minutes of Conference*, i. p. 58, ed. 1812.]

By this time, however, John Wesley had become intimately acquainted with the Moravians and their system, having visited their settlement at Herrnhut in 1738, and having taken part in the services of their chapel in Fetter Lane for more than a year after his return. This association had tended greatly to weaken Wesley's hold upon the system of the Church, and although to the latest day of his life he earnestly repudiated the idea of separating from it, yet his movement from that date distinctly and progressively tended towards the formation of a religious community independent of the Church. The impetus of this sectarian movement grew with every year of his life, and after his death Methodism at once passed beyond the borders of the Church of England, and was developed into a separate body by the lay-preachers, whose authority then took the place of that so long exercised by the clerical head of their Society.

The first step which Wesley himself took in this direction was that of building "preaching-houses," the object of which was very similar to that of modern "mission chapels," but which differed from the latter in the important point of being set up without any sanction, obtained or sought, from the clergyman of the parish or the bishop of the diocese. This first step offers one illustration among many of the way in which Wesley, though exacting the strictest obedience from those who were set *under* him, disregarded the authority of those who were set *over* him whenever obedience clashed with his plans. "How far," he asks, in 1744, "is it our duty to obey the bishops?" His reply is, "In all things indifferent. And on this ground of obeying them, we should observe the canons, so far as we can with a safe conscience." [*Min of Conf* i 8.] Thus, while professing to be earnestly devoted to the system of the Church of England, and laying great stress upon his position as a priest of that Church, he began the organization of his Society by acting as if such a thing as Church laws had no existence, and recognising no authority except his own. When he was asked, a quarter of a century later, by what authority he acted, his reply was, "By the authority of Jesus Christ, conveyed to me by the now Archbishop of Canterbury, when he laid hands upon me and said, Take thou authority to preach the Gospel" [Wesley's *Works*, xxvii. 88]. But he garbled these words by omitting the important ones which

was to the physician who treated his patients according to a scientific system [Μεθοδικός] as opposed to the empiric, who depended chiefly on practical experience. This use of the word still existed at the end of the seventeenth century, being found in the works of Boyle [ii. 245] and Hammond [iv. 577].

complete their sense, namely, "in the congregation where thou shalt be lawfully appointed thereunto," and this omission gives the key to Wesley's life

The first preaching-house was begun at Bristol on May 12th, 1739, but before it was completed Wesley had fitted up for the purpose an old cannon-foundry in Moorfields, and this was opened under the name of "The Foundry," and as the headquarters of the Methodist movement, on November 11th, 1739, which may be regarded as the birthday of the sect, though many years elapsed before its position as a separate family from the Church of England was fully established

The second step towards the organization of Methodism as a sect was the appointment of lay preachers The preaching-houses were originally intended as places where Wesley and other clergymen who co-operated with him might officiate at any time without asking for the use of a church, or being necessarily driven to preach in the open air They also, doubtless, offered greater freedom for extempore prayer, and many customs could be permitted in them which Wesley and his clerical friends would have shrunk from countenancing in a consecrated building But an uneducated young layman named Thomas Maxfield,[1] whom Wesley had appointed to pray extempore in the preaching-house at Moorfields during his own absence at Bristol, thought himself as well able to preach as to pray, and was encouraged to do so by Lady Huntingdon [*Life of Lady Hunt* i 3] "He is," she wrote to Wesley, "one of the greatest instances of God's peculiar favour that I know He has raised from the stones one to sit among the princes of His people"—"princes" being apparently interpreted "preachers" by this rather silly Countess He hastened to London to put a stop to the innovation, of which he very strongly disapproved, but his mother's persuasions were added to those of Lady Huntingdon, and feminine influence so far overcame Wesley's better judgment, that he was persuaded to sanction Maxfield's performances with the questionable explanation, "It is the Lord, let Him do what seemeth Him good" From that time [A D 1741] lay-preaching became part of the Methodist system, and by means of it the Methodists were rapidly withdrawn from the influence of the Church system, for the ministrations of an ordained clergy became less and less necessary in their eyes the more they became familiar with the sight of laymen in the pulpits of their preaching-houses

Wesley apologized for this innovation on the ground of necessity, for "what could they do in a case of so extreme necessity, where so many souls were at stake? No clergyman would assist at all" But his writings in the Minutes of Conference and elsewhere give abundant evidence

[1] Maxfield was ordained some years afterwards by the Bishop of Derry, with the words, "Sir, I ordain you to assist that good man, that he may not work himself to death" Eventually he seceded from Wesley on the question of Calvinism, and having become rich by marriage, he built a chapel for himself in Moorfields, where he officiated for twenty years

that the system thus forced upon him was one which he never heartily accepted, and that the preachers were often too strong for the power of even his will to keep close to the pattern of his own orthodox teaching Ever afterwards, also, he was in dread that they would end by severing that connection with the Church which he still claimed for his Society "Do we separate from the Church?" he asked in the conference which was held three years after lay-preaching had been established His answer was "We conceive not We hold communion therewith for conscience' sake, by constantly attending both the Word preached and the Sacraments administered therein" [*Min of Conf* i 9] But the "we" included a very small number, if any, of his preachers, and the growing secession from the Church became so evident, that in 1749 he issued the following remonstrance and admonition to them, the language of which, even under its catechetical veil, clearly indicates the circumstances of the case. "In every place," he writes, "exhort those who were brought up in the Church constantly to attend its service And in visiting the classes, ask every one, 'Do *you* go to Church as often as ever you did?' Set the example yourself And immediately alter every plan that interferes therewith Is there not a cause for this? Are we not unawares, by little and little, tending to a separation from the Church? Oh! remove every tendency thereto with all diligence [1] Let all our preachers go to Church [2] Let all our people go constantly [3] Receive the sacrament at every opportunity [4] Warn all against niceness in hearing, a great prevailing evil [5] Warn them likewise against despising the prayers of the Church [6] Against calling our Society *a church* or *the Church* [7] Against calling our preachers *ministers*, our houses *meeting-houses*, (call them plain preaching-houses) [8] Do not license them as such The proper form of a petition to the judge is, 'A B desires to have his house in C licensed for public worship' [9] Do not license yourself till you are constrained, and then not as a *Dissenter*, but a *Methodist* preacher It is time enough, when you are prosecuted, to take the oaths Thereby you are licensed" [*Min of Conf* i 57]

The third step towards the separation of Wesley's Society from the Church was a personal act of schism, of the gravest possible character, on the part of Wesley himself, for on September 2nd, 1784, a new plea of necessity induced him to assume the office of a bishop by going through the form of consecrating Dr Coke and Mr Asbury as bishops, and others as priests, for his missions in North America Dr Coke being already a priest of the Church of England The shocking character of this assumption he attempted to veil by calling the pretended bishops "superintendents," and the others "elders," and by alleging "Lord King's account of the Primitive Church convinced me many years ago that bishops and presbyters are the same order, and consequently have the same right to ordain" and this when Lord King himself had recanted his unhistorical notion He also excused himself on the following grounds "It has, indeed, been proposed to desire the English bishops to ordain part of our preachers for America But to this I object [1] I desired the Bishop of London to ordain only one, but could not prevail [2] If they consented, we know the slowness of their proceedings, but the matter admits of no delay [3] If they would ordain them now, they would likewise expect to govern them And how grievously would this entangle us! [4] As our American brethren are now totally disentangled, both from the State and from the English hierarchy, we dare not entangle them again either with the one or the other They are now at full liberty simply to follow the Scriptures and the Primitive Church And we judge it best that they should stand fast in that liberty wherewith God has so strangely made them free" [*Min of Conf* i 179] But this professed confidence for "many years" in his power as a priest to act as a bishop, had never yet been sufficiently strong to induce him to go through the same forms of ordination with his preachers, though he was "for many years importuned" to do so It is not too much to say, 1 that he had far too great facility in convincing himself that what he wished to do was right to do, and 2 that his respect for his preachers was not strong enough to stimulate his wishes to the point of raising them to the same ministerial level with himself in England [1] The wise Alexander Knox, his intimate friend, wrote that Wesley was "the dupe of his own weakness, and of other men's arts" [*Remains of Knox*, iii 470 ed. 1837], which seems to be the plain and straightforward explanation of the matter It was the occasion of a sarcastic epigram from the pen of Charles Wesley —

> "How easy now are Bishops made,
> By man or woman's whim,
> Wesley his hands on Coke hath laid,
> But who laid hands on him?"

And although the loving spirits of the two could not be alienated from each other, Charles Wesley ceased for the remaining four years of his life to take any further part in the affairs of the Methodists beyond that of paying his brother's debts

The fourth and last step taken by Wesley towards organizing his followers into one independent sect was that of authorizing the preachers to use the Book of Common Prayer in the preaching-houses This he did first about the beginning of 1786, his rules respecting the permission being given in a paper dated from Bristol on July 22nd of that year "Perhaps there is one part of what I wrote some time since which requires a little further explanation In what cases do we allow of service in Church hours? I answer [1] When the minister is a notoriously wicked man, [2] When he preaches Arian, or any equally pernicious doctrine, [3] When there are not churches in the town sufficient to contain half the people, and [4] When there is no church at all within two or three miles. And we advise every one who preaches in the Church hours to read the Psalms and Lessons, with part of the Church prayers because we apprehend this will endear the Church service to our brethren, who probably would be prejudiced against it if they heard none but extemporary prayer" [*Min of Conf* i 191]

But these vague limitations were superseded shortly afterwards, in 1788, by the following general order "The assistants shall have a discretionary power to read the Prayer Book in the preaching-houses on Sunday mornings, when they think it expedient, if the generality of the society acquiesce with it, on condition that Divine Service never be performed in the Church hours on the Sundays when the Sacrament is administered in the parish church where the preaching-house is situated, and the people be strenuously exhorted to attend the Sacrament in the parish church on those Sundays" [*ibid.* 208]

These four steps towards making the Methodists a sect (in spite of his frequent and vigorous protests against their separation from the Church) bore their fruit, even in their founder's lifetime The preachers had importuned Wesley in vain to ordain them, but by permitting them to preach and to use the Book of Common Prayer he had given them a position which, to their ignorant minds, seemed almost the same as that of clergymen One thing only seemed to them to be wanting to complete their sacerdotal character, and that was permission to administer the Holy Communion. Wesley stopped these demands at first by expelling those who made them from his society [*Centenary of Meth* 38], but they increased so greatly in number that this course became no longer possible without breaking up the work of his life Some of his last words shew better than any others can do how vigorously he resisted this final attempt to make the Methodist Society independent of the Church

"In 1744, all the Methodist preachers had their first Conference, but none of them dreamed that the being called to preach gave them any right to administer Sacraments, one of our first rules was given to each preacher 'You are to do that part of the work which we appoint' But what work was this? Did we ever appoint you to administer Sacraments? to exercise the priestly office? *Such a design never entered into our mind, it was farthest from our thoughts*, and if any member had taken such a step, we should have looked upon it as a palpable breach of this rule, and consequently as a recantation of our connection I wish all you who are vulgarly termed Methodists would seriously consider what has been said, and particularly you whom God has commissioned to call sinners to repentance It does by no means follow hence, that you are commissioned TO BAPTIZE AND TO ADMINISTER THE LORD'S SUPPER. Ye never dreamed of this for

[1] When they had complained in 1766 that he was "shackling free-born Englishmen by not permitting them to vote in the Conferences," his reply was, "I answer, it is possible, after my death, something of this kind may take place but not while I live," and when he was charged with making himself a Pope, he replied, "I see no hurt in it" [*Min. of Conf* i 60]

Methodists

ten or twenty years after ye began to preach, ye did not then, like Korah, Dathan, and Abiram, seek the priesthood also, ye knew no man taketh this honour unto himself but he that is called of God, as was Aaron Oh, contain yourselves within your own bounds" [*Armin Meth Mag* 1790]

John Wesley died on March 2nd, 1791, at the great age of eighty-eight His personal holiness had gained for him the veneration of all who knew him, his vast industry in preaching had led multitudes to a better life, his great powers of organization had formed a Society whose ramifications extended through every part of England and Wales, and across the Atlantic, his strong will had kept that Society under control far beyond anything that could have been expected when it is considered of what social elements it was composed But when the influence of his holiness, industry, and strong will were removed, the revolution which had been impending among the Methodists for so many years immediately broke out, and exhibited at once the weak point in his organization, that of making it dependent on a personal influence that must soon pass away, instead of resting it on the corporate system of the Church, which has a continuous existence If Wesley had possessed more faith in the Episcopate as a system, and less confidence in his own power of organization, he might have reformed the Church of England instead of founding a sect[1]

But that Wesley had founded a sect became only too evident immediately after his death The younger generation of Methodists had long accepted such a position for themselves, and as soon as their head was taken away from them they began their endeavours to force the whole body to take up definitively and officially a similar position. Within two months of Wesley's death, his Society was racked with dissension on two questions, the one relating to its government and the other to the administration of the Sacraments independently of the Church The younger party wished to restrict the power of the preachers by admitting "laymen" to a larger share in the general and the detailed management of the Society, and to remove every restraint as to the times of service and the administration of the Sacraments in the preaching-houses Opposite to these was a party that desired to return to the original idea of Methodism as an organization supplementary to the Church system, and not supplanting it A third and intermediate party, led by those into whose hands the power of Wesley was passing, desired to stereotype Wesley's latter plans, only permitting the Methodist chapel to be a complete rival to the parish church in particular cases, and reserving to the Conference the power of licensing it to become so This latter party was entirely opposed also to any extension of lay influence in the Conference, or in the minor organizations of the Methodist body

After much preliminary pamphleteering and wrangling, the Conference met at Manchester on July 26th, 1791, when a letter was produced which Wesley had written on April 7th, 1785, and committed to the charge of his travelling companion or secretary, in which he besought the Conference to let all things go on, as far as circumstances would permit, exactly in the same manner as during his lifetime [*Min of Conf* i 234] A president was therefore elected from the intermediate party The Conference took upon itself the government of the body without any further change than that of arranging the "circuits" into "districts," and then

[1] His views on the subject are further illustrated by the following letter, which is in the possession of Mr Henry J Mills of Bristol, the lady to whom it is addressed having become the second wife of Mr Mills' grandfather

"*London, Oct* 10, 1778

"My dear Miss Bishop,—I am not unwilling to write to *you*, even upon a tender subject, because you will weigh the matter fairly And if you have a little prepossession (which, who has not?) yet you are willing to give it up to reason

"The original Methodists were all of the Church of England, and the more awakened they were the more zealously they adhered to it in every point, both of Doctrine and Discipline Hence we inserted in the very first Rules of our Society, 'They that leave the Church leave us' And this we did, not as a point of prudence, but a point of conscience We believed it utterly unlawful to separate from the Church, unless sinful terms of communion were imposed, just as did Mr Philip Henry, and most of those holy men that were contemporary with them

"'But the ministers of it do not preach the Gospel' Neither do the Independent or Anabaptist ministers Calvinism is not the Gospel, nay, it is further from it than most of the sermons I hear at Church. These are very frequently unevangelical, but those are anti evangelical They are (to say no more) equally wrong, and they are far more dangerously wrong Few of the Methodists are now in danger of imbibing error from the Church ministers, but they are in great danger of imbibing the grand error—Calvinism—from the Dissenting ministers. Perhaps thousands have done it already, most of whom have drawn back to perdition I see more instances of this than any one else can do, and on this ground also exhort all who would keep to the Methodists, and *from* Calvinism—'Go to the Church and not the meeting'

"But, to speak freely, I myself find more life in the Church prayers than in the formal extemporary prayers of Dissenters Nay, I find more profit in sermons on either good tempers or good works than in what are vulgarly called *Gospel sermons* That term is now become a mere *cant* word. I wish none of our Society would use it It has no determinate meaning Let but a pert, self-sufficient animal, that has neither sense nor grace, bawl out something about Christ and His Blood, or justification by faith, and his hearers cry out, 'What a fine Gospel sermon!' Surely the Methodists have not so learnt Christ? We know no Gospel without salvation from sin

"There is a Romish error which many Protestants sanction unawares It is an avowed doctrine of the Romish Church that the '*pure intention* of the minister is essential to the validity of the Sacraments' If so, we ought not to attend the ministrations of an unholy man, but in flat opposition to this, our Church teaches, in the 28th Article, that 'the unworthiness of the minister does not hinder the validity of the Sacraments' Although, therefore, there are many disagreeable circumstances, yet I advise all our friends to keep to the Church God has surely raised us up for the Church chiefly, that a little leaven may leaven the whole lump

"I wish you would seriously consider that little tract, 'Reasons against a Separation from the Church of England.' Those reasons were never answered yet, and I believe they never will be

"I am glad you have undertaken that labour of love, and I trust it will increase both your spiritual and bodily health

"I am, my dear Miss Bishop,
"Yours very affectionately,
"J WESLEY"

pledged itself to a conservative policy in the words, "We engage to follow strictly the plan which Mr Wesley left us at his death" [*Min of Conf* i 246.]

It is needless to go into any detail respecting the bitter wranglings which ensued during the next few years, in consequence of the position thus taken up by the Conference Ignoring this, we may see the plain history of the case indicated by the following extracts from the minutes of the following year "*Q* 23 What rules shall be made concerning ordinations? *A* 1. No ordination shall take place in the Methodist Connexion without the consent of the Conference first obtained 2 If any brother shall break the above-mentioned rule, by ordaining or being ordained, without the consent of the Conference previously obtained, the brother so breaking the rule does thereby exclude himself *Q* 24 What rule shall be made concerning the administration of the Lord's Supper? *A* The Lord's Supper shall not be administered by any person among our Societies in England and Ireland, for the ensuing year, on any consideration whatsoever, except in London *Q* 26 What rule shall be made concerning the service in the Church-hours? *A* The service shall not be performed in any new place in the Church hours in future, without the consent of the Conference first obtained *Q* 27 Expressions have been used by some, through a false zeal for their own peculiar sentiments, which were very unjustifiable How shall we prevent this in future? *A* No person is to call another heretic, bigot, or by any other disrespectful name, on any account, for a difference in sentiment" [*Min of Conf* i 259]

In 1793 a resolution was passed by the Conference, "That the Sacrament of the Lord's Supper shall not be administered by the preachers in any part of our Connexion, except where the whole Society is unanimous for it, and *will not be contented without it*, and, in even those few exempt Societies, it shall be administered, as far as practicable, in the evening only, and according to the form of the Church of England" [*Min. of Conf* i. 279]

At the same time an Address was printed in which the Conference said, "We are determined, as a body, to remain in connexion with the Church of England We have never sanctioned ordination in England, either in this Conference or in any other, in any degree, or ever attempted to do it." [*Min of Conf* i 281]

In 1794 other resolutions were passed on the same subject, as follows "1st, All ecclesiastical titles, such as *Reverend*, &c, shall be laid aside, as also gowns, bands, &c, agreeably to the resolutions of the Conference held at Leeds in 1793[1] 2ndly, Preaching in Church hours shall not be permitted, except for special reasons, and where it will not cause a division 3rdly, As the Lord's Supper has not been administered, except where the Society has been unanimous for it, and would not have been contented without it, it is now agreed, that the Lord's Supper shall not be administered in future where the union and concord of the Society can be preserved without it 4thly, The preachers will not perform the office of Baptism, except for the desirable ends of love and concord, though Baptism, as well as the burial of the dead, was performed by many of the preachers long before the death of Mr Wesley, and with his consent" [*Min of Conf* i 299]

The final settlement of the question was effected in the year 1795, when eighteen "Articles" respecting the Sacraments and Discipline were set forth, the ten first, relating to the former subject, being these —"Articles of agreement for general pacification [I] Concerning the Lord's Supper, Baptism, &c 1 The Sacrament of the Lord's Supper shall not be administered in any chapel, except the majority of the trustees of that chapel on the one hand, and the majority of the stewards and leaders belonging to that chapel (as the best qualified to give the sense of the people) on the other hand, allow of it Nevertheless, in all cases, the consent of the Conference shall be obtained before the Lord's Supper be administered 2 Wherever there is a society, but no chapel, if the majority of the stewards and leaders of that society testify that it is the wish of the people that the Lord's Supper should be administered to them, their desire shall be gratified provided, that the consent of the Conference be previously obtained. 3 Provided, nevertheless, that in Mount Pleasant Chapel in Liverpool, and in all other chapels where the Lord's Supper has been already peaceably administered, the administration of it shall be continued in future 4 The administration of baptism, the burial of the dead, and service in Church hours, shall be determined according to the regulations above mentioned 5 Wherever the Lord's Supper shall be administered according to the before-mentioned regulations, it shall always be continued, except the Conference order the contrary 6 The Lord's Supper shall be administered by those *only* who are authorized by the Conference, and at such times, and in such manner *only*, as the Conference shall appoint 7 The administration of Baptism, and the Lord's Supper according to the above regulations, is intended only for the members of our own Society 8 We agree, that the Lord's Supper be administered among us on Sunday evenings only, except where the majority of the stewards and leaders desire it in church hours, or where it has already been administered in those hours Nevertheless, it shall never be administered on those Sundays on which it is administered in the parochial church 9 The Lord's Supper shall be always administered in England according to the form of the Established Church, but the person who administers shall have full liberty to give out hymns and to use exhortation and extemporary prayer 10 Wherever Divine Service is performed in England, on the Lord's day in Church hours, the officiating preacher shall read either the service of the Established

[1] The President of the Conference has recently been styled "Right Reverend"

Church, our venerable father's abridgment, or at least the Lessons appointed by the Calendar But we recommend either the full service, or the abridgment" [*Min of Conf* i 322]

During the few following years the petitions for permission to administer the Sacraments were very numerous, and it was not long before the practice became almost universal in Methodist chapels The usual mode of "ordination" adopted until the year 1836 was that of "setting apart" with prayer. In that year imposition of hands was introduced, and this has been the only important change in the practice of the Methodists since their final settlement as a body distinct from the Church by the above "Articles of Pacification"

The later history of the sect has not been distinguished by any other events of importance except the formation of other sects from the original one These have been the "New Connexion," which separated under the leadership of Alexander Kilham, on the questions of the Sacraments and lay influence, in the year 1797 [METHODISTS, NEW CONNEXION] the Primitive Methodists, who separated in the year 1810, who claimed, but were forbidden, the right to use the original exciting methods of promoting conversion [METHODISTS, PRIMITIVE] the Bryanites, or Bible Christians, who formed a sect in Cornwall in 1815 [METHODISTS, BRYANITE] the "Wesleyan Association," which was formed in 1835, and the "Wesleyan Reformers" in 1839, both of which have since been united in one sect [METHODISTS, UNITED FREE CHURCH]

III THE ORGANIZATION OF THE METHODISTS The most distinctive feature of the system established by Wesley was its organization for the purposes of religious discipline, finance, and ecclesiastical government, an organization which was admirably adapted to the habits of the classes out of whom his community was formed

1] *Bands* The unit of this system is a small body of from five to ten persons called a "band"[1] It is not compulsory on every Methodist to belong to one of these bands, but it was Wesley's original intention that all should so associate themselves voluntarily His object was to keep up a sense of sin in the members of his confraternity, and to assist them in overcoming temptation, by means of mutual confession. "The design" of the bands, he writes, "is to obey that command of God, 'Confess your faults one to another, and pray one for another that you may be healed' The chief rules are [1] To meet once a week. [2] To come punctually [3] To begin with singing or prayer [4] To speak each of us in order, freely and plainly, the true state of our soul, with the faults we have committed in thought, word, or deed, and the temptations we have felt since our last meeting [5] To desire some person among us (thence called a leader) to speak his own state first, and then to ask the rest in order as many and as searching questions as may be concerning their state, sins, and temptations" Two questions are to be asked occasionally, thus —"Do you desire we should come as close as possible, that we should cut to the quick, and search your heart to the bottom? Is it your desire and design to be on this and all other occasions entirely open, so as to speak everything that is in your heart, without exception, without disguise, and without reserve?" Four questions are, however, to be asked at every meeting of the band —[1] "What known sins have you committed since our last meeting? [2] What temptations have you met with? [3] How were you delivered? [4] What have you thought, said, or done, of which you doubt whether it be a sin or not?" [Wesley's *Works*, xv 212, 1st ed]

These "bands" were considered of great importance for the spiritual discipline of his followers by Wesley "As soon," he wrote to his preachers in 1768, "as there are four men or women believers in any place, put them into a band These need to be inquired of continually, and the place of any that do not meet supplied In every place where there are bands, meet them constantly, and encourage them to speak without reserve" [*Min of Conf* i 79] "Exhort the leaders of bands to speak to those with them in the closest manner possible" [*ibid* 73].

"An objection boldly and frequently urged is, 'all these bands are mere popery' A very stale objection, which many people make against anything they do not like, and which betrays the gross ignorance of those who make it in two respects the confession we practise (in bands) Papists do not, the confession they hold (*i.e* private to a priest) our Church holds also" [Wesley's *Works*, xv 214] The band meetings were considered as private and confidential and the nature of the confessions required at them was, of course, such as obliged the bands for each sex to be held separately It was also contrived that each band should consist of persons occupying similar positions in life, and of about a uniform age, so that they might speak their minds with the less embarrassment. After Wesley's death the band part of his system greatly fell off [*Min of Conf* iii 294]

2] *Classes* The next step in the system is that of "classes," consisting of from twelve to thirty persons, to one of which every Methodist must necessarily belong, several of these classes making a "society" or congregation The mem-

[1] This system of "bands" was copied from the Moravians, having been established by Zinzendorf in 1727 "The Societies called bands," said Zinzendorf, speaking in 1747 of what had occurred twenty years before, "consist of a few individuals met together in the name of Jesus, amongst whom Jesus is who converse together in a particularly cordial and childlike manner on the whole state of their hearts, and conceal nothing from each other, but who have wholly committed themselves to each other's care in the Lord Cordiality, secrecy, and daily intercourse is of great service to such individuals, and ought never to be neglected, but whenever slothfulness creeps in, the individuals ought to feel ashamed of it and amend" [Spangenberg's *Life of Zinzendorf*, Jackson's transl 87] "Love feasts" were also established at Herrnhut in 1727, originating in little companies that were provided with "something from the Count's kitchen for dinner, which they ate together in love" after returning from receiving the Communion [*ibid* 89]

bers of these classes are required to meet, under a leader of their own election, once a week, when, after a hymn and a prayer, each member of the class is expected to follow the leader in telling his spiritual "experience" during the week preceding This practice has been found to degenerate into unreal exaggeration, in which persons often magnify the depths of wickedness out of which they have escaped, and mostly the heights of goodness to which they have attained And it seems impossible that ordinary persons could be trusted to tell their "experience" without such unreality arising, partly from a supposed necessity of saying something, partly from the difficulty of making a true "diagnosis" of one's own case, and partly from emulation in the ostentation of humility

The class-meeting is, however, a very essential part of the modern Methodist system "Whatever may be alleged," says the Conference of 1870, "against that mode of Christian fellowship which is in use among ourselves, it was the origin of Methodism The peculiar features of our system have grown out of the class meeting . We exhort you on every ground to value the pearl of Methodist privileges To surrender the class meeting is to take the heart out of Methodism, to esteem it lightly is to enfeeble the pulsations of that heart" [*Min of Conf* 1870, p 216] In the next year, however, the Conference "cannot but mourn over the report this year of a diminished number in our classes," and they associate this diminution with the "spiritual depression" of Methodists [*Min of Conf* 1871, p 227] It is also to be observed that the class meeting has an important bearing on the financial prosperity of the Methodist community, since every member of a class is required to contribute at least one penny weekly, and one shilling quarterly to the general fund, out of which ministers are paid This Wesley calls his "original rule" [*Min of Conf* p i 159, ed 1812]

3] *Circuits* Several of the "societies" (or congregations formed by the union of several classes) are organized into a "circuit," which generally comprehends the chapels in some market town and the villages for ten or twelve miles round. To each of these circuits are appointed from one to five ministers, and a number of lay or "local" preachers, the ministers being technically called "travelling preachers," because they are not allowed to continue in the same circuit for more than one or two years, the local preachers always remaining in the circuit to which they belong The senior minister of each circuit is called the "superintendent" of it, and to him is committed the general supervision of all the societies and the preachers within its boundaries These superintendents were originally called "assistants" to Wesley

4] *Districts* The circuits are again organized into "districts," of which there are thirty-three in England and Scotland, each containing on an average eighteen circuits. These districts (which were arranged by the Conference after Wesley's death) are organized chiefly for the purpose of gathering the preachers together in meetings at appointed times for financial and disciplinal objects. Of the district meetings thus gathered each one acts as a kind of local committee of the Conference, when that body is not sitting, having authority to suspend preachers for misconduct or insufficiency, to authorize the building of chapels, and to superintend the finances of the district Every district has its chairman and financial secretary

5] *The Conference* This is the central governing body of the Methodist community It consisted originally of those travelling preachers whom Wesley invited to meet him once a year for consultation respecting the affairs of the community, and to assist him in making and enforcing arrangements for its government In the year 1784, this annual Conference was formed into a body, recognisable in Courts of Law by a "Deed of Declaration," drawn up under the advice of counsel, and properly enrolled in the Court of Chancery Under this deed, "The Yearly Conference of the people called Methodists" consists of one hundred of the travelling preachers originally nominated by Wesley, its succession being, however, provided for by directing that after his death vacancies should be filled up by the Conference itself It meets once a year in London or some large provincial town, for a session not to exceed three weeks, or to last less than five days, and appoints committees for carrying on the details of business connected with the various institutions of Methodism during the interval between its meetings Although the Deed of Declaration limits this body to the number of one hundred, every preacher who has been admitted into "full connexion," after five years' itinerancy, is permitted to attend, and to vote in its proceedings The presidency of the Conference is the post of highest honour in the Methodist community, having been filled by Wesley himself for forty-seven years

The principal business of the Conference is the reception of probationers on trial for the ministry, the ordination of those preachers whose term of probation has expired, the appointment of preachers to every circuit for the ensuing year, and the general supervision of the affairs of Methodists throughout England The results of its proceedings are ultimately published in the form of "Minutes of Conference"

IV THE THEOLOGY OF THE METHODISTS has been from the beginning of their existence as a community, and still is, formally that of the Church of England John and Charles Wesley were, like their father and their elder brother, High Churchmen of the Laudian school, they, like Laud and other opponents of Calvinism, being called "Arminians" John Wesley accepted the title of Arminian, but the jejune creed of the true Arminians was far from being his creed, and he accepted it only in the modified sense of anti-Calvinist, being very imprudent in accepting at all a name which merely represented one controversial facett of his theology [1]

1 Wesley's almost morbid aversion to Calvinism might be illustrated by very many passages from his works.

It is not unfrequently alleged, indeed, that the theology of Wesley in his later life was very different from that of his earlier days But those who knew him well thought differently, and his own words agree with their testimony Alexander Knox wrote, "In his prevalent tastes and likings, as an individual, he was a Church of England man of the highest tone, not only did he value and love that pure spirit of faith and piety which the Church of England inherits from Catholic antiquity, but even in the more circumstantial part there was not a service or a ceremony, a gesture or a habit, for which he has not an unfeigned predilection" "I am now," he himself writes in his last years, "and have been from my youth, a member and minister of the Church of England, and I have no desire nor design to separate from it till my soul separates from my body" "I have uniformly gone on for fifty years, never varying from the doctrine of the Church at all" "I have been uniform both in doctrine and discipline for above these fifty years, and it is a little too late for me to turn into a new path now I am grey-headed' Abundant illustrations have also been given from his works to the same effect [*John Wesley and High Churchmen*, by an old Methodist, 1866], shewing that his teaching on the subject of the Sacraments of Baptism and the Holy Communion, and on other chief doctrines of Christianity, was distinctly that of the Church of England as interpreted by theologians of the present day [1] His very first principle was indeed that of maintaining such a position "I hold all the doctrines of the Church of England," he wrote in 1790, "and I love her Liturgy, I approve her plan of discipline, and only wish it could be put in execution" [*Armin Mag* 1790, p 287] It was in this sense also that he accepted the names "Precisian" and "Methodist," writing that a "a true Methodist" was "none other than a true Churchman," precise and methodical in his observance of Church rules respecting the practice of personal piety [Wesley's *Works*, xvi 10]

The standard of Methodist theology is still formally the same, being based on Wesley's Sermons and his Notes to the New Testament, to both of which the preachers of the "Old Connexion" are obliged to subscribe The Thirty-nine Articles of Religion are accepted by Methodists, as is also the Book of Common Prayer, the sacramental offices of which are used entire, although those of Morning and Evening Prayer are usually abridged No standard of doctrine other than that of the Church of England has ever been imposed upon the Methodists either by Wesley or by the Conference, and what variations from it there may be in the teaching of some of their ministers are the variations of individual opinion only, which have no sanction from any authoritative Methodist formulary of faith

V The Practical System of the Methodists Apart from the usurpation of the sacerdotal office by their ministers, the Methodists have not anything in their practical system which is inconsistent with the principles of the Church of England It met with the disapprobation of many in former days on account of its "enthusiasm," but much of what is called enthusiastic in the practices of the Methodists results from a sincere zeal in the pursuit of personal religion, and its faults are rather those of stilted language and general bad taste than those of unorthodoxy The discipline adopted by them in their "classes" is simply a form of pastoral superintendence, and though the "class-meetings" at which they "tell their experience," have often been made occasions for the display of spiritual vanity and pride, their real object is exactly that of confession—the unburdening of conscience Such practices were strange enough to the "donnish" bishops and other prominent persons who were taken as exemplars of the Church of England down to quite a recent period, but the revival of personal religion and devotional earnestness which was effected by the Evanglical and Tractarian movements has naturalized the zeal and the confessional system of the Methodists and has also shewn that stilted language and bad taste in religion are merely class peculiarities, which must be borne with until they pass away under the influence of sound religious education

The practical system of the Methodists is founded on a set of rules which were drawn up by the two Wesleys in the year 1743, and as these offer a full illustration of it in the present day, as well as in the early days of Methodism, they are given at length

The following is taken from the Minutes of 1776 "*Q* 26 Calvinism has been the grand hindrance of the work of God What makes men swallow it so greedily? *A* Because it is so pleasing to flesh and blood the doctrine of final perseverance in particular *Q* 27 What can be done to stop its progress? *A* 1 Let all our preachers carefully read our tracts and Mr Fletcher's and Mr Sellon's 2 Let them preach Universal Redemption frequently and explicitly, but in love and gentleness, taking care never to return railing for railing Let the Calvinists have all this to themselves 3 Do not imitate them in screaming, allegorizing, calling themselves ordained, boasting of their learning, college, or 'my lady'" The Countess of Huntingdon was the great patroness of Whitfield and the Calvinistic Methodists The rivalry of John Wesley and "my lady" was so well known that they came to be called "Pope John" and "Pope Joan"

[1] The tone of Wesley's churchmanship may be illustrated by the following memorandum in his own handwriting, written when he was about forty years of age —

"I believe [myself] it a duty to observe, so far as I can [without breaking communion with my own Church]

"1 To baptize by immersion

"2 To use Water, Oblation of Elements, Invocation, Alms, a Prothesis, in the Eucharist

"3 To pray for the faithful departed

"4 To pray standing on Sunday in Pentecost

"5 To observe Saturday and Sunday Pentecost as festival

"6. To abstain from blood, things strangled

"I think it prudent (our own Church not considered)

"1 To observe the Stations.

"2 Lent, especially the Holy Week

"3 To turn to the East at the Creed."

[Urlin's *Wesley's Place in Church Hist* 69]

"RULES OF THE SOCIETY OF THE PEOPLE CALLED METHODISTS

"1 In the latter end of the year 1739, eight or ten persons came to me in London, who appeared to be deeply convinced of sin, and earnestly groaning for redemption. They desired (as did two or three more the next day) that I would spend some time with them in prayer, and advise them how to flee from the wrath to come, which they saw continually hanging over their heads That we might have more time for this great work, I appointed a day when they might all come together, which, from thenceforward, they did every week, viz, on Thursday in the evening To these, and as many more as desired to join with them (for their number increased daily), I gave those advices from time to time which I judged most needful for them, and we always concluded our meetings with prayer suitable to their several necessities.

"2 This was the rise of the UNITED SOCIETY, first in London, and then in other places Such a society is no other than 'a company of men having the form, and seeking the power, of godliness, united in order to pray together, to receive the word of exhortation, and to watch over one another in love, that they may help each other to work out their salvation'

"3 That it may the more easily be discerned whether they are indeed working out their own salvation, each society is divided into smaller companies, called classes, according to their respective places of abode There are about twelve persons in every class, one of whom is styled the leader It is his business,

"[1] To see each person in his class once a week, at least, in order

"To inquire how their souls prosper,

"To advise, reprove, comfort, or exhort, as occasion may require,

"To receive what they are willing to give towards the support of the Gospel

"[2] To meet the ministers and the stewards of the society once a week, in order

"To inform the minister of any that are sick, or of any that walk disorderly, and will not be reproved,

"To pay to the stewards what they have received of their several classes in the week preceding, and

"To shew their account of what each person has contributed

"4 There is one only condition previously required of those who desire admission into those societies, viz, 'a desire to flee from the wrath to come, and be saved from their sins.' But wherever this is really fixed in the soul, it will be shewn by its fruits It is therefore expected of all who continue therein that they should continue to evidence their desire of salvation,

"First, By doing no harm, by avoiding evil in every kind, especially that which is most generally practised Such as

"The taking the name of God in vain

"The profaning the day of the Lord, either by doing ordinary work thereon, or by buying or selling·

"Drunkenness, buying or selling spirituous liquors, or drinking them, unless in cases of extreme necessity·

"Fighting, quarrelling, brawling; brother going to law with brother, returning evil for evil, or railing for railing, the using many words in buying or selling

"The buying or selling uncustomed goods

"The giving or taking things on usury, viz. unlawful interest

"Uncharitable or unprofitable conversation, particularly speaking evil of magistrates or of ministers

"Doing to others as we would not they should do unto us

"Doing what we know is not for the glory of God, as,

"The putting on of gold and costly apparel,

"The taking such diversions as cannot be used in the name of the Lord Jesus,

"The singing those songs, or reading those books, which do not tend to the knowledge or love of God.

"Softness, and needless self-indulgence

"Laying up treasure upon earth

"Borrowing without a probability of paying, or taking up goods without a probability of paying for them

"5 It is expected of all who continue in these societies, that they should continue to evidence their desire of salvation

"Secondly, By doing good, by being in every kind merciful after their power, as they have opportunity, doing good of every possible sort, and as far as is possible to all men·

"To their bodies, of the ability that God giveth, by giving food to the hungry, by clothing the naked, by helping or visiting them that are sick, or in prison·

"To their souls, by instructing, reproving, or exhorting all we have any intercourse with trampling under foot that enthusiastic doctrine of devils, that 'we are not to do good, unless our hearts be free to it'

"By doing good, especially to them that are of the household of faith, or groaning so to be, employing them preferably to others, buying one of another, helping each other in business, and so much the more, because the world will love its own, and them only

"By all possible diligence and frugality, that the Gospel be not blamed

"By running with patience the race that is set before them, denying themselves, and taking up their cross daily, submitting to bear the reproach of Christ; to be as the filth and offscouring of the world, and looking that men should say all manner of evil of them falsely, for the Lord's sake.

"6 It is expected of all who desire to continue in these societies that they should continue to evidence their desire of salvation.

"Thirdly, By attending upon all the ordinances of God. such are

"The public worship of God,

"The ministry of the Word, either read or expounded,

"The Supper of the Lord,

"Family and private prayer,

"Searching the Scriptures, and

"Fasting or abstinence

"7 These are the general rules of our societies all which we are taught of God to observe, even in His written Word,—the only rule, and the sufficient rule, both of our faith and practice And all these we know His Spirit writes on every truly awakened heart If there be any among us who observe them not, who habitually break any of them, let it be made known unto them who watch over that soul, as they that must give an account We will admonish him of the error of his ways we will bear with him for a season But then, if he repent not, he hath no more place among us We have delivered our own souls.

"JOHN WESLEY,
"CHARLES WESLEY

"May 1, 1743"

These rules might just as well be called those of "the people called Churchmen" as those of "the people called Methodists," and when the Wesleys framed them, the two zealous brothers were but working out in their own way a good system of pastoral work such as is mapped out in Bishop Burnet's *Pastoral Care,* or George Herbert's *Country Parson,* and a good system of personal holiness such as was illustrated by the lives of the Ferrars, and has been illustrated by many others before and since, both in the Church of England and in Catholic Churches elsewhere

In conclusion, it may be said that there is nothing which really differences the Methodist community from the Church of England, except the assumption of the sacerdotal office and sacerdotal functions by its ministers This is an error of a very grave character, but it is one which has partly resulted from the incomplete manner in which the nature of the priest's office was set forth by theologians of a past day, and it is, therefore, one for which much excuse may be made The day may come when the better instructed Methodist preachers may seek and obtain episcopal ordination, and when the less educated class may also have work assigned to them analogous to their present work, but not sacerdotal, under similar authority A general movement of this kind would go far towards ending the sectarian position of the Methodist body and restoring it to the position which it was intended by its founder to occupy The two streams of practical godliness which now flow in the two separate channels of the Church of England and of the Methodist community, might then combine to form one great river whose broad expanse would represent an unity consistent with the varieties of English character and habit, and whose almost irresistible force would mould the religion of English-speaking people throughout the world

VI STATISTICS OF THE WESLEYAN METHODISTS At the time of Wesley's death in the year 1791, his Societies in various countries numbered 136,622 members Of these there were 60,000 in Great Britain, and 11,000 in Ireland, far the greater proportion of the former, 35,000 in the north and 12,000 in the west, being among the people of the northern and western counties The number of ministers in Great Britain was then about 300, not including the local preachers

In the year 1871, there were in England and Scotland 347,090 members of classes, and 18,126 on trial, the number of ministers being 1,649 These numbers shew a decrease during the previous twelve months of 1,381 members of classes and 2,307 on trial A growing decrease in numbers is conspicuous in the iron and cotton districts, in the metropolis and in Scotland, as is shewn by the following table, and in populous districts it amounts to nearly 2 per cent per annum diminution of actual members

	1870	1871	Decrease
Metropolis,	20,252	19,593	659
Lancashire,	29,659	29,431	228
Birmingham Iron district,	11,915	11,416	499
Durham, Cumberland, and Northumberland,	29,862	29,664	198
Scotland,	5,722	5,456	266
Total,	97,410	95,560	1,850

Other districts also are decreasing in numbers, but there is a partial counterbalance on the whole of some increase in Yorkshire, Wales, and the Eastern Counties The whole number of members throughout the British Empire amounted in 1871 to 576,000, those on trial numbering 39,000, there being an increase of 5,000 in Canada and Australia during the preceding year

The Methodists formerly did but little in the work of educating their poor, considering their great resources, but since the formation of the "Wesleyan Education Committee" in 1837, they have been much more active in this direction, especially in recent years In 1863, their week-day schools were 556 in number, with an attendance of 79,582 scholars In 1871, the schools were 889, and the scholars 150,765 The number of Sunday scholars is about four times as large, and there is a teacher for every six children

The Wesleyan Methodist Missionary Society employs upwards of 1,000 missionaries, for whose education a College has recently been established at Richmond near London The expenditure of the Society on its missionary work amounts to £150,000 a year

There are also two other Colleges for the education of Wesleyan ministers, one at Didsbury near Manchester, accommodating seventy students, and another for forty at Headingley near Leeds

[*Minutes of Conference* Wesley's *Works,* ed 1773 and 1829 Myles' *Chronological Hist Meth* Warren's *Digest of Meth Laws and Regul* Coke and Moore's *Life of Wesley* Tyerman's *Life of Wesley* Smith's *Hist of*

Meth. Steven's *Hist. of Meth* DICT. *of* THEOL METHODISM.]

METHODISTS, CALVINISTIC Another branch of the great stream of religious revival, which flowed off from that of Wesley under the guidance of George Whitfield in the year 1741.

While he was a young servitor at Pembroke [A D 1732-1736], Whitfield had become known to Charles Wesley, who was then a student of Christ Church, and through him to his brother John, who was a Fellow of Lincoln He had thus been brought into association with the Methodists in the University stage of their existence, and when he was ordained deacon, in 1736, he very soon gave up his dull Hampshire curacy at Dummer, and assumed to himself a roving commission as a preacher wherever he could get people for hearers After two years of such work, he left the shores of England for missionary work in Georgia just as Wesley was returning to them after his failure there Reaching Georgia in May 1738, he was back in London on Dec 8th of the same year, and on January 11th, 1739, was ordained priest He sailed again for his living at Savannah in August, after much itinerant preaching in England, but towards the end of 1740, being suspended by the Episcopal Commissary in Georgia for ecclesiastical irregularities, he appealed home, and returned thither himself by March 11th, 1741, marrying a widow ten or twelve years older than himself shortly afterwards The thirty-four years of his ministry were all spent in a similar restless manner, for during that time (of which he lived half in England and half in America) he made thirteen voyages across the Atlantic, and seldom remained many days together in one place, either in the old country or the new

It was while Whitfield was in America in 1740, that he received information respecting Wesley's "Arminian" preaching of Universal Redemption from John Cennick, one of the Methodist lay-preachers, who accompanied his information with an earnest entreaty that he would return home to oppose the "heresy" of their master A controversy at once arose between Wesley and Whitfield, and they preached and printed sermons against each other across the ocean On his return to England Whitfield immediately began preaching on Kennington Common, and in Moorfields, not far from Wesley's "Foundry" chapel Once he was invited to preach in the chapel itself, and using the opportunity for the proclamation of his Calvinistic views respecting the eternal decree of some to damnation as well as of some to salvation, he was not permitted to preach there any more For this he consoled himself with some words in Beza's Life of Calvin, "Calvin turned out of Geneva, but behold a new Church arises," and the omen was fulfilled by some of his admirers erecting a temporary wooden "Tabernacle" for him in Moorfields, shortly to be superseded by a permanent building [1]

From this date, 1741, the Methodists who dissented from Wesley on the ground of his opposition to Calvinism, looked to Whitfield as their theological leader for thirty years, but the practical leadership of the party drifted into the hands of the enthusiastic Countess of Huntingdon, and most of them in England became members of the Low Church sect which she established, half within and half without the Church of England [HUNTINGDON CONNEXION] Whitfield died at Newbury-Port near Boston, in New England, on September 30th, 1770 He had no power whatever of organization, his one talent being that of impassioned preaching, and consequently his followers were never formed into a compact society by him as the Wesleyan Methodists were Adam Clarke records a saying of Whitfield's illustrating this fact "My brother Wesley acted wisely The souls that were awakened under his ministry he joined in class, and thus preserved the fruits of his labour This I neglected; and my people are a rope of sand" [2] Some part of the sand agglomerated in the formation of Lady Huntingdon's sect but a large portion of Whitfield's followers were absorbed into the Church, to form the nucleus of the "Evangelical" school [LOW CHURCHMEN] Some of their chapels were, however, kept up in a few places independently of the Church, yet following its usages so closely as to be mistaken for Episcopal chapels Before the revival of Church building, not a few of them were found in which the Prayer Book, the surplice, and all Church customs were adopted in the same manner as in Lady Huntingdon's Connexion, although the ministers were not ordained in the Church Such were Surrey Chapel, where the well-known Rowland Hill, brother of the great Lord Hill, was minister (who was, however, in deacon's orders), and Ranelagh Chapel, Chelsea, so well known at a later date as the Court Theatre Most of these, however, have given way before Church extension, and the few scattered congregations of Calvinistic Methodists which still remain adopt the name of "Independent Methodists," and the usages of the Independents

METHODISTS, WELSH CALVINISTIC A large community of Methodists which owes its origin indirectly to Wesley, and has adopted his system of organization, but which follows the Calvinistic theology of Whitfield

[1] "Tabernacle" was a term used for the wooden sheds set up for Divine worship after the Fire of London It is also used by Tillotson in 1688 in a letter to Lady Russel, and as synonymous with "chapel of ease" in the report of Convocation to Parliament respecting the scheme for new churches in 1710

[2] Wesley records his conviction, on August 25th, 1763, that the work of the Calvinistic Methodists was a "rope of sand" in spiritual matters also "I was more convinced than ever that the preaching like an apostle, without joining together those that are awakened and training them up in the ways of God, is only begetting children for the murderer How much preaching has there been for these twenty years in Pembrokeshire! But no regular societies, no discipline, no order or connection And the consequence is, that nine in ten of the once awakened are now faster asleep than ever" [Wesley's *Journ* xii 33]

The direct originator of Welsh Methodism was an Oxford disciple of the Wesleys and friend of Whitfield named Howell Harris [A D 1714-1773], a young man of some property at Trevecca. Harris left Oxford without taking his degree, and when (being under twenty-three years of age) Bishop Clagett declined to ordain him [A D 1736] he began to emulate the career of Whitfield as an itinerant preacher among his countrymen, and formed societies similar to those of Wesley. This work he continued in spite of much opposition, and before 1742 he had won over ten clergymen to co-operate with him, among whom the most effective fellow-worker was Daniel Rowlands, Rector of Llangeitho, near Cardigan, and Chaplain to the Duke of Leinster, whose grand presence and voice gained him the name of "the Thunderer' among his excitable countrymen Rowlands was suspended by his bishop after some years of irregular ministration, and for the rest of his life he followed the course of Wesley and Whitfield, travelling from one end to another of Wales, and continually preaching to multitudes with vehement energy until a little before his death, which took place in 1790, when he was seventy-seven years old The work of Harris and Rowlands in South Wales was taken up in North Wales by Thomas Charles, Curate of Bala, one of the founders of the Bible Society He was offered several benefices in the Church, but he preferred the position of authority which he acquired over a large number of his countrymen by following in the footsteps of Rowlands Before his time the Welsh Methodists had not actually coagulated into a sect, although long practically dissociated from the Church, but in 1811, Mr Charles completed their sectarian organization by "ordaining" a number of their lay-preachers, and establishing a settled system of rules for the government of the Society In 1823, a "Confession of Faith" was agreed to, which was founded on the Calvinistic Confession of the Westminster Assembly of Divines

At the present time the actual members of the Welsh Methodist sect number about 60,000, but many who are not Methodists attend their chapels They have 200 ministers, 250 lay-preachers, and between eight and nine hundred chapels In estimating the number of chapels, however, it must be remembered that some of them represent a body of a dozen or two only of attendants "I am not sure," says a recent correspondent in a Welsh Methodist Magazine, "that some chapels are not erected and small branches separated from the mother Church to be independent churches, from desire of office and a spirit of ambition Some persons feel—Oh! there is no possibility of my being a leader in this Church as it is, no one here sees any need of me, but we will have a little Church of our own, and we will be heads over it The great poet Milton puts in the mouth of Satan, 'Better to reign in hell than serve in heaven' The language of some men's conduct is, 'Better to reign over a society where there are no more than five members, than serve in a Church where there are 300'" The Welsh Methodists have training colleges for their ministers at Trevecca and at Bala.

METHODISTS, NEW CONNEXION This body of Methodists seceded from the original connexion under the leadership of Alexander Kilham, in the year 1797, and are hence known also as "Kilhamites" On their first separation they were also called "The New Itinerancy"

The New Connexion was formed by about 5000 Methodists, who were discontented because the following claims were not granted by the Conference [1] The right of the people to hold their public religious worship at such hours as were most convenient, without their being restricted to the mere intervals of the hours appointed for service in the Church [2] The right of the people to receive the ordinances of baptism and the Lord's Supper from the hands of their own ministers, and in their own places of worship [3] The right of the people to a representation in the district meetings and the annual Conferences, and thereby to participate in the government of the community and in the appropriation of funds [4] The right of the people to have a voice, through the local business meetings, in the reception and expulsion of members, the choice of local officers, and in the calling out of candidates for the ministry

The growing discontent had been much fostered by the anonymous publications and avowed opposition of Kilham, a Methodist from Wesley's own village of Epworth, who had done good service in the Channel Islands The position of Kilham at last became so dangerous to the preachers who ruled the Society, that it was resolved to accept the risk of expelling him, notwithstanding the number of those who would follow, rather than that of allowing him to break up their oligarchy At the Conference held on July 26th, 1796, Kilham was therefore required to subscribe afresh to the canon law of Methodism, the "rules of the large minutes" of Conference His reply to the demand was "I agree to them as far as they are agreeable with Scripture" The answer of the Conference was, "We all agree with the Koran of Mahomet with the same limitation, namely, as far as it is agreeable to Scripture, but we agree to these rules because we believe them to *be* agreeable with Scripture" As the accused, or already condemned, preacher had nothing further to say, he was expelled by the following sentence of excommunication "Whereas Mr Kilham has brought several charges against Mr Wesley and the body of the preachers of a slanderous and criminal nature, which charges he declared he could prove, and which, upon examination, he could not prove even one of them, and also considering the disunion and strife which he has occasioned in many of the societies, we adjudge him unworthy of being a member of the Methodist Connexion" Kilham protested against this sentence, and a Committee was sent to him to see whether he would subscribe the "Articles of Pacification," but as he refused to do so, the sentence was confirmed, with the declaration of the Conference, that "he could have no place in the Connexion while he continued in his present opinions" [*Min. of Conf* i 347]

Kilham being a man of some power and great energy, soon gathered around him a large body of seceders, 167 class-leaders in Leeds alone coming to his side; some of the circuits in Yorkshire, Lancashire, and Nottinghamshire retained hardly any members of the Old Connexion, and the first census of the New one shewed as many as 5000 members The disgusted Conference issued an Address, which contains the following passage. "We shall lose all the turbulent disturbers of our Zion,—all who have embraced the sentiments of Payne, and place a great part of their religion in contending for (what they call) liberty The vine which the Lord has planted among us with His own right hand needed to pass through this pruning and purgation At the same time, all our watchfulness and diligence should be employed, that the wheat may not be destroyed with the tares For the loss of the latter we have reason to be thankful to God And we trust and believe that He will preserve our dear faithful brethren from all the attacks of Satan and His emissaries The Captain of our salvation is stronger than the demon of discord, and He will in His good time drive him back to the hell whence he came" [*Min of Conf* i 388] But there is no reason to think that there was any such Atheism among the seceders as they are here charged with nor was the religious liberty for which they seceded at all inconsistent with the principles of Methodism as they had by this time become developed The fact is, that the ruling preachers inherited Wesley's intolerance of opposition, and his custom of assuming that all who opposed him were necessarily influenced by the powers of darkness

The New Connexion Methodists at once adopted the practice respecting the Sacraments which were only gradually adopted by the parent sect, and they also introduced the "lay element" freely into the organizations of their Society from the class upwards to the Conference This latter point is now the only one in which they differ from the Wesleyan Methodists of the older stock

Their numbers are not very large In the year 1870 there were 22,633 members in England and Wales, with 419 chapels and rooms, and 149 preachers This was a decrease of 605 members during the preceding twelve months, the diminution in London being 132, in the Northern counties 412, and in Cornwall 177, counterbalanced by a small increase in some other parts of England The sect is distributed chiefly over the northern counties, where they number 13,568, in Lancashire, Yorkshire, Durham, and Northumberland It expends more than £5000 a year on foreign missions, and numbers 9000 members out of England

METHODISTS, PRIMITIVE Shortly after the secession of the New Connexion from the main body of the Methodists, extensive attempts were made to recruit the ranks of the latter by means of "revival services," especially in Cornwall, Lancashire, and Staffordshire In 1807 these efforts were assisted, in the last-named county, by Lawrence Dow, an American Methodist who had previously been engaged in the same kind of work in Ireland as well as in the United States To him is traced the origin in England of the well-known "camp-meetings," the first of which was held at Mole Cop, near Newcastle in Staffordshire These were extensively promoted by two local preachers named William Clowes and Hugh James Bourne, who had long advocated a revival of the original methods by which Wesley, Whitfield, and other field-preachers had won so many converts sixty years before The Methodists were now, however, established in a position of more dignity than in those long-gone days, and they looked upon a revival of old Methodist habits much as a parvenu looks upon the trade of his grandfather The Conference of 1807 asked itself, therefore, "What is the judgment of the Conference concerning what are called camp-meetings?" and answered, "It is our judgment that, even supposing such meetings to be allowable in America, they are highly improper in England, and likely to be productive of considerable mischief. And we disclaim all connection with them." [*Min of Conf* ii 403]

In 1808, Bourne was expelled from the Methodist body by the Burslem Quarterly Meeting, and in 1810 this expulsion was followed by that of Clowes These two local preachers, being thus made the victims of a generation of travelling preachers who had learned to despise the origin of Methodism, at once began to form a new sect, and were joined by sixteen congregations and twenty-eight preachers in Lancashire and Cheshire Thus a nucleus was formed for an organization which has numbered more than all other offshoots of the parent body put together, and which has been its most dangerous rival Within twenty years, in 1830, the Primitive Methodists numbered 36,000, which was 6,000 more than the original Methodists had numbered in England in 1774, after thirty years of Wesley's vigorous preaching and organizing, and at the present time they reckon 30,000 more members than the original community did in 1804, when it had been in existence for the same number of years By the statistics published in their Minutes of Conference, the Primitive Methodists numbered in 1870 as many as 150,169 in England, and 12,000 elsewhere, being an increase of 1152 during the previous twelve months Their chapels were reckoned as 6,397, their travelling preachers as 961, and their local preachers as 14,332 Of day schools they counted only 41, with 2,717 scholars, but their Sunday scholars were 271,802 in number, with 47,379 teachers. The distribution of the sect in England is 32,916 in the southern and western counties, 12,609 in the eastern counties, 20 981 in the Birmingham iron district, and 83,663 in the northern counties.[1]

[1] The Primitive Methodists still keep up the early habits of the original followers of Wesley, as will be seen

METHODISTS, PRIMITIVE IRISH This name is used in Ireland as descriptive of those Methodists who still adhere to Wesley's system of making their Societies part of the Church system

METHODISTS, BRYANITE. This sect of Methodists, which is also known by the vague name of "Bible Christians," owes its origin to a local preacher of Cornwall named O'Bryan, who separated from the main body of the Methodists in the year 1815 and returned to it again in 1829 There are no substantial differences whatever between their doctrines and customs and those of the sect from which they seceded, except that they permit women to preach, and that the preachers form a smaller portion of their governing bodies The Bryanites are especially a West-country sect, the distribution throughout England in their circuits and home missions in 1870 being as follows —

	Chapels	Members
Cornwall and Devonshire,	370	13,000
West Somersetshire and Wales,	60	2,000
Sussex, Hampshire, and other Counties,	114	3,466
Total,	544	18,466

It thus appears that there is a chapel to every 33 members of the sect There are also about 7000 Bryanites in Canada and Australia. [*Min of Conf of Bible Christ* 1870]

METHODISTS, ASSOCIATED [METHODISTS, UNITED FREE CHURCH]

METHODIST REFORMERS [METHODISTS, UNITED FREE CHURCH]

METHODISTS, UNITED FREE CHURCH This sect of Methodists has been organized in its present form since the year 1857, but previously to that time the two bodies by whose union it was formed had existed, the one from 1835, the other from 1849

The first secession, that of the WESLEYAN METHODIST ASSOCIATION, arose out of a dispute respecting the establishment of the Wesleyan Theological Institution Dr Samuel Warren (best known as the father of the author of *Ten Thousand a Year*) taking a part in this quarrel which was objectionable to the other members of the Conference, that body secured his expulsion by the district meeting from the Manchester chapel of which he was the minister, the act being sustained by the Vice-Chancellor, and eventually by the Lord Chancellor [*Min of Conf* 1835] Dr Warren was then expelled from the Methodist body by the Conference, and within two years about 20,000 had joined him in forming the sect of "Associated Methodists" The founder of the secession eventually took holy orders, and became Incumbent of All Souls' Church in Manchester, and from that time its numbers began to diminish

The WESLEYAN METHODIST REFORMERS, the second of these two sects, originated in a quarrel of a still more trivial and personal character Some anonymous pamphlets entitled "Fly Sheets" were published at intervals from 1844 to 1848, in which the proceedings of the Conference were severely criticised, and some rough personalities used towards Jabez Bunting, the President. With its usual intolerance this body of preachers expelled the supposed authors, three in number, from the Methodist body, and, as usual, stigmatized the agitation against themselves in terms that would have been more appropriate to the condemnation of blasphemy The excommunication of the three preachers, however, raised a storm of indignation, and 400 delegates from those who sympathized with them assembled in London just before the meeting of the Conference At the latter a petition was presented for the redress of certain specified grievances, to which more than 50,000 Methodists had signed their names The Conference was at once seized with the desperate instinct of self-preservation, and excommunicated all who had been in any way concerned in the meeting of the delegates, as well as whole "classes" and "societies" of those who had been most conspicuous in criticising their authority This great multitude of excommunicated Methodists soon became a flourishing body, reporting itself as possessing 339 chapels, with an attendance of about 35,000 persons at their services

In the year 1857 the Association and the Reformers joined together in the formation of a new body, which calls itself "The United Methodist Free Churches," which numbered in 1870 as many as 62,898 members of classes, with 5786 on trial, and 5000 elsewhere than in England. The chapels and preaching-rooms of the community are 1460 in number, which are provided with 282 travelling and 3309 local preachers

It has 61 day schools, with 6117 scholars The Sunday schools are 1142, with 150,560 scholars, and 23,726 teachers The members of the sect are distributed over England in the following proportion —In London and the south-eastern counties, 8171 , in Dorset, Devon, and Cornwall, 10,027 , in the Birmingham iron district, 6058 , and in the northern counties, 38,642. There was a net decrease in 1869-70 of 120 members , but the decrease in Cornwall was 195, in Northumberland and Durham, 195, in Nottinghamshire and Derbyshire, 212 These districts contain one-third of the whole number of members, and thus the decrease amounts to 3 per cent in those counties.

by the following particulars, very moderately stated by the *Primitive Methodist Magazine*, of occurrences in Durham, so recent as 1871 —"On the 5th of March last, Mrs Thompson, formerly Miss Hyde, commenced a series of special services, which extended over six weeks The chapel will seat 600 persons, and on the week evenings it was often crowded On the Sabbath evenings scores could not find admission Individuals often lay prostrate for hours during the services, and some were restive, and in a trance like state with closed eyes would walk about the chapel, and even stand upon the pew backs, and if not held, appeared as though they would come over the front of the gallery Scores were converted The city membership rose from 58 in March to 110 in June The numbers were taken again in August for September, and there were 106 Several have joined since the numbers were made up. There is converting power in the services Prostrations are still experienced, and moving about in the service at times, but it does not excite so much attention as at first " These "individuals" appear, from other reports, to have been all, or nearly all, young women

METHODISTS, AMERICAN The rise of Methodism in America was simultaneous with its early spread in England, Whitfield carrying thither his fervid zeal in the year 1738, just as Wesley was returning to his native shores from his unsuccessful missionary work in Georgia Whitfield spent at least one-third of his life for thirty-two years [A D 1738-1770] in America, but he himself organized no separate sect there any more than he did in England, leaving his converts to the ministrations of the Church, or of the sects already existing The first Methodist congregation was, in fact, formed not by Whitfield's followers, but by some Irish emigrants who landed in New York in the year 1766 But although they had a local preacher, Philip Embury among them, they did not set themselves up as a separate community until stimulated to do so by a female emigrant of a more energetically sectarian disposition, who arrived in the following year, and through whose exertion the first Methodist chapel in America was erected in John Street, New York, in 1768. The small community thus formed entreated Wesley to send them preachers from England, and ten being sent out at various times, the Methodist Societies in New York and Philadelphia numbered in 1773 about 1200 members When the War of Independence broke out, all the English preachers returned home, but the increase of the sect proceeded so rapidly, that at the close of the war in 1783 they numbered 43 preachers, and 14,000 members

METHODIST EPISCOPAL CHURCH. In the year 1784 the sect so formed received a new constitution from Wesley Assuming to himself the authority of an apostle, Wesley laid hands on Dr Coke (a priest of the Church of England), and Mr Asbury (one of the missionaries who had fled from America ten years before), sending them out with the name of "superintendents," but for the purpose of acting as bishops [See page 315] He also enjoined upon the American Methodists the use of his abridged Book of Common Prayer, and gave them twenty-five articles of religion as the standard of their doctrine Thus reorganized, the sect assumed the name of "The Methodist Episcopal Church," and it has ever since retained the constitution thus given to it by Wesley, its general organization being that of the English Methodists, its ministerial being that of so-called bishops, elders, and deacons

In the Northern States this body of Methodists numbers three-quarters of a million of members, with more than 11,000 preachers In the Southern States, before the war, the number of members was more than half a million, with about 6000 preachers [Stevens' *History of the Meth Episc Church*, New York, 1864]

METHODIST REFORMED CHURCH This sect of American Methodists separated from the main body in the year 1814, giving up the form of Episcopacy and reverting to the original characteristics of Methodism They made much of the early Methodist doctrine of Christian perfection, and also of that respecting the power of faith, which latter they considered capable of restoring the sick to health as in Apostolic days. They were also strongly opposed to slavery, not permitting any person who countenanced it to remain in their community. To these distinctive principles of the sect has lately been added that of "temperance" In the year 1843, it developed into a much larger body by union with a number of Methodists who again seceded from the parent sect on the questions of episcopacy, slavery, and intemperance They now consider themselves the true Wesleyan Methodists of America, but their numbers are not large as compared with the original sect, amounting only to about 25,000 members, and 600 preachers

AFRICAN EPISCOPAL METHODISTS. This is an offshoot of the original sect formed by the secession of its black members in Philadelphia and Baltimore in the year 1816 They profess to hold precisely the same doctrines, and to practise the same discipline as the body from which they seceded, their only reason for separation being the contemptuous treatment which they received from their white brethren

ZION WESLEY METHODISTS This is another community of black seceders from the original Methodists of the Northern States They established separate chapels in the end of the last century, but continued under the control of the Conference of the Episcopal Methodists until 1820 In the latter year disputes arose with the Conference respecting the authority of the latter over the chapel property and the ministers' salaries of the Zion Methodists, and this led to an entire separation

METHODIST SOCIETY. A secession from the Episcopal Methodists which took place in 1820, on a question respecting the administration of local collections of money It was a small body, and was ultimately incorporated with the

METHODIST PROTESTANT CHURCH, a similar secession which was formed in the year 1830, on the question of lay-representation in the Conferences The united bodies now number about 100,000 members, with 2000 preachers

MICHELHAHNITES [MICHELHAHNER] A Pietistic sect of the Evangelical Lutherans of Wurtemberg, said to number about 30,000, and professing to maintain the true principles of the body from which they have separated. They take their name from Michael Hahn, a farmer of Wurtemberg [A.D. 1758-1819], who pretended to receive special inward illuminations, and who gave up his original calling for that of a travelling preacher The Michelhahnites are zealous Millenarians, and expect a "restoration of all things" that is, the salvation of fallen angels and men From among them arose the KORNTHALITES, under the elder Hofmann, immediately after the death of Hahn

MILITES This name is given by Philaster as one of the names by which the FLORINIANS were known [Philast *Hær* lxvi] Epiphanius also says that the Gnostics were called Στρατιωτικοί in Egypt [Epiphan *Hær* xxvi 3] a statement in which he is followed by Theodoret

[*Hær fab* i 23] and St John Damascene [*Hær* xxvi]

MILITZ or MILICZ One of the precursors of Huss and the Calixtines, who was the leader of a great spiritual reformation in Prague between the years 1363 and 1374, but provoked a charge of heresy against himself by wild declarations respecting the immediate approach of Antichrist and the end of the world.

Militz was a native of Cremisia in Moravia, but became Archdeacon of Prague, and Secretary to the Emperor Charles IV, King of Bohemia His ascetic habits led him to give up his offices in the year 1363, and retire to the little town of Bischofteinitz, where he spent six months as assistant to the parish priest He then returned to Prague, and began to take up a position similar to that of Wesley four centuries later, zealously preaching to the people in their native tongue, with stirring exhortations to amendment of life Bohemia, and especially the new city of Prague, was then full of vice, one quarter of the city being called "Benatky" or "Little Venice," because it was wholly occupied by houses appropriated to purposes of profligacy Among the inhabitants of this quarter the preaching of Militz had so good an effect that the name of Little Venice was exchanged for that of "Little Jerusalem," his movement being combined with the use of confession, and of frequent and even daily communion by his penitents

Like so many reforming ascetics of that age, Militz at last wandered into fanaticism on the subject of Antichrist and the Second Advent, which he declared to be immediately at hand In the year 1367, he went to Rome that he might proclaim this belief at the very centre of Christendom, and the Pope, Urban V, being still at Avignon, he affixed a notice to the pillars of St Peter's Church declaring his intention of doing so This led to his being confined for a time within the walls of a Franciscan monastery, but on the Pope's arrival he ordered him to be liberated, to be entertained by one of the cardinals, and eventually to be sent home to Prague His fanaticism, however, growing more dangerous, Gregory XI issued bulls condemning the teaching of Militz, and he was summoned to Avignon to answer the accusations made against him There he died, while his cause was still pending, in the year 1374

There is extant a Life of Militz, written by his disciple Matthias of Janow, from which Neander has made many quotations in his Church History Another is also extant in Balbinus the Jesuit's *History of the Kingdom of Bohemia*, printed in 1682

MILLENARIANS The Millenarian heresy is the retention in Christianity of the low Judaic notion of a Millennium of mere earthly blessedness This unworthy conception of the last stage in the world's history is not, it must be remarked, true Judaism Judaism had indeed a system of temporal promises, but it possessed also elements of spirituality by which its teachers, had they been true successors of the prophets, would have placed due limitations to those promises and have risen above the old and temporary covenant Such instructors were wanting, and the later Jews, as they looked only for a temporal deliverer in the Messiah, looked only for a temporal Messianic reign Christianity, giving the true conception of the kingdom of heaven, corrected this unworthy belief, and introduced a conception of a final stage in this world's progress, in which not only shall things temporal be subordinated to things spiritual, but nature itself shall be rendered a willing instrument of the perfect man, that is, of the righteous who are raised from the dead

It is needless to repeat here the statements of the Dictionary of Theology [MILLENNIUM] regarding the evidence of a belief in the Millennium in the early Church Those statements shew, to say the least, that such belief, if it be not formally sanctioned by the Church, has on its side a preponderance of early testimony At present it is proposed to shew [1] the essential difference between the Christian doctrine and the perverted Judaic doctrine, and [2] that the condemnation of Millennial doctrine attaches only to the latter

The former of these points is worked out by Dorner [*On the Person of Christ*, div i vol i app note AAA] The Jews represented the Millennium as the triumph of Israel according to the flesh, of Jerusalem that now is Christianity represents it as introduced by Jesus of Nazareth Who was crucified and is now exalted, as including believing Jews and Gentiles, as superseding Israel according to the flesh by Israel according to the spirit, the Jerusalem of the Jews by the city of God which comes down from heaven The Jews taught that Messiah would found His kingdom of earthly blessedness immediately on His first appearance, and evaded that which is essential in Christian doctrine, that the exalted one should be identical with the sufferer In their view the kingdom of earthly blessedness was not merely a prelude to heavenly blessedness, but was itself substantially the goal and final consummation [Compare Mede's remark on Jewish ignorance of the second resurrection, DICT *of* THEOL, MILLENNIUM, 471, col 2] In the Christian view, the Millennium is but a prelude to the blessedness of heaven, the final stage of the world in which all the senses and all nature shall be subdued to the spirit, the spirit exerting not an annihilating but an ennobling power on the first nature or creation. Without this, it was thought that God cannot be said to reconcile all things to Himself by Christ. "It is fitting," said Irenæus, "that the creation itself, being restored to its primeval condition, should without restraint be under the dominion of the righteous, and the Apostle has made this plain in the Epistle to the Romans when he thus speaks, 'For the expectation of the creature waiteth for the manifestation of the sons of God . The creature itself shall be delivered from the bondage of corruption into the glorious liberty of the sons of God'" [Iren *cont Hær.* v 32].

To the Jewish perversion of the Millennium the Christian Millennium was distinctly antagonistic, and those who retained or fell back into the Jewish perversion were unsparingly condemned. Origen led the way He states that certain men think that the promises of the future are to be looked for in bodily pleasure and luxury, describing the sensual gratifications, the earthly pomp, the temporal dignities which they expect "Such," he says, "are the views of those who, while believing in Christ, understand the Divine Scriptures in a sort of Jewish sense, drawing from them nothing worthy of the Divine promises" [Orig *de Princip* ii. 11] We do not assert that, in the sections which follow these words, Origen enounces on the other hand a Christian Chiliasm but we assert that his doctrine of the intermediate state with its several abodes is not inconsistent with Chiliastic doctrine

So Jerome "Judæi et nostri Semijudæi, qui auream atque gemmatam de cœlo expectant Jerusalem Hæc illi dicunt, qui terrenas desiderant voluptates, et uxorum quærunt pulchritudinem, ac numerum liberorum" [*Comm in Is* cap lx 1, 2, 3] In the commentary on the fifty-ninth chapter, Jerome had mentioned the belief that circumcision was to be restored Gregory Nyssen "entirely disclaims the expectation of a voluptuous Millennium, the renewal of Jewish sacrifices, and a terrestrial Jerusalem adorned with precious stones" [Lardner, *Credib* chap c 8] It is not denied, however, that through opposition to these carnal notions, true Chiliastic doctrine was very generally abandoned Andrew, Bishop of Cæsarea in Cappadocia, is a witness to this In his Commentary on the Revelation [cap xx. 7], he states that some interpret the thousand years of the period of our Lord's ministry · "others think," he adds, "that after the completion of six thousand years shall be the first resurrection from the dead, which is to be peculiar to the saints alone, who are to be raised up that they may dwell again on this earth, where they had given proofs of patience and fortitude, and that they may live here a thousand years in honour and plenty · after which will be the general resurrection of good and bad But the Church receives neither of these interpretations" Consequently he interprets the thousand years of the time of the Gospel dispensation

The writers on heresies confine themselves to the denial of a sensual Millennium [Philaster, lix , August viii , Isid cap vi *Hær.* viii] Augustine at one time held Chiliastic doctrine and when he had relinquished it, still allowed it to be tolerable. [Dict *of* Theol, Millennium] Epiphanius, arguing against Apollinaris, urges, as Jerome did, the absurdity of supposing a return to the rite of circumcision [*Hær* lxxvii cap 38]

It is in the writings of the doctors of the Church, not in conciliar decrees, that the condemnation of a perverted Chiliasm is to be sought So, on the other hand, there are no authoritative decrees against true Chiliasm, while it is at the same time confessed that after the first ages there has been a noticeable abandonment of the doctrine The English Articles of the year 1553 contained a condemnation of Millenarianism, couched in language agreeing with that which has been quoted from Origen and Jerome "They that go about to renew the fable of heretics called Millenarii, be repugnant to Holy Scripture, and cast themselves headlong into a Jewish dotage" [art xli] This article was directed, as is well known, against the Anabaptist teaching [compare Augsburg Confession, 1531 and 1540, art xvii] It was dropped in 1562, owing, it may be, to the suppression of fanatic teachers who had formerly converted Millenarian expectations into pretexts for licentiousness, both moral and political [Hardwicke, *Hist of Art* p 131] With the omission of the article must be connected, however, the appearance of Chiliastic doctrine in Edward VI's Catechism, printed in the same year as the Articles. It may have been thought that the article would be considered to condemn all Chiliastic doctrine whatever

In conclusion, it may be said that Millenarianism is to a certain degree not unorthodox, but that Millenarians who uphold the doctrine of a sensual or Judaic Millennium are unequivocally condemned by theologians

MILLENNIAL CHURCH [Shakers]

MILLIARII [Millenarians]

MILLIASTÆ. [Millenarians]

MODERATES. This name was given to the party dominant in the Established Kirk of Scotland during the eighteenth century, which (by a reaction, consequent upon the Revolution settlement, from the fervid fanaticism evoked by the ecclesiastical struggles of preceding years) regarded with indifference many of the points held cardinal with the old Covenanters, acquiesced in, and approved of, the system of absolute lay patronage, preached more on morals than on faith, and was generally Latitudinarian in doctrine, Erastian in policy, and worldly in tone of life It quieted controversies by treating them alike with indifference, and went so far in its aversion to any exertion of spiritual life, as to reject in the General Assembly of 1796 an overture in favour of Missions, partly on the ground alleged by a minister that the preaching of the Gospel was likely rather to hinder than advance the simple virtues of the untutored savage, and partly on that alleged by a lay elder, panic-struck at the progress of French revolutionary ideas, that the funds collected for such an object would "certainly" in time "be turned against the Constitution" The party, however, was not without many members who possessed a more evangelical spirit, and to whom the term "moderate" attached in a far better and higher sense, while with regard to intellectual ability the names of Blair and Robertson (by the latter of whom the proceedings of the Assembly were directed for many years with great tact and prudence) give to it no mean distinction But as the prevalence of a similar party in England gave rise to Methodism, so the opposition to the Moderates in Scotland found vent in the Secession and Relief Synods, and finally rent the Kirk in twain by the Free Church movement of the present century

MOLINISTS. An anti-Augustinian school of Jesuit theologians, originated by the Spanish Jesuit Molina, in the latter part of the sixteenth century

Lewis Molina [A D 1535-1601] was a professor of divinity in the Portuguese university of Evora, where he promulgated opinions on the subject of grace and free-will which were opposed to the received theology of St Thomas Aquinas, and to that of St Augustine, on which the arguments of Aquinas are grounded These opinions were published by Molina in the year 1588, in a book first printed at Lisbon, and in an enlarged form at Antwerp in A D 1595, under the title of a "Harmony of Free Will with the gifts of Grace," &c [*De Liberi Arbitrii Concordia cum Gratiæ Donis, Divina Præscientia, Providentia, Prædestinatione, et Reprobatione*] The book was immediately attacked by the Dominicans as being of a Pelagianizing tendency, and before the second edition of it had been brought out, the controversy between them and the Jesuits, who sided with Molina, had become so dangerous, that, in 1594, Pope Clement VIII. enjoined silence on both parties, and promised to commit the decision of the dispute to a congregation of theologians Upon this the Dominicans used their influence with Philip II to induce the Pope to re-open the question at once, and the King's persuasions prevailed on Clement to convoke the promised assembly early in the year 1598. It consisted of a president, Cardinal Madrucci, the Bishop of Trent, of three other bishops, and seven theologians of different fraternities, and its meetings continued for three years under the title of "Congregationes de Auxilus," or "Congregations concerning Divine Grace" At the third of these, held on January 16th, 1598, the opinions of Molina were thus summarized —

[1] A reason or ground of God's predestination is to be found in man's right use of his free will. [2] That the *grace* which God bestows to enable men to persevere in religion may become the *gift* of perseverance, it is necessary that they be foreseen as consenting and co-operating with the Divine assistance offered them, which is a thing within their power [3] There is a mediate prescience, which is neither the free nor the natural knowledge of God, and by which he knows future contingent events before he forms his decree [1] [4] Predestination may be considered as either general (relating to whole classes of persons) or particular (relating to individual persons) In general predestination there is no reason or ground of it beyond the mere good pleasure of God, or none on the part of the persons predestinated, but in particular predestination (or that of individuals) there is a cause or ground of it in the foreseen good use of free will

The Jesuits did not adopt these opinions, but they maintained that they were not Pelagian, and that they were permissible, the Dominicans, on the other hand, identified them with Semi-Pelagianism, and opposed to them the theology of Aquinas, the great theologian of their order and of the whole Church and the decision of the divines to whom the controversy was committed was given in favour of the latter view in the year 1601

Notwithstanding this decision, however, the Jesuits succeeded in prevailing on Clement VIII to re-open the case, and a new congregation was appointed, consisting of fifteen cardinals, five bishops, and nine doctors, over whom the Pope himself presided on seventy-eight separate occasions between March 20th, 1602, and January 22nd, 1605 but just as he was ready to pronounce his sentence in the cause he died, within six weeks of the last session The congregation met again under the presidency of his successor Paul V between September 1605 and March 1606, but ultimately it was determined that no sentence should be pronounced on either side, public policy requiring, probably, that the Pope should not make an enemy of France by deciding against the Jesuits, or of Spain by deciding against the Dominicans The views of the latter were shortly afterwards developed in their extreme form in the "Augustinus" of Cornelius Jansen while the "scientia media" of the Molinists has been substantially adopted by Jesuit theologians [Fleury's *Eccl Hist* clxxxiii 4 Le Clerc's *Bibl Univ et Hist* vol xiv Aug le Blanc's *Hist Congreg de Auxil gratiæ Divin.* (Dominican) Meyer's *Hist Controv de Divin Gratia Auxil.* (Jesuit)]

MOLINOS [QUIETISTS]

MOLOKANES [MALAKANES]

MOMMIERS A nickname given to those who represented a revival of "Evangelical" Christianity in Geneva about the year 1818, under the ministrations of Cæsar Malan and Robert Haldane, the former a Calvinistic pastor at Geneva, the latter an English clergyman Mr Haldane established a class of theological students at Geneva in 1817 (of whom Merle d'Aubigné was one), which gradually developed a better description of pastors than had been hitherto known in Geneva The prayer-meetings held by these (after the custom of the Methodists and Evangelicals in England) gained for them the absurd name of "Mommiers," but in the year 1831 the party was strong enough to form an organized body, with a theological college, and it then became known as "The Evangelical Society of Geneva" A similar Society was afterwards formed on the opposite shore of the Lake for the Canton de Vaud

MONARCHIANS By this euphemistic name are called those heretics who deny the distinction of Persons in the Divine Nature They pretended that they alone held a true μοναρχία, in the same manner as modern Unitarians pretend that they alone hold the Unity of God

The term μοναρχία this party used not in the

[1] In Molina's theology the "natural" knowledge of God is that of what He effects by His direct power or by second causes, His "free" knowledge is that of what He purposes of His own free will, His "mediate" knowledge ("scientia media") is that of what will depend on the free will of His creatures, whose actions He foresees by a knowledge of all the forces by which those actions will be brought about and controlled

Catholic sense, as maintaining that there is one only ἀρχή, source or fountain of Deity, the Father, which sense implies the existence of the Begotten Son and Proceeding Spirit as distinct Persons nor in the sense of unity, for unity can only be asserted when there is plurality (in which lies the misuse of the term by Unitarians) nor again in the sense of God's sole government, which affirms nothing concerning the existence or non-existence of a distinction of Persons in the Godhead, but in the sense of simple oneness, from which oneness they argued that the Godhead is so simple a Being as to be μονοπρόσωπος, a solitary, single Hypostasis They charged the Trinitarians accordingly with Tritheism "Monarchiam tenemus," they boasted [Tert *adv Prax.* 3], i e (Rigault remarked) μοναρχικὴν θεότητα, nam alias incidimus εἰς τὴν ἄθεον πολυθεότητα. That this was the meaning in which they used the term is apparent on the very face of the controversy Tertullian goes on to assert that Monarchia means nothing else than "singulare et unicum imperium" So far then as his arguments rest on this assertion, it seems that they are not to the purpose, being directed really against a misuse of the word, not against the thing the Monarchians intended by it

Dionysius of Rome uses the word of the Unity of God, speaking of those who in their opposition to Sabellius, by division of the Persons, destroy τὴν μοναρχίαν, τὴν ἁγίαν Μονάδα [Routh, *Reliq Sac* iii p 373-4]

The heresy of the Monarchians, who thus misused the term Monarchy, may be traced in the very earliest times of Christianity Justin Martyr expressly denounces it, and his notice guides us to its source for he finds the heresy to exist both among Jews and Christians He condemns the Jews for thinking that when God was said to have appeared to the patriarchs, it was God the Father who appeared. Such, he says, are justly convicted of knowing neither the Father nor the Son, for they who say that the Son is the Father are convicted of neither understanding the Father, nor of knowing that the Father of the universe has a Son, who being the first-born Logos of God is likewise God [*First Apol* ch lxiii] In the Dialogue with Trypho he handles the same topic, and extends the charge to Christians "I am aware that there are some who wish to meet this by saying that the power which appeared from the Father of the universe to Moses, or Abraham, or Jacob, is called an Angel in His coming among men, since by this the will of the Father is made known to men, He is also called Glory, since He is sometimes seen in an unsubstantial appearance, sometimes He is called a man, since He appears under such forms as the Father pleases, and they call Him the Word, since He is also the bearer of messages from the Father to men But they say, that this power is unseparated and undivided from the Father, in the same manner that the light of the sun when on earth is unseparated and undivided from the sun in heaven, and when the sun sets the light is removed with it, so the Father, they say, when He wishes makes His power go forth, and when He wishes He brings it back again to Himself" [*Dial. c Tryph.* cc 127, 128]. It appears, then, that there were persons in Justin's time who called themselves Christians, but who believed that the Son was merely an unsubstantial energy or operation of the Father [See Bull, *Def Fid Nic.* II iv. 4, Burton, *Bampt Lect* note 103]

Now, in this the Jews had deserted the better teaching of their earlier Rabbis. For these ascribed a Divine Personality to the Angel of the Presence, and the doctrine of the Holy and Undivided Trinity subsisted, though in a less developed form, in the synagogue of old [see Mill, *Panth Prin.* part ii pp 92-99] The cause of this declension in doctrine was, that opposition to the Incarnate Word when He really appeared predisposed them to accept a heathen philosophy, and to represent the Logos, as Philo did, as the manifest God not personally distinct from the concealed Deity This error found its way into Christianity through the Gnostics, who were largely indebted to the Platonic school of Alexandria It appears as the foundation of the system of Simon Magus, who taught that the originating principle of all (which he asserted to be Fire, for "God is a consuming fire") is of a twofold nature, having a secret part and a manifest part, corresponding, as Hippolytus remarks, to the potentiality and energy of Aristotle If this be nothing else than Philo's representation of the Logos, there is some sure ground for the notion that Simon held the heresy afterwards called Sabellian Burton rejects the notion, inasmuch as the doctrine of emanations is not to be confounded with the theory of Sabellius, but Hippolytus (whom Burton did not possess) shews that the Logos, in Simon's theory, employed certain portions of the Divine fulness, which portions he called Æons, and that the Logos, although Simon uses the word Begotten, is really the manifest God not personally distinct from the concealed Deity [Burton, *Bampt Lect* note 46] Although therefore the doctrine of emanations is not to be confounded with the doctrine of Sabellius, it had in its original form as constructed by Simon a foundation of Sabellianism Traces of Sabellianism are found even in the later schools of Gnostics, and the later Sabellianism approached to an emanation theory A resemblance has been noticed between the tenets of Valentinus and those of Sabellius [Petavius, *Dogm Theol.* II i. 6, Wormius, *Hist Sabel.* ii 3], and Neander is inclined to think that Marcion may have adopted some of the Patripassian doctrines in Asia Minor [*Allgem. Geschichte,* i p 796 Burton, *Bamp Lect* note 103]

The leading tenet of the Monarchians thus appears to have been introduced into Christianity principally through the Alexandrian Jews and the Gnostics It may also have been derived immediately from heathen philosophers, as in the case of Noetus it is ascribed by Hippolytus immediately to Heraclitus [NOETIANS]

The tenet rests on the sophism, Either the Son is the same as the Father and not distinct in-

Person, or we must say that the Divine Substance is divided into two parts, of which the one constitutes the Person of the Father, the other the Person of the Son This follows evidently, Bull remarks, from the passage of Justin Martyr which has been quoted [*Def Fid Nic* II iv 4] The Monarchians asserted, that is, that we cannot distinguish the Persons without dividing the Substance

From this error it follows logically that the Divine Nature in our Blessed Lord is either denied, or asserted to be the very nature of the Father The Monarchian, to be consistent, must be an Arian or a Patripassian And all who denied the distinction of Persons in the Godhead did adopt one of the varying forms of the heresies of Sabellius, Paul of Samosata or Arius In the forms of some of these different sects the Monarchian controversy agitated the Church of Rome, especially during the episcopates of Zephyrinus and Callistus, during the third century, and passed into the great controversies which agitated the whole Church in the fourth century, and called for the two great Councils of Nicæa and Constantinople

The history of the Monarchian sects shews an endeavour to escape from the revolting tenet of Patripassianism, and to retain or supply that which the nature of man almost instinctively requires, a superhuman mediation and atonement The working of these two motives, as the Monarchian adopts either the Arian or the Patripassian alternative, is very remarkable, inasmuch as the return to Catholicity appears to be much easier in the school which adopts the former alternative When Patripassianism is at once and decisively rejected it is open to the Monarchian to satisfy the need for a Mediator by magnifying the Divine element in our Lord, which at first he considered to be only the highest degree of prophetic grace, and passing through stages of Arianism and Semi-Arianism to approach nearer and nearer to the truth Whereas, when Patripassianism has been adopted, and the need is felt for freeing the mind from a tenet at which one shudders, it is only done by diminishing the Divine Nature in our Lord, through the stages of supposing it a portion of the Divine fulness, then an emanation from the Godhead. The result is a deliberate Psilanthropism

Regarding the heresy itself of Pseudo-Monarchianism, the main points for consideration are the following First, An eternal Mind must needs have in it from eternity an ἔννοια or λόγος, *a notion or conception of itself*, which the schools term *verbum mentis*, nor can it be conceived without it "This Word in God cannot be, as it is in us, a transient vanishing accident, for then the Divine nature would indeed be compounded of substance and accident, which would be repugnant to its simplicity, but it must be a substantial, subsisting Word" [Bull, *Cath Doct concerning the Blessed Trinity*] The Monarchians denied this Τελειότατον καὶ ζῶντα καὶ αὐτοῦ τοῦ πρώτου νοῦ λόγον ἔμψυχον Denying this, they denied also that substantial *vinculum Charitatis* in which the Father and the Son are One ἑνότητι Πνεύματος. Secondly, Thus is destroyed that αὐτάρκεια which we attribute to God, *i e* His self sufficiency and most perfect bliss and happiness in Himself alone, before and without all created beings For this we cannot well conceive without acknowledging a distinction of Persons in the Godhead The Monarchians denied the Individual Society of the Ever-blessed Trinity.

MONARCHY MEN [Fifth Monarchy Men]

MONOIMUS An Arabian heretic of the second century, who appears to have been a follower of Basilides He is mentioned by Theodoret, but the particulars of his system, which was formed of strange geometrical and arithmetical speculations respecting the origin of the world, are given only by Hippolytus The substance of these is that primal man is the universe that the universe is the originating cause of all things, he himself being unbegotten, incorruptible and eternal, that a Son of the primal man was generated independently of time, that the Son of Man is a monad represented by the iota and the tittle, that is the Greek figure 10 [ί], that all things have emanated from the substance of this monad, that cubes, octahedrons, pyramids, and all such figures, out of which crystallize fire, water and earth, have arisen from numbers which are comprehended in the number ten In a letter from Monoimus to Theophrastus, which is quoted by Hippolytus, the former avows that he believed in no God separate from man's own self [Hippol *Refut Hær* viii 5-8, x 13 Theodor *Hær fab* i 18]

MONOPHYSITES [Μονοφυσῖται] A sect which separated from the Orthodox Eastern Church upon the condemnation of the Eutychian heresy in the year 451 by the Council of Chalcedon, gradually extending itself to every part of Eastern Christendom, and being represented after the sixth century by the Jacobites Their distinctive tenet was developed out of the heresy of Eutyches, but was not identical with it Eutyches maintaining that the Union of Christ's Divine and Human Natures in the Incarnation resulted in the ultimate extinction of the latter, so that the glorified Saviour is wholly and only Divine, while the Monophysites held that the two Natures were so united, that although the "One Christ" was partly Human and partly Divine, His two Natures became by their union only one Nature (μόνη φύσις)

The modification of the opinion of Eutyches [Eutychians], which thus acquired the name of Monophysitism, originated with Dioscorus, the successor of St Cyril as Patriarch of Alexandria. He presided at the Council of Ephesus, which was summoned in the year 449 to consider the opinions of Eutyches, and which from the murderous violence shewn by his Egyptian partizans was called the "Latrocinium" or "Robber Synod" Under the influence of Dioscorus, who wished to gain a victory over the patriarchs of Antioch and Constantinople, the chief opponents of Eutyches, the assembled bishops were persuaded or forced to give their decision in favour of Eutyches, the key-note to that decision being struck by the passionate exclamation of Dioscorus, "Will you endure that two Natures should be spoken of after the Incarnation" [Mansi, *Concil* vi 503] The decision so given was not, however, accepted by the Patriarch of Antioch nor by Flavian the Patriarch of Constantinople (who died in exile shortly afterwards from the wounds which he received at the last riotous meeting), nor by Leo, Bishop of Rome, and another Council was summoned by the new Emperor Marcian in the following year, which assembled first at Nicæa, but eventually at Chalcedon, from which latter city it received its name At this Council, composed of 630 bishops (a much larger number than had attended any previous general council), the opinions which the martyred Flavian had maintained against Eutyches were declared to be orthodox, and Dioscorus, by whom he had been deposed, and through whose encouragement of violence he had been murdered, was himself deposed At the moment of his condemnation he reiterated his opinion in the cry, "They are condemning the Fathers as well as me, I have passages from Athanasius and Cyril which forbid us to speak of two Natures after the Incarnation" [Mansi, *Concil* vi 590] He was, however, banished by the Emperor to Gangra, in Paphlagonia, and Proterius, Arch-priest of the Church of Alexandria, was [A D 452] elected patriarch in his stead, great riots ensuing among the people of Alexandria, a large number of whom were the partizans of the banished patriarch He never returned from exile, but died at Gangra some time in the year 454

As the initiation of the Monophysite schism was signalized by the murder of its opponent, so was its consummation The leading adversary of Proterius was Timotheus Ælurus, who organized some of the Monophysites into a separate body, with places of worship of their own, and who acquired his nickname of "the cat" by climbing up to the windows of the monks, and pretending that he was a messenger sent from Heaven to bid them forsake the communion of Proterius, and make himself patriarch in his stead On the death of the Emperor Marcian, Timothy collected a body of monks and other followers, seized on the Church of Cæsarea, and was there consecrated patriarch [A D 457] by two bishops who had been condemned by a council and exiled by the Emperor A few days after some of his partizans attacked the house of Proterius, and when he fled to the baptistery, where the baptisms of Holy Week were going forward, for safety, he was followed by the mob, who stabbed him to death, dragged his body round the city till it was torn to pieces, and having burned what remained on the shore, scattered his ashes in the sea, treating him in the same savage manner as Hypatia had been treated not long before

From this time there was an unbroken succession of Monophysite patriarchs in Alexandria The orthodox succession was revived in Timothy Salofaciolus for twelve years [A D 468-482], and afterwards for a short time in John Talaia, who, however, was soon driven away from Egypt, and died Bishop of Nola near Rome There was then a vacancy in the see for more than half a century, when, in the year 539, a new race of nine orthodox patriarchs began which lasted until about A D 640 From that time the patriarchate of Alexandria lapsed into the hands of the Monophysites through the favour which was shewn to them by the Mahometan conquerers of Egypt, and although an orthodox succession was restored in the eighth century, the original Church of St Mark sunk into insignificance, and has become little more than a dependant on that of Constantinople

At the same time that the Monophysite sect was thus beginning to take possession of Egypt it acquired a strong hold on Palestine through the usurpation of the see of Jerusalem by a monk of the party named Theodosius, who seized on the patriarchal church and throne during the absence of Juvenal, the reigning patriarch, and consecrated Monophysite bishops in opposition to the orthodox bishops throughout Palestine, a similar schism being not long after established by Peter Fullo, or the Fuller, at Antioch and thus a large portion of the Eastern Church was confronted by a bitter sectarian rival, before the successful progress of which the orthodox Christians came to be looked upon as a mere Church party under the name of "Chalcedonians," or even a mere State party under the name of "Melchites," or Royalists

The first great success of the sect was attained through an imperial edict which was issued by Basiliscus, the usurper who for a short time succeeded Marcian, at the persuasion of Timothy Ælurus. In this edict [A D 476] the Emperor professed his adherence to the three Œcumenical Councils of Nicæa, Constantinople, and Ephesus, and rejected that of Chalcedon To this profession of faith Ælurus himself, Anastasius of Jerusalem, and Peter Fullo of Antioch, all added their subscriptions, and they were followed by nearly 500 other bishops, so strong had the sect grown [Evagr. *Hist Eccl* iii 5]. Under Timothy Ælurus the Monophysites were led back a degree nearer to orthodoxy Dioscorus had followed Eutyches in denying our Lord's human nature to be of the same kind as that of ordinary men, but when Timothy was on a visit to Constantinople, and some Eutychian monks desired to join his communion, he took the opportunity of disclaiming this part of their belief, and declared the conviction of himself and his followers to be that the Saviour became consubstantial with men according to His Human Nature, as He had ever been consubstantial with the Father according to his Divine Nature. In this particular the Monophysite followers of Timothy, who were hence called "Timotheans," as the opposite party were called "Dioscorians," returned to the Creed of St Cyril, which his deacon and successor Dioscorus had forsaken.

When the Emperor Zeno had returned to Constantinople and deposed Basiliscus, he for a time discouraged the Monophysites, but was at length persuaded by Acacius, the patriarch of Constantinople, to attempt a reunion between them and the Church by means of an edict similar to that of Basiliscus, and called from its object the "Henoticon," or Formula of Concord [*ibid* 14] This was accepted by Peter Mongus, the successor of Timothy Ælurus, and the orthodox patriarch, John Talaia, having then fled from Alexandria to Italy, many members of the forsaken Church were willing to accept the Monophysite bishop for their head, so that he and his successors became sole Patriarchs of Alexandria for fifty-seven years [A D 482-539], only a few holding out, weakened and persecuted, and known as "Proterians" At the same time another schism broke out among the Monophysites, for while Mongus was professing great zeal on the one side, by inserting the names of Dioscorus and Timothy Ælurus in the diptychs, he was also professing to the patriarchs of Constantinople and Rome that he accepted the decrees of Chalcedon Hence the old Dioscorian party separated from him entirely, and reverting to the original principles of Eutyches, formed the sect known as the ACEPHALI, or those who had separated from their episcopal head, and had no bishop of their own

The Monophysites were again broken up into two sects about the year 520 Severus having been deposed from the see of Antioch, and Julian from that of Halicarnassus, by the Emperor Justin, both sought refuge in Egypt There Severus headed that division of the sect which was called by the name of Severianists, PHTHARTOLATRÆ, or Corrupticolæ, and which maintained the corruptibility of Christ's Human Nature, or its identity with that of ordinary pain-suffering, weak, and mortal manhood, while Julian became the leader of the Julianists, or APHTHARTODOCETÆ The theology of Severus eventually became that of the Monophysites at large, while that of the Julianist party soon ceased to have any supporters The memory of Severus is so bound up with the traditions of the sect, that a festival is set apart in the Jacobite calendar to commemorate his arrival in Egypt From the time of Severus the tenets of the Monophysites receded therefore another stage further from Eutychianism, and although they still maintained that our Lord after His Incarnation was of one Nature only, the doctrine was henceforward held in such a way as not to be so extremely divergent from that of the Church For, in the theology of Severus, the qualities of human nature were all retained in our Lord after the Incarnation, although that nature was in Him so amalgamated with the Divine Being that it could not be said to possess any being or identity of its own Thus the Monophysite conception of Christ's Person settled into that of a Theandric or composite Nature, analogous to that composite action of His Person which later divines have called a Theandric operation (θεανδρικὴ ἐνέργεια) But belief in such a composite Nature is inconsistent with the Nicene Creed, which asserts that our Lord Jesus Christ is "of one Substance with the Father," and since the Father is not of such a composite Nature, to declare the Son to be so is to declare Him to be of a different substance from Him. Thus, the intellectual form which Severus gave to Monophysitism cannot escape from the charge of heresy any more than that earlier form of opinion which was condemned at Chalcedon

The instability of opinion, when dissociated from the safeguard of the Nicene Creed, was also strikingly illustrated in the case of the later Monophysite school, as well as of the earlier Severus himself held views respecting the Soul of the united Natures of Christ which were not logically consistent with the theology respecting their oneness, and thus it was only one step forward for Themistius, his deacon, to invent the tenet of the AGNOETÆ, that the human soul of Christ was like ours in everything, even in its want of omniscience, or "ignorance" When, again, Severus maintained that the Divine and the Human Wills in the united Natures were also so united that there could be no volition of the one nature one way and the other nature in another direction, he was preparing the way for that development of his opinion which was made by the MONOTHELITES, who maintained that there was only one will in Christ as well as only one nature

After the death of Severus, and of Timothy II, who was sole patriarch of Alexandria during the fifteen years in which Severus was so prominent a leader of the Monophysites, a new schism broke out among the latter, the clergy and men of wealth choosing Theodosius, a disciple of Severus, as successor to Timothy, the monks and the lower classes electing Gaianus, the leader of the Aphthartodocetæ, whose party took the name of GAIANITES This division, and the energy of the Emperor Justinian in supporting the orthodox cause, led to a revival of the orthodox episcopate in the person of Paul, who was consecrated in the year 539, and who began a new Catholic succession of patriarchs, beside which the patriarchate of the Monophysites ran parallel for a century During the greater part of Justinian's reign [A D 527-565], the sect was much depressed, and broken up into a great number of parties Its principles were condemned in synods held at Constantinople in the years 536 and 553, and the Emperor himself, who eventually adopted the opinions of the Aphthartodocetæ, was always personally opposed to the Severian, or predominant, party of the Monophysites, and wrote against them [Justin Imp *contr Monoph in Galland Bibl Patr* xii 292] But towards the close of Justinian's reign a disciple of Severus, Jacobus Baradæus, or Zanzalus, Bishop of Edessa, [A D 541-578] began an energetic revival of Monophysite opinions in Syria, a revival which spread to Egypt also From that time until the Mahometan armies began to overrun the East, the "Jacobites," as they now began to be called from the revivalist just named, were again a prosperous and important sect; and they so easily went over from the side of the orthodox Greek Emperors to that of the infidel conquerors, that the latter shewed them much favour, and eventually established them as the recognised Christianity of the new empire in Egypt [JACOBITES. Evagr *Hist Eccl* Renaudot, *Hist Patriarch. Alex* Assemann *Diss de Monoph in Bibl Orient* ii Gieseler's *Commentatio qua Monophysitarum variæ opiniones illustrantur* Neale's *Hist East Ch Patriarch Alexandr* Dorner's *Person of Christ* II i Clark's transl]

MONOTHELITES [Μονοθελῆται] An heretical school developed within the Eastern Church in the earlier half of the seventh century, through an attempt to harmonize the orthodox doctrine of the Incarnation with the opinions held by the Monophysite sects The distinctive tenet of the Monothelites was that the Divine and Human Natures of Christ did not possess separate Divine and Human Wills, but one Will (*μόνον θέλημα*) partly Human and partly Divine

The name of the Monothelites first appears in the writings of St John of Damascus in the middle of the eighth century, but the origin of their opinion may be traced as far back as to Severus, the deprived patriarch of Antioch, who, during the last fifteen years of his life [A D 520-535] resided in Alexandria, and became the founder of the later school of Monophysites In some fragments of his writings which have come down to modern times, Severus remarks that our Lord's words, "Not My will, but Thine be done" [Luke xxii 42], do not prove the existence of a will distinct from the Divine Will, nor that there was any struggle or resistance on the part of the Saviour's Soul as if He had a human fear of death or a human unwillingness to die, but that the words are so set down by way of accommodation, and for Christian instruction [Mai, *Coll. Nov* vii. 288] But the distinct formulation of the Monothelite dogma is attributed to Theodore, Bishop of Pharan in Arabia Although not a Monophysite, Theodore taught that all the acts of Christ proceeded from one principle, originating in the Word, and operating through the human soul and body Hence, though the Logos and the Manhood were distinct natures, they were both acted upon by one and the same *ἐνέργεια*, and there being one activity, there was one will by which it was moved, that will being divine [Αὐτοῦ γὰρ τὸ θέλημα ἕν ἐστι, καὶ τοῦτο θεικόν Mansi, *Concil* xi 568]

Athanasius, the Monophysite patriarch of Antioch, was a zealous convert to the opinion of Theodore, and laid it before the Emperor Heraclius as offering a basis for such a compromise between his sect and the Church as might enable them to reunite in one communion. The idea of reunion was taken up with enthusiasm both by the Emperor and by Sergius, the patriarch of Constantinople, and the see of Alexandria becoming vacant [A D 630], Cyrus, Bishop of Pharis, was translated thither for the purpose of effecting it in that city, which was the intellectual stronghold of the Monophysites Immediately after his appointment, Cyrus held a council, at which terms of reunion were arranged in nine articles, all of which were orthodox except the seventh, in which the opinion of Theodore was affirmed in the words *τὸν αὐτὸν ἕνα Χριστὸν καὶ υἱὸν ἐνεργοῦντα τὰ θεοπρεπῆ καὶ ἀνθρώπινα μιᾷ θεανδρικῇ ἐνεργείᾳ* [Mansi, *Concil* xi 565], where the theandric operation appears intended to comprehend the idea of one will alone, as expressed by Theodore in the passage previously quoted This canon was protested against by a learned monk named Sophronius, who declared that it revived the Apollinarian heresy which made the Divine Nature of Christ to be the Soul of His Human Nature, but Cyrus disregarded this protest, and a formal reunion of the Monophysites and the Church was effected in the spring of A D 633 This was looked upon as a victory over orthodoxy by the former, and many of the orthodox were alienated

In the following year Sophronius was appointed Patriarch of Jerusalem, and at once embarked in a controversy respecting the new dogma. His opposition was so formidable, that Sergius, the Patriarch of Constantinople, thought it desirable to obtain the countenance of Honorius, Bishop of Rome, to whom he wrote a detailed account of the origin and progress of the controversy including the nine canons which had formed the basis of reconciliation The Roman Pope replied in terms approving of the policy which had been adopted, and assenting to the Monothelite dogma, though regarding it as an unpractical piece of controversy But Honorius seems even to have gone further than Sergius in assenting to it, for whereas the latter and Cyrus, with the canon passed in the council, had only spoken of one activity or *ἐνεργεία*, Honorius writes "Inasmuch as the Humanity was naturally united with the Word, and Christ is therefore One, we acknowledge one will of our Lord Jesus Christ—unam voluntatem fatemur Domini nostri Jesu Christi" [Mansi, *Concil* xi 539] Sophronius appealed to Honorius, sending to him Stephen, Bishop of Dora and entreating him to oppose the growing heresy, but he only met with a sharp rebuke from the Pope, who admonished him to submit his opinion to that of Sergius, and no longer to teach that there was a duality of wills in Christ Shortly afterwards Antioch was in the hands of the Saracens, and no more is heard of Sophronius

Within a few months after the correspondence with Honorius, the Emperor Heraclius followed the example of Zeno and Justinian by publishing [A D 638] an edict composed by Sergius, which contained an exposition of the faith, and hence received the name of the "Ecthesis" ("Ἔκθεσις τῆς πίστεως) This forbad discussion on the subject of the unity or duality of the *ἐνέργειαι*, but laid down positively that the Catholic faith required the acknowledgment of one only will in Christ, thus substantially embodying the statements which Sergius had received from Honorius, though in some parts using the words of the epistle which Sergius himself had written to Rome [Mansi, *Concil* x 992]

The Ecthesis was quietly received in the East, but John IV, the successor of Honorius, rejected and condemned it in a council which he held at Rome in the year 641 He also wrote against it to the Emperor Constantine (son and successor to Heraclius), and to Pyrrhus, the successor of Sergius [Theophan *Chronograph* i 508, Mansi, *Concil* x 682, xi 9], but his remonstrances produced no effect upon either emperor or patriarch In a few years, however, the edict was withdrawn by Constans II, and its place supplied [A D 648] by another called the "Type" [τύπος τῆς πίστεως], which strictly forbad, under penalties, all controversy respecting the mode in which Christ's will or energy is exercised, and required both clergy and laity to keep within the bounds of conciliar statements [Mansi, *Concil* x 1029] This penal suppression of truth, as well as falsehood, was so unacceptable at Rome, that Martin, who was then Pope, immediately summoned a council to meet at the Lateran, which, in A D 649, condemned the Monothelite heresy, the Ecthesis and the Type, and anathematized Theodore, Sergius, Cyrus, Pyrrhus, and also Paul, the reigning patriarch of Alexandria The Emperor was so indignant at this disregard of his authority, that he caused the Pope to be treated with great severity He was carried to Constantinople as a criminal, tortured and banished to the Crimea, where he died in the year 655, to be numbered among the martyrs of the Western and the Confessors of the Eastern Church His great intellectual supporter at the council had been a Greek abbot named Maximus and he too underwent a long persecution, being scourged, having his tongue cut out, and at last dying a death little short of martyrdom just as he had reached his place of exile, A D 662

The final and authoritative condemnation of the Monothelite heresy took place at the Sixth General Council held at Constantinople in the year 680 This council was summoned by Constantine Pogonatus [A D 668-685], the successor of Constans II, and sat from November 7th, 680, to September 16th, 681, the Emperor himself sometimes presiding The English bishop Wilfrid was present, and brought home the acts of the council to be accepted by the Church of England at the Council of Hatfield [Haddan & Stubbs' *Councils*, iii 140] An exact and laborious inquiry was made into the arguments which were alleged by Macarius, Patriarch of Antioch, on the Monothelite side, and those of Pope Agatho's deputation on that of the orthodox faith, but it was not until the thirteenth of its eighteen sessions that the council arrived at any decision At last it was ruled that there are in Christ "two natural wills and two natural operations, without division, without conversion or change, with nothing like antagonism, and nothing like confusion," but that at the same time the Human Will of Christ could not come into collision with His Divine Will, but is in all things subject to it An anathema was also pronounced on Theodore, Sergius, Honorius, and all who had maintained the heresy this anathema being confirmed by Leo II, who wrote to the Emperor respecting his own predecessor in the See of Rome "Anathematizamus . . necnon et Honorium qui hanc apostolicam ecclesiam non apostolicæ traditionis doctrina lustravit, sed profana proditione immaculatam subvertere conatus est" [Mansi, *Concil* xi 631-637, 731] This anathema of Pope Honorius was repeated by his successors for three centuries

After this œcumenical condemnation of Monothelitism little more is heard of the heresy The controversy which had risen respecting it was soon supplanted by that of the Iconoclasts, and the only Monothelites known in recent times are the small community of the MARONITES, who inhabit the Lebanon and Anti-Lebanon [Combefis *Hist hær Monothelit* Paris, 1648 Assemann, *Bibl. Orient* Dorner's *Person of Christ* II i. Clark's transl Neale's *Hist East Ch. Patriarch Alex*]

MONTANISTS A sect of the second century which claimed, in virtue of new revelations, to introduce a dispensation of the Spirit superior to that of Christ and His Apostles, and to perfect accordingly the discipline of the Church in the matters of the power of the keys, the rule of marriage, the rules of food and fasting, and the permission to save life in time of persecution

This sect is now usually called Montanist [as it was by Theod *Hær fab* iii 2], from its founder Montanus, a native of Ardaba, a village of Mysia adjoining Phrygia [anon author in Euseb *H E* v 16], but of old more commonly Phrygian or Cataphrygian [so Eusebius, v 14, Epiphanius, xlviii, Augustine, xxvi, Philastrius, xlix] from the country, sometimes (or more properly a branch of them) Pepuzians, from Pepuza, a town in Western Phrygia, in which they located the heavenly Jerusalem [Epiph xlviii 14]

The author[1] whom Eusebius quotes dates the rise of Montanus in the proconsulship of Gratus in Asia, but the year of this proconsulship has not been ascertained, Eusebius [*Chronicle*] in the twelfth year of Marcus Antoninus, *i e* A D 171, which agrees with Eusebius' narrative [v 3] of the letters of the churches of Vienne and Lyons Epiphanius gives the date A D 156, and Pearson and Beausobre follow him Eusebius, however, is more correct in his chronology than Epiphanius, and the later date is much more consistent than the earlier with the appearance of Montanism in Rome.

Gieseler and Milman remark that the national character of the Phrygians impressed itself on their Christianity, and led to a sensuous enthusiastic worship of the Deity and to a wild mysticism But this cannot have been the cause of the Montanist movement, it can only have given a peculiar character to the movement, and influenced its details For Montanism is but one of a number of similar movements in the Church At intervals, throughout the annals of Christianity, the Holy Ghost has been summoned by the hopes, felt as present by the kindled imaginations, been proclaimed by the passionate enthusiasm of a few, as accomplishing in them the imperfect revelation, as the third revelation which is to supersede and to fulfil the Law and

[1] Not Asterius Urbanus, who is an older writer quoted by the anonymous author whom Eusebius cites [Routh, *Rel Sacr* ii p 209]

the Gospel This notion appears again in the Middle Ages as the doctrine of the Abbot Joachim, of John Peter de Oliva, and the Fratricelli, in a milder form it is that of George Fox and of Barclay [Milman, *Latin Christ* i 1] In the Irvingites of our day the same notion is but slenderly disguised For if God restores Apostles to His Church, it is quite open to the Irvingites to argue that as the Church developed itself from St. James of Jerusalem to St. Paul of Antioch, so it may develope itself beyond the Gospel of St Paul under later Apostles. In all these cases there is a striving, but a misguided striving, after a higher standard This striving is at first, it may be, an endeavour to raise the Church above that which is its normal condition since Apostolic days to the extraordinary condition of those days, not only in piety and charity, which is the endeavour of every good man, and tends to a true revival of religion, but in apostolic and prophetic mission, in the extraordinary χαρίσματα of the Holy Spirit As human infirmities and passions enter more and more into such a misguided endeavour, as knowledge puffeth up, as pride and the love of pre-eminence are engendered, as fanaticism begins and grows, new revelations are asserted, and a claim set up that a new dispensation of the Spirit, in a new Gospel, is begun. Such a movement could hardly fail to take place at a time when the miraculous powers and gifts which marked the introduction of the Gospel were ceasing An enthusiast would be naturally tempted to connect a low standard of holiness, a decline of faith and love, with the cessation of those gifts, and therefore to seek their renewal To suppose such an origin of Montanus' career is both more just to all parties concerned and more in accordance with history, than to suppose him from the first an impostor Montanus and Alcibiades and Theodotus raised up in many an opinion that they prophesied and this belief was so much the more increased concerning their prophesying, for that as yet in several churches were wrought many and stupendous effects of the Holy Spirit [Euseb *H E* v 3] Origen, about seventy years later, notes that the prophetic power had all but ceased, that only some traces of it were in his time to be seen [*cont Cels* viii p 337, Spencer, 1677] The esteem in which Montanus was at first held by the Bishop of Rome, and Tertullian's joining his party, are thus best explained Montanus, then, as an enthusiast passing into an ecstasy, announced that the Holy Spirit had imparted Itself to him for the purpose of raising the Church to perfection.[1]

That these ecstasies were a mere simulation there is no reason whatever for asserting In Eusebius they are thus described "Montanus, in the excessive desire of his soul to take the lead, gave the adversary occasion against himself, so that he was carried away in spirit, and wrought up into a certain kind of frenzy and irregular ecstasy, raving, and speaking, and uttering strange things." In Tertullian they are described thus (in the case of one of the prophetesses) "Nam quia spiritalia charismata agnoscimus, post Joannem quoque prophetiam meruimus consequi. Est hodie soror apud nos revelationum charismata sortita, quas in Ecclesia inter Dominica solemnia per ecstasin in spiritu patitur, conversatur cum angelis, aliquando etiam cum Domino, et videt et audit sacramenta, et quorundam corda dignoscit, et medicinas desiderantibus submittit Jam vero prout scripturæ leguntur, aut psalmi canuntur, aut adlocutiones proferuntur, aut petitiones delegantur, ita inde materiæ visionibus subministrantur Forte nescio quid de anima disserueramus, cum ea soror in spiritu esset Post transacta solennia dimissa plebe, quo usu solet nobis renunciare quæ viderit," etc [*de Anima*, c ix p 311, ed 1641] These appear to be genuine ecstasies of fanaticism, which, at a time when Charismata had not altogether ceased, and in men who earnestly coveted those Charismata, would naturally ape the Charisma of prophecy. They were pseudo-prophetical raptures Chrysostom laid down this difference between true and false prophets. It is the property of a diviner to be ecstatical, to undergo some violence, to be tossed and hurried about like a madman But it is otherwise with a prophet, whose understanding is awake, whose mind is in a sober and orderly temper, who knows everything that he saith [*Hom* 28, 1 *Cor*] This sobriety of mind and evenness of temper does not exclude the strong emotions, varying perhaps according to the subject-matter of the prophecy, which appear so frequently in the Old Testament [Jer xxiii. 9, Ezek. iii 14, Dan x 8], but the prophet does not lose his self-control The spirits of the prophets are subject to the prophets

The Charisma of prophecy, the true prophetical spirit, seated itself as well in the rational as in the sensitive powers, it did not alienate the mind, but informed and enlightened it The pseudo-prophetical spirit was seated in the imaginative powers and faculties inferior to reason, upon these the foreign force acted (if foreign force there were, such as the lying spirit of 1 Kings xxii 21), or from the natural excitement of these the pretended spirit of prophecy was engendered Thus the true prophetical influx and a mistaken enthusiasm had this in common, that both made strong impressions upon the imaginative powers, and required the imaginative faculty to be vigorous and potent Considering this common element, considering too that the true gift of the spirit was subject to the control of him who possessed it, and might be used "decently and in order" [1 Cor xiv 4], and therefore might also be used indecently and disorderly, it is easy to imagine that there was difficulty in distinguishing between the true and the false, and that a true Charisma wrongly used might be withdrawn, and the enthusiasm of him who had possessed it might continue an imitation of it. The true prophet might pass into the false prophet, and be for some time undetected

[1] This statement is obtained by correcting the anonymous author in Eusebius by the more charitable language of the martyrs' letters [Euseb v 16 and 3. Regarding the ecstasy, see Gieseler's note, i p 147]

The Fathers gave it as the mark of the false prophets that they spoke in an ecstasy But among the lies (writes Clement of Alexandria) the false prophets also told some true things In reality they prophesied in an ecstasy as the servants of the Apostate [*Strom* I xvii] This test was applied to the pretensions of Montanus by the historian Miltiades "The false prophet," he wrote, "is carried away by a vehement ecstasy" . "They will never be able to shew that any in the Old or New Testaments were thus violently agitated and carried away in spirit" [Euseb *Hist Eccl* v 17] So too by Jerome "Non loquitur propheta ἐν ἐκστάσει, ut Montanus et Prisca Maximillaque delirant" [*Proœm in Nahum* See also the prefaces to Isaiah and Habakkuk][1]

It is impossible now, and probably was impossible during Montanus' career, to say whether he was knowingly a deceiver, but the marks of enthusiasm passing into fanaticism are much stronger than the marks of imposture In this case, as in many others, the more charitable judgment which refers Montanus' career to mistaken enthusiasm, is probably more just than that which refers it to disappointed ambition

That these new revelations announced a new dispensation or at least were so interpreted, is clear from Tertullian's distinguishing the times of the Paraclete from the times of Christ Tertullian argues that as Christ took away what Moses commanded, the Paraclete may have forbidden the indulgences which Paul allowed Hardness of heart occasioned certain precepts of Moses, infirmity of the flesh certain indulgences of Paul [*de Monogam* p 686]. The time of the Paraclete is the time of Montanus In the beginning of the same tract our Lord's words, "When the Spirit is come, He will guide you into all truth," are explained in the same way of the new revelation of discipline [pp 673-4], and expressly also in the tract, *de Virg. Vel* [p. 192] "Quæ est ergo Paracleti administratio nisi hæc, quod disciplina dirigitur, quod scripturæ revelantur, quod intellectus reformatur, quod ad meliora proficitur? " "Justitia primo fuit in rudimentis, natura Deum metuens dehinc per Legem et Prophetas promovit in infantiam dehinc per Evangelium efferbuit in juventutem *nunc* per Paracletum componitur in maturitatem" [p 193]

Consequently, Christians before Montanus were only Psychici "Et nos quidem postea agnitio Paracleti atque defensio disjunxit a Psychicis" [*adv Prax* p 634] The followers of Montanus were Spiritales, πνευματικοὶ

Excepting this infringement of the doctrine of the Holy Catholic Church, Montanus and his followers were orthodox. Jerome [*Epist* liv *ad Marcellam*], Socrates [i 23], Sozomenus [ii 18], attribute Sabellianism to them Such statements are true of the sect in a second stage (as will be hereafter noticed), but that they are not true of Montanus himself and his immediate followers we may believe from Tertullian's works, especially his Treatise against Praxeas, and from the testimony of Epiphanius [xlviii 1], and Theodoret [*Her fab* iii 2 See Bull, *Defen Fid Nic* II i 15, and vii 7]

The prophesyings of Montanus, Prisca, and Maximilla, accepted by their followers as revelations, related to the discipline of the Church

I St John's words, "a sin not unto death," and a "sin unto death," were held to divide sins as regards the outward act, into two classes, for the former of which alone the sacrament of penance was appointed, and in which alone the absolution of the Church might be given The latter (it was not denied) were remissible by Almighty God, but no ministration of forgiveness was appointed for them "Causas pœnitentiæ delicta condicimus Hæc dividimus in duos exitus Alia erunt remissibilia, alia irremissibilia Secundum quod nemini dubium est alia castigationem mereri, alia damnationem" And again, after naming St Paul's obtaining mercy for what he had done ignorantly in unbelief, Tertullian continues "Quod si elementia Dei ignorantibus adhuc et infidelibus competit, utique et pœnitentia ad se clementiam invitat, salva illa pœnitentiæ specie post fidem, quæ aut levioribus delictis veniam ab Episcopo consequi poterit, aut majoribus et irremissibilibus a Deo solo" [Tert *de Pudicit* pp 717, 738] These "capitalia delicta" are called also, in a like sense, "inconcessibilia," "immundabilia" [pp 726, 742]. In the Montanist system, then, such sinners ceased, *ipso facto*, to be members of the Church

II Second marriages were altogether condemned by Montanus They were held to be no other than fornication, and to have been permitted by St Paul in consequence of his knowledge and prophecy having been only in part [Auctor Prædestinati, *Hær* xxvi , Tert *de Monogamia*, pp 669, 675, 681, *de Exhort Castit* pp 664, 670]

Apollonius, quoted by Eusebius [*H E* v 18], adds that Montanus taught λύσεις γάμων, dissolution of marriage, and that Prisca and Maximilla, as soon as they received the Spirit, abandoned their husbands Wernsdorf [see Routh's note, *Rel Sac* i 473] observed that this teaching was not by precept, but by the examples of the two prophetesses It is contrary to Tertullian's principles, who defended the one marriage as honourable and holy [Tertull *adv Marc* i 29, p 452] It is doubtful whether Apollonius' evidence regarding the two prophetesses can be implicitly relied upon

III Montanus appointed two Lents in the year besides that observed by the Church, and two weeks of Xerophagy [Hieron *Epist* liv *ad Marcellam*, *Comm. ad Cap* i *Aggæi*, Tert *de Jejuniis*]. Kaye sums up the differences between the orthodox and Montanists on the

[1] "Neque vero (ut Montanus cum insanis feminis somniat) prophetæ in ecstasi sunt locuti, ut nescirent quid loquerentur, et cum alios erudirent, ipsi ignorarent quid dicerent" [Hieron *Proœm in Esai*] "Adversum Montani dogma perversum intelligit (propheta) quod videt nec ut amens loquitur, nec in morem insanientium feminarum dat sine mente sonum Ex 1 Cor xiv intelligitur, prophetam posse et loqui et tacere cum velit Qui autem in ecstasi, id est, invitus, loquitur, nec tacere nec loqui in sua potestate habet" [*Proœm. in Habacuc* v p 185, ed 1616]

subject of fasting thus: "With respect to the Jejunium or total abstinence from food, the orthodox thought that the interval between our Saviour's Death and Resurrection was the only period during which the Apostles observed a total fast; and consequently the only period during which fasting was of positive obligation upon all Christians At other times it rested with themselves to determine whether they would fast or not The Montanists, on the contrary, contended that there were other seasons during which fasting was obligatory, and that the appointment of those seasons constituted a part of the revelations of the Paraclete With respect to the *Dies Stationarii*, the Montanists not only pronounced the fast obligatory on all Christians, but prolonged it until the evening, instead of terminating it, as was the orthodox custom, at the ninth hour In the observance of Xerophagiæ, the Montanists abstained not only from flesh and wine like the orthodox, but also from richer fruits, and omitted their customary ablutions" [Kaye, *on Tertull* p 416] Apollonius [in Euseb *H E* v 18], in this particular, simply notices of Montanus, "This is he who laid down laws of fasting," pointing out in these words that Montanus' offence was not the change of one law for another, but the imposition of a law where there had been liberty

IV Men are not to flee in persecution For if persecution proceeds from God, it is no way their duty to flee from what has God for its author it ought not to be avoided, and it cannot be evaded [Tert *de Fuga*, sec iv pp 691, 692] Our Lord's command [Matt x 23] was a special command to the Apostles, that they might fulfil their mission Our Lord's own conduct was ruled by the same principle And if we may not flee, neither may we buy off persecution, "Sicut fuga redemptio gratuita est, ita redemptio nummaria fuga est" [pp 693-697] The anonymous author in Eusebius asserts, however [*H E* v 16], that there had been no Montanist martyrs

In these rules of discipline there is little that had not been already advocated, or at least prepared for, in one or another part of the Church St Cyprian mentions that some of his predecessors had denied penance and reconciliation to adulterers [Epist *ad Antonian* p 110, Fell], and his letter being written A D 252, this may reach back to the time of Montanus The refusal however was, as Augustine remarked in a like case, "non desperatione indulgentiæ, sed rigore disciplinæ" [*Epist ad Bonifac* See Marshall's *Pen Disc* p. 86] An undue estimate of celibacy and marriage was far from uncommon Athenagoras had declared that a second marriage was but a cloked adultery [*Legat.* cap xxxiii]. Ascetic practices were considered neither unusual nor blameable, and the Church had its laws of fasting, of which the rules of Montanus were an extension.

In what respect then was Montanus a heretic? His heresy lay not in the rules themselves, but in the foundation on which they were made to rest The rules themselves, although in some respects an unwarrantable narrowing of Christian liberty, and in other respects an unwarrantable denial of divinely-appointed means of reconciliation, were yet such as need not interrupt communion between a church which adopted them and a church which refused them, if adopted only as disciplinary Nor was there anything heretical in the simple doctrine that Charismata had not ceased in the Church But that these Charismata introduced a new dispensation superior to that of Christ and His Apostles is a doctrine in a high degree heretical That Christ who came to fulfil the Law and the Prophets, and promised His Holy Spirit to His Apostles to guide them into all truth, bequeathed to His Church only an insufficient morality, and a dispensation which needed to be supplemented by the Paraclete of Montanus, is utterly inconsistent with a true reception of the doctrines of the Catholic Church, and of the Holy Ghost who spake by the Prophets. The distinction in Montanus' system between the Paraclete and the Holy Ghost is not a distinction (or difference rather), of Person or Nature, but the distinction of a plenary bestowal for a complete revelation following a partial bestowal for an imperfect and temporary revelation It may be compared, and is virtually compared by Tertullian in the passages cited above from the treatises *de Monog.* and *de Virg Vel*, to the distinction drawn by St. John when he says, "The Holy Ghost was not yet given." It was the same Spirit in the Mosaic and the Christian dispensations, yet might be called another on account of the different and larger grace of the Christian dispensation So the Paraclete is in Person and Being identified with the Holy Ghost, but the larger measure of the Spirit given for the completion of Christianity introduces a distinction by which the Holy Ghost bestowed on the Apostles is inferior to the Paraclete. The Paraclete is undeniably identified with the promised Spirit of Truth, *i e.* the promise of our Lord, which the Church believes to have been fulfilled on the first Pentecost day, was not fulfilled until the Spirit came on Montanus [1] Mosheim [cent ii p ii cap v sect 23, note], we must take the liberty of saying, entirely mistakes the nature of the distinction, if his words imply, as we understand them to imply, a teacher other than the Third Person of the Blessed Trinity This heresy gave a character to the new disciplinary rules. It introduced also schism in its most aggravated form, asserting that the party of Montanus alone was the true Church, the Pneumatici, all other nominal Christians being Psychici [2]

It is consistent with this that Montanus,

[1] Tertullian's words are [*de Virg Vel* p 292] "Cum venerit ille spiritus veritatis, deducet vos in omnem veritatem, et supervenientia renunciabit vobis Sed et supra de hoc ejus opere pronunciavit Quæ est ergo Paracleti administratio nisi hæc?" &c. The Paraclete is the promised Spirit of Truth

[2] "Nos—quos Spiritales merito dici facit agnitio spiritalium Charismatum" [*de Monog* p 673]

Prisca, and Maximilla had no successors If they had pretended to ordinary Charismata, they might have had successors—as the plenary prophets of a complete revelation there was no room for successors

Such was Montanism in its first stage The Catholic writers who opposed the heresy in its early form did not deny the possible or actual continuance of Charismata in the Church, but the genuineness of the Montanist prophesyings And they rested this question on the difference between an ἔκστασις and a true prophetic rapture. There were also many synods held in which the novel doctrines were examined and rejected, and those who held them excommunicated [Euseb *H E* v 16] One of these was held at Hierapolis [A D 173] by Apollinarius, with twenty-six bishops It is named by the author of the *Libellus Synodicus*, an authority to which Cave says he should not have trusted had it not been for the statement of Eusebius that such councils were held If the date of this council be correctly given it is almost necessary to adopt an earlier date than A D. 171 for the commencement of Montanus' prophesyings

The second stage of Montanism is clearly marked by an alteration in the formula of Baptism Montanus himself had retained the Catholic form For this we have the evidence of Athanasius, who writes Φρύγες . τὰ ὀνόματα λέγοντες οὐδὲν ἧττόν εἰσιν αἱρετικοί [*cont Arian Or* ii 43] He is writing of Baptism, and the "names" are the Names of the Persons of the Holy Trinity. Even without this evidence we should have been slow to think that Tertullian could have fallen so low as to baptize in the Name of the Father, of the Son, and of Montanus That this was done in the second stage of the heresy is stated by Basil [*Epist* clxxxviii *Canon Prima*, iii 268, Paris 1730] and Theophylact [*in Luc* xxiv 45-53], and their statements are corroborated by the decrees of the Councils of Laodicea and Constantinople, that the Montanists be baptized for reception into the Church [*Laod* viii , *Constant* vii] Athanasius did not deny the validity of the baptism he names, but asserts the heresy of the sect It appears, then, to be true that the later sect actually held that Montanus was the Paraclete, in which case Jerome's statements are explained and verified [*Epist* liv *ad Marcellam*] He says, that the Montanists, following the opinion of Sabellius, bring the Trinity to the narrow restraints of One Person that, in their system, God at first intended to have the world by Moses and the Prophets, but because He could not effect His design that way, He assumed a body of the Virgin, and preached in Christ, under the species of a Son, and suffered death for our sakes And because by these two degrees He could not save the world, at last He descended by the Holy Ghost into Montanus, Prisca, and Maximilla The assertion that Montanus was the Paraclete can only have been made on the notion that the Paraclete was a manifestation of Deity, embodied in Montanus, or which is tantamount to it, one of the Simonian Roots taken from the Deity [SIMONIANS] Æschines is named in the Appendix to the *de Præscriptione Hæreticorum* as at the head of this later heresy

It is needless to attempt to follow the sect into its obscure subdivisions Besides their usual names, Montanists and Cataphryges, other appellations were applied to them, some of which may have referred to particular sections, while others were mere names of derision [Gieseler] The Montanists had their peculiar ecclesiastical constitution Jerome writes "Habent primos de Pepusa Phrygia Patriarchas secundum quos appellant Cenonas atque ita in tertium, i e pæne ultimum locum Episcopi devolvuntur" [*Ep* liv *ad Marcellam*] No explanation is given of the word "Cenonas" It may be that the office is specially referred to in the words εἰ καὶ μέγιστοι λέγοιντο of the Laodicean canon This constitution continued down to the sixth century The last laws against them proceeded from Justinian [A D 530 and 532 see *Cod* lib i tit 5, l 18-21 Gieseler] At this time, if Procopius' *Historia Arcana* may be trusted, some Montanists in Phrygia, driven to desperation, shut themselves up in their conventicles, set fire to them, and perished in the flames [*Hist Arc* ii pp 34, 35]

It has been noticed incidentally that the early movement of Montanism was not regarded unfavourably at Rome The letters of the Lyonese martyrs to the Asiatic Churches, and to Eleutherus, Bishop of Rome, appear to have been at least apologetic, if not recommendatory of Montanism [Euseb *H E* v 3] Elaborate statements of the resemblance of Montanism to orthodoxy, and of the probable holiness of Montanus, may be seen in Baronius, and in Rigaltius' *Preface to Tertullian* It appears further, from Tertullian, that the Bishop of Rome, probably Victor, was on the point of formally recognising the new prophets, when Praxeas, a confessor, came from Asia to Rome, and by his reports of the character of the pretended revelations, induced the bishop to change his opinion, and to renounce communion with the Montanists [*adv Praxeam*, p 634]

Praxeas proving himself a heretic [PRAXEANS], Tertullian had the controversial advantage, which he was not slow to seize, of representing the heresy and the opposition to Montanism in the same light. "Ita duo negotia diaboli Praxeas Romæ procuravit, prophetiam expulit, et hæresim intulit, Paracletum fugavit et Patrem crucifixit" Victor however took decided measures against Montanism, the most important particular of which is given by Tertullian · "Audio etiam edictum esse propositum et quidem peremptorium Pontifex scilicet Maximus, Episcopus Episcoporum, edicit ego et mœchiæ et fornicationis delicta pœnitentia functis dimitto" [*de Pudicit* cap i] Separate Montanist churches were formed in the West Augustine relates that in his time the remnant of the Tertullianists in Carthage returned to the Catholic Church [*Hær.* lxxxvi] The author of *Prædestinatus* infers that the Tertullianists had formed a peculiar sect separated from the other Montanists Gieseler denies the correctness of this inference [*Compend* i p 214, note 6] But, considering what later Montanism was, disciples of Tertullian cannot but have separated themselves from the main body · and that the main body fell into the deeper heresy which has been named, the testimonies given above prove conclusively

It is evident that Montanism was in no inconsiderable part a carrying out of orthodox principles, that on this account it was at first well received in Rome, that as such it has left its mark on the Church at large Dr Newman observes "that while it is chiefly in Tertullian's Montanistic works that strong statements occur of the unalterableness of the Creed, yet, on the other hand, the very foundation of Montanism is developement, not of doctrine, but of discipline and conduct In its whole system Montanism is a remarkable anticipation or presage of developements which soon began to show themselves in the Church, though they were not perfected for centuries after The prophets of the Montanists prefigure the Church's doctors, and their inspiration her infallibility, their revelations her developements" [Newman's *Essay on Developement*, pp 349-352] Since these words were written a new significance has been given to them by the proceedings of the Vatican Council, which has associated with the individual person of the Pope an infallibility that has hitherto been associated only with the collective Episcopate of Christendom The principle of Montanism has thus been revived in a remarkable manner, and grave apprehensions may be felt whether its revival may not ultimately be developed to a still further extent in the direction of that fundamental error respecting the Holy Spirit which characterized the heresy of Montanus

MONTENSES This name seems to have been a local name of the Donatists St Augustine saying distinctly that in his time those heretics were called "Montenses" at Rome [Aug. *Hær* lxix] Epiphanius and Theodoret both associate the name, on the other hand, with the Novatians [Epiph *Hær* lix, Theodor *Hær fab* iii. 5] In the early list of heresies which goes by the name of St Jerome it is said that the Montenses were found chiefly at Rome, and that they were so named because they had concealed themselves in the hill-country during a time of persecution This author speaks of them as distinct from the Donatists and the Novatians, but as adopting the heresy of the one as to the rejection of penitents and of the other as to re-baptism [Pseudo-Hieron *Indicul de Hæres* xxxiv] In one of the canons of the African code which directs the mode of receiving a person into the Church when coming "de Donatistis vel de Montensibus," the two names seem to be used as synonymous [Donatists]

MORAVIANS The sect originally known by the name of "Moravian Brethren" was part of that more moderate section of the Taborites, which began to shew itself in Prague about the year 1450, under the protection of John Rokyczana, the Calixtine Archbishop of Prague, and which, assuming the general name of "Brethren," or "Brethren of the Law of Christ," was distinguished in Bohemia and Moravia respectively by the prefix "Bohemian" or "Moravian" On the subjugation of the Taborites in 1453, a large number of them came round to this moderate party, and it spread widely through Moravia, many doubtless flying there to escape from the persecution of George Podiebrad, who came to the throne of Bohemia in 1461, and who, with Rokyczana, was then endeavouring to bring about a reconciliation between Rome and the Calixtines. During this persecution the "Brethren" hid themselves in caves and underground dwellings, and were thus contemptuously called "Jamnici," or 'Burrowers" ["Grubenheimer"]

The Bohemian and the Moravian part of the sect appear to have had a common organization, and to have co-operated together, whether in time of peace or of persecution, under the name of "Unitas Fratrum" They continued to increase notwithstanding the latter, and in the year 1467 they constituted themselves into a formal sect by electing "elders" in an assembly held at Lhota This election was made by lot, the assembly first selecting twenty names from which to choose, reducing these to nine, and then writing on three slips of paper the word "Est," and mixing them with nine other slips which were left blank The three lots fell to Matthias of Kunewald, Thomas of Prschelanz, and Elias of Krschenow The persons thus chosen were not ordained by bishops, nor is anything said of any ceremony of ordination whatever a point of importance to remember in connection with the claims to an episcopal ministry which are asserted by modern Moravians Shortly afterwards, at another synod, a discussion arose as to whether the persons so chosen by lot were really presbyters, or whether the office of a bishop was not necessary for that purpose. It was decided that a bishop's intervention was not necessary but was expedient, and therefore "to put it out of the adversaries' power to dispute the validity of their office they would seek to obtain an episcopal ordination" Three of the "elders" were therefore sent to Stephen, a "Bishop" of the Waldenses, who had been banished from France, and was now settled in Austria, and by him and his chorepiscopus, they were not only ordained as priests, but consecrated as bishops, Michael of Szamberg being one of the number. Shortly afterwards Stephen was burnt as a heretic at Vienna [Camerarius, *Historica narratio de Fratr Orthod eccl in Bohemia, Moravia, et Polonia.* Comenius, *de Eccl Fratr in Bohem et Morav* 116] This consecration by a Waldensian bishop is alleged as conveying to the Moravian Brethren an apostolical succession But it must be remembered that the Waldenses did not originally, or perhaps ever, make any claim to such a succession in its ordinary sense, having no ground whatever for doing so They alleged that as the Apostles were all bishops though not ordained by men, so their founder Waldo, having a divine mission as an apostle, had the same authority as the Apostles of our Lord had received twelve centuries before, that of consecrating successors in the newly established ministry [Gieseler's *Eccl Hist* iii 466, n 29, Clark's tr] The claims of the Waldenses to an episcopal ministry were, in fact, based on a similar foundation to that of the Irvingites in a later age, and when Stephen handed on a ministerial succession to the Moravians he handed on that which had been derived from the layman Waldo, just as the Irvingites hand on that which they have derived from a layman of their own body [IRVINGITES] Whether those laymen were entitled to be accounted apostles is a separate question

In the year 1481 the Brethren were made the subject of fresh persecution and were banished from Moravia, whence they emigrated through Hungary and Transylvania to Moldavia After six years a large proportion of them returned to Moravia, but some descendants of the original emigrants are still believed to exist among the mountaineers of the Caucasus The doctrines of the Brethren at this time are stated in three apologies which were sent by them to King Ladislaus, between the years 1504 and 1508 [Brown's *Fascic* i 162, 172, 184] They repudiated the Roman doctrine of Purgatory, believing the true Purgatory to be in this world They also rejected the worship of Saints, and the dogma of Transubstantiation But they did not hold the doctrine of Protestants respecting the Eucharist, believing the consecrated elements to be really the Body and Blood of Christ "Corpus Christi, verum, naturale, ex castissima virgine sumptum, similiter vinum sanguis est naturalis corporis ejus "

In the beginning of the sixteenth century the Brethren numbered two hundred congregations in Bohemia and Moravia They were about that time joined by many of the Calixtines, and some of the Calixtine nobles built them places of worship in the towns and villages over which they had authority But after many vicissitudes they were driven from both Bohemia and Moravia in the year 1627 Their estates, their churches, and their schools were confiscated, and if any of the Brethren remained in either country they were only those whose poverty and insignificance concealed them from the notice of the authorities Their last minister who professed to exercise the office of bishop was the learned John Amos Comenius [A D 1592-1671] Towards the close of his life Comenius did indeed give authority in writing to Daniel Vetter, "his co-senior," to consecrate Nicolas Gertichius as Bishop for the Brethren dispersed through Poland (where most of them resided), and Paul Jablonsky for those elsewhere, but he himself took no further part in the act than this, and Jablonsky dying before himself he made no attempt to secure a successor [Crantz' *Hist. of the Brethren*, La Trobe's transl p 76] After the death of Comenius the Brethren subsided into an ordinary Presbyterian organization, holding Lutheran tenets; and the only relic of episcopacy which they retained was the occasional use of the name bishop for their "senior," which was the official title of their presiding elder [1]

MODERN MORAVIANS HERRNHUTTERS, or ZINZENDORFIANS This sect is a revival in name only of the ancient Brethren whose history has been sketched above, and there is no real historical association between the two The Modern Moravians were originally a Lutheran community on the plan of Spener's "houses of piety," established on his estate of Bertholdsdorf in the year 1722 by the young Count Zinzendorf, who was a godson of Spener, and whose father was one of Spener's intimate friends and admirers This community was originally called "Bethel' by Zinzendorf, and afterwards received the name of Herrnhut, the "watch of the Lord" The members of it eventually assumed the name of "Moravian Brethren" when they separated from the Lutheran establishment in 1727, that name being suggested by the presence of several Moravian families among them, especially that of their leading man, Christian David [2]

Zinzendorf [A D 1700-60] became acquainted with David (a shrewd working carpenter of Gorlitz, who had left Moravia some time before), while he was an enthusiastic young man of twenty-one, who had just resolved "faithfully to take charge of poor souls for whom Christ had shed His blood, and especially to collect together and protect those that were oppressed and persecuted" [Spangenberg's *Life of Zinzendorf*, Jackson's transl 36] Christian David availed himself of this resolution of the young nobleman by fetching from Zauchtenthal in Moravia two of his friends who were cutlers, and unable to earn a living, that they, with their wives and six children, might be the nucleus of such a settlement as his keen eye saw the possibility of founding on Zinzendorf's recently acquired estate at Bertholdsdorf in Upper Lusatia, where the Count was then building a house. These two men, Augustine and Jacob Neisser, under the guidance of David, built timber-houses for themselves at Hutberg ("the Watch hill") near to the Count's residence, in 1722, and marked out the lines of a considerable village David then went again to Moravia and persuaded five more of his friends, three brothers named

[1] "A Polish nobleman, a Protestant, residing in London, whose father in a manner has protected these Calvinists, reports of them, "that all their ministers are on an equal footing, that the oldest of them, without having respect to the importance of his cure, is always chosen a 'senior' or 'elder,' for the sake of performing ordinations, that he is nothing else but *primus inter pares*, having not the least jurisdiction or authority over the other clergy, and that he never heard there a minister presume to give himself out for a bishop, which besides was inconsistent with the Polish constitution " [Rimius' *Supplement to the Candid Narrative of the Rise and Progress of the Herrnhutters*, p xxxii n]

[2] "That which first gave rise to the institutions in Upper Lusatia was Spener's idea of planting little churches in the great Church " [Spangenberg's *Life of Zinzendorf*, 41]

Nitschmann, and two others, to return with him to his new settlement, which they did in 1724 From that time the village rapidly increased under the management of David, and in ten years from its first foundation his expectations were so far realized that it contained as many as six hundred inhabitants During most of this time Zinzendorf, who had married and held office at court, resided principally at Dresden, having at the outset presented to the parish of Bertholdsdorf, of which the new settlement of Hutberg formed a part, a zealous young Pietist named John Andrew Rothe, with whom, for some years, his own sentiments and those of his dependants were in agreement

Up to the year 1727 the settlement at Hutberg was thus, as to its religion, simply a community of Lutheran Pietists, and nothing was heard of any religious association between it and the ancient "Unitas Fratrum" About that time, however, some of the community began to forsake their parish church, and to have separate services in the great hall of the community, and about the same time a distinctive religious name began to be given to the settlement by changing that of Hutberg for Herrnhut ("The Watch of the Lord") Disputes arose among them as to the doctrines of Election and the Lord's Supper, some being Schwenkfeldians, though the majority were Lutherans, and it seems likely that the revival of the name "Unitas Fratrum" for their new sect was originally suggested to the Moravian members of the community by the reconciliation of the two parties The revival of the old sect may also have been suggested by the need of some organized ministry, for they adopted precisely the same plan for forming it, that of choosing "elders" by lot, which had been adopted in 1467 by the Brethren themselves Four were thus chosen out of twelve, Christian David and Melchior Nitschmann being two of the four [Spangenberg's *Life of Zinzendorf*, 84]

The ecclesiastical relation in which Zinzendorf stood to the community at Herrnhut had hitherto been that of catechist, in which office he acted as deputy to Rothe, the pastor of the parish But on coming to reside more permanently on his estate, he styled himself "guardian," "warden," or "trustee" of the community In 1734, however, he was himself ordained as a Lutheran pastor at Tubingen As the community separated more and more from the Lutheran establishment, the question was agitated whether the episcopal system of the old Brethren should not be established among their professed representatives Zinzendorf had hitherto discouraged the attempts in this direction, but he now assented to the plan, and David Nitschmann, being chosen by lot for the office, he was despatched to Berlin to be "consecrated" by Daniel Ernest Jablonsky, chaplain to the King of Prussia, who was "senior" to the dispersed Brethren This act of Jablonsky was at the time assented to by letter by Christian Sitkovius, the senior of the Polish Brethren

In 1736 Zinzendorf was banished from Herrnhut and from Saxony, his proceedings having been so mixed up with political intrigues that they were considered to be dangerous to the State From that time until his death, a quarter of a century afterwards, he spent much of his time in travelling about Europe, establishing many settlements similar to the original one, and organizing the missionary work of his sect Among other countries he visited England in 1737, and became acquainted with Charles Wesley, but the influence which the Moravian system had upon that of the Methodists was exercised through the subsequent intimacy of John Wesley with Peter Bohler on his voyage to Georgia, and of a visit which he paid to Herrnhut [DICT *of* THEOL, METHODISM] Having made a short stay in England, Zinzendorf went to Berlin, where, on May 20th, 1737, he was ordained bishop by Jablonsky and Nitschmann in the private house of the former, with the consent of the King To this act of Jablonsky also Sitkovius gave his consent by letter, but he afterwards considered that he had been imposed upon, and disclaimed all intention of assenting to either ordination in any other sense than as making Nitschmann and Zinzendorf "seniors" or presiding presbyters [1] [Rimius' *Suppl to Candid Account*, xxxii] Shortly afterwards the Count-Bishop was permitted to return to Herrnhut, but he was again banished from Saxony in the following year, and took up his residence at Berlin, where he opened his house for religious services, the clergy declining to admit him to their pulpits In subsequent years he visited the West Indies, and nearly every European country, forming Moravian settlements and missions, or inspecting those already in existence

Such a settlement was projected and partly carried out by Zinzendorf in England in 1749 He purchased of the Duke of Ancaster a mansion on the banks of the Thames at Chelsea, named Lindsey Place, a former residence of Lord Lindsey, securing with it, on a ninety-nine years' lease, most of the site and the outbuildings of Beaufort House, the old residence of the Dukes of Beaufort, the Duke of Buckingham, and Sir Thomas More, which had been demolished in 1740 by Sir Hans Sloane, the destroyer of the ancient Court suburb The stables of Beaufort House were turned into a Moravian chapel, with a burial-ground adjoining, and Lindsey Place was repaired and enlarged for the purpose of making it a residence for three hundred families, receiving the new name of "Sharon" [2] This great scheme was never accomplished, but for twenty years Lindsey House became the headquarters of the Moravian body, and some of its managing heads

[1] The "Instrument of Consecration" runs "Quod majus est, non sua solum, sed et *seipsum* ita Deo et Ecclesiæ vir Illustrissimus *consecravit* ut Antistitis et Episcopi vices in Ecclesiis Bohemo Moravica in se suscipere sit dignatus," &c. [*Acta Fratrum Unitatis in Anglia*, 1749, p 63]

[2] The next house westward was that of Lady Huntingdon, afterwards known as Cremorne House, and then as Cremorne Gardens, where Whitfield first began his mission work among the London gentry

lived in the splendid mansion It was then used as an orphanage until it was sold in 1770, ten years after Zinzendorf's death. Besides the chapel adjoining this mansion, there were others in Fetter Lane and White's Alley, and several in country towns.

While Zinzendorf was in England he procured an Act of Parliament to be passed [22 Geo II c 30] exempting the Moravians from military service He also attracted much attention to them by an unscrupulous misrepresentation of their claims to apostolical succession and a genuine episcopacy, printing a thin folio volume of documents, which were put together with more cleverness than candour, and published in 1749 under the title of "Acta Fratrum Unitatis in Anglia." Archbishop Wake, in his zealous endeavours after unity with foreign churches, was rash enough to write strongly in favour of the claims made by Zinzendorf, and Bishop Wilson accepted the appointment of "Administrator of the Reformed Tropus in the Unity of the Brethren" A tradition thus grew up respecting the Catholic position of the Moravians which, as is shewn above, is altogether groundless

Since the death of Zinzendorf in 1760 the sect which he founded has maintained a quiet and unassuming position among Christian communities apart from the Church, which has won great respect for its members Some of the quaintness and simplicity of German country life have clung to them everywhere, and while they are characterized by an earnest mission spirit as regards the heathen, they are entirely unaggressive as regards other sects Their theological position is identical with that of the Evangelical Lutherans, and their sympathies have always been strong towards the Low Church School in the Church of England The whole number of them in Europe, including children, is said to be only about 12,000, but they reckon as many as 70,000 in their missions, which are chiefly among the Negroes, the Hottentots, and the extreme northern people of Europe and America. The parent settlement at Herrnhut still exists, with many others in Germany, and the next in importance to these are Fulneck near Leeds, Fairfield near Manchester, Ockbrook near Derby, with Bethlehem, Nazareth, and Lititz in Pennsylvania, and Salem in North Carolina

MORELSTSCHIKI A name signifying "self immolators," and given to a fanatical sect of Russian Dissenters, whose wild and savage practices are more like those of the ancient Scandinavians than of professing Christians of the nineteenth century Their custom is to meet together on a certain day in the year in some retired place, and having dug a deep pit, to fill it with wood, straw, and other combustibles, while they are singing weird hymns relating to the ceremony Fire is then applied to the piled-up fuel, and numbers leap into the midst of it, stimulated by the triumphant hymns of those around, to purchase a supposed martyrdom by their suicidal act These fanatics are found chiefly in Siberia, and the Russian government has endeavoured to discover and suppress them by means of very severe measures, but has not yet succeeded in doing so

MORISONIANS An offshoot from the United Secession body in Scotland, which originated in 1841 in the defection of a small minority from the high Calvinism maintained by the parent sect In that year James Morison, a young minister at Kilmarnock, but afterwards of Glasgow, was deposed for maintaining the universality of the Atonement. In opposition to the view that Christ died in purpose and effect only for those who are by an irreversible decree the elect, although the benefits of His death are also freely offered to those who reject them, he taught that Christ died equally for all men, and that by His death He has removed all obstacles to forgiveness, that every one who will simply believe that Christ died for him is at once saved, that holiness, grace, and a spirit of devotion are at once comprehended in this belief, that repentance is not sorrow for sin, but simply the change of mind from disbelief in salvation to belief, that those who ultimately will be condemned, will be condemned only for disbelieving the truth of Christ's dying for them, and consequently failing to secure forgiveness through Him, that all men are able of themselves to believe, and that Adam's fall has not so corrupted mankind as to render them liable to eternal punishment on account of his sin From the extreme of Calvinism the rebound was thus made to Pelagianism, while the exaltation of the simple act of faith as all-sufficient has a strong tendency to develope Antinomianism in practice Morison was joined in the course of a few years by several other ministers, chiefly from amongst the Independents, and a body was constituted which styles itself "The Evangelical Union and affiliated Churches," although often called by others after the name of its originator The sect is of the Congregational kind, each separate congregation maintaining individual freedom, and consequently, although generally agreeing in maintaining Morisonian views, there is not in it any necessary unanimity in opinion At the census of 1851 the sect was returned as possessing 27 places of worship in Scotland, with a total attendance of 10,192 persons at morning, afternoon, and evening service There are now eighty congregations, of which four are in England and two in Ireland

[Morison's *Extent of the Propitiation* and *Way of Salvation*, two tracts *United Secession Magazine*, 1841 Eadie's *Ecclesiastical Cyclopædia*, 1862 *Religions of the World*, ed 1870]

MORMONS The usual title of the adherents of a religion founded, A D 1830, in the United States of America, by Joseph Smith They derive the above name from one of their sacred books; but they call themselves "The Church of Jesus Christ of Latter-Day Saints," or briefly "Latter-Day Saints" They number about 250,000 persons, 80,000 of whom live in the territory of Utah, in the United States, between the Rocky Mountains and California, the rest are scattered over the world

I *History.* The founder, Joseph Smith, was born, of poor and somewhat disreputable parents, in Sharon, Windsor County, State of Vermont, December 23rd, 1805 In 1819 the family removed to Manchester, State of New York, where soon afterwards a religious "revival" took place Joseph took advantage of the excitement to declare that he had seen a vision Two heavenly personages appeared to him, who, declaring themselves to be God the Father and God the Son, bade him join no religious sect then existing, for they were all in error This story only met with ridicule, and for some years Smith lived an idle, discreditable life In September 1823, he alleged that another vision had been vouchsafed to him A glorious personage appeared to him three separate times in one night, and told him that his sins were pardoned, that the time was now come for the Gospel to be fully preached, and that God had a great work for him to do Directions were then given to him where he should find, buried in the earth, some golden plates, inscribed with the writings of ancient prophets, together with an instrument whereby they could be read and translated He was also warned, on pain of death, to shew the plates only to those persons who should be pointed out to him, and not to indulge a worldly or covetous spirit in his thoughts of or dealings with the plates. [See also Book of Mormon, *Mormon*, iv 2, p 510] From this time he professed to receive constant messages from heaven Smith alleges that he found the plates in the spot indicated, but that he was not yet allowed, owing to his want of holiness, to possess them they were, however, after three yearly visits to the place, committed to his charge in September 1827 These plates are asserted to have been of fine gold, about 8 inches long by 7 broad, a little thinner than ordinary tin, bound together in a volume, and fastened at one edge by three rings running through the whole The volume was about six inches thick, but part was sealed up, so that it could not be opened or read The plates were beautifully engraved with small characters in an unknown tongue, called in the work itself the Reformed Egyptian [Book of Mormon, *Mormon*, iv 8, p 515] With them were found "two smooth three-cornered diamonds set in glass, and the glasses set in silver bows, which were connected with each other in much the same way as old-fashioned spectacles" [*Biogr Sketches*, 101] This was the Urim and Thummim, the possession and use of which constituted seers in ancient times, and God had prepared it for the purpose of translating the plates [See Book of Mormon, *Ether*, i 7-11, pp 520-522] Besides these, there was a curious breastplate of metal, apparently copper, and a sword, formerly used by Laban, one of the personages in the Book of Mormon [*Nephi*, i 20, p 5, *sq*] No one else professes to have seen the plates till, two years after [A.D 1829], in accordance with a revelation, they were shewn to three persons, and subsequently, when or how is unknown, to eight others The testimony of these eleven persons is prefixed to the printed copies of the book Two of the first three witnesses afterwards apostatized; of the eight five were relations of one of the former three, the others were the father and two brothers of Smith himself The "Urim and Thummim" was shewn to a few people, the breastplate only to Smith's mother, the sword to no one They were all, according to Smith's statement, afterwards returned to the angel, and never seen more In the beginning of 1827, Smith told his story to one Martin Harris, a farmer of Palmyra, State of New York, a person of much credulity and some property This man at once agreed to aid in supporting Smith while he translated the plates, and the great work was begun Smith sitting behind a blanket, hung up as a curtain lest the plates should be seen by unholy eyes, dictated the translation to Harris When a small portion was finished, Harris was sent to lay it, together with a copy of the characters on one of the plates, before Prof Charles Anthon, of New York The Mormons assert that the Professor declared the characters to be Egyptian, Chaldaic, Assyrian and Arabic, and asked to see the original [*P of G P* 45] Prof Anthon himself states that he saw at once that the engraving was a deceit, and warned Harris against being the victim of roguery [*Letter*, in Mackay, 32-34] A facsimile, alleged to be identical with that shewn to Prof Anthon, is published in the *Millennial Star* [xv 540, also in Rémy, i 244] This has no resemblance to any existing characters, and is like nothing but the scratches made by children for amusement when they begin to learn writing. Harris however returned to Smith, and continued his labours as secretary When about 116 pages were finished, Harris was permitted to take the MS home to read to his wife, but with her connivance it was stolen On this Joseph produced a revelation ordering him not to translate again the portion lost, lest the wicked, finding the two translations to differ, should scoff at God's work [*D and C* xxxvi p 178, *sq*] Harris was soon after replaced in his task by Oliver Cowdery, a village schoolmaster, who professed to believe in Smith A vision was soon granted to these two A heavenly messenger, declaring himself to be John the Baptist, appeared to them as they prayed in a wood, and, laying his hands on them, consecrated them, in the name of Jesus Christ, "Priests of the order of Aaron," and commanded them to baptize each other by immersion As soon as they were baptized "the Holy Ghost fell on them, and the spirit of prophecy was granted them" [accounts by Smith and Cowdery, *P of G P* 46, 47] The new gospel was made known to several persons, some believed, and aided Smith with hospitality and money, others, knowing his character, scoffed at it, and annoyed him in various ways When the translation was finished [A D 1829], Harris undertook to bear half the cost of printing it, having, in obedience to a revelation [*D and C* xliv. 3, pp 194, 195], sold his farm for that purpose. Meanwhile the "Church of Christ," as it was at first called, was being organized through numerous and minute revelations, and on Tuesday, April 6th, 1830, it was formally started at La Fayette, State of New York Six members were present, who ordained each other, after which they received the Communion, and were "confirmed in the Church of Christ by the Holy Ghost," who granted them the gift of prophecy. Several persons present as spectators were converted and baptized, among them the Prophet's father and mother About the same time the Book of Mormon was published This work was really written about 1809, by Solomon Spaulding, who had been a preacher of some obscure sect, and had afterwards failed in business The discovery of some remains of an extinct race led him to write a romance connecting this race with the Jews on the one hand and the American Indians on the other The MS was entrusted for publication in 1812 to a bookseller named Paterson at Pittsburg, Pennsylvania Before, however, the arrangements were completed, Spaulding died The MS remained with Paterson, who, it would seem, allowed a copy of it to be taken by Sydney Rigdon, one of his compositors, a man of some ability and a preacher of the CAMPBELLITES It is supposed by some that Rigdon was an accomplice of Smith in concocting the story of the plates and the plan of a new religion, but the two appear not to have met till after the Book of Mormon was published It is therefore probable that Smith obtained Spaulding's MS, or a copy of it, in some other way, and that it was the knowledge of the origin of the pretended Holy Book that drew Rigdon to him There is no doubt that several persons, including the widow, the brother, and the partner of Spaulding, recognised in the Book of Mormon Spaulding's fiction The same names, incidents, and peculiarities of style were found in it, with such additions as suited the imposture The story of the gold plates was probably suggested by the discovery by Smith of some ancient remains, such as are often found in North America It was at first apparently intended as a hoax, but the credence which it obtained induced Smith to carry it further, and to use Spaulding's MS to support his story The publication of the Book of Mormon, and some alleged miracles, attracted several converts, and at the First Conference of the Church [June 1st, 1830] thirty members were present Missionaries were sent forth through the States, and had no small success, among their converts being Brigham Young, Smith's successor as president, and two brothers named Pratt, both clever men Rigdon also openly joined Smith, and at once became his confidential counsellor The affairs of the Church were entirely directed by revelations Many of these were simply to serve Smith's idleness and greed For instance, one [dated July 1830] orders the Church to support him [*D and C* ix 4 p 112], another [February 1831] declares "It is *mete* that my servant Joseph Smith, jun, should have a house built" [*D and C* lxi 3, p 214], a third bids that he be provided "with food and raiment, and whatsoever things he needeth to accomplish the work *wherewith* I have commanded him" [*D. and C* xiv 3, p 131] The success of the Prophet roused great animosity, his previous conduct and character were cast in his teeth, charges of fraud were brought against him, and when he was acquitted in the district courts, he and his friends were threatened with violence. In the beginning of 1831, therefore, the saints in a body removed to Kirtland, Ohio, where Rigdon had made many converts Here the Prophet resided for some years, employing himself, with the help of Rigdon and others, in elaborating, by revelation, the doctrines and discipline of the sect He also pretended to make, with the help of the Urim and Thummim, a new translation of the Bible In this year the Melchisedek Priesthood was established Soon after his arrival in Kirtland, Smith, seeing that he could not carry out his plans in the more settled States, set out with several companions westward in search of a fitting settlement He pitched upon a spot in Jackson County, Missouri, on the banks of the Missouri River, which was declared to be "Zion, the New Jerusalem, where Christ would shortly reign in person" The saints were ordered by revelation to settle there, and buy up the land, and in a short time nearly 1200 persons had removed thither After a stay of about six weeks the Prophet returned to Kirtland In addition to his duties as "Prophet, Seer, Revelator, and Translator," he managed a store, a mill, and a bank, and he also occasionally went on missionary tours through the States, where, by preaching and pretending to work miracles, he gained many converts But persecution, arising partly from jealousy of the Saints' prosperity, partly from disgust at their teaching, soon broke out at Kirtland also In March 1832, Smith and Rigdon were torn from their beds by a mob, and tarred and feathered Rigdon was treated so roughly that he was for some days insane, Smith, however, on the next day preached to a great crowd and made three converts [*Biogr Sketches*, 192-194] In the next year [A D 1833] the first edition of "The Book of Doctrine and Covenants" was published Troubles now came on the new colony in Missouri The Mormons in their enthusiasm declared that all unbelievers would be rooted out from the State, which would soon be theirs Their newspaper also put forth abolitionist views The people, enraged by these proceedings, and by charges against the Saints of communism of goods and wives, resolved on their expulsion After enduring mob violence for some months, and receiving no protection from the authorities, the Mormons were compelled to forsake Zion in the midst of winter They settled ultimately at Liberty, Clay County On the news of this outbreak, Smith, with 150 men, set out from Kirtland to aid his followers Before starting, he established, in order to appease some jealousies, the first presidency of three members, himself being first and Rigdon second, and the High Council of 12, and as the ruling authorities of the Church The formal title of "The Church of

Jesus Christ of Latter-day Saints" was also adopted [May 1834] The Prophet and his "company for the redemption of Zion" suffered much hardship in their journey, the cholera also broke out among them, which Smith, to the scandal of the Saints, was unable to cure by the laying on of hands On their arrival, they found themselves too few for their purpose, the Prophet therefore returned, after a fortnight's stay, to Kirtland The Mormons now remained unmolested for nearly four years [1834—end of 1837], and, through their missionary zeal, their numbers largely increased. The institution of tithes was now [November 1834] set on a regular footing In 1835, Smith obtained some Egyptian papyrus rolls, of which he published translations, obtained by the Urim and Thummim The first foreign mission was despatched to England in 1837, the first conference of converts was held at Preston, Lancashire, December 25th of that year Smith still carried on his trading enterprises, obtaining the capital required from the tithes and contributions of the Saints, while the profits were made over chiefly to his own family, who were not sparing in their demands Accordingly, in the autumn of 1837, the business failed, and the bank, which had issued notes to a large amount, stopped payment Smith and Rigdon were at once indicted for swindling, and to avoid the writs fled by night to their friends in Missouri Here also troubles soon arose, both within and without the Church, and the dissensions reached such a pitch, that Cowdery, Harris, Rigdon, and other Mormons of long standing were [A D 1838], expelled from the Church Rigdon, however, who knew too much to be made an enemy of, was soon pardoned and re-admitted During their respite from persecution, the Mormons, through their industry, had prospered much. With success, their arrogance also returned The Prophet is said to have declared that he would yet trample on the necks of his enemies, and that as it was with Mahomet, "The Koran, or the sword," so it should soon be "Joseph Smith and the sword" About this time also a band of men, called Danites, or Destroying Angels, was secretly organized to defend the First Presidency by any means, fair or foul, and there is little doubt that, up to a recent time, many murders and other acts of violence were committed by them on opponents and apostates Persecution again began, the Mormons retaliated, and regular warfare, with much destruction of property and some bloodshed, ensued At length the State militia were called out, nominally to preserve the peace, really to crush the Mormons After much loss and suffering, especially at a place called Hawn's Mill, where several Mormons were massacred, the Saints were driven, in the depth of winter, across the Mississippi into Illinois [A D 1838] The Prophet, his brother Hyram, and other leading Mormons, were seized, and sentenced by court-martial to be shot, but the sentence was not carried out, and after some months' close confinement, they all escaped into Illinois [April 1839] A third settlement was there formed, and named Nauvoo, explained as Hebrew for "beautiful" Numerous converts assembled, and the Saints soon amounted to 15,000 In 1840 a charter of incorporation was obtained, the militia, consisting of all able-bodied men, with Smith for General, was organized, under the name of "The Nauvoo Legion," and a mansion was built, where the Prophet and his family were maintained at the public cost A revelation of great length [*D and C* 103, p 298, *sq*] gave directions for the building of a splendid temple, the first stone of which was laid with great pomp on April 6th, 1841 The Anti-Mormons now tried another mode of attack During the next three years Smith was several times brought to trial on charges of libel, swindling, treason, and inciting to murder He was, however, always acquitted, though he had a narrow escape in 1842, when accused of bribing a ruffian to shoot Governor Boggs of Missouri, one of his chief opponents The Mormons still increased in wealth, numbers, and audacity The corporation assumed an independent jurisdiction, and passed an ordinance imposing imprisonment on any person who should speak disrespectfully of the Prophet, all legal documents were declared to be void unless backed by his signature Smith was now absolute ruler, both in spiritual and temporal things, over 20,000 persons, and his converts, both in America and elsewhere, were rapidly increasing in numbers It is stated that in 1843 there were 10,000 in Great Britain alone, and in the following year a copy of the Book of Mormon was presented to the Queen Smith used his prosperity for the gratification of his greed and lusts He exacted large contributions in money and kind, and, with his chief followers, he began, under cover of a theory of "Spiritual Wives," secretly and cautiously to teach polygamy Some of the women to whom proposals were made informed their friends, rousing thereby great indignation Meanwhile, in 1844, Smith went so far as to offer himself as a candidate for the Presidency of the United States But his proceedings raised against him many bitter enemies, including some of his former partisans At length the Anti-Mormons established a newspaper in Nauvoo itself, in the first number of which were published affidavits from sixteen women, stating that Smith, Rigdon, and other prominent Mormons had attempted to seduce them A council of the Saints promptly declared the journal a public nuisance Smith ordered the nuisance to be abated, and a mob of Mormons destroyed the office, papers, and furniture The owners obtained warrants against Smith and others concerned the Mormons resisted their execution the whole neighbouring population rose in arms against them the governor called out the militia, and finally, to avoid a general massacre, and on the governor pledging his word and the honour of the State that they should be protected, Joseph Smith, his brother Hyram, and some others, surrendered, and were lodged in prison at Carthage, the State capital. All was quiet for a time, but a rumour arose that the governor wished their escape. At 6 A.M., June 27th, 1844, 200 men, disguised and painted as Indians, overpowered the guard, broke into the prison, and shot the Smiths dead, severely wounding their companions. [Accounts from Mormon eye-witnesses, in Burton, app. iii.; Mackay, 189, *sq.*] Joseph Smith was thirty-eight years of age, and left a widow, with several children. His character and whole career is that of a low-minded, lustful impostor, with little education but much shrewdness, led on by circumstances to play the part of a religious leader. There is not the slightest evidence that he was, as some have maintained, a misguided enthusiast. He used his power simply for his own personal ends; and his zeal and endurance under persecution were prompted by keen-sighted views of the future, and in some degree also by natural firmness and resolution. [For the life of Smith, see *Biographical Sketches of Joseph Smith the Prophet and his Progenitors*, by Lucy Smith, mother of the Prophet; *The Autobiography of Joseph Smith*, in *Mill Star*, xiv. xv.; *The Book of Doctrine and Covenants, passim.*]

At first it seemed that the death of the Prophet would cause the ruin of his religion. Four claimants for the vacant presidency arose; but the twelve apostles unanimously elected Brigham Young their president; and the choice was generally accepted. Rigdon, who ventured to resist, was, with some adherents, finally excommunicated. The "Saints" were for a time left in peace; but their rejoicings and boastings at the laying the capstone of the temple again roused the populace against them. After much loss of life, the leaders resolved to remove from the civilized world beyond the Rocky Mountains. They agreed to leave Illinois altogether in the course of 1846, and a promise was made that they should be allowed to sell their property and retire in peace. An exploring expedition, setting out in February 1846, after much hardship reached Iowa. Here circumstances compelled them to wait till they were recruited by fresh parties from Nauvoo. Meanwhile those who remained in the city, while preparing for their removal, pressed forward the building of the temple, which was solemnly consecrated in May 1846. This proceeding was regarded as a sign that the Saints intended to remain or to return hereafter. The populace again rose; and after three days' bombardment, the remnant of the Mormons were driven out of Nauvoo by the sword, in the greatest misery. The city, which had contained 20,000 inhabitants, was left desolate. The temple, having been dismantled by the departing Mormons, was set on fire by an incendiary, November 19th, 1848; and the bare walls were blown down by a hurricane, May 27th, 1850. From the camp in Iowa an advanced body, with the president, after marching for three months, reached the valley of the Great Salt Lake; and, guided, as they said, by an angel, fixed on this for their new home. Here they were soon joined by the main body. They suffered terribly in their long march, and during the autumn and winter after their arrival. A circular letter from the twelve apostles called all the Saints to the new "Zion," which was named Deseret, interpreted to mean, in the "reformed Egyptian" language, "Honey-bee" [Book of Mormon, *Ether*, i. 3, p. 518]. Public buildings (including a tabernacle, or temporary place for public worship), manufactures and shops were soon established; and a system of emigration was organized, with a fund to help the Saints on their way, who flocked thither, enduring much privation from the journey. In 1850, the district—part of that ceded by Mexico in 1849—was admitted into the United States as a territory, with the name Utah, a claim that it should be erected into a State being rejected. Brigham Young was named the first governor. In 1852, the "Celestial Law of Marriage," authorizing polygamy, was promulgated, and at once acted on; and in 1853 the corner-stone of the temple, the plan of which with all its details was "revealed" to the president, was laid; it is not [A.D. 1873] nearly finished. Difficulties soon arose with the judges and other officers appointed by the United States President; and twice, in 1854 and 1856, they were all compelled to fly to Washington. The first difficulty was smoothed over; but in 1857, 2,500 troops were sent to enforce submission. The Mormons prepared to resist, but, after some skirmishes, gave way. The troops were withdrawn in 1860, but in 1862 it was found necessary to form a permanent camp at Douglas, close to the city, to overawe the Mormons. The governor forbade the annual muster of the militia, and tried to prevent the packing of juries; his death soon after was considered by the Saints as a judgment. His successor, supported by the judges, continued this policy; and in consequence the Mormon periodicals are full of complaints of injustice, corruption, and personal profligacy. In 1871 some of the Mormon leaders were indicted under the United States law against bigamy; in the first case, the defendant was convicted, whereon the president was arrested for bigamy and inciting to murder. On appeal, however, the proceedings were quashed, to the great joy of the Mormons, who look on this result as due to a special interference of Providence. They declare their resolve to resist to the death all attempts to put down polygamy, and their firm belief that God will work miracles for them, as for his ancient Saints, the Jews [Rae, 116, *Mill Star*, vol. xxxii. *passim*, esp. p. 328]. The opening of the Pacific Railway [A.D. 1869], by giving a great impulse to mining, has largely increased the number of "gentiles," and this fact will probably greatly influence the future fortunes of the Mormons. Recent events [May 1873] shew symptoms of a design to leave Utah for some spot where a more complete isolation can be maintained.

II. *Sacred Books.* The alleged discovery and real history of the "Book of Mormon" has been already described. In its published form it is a duodecimo volume of 563 pages of small print.[1] It is divided, in imitation of the Old Testament, into fifteen books of unequal length, bearing the names of their supposed authors,—Nephi [*cf* 2 Macc i 36], Jacob, Enos, Jarom, Mosiah and the like, each book being divided into chapters and numbered paragraphs The work contains the history of three peoples who came from the East to America, the earliest after the dispersion of Babel, the others setting out from Jerusalem in the reign of Zedekiah Lehi [*cf* Judg xv 19], a righteous Jew of the tribe of Joseph, warned by God to flee from the approaching destruction of Jerusalem, was, with his wife and four sons, divinely guided to America From this family sprung two nations, the righteous Nephites and the wicked Lamanites, who were continually at war with each other The latter were finally punished by the loss of their fair skins, and were allowed to sink into barbarism, becoming the Red Indians The history of the Nephites is given at length In the fifth century after their arrival, the Nephites, under Divine guidance, found and united with a people of the tribe of Judah, whose ancestors had left Jerusalem after its capture by Nebuchadnezzar This people possessed plates containing the history of the family of Jared, who had come to America after the dispersion of Babel From this family sprung great nations, who mutually destroyed each other A number of prophets arose among the Nephites, who foretold the redemption through Christ, and instituted baptism in His Name At the time of the Crucifixion the Nephites were visited with terrible convulsions of nature, and a voice from Heaven commanded the people to repent and believe After the Ascension, Jesus Christ thrice appeared to them, converted all the nation, appointed twelve disciples, instituted the two sacraments, performed many miracles, and ascended again into Heaven After a long period of piety and prosperity wickedness and troubles again arose, and finally, all the Nephites but one were slain by their enemies the Lamanites. So all true religion perished, miracles and gifts of grace ceased The chronicles of the Nephites were kept on gold plates, handed down from generation to generation The final possessors of them, Mormon, and Moroni his son, at God's command, made an abridgment of the history, and hid it in the place where it was found by Joseph Smith With the history are mixed up long exhortations, visions, parables, religious meditations, in language imitating that of the English Bible, from which many passages are directly copied, sometimes with slight variations which do not improve the sense, including large portions of Isaiah, the Sermon on the Mount, and some verses of St Paul's Epistles The narrative is most tedious, there is not a trace of any elevated, poetic, or religious feeling The style is that of an uneducated person, glaring grammatical errors appearing on nearly every page, besides the grossest absurdities and anachronisms. Beyond the assertions that the Book is the work of inspired writers teaching true religion, and that revelations, miracles, and gifts of tongues are ever with the faithful, few of the doctrinal peculiarities of Mormonism appear Materialistic notions of the Deity are hinted at [*Ether*, i 8, p 521, 522], and infant baptism is forbidden [*Moroni*, viii 2, pp 557]

The chief authority on doctrine is *The Book of Doctrine and Covenants of the Church of Jesus Christ of Latter-day Saints, selected from the Revelations of God*, by Joseph Smith, President The first edition, published in 1833, differs much from the later ones, and was subsequently suppressed [2] This work consists of two distinct parts Pp 1-64 contain seven lectures on faith, originally delivered before a class of elders at Kirtland, and it seems probable that they were written by Rigdon In them are some very curious statements For instance, it is inferred from Heb xi 3, that faith is "the principle of power existing in the bosom of God by which the worlds were framed, and that if this principle or attribute were taken from the Deity, He would cease to exist [Lect i 13-17, p 3] Again, "When a man works by faith, he works by mental exertion, instead of physical force It is by words, instead of exerting his physical powers, with which every being works, when he works by faith" [Lect vii 3, p 55] Many peculiar doctrines are here set forth The second part, entitled *Covenants and Commandments*, consists of the revelations given to Smith at various times, and is evidently by a different hand from the "Lectures" The style and grammar betray the interpolator of the Book of Mormon The "Covenants and Commandments" resemble in form the Koran, both works contain Divine revelations, much in both is only of temporary interest, and both afford undesigned materials for the life of their authors But all the merits of the Koran are absent and all its defects present in the work of Joseph Smith The revelations were given to a great number of persons, but always through the medium of Smith They refer to various subjects the organization, worship and hierarchy of the Church, instructions in faith and morals, prophecies, visions, parables, interpretations of Scripture, directions to individuals about their acts, preachings, journeyings, for the promotion of the faith, and concerning the affairs and needs, spiritual and temporal, of the Church There are also two addresses of the Prophet to the Saints in Nauvoo, delivered in writing only, minutes of the High Council [February 17th, 1834]; declarations of the Church on marriage, and governments, and an account of the martyrdom of Joseph Smith and his brother Those sections relating to the organization of the Church and the duties of the ministry are placed first, then the portions chiefly treating of faith and practice, lastly, those that relate chiefly to individuals and to temporary circumstances

[1] The edition here referred to is the sixth European, Liverpool, 1866. The first figure denotes the chapter, the second the paragraph

[2] The edition used is the sixth European, 1869 It is referred to as [*D and C*] When there are two figures, the first denotes the section, the second the paragraph

Many other revelations, translations, prophecies addresses, etc, of Smith were published in the periodicals of the sect, all of which are regarded as of authority Some of these have been collected into a pamphlet, entitled *The Pearl of Great Price*, being a choice selection from the revelations, translations, and narrations of Joseph Smith, Liverpool, 1851 [referred to as *P of G P*] In this book is set forth the theory that Mormonism is a revival of the primitive religion revealed to Adam [see also *D and C* Lect ii p 8, *sq*, *Coots and Comm.* iii 18-29, p 78] A similar theory is found in the Koran Here also appears a translation, with facsimiles, of some Egyptian papyrus rolls, procured from a travelling showman Smith declared these rolls to be written by Abraham, narrating his stay in Egypt An eminent French Egyptologer, M Déveria, before whom the facsimiles were laid, shewed that they represented the resurrection of Osiris, a funerary disk, and a painting from a funerary MS [For full details see Rémy, ii. 536, *sq*] In this pamphlet two different accounts of the creation are given, both made up out of Gen i A translation is given of Matt xxiii 39 and xxiv differing from the Authorized Version in containing additions to the extent of one-third, entirely unsupported by any MS or version There are some other fragments, absurd but unimportant, except as shewing the audacity of the author The "translations" are portions of a translation of the whole Bible, said to exist in MS in the hands of the Mormon leaders. Some further extracts have appeared in periodicals the text is altered to suit Mormon doctrines, and large additions made It is asserted by the Mormons, that the Authorized Version has been fraudulently corrupted, and that this "translation" alone represents the original and true form Other revelations are also said to exist in MS, to be published when the world is ripe for them

III *Doctrines* It is difficult to set forth exactly and clearly the principles of Mormon theology, first, from the theory of continuous revelation abiding in the Church [see preface to *Hymn Book*, 1856, quoted in *Qu Rev* cxxii. 477, also *Spencer*, Lect. ii, *Compendium*, 43-47], secondly, Mormon theology has neither scientific form nor leading idea, being a disorderly mixture of doctrines and superstitions borrowed from many different sources The only document at all resembling a creed is published in *P of G P* [p 55, see also Burton, 467-480], which nearly represents the form in which Mormonism is usually preached Faith in Joseph and his successors, repentance, baptism for the remission of sins, reverence for the Bible and the sacred books described above, the payment of tithes, absolute obedience to the president and the priesthood, this is nearly all that is required of the orthodox, while farms at Utah and the attractions of polygamy are held out to gain converts The deeper doctrines are reserved for the intelligent and inquiring

The Mormon faith is based on very gross Materialism, in some points verging on Pantheism. All that exists is material, matter therefore is eternal, and is in fact only one substance of which all existing things are modifications The Supreme Deity then is material, originating in the union of two elementary particles of matter · passing through the human stage, He has by constant development attained omnipotence This Supreme Godhead is threefold its nature may be understood by comparing it to a council of three, each of whom is separate and distinct from the others, equal in knowledge, truth, power, and all other respects, but yet the three compose but one body These three persons are called Elohim, Jehovah, and Michael, who is the same as Adam, and they "organized" the world out of previously existing matter This God has also a wife, a female Deity, and from these two have sprung, by a celestial mode of generation, countless gods of both sexes, differing in dignity and power, also angels and the spirits of men No spiritual being therefore is created, all are begotten "God," said Smith, "never did have power to create the spirit of man at all The very idea lessens man in my estimation I know better" [Last sermon in *Mill Star*, v 87, *sq*] The gods possess both body, parts, and passions, and therefore are not omnipresent A Mormon hymn [No 349] begins—

"The God that others worship is not the God for me
He has no parts nor body, and cannot hear nor see"

[See also Spencer, *Lett* viii, *Compend* 140-146] The gods therefore have local residences, the Supreme Deity lives "in the planet Kolob" [*P of G P* 24, *Compend* 199-200] The revelation which the Trinity, Elohim, Jehovah, Michael, bears to the Christian Trinity is not very clear It is said that "these three in organizing element are perfectly represented in the Deity as Father, Son, and Holy Ghost" [*Compend* 153] God the Father, like the other gods, has the form and body of a man, and in fact once inhabited this earth, but by development has become the model or standard of perfection to which man is intended to attain Jesus Christ, the Son of God, was born of the Virgin Mary, the latter having been duly married after betrothal by the Angel Gabriel Yet He had a previous existence in the bosom of the Father, and "He is called the Son, because of the flesh" [*D and C*, Lect v 2, p 45] The Father is a personage of spirit, glory and power, possessing all perfection and fulness, "but the Son is a personage of tabernacle, made or fashioned like unto man, or being in the form and likeness of man, or rather man was formed after His likeness and in His image" [*ib*] There are two personages in the Godhead, the Father and the Son [*ib* p 47] The Holy Spirit also is a member of the Godhead, being the mind of the Father and the Son, but while the other two persons have bodies of flesh and bones, the Holy Ghost has not, but is a personage of Spirit [*Compend* 154] Yet His substance is material, subject to the necessary laws which govern matter He has therefore parts, which are infinite and spread throughout all space, and so is He virtually omnipresent The Father and the Son, as persons, are not omnipresent, but only through the Spirit [*Comp* 140-148] He may properly be called God's minister, to execute His will in immensity He is therefore the worker of miracles, the source of grace, and even the cause of increase, being in every person upon the face of the earth, for the "elements that every individual is made of and lives in possess the Godhead" [B Young in *Compend* 148] As God is in the form of a man, so man was created to become a god The Divine beings are constantly producing souls by generation, these are destined to become gods, which they can only do by obtaining bodies Hence, Michael, or Adam, and Eve his wife, who were immortal, assumed humanity to provide tabernacles of flesh for the disembodied spirits They and their offspring would not have been subject to death but for the Fall, which necessitated redemption by the death of Christ. They have now become gods, and with the other deities continue to bear disembodied souls, which are waiting for bodies, in order that they may attain perfection This can only be effected through the agency of men He who has few or no children is injuring these souls, and the more wives and children a man has, the greater will be his glory in the next life as a god Thus one of the hymns [326] says,—

> "Through him who holds the sealing power,
> Ye faithful ones who heed
> Celestial laws, take many wives,
> And rear a righteous seed
>
> "Though fools revile, I'll honour you,
> As Abraham my friend,
> You shall be gods, and shall be blessed
> With lives that never end "

Jesus Christ had several wives, among others Mary and Martha, the sisters of Lazarus Joseph Smith will be a chief god Hence it is said of him [Hymn 252] "Mingling with gods, he can plan for his brethren," and [290], "His home 's in the sky, he dwells with the gods" The angels have been men, who have not fulfilled the law of their life, nor spent their strength in perfect obedience to God, like Abraham, and other scriptural friends of God, *i e* have not taken many wives Hence they will never become gods.

This theology is supported by the most absolutely literal interpretations of Scripture, and also by the doctrine that the Mormon faith, through the continuous revelations granted to the priesthood, is the supplement and perfection of Christianity, standing in nearly the same relation to it as Christianity to Judaism [Spencer, *Letters*, 55] At the same time, Mormonism is a revival of primitive Christianity, with all its miraculous powers, the gifts of tongues, healing, etc, which were suspended through the failure of faith till Smith came. Many accounts of miraculous cures are given [*Mill Star*, v 32, 1870, 445, 475, 494, also Hymn 243] As the Jews were bidden to separate themselves from the Gentiles, and the early Christians (the Ancient Saints) from the heathen, so the Latter-Day Saints are called forth from a wicked world, doomed to almost immediate destruction which is indeed already beginning, to the Zion of the latter-days on the Western Continent. When the Gospel has been preached to all the world, and the elect have assembled at Zion, then all unbelievers will be destroyed, the kingdom of heaven will be set up on the earth, and God will reign in Zion in person

IV *Ordinances* The "Ordinances of the Gospel" are five [1] *Faith*, which is very strangely described, see quotations from *D and C* above, [2] *Repentance*, *i e* sorrow for sin, and resolution to lead a good life, [3] *Baptism*, administered by immersion, to none younger than eight years, that being regarded as the age at which moral responsibility begins [*D and C* xxii 4, p 160] Infant baptism is declared to be a "solemn mockery, because little children have no sins to repent of, and are not under the curse of Adam" [Mormon, *Moroni*, viii 2, 3, p 557] The rite is administered as follows "The person who is called of God, and has authority from Jesus Christ to baptize, shall go down into the water with the person who has presented him or herself for baptism, and shall say, calling him or her by name 'Having been commissioned of Jesus Christ, I baptize you in the name of the Father, and of the Son and of the Holy Ghost Amen' Then shall he immerse him or her in the water, and come forth again out of the water" [Mormon, *Nephi* v 8, p 457, *D and C* ii 21, p 73] The effect of baptism, when administered to and by a qualified person, is declared to be the remission of sins, the gift of the Holy Ghost, and a title to eternal life It is regarded as absolutely necessary to salvation, without it, neither repentance nor faith avail [*D and C.* iv 12, p 87] To supply the deficiency of those who through ignorance or other involuntary defect have died unbaptized in the Mormon faith, the practice of baptism for the dead has been ordained The faith is preached to the dead in Hades by departed Saints, and the benefit of baptism is obtained for them by proxy Any believer may be baptized for his departed friends, relations, and ancestors to the most remote ages, and, in the perfect state, those for whom a person has been thus baptized will be added to his family and subjects [Spencer, *Letters*, 162-164, *Mill Star*, v 87, *sq*] A careful record of the persons vicariously baptized is kept by duly appointed registrars These records are the books spoken of by St John [Rev xx 12], the book of life being a record kept in heaven to verify those kept on earth [*D and C.* cvi 6, 7, p 319] [4] *Laying on of hands* for the gift of the Holy Ghost, sometimes called baptism by fire as distinguished from baptism by water It is usually administered immediately after baptism, of which it is regarded as the completion By it the spirit of prophecy, the gift of tongues, and the power to work miracles are given [5] *The Sacrament of the Lord's Supper*, originally administered in bread and wine, as Christ Himself ordained when He appeared to the Nephites [Mormon, *Nephi*, viii 6, p 469]

In 1833, it was revealed to Smith that "strong drinks are not for the belly, but for the washing of your bodies," and that wine was only to be used in this ordinance if it was the pure juice of the grape, and made by Mormons [*D and C.* lxxxi 1, p 240] Water only, therefore, is now used The rite is administered every Sunday, the water, having been blessed, is handed round in tin cans, together with the bread [Rae, 106]

Of other rites, the most important is that of marriage The present service is of some length, containing, in the case of all marriages after the first, certain ceremonies by the first wife [Conybeare, 74, 75] There are two kinds of marriage —for eternity and for time. A marriage for eternity holds good not only during this life, but for ever, and is not necessarily consummated here, but those thus married will produce souls in the world to come Marriages "for time" are in order to produce children in this world, hence a woman may be married, or "sealed," to one man for eternity, and to another for time, or may be married to the same man both for time and for eternity Marriages for time only are dissolved by death, and the children in the perfected state are added to the family of the husband for eternity, increasing his glory The faithful Mormon who in this life has been prevented by some involuntary cause, such as an early death, from doing his duty as a child-producer, may have wives "sealed" to him In this case another person, appointed by the president, acts for the dead man, and if any children are born they are reckoned to the latter Divorce is common, and marriage is allowed within near degrees, a man may marry two sisters, a niece, a mother and daughter, and even a half-sister The consequence of this doctrine of marriage is the utter degradation of woman, by herself she is useless and meaningless, all her honour, both in this life and the next, comes from the husband, an unmarried woman has only the very lowest place [1] The public profession of polygamy, or, as it is officially called, "plurality," is a later development of Mormonism Suspicions were early aroused by the life of Smith and other leading Mormons, and the charge of teaching this practice was frequently thought to excite public odium The accusation however was vigorously denied Passages from the Book of Mormon [*Jacob*, ii p 118, *sq*] were quoted against it a public declaration of the Church [A D 1841] stated, "We believe that one man should have one wife, and one woman but one husband" [*D and C.* cix 4, p 331] The *Millennial Star* [Aug. 1842] declares, "No such principle ever existed among the Latter-Day Saints, and never will" [*Mill Star*, iii 74] It is however now alleged, that in 1832 it was, in answer to an inquiry, divinely revealed to Joseph that the principle of "plurality" is true, but that the time had not yet come for it to be practised, and that, on July 12th, 1843, the Prophet, then at the height of his power in Nauvoo, received a long revelation on the subject [See Burton, 451] This document, if genuine, was kept secret till August 29th, 1852, when it was published at a great meeting at Utah [Rémy, ii 112-130] The Prophet's widow at once denounced it as a forgery, and, with four of her sons, headed a schism On the other hand, several women publicly declared that they had been married to Joseph, while the president and others stated that they had been taught the doctrine by him [*Mill Star*, xxxii 327, 333, etc] The practice is now carried to great lengths, the leading men having from fifteen to forty wives each, and it is preached as the one thing needful to regenerate a world steeped in wickedness Many plausible and paradoxical arguments are urged in its favour [See Conybeare, 76-83, Rémy, ii 97-109, Burton, 525 *sq*, Ollivant, *App B* 148-151, and *Mill Star, passim*] For burial there appears to be no prescribed ritual The ordinary worship consists of prayers, with addresses, often of a very homely character, and hymns The chief peculiarity of the services is the absence of any true devotional element. The duties of private prayer, meditation, communion with God, self-examination, are seldom or never spoken of, and very gross irreverence is often shewn during public worship [*Qu Rev* cxxii 486-488, Ollivant, 54, and *App A* 119, 147, Rae, 106, *sq*] When the temple is completed, it is intended, as the founder ordered, to establish sacrifices and every ordinance belonging to the priesthood, as they existed prior to Moses' day [*Compend* 177] There are also some ceremonies, which are most carefully kept secret and of which very different accounts have been given.

V. *Hierarchy* This is very elaborate, and the ministers possess very great power. About one-fifth of the male members hold some church office. "The priesthood," said the Prophet, "is the channel through which the Almighty commenced revealing His glory at the beginning of the creation of this earth, and through which He has continued to reveal Himself to the children of men to the present time, and through which He will make known His purposes to the end of time" [*Compend* 176] There are two grand divisions of the priesthood, the Melchisedek and the Aaronic or Levitical To the former belong the first presidency, the patriarch, the apostles, the seventies, the high-priests, the elders, to the latter, bishops, priests, deacons, teachers The Melchisedek priesthood is so called "because Melchisedek was such a great high-priest" [*D and C* iii 1, p 74] Its power and authority is thus described "To hold the keys of all the spiritual blessings of the Church—to have the privilege of receiving the mysteries of the kingdom of heaven, to have the heavens opened to them—to commune with the general assembly of the first-born, and to enjoy the communion and presence of God the Father, and Jesus the Mediator of the new covenant" [*D and C* iii. 9, p 76] The Aaronic priesthood ought to consist of literal descendants of Aaron, pointed out

[1] For the practical working of polygamy see *A Lady's Life among the Mormons*, London, 1873.

by revelation; but, in default of such, others may be appointed [*ibid* iii 8, p 75] The power and authority of this priesthood is "to hold the keys of the ministering of angels, and to administer in outward ordinances the letter of the Gospel—the baptism of repentance for the remission of sins" [*ibid* iii 10, p 76] The highest office in the Church is *The First Presidency*, consisting of three members, the successors of Peter, James and John among the Apostles Of these the first president is supreme, being ex officio seer, revelator, and prophet, he is "the presiding high-priest over the high-priesthood of God, and, under God, holds the keys of heaven and hell." From his decision there is no appeal; for the other two presidents are only his councillors The first presidency is said to be appointed by revelation, but at the General Conferences, held twice a year, a vote is passed to sustain the existing holders *The Patriarch*, also called "Father of the Church," is appointed by the Church for life His sole duty is to administer blessings The *Twelve Apostles*, or Second Presidency, are "the special witnesses of the Name of Christ in all the world" [*D and C* iii 11, p 76], being mainly for missionary purposes Their duty is to build up the Church, and to ordain and set in order all inferior ministers, they take the lead in all meetings, except in presence of a president, and may administer all ordinances An apostle presides over the most important foreign missions and churches The *Seventies* are a number of committees, so called because each consists of seventy persons The first seventy, like the apostles, are chosen by the Church in conference at Utah, of these seven are appointed presidents, with a chief, "the president of all the seventies" The presidents appoint seventy others, and these again seventy more, "until seven times seventy, if the work in the vineyard so require" Thus the number of "the seventies" amounts to many hundred, though the number of seventy is rarely complete Their duty is to assist the apostles, under their direction, in building up the Church, and they are in fact travelling ministers *The High-Priests*, after the order of the Melchisedek priesthood, form the highest class of ordinary ministers, they exercise spiritual authority under the general direction of the first presidency, and the control of a president of their own order, they may officiate in all offices of the Church The *Bishops*, the highest order of the Aaronic priesthood, have chiefly temporal duties, though in spiritual matters they have authority over the lower ministers Their work consists mainly in the management of the Church funds, obtained by tithes and offerings, in relieving the wants of the ministers, aiding needy Saints, &c A bishop is the local authority in each of the wards of Utah and the settlements in the neighbourhood The *Elders*, the lowest rank of the Melchisedek priesthood and the most numerous class of ministers, conduct the ordinary meetings, except in presence of one of higher rank, and execute the ordinary ministerial duties—the administration of the ordinances, preaching, teaching, visiting from house to house, and privately exhorting the Saints The *Priests* have the same duties as the elders, and may also ordain other priests, teachers, and deacons in subordination to the elders The *Teachers* usually assist the other ministers, they exercise a general supervision over the members, may expound, exhort and teach at meetings, but may not administer any ordinances The *Deacons* assist the bishops in their temporal duties, as collectors, treasurers, etc; they may officiate in the absence of other ministers, but only as preachers and expounders

Besides these office-bearers, there is also *The Standing High Council*, to settle difficulties among believers This consists of eighteen (at first twelve) high-priests, appointed by ballot, with one or three presidents, being the first president alone, or with his assessors After the evidence has been heard, and the accusers, accused, and a certain number of councillors, from two to six, according to the gravity of the case, have spoken, the president gives his decision, and calls on the other members to sanction it Sometimes a case is reheard, in special difficulties recourse is had to revelation Every "stake" and separate church is governed by its own "High Council," with a similar constitution and procedure, and with an appeal to the Supreme High Council

General affairs are managed by conferences, held April 6th and December 6th in each year At these, which sometimes last several days, the first presidency and other office-bearers are sustained in office by the vote, always unanimous, of the meeting, vacancies are filled, reports on various subjects are read, prayers are offered, addresses delivered, hymns and anthems sung, etc [*Mill Star, passim*, Burton, 367, *sq*, *Qu Rev* cxxii 488]

Missions are a great feature of Mormonism Any member of the priesthood is liable to be sent, at the will of the president, on a sudden impulse, at short notice, to "preach the Gospel to the Gentiles" The missionaries are sent forth moneyless, or with only sufficient funds to take them to their destination, and have to work for their living till they can be supported by the offerings of converts The Book of Mormon has been translated into Welsh, French, German, Italian, Danish, Norwegian, and other languages, churches have been founded in Great Britain, Denmark, Norway, several parts of Australia Gibraltar, Malta, Switzerland, France, and Germany Missions to Sweden, Austria, Chili, China, Hindostan, have been unsuccessful The converts are numerous, most being from the North of England, Wales, Norway, Denmark, and the seaboard States of the Union, almost all have belonged to some Protestant sect, and all are from the indigent and hopelessly ignorant classes Every inducement is held out to them to go to Utah, and an excellent system of emigration has been established [Conybeare, 56, *Ed Rev* No 233, pp 188, 189] For this, and other purposes, every Mormon is bound to pay tithe from his income to the Church, and is exhorted to give liberally besides The tithes are supposed to be devoted to the building of the temple [Hymn 218], but are absolutely at the disposal of the president

The Mormon system is an almost unlimited temporal and spiritual despotism "The people," it is said, "will be as much condemned if they do not obey Brother Brigham as they would if they should disobey the Lord God were He here in person" [*Compend* 42] "When the Lord comes, He will take vengeance on those who obey not His priesthood The word of Brother Brigham is the word of the Lord" [*ibid* 43] The whole duty of a Mormon consists in thinking and doing as he is told, even as regards his most private and personal affairs The president may order, or forbid, a man to marry, a bishop may at any time enter any Mormon's house and issue what orders he pleases All are compelled to deal only at the authorized shops and stores, which are managed on the co-operative principle for the benefit of the Church, *i.e* the enrichment of the leaders By means of a constant system of espionage, any breach of rules is promptly noticed, and if it be persisted in, the offender is cut off from the Church, and every means are used to crush him Persons are even excommunicated without any reason assigned, and, on complaining, are told that their crime will in due time come to light, it being held that if any man fails in obedience to the priesthood in any respect he must have committed some great sin, whereby he has lost the Spirit of God [Ollivant, 86, 87] All the arrangements at Utah are admirably suited to maintain obedience Every means are adopted to prevent any but the chief men from accumulating money, so that while a man can live from hand to month in some comfort, he cannot save anything, hence in no place are there more people, who can just hang on, short of absolute poverty [Ollivant, 47, 101] The majority, therefore, are virtually prisoners in Utah If any man secedes, or is cast out, all Mormons are forbidden to have any intercourse with him, even to give him food or shelter, sometimes violence, even to death, has been used, and in such a way that it cannot be easily proved, moreover, accused Mormons are usually acquitted by packed juries All "Gentiles" are suspected, and every means are used to keep or drive them away [See Rae, 118-120, *Fraser's Mag* for June 1871, p 692]

The *prospects* of Mormonism in its present form do not seem favourable The Republican party in the States have made it part of their platform "to put down the Saints," and though the first attempt has failed, it will doubtless be repeated with greater caution and success In that case, the Mormons would have to choose between abandoning polygamy or Utah If the former were done, they might still linger on among the chaos of sects in America If the latter, they might for a few years retain their attractions for the sensual and the fanatic The influence of the two schisms is considerable in causing disaffection, and the younger people are said, partly from education, partly through intercourse with Gentiles, not to be, as a body, very zealous for the faith An Episcopal Mission, established in 1866, has had some success, chiefly through the excellence of its schools

The *causes of the success* of Mormonism may be briefly summed up [1] Its appeal to that unreasoning reverence for the *letter* of the English Bible fostered by popular Protestantism in the uneducated [2] The claim to be "the Lord's own people," appealing to the feeling of spiritual pride, and the idea that God is ever interfering, by miracles and extraordinary gifts, in their behalf [3] Its earthly character, as a religion—not above, but on a level with low and carnal desires, offering the full present enjoyment of this life, and a life to come, which is only a continuation of that enjoyment [4] The pictures held out by preachers of the wealth and comfort to be obtained at Utah, and the allurements of polygamy

Two schisms have taken place from Mormonism The first, whose headquarters are in Illinois, with the title of "The Reorganized Church of Jesus Christ of Latter-Day Saints," was led, in 1852, by the widow and sons of the founder, on the publication of the revelation authorizing polygamy, the genuineness of which they denied Their chief feature is the rejection of that practice and the doctrines connected therewith The second secession arose in 1869, in Utah itself, with the title of the "Church of Zion," it advocates freedom of thought and action, as opposed to the despotism of the president and the priesthood Many old and prominent Mormons have joined this body [Rae, 157, *sq*, Ollivant, 82-90] Both these schisms cause much trouble to the Mormon leaders

[*A Compendium of the Faith and Doctrines of the Church of Jesus Christ of Latter-Day Saints* Liverpool and London, 1857. *Letters exhibiting the most prominent Doctrines of the Church, etc*, by Elder Orson, Spencer, 5th ed 1866. *Sacred Hymns and Spiritual Songs for the Church etc*, 12th ed 1863 Tracts, chiefly by Orson Pratt *The Millennial Star*, a periodical published at Liverpool W J Conybeare, *Mormonism*, repr from *Edin Rev* No 202 Olshausen, *Geschichte der Mormonen* Bennett, *Mormonism Exposed*, Boston, U S 1842 Mackay, *The Mormons*, 4th ed Chandless, *A Visit to Salt Lake* Burton, *City of the Saints* Rémy, *A Journey to Great Salt Lake City* Dixon, *New America* Rae, *Westward by Rail* Ollivant, *A Breeze from the Great Salt Lake* Articles Herzog, *Encyklopadie*, art *Mormonen* *Revue des deux Mondes*, Sept 1853, Feb 1856, Sept 1859, April 1861 *Edin Rev* No 233, p 185, *sq* *Quart Rev* vol cxxii p 450 *Fraser's Mag* vols iii and iv, new series, June and July 1871]

MUGGLETONIANS A sect originated during the Great Rebellion by Ludovick Muggleton [A D 1609-1697], a journeyman tailor of London, and an associate named Reeves

Muggleton set forth that he and his accomplice were the two witnesses spoken of in Rev xi 3-6, and that it was their mission to prophesy during the last days, which had then arrived They professed to have special revelations from heaven, and that they had received power to destroy any who opposed them The fanatics also taught strange notions, that look as if they were confused memories of some Gnostic heresies,—as that earth and water were not created, but self-originated, that the Evil One became incarnate in Eve, that the Father was the Sufferer upon the Cross, having left Elijah to govern heaven, while He came to earth to die, that Reeves represented Moses, and Muggleton represented Aaron

Reeves died many years before Muggleton and after his death the latter claimed to have a double portion of the Spirit bestowed upon him He himself died in the year 1697, and was buried in Spinningwheel Alley, Moorfields, where the following inscription was placed upon his tomb —

"Whilst mausoleums and large inscriptions give
Might, splendour, and past death make potents live,
It is enough briefly to write thy name
Succeeding times by that will read thy fame,
Thy deeds, thy acts, around the world resound,
No foreign soil where Muggleton 's not found"

The sect of the Muggletonians just survived until within the last few years [Chamberlain's *Pres State of Eng* 1702, p 258 *The Snake in the Grass* *Transact Liverpool Lit and Phil Soc* 1868-70]

MUNSTER, PRESBYTERY OF A secession from the main body of the Presbyterians of Ireland, consisting of ten congregations in Dublin and the South of Ireland

MUNZER [ANABAPTISTS]

MUSTITANI A small and obscure sect of Donatists, condemned by the three hundred and ten bishops of that schism, who met at Bagai or Vaga in Numidia, A D 398 [S Aug *contra epist Parmeniam*, lib iii cap 29]

MYSTICS, so called from *μύστικον*, that which pertains to mysteries from which the uninitiated are excluded The term applies at the present day to that union with the Deity which the rapt soul is believed to attain by ecstatic contemplation Mysticism, in this sense, lies at the root of every form of religious enthusiasm, and by easy degrees may pass on into fanaticism "Mysticismus haud raro obit in fanaticum furorem" [Wegscheider] Where mysticism is the dominant power of the will it is fanaticism, as mixed up with the imagination it is enthusiasm, and where it has attempted to engraft the religious idea on anciently received forms of philosophy, it has been definitely known as theosophy In every case it claims to set itself above the moral guidance of principle, the feelings of the heart and the purblind impulse of the imagination being its only law

But a distinction may be drawn between the mystical principle, holding the verity of the soul's union with God, and mysticism in its exaggerated and morbid condition [Nitzsch, *Syst d. Chr Lehre*, Sack, *Polemik*], and certainly, so far as the inner life of the soul, in direct communion with God, is to be distinguished from the action of the same soul in its relation with the world, a distinct phase of spiritual power is to be recognised, whether it be termed the mystical principle of the soul, or the divine union of the soul with God, or the Life of God in the soul of man Mysticism is the intensified application of this principle, carried out to lengths that are inconsistent with the everyday duties of life Mysticism has so far no necessary connection with practical piety It aims at the absorption of the life of man in the Divine, while a rational piety seeks its blessing in representing the Divine Life faithfully in every relation with the world, that is, in every phase and minute ramification of daily duty The tendency of mysticism is towards a pantheistical summing of all in the Deity, whereby the sense of distinct personal existence, whether in the human or divine substance, becomes confused Yet the mystical principle is to a certain extent inseparable from a deep appreciation of the religious idea The soul's yearning for the invisible finds the object of its aspiration in a sacramental union with the object of its desire Jacob's realisation of the Divine presence at Bethel was as the mystic ladder of communication, on which the angels of God passed to and fro between earth and heaven By a deeper generalization Solomon saw in the wisdom of God the bond of union that connects the Spirit of the universe with the Spirit of God The religious idea had at that early date its obverse side of mystic impress In the cognate theology of St John, the Word is the middle term between earth and heaven, and being God from the beginning, He is still the Light that lighteth every man that cometh into the world Hence the mystic principle is inseparable from true religion, so far as it sets the Invisible before the eye of faith, and enables the soul to anticipate the future for which it was created Hence also the less true forms of religion have one and all embodied the mystic principle, as involving the very essence of religion Therapeutic contemplation was the obverse of Mosaic ordinance, the Cabbala refined upon the Talmud, and Persian Sufism is as the spirit of which the Koran is the letter.

In the Church of the sixth century the pseudo-Dionysian mysticism was a reaction upon the dogmatic teaching forced upon the Church by heresy, much as the mysticism of the ALOMBRADOS or Illuminati of Spain, in the sixteenth century, was called forth by the rigid orthodoxy of the Inquisition, and Jansenist and Quietist tenets by Jesuitism Mysticism has still been the most usual form in which the expiring flame of religion has flickered up from its embers Theosophical mysticism may be referred back to the allegorizing exegesis of the Alexandrian school of theology, the remote source of which may be found in the writings of Philo The historical treatises of this writer were evidently composed for Hellenistic readers, and set forth such facts of Jewish history as were known to every child under synagogal discipline His allegorizing treatises[1] were addressed to that particular phase of the Jewish mind that is dimly indicated in the Proverbs of Solomon, more clearly in the writings of the Son of Sirach, and which became a rule of life in the Therapeutæ of Alexandria At Alexandria the literary Jew added the study of Plato to the teaching of the Law, and learned to qualify the anthropomorphism of the latter by the transcendental notions of the Deity conveyed by the purest form of Greek philosophy By a natural progression the anthropopathic descriptions of the Sacred Books were spiritually interpreted as divine allegory, and in time the whole letter of the Law was regarded only as a veil that screened deep mystical truths from the vulgar gaze, σχεδὸν τὰ πάντα ἀλληγορεῖται are the words of Philo This is the true origin of the allegorizing school of exegesis that was developed in the catechetical school of Alexandria by Clement and Origen, and continued elsewhere by Theophilus of Antioch, Hilary, Cyril of Alexandria, Ephrem Syrus, and the elder Macarius The authority principally followed by mystics of succeeding ages was that of Dionysius the Areopagite, said to have been the first Bishop [St Denys] of Paris,[2] in the "Mystical Theology," the "Divine Names," the "Heavenly Hierarchy," and the "Ecclesiastical Hierarchy" The object of this writer was to give a Platonic development and colouring to the deep mysteries of the Christian faith, and to lead the soul on by contemplative energy to adunation with the Deity The highest attainment in Christian philosophy was to behold in spirit, and to become one with, God, Who is neither darkness nor light, neither negative nor positive Three steps lead to this blissful consummation purification, illumination, and vision (ἐποπτεία), terms adopted from the various grades of Eleusinian initiation [Plut *Demetr* 26] A more direct application of the terminology of heathen mysticism was made by this writer when he gave its title to the work "De Mystica Theologia"

The works of Dionysius exercised a considerable influence on the Latin Church of the Middle Ages. John Scotus Erigena translated them into Latin by the command of Charles the Bald, and left them as a model, of which the St Victoire schoolmen afterwards made much use These writings are referred by Dr Westcott [*Contemp Rev* May 1867] to some writer of the Edessene school at the latter end of the fifth or commencement of the sixth century The immediate source of Dionysian mysticism was the Symposium of Plato, in which the function of Eros is described as the medium of intimate communication between God and men, filling every void place throughout the universe, and binding together all its parts, celestial and mundane, in one compact body of love [*Symposium*, 202 E] Dante, himself an exponent of the Symposium, perhaps drew from thence the inspiring thought of his Beatrice The further development of the Platonic idea by the Neo-Platonists, Plotinus, Porphyry and Proclus, is closely copied in the abstraction from mundane grosser thought, and in the unity of divine contemplation to which Dionysius aspired He ploughed, as Fabricius says, with the Neo-Platonic heifer [Fabr *in vit Procli*, Proleg xii., Lupton, *Introd to Dean Colet's two Treatises on Dionys* xln] The great end at which he aimed was to shew how, by means of an intermediate and mediatorial hierarchy, man may hold communion with these celestial powers, order above order, until he reposes on the immediate contemplation of God Himself But he seems to wander beyond the pale of the Church The celestial hierarchy in this scheme replaces the mediatorial functions of the Redeemer of Mankind He himself defines this hierarchy [*Cœl Hier* iii 1] as a divine order, science and energy, standing in closest connection with the attributes of Deity, it is in fact an exact reflex of those attributes The works of Dionysius were explained as genuine in a commentary by Maximus the monk, of Constantinople He composed also an allegorizing work on the Liturgy, with the title of Mystagogia, in close connection with Dionysian views This work still has a value as exhibiting the Liturgy of the Greek Church of the seventh century Maximus forms a middle term between the so-called Areopagite and Erigena We find in his Scholia on Gregory of Nazianzum the same transcendental notions of the Deity, and of the Divine Immanence in the world of matter, which only *is* by virtue of that Immanence[3] As supra-substantial (ὑπερούσιος) God has nothing in common with any[4] known thing, but so far as the one is manifested in Being it is multiform, and conversely, the multiform by involution is substantially one[5] It anticipates the Spinozist "Alles ist Eins, und Eins ist Alles" Man having had an eternal existence in the Ideality of the Divine Being, partakes of that Being[6] From the Divine Substance he comes forth and

[1] *E g.* the Books on the Allegories of the Law, the Treatises on the Cherubim, on the Sacrifice of Cain and Abel, the Good plotted against by the Evil, on the Posterity of Cain, on the Giants, on the Immutability of God, and other Books, having for their theme subjects from the Mosaic records The tone of thought represented in these books was scarcely originated by Philo he made application of existing material

[2] Hunc alii moderni temporis asserunt, a Papa Clemente in partes Galliarum directum fuisse, et Parisiis martyrii gloria coronatum fuisse [J Scot Erig *Præf in Dion Areop*]

[3] *Εἰς ἑαυτὸν τὰ πάντα ανακεφαλαιούμενον, καθ' ὃν τό τε εἶναι καὶ τὸ διαμένειν καὶ ἐξ οὗ τὰ γεγονότα ὡς γέγονε μετέχει Θεοῦ πάντα γὰρ μετέχει διὰ τὸ ἐκ Θεοῦ γεγενῆσθαι αναλόγως Θεοῦ, ἢ κατὰ νοῦν, ἢ κατὰ λόγον, ἢ αἴσθησιν, ἢ κίνησιν ζωτικήν, ἢ οὐσιώδη καὶ ἐκτικὴν ἐπιτηδειότητα* [*Schol in Greg Theol* Oxford ed p 14]

[4] The soul in the same way is, as Maximus says, beyond conception, we know its existence only by its effects, in the same way we see the occult Divine Intellect in the works of Creation

[5] *Schol in Greg Theol* 14-17 Compare Schol Dionys *de div Nom Schol* Corderius, ii 92

[6] *Αὐτῷ τῷ καθ' ὃν ἐκτίσθη λόγῳ τῷ ἐν τῷ Θεῷ ὄντι καὶ πρὸς Θεὸν ὄντι, μοῖρα καὶ λέγεται καὶ ἔστι Θεοῦ, διὰ τὸν αυτοῦ προόντα ἐν τῷ Θεῷ λόγον* [*Schol in Greg* 14.]

into that Substance he returns, a consummation apparently but little removed from the Nirwâna of the Indian theosophy Man, both in his origin and in his future destiny, is impersonal As uniting in one the material and intellectual, he is a microcosmic representation of the universe;[1] as the crowning effort of creation, he embodies in himself the future recapitulation of all things in God Substantive union with the Deity is only possible in Human Nature, and it was made possible to all by the union of the Manhood and Godhead in Christ Thereby man's spirit soars up to God through the energy of the will, and the Incarnation of the Word is perpetuated in the individual By means of his own free will, man may be raised more and more above the trammels of the body, and be formed in God As God is man by Incarnation, so man through grace is divinely formed, and is one with God God through love became Man, man through love, and by virtue of the Incarnation, becomes God It is not once for all, but by an indefectible continuance in all and through all the whole mass of humanity, that the mystery of the Incarnation is perfected[2] The writings of Maximus, with Erigena's translation of Dionysius, helped to raise scholastic thought from its dry dialectics, and to create a taste for spiritual contemplation Thus St Bernard, in his deep appreciation of things unseen, stands forth in strong contrast with the materialism of Abelard and Gilbert de la Porrée Two canons of St Victoire, selected apparently for their kindred tone of mystic thought—Hugo de St Victoire being of Saxon, Richard of Irish extraction—threw a fervour into the theology of the schools, the cold reasoning of which was seen by them to kill down religious warmth. The conception of Hugo in every other subject was "moulded by his theology, and that theology is throughout sacramental" [Maurice, *Mediæv Phil* iv 44] Mysticism, as applied to this school, means a deep appreciation of the things of faith, a realization by the spirit of the unseen world, and is very far from implying the unintelligible musings of the enthusiast, or any other "cold formal generalization of a later period" [Maurice, *Mediæv. Phil* iv 41] Hugo stands at the head of this school as its founder Walter's mysticism stood in direct antagonism with the scholastic system, his work, *Contra quatuor Labyrinthos Galliæ*, being a running invective against the principles developed by the four principal Gallican schoolmen, Peter Abelard, Gilbert de la Porrée, Peter Lombard, and Peter of Poictiers Joachim à Floris opposed an apocalyptic mysticism to the dialectical theology of the schools In Bonaventura and Gerson the mystic and dialectic elements flowed on once more in harmonious action In the fourteenth century the mystic tone given by the HESYCHAST monks of Mount Athos to the Greek Church was approved by three councils held on the subject at Constantinople [A.D 1341, 1347, 1350] They drew their inspiration from the writings of Maximus, the annotator of the *Celestial Hierarchy* In the controversy that arose in the Greek Church, Nicolas Cabasilas [Archbishop of Thessalonica, A D 1354] stood forth as the Hesychast champion, and his *Seven Discourses of Life in Christ* is one of the most effective works that mystical theology has produced The mysticism of St Hildegard in the twelfth century, of the Swedish saint Birgitta, and of Catherine of Sienna in the fourteenth, all form part of the same wave of thought PAULICIANISM, the remote germ of the Waldensian and Albigensian sects, was rooted in a dualistic mysticism, and the Quietists of the seventeenth century were still true to the Alombrado stock from whence they sprang

Asceticism not unfrequently issued from the mystical religious life, its highest instance being that of St Francis of Assisi, the founder of the Franciscan Order The FRATRICELLI of the thirteenth century were an offshoot from this stock The Beguine establishments, originally asylums for the widows and daughters of Crusaders, became convents of mystical devotees, with more or less of heretical taint. [BEGHARDS] Germany has been peculiarly the seat of mysticism before and since the Reformation period On the Rhine, in the thirteenth century, the Brotherhood of the "Free Spirit" gave a wide impulse to the pantheism of Amalric of Bena and David of Dinant In the fourteenth century the pantheistic theory of J Scotus Erigena was revived by Eckhart, provincial of the Dominican Order in Saxony, the "Doctor Ecstaticus," a man of unblamed purity of life and great earnestness of character The boldest metaphysical speculations were united in his system with a severe asceticism It was a period that particularly favoured the development of mystical or spiritual theology The distraction of party warfare in State matters, the hostile attitude of the Emperor towards the Court of Rome, and the increasing divergence of religious opinion, gave an opportunity that was not thrown away by the mystic theologian Without adopting any party in particular, the mystic devotee could combine his higher spiritual aspirations with the most opposite political and religious theories, and gain a willing ear from all The whole heart of the people was open to him Hence the success of Tauler as a preacher in the fourteenth century He was termed "Doctor Illuminatus," as being the most enlightened preacher of his age A living faith in the pure word of God, he said, was better than mass attendance or bodily mortification, the sincerely pious man alone was free, the friend of God, over whom the Pope had no spiritual power, for God had enfranchised and sanctified him to his free service, the spiritual and political powers were essentially distinct, neither, if the former was ever on ill terms with the civil governor, had it authority to lay his subjects under a ban. In Tauler, the mystic principle was exhibited on its most practical side, and in

[1] *Λόγον ἀνθρώπων λόγον πάντων τῶν ἐκ Θεοῦ τὸ εἶδος λαβόντων* [*ib*] So also Erigena, *de Divis Nat* ii 3, 4, iii 39.

[2] *Schol in Greg* 18.

many of his views he was the harbinger of that school of thought that brought about the Reformation of the sixteenth century, and which was represented by Wycliffe in England, Huss in Bohemia, Savonarola in the Ferrarese, and John Wessel of Groningen more ubiquitously throughout the Continent [FRIENDS OF GOD]

With Tauler must be associated the name of Henry Suso, his friend and ardent admirer, a pupil of Eckart [A D 1300—1365] Mysticism with him was a matter of feeling rather than of speculation Wisdom as personified by Solomon was his theme, identified at one time with Christ, at another with His Virgin Mother To make himself worthy of the object of his adoration he practised severe austerities, and claimed to be frequently favoured with divine visions His was no connected system, but a tissue of rhapsodical applications of the mystical theology of the preceding period, which he invested in fantastic and visionary forms He adopted the view which led the schools so closely to the verge of Pantheism, that all created nature is a mirror in which the Deity is reflected Creation was eternally in God as the universal exemplar No name can sufficiently declare the Deity As Basilides termed the Divine Principle οὐκ ὤν, and as Hegel in modern times has said the same thing, so Suso declared that the Deity might with equal propriety be termed an Eternal Nothing, as a self-existent entity He is as a circle whose centre is everywhere, whose circumference is nowhere Imitation of Christ's sufferings is the true mean of man's regeneration Three principal steps lead on to union with the Deity, purification or expulsion of all mortal desire illumination, which fills the soul with divine forms, and perfection, to which is accorded the fullest enjoyment of heavenly good If Eckart was the philosophic mystic, and Tauler the more practical devotee, Suso was more poetical in his enthusiastic adoration of Eternal Wisdom

In all ages a yearning for more spiritual forms of religion has driven more ardent spirits into mysticism Thomas à Kempis [Thomas Hamerken of Kempen, near Cologne, A D 1380—1471], in his *Hortulus Rosarum*, *Vallis Liliorum*, *de Tribus Tabernaculis*, and above all in his *De Imitatione Christi*, gives sufficient indication of the mystic spirit Molinos of Saragossa, a resident at Rome from A D 1669, published his *Guida Spirituale* A D 1675, of a similarly mystical cast The Père La Chaise, confessor of Louis XIV, brought it under the notice of the Pope as a production of a kindred spirit to the Beghards of the Netherlands or the Spanish Alombrados, who laid the whole work of religion in silent prayer, to the neglect of external ritual Sixty-eight heretical propositions were found in it, and the book was condemned by Innocent XI [A D 1677] Molinos, notwithstanding his confession of error, was confined in a Dominican cell, under a tedious course of lifelong penance His followers were termed "Quietists," and as the Pietism of Germany was copied from them, they may be considered to be a link of connection between Catholicism and Protestantism Pope Innocent, before the denunciation of Père La Chaise, had received much edification from the work of Molinos which he afterwards condemned Fénélon also, Archbishop of Cambray [A D 1694], was more consistent in his appreciation of the mystic principle, as shewn in his Reflections and Meditations on the inner life of the Christian His rival, Bossuet, Bishop of Meaux, complained of his metropolitan to the King, and the matter was referred to the Court of Rome, where twenty-three propositions of doubtful character were declared to be erroneous Fénélon submitted with humility to the papal decree, himself published the judicial bull, and proscribed his own writing But there was nothing about him of the Protestant Pietist, one must be either Deist or Catholic was rather his theory

There was also an unsuspected strain of mysticism about Pascal, the scourge of Jesuitism, for after his death an iron belt rough with nails[1] was found to encircle his body, and a folded parchment sewn within his dress, Pascal's "amulet," on which was a figured cross and the following writing —"In the year of grace 1654, Monday, Nov 23rd, Feast of St. Clement, pope and martyr, and others of the martyrology, vigil of St Chrysogone, martyr, and others, from about half-past ten in the evening till about half-past twelve at night, Fire

"God of Abraham, God of Isaac, God of Jacob [Exod iii 6, Matt xxii 32], not of wise men and philosophers Certainty, certainty, feeling, joy, peace

"The God of Jesus Christ 'My God and your God' [John xxii 17] Thy God shall be my God [Ruth i 16] Forgetfulness of the world and of all beside God He is found only in ways taught of the Gospel Dignity of the human soul Righteous Father, the world hath not known Thee, but I have known Thee [John xvii 25] Joy, joy, joy, tears of joy

"I have separated myself from Him 'Dereliquerunt me fontem aquæ vivæ' [Jer ii 13] O God, wilt thou forsake me? [Matt xxvii 46] May I not be separate eternally! 'This is true life, that they may know Thee, the only true God, and Jesus Christ Whom Thou hast sent' Jesus Christ! Jesus Christ! I have separated myself from Him, I have fled from Him, renounced, sacrificed May I never be separated from Him! Safety is alone in the ways taught by the Gospel. Self-renunciation, total and sweet Total submission to Jesus Christ and my guide Everlastingly in joy, for one day of trial upon earth 'Non obliviscar sermones tuos' [Ps cxix 16] Amen"

If this was mysticism,[2] it may find its parallel in the conversion of St Augustine [*Conf* viii 11, 12] Both had sought peace in philosophy, the Father in Plato, the Jansenist in Descartes it their respective masters could demonstrate the

[1] *Vie de Pascal*, vii.

[2] Compare also Faugère's newly-recovered fragment by Pascal, ed Havet, p. 397, being a meditation on the various circumstances of the Passion

existence of the Deity, they could not lead the soul to the Eternal, the revelation of the way the truth and the life was in either case attended with the same effects; tears, vision, light, joy, peace They were mystics according to Montesquieu's definition, "Les dévots qui ont le cœur tendre."

The "German Theology" had a great effect on the inner religious life of Germany at the time of the Reformation, and gave to it a mystic tone It is the title of a work that was first brought under public notice by Luther, and published by him, A D 1518, as *Eyn edels Buchlein, von rechtem Vorstand was Adam und Christus, sey und wie Adam yn uns sterben und Christus ersteen soll* Since that time it has been frequently translated and republished, and has been a great favourite in Lutheran Germany All that is known of the author is that he was Custos of the Deutsch Herren Haus at Frankfort, or rather across the Maine at Sachsenhausen, and a member of the society of "God's Friends," Catholics of mystical principles, who disappeared from the scene at the close of the fourteenth century The style of the book is quite similar to that of Tauler and Suso The book inculcates the necessity of completely merging the will of man in the will of God, and of practising the most complete self-denial and mortification of the natural inclinations It is self-will that stands as a wall of separation between man and God, it converted angels into devils, and is as the fire that never can be quenched. voluntary humiliation is its remedy Of the high conceit and lax morals of the "Brethren of the Free Spirit" it speaks with much severity, as the very spirit of Antichrist Enlightenment, in which mysticism has always professed to initiate its votaries, is not to be attained by talk or study, but by steady acts of self-devotion, and the practice of active virtue Love and no taint of self-seeking must be the spring of all his actions, and a man can only hope to attain perfection when he renounces as unworthy all wish for earthly reward The same mind must be in him which was in Christ Jesus, a self-devoting, self-sacrificing spirit The tone of the book shews no symptom of disrespect for the Church, but its free application of Bible principles in a neoterizing spirit scarcely failed to prepare the way for the Reformation In some respects it exhibits also the germ of the *Reine Vernunft* of Kant The book was always a great favourite with Luther, who ranked it in the third place after the Bible and the works of St Augustine

At the Reformation period, Paracelsus [Theophrastus Bombast of Hohenheim, born A D 1493, d 1541] was the first who shewed a decided leaning to mysticism, though medicine, not theology, was his peculiar faculty He was by no means a partisan of Luther, although he was himself a zealous reformer. His theological mysticism was mixed up with medicine, astronomy, astrology, alchemy, and natural history. from a similar medley Jacob Behme, at a later date, extracted religious comfort But the first of the Reformed party who gave to mysticism a definite shape was Valentine Weigel, minister of Ischopping, near Meissen in Saxony, who died A D 1588. Mysticism has often made a close approach to Pantheism, and so in his system he said that God had pity on Himself in pitying man For since the believer is by his act of faith raised above himself and abandons the soul to God, so God is conscious of His own being in man So Spinoza declared that God is only self-conscious in the self-consciousness of man Man is a microcosmal power, and in him the world is exhibited in miniature reflexion During his life Weigel had the worldly wisdom to keep his thoughts to himself, and subscribed the "Formula Concordiæ" as a good Lutheran, to avoid inconvenience, as was found stated in a posthumous writing, and not from inner conviction In his Postils he complains earnestly of the sluggish spirit of the existing schools of theology, their bulky bodies of doctrine, their confessions, their commonplaces and table-talk, as well as their famed Formula of Concord All such beggarly elements of instruction he would sweep away, and go to the word of God alone for light Imputed righteousness was a doctrine he said that could only have been devised by Antichrist Thus he also, though a professed reformer, was in many points at direct antagonism with Luther and Melanchthon

But the most unintelligible of mystics was Jacob Bohme, a cobbler of Gorlitz, on the Saxon boundary of Silesia, who died A D. 1624 Light, he declared, had been revealed to him that rapt him into a state of ecstatic rest, and thoughts were inspired by the revelation that he seems never to have had the power of communicating to others After a silence of fifteen years he wrote the *Aurora* [A D 1612], which was followed by other similar coruscations. His reveries shew a strange mixture of the naturalism afterwards developed by Schelling and the wilder theosophy of the ancient Gnostics Thus he affirmed God and nature to be essentially one, and this dualized principle, without which neither nature as a whole nor any integral portion of it can exist, is the Deity As to be self-engendered is of the essence of the Deity, so nature and the external world is the substance of that self-generation In the fall of Lucifer, where a spirit of light should have been engendered, there issued forth a spirit of fire It is the principle of life of all creatures, the very heart of their existence All that is gross and hard, dark and cold, terrible and evil, has its origin in the fall of Lucifer, the Prince of this world But intimately as his spirit interpenetrates the mass of existence, he is not wholly one with it The spirit of life is there also, held captive as it were under the covenant of death, yet not extinguished The confines of the rival kingdoms touch each other in man, and keep up a perpetual contest between Love and Rage. In the material world the Creator is born as creature in the quickened life of the spirit, the stars are nothing else than powers of God, and all three Persons of the Trinity are ever-present in the universe. The Father is the occult foundation of all, the Son in the heart of the Father is the quickening spirit of life and love, of tenderness and beauty The Spirit is universally present From nature and its internal development Bohme professed to have gained his knowledge of philosophy and astrotheology He was indebted to no human lore, his only book was the book of nature, ever open before his soul Fr Schlegel has been able to trace in these ravings the afflatus of a poetical mind of high order, and he does not scruple to rank Bohme with the master minds who have taken their theme from the unseen world, Dante, Milton, and Klopstock Hallam can see in them nothing better than the incoherence of madness [*Lit M A* III iii 20]

J. Arndt's mysticism was of a very different stamp It meant in him thoroughly spiritual religion. He was a Lutheran preacher in Anhalt, and when that province adopted Calvinism, he resigned his post rather than give up baptismal exorcism, which since the time of Luther had been a badge of the party He died A.D 1621. His principal works are the four books of *True Christianity*, and his devotional collection, the *Paradise of Christian Virtues* They maintain their high character, and are still used in many households throughout Germany But they encountered a vehement opposition when they first appeared, and more especially from Osiander the younger, who managed to extract from them eight several heresies the main gravamen being, that Arndt threw a slight on school learning by his advocacy of practical piety and of such "popish" mystics as Thomas à Kempis and Tauler Moreover, by his doctrine of the illumination and indwelling of the Holy Spirit, he trenched upon the Lutheran theory of justification by faith alone, and the orthodox doctrine of grace

J Gerhard's *Meditationes Sacræ* [A D 1606], his *Schola Pietatis* and *Postils*, are works of a similar tone of thought to Arndt's, but they met with the same reception at first; as Gerhard said, "If any writer upholds pious practical Christianity, and aims at something higher than mere theological learning, he is straightway branded as a Rosicrucian or Weigelian"

J Val Andrea, grandson of Jacob Andrea who took a prominent part in setting up the Lutheran *Formula of Concord*, was of the same school In his younger years he accepted the Rosicrucian [1] mystery [A D 1602], but more in jest than earnest His later writings [A D 1617-1619], are written in a spirit of mystical piety His endeavour evidently was to expose and put down the religious and political follies of the age, and to uphold what he deemed to be spiritual Christianity But he wrote in the spirit of Lucian, and it is often difficult to see where irony ends and earnest principle begins. His more liberal acceptation of the ancestral *Formula Concordiæ* made him many enemies among the high orthodox Lutherans The Pietist Spener said of him, "If I could raise any from the dead for the good of the Church it should be Valentine Andrea" It was owing to Arndt's influence that the mocking, scoffing spirit that seemed natural to Andrea was replaced with something higher and worthier of a Christian man

Enough has now been said to shew that the Theology of the true Mystics exhibits two distinct phases, a side towards earth on which the legend of the medal is obscure and without meaning, and an obverse side bright with the light of heaven, union with the Eternal through sacramental grace is its impress of truth, and, flowing from that grace, a loving exercise of the great duties of Christian life It is closely allied with QUIETISM A very different kind, and yet an essential form of Mysticism, is that avowed by Schlegel, one closely similar to the rhapsodical notions of Plotinus, when he says that whereas human consciousness, in which subject and object are inseparably blended together in idea, cannot form to itself a notion of the Absolute, which is unity, still an adequate idea of the Absolute may be gained by the contemplation or intuitive faculty, independently of thought or consciousness, it is a rapid illumination, a sudden rapture, too fleeting for analysis, for it eludes reflection and baffles consciousness Reflection is in fact its death In this mystical condition of the mind all distinction between subject and object vanishes There is no longer the Deity on the one hand, the soul on the other The soul identifies itself with the Deity It is on this side that Mysticism passes into Pantheism

[Helfferich, *d. Christliche Mystik in ihrer Entwickelung u in ihren Denkmalen.* Tholuck, *Blumensammlung aus der morgenlandischen Mystik* R Law, *Elucidations of Bohmen and Freher* J. Behmen, *Mysterium Magnum* Conybeare, *Bampton Lect* 1824]

[1] The name was suggested by the family device of Andrea, a cross quartering four roses with the legend

"Des Christen Herz auf Rosen geht
Wenn's mitten unterm Kreuze Steht."

It became the favourite device of alchemy

N

NAASSIANS [OPHITES]

NATURALISTS This name, which has now become nearly obsolete in a theological or philosophical sense, has been used to designate two sections of the antichristian school which rejects belief in supernatural causes or operations [1] The name has been mostly used by German writers for those who identify God with nature, but who are now more generally known as Pantheists [2] By English writers it is generally taken as signifying those who consider natural religion to be sufficient for man's guidance and happiness without any supernatural revelation But these latter may be subdivided also into two classes, the *first* of which has received the name of "philosophical naturalists," rejecting altogether belief in revelation, the *second*, that of "theological naturalists," who accept revelation as containing truth, but as being at the best only a republication of natural religion, and so unnecessary

The name is rarely found in works written later than the seventeenth century, when it was used by Kant in Germany and by Boyle in England; and the school formerly known as Naturalists are now called PANTHEISTS and RATIONALISTS

NAZARÆANS A Jewish sect mentioned under this name only by Epiphanius [*Hær* xviii] The name is probably derived from Netsir, a branch (Epiphanius writes it also Nasaræans, and Nassaræans), and, if we are right in identifying this sect with the Genistæ, signifies branches of the true stock The sect aimed at a patriarchal religion in place of a Mosaic Judaism They canonized the patriarchs, and did not exclude Moses and Joshua from that society, they allowed that a law was given to Moses, but asserted that law to have been lost, and the Pentateuch to be corrupt or supposititious. They practised circumcision, kept the Sabbath and the Jewish festivals, rejected the sacrifice of animals, and ate no flesh It follows from this that they rejected the history of Genesis as well as the laws of Moses, but whether they professed to found their doctrine on tradition or on a new revelation is not told They were found in Galaaditis, Basanitis, and other parts beyond Jordan

NAZARENES Jewish Christians who continued to observe the law of Moses after the mother Church of Jerusalem had abandoned it. The sect was the Pella branch of the Jerusalem Church [JUDAIZERS], which did not join in the change made upon the appointment of Marcus, the first Jerusalem bishop of the uncircumcision The Nazarenes are not named by the earlier historians and Fathers of the Church, Irenæus, Hippolytus, Tertullian, Origen, Clement, and Eusebius being silent regarding them and the accounts and notices which we have of them are by Epiphanius, Augustine, Theodoret, Philaster, Jerome, and Isidore.

I Epiphanius states that the Nazarenes flourished principally in Berœa, in Cœle-Syria, in Decapolis at Pella, and in Basanitis, and that from hence, after the retreat from Jerusalem, the sect had its beginning Epiphanius adds that he could not ascertain the date of the sect as compared with the Simonians, Cerinthians and others, a statement which points to a sect not formed by one leader whose date could be ascertained, but to a party gradually separating from the Church Jerome speaks [*Catal Scriptt Eccl*, *Matthæus*] of the Nazarenes who dwell at Berœa, using St. Matthew's Hebrew Gospel, and this implies an early formation of the party Epiphanius, in his prefatory index, defines the Nazarenes as confessing Jesus to be Christ and the Son of God, but as living in all things according to the law And Augustine [*Hæres* ix] describes them as confessing Christ to be the Son of God, but observing the law, which Christians are taught to keep not carnally but spiritually

From all this it is clear that the Nazarenes were Jewish Christians, forming themselves into a party in Pella and its neighbourhood after the retreat from Jerusalem, and passing by degrees into a distinct sect But there were two classes of Jewish Christians, the one apostolic and orthodox, who did not impose the observance of the law as necessary to salvation, who acknowledged the mission of St Paul and recognised the communion of the Gentiles, the other Pharisaic and sectarian, who maintained the universal obligation of the law, and denounced St Paul as a transgressor In inquiring to which of these two classes the Nazarenes belonged, it must be noticed, in the first place, that the community at Pella was composed of those converts who joined the Church of Jerusalem in her exile, of those Hellenist fugitives whose national feeling and love of their city was not so strong as in the native Jews, and of those native Jews who had formed connections in their new residence which overpowered their national feeling It was a community predisposed to accept in the spirit as well as the letter the decree of the Council of Jerusalem In the next place, the Ebionites and the Nazarenes are contrasted But it was the Ebionites who held the universal obligation of the law [EBIONITES] When therefore we read in Jerome [*in Is* i t 3, p 4, ed 1616], "Audiant Ebionæi, qui post passionem abolitam legem putant esse servandam Audiant Ebionitarum socii, qui Judæis tantum, et de stirpe Israelitici generis hæc custodienda decernunt," it can hardly be doubted that the "Ebionitarum socii" are the Nazarenes

This sect is thus identified as, in its origin at least, a branch of the orthodox Church of Jerusalem The Church of Jerusalem had been under the Apostles of the Circumcision, and at the time of the retreat to Pella had "a literature consisting on the one hand of most of the New Testament, except the Gospel of St John, and on the other of much studied of old Halachah and Haggadah—law and poetic fancy," [DICT *of* THEOL *s v*] "with rites wherein Jewish and Christian practices are still found side by side, circumcision and baptism, hallowing of the Sabbath and of the Lord's day, Passover perhaps, and Eucharist, —these are the surroundings amid which we place" the sect of the Nazarenes in its origin [Sinker, *Testamenta XII Patriarcharum*, Camb 1869, p 124]

This quotation, the words of which were used with reference to the author of the *Testaments of the Twelve Patriarchs*, leads us to a remarkable book which proceeded from the school, and probably from the very sect under consideration This book, and the writings of the Ebionite school, have been much studied of late, and in the hands of German scholars have thrown considerable light on the history of the early Church In noticing it as an example of the theology of the Nazarenes, it must be remembered that we are entirely ignorant of its author, of the position he held in the Judæo-Christian Church, and of the degree of acceptance the book met with In short, we are not entitled to assume that it is a representative book But it is known from other authority that the author was of the Nazarene school, and we are thus entitled to gather from his book the broad and distinctive characters of the school Finer shades of doctrine, and doctrines that are not distinctive, must be referred to the standard formed by the teaching of the Apostles as supervening upon the tenets of the Jewish Church

Lardner's summary of the writer's doctrine may be first given "The writer speaks of the Nativity of Christ, the meekness and unblameableness of His life, His Crucifixion at the instigation of the Jewish priests, the wonderful concomitants of His Death, His Resurrection and Ascension He represents the character of the Messiah as God and Man, the Most High God with men, eating and drinking with them, the Saviour of the world, of the Gentiles and Israel, as eternal High-Priest and King He likewise speaks of the effusion of the Holy Spirit upon the Messiah, attended with a voice from heaven, His unrighteous treatment by the Jews, and their desolations and the destruction of the Temple upon that account, the call of the Gentiles, the illuminating them generally with new light, the effusion of the Spirit upon believers, but especially, and in a more abundant measure, upon the Gentiles Here little notice is taken of our Lord's miracles, however, he speaks of the Messiah as a 'Man who renews the law in the power of the Most High,' in which expressions the working of miracles seems to be implied Here are also passages which seem to contain allusions to the Gospels of St Matthew, St Luke, and St John, the Acts of the Apostles, the Epistle to the Ephesians, First to the Thessalonians First to Timothy, the Epistle to the Hebrews, the First Epistle of St John, and the Book of the Revelation And, as far as was consistent with his assumed character, the author declares the canonical authority of the Acts of the Apostles and the Epistles of St Paul" [Lardner's *Credibility*, etc ii 363]

Here the recognition of St John's Gospel and Epistles, and of St Paul's Epistles, shews that Nazarenes, at the later period of this book, were not without the teaching of full Catholic Christianity The question will arise again, with regard to a still later period, "What was Nazarene doctrine respecting the Divinity of our Lord?" At the period we have now before us, it is just to the Nazarenes, as Jewish Christians, to assimilate their confession, that Jesus is Christ and the Son of God, to St. Peter's confession,[1] without attributing to them any limited meanings of the term, such as were devised at a later time The passages may be seen quoted and commented in the third chapter of Sinker's work, in which Dorner's remark is quoted, "that the words," from Levi 18, "imply that the relation of Christ to the Father is as close as is that of a human son to his father"[2]

Our Lord's birth of a Virgin is referred to in Josh 19 His pre-existence in Dan 6, Sim 6 On these points we may believe the Nazarenes to have been orthodox The Ethics of the *Testaments* are sufficiently characterized in the remark, "that the view held as to the law of God is the same which we find in St James' Epistle, the old Mosaic law completed and developed by Christ, and that thus the author recognises the moral bearing of Christianity, not as a contrast, but as a continuation of the old religion" [Sinker's *Testam XII Patriarch* 121]

[1] Athanasius says that the Apostles of Christ, well knowing the Jewish prejudices on this head, with great wisdom first instructed them in our Saviour's humanity [Athanas *de Sent Dion* i 248 C, Paris, 1698] Chrysostom and Augustine speak also of the three Evangelists, and of the Apostles in their earlier teaching, insisting chiefly upon our Lord's humanity

[2] See Grabe's *Testimonia pro Deitate Christi adducta ex Testamentis XII Patr* in *Annot on Bull's Defensio Fid Nic*, Bull's *Works*, Burton's ed v 176

Nazarenes

The subject of priesthood, the priesthood of our Lord primarily, of the ministers of the Gospel secondarily, requires a more distinct notice. Judah (sect 21) is made to say, "God gave Levi the priesthood, to me the kingdom, and subjected the kingdom to the priesthood To me He gave things of earth, to him things of heaven As heaven surpasses earth, so God's priesthood surpasses an earthly kingdom" The *Testaments* represent our Lord as combining in Himself the offices of High-Priest and of King, and state consequently that He is to spring from the tribe of Levi as well as from the tribe of Judah [Sim 7, Dan 5] This identifies, or at least tends to identify our Lord's Priesthood with the priesthood of Aaron, contrary to the teaching of the Epistle to the Hebrews

This opinion of the descent of the Blessed Virgin Mary from both Judah and Levi might doubtless be held by men of piety and Catholicity, who might further repudiate the inference to which it seems naturally to lead, but, on the other hand, it is certain that the opinion, made to rest, as it must be, upon much legendary matter, would connect itself with heresy more readily than the historical Davidic genealogy [1] It would suit the purpose of those who denied that the Word was made Flesh to represent the genealogy as a myth setting forth a transmission of office This would be more complete if it set forth a transmission of the priesthood as well as of the royalty of our Lord The Gnostics were all of them Docetæ [Iren iii 11], and there is nothing unreasonable in the supposition that Docetic teachers in later times laid hold of this opinion, if it were current in the community of the Nazarenes, and endeavoured through it to instil their heresy In which case we should have a reason for the disquisition regarding the priesthood and the royalty, with which Epiphanius introduces his account of the Nazarenes, the relevancy of which is otherwise not very clear

The opinions of the author of the *Testaments* regarding the ministry of the Church are stated clearly in the Testament of Levi In sect 3 the universe in the times of the Gospel is described as of seven spheres [2] Three represent the outer world, the world of unbelievers, the third containing the encampments of the ministers of retribution on the ungodly The fourth, fifth, and sixth represent the Church, taking the word church in its widest sense, the fourth being the sphere of the saints, the fifth of the ministry, the sixth of the ministering angels of intercourse The fifth is occupied by angels of the Face of God [3] They minister and make atonement before the Lord for all the ignorances (ἀγνοίαις) of the just They offer to the Lord the reasonable service of a sweet-smelling savour, and an unbloody offering Again, in sect 8, after the robing of Levi, it is said that Levi's offspring shall be divided into three ranks of office Two appear to belong to the body of Levites, and to the Aaronic priesthood; the third clearly belongs to the Christian ministry For the third possesses a new name a King arises from Judah, and creates a new priesthood, which is κατὰ τὸν τύπον τῶν ἐθνῶν, εἰς πάντα τὰ ἔθνη The Ethnic type is the priesthood of Melchisedek A passage in Theophilus of Antioch makes this designation easier "Melchisedek was the first priest of all the priests of the Most High God From his time priests were found in all the earth" [*To Autol* ii cap. 31] This new priesthood shall set in order the table of the Lord, and of it shall be priests, judges, and scribes, priests, *i e* in ministering, judges in discipline, scribes in teaching The only objection which can be made to this description is that the Christian ministry is made to descend from Levi If the newness of their priesthood were lost sight of, the Christian ministry would be at once identified with the Aaronic priesthood From this affiliation of the ministers of the Gospel to Levi we are inclined to contend, supposing that the Testaments justly represent the belief of the Jewish Christians, that the lower or spurious sacerdotalism, which has found place in the Church, is of Judaic, not of Gentile, origin That the Hebrews found a difficulty in appreciating the true import of the history of Melchisedek is clear from the Epistle to the Hebrews A sense of this difficulty may have led the author of the Testaments to refrain from an explicit mention of Melchisedek Of another writer of this school, Aristo of Pella, we have very short fragments [Routh, *Rel* i pp 93-97] One fragment is important Aristo speaks of Jesus as the Son of God, the Creator of the world [See Westcott, *On the Canon*, pp 105-107 and Professor Lightfoot, *St Paul and the Three*, n 2, p 294]

II It may next be inquired whether the Nazarenes in later times fell into heresy Augustine accuses them only of Judaizing [Aug *de Hæres* ix, *contr Faust* xix 4, *contr Crescon.* I xxxi 36, *Epist. ad Hieron* lxxxii, ii 16, *de Bapt contr Donat* vii 1] Epiphanius having briefly defined them in the prefatory index as Judaizers, begins in the work itself [*Hæres* xxix] with stating that they hold the same opinions as the Cerinthians, but in his seventh chapter he professes his inability to say whether they did or did not hold Cerinthian doctrine regarding our Lord This quite sets aside his previous statement, which may be

[1] Compare the Manichees' rejection of the Davidic descent of our Lord for the Levitical, for which see Mill on *Panth Principles*, part ii p 206, n 58 In the fragment, preserved by Augustine [*cont Faust* xxiii 4], of the History of the Nativity of the Virgin Mary, written by Leucius, who is said by Jerome to have been a Manichee, Mary is called the daughter of Joachim, a priest

[2] Aristo of Pella names seven heavens, but his belief regarding them does not appear Routh, *Rel Sac* i p 96, and note p 106 Irenæus [I v sect. 2, trans in *Ante Nicene Library*] writes that the Valentinians affirm that the Demiurge created seven heavens, in which he exists, that these seven heavens are intelligent, that they speak of them as being angels, that Paradise, situated above the third heaven, is a fourth angel possessed of power, from whom Adam derived certain qualities while he conversed with him The Vision in the Testaments is entirely different from the Valentinian scheme.

[3] The presidents of Jewish synagogues were called angels, and in the Apocalypse we have Angels of the Churches

referred to his well-known proneness to make charges of heresy. In his Commentary on Isaiah Jerome calls the Nazarenes the Hebrews that believed in Christ [Hieron *in Isa* cap ix t 3, p 33, ed. 1616], giving the Nazarene explanation of the prophecy, that Christ's doctrine delivered the land of Zebulon and Naphtali from . . Jewish traditions, that by St Paul's preaching the Gospel shone among the Gentiles, and at length the whole world saw the clear light of the Gospel. [See also *ad August Ep.* 89, t ii p 266, ed 1616.] Accordingly Lardner[1] writes "It might easily be shewn that the Nazarean Christians did not reject St. John's Gospel, nor hold any principles that oblige them to reject or dislike it" [Lardner's *Jewish Testimonies*, cap i vol vi p 387, Kippis' ed 1861]. On the other hand, Theodoret [*de Hær fab* ii 2] accuses the Nazarenes of denying our Lord's divinity, but the later authority of Theodoret cannot outweigh the mass of earlier testimony in their favour.[2]

III Adopting then the conclusion that the Nazarenes retained their orthodox creed, it remains to be asked whether they retained their position in the Church, or whether, while free from heretical error, they were yet sectarian. There is no historical information to enable us to answer this question, but there does not appear to be any sufficient reason why the Church of Jerusalem, when it renounced Judaism, should exclude the Church of Pella from communion simply for its retention of national customs, and certainly there was no reason why the Church of Pella should renounce communion with Jerusalem. The general observance for some centuries of the decree of the Council of Jerusalem [JUDAIZERS], enforcing on Gentiles abstinence from things strangled and from blood, implied also (it may be fairly argued) a liberty to the Jews to continue in the observance of their national law, while canons intended to prevent Gentile Churches from adopting Jewish customs do not apply to the Nazarenes. On the other hand the strong condemnations of the Nazarenes as heretics, by Epiphanius and Augustine, can be fully explained only on the supposition that the Nazarenes had become the authors of a schism by renouncing communion with the Church. Augustine states in several places that the Nazarenes were called by some Symmachians.

NECESSITARIANS. This term is used [1] in a wide sense as the name of those who believe in Fatalism, or that everything happens according to fixed laws which cannot be changed by the will of God or the will of man, and [2] in a more restricted sense for those who believe that man's will is not free to control his actions, but that all the latter proceed necessarily and inevitably from the direction given to them by the will of his Creator.

These two classes of Necessitarians are, however, closely allied with each other, and if the opinion of the second class is carried to its logical terminus, it will be found not really to differ from the simple Fatalism of the first. Thus the Stoics, who professed to allow free will to man, although all beyond the will of man was Fate, and the Mahometans, who deny all free will to man, and yet speak habitually of the will of God, although they represent two phases of fatalism, do in reality represent the same general principle, the substitution of inevitable law in a higher or a lower portion of that sphere of intelligence, where the effects of will in one region are manifestly interwoven with its effects in the other, and the free will of man exhibited as the image of the free will of God.

The school of modern Necessitarians takes its origin from HOBBES, the founder of the English Deists, and one whose influence extended far beyond his country or his age. "Liberty and necessity," he writes, "are consistent. As in the water, that hath not only liberty but a necessity of descending in the channel, so likewise, in the actions which men voluntarily do, which, because they proceed from their will, proceed from liberty, and yet, because every act of man's will, and every desire and inclination, proceedeth from some cause, and that from another cause, in a continual chain (whose first link is in the hand of God, the first of all causes) proceed from necessity. So that to him that could see the connection of those causes, the necessity of all men's voluntary actions would appear manifest. And therefore God, that seeth and disposeth all things, seeth also that the liberty of man, in doing what he will, is accompanied with the necessity of doing that which God will, and no more nor less. For though men may do many things which God does not command, nor is therefore the author of them, yet they can have no passion, will, or appetite to anything of which appetite God's will is not the cause. And did not His will assume the necessity of man's will, and consequently of all that on man's will dependeth, the liberty of men would be a contradiction and impediment to the Omnipotence and liberty of God." [Hobbes' *Leviathan*, 108.]

Contemporary with Hobbes was SPINOZA, whose broad Materialism admitted no other view respecting nature and the mind than that of mechanical law. Against this extreme Materialism Leibnitz opposed himself with considerable vigour, but in the theory of Leibnitz the whole universe was as much a machine as in the theory of Spinoza, the only difference being that the one admitted an original moving Divine Power, while the other made this power a part of the machine itself. Hence in the spiritual machine which Leibnitz called mind, the freedom of the will of man was entirely rejected, and the freedom of the will of God was restricted to the imposition of the original

[1] It must be remembered that Lardner was a Socinian. He puts a Socinian interpretation on Acts ii 22, 36, x 38, xvii 31, Col ii 3 9, 1 Tim ii 5, and argues that this was the sentiment of the Nazarene Christians. *Letter on the Logos*, x pp 101, 102. But his authority is good to the point that the Nazarenes did not reject the Fourth Gospel.

[2] See a full defence of the orthodoxy of the Nazarenes in Bull's *Judicium Eccl Cath* ii 10 16.

law out of which human actions developed themselves from the original spiritual monad [LEIBNITZ] According to him, therefore, no event that ever happened in general history or in individual action could ever have taken place otherwise than it did This theory of Necessity pervades the scattered writings of Leibnitz, but it was specially developed in his *Essais de Théodicée sur la bonté de Dieu, la liberté de l'homme, et l'origine de mal*, which were published in the year 1710. Leibnitz was met by an able antagonist in Dr John Clarke, Dean of Salisbury, with whom he was in correspondence at the time of his death

A little later Dr Clarke met with another opponent in Anthony Collins, the founder of the FREETHINKERS, who printed a *Philosophical Inquiry into Human Liberty*, in which he maintained the doctrine of Necessity in its extreme form as regards the will of man, and although he was himself as nearly an Atheist as any one probably can be, asserted with the greatest effrontery that the doctrine of the freedom of the will led to Atheism Collins argues for Necessity on five grounds [1] Our experience gives us a consciousness that our actions are not controllable by our will, but by an inevitable force external to ourselves [2] Liberty is impossible, for all man's actions have a beginning, and "whatever has a beginning must have a cause, and every cause is a necessary cause If anything can have a beginning which has no cause, then nothing can produce something And if nothing can produce something, then the world might have had a beginning without a cause, which is an absurdity not only charged on Atheists, but is a real absurdity in itself . Liberty, therefore, or a power to act or not to act, to do this or another thing under the same causes, is an impossibility and atheistical" [3] The Divine Prescience takes in from the beginning the particular actions of all men, and therefore they are foreordained in stating which argument the writer forgets that God's own actions also are foreseen, and that if His Prescience of men's actions takes away their freedom, so also is His own freedom of will and act destroyed by the same prescience [4] The nature and use of rewards and punishments [5] The nature of morality His arguments were all answered effectively in the Boyle Lectures of Dr. Clarke for 1720 and 1721, on the Origin of Evil

The writings of Collins, superficial as they are, much affected the generation in which he lived He was the intimate friend of Locke, and the latter seems to have paid much deference to his opinions Locke was also trained in the school of Hobbes, and although in words he maintained the free agency of man, yet deference for the opinions of his predecessor and his contemporary led him to make such concessions to their theories that Priestley not unjustly ranks him among those who really adopted the doctrine of Necessity while verbally repudiating it This is especially evident in Locke's doctrine of Power and the general influence of Collins on the thought of the day is indicated by two lines in Pope's *Essay on Man* —

> "The general order since the whole began
> Is kept in Nature and is kept in Man"

But modern Necessitarians found their most effective champion in Priestley [A D 1733-1804], who took up the Materialistic theories of Spinoza, and deduced from them their logical consequence of a mechanical, which he called a "philosophical," necessity This he worked out in a treatise entitled *The Doctrine of Philosophical Necessity Illustrated*, which was published in the year 1777, in which he argued out the main doctrines of Christianity on the groundwork of the theory that whenever the human mind is in a particular state, and under the influence of particular circumstances, it will always act uniformly, as the same weight will always act in the same manner upon the balance and that thus man can have no such liberty as is implied in the doctrine of free will, any more than the weight or the balance have power to change their mode of action and its results Such a theory destroys at once all moral responsibility, makes prayer useless, and abolishes the idea of future reward and punishment.

About the same time the writings of an American divine, which were of a more popular character than those of Priestley, began to be known in England, and helped to spread the doctrine of Necessity among Socinians without and within the Church This writer was Jonathan Edwards, President of Princeton College [A D 1703-1758], who, towards the close of his life, had printed two works, entitled *An Enquiry into the Freedom of the Will*, and on *The Doctrine of Original Sin*

Since Priestley there has been no writer of distinction among those who have maintained the doctrine of Necessity, but it has been extensively held by the Unitarians and the Rationalists [Copleton's *Inquiry into Necessity*, etc.]

NEOLOGIANS [RATIONALISTS]

NEONOMIANS A controversial name given to their opponents by the CRISPITES A Neonomian is defined by one of their writers as "One that asserts the Old Law is abolished, and therein is a superlative Antinomian, but pleads for a New Law, and justification by the works of it, and therefore is a Neonomian" [Chauncy's *Neonomianism Unmasked*, 1692]

NEO-PLATONISTS It will be the object of this article to set forth—[I.] The history, and [II] The principles of Neo-Platonism, as affecting Christian thought.

[I] It has exercised a very decided influence on intellectual Christianity in ancient, mediæval and modern times It has had its positive and negative side, an attracting as well as a repelling pole It took its rise at Alexandria This important city and centre of civilization having been built by Alexander, was colonized by the representatives of every quarter of the globe—Macedonians, Greeks, Romans, Jews, Syrians, and Persians The religious and philosophical opinions of this motley population were fused together in the various schools which had a common centre in the Museum An age of philosophic scepticism, in the century preceding and in the first two hundred years of Christianity, had thrown a doubt upon every existing intellectual system, but a neutral condition of doubt is alien to the mind of man, and is sooner or later displaced by positive teaching Doubt, as the first principle of Descartes, leads to the definite axiom, "Cogito ergo sum," and Pyrrhonism was gradually displaced by a syncretic fusion of conflicting elements, which were reduced into system at Alexandria Points of agreement were noted between the great masters of Grecian thought; Truth was no longer held to be confined to any one school, Chaldæan lore, worked into cabbalistic form by the learned Jew, Zoroastrian theosophy, Egyptian symbolism, and the reasonings of the Indian Gymnosoph, founded upon theories reaching back to the cradle of the human race, were each and all admitted to a co-ordinate respect with the more familiar Platonic and Pythagorean teaching The Amshaspands and Ferouers of the Persian system, forming an intermediate world of intelligence between the soul of Man and the Infinite ONE, were seen to have points of analogy with Greek mythology, and the fables of the poets were treated as allegories—pregnant with meaning, and veiling important truths from the gaze of the vulgar The teaching of Christian truth, also, was too remarkable as a moral restorative to be neglected, and one of the greatest perils to Christianity was the risk of having the pure doctrines of Christ and His Apostles confounded with hybrid counterfeits Philosophy at Alexandria, thus variously tinctured, became more closely identified with Oriental theosophy, and it gained from it a religious element in mysticism, which may have facilitated in the end the reception of Christian truth, but in its earlier stages it stood in complete antagonism to the Cross of Christ This syncretic fusion at first gave rise to various phases of Gnosticism, in which the Oriental theory of emanations formed a conspicuous feature, but these outrageous absurdities had no charm for the philosophic mind, though it accepted the eclecticism on which they were based. Among Christian teachers, Clement of Alexandria openly professed the eclectic scheme, afterwards known as Neo-Platonism "By philosophy," he says, "I mean not Stoic, Platonic, Epicurean, or Peripatetic theories, but all sound teaching of the collective schools, all precepts of virtue that have connection with religious knowledge This eclectic aggregate, πᾶν τὸ ἐκλεκτικόν, I call philosophy" [*Strom* i 7] Philo, contemporary at Alexandria with St Mark, claimed for his race priority of civilization and science, while he gave to his Shemitic notions an Hellenic colouring Plutarch, advancing the same claim in favour of Greece, had no prejudices as regards barbarian tones of thought, but assimilated them eclectically with analogous theories of Plato and Pythagoras Apuleius, however, was the most completely representative man of the early Neo-Platonic school Deeply read in Greek and Roman literature, at once a scholar, naturalist, and philosopher, versed in the resources of dialectics, and in the special pleading of forensic practice, enlightened, and at the same time superstitious; sceptical and credulous, initiated in every mystery, disciple of every school, he did more than any other votary of the philosophy of the period to found the new school of eclectic Neo-Platonism. Thus, in the second century, the disengaged elements of newly-awakened thought were reduced to system, and the first weak attempt of Potamo received a rapid development at the commencement of the next century under Ammonius Saccas, the sack porter His principal aim was to harmonize the theories of Plato and Aristotle, whose followers had already begun to tamper with the master's text Numenius, apparently of Hebrew extraction, succeeded him, and cast the Mosaic account into the crucible, as another element for amalgamation, saying that Plato was only an Atticizing Moses Longinus followed, and then Plotinus consolidated the new school of interpolated Platonism Ammonius had been his only guide and instructor From Longinus he gained nothing, philology rather than philosophy having been his study

The transcendental teaching of Plato with respect to the Deity was greatly exaggerated by Plotinus That which men term Deity, he said, is the negation of every conceivable idea It has neither quality nor quantity, is neither intellect nor soul, is neither motive nor quiescent, uniform yet unformed, pure Being, but without the accidents of being we can affirm and deny nothing, he said, with respect to the Deity, the soul can only realize its mode of affection towards the Absolute by ecstatic progression from its own centre No appellative befits the One, the First, the Best not even Thought, for so there should be the antinomy of discrimination All that we know is, that a power external to Nature underlies all other existence which it thereby upholds From this school has proceeded the negative notion of the Deity, which was adopted in due course by Dionysius the so-called Areopagite [MYSTICS], J Scotus Erigena, and in later days by Hegel and his school The emanational theory, also, of Plotinus gave rise to the celestial Hierarchy of Dionysius The overflowing redundancy of the First Principle evolves the Second, yet without change or loss of glory, as the sun remains unchanged, though an infinity of rays for ever speed from its substance This Second Principle is Intellect, the express image of the Primeval First, and from whence, equally without change, the Soul of all Nature proceeds Neo-Platonism is only semi-Christianized, and the intermediate divinities and spirits of Proclus are the angelic series of Dionysius The two systems, however, differ in this, that the emanation theory of Dionysius was purely spiritual [*Ep* viii 2, *Demophilo Monacho*] That of the former, as in the Gnostic scheme, issued in the plastic principle of the material world.

A few words will suffice for the other names

of authority in the Neo-Platonic school Porphyry [Malchion, b at Tyre A D 232—d at Rome A D 304], and Jamblichus, a Cœle-Syrian [A D 363], at Alexandria, exhibited the Plotinian theory in a more popular form, giving an allegorical application to Hellenic myths Porphyry was the bitter enemy of Christianity, allowing Christ to have been a pattern of the highest virtue, but imputing to His followers thorough delusion [Aug *Civ Dei*, xix 23] He attacked Scripture from every point of view, more especially denying the genuineness of the Book of Daniel He was an enthusiast perhaps rather than an impostor, for if, like the theurgical juggler Jamblichus, he professed to prepare himself for communion with the Deity by familiar converse with subordinate demons, he actually macerated the body with rigid asceticism [*de Abstin*] Extreme contempt and neglect for the body, as the prison-house of the divine spirit, was always a constituent element in the teaching of this school Julian the Apostate did his utmost to support Neo-Platonism by restoring heathen worship He rebuilt the temples and heaped up hecatombs But the great Pan was dead The system at once collapsed, and in revenge he became persecutor A more systematic arrangement of Plotinian subtlety was made by Proclus [A D 450] giving to Neo-Platonism a dialectical and scientific character that commended it to the schoolmen

Earlier in the same century Hypatia was head of the school at Alexandria, of rare beauty, and spotless purity of character, but a determined foe of Christianity Her mission she considered to be the reconciliation of Plato and Aristotle It has been said that Cyril, Patriarch of Alexandria, caused her death through jealousy of her popularity, but it is referable rather to the reader named Peter, who thus revenged the death of a monk killed by a mob of fanatics At the head of a body of monks Peter dragged his victim into the church, where she was stoned to death, and her mangled limbs were afterwards burned in public by the people

Notwithstanding the Neo-Platonic hatred for Christianity, its theory of the divine origin of the soul, and its lofty aspiration, always proved attractive to the more philosophical sons of the Church Origen was a hearer and an admirer of Ammonius Saccas Clement was eminently eclectic Augustine was thoroughly imbued with one phase at least of the Plotinian teaching [1] Basil, Theodoret, Synesius, all made free use of Plotinus While in the writings of Pseudo-Dionysius Neo-Platonic opinion gained a weight that has told sensibly upon the more fervid spirits of the Church, Neo-Platonism maintained an uneven contest with Christianity till the schools of philosophy were finally closed by Justinian, A D 519 Its votaries then found a temporary asylum at the court of Chosroes, but it had finally died out before the middle of the century Neo-Platonism had a firm hold upon the minds of learned men about the time of the Reformation, Florence being its stronghold, and Ficinus and Picus Mirandola being its exponents, when courtiers, warriors, statesmen, and poets were Neo-Platonists There is much in the Pantheistic philosophy of modern days that altogether harmonizes with the teaching of the Neo-Platonic school, as will be shewn in its proper place

[II] Neo-Platonism is thus seen to have been a combination of mysticism and eclecticism, and hence it had a transitional character its eclecticism connected it with the various intellectual phases of the past, its mysticism gave a starting-point to religious theories of the future Its main deficiency, until the time of Proclus, was a total absence of critical and scientific principles At Alexandria it chiefly occupied itself with the nature of the Deity It fused together a conception of the active disponent Deity of the Timæus with the metaphysical Deity absorbed in the contemplation of his own perfections, and the Absolute Unity of the Eleatic School An inactive Deity was seen only to have an hypothetical existence, yet unmoved Intelligence must itself be superior to all movement The subtle distinction was acknowledged of a Perfect Essence, apart from every other being, shrouded in impenetrable mystery, wholly inaccessible to reason, and infinitely exalted far above the most simple and ineffable of universal principles The antinomies of these reasonings on the Divine nature were manifest Neo-Platonism professed to resolve them First, it is impossible to conceive this Absolute Unity superior to Essence—Ineffable, and, therefore, relatively to any known mode, Non-Existent Secondly, the affirmation of an Eleatic Unity is the negation of Divine Essence; but to declare with Plato and Aristotle that God is the Primary Intelligence, is to make God one with Essence, since Intelligence is identical with Essence And further, since movement is inconsistent with Infinite Perfection, Divine Intelligence must be itself unmoved, although it is affirmed, per contra, that the Deity, without loss of perfection, is the active principle of all movement Hence, the Neo-Platonic theory made a distinction in the nature of the Deity, without touching the Divine Unity, after the manner of those Oriental trinities that have very possibly descended as a faint echo of the faith of humanity from the very cradle of the race Thus it recognised a Divine Unity in the Absolute, Intelligence or Self-Existent Essence, and Soul, as the efficient cause of all Will, Mind, and Power Reason, it was conceded, cannot fathom or declare the Divine Nature But it is brought home to the soul and spirit of man, and made one with his own self-consciousness, by another principle than that of reason—by an ecstatic union with the Deity, whereby the spirit of man travels, as it were,

[1] He has observed that Plotinus helped to lead some on to Christ "Plotini schola Romæ floruit, habuitque condiscipulos multos acutissimos et solertissimos viros Sed aliqui eorum magicarum artium curiositate depravati sunt, aliqui Dominum Christum Jesum ipsius veritati atque sapientiæ incommutabilis, quam conabantur attingere, cognoscentes gestare personam, in ejus militiam transierunt" [*ad Diosc Ep* 118]

beyond itself, and, apart from all sublunary matters, becomes one with its sublime object The Absolute is thus known independently of reason, and by abstract intuition, but this ecstatic mean stands in no antagonism with reason it is rather reason in its highest and most perfect condition, as involving oneness with Absolute Truth, whereby Thought and its object are one

Further, this mysterious power of the Soul shews the non-permanence of individual existence, since by ecstasis self goes forth from and returns again to its own being Man in this is a microcosmic counterpart of the universe The whole world of creation is an aggregate of phenomena distinct from God, and yet resolvable again into His nature They emanate from Him, and yet they have their immanence in His Being Two currents are ever in flux and ebb throughout the universe, productive and absorbent of life, which they at the same time serve to interpret The one is an emanative series, whose progression is from unity to multiplicity, from the perfect to the imperfect, the other is the law of re-absorption, whereby all being returns to its source, so that it be not defiled in its exodus, and be deemed worthy to re enter into the bosom of the Parent of all The Divine Being is that continued systole and diastole, which is life These notions, in their several elements, were confessedly reproduced in Christian mysticism, and in the pantheism of subsequent intellectual systems As a corollary, also, extreme contempt and neglect of the body, the prison-house of the soul, became a necessary principle of philosophy.

The conditions whereby the visible world thus proceeds forth from the Divine Unity are determined by matter This is wholly a negative quantity, to speak algebraically,—without form, without substance or attribute, a nonentity, which can only become an object of thought as an abstract privation of form and individual property, a wholly unintelligible quiddity As the antagonism of the Eternal Good, it is the matrix of evil, τὸ πρώτως κακόν The One, through the mundane soul, having His issue in this abstract negation, fills the material world with life and being, which, howbeit inseparably combined with evil, thence becomes the counterpart of the ideal forms of Intellect There is a manifest analogy between this theory and Gnostic notions, only whereas these early heretics wholly vilified matter and everything material as inherently and entirely evil, of which the Demiurge was the active principle, the Neo-Platonist, with a higher religious tact, commended it as exhibiting the providential wisdom of the Deity, and as giving scope to the good that still abounds in the world This providential wisdom is not merely care and order, but it is the very law of the universe, binding everything together in harmonious action, the reflex image of the Soul that quickens all, and creates in all a yearning and tendency to revert to the Unity from whence it sped If better exists, so then must the worse, and evil in this system has its destined part to play as the relative shadow of good All existence is as a tree of life the One Sole Being is as the root, Intellect as the stem that contains within itself the germ of an endless sequence of results, the Soul is as the branches breaking forth into a rich profusion of leaf and flower and fruit The latent pantheism of such a system cannot escape detection

NEPOS An Egyptian bishop of the third century, whose teaching respecting the Millennium made a temporary schism in the Church of Alexandria He himself is spoken of with great respect and affection by Dionysius, the bishop of that see, who, calling together to Arsinoe the clergy and laity who had been led away by a priest named Coracion [A D 255], expounded to them the true apocalyptic teaching of St John for three days together, and persuaded them, including Coracion, to retract their opinions and return to the communion of his see The Book of Nepos, on which the Chiliastic opinions of his followers were grounded, was entitled Ἔλεγχος τῶν ἀλληγοριστῶν, a refutation of the Allegorists, but it has not been preserved From Theodoret's notice of the work it appears to have been of a Judaizing character [Euseb *Hist. Eccl* vii. 24, Theod *Hæret fab* iii 6]

Timotheus Presbyter speaks of a sect as "Nepotiani a Nepote Elcesæo," but gives no particulars [Timoth Presb *Hær* vi]

NESTORIANS These heretics derived their name from Nestorius, Patriarch of Constantinople [A D 428] Like many other heresies this was in part a reaction against previous heresies The confusion of the two Natures in Christ by the Apollinarians had caused others to insist so strongly on His Human Nature as to tend to a separation of Persons in Him This is what constitutes the Nestorian heresy, the denial of what is called in theology the Hypostatic Union In the history of the controversy this main point is frequently obscured; and Nestorius himself, as well as his followers, did as other heretics have done, so wrapped up their doctrine in verbiage as to make it uncertain what they really meant to teach

Nestorius was a Syrian by birth, and at the time of his appointment to the see of Constantinople a presbyter of Antioch In the first year of his patriarchate the heresy was propounded Anastasius, one of his presbyters at Constantinople, being the first who gave utterance to these unsound opinions In a sermon preached in the presence of Nestorius, at Advent [A D 428], he maintained that the title Θεοτόκος was inapplicable to the Blessed Virgin Mary, inasmuch as God could not be said to be born of a human creature This term, Θεοτόκος, had been in use for many years It was brought into prominence at the time of the Arian controversy by Alexander, Bishop of Alexandria, in a letter to Alexander, Bishop of Byzantium It had been adopted by many others, and appears at the beginning of the fifth century to have been generally established [DICT. *of* THEOLOGY, THEOTOKOS] The term was meant to express the catholic doctrine of the two Natures in the one Person of Christ, and had nothing whatever to do with additional honour or dignity thereby accruing to the Blessed Virgin herself The ostentatious rejection of this term by Anastasius created a great disturbance Not very long afterwards the archbishop himself preached on the same subject, entirely upholding the view advanced by Anastasius The first to take upon himself to defend the Catholic doctrine against Nestorius was Cyril, Bishop of Alexandria. Having discussed the matter in synod, Cyril sent two letters of admonition to Nestorius In the former of these letters he referred to a letter to the same purport which had already been sent from the See of Rome John, Bishop of Antioch, also appealed to Nestorius upon the subject The Patriarch of Constantinople, disregarding these admonitions, and treating them with contempt, fell into general disfavour With those expostulations the year 429 was taken up Early in the following year another hortatory letter arrived from Cyril, and a more pronounced one from Celestine, Bishop of Rome In this latter it was announced that the error of Nestorius had been examined and condemned in a synod at Rome, and unless he recanted within ten days he was to be excommunicated, "ab universalis Ecclesiæ Catholicæ communione" dejectus Nestorius having at length replied to Cyril, and exhibiting no disposition to retract, but on the contrary accusing Cyril of having fallen himself into the opposite error to that which he meant to condemn, Cyril drew up twelve anathemas, which were approved at a synod of all Egypt, held at Alexandria, and transmitted them with a letter to Nestorius John of Antioch took exception to this letter, and began to sympathize with Nestorius, considering that Cyril himself, as had been alleged by his opponent, immoderately opposing the unsound views of Nestorius, had fallen into the Apollinarian heresy The Bishop of Antioch had from the first interfered only in the interests of peace, and he still urged Nestorius so to qualify his expressions and statements that he could be pronounced orthodox; but this he could not be persuaded to do Nestorius now appealed to the Emperor Theodosius, who wrote upbraidingly to him, but consented to convene a general council, which his opponents also demanded It was appointed to meet at Ephesus, at Pentecost, A D 431. Celestine of Rome had deputed Cyril to act on his behalf and carry out the sentence of the Roman council of the preceding year, and Cyril's assembly of his bishops, and further proceedings, brought matters to the crisis

The Bishop of Hippo, St Augustine, was to have presided at the council of Ephesus, but he died in the latter part of the year 430 By the appointed time all the bishops summoned had arrived, except those from the East A fortnight's delay was assented to in the hope of their arrival, but at the end of that time a message from John of Antioch having been received, which begged them to proceed with the business if the Syrian bishops were still detained, it was resolved to wait no longer Upward of 200[1] bishops met under the presidency of Cyril, but Nestorius was not of the number Messengers were sent to his house, but brought back his refusal to appear. The reason he assigned was not any objection to the constitution of the council, but the continued absence of the Syrian party The assembled bishops accordingly, in his absence, read Nestorius' writings, and discussed the term Θεοτόκος The council was unanimous in its condemnation of the patriarch's doctrines, and in its enunciation of the Catholic doctrine of the Hypostatic Union, "that Christ was one Divine Person in Whom two Natures were most closely and intimately united, but without being mixed or confounded together" The council then passed formal sentence of excommunication and deposition In less than a week John of Antioch, with his bishops, in number about 33, arrived Messengers were sent to inform him of the proceedings of the council, but were not received He presided over a schismatical council of his own party, at which Cyril and Memnon of Ephesus were condemned Fresh arrivals having taken place, there was a final meeting of the council under Cyril, entirely confirming the former decision, and passing sentence of excommunication upon John and the Syrian party At this meeting letters were drawn up and sent to the Emperor and the clergy

In the first instance the Emperor confirmed all the condemnations, but upon being better informed, he directed Nestorius to be dismissed, and the other bishops to return to their respective dioceses The Syrians, on their arrival at home, were again summoned to meet by John, and they again condemned Cyril, by this time at Alexandria. Nestorius himself was banished to Egypt and the town where he lived being attacked, he wandered about in want and misery till he died [See Hey's *Lectures*, bk. iv 21, 16] He survived his deposition barely four years

It has been stated above that the original Nestorian party obscured their real sentiments by a hazy use of words Nestorius himself used to complain that inferences were by his opponents drawn from his words which they were not intended to convey Dupin [*Bibliothèque*, i. 442, ed. 1722] thus summarizes his views, as expounded by himself [1] He expressly rejected the error of those who said Christ was a mere man, as Ebion, Paul of Samosata, Photinus [2] He maintained that the Word was united to the humanity in Christ Jesus, and that this union was most intimate and strict [3] He maintained that these two Natures made one Christ, one Son, one Person [4] And that this Person may have either divine or human properties attributed to Him

But his words contradicted this formal enunciation of his doctrine His illustrations proved that he did not allow the Hypostatic Union, but admitted a moral union only A contemporary writer [Marius Mercator, *Opera*, Paris 1673, ed

[1] The numbers are not always given alike Liberatus says 200, Mercator 275

Garner], who lived in the first half of the fifth century, says that Nestorius was sound in most of the Catholic truths on this question taken seriatim He was sound "de persona divina assumente," also "de natura humana assumpta," and also "de tempore, quo primum extitit unio," all these positions being demonstrated by extracts from extant sermons and other writings of Nestorius But he was unsound "de genere unionis" He certainly allowed only a moral union, "Deus et homo unum tantum moraliter" Hence the Incarnation, according to him, was *ἐνοίκησις, ἀνάληψις, ἐνέργεια, ἐνανθρώπησις* There were two Natures in Christ, and the properties of each should be very carefully distinguished, "duæ in Christo reipsa hypostases, secernenda singulorum idiomata" Nor would he allow human attributes to be predicated of the Divine Nature, or divine ones of the Human Nature of Christ. "Nec quæ unius tribuenda alteri, nisi *καθ' ὁμονυμίαν*, vel *σχετικῶς*" Rogers [*Parker Soc* 55] quotes an apposite passage in this connexion *Φησὶ γὰρ ἑνωθῆναι τὸν Θεὸν λόγον τῷ ἐκ Μαρίας ἀνθρώπῳ, ὥσπερ εἴ τις φίλος φίλῳ ἕνωσιν διὰ σχέσεως ποιοῖτο* [Nicephorus, xviii 48] He refused therefore to say that God the Son had endured human suffering or gone through human experiences He necessarily rejected, according to the above view, the term Θεοτόκος, and proposed Χριστοτόκος as an alternative There is abundant proof from his works of his denial of the Hypostatic Union He compared the union of the two Natures in Christ to a marriage he spoke of Christ's Humanity being the Habit, the Temple, of His Divinity He said that Thomas had touched Him that was risen again and honoured Him that raised Him up He believed "hominem Deificatum, et non verbum carnem factum" that Christ became God by merit, and was not God by nature At some meetings at Ephesus preliminary to the council, Nestorius said he would not admit that a child could be God Acacius, bishop of Melitana, at the council, said that he had heard a bishop of the party of Nestorius say, "that He that suffered for us was a distinct Person from the Word" [Dupin, i 640] Nestorius proposed an alteration of phraseology in order to overcome his difficulty He suggested that there would be no difficulty if we said the Divine Jesus Christ knew men's thoughts, the Human Jesus Christ was hungry, and the like [See Dr Hey's *Lectures*, iv He speaks of the cruelty of the persecution of Nestorius, and does "not scruple to say that the Council of Ephesus erred in treating Nestorius with too great severity"] Practically it became clear that his doctrine amounted to teaching that there were two Persons in Christ, and it was so felt at the time.

Including the diocesan synods and the schismatical assemblies, there were not less than nineteen or twenty meetings during the first twenty years of the controversy. Mercator gives them in order he makes out that there were four at Rome, at Alexandria, and at Constantinople, two at Ephesus, two at least held by the Orientals, and others at Antioch, Berœa, and elsewhere. Most of these have been already spoken of The second at Constantinople, held 25th October 431, was for the election of Maximian in succession to Nestorius and the third, which was rather a consultation of bishops with the Emperor, was for considering the best means of re-establishing the peace of the Church. The Council of Chalcedon [A D 451] assembled to condemn the opposite heresy, that of Eutyches it not only did so, but incidentally confirmed the decision of the Council of Ephesus, and expressly adopted the term Θεοτόκος Two years later a council at Constantinople, among other things, condemned a letter of Ibas of Edessa that had renounced the term Θεοτόκος Gelasius, Bishop of Rome [A D 492-496], also synodically condemned the Nestorians Pope Anastasius II, who succeeded Gelasius, is said to have been inclined to favour the Nestorians At the beginning of the fourteenth century Pope John XXII made a vigorous effort at their total suppression He sent letters to the Patriarch of Jerusalem on the subject [A D 1326] By this time both Nestorians and Jacobites (who held the Eutychian heresy that there was but one Nature in Christ) had extensive establishments In the Pope's letter it is stated that both these sects, "habentes illic distinctas ecclesias, in quibus errores et hæreses hujusmodi, non sine magnis suarum et multorum aliorum animarum periculis, publice dogmatizant" The patriarch is accordingly urged to exterminate them

It need hardly be said that the Nestorians repudiate the councils of Ephesus and Chalcedon Timotheus, then patriarch, in a national synod [A D 786, confirmed A D 804], pronounced "Anathematizatas fuisse Synodos Ephesinam et Chalcedonensem ex eo, quod duas personas in unam coaluisse docuerint" [Asseman, *de Catholicis seu Patriarchis Chaldæorum et Nestorianorum Commentarius*, 1775, pref xliv]

After the death of Nestorius the sect largely increased, especially in Northern and Eastern countries They still exist in the East, and have a patriarch in Seleucia and elsewhere They are not now quite identical with the old Nestorians The modern Chaldæans or Nestorians are very numerous, and have spread over Mesopotamia, India, Tartary, and China Those of India in the twelfth century settled under the Tartar Khans They officiate only in Chaldee or Syriac Many learned men doubt if they are now tainted with the original heresy, having by several confessions of faith cleared themselves They are believed in the main to agree with the Roman Church on the Incarnation, though they express the doctrine in different terms Some on the coast of Malabar are not conformed to the Church of Rome, but others, as at Diarbekir, are professed Roman Catholics

It has been shewn that the great opponent of the heresy was Cyril. He has written five books against Nestorius, and a dialogue to prove that the Blessed Virgin Mary was Θεοτόκος, and not Χριστοτόκος But there are, besides, a great number of writers against this heresy whose works are extant Among them are Philastrius, Epiphanius, Theodoret, Faustus, Leontius of Byzantium, Maxentius, Marius Mercator, and many others The works on the history of the sect are very numerous In Malcom's *Theological Index* is a long list of such works, the most important being Doucin, *Histoire du Nestorianisme*, Franzius, *Notholti Dissertationes*, Le Quien, *Oriens Christianus*, Schroeder, *Liberati Historia controversiæ Nestorianæ* In the foregoing account, besides the usual materials, the Breviarium of Liberatus, who was Archdeacon of Carthage, written c. A D 564, and the works of Marius Mercator, have been found very valuable Malcom gives also a list of modern writers on the subject On the Nestorian side appear the Sermons of Eutherius; and Asseman [quoted by Dr Hey, bk iv art ii sec 9] gives a catalogue of 198 writers, with more in an appendix, who are called Syrian Nestorian writers. "but the New Testament is one book reckoned, and Clemens Romanus one author" [Dict *of* Theol., Councils, Nestorianism, Theotokos Badger's *Nestorians and their Rituals* Broughton's *Dict* Grant's *Lost Tribes of Israel*]

NETOVTSCHINS. A sect of Russian Dissenters, whose leading tenet is that Antichrist has begun his ruin of the Church, and that a gradual extinction of all holiness is now going on. They assume the name of Spasova Soglasia, the Union for Salvation, and appear to be an offshoot of the Pomorane [Platov's *Present View of Russian Church*, Pinkerton's transl]

NEW-BORN, THE An American sect of Antinomians, which existed for about twenty years during the first half of the eighteenth century. It originated with a German emigrant named Matthias Bowman, who settled in Berks County, Pennsylvania, in 1719, and died there in 1727. He and his few followers professed to have been regenerated by inspiration and by visions, and thus to have received the new name of the Apocalypse They also held the Familist opinion of the deification of humanity, and its Antinomian consequence, that of the impossibility of any act being sin in persons so deified

NEW CHURCH [Swedenborgians]

NEW CONNEXION GENERAL BAPTISTS [Baptists]

NEW CONNEXION METHODISTS [Methodists]

NEW ITINERARY [New Connexion Methodists]

NEW JERUSALEM CHURCH [Swedenborgians]

NEW LIGHTS [Fifth Monarchy Men]

NEW LIGHTS [Free Will Baptists]

NEW LIGHTS [Separates]

NEW LIGHT BURGHERS. [Burghers.]

NEW LIGHT ANTIBURGHERS [Antiburghers]

NEW PELAGIANS. After the Reformation a body of persons arose, chiefly in Holland, holding Pelagian views on grace and free will They are sometimes called "Pelagiani Novi," but sometimes "Comarista," from Theodore Comarius, secretary to the States General, who died c A D. 1595

NEW SCHOOL PRESBYTERIANS [Presbyterians]

NICOLAITANES. Two of the seven churches of Asia, Pergamos and Thyatira, are charged in the Apocalypse with allowing among them some who taught "the doctrine of Balaam, to eat things sacrificed unto idols, and to commit fornication," and the doctrine is named "The doctrine of the Nicolaitanes" [Rev ii 13, 14] The name shews that there was a distinct heretical party which held the doctrine, while the terms of both the Epistles to the Churches shew that these heretics had neither formally separated themselves from the Church nor had been excommunicated

In considering this heresy it will be assumed that the Apocalypse was written before the destruction of Jerusalem A book so "thoroughly Jewish in its language and imagery," and yet so pregnant with the ideas of catholic Christianity, can only be the last inspired utterance of the Judæo-Christian Church "The Apocalypse winds up St John's career in the church of the circumcision, the Gospel and the Epistles are the crowning result of a long residence in the heart of Gentile Christendom" [Lightfoot's *Dissertation*, "*St Paul and the Three*," *in Comm on Galatians*, p 334 Compare, as on a kindred topic, Mill's remarks on the Benedictus in *Observations on Pantheistic Principles*, part ii p 43]

Before the year 70, then, there was a distinct heretical party, the matter of whose heresy had entered into the decree of the Council of Jerusalem nearly twenty years before The subject-matter being so plainly the same, it is of little moment whether or not we assume in the Apocalypse a reference to the council, but the words "I will put upon you none other burden" appear to be rather a quotation from the decree than a mere reference to it.

The decree probably shews that the evil denounced was even then in existence The council determined, on the one hand, that it was not necessary to be circumcised and keep the law of Moses; on the other hand, it prescribed what, in things indifferent, ought to be conceded to the scruples of the Jewish Christians, who still adhered to their national customs. Into this latter part of the decree so grave a moral evil as fornication could hardly have been brought, unless [1] the existence of the evil had been shewn, and [2] it had been connected with the other topics of the decree by an assertion that the abrogation of the Mosaic law had made the practice permissible. How such a pretence could be made, and the nature of the crime, are important points for investigation.

The identification of the doctrine of the Nicolaitanes with the doctrine of Balaam [Rev ii 14] proves that the fornication spoken of is not that crime under ordinary circumstances, but fornication connected with religious rites Until the return from Babylon, the Jews had been familiar with this odious practice. Among the Hebrews, as previously among the Canaanites

[Gen xxxviii. 21, 22, Deut xxiii. 18], a prostitute was termed "consecrated," and notwithstanding the laws of Moses and the denunciations of the Prophets, "consecrated" women and even boys were at times kept in the temple itself [2 Kings xxiii 7] This dreadful custom was spread in different forms over Phœnicia, Syria, Phrygia, Assyria, Babylonia [Hos iv 14, and Pusey's note; Apocr Letter of Jeremiah, vv 42, 43, Herodotus i 199, Michaelis on *Laws of Moses*, art 268] The licentiousness mixed up, by the Greeks and Romans, with the worship of Dionysus and Aphrodite is well known, and needs no detail

In two ways this evil might enter into Christian worship first, through the pretence that by the abrogation of the Mosaic law the statute imposed in Deut xxiii 17, 18 was repealed, that men were at liberty to follow a national custom, the sanction of long-established national custom doing away the criminality of the act, or, secondly, by the fanaticism of professors of religion dwelling with erotic fulsomeness on the ties of human love, as setting forth heavenly love and heavenly communion, until lust conceived and brought forth sin This fanaticism appears, as we shall see, in the second century In the apostolic times and conditions of the Church, the former mode of the entrance of sin is the more probable, and the comparison of the epistles to Pergamos and Thyatira with the decree of the council, and the occasion of the calling that council, leads to the conclusion that the apostolic decree is to be regarded, in this part, not primarily as a denunciation of fornication in general, but as a denunciation of religious prostitution, whether in the idol-feasts of the nation or imported thence into the Christian love-feasts.

Other scriptures confirm this conclusion St Paul indeed treats the three elements of the question—the eating idol-sacrifices, the Christian love-feast, and fornication—each on its own independent ground But Nicolaitane doctrine does not appear to have reached Corinth The apostolic decree of Jerusalem was directed only to Judæo-Christian churches, and in any case the mind of St Paul preferred the more general treatment of the subject Both St Jude and St Peter, however, follow the more limited treatment, which was afterwards adopted in the Apocalypse

St Jude describes these filthy dreamers as defiling the flesh with Balaam, despising dominion[1] with Cain, and speaking ill of dignities, or church rulers, with Korah He specifies the Agape as the scene of their wickedness, and points out the separation from the Church which was taking place St Peter's words are a re-casting of St Jude's words He too gives the same threefold description, omitting the parallels of Cain and Korah, but dwelling on the typical example of Balaam He at least points to the love-feast,

[1] Cain despised and forfeited the lordship belonging to the first born, which was assured him on the condition of well doing [Gen iv 7] These evil doers despise and forfeit their sonship in the Christian Covenant Baronius refers these passages of SS Jude and Peter to the Nicolaitanes.

for the words "while they feast with you" can be interpreted only of the Agape, even if we do not adopt the probable correction of *ἀγάπαις* for *ἀπάταις* In these four Scriptures then is described the growth in apostolic times of the heretical party of the Nicolaitanes. And thus far their doctrine appears to be a doctrine of libertinism in religious ordinances

But St Peter mentions also teachers of the false doctrine, who denied the Lord that bought them These words may be interpreted either of a denial in works, such as is named in Tit i 16, or of a formal denial of the divinity of our Lord Irenæus states that St John wrote his Gospel to remove the errors of Cerinthus, which had a long time previously been disseminated by the Nicolaitanes[2] But again, having named Cerinthus and the Ebionites, he describes the Nicolaitanes simply as they are represented in the Apocalypse, without attributing to them Cerinthian errors [Iren *adv Hær* III xi 1, I xxvi 3] These two statements are not altogether consistent Comparing them, and collating them with other notices which will be presently given, the most probable conclusion is, that Nicolaitane doctrine is simply, as described above, a doctrine of libertinism,[3] and that it attached itself before long to other heresies

Whether the Nicolaitanes rightly claimed Nicolas the Deacon, and proselyte of Antioch, as their leader, has been much disputed The balance of early testimony appears to be in favour of their claim, and to shew that one of the seven became a heresiarch Irenæus and Hippolytus state it unhesitatingly [Iren *adv Hær* i 26, Hippol *Refut Hær* vii 24], and Hippolytus does not appear to have rested on the authority of Irenæus, but to have given an independent account On the other hand, Clement of Alexandria defends Nicolas from the charge, Eusebius follows him, merely transcribing his words [Clem Alex *Strom* ii. 20, iii 4, Euseb *Hist Ecc* iii 29] In this defence Clement tells a story (and tries to put a good interpretation upon it) which is incredible It is that Nicolas having a beautiful wife, and being reproached with jealousy by the Apostles, conducted her into the midst of them, and permitted any one that wished to marry her, and that he used the expression, "Every one ought to abuse his own flesh" Epiphanius [*Hæres* xxv 1] tells a different story, that Nicolas refrained from living with his wife that he might devote himself to religion, but could not persevere in his resolution, and gradually sank into sin, and invented a doctrine that luxury was necessary to salvation Both stories may be dismissed [Ittig *Diss de Hæres* I ix 4] The doctrine however which Epiphanius attributes to Nicolas appears

[2] Augustine also attributes to them Cerinthian errors regarding the creation of the world [Aug *Hæres* v]

[3] The author of Prædestinatus attributes to the Nicolaitanes this doctrine of libertinism only He says that Nicolas began to teach it when he was blamed for jealousy of a very beautiful wife A doctrine of promiscuous intercourse is not likely to spring from such a cause [*Præd* i 4]

to be the fanatical doctrine to which Clement passes on after describing the libertinism of the Nicolaitanes: Εἰσὶν δ' οἱ τὴν πάνδημον Ἀφροδίτην κοινωνίαν μυστικὴν ἀναγορεύουσιν [Clem Alex *Strom* iii 4]

Eusebius [*Hist Eccl* iii 29] states that the heresy of the Nicolaitanes lasted but a very short time. The explanation of this, as compared with other notices, is that a doctrine of libertinism easily attaches itself to other forms of heresy, and, as far as the name goes, is lost in them. Thus Tertullian says [*de Præscr* ch xxxiii] "Johannes vero in Apocalypsi idolothyta edentes, et stupra committentes jubetur castigare Sunt et nunc alii Nicolaitæ, Caiana hæresis dicitur" The author of the continuation of the *de Præscr.* connects the Nicolaitanes with the Gnostics Hippolytus [vii 24] writes that Nicolas was the cause of the widespread combination of the wicked Gnostics Clement of Alexandria [*Strom* iii 2] speaks of the Carpocratians abusing love-feasts to licentiousness, and is of opinion that St Jude wrote prophetically of them Justin Martyr [*Trypho*, xxxv] speaks of certain calling themselves Christians, Marcians, Valentinians, and others, partaking in nefarious and impious rites Agrippa Castor [Euseb *Hist Eccl* iv 7] charged the Basilidean Gnostics with holding the indifferency of things sacrificed to idols Hippolytus speaks of the Nicolaitane practices of the Simonians [Hippol. *Refut Hær* vi 14] Epiphanius derives the Gnostics from the Nicolaitanes It is more probable that they had a separate origin, and adopted Nicolaitane teaching and practice.

Thus the doctrine of the Nicolaitanes was extended into several other heresies, while the sect, as a distinct body, lasted but a short time And upon the whole it may be concluded that Nicolaitane doctrine was a doctrine of libertinism in religious rites, passing quickly into a doctrine of general libertinism, defending itself under a shew of fanaticism, and attaching itself soon to other heresies

NICOLAS OF BASLE [FRIENDS OF GOD]

NICOLAS, HENRY [FAMILISTS]

NICONIANS A name applied by Russian dissenters to the orthodox members of the Established Church who accepted the reforms introduced by the Patriarch Nicon in the year 1654

NIHILISTS A school of theologians who taught that God did not become anything through the Incarnation which He was not before This proposition is founded on the doctrine of the unchangeableness of the Divine Nature, from which it is deduced that since God can never be otherwise than God, therefore it cannot be true to say that He became man Peter Lombard [A D 1160] stated this theory in the third book of the Sentences [Lombard, *Sent* iii *dist* 5-7], but it was of earlier date, being traceable to Abelard in the twelfth century [Abelard, *Theol Christi* in Martene, *Thes* v 1307], and even to the early theology of the school of Antioch, which maintained that God clothed Himself with humanity as with a garment. The more advanced Nihilists held the opinion in such a form as to make the Incarnation nothing more than a theophany, in which without becoming man the Son of God made Himself appear as man to the eyes of men The proposition, in the form "Deus non factus est aliquid," was laid before the Council of Tours [A D 1163], and rejected [Mansi, *Concil* xxii 239] A work was also written against it by an Englishman, John of Cornwall, about the same time [Joann Cornub in Martene, *Thes* v 1658], and by Walter St Victor, who charged Peter Lombard with the extreme form of Nihilism It was finally condemned in the year 1179 at the Council of Lateran [Mansi, *Concil* xxii 426]

NIOBITES A party of Alexandrian Monophysites formed under the leadership of a Sophist named Stephen Niobes, who attempted to revive the older Monophysite doctrine in opposition to the modified form of it maintained by Damian, Monophysite Patriarch of Alexandria [A D 570-603], who belonged to the school of Severus and the PHTHARTOLATRÆ.

The particular opinion brought forward by Niobes was that the qualities belonging to human nature could not continue in the Human Nature of Christ after its amalgamation with or absorption into the Divine Nature. He thus took up the position that there was no logical ground for the Severian compromise between orthodoxy and Monophysitism, and that the Jacobites ought to revert to the creed which they held before Severus came to Egypt, that which Dioscorus had maintained in opposition to the Council of Chalcedon The Niobite party was driven out of Alexandria by Damian after the death of Niobes, and settled at Antioch, where, before the death of Damian, they gradually came round to orthodox opinions, and were energetic supporters of the Chalcedonian doctrine. [Assemann *Bibl. Orient* ii 72]

NJETOWSCHITSCHINI [NETOVTSCHINS]

NOETIANS A sect, both heretical and schismatic, of the beginning of the third century, belonging to that branch of the Monarchians which maintained that there is a Divine as well as a Human Nature in the Person of our Lord They avowed the Patripassianism which results from this recognition of a Divine Nature in our Lord when conjoined with the erroneous view of the Monarchy In this respect they went beyond the Praxeans

Of Noetus himself nothing more is known than the few particulars which follow He was a native of Asia Minor, Hippolytus [*Ref* ix 11] and Epiphanius [*Synopsis*, I ii 11] say of Smyrna, but Epiphanius in the body of his work says of Ephesus [*Hær* lvii] perhaps a native of Ephesus, and a presbyter of Smyrna At Smyrna he advanced his heresy, and was summoned before the synod of presbyters, when he denied or evaded the charge, but presently, encouraged by gaining about ten associates, he openly maintained the doctrine charged to him, and on a second summons before the synod avowed it. He was excommunicated, and then gathered followers, and formed a school for the propagation of his opinions, shortly after which he died [Hipp *Disc against Noetus*, Epiph *Hær* lvii] The author of Prædestinatus states that he was condemned also by Tranquillus, Bishop of the Chalcedonians in Syria [Prædest *Hær* xxxvi]

From Hippolytus we learn that Epigonus, a disciple of Noetus, aided by Cleomenes, a disciple of his own, disseminated the heresy at Rome in the episcopate of Zephyrinus Zephyrinus, an illiterate and covetous man, was bribed into licensing Cleomenes as a teacher, and then became his convert [Hipp *Ref* ix 2, Wordsworth, *Hipp and his Age*, pp 84-91] Irresolute however as well as ignorant, governed generally by Callistus, who tried to hold a balance between the orthodox and the heretics, but acted upon now by Cleomenes, now by Sabellius, Zephyrinus was swayed to and fro There was endless conflict and confusion throughout the remainder of his long episcopate [see Milman, *Lat Christ.* I. i p 53, ed 1867]

The time at which Noetus formed his heretical school at Smyrna must be gathered from this history, for the date assigned by Epiphanius is clearly inadmissible The tenor of the narrative of Hippolytus leads to the conclusion that Zephyrinus fell into heresy some time before his death, which was in A D 219 Allowance must be made for the action of Epigonus and Cleomenes before Zephyrinus joined them, and for that of Epigonus alone Consequently the establishment of the Noetian school may be well placed at A D 205-10, and Praxeas, who came to Rome in the time of Victor, A D 192-201, was probably one of the earlier disciples of Noetus

Noetus denied the distinction of Persons in the Godhead, and there can be no doubt that he avowedly held what may be called the simpler form of Patripassian doctrine, the form namely which is obtained by substituting in the Person of our Lord for the Divine Nature of the Word the one undistinguished Nature of Deity which the Monarchians called the Father The sum and substance of this is thus well set down by Victorinus "Patripassiani Deum solum esse dicunt, quem nos Patrem dicimus, ipsum solum exsistentem et effectorem omnium, et venisse non solum in mundum, sed et in carnem, et alia omnia quæ nos Filium fecisse dicimus" [Pearson, *On the Creed*, p 158, fol 1741]

But the statements of Hippolytus appear to make it probable that Noetus went even beyond this in heresy, that he held the truly appalling doctrine that the Father, the One Primary Principle, suffered on the cross, not in the way in which the Catholic Faith teaches that Christ suffered, but from a passibility attributed to the Divine Nature itself In stating the catholic doctrine that the Son of God suffered, it is not said that the Word is in His own Nature passible, nor is it said that Christ suffered "ratione divinæ naturæ," but "ratione humanæ naturæ, quæ sola passibilis erat" But do not the statements of Noetus' doctrine begin with ascribing passibility to the Divine Nature itself? The Noetians "advance statements after this manner—that one and the same God is the Creator and Father of all things, and that when it pleased Him, He appeared to just men of old" "Wherefore it is that, according to the same account, He is invincible and vincible, unbegotten and begotten, immortal and mortal" The subsequent statements it is true refer these positions to the supposed incarnation of the Father, but it may be asked, whether that supposed incarnation, with its consequences, is not in accordance with a presupposed attribute of passibility in the Deity itself.

On no other supposition can the derivation of Noetianism from the doctrine of Heracleitus be made good, a derivation which Hippolytus insists upon very strongly The original principle of the universe Heracleitus believed to be living, æthereal fire, self-kindled and self-extinguished. In the following passage he asserted, as Hippolytus states, that the primal world is itself the Demiurge and Creator of itself "God is day, night, summer, winter, war, peace, surfeit, famine" He says that the universe is divisible and indivisible, generated and ungenerated, mortal and immortal, reason, eternity, Son, Father, Justice, God In this passage the manifestations or developments of the Primal Principle in time are contrasted with its nature and existence in eternity And the derivation of Noetian doctrine from the doctrine of Heracleitus will scarcely hold good unless Noetus be understood to attribute to the Godhead itself that which Heracleitus attributed to the Primal Principle. Whence, after quoting the pantheistic passages from Heracleitus, Hippolytus stated the Noetian doctrine that, according to the same account, the Father is unbegotten and begotten, immortal and mortal Is it not to be inferred that to be unbegotten and begotten, to be immortal and mortal, was attributed by Noetus to the Godhead itself independently of the supposed incarnation of the Godhead, in short, that he held the Father to be visible and passible, so that there was required the addition to the Creed which was made by the Church of Aquileia, affirming the Father to be invisible, impassible?

A further proof of this is found in the 12th anathema of the Synod of Sirmium, A D 351, which, summoned to deal with Photinus, condemned the various errors of the Sabellian school. It can hardly be doubted that the following words were directed against the Noetians, who were Sabelliani ante Sabellium. "Si quis unicum Filium Dei crucifixum audiens dealitatem[1] ejus corruptionem vel passibilitatem aut demutationem aut deminutionem vel interfectionem sustinuisse dicat anathema sit"

The Monarchian controversy arose from the intrusion into Christian doctrine of heathen philosophy, and the affiliation of Noetus to Heracleitus is a strong proof of the truth of this assertion

In the Refutation no notice is taken of that

[1] θεότητα. The word is used by Arnobius Junior

which is mentioned in the Discourse, and by Epiphanius, that Noetus alleged himself to be Moses and his brother to be Aaron—or as Philaster gives the assertion—Elias, and it was probably nothing more than an arrogant comparison It does not appear that there was any attempt to maintain the sect by a separate episcopal succession and in Augustine's time the name of Noetus was almost unknown

NOMINALISTS A school of mediæval theologians which arose in the latter half of the eleventh century, maintaining the opinion that objects exist only as individuals, so that genera, species, or "universals" (the term then in use) are but several or many individual objects collectively brought under one common name, or thought of under one common idea The Nominalists thus opposed the position of the Realists, that universals have an abstract existence distinguishable from the existence of the individuals related to them, and they took as the formula of their school "universalia post rem" The extreme application of the theory is seen in the opinion of some Nominalists that the Three Names of the Holy Trinity are the Names of Three individual Substances, and that the Unity of the Trinity is but a verbal expression and not a Unity of Three consubstantial Persons

The founder of the Nominalist school was Roscellin, Canon of Compiègne [*circ* A D 1089], whose opinions respecting the Trinity were carried to the tritheistic extent just indicated [ANTITRINITARIANS, p 36], and who was compelled to retract them at the Council of Soissons in the year 1092 The next distinguished leader of the school was his pupil Abelard [A D 1079-1142], who modified the tritheistic opinion of Roscellin into a Sabellian form, defining the Three Persons as God's power, wisdom, and goodness, but yet not altogether denying the personality of those attributes. After his time Nominalism was little regarded by theologians until the fourteenth century, when it was revived by William of Occam [* —1347], the pupil of Duns Scotus Henceforward the Nominalists may be recognised as the school of progress, inquiry, and criticism, out of which the Reformation arose a school which so far tended towards scepticism that it overvalued the truth which it arrived at by reasoning, and undervalued that which it received by revelation; thus being disposed to believe only after demonstration In later times the Nominalist theory was adopted by Hobbes, Hume, and Dugald Stewart [REALISTS SCHOOLMEN]

NONCONFORMISTS Presbyterian, Independent, and other non-Episcopal ministers, who held benefices by authority of the Revolutionary Parliament during the Great Rebellion, and were deprived of them by the Restoration Parliament The name has also been occasionally used—as by Bishop Bancroft at the Hampton Court Conference—for those Puritan priests and deacons who refused to conform to the ritual customs of the Church of England during the reign of Queen Elizabeth, but who are more generally known by the familiar name of PURITANS

To understand the position of the Nonconformist ministers of 1662, it is necessary to trace out the circumstances under which they came to occupy the churches and parsonages, and to receive the incomes which were appropriated, under the old established endowment system, to the clergy, of the Church of England [1] These have been noticed at some length in the article on the Puritans, in which it is shewn that the overthrow of the Episcopal system in the middle of the seventeenth century was the climax of a movement which had been going on within the boundaries of the Church for about 120 years, and that this movement was for the purpose of establishing the Presbyterian system, instead of that which was inherited by the Reformed Church of England from that of Mediæval, Saxon, and Primitive times It may now be observed more particularly that the post-Reformation system was as distinctly and uncompromisingly episcopal as that which had preceded it, and that none but clergy ordained by bishops were recognised by it

I In November 1549, Parliament passed an Act [3 & 4 Edw VI c 12] declaring that, "forasmuch as concord and unity to be had within the King's Majesty's dominions, it is requisite to have one uniform fashion and manner for making and consecrating of bishops, priests, and deacons, or ministers of the Church Be it therefore enacted by the King's Highness, with the assent of the Lords spiritual and temporal, and the Commons in this present Parliament assembled, and by the authority of the same, that such form and manner of making and consecrating of archbishops, bishops, priests, deacons, and other ministers of the Church as by six prelates and six other men of this realm, learned in God's law, by the King's Majesty to be appointed and assigned, or by the most number of them, shall be devised for that purpose, and set forth under the Great Seal of England before the first day of April next coming, shall by virtue of the present Act be lawfully exercised and used, and none other, any statute or law or usage to the contrary in any wise notwithstanding" There was a strong Germanizing party which wished to introduce Presbyterian ordination, Poynet desiring to abandon the very name of bishop, Grindal calling consecration a mummery, and Jewel and Hooper

[1] The endowments of the Church of England before the Reformation were as follows —

1 Episcopal and Capitular Estates, a large proportion of which were given by the Crown in times before the Conquest

2. Tithes and lands, the former given in times beyond record, and the latter mostly in times before the Conquest, for the use of the parochial clergy

3 Monastic Estates, chiefly given in times subsequent to the Conquest, for the use of the monks and nuns

4 Chantry Estates, chiefly given in the fourteenth and fifteenth centuries, for the use of chantry priests (not parochial clergy) to offer masses for the dead.

The two latter descriptions of property were entirely appropriated by the Crown, and given away by the Crown, (chiefly to courtiers and political adherents,) in the reigns of Henry VIII and of Edward VI The two former descriptions of property were (with some diminution) retained by the clergy being almost as much opposed to the continuation of the old customs But the Ordinal now in the Book of Common Prayer had already been substantially constructed under a commission issued by the Crown in 1548, and this was published, under the authority of the Act which has been quoted, in March 1549-50 The Preface to this Ordinal (probably written by Archbishop Cranmer) enacts that "no man shall be accounted or taken to be a lawful bishop, priest, or deacon, in the Church of England, or suffered to execute any of the said functions, except he be called, tried, examined, and admitted thereunto according to the form hereafter following, or hath had formerly episcopal consecration or ordination" The whole of the Prayer Book, including the Ordinal, and therefore this unambiguous enactment respecting episcopal ordination, was incorporated into the second Act of Uniformity [5 & 6 Edw VI ch 1, A D 1552], and when that had been repealed by Queen Mary's Parliament, it was again incorporated into the third Act of Uniformity [1 Eliz ch 2, A D. 1559] Efforts were made to override this provision of Church and State in the cases of Whittingham, titular Dean of Durham, and Travers, the opponent of Hooker, who had neither of them received episcopal ordination but it is clear that the principle was not conceded, although some latitude was permitted to them because they had been set apart as ministers abroad by foreign, and not at home by English, Presbyterians [Strype's *Ann* ii pt. 2, pp 168, 622, *Life of Whitgift*, iii 182] In fact it was an article of enquiry of the churchwardens at episcopal visitations, "Whether doth your minister or any other take upon them to read lectures, or preach, being mere lay persons, or not ordained according to the laws of this realm?" [Cardwell's *Docum Ann* ii 22] In spite of all such enactments and care, some "counterfeit ministers," as Archbishop Whitgift called them [*ibid* 29], did probably obtain a footing in a parish here and there, but this was only by breaking the law, and the rule was never authoritatively relaxed except in the case of a very small number of foreign Lutherans or Calvinists, to whom Puritan bishops gave preferment Even those extreme Puritan clergy who submitted to the system of "calls" mentioned in the article on "Puritans," were always careful to be ordained by bishops and probably there were no persons beneficed in the Church of England at the time when the Great Rebellion began who had not been episcopally ordained [1]

II It need hardly be said that the strict system of episcopal ordination thus maintained from the Reformation to the Rebellion was never altered by any act of the Church But on November 8th, 1645, an "Ordinance" was passed by the Lords and Commons, who then claimed to be the Parliament of England, declaring that "the word 'Presbyter,' that is to say 'Elder,' and the word 'Bishop,' do in the Scripture intend and signify one and the same function," and that it being an usurpation on the part of bishops for them alone to ordain, henceforth ordination was to be given by presbyters, under certain rules respecting examination and trial which were laid down in the Ordinance and then it was enacted that all persons who shall be ordained presbyters according to this Directory, "shall be for ever reputed, and taken to all intents and purposes, for lawful and sufficiently authorized ministers of the Church of England" [Rushworth's *Hist Coll* vii 212] At this time the parochial clergy were being rapidly and very generally driven away from their parishes Many were notoriously loyal to the Crown and to Episcopacy, and had to fly for their lives, because they would not take the Covenant and the Engagement, many were imprisoned (some with circumstances of great cruelty, as when twenty were kept under hatches in a ship on the Thames), and it is believed that not a few were "sent to the plantations" to slavery as the early Christians were sent to the mines There were also "Committees for enquiry into the scandalous immoralities of the Clergy," and as the least taint of loyalty to Church or King, the use of the Prayer-Book or the refusal of the Directory, was scandalous and immoral in the estimation of these Committees, they turned out most of those clergy who were not got rid of by other means The consequence of all these rigid measures was, that nearly the whole of the Episcopal clergy were turned out of their benefices during the early years of the Great Rebellion. A few temporized, a few were protected by influential laymen, and a few escaped notice, but the number of those who thus retained their places was very small, and it is probable that the popular estimate which put down the number of the clergy ejected by the Parliamentary party at from 8,000 to 10,000 was correct.

As the episcopally ordained clergy were thus driven away from their churches, their parsonages, their tithes and their glebes, the Presbyterians and Independents stepped into the vacated benefices, and were settled in them securely by the authority of the Ordinance of Parliament which is quoted above. Thus it came to pass that between the years 1643 and 1660 most of the parishes throughout England and Wales received for their incumbents men who had not received episcopal ordination, the number of such amounting to about 10,000 at the time of the Restoration

III The Restoration of the civil constitution of the country was accompanied by the restoration of its ecclesiastical constitution almost as a matter of course Attempts were made, indeed, by a comparatively small but yet noisy party, to prevent the re-introduction of the Episcopal system in its integrity, but the great body of the laity were heartily weary of Presbyterianism, Independency, and of the fanatical sects which had sprung

[1] Some exceptional instances might perhaps be found in very out-of-the-world places in the hill and fell districts of the North of England It is said there are several parishes in Yorkshire in which the news of the Reformation was only received in the eighteenth century and Bishop Watson found parishes in Cumberland where a clergyman was never known

up like mushrooms during the supremacy of these two principal ones, and lay influence being consequently exercised strongly against this attempt it was at once defeated One of the first proceedings of the restored Parliament was to pass an Act for the confirming and restoring of ministers [12 Car II ch 17], which enacted that every minister of the Church of England who had been ejected by the authority of the Rebellion Parliament should be restored to his benefice by December 25th, 1660, provided he had not justified the King's murder or declared against Infant Baptism Under this Act many of the non-episcopal ministers had to retire from the livings into which they had been intruded, that the old, persecuted, poverty-struck clergy, who had been turned out of them fifteen or sixteen years before might be restored to their homes and their flocks. Some even of those who had been episcopally ordained had also to retire, and thus Richard Baxter had to make way for the return of the old and rightful Vicar of Kidderminster, whose place he had not unworthily held for half a generation But half a generation of exile, war, persecution, poverty and hardship, had not left many of the old clergy to return to their parishes, and most of these were still occupied by non-episcopal incumbents until the Act of Uniformity came into force on August 24th, 1662

This Act of Parliament [14th Car II ch 4] was no novelty, being the fourth Act of Uniformity which had been passed since the Reformation, and having its parallel in several "Ordinances" of the Parliament which were passed during the Rebellion It was, moreover, absolutely necessary that if the Church system was to be restored some enactment should be made enforcing the first principle of the system, that of episcopal ordination But it was under the consideration of Parliament (especially of the House of Lords, which received a formal request to hasten it from the House of Commons) for several months, and it was so constructed as to deal considerately with the non-episcopal incumbents as well as to deal justly with the principles of the Church The former were not, therefore, "ejected" as it has been so often represented, but opportunity was given to them of retaining the benefices which they held without any difficulty if they were willing to conform to those principles which had always been maintained, and which could not be given up, respecting episcopal ordination, the use of the Prayer Book, and decent loyalty to the Crown The conditions thus imposed were stated as follows in the Act of Uniformity —

1 "Every parson, vicar, or other minister whatsoever, who now hath and enjoyeth any ecclesiastical benefice or promotion within this Realm of England, . . . shall openly and publicly, before the congregation there assembled, declare his unfeigned assent and consent to the use of all things in the said Book contained and prescribed, in these words, and no other 'I, *A B*, do here declare my unfeigned assent and consent to all and everything contained and prescribed in and by the Book intituled The Book of Common Prayer,'" etc.

2 Every such incumbent, or any one to be admitted to an incumbency thereafter, was required to subscribe the following declaration "I, *A B*, do declare that it is not lawful, upon any pretence whatsoever, to take arms against the King, and that I do abhor that traitorous position of taking arms by his authority against his person, or against those that are commissioned by him, and that I will conform to the Liturgy of the Church of England, as it is now by law established And I do declare that I do hold, there lies no obligation upon me, or on any other person, from the Oath commonly called 'The Solemn League and Covenant,' to endeavour any change or alteration of government either in Church or State and that the same was in itself an unlawful oath, and imposed upon the subjects of this realm against the known laws and liberties of this Kingdom"

3 It was also provided that "no person who now is incumbent, and in possession of any parsonage, vicarage, or benefice, and who is not already in holy orders by episcopal ordination, or shall not before the feast of St Bartholomew be ordained priest or deacon according to the form of episcopal ordination, shall have, hold, or enjoy the said parsonage, vicarage, benefice with cure, or other ecclesiastical promotion, within this kingdom of England, or the dominion of Wales, or town of Berwick-upon-Tweed, but shall be utterly disabled, and *ipso facto* deprived of the same, and all his ecclesiastical promotions shall be void as if he was naturally dead"

The Act of Uniformity, therefore, to secure the integrity of the Church system on the one hand, and to secure the vested interests acquired by long possession on the part of the non-episcopal incumbents on the other, offered to the eight or nine thousand of the latter who still remained, that if they would be ordained, accept the Prayer Book, and renounce their engagement to destroy Episcopal government [COVENANTERS], or to bear arms against the Crown, they might retain their benefices The great majority accepted the terms that were thus offered, so legalizing their position, and qualifying themselves to carry out the system of the Church of England according to its long-established principles

The "Nonconformists" who did *not* accept these liberal terms offered by Parliament have been paraded before the world for two centuries as amounting in number to 2,000 Contemporary writers of authority—as for example Bishop Kennett in his "Register and Chronicle," the great storehouse of information respecting the years 1660-2—often denied that the number was so large, but Calamy published an "Abridgment of Baxter's Life and Times" in 1702, the ninth chapter of which is occupied with biographical notices of some of the Nonconformists, and in which he gives the number of 2,000 as correct When this chapter was answered in 1714 by Walker's folio volume on the "Suffering of the Clergy," Calamy compiled a "Continuation" of his former work, which was published in 1721 in two volumes, and in which he still maintained that 2,000 Nonconformists were "ejected" by the Act of Uniformity. A critical examination of Calamy's evidence shews, however, that he has much overstated his case, the number being not much more than one third of what he alleges it to be, and as so much has been made of the matter by dissenting writers, it is worth while to shew what is the real conclusion furnished by his evidence

The list of ejected ministers printed by Calamy may be distributed under the seven following heads [1] Those who were actually dead before the time of ejection arrived, [2] Those who yielded up their places to the dispossessed Episcopal incumbents, [3] Curates and lecturers whose appointments were not benefices, and who were not therefore "ejected" from any by the Act, [4] Cases in which the list sets down two incumbents for the same benefice, [5] Cases in which Bishops' registers shew that other men than those named in the list were in possession, [6] Those who, on Calamy's own shewing, had no benefices to be lost, but whom he includes among those ejected from benefices, [7] Those who may have been deprived by the operation of the Act of Uniformity

By the help of Newcourt's "Repertorium" of the diocese of London, those ministers whom Calamy names as ejected from benefices in that diocese may be distributed under these seven heads as follows

	Number given by Calamy	1	2	3	4	5	6	Number possibly ejected
London,	119	2	21	8	3	12	22	51
Middlesex,	31		3	8		14		11
Essex,	127	2	23	1	6	15	18	62
Herts,	16		5			8		3
Total	293	4	52	12	9	49	40	127

The number of those of whom it is possible that they may have been ejected is thus, taking the general average, only 43 3 per cent of the number given by Calamy for the diocese of London If this proportion be taken as regards the alleged number ejected throughout England and Wales, that number will thus be reduced from 2,000 to 867 It seems improbable, therefore, that the number of Nonconformist ministers who were "*ipso facto*" deprived of their parishes on St Bartholomew's Day was much, or any, over 800, and, as contemporaries allege that some of these were men of property, that some made good marriages, that some returned to the trades which they had given up for the pulpit, and that great kindness was shewn to those who were poor by the bishops and the nobility [Kennett's *Register*, 888, 919], it may be concluded that much exaggeration has been used by those who have used the event to the discredit of the Church

Among those who thus refused to accept the terms offered by the Act of Uniformity there was also a large number who continued to attend the ministrations of the Church, and whom Baxter calls "Episcopal Nonconformists" These, he says, "are for true parish churches and ministers reformed, without swearing, promising, declaring, or subscribing to any but sure, clear, necessary things, desiring that Scripture may be their canons, taking the capable in each parish for the communicants and Church, and the rest for hearers and catechized persons desiring that the magistrate be judge whom he will maintain, approve, and tolerate, and the Ordainer judge whom he will ordain, and the people be free consenters to whose pastoral care they will trust their souls, desiring that every presbyter may be an overseer over his flock, and every church that hath many elders have one incumbent president for unity and order, and that godly diocesans may (without the sword or force) have the oversight of many ministers and churches, and all these be confederate and under one government of a Christian king, but under no foreign jurisdiction, though in as much concord as possible with all the Christian world And they would have the keys of excommunication taken out of the hands of laymen (chancellors or lay brethren), and the diocesan to judge in the synods of the presbyters in cases above parochial power" [Baxter's *Life and Times*, App 71, ed 1696] These were probably a large class among the laity for some time after the Restoration

Three years after the Act of Uniformity had caused the ejection of these 800 Nonconformist ministers, Parliament passed a severe law against them called the "Five-Mile Act" [17 Car II ch 2], which prohibited them from dwelling within five miles of any city or corporate town, or from even coming within that distance of any such town except in the course of travel, thus placing them in a much more unfavourable condition than ordinary Dissenters This Act soon fell into disuse, and the few Nonconformists who remained alive at the Revolution were relieved from its operation altogether by the Toleration Act

NONCONFORMISTS A term which has come into use, in quite recent times, as a general designation of Protestant Dissenters This new application of an old word causes some inconvenience, as confusing modern Dissenters of all sorts with the ministers who declined to conform to the Act of Uniformity, and so were deprived of the benefices which they had got into their hands during the Great Rebellion, as narrated in the preceding article

NON-INTRUSIONISTS [Free Kirk]

NONJURORS This name was originally given to those bishops and other clergymen who were ejected from their benefices in 1689-90 for refusing to take the oath of allegiance to William and Mary while they were still bound by that which they had taken to James II It subsequently designated those of the party who, in the year 1693, organized an Episcopal sect of Non jurors, which lingered on until the beginning of the nineteenth century

I When the Prince of Orange invaded England with a Dutch army (of whom 4000 were Papists) in September 1686, at the instigation of the unpatriotic statesmen who then held the reins of government, it was supposed by many that he would merely act as an armed arbitrator between King James and the discontented portion of his subjects The King, however, having reason to fear from his son-in-law the same fate which his father had met with at the hands of Cromwell, did, on December 24th, 1688, what his father had taken care never to do, fled from his own dominions and took refuge in a foreign kingdom Under these circumstances a general desire arose that the Prince of Orange should be appointed Regent during the absence of the King, but as the Princess of Orange had ceased to be heir-apparent to the English throne through the birth of her brother on the preceding June 10th, the Prince was unwilling to lose the new chance of a kingdom which had thus fallen into his hands, and refused to accept the government of it on any other condition than that of becoming its sovereign, threatening that, if any other settlement was attempted, he and his army would return to Holland The crown was therefore offered to him on February 7th, 1688-9, by a body of Lords and Commons who had formed themselves into a joint committee, to which the name of a "Convention" was given, and on February 13th, seven weeks after King James had left England, the Prince and Princess were proclaimed its King and Queen.

The change of sovereigns having been thus effected, it was thought necessary that all persons holding office in Church or State should take an oath of allegiance to those who *de facto* occupied the throne, and this Oath was imposed in the form, "I, *A B*, do sincerely promise and swear to bear true allegiance to their Majesties King William and Queen Mary" A new Oath of Supremacy was also imposed, which ran in similar terms The Act of Parliament by which the new oath was imposed required that it should be taken by all ecclesiastical persons[1] before August 1st, 1689, under pain of suspension, and if they still refused to take the oath, their benefices were to be declared vacant on February 1st, 1689-90

The position which the clergy were thus placed in was a very difficult one, for they had already promised to bear true allegiance to King James, and although many persons thought that his departure from the kingdom had released them from that allegiance, there were others who considered the oath to be still binding, and the more so because it bound them to the King's direct heir as well as to himself, that heir being now the infant Prince of Wales, and not the Princess of Orange. Some, on reflection, adopted the principle indicated (though at a much later date) by Nicolson, Bishop of Carlisle "Whenever," he writes, "a sovereign *de facto* is universally submitted to and recognized by all the three Estates, I must believe that person to be lawful and rightful monarch of this kingdom, who alone has a just title to my allegiance, and to whom only I owe an oath of fealty" [Bp Nicolson's *Epist Correspond.* ii 387] But although in modern times this principle might be conceded by many persons without hesitation, it was not so easy to act upon it in an age when the displacement of one sovereign by another was a rare occurrence Hence the clashing of the two oaths was a real difficulty to the consciences of a large number of the clergy, as well as to some of the official laity This difficulty is well stated in a letter written by Dr Fitzwilliam, Canon of Windsor and Rector of Cottenham, to Lady Russell, and dated May 13th, 1689 "What now I shall do in this present emergency I am ir-resolved but if having first debated it with myself and advised with my friends, it shall seem most expedient to make such a retreat, I will depend upon your honour's mediation for that favour It may be I have as sad thoughts for the divisions of the Church, and as ardent desires for its peace as any, and let my tongue cleave to the roof of my mouth if I prefer not Jerusalem before my chief joy But I cannot esteem it a good way to seek the attainment of this by any act which shall disturb my own peace In the meantime I entreat you, very good madam, not to call boggling at an oath, clashing against another, as far as I can discern, which I formerly took, an unnecessary scruple I believe, were you under such an engagement, your tenderness and circumspection would be rather greater than mine

"The former oath of allegiance runs thus —'I will bear *faith and true allegiance* to his Majesty King Charles, or King James, *and his heirs and successors, and him and them* will defend.' Of supremacy, 'I will bear *faith and true allegiance* to the King's Highness (Charles or James), *his heirs and lawful successors*, and to my power shall assist and defend all jurisdictions, privileges, pre-eminences, and authorities granted or belonging to the King's Highness, his heirs and successors, or united and annext to the imperial crown of this realm'

"Now I am informed by the Statute 1 Jac c 1 that lineal succession is a privilege belonging to the imperial crown, and by 12 Car II c 30, § 17, that by the undoubted and fundamental laws of this kingdom, neither the Peers of this realm nor the Commons, nor both together, in Parliament, or out of Parliament, nor the people collectively nor representatively, nor any persons whatsoever, hath, or ought to have, any coercive power over the kings of this realm

"The present oath runs thus: 'I will bear true allegiance to their Majesties King William and Queen Mary' Now let any impartial person resolve me whether one of these, King James having abdicated, be his heir or lawful suc-

[1] It should be remembered that the clergy are not required, by the ordinary Statute law, to take the Oath of Allegiance at the accession of a Sovereign, but only when being admitted to benefices

cessor, or could be made so, had the people met either collectively or representatively, which they did neither" [Lady Russell's *Letters*, ed 1792, p 458]

No one can complain that men who had such scruples of conscience on this subject should be willing to give up their bishoprics and their parishes rather than do an act which they considered as wilful perjury And that they did so consider is shewn not only by the costly acts of self-denial to which they submitted, but by the dying words of two bishops of the number "If the oath had been tendered," said Bishop Lake, "at the peril of my life, I could only have obeyed by suffering" "If my heart do not deceive me," said Bishop Thomas, "and God's grace do not fail me, I think I could suffer at a stake rather than take this oath." [*Life of Kettlewell*, 199, 206]

When the first date named in the Act had arrived, seven bishops and a large number of the clergy declined to take the oath, and were consequently suspended from the performance of their duties, but it does not appear that this was done by any proper ecclesiastical process Thomas, Bishop of Worcester, and Cartwright, Bishop of Chester, would have been added to the number, making nine bishops, but they died a short time before During the six months that followed, Lake, Bishop of Chichester, also died, as did some of the inferior clergy, the numbers of the latter being also diminished by the compliance of many under the influence of argument and persuasion The six bishops who remained alive on February 1st, 1689-90, were Sancroft, Archbishop of Canterbury, Ken, Bishop of Bath and Wells, Turner, Bishop of Ely, White, Bishop of Peterborough, Lloyd, Bishop of Norwich, and Frampton, Bishop of Gloucester These were followed by about 400 clergy, the best blood of the Church, the names of most of whom have come down to us [*ibid* App v] A large number of the laity took the same view of the oath of allegiance as that taken by the Nonjuring clergy, but as it would only be tendered to those who were in the service of the Crown, none among them but the latter were called upon to make any sacrifice on account of their opinion

II Some of the Nonjurors looked upon their position as simply a political one, which did not affect their spiritual relations to the Church But the more ardent of them took a different view, and mixed up the idea of the oath with that of orthodoxy, in such a manner as to make it appear that only those were true to the Church who refused to take it. The only shadow of reason for this latter view was, that continued communion with the Church seemed to entail some recognition of the prayers which were offered for the new sovereigns But although it is easy to see that these prayers must have been a burden to the consciences of those Nonjurors who were present at the services of the Church, it is not easy to see how they could constitute so heavy a burden as to make such presence impossible still less, to see how the insertion even of an usurper's name in the prayers—to put the matter in the strongest light possible—could in itself affect the catholicity of the ancient Church So strongly, however, did some of the Nonjurors feel on this point, that they not only declined to attend the services of the Church, but they advocated the immediate formation of a separate communion, for the purpose of continuing what they believed to be the true ancient Church of England, as represented by themselves, in contradistinction to the body which occupied the sees and parishes of the land

Thus far the position assumed by the Nonjurors appears to be justifiable by no reasonable argument but when the sees of the six bishops and the parishes of the 400 clergy were filled up by other bishops and clergy, during the lifetime of incumbents who had not been displaced by any sufficient ecclesiastical process, there was much to be said for those who refused to consider the new-comers in any other light than as schismatical intruders When it was stated by the Nonjurors, for example, that Archbishop Sancroft was really and truly the ecclesiastical head of the Church of England, and that nothing could make Tillotson such during Sancroft's lifetime, they could only be answered by the counter allegation that those who consecrated Tillotson had ecclesiastical authority to give him mission to the see of Canterbury, because the latter had been made vacant by the operation of an Act of Parliament But if an Act of Parliament can thus destroy the spiritual mission of a bishop [DICT *of* THEOL, JURISDICTION], Parliament is indeed supreme, and there seems no good reason left for rejecting its dictum, when it alleged that ordination by presbyters was the same thing as ordination by bishops [NONCONFORMISTS] What is thus said of Tillotson applies also to Kidder, who took possession of the see of Ken (which Beveridge altogether refused to do), and of all the other bishops who assumed spiritual jurisdiction over dioceses the true bishops of which were still living And what is thus said of the bishops is also applicable, in its degree, to those who took the places of the ejected parochial clergy, not one of whom can be considered as lawfully deprived of the cure of souls committed to him Those who framed the Act of Parliament had, in fact, made a great mistake, such as lawyers often make when dealing with ecclesiastical matters, for they omitted to insert a provision directing that Nonjuring clergy should be deprived of their spiritual jurisdiction by a proper ecclesiastical process If the Nonjurors had been thus deprived, there could have been no doubt as to the position of their successors, and though the deprivations might have been still open to the charge of injustice, they would not have been open to the charge of nullity, as they actually were

But notwithstanding this grave error, which left the Nonjuring bishops still responsible for the cure of souls in their dioceses, and the Nonjuring priests for the cure of souls in their parishes, there does not seem to be any instance on record of either bishop or priest endeavouring to carry out their responsibilities in any such complete manner as to justify the claims which they made, or which were made on their behalf Sancroft issued a commission to three of his suffragans to consecrate Burnet to the bishopric of Salisbury, and under this commission the consecration took place on May 31st, 1689. But after the Act of Parliament had come fully into force, Sancroft made no further attempt to carry out his duties, or to assert his spiritual jurisdiction, only remaining at Lambeth until he was turned out, which was little if anything more than an assertion of his temporal rights to his benefice, rights which possibly an Act of Parliament could really extinguish Nor does it appear that any of the other bishops, or any number of the clergy, took this ground They seem to have been surprised into yielding their spiritual charges, and so letting their sees and parishes practically lapse into the hands of those whom they considered unlawful intruders They vacated their spiritual charges as James had vacated his throne, and yet claimed to be still the rightful occupants of the posts they had vacated Thus, if there was a grave error on the part of Parliament in omitting to provide for others doing what Parliament itself could not do, in omitting to release the Nonjuring clergy from their spiritual responsibilities, there was also a grave error on the part of the latter in acting as if they had been so released And while this latter course went far to cut the ground from under their feet, as regards the claim which the Nonjurors asserted to be still the only rightful representatives of the Church in the dioceses and parishes committed to them, so it went far to justify Tillotson and the rest of the intruders in assuming themselves to be rightfully possessed of posts which had thus been suffered to lapse into their hands Even so far the Nonjurors cannot be altogether exonerated from a share in the confusion—very nearly approaching if not actually amounting to schism—which was caused in the six dioceses and 400 parishes, when they were thus provided each with two pastors But many of them, doubtless, took the same line that was taken by Bishop Ken, and quietly retiring from their posts refused to take any part in setting up a rival communion

III The first step which was taken towards placing the Nonjuring clergy in a schismatical position was an imprudent act which Sancroft himself was persuaded to perform, that of delegating to Lloyd, the ejected Bishop of Norwich, that archiepiscopal jurisdiction which he declined to exercise personally This was done by an instrument dated February 9th, 1691-2, when he had allowed his authority to lie dormant for eighteen months, during half of which time Tillotson had been consecrating suffragans for the province, and ordaining and confirming within the diocese of Canterbury, while Sancroft himself had been living the life of a hermit on a small property which he possessed at Fresingfield Under the authority thus delegated to him, Lloyd shortly afterwards took steps for consecrating two bishops, and the consent of the exiled King having been obtained, Hickes, the deprived Dean of Worcester, was consecrated suffragan Bishop of Thetford, and Wagstaffe suffragan Bishop of Ipswich, on February 24th, 1693-4, the consecrating bishops being those who had previously occupied the sees of Norwich, Ely, and Peterborough The consecration took place secretly in a private house, but was witnessed by the Earl of Clarendon, it was known to very few persons, and those in confidence, until the latter part of the year 1710, when all the deprived bishops but Ken being dead, and he having resigned his see, a discussion arose among the Nonjurors as to the continuance of their separation

Upon the death of Ken, that saintly bishop departing to his rest on March 19th, 1710-11, many of the Nonjurors, among whom were Nelson, the well-known author of "Fasts and Festivals," and the learned Henry Dodwell, began again to frequent their parish churches, and gave up all formal connection with the separated party. But another section, led by Hickes, determined to perpetuate the secession, and for that purpose to continue the succession of bishops Hickes and Wagstaffe had been consecrated only as suffragan bishops to Bishop Lloyd, and had therefore no authority after his death in 1710 Wagstaffe himself died in 1712, and Hickes, being thus left as the sole episcopal representative of the Nonjurors, and being then 71 years old, called in the assistance of two Scottish bishops, Campbell and Gadderar, and on Ascension Day, in 1713, these three consecrated Jeremiah Collier, Samuel Hawes, and Nathaniel Spinckes, Scotland thus once more contributing an element of schism to England Hickes died in 1715, and Collier becoming the leader of the now formally constituted sect, Henry Gandy and Thomes Brett were consecrated by him and the other two schismatical bishops on January 25th, 1716

In the following year began the dispute among the Nonjurors respecting the "usages" Collier wrote a tract entitled "Reasons for Restoring some Prayers and Directions as they stand in the Communion Service of the first English Reformed Liturgy," etc. In this he advocated the reintroduction into the Communion Service of the mixed cup, of the Invocation of the Holy Ghost, of the Prayer of Oblation, and of Prayers for the departed, these always having been used by Hickes, who celebrated with the Communion Office of Edward VI First Book, and by Collier himself, while Brett and the Scottish bishop Campbell strongly supported the practice A division thus sprung up in the now small body of Nonjurors, Spinckes and Gandy leading one party, which wished to retain the use of the last Book of Common Prayer, Collier and Brett leading another section, which used the First Book the former party being called "Non-Usagers" and the latter "Usagers" The two parties remained separate, each consecrating several bishops, from the year 1718 to 1733, when a reconciliation took place, though some still continued to be "Usagers" and others "Non-Usagers"

The sect lingered on during the whole of the

eighteenth century, but with continually diminishing numbers and with continually increasing divisions Few priests seem to have been ordained among its members, but the consecration of bishops was kept up, at last in a very irregular and reckless manner, until nearly the close of the century [DICT *of* THEOL. p 515] Among them were many men of great learning, and whose works have been of high value to the Church, especially Hickes and Dodwell as theologians, Collier and Carte as historical writers, Brett as a high authority in liturgical theology, Kettlewell, Nelson, and Law as devotional writers whose influence deeply affected the religion of the Church for a century and a half The Nonjurors appear to have always held their services in private houses, and many of their clergy practised medicine or followed some trade Gordon, the last of their regular bishops, died in 1779, Cartwright, one of the last of the irregular section, practised as a surgeon at Shrewsbury, and was reconciled to the Church at the Abbey there in 1799, by a clergyman who mentioned the circumstance, in his old age, to the present writer Boothe, the last of all their bishops, died in Ireland in 1805, but some small congregations of Nonjurors are said to have existed some years later Many of the last of the Nonjurors, however, attended their parish churches, only reserving to their consciences the privilege of using Prayer Books which had been printed before the Revolution

A strong intimacy was always kept up between the Nonjurors of England and the Episcopalians of Scotland, and they were mostly mixed up with the Jacobite party to a dangerous extent, some of them even suffering for high treason in 1716 and 1745 Not a few of them seceded to the Roman Catholic sect, and when an Act was passed against Recusants, the Nonjurors were included The strong desire for Catholic reunion, which thus impelled them to seek it somewhere, although their political feelings would not permit them to seek it in the Church of England, also led to an attempt being made in 1716 to bring about "a concordat betwixt the orthodox and catholic remnant of the British Churches and the Catholic and Apostolic Oriental Church " The full particulars of this have been printed in Williams' *Orthodox Church of the East in the 17th century*, but the correspondence on the subject fell through in 1725 [*Life of Kettlewell* Bowles *Life of Ken.* D'Oyley's *Life of Sancroft* Lathbury's *History of the Nonjurors*]

NONJURORS, SCOTTISH A party in the Scottish Establishment became known by this name in 1712, on their refusing to take the Oath of Abjuration as enjoined in the Toleration Act passed in that year The oath recognised by implication the conditions of the Succession Act, among which were the provisions that the Sovereign should always be of the communion of the Church of England, and should swear to maintain that Church as by law established Hence, by many amongst the more rigid Presbyterians, the refusing the oath was regarded as a criterion of ministerial faithfulness, and almost as a test of communion In 1719 the oath was modified, in accordance with an address from the Nonjurors themselves, but a few (including T Boston, who wrote *Reasons for refusing the Abjuration Oath in its Latest Form*) still resolutely declined it [CAMERONIANS MARROW MEN.]

NON-USAGERS [NONJURORS]

NORWEGIAN PROTESTANTS [DANISH PROTESTANTS]

NOVATIANS or NOVATIANISTS. A sect which arose at Rome, in the middle of the third century, from a simple spirit of insubordination, and then adopted, as if for its justification, the tenet that the means of grace and reconciliation entrusted to the Church are inapplicable to those who have fallen from the faith in persecution, and to those who have after baptism committed mortal sin

The sect organized itself into a body, and the schism became complete when Novatian, from whom it is named, fell off from Catholic unity, and assumed the position of bishop of Rome, in the reign of the Emperor Decius A succession of schismatic bishops was kept up for nearly three hundred years, not in Rome only, but almost throughout Christendom The sternness of Novatian's refusal to admit the lapsed to penitence was extended by his followers, if not by Novatian himself, to other cases of heinous sin, and to some cases treated as sinful by a mistaken asceticism, such as second marriages In this matter the sect which in other respects of doctrine was orthodox, must be judged heretical From this attempt to enforce a more rigid discipline, they took the name "Cathari,' the Pure, and shewed their schismatic spirit by unchurching the body from which they separated, denying even the validity of the Catholic baptism The spirit of schism manifested itself also, as is usual, in an alliance with the secular power They gained the favour of the heathen government, treated the banishments of bishops by the government as if they were canonical depositions, and thus virtually surrendered the liberties of the Church to the secular arm

Thus the schism of the Novatians involved these three cardinal points · the constitution of the Christian Church, its use of the means of grace and reconciliation, and its relation to the secular power Considering this, and considering the wide extent and long duration of the schism, it is remarkable that there does not remain from original authority any detailed account of its rise and progress Its history must be gathered from unsystematic notices in Cyprian's epistles, from some few epistles of particular bishops and doctors of the Roman, African, and Eastern Churches extant among Cyprian's works, from the remains of some tracts and epistles of Dionysius of Alexandria preserved by Eusebius, from Pacian's epistles, from Ambrose's treatise, *De Pœnitentia*, from a few conciliar determinations, from the occasional notes of Socrates and Sozomen, and from statements of particular points of doctrine or history by Jerome, Augustine, and Basil. By far the greater part of this information comes from opponents, and in the consideration of it, this chapter of Church history, more perhaps than other chapters, is liable to be distorted by the prepossessions of the historian.

The history of this schism must begin with the Carthaginian presbyter Novatus,[1] for with him began the rebellion against episcopal authority That in opposition to Cyprian he advocated lenity, in opposition to Cornelius he advocated rigour, shews that his mercy and his severity arose from his love of rebellion The election of Cyprian to the bishopric of Carthage was opposed by a small but relentless minority Five presbyters in particular carried on their opposition after his consecration [Cypr *Ep* xliii] Whether Novatus was one of these five, is disputed, but if the expression in Ep xliii regarding the five presbyters, "Antiqua illa contra episcopatum meum venena retinentes," be compared with Ep xiv, in which are given the names of four of the schismatical presbyters, Novatus being among them, there will be little doubt of the "existence of only one anti-Cyprian party from the very beginning—a party which held together, and in which Novatus took a conspicuous part" [Neander's *Ch. Hist* Rose's transl i p 241] Novatus first set himself in open opposition to his bishop by procuring the ordination of Felicissimus, and appointing him his deacon, without Cyprian's permission [Cyp *Ep* lii][2] Novatus was now accused of heinous crimes It was said that he had robbed widows and orphans, that he had kicked his wife during her pregnancy and caused the death of her child, that he had allowed his father to starve, and then remain unburied On these charges he was to be tried, but the Decian persecution prevented the trial [Cypr *Ep* lii] Of these charges it can only be said that they are not proved It is as unjust to Cyprian to attribute them to blind passion, to the rancour of controversy, as it is to Novatus to assume them to be true, in their full extent, because Cyprian believed them From Epistle xiv, written during the persecution, after Cyprian had left Carthage, it appears that Novatus and three other of the presbyters wrote to Cyprian concerning the affairs of the diocese A good deal of stress has been laid on the fact that Cyprian calls these four "compresbyteri nostri" He was too just to deny Novatus this title before trial and proof of the charges and sentence given And the inference from these several notices appears to be, that Novatus was waiting trial when the persecution broke out—that the persecution prevented the trial coming on—that Novatus did not immediately flee, which would naturally tell in his favour in the mind of the bishop—that a lull of persecution rendered it likely the trial might come on—that Novatus then retreated—that (as is always the case when men avoid trial) further evidence against him came to light, and convinced Cyprian of the guilt of his presbyter, and caused the stronger language of the later Epistle, the fifty-second Cyprian's retreat from persecution was justifiable, but was open to doubt, and very liable to misrepresentation[3] His opponents were not slow to take advantage of it, and besides traducing the character of their bishop, they increased their numbers by receiving on easier terms than Cyprian would have allowed those who had denied the faith and offered sacrifice, and those who without actually sacrificing had bought certificates of submission Felicissimus was now at the head of the party He resisted Cyprian's commissioners, who were empowered to visit the church and regulate the distribution of the church funds Upon Cyprian's return, he with his party was condemned in a synod of the North-African Church Instead of yielding, he procured the consecration, as rival bishop, of Fortunatus, one of the five presbyters Our subject requires us not to dwell on these events, but to follow Novatus to Rome.

Novatian, whose party Novatus now joined, a presbyter of Rome, had, according to Cornelius' account, been possessed by a devil, had been aided by exorcism, and after a long illness had received baptism as a clinic, but upon his recovery had neglected the rite of confirmation [Cornel *Epist*

[1] Novatian, the presbyter of Rome, is generally called Novatus by the Greek writers Lardner argues that his real name was Novatus [*Credib* note on chap xlvii] It has been said that Lardner confounded the two [Smith's *Dict*, *Novatianus*] This is a mistake Lardner writes, "Novatus of Carthage came to Rome, and joined the party of the Roman presbyter of that name" [*Credib* ch xlvii iii] But the two have often been confounded Natalis Alexander states that Eusebius, Epiphanius and Theodoret confound them, and so Sirmondi writes "Subtilius de Novatianorum conditore disputant Patres Latini, qui Novatum Episcopum Africanum, distinguunt a Novatiano Presbytero Romano Utrumque pro uno habuerunt plerique Græci" [Note in Theod *Hær fab* III v] But it appears only that they called Novatian Novatus They do not ascribe to Novatus of Rome anything proper to Novatus of Carthage

[2] Cyprian's words are "Ipse est qui Felicissimum satellitem suum Diaconum, nec permittente me, nec sciente, sua factione et ambitione constituit" Many historians understand by this a presbyterian ordination by Novatus himself Neander writes that Novatus, with his views, and according to his presbyterian system, might think himself qualified, as a presbyter and president of a church, to perform this It does not seem at all probable that Cyprian would have brooked a presbyterian ordination, though he might be obliged to pass over the irregularity of the ordination by another bishop He allowed Felicissimus to remain in office Bingham's interpretation is therefore adopted [*Antiq* II iii 7] So Pearson also understands Cyprian's words [*Ann. Cypr* p 25] Some have argued, but without sufficient ground, that Novatus was a bishop See the quotation from Sirmondi in foregoing note So also Baronius, Petavius, Labbæus

[3] In considering Cyprian's conduct in this particular, it must be remembered that the persecution was begun by the people, not by the Emperor's edict, which was not issued by Decius until a year after Reasons will be given below for thinking that Cyprian's Christian opponents joined in the popular cry against him In such a state of things there may have been more to justify his retreat than would have been if the persecution had arisen from the edict His remaining with his flock might have provoked the unbelievers to greater violence against them See Cypr *Ep* xliii xiv lix "Oportet nos tamen paci communi consulere, et interdum, quamvis cum tædio animi nostri, deesse vobis, ne præsentia nostri invidiam et violentiam gentilium provocet" [*Ep.* vii]

in Euseb *Hist Eccl* vi 43] There is probably some truth in the reproach of Cornelius (exaggerated as we must believe his letter to be, and uncharitable in several respects as we must feel it), that Novatian was a man of unsocial and savage habits[1] The alleged possession by the devil was—or accompanied—an attack of the solitary and gloomy hypochondriasm of a hard nature, to the unsociability of which the wrestlings of a mind labouring after knowledge would naturally contribute. The rejection of the further means of grace in the ordinances of the Church —the neglect of confirmation implies also the neglect of the Holy Eucharist—indicates a want of humility and true self-knowledge, the proud self-reliance of one who had not altogether unlearned the lessons of heathen philosophy Cyprian's words make it at least very probable, though they do not certainly prove, that Novatian had been trained in the Stoic school[2] [Cypr *Epist* lv] How long this standing aloof from Church communion lasted we do not know But we know that Novatian distinguished himself by his writings in defence of the Catholic faith, and by an ascetic life Fabian, Bishop of Rome, ordained him priest notwithstanding the remonstrance of the clergy, who alleged the law of the Church, that no clinic should be ordained[3] [Cornel *Ep*] As a presbyter Novatian gained much esteem and influence. In the year 250, during the vacancy of the see after the death of Fabian, he was commissioned by the Roman clergy to write a letter in their name to Cyprian [Cypr *Ep* xxx , see *Ep* lv p 102] In this letter, it must be carefully observed, Novatian does not deny absolution to the lapsed at the point of death He argues strongly against hasty absolution, he urges the propriety of doing nothing new before the appointment of a bishop, and says that the Roman clergy " believe that in the meantime, while the grant of a bishop is withheld from them by God, the cause of such as are able to bear the delays of postponement should be kept in suspense, but of such as impending death does not suffer to bear the delay . . to them such cautious and careful help should be ministered, . so that neither ungodly men should praise our smooth facility, nor truly penitent men accuse our severity as cruel" Cyprian quotes the substance of this in brief, "that peace ought to be granted to the lapsed who were sick and at the point of departure "

The story told by Cornelius that Novatian shut himself up in the time of the persecution, and refused to go to the assistance of the sufferers, saying " that he wished to be presbyter no longer, but to follow a different philosophy," if true, is very discreditable. But it does not appear to be consistent with Novatian's character, and is probably, to say the least, much distorted. [See Evans, *Biography of Early Church*, ii p 259]

So stood matters when Cornelius was elected bishop in June 251. Novatian had assured the Church with a solemn oath, that he did not desire the office He was taken at his word There was also good reason for passing him by His literary qualifications would not compensate for the gloomy and unsocial disposition, which was unsuitable to the active and practical nature of the bishop's duties Cornelius was made bishop by the testimony of almost all the clergy, and by the suffrage of the people then present [Cypr *Epist* lv] The exact time of Novatus' appearing in Rome is not known, but it was probably in the beginning of the same year That he joined the party of Novatian in opposition to Cornelius there is no doubt, as to the extent of his influence there is considerable doubt. "The Greek writers, who appear to be well acquainted with the Novatian sect, say nothing of this African Novatus, nor does Cornelius, in the fragments of his letter to Fabius of Antioch preserved by Eusebius, take any notice of him. Indeed, Cornelius, in a letter to Cyprian, mentions this person among other legates in the second deputation sent by his rival from Rome to Africa, but he does not lay anything particularly to his charge and he there actually calls another person (Evaristus) author of the schism[4] [Cypr *Ep* l] It is also apparent from Cyprian's answer to that letter that Cornelius had never sent him any account of the conduct of the African Novatus" [Lardner, *Credib* xlvii. 111] From this silence regarding Novatus it is inferred by Lardner that Cyprian had an exaggerated notion of the powers and importance of the man who had given him so much trouble, and that his statements, such as, *e g*, that Novatus made Novatian bishop as he had made Felicissimus deacon, cannot be relied upon Others, as Neander, accept Cyprian's statements of Novatus' influence, and suppose that it was Novatus' mode of proceeding to be the moving-spring of all troubles, and yet not to set himself but another at the head of the party

Of far greater consequence than the determination of this point is a correct judgment of the change which took place in Novatian's principles His letter, which has been already quoted, allows the reception of penitents in prospect of death, it urges the propriety of waiting for the election of a new bishop before any new rule is made Then he is joined by Novatus, who at Carthage had been on the side of lenity, a bishop is appointed with whom the majority of the Roman clergy agreed, yet we presently find Novatian at

[1] Cornelius relates τὴν ἀκοινωνησίαν αὐτοῦ καὶ λυκοφιλίαν "τὴν ἀκοιν Ita loqui videtur Cornelius propter peculiarem Novatiani opinionem " Constantius, in *Romanorum Pontificum Epistolæ*, quoted by Routh, *Reliq Sac.* iii 53 but the term λυκοφιλία does not seem to agree with this interpretation

[2] "Novatiani philosophiam, per quam ille in naufragium religionis incurrit" [Pacian, *Ep* ii p 197] Ambrose states that the Stoic doctrine of the equality of sins led Novatian to deny penance to lesser sins as well as greater [*de Pœn* I ii]

[3] The existing canon to this effect is of later date, Neocæs xii A D 315 But that it was a re-establishment of the old law of the Church is shewn by the testimony of the Roman clergy It admits an exception, "unless it be for his fidelity and diligence afterwards "

[4] Evaristus was probably one of the consecrators of Novatian [See Routh's note, *Reliq Sac.* iii p 35.]

the head of a party which had altered its principles so entirely as to deny the power of the Church to grant absolution even *in articulo mortis*, and which insisted on its new principle so rigidly as to assert, that the church which did grant this absolution was apostate, and became no church at all This change of principle on the part of Novatian is not to be classed with the changes of Cyprian and Cornelius These were only changes of degree, of more or less strictness or lenity Novatian's change was from a recognition to a denial of the power of the Church The inference to be drawn from the facts is, that the heresy was on account of the schism, not the schism for the sake of the heresy.[1] Jerome's apophthegm is proved true by Church history "Nullum schisma non aliquam sibi confingit hæresim, ut recte ab ecclesia recessisse videatur" [Hieron in *Ep ad Tit*], and Novatian's heresy appears to be no exception Pacian speaks very expressly to the point St Ambrose concurs with him Dionysius of Alexandria puts the schism first St Basil says that "the beginning of their separation was by schism," as distinguished, *i e.*, from heresy [2] These testimonies will outweigh the account given by Socrates, who says that the Novatians deserted Cornelius because he received into communion those who in the time of the Decian persecution had sacrificed to idols [Socrat *Hist Eccl* iv 13] How little the denial of the power of the Church to receive the lapsed was the cause of the schism may be seen from this, that Maximus, who was Novatian's legate from Italy to Africa, and was excommunicated there by the Catholics, was by the Novatians made a bishop in Africa though he had sacrificed [Cypr *Ep* lix pp 132, 133], and from this, that in the year 253, the Novatians communicated with the Lapsi [Cypr *Ep* lxv] We are led therefore to describe the consecration of Novatian as an act of pure schism, without the excuse which a principle put forward, as for the maintenance of holy discipline, might seem to lend it [3] The Novatian doctrine of repentance was a new heresy upon a schism Pacian writes that Novatian was first stimulated and provoked by his envy, and could not endure Cornelius' episcopal government over him, whereupon he gave himself up to Novatus [*Ep* ii *ad Sempron*]

Under these circumstances we may well believe that Novatian's consecration was procured by secret, underhand and treacherous dealings. The account which Cornelius gives of the transaction is, that Novatian's agents persuaded three distant Italian bishops to come to Rome to act as mediators between the two parties, feasted and intoxicated them on their arrival, and then compelled them to perform the consecration[4] [Euseb *Hist Eccl* vi 43] Cyprian, contrasting the conduct of Cornelius and Novatian, states that the latter used force and violence "Non, ut quidam, vim facit ut episcopus fieret, sed ipse vim passus est, ut episcopatum conatus acciperet" [Cypr *Ep* lv] Of the three consecrators, one not long afterwards, returned to the Church, mourning and confessing his error He was admitted to lay communion The other two were deposed Many of the Roman confessors had sided with Novatian Cornelius was soon able to inform Cyprian of their return to the unity of the Church [Cypr *Ep* xlix]

Novatian and Fortunatus[5] followed the custom of the Church in notifying their election to other sees, and Novatian was anxious to be recognised by the three great Churches of Carthage, Antioch,

[1] The controversy no doubt had arisen before Novatian's consecration [see Routh's note, *Reliq Sacr* iii p 42], but it would not have assumed such importance, the point in dispute would not have been made the "articulus stantis vel cadentis ecclesiæ," except for the sake of justifying the schism

[2] "Tu postquam a reliquo corpore segregatus es, et a matre divisus, ut facti tui rationem redderes totos librorum recessus, assiduus scrutator, inquiris. Occulta quæque solicitas, quicquid exinde securum est inquietas" [Pacian, *Ep* iii p 199] Again, having related Novatian's earlier opinions, as shewn in his letter to Cyprian, Pacian writes "Si nemo vobis Cornelium prætulisset, maneret illa Novatiani scribentis auctoritas, nunc displicet tota sententia" [*ib* p 202] 'Qui ideo, ut dicitis, in ecclesiam non convenitis, quia per pœnitentiam tributa spes fuerat his qui lapsi sunt, revertendi Sed hoc prætentum est specie Ceterum episcopatus amissi dolore succensus Novatianus schisma composuit" [Ambr *de Pœnit* I xv 85, Bened edit Eusebius *H E* vii 8 Basil, *Can. Epist* i, *ad Amphil*] This conclusion agrees with the tenor of Cyprian's letter to Antonianus [*Ep* lv] Pacian states that he took his narrative from Cyprian's Epistles, and he appears to have had access to letters not now extant See *Historical Collections conc District Successions*, p 179, and the note in Benedictine edit of Ambrose, *loc. cit*

[3] Pacian states that Novatian assumed episcopal authority upon the receipt of a letter from the confessors, without consecration "Novatianus quem absentem Epistola episcopum finxit, quem, consecrante nullo, linteata sedes accepit" [ii p 196] "Sine consecratione legitima episcopum factum, ideoque nec factum per Epistolam eorum qui se confessores esse simularent" [p 198] "Novatus ex Africa Romam venit, et cum apud Carthaginem, urgentibus in ecclesia fratribus, dies cognitionis ipsius immineret, et hic latitavit · nec multo post Novatianum istum episcopatu Cornelii anxium, (nam sibi speraverat) cum aliquantis, ut in tali re solet, ex sua parte fautoribus nutantem impellit, dubitantem fovet, invenit aliquos ex eorum numero qui tempestatem persecutionis illius evaserunt, apud quos hanc ipsam de lapsis receptis Cornelio conflaret invidiam dat eorum Epistolas ad Novatianum ille ex auctoritate epistolarum, sedente jam Romæ Episcopo, adversum fas, sacerdotii singularis alterius Episcopi sibi nomen assumit Cornelium lapsis communicasse arguit se vindicat innocentem" [iii p 202] This account is quite compatible with that given above Novatian thus assuming the title of bishop, would soon find a consecration necessary, and procure it by any means The account indicates (if true) not settled presbyterian principles, but a disbelief of the necessity of any ordination whatever Theodoret states that Novatian went himself into Italy to find and bring the three bishops This is contradicted by Cornelius' account of the transaction

[4] Cornelius describes the conduct of the principal thus οὗτος γὰρ ὁπηνίκα περισπᾶσθαι τε καὶ ὑφαρπάζειν τὴν μὴ δοθεῖσαν αὐτῷ ἄνωθεν ἐπισκοπὴν ἐπεχείρει, κ τ λ of the agents, ὥρᾳ δεκάτῃ μεθύοντας καὶ κραιπαλῶντας μετὰ βίας ἠνάγκασεν. It appears to be the ordinary case of agents effecting the principal's wishes by means he had not directly sanctioned The proportions of guilt man cannot assign

[5] Fortunatus sent Felicissimus and others to Rome on this errand [Cypr *Ep* lix]

and Alexandria His legates arrived at Carthage while a council was sitting, and were at once repelled [Cypr *Ep* xliv], upon the representation of four African bishops, who at the same time returned from Rome, where, with fourteen others, they had been present at the election of Cornelius, and now bore testimony to the validity of that election [1] The letter of Cornelius to Fabius of Antioch, which has been quoted so often, was probably a reply to inquiries of Fabius in consequence of a missive from Novatian Dionysius of Alexandria answers Novatian, "If as you say, you were forced against your will, you will shew it by retiring voluntarily" [Euseb *Hist Eccl* vi 45]

The Novatians now endeavoured to support their cause by assuming the appearance of superior sanctity They restricted the power of the keys, denying at first its extension to those who had apostatized in persecution, then to those who committed certain greater crimes after baptism The power of binding and loosing was in fact ultimately limited to the remission of sins in baptism [2] They took the title of Cathari, and asserted that all besides themselves had forfeited their catholicity They rebaptized those who joined them This shew of sanctity and rigour of discipline doubtless prevailed with some some it alienated, of whom an example is given by Socrates, who reports that Atticus of Constantinople drew the distinction between Novatian and his followers, approving the refusal of communion to those who had sacrificed, condemning the refusal to the laity who had been guilty of less heinous crimes [Socrates, *Hist Eccl* vii 25]

The great cause of the rapid increase of this sect was that they gained the secular power to their side, enabling them to form themselves into a corporation to purchase lands and build churches, and further protecting them by law in invading not only the sees of the Catholics and their spiritual rights, but their temporalities also, which the schismatics were enabled to use for carrying on their schism This appears from Constantine's edict of restitution, which will be quoted below Decius declared his mortal and irreconcilable hatred to Cornelius He had put Fabian to death, and "would rather hear of a rival prince than of a priest of God setting himself up at Rome" [Cypr *Ep* lv]

From the tenor of Dionysius' reply to Novatian it appears that Novatian asserted (with what truth we are not able to say) that he was compelled by the Emperor's threats to accept the bishopric, for Dionysius tells him it is a duty to suffer anything, even martyrdom, rather than to afflict the Church of God Novatian could not have pretended that he was in danger of martyrdom from the Roman clergy if he refused to be made bishop But it is uncertain how far Novatian's letter of excuse told the whole truth The exemption of the Novatians, however, from persecution under Gallus and Volusianus can hardly be accounted for on any other supposition than that of favour shewn from the first to Novatian as the rival of Cornelius Decius' death was late in the year 251 Persecution then ceased for about seven months, and recommenced upon the refusal of the Christians to sacrifice at the heathen altars of propitiation In August 252, Cyprian wrote to Cornelius, who was then in exile, and his letter contrasts the sufferings of the Catholics with the rest the heretics enjoyed [*Ep* lx] Now we do not suspect the Novatians of sacrificing, and that their refusal to sacrifice was overlooked can be attributed only to some earlier concordat with the government If they had been persecuted under Decius' government, although they were Cornelius' rivals, it is difficult to assign the ground on which such a concordat can have been made in the seven months of rest It is far easier to suppose that they were favoured from the first as enemies of Cornelius Novatian retired from Rome, it is true, at the time of the Decian persecution, but if he left his followers under persecution, a letter on Jewish meats, without one word of exhortation to constancy and patience, was surely a singular mode of seeking to edify them His retirement may have been only to save appearances

In Carthage, early in the year 251, the five presbyters who opposed Cyprian were associated with the magistrates in an edict, says Cyprian, that they might overthrow our faith, and turn away the hearts of the brethren [*Ep* xliii] This makes it more probable that a like course was pursued at Rome Cyprian's *Epistle to Lucius* [lxi] speaks also of the freedom which the Novatians enjoyed, God's secret ordering so contrived it, he says, that the punishment was a test which distinguished the true Church, the devil attacked only the soldiers and fortresses of Christ, he passed by the heretics once prostrated and already made his own He expressly limits the persecution to the Church of Christ and its bishop Cornelius

It is to feared then that, as at Carthage the heretical presbyters joined the magistrates against Cyprian, so at Rome the Novatians joined the secular power in this persecution for the sake of removing the Catholic bishops, and setting themselves as successors in their sees How far the Novatians profited by the persecution and availed themselves of it, is at least clear from the laws we are now to name, which prove that they had churches, cemeteries, and houses, possessed by them a long time as their freehold, even from the beginning of their schism, some of which belonged to the Catholic bishops and clergy.

[1] Fabius at first seemed to incline to the new schism, but was saved from it by Dionysius A council met at Antioch, where certain persons were trying to establish the schism [Euseb *H E* vi 44, 46]

[2] Novatian wrote circular letters to the churches, urging them to refuse communion with those who had sacrificed, but the terms of the letters included all cases of the commission of "peccata mortalia" [Soc iv 18] Neander accordingly writes that Novatian had probably intended from the first this whole class of sins Accordingly the office of penitentiaries was abolished or dropped by them *οἷς οὐλόγος μετανοίας, οὐδὲν τούτου ἐδέησεν* [Sozom *H E* vii 16]

Constantine's law is rather favourable than otherwise to the sect. "Novatianos non adeo comperimus prædamnatos, ut iis, quæ petiverunt, crederemus minime largienda Itaque ecclesiæ suæ domos et loca sepulchris apta sine inquietudine eos firmiter possidere præcipimus ea scilicet, quæ ex diuturno tempore vel ex empto habuerunt, vel qualibet quæsiverunt ratione Sane providendum erit ne quid sibi usurpare conentur ex his, quæ ante dissidium ad ecclesias perpetuæ sanctitatis pertinuisse manifestum est" Dat vii Kal Oct Spoleti, Constantino A vii, et Constantio C Coss [A D 326][1] The law of Theodosius the younger and Valentinian III is general "Hæreticorum ita est reprimenda insania, ut ante omnia quas ab orthodoxis abreptas tenent ubicunque ecclesias, statim catholicæ ecclesiæ tradendas esse non ambigant, quia ferri non potest, ut, qui nec proprias habere debuerant, ab orthodoxis possessas aut conditas suaque temeritate invasas ultra detineant" Section 2 proceeds "Posthæc quoniam non omnes eadem austeritate plectendi sunt, Arianis quidem, Macedonianis et Apollinarianis, quorum hoc est facinus, quod nocenti meditatione decepti credunt de veritatis fonte mendacia, intra nullam civitatem ecclesiam habere liceat, Novatianis autem et Sabbatianis (the Sabbatians were the Judaizing Novatians) omnis innovationis adimatur licentia, si quam forte tentaverint, Eunomiani vero . . . et Manichæi nusquam in Romano solo conveniendi orandique habeant facultatem," Dat iii Kal Jun Constantinopoli, Felice et Tauro Coss [A D 428]. [*Cod Theod* lib xvi. tit v legg I 65] The first and third clauses of this latter section referring to holding places of worship, the meaning of "innovatio" in the second clause must be trespass upon the Catholic churches, and change of their destination from Catholic worship to heretical

The sixth title also of the same book, "Ne sanctum baptisma iteretur," appears to refer primarily to the Novatians, as the chief sect which then rebaptized The first law of Valentinian and Valens [A D 373] declares the Antistes who rebaptizes to be unworthy of the priesthood, the second, of Valens, Gratian, and Valentinian [A D 377], condemning rebaptism, proceeds, "Eos igitur auctoritas tua erroribus miseris jubebit absistere, ecclesiis, quas contra fidem retinent, restitutis catholicis." The law is directed "ad Flavianum Vicarium Africæ."[2] From all this it may be concluded that the Novatians did what the Donatists and Arians did—the Donatists courted Julian the Apostate, the Arians complied not only with the Meletian schismatics, but with the heathens, to make their party stronger. [DONATISTS ARIANS] It is indeed the natural and common course of schismatical action

To this favour shewn by the emperors and their governments is to be attributed the increase of the sect, after the severe blow which it received when the confessors returned to the Catholic Church[3] The error of the confessors it is not difficult to understand "It is natural for men who have distinguished themselves in any way from the rest to consider themselves an exclusive party Where this distinction is of a dangerous nature they consider themselves as the elect, and are fain to shew their election visibly to the world, as well as palpably to represent it to themselves, by drawing a line between themselves and the general body The martyrs, therefore, sometimes as weak in understanding as they were strong in resolution, were a ready prey to the flattery of such as wished to use them for the instruments of schism" [Evans' *Biog of Early Church*, ii. p 273][4] The error lasted but a short time Cyprian's interposition was successful, the confessors publicly acknowledged their fault, and submitted to the rightful authority of Cornelius [Cypr *Ep* xlvi. xlvii xlix]

The letter of Dionysius of Alexandria, given by Eusebius [*H E* vii 5], and Eusebius' words introducing it, have been quoted to prove a rapid decline of the party We venture to think that this arises from misinterpretation Eusebius represents the Churches of the East as averse to the innovations of Novatian, and as at peace among themselves, that is, on the point of the re-baptism of heretics This question had caused an interruption of communion and the restoration of communion among themselves, not the return of the majority of the Novatians to the Church, appears to be the peace which Dionysius refers to There are many proofs of the wide extension of the Novatian body Cyprian writes thus "Per plurimas civitates novos apostolos suos mittit . ille super episcopos in persecutione proscriptos creare alios pseudo-episcopos audet" [*Ep* lv] We have no complete catalogue of these intruding bishops, but we meet with them frequently in history. Maximus at Carthage [Cyp *Ep* lix], Acesius of Constantinople [Socr *Hist Eccl* I vii], Agelius of Constantinople [*ibid* v 12], Leontius of Rome [*ibid* v 14], are examples "Socrates speaks of their sees at Constantinople, Nice, Nicomedia, and Cotiæus in Phrygia, as the chief sees of the sect in the fourth century, in the East at least, for

[1] Sozomen mentions a severe law of Constantine, about the year 331, in which the Novatians are placed at the head of the worst heresies, the Montanists, Valentinians, Marcionites, Paulianists, all these are forbidden to hold public or private assemblies, their oratories are confiscated, their leaders banished [Sozom *Hist. Eccl.* ii 30]

[2] Jerome speaks of Novatian's remaining at this time "nudatus et pene solus"

[3] It would appear from Eusebius that Moses, confessor, and afterwards martyr, renounced communion with Novatian and his five presbyters after their formal schism had taken place [Euseb *Hist. Eccl* vi 43] But see Pearson's *Ann Cyp*, *anno* 251, for the date of Moses' death

[4] Evans ascribes to the desperation which Novatian felt at his adherents thus deserting him, the impiety, which Cornelius relates, of forcing communicants in the Holy Eucharist to swear that they would not return to Cornelius [*Biogr Early Church*, ii 283] It is difficult to believe the story, and the tone of Cornelius' letter makes one judge that he would not be very careful in examining the evidence on which it rested.

he supposeth them besides very numerous in the West The pieces written against them by St Ambrose, Pacian, the anonymous author of the Questions out of the Old and New Testament, the notice taken of them by Basil, Gregory Nazianzen, the accounts given of them by Socrates and Sozomen, are proofs of their being numerous, and in most parts of the world, in the fourth and fifth centuries Eulogius of Alexandria wrote against them not long before the end of the sixth century ' [Lardner, *Credib* part II ch xlvii]

In Phrygia, where on account of the national character and manners of the people the Novatian sect greatly flourished, a subordinate schism took place through the introduction of the Quartodeciman dispute It began under Valentinian and Valens, *i e* about A D 270, when a small synod at Pazus, a village at the source of the Sangaris, decreed that the Jewish Paschal reckoning should be adopted The leading Novatian bishops were not present at this synod, and the matter appears to have rested until, under Valentinian II and Theodosius, the question was again brought up by a presbyter, Sabbatius, a convert from Judaism Marcian, his bishop, called a council to consider the subject. The council declared the point to be indifferent, and no just cause of separation or of breach of communion Sabbatius would not yield He gathered followers, and was made bishop (by what consecrators does not appear), although he had before taken an oath that he would not be consecrated [Socr *Hist Eccl* iv 13, v 20, Sozom *Hist Eccl* vi 24, vii 18] These Quartodeciman Novatians appear to have coalesced with the Montanists, their notions of discipline being nearly the same, but we are not told whether in this coalition the Novatians adopted the Montanist new prophecy, or the Montanists abandoned it.

The formal action of the Church regarding the Novatian sect was as follows Immediately upon the consecration of Novatian a council was called at Rome by Cornelius in the year 251 Sixty bishops and as many presbyters assembled Novatian and his followers were declared to be separated from the Church, and it was decreed that the brethren who had fallen were to be admitted to the remedies of repentance [Euseb *Hist. Eccl* vi 43] Eusebius states that the epistles of Cornelius shew not only the transactions of the Council of Rome, but the opinions of all those in Italy and Africa The opinions of the Africans were delivered in a council, A D 251, mentioned by Cyprian, *Ep* lvii , and Jerome speaks of three councils, supposing that the opinions of the Italians were formally delivered also in an Italian Council At Antioch also a council was held, A D 253, which came to the same determination It was summoned by Fabius, but he died before it met, and it was held by his successor Demetrianus [Euseb *Hist. Eccl* v 46]

The Council of Nicæa assigned to the Cathari their place in the Church upon reconciliation Canon viii decreed that those already ordained should continue to rank among the clergy,[1] upon written promise that they would adhere to the decrees of the Catholic Church, that is, that they would communicate with those who had married a second time, and those who had lapsed under persecution, to whom a term of penance had been assigned In places where there were no other clergy they were to remain in their order; where there was a bishop or priest of the Catholic Church that bishop was to retain his dignity, the Novatian bishop having the honour of a priest, unless the bishop should think fit to allow him the nominal honour of episcopate, otherwise the bishop was to provide for him the place of a chorepiscopus, or of a priest, so that there should not be two bishops in one city [2]

The Council of Laodicea, A D 367, directs that the Novatians are not to be received until they have anathematized all heresy, especially that in which they have been engaged Their communicants, having learnt the creeds and having been anointed with the chrism, may then partake of the holy mysteries [can vii] The Council of Constantinople, A D 381, receives "the Sabbatians and Novatians who call themselves Cathari,[3] if they give in a written renunciation of their errors, and anathematize heresy, by sealing them with the holy chrism on forehead, eyes, nose, mouth, and ears, with the words, *The Seal of the Gift of the Holy Spirit*" [can vii] The Council of Telepte (Thala in Numidia), A D 418, decreed "Ut venientes a Novatianis vel Montensibus per manus imposi-

[1] ὥστε χειροθετουμένους αὐτοὺς μένειν οὕτως ἐν τῷ κλήρῳ There is considerable doubt as to the meaning of these words Balsamon, Zonaras, and after them Beveridge and Routh, understand them in the sense given above Routh [*Opusc* ii p 437] adopts Beveridge's note Dionysius Exiguus, Justel, and lately Robertson [*Hist of Church,* i p 123], understand that the Novatian clergy are to be admitted by imposition of hands, that is, the validity of their orders is to be allowed, and the imposition of hands is a ceremony of reconciliation But again, Theophilus of Alexandria, about A D 385, in the exposition of canons, or supernumerary canons, states that the Council of Nicæa ordered such to be reordained, and directs this rule to be followed if their life be upright This makes the Novatian orders in themselves null, but allows them to be a title for Catholic orders [Hardouin, i 2000]

[2] It may be noticed that the *Præfatio Arabica* mentions the washings, purifications, and fastings of the Cathari , and states that, while they preserved the faith and retained the Scriptures, they asserted that there was no place for repentance of sin after baptism, and consequently admitted none to absolution [Hardouin, *Concil* i 1018 B]

[3] In Cardinal Pitra's *Juris Eccl Græc Historia et Monumenta* is the following note, i p 438 "Catharos hic vocari Novatianos non dubitatur, tum etiam impositionem manuum non de confirmationis sacramento juxta Morini sententiam, sed de ecclesiastica ordinatione esse intelligendam Cave autem ne vetere deceptus interprete ad iteratam referas quæ recte ad receptam antea a Novatianis ordinationem pertinent '*Placuit magnæ synodo eos jam ordinatos sic manere,*' id est, sic ut sunt ordinati Ita recte synodus vi Carthagin Græca verti jussit. Vid imprimis Ballerini in Ep S Leonis 167, not 13 Innocentius vero I pp rom tetigit hunc canonem in epist apud Sozom viii 26, tum etiam Augustinus in Epist 100, qua candide fatetur se quid hic prohiberetur, ignoravisse "

tionem suscipiantur, ex eo quod rebaptizant" [Brun's *Canones Apost et Concil* i p 154] The sixth of Carthage [A D 419] enforced and explained Nic I viii, see last note The second of Arles [A D 452] directs that a Novatian shall not be received into communion without undergoing penance for his disbelief, and condemning his error [can ix] Of these the Constantinopolitan canon is to be noticed as determining, against St. Basil, the validity of Novatian baptism [1] In Basil's first canonical epistle, to Amphilochius, canons i and xlvii involve this point There are several difficulties regarding their interpretation, but thus much seems to be clear that Basil proceeded on the general principle of the invalidity of lay baptism, and, arguing that the Cathari had no longer the communication of the Holy Ghost, having broken the succession, that being schismatics, they were become laymen, he ordered them (at least such of them as had received only Novatian baptism) to be received into the Church by baptism The first Council of Arles [A D 314] had laid down the principle that those baptized in the name of the Holy Trinity should be received by imposition of hands [can. viii.].

There must be noticed, lastly, the conduct of several distinguished prelates towards the Novatians as recorded by Socrates. Cyril of Alexandria, we are told, shut up their churches, and took away all their sacred vessels and ornaments, and deprived Theopemptus, their bishop, of all that he had Innocent I persecuted them at Rome, and took from them many churches. Celestinus followed the same course [Socrat *Hist Eccl* vii 7, 9, 11] The particulars of these transactions we do not know, but after the proofs we have had of the violent intrusion of the schismatics into Catholic churches, it is as easy to suppose, and is far more likely, that what Socrates represents as persecution and robbery was only discipline and restitution The Novatians suffered together with the Catholics in the Arian persecution under Constantius about the year 356

Such are the main points which have come down to us of the history of the Novatians From this contention the Catholic system of the Church, deeply rooted and thoroughly compact in all its parts, came forth victorious, and the Novatians were reduced to an inconsiderable party about the middle of the fifth century

[1] We have called this canon a Constantinopolitan Canon, as it is usually so classed, but probably it was not passed by any council before the Quinisextine See Beveridge's note One of Beveridge's arguments is founded on the mention of the SABBATIANS

It remains only to define the heresy which was superadded to this schism. Several authors have ascribed to Novatian a denial of the possibility of salvation to those who after baptism fall into the greater or deadly sins That this is an exaggeration is shewn by Petavius, and our limits compel us simply to refer to his Essay Novatian denied that the Church can reconcile them. It has already been pointed out that Novatian's change of opinion on this point was not a change of degree of rigour of discipline, but a change of principle, and his new principle must be judged heretical Cyprian did not scruple to call Novatian a heretic, and the great Dionysius, whose proceedings were both cautious and charitable, wrote thus —"It is with good reason that we detest Novatian for rending asunder (as he has done) the Church, drawing some of the brethren into impieties and blasphemies, introducing a novel and most impious doctrine respecting God, traducing our most kind Lord Jesus Christ as devoid of pity, and in addition to all this, setting at nought the holy laver, subverting the faith and confession which precedes it, and utterly putting to flight from among them the Holy Spirit" [Euseb *Hist Eccl* vii 8]

The Church being the Body of Christ, where there is a possibility of salvation there must be in the same degree the possibility of reconciliation to the Church The means of grace being in and through the Church, repentance has by God's promise a valid title to be met by the ordinances of the Church. Holy men will differ as to the due period of penance to refuse reconciliation and the means of grace altogether, involves a denial of God's mercy either primarily, which in terms Novatian was not guilty of, or secondarily, in the denial of His mercy through the Church And those who consider the office and nature of the Church, and the extent of the power of the keys, cannot but judge it heretical to assert that the covenant of mercy in the Church has narrower limits than the primary mercy of God in Christ.

NUDIPEDES [EXCALCEATI]

NYCTAGES A name derived from νυστάζειν or νυκτάζειν, and given to those who repudiated the night hours of prayer, on the ground that as the day is divinely ordained for work, so the night is equally ordained for rest and sleep [Isidor *de Hæres* lxiv, Paulus, *de Hæres* lii, Ebrard *in Bibl Max.* xxiv. 1577] They are also spoken of under the name of Dormitantes by St. Jerome in his treatise against Vigilantius.

O

OCCAMITES The school of English Nominalists, or rather the revivers of Nominalism, who followed William of Occham's lead in the first half of the fourteenth century, and whose opposition to Realism brought about the decline of scholastic philosophy [SCHOOLMEN]

OCKWALLISTS [UCKWALLISTS]

ODIANS. [AUDIANS]

OLD BELIEVERS [STAROVERTZI]

OLD CATHOLICS The Old Catholic movement originated in Germany, where it still has its headquarters, though it now extends over other Catholic countries of Europe, and beyond it And it is necessary, in order to understand its true nature and significance, to go back some years and examine briefly the remoter causes out of which it sprung When both Catholic and Protestant theology woke from the long religious sleep of the last century, they were at once brought face to face with each other in their revived energy in the mixed religious society and mixed universities of Germany, and thus a spirit of honest scientific inquiry was engendered, which soon came to be viewed with great jealousy at Rome. The Congregation of the Index, whose arbitrary and unintelligent method of procedure was exposed some years ago in the posthumous Letters of one of its Austrian Consultors [*Briefe aus Rom* von Dr Flir, Innsbruck, 1864], was set to work, and few distinguished names among the Catholic divines of Germany, such as Hermes and Gunther, escaped its censure As a rule they were condemned unheard, without explanation of reasons or opportunity of appeal, and for the most part they made a formal submission, and so the matter ended Some years ago, however, a book on the Soul was published by Dr Froschammer, of Munich, based on copious authorities from Fathers and Catholic divines, which for some unexplained reason was placed on the Index He requested information as to the grounds of the sentence, which was, as usual, peremptorily refused, and on his declining, under these circumstances, to make an unconditional *ex animo* submission, he found himself (in 1863) *ipso facto* excommunicated This occurrence may have helped to precipitate the crisis, though Dr Froschammer, who has now abandoned the standpoint of Christian belief altogether, never had any connection with the Old Catholic movement, except as its bitter assailant both in the *Contemporary Review* and in various German periodicals In September 1863 a Conference of about a hundred Catholic scholars and divines (which Dr Froschammer did not attend) was held in the Benedictine abbey at Munich, under the presidency of Dr Dollinger, and with the full sanction of the archbishop, who sang high mass at the opening It was designed at once to form a bond of union between the Catholic divines of Germany and to illustrate the real harmony of scientific and religious truth The president's inaugural address [*Die Vergangenheit und Gegenwart der kath Theologie*], which has unfortunately never been translated into English, but of which an excellent summary appeared in the *Home and Foreign Review* for January 1864, contains a masterly sketch of the growth of Catholic theology from the Alexandrian school of the second century down to our own days It was however unfavourably received by the party who have the ear of Rome, and early in 1864 a Papal Brief was addressed to the Archbishop of Munich, denouncing the methods and spirit of German theology, and asserting the absolute supremacy of scholasticism and of the Roman Congregations. This was understood on all sides as a censure of the Munich Conference, which accordingly did not meet again in that year, as had been intended, and when, some months later, the now famous *Syllabus* was issued, it was felt that war to the knife with Catholic Germany had been proclaimed by the authorities at Rome

It was not to be expected that the German Catholic divines would acquiesce in the finality of a verdict almost avowedly intended to suppress them It could only become final on the assumption of Papal infallibility, which they had never accepted, and which, though a popular Ultramontane opinion, was no doctrine of the Church But the Jesuits, who for the last twenty-five years have been supreme at Rome, were resolved to enforce, in its fullest and most obnoxious sense, the teaching of the *Syllabus*, which, in fact, was their own work [see *Stimmen aus Maria Laach*, Freiburg im Breisgau, 1868-70], and they had for years been sedulously pioneering the way for a definition which would summarily dispose of all controversies by the infallible arbitrament of Rome The main outlines of their policy are traced in the earlier pages of Janus [*The Pope and the Council*, Rivingtons], and its results may be studied at length in the *Letters of Quirinus* [Rivingtons],

Old Catholics

which Bishop Strossmayer has declared to be "the truest compendium of the proceedings of the Vatican Council" which he has seen When in 1868 a General Council was summoned for the ensuing year, there could be little doubt of its real object, though no hint of it was given in the Bull of Indiction, and a series of papers which appeared early in 1869 in the *Civiltà Cattolica*, the authorized Jesuit organ of the Holy See, raised suspicion into moral certainty A Catholic writer in the *Allgemeine Zeitung* replied in what now forms the earlier portion of *Janus*, and in the summer of the same year an influentially signed address from Catholic laymen at Coblentz, combating the Jesuit programme for the Council, was presented to the Bishop of Trèves In September the German bishops issued a joint Pastoral from Fulda, declaring against any doctrinal innovations It is not our business here to write the history of the Vatican Council, which met on December 8th, 1869 Suffice it to say, that the 55 *Schemata* to be laid before it had been carefully prepared beforehand, in strict secrecy, under Jesuit auspices Two of them, after undergoing some modifications, were passed—the *Schema de Fide*, on April 24th, and the *Schema de Ecclesiâ*, including the chapters on the supreme universal jurisdiction and infallible teaching of the Pope, on July 13th, by 451 *placets* against 88 *non-placets*, and 61 conditional votes, while 91 members abstained from voting at all The minority bishops handed in a protest, and left Rome before the Solemn Session of July 18th, when the voting was of course all but unanimous Their objections, both to the dogma and the validity of the Council, may be seen at length in the official *Synopsis Analytica Observationum*, reprinted in Friedrich's *Documenta ad Illustrandum Conc Vat* [Nordlingen 1871], and summarized in Lord Acton's *Sendschreiben an einen deutschen Bischoff* [Nordlingen 1870] Nevertheless, within a short time, nearly all of them outwardly succumbed, though the Austrian bishops and some others have never made any pretence of enforcing the decrees Bishop Hefele held out for nearly a twelvemonth, when he was reduced by a refusal to renew his quinquennial faculties, Archbishop Darboy was murdered by the Commune, Bishop Strossmayer still remains firm In August 1870 the North German bishops assembled at Fulda, and issued a Pastoral promulgating the Vatican decrees, thereby, as Professor Reinkens has expressed it, "affirming the precise opposite of their Pastoral of the previous year, and of their declarations at Rome" This public announcement that no help could be looked for from the bishops proved the signal for a vigorous resistance to the new articles of faith Lord Acton's Letter, already referred to, appeared a month afterwards, and in the same month appeared what may be called the first Old Catholic manifesto, publicly rejecting the Vatican decrees, issued by a large body of Catholic professors at Nuremberg It may be found at length in the article on "The Altkatholik Movement" in the *Theological Review* for Jan 1872

The time was now come for Dollinger, whose studious and Conservative instincts and his habitual deference to authority would have made him shrink from courting such a position, to be forced to the front of the contest The Archbishop of Munich, on his return from Rome, had summoned the Theological Faculty, and called on them for their adhesion to the Vatican decrees, which was refused [Friedrich's *Tagebuch*, pp 389, *sq*], but all except two had subsequently succumbed, including Haneberg, Abbot of St Boniface, who has since been made Bishop of Spires By the end of March [1871] the two recalcitrants, Dollinger and Friedrich, were required to make their formal submission, and on March 29th Dollinger handed in his famous *Erklarung* (a full translation of which may be read in the *Union Review* for May 1871), which at once struck a chord that vibrated throughout Catholic Germany It announced his definite rejection of the dogma of papal infallibility, as contrary to Scripture and Tradition, based on spurious authorities, condemned by the Councils of Constance and Basle, and incompatible with the existing civil order of European States On Palm Sunday [April 2nd] a Pastoral was read in all the churches of Munich condemning his views He pontificated for the last time on Easter Sunday in the Chapel Royal, and received on the same day an address of sympathy from the Catholic Professors of the University On Easter Monday a public meeting to express sympathy with him was held in the Museum, and an address to the King denouncing the new dogma received 12,000 signatures The Archbishop declared all the signataries to be *ipso facto* excommunicate, and on April 18th pronounced the greater excommunication against Dollinger by name, as a formal heretic Friedrich had been already excommunicated The "venerable Nestor of Catholic theology" was thus placed, by no choice of his own at the head of the movement which was now fairly begun In Whitsun week he presided over a preliminary conference of Catholic divines from various parts of Germany held at Munich, which set forth the aims and principles of the movement in a programme forming the basis of that afterwards adopted by the first Old Catholic Congress In this document the validity of censures pronounced on priests or laymen for rejecting the Vatican Council is openly denied And accordingly, when a Munich professor who died in the following June, Dr Zenger, was refused the last sacraments by his parish priest, on account of his having signed the address to Dr Dollinger, Dr Friedrich administered them to him, and performed the rites of burial in the presence of 20,000 persons, including nearly all his colleagues in the professoriate. He was also called on to marry couples who were refused on similar grounds by the parish priests, and a petition with 18,000 signatures, chiefly of heads of families, was presented to the Government on the subject But although several members of the Bavarian Chambers and Cabinet had taken part in the Whitsuntide meeting, and the Government had declined the request of the bishops to set aside Dr Dollinger's election in July as *Rector Magnificus* of the University, by the unprecedented majority of 54 votes against 6, it was not till the end of August that an official note was issued by Herr von Lutz, the Minister of Worship, intimating that the Government did not recognise the legal validity of the Vatican decrees, and would maintain the rights of its Catholic subjects, whether clergy or laity, who rejected them The action of the Government has however throughout been undecided and evasive, and Professor Huber observed at the Congress of Cologne last September [1872] that if they had talked less and done more, half Munich would long ago have openly joined the movement.

The first Old Catholic Congress met at Munich on Friday, September 22nd, 1871, and sat for three days Schulte, Professor of Canon Law at Prague, but a Prussian by birth, presided, and the Committee for drawing up the resolutions consisted, besides himself, of Professors Maassen of Vienna, Langen of Bonn, Reinkens of Breslau, Huber of Munich, and Dollinger The Vice-presidents were Keller of Aarau, and Professor Windscheid of Heidelberg, Professor Schwicker of Ofen and Stumpf of Coblentz were secretaries Deputies were present from every part of Germany, and the meeting was in fact the response of Catholic Germany to Dollinger's Declaration of the previous March, but there were also representatives of nearly every European country and of North America and Brazil, together with three priests of the so called Jansenist Church of Utrecht, and Dr Ossinin, a theological professor at St Petersburg The main part of the programme, agreed upon after full and minute discussion, ought to be put on record here, defining as it does the doctrinal basis and scope of the movement, and thereby clearly establishing its distinctively Catholic character

"I In the consciousness of our religious duties we hold fast to the ancient Catholic faith as witnessed in Scripture and Tradition, and the ancient Catholic worship We therefore claim our full rights as members of the Catholic Church, and refuse to be thrust out of Church communion or of the ecclesiastical and civil rights appertaining thereto We declare the Church censures inflicted on us for our loyalty to our faith to be objectless and arbitrary, and shall not be disturbed or hindered in conscience thereby in our active participation in Church communion From the standpoint of the confession of faith contained in the Tridentine Creed, we reject the doctrines introduced under the pontificate of Pius IX, in contradiction to the teaching of the Church, and the principles observed from the Apostolic Council downwards, especially the dogma of 'the infallible teaching office' and 'supreme ordinary and immediate jurisdiction,' of the Pope

' II We adhere to the ancient constitution of the Church We reject every attempt to thrust out the bishops from the immediate and independent government of the separate churches We reject the doctrine embodied in the Vatican decrees, that the Pope is the sole divinely ordained depositary of all ecclesiastical authority and official power, as contradicting the Tridentine canon, according to which the divinely ordained hierarchy consists of bishops, priests, and deacons We acknowledge the primacy of the Roman Pontiff, as it was acknowledged on the ground of Scripture by the Fathers and Councils of the ancient undivided Church

"[1] We declare that articles of faith cannot be defined simply by the decision of the existing Pope, and the express or tacit assent of the bishops, who are pledged by oath to unconditional obedience to him, but only in harmony with Holy Scripture and the ancient tradition of the Church, as contained in the acknowledged Fathers and Councils Even a Council not deficient, like the Vatican, in essential outward conditions of œcumenicity, and where the breach with the fundamental principles and past history of the Church is consummated by the unanimous vote of its members, could not issue decrees binding on the conscience of any members of the Church

"[2] We maintain that the dogmatic decisions of a Council must be shewn to agree with the original and traditional faith of the Church in the consciousness of the Catholic people and in theological science We reserve to the Catholic laity and clergy, as also to scientific theology, the right of bearing testimony or of objecting in the establishment of rules of faith

"[3] We desire by the aid of theology and canon law, and in the spirit of the ancient Church, to effect a reform which shall remove existing abuses and defects, and fulfil the legitimate desires of the Catholic laity for a constitutional participation in Church affairs, whereby national views and needs may be recognised without prejudice to doctrinal unity We declare that the charge of Jansenism has been unjustly brought against the Church of Utrecht, and that consequently there is no dogmatic difference between us We hope for a reunion with the Oriental and Russian Churches, whose separation had no urgent cause, and is based on no irreconcilable dogmatic differences In view of the reforms we are striving for, and in the way of science and advancing Christian culture, we look for a gradual understanding with the Protestant and the Episcopal Churches"

The remaining paragraphs deal with the necessity of searching reforms in clerical education and discipline, the political aspects of the new dogma, and the pernicious moral and social results of Jesuit teaching, which ought therefore to be suppressed, and the last clause affirms the full civil rights of the *Altkatholiken* "to all real property and possessions of the Church" It was further resolved that unions (*Vereine*) for organizing the movement should be formed throughout Germany, and religious congregations (*Gemeinde*) wherever circumstances required it One such congregation had already been established in the Church of St. Nicholas at Munich, and they are now spread over the country, the first effect generally being that, wherever an Old Catholic church is opened, the regular parish priests at once cease from asking any questions about the new dogma in the confessional In Austria, where no difficulty is made about giving the sacraments to Old Catholics, separate congregations have not been established Dr Schulte, who presided at both the first and second Old Catholic Congress, continued to live on intimate terms with the Cardinal Archbishop of Prague (Schwarzenberg) until he quite recently migrated to Bonn, where a chair had been offered him The Munich Congress, which first gave to the movement a definite organization, established two points beyond possibility of doubt, viz that it represents no mere local or temporary phase of opinion, and that it does not aspire, like the so-called "German Catholics" or *Lichtfreunde* of a quarter of a century ago, to add one more sect to the multitudinous progeny of the Reformation, but is a *bona fide* attempt to fulfil the design, again and again proclaimed since the Council of Constance by some of the wisest and holiest of her sons, to effect from within a genuine "reform of the Catholic Church in her head and in her members" It claims to represent the Catholic faith as held up to July 18th, 1870 At the same time it does express what has long been a strong and growing conviction in Germany in favour of restricting Roman influences to what is necessarily involved in the idea of the primacy, and that as well from a deep moral indignation against the habitual policy of the *Curia*, as with a view to facilitate the reunion of religious bodies separated from the Church Dollinger himself has avowed his conviction that "Philoctetes has received his death wound, and it is now only a question of time when the movement shall triumph over the curialistic system" And Archbishop Darboy has embodied in the brief but pregnant pamphlet he published towards the close of the Vatican Council [*La Dernière Heure du Concile*] a similar sentiment "Les Spartiates, qui étaient tombés aux Thermopyles, pour défendre les terres de la liberté, avaient préparé au flot impitoyable du despotisme la défaite de Salamine" The Congress closed with two public meetings held in the Glass Palace, where addresses were delivered to some thousands of persons by Schulte, Huber, Michelis, Reinkens, Hyacinthe, Van Thiel (from Utrecht), and other speakers, the whole assembly joining in a final tribute to the steadfastness and courage of "the great Nestor of German theology," Dr Dollinger

We must pass rapidly over the year intervening between the first and second Congress, which was marked by an extensive development of the movement both in Germany and Switzerland, and the appearance of several learned and able publications in connection with it The Prussian Government meanwhile expelled the Jesuits and adopted other measures, which it does not fall within the scope of this article to criticise, hostile to Ultramontane interests Bishop Ketteler of Mayence, who was a leading member of the Opposition at Rome, and the inspirer and disseminator of a powerful work [*Quæstio*] against papal infallibility, soon became the most influential champion of Ultramontanism in the German Episcopate, who assembled again at Fulda in September 1872, and addressed a memorial to the Government endorsing, while it ingeniously misrepresented, the Vatican dogmas. A reply was published, drawn up by the Standing Committee of the Cologne Congress This memorial seems to have given the immediate occasion of Prince Bismarck's ecclesiastical legislation, which was soon afterwards introduced into the Prussian *Landtag* In France Dr Michaud served the cause by the issue of a remarkable series of eight pamphlets [Paris, *Sandoz et Fischbacher*], and in the spring of the year Dr Dollinger delivered at Munich his *Lectures on the Reunion of the Churches*, since translated into English In Prussia, Archbishop Melchers of Cologne, and Bishop Crementz of Ermeland, both members of the Opposition at Rome, led the crusade against the anti-infallibilist clergy and professors In March, four Catholic professors at Bonn, three of whom were priests, were excommunicated by the Archbishop of Cologne—Hilgers, Reusch, Langen, and Knoodt—and vindicated their position in a spirited and telling reply Shortly before, Mother Augustine (Amalie de Lasaulx), Superior of the Sisters of Charity at Bonn, who was so beloved and revered throughout the Rhineland for her holiness and works of mercy as to be popularly credited with miraculous powers, had been excommunicated and turned out of her convent during her last illness for refusing to accept the Vatican decrees, and was refused the last sacraments and the rites of Christian burial A weeping crowd followed her to the grave on January 30th, when Dr Reusch, formerly confessor of the convent, said a few prayers It was well known that numbers both among the clergy and laity, who lacked the courage or the occasion for openly avowing their sentiments, were of the same mind The Theological Faculty of Tubingen, *e g* have never submitted, and the venerable Dr Kuhn, who is at the head of it, has written a work against the dogma, which is only withheld from publication for a time to spare further embarrassment to his diocesan, Bishop Hefele To the immense majority of the clergy, who are absolutely at the mercy of their bishops in the present abnormal state of the law, resistance would mean starvation, whence the term *Hungerdogma* has come to be applied to the new article of faith; and there are large classes of the people, as was pointed out at the Cologne Congress by Reinkens, who are dependent on Ultramontane patronage, and would be exposed to ruin or serious loss if they ventured to speak out The professed Old Catholics form therefore the centre and nucleus of a movement which has a wide circumference The defection of the German bishops of the minority has supplied the ground and example of an outward conformity, which in numberless cases represents no inward belief.

Notwithstanding these serious difficulties the movement, first organized at the Munich Congress of 1871, had enormously extended its range and influence when the second Congress met at Cologne on September 20th, 1872 The mere fact of its migration from a court and university city like Munich to a busy commercial centre of North Germany, the chief Catholic city of the Rhineland, illustrated the advance made during the past twelvemonth, of which another indication was seen in the presence of the Archbishop of Utrecht[1]—who had already held a series of confirmations for Old Catholics in Germany—and of the Bishops of Lincoln, Ely and Maryland, and the Russian Archpriest Janyschew Letters of sympathy were read from two Eastern Archbishops and the Bishop of Lichfield, and from several distinguished English clergymen and laymen who were unable to be there In all, about 500 deputies and invited guests from Belgium, Switzerland, Hungary, and Italy, as well as various parts of Germany, took part in the business sessions, and from 3,000 to 4,000 persons attended the two public meetings and the services and sermons in St Pantaleon's Church Schulte again presided, with Petri of Wiesbaden and Cornelius of Munich for vice-presidents This time there was no programme to be drawn up, and the Congress was entirely occupied with practical business, the main points being the further organization of worship and cure of souls (*Seelsorge*) for Old Catholics, and of means for maintaining their civil rights, and for extending the movement, the appointment of a Committee to make arrangements for appointing one or more Bishops, who will receive consecration at Utrecht, and of a Committee of ten members to promote Reunion, with Dollinger for chairman, Friedrich, Reinkens, Michelis, and Michaud among its members Two Central Committees were nominated for North and South Germany respectively, and it was resolved that the Congress should be held in alternate years at Munich and Cologne For a full report of the very interesting speeches delivered both at the private and public sessions, we must refer our readers to the official *Acts* [*Verhandlungen des zweiten Altkath Congresses*], or for an English summary of them to the last article of the *Union Review* for March 1872 It should be noticed that the same Conservative spirit prevailed as at the first Congress Advocates of extreme measures, like Bauer and Kaminski, found no support, and Hyacinthe, whose unauthorized marriage had discredited him, was not invited to speak, while the question of organic reforms, as in the law of celibacy, was expressly reserved for "the constitutional organs of the Church" The President began by defining their "stand-point" as "the Catholic one," and added, "Those who do not hold to the ground of positive believing Christianity, as contained in the Scriptures and the truly Œcumenical Councils, we cannot regard as Catholics, nor can they have any active participation in our work" And the Archbishop of Utrecht insisted amid general applause on the necessity of maintaining Catholic unity

At the time of the Congress the movement had made little progress in Switzerland, but it has since advanced rapidly, especially in the diocese of Basle, where several *Altkatholik* congregations have now been formed During the first fortnight of December, Reinkens, in compliance with urgent invitations addressed to him, visited Olten, Soleure, Berne, Rheinfelden, and Lucerne, where he addressed enthusiastic audiences, on his departure six parishes had openly joined the movement, and several more have since followed their example Meanwhile the bishop, Mgr Lachat, who had made every effort to enforce the Vatican decrees by suspension and excommunication, became involved in disputes with the Diocesan Conference of the seven Cantons under his jurisdiction, and eventually with the Government In February last Reinkens and Michelis addressed a meeting of 3,000 persons in the Old Council Hall of Constance, and one of the churches there is now assigned to the Old Catholics On June 4th a select body of clergy and laymen, assembled at St. Pantaleon's Church, Cologne, elected Dr Reinkens, late Professor of Ecclesiastical History at Breslau, Missionary Bishop for the Old Catholics of Germany, and he was consecrated at Rotterdam by the Bishop of Deventer on August 11th, 1873, according to the Roman rite, but without any recognition of the Pope's supremacy He is a man of great learning and eloquence and profound earnestness, and has contributed to the pending controversy an able treatise on the *Papal Decrees of July 18th*, 1870, in six parts Until a bishop was appointed the movement, successful as it has already proved, could not be considered to have passed beyond its tentative and initial stage

We have not spoken of Italy, as the movement has not yet taken shape there, but Mr Chauncey Langdon, American chaplain at Florence, bore testimony at the Cologne Congress to the sympathy felt for it among both ecclesiastics and laity, and they have an organ in the *Rinnovamento Cattolico* at Florence Signor Mamiani, a member of the Italian Parliament, also wrote to express his sympathy In France political events have conspired with episcopal absolutism to repress any outward resistance to the dominant Ultramontanism But there is practically no interference with the widespread personal disbelief in the Vatican dogmas, and many of the bishops are with good reason suspected of retaining the convictions they so emphatically expressed at the Council

It will be a convenience to those who desire further information if we append to this necessarily brief sketch some references to works bearing on the antecedents, history, and character of the Old Catholic movement The English reader may profitably consult *The Pope and the Council*, by Janus, *Letters from Rome on the Council*, by Quirinus, *The Church of God and the Bishops*, by Liaño; *Lectures on Reunion of the Churches*, by Dollinger (Rivingtons), *Home and Foreign Review*, January 1864, art. "Munich Congress,"

[1] Archbishop Loos, who had held the See of Utrecht since 1858, died June 4th, 1873, leaving the Suffragan Bishop of Deventer to carry on the succession.

Theological Review, January 1872, "Altkatholik Movement" (Williams and Norgate), *North British Review*, October 1870, "Vatican Council" (Edmonston and Douglas), *Union Review*, May 1871, "Liberal Catholics of Germany," *ibid* January 1872, "Catholic Congress of Munich," *ibid* March 1873, "Russian View of the O C Congress," "Second O C Congress," *Letters to Mgr Deschamps*, by A Gratry (Hayes), *Contemp Rev* November 1872, "O C Congress," by Dr Littledale, to which may be added a series of articles bearing on the subject in the *Saturday Review* during the last four years Among the mass of original authorities, illustrating the history of the movement, may be specified *Documenta ad Illustrandum Conc Vat*, von Friedrich, *Tagebuch*, Friedrich (Nordlingen), *Stenographischer Bericht des Congresses*, 1871 (Munchen), *Die Verhandlungen des zweiten Altkath Congress* (Koln und Leipzig 1872), *Erklarung an den Erzbischof von Munchen*, von J Dollinger (Munchen 1871, Lord Acton's *Sendschreiben an einen deutschen Bischof*, Nordlingen 1870) The following works, among many others, exhibit or illustrate its principles. *Das Vatican Dogma*, von J Langen (Bonn 1871), *Die papstlichen Dekrete*, von H Reinkens (Munster 1871), *Die Stellung von Concilien, Papsten und Bischofe*, von J F Schulte (Prag 1871), *Stimmen aus der kath Kirche* (Munchen 1870), *La Dernière Heure du Concile* (Munchen 1870), *Einige Worte uber Unfehlbarkeit*, von J Dollinger (Munchen 1870) Some other works have been already referred to in the course of the article

OLD FLEMINGS [FLEMINGS]

OLD LIGHT ANTIBURGHERS [ANTIBURGHERS]

OLD LIGHT BURGHERS [BURGHERS]

OLD LUTHERANS Those Lutherans of Prussia are so called who have not joined the UNITED EVANGELICAL CHURCH

OLD SCHOOL BAPTISTS A party among the American Baptists who adhere to the original strict notions respecting predestination and election, in opposition to the tendency which the younger generation of the sect shews towards the doctrine of free will and towards universalism The Old School Baptists deny that the salvation of souls can depend on human effort, and maintain the strictest Calvinism in regard to the doctrine of election

OLD SCHOOL PRESBYTERIANS [PRESBYTERIANS]

OMISH CHURCH A sect of American strict Mennonites, who are said to take their peculiar name from Jacob Amen, a Swiss Mennonite preacher of Amenthal, of the seventeenth century, and to have been originally called "Amenites" Some still remaining in Switzerland are called "Hook Mennonites" or "Button Mennonites" according as they wear hooks or buttons on their coats. The American sect is analogous to that of the FLEMINGS or "Fine" Mennonites of Holland

'ΟΜΦΑΛΟΨΥΧΟΙ [HESYCHASTS]

OPHITES [Ὄφις] An Egyptian sect of very early date, the principles of which appear to have been a compound of the mysteries of Isis, and of the involved fancies of Oriental mythology, mingled with corrupt notions of Christian history and doctrine St Cyprian mentions them by name [Cypr *Ep* lxxiii 4], and the last chapter but one of Irenæus' first book is supposed to be written against them and the SETHIANS [Iren *adv Hær* i. 30] Origen calls them "a very obscure sect," and denies that they were Christians, saying "that no person was allowed to join their assemblies till he had uttered curses against Jesus" [Orig *contr Cels* iii 13, vi 24] He also says that they were founded by a man named Euphrates [*ibid* vi 28], a name mentioned by Theodoret as that belonging to the founder of the heresy of the PERATÆ [Theodor *Hær fab* i 17], but which in the account of the Naasseni or Ophites given by Hippolytus is taken as the name of the mystical water of life spoken of in John iv 10 Hippolytus looks upon the Ophites as the originators of all heresies, and associates them both with the Jews and the Gnostics, for he writes of them under the Hebrew form of their name as "the Naasseni" [from נָחָשׁ nachash], "who call themselves Gnostics" [Hippol *Refut* v. 6] Philaster places them first in his list of heresies before Christ [Philast *de Hær* i], while Epiphanius and St Augustine say that they were alleged to have been derived from the Nicolaitanes or the Gnostics [Epiphan *Panar* xxxvii Aug *de Hær* xvii]

The author of the Treatise against all Heresies which goes by the name of Tertullian says of the Ophites that they derived their name from the reverence which they entertained towards the tempter of Eve, who brought into the world the knowledge of good and evil It was in reference to his power and majesty, they alleged, that Moses set up the brazen serpent, and they brought our Lord's words [John iii 14] in support of this notion, thus shewing their acquaintance with the New Testament The same writer also states that they introduced the serpent into their assemblies to bless the Eucharist [Tertull *adv Hæres* ii], a horrible ceremony, in which, as Epiphanius, St Augustine, and other writers affirm, they caused the serpent to trail over the bread of which the communicants were about to partake, each person also kissing the serpent before receiving

The heretical philosophy of the sect is given by Hippolytus and by Epiphanius as above quoted The former says that they professed to derive it from James the brother of our Lord, who handed it down to Mariamne He also quotes from a "Gospel according to Thomas," which was in use among them, which seems to be the "Gospel according to the Egyptians," mentioned by Epiphanius in his twenty-sixth book, among the Gnostic Apocrypha In addition to these sources of information there is also an account given by Origen of their "Diagram," a tablet on which they set forth their doctrines in a hieroglyphical form [Orig *contr Cels* vi 33] The chief points of their profane belief, apart from the intricate and fanciful system of dualistic philosophy which they adopted, were · that the serpent was Christ, that He Who was born of the Virgin was Jesus alone, upon whom Christ afterwards descended They held the Valentinian theory of a Demiurge, whom they named Jaldabaoth, and who was set forth as begetting six beings, the spirits of the seven planets By these six beings man was created after their common image, a body without a soul, and they brought him to Jaldabaoth, who breathed into him a living spirit At the sight of man's perfection Jaldabaoth became envious, and gave him a command which the serpent led him to disobey Hence the conflict of good and evil in the world, the good being represented by the serpent The mythic Christ of the Valentinians is the opponent of Jaldabaoth, and is ever endeavouring to defend man from his envy

The sect continued to exist after other forms of Gnosticism had died out, the Emperor Justinian enacting laws against them [Cod I v 1, 18, 19, 21] so late as A D 530

ORDIBARII This name appears in the treatise of Reinerius against the Waldenses, in close association with the sect of the Ortlibenses [*Bibl Max* xxv 266], but Gieseler states that the reading of an authentic manuscript gives the word as "Ortlibarii" The context of the passage gives no reason for supposing that Reiner was writing of two sects, all that he says applying to the Ortlibenses In Pluquet's *Dictionnaire des Heresies*, and in the Index to Sianda's *Lexicon Polemicum*, the name is printed "Orbibarii," which offers a further illustration of the way in which the original name may have been corrupted [ORTLIBENSES]

OREBITES [HOREBITES]

ORIGENISTS Those of the immediate disciples of the great Origen, and those subsequent students and admirers of his works who developed heretical opinions out of the bold philosophical speculations which he mingled with his allegorical interpretations of Scripture

The father of philosophical Christianity from whom these errors were said to have sprung—Origen [A D 185-253] the Adamantine ['Ἀδαμάντιος] and the "brazen-brained" [χαλκέντερος]—was pupil and successor to St Clement in the school of Alexandria, being appointed by Demetrius the Patriarch on the flight of St Clement during the persecution of Severus, and before he had reached the age of twenty [Euseb *Hist Eccl* vi 3] He had already adopted the life of an ascetic, and of a hard, untiring student, endeavouring to carry out the Counsels of Perfection literally [Matth xix 12], going barefoot, having but one coat, sleeping on the bare floor, and restricting his diet to the humblest vegetable fare Four years of such a life as this, combined with the daily labour of instruction, compelled him to retire for a time from Alexandria to Rome, but in the year 212 he was again at his post Three years afterwards he visited Palestine, and although not ordained to the priesthood, was invited by the Bishops of Jerusalem and Cæsarea to preach in the churches of those cities This led to a remonstrance on the part of his own bishop, Demetrius, and he returned to Alexandria A few years afterwards he again visited his friend and pupil, Alexander, the Bishop of Jerusalem, and was ordained priest by him, when he was about forty-four years of age. This ordination was uncanonical in two ways Origen having incapacitated himself for the priesthood by his early self-mutilation, and it being contrary to all rule for a bishop to ordain a person belonging to another diocese without letters commendatory from the bishop of the latter An angry discussion arose, in which the clergy of Palestine took the side of Origen, and those of Alexandria that of Demetrius The latter summoned a council, before which it was represented that the great catechist had been guilty of teaching heresy as well as of violating the canons, and he was condemned and excommunicated in A D 232, being at the same time deposed from his office as the head of the Catechetical School [Euseb *Hist Eccl* vi 26] This sentence was afterwards, perhaps, withdrawn [Huet's *Origeniana* I iii 10], and it was certainly disregarded by the bishops of Palestine, Arabia, and Greece, but Origen never returned to Alexandria Labouring for the conversion of heretics [BERYLLUS, ARABICI] in the three countries named, he at the same time accomplished literary labours so vast that he is said to have been the author of 6000 separate books and tracts (most of which are lost), to have dictated to seven amanuenses, and, as it is put by St Jerome, to have written more than any other man could read Among such a multitude of writings it would not be difficult, probably, to find materials out of which to frame charges of heresy, yet the opinions on which these charges are chiefly founded are contained in a work on First Principles [Περὶ ἀρχῶν], which was written while he was at Alexandria, but of which only a Latin version has been preserved When he was sixty-six years of age, Origen was imprisoned and put to the torture during the Decian persecution, and before he was seventy his life was brought to a close at Tyre

The writings of Origen are so corrupted with interpolations of a later date, and so many of them have been lost, that it is impossible to determine with anything like certainty how far he was responsible for the extreme form in which his peculiar opinions now appear It is true that he was convicted of erroneous opinions as well as of uncanonical conduct by a synod of Egyptian clergy, and that the Bishop of Rome concurred in this conviction, but it is also true that many bishops refused to recognise this decision, and that this refusal diminishes greatly the force which it might otherwise have It is true, too, that opinions attributed to Origen are refuted by St Jerome and others, especially by Epiphanius, but it is also certain that (as Origen himself complains) his opinions were greatly perverted by some of his hearers and readers,[1] and

[1] "Plerique dum plus nos diligunt quam meremur, hæc jactant et loquuntur, sermones nostros doctrinamque laudantes, quæ conscientia nostra non recipit Alii vero tractatus nostros calumniantes, ea sentire nos criminantur

all critics agree in considering that his works were corrupted by heretics at a very early date, that they might gain the weight of his name to their side The great deference which he shewed for Holy Scripture, at the study of which he laboured during twenty-eight years for his "Hexapla" edition of the Old Testament, as also his respect for the tradition of the Church, make it very improbable that Origen wandered into actual heresy, but, at the same time, he began to teach and write very early in life, and wrote so abundantly, that some of his productions must have been hastily sent into the world, and may have contained many ill-considered statements His profound speculations on the nature of God and created beings, and on their relations to each other, offered, too, a tempting field for wilder and less learned speculators to work in, and it is easy to see that heresies might thus be manufactured out of his words by others for which he himself was not in reality responsible

The opinions which Origen was charged with holding, and which those called Origenists professed to draw from his works, were chiefly these [1] That there is an inequality between the Persons of the Holy Trinity, [2] That human souls pre-existed before the creation of Adam; [3] That the soul of Christ pre-existed with other human souls, [4] That the resurrection nature of mankind will not include material bodies, [5] That the punishments of the wicked and of evil spirits will not be eternal, [6] That all intelligent beings tend towards re-absorption into the One Fountain of Being from which they sprung

These opinions are part of a methodical system, the materials of which are to be found, for the most part, in the *de Principiis* of Origen, but some of them are only known as his from the statements of St. Jerome and others who wrote against them, these authors, no doubt quoting from works which are not now extant, but which were known to be—whether corrupted or not cannot now be discovered—his authentic productions Taking them in the order in which they are given above, the system which they form is as follows —

[1] The Divine Nature consists of three *ὑποστάσεις, first,* the Father, who is the one original essence, and the one source of all other being, *secondly,* the Son, who is necessarily generated eternally by the Father as an eternal Brightness proceeding from an eternal Light, or as an ever-flowing stream from an inexhaustible Fountain, and *thirdly,* the Holy Spirit, a Spirit created by the Son, and yet united in the Unity of Trinity with the other two Divine Persons [Hieron *ad Avitum,* Ep lix *ad Pammach et Ocean* Ep lxv, Justinian Imp *adv Origen* in Mansi, *Concil* ix 487.] Here it is to be observed that the Son is also alleged to be inferior to, and different from the Father, although the primary emanation from Him and His minister in the work of creation, while the Holy Spirit is accounted inferior to both This doctrine of Subordination was never accepted by the Church, and its promulgation by Origen led some writers to charge him with being the father of Arianism On the other hand, he was the first to formulate the doctrine of the Eternal Generation, and this has ever since been received, in the words of the Nicene Creed, *τὸν Υἱὸν τοῦ Θεοῦ τὸν μονογενῆ, τὸν ἐκ τοῦ Πατρὸς γεννηθέντα πρὸ πάντον τῶν αἰώνων . Φῶς ἐκ Φωτός*

[2] The pre-existence of human souls is associated with the tenet that creative energy is a necessary quality of Omnipotent and ever-ruling Deity, and must therefore have been exercised by God from all eternity Hence the existing creation is one of a successive order of creations, each of which has been part of the eternal kingdom of the eternal Ruler, and each peopled with living intelligences These spiritual beings were all originally of one order, partaking, in a lower degree, of the Divine nature from which they had originated but being endowed with free will they were capable of falling, and thus while some fell to become evil spirits, others degenerated into the condition of souls, which were afterwards imprisoned in mortal bodies as a punishment for their sins

[3] The pre-existence of the soul of Christ is taken as an antecedent of the Incarnation The eternal Logos, determining upon a work of restoration on behalf of the fallen, united His Divine nature to one of the perfect intelligences, and was thus able to acquire a soul capable of being united with a human body, and capable also of redeeming fallen intelligences of every degree

[4] In respect to the resurrection of the body, the Origenists held that the material bodies of the saints will be renewed in a less material substance, a resurrection body more pure and subtle than the natural body Thus the risen body of Christ was believed by them to be already a glorified body, (a belief strongly repudiated by some of the Fathers, but accepted by others) and as such a pattern of the resurrection bodies of Christians

[5] The future life, whether of blessedness or of misery, was considered by the Origenists to be still a life of probation, in which the exercise of free-will gives to all the power of going forward to a higher condition or of going backward to one that is lower Hence the punishment of the wicked is not eternal, the work of the Saviour extending to them and even to the fallen angels, to enable them to rise from the depths to which they have fallen, and ultimately to attain the condition of the blessed This belief is referred to by St Jerome when he writes, "And though Origen declares that no rational being will be lost, and gives penitence even to the Evil One, what is that to us who believe that the Evil One and his satellites and all the wicked will perish eternally, and that Christians, if they have been cut off in sin shall, after punishment, be saved"[1] [Hieron. *contr. Pelag* ii 712, ed 1737]

quæ nunquam sensisse nos novimus Sed neque hi qui plus diligunt, neque illi qui aderunt, veritatis regulam tenent, et alii per dilectionem, alii per odium, mentiuntur" [Origen, *Hom* xxv *in Lucam.*]

[1] This passage is illustrated by another in the writings of the same Father "I believe that after the resurrec-

[6] Lastly, the Origenists held the opinion that the advancement of spiritual life after the resurrection removes the nature of the saints more and more from the sphere of material existence, and draws them nearer and nearer to that of the highest spiritual existence Thus the progress of spiritual life in heaven is in reality a step onward towards a continuous process, by which created beings are being absorbed into the uncreated, until God becomes all in all

Although a school of Origenists arose in the Church after his death, among the many who were educated by him and by his works, the most distinguished of those belonging to it being Gregory Thaumaturgus, Pamphilus, and Eusebius the historian, it was only on the revival, in the sixth century, of the controversy respecting his principles, which had been long dormant, that those principles were brought before a council The attention of the Emperor Justinian having been drawn to the writings of Origen, he wrote a long treatise against them, addressed in the form of an edict to Mennas, the Patriarch of Constantinople [Justin Imp *adv Orig* in Mansi, *Concil* ix. 487]. In this edict the Emperor directs Mennas to convene a synod for the purpose of anathematizing Origen. It was at this synod [A.D 544], as is supposed, that fifteen canons, which are extant, were passed, condemning the tenets mentioned above, and some other opinions of less importance [*ibid* 395] When the fifth general council met, in the year 553, it did not take any notice of these canons or of the Origenist opinions which had been condemned, and notwithstanding the agitation raised respecting the THREE CHAPTERS, the only conciliar condemnation of those opinions was in the obscure synod referred to

[A very able defence of Origenist opinions was printed anonymously, in the year 1661, by Rust, Bishop of Dromore, under the title *A Letter of Resolution concerning Origen and the chief of his Opinions, written to the learned and most ingenious C L Esquire, and by him published* A good account of the controversy will be found in Natalis Alexander, *Hist. Eccl* iii. 648, 761-780]

ORIGENISTS From Epiphanius it appears that there was a sect of Origenists who were followers of some unknown Origen, a person quite different from the Father of the second and third century In one place indeed Epiphanius (a very bitter opponent of Origenist opinions) says he is ignorant whether or not the sect was derived from him [Epiph *Panar* lxiii lxiv], but in another he speaks of them without doubt as followers of some other Origen [Epiph *Anacephal*] These Origenists are spoken of as given to shameful vices, but nothing farther is mentioned of them There was an Alexandrian philosopher of the same name contemporary with the great Origen, but there is nothing known which connects him with the sect Philaster is silent about them, while Augustine and Prædestinatus are only able to repeat the statement of Epiphanius

ORIGINAL BURGHERS [BURGHERS]

ORIGINAL CONNEXION METHODISTS [METHODISTS]

ORIGINAL SECEDERS. [UNITED ORIGINAL SECEDERS]

ORPHANS A party of the Hussites, which refused to follow Procopius, or to elect any special leader after the death of Ziska, alleging that there was no one man fit to succeed him, and hence calling themselves Orphans, as those who had lost their father They kept to their camps, fortified with their waggons, and associated little with the Taborites and the Horebites, the remaining followers of Ziska [HUSSITES]

ORTLIBARII [ORTLIBENSES]

ORTLIBENSES This was the original name of the sect of heretics afterwards known as the BRETHREN OF THE FREE SPIRIT It occurs in the treatise of Reinerius against the Waldenses [*Bibl. Max* xxv. 266], where also they are called, but apparently by a false reading, "Ordibarii" They appear to have been a party of the disciples of AMALRIC of Bena, who formed into a sect under the influence of a leader named Ortlieb at Strasburg early in the thirteenth century [Gieseler, *Compend. Eccl Hist* iii 467, Clark's ed] Reiner describes them as repudiating nearly all the articles of the Christian faith; the doctrines of the creation of the world by God, of the Trinity, of our Lord's miraculous conception, and of the Sacraments He also accuses them of not receiving the Holy Scriptures, on the ground that they had a divine inspiration which made them independent of the Bible, and of holding extreme Antinomian opinions on all subjects connected with morals These heresies seem to be closely associated with the Pantheism of Amalric, and with his theory as to the Incarnation of the Holy Spirit, and thus to bear out the view taken by Gieseler The only account of the sect under the name Ortlibenses is that given by Reiner,

OSIANDRIANS A section of the early German Protestants who followed Andrew Hosemann (exalted by Latin transformation into Osiander) rather than Luther Osiander maintained that the Atonement was wrought by the power of the Divine and not of the Human Nature of Christ, the exact converse of this opinion being that of the STANCARISTS Osiander became head of the newly-founded University of Konigsberg in A D 1548, but his followers were never numerous His opinions were maintained by Funch, his son-in-law, but when the latter was executed for high treason in the year 1566, they ceased to have any influential supporter, and the sect was absorbed by Lutheranism. The sixth volume of Schlusselburg's *Hæreticorum Catalogus* consists of 259 pages "De secta Osiandristarum "

OSSENES or OSSENIANS. The name given to the ESSENES by Epiphanius

OWENITES [SOCIALISTS.]

tion from the dead we shall still need a Sacrament to advance and purify us, for none will be able to arise pure from stain, nor will any soul be found which shall at once be free from all faults " [Hieron *in Lucam Hom.* xiv vii 288, ed 1737]

P

PACIFICATORS A name assumed by the Imperial party which supported the Henoticon of Zeno in the year 482 [HENOTICON MONOPHYSITES]

PÆDOBAPTISTS A name given by the Anabaptists of the sixteenth century, and by Baptists of later date, to those who baptize infants or little children [παῖδες]

PALAMITÆ [HESYCHASTS]

PANTHEISTS Those who hold the opinion that God is everything, and everything is God This heresy presents itself to us under a double aspect It is either a quasi religious creed, or it represents a philosophical tenet, in either case it may be clearly traced into the emanational theories of oriental antiquity. The notion is old, but the term Pantheism is of very recent date The Deist Toland was the first to use it in his *Socinianism truly stated by a Pantheist to his orthodox Friend* [A D 1705], and at a later date he published his *Pantheisticon* [A D 1720] Toland said expressly that he had borrowed his notion from Linus, which the motto of his *Pantheisticon* expressed as "ex toto sunt omnia, et ex omnibus est totum;" briefly put by his antagonist Fay as "Pantheistarum Natura et Numen unum idemque sunt" Pantheism is little else than the oriental emanation notion imported into the West for the purpose of superseding the religious idea of a personal Deity first creating out of nothing and ever after overruling the course of the world Creation designates the summoning into existence of that which before was not Emanation is a mere modification of that which is, it maintains the selfsame existence, though after other forms and other conditions, it is the developed fruit of the quickened germ It supposes an Infinite Eternal Substance, which arouses itself into action by a self-energy, and clothes itself in a multiplicity of forms, that in the aggregate make up the universe Thus the Divine Idea as the Whole is All things, and All things are the Whole, and in the end All things will return once more into the Inscrutable Oneness from whence they came forth

Such was the groundwork of the Brahminical system, and of the cosmogony of the most ancient Indian writing, the *Institutes of Menu.* Brahm the primal substance, the Absolute, awakening into consciousness, gave birth to Maja, spectral matter, the illusive source of all that appears to exist A threefold manifestation of himself is put forth by Brahm, Brahma the Creator, Vishnu the Preserver, and Siva the Destroyer All creation proceeded forth from the joint energy of Brahma and Maja, being concentrated under a twofold originative power, Mahabhava, the principle of spiritual concretion, and Pradjapati, the condensation of all less ethereal elements. All at first was a void nullity, when Tad ("*He*" the Cabbalistic מי who?) breathed upon Sudda ("*Her*"), who existed only in him, and nothing which has since been called into being has existed otherwise than in Him Thence the world of spirits and of men was evolved The Vedantic philosophy is equally pantheistic After making all allowance for interpolation and corruption, the fundamental principles of both remain the same. Knowledge alone is that which can raise the spirit of man to the unchangeable To see in creation material forms separate from Brahma is to dream, only when a man recognises All things in Brahma does he wake up from his dream, and gain the use of thought Brahma is the vast ocean of which the surface waves are the whole external form, the foam and surge that go to make up his substance He is at once active and passive, active, in the continued evolution of emanations that degenerate more and more from original perfection; and passive, as being himself the degenerating emanations that are evolved All too is Maja, illusion, light yearned for increase, and its multiple became water, water similarly produced earth The more visible creation becomes, the more it degenerates, and the more is illusion intensified It is only by contemplation that all forms and names and illusive appearances vanish, the one real substance is perceived, and the truth is apprehended that the contemplative mind is one with the Infinite.

So again, in the Egyptian system, One Inscrutable Being gives a first impulse to creation by the evolution of intelligence, Cneph, the conceptive Demiurge, and next of Phtha, the organizer of the world, the vital principle of fire and warmth The various succeeding emanations in ogdoads and decads and dodecads are by pairs or syzygies, whereof the secondary principle is more or less antagonistic of the primary, representing the various phenomena of nature, such too were the φιλία and νεῖκος of Pythagoras and Empedocles Thus Osiris, radiant with white light, was combined with Isis in the many-tinted robe of nature; and Typhon, the principle of evil, by union with Nephthys, the ideal of consummate beauty, produced the chequered state of good and evil which is the world of man Life, as the spirit that pervades all nature, could never again be extinguished, its deification is read clearly in deciphered hieroglyphics, and death is only the narrow doorway that leads back to the fresh life of perpetual youth In all this we see the remote elements of Gnosticism In the Egyptian therefore, as in the Indian system, the world of matter, whether real or phantasmal, emanates from and is in fact one with the Deity The antagonisms of the Egyptian theogony became a dualistic system in Chaldæa and Palestine, where Bel and Nebo or Nergal, Matter, were made to proceed from the procosmic Ur, Light, and in Persia, as seen in the antagonism of Ormuzd and Ahriman The sect of Sipari, adorers, claiming to return to præ-Zoroastrian truth, professed a modified Zabianism that was wholly pantheistic The Dabistan (school of morals), a work on all the Oriental forms of religious belief—Magianism, Brahmanism, Judaism, Islam, Christianity, and that which the author, Moshan-Fani, terms the "religion of philosophers"—names other pantheistical sects [Dabistan, *Orient Tr Comm* i 203], but they have had nothing to do with the origin of similar principles in Europe

Greece received its first ideas of civilization from Egypt and the East Thales indeed professed the dualism of Chaldæa and Egypt, but Linus, in a passage that has been preserved by Stobæus, exactly expresses the notion afterwards adopted by Spinoza "One sole energy governs all things, all things are unity, and each portion is All, for of one integer all things were born, in the end of time all things shall again become unity, the unity of multiplicity" Orpheus, his disciple, taught no other doctrine [Cudw *Intell Syst* ii 94] Pythagoras, an adept in ancient Orphic theology, impressed the same character on the nascent philosophy of Greece [Creuzer, *Symbolik*, Irenæus, Cambr ed introd xlii-xlv] His numerical theory was only an illustration of the emanative system One is all, and all is a wide development of the unit The monad produces the dyad, the two constitute the triad, and the product symbolizes the absolute unity that holds, as it were, in free solution spirit and matter Unity becomes a multiple of itself by factors of increasing power, and this multiple is the universe, the very being of the Divine Unity, quickened in all its parts with the Divine Life The soul of the world is the Divine energy that interpenetrates every portion of the mass, and the soul of man is an efflux of that energy The world too is an exact impress of the Eternal Idea which is the mind of God A poetical theogony was easily engrafted on such notions, and a polytheistic religion for the people

In more savage tribes Fetichism is only Pantheism in its grossest form, deeming "either fire, or wind, or the swift air, or the circle of the stars, or the violent water, or the lights of heaven, to be the gods that govern the earth" [Wisd xiii 2] The deification of gross matter was the earliest error of humanity, as the deification of man's moral nature has been the latest phase of Pantheism

The Eleatic school was founded by Xenophanes, the contemporary of Pythagoras, on purely pantheistic principles Matter was uncreate, for nothing can come of nothing Neither was continuous production possible, for in whatever respect the product differed from its antecedent type, it was causeless, and therefore impossible But all substance has its pre-existence in absolute unity, and that which has pre-existed is in no sense produced All that really exists is eternal, unchangeable, and must continue for ever to exist. All is one, there can be no variety of substance, and any apparent diversity is only illusion. Existence is unique, and the thinking mind is the only real, persistent, unchangeable substance Omnipotence and intelligence are the only two positive attributes of the universal whole, otherwise it can only be defined relatively by a process of negative elimination [Aristot *de Xenophane*, iii, Diog. Laert ii 19, De Gérando, I. vi]. Parmenides gave a further development to the pantheistic notion, viewed on the side of the universe rather than of its source, of existence rather than of its cause The only reality, he said, was absolute intelligence, the finite external world was only a phantasm of the mind, all was false and hollow that was based upon the suggestions of sense Thought and its object are identical Zeno, in defending the same system, gave its first impulse to dialectical reasoning, hence also to the school of Sophists It was now denied that simple substance can fill space, next, it was stripped gradually of every attribute, until it reached the vanishing point of the pantheistic perspective, substance then, being wholly neutral and void of colour, ceased to have any appreciable quality, and the schools of philosophy subsided into the blank atheism of Leucippus and Democritus, whose atomic fatalism finds a close parallel in the Zabianism of the Babylonians, Phœnicians, with other idolatrous offsets of the Shemitic stock The deepest questions that can occupy the human intellect were bandied to and fro in sophistical discussion, all was problematical, all was doubt, and the only principle which met with universal acceptance was the sceptical maxim, μέμνασο ἀπιστεῖν Socrates once more asserted the claim of sound reason to be heard, and Pantheism vanished from the scene, to reappear after many generations in the Eclectic and Gnostic schools [ECLECTICS GNOSTICS ZABIANS]

Gnosticism was either monarchical, believing in one principle, and purely pantheistical, as were Apelles, Valentinus, Carpocrates, Epiphanes, or dualistic, making two eternal principles, Mind and Matter, as did Saturninus, Bardesanes, and Basilides, whose systems were borrowed from Zoroaster and issued in Manichæism, and were forms of Gnosticism that were scarcely pantheistic These were all of Oriental or Egyptian origin, and made their attacks upon the faith, not by the methodical approaches of dialectical warfare, but as a disorganized rout of fanatics, with imagination for their guide and rhapsody for their best weapon of offence The Jewish CABBALA, a collateral descendant from the philosophy of Zoroaster learned at Babylon, was decidedy pantheistic

Neo-Platonicism was the form assumed by the last expiring attempt of the heathen schools to make head against Christianity [ECLECTICISM] Professing to combine the salient characteristics of every other system, it fixed upon the principle that was common to the most ancient forms of philosophy, and was essentially pantheistic Plotinus had accompanied the Emperor Gordian on his Persian expedition, and made good use of his opportunities for mastering the emanative theories of the East, these he made the basis of his system, tempered by a mixture of Christian Trinitarianism. His absolute Unity is as the Monad of Pythagoras, or the Bythus of the Gnostic, the inscrutable Ut of the Chaldæan mage, first source of Bel and Nebo. This Unity is the substance of all that is real, nothing external to it has any reality, or in fact any existence It can neither be described as Being nor Intellect in an ineffable manner it is far removed above both From this Unity proceeded Mind as a second principle, perfect although subordinate, pure reflex of the pure, transcendental glory of the transcendental. The universal Soul is the third principle, subordinate to both the preceding, the manifestation as well as energy of Mind, and these three form one Being of co-equal and co-eternal glory It is impossible that heathen philosophy should have thus expressed itself before the day of Christ. This triad of Plotinus constitutes the ideal or intelligible universe, identically one with the Deity, type of the world of sense, and alone real and true It was the origin of the Realism of the schools, the link that connected the teaching of some of the most eminent schoolmen with Pantheism, Porphyry and Boethius having been the medium of communication [SCHOLASTIC THEOLOGY] From the Supreme emanates the soul of all things, of gods and men, of animals and brute elements Matter was also evolved, but it is as the dregs of deteriorated efflux, beyond which it is impossible that emanation should be carried The unity that maintains all-else in combination with the Divine is here dissipated, and perfection is converted into corruption Matter involves only negative attributes, and can only be qualified for good by ideas and souls that are themselves factors of the universal Thus all things come forth from the One, in themselves multiplicate and divisible, typal form and grosser matter These products also are eternal, for as the One has never existed apart from Intellect and Soul, so it has eternally produced the universe and every form of existence that it contains The absolute identity of all things with the Deity is the basis of the Plotinian scheme True knowledge is oneness of the percipient with the perceived If in high acts of contemplation we perceive the Supreme, it is our own selves that we perceive, if we gain knowledge of other intelligences, it is still ourselves that we know in them

The system of Proclus was similar to that of Plotinus, though differing somewhat in terms It was a self-consistent scheme of unity The Supreme emits from a centre of light every form of life, all of which are one, as partaking of the nature of the One; yet various in power, as scintillations from the source of ever-varying life The force with which these speed from the central Unit carries them back again to be reabsorbed in Unity The Cabbala has also borrowed this idea from Orientalism. Thus the Pythagorean doctrine of a transmigration of souls was a distinguishing feature of ancient Pantheism Neo-Platonicism had an especial aversion for Christianity, and was eventually suppressed by Justinian, who closed the school of Athens, when many of its disciples betook themselves to kindred spirits in the East.

Another void occurs in the history of Pantheism till the foundation of schools of learning by Charlemagne [SCHOLASTIC THEOLOGY] John Scotus Erigena restored Neo-Platonic ideas in the ninth century, and with it Pantheism, by his translation of the mystical writings of Pseudo-Dionysius the Areopagite He stands midway between the more ancient and modern Pantheists, the corner-stone of the old system was the foundation of the new His book *de Div Naturæ* is remarkable for its outspoken Pantheism [*ibid*] It describes the Universal as a mighty river flowing from its source in an indefinite stream, quickening all things in its course, and carried back to the fountain-head by natural exhalation and condensation, to be again rolled forth as before [*de Divis Nat.* iii. 103] "All is God and God is All" The divine progression through all things is resolution, the return of all to the source is deification [De Gérando, iv 363]

Again two centuries, and William of Champeaux, the immediate precursor of the scholastic system, broached a theory that, if it was not Pantheism, led straight to it His notion of Universals, borrowed from Plotinus, taught that all Individuality is one in its substance, and varies only in its non-essential accidents and transient properties Amalric of Bena and David of Dinant followed the theory out into a thoroughgoing Pantheism, and were condemned [A D 1210] Gerson gives as the heads of Amaurism "All is God and God is All The Creator and the creature are one Ideas are at once creative and created, subjective and objective Being God is the end of All, and All return to Him As every variety of humanity forms one manhood, so the world contains only individual forms of one eternal essence" David of Dinant only varied upon this by imagining a corporeal unity. Although body, soul, and eternal substance are three, these three are one and the same Being Latin versions of the Arab philosopher Averroës (Ibn Roshd), and orientalized paraphrases of Aristotle, tended to give a still more decided pantheistic tinge to scholastic theology [*Encycl Metr.* xi. 809] Albertus Magnus, Duns Scotus, and Raymund Lully, were the principal delinquents. [SCHOOLMEN.]

The fermentation of philosophic thought had brought the scum of Pantheism once more to the surface

In the latter half of the sixteenth century Bruno Giordano, who first introduced a knowledge of the Copernican system into England [Whewell, *Intr to Ind. Sc* i 385], an obscure and inconsistent reasoner, formed a mixed system which was partly Pythagorean, partly hylozoic, and partly was borrowed from the writings of Proclus He and his books were burned at Rome, and in consequence his writings are scarce, but copious extracts are given by Hallam [*Introd to Lit of Eur* ii 146-154] God, he said, is the Universe, and the Universe is God The Pythagorean method of illustrating the emanation of all things from God by arithmethical development expressed the truth, according to his view, better than any other The world of sense is a vast animal having the Deity for its living soul It was the old Stoic theory revived Birth is expansion from the one centre of life, life is its continuance, and death is the necessary return of the ray to the centre of light

Baruch (Benedict) Spinoza, born of Jewish parents at Amsterdam [A D 1632], gave its first impulse to the Pantheism that has formed the main staple of German philosophy in modern times, as exhibited by Fichte and Schelling, Hegel and Strauss His system, suggested by the CABBALA of Judaism, is briefly set forth under SPINOZISM, it is sufficient therefore to say here, that in this orientalizing notion the Deity and the universe are said to be but one substance, at the same time spirit and matter, thought and extension, which are the only known attributes of the Deity He was a disbeliever of the world rather than of God, an Acosmist, to use Jacobi's expression, rather than an Atheist, as Bayle has erroneously termed him His "natura naturans" expresses the extended Deity, life is the divine expansion, thought is an attribute of the Deity, rather it is the Deity itself as sentient substance, though perfectly passive and impersonal To do away with the notion of a personal Deity has ever since been the aim of German philosophy His scoff upon the Christian doctrine of the Incarnation is best expressed in his own words "Quod quædam ecclesiæ his addant quod Deus naturam humanam assumserit, monui expresse me quid dicant nescire imo, ut verum fatear, non minus absurde mihi loqui videntur, quam si quis mihi dixerit quod circulus naturam quadrati induerit" [*Ep* 21, *ad Oldenb*] To speak of the Intelligence or the Will of the Deity is to speak of Him as of man, it is as absurd as to ascribe to the Deity bodily motion There is nothing whatever in common between the Divine Mind and human intelligence "Cogitatio Deo concedenda, non intellectus" There is no such thing as freedom of thought or will, everything is one extended chain of consequences, and thought begets thought by a necessity that is under no other control than the fatal law of its own being Evil is inconceivable where all is equally divine and necessary, and where liberty is null. All is good where all is order, it is our own ignorance of ultimate results, and of the necessary relation of things, that makes us think things ill that are not substantially so What man terms evil in its worst forms is only a contradiction to the laws of his own nature, not of laws that are universal Spinoza speaks mistily of a future state, and is unable to imagine the soul separate from the body Immortality consists in a return to God, to the annihilation of all personal and individual existence, it was the idea of Averroes again revived The more intellectual theory of Spinoza was only distilled off from the dead dregs of primitive Pantheism, it added little to the Vedantism of India, the same matter was manipulated, but with a more scientific consistency and a more cold-blooded rationalism, it was in close alliance with the Eleatic theory Spinoza, like Erigena, was never the representative man of a school, yet he has exercised an undoubtedly powerful influence over German modes of thought He first declared that all ideas have their negative side, and succeeding reasoners gave a full development to this germ of thought Thus there is an inherent contradiction in the notion of Deity on the side of attribute, for attribute implies definition, and definition the negation of all that it does not comprehend Extension is in antagonism with non-extension, thought with void Schelling, following out the hint, made "I" in its positive and negative aspect one reality Hence, too, the identical contradictories of Hegel, "Being" identical with "Nil," the Finite with the Infinite, Life with Death, of which more will be said in its place. Spinoza was warmly patronized by Lessing, whom Mendelssohn defended loyally as a friend from the charge of Spinozism, Schleiermacher also has all but canonized the renegade Jewish philosopher

There is nothing pantheistic in the sceptical philosophy of Kant, but he struck out new modes of thought that were easily worked into their systems by Fichte and Schelling and Hegel, the three hierophants of Pantheism in modern Germany The mutual relations and functions of subject and object according to Kant form a primitive duality. Subject is the absolute ideal, surrounded by every attribute that pertains to it as an impression on the mind in its most abstract form, Object is the idea invested in its appropriate form in man's world of action, it is a "fait accompli," external to the mind, but of universal cognizance, thus, if St Paul speaks of faith, St James shews that subjective faith cannot save a man, its reality must be demonstrated objectively as a "fides formata," and give actual tangible proof of its existence to other minds He exhibits the two different phases of the same quality The subjective is of the secret essence of our mental perceptions As the perceptive faculty of thought, it suggests the conditions of perception, as the initiative faculty of knowledge, the conditions of judgment The objective is the material substratum of our perceptions, the realization of phenomenal experience All knowledge involves the union of form and matter, the coincidence of subject and object These two principles have no substantial reality in themselves, but stand merely in reciprocally dependent relation; we know nothing of any absolute nature that they may possess, it is to us as the unknown quantity x Reason is a function of ideas that are unconditional and absolute, it is a generalizing power, perception that is invested with the highest possible degree of unity The objective plays so subordinate a part in the transcendental idealism of Kant, that by an easy transition the next step in German philosophy was to blot it out altogether as a separate factor in mental philosophy This was done by Fichte According to his theory subject is the sole source of all absolute reality To form a true conception of identity, that I (Ich, Ego) = I, abstraction from every external idea is requisite, thought reverts upon itself and occupies itself with that which is thus wholly abstracted, the subjectively thinking being and the objectively conceived thought are identically the same; that which is thus subjectively known is the only real existence He recognised alone as real the subjective I, and eliminated the objective or external world. It was a system of pure Idealism By abstraction and reflection, then, that purely free and plastic energy is attained whereby the individual I gains a conception of itself, and proceeding onwards in the same direction, it improves upon that conception by grasping the idea of the Absolute It is the intuition of intelligence Thus, I is All and All is I The notion of matter is from the first annihilated, intelligence alone exists and is generative of all else The production of the external world is the manifestation of self-unity The Deity is moral order, the consolidation of the ideal in the real, of reason in results It is the soul of all human progress, of which Fichte declared to his class with blasphemous hardihood, "Gentlemen, I will now proceed to create the Deity"[1] There is a close parallel to Fichteism in the Buddhist system, which represents I as the Eternal, the Creator, who draws from self-resource all the phenomena of nature Thus, the ethical Theism of Kant was converted into ethical Pantheism by Fichte

Schelling was the exponent of the "Philosophy of Nature" [*Darlegung des wahren Verhaltnisses d Naturphil z Fichtischen Lehre*] Subject and object he said, with Kant, are relative terms, they reciprocally involve each other's existence, do away with the one and the other vanishes Truth is not absolute subjectivity, and absolute subjectivity is not the truth pure and simple, but truth is alone to be found in the Absolute, which is the one Eternal unchangeable Being, and is developed in the ideal God is identically one with reason The Absolute is not to be apprehended by abstraction or reflection, but by direct intellectual intuition, as some of the St Victoire schoolmen also asserted By intuition that plastic energy is gained at once which associates the spirit of man with the Absolute All being is one and the same. Knowledge and Being are one perfect unity There is a like identity between form and matter Yet there is an apparent antithesis in Being, consisting as it does at the same time of unity and multiplicity But unity *qua* unity, and multiplicity *qua* multiplicity have no proper being, the alone Existence is the copula that unites them, which is Being God is unity, and He is all things The universe and God are the selfsame substance Variety and multiplicity are only apparent, they have no reality in Being Nature sleeps in the plant, dreams in the brute creature, but wakes up in man Spirit and matter interpenetrate each other, and there is a species of "communicatio idiomatum" between them, for intellect is only matter lit up and etherealized, matter is only intellect darkened and crassified. Thus Schelling caused every other essence to pass over under his manipulation, and a "caput mortuum" of existence, neutral and colourless, was all that remained in the alembic. His system was a transcendental idealism based upon pure Pantheism, which affected every phase of life, whether private or public Moral law is a tendency in the direction of the Absolute, science is a knowledge of the Absolute, art is its terrestrial image, the body politic is the realization of public life ordained with reference to the Absolute, history involves the idea of an indefinite progressiveness, of perfectibility in the Absolute, of which it is a continuous revelation Blessedness is final absorption into Being, like the Nirvána of the Buddhist Men may seem to act spontaneously of their own free will, yet they only carry out a predetermined order of things, and are under the constraint of a secret necessity The Deity is not in this or that man, but is in the sum total of humanity Religion in every varying aspect is the measure of Divine development in the soul of man No one religion *per se* can convey an adequate idea of God, but religious systems are complete as a whole in supplementing each other's deficiencies An adequate notion of the Deity will at some time be the result The golden age of religion is not in time past, but future Thus Schelling carries back our thoughts to the Eleatic and Neo-Platonic schools, in which knowledge was identical with Being Xenophanes and Parmenides, Plotinus and Proclus, described pure existence as absolute unity All things with them were one, as in the subjective Idealism of Schelling

Hegelism is a further development in the same direction, but it is Idealism in a more absolute sense, like Buddhism Its basis is unity, Being is identical with Thought More thoroughgoing than his predecessors, possibly also with more consistency, Hegel professes to exhibit the law which bands together the various modifications of this unity By its own inherent energy, unity comes forth from its absolute re-

[1] It was an improvement, as he doubtless thought, upon the concluding words of Spinoza's first book of Ethics, where he says with consummate effrontery, "I have now explained the nature of the Deity.".

pose, and subjects itself to every condition of transformation and limitation Yet it remains Unity This "Prozess" of modern German thought is a reflex of Oriental emanation theories The Idea antecedent to all successional product is a cold abstraction, its first offsets are of like character, Being and non-Being, shortly to be explained, quality, quantity, measure, identity, difference, and so forth, express a gradational "Becoming" (das Werden) of that which was not before, and constitute a chain the first link of which is Being. The Absolute includes the ideas of Extension and Thought, at once pure Being and pure Notion, the Ideal and the Real Idea and Notion, Being and Absolute, all being convertible terms

Hegel's determination of his Laws of Idea is laid down in the *Logic*, deduced from one fundamental principle, the "Law of Contradictories" Giving a further development to Spinoza's idea, he affirmed that every notion involves a contradiction antithesis is an essential element of ideal constitution, thus mind and matter form the individual man Will and foreknowledge, though antagonizing qualities, in no way interfere with the Divine Unity The universe involves the same contradiction, for Nothing as well as All Things emanated from the Divine Idea. Darkness is the shadow of light, the mingling of the two by abstraction of various beams gives the semblance of colour Being is antagonized by non-Being Every idea then involves three elements, or, in Hegelian language, "moments" An idea may be considered as it is in itself, or as it is in contrast with its antagonism, or as it is in joint relation with both its positive and negative side The first represents the Idea or Deity, the second the Deity as Nature, in which "to become" distinguishes Being from non-Being, and gives the basis of natural science, and the third is Spirit, resulting from the recombination of the two in one moral and æsthetic world, of which religion and philosophy, arts and social institutions are the various phases The "logical" emanations of Hegel having a real being assigned to them, are suggestive of Gnosticism, "Deus est in fieri," it was a process of daily development, but there is a strong Neo-Platonic cast in other terms of his system, such as his rejection of the experience on which Kant so strongly insisted, and his claim of direct intuition, the identity of thinking mind and its object, the triune character of his theory, the profession of leading the initiated on to Absolute Truth, and other points of analogy with the teaching of Plotinus

The principles of Strauss are Hegelian utterances in their most exaggerated form, under their guidance he professes to apply to Gospel history the critical method of Niebuhr, whose freethinking however never reached beyond the domain of history Such history at the best he declares to be *nil* The work of the Spirit is present, and is not to be sought out in the far-distant dreamy visions of bygone ages Like Hegel, Strauss draws no distinction between the Spirit of God and the spirit of man All is one Spirit The Vedantists of India also identified the spirit of man with the spirit of the universe But they rose to a much higher level than modern Pantheists At the present day, union with the Deity means little more than the transcendental march of intellect, the Vedantist taught that it was oneness with all that is pure and holy in the spiritual world of blessedness [Mill, *Panth Princ* 41] According to Strauss, religion is the human and revelation the divine side of that unity that constitutes all things one The universality of human souls, an idea taken from Averroes by Amalric of Bena and David of Dinant, and condemned at Paris A D 1210, is reproduced by Strauss as it was by Spinoza "Without World God is not God" (ohne Welt ist Gott nicht Gott) is the teaching of both Hegel and Strauss Their God is not a person but vague personality, and cannot interfere with the established order of the world's progress The Christology of Strauss, like that of Hegel, treats with contempt the thought of the personality of Christ, which is a "purposeless residuum" Humanity is the Anointed of the Lord The Incarnation means, not the union of two natures in one personal subsistence, but union through the spirit of the Absolute and the Finite, the Deity thinking and acting in universal humanity Spinoza had already said as much The Resurrection and Ascension are a mere representation of human progress by a double negation, the negation of all that is worth the name of life, followed by a resolution of that negative condition through quickened union with the Absolute. Thus there is no room for faith or trust, no sense of individual support, no hope of answered prayer in this soulless and hopeless system The "sting of death" is ignorance of Straussian and Hegelian ideas, its removal is the only "resurrection to life" Other points of the Strauss theory, as of German philosophy, need not to be touched upon here, which have less palpable points of contact with Pantheism, being reserved for a subsequent article [RATIONALISTS]

The foregoing account will have shewn that the entire system of German metaphysics, as represented by the writers instanced, is a reproduction of ancient Pantheism It is the Theosophy of the East imported into the West, an avowed attempt to displace the religious idea that God stamped upon the soul and conscience of humanity from the very cradle of the race in Paradise The personality of the Deity and of Christ, with the individual responsibility of man, are the weighty questions upon which men's minds are to be unsettled There is nothing original in the means adopted, unless indeed in their higher sublimation from all earthly taint of common sense, "Insana magis quam hæretica," the present deification of man is the last word of German philosophy, which begins with the Scepticism of Kant and ends in the Pantheism of Hegel and Strauss "J'ai assez lu," says Saisset, as the conclusion of his comparison of the successive systems of German philosophy [*Essaie de Phil. Rel*], "j'ai assez discuté, l'âge mûr arrivé, il faut fermer ces livres, me replier au dedans de moi, et ne plus consulter que ma raison "

[Maret, *Essaie sur le Pantheisme* Dr Mill's *Observations on Pantheistic Principles*, etc Saisset, *Essaie de Phil Relig* and *Descartes*. Cudworth's *Intellectual System* Franck, *Etudes Orientales* and *La Cabbale* Baur, *K Gesch d XIX Jahrh* Dr R Williams, *Christianity and Hinduism* Herzog and K Lexicon, Art *Pantheismus* Renan, *Averroes* and *Etudes de Phil Relig* Ritter, *Gesch d Philosoph* Fischer, *Gesch. d neueren Phil* De Gérando, *Histoire Comparée* Milman, *Hist. Jews*, bk xxviii Leibnitz, *Crit Rem on Spinoza* Schleiermacher, *Gesch d Philosoph* Biogr Univ *Spinoza* Christlieb, *Leb u Lehre Joh Scot Erig* Staudenmayer, *J Scot Erigena* Helfferich, *Spinoza u Leibnitz*. Richter, *Pantheismus* Romans, *Pantheismus* Barchou de Penhoen, *Philos Allemande* Ancillon, *Fichte et Schelling* Bohmer, *de Panth. nom. et orig.* Tholuck, *die Lehre v d Sunde*]

PAPELLARDS A term used in the thirteenth century to designate the party which uncompromisingly supported the Papacy. It was applied chiefly to the mendicant friars and their adherents, and with special reference to their pietistic affectation of poverty and their arrogant pretence of humility William of St Amour [A D 1255] uses it not only with reference to the mendicant friars, but also to "those young men and maidens itinerating about in France, who, under pretence of living only for prayer, had really no other object in view than to get rid of work, and live on the alms of the pious" When Louis IX was almost persuaded by the Dominicans to enter their order, he was nicknamed "Rex Papellardus" [Gulielm de Sancto Amore, *De periculis novissimorum temp*, quoted in Neander's *Ch Hist* vii 396, Bohn's ed] It was also a name given to the Beguins [Robert de Sorbonne in *Biblioth Max Lugd* xxv 350]

PARKER, THEODORE. [RATIONALISTS]

PARMENIANI or PARMENIANISTI The usual name of the Donatists in the interior of Africa, derived from Parmenian, a Donatist bishop [Prædestinati, lib cap. 69]

PARSEES The name given to the adherents of the ancient religion of Media and Persia, founded, probably not later than B C 1000, by the Bactrian Zarathrustra Spitama, or Zoroaster They now number not more than 150,000 persons, some living in the north of Persia, in the town of Yezd and the surrounding villages, but the greater number in Hindostan, in the city of Bombay and its neighbourhood, and in some cities of Gujerat Many have of late years settled, for purposes of trade, etc, in Calcutta, and other cities of Hindostan, in China, and in Great Britain. The name "Parsees" signifies "Inhabitants of Fars," or Persia Other names by which they are known are, "Zoroastrians," from their founder, "Magians," properly the name of another religion incorporated with that of Zoroaster, "Ghebers" or "Guebers," applied in contempt by the Mahometans to the small remnant in Persia, and said, in violation of all linguistic laws, to be derived from the Arabic Kafir, an unbeliever, perhaps it was the name of some tribe, sect, or city.

This religion arose out of a schism from, and a revolt against, the primitive Aryan worship of nature-powers, known to us from the earliest portions of the Vedas [BRAHMINS] The common origin of these two religions is shown by the similarity of many of their rites—the offering of the juice of the homa or soma plant, and the effects ascribed to drinking it, the sacrifice of the horse, the investiture at initiation with the sacred thread The legends of the sacred books strikingly resemble each other, even to the names of those of whom they are related. Their antagonism is shewn in the titles of the sacred Beings In the oldest form of Brahminism, these, regarded as powers rather than persons, are known indifferently as Ahuras, or Asuras, and Devas But the later development, after the rise of Zoroastrianism, confined the name Deva to the good powers, assigning that of Asura to the evil beings. Zoroastrianism, recognising spiritual personal existences, reverses the names, calls the good spirits Ahuras, the evil Devs, while most of the beings hitherto worshipped are included among the Devs There are very plain indications of the struggle both in the Zend-Avesta and in the Brahmanas The causes of the schism have been plausibly conjectured to be of both a social, political, and a religious nature It is probable that a portion of the ancient Aryans, abandoning their previous pastoral and nomad life, settled as agriculturalists in Bactria and other suitable districts These, in consequence, became estranged from the other Aryan tribes, who still clung to their ancestral mode of living The latter, allured by hope of plunder, attacked and devastated the settlements of the former The hatred which arose naturally extended to religion, devotion to which was regarded as the cause of success Hence arose a divergence of views, and, in the end, each regarded the religion of the other as the source of all mischief and wickedness [See Haug, *Essays*, 248, 249] He who gave a distinctive form to the new faith of the Bactrian tribes was Zarathrustra (the Greek Ζαραστράδης, Ζωροάστρης, the Latin Zoroaster, Modern Persian Zerdoscht, Zerdusht), usually distinguished from those successors in the priesthood who bore the same title by the addition of his family name, Spitama. The date assigned to him varies enormously B C 3000 [Bunsen, *God in History*, i 276], B C 1500 [Haug, *Essays*, 254, 255], 6th century B.C , but this last date is certainly too late, and arose from a mistaken identification of the King Vistaspa, under whom he lived, with Darius Hystaspis The details of his life, as handed down to us, are entirely legendary and unhistorical. We only know that he was a native of Bactria, living under a King Vistaspa, that he was married, and had children In the Vendidad he is represented as possessing supernatural and even divine powers, being superior to the Amshashspands, and next to the supreme Deity himself. He is styled "The master of the whole living creation," "The abyss of knowledge and truth" His religion became predominant in ancient Irania, including Bactria, Media, and Persia, being, in course of time, adopted as the official religion of the two latter empires, but undergoing various modifications and developments It received a great blow from the conquests of Alexander the Great, and under the Greek, semi-Greek, and Parthian kingdoms which were successively built upon the ruins of his empire, it lost almost all its influence and power But on the restoration of the Persian monarchy by the Sassanidæ [A D 226], the religion of Zoroaster was revived, purified, and re-established as the State religion The remains of the sacred books were collected, and translated into the vernacular Pehlevi from the obsolete Zend It was finally overthrown by the Mahometan conquest [A D 651], and soon almost exterminated Its votaries were forcibly converted, or expelled from Persia Some took up their abode to the north of that country, where a few thousands, in the most wretched condition, still remain, others removed, first to the shores of the Persian Gulf, and then [eighth century A D.] to Hindostan

The doctrines of the Parsee religion are contained in the remains of the sacred books, called the Zend-Avesta, or, more properly, Avesta-Zend, a contraction of Avesta-u-Zend, "Text and Commentary" They consist of a text, with an authorized commentary, equally sacred with the text, written in the language called Zend—a sister to Sanscrit, closely resembling the oldest form of Sanscrit, and, like it, now a dead language A translation of the Zend-Avesta into the Pehlevi language, a corruption of Zend by Semitic elements, was made about the third century A D, under the Sassanidæ, when Pehlevi became the national speech, and a further translation and explanation was, at a later time, made into Pazend or Parsee, a language closely resembling modern Persian

Only a very small portion of the original Zend-Avesta now exists, the remainder having been destroyed, partly through the conquests of Alexander, but still more through the Mussulman conquest of Persia, A D 651 The Zend-Avesta proper contained twenty-one Nosks or books, each consisting of text and commentary Of these the names and subjects alone are preserved, except the 20th, called Vendidad, which is entire, and some fragments There are also other works included in the present Zend-Avesta, which either are not mentioned among the Nosks at all, or only imperfectly indicated Of these the most important are the Yaçna, or Izeschne, and the Visparad, which are more ancient than the Nosks, bearing the same relation to them as the Vedas to the Shastras and Puranas [Haug, *Essays*, 128] The most important of all is the *Izeschne* or *Yaçna*, which consists of two parts, divided into seventy-two chapters The second part, containing five Gâthas, or songs in metre, is by far the most ancient of the Zoroastrian writings, and is plausibly attributed to the founder himself, or his immediate followers The Yaçna consists of prayers to be recited at the sacrificial rites The *Visparad*, in twenty-three chapters, is a collection of prayers, of later date, to be used on the same occasions The *Vendidad*, the code of religious, civil and criminal laws, above mentioned, ranks next It is apparently fragmentary, and is evidently the work of many hands and times It is composed of twenty-two Fargards or sections, and may be divided into three parts The first part (Farg 1-3) is introductory, containing an enumeration of regions successively created by Ormazd, and spoiled by Ahriman, probably indicating the countries over which Zoroastrianism had spread, legends of a certain king Yima, and recommendations of agriculture The second part (4-17)—the groundwork—contains laws, ceremonies, and observances, treated without observing any order or arrangement The third part (18 to end) is a sort of appendix on various subjects, such as spells against diseases The foregoing works form the Vendidad Sadè, or Liturgy, and are arranged as a manual for the use of the priests The *Yashts*, twenty-four in number, are hymns in praise of sacred persons, or ministers of Ormazd, and sacred objects—the sun, the stars, the homa juice, etc There are also smaller collections of prayers, praises, and blessings, etc, for various occasions, which, with the Yashts, compose the Khordah-Avesta, or little Avesta, for the use of the laity According to Parsee tradition, the whole of the Zend-Avesta was composed by the Deity, and delivered to Zoroaster to be given to mankind This claim to a divine origin is unsupported by internal evidence, and probably arises from the fact that Zoroaster is a collective name, indicating the school of successors of the founder as high priests, from whom the Zend-Avesta chiefly proceeded The text, in its present form and arrangement, cannot be earlier than the time of the Sassanidæ [A D 226]; but the different parts are many centuries older The Gâthas, the earliest part, are probably at least as early as B C 1000 To the Zend-Avesta proper is added, as a sort of appendix, the *Bundehesh*, now existing only in Pehlevi, a compilation of extracts and fragments of very different dates, treating of the constitution of the universe, and in its present form not earlier than the 7th century A D

The modern Parsees also use other works of later date, mostly post-Christian, which are not canonical, such as the Sadder, a manual of doctrine and practice, and various catechisms, and other works

DOCTRINES. The religion of Zoroaster, so far as can be gathered from the earliest Gâthas, was a pure Monotheism The highest object of adoration is "Ahura Mazdao," i e that Ahura which is Mazdao The name appears in later times under the forms Auramazda (cuneiform inscriptions), Ὡρομάσδης in Greek writers, Ahurmazd under the Sassanidæ, Ormazd among the modern Parsees Its meaning has been variously explained as "The living wise One," "The living Creator," "The great Giver of Life" [Rawlinson, *Five Monarchies*, iii.

96, note 10 Smith, *Ancient Hist of East*, 384, note 11] The conception of the supreme Deity is sublime All the highest attributes, except that of Fatherhood, are assigned to him He is the Creator and Lord of the whole universe, the Creator of earthly and spiritual life He is the Holy God, the Father of all Truth, the "Best Being of all," the Master of Purity He is supremely happy, possessing every blessing, health, wealth, virtue, immortality, wisdom, and abundance of every earthly good All these he bestows on the good man who is pure in thought, word, and deed, while he punishes the wicked All that is created, good or evil, fortune or misfortune, is his work He is to be served by purity, truth, and goodness, in thought, word, and deed, by prayers and offerings The works of agriculture are especially pleasing to him No images of him were allowed In spite of some mixture of physical ideas, the ascription to him of health, the conception of him as in some sense light, the notion of Ahura-Mazda is truly spiritual Under the Supreme Being are the Genii, who stand between God and man—Sraosha, the instructor of the prophet, the friend of God, and the protector of the faith, and Armaiti, the genius of the earth, and the guardian of piety, and perhaps some others The existence of evil was accounted for by the supposition of two primeval causes, which, though opposed to each other, were united in every existing being, even in Ahura-Mazda himself, and by their union produced the world of material things and of spiritual existences The cause of good is Vohu-Mano, the good mind, from which springs Gaya, or reality, to it all good true, and perfect things belong The evil cause is Akem-Mano, "naughty mind," from which springs non-reality (Ajyaiti), to it all evil and delusive things belong But, as united in Ahura-Mazda, the two principles are called Spento-Manyus the white or holy spirit, and Angro-Manyus, the dark spirit No personal existence is ascribed to these; they both exist in Ahura-Mazda, but they are opposed to one another as creators of light and darkness, of life and death, of sleep and waking Such were the original Zoroastrian doctrines But, in course of time, through the operation of the principle whereby abstractions become personified, this primeval doctrine became corrupted into a systematic Dualism, which is seen fully developed in the Vendidad The two causes appear as distinct and opposed personal beings, Ahura-Mazda or Ormazd, of whom Spento-Manyus is a title, and Angro-Manyus or Ahriman These two existed separately and independently from all eternity, each ruling over a realm of his own, and constantly at war with and striving to overthrow the other All the good and pure creations of Ormazd are defiled and spoilt by those of Ahriman, who cannot create independently, but only brings evil into being to counterwork, spoil, and destroy the good works of Ormazd Under each principle is a hierarchy of ministers, personal beings created by their respective lords, whom they serve and obey in every way The first created and chief of these to Ormazd are his six councillors, in later times made seven by including Sraosha or Ormazd himself They are called Amesha-Spentas (among the modern Parsees Amshashpands), or "immortal saints," and each rules over a special province of creation. These are in their origin personifications of abstractions representing the gifts of Ormazd to his worshippers Ahriman has also a council of six (later, seven) evil beings, the counterparts of Ormazd's councillors, who work evil in the spheres over which the latter preside. Under these, on each side, are hosts of other spirits Those of Ormazd are the Yazatas (modern Yezds), good spirits, headed by Sraosha and the Fervers, invisible protectors of all created beings Ahriman has the Devas or Devs, the exact contraries to these The two principles are regarded as coequal and coeternal in the past, neither is absolutely victorious as yet. Their strife extends throughout all creation, every existing thing is ranged on one side or the other, nothing can be neutral But at the last three prophets, sprung from Zoroaster, will appear, will convert all mankind to Zoroastrianism, evil will be conquered and annihilated, Ahriman will vanish for ever, and creation will be restored to its pristine purity A later development still was made by the Zarvanian sect, probably about 350-300 B C These, to save the unity of the Supreme held that the two principles emanated from a being called Zarvan-akarana, time without bounds, into whom they will again be in the end absorbed This doctrine rests on a misinterpretation of texts in the Zend-Avesta [See Haug, *Essay*, etc pp. 20, 21, 264] It is, however, still held by the Parsees and Guebres Man is represented as created by Ormazd in purity and holiness, but through the temptation of the Devs he fell, and became exposed to sin and evil Every man is bound to choose whether he will serve Ormazd by good deeds, industry, and piety, or Ahriman by the contrary vices According as he chooses, so is he rewarded or punished in another world On the day following the third night from death, the souls of the dead are collected, and have to pass over an exceedingly narrow bridge, stretched over hell, leading to heaven, called Chinvat Peretu, "the bridge of the judge" or "gatherer" The wicked fall into the gulf below, where they are received with scoffs and scorn by Ahriman and his ministers, and live in misery, feasting on poisoned banquets, till the time of restitution The good, upheld by good spirits, and aided by the prayers of their friends, pass into heaven, are received by the archangels, and dwell with Ormazd and the Amshashpands According to some authorities it is taught, that at the final restitution the body will rise again and be reunited to the soul, but this is probably a later addition from Christian or Jewish sources [See Haug, *Essay*, etc 196, 266, Pusey *on Daniel*, 508, *sq*] The morality of Zoroastrianism is simple, pure, and practical The great duty of the faithful is to aid Ormazd in the struggle with evil, both within the soul and without it Truth, purity, piety, and industry are the highest virtues, suicide, impurity, and lying the most horrible crimes Virtue in thought, word, and deed is equally required The religious rites consist in the acknowledgment of Ahura-Mazda, and the spiritual hierarchy under him, in frequent prayers, praises, and thanksgivings to them in sacrifices, and purificatory ceremonies Originally images were forbidden, but the faith was corrupted in this respect under the later Persian kings by the adoption of foreign deities and idols, especially of Mithra, originally one of the Yazatas, afterwards looked on as the Sun-God, and Anaitis The Sassanian reform restored the primitive purity in this respect Luminous objects, the sun, moon, planets, fire, are reverenced as symbols of Ormazd, to one of these believers turn in prayer In the temples are altars fed by sacred fire ever kept burning, the sullying of which is punished by death The priests wear masks when they approach it, and only touch it with holy instruments Great reverence is also paid to the other elements, earth, air, and water These may not be defiled by the dead, which are therefore exposed on a grating at the summit of towers (called towers of silence) to the birds of prey and the weather When the bones are stripped they fall through a grating to a vault beneath It is much disputed whether this reverence to the elements belonged to the religion of Zoroaster, or whether it is a later addition arising from the fusion with it of the Turanian elemental worship of the mountain regions, Armenia, Kurdistan, etc, of which the Magi were the priestly caste. Dr Haug [*Essays*, 250, 251] advocates the former view, holding that Zoroaster himself was a "fire priest," Prof Rawlinson, and others, for whom the evidence seems to preponderate, the latter [See Rawlinson, *Five Monarchies*, iii 122, 136, iv 340, 347, and *Herodotus*, App to Bk I. Essay V; and the article "Magier" in Herzog's *Encyklopadie*, vol viii pp 675, *sq*] The sacrifices consist of the slaying of animals, a portion of whose flesh is shewn to the fire, and then the whole victim eaten by the priests and worshippers There is also the Homa ceremony, consisting in the extraction of the juice of the homa plant during prayers, the presenting it to the fire, and the consumption of it by the priests and worshippers This was thought to confer immortality and other great gifts A sacred meal is on certain occasions eaten with special blessings, prayers, and ceremonies, in honour of Ormazd and the good spirits Confession of sins to the priests is practised, but ascetisism is expressly discouraged Impurity is cleansed by the ceremonial washing with nirang, *i e* cow's urine, accompanied by prayers There are now two orders of priests, the Destoors and the Mobeds over all is a chief Destoor The Modern Parsees are very exclusive in their customs, they will eat no food cooked by one of another religion, and only marry among themselves Polygamy is forbidden, and divorce only allowed after nine years of barrenness. Of late years a party has arisen to advocate reforms in their customs and habits, such as the abolition of exclusiveness, of marriages of consanguinity, and of the use of the nirang, and this movement has caused much controversy among them [On the present state of the Parsees, see *Manners and Customs of the Parsees, and the Parsee Religion*, by Dadabhai Navroji, *The Parsees*, by Dosabhoi Framjee, Max Muller, *Chips*, I art vii viii] It has been strongly urged by recent writers that many of the scriptural doctrines, *e g* the resurrection of the body, the nature of the angels, were borrowed from Parseeism For a complete refutation of this theory see Pusey's *Daniel*, Lect ix, Hull's *Myth Interp* 124, *sqq* But very plain indications of its influence may be found in the later Jewish theology set forth in the Talmud [*Quart Rev* cxxiii p 456, *sq*] The religious Jews were naturally more favourably inclined to Zoroastrianism than to the other religions with which they were brought in contact, resembling their own faith as it did in its Monotheism, its hatred of idolatry, and the purity of its moral precepts From it was derived the dualism of the Manichees and other heretics [Milman, *Hist Christianity*, i 62, ed 1867] Mahometanism borrowed largely from its tenets, even to minute details [Mahometans]

[Hyde, *De Relig vet Persar*, *Essays on the Sacred Language, Writings, and Religion of the Parsees*, by Dr Martin Haug, Rawlinson, *Five Great Monarchies*, iii 93-136, iv 328-347, and *Translation of Herodotus*, App Essay V vol i 346, "The Sacred Books of the Zoroastrians" in Miss Cobbe's *Studies New and Old of Ethical and Social Subjects*, pp 89-143, Bunsen, *God in History*, bk iii ch 6, and App notes D, E, *Egypt*, iii 474, *sq*, Max Muller, *Chips from a German Workshop*, arts iii v-viii, Milman, *Hist Christianity*, i 62, *sq*, ii 247, *sq* ed 8167, Pusey, *Daniel the Prophet*, Lect ix; *Theological Review*, No 32, for Jan 1871, pp 96-110, the articles *Magier*, viii 675, *sq* and *Parsismus*, xi 115, *sqq* in Herzog's *Real Encyklopadie* There are editions of the Zend-Avesta by Westergaard and Spiegel, and a German translation by Spiegel]

PARTICULAR BAPTISTS [Baptists]

PASAGIANS A sect of Judaizing Catharists which appeared in Lombardy late in the twelfth or early in the thirteenth century, but which probably originated in the East, and took its name either from the fact of the emigration and wandering life of those who composed it, as if they were "passaggieri," birds of passage, always on the move either from habit or from fear of persecution, or from some association with the Crusades, for which "pasagium" was an ordinary name They observed the law of Moses except as to sacrifices circumcision, the Sabbath, and distinctions of clean and unclean food, all forming part of their system, and hence they were also called "Circumcisi" Their Christology only allowed Christ to be the highest of created beings, and they seem to have considered Him a kind of Demiurge by whose work all other creatures were brought into being.

The Pasagians appealed to the Scriptures of the Old and New Testaments in support of their doctrine, a fact which is met thus by Bonacursus, the chief authority for their history "Sed quia hunc suum errorem Novi Testamenti ac prophetarum testimonio nituntur, proprio illorum gladio, Christi suffragante gratia, sicut David Goliam, eundem suffocemus" [Bonacursus, *Vita Hæret seu Manifestatio hæres Catharorum*, in D'Achery's *Spicileg* i 211 Gerhard Bergam in Murator *Antiqq Ital Med Ævi* v 152]

PASAGINIANS [PASAGIANS]

PASCAL [JANSENISTS]

PASCHAL CONTROVERSY The dissension which arose between the early Churches of the East and West respecting the days on which our Lord's Death [πάσχα σταυρώσιμον] and Resurrection [πάσχα ἀναστάσιμον] were to be commemorated

Whether there was originally one universal custom respecting the observance of these days is uncertain, but the difference is found in the second century, and since at that early date the Asiatic Churches alleged that they followed a rule laid down by St John and St Philip, while the Roman Church alleged the authority of St Peter and St Paul, it is probable that the want of uniformity out of which the controversy arose had existed even in the first century

The *Eastern custom* was to commemorate the Death of our Lord on the day of the year which answered to the 14th day of the Jewish month Nisan (that being the actual day on which it occurred), and the Resurrection on the third day following (or that answering to the 16th of Nisan), without any regard to the time of the week on which these days fell [QUARTODECIMANS]

The *Western custom* was to keep as Easter Day the Sunday following the 14th day of Nisan, and to commemorate the Death of our Lord on the preceding Friday

The history of this controversy is given at length in the DICTIONARY *of* THEOLOGY. it is sufficient here to say that the subject of it was one of the two which were placed by Constantine before the Council of Nicæa [A D 325], and that the original controversy was substantially settled by the decision of the bishops there assembled that Easter Day should always be a Sunday The Sunday fixed by the Council was that which follows the vernal equinox, and the Church of Alexandria was directed to give good notice every year what Sunday that would be in the year following Uniform accuracy was not obtained, however, for many years, and in England the use of one cycle in the North and West and of another in the South and South-east caused Easter Day to be kept on different Sundays so late even as the year 664, when an uniform custom was established by the Council of Whitby

PASCHASIUS RADBERTUS. The originator of the theory that bread and wine no longer exist in the elements of the Holy Eucharist after the Body and Blood of Christ have become present there by the act of consecration He may thus be said to have raised a controversy which has disturbed the Western Church for more than a thousand years

Paschasius Radbertus first comes into notice as a monk of Corbey in Aquitaine [A D 831] He afterwards became abbot for a few years [A D 844 851], but resigning the office, died there as a simple monk [A D 865] A former pupil, named Warin (whom he addresses as Placidius), having become Abbot of New Corbey in Saxony, requested his old instructor to draw up a treatise on the Holy Eucharist for the guidance of his young community In the year 831, therefore, Paschasius Radbertus wrote his work, *de Sacramento Corporis et Sanguinis Christi*, of which he presented an enlarged copy to the Emperor Charles the Bald in the year 844 at the Emperor's own request or demand, when it had become the subject of controversy.

In this treatise Radbert sets forth the ordinary doctrine of the Church respecting the true and real presence of our Lord's Body and Blood in the consecrated elements, but he goes far beyond all previous writers in defining the mode of that presence, and its consequences There had been scarcely any controversy hitherto on the subject of the Holy Eucharist, although St John Damascene [circ A D 740], followed by the second Council of Nicæa [A D 787] and the Council of Frankfort [A D 794], had seen cause to censure the application of the terms "type" and "figure" to the elements, while a Council of Constantinople [A D 754] had asserted their legitimate use which shews the dawn of such a controversy The dialectical subtlety which had been employed on doctrines concerning the Person of our Lord and the Holy Trinity was now, however, to be engaged for many a generation on those connected with the Sacrament of our Lord's Body and Blood, and the full tide of strife was set flowing by the clear and uncompromising statements of Radbert.

The substance of these statements is as follows. [1] That the very Body of Christ which was born of the Virgin Mary, and which was immolated upon the Cross, together with the very Blood that belonged to that Body and was shed upon the Cross, are that which the communicants receive (and he does not hint at receiving in one kind only) in receiving the consecrated elements of the Holy Eucharist [2] That the bread and the wine which are consecrated are wholly and entirely converted into the Body and Blood of Christ, so that they are no longer to be spoken of as being in any natural sense bread and wine. [3] That this conversion ordinarily takes place in such a manner that it is not made known to the senses, God permitting the appearance and taste of the bread and the wine to remain as a veil to the great miracle which He has wrought [4] But that under special circumstances—to confirm the faith of doubters, or to satisfy the devotion of saints—the fact of the conversion is made apparent to the senses by the substance of Christ's Body and Blood becoming visible, either in the form of a lamb, or presenting the colour and appearance of flesh and blood Only one such instance is narrated, but it is said to be one out of many [Pasch Radbert *de Sacram Corp et Sang Christi* in *Bibl Max Lugd* xiv 729, Martene, *Vet Script Collect* ix 367, Migne, *Patrol* cxx.]

This precise definition of the nature of the Eucharist was a novelty in the Church, as is shewn by the catenæ of authorities respecting that Sacrament which have been collected by Pamelius in his *Liturgicon*, and by Guéranger in his *Institutions Liturgiques* It raised a controversy at once among the theologians of the Benedictine order, and Radbert endeavoured to prove his statements in a letter addressed to one of his monks named Frudegard, in which he collected passages from the Fathers [Pasch Radbert *Opp Bibl Max Lugd* xiv 749, Migne's *Patrol* cxx 1351] The first to write against the novel opinions or definitions was Rabanus Maurus, Abbot of Fulda [A D 822-847], and afterwards Archbishop of Mentz [A D 847-856], in an epistle to a monk named Egil, which has been lost [*cf.* Mabillon, *Act Sanct Ord Bened* sæc iv II 591] When the controversy attracted the attention of the Emperor Charles le Chauve he required Paschasius Radbertus to place a copy of the treatise in his hands, and this was delivered to another monk of Corbey, Ratramnus, or Bertram, for examination The result was an answer by Ratramnus in the form of a treatise bearing the same title as that of Radbert, the point of which is to prove that there is a difference between the manner of Christ's Presence when on earth and that of His sacramental Presence in the Eucharistic elements, that in the latter "est quidem Corpus Christi, sed non corporale, sed spirituale," maintaining however, as strongly as his opponent, the reality of that presence [Ratramn *de Corp et Sang Domini*, Migne's *Patrol* cxviii 815, Oxford ed 1838] The great liturgical commentator, Walafridus Strabo, was also an opponent of Radbert, and that portion of his work which deals with the subject is much more in accordance with the writings of their Catholic predecessors [Walaf Strab *de Reb Eccl* xvi xvii] Another opponent was Erigena, but his opinion seems to have been utterly at variance with that of the Church, being that the Eucharist is a mere memorial of Christ's Death in past time, and not of His Presence in the Sacrament, a typical act of feeding by which the mind of the faithful communicant intellectually and piously reminds him of the work of his Lord [Dollinger's *Ch Hist* iii 73, Cox's transl]

This epoch of the thousand years' controversy does not appear to have been prolonged beyond the death of Paschasius Radbertus Its revival by Berengarius and Lanfranc in the twelfth century shews, however, that it must have been extending its effects far and wide on the popular mind and the views of Radbert were finally stamped upon the authoritative theology of the Roman Church, under the name of Transubstantiation [DICT THEOL *s v*], by the fourth Council of Lateran in the year 1215 [BERENGARIUS]

PASSALORYNCHITÆ. A sect of early mystics who derived their name from πάσσαλος, a gag, and ῥύγχος, a muzzle, it being their custom to place a finger across their lips and nose to prevent themselves from breaking silence during worship and meditation, as a literal fulfilment of the words "Set a watch, O Lord, before my mouth, and keep the door of my lips" [Ps cxli 3] St. Augustine wished to change the name of the sect to that of "Dactylorynchitæ," unaware apparently that the Greek word was sometimes used for a gag as well as for a stake The sect was probably the same as that called Tascodrungitæ [Philast *Hær* lxxvi, Aug *Hær* lxiii, Prædestinat *Hær* lxiii]

PASSIONISTS [PATRIPASSIANS]

PASTORELLI [PASTOUREAUX]

PASTOUREAUX These fanatics first appeared in the north of France about 1251 A D Their rise was due partly to the growing hatred of the clergy, who already in the thirteenth century were, in the minds of the peasants, associated with the tyrannous lay proprietary, partly to the crusading frenzy, to which the piety of St. Louis had given a marked impetus They also expressed, in an irrational way, the peasants' genuine loyalty to their king, whose absence in Egypt served to aggravate their misery Their name originated in the fact that most of those who took part in the movement were shepherds

This movement commenced in Flanders Suddenly a mysterious personage, who bore the name of "the Master of Hungary," appeared in the villages, inviting all shepherds, herdsmen, and labourers to join in the work of the rescue of the King and the recovery of the Holy Sepulchre He was an aged man with a long beard and pale emaciated face, who, it was said, spoke all languages by miracle, and claimed to act by direct authority of the Virgin When he preached, the divine letter containing his instructions was kept clasped in one of his hands, the fingers of which were never even for a moment unclosed, lest he should lose the supernatural commission This conduct readily imposed on the credulous multitude, while terror amongst the higher orders spread the wildest rumours as to his origin and character He was said to be an apostate Cistercian monk, in his youth he had denied Jesus Christ, he had been, nay, was a Mahometan, he it was that in his youth had led the crusade of children who had plunged by thousands into the sea or been sold in slavery to the Saracens, finally, he was an emissary of the Soldan of Egypt Most of this is manifest fable, but this person's facility for preaching makes it probable that he was really a monk, while his title, "the Master of Hungary," leads to the suspicion that he was in some way connected with the Bulgarian Manichees He certainly had great powers of organization, for, as he proceeded through France, and as his following of credulous boors was augmented by numbers of profligate desperadoes, he appears to have instituted and maintained a tolerable discipline Two lieutenants, who bore the title of masters, and numerous captains of thousands, received his orders and transmitted them to the obedient multitude

Marching through Flanders and Picardy, he entered Amiens at the head of thirty thousand men, thence he passed to the Isle of France, gathering the whole labouring population in his wake. None of the cities dared to close their gates against him, the horde of shepherds had become an army On their banners were emblazoned the Lamb and the Cross, the Virgin with her angels appearing to the Master In battle array they reached Paris to the number of one hundred thousand men Blanche, the Queen Regent, in some wild hope that these fierce peasants might themselves aid in achieving, or compel others to achieve, the deliverance of her son, suffered them to be admitted into the capital

But now their hostility to the Church became apparent They not only usurped all the priestly functions, performed marriages, distributed crosses, offered absolution to those who joined their crusade, but they inveighed against the vices of the priesthood "They taunted," says Matthew Paris, "the Minorites and the Friar preachers as vagabonds and hypocrites, the White Monks" (the Cistercians) "as covetous of lands and the robbers of flocks, the Black Monks" (the Benedictines) "as proud and gluttonous, the canons as half-laymen given to all manner of luxury, the bishops as hunters, hawkers and voluptuaries" It is noteworthy that the popularity of the Pastoureaux, at least in the cities, was won by thus heaping reproaches on the mediæval clergy

The Master, emboldened by impunity (he had actually been admitted into the presence of the Queen), now worked his will in Paris Mounted in the pulpit of the Church of St Eustache, wearing a bishop's mitre, he preached and blessed and consecrated, married and granted divorces, while his swarming followers mercilessly slew the priests who endeavoured to oppose them After a short stay they quitted the city The unwieldy host divided into three bodies One went towards Orleans and Bourges, one towards Bordeaux, one to the Mediterranean coast. The first troop, led by the Master in person, entered Orleans, notwithstanding the resistance of the bishop and the clergy Finding the populace favourable to the insurgents, the bishop issued his inhibition to all clerks, ordering them to keep aloof from the profane assembly Unfortunately the command was not obeyed Some of the younger scholars were induced to attend the preaching which had awed Paris and her University One of them foolishly interrupted the preacher, he was immediately struck down, the scholars were pursued, many were killed The bishop laid the city under an interdict and fled Leaving Orleans they shortly reached Bourges, where, penetrating into the Jewish quarter, they plundered the houses, and massacred the inhabitants. Here the executive, at length convinced of their danger, decided to act The moment selected was judicious, for the Pastoureaux were not expecting opposition The Master was about to, or had failed to, perform some pretended miracle when the assault was commenced A soldier rushed forth and clove the head of the Master, the royal bailiff and his men-at-arms fell on the panic-stricken followers, the excommunication was read, such of the shepherds as were not massacred were hanged Simon de Montfort at Bordeaux adopted similar measures with the second division Their leader was seized and thrown into the Garonne, his followers cut down by the soldiery or hanged by the magistrates The third division, which reached Marseilles about the same time, met with a similar fate

Seventy years later, in the time of Philip V, this spasm of fanaticism was repeated This rising, which was almost identical in character with that already described, took place under the same pretence of a crusade, though under a very different king Again the leader was a priest and monk who claimed supernatural gifts, again the disciples were found amongst the miserable peasants The insurrection, perhaps more extended in scope, meeting with no encouragement, was less terrible in result These enthusiasts commenced their career as mere mendicants, and it was not until many of them had been hanged that, in self-defence, they displayed any violence. It was with this object that the large body which reached Paris in the spring of 1320 A D commenced hostilities Encamping in the Pré aux Clercs they claimed the release of their imprisoned brothers, and, in default, forced the prison of St Martin, St Germain, and the Chatelet, and set at liberty the inmates Having succeeded in this rescue they set off southward This time they appear to have passed by the great cities of Central France, but 40,000 entered Languedoc and commenced a massacre of the Jews At Verdun, on the Garonne, a royal castle whither the Jews had fled for protection, a frightful butchery took place At Auch, Gimont, Castel Sarrasin, Toulouse and Gaillac, similar cruelties were perpetrated They then hurried to Avignon, but failed to enlist the sympathies of the Pope John XXII excommunicated them, alleging as the ground of this measure that they had taken the cross without papal authority Further, he invoked the civil power, and found the Seneschal of Carcassonne only too obedient By his orders all the roads in the district were rendered impassable, all the supplies of provisions stopped Thus hemmed in on all sides, in a malarious and barren country, the greater part of the Pastoureaux perished of famine and disease, and the survivors were put to death So suddenly began and ended these two outbreaks of religious Jacquerie

Literature of Pastoureaux The original authorities as to the earlier fanatics are Matthew Paris and William of Nangis, of the latter the *Continuator Nangii* Of modern accounts

Sismondi's *History of France*, vols vii and ix, and Velly's, v and viii, are the best See also Du Cange, *s v Pastorelli*

PATERINI An Italian name for the Paulicians, or Manichæan heretics who migrated from Bulgaria to Italy in the eleventh century The name was used as a common designation of heretics in the twelfth and thirteenth centuries, and was also given by married priests to those who opposed the marriage of the clergy, as if such opposition indicated a Manichæan view of marriage [Mosh *Eccl Hist* ii 33, n 2, Stubbs' ed] As the word "pataria" signifies, in the dialect of Milan, "a popular faction," it has been supposed by some that the opponents of the clergy were called Paterini on account of their popularity, and that these being generally infected with the Albigensian errors, the name became a common designation of heretics [Neander, *Eccl. Hist* vi 67, Bohn's transl] The Patarins were among the sects condemned by the Council of Lateran, A D 1179 [Harduin's *Concil.* vii 163]

PATERNIANI A sect of Manichæan heretics mentioned by St Augustine and Prædestinatus as believing that the upper or intellectual part of the body was created by God, and the lower or sensual part by the Evil One They were also called Venustians, and were condemned for their immorality as well as their heresy by Damasus in a council held at Rome in A D 367 [Aug *Hæres* lxxxv, Prædest *Hæres* lxxxv, Labbe's *Concil* ii 1038]

PATRICIANI A sect named by all the early heresiologists as followers of a heretic named Patricius, whom Philaster describes as a Roman [Philast *Hæres* lxii] They maintained the principle afterwards common to all Manichæan heretics, that the substance of the body was created by the Evil One and not by God, and this they carried to such a length that they justified self-destruction as a righteous act, by which a man becomes perfect through separation from his evil body [Aug *Hæres* lxi, Prædest *Hær* lxi] St Augustine also classes them with Basilides, Carpocrates, Marcion, and other precursors of the Manichees, as repudiating the Holy Scriptures [Aug *contr Adversar Leg et Proph* ii] Nothing is known of Patricius beyond the bare statement of Philaster, and as the heresy of which he is said to be the founder is not mentioned by Epiphanius, Danæus thinks it probable that it arose after his time, perhaps about A D 380 Prædestinatus says that the Patricians sprung from the northern parts of Numidia and Mauritania

PATRIPASSIANS As their name imports, the Patripassians held that God the Father became incarnate, and suffered for the redemption of man. This heresy presupposes a denial of the distinction of Persons in the Godhead [MONARCHIANS], and the word Father, in the statement of the Patripassian tenet, is not used to signify the Father of the Begotten Word, but to signify the Godhead, One single Hypostasis, the Father of all

It will be readily seen that there may be two forms of Patripassianism, one, which in the Person of the Redeemer substitutes for the Divine Nature of the Word the one undistinguished God, the other, which attributes a capacity of suffering to the Godhead itself The former asserts that the Father of all becoming incarnate, suffered in the same way as Catholic doctrine asserts that Christ suffered, namely, as to the Human Nature, not as to the Divine Nature, which is itself impassible the latter, not excluding this suffering of the One Person constituted of Two Natures, asserts that the very Nature of the Godhead is itself passible The former of these two doctrines was ascribed to the Praxeans and Sabellians, and it followed so directly from their Monarchian tenets, compared with their estimate of the Person of the Redeemer, that it may be doubted whether their denial of Patripassianism was really anything more than a denial of the latter doctrine The former doctrine again was avowed by the Noetians, and there is some reason to think that they held also the latter [PRAXEANS SABELLIANS NOETIANS] The latter doctrine is also involved in the Arian and Apollinarian heresies Pearson has pointed this out as a thing not generally understood To his words, *The infinite Nature cannot, by any external acquisition*, i e by the assumption of humanity, *be any way changed in its intrinsical and essential Perfections*, he subjoins the note, *That Arius made the Nature of the Word to suffer in the Flesh is not so frequently and plainly delivered as his heresy, condemned at Nice, is known* [*Expos of the Creed*, Art iv p 187, ed 1741] To the authorities which Pearson gives may be added that of Athanasius, who says of the Apollinarians that they must either with Marcion make the Death and Resurrection a mere appearance, or with Arius declare the Godhead of the Logos to be passible [*cont Apollin* ii 12] Of these two forms of error, the former is repugnant to the Christian mind rather from the antecedent error of the denial of the Persons of the Godhead [MONARCHIANS], than from the consequent error itself. For this consequent error, great as it is, does not of itself violate the sanctity of the Godhead, as the second form of Patripassianism does, inasmuch as it attributes to the θεότης of the single Hypostasis that (and no more) which Catholic doctrine attributes to the θεότης of the Word But the second form of Patripassian error "harbours so low an estimation of the Divine Nature as to conceive it capable of diminution It makes the Essence of the Godhead subject to the sufferings of the flesh" [Pearson, *loc cit.*].

The Aquileian Church added to its *Credo in Deum* the words *Invisibili et Impassibili.* Rufinus states this was done to meet the Sabellian heresy. His commentary applies the words to the denial of the two forms of Patripassianism which have been named But, regarding the Aquileian Creed, see Ffoulkes on *The Athanasian Creed*, ch i

PATTALORYNCHITES [PASSALORYNCHITES].

PAULIANISTS The followers of Paul of Samosata. [SAMOSATENES]

PAULIANISTS. [PAULITÆ]

PAULICIANS These heretics were a Manichæan sect of Asiatic origin, and first appeared in the western part of Armenia in the seventh century At that period the primitive Manichæanism of Africa, directly derived from the teaching of Mani, (and which at no time possessed continuous communication with the East,) had been for more than a century crushed or dispersed by Roman persecution, and the sources of Paulicianism must be sought therefore in the body of Manichæan influence and belief, which, after the execution of Mani, found a refuge from proscription within the eastern frontier of the Roman Empire There, for more than three centuries, the heresy learned to modify its language and institutions in accordance with the requirement of an orthodox but unsettled country, and when it appears in the seventh century under the name of Paulicianism, it is found to bear evident traces of this modification Thus we find the Paulicians, while retaining the characteristic errors of Manichæan dualism, both renounced the dangerous dogma of the apostleship of Mani and explained or rejected the more odious portions of his teaching, and it is thus that the Paulician heresy may be said to represent a reformed or schismatic development of Manichæism

The precise origin and date of the title "Paulician" is wrapt in some obscurity, but, at any rate, the name is not older than the seventh century and the reign of Constans II Its origin is attributed to one Paul, the son of a Manichæan woman named Callinice, who with his brother John is said to have preached the reformed heresy in the country lying near the sources of the Euphrates This story however rests on no solid foundation, and is probably a Western invention Even if such a person as this Paul did exist, his fame has been eclipsed by the more fruitful labours of Constantine, who must be looked upon as the real founder of the Paulician sect. For seven-and twenty years (that is, from about the year 660 to 687 A D) this Constantine, or Sylvanus, as he was afterwards called, laboured to erect the Paulician church Starting from Mananalis, near Samosata, he preached throughout Armenia and Pontus, and the success of his missionary enterprise was so great that it at length provoked the interference of Constantinople An imperial commissioner, by name Simeon, was despatched by Constantine Pogonatus, the fourth of the Heraclian emperors, to Colonia, the scene of this preacher's latest success; but the conduct of the Paulicians so favourably affected him that he exchanged the *rôle* of persecutor, first for that of convert, subsequently for that of martyr An apostate (Justus) betrayed his former brethren, and enabled the Byzantine government everywhere to detect and punish the heresy Though marked with the usual circumstances of cruelty on the part of the imperial authorities, and of devotedness on the part of the heretics, the persecution was wholly ineffectual, and in the reign of the emperor's successor another Paul revived and extended the heresy in Cappadocia

Whatever was the precise origin of the Paulician name, it is certain that these heretics claimed the special protection or a monopoly of the pure doctrine of the Apostle of the Gentiles, but notwithstanding this claim, and notwithstanding the invariable assumption by their leaders of names which (like Sylvanus, Tychicus, Titus, and Timothy) are peculiarly connected with the ministry of St Paul, the tenets of the Paulicians were distinctively Manichæan and by no means Pauline They however emphatically repudiated the apostleship of Mani [*προθύμως ἀναθεματίζουσι Σκυθίανον Βουδδᾶν τε καὶ Μάνεντα*, Photius, i e 4], but, except that they rejected his individual inspiration, they differed as to no material dogma from the old Manichæans They taught the essential evil of matter, the eternal hostility of the two principles, they denied the inspiration of the Old Testament and the Deity of the Jehovah, they despised the Cross, and, holding the Valentinian doctrine that the spiritual Christ passed the body of the Virgin like water through a pipe, were naturally accused of insulting her memory, they taught a purely illusory baptism, and had no Eucharist at all, they excluded their ministers or scribes (who bore the humble title of *συνέκδημοι*, or fellow-voyagers) from all government in their community, above all, they were iconoclasts, and placed the Scriptures in the hands of the laity The greater part of these errors were, it will be seen, shared by the early disciples of Mani The abandonment of the Eucharist, of which the older sectaries retained but a meaningless profanation, is but the natural development of the leading tenets of dualism, and the subordination of the clergy is only a matter of discipline An apparently graver difference exists in the fact that the Paulicians blended the two orders of virtue, the "perfect" and the catechumen, but this was a modification natural enough in a comparatively barbarous community, nor is it other than a reasonable development of that equality between the lay and clerical perfect which was a fundamental principle, or, at least, an invariable usage of ancient Manichæism These changes had moreover the specific advantage of giving to the Paulicians a more consistent and rational creed, and a more united and enthusiastic communion They were enabled, too, in this way, to combine the discordant elements of democracy and sacerdotalism, for each Paulician respected in himself the sacredness of an individual "perfect" But few differences existed in the two canons the Paulicians certainly, the Manichæans possibly, excluded the Petrine Epistles, and the former, while including the Acts of the Apostles and the epistle of the Paulician Sergius, rejected the works of Mani, which indeed had probably early disappeared, or at least were not easily accessible in Armenia Finally, by substituting for the crude method of denial of the authenticity of adverse scripture the more convenient system of metaphorical explanation, they avoided the charge, if not the punishment, of sacrilege

 Paulicians

From the close of the seventh century to the middle of the ninth the Paulicians suffered continuous and unremitting persecution If we except, as a measure of kindness, the transportation in the eighth century by the Emperor Copronymus of a small colony from Asia to Thrace, and perhaps one short time of truce in the reign of Nicephorus Logotheta, the treatment which the Asian Paulicians, from the time of their first appearance, received from the emperors fully justifies their subsequent revolt Even heretical emperors were unable to afford them much protection, for as iconoclasts they were too unpopular to venture on the open toleration of an odious heresy, and the orthodox princes had no temptation to be lenient Constantine Pogonatus and Justinian II head the list of persecutors, while Leo the Armenian and the glutton Michael, who eclipsed their fame, were in turn cast into the shade by the Empress Theodora, who, while she restored the images to the Eastern Church, promised it the absolute extirpation of the Manichæan heretics During her brief reign no less than 100,000 Paulicians perished by the imperial cruelty The whole sect revolted Led by Karbeas, himself an officer of the imperial army, whose father had been impaled by the imperial executioner, they established themselves at Tephrice, a fortress in the mountains of Trebizond, and there, in alliance with the Saracen emir, they preserved their independence, and harassed the dominions of the Emperor The imperial forces, led by Michael the drunkard, were quite unable to cope with the enthusiasts, and suffered at their hands a shameful defeat under the walls of Samosata On the death of Karbeas, the place of leader was supplied by Chrysocheir, a heretic of equal ability and greater fierceness Under his standard the Paulicians enjoyed the pillage of Nice, Nicomedia, and Ancyra, and stabled their horses in the famous church of the Ephesians, but he at length fell in an obscure skirmish, and Basil the Macedonian reduced the impregnable Tephrice From that time, though far from being exterminated, and always dangerous by their alliance with the Mahometan sultans, they never again seriously threatened the peace of the Empire Throughout these troubles the Paulician colony of Copronymus had remained unmolested in its Thracian home By the close of the ninth century the Paulician preaching had perverted the faith of the Bulgarians, and caused alarm and sorrow to the provincial archbishop In the next century (the tenth) they were reinforced by a large and powerful colony, which John Zimisces transported into Thracia from the mountains of Pontus They soon obtained possession of Philippopolis, their courage made them favourites with the Bulgarians, on whom they conferred their heretical faith, and with whom they were confounded in their national appellation Their valour made them respected by the Government, but their missionary zeal was terrible to the Church The close of the tenth century is marked by the rise in Bulgaria of an obscure body of dissenting heretics, a circumstance strongly testifying to the robust condition of Paulician Manichæism [BOGOMILES]

The last persecution of the Paulicians, which was comparatively bloodless, was undertaken by Alexius Comnenus at the close of the eleventh century. He had more than once recognised the valour and punished the independence of his Bulgarian troops He now adopted a characteristic scheme of conversion Fixing his winter quarters near the Paulician capital, he superintended the erection of an orthodox rival in the city of Alexiopolis Thence for many weeks the Emperor τρισκαιδεκατὸς ἀπόστολος, as his daughter devoutly terms him, preached and argued against the dangers of heresy Honours and emoluments were showered on the converts, the obstinate suffered imprisonment and confiscation The new city built expressly for those who yielded to the imperial persuasion was enriched with every privilege the Empire could bestow Many converts were made, for the greedier and less zealous Paulicians readily accepted the gold and the orthodoxy of the Emperor Philippopolis, divided against itself, was wrested from their hands, the leaders who were faithful to their error were imprisoned or exiled, and their property distributed among their less faithful brothers For once cruelty was absent from the councils of the imperial inquisitor, and the only heretic who suffered death was Basil, the deluded founder of the wretched Bogomiles On the departure of Alexius from Bulgaria, an event soon followed by his death, most of the converted heretics recanted, and the old faith of Paulicianism recovered its former influence, but its missionary zeal was on the wane, and with its loss of activity its distinctive character disappears Before the thirteenth century it seems to have succeeded in establishing relations with the sects of Italy and France, the scene of the latest development of revived Manichæism But from the close of the eleventh century Paulicianism as such ceases to be significant

After the eleventh century the history of Paulicianism is involved in obscurity, and confused so much by the rise, development and destruction of the Albigensian movement that it is difficult to decide how much of later Manichæism can properly be called Paulician At the end of the twelfth century Matthew Paris informs us that a Paulician pope or primate named Bartholomew governed from some spot on the confines of Bulgaria affiliated societies in France and Italy This probably is the error of an ill-informed person, although it is reasonably clear that community of creed and interest had at that date brought the Manichæism both of East and West into communication After the destruction of the Albigensian heresy [ALBIGENSES] Western Manichæism in its ineffectual life in Bosnia must have drawn much of its vitality from Paulician sources, but in the absorbing interest of the struggle between Christian and Mahometan the existence of these inhabitants of a barbarous district was almost forgotten In the middle of the fifteenth century two "Way-wodes," or native princes of Bosnia, are recorded as having supported the Manichæan heretics, and in the same century these Paulicians (if they may be so termed) tasted for the last time genuine orthodox persecution This persecution, commenced by Stephen Thomas, King of Bosnia, in A D 1420, was carried on by Stephen Thomas, his successor, and was terminated about the year A D 1463 by the conquest of the country by the Ottoman Turks. From time to time various dignitaries, of whom the most renowned was the Cardinal Carvalho, have claimed the honour of having converted the Paulicians, and it is certain that they attracted the attention both of Nicolas V and Pius II The latest missionary efforts directed towards them were due to Deodatus of Sophia, who attempted the conversion of some Manichæans on the borders of Bulgaria about the close of the seventeenth century At the present day a few barbarous heretics still hold dualistic opinions in the Danubian provinces, and these have also been classed with the Paulicians, but they are known to practise bloody sacrifices, and by their barbarism they would seem more akin to the Bogomiles than to the Paulicians At present an accurate account of their religion and opinions is wholly wanting

[Petrus Siculus, *Historia Manichæorum*, Photius, *contra Recentiores Manichæos*, Constantini Porphyrogeniti, *Continuator*, Anna Comnena, *Alexias* Some very curious information is also to be found, particularly in relation to the atrocious charges made against all Manichæans, in Johannes Philosophus Ozniensis, *Armenorum Cathol Opera*, ed Hucher. Mosheim, *Ecclesiastical History*, cent IX, and Gibbon, *Roman Empire*, chap liv, give the best modern accounts]

PAULI JOANNITES A name given to the ATTINGIANS, and sometimes to the Paulicians in general, from Paul and John, the founders of the heresy

PAULITÆ An obscure sect of the Acephali, followers of Paul, a patriarch of Alexandria, who was deposed by a council [A D 541] for his uncanonical consecration by the Patriarch of Constantinople, and who, after his deposition, sided with the Monophysites [Niceph *Hist Eccl* xlix] They are mentioned under the name of Paulianists in the treatise on the reception of heretics which was written by Timothy of Constantinople [Timoth *de Triplici Recept Hæret* in Cotelerii *Monument* iii 377]

PAULUS [RATIONALISTS]

PAUPERES CATHOLICI A society formed under the auspices of Innocent III [A D 1198-1216], composed of Waldenses who had returned to the Church, and intended as a missionary community for the conversion of others The ecclesiastics and better educated were to busy themselves with preaching, exposition of the Bible, religious instruction, and controversy with the sectarians. Others not qualified to undertake such work as this were to live in communities by themselves, occupied in devotion and good works. The Pope granted them several concessions, in accordance with the prejudices of the Waldenses; as, for example, that they should not be called upon to take up arms except against the heathen, nor to take an oath in courts of law in any but criminal causes The society was originated by Durand of Osca, and maintained itself for many years in Catalonia under his guidance But it seems never to have met with the success that it ought to have done, the wrong-headedness of the Waldenses, like that of the later Puritans, standing in the way of all reasonable schemes of comprehension [Neander's *Eccl Hist* vii 361]

PAUPERES DE LOMBARDI [WALDENSES]

PAUPERES DE LUGDUNO [WALDENSES]

PECULIAR PEOPLE A quite recent sect of very ignorant people, found chiefly in Kent, whose principles are very similar to those of the American TUNKERS The characteristic which has been most prominently brought forward is their refusal to adopt any material means for recovery from sickness, their dependence being placed entirely on prayer

PELAGIANS An influential school which sprang up early in the fifth century, and which derived its appellation from its founder Pelagius Its distinctive feature was the denial of original sin and its consequences

[I] The Greek name by which the founder of this school is familiarly known is merely a translation of the Latin "Marigena," or the Welsh "Morgan," and he is sometimes called "Brito," either to denote his nationality or to distinguish him from another Pelagius of Tarentum St Jerome says that "by descent he belonged to the race of the Scots in the neighbourhood of the Britons," [1] that "he was heavy from feeding on Scotch porridge" [2] A Christian poet describes Pelagianism as—

"Dogma quod antiqui satiatum felle draconis
Pestifero vomuit coluber sermone Britannus"
[Prosper *de Ingrat* cap I]

Some description has also reached us of his personal appearance, he had broad shoulders, a thick neck, and a fat face,[3] and these physical characteristics may have suggested the charge of voluptuousness,[4] which is not supported on any other grounds The exact time and place of his birth are uncertain, although tradition fondly pointed to the year B C 354, the date of the birth of his great future antagonist St Augustine [Dempster, *Eccles Hist of Scotland*] He embraced the monastic profession, and became a monk in the famous abbey of Bangor, or, according to another account, its abbot, with two thousand or more monks obedient to his rule [Ussher, *Eccles Brit Antiq* cap viii] [5] There is no historical ground for the belief that Pelagius resided

[1] "Habet enim progeniem Scoticæ gentis, de Britannorum vicinia" [Hier in præfat lib 3, *in Jeremiam*]

[2] "Scotorum pultibus prægravatus" [*ibid*]

[3] Balneis epulisque nutritus, latos humeros gestans robustamque cervicem, præferens etiam in fronte pinguedinem" [Paulus Orosius in *Apolog* c 27]

[4] "Monachus voluptuosus" [Isidore of Pelusium, quoted by Baronius, *Ann* v p 305]

[5] Several other facts of a legendary character in the life of Pelagius are recorded in Ussher's *Eccles Brit Antiq* cap viii ix

in early life in Eastern Europe, or that he is to be identified with a monk of the same name whom St Chrysostom alludes to as having gone astray [Chrysost Ep iv tom iii p 567], it seems to have been based on [*a*] his acquaintance with the Greek language, [*b*] his oriental tone of thought, and [*c*] the intellectual rather than practical character of the heresy, all of which may be only proofs of the intimate connection which early existed between the British and Eastern Churches Towards the close of the fourth century he left Britain for Italy, and took up his quarters at Rome, where he became acquainted with several of the leading ecclesiastics of the time, among them the saintly Paulinus, afterwards Bishop of Nola [A D 409-421], Rufinus of Aquileia, Cœlestius, variously described as an Italian or a Scotchman, his future companion in thought and travel, and almost equally famous with himself In the year 411, after the sack of Rome by the Goths under Alaric, Pelagius and Cœlestius left Italy in company for Africa, where, after a very few years together, Pelagius left his companion encountering the strong opposition of the African prelates, and took up his abode in Palestine, where he first found a friend and then a foe in Jerome, at that time resident in Bethlehem Pelagius had by this time acquired both a fame for his learning and a reputation for his piety This is frequently and candidly admitted by St Augustine [*de Peccat Mer et Rem* iii 1, Ep clxxxvi 1, etc], and is attested by the fact that he was requested by Juliana, a noble Roman lady of the Anician family, then an exile in Africa, to write a letter to her daughter Demetrias on her profession of virginity In this letter, which is extant among Jerome's works, he for the first time expressed his views in print in such a manner as to cause letters of remonstrance and confutation to be composed by St Augustine, and Alypius, Bishop of Tagaste Soon afterwards [A D 415], he was publicly accused of heresy by Paulus Orosius, a young Spanish ecclesiastic sent into Palestine by St Augustine, nominally to study under Jerome, but in reality to raise opposition against the teaching of Pelagius The synod before which the charge was investigated was held at Jerusalem, and presided over by its bishop John, who was extremely partial, if not friendly to the accused, and inclined to resent the vehement conduct of Orosius Much difficulty was caused by the inability of Orosius to speak Greek and of the Council to speak Latin, while Pelagius, who was acquainted with both languages, was placed in a position of advantage It was eventually resolved to refer the whole controversy to Pope Innocent I, which was tantamount to shelving it at least for the present But it was not to sleep. About this time Jerome published his three books against Pelagianism, in the form of dialogues between Atticus and Critobulus, the former a Catholic and the latter a Pelagian [printed in S Aug *Opp* vol x Benedict edit] A fresh accusation was laid against him within the same year, at the instance of Heros of Arles and Lazarus of Aix (Aquæ), two deposed Gallican bishops, before Eulogius, metropolitan of Cæsarea A synod of fourteen bishops was held at Diospolis (Lydda) for its investigation—the *Synodus Miserabilis* of Jerome [Epist 79, edit Vellars] Neither of the accusers appeared, pleading illness as an excuse Orosius also was absent, and Pelagius, skilled in controversial tactics, succeeded in securing his own acquittal on consenting to disavow the opinions held by Cœlestius, and condemned at the Synod of Carthage [A.D 412] Even this he did in an equivocal manner In the first place, he would only find fault with them as foolish instead of erroneous, in the second place, he adopted hypothetical language, "whether these are Cœlestius' sayings or not, let them look to it that say they are his I never held so, and I do anathematize any one that so holds" Pelagius was very pleased with this result, he wrote exultingly to announce it to St Augustine, and was encouraged to bring out his work on Free-will But the African Church was not content with the verdict of the small assemblage of Diospolis Several synods were convoked, one at Carthage attended by sixty-eight bishops, another at Milevum by sixty-one bishops; at both, in consequence mainly of information afforded by Orosius, Pelagius was condemned, and Pope Innocent I, on being appealed to by such leading prelates as St Augustine of Hippo, Alypius of Tagaste, and Aurelius of Carthage, yet without asking or receiving any explanation from the Pelagian party, confirmed their verdict But in the next year Innocent died [A D 417], and was succeeded on the papal chair by Zosimus Cœlestius forthwith appeared at Rome with letters in his favour from Praylius, who had lately succeeded John in the see of Jerusalem, and Pelagius He was granted several private interviews, at which he tried to persuade the new pope that certain of Pelagius' views about original sin were mere superfluous speculations [St Aug *Opp* vol x app p 97], and in proof of whose orthodoxy he presented a long creed, the two last clauses of which are here quoted, to prove in how nearly orthodox language the Pelagians were ready to express their views on free-will, and how humble an attitude they were ready to assume before a favourable pope

"Free-will we do so own as to say that we always stand in need of God's help [St Aug criticises this as insufficient *de Gratia Christi*, cap 33] and that as well they are in an error who say with the Manichæans that a man cannot avoid sin, as they who affirm with Jovinian that a man cannot sin For both of these take away the freedom of the will But we say that a man always is in a state that he may sin or may not sin, so as to own ourselves always to be of a free-will

"This is, most blessed pope, our faith which we have always learned in the Catholic Church, and have always held In which, if there be anything which is perhaps unwarily or unskilfully expressed, we desire it may be amended by you (si quispiam ignorantiæ error obrepsit vestrâ sententiâ corrigatur), who do hold both the faith and see of Peter And if this our confession be approved by the judgment of your apostleship, then whoever shall have a mind to find fault with me will shew not me to be a heretic, but himself unskilful, or spiteful, or even no Catholic"

The Pelagian party thus fortified, and with this professed readiness to anathematize all that was condemned by the papal see, succeeded in carrying their point. Zosimus declared their orthodoxy unimpeachable (tales etiam absolutæ fidei), and addressed a circular letter to the whole African episcopate, demanding either that their accusers should appear personally at Rome within two months or that the charges should be abandoned But the dogma of papal infallibility having not yet been invented, the decree of Zosimus did not meet with unquestioning acquiescence or respect In the East, Theodotus, Bishop of Antioch, held a synod at Jerusalem, to which Pelagius was cited, and where his views were condemned [Marius Merc *Common* cap 3, Tillemont's *Mém* xiii p 756] In Africa, Aurelius, Bishop of Carthage, refused to comply with the directions of Zosimus, and was supported in this course not only by two local synods but also by a third and provincial council, attended by two hundred and fourteen bishops, who, after asserting their independence of Italy, proceeded to pass nine canons in condemnation of Cœlestius and Pelagius [a detailed description of which will be found in Tillemont's *Mém* vol xiii p 739] When news of these various proceedings reached Rome, whither also the Carthaginian canons had been despatched, the papal policy changed, and both the civil and ecclesiastical authorities combined in condemnation of Pelagius Several edicts were issued by the Emperor, apparently at the request of the North African bishops, one of them being addressed to Aurelius himself Theodosius and Honorius agreed to publish a joint rescript [for the full text see Ussher, *Brit Eccles Antiq* cap x p 272] banishing Pelagius and Cœlestius and all who held their views Zosimus, too, excommunicated them, not without being justly taunted for his tergiversation by the condemned party [August *contra Julian* lib vi sect 37], and ineffectually whitewashed by the more orthodox writers The majority of the Italian bishops acquiesced in this decision, but nineteen who refused to subscribe the papal document were deposed from their sees, among them one who became a leading controversialist on the Pelagian side, Julian, Bishop of Eclanum[1] (Avellino), against whom Augustine wrote six books, and whose remonstrance against the arbitrary character of these proceedings is still partially extant in the form of a letter addressed by him to Rufinus, Bishop of Thessalonica [quoted by August. *contra Duas Ep Pelag* lib iv. sec 20] The ejected party next demanded, but unsuccessfully, a general council to decide the question, in a letter declaratory of their faith, composed by Julian, and addressed to the Pope. Baffled on this point they appealed for sympathy in more distant places, Constantinople, Ephesus, Thessalonica, but were everywhere condemned, especially at a synod held in Cilicia [A D 423], and presided over[2] by Theodore, Bishop of Mopsuestia [A D 392-428] The latter appears, however, before his death to have inclined to Pelagian views, and to have been the author of a book, of which an abstract is given by Photius, Patriarch of Constantinople [A D 858-891], entitled, "Against them that say men sin by nature and not by will," and from a careful analysis of whose system Neander proves its identity in many points with Pelagianism [vol iv 420-427] Other prominent holders of Pelagian views were Leporius, a monk and priest of the South of France, who, on being compelled to flee his native country, passed over to Africa, where he was led to abjure his heretical notions by Augustine [A D 426], and Anianus, a Deacon of the Church at Celeda in Italy, the author of several tracts, the translator of some of the Homilies of St Chrysostom, and one of those clergy who was deposed by the sentence of Zosimus, A D 418 Pelagianism received its "coup de grace" at the third General Council of Ephesus [A D 431], being alluded to in the Synodical Letter prefixed to the acts of that assembly, and in the first and fourth canons, the latter of which runs thus

"The holy Synod gives it in charge that all who fall away, and either publicly or privately adhere to the opinions of Nestorius and Cœlestius, be deposed"

Throughout the remainder of this century occasional allusions are found to the continued existence of the views thus condemned Letters are extant written by Pope Leo [A D 440] to the bishop of Aquileia warning him not to admit Pelagians into that communion for which they clamoured, and to the bishop of Altino in Lombardy on the same subject [A D 444] Two letters also were sent by Pope Gelasius to Honorius, Bishop of Dalmatia, complaining of their increase in that province [A D 495] Nothing is known with certainty of the time or place or manner of the death of Pelagius himself By some that event is placed in A D 418, by others a few years later, while others maintain that he lingered on for a long time after his excommunication in obscurity There seems to be no historical ground for the vague expression of Sianda and other lexicographers, "miserabiliter decessit" It has been supposed that he revisited Britain, but this rests only on the slender ground that Germanus, Bishop of Auxerre, and Lupus, Bishop of Troyes, were sent over to England [A D 429] to combat the growing tendency to Pelagianism [Bede, *Eccl Hist* lib i 17]

[1] A full history of the life and views of Julian is to be found in Tillemont's *Mémoires*, vol xiii art cccvii cccx His course was marked by boldness and an unwillingness to shroud his views under the ambiguities of language Hence he is called "jactantissimus Pelagiani erroris assertor" [Prosper, *in Chron* ad ann 439]

[2] Marius Mercator, *Common.* cap 1

The moral character of Pelagius, in spite of the aspersions previously alluded to, was above suspicion St Augustine himself candidly allows his adversary to have been a good and praiseworthy man [1] His learning, too, was beyond dispute, and is evidenced by the many works of which he was the author, but none of which are extant with the exception of his Commentaries on St Paul's Epistles, an Epistle on Virginity, and his Confession of Faith, which have been accidentally preserved among the works of St Jerome

[II] There is some difficulty in ascertaining what Pelagius really taught, for several reasons [1] Because we gain our information almost exclusively from his adversaries, especially from St Augustine's works, and from St Jerome's letter to Ctesiphon and his Dialogues, or from the long letter addressed by Pope Cœlestius to the Gallican bishops [A D 431], preserved in the appendix to vol x of the Benedictine edition of St Augustine's works, p 133, or from the Commonitorium of Marius Mercator, a layman resident in North Africa, or still later in the confutation of Julian's views found among the Venerable Bede's works in the Preface to the Canticles [2] From a willingness on Pelagius' part to adopt the most orthodox language, provided that he might interpret it in his own way Thus using "grace" not in the Augustinian sense, but to denote all the moral and spiritual powers which God has conferred *ab initio* on human nature, he was willing to subscribe to such a sentence as the following "I do anathematize any one who says or thinks that the grace of God, by which Christ came into the world to save sinners, is not necessary both every hour and moment, and also in every action, and they that deny this grace incur eternal punishment" [Aug *de Pecc Orig* cap 22]

Keeping in view these circumstances, the general account of Pelagianism seems to be as follows. The prevailing tendency which Pelagius found in the monastic system, under which he was brought up, was an over-reliance on the sacraments and sacramental ordinances of the Church, and, in spite of these spiritual privileges, considerable, sometimes habitual, deviation from the laws of rectitude The remedy he thought would be a creed which made man more dependent on his own exertions, and this view he proceeded to develope into a logical system As a foundation it was necessary to assume that a just God would not visit the sins of one man on the heads of others, and that therefore neither the free-wills nor the moral lives of mankind could be affected by Adam's fall Men came into the world pure, disease and death being not due to sin, but the natural accompaniments of the elements of which human bodies are formed, and baptism being not a cleansing rite, but a form of admission into God's kingdom Internal grace was neither necessarily nor usually bestowed, because God had been sufficiently bountiful, in granting us the privilege of using our natural faculties, in giving us a revealed gospel, and in intrusting His Church with the power of dispensing forgiveness for sins committed With such aids, which were not what the Catholic party meant by grace, though the Pelagians made the controversy a complicated one by so terming them, man by his own free-will would be able to keep all God's commandments, and if he failed it was his own fault, and if he succeeded it was his own merit Thus underlying the whole dispute there were these general and irreconcilable grounds of difference There were two wholly distinct modes of contemplating human nature in its present condition St Augustine started from the position that man finds himself here in a state of inherited corruption, a point of view of which Pelagius repeatedly expressed his rejection The former would only regard human nature in one of two conditions either as it existed in its unfallen state in Paradise, in communion with the original Source of goodness, or as it exists now, estranged from the Source of all goodness, and enslaved by the foreign power of evil Pelagius placed human nature, furnished by God as its Creator with the moral faculties, in a middle and unbiassed position between good and evil The further deduction of St Augustine was, that since the first man by his free-will became alienated from God, this free-will, once the fountain of all good, was now only active to sin, and that man therefore needed a new supervenient grace in order to be brought back to goodness The ultimate deduction from Pelagian principles was, that there was no room for the recognition of anything supernatural, that God, having once for all created human nature, and provided it with all the powers requisite for its preservation and development, permitted it to go on with the powers bestowed upon it, and according to the laws implanted in it, so that the continuous operation of the Divine agency was with reference only to the preservation of its powers and capacities, not to any concursus in order to their development and exercise

[III] Such being a general survey of the two positions occupied by Pelagianism and Augustinianism, it will be useful to enumerate separately the erroneous elements of the former

1 *The denial of original sin*, and, as a necessary consequence, of its remission in baptism.[2] This denial was supported by such arguments as, that its existence would imply the doctrine of the propagation of souls as well as bodies, that it was inconsistent with the freedom of the will, that it made marriage sinful, a charge which is entered into at length by St Augustine in his letter "de Nuptiis et Concupiscentiâ," addressed to the Consul Valerius The Pelagians in their turn were hardly pressed with the argument drawn from infant baptism The Catholics argued, "that infants have sin is proved from

[1] "Vir bonus et prædicandus" [*de Pecc. Mer et Remis* lib iii 3]

[2] August *de Pecc Orig* c 17, 18 The orthodox party were called Traducianists by the Pelagians, in connection with the doctrine of the transmission of original sin

the need they have of baptism, and other than original sin they cannot have" The Pelagians did not deny the necessity of infant baptism, but rejoined sometimes that they were not baptized for forgiveness but for something else, sometimes that though they were ostensibly baptized for forgiveness, it was not that they had any sin, but that the uniformity of words might be preserved, or because they were baptized into the Church, where forgiveness was to be had for those that wanted it, or because they were baptized with a sacrament which had the means of forgiveness for any that had sinned or should sin, or because infants actually had sin, not by propagation from a sinful stock, but either before they were born, in a former state, or since birth by peevishness and such like imperfections On other occasions Pelagius sought an escape by this argument "If baptism takes away original sin, then children who are born of parents both baptized must be without that sin" [Aug *de Grat Christi*, c 8], to which St Augustine replied, that as a circumcised parent begets an uncircumcised child, as pure wheat, when sown, produces both wheat and chaff, so a parent who is spiritually cleansed begets a son that resembles him, not according to that state in which he is by spiritual regeneration, but according to the state in which he is by carnal generation Another argument of Pelagius was that if only the body and not the soul was derived from the parents, how was it consistent with our conception of divine justice that the *soul* should be involved in the guilt of original sin? [Aug *de Pecc Mer* lib III 10] St Augustine, in reply, contented himself with mentioning various other difficulties which we are not permitted to solve, and pointed out the rationalistic tendency of all such inquiries.

2 *The denial of the necessity of grace.* At the same time that Pelagius denied the necessity of divine grace in the Catholic acceptation of the term, he admitted it as God's gift in these subordinate senses 1 In His giving us a free-will 2 In giving pardon for past sins, and encouragement to avoid future shortcomings—a limited sense which was condemned by the fourth canon of the Council of Carthage [A D 418], which asserted those to be accursed who said, "that the grace of God, by virtue of which we are justified through Christ, refers merely to the forgiveness of past sins, and not to assistance to secure us against falling under sin for the future" 3 In opening our understanding by giving us the law and the light of the Gospel—a narrow view condemned by the fifth canon of the same council "Let him be accursed who teaches that this grace helps us to keep from sinning, only so far as it opens our minds to a knowledge of the divine commands, so that we are made acquainted with what we must strive after and what we must avoid, but that it does not bestow on us a disposition to love and a faculty to practise such commands." 4 The grace of baptism wherein an adult person that has sinned obtains the remission of sins, and the inheritance of the kingdom of God 5 In bestowing the kingdom of heaven as a reward to encourage us 6 In generally facilitating and assisting us by doctrine and revelation, in declaring to us the things that shall be hereafter, that we may not be wedded to the present, in discovering to us the wiles of the devil, in enlightening our understanding by the means of His grace. Julian summed up these various effects of grace when he said that God helped us by commanding, blessing, sanctifying, chastising, inviting, enlightening Pelagius recognised three progressive forms of righteousness [1] that of the heathen, achieved by Socrates and other illustrious pagans, [2] that of the Jews who lived under the law, [3] that of Christians who live under grace Augustine, on the contrary, traced all that was really righteousness to the same source The virtues of the heathen were only seeming virtues, and were dictated by vainglory or other personal motives The righteousness of the saints of the Old Testament was due to faith in a promised Saviour, as that of Christians was due to a faith in the same Saviour already come Or the difference of view may be gauged by analyzing an action into its three constituent parts, the capacity, the will, and the act, the posse, velle, and esse In the Augustinian system, the two first were attributed to grace, and the latter only to free-will, in the Pelagian system, the two latter were attributed to free-will, and the first only to grace The strong expressions with which Holy Scripture abounds, favouring, in their literal interpretation, the views of St Augustine, were explained away to suit the requirements of the Pelagian scheme "I will have mercy on whom I will have mercy, and I will have compassion on whom I will have compassion" [Rom IX 15], was interpreted to mean, "I will have mercy and compassion on those who, I have foreseen, will by their actions merit mercy and compassion" The passage in the Epistle to the Philippians, "It is God that worketh in us to will and to do" [II 13], was explained as meaning only, "He works in us to will what is good and holy, when He consumes what is offered to our earthly desires by the greatness of the future glory and the promise of rewards, when He excites the prayerful will to longing after God by the revelation of His wisdom, when He counsels us to all goodness" [Aug *de Grat Christi*, cap 10]

3 *The assertion of complete free-will* As the Pelagians denied the original corruption of human nature, so they magnified the present freedom and goodness of it Some of them presumed so far on the freedom of the will, as to assert that we have no need to be assisted by God to avoid sin, after He has once granted to our nature the power of free-will Hence the offence which Pelagius is said to have taken when he heard a bishop utter, as expressive of his own feelings, the words of a prayer in St Augustine's Confessions, "My God, bestow on me what Thou commandest, and command what Thou wilt," "Da quod jubes et jube quod vis"

[*Confess* lib x. 29] In support of their position all the old dilemmas of the Sophists were reproduced and raised, "God's commands are either possible or impossible." "Sin is either a thing that can be avoided or that cannot be avoided," "Sin is either a thing of will or of necessity," etc, most of which were answered seriatim by St. Augustine [*Lib de perfect. Just*, *Hom ad Eutropium*] If the grace of God was necessary to every good action, there was no room, urged Pelagius, for free-will, and to avoid this, instead of denying grace, he sometimes sought to identify it with free-will, although by this process the difficulty, instead of being solved, was only thrown further back The Augustinian theory seemed to imply that God had a predilection for some of His creatures more than others, and bestowed grace on men in varying degrees, as a free gift, and not as a reward of their merits If there is a difficulty in accepting this doctrine, how is it removed by the identification of grace with free-will, that is, with man's natural power of doing good? That power must be the gift of the Creator, yet it is not equally possessed by men, some are born with more spirit, or with a better character, or with a stronger inclination to virtue, or with less violent passions than others A predilection on God's part is equally implied Such powers are still a purely gratuitous gift at His hands which cannot have been merited by mankind before they were born, though its bestowal must have been predetermined by Omniscience

4 *The possibility of a perfectly sinless man* This was a logical deduction from the previous positions When Pelagius found persons excusing their shortcomings on the ground of the weakness of human nature, and the impossibility of keeping the Divine commands, he said that instead of attributing their faults to a source which reflected on the Creator Himself, they should seek the cause in the feebleness of their own wills By way of encouragement he proceeded to name certain persons whom he asserted to have been without sin, Abel, Enoch, Melchizedek, and about twenty more, also certain women, Deborah, Hannah, Judith, and above all the Blessed Virgin, in confessing whom to have been without sin he anticipated the modern Church of Rome, and he disagreed with St Augustine in considering the tenet to be *de fide* [Aug *de Nat et Grat* cap 36] His argument was a curious one No sins are recorded as having been committed by these persons, therefore we may conclude that they were sinless, at least to assert otherwise would be to make a statement unauthorized by Holy Scripture [1]

[1] The actual words are worth quoting "Certe primo in tempore quatuor tantum homines fuisse referuntur Peccavit Eva, scriptura hoc prodidit Adam quoque deliquit, eadem scriptura non tacuit sed et Cain peccasse, quia aeque scriptura testata est, quorum non modo peccata, verum etiam peccatorum indicat qualitatem Quod si et Abel peccasset, et hoc sine dubio scriptura dixisset, sed non dixit, ergo nec ille peccavit, quin etiam justum ostendit Credamus igitur quod legimus, et quod non legimus nefas credamus adstruere [Aug *de Nat et Grat* sec 44]

5 *The existence of a middle state for infants dying unbaptized* Pelagius considered that new-born infants were in the same condition as Adam before his fall What became of them in case of their death? Sometimes he was content with the ambiguous reply, "Whither they do not go I know, whither they go I know not" Sometimes he taught the existence of a threefold state, damnation for sinners, heaven for baptized persons who lead a holy life, and a middle existence of neither pain nor pleasure, "Limbus Infantium," for infants dying unbaptized, before they have committed actual sin

6 *That Adam's fall injured himself only, and not mankind* The commonly received theory of the physical and moral consequences of the transgression of the first man on the entire race was rejected as encouraging moral indolence, as inconsistent with the justice of God, and as conflicting with the Pelagian theory of the absolute freedom of the will "Even the individual," argued Julian, "cannot by means of a simple transgression suffer a change in his moral nature, he retains the same freedom of the will; the past sin no longer injured the first man when he had repented of it How then was it possible that the entire human nature should be corrupted thereby?" The only sense in which it could be allowed to have been injurious to the human race was by its evil example That death which Scripture asserts to have entered the world through the fall [Rom v 12], was interpreted to mean spiritual death only [2] This partial view of the effects of the fall led to a correspondingly deficient conception of the effects of the Atonement, not always boldly asserted, but inevitably implied by the preceding positions, namely—

8 *That as neither death nor sin passed upon all men by the fall of Adam, so neither are righteousness or life necessarily due to the death and resurrection of Christ* The redemption was not necessary to man's salvation, but was beneficial, as the Fall had been injurious, by the example afforded by the life of Christ Man was as capable of securing salvation by the proper use of his own powers, as of drawing on himself damnation by their misuse, God having given him a law which prescribes nothing impossible, and to which He therefore expects a perfect personal obedience Thus Pelagianism, fully developed, and in its worst aspect, made the atonement superfluous, and altered the character of Christ, while in its best aspect it fell far short of that idea of sanctification which is only the work of Christ, and that inner connection between Christ and the faithful resulting in their justification by Him

Besides the above generally received views of Pelagius, a few doctrines of an eccentric character were held by some of his followers in Sicily

[2] The last words of this verse ἐφ' ᾧ πάντες ἥμαρτον, which St Augustine, following the Latin version, translated into "quo (sc Adam) omnes peccaverunt" was more correctly translated by Pelagius "forasmuch as (= ἐπὶ τούτῳ ὅτι) all have sinned," though at the cost of consistency with his doctrine of the impeccability of certain persons

Hilary writing thence [c A D 410], enumerates the following, and asks St Augustine's opinion on them

1 That a rich man, if he keeps his wealth, and does not sell all he has, cannot enter into the kingdom of God, and that it will not avail him if he uses his riches well

2 That it is not lawful to swear under any circumstances

3 That the church of which it is written that it has neither spot nor wrinkle, is the church in which we now live [Usher, *Brit Eccles. Antiq* p 229 Aug *Ep* 88]

Arminians have been frequently charged with verging on Pelagianism The Remonstrants at the Synod of Dort [A D 1618-19], rebutted the charge by confessing that Divine grace was necessary, not only as it illuminates the understanding, but as it gives strength to the will to avoid sin, not only as it teaches us what we ought to do, but also as it gives us desire and power to do that which we ought

[Pelagianism is treated of at length by St Augustine in the following books *de Nuptiis et Concupiscentia, ad Valerium*, lib ii, *contra Duas Epistolas Pelagianorum ad Bonifacium* lib iv, *Enchiridion*, lib i, *de Gratia et Libero Arbitrio*, lib i, *de Correptione et Gratia*, lib i, *de Prædestinatione Sanctorum*, lib i, *de Dono Perseverantiæ* lib i, *contra Julianum Pelagianum*, lib xii, *de Gestis Pelagii*, lib i, *de Octo Dulcitii Quæstionibus*, lib i, *Comment in Psalm* li, *Sermo* x *item* xiv *de verbis Apostoli item in Sancti Johannis Nativitatem* *Epistolæ ad Paulinum, Optatum, Sextum, Cœlestinum, Vitalem, Valentinum, etc* Also in G J Vossius, *Historia Controversiarum Pelagianarum* Patouillet, *Vie de Pélage*, 1751 Leutzen's *Dissertatio de Pelagianorum Doctrinæ Principiis*, 1833 Wigger's *Pragmatische Darstellung des Augustinismus und Pelagianismus*, 2 vols Hamb 1833, Eng translation by Emerson, New York 1840 *Varia Scripta et Monumenta ad Pelagianorum Historiam pertinentia*, to be found at the close of vol x of the Benedictine edition of St Augustine's works, and containing a large amount of miscellaneous information *Commonitorium Marii Mercatoris contra Pelagianos* Pauli Orosii *Liber Apologeticus contra Pelagium, de Arbitrii Libertate* Walch, *Historia der Ketzereien*, iv 735 Usserii *Britann Eccles Antiquitates*, caps viii ix x xi Baronius, *Annales*, Antwerp. 1593, vol v pp 303-682 Tillemont's *Mémoires*, art cclix cclxxxvi Prædestinati, *Liber de Hæres* c lxxxviii Prosperi Aquitani *ad Rufinum Epistola de Gratia et Libero Arbitrio* Wall, *Infant Baptism*, vol i cap xix Cardinal Noris, *Historia Pelagiana*]

PEPUZIANS [MONTANISTS]

PERATÆ A very obscure sect, first named by Clement of Alexandria, and described in some detail by Hippolytus, the latter being followed by Theodoret, without any fresh information about them being added by him [Theod *Hæret fab* i. 17]

They appear to have been called Peratæ, or Peratici, in the first instance from the country to which they belonged, Eubœa, i e the land beyond [πέραν] the continent, as Peræa was the district beyond Jordan, and this is the only fact stated about them by Clement of Alexandria [Clem Alex *Strom* vii 17 *ad fin*] But they afterwards gave another meaning to the name, that of "Transcendentalists" [Περᾶσαι], because through their knowledge of divine mysteries they were qualified to "proceed through and pass beyond destruction" Hippolytus says that they originated with Euphrates the Peratic, and Celbes the Carystian, the latter being also called Ademes and Acembes the Carystian both by Hippolytus and Theodoret, but no particulars are given about either

The Peratæ appear to have been a local sect of Gnostics, whose peculiar γνῶσις was a recondite philosophy founded on theories associated with the constellations of astronomers, and on serpent-worship Hippolytus says that they and their doctrines had been very little known until he described them, and that the latter were so intricate that it was difficult to give a compendious notion of them But, after stating many details of their strange system, he goes on to sum it up in the following terms According to them the universe is Father, Son, and Matter, each of the three having endless capacities in itself Intermediate between Matter and the Father sits the Son, the Logos, the Serpent, always being in motion towards the unmoving Father and towards moving Matter At one time the Son is turned towards the Father, and receives powers into His own Person, at another time He takes up those powers and turns towards Matter Then Matter, devoid of attribute and being unfashioned, moulds itself into forms from the Son which the Son moulded from the Father They believed further in a Demiurge who works destruction and death, and that men could be saved from his power only through the Son, Who is the Serpent.

But in addition to this fundamental corruption of Christianity, the Peratæ had also many secret mysteries, which Hippolytus says could not be mentioned by him on account of their profanity [Hippolyt *Philosoph* v 7-13, x 6]

PERÆANS [PERATÆ]

PERATICÆ [PERATÆ]

PEREMAYANOFTSCHINS A sect of Russian dissenters, which takes its name of "re-anointers" from the practice of re ordaining those popes or priests who secede to them from the Church The Peremayanoftschins are a branch of the POPOFTSCHINS, the practice of re-ordination being their chief distinction

PERFECTI A name assumed by the stricter Catharists of the twelfth and thirteenth centuries Reinerius, who had himself been a Catharist, and who speaks of a census of the sect taken by themselves, says that there were only 4000 of these, although the "Credentes," or general body of the Catharists, was innumerable These "Perfect" Catharists were analogous to the Manichæan "Elect," professing to live an extremely strict life, in imitation of Christ and His Apostles From among them were taken their bishop, "Filius major," "Filius minor," and deacon, some of whom were brought up from their childhood on a rigid fish and vegetable diet [Reiner *contr Waldens* in *Bibl Max* xxv 266, 269] The Perfecti also called themselves "Consolati" and "Boni Homines"

PERFECTIBILISTS A controversial designation of those who hold the doctrine that Christian perfection is attainable during the present life

Among ill informed persons this doctrine has often been taken up on the ground of those passages in St Paul's Epistles in which he refers to the τέλειοι [1 Cor ii 6], or those who having been first among the Catechumens, then among the Baptized, were at last received among the ranks of Christians, who were entitled to the highest grace that could be given, τὸ τέλειον, the Holy Eucharist But many mystical divines have believed that a life of profound devotional contemplation leads on to such an union with God that all which is base and sinful in the Christian's soul becomes annihilated and there ensues a superhuman degree of participation in the Divine perfection Such a doctrine was held by the great mystic whose works pass under the name of Dionysius, and from him was handed down to the Hesychasts, the strict Franciscans, the Molinists, the Jansenists, and the German Mystics, from whom it passed on to the English Methodists, among whom it has always been a special tenet that sanctification may, and ought to, go on to perfection

But Perfectibilists in theory are very often Antinomians in practice Thus the Fraticelli, the Brethren of the Free Spirit, the Beghards, the Anabaptists, and the Familists, all claimed to have attained a state of perfection in which no act, however evil in others, could in them be condemned as sinful Similar opinions have been held by great numbers of Methodists, and in quite recent times the PERFECTIONISTS of America and the PRINCEITES of England have carried the doctrine of perfectibility on to Antinomianism in as extreme a form as it was carried by the Familists

PERFECTIONISTS A licentious American sect of Antinomian Communists, established about the year 1845 by John Humphrey Noyes They are also known as "Bible Communists" and "Free Lovers"

Noyes was an Independent preacher at Yale College New Haven, when he professed to have discovered from the writings of St Paul that the Christian Church and all the sects are alike in error, and determined to set up a new church of his own Being a man of a not uncommon class, susceptible of strong religious feelings, while at the same time ready to give unbridled license to his passions, his new community was to be professedly under the entire control of the highest religious principle, and yet entirely free from the control of the ordinary rules of morality He accordingly established a community (somewhat similar to those of the Shakers), at Oneida Creek, in which the following four principles are recognised · [1] that all its members are reconciled with God, [2] that being so reconciled they are saved from sin, [3] that man and woman are entirely equal, [4] that there should be a perfect community of goods The "reconciliation" on which the system is grounded is simply an assurance of faith that such a reconciliation has been effected, so that if a man or woman feels this, the feeling is full evidence upon the subject Being so reconciled, the person declares the fact before the community, and is then said to "stand up and confess holiness" Having so confessed holiness, they are accounted, and are to account themselves, "perfect," so that they can neither go backward into unholiness or forward to greater perfection Henceforth also all that is done by the person confessing holiness must necessarily be good, because done by a perfect person, to whom all things are pure, and to whom all things are consequently permitted

On this principle an iniquitous system of "free love" or "complex marriage" has been established as the true interpretation of equality of the sexes This is, in reality, an open and shameless abolition of monogamy and of the marriage bond, and the substitution for marriage of a community of women which is subject only to such social restrictions as are necessary to obtain free inclination on both sides, and to secure the peace of the community The latter is effected by obtaining the general consent of the community to every licentious union, and to every fresh partner in licentiousness, that is entered into

There are three settlements of this antichristian sect in America, one of about 300 persons at Oneida Creek, and two smaller ones at Brooklyn and Wallingford Assuming to be "perfect," the members of it practically discard all positive religion or devotion, and their place of worship at Oneida is described as "a chapel, a theatre, a concert-room, a casino, a working-place, all in one, being supplied with benches, lounging chairs, work-tables, a reading-desk, a stage, a gallery, and a pianoforte" The English sect of the PRINCEITES is of an analogous kind [Dixon's *New America*, 213, 6th ed]

PETER THE FULLER. [MONOPHYSITES]

PETILLIANISTS Those who adhered to the party of Petillian, the Donatist Bishop of Carthage, in his controversy with St Augustine

PETRITES The followers of Peter Mongus, the Monophysite Patriarch [A D 477-490] of Alexandria [Timoth Presb in *Combefis Hist Monothelit* MONOPHYSITES]

PETROBRUSIANS The sect of the Petrobrusians, or as they are commonly, but less correctly called, Petrobussians, was the earliest of the anti-sacerdotal communities which the profound discontent inspired by the tyranny of Rome called into existence at the beginning of the twelfth century. They were the followers of an eloquent but ignorant heretic named Peter de Brueys The date of his birth is unknown, nor are we better informed as to his family, early life, or personal character All the information which has reached us of this remarkable person is contained in a tract or epistle composed for the refutation of his doctrines, and addressed to certain Bishops of Dauphiné and Provence (at that time fiefs of the Holy Roman empire) by Peter the Venerable, Abbot of Clugny, afterwards renowned as the protector of Abelard Although the account of an enemy is always to be read with suspicion, the high and disinterested character of the Abbot of Clugny gives more than ordinary value to his narrative The time of the composition of the preface to the refutation (the body of which was of earlier date) was shortly after the death of De Brucys, which took place about A D 1125 At this time, the author tells us, the heresy had been flourishing for twenty years

Like many others of the reformers, Peter de Brucys was an ecclesiastic, apparently one of the secular clergy, and it would seem the possessor of a benefice in some diocese in Southern France, a region where the degradation of the clergy had reached its lowest point of infamy An ambitious man, he quitted his meagre benefice and unhonoured profession for the popular *rôle* of reformer His principal doctrines, which (with one exception, his repugnance to the Cross) were more ably extended by his more powerful successor, Henry the Deacon [HENRICIANS], were partly Rationalistic, partly what is in this day termed Evangelical At first the preaching of Peter seems to have been confined to the inculcation of a loose system of general morality, but time and impunity so favoured heretical cultivation that the seeds of dogmatic errors "per xx fere annos sata et aucta quinque præcipua et venenata virgulta produxerunt"[1]

The capital charges upon which he is arraigned are [1] He rejected infant baptism, alleging that no miraculous gifts were possible in that ceremony, which he declared to be wholly void when performed on the person of an irresponsible infant [2] He denied that any special sanctity resided in consecrated buildings, forbidding the erection of churches, and directing that such churches as did exist should be pulled down. [3] In particular he objected to the worship of the Cross, alleging that the accursed tree should be held in horror by all Christians as the instrument of the torture and death of the Redeemer [4] He denied any sort of real presence in the Eucharist Whether or not he retained the office of the communion as a memorial rite is unknown, but as his rejection of the Eucharist as such seems inevitable, it is reasonable to suppose that he proscribed it altogether [5] He was bitterly opposed to prayers, oblations, alms, and other good deeds done on behalf of the dead. Besides these five capital errors, which form the subject of the Clugniac Abbot's refutation, must be added a total prohibition of chanting and all use of sacred music Puritanical as some of these tenets seem, de Brucys was no lover of asceticism He inculcated marriage, even of priests, as a high religious usage, and would have abolished all the fasts of the Church The deleterious effects of his teaching are thus summed up by the authority we have quoted "The people are re-baptized, churches profaned, altars overturned, crosses are burnt, meat eaten openly on the day of the Lord's Passion, priests scourged, monks cast into dungeons, and by terror or torture constrained to marry" The scene of the labours which had this result was the ancient Narbonensian Province The dioceses of Arles in Provence, Embrun, Die and Gap in Dauphiné, and some districts lying further east, were the greatest sufferers from his preaching Strangely enough this popular heretic met his death at the hands of the people Seized by a mob in an émeute caused by his preaching (but which some assume to have been organized by the ecclesiastical authorities) he was committed to the flames at St Gilles in the Arelatensian diocese His career, which commenced about A D 1104, was thus terminated about A D 1125

PETRO JOHANNITES A name given to the partizans of Peter John Olivi [A D 1279-1297], a monk of Bezieres, the founder of the Fraticelli schism among the Franciscans He was a disciple of the Abbot Joachim, and following in the steps of his master, wrote a Commentary on the Revelation containing interpretations of a similar character to the prophecies of Joachim From his birthplace he is called Peter of Serignan, and from his monastery Peter Biterrensis When Pope Nicolas III issued a new interpretation of the Rule of St Francis [A D 1279], with the view of suppressing the fanaticism which was rising among the "Spirituals" of that order, a party was formed to resist it under the leadership of Olivi, and this party of Petro-Johannites, or strict Franciscans, became after his death the party out of which the FRATICELLI took their rise [Wadding, *Annal. Min Frat.*, Oudinus, *de Scriptor Eccl* iii 584 Baluze, *Miscellan* i 213]

PETZELIANS An obscure sect of Socialists which existed for a short time in Upper Austria under the leadership of a priest named Petzel, but was put down by the Government as being more of a political than a religious character

PHANTASIODOCETÆ A term used by Theophylact in his commentary on the fourth chapter of St John [DOCETÆ]

PHANTASIASTS [DOCETÆ]

PHARISEES A religious party among the Jews which grew up during the last two centuries of their national existence, and which represented strict Judaism They are first heard of under

[1] *Petri Venerabilis, Abb Cluniac Epist ad Arelatensem Ebredunensem Archiepisc Diensem Vapincensem Episc adv Petrobrusianos Hæreticos* in *Max Bibl Patr Lugdunens* xxii 1033, *et seq* The argument of de Brucys upon the question of the sacrament is noteworthy "Nolite, o populi, Episcopis Presbyteris seu clerico seducenti credere qui in altaris officio vos decipiunt Mentiuntur plane Corpus enim Christi semel tantum ab ipso Christo, in cœnâ ante passionem factum est, et semel, hoc est tunc tantum, discipulis datum est Exinde neque confectum ab aliquo neque alicui datum est"

the name of "The Assidæans" [*Chasidim*, i e "The Pious"], who are described as "mighty men of Israel, even all such as were voluntarily devoted to the law" [1 Macc ii 27, 42], and as joining the army of Mattathias in the early part of the Maccabæan struggle for national freedom [B C 166] At a later time the name of Pharisees [*Perishim*, i e "Separatists"] was probably given to them by their opponents, the Sadducees, who held the reins of political power, much as the representatives of the ancient Muscovite Church, the "Staroverzi," or "Old Believers," are regarded as Separatists by the modern rulers of Russia.

At the time this party of strict Jews first arose a strong effort was being made by Antiochus Epiphanes [B C 175-164] to destroy the national character of the Jews, and among the latter themselves there were many young men who were willing to promote his objects, being captivated by the Greek customs with which they were beginning to become acquainted These Hellenizing Jews paid Antiochus 440 talents of silver to depose Onias the high-priest, and appoint for his successor one of their own party named Jeshua The new high-priest at once changed his honourable Jewish name for the Greek name Jason, and as one proof of his determination to break down the distinctive nationality of the people, he caused the "chief young men" to "wear a hat' or "fez' in the place of the ancient turban He then paid Antiochus 150 talents of silver more for the privilege of building "a place for exercise" or gymnasium, in which the young Jews might be trained up to the athletic sports of the Greeks, and for the further privilege of calling "them of Jerusalem by the name of Antiochians"[1] When this place of exercise was completed its attractions were so great that the priests actually forsook their duties in the Temple to waste their time over "the game of Discus" Thus Jason "forthwith brought his nation to the Greekish fashion, and putting down the governments which were according to the law, he brought up new customs against the law" To such an extent did this high-priest carry his contempt for the old national faith that he actually sent an offering of "300 drachms of silver to the sacrifice of Hercules" at the annual games of Tyre, an act which so scandalized even his own messengers, "who were Antiochians,' that they diverted the offering from its purpose, and gave it as a contribution towards "the making of galleys" [2 Macc iv 7-20] It was shortly after the death of this Hellenizing high-priest that Antiochus Epiphanes polluted the great altar by a mock sacrifice of swine, and turned the Temple into a temple of Zeus or Jupiter Olympius [1 Macc i 47, 2 Macc vi 2] He then issued a decree "to his whole kingdom, that all should be one people, and every one should learn his laws," when "many of the Israelites consented to his religion" [1 Macc i 42, 43]

It was when "the abomination of the desolation" was thus set up in the shape of an idol altar on the great altar of the Temple, and other idol altars throughout Judæa, that "The Pious" and courageous among the Jews banded together to restore the national worship and the national law This was effected under the leadership of Judas Maccabæus, and the Feast of "the Dedication," which was kept in the time of our Lord [John x 22], was a lasting memorial of the good work which the Assidæans, or early Pharisees, had effected by their valour, commemorating as it did the day when, nearly two centuries before [B C 166], the Temple service was restored, and "there was very much gladness among the people, for that the reproach of the heathen was put away" [1 Macc iv. 55]

This restoration marks, probably, the beginning of the transition from the military to the simply religious phase of the party, the Assidæans, whose zeal restored pure Judaism by means of the Maccabee wars, becoming in the next generation the Pharisees, whose zeal defended it by their teaching They became the educated, scholarly, class among the Jews, men of whom St Paul, "a Pharisee, the son of a Pharisee" [Acts xxiii 6], "taught according to the perfect manner of the law of the fathers, and zealous towards God" [Acts xxii 3], was a fair specimen. Hence they received the name of "Scholars" [*Chaberim*] or Divines, because they made the knowledge and practice of the divine law the one great object of their life It was in the pursuit of this object that the Pharisees investigated and collected the great body of tradition respecting the law and its observances, which was always current—partly by word of mouth, and partly by written commentaries—among the educated Jews The Sadducees rejected all interpretation of Scripture but that which came from each man's own mind, professing to stand by the simple letter of the law, but the Pharisees strove to gather up the wisdom of all preceding generations, as well as to make the best use they could of their own reason, and looked upon the Word of God as a mine of wealth which no ages of human research could ever exhaust It was out of the midst of their body that the great Scribes and Doctors arose, men, like Gamaliel, whose pious wisdom in the Sanhedrim [Acts v 34 40] sounds almost like the words of an old prophet, and to whose training the Christian world is indebted, so far as human learning and the developement of intellectual power are concerned, for the greatness of St Paul

In the times of the New Testament, the Sadducees were the ' rulers of the people," but the Pharisees were the teachers of the people They had not, however, escaped from those influences which wrought so much degeneration in the Jewish character during the last generations of their national existence, and they were not excepted from the denunciations which St John the Baptist and our Lord so freely poured out upon the Jews of that time There were, especially, many among them who lost sight of practical religion in theoretical religion, who made much

[1] Probably the germ of the party known in our Lord's time as "Herodians," the Erastian party.

of lesser duties, such as tithing "mint, rue, anise, and cummin," and neglected greater duties, the "weightier matters of the law," who exaggerated the value of their interpretative system to such an extent that they made "the Word of God of none effect" by their traditions, who made long prayers out of mere ostentation, and who as to their morals were but "whited sepulchres" The existence of a large body of such "hypocrites" among the Pharisees shews that the Pharisaic system was, like all else belonging to the Jewish nation, in a condition of mortal decay Many years before, the more ascetic element of the party had broken off into a sect, the ESSENES, and it is not unlikely that their schismatical position had brought discredit upon asceticism in general But without an almost ascetic severity and self-denial, a strict practical observance of Judaism was impossible, however strictly its rules might be laid down in theory Yet there is no evidence that the Pharisees were morally below the level of the Jewish people at large, and the popular identification of the words "Pharisee" and "hypocrite" is a popular error which is very inconsistent with the true history of a body of men who were probably at all times the best men among the Jews St Paul did not speak in condemnation of his former life when he said to Herod Agrippa, "After the most straitest sect of our religion I lived a Pharisee" [Acts xxvi 5]

In the last great struggle of the Jews for their lost freedom, a class of military Pharisees arose under the name of "Zealots," in whom the ancient self-devotion of the Assidæans was revived But Christianity had absorbed the best elements of the Jewish nation, and the fanatic Zealot was but a degenerate representative of the heroic Assidæan After the fall of the nation, Judaism and Pharisaism became substantially identical; the traditions of the Talmud and the Mishna representing that cumbrous overlaying of the Word of God for which the learned Jews were condemned even in the time of our Lord [DICT *of* THEOL MISHNA TALMUD]

PHEMIOZITÆ [BARBELITES]

PHIBIONITÆ A local name of the Gnostics [Epiph *Hær* xxvi 3] As Valentinus was said to be a native of Phrebonitis, on the coast of Egypt [Epiph *Hær* xxxi 2], it is not improbable that his sect was at first called by the name of Phrebonitæ, and that this was afterwards corrupted into Phibionitæ.

PHILADELPHIAN CHURCH [SOUTHCOTTIANS]

PHILADELPHIANS A society of Theosophical Pietists founded in the year 1695 under the name of "The Philadelphian Society for the advancement of Piety and Divine Philosophy" It originated with an aged lady named Jane Lead, who died in 1704 at the age of eighty-one She had spent many years in the study of Jacob Boehm's works, and herself wrote many books, the mystic character of which is indicated by the title of one published in 1695, "The Wonders of God's Creation manifested in the variety of Eight Worlds, as they were made known experimentally to the Author" In establishing the Philadelphian Society she was assisted by a physician named Pordage, who was in Holy Orders, but had taken to the practice of medicine when ejected from his benefice as a Nonjuror He was the author of "Divine and True Metaphysics," in three volumes, and also of "Theologia Mystica," and some ascetic works Another of the Philadelphians was the learned physician Francis Lee, who contributed the historical Prolegomena to Grabe's Septuagint, and the "Occasional Annotations" on physiological and other scientific subjects to Parker's admirable but unfinished commentary, entitled "Bibliotheca Biblica" Dr Lee edited the "Theosophical Transactions" of the Society, and also the later works of Mrs Lead, who in her old age was blind A third physician who became an active member of the Society was Lot Fisher, who caused all the works of Mrs Lead and her associates to be translated and splendidly published in Dutch A fourth principal coadjutor was Thomas Bromley, author of "The Sabbath of Rest," and of some works on Biblical subjects

The Philadelphian Society contributed largely to the spread of that mystical piety which is so conspicuous in the works of the good and learned William Law, and which affected in no small degree the early stages of Methodism Mrs Lead herself, however, combined much fanaticism with her pietism, professing (like Swedenborg in a later generation) to hold intercourse with spirits This fanaticism imparted itself to many members of the Philadelphian Society, and imaginary apparitions of good and evil angels became, for a time, a prominent feature of their religious life In other respects their mysticism was of the ordinary character, making the contemplative life the basis of religious knowledge and practice

A small work entitled "The Principles of the Philadelphians," published in 1697, gives a curious exposition of their mysticism

PHILETUS A heretic of Apostolic times, who is coupled with Hymenæus by St Paul as one of those who "concerning the truth have erred, saying that the resurrection is passed already" [2 Tim ii 17, 18] Nothing further is known respecting him than what is recorded in the few words of the Apostle [HYMENÆUS]

PHILIPOFTSCHINS A small sect of Russian dissenters, who, after the disturbances at Strelitz under Peter I [A D 1689-1725], in which they had taken part, fled for refuge to Lithuania, where they formed a new denomination under the leadership of a monk named Philip, known among themselves as Pustos-Wiat, or the Saint of the Desert They are sometimes called *Brûleurs* or *Tueurs* from their tendency to suicide, which they considered meritorious, and which they accordingly courted, sometimes burying themselves alive, sometimes starving themselves to death It was rather on points of practice than of doctrine that they differed from the orthodox church, whose baptism they only rejected as invalid, because "Amen" was repeated four times in the course of the service Without a regular priesthood [STAROVERTZI], they elected one of their number as an elder, who was called the Starik, who occupied the position of a pope or priest, and remained unmarried, but the duty of preaching was left open to any one who felt himself "called by the Spirit" to undertake it Accusations of laxity of morals were brought against them, of renouncing marriage, and living in spiritual brotherhood and sisterhood, the truth of which was never clearly established, for when the Empress Anne [A D 1730-1740] sent commissioners to inquire into the state of their monasteries, they shut themselves up and burnt themselves alive within their own walls rather than give any evidence on the subject

PHILIPONIANS [PHILIPOFTSCHINS]

PHILIPPISTS The party of moderate and conciliatory Lutherans who sided with Philip Melanchthon against the rigid Lutherans headed by Flacius Illyricus, the dispute between whom acquired the name of the Adiaphoristic Controversy The Philippists were strongest in the University of Wittenberg, the opposite party in that of Jena The former were in the end accused of being Calvinists at heart, and were much persecuted by the ultra-Lutheran party [ADIAPHORISTS]

PHILIPPINS [PHILIPOFTSCHINS]

PHILOPONISTS A section of the Tritheists of the sixth century who followed John Philoponus, a layman of Alexandria, famous as a grammarian and philosopher The Philoponists formed the main body of the Alexandrian Tritheists, being, however, divided from the CONONITES on the subject of the resurrection of the body Philoponus maintained that both the matter and form of bodies will be restored at the resurrection, but the Cononites limited the restoration to their matter only. John Philoponus received his surname, "The Laborious" [ὁ φιλόπονος], on account of his great literary industry He wrote a work on the Hexæmeron, another on Easter, a treatise against the materialism of Proclus, another against the work written by Jamblichus in favour of Image-worship, a book on the Resurrection, and another on the Trinity, together with Commentaries on Aristotle and other secular works [Niceph *Hist Eccl* xviii 45-48 Joann Damasc *de Hæres* lxxxiii Walch, *Hist Ketz* viii 702 Cave, *Hist Liter* i 267]

PHOTINIANS A sect of Sabellian heretics which arose in the fourth century, under the leadership of Photinus, Bishop of Sirmium in Lower Pannonia Photinus was a native of Galatia, and a disciple of Marcellus of Ancyra, under whom he served as deacon [Hieron *de Vir Ill* iii 107, Hilar Pict *Frag Hist* ii 19], but the dates of his birth and consecration are not known The councils in which he was condemned on the appearance of his heresy range from A D 336 to 351 His tenets were nearly identical with those of Paul of Samosata [1]

Photinus held the tenet of an Antitrinitarian Monarchia, and that Jesus Christ was born of the Holy Ghost and the Virgin Mary, that a certain portion of the Divine Substance, which he called

[1] Philaster and the author of Prædestinatus assert the entire identity of Photinian and Samosatene doctrine Rufinus calls Photinus Paul's successor Epiphanius says he held the same, or even worse doctrines than Paul concerning the Son of God, that he was of the faction of Paul [Pearson appears to take ἀπὸ μέρους to mean partially *on the Creed*, note p 119, fol edit], Socrates and Sozomenus class together Sabellius, Marcellus, Paul, and Photinus, Theodoret says that Photinus differs from Sabellius only in phraseology Hilary of Poitiers, Jerome *loc cit*, Pseudo-Hieronymus [*Hær* xxxvi], Isidore of Hispalis [*Hær* xxxviii], Honorius [*Hær* liii], Pope Damasus [Theod *H E* v 11], say that Photinus revived the heresy of Ebion. This statement, in any accurate sense, we may dismiss, as Pearson does [EBIONITES] Sulpicius Severus [*Chron.* ii 37] having said that Marcellus asserted the Sabellian heresy, adds that Photinus introduced a new heresy, "a Sabellio quidem in unione dissentiens, sed initium Christi ex Maria prædicabat" The evidence that Photinus held the "Unio" outweighs the testimony of Sulpicius So, too, Marius Mercator must be held in error in stating that Photinus denied the miraculous birth of our Lord [*Diss de XII Anath* n xvii t ii p 128, Garner] Of greater weight than any authority yet named must be the authority of Hilary of Poitiers, and those who identify Photinianism with an advanced Sabellianism must be able to give a reasonable explanation of Hilary's statements For Hilary expressly confronts both Sabellius and Arius with Photinus The passage is long, but it must be given in full "Jam vero qua fidei nostræ victoria Hebion, qui Photinus est, aut vincit aut vincitur dum Sabellium arguit, cur hominem neget filium Dei, dum ab Arianis confutatur, cum in homine nesciat Dei filium Adversum Sabellium Evangelia sibi ex filio Mariæ defendit Arius ei Evangelia pro solum Mariæ filium non relinquit Adversum hunc, qui filium negat, homo ab eo usurpatur in filium Ab hoc ei, qui ante sæcula filium nesciat, filius Dei solum negatur ex homine Vincant, ut volunt, quia se invicem vincendo vincuntur dum et hi, qui nunc sunt, de natura Dei confutantur, et Sabellius de sacramento filii refellitur, et Photinus natum ante sæcula Dei filium vel ignorare arguitur, vel negare Sed inter hæc Ecclesiæ fides, evangelicis atque apostolicis fundata doctrinis, et adversus Sabellium tenet filii professionem, et adversus Arium Dei naturam, et adversus Photinum sæculi creatorem et hoc verius, quod hæc ab his invicem non negantur Naturam enim Dei in operibus Sabellius prædicat, sed operantem filium nescit Hi vero filium nuncupant, sed veritatem in eo naturæ Dei non confitentur Hominem autem Photinus usurpat, sed in usurpato sibi homine nativitatem Dei ante sæcula ignorat" [*De Trin* vii 7] Here Photinus is said to hold a Sonship beginning from Mary, while Sabellius allows none at all The later part of this assertion is clearly contradictory to the statements of Epiphanius, which are supported by Augustine and others, for these aver that Sabellius taught that the Son came into the world as a Ray from the Father By comparison with these statements the "Deus protensus usque ad Virginem" named by Hilary is referred by commentaries to Sabellius [SABELLIANS] According to these statements Sabellian doctrine and Photinian doctrine, as condemned at Sirmium, are perfectly equivalent as regards the Sonship of our Lord But Hilary's assertion is true of the first stage of Sabellianism, in which there was held to be, properly, no Son at all, the Father being Son Accordingly Pearson remarks that Photinus differs from Sabellius, being far from a Patripassian Understand then Hilary, in the chapter which has been quoted, to be speaking of the first or Patripassian stage of Sabellianism, and the chapter becomes clear The only question remaining undecided is the comparatively unimportant one, whether Sabellius himself passed into the second stage into which his school undoubtedly passed, as Epiphanius asserts him to have done, or, whether, as a strict interpretation of Hilary would lead us to think, he continued to hold Patripassian doctrine, and the doctrine of the "Deus protensus" is not really his, but belongs only to his followers who deserted him The evidence before us leads to the conclusion that Sabellius did pass out of the Patripassian stage, and that Hilary, in the somewhat rhetorical passage we have quoted,

the Word, descended upon and acted through the man Jesus Christ, that on account of this association of the Word with the human nature Jesus was called the Son of God, and even God Himself, that the Holy Ghost was not a distinct Person, but a celestial virtue proceeding from the Deity [Epiph *Hær* lxxi, Hilar *de Trin* vii 3, 7, viii 40, Rufinus, *Comm in Symb* § 39, Socr *H E* i 18, 19, 30, Sozom. iv 6, Theod *Hær fab* ii 11, *Dial* ii vol iv p. 52, ed 1642, August *Ep* 1 *ad Bonif* and *Serm in Matth* xii] These tenets are sufficiently stated in the article SAMOSATENES, and other articles regarding the various Monarchian sects, and it will be requisite only to point out wherein Photinus differed from Paul In this Marius Mercator is our first authority [1] Marius writes (in words which Lardner said the learned would more easily understand than he could translate) "Differentia itaque inter Samosatenum et Photinum ista sola est, qua Paulus Verbum Dei προφορικὸν, καὶ πρακτικὸν λόγον καὶ ἐνεργητικόν, id est, prolativum et potestatis effectivum Verbum sensit, non substantivum, quod Græci οὐσιῶδες dicunt" [*Diss de XII Anath Nestorii*, Num xix] This statement of Paul's doctrine agrees exactly with the statement in the article Samosatenes in the words of Athanasius Marius asserts that Photinus held the Divine element that acted in our Lord's Person to be "substantivum, or οὐσιῶδες" Now Photinus denied the personality, and consequently the Sonship of the Word, but allowed Its eternity as existing in the one undistinguished God We are therefore thrown back upon the tenet described in SABELLIANS as the division of the Union, namely, that the "Deus protensus," not being a distinct Person, is separable from the Godhead, or that a certain portion of the Divine Substance added to the human nature formed Jesus Christ the Son of God

The conclusion that this was the doctrine of Photinus is supported by a remarkable chapter in Philaster (the chapter which has some of the language of the Athanasian Creed), the 93rd, "Est hæresis quæ dicit veluti triformem Deum esse et compositum, ut quædam pars Patris, quædam Filii, quædam Spiritus Sancti sit." Philaster enounces the doctrine of the Three Persons of the One God, and proceeds, "Immensibilis est igitur hæc Trinitas, invisibilis," etc "Cum enim dicit mittere Patrem Filium, et Filium mittere Spiritum Sanctum, personarum causa dicit, non loci separatione disjunctos ostendit, propter Sabellium scilicet et Photinum hæreticos" Then he speaks of Sabellius "Cum ergo dicit misisse Patrem, et missum fuisse Filium, personarum causa dicit, ne quis aut ipsum Patrem aut ipsum Filium esse æstimet, quod ita sentiens delirat Sabellius" He turns to the other error, namely of Photinus, "Et ne iterum missus Filius de cœlo æstimetur non esse ubique in Patre, dixit quidem se missum a Patre, ubique tamen esse cum Patre ostendit, dicens, Pater qui me misit mecum est Non ergo separationem loci dixit" A belief in a local separation of one part of the "triformis Deus" is attributed to Photinus, and it is rightly noted that this belief denies the attribute of God, that He is Immensus, ἄπειρος, ἀμέτρητος The fourth Lateran Council [A D 1215] declaring that God is "Immensus," is said to have had in view this heresy of Photinus [Dec i, *de Fide Catholica*]

The description of this sect by Vincent of Lerins is thus found to be correct as far as it goes, but incomplete in that it does not define the nature of the Divine element which Photinus conceived to be superadded to the man Jesus to constitute Him the Son of God Vincent says "Photini ergo secta hæc est Dicit Deum singulum esse et solitarium, et more Judaico confitendum Trinitatis plenitudinem negat, neque ullam Dei Verbi, aut ullam Spiritus Sancti putat esse personam Christum vero hominem tantummodo solitarium asserit, cui principium adscribit ex Maria, et hoc omnibus modis dogmatizat, solam nos personam Dei Patris, et solum Christum hominem colere debere" [Vincent Lirin *adv Hær* xvii] If to this we add from the second stage of Sabellianism the tenet, that there acted in and through the man Jesus an element from the nature of the Deity, impersonal, yet substantive, which is to be again resumed into the Deity, our conception of Photinianism will, it is thought, be complete

The statements of the errors of Photinus made by the councils which condemned him (so far as the acts have come down to us) have been left for verification Photinus was, first, condemned with Marcellus [Sulpic Sever ii 36] This was probably at Constantinople, [2] A D. 336, for then the Arians in synod deprived Marcellus [Socr i 36, Sozomen ii 33] Secondly, in the Semi-Arian Council, the second of Antioch, A D 344 [Socr ii 19] Thirdly, in the Council of Sardica, A D 347, when Marcellus was acquitted, but the sentence against Photinus was not reversed [Sulpic Sever ii 36, Epiph *Hær* lxxi] Fourthly, in a council at Milan in the same year [Hil *Frag Hist* ii 19, Socr ii 36, Valesius' note] Fifthly, by a council at Rome, A D 349 [see authorities in Cave's *Hist Lit ad ann* 349] Sixthly, in a Synod at Sirmium, A D 349, when he was deposed by the Western Bishops, but through the affection and opinion of the people could not be removed [Hilar *Frag Hist* ii 21] Seventhly, at the second Synod of Sirmium, A D 351, by the Eastern Bishops, when, being convicted by Basil of Ancyra, he was banished [Socr ii 29, Sozom iv 6, Valesius' note in Socr for the date] The foregoing enumeration is that of Pearson, except that the Roman synod is added [*cf* Newman's *Treatises of Athanas* i 160 *n*]

argues upon his earlier tenets, which doubtless would be in such a case rather quietly ignored than formally recanted We much miss on this point Ittigius' promised dissertation [*Hist Photini* cap. ix] Besides the difference in their conception of the Logos, Photinus appears to have believed that the Logos inhabited Christ from the time of the Nativity, Paul, that the Logos did not descend into the Son until He had merited the gift by His holy life [See Stillingfleet *on the Trinity*, p 50]

[1] See regarding Marius Mercator, Natalis Alex *Sæc* iv cap. v art 8

[2] See a discussion of the question in Ittigius [*Diss* p 440], and a notice of all the synods

Out of these, the second-named council, which issued the Macrostiche, anathematized Paul of Samosata, and further, those who hold the doctrine of a Logos, impersonal and unsubstantial, now προφορικὸς, now ἐνδιάθετος, who say that Jesus Christ was not before the world, but only from the time of Mary, when His kingdom began, which kingdom is to have an end Of which sort they say, are the followers of Marcellus and Photinus, who do away the existence of Christ before the worlds, and His divinity, that they may seem to establish the "Monarchy"

Here, it will be observed, no distinction is made between πλατυσμός, strictly taken as a "dilatatio substantiæ," and the Marcellian πλατυσμός, which consisted in the ἐνεργεία of the Λόγος [MARCELLIANS] But the language of the Council of Sirmium [A D 251] is very explicit "Si quis dilatatam substantiam Dei Filium dicat facere, aut latitudinem substantiæ ejus Filium nominet, anathema sit" There can be little doubt that this is directed specially against Photinus The fifth article (which Pearson says aims clearly at Photinus) is really more general, it is directed against those who say that the Son existed before Mary only in the foreknowledge and purpose of God Then follow articles against two classes to whom the former would apply, those who held the "dilatatio substantiæ," and those who held the "prolativum verbum," the Photinians and the Marcellians The last article, as directed against the head and front of the heresy, must be quoted "Si quis Christum Deum Filium Dei ante sæcula subsistentem et ministrantem Patri ad omnium perfectionem non dicat, sed ex quo de Maria natus est, ex eo et Christum et Filium nominatum esse, et initium accepisse ut sit Deus, dicat anathema sit" One observation may be made with regard to what has been said of Hilary's putting Photinus in opposition to Sabellius The synod was called against Photinus Hilary says "to meet the heresy which was *renewed* by Photinus" Now it is clear that the errors denounced are those of the different branches of Sabellianism The Patripassianism of Noetus, *e g* is condemned in Art xii Now when we find the earlier articles which have been named (v to viii) clearly applying to a developed Sabellianism, it follows surely that the opposition stated by Hilary was, as was argued, only to the early stage [Hilar *de Synodis* 1174, *et seq*] The Bishops of Italy, in their letter to the Illyrian Bishops, say that Photinus was condemned "partiaria Sabellii hæreditate" [Hil *Frag Hist* xii]

Next after these decisions, there meets us the seventh Canon of Laodicea There appears to be no sufficient reason for excluding "Photinians" from this canon, and the mention of them proves beyond doubt that the council cannot be of the early date, A D 320 assigned to it by Baronius and Binius We adopt therefore the later date, 366 It is ordered that catechumens or communicants converted from Photinianism shall not be received without anathematizing all heresy, especially that in which they have been engaged, and that the communicants having learned the creeds, and being anointed with the chrism, may receive the Holy Mysteries

The General Council of Constantinople, A D 381, beginning with a general condemnation of heresies, named Photinians after Sabellians and Marcellians [Can I], and sanctioned the addition to the Creed of the clause, "Whose kingdom shall have no end" The contrary opinion was held by Marcellus as well as Photinus It appears from Cyril's Catechetical Lectures that the clause had been already added to the Creed by some of the Eastern Churches The Allocution of the Fathers of Chalcedon to the Emperor Marcian, A D 451, describes Photinus and Marcellus as introducing a new blasphemy against the Son, denying His existence, and reducing the Trinity to a Trinity of names Against them therefore the Fathers have declared the dogma of three Hypostases [Harduin, *Conc* ii 645] The second Council of Arles, A D 452, decreed "Photiniacos *sive* Paulianistas secundum Patrum statuta baptizari oportere" The "statuta Patrum" are the Apostolic Canon XLVI [XLVII], and particularly the 8th Canon of the first of Arles, and as the principle of that canon is applied by the second council to the case of the Bonosiacs, who coming from the same error yet retain the Catholic form, and are not to be baptized, it appears to follow without doubt that the Photinians had changed the form Further, since at Laodicea Photinian baptism was allowed, it follows that the form was changed between the times of these two councils In the 7th Canon of Constantinople, which treats of Baptism, the Photinians are not specified, but Sabellians are ordered to be baptized, and all other heresies, especially such as come from the country of the Galatians The council evidently proceeded on the same rules as the councils of Arles

Photinians are specified in the Constitution of Gratian, Valentinian and Theodosius, A D 381, against heretical conventicles and for restoring churches to Catholics Also in that of Theodosius and Valentinian, A D 428, to the same purpose as the former, and imposing on heretics severe civil disqualifications [*Cod Theod* XVI v 6, 65]

PHTHARTOLATRÆ One of the two principal divisions into which the sect of the Monophysites broke up in the early part of the sixth century The name was given to them by their opponents the Aphthartodocetæ, and was compounded of the Greek words for "corruptible" [φθαρτός] and "worship" [λατρεία], indicating the tenet of the sect, that the human body of the Saviour was subject to the corruptibility incident to ordinary human nature The sect was known in Antioch by the name of "Severians," from Severus its founder, the deprived Monophysite patriarch, in Egypt by the name of "Theodosians," from a rhetorician of Alexandria who became a disciple of Severus, and the leader of his sect in that city after his death [A D 535] The sect was known among Western writers by the name of "Corrupticolæ"

Severus became Patriarch of Antioch in the year 511, and was deposed by order of the

Emperor Justin in the year 520 He fled to Egypt after his deposition, finding Alexandria a safe place of retreat, and so greatly is his memory venerated by the Jacobites even to this day as one of the chief founders of their sect, that the day of his entrance into Egypt is observed as a festival While at Alexandria, Severus was brought into controversy with Julian, the deprived Monophysite bishop of Halicarnassus, the founder of the Aphthartodocetæ, and maintained against him the opinion that the natural body of Christ was necessarily subject to the natural wear and tear to which all human bodies are liable and hence to the necessity of food and rest If it were not so, Severus contended, the truth of His Passion would be denied, and an additional support would be given to the heresy of Manes, who followed the Docetæ in asserting that our Lord took merely the semblance of a body, and not a real and substantial one The Phthartolatræ, however, never went the length attributed to them, as a consequence of their argument, by their opponents—that the body of Christ was capable of corruption after death.

The tenets of the Phthartolatræ were those which eventually prevailed among the Monophysites in general, notwithstanding an edict of Justinian in the year 563 in favour of their opponents But a large party among them had early adopted the opinions of Themistius, and, driving the doctrine of Severus beyond its proper limits, had attributed imperfection to the soul of our Lord, and earned for themselves the name of AGNOETÆ [Evagr *Hist Eccl* iv 11 MONOPHYSITES. APHTHARTODOCETÆ]

PHRYGIANS [MONTANISTS]

PHUNDAITES The Bogomiles were so called from the peculiar "phunda" or girdle which they wore [BOGOMILES]

PHYGELLUS One of those of whom St Paul writes to Timothy, "This thou knowest, that all they which are in Asia be turned away from me, of whom are Phygellus and Hermogenes" [2 Tim i 15] The Apostle seems to speak of them as in some way deserting him in his missionary work rather than as forsaking the faith Tertullian, however, in the next century, speaks of them as "erring concerning the truth," in respect to the resurrection of the body [Tertull *de Resurr Carn* xxiv], and Epiphanius classes them with Cerinthus, Ebion, and others who denied the Divine Nature and miraculous conception of our Lord [Epiphan *Hær* li 6]

PICARDS [BEGHARDS]

PIETISTS [1] The specific appellation of a party of Reformers in the Lutheran Church, who appeared in Germany towards the close of the seventeenth century, and were in fact the Methodists of that country They cannot be strictly described as a sect, for they neither claimed nor desired any severance from the main body of the Lutherans, nor did they promulgate any special theological doctrines But the party is important, for amongst their numbers were many distinguished persons whose opinions strongly influenced the subsequent teaching of Protestantism In this way the Pietistic tendency was specially noteworthy first, because it was indifferent to all scholastic definition, when such differences of opinion were considered points of cardinal importance, secondly, because it laid great stress upon the duties of active morality at a time when morality was particularly neglected Historically, Pietism may be described as the formularization of the popular discontent at the arid dogmatism which the Church's continuous conflict with Geneva and Rome had made endemic in the Lutheran pulpits, and it was at the same time a protest against the low state of public morals engendered by the miserable delays of the Thirty Years' War

The leader of the movement, Philipp Jakob Spener (who has been called the Fénélon of Germany), was born at Rappolzweiler, in Elsass, in the year 1635 He was educated in Strasburg in the strictest sect of the Lutherans, under the eye of the famous professors Sebastian Schmidt and Conrad Dannhauer After completing his theological education at the various seats of Protestant learning, he was appointed public pastor at Strasburg in 1662, whence after a few years, he passed by invitation to Frankfort There his career as a preacher was at first marked by a violent advocacy of the teachings of Luther, and an equally violent denunciation of the opinions of Calvin Serious remonstrance from some influential Calvinists followed, and, strange to say, the remonstrance was listened to Indeed, Spener appears to have soon convinced himself that these polemical addresses were undesirable, and that the need for virtue was more urgent in Germany than that for sound doctrine Acting upon this conviction, and to the grief of the more zealous Lutherans, he turned the current of his powerful eloquence from the exclusive denunciation of Calvinism to the exclusive advocacy of morality It was in this cause, and in an endeavour to evangelize his congregation, that he established those meetings which, under the name of "Collegia Pietatis" or "Collegia Biblica," formed, subsequently, the distinguishing feature of Pietism

About 1670, Spener, being at that time pastor in Frankfort, set on foot, first at his private residence, and subsequently in the church, gatherings, where all his congregation were welcomed to hear the pure Scripture read and its difficulties explained The name of "Collegia"

[1] The name of Pietists is frequently, but hardly accurately, bestowed on other bodies besides that here described It has in fact been applied generally to designate sects which, like the Beghards and Cathari, have laid claim to abnormal piety Latterly, too, it has been used to denominate many classes of mystics having no pretensions resembling those of the followers of Spener For this use reference may be made to the well known work *Manipulus Observationum Antipietisticarum* On all these bodies the name has been fathered by the contempt of their opponents, it is, however, the proper appellation of a small missionary society founded in 1678 by Nicolas Barre, and otherwise known as "the Brethren and Sisters of the Pious and Religious Schools" The aim of this society was in no way sectarian, but directed wholly to the education of the poor.

was adopted for these meetings from the resemblance to the gatherings of the Mennonites of Holland, who were known in Germany under the name of COLLEGIANTS This practice of Spener's was well received, and became popular with the laity, particularly with the poorer classes, though regarded with jealous eyes by the old Lutheran and aristocratic party, nor was this mistrust diminished when Spener's admirers began to attract notice by their ostentatious asceticism of dress and demeanour, and their absence from all, even the most innocent, amusements Nevertheless, during a long series of years, no overt act of hostility interrupted Spener's evangelical labours, and it was during this period that he composed his celebrated *Pia Desideria*, a work which sufficiently sets forth the modest aims and genuine piety of the founder of Pietism The full title of the book, originally intended for a preface to a republication of Professor Arndt, but subsequently printed in a separate form, is "Pia Desideria, or Earnest Wishes for the Good Improvement of the True Evangelical Church, with some Christian Proposals for that end" It consists mainly of an expression of the need of reform in education, particularly with reference to the Bible, and of regret at the injury which the incessant preaching of dogma was effecting on the public morals The work added greatly to the fame of the author, and assisted the spread of the peculiar opinion of Spener, that a virtuous life was of greater importance than a correct creed The revivalist feeling spread rapidly through Germany, where the institution of "Collegia," being in complete accord with the national instinct, soon attained great popularity. Up to this time Pietism had spread without exciting commotion, no persecution having yet been attempted, but this fortunate state of things did not long continue

In 1686 Spener removed to Dresden, where he was high in favour with the Electoral Prince Thither he brought with him numerous theological students, amongst whom were Francke, Antony and Schade, destined to be the shining lights of Pietism Some of these shortly afterwards removing to Leipsic, commenced lecturing in Collegia in imitation of their leader's practice, giving in their lectures particular prominence to the correction of the errors contained in Luther's translation of the Bible As this translation was regarded as little short of inspired by the body of educated Lutherans, this freedom of criticism was far from popular It was in particular badly received by the older members of the University, who also took umbrage at the delivery of these lectures in the vulgar tongue All kinds of adverse rumours were spread abroad, and opinion was further irritated by the conduct of the Pietist audience, who, with the ardour of new converts, changed their dress and manners of everyday life for a marked and ascetic habit. Considerable disturbances arose from time to time, and on one of these occasions (it is said at a funeral discourse delivered at the grave of one of Francke's congregation) the term "Pietist" was finally fixed and adopted as the sobriquet of Spener's admirers In the end the lecturers were accused of heresy, and a commission was directed to investigate the matter The learned Thomasius—who was a fervent admirer of Spener—undertook the defence, but although Francke and his friends were triumphantly acquitted, the biblical lectures were prohibited This inopportune prosecution made the fortune of Pietism, and Collegia sprang up rapidly in every considerable town with a German-speaking population In Hamburg and Giessen, Frankfort, Gotha, and the towns of Switzerland, the revival was more than ever successful, and to such an extent was the old party at Leipsic enraged by this success, that the acquitted Pietists and their advocate were driven from the University by threats of personal violence

The leader of Pietism himself had at this time left Dresden, having given offence to the Elector by rebuking him for drunkenness, and was now in 1691 at Berlin, under the protection of the Duke and future King of Prussia There his influence was sufficient effectually to succour his expelled followers, and under his patronage the exiles founded the University of Halle as the home for the proscribed opinions Meanwhile a serious attack was made on Spener by the Wittenberg divines, who at length formally arraigned him for false doctrine and impiety Spener energetically and successfully defended himself, and his work, "The True Agreement with the Confession of Augsburg," which sets forth a complete justification of his teaching, became the leading authoritative treatise on ultra-evangelical Lutheranism These persecutions and this defence set the seal to the division of the Lutherans into what may be properly called a right and left party—a division which, with more or less continuity, has ever since existed in that communion

It was not, however, from men of learning like Francke and Spener, nor from the Universities that Lutheranism had anything to fear But in the practice of the Collegia there was a genuine source of danger Ignorant and fanatical persons, arrogating to themselves an insight to which they had no claim, gave the rein to their fancies, and mistook them for the prompting of the Holy Spirit Thus they went so far as to speak of the Lutheran Church as Babylon, and prophesied its impending dissolution Spener died in 1705, and, shortly afterwards, the commotions at Augsburg, Giessen, Dantzig, Hamburg, Erfurt, and other places, had become so intolerable, that the executive interfered by the imposition of severe penal laws, and finally proscribed the overt exercise of Pietism Thus all opportunity for the development of the Pietists into a completely organized sect was effectually destroyed

The principal reforms demanded by the Pietists, to be gathered from the writings of their leaders, were these First, that the theological schools should be reformed by the abolition of all systematic theology, philosophy, and metaphysics, and that morals and not doctrine should form the staple of all preaching, secondly, that only those persons should be admitted into the Lutheran ministry whose lives were examples of living piety In support of this last proposal, they urged the quasi-Wickliffite doctrine, that the theology of the wicked cannot be a true theology, and (some of them at least) added that the ministrations of the wicked are inefficacious Other doctrines, some of them of a violent character, are attributed to certain men of mark who were connected with the Pietistic movement, such as Arnold Dippel and Petersen, but these were for the most part either the result of hatred for the Lutheran order, or, as in case of the last-named writer, of simple delusion An exception must be made of Schade, who, undoubtedly, opposed the Lutheran practice of confession Though an undoubted Pietist, he was singular in this opinion It deserves mention that the Pietists were accused of impugning the special Lutheran view of the doctrine of justification by faith only, but the accusation was unfounded Spener and his followers never denied that good works were unnecessary to salvation, they only desired that this difficult doctrine should not be preached to the congregation

Debarred from the exercise of special external ceremonies, Pietism has, from the beginning of the eighteenth century, preserved a meagre and unimportant existence up to the present time First, the Wolffian philosophy, secondly, that of the Encyclopédists, finally, modern Rationalism, has, since the death of Spener, given to Lutheran Christianity opponents of a calibre sufficient to employ all its powers of resistance, and this has made it perhaps unwilling to renew a frivolous and internecine conflict

The dead formulism of Halle indeed long continued, and may, in a sense, still be said to preserve the tenets of Spener in a fossilized condition, but the quickening ardour of the leaders of the movement that made Pietism a force has long since disappeared A temporary reanimation is to be noted, commencing about 1827 by the appearance of a publication edited by Hengstenberg, but the movement was quite unimportant, and since 1835 European attention has not been attracted to the Evangelicalism of Spener [The best account of Pietism is to be found in Hossbach, *Spener und seine Zeite*, Illgen, *Historia Collegii Philobiblici*, Bretschneider, *die Grundlage des Evangelischen Pietismus*, Marklin, *Darstellung und Kritik des modernen Pietismus*, with which Binder's *Des Pietismus und die moderne Bildung*, Brucker's *Historia Critica Philosophiæ*, Shroeckh's *Kirchen nach der Reform* can be advantageously compared]

PILGRIMS AND STRANGERS [SIONITES]

PIPHILES A name given to the Flemish Albigenses [Ekhert *adv Cathar* in *Bibl Max Lugd* xxiii 601]

PIRNENSIANS A mediæval sect, taking its name and origin from John Pirnensis, an anti-sacerdotalist schismatic of Silesia, A.D 1341. His principles were those common to the mediæval sects, and illustrated especially in the BEGHARDS and the BRETHREN OF THE FREE SPIRIT It is thought probable that they were in some way connected with the STRIGOLNIKS of Russia, although the latter belong to a much more recent time [Krazinski, *Reform in Poland*, i 55]

PLOTINUS [born A D 205, died A D 270] A native of Egypt, the most celebrated follower of Ammonius Saccas, although a bitter foe of Christianity, closely connected with its schools on the side of Mysticism Where doubt had been considered to be the true atmosphere of philosophy he aspired to give certainty To Pyrrhonism he opposed a system of pure intellectualism, and engaged to lead his followers into positive truth The soul, he said, is in a state of debasement through contact with a body of matter, it is alienated from the eternal and infinite Source of its being, in whose nature it still participates It is the mission of a true philosophy to restore this interrupted union, and to lead back the soul to a blissful oneness with the Source of all goodness and unity He affirmed with his dying breath, "I am striving to bring the God Which is in us into harmony with the God Which is in the universe" But he did it by confusing subject and object, in the same manner as Fichte and Hegel and modern pantheists That harmony is true knowledge, and philosophy alone can teach it It is a knowledge, he said, that is more than philosophy, to which he only possessed the clue, existing not in the imagination, but as absolute verity, not in set words and phrases, but in subjective truth It is cognizable by a higher power than mere intellectual thought, this power is self-consciousness, νοησις, the knowledge which reason possesses of its own being, that itself is the truth and the substantive existence of the being man This knowledge is not to be reasoned out as though its object were without the percipient soul, but it is of such a nature as to fuse together all distinction between the subject and object of knowledge We do not discern reason, but reason discerns itself It is perceptible in no other way Supersensate truth can only be known in the spirit Philo had already held similar opinions with respect to union of the soul with God However great, he said, the gulf may be between man and the Deity, it may be bridged over through the manifestation of God to the soul It is not only that the mind mirrors out to itself God the Creator and Preserver of the sensible world of matter,[1] whereby is gained a consciousness only of the existence of the Deity, but no adequate idea of His Being or Nature To aspire to know this were mere folly,[2] man cannot see God, but God reveals Himself to man in the reasonable soul,[3] and this revelation consti

[1] Ὡς γὰρ διὰ κατόπτρου φαντασιοῦται ὁ νοῦς Θεὸν δρῶντα καὶ κοσμοποιοῦντα καὶ τῶν ὅλων ἐπιτροπευοντα [*de V contempl* 10, p 484, and compare *de Decal* 21, p 198, Mangey]

[2] Περαιτέρω δὲ καὶ σπουδάζειν τρέπεσθαι, ὡς περὶ οὐσίας ἢ ποιότητος ζητεῖν ὠγύγιος τις ἠλιθιότης [*de Poster Cain* 48, p 258]

[3] Ὃς ἕνεκεν φιλανθρωπίας ἀφικνουμένην τὴν ψυχὴν ὡς αὐτὸν οὐκ ἀπεστράφη, προυπαντήσας δὲ τὴν ἑαυτοῦ φύσιν ἔδειξε, καθ' ὅσον οἷόν τε ἦν ἰδεῖν τὸν βλέποντα διὸ λέγεται, οὐχ ὅτι ὁ σοφὸς εἶδε Θεόν, ἀλλ' ὅτι ὁ Θεὸς ὤφθη τῷ σοφῷ Καὶ

tutes his highest happiness We have here the germ of all those semi-fanatical aspirations after a union with the Deity that afterwards became the soul of mystical theology, descending through the Neo-Platonic school and Dionysius (Pseudo-Areopagita) to the school of St. Victoire, and thence to Bonaventura, Eckhart, and Gerson[1] Where this is accorded to man, his soul is no longer led by the subordinate powers of divine relation nor by angelic influence, but by God Himself, and man, though "a little lower than the angels," is raised to a level with them Numenius also defined the divine Unity as Reason and Goodness, and said that the soul was capable of such a close union with it as to involve positively no diversity[2] The outer rays of the Divine Nature nourish and support our bodily nature; by internal contemplation of the Deity we rise above the body and emerge into the purer life of reason, being made partakers of a blessed existence. It was a prolepsis of Fichtean and Hegelian Pantheism Plotinus fairly outsoars his predecessors Intellect as the principle of unity does not satisfy him, something yet more recondite there must be from which it emanates, which Plotinus names "the First," or "the undefined and undefinable, the source of motion and rest, itself devoid of either as being infinite" Such human notions as Thought and Will are wholly inapplicable to the Absolute, with which nothing else can have relation, and whom no attribute can limit. Itself nothing in respect of all things, it is yet the power and energy of all Plotinus aspired to reach back to this principle through the contemplative faculty of the soul itself, an emanation from intellect the second principle, as light proceeds from the sun by effulgence rather than emanation Intellect, as the source of every living principle, contains within itself the principle of multiplicity, in it are stored the universal ideas that are spirit and life, the intelligible world—*κόσμος νοητός* Nothing of human reason, nothing of material sense, can have anything to do with union of the soul with its origin, for the One is an incomprehensible essence The soul united with it exists in a divine ecstasy, it is then conscious of nothing earthly, mortal sense has no part in that which transcends all human reason The whole soul is filled with a God-like delight, it is one with the Beautiful, which is no longer external to it but inherently one.[3] The soul is distracted at such a time with no earthly thoughts, but as the divine vision comes and as it goes it is wholly absorbed in it[4] Such moments of privileged existence are few and short, but they portend the bliss that awaits the soul when released from matter If the Divine Principle is the centre of all, the rapt soul is concentric with it, *ὥσπερ κέντρῳ κέντρον συνάψας* The nature of the vision may not be disclosed to the uninitiated, *τὸ μὴ ἐκφέρειν εἰς τοὺς μὴ μεμυήμενους*, and when it is enounced in such terms as Sight and Vision, this is only in default of adequate means of expression Also, when we speak of the Deity as perfect goodness, it is a goodness that is inconceivable by us, who have no other gauge to apply than human virtues that can have no place in the Deity Courage involves the possibility of fear, self-restraint the notion of some object of desire, moderation is the antithesis of excess Virtue therefore is not the final good at which the soul must aim, but it is the means of attaining that end, and the soul in pursuing it emerges into a higher state of being, an ecstatic condition, a reduction of the soul into its first simple elements, a surrendering of itself wholly to the essence of its contemplation,[5] but the Divine Principle only exists in a man in the degree to which he is conscious of the indwelling principle within him The Third Principle, in subordination to the First Good and to Intellect, is the supramundane and vital Soul of the universe, the Source of all life, subsisting with the Intellect, of which it is the animal counterpart in the Divine Substance, and impressed with the forms of eternal ideas, by it unconsciously conceived and propagated The three principles are co-eternal, forming a kind of hierarchy of order and dignity, from whence the pseudo-Dionysian notion of a celestial hierarchy was derived, and with which different gradations of excellence—gods, demons, genii and heroes—are connected. There are three steps of access towards the highest good harmony, that occupies itself with lower matters of sensation, love, that contemplates the immaterial and vast, and finds its only repose in full possession of its object, and wisdom, that becomes absorbed in communion with the First Good Their representative characters are the musician, the lover, and the philosopher No glimpse of truth is attainable by the common herd Purifications, prayers, and spiritual exercises are the means whereby the soul learns to soar far above all earthly considerations, not merely into the presence, but into actual union with the Deity, where intellect becomes one with essence This Trinity of principles and powers, devoid of all hypostatic individuality, may have been borrowed from the Christian faith but it has nothing else in common with it, in fact, in the hands of Plotinus, it was a formidable weapon of attack upon Christianity, and in an opposite direction his conversion of the old heathen mytho-

γὰρ ἦν ἀδύνατον καταλαβεῖν τινὰ δι' αὑτοῦ τι πρὸς ἀλήθειαν ἂν μὴ παραφήναντος ἐκείνου ἑαυτὸ καὶ παραδείξαντος [*de Abr* 17, p 13, and compare *de Poster Cain* 5, 229]

[1] *Ἔστι δέ τις τελεώτερος καὶ μᾶλλον κεκαθαρμένος νοῦς, τὰ μεγάλα μυστήρια μυηθεὶς, ὅστις οὐκ ἀπὸ τῶν γεγονότων τὸ αἴτιον γνωρίζει, ὡς ἂν ἀπὸ σκιᾶς τὸ μένον, ἀλλ' ὑπερκύψας τὸ γέννητον ἔμφασιν ἐναργῆ τοῦ ἀγεννήτου λάμβανει ὡς ἀπ' αὐτοῦ αὐτὸν καταλαμβάνειν καὶ τὴν σκιὰν αὐτοῦ, ὅπερ ἦν τόν τε λόγον καὶ τόνδε τὸν κοσμον* [*Leg alleg* iii 33, 187]

[2] *Ἕνωσιν μὲν οὖν καὶ ταυτότητα ἀδιάκριτον τῆς ψυχῆς πρὸς τὰς ἑαυτῆς ἀρχὰς πρεσβεύειν φαίνεται Νουμήνιος* [Jambl *ap Stob Ecl* i]

[3] *Οἷον οἰνωθεῖσι καὶ πληρωθεῖσι τοῦ νέκταρος, ἅτε δι' ὅλης τῆς ψυχῆς τοῦ κάλλους ἐλθόντος Οὐ γὰρ ἔτι τὸ μὲν ἔξω, τὸ δὲ αὐτὸ θεώμενον ἔξω, ἀλλ' ἔχει ὁ ὀξέως ὁρῶν ἐν αὑτῷ τὸ ὁρώμενον* [Enn v 8, 10, 11].

[4] *Εἶναι δὲ τὸν νοῦν τὸν ἐλθόντα, καὶ τοῦτον εἶναι καὶ τὸν ἀπιόντα* [Enn v 8]

[5] *Τὸ δὲ ἴσως ἦν οὐ θέαμα, ἀλλὰ ἄλλος τρόπος τοῦ ἰδεῖν, ἔκστασις καὶ ἅπλωσις καὶ ἐπίδοσις αὑτοῦ, καὶ ἔφεσις πρὸς ἁφὴν καὶ στάσις καὶ περινόησις πρὸς ἐφαρμογήν, εἴπερ τις τὸ ἐν ἐν ἀδύτῳ θεάσεται* [vi 9, 10, 11]

logical notions into allegory, as a gradational element in the hierarchy, helped to give new life to the expiring theories of heathenism In either case his teaching was equally prejudicial to the cause of truth As Intellect is one, though infinitely varied, so the soul of Nature is one, yet teems with a multiplicity of life. The same mysticism runs through the writings of the Neo Platonic school[1] In Jamblichus, and afterwards in Proclus, mysticism took a more theurgical direction, the First God, or the Absolute, in more modern phrase, was represented as infinitely remote, certain intermediate δαιμόνια alone afforded the possibility of communion with Him [Proclus, *Theol Plat* iii 14] It may be observed that the entire new Platonic school has been divided by de Gérando into three branches Plotinus [A D 250] and Porphyry [A D 280 *Syriace*, Malchus] representing the Roman branch, which exhibited an essentially philosophic eclecticism, and was only so far tinctured with Oriental tradition as it taught the mystical union of the soul with God as an essential truth, the school of Alexandria had Jamblichus [A D 363] and Hierocles [A.D 485], the harmonizer of Plato and Aristotle, as its main lights, and by its union with the theosophy of the East served as the main basis of mystical theology, while the school of Athens, where Plutarch and Syrianus taught, and of which Proclus [A D 450] is the exponent, affected to revert to the ancient sources of Greek wisdom as embodied in the Orphic hymns

The writings of Plotinus, as arranged by Porphyry, are contained in six books, each book being subdivided into nine sections or Enneads Their general object may be stated to be an exposition of the Absolute Unity, the source and origin of all the successional development exhibited in the varied phenomena of the universe Their style, obscure in the extreme, has aggravated the confusion of these writings Plotinus seldom delivered his lectures from written notes, his pupil Porphyry therefore persuaded him to compose some work as a standard of authority on the abstruse topics that he handled His neglect of revising that which he wrote, and his want of scientific method, have added to the obscurity of the books that bear his name But for the friendly aid of Porphyry in revising and correcting this obscurity would probably have been hopeless Longinus plainly confessed that many of the subjects handled by Plotinus[2] were beyond his comprehension No writing of Plotinus has come down to us which openly attacks Christianity, though it is very possible that the Ennead κατὰ γνωστικούς [ii 9] may have been partly levelled against the teaching of the Church

PLYMOUTH BRETHREN A sect which originated almost simultaneously in Dublin and Plymouth, about the year 1830, the members of which, calling themselves "The Brethren," came to be called from their headquarters in England the "Plymouth Brethren" The principal founder of the sect was a clergyman, who had been a barrister, named Darby, from whom the Plymouth Brethren are sometimes called "Darbyites" Giving up his ministrations in the Church of Ireland, he established a small sect in Dublin under the name of SEPARATISTS, and then came to England, and went about as an independent preacher, organizing small societies of the strictest Calvinistic type of Evangelicalism for the promotion of personal piety, which were soon converted into congregations claiming to be independent of all other religious communities The chief peculiarity of these congregations is that they are without any separate ministry, every "brother" and "sister" being considered to have a full right to 'prophesy" or preach whenever he is moved to do so They also administer baptism to all adults, whether baptized before or not, and substitute a kind of weekly love-feast, in which bread and wine are passed round from one to another for the Holy Eucharist. Like many other small sects the Plymouth Brethren maintain that true Christianity is not to be found in the Church or among the sects, but only among themselves. They are also strong Predestinarians and Millenarians In their own phraseology they are "the assembly of God," not meeting together by human will, but "gathered to Jesus by the Holy Ghost" Hence they consider that they need no human ministry, but are under immediate Divine presidency, which is the fulfilment of the promise, "Where two or three are gathered together in My Name there am I in the midst of them" This they call the "many-men ministry" in contradistinction to the "one-man ministry" of ordinary Christian congregations

The Plymouth Brethren are a rather widely spread and growing sect, but they have little organic unity, being broken up into many sections by the differences of opinion (often followed up with great animosity and bitterness) arising from their "many-men" ministry At the same time there is much attraction for the leisurely class of what may be called semi-professional society which is found in towns inhabited by retired officers, etc, in the system of every one having a psalm or an interpretation, and the sect is largely recruited from this class of persons [Guinness' *Who are the Plymouth Brethren?* Dennett's *Plymouth Brethren, their Rise, etc*]

PNEUMATICS [AMBROSIANS]

PNEUMATOMACHI The name "Adversaries of the Holy Spirit," given to that party which, upon the subsidence of the Arian controversy, was distinguished by the denial of the Catholic faith regarding the Third Person of the Holy Trinity, some denying His Divinity, others His Personality also

The heresy of the Pneumatomachi is commonly connected with the name of Macedonius, but since Macedonius was so closely connected with the Semi-Arian party that the term Macedonian was used as equivalent to Semi-Arian,[3] and since there were others than Semi-Arians who held the

[1] Porphyry, *de Abstin* i 38, 57 Jamblichus, *de Myst Æg* i 10, iii 3, iv 3.
[2] Porphyry, *Vit. Plotin*

[3] "Pneumatomachi ipsi sunt Macedoniani, similes Homunciomtis" [Pseudo Hieron *Hæres* xxix.] *Cf* HOMUNCIONITÆ

heresy, the more comprehensive name is to be preferred The appearance of the party is to be dated A D 360, when Athanasius wrote against them, giving them the name here adopted Athanasius was then in the deserts of Egypt, and Serapion, Bishop of Thmuis, in Lower Egypt, requested his interposition The heresies themselves were no novelties It was a part of the Arian creed that the Holy Spirit was a created being, superior it might be in dignity, but nowise different in nature from the angels and in the Gnostic systems we meet with Christ and the Holy Ghost as Æons [VALENTINIANS], the latter being held, in some cases at least, to be not a distinct Person, but a divine energy diffused through the universe But there was a great difference in the mode in which these heresies were held They then appeared, not as proceeding from a special opposition to the greatness of the Holy Spirit, but as deductions from some other leading heresy to which they were subordinate Thus in the case of the Arians, with which our present subject is concerned, the denial of the divinity of the Holy Spirit follows upon the denial of the divinity of the Son For as it is impossible to advance the Third Person of the Trinity above the Second Person, the controversy turned therefore on the divinity of the Second Dealing with this, the Council of Nicæa did not deal specifically with the subordinate heresy, but left it to stand or fall with the leading one But when the leading heresy was abandoned, and yet the subordinate heresy retained, then the latter not only became prominent, but was seen to be adopted on its own independent grounds, for its own sake The Arian half converted to Catholicity was properly a Pneumatomachist Such were those whom Athanasius dealt with in his letter to Serapion They were seceders from the Arians who had embraced the true faith regarding the Son, but retained their error regarding the Holy Spirit[1] They were consequently opposed both by Catholics and Arians, but their true controversy was with the former their contest with the latter (Athanasius urges) could be only pretended, inasmuch as both agreed in opposing the doctrine of the Trinity [*ad Serap* i 1, 2, 9, 32] This class then differed from the later Macedonian class it held Homoousian doctrine regarding the Son, whereas the Macedonians were Homoiousians Athanasius calls them also TROPICI, from their figurative interpretations of Scripture, but this is rather an epithet than a proper name

In comparison with the Macedonian party, this earlier party can have been but small It was however reinforced a few years later, as we shall shew, upon the return of a large portion of the Semi Arian body to catholicity The adoption of the truth concerning the Son leads almost necessarily to the adoption of the truth concerning the Holy Spirit The arguments of Athanasius [*ad Serap* i 29, iv 7] shew forcibly how untenable a position is that which maintains a Duality instead of a Trinity The original Monarchian tenet from which the Arians started is much more easily admissible

The Pneumatomachi of the Macedonian school were the Semi-Arians left behind in schism when, in the year 366, the majority of the sect gave in their assent to orthodoxy, and were received into the Church Before this time Macedonius had joined the Semi-Arian party He had been appointed Bishop of Constantinople by the Arians, being then an Anomœan or Acacian [Phot *Bibl Cod* 257], but professing Semi-Arian opinions, was deposed by the Arian Council of Constantinople, A D 360 [Theod *Hist Eccl* ii 6] He then invented the artifice of the "Homoion," and connecting himself closely with the Semi-Arian party, gave them his name [Theod *Hær fab* iv 5] At first therefore the term Macedonian was simply equivalent to Semi-Arian, and Socrates calls the reply of Liberius to the Semi-Arian legates a letter to the bishops of the Macedonians [Socr *Hist. Eccl* iv 12] The name of Macedonius appears in this reply The good faith of this transaction is (to say the least) very doubtful,[2] and we are in uncertainty as to the opinions which Macedonius really held at the close of his life But there is no uncertainty as to the course of the heresy The letters of Liberius were exhibited at the Council of Tyana, and the deputies who presented them were acknowledged as members of the Catholic body This was probably in A D 368 A council was appointed to meet in Tarsus to complete the work of reconciliation, but just before the meeting thirty-four Asiatic bishops assembled in Caria, refused the Homoousion, and Valens, at the instigation of the Arian Eudoxius, by whom he had been recently baptized, forbad the council [Sozom *Hist Eccl* vi 12] From this time however Semi-Arianism disappears from ecclesiastical history The controversy regarding our Lord's divinity was ceasing, and the denial of the divinity of the Holy Spirit became the distinguishing tenet of the Semi-Arian party, the tenet thus becoming associated with the name Macedonian, which the Semi-Arians had recently acquired Many called them Marathonians, saying that Marathonius, Bishop of Nicomedia, had introduced the term Homoiousion [Socr *Hist Eccl* ii 45]

It is to be noticed here that several writers, when treating of the present heresy, use the word Semi-Arian in another sense than that now given it Philaster [*Hær* lxvii] defines the Semi-Arians thus "Hi de Patre et Filio bene sentiunt, unam qualitatis substantiam, unam divinitatem esse credentes, Spiritum autem non de divina substantia, nec Deum verum, sed factum atque creatum Spiritum prædicantes" And Augustine [*Hær* iii] "Macedoniani de Patre et Filio recte sentiunt, quod unius sint ejusdemque substantiæ vel essentiæ, sed de Spiritu Sancto hoc nolunt credere, creaturam eum esse dicentes Hos potius quidam Semi-Arianos vocant, quod in hac quæstione ex parte cum illis sint, ex parte nobiscum" This use of the term Semi-Arian is now to be

[1] For this Arian error see Athan *Orat* iii. *cont Arian* sec 15

[2] See the notes on the chapter of Socrates in *Variorum Annotationes* in Reading's edition of Valesius

avoided, the distinctive mark of that party being the Homoiousion But these two authorities shew that the original Pneumatomachi, against whom Athanasius wrote, must have been largely reinforced from those who joined the church under Liberius This appears also from Epiphanius [*Hær* lxxiv], who states that the Pneumatomachi proceeded partly from the Semi-Arians and partly from the orthodox In the preceding article he had defined the Semi-Arians by the Homoiousion, and the "orthodox," it cannot be doubted, were not the old Nicenes, but those who from the Arians had come over to the Homoousion and had been accepted by Liberius as orthodox Thus of the Pneumatomachi some were orthodox regarding the divinity of the Son, some retained the Homoiousion, and these latter are properly Macedonians, being Semi-Arians

All these started with the tenet of the sect from which they sprung, namely, that the Holy Spirit is a created being, of the same order as the created angels [Theod Epiph *l c*] And the authorities of Philaster and Augustine are sufficient to shew that this was retained by the majority of the party But another opinion arose early It proceeded—Eustathius of Sebastia being an example [Socr *Hist Eccl* ii 45]—from a reluctance to call the Holy Spirit a creature But as they who felt this reluctance would not consent to call Him God, it followed necessarily that they were obliged to deny His Personality Still they assigned to the impersonal Spirit that which is assigned to the Personal Spirit by Catholics, to be the Vinculum[1] of the Persons of the Godhead This is noted by Augustine [*Hær* lii] "Quamvis a nonnullis perhibeantur non Deum, sed Deitatem Patris et Filii dicere Spiritum Sanctum, et nullam propriam habere substantiam" And what Catholics regard as God the Holy Ghost working in the world, they regarded as a divine energy diffused through the world Mosheim represents this, it appears upon insufficient grounds, to be the tenet of the Macedonians in general [Walch, *Hist der Ketz* iii p 98]

The heresy of the Pneumatomachi was condemned, first, in a synod at Alexandria, A D 362, held by Athanasius on his return [Athan *Synod Epist ad Antioch*],[2] secondly, in a synod in Illyricum, A D 367 [*Epist Synod ad Orient*,[3] Harduin, *Concil* i 794, Sozom *Hist Eccl* vi 22], thirdly, in a synod at Rome, A D 367 [Damasi *Epist* ap Theod *Hist Eccl* ii 22], fourthly, in another synod at Rome, A D 382 [Damasi *Epist* ap Theod *Hist Eccl* v 11, Vales, *n*], and lastly, in the Council of Constantinople, A D 381, by which, in opposition to the heresies of Macedonius, Apollinaris, and Eunomius, the Nicene faith was confirmed and more fully stated The first canon anathematizes the "Semi-Arians or Pneumatomachi," the seventh canon uses the name Macedonians, and orders the admission of converts from this heresy to be by unction To the simple article of the Nicene Creed, "I believe in the Holy Ghost," were added those clauses (excepting the Filioque) which stand at present as the complement of the Catholic faith

The Macedonians were invited to the Council of Constantinople in the hope that the reconciliation interrupted at Tarsus might be effected, but the hope was not realized [Socr *Hist Eccl* v 8, Sozom *Hist Eccl* vii 7][4] The council completed the work which was begun at Nicæa, and finally declared the Catholic faith regarding the Holy Trinity Against its determination the Semi-Arian, now the Pneumatomachist, party was not able to make any effectual resistance

PODONIPTÆ [FLEMINGS]

POLEMIANS [SYNUSIASTÆ]

POLISH BRETHREN [SOCINIANS]

POLISH PROTESTANTS The Reformation did not succeed in finally establishing itself in Poland, in consequence not so much of the opposition of the Government as of the dissensions among the Protestants themselves During the reign of Sigismund I [A D 1506-1548] Lutheran congregations began to be secretly held in Cracow and other chief cities, but the movement did not become of public importance till the days of his successor Sigismund Augustus II [A D 1548-1570] Several circumstances then combined in its favour In the very first year of the new reign a large number of refugees, expelled from Bohemia by Ferdinand on account of their religious tenets, settled in Poland These BOHEMIAN BRETHREN, as they are called, were akin to the Waldenses in their views, and a branch of the older Hussites Secondly, the King himself, although not prepared openly to desert the Catholic Church, was by no means unfavourable to the Reformed opinions He would listen to the exhortations of the famous Polish ecclesiastic Laski (John à Lasco), Melanchthon wrote letters to him, Calvin dedicated to him his Commentary on the Epistle to the Hebrews In the year A D 1560 he granted full liberty of opinion to Dantzic, Thorn, and Elbing, towns in Western or Polish Prussia, a district which, having voluntarily submitted to Casimir III [A D 1333-1370], had been finally incorporated with Poland [A D 1466], and in which Knade, Beuchenstein, and a Dominican friar named Klein had, in the earlier part of the sixteenth century, created disturbances by their Lutheran preaching On the death of Sigismund the Polish monarchy became elective, and the bias of subsequent rulers was

[1] See Bull, *Def Fid. Nic.* ii 3, 13, Augustine, *de Fide et Symbolo*, sec 19

[2] The Epistle states that Arians, on their reception into the Church, are to anathematize those who say that the Holy Spirit is a created being and divided from the substance of Christ A true renunciation of Arian doctrine is to abstain from dividing the Holy Trinity, from saying that one of the Persons is a created being

[3] "We write that you may know the Arians are condemned, who assert that neither the Son nor the Holy Spirit are of the substance of the Father" The Synod was held at Valentinian's order, who had heard of controversies in Asia and Phrygia [Theod *H E* iv 7]

[4] Facundus states that Macedonius himself was invited to the council This is no doubt an error The exact date of Macedonius' death is not known, but it appears to have been soon after the Council of Tarsus [See Tillemont, *Hist* ix]

generally Romish, especially in the case of Sigismund III [A D 1587-1632], during whose reign Protestantism became nearly extinct. Its overthrow was due partly to the fierce persecutions which it was made to pass through during the greater part of the seventeenth century, but largely also to the dissensions existing between its four chief parties, the Lutherans, the Swiss, the Waldensians, and the Socinians, although an attempt at reconciliation had been made, and a consensus drawn up between the first three bodies at a synod held at Sandomir A D 1570, and again at Vlodislaw A D 1583

According to statistics obtained in Poland A D 1855, out of about four million inhabitants a quarter of a million belong to the various Protestant communities

[Krazinski's *Sketch of the Rise, Progress, and Decline of the Reformation in Poland*, London, 1838 Kantz, *Præcipua Relig Evang in Polonia*, Hamburg, 1738]

POMORANE A small Russian sect, "dwellers by the sea," so called from their proximity to the Lake Ladoga and the White Sea, or from Pomori, a village in the government of Olonetz, where they appear to have originated [c A D 1675] They form a subdivision of that class of Russian Dissenters who reject the theory of a settled ministry [BEZPOPOFTSCHINS], and are themselves split up into numerous small factions, called Feodorians from their leader Feodorius, Abacumians from Abacun, etc They reject the reforms of Nikon with as much rigidity as the Starovertzi, and rebaptize all who join their sect from the Church or from other communities

POMOREYANS [POMORANE]

PONGILUPUS The Franciscans attribute the origin of the FRATICELLI to Hermann Pongilupus of Ferrara, who died A D 1269, and at whose tomb in the principal church of that town miracles were said to be wrought. In his lifetime he had practised great austerity as one of the CONSOLATI but some years after his death [A D 1300] charges of heresy were brought against him, and a judicial process having been brought against him, his bones were burnt and his tomb demolished by order of Boniface VIII , the object being to put an end to the extravagant veneration shewn to his memory by the populace Mosheim considers that it is an error to connect Pongilupus with the Fraticelli, and says that he was one of the BAGNOLIAN sect [Mosh. *Eccl Hist.* ii 207, Stubbs' ed] Natalis Alexander speaks of him as reviving several vile practices of the Gnostics [Wadding, *Annal Minor Fratr.* vi 279 Natal Alex *Hist Eccl* viii 87]

POOR OF LYONS [WALDENSES]

POOR PRIESTS This name was given to, or assumed by, Lollard clergy of the fourteenth and fifteenth century, who wandered about the country holding what are called in modern times "missions" wherever they pleased, without any cure of souls being given to them, or license by the bishop of the diocese The name "poor" seems to shew an association of idea with the "Pauperes Catholici" and the "Poor of Lyons"

POPLICIANI A common name for the Catharists of France It is probably a corruption of Pauliciani The name is given by Matthew Paris, "Gallice etiam dicuntur ab aliquibus Popelicani." [Matth Par *ad ann.* 1236.]

POPOFTSCHINS That division of Russian Dissenters which retains the office of "pope" or priest in its ministrations and services This is done in a large degree by means of priests who secede from, or are no longer permitted to minister in, the Church The Popoftschins are divided into five principal sects, the Starovertzi, the Diaconoftschins, the Peremayanoftschins, the Epefanoftschins, and the Tschernoboltsi

PORPHYRIANS This name was given to the Arians in an edict of the Emperor Constantine issued in the year 325, the reason stated being that, as they had emulated the impiety of Porphyry in their errors, so they ought to be named after him [Socrat *Hist Eccl.* i 6] This decree was afterwards quoted as a precedent by Theodosius the Younger, who ordered that the Nestorians should, in a similar manner, be called Simonians It may be doubted whether either name extended much beyond the four corners of the edicts in which they were given [Baron *Annal ad ann* 325, lxxxiv lxxxv]

PORPHYRY [NEO-PLATONISTS]

PORRETANUS The Latinized name of Gilbert de la Porée, Bishop of Poictiers, who held opinions respecting the personality and the essence of the Holy Trinity analogous to those of the Tetratheitæ or DAMIANISTS of the sixth century Porretanus distinguished the Divine Essence from the Three Divine Persons, and each Person from His attributes and as a consequence of this distinction he seems to have gone far towards a denial of the Incarnation, respecting which he ventured to set forth the proposition "Quod Divina natura non esset incarnata" Porretanus was accused by two of his clergy of teaching blasphemy, and his opinions were brought before Pope Eugene III by his archdeacons Arnald and Calo, and by St Bernard A council was held at Paris in the year 1147, and another at Rheims on March 21st, 1148, and his opinions being condemned at the former, Porretanus recanted them at the latter It does not appear that any large party was formed by Porretanus, but some are spoken of under his name as his followers [*Gallia Christiana*, ii 1175 Harduin, *Concil* VI ii 1297 Mansi, *Concil* xxi 712]

PORT-ROYALISTS [JANSENISTS]

POSITIVISTS A modern school of sceptics which owes its origin to Auguste Comte [A D 1797-1857], and which holds for its fundamental principle that nothing is to be believed but that which can be positively demonstrated It is a philosophy rather than a religious system, although from his philosophical deductions Comte professes to form a religion of his own

The Comtean philosophy aims at effecting that for the entire group of sciences which the Baconian method did for knowledge generally to apply inductive generalization to the laws that govern the several sciences, and by reducing them under the head of general principles, to bring all under one category of unity. The idea is grand and vast, and he advanced so far on the path towards demonstration as to shew that there is no innate inconsequence in the idea It was a recapitulation of every antecedent philosophical development, as Bacon's Inductive Method was a comprehensive generalization of all that had come to hand two centuries before It was perhaps this analogy between the systems of Comte and Bacon, as an interrogation and interpretation of experience, that gave to the former a reputation among English thinkers, such as Dr Brown,[1] Bentham and James Mill, almost before his system was known in France

Comte professed to evolve no new principle, he claims only to adhere to the traditions of the greatest masters of thought, Descartes and Leibnitz, Bacon and Newton. His theory of antecedents and succession in lieu of cause and effect was that of Hume, our ignorance of real substances and real causes was declared by Kant Positivism aims at unity, the working out of a system sufficiently general to affect every variety of scientific idea, and so irresistibly convincing to the reason as to be absolutely "positive." To make a science positive in the Comtean sense is to give to it its final scientific constitution, by pursuing to their logical consequences those of its truths which link it with the rest. Positivism raises each science in succession from its empirical condition, and incorporates it with every other positive science as a co-ordinated and coherent body of doctrine Knowledge, it affirms, can only be co-extensive with the range of phenomena We can neither know the essence of things, nor understand their real mode of production, our ideas of phenomena also are purely relative, succession and resemblance being the principal data. These relations are exact and undeviating, ever succeeding as similar results under the operation of similar circumstances These resemblances and unvarying sequences constitute the laws of phenomena, and give to us our only means of knowledge Essence and causation, whether effective or final, are equally beyond our powers of observation, however true an existence they may have Our power of controlling phenomena consists ultimately in the accuracy of our observation of their natural sequences Foresight depends wholly upon this fact The various sciences are assumed by the Positivist to have reciprocal points of relation, which will bring them eventually under the same category But circumstances hitherto have kept these relations in the background so that they have eluded detection Thus all is linked together in one continuous chain. Nature has no breaks The entire cycle of sciences is in harmony with itself, but the harmonizing elements have been kept in abeyance by the incompetence of its professors to deal with them in a large inductive spirit Each man of science has his own speciality, and however expert he may be in dealing with the arcana of his own particular faculty, he is usually a bad generalizer, blind to the mutual relation of the respective sciences, and unable to seize the universal principles that pervade them all The very division of labour that assigns to each man his own particular portion of the field of knowledge for cultivation prevents him from taking a comprehensive view of all. Men of science have not the philosophy, and philosophers have not the science that together enable the intellect to work out the positive principles that lie in the depths of attainable knowledge The "Natur-philosophie" of Schelling and Hegel is an instance in point, even Newton could not conceive the existence of gravitation without a subtle ether through which it might act. This anarchy M Comte held could alone be reduced to system and order by a doctrine that should be "positive," as educed from the positive sciences, and at the same time as wide in its generalizations as metaphysical reasoning, though free from the indeterminate vagueness of metaphysics If, therefore, Bacon's was a "Nova Instauratio," Comte's is "Novissima," both with a telescopic sweep collect inductively the materials for deduction—the one affecting facts, the other positive doctrines and vital principles His system is purely utilitarian. Intellect is to have the general good as its only aim, any private end is selfish and immoral All independent thought is a reaction from Positivism, and cultivation of abstract science is useless, beyond the point at which one science lays the foundation of the science next in order Astronomy, for instance, needs only to be pursued so far as the planetary system is visible to the naked eye, and exercises a perceptible gravitative or irradiating influence on the earth Comte had an intense hate for all abstract reasoning as morally dangerous in fostering pride, and as being to the many essentially dry and repulsive.

In working out his Positivist system Comte establishes with logical precision one step after another Positive philosophy includes science in all its relations The same *method* applies to all investigations physics, ethics, politics, and the subordinate sciences, all fall under the same category *Classification* marshals the several sciences in the natural order in which they must be attacked The simpler come first, as paving the way for the more complex and difficult Mathematics are the foundation of astronomy and physical science, and chemistry stands in the same relation to biology which this latter occupies with respect to sociology, itself the wide basis of religion The order of *evolution* is as a fundamental law. All human science has had its orderly progression, and through the successive stages of the theological, the metaphysical, and the positive phases The terms are not happily chosen by Comte to express his particular ideas, but they are his[2] Metaphysics with him is a comprehensive term of condemnation, an intermedi-

[1] Brown's *Philosophy of the Mind* is eminently Positivist. "No better introduction to Positivism than the early part of Brown's lectures has yet been produced" [T S Mill]

[2] Mr J S Mill proposes to substitute on the score of clearness, for theological, the personal or volitional explanation of nature, for metaphysical, the abstractional

ate limbo to which he condemns all attempts at positive science which are unscientifically misdirected Transition from one condition to another has been determined in different cases with more or less rapidity By theology Comte means a belief in supernatural power, either in philosophy or in religion Beginning as the merest Fetichism, it becomes first Polytheism, and rises eventually into the belief of one God, the Ruler and Governor of the universe, to Whom the disposal of events that are ruled by the inevitable operation of their own laws is ascribed by the untutored mind Under its metaphysical phase, philosophical thought passes on from the idea of a supernatural Being overruling all things throughout the universe to that of abstract forces inherent in the various cosmic substances, and giving rise to those phenomena which, under the preceding phase, had been ascribed to a Divine will This leads to the positive, in which the mind, divorcing itself from all inquiry into causes and essences as utterly futile and vain, applies its energies to the diagnosis and classification of the laws which regulate effects; the definite and invariable relations of sequence and analogy in which all things stand to each other The highest flight of the human intellect will be, at some future time, the demonstration that all phenomena issue forth from one general principle Thus the several sciences have had this uniform progression, the Sun-god of heathen mythology made way for the harmony of the spheres, and the mystical properties of numbers under Pythagoras, to be succeeded in due course by the positive result of the discovery of the law of gravitation and of attraction A knowledge of dynamics and gravitation raises astronomy as a science to so completely positive a condition, that the recurrence of celestial phenomena may be predicted as certainly as the position of the sun at any given hour to morrow, the incidence of an annular eclipse is so certainly foreknown that astronomers betake themselves to the exact spot upon the earth's surface from whence it may be best observed The sequence of the occultation of Jupiter's satellites is so unvarying that the seafaring man has no better method for determining his exact position on the pathless deep Nothing can be more positive than a science that can shew such results as these. So also meteorology, already advanced in some degree in the same direction, will become absolutely positive, when its laws and invariable sequences are wholly known "Snow and vapours, wind and storm, fulfilling His word," will be found to be determined in their most capricious phenomena by laws that in principle are one with those of every other law of Nature Thunder, ascribed of old to the nod of Jove, and in the Italic school to the whirl of the spheres reaching us through the rent clouds, is by positive science identified with electricity, but a yet wide generalization may bring the laws both of gravitation and electricity under the operation of one and the self-same principle Even mathematics has had its theological phase in the mystical properties applied to numbers by Pythagoras, and adopted by the Gnostics, also in the deification of geometrical properties by the Egyptians [Plut. *de Is et Os* 56, compare 47, and Irenæus, Cambr ed introd pp xxiv xxv]

The positive system, therefore—discarding all notion of supernatural power and of forces interposing between phenomena and their evolution, as in fact Descartes had already done—takes account solely of phenomena, it traces down their laws—that is, the unvarying character of their sequences, their tendencies and reciprocal analogies The determination of those laws is henceforth to be the highest aim of the human intellect Positive philosophy is content with the demonstration of such laws, it troubles not itself with their cause Things as yet are only tending that way Biology is in its metaphysical stage, and metaphysicians weary themselves with vain attempts to reach back to the first cause of life, and to discover whether the vital principle consists of electricity or galvanism or some neuro-chemical action Sociology also is still in its primitive theological state, and men persist in believing that human actions are rewarded and punished by a Supreme Governor, whom they have never seen and cannot know If there be a Supreme Being He must be bound by the laws that uphold the regular course of Nature Positivism will eventually enable men to predict the occurrence of phenomena in every science as infallibly as in the forecasting of astronomy

Comte's classification of the fundamental sciences, as preliminary to the successful investigation of their laws, is certainly remarkable As in mathematics, principle is evolved from principle, and the most intricate and complex proposition depends ultimately on simple postulates and axioms, so is it with the sciences All have the orderly progression. The phenomena exhibited by each determine their mutual relations, and the order of their dependence is defined by the simplicity or generality of those phenomena—the most simple are the most general Proceeding, therefore, from the study of the most simple or general phenomena, the Positivist must advance onwards towards the mastery of those that are in the highest degree complex The sciences have their scale of subordination, and must be taken methodically, and this not with the mere view of facilitating study, but as an essential element of Positivist discipline

Philosophy is reducible into abstract and concrete sciences abstract science involving the laws that govern the rudimental phenomena of nature in every possible form, while concrete science affects the individual phenomena Abstract science, as coming first in natural order and as the basis of concrete science, is of earlier development. It forms a group of six, their order is determined by successive accretion

1 MATHEMATICS, including the science of num-

or ontological, and for positive, in its objective aspect, phenomenal, and subjectively, experiential.

ber, arithmetic and algebra, extension, geometry; dynamics, statics, and mechanics

2 ASTRONOMY, based upon 1 + {gravitation and attraction}

3 PHYSICS, depending upon 1 + 2, natural phenomena being affected by planetary movement and influence, heat, light, electricity, etc

4 CHEMISTRY depends on 1 + 2 + 3, especially on the last named phenomena

5 BIOLOGY depends on 3 + 4 + its own laws

6 SOCIOLOGY involves in a greater or less degree all the preceding

Of these, Physics include a group of sciences, such as barology, the science of weight, thermology, of heat, acoustics, optics and electrology Barology ranks first, as being connected with astronomy, and electrology last, as preparing the transition to chemistry Chemistry entered into its positive stage under Lavoisier about the middle of last century. Sociology has not become in any degree positive, theological and metaphysical modes of thought still retard its progress

There is certainly comprehensiveness in the grasp that Comte has taken of the cycle of sciences that bears a favourable comparison with the generalizations of the greatest thinkers But when we follow him into the region of sociology, and master his draftings of the laws that should regulate man as a social and religious being, the result is utter disappointment All is an Utopian optimism, moral standard there is none, unless indeed it be in the entire denegation of self that he enforces Its only other redeeming point is his connected view of universal history, filling two out of the six volumes of which his *Cours de Philosophie Positive* consists, and which are remarkably rich in ideas and analytical power The philosophy of history in his hands becomes a science

Comte would devise a religion that should embrace every form of belief, incorporating Judaism and Mahometanism with Christianity Practically his religion, "teneatis risum," is gynolatry The idea of a Deity, he declares, only grew out of Fetichism, in Baconian phrase, it is an "idolum specus," a fond notion of the superstitious past Still there must be some concrete object round which religious veneration must gather The unseen Benefactor is the abstract idea of Humanity, the "Grand Etre," which includes also man's humble companions, his dog, his horse, and his cat But the object of Positivist adoration must be something thoroughly well known to the intellect, and have a warm life in the affections, something that needs our service, which Omnipotence does not From whence does man derive holier lessons of love and affection than from his female relations? wife, mother and daughter representing the present, past and future. Therefore they are only fitting objects of Positivist adoration They are our guardian angels, and if such relations are denied to any lone being, or are unfortunately unsuited for religious cultus, any other type of womanhood, even historical so that it be real, may be substituted Mental commemoration of these concrete feminine virtues is the great devotional act Two hours daily, and variously divided, are to be given up to such edifying contemplation Prayer also must be offered to the idolized ideal, an outpouring of feeling, such as mysticism endeavours to realize as its evidence of union with the Invisible Comte in his matrimonial relations was singularly unfortunate, he was separated from his wife, and formed a liaison with a married woman, Clotilde de Vaux, who died within the year He would allow of divorce only in the solitary case of infamy contracted by a judicial punishment It was the misfortune of his Clotilde to have been thus qualified Second marriages also were discouraged, matrimony being held strictly to make of two one flesh, and to involve a vow of perpetual widowhood on the part of the survivor, for remembrance is as life to the deceased, and in the case of the wife it is her apotheosis of posthumous adoration. Under the head of religious cultus must be mentioned also the Positivist red letter days A collective worship is due to the "Grand Etre," Humanity This public service employs seven days altogether per month The Positivist calendar perpetuates its benefactors It excludes the French "philosophes" of the last century, though Voltaire and Diderot have their niche Protestants also are rigorously excluded Comte mimicked wherever he could ecclesiastical rites and institutions, he had his infidel travestie of Church sacraments, the ninth and last being a public judgment by the spiritual power of the life of the departed, and, if merited, incorporation into the 'Grand Etre" is decreed, and the newly canonized is added to the objects of Positivist adoration This surviving memory of the departed is the only futurity recognised in the wretched craze termed Positivist religion It knows no future life whatever beyond this change through death from objective to subjective existence in the memory of survivors To be worshipped in the "Grand Etre"—Humanity—is a sufficient immortality

The Positivist religion also has its hierarchy There are two powers in the State [1] The spiritual, consisting of the theoretical class, "proletaires" or workmen, and the women and children This includes the clergy or the educational, and the philosophical, legal and medical sub-classes, which are maintained by a small State stipend, with which they are to be content, for to have the confidence of the masses, who are poor, its members must themselves be poor [2] A supreme pontiff is to be head of this hierarchy for the whole human race, divided into small kingdoms no larger than Belgium, with Paris as the metropolis of the world All functionaries have the power of naming their successors, to get rid of the elective principle, for which, and for deliberative assemblies, Comte had a supreme contempt, neither had he any respect for learning, and for the sake of "hygiène cérébrale" he would burn all books in existence, with the exception of about a hundred, chiefly of the poetical class Such is Positivism in its scientific and religious aspects Comte's theory with respect to capital and labour is pure Socialism, in which principles, as a St Simonian, he was brought up But he demanded a more complete abnegation of self than any ascetic devotee "Vivre pour altrui" was his motto, and this, his great moral principle, he termed "altruism" To love our neighbours as ourselves is egotism We must not love ourselves at all, but aim at the highest perfection by bestowing all our love upon others Ascetic discipline is only to be restricted by the consideration of health, to preserve the healthy exercise of every faculty is the Positivist's first duty Indulgence in food, or in anything not necessary for bodily vigour, is immoral, and every gratification of sense, however casual, is an "inevitable infirmity" Still a moderate "luxe" is to be allowed to the rulers of the Positivist state on account of their arduous duties. [Aug Comte, *Cours de la Ph Pos*, and Miss Martineau's translation *Catéchisme Pos*, translated by Congreve *Positivist Calendar* Lewes, *Comte's Phil of the Sciences*, *Biographical Hist of Ph* J S Mill, *Positivism*]

PRAXEANS Of those Monarchians who retained or tried to retain the Catholic faith that our Lord Jesus Christ is God and Man, Praxeas, the founder of this heresy, is the first named in history [MONARCHIANS] The heretical tenet that there is no distinction of Persons in the Godhead, coupled with the acknowledgment of a Divine Nature in our Lord, leads logically to the conclusion that the Father was incarnate and suffered Whence, although he himself shrunk from the inference, Praxeas is reckoned with the Patripassians He did not form a schismatical party Philaster states that the Sabellians, called also Patripassians and Praxeans, were cast out of the Church [*Hær* liv], but we cannot infer from this that Praxeas himself was excommunicated

Our knowledge of Praxeas is derived almost entirely from Tertullian's treatise against him Augustine, as well as Philaster, names him and his followers under the heresy of Sabellius; and excepting from Tertullian, we have only the bare mention of his name as a heretic From Tertullian it appears that he came to Rome from Asia, and the words of Tertullian, "œconomiam intelligere nolunt etiam Græci," appear to contain an allusion to his nation It is probable that he learnt his heresy from a school in Proconsular Asia which produced Noetus [NOETIANS] If he held his heresy while in Asia he can scarcely have been, as he is often said to have been, a Montanist There was a connection between the later Montanists and the Sabellians, but the earlier Montanists were free from Sabellianism Tertullian's words imply no more than that Praxeas had in Asia become acquainted with the character of Montanist pretensions and doctrine. [MONTANISTS] In Asia Praxeas had suffered imprisonment ("de jactatione martyrii inflatus, ob solum et simplex et breve carceris tædium," is the polemical notice of it), and with the credit attaching to a confessor he preached his false doctrine at Rome Whether the doctrine met with resistance, toleration or favour is not told,[1] but that Praxeas' endeavours to propagate it had but little effect we are entitled to infer from the silence of Hippolytus. The Refutation of Heresies was called forth by this very controversy, and Hippolytus details carefully the tenets of Noetus, and the action of the Bishop of Rome with regard to them Had Praxeas prepared the way to any considerable extent for Noetus, some notice of his influence would surely have been given, whereas all that can be said is, that in the separate tract against Noetus, the opening words will include, but without naming, disciples of Praxeas joining Noetus It is easy to suppose that Victor, discovering the heresy of Praxeas, and not wishing, for his own sake, to disgrace one upon whose information he had acted, and by whom perhaps he had been influenced in the matter of the Montanists, quietly sent Praxeas from Rome From Rome Praxeas went into Africa[2] There he held a dispute, probably with Tertullian, acknowledged his error, and delivered to the Church a formal recantation But he returned again to his errors, and Tertullian, now a Montanist, wrote his Tract in confutation of them

The date at which Praxeas arrived at Rome, and the length of his stay there, are not accurately known, but he reached Africa before Tertullian became a Montanist [Tertull *adv Prax.* 1] Different dates, from A D 199 to 205, are assigned for this latter event. The history of the Montanists is best understood by supposing Praxeas to have been at Rome in Victor's time, and the date of Tertullian's Montanism to have been the earlier date

Praxeas held that there is only one Divine Person, that the Word and the Holy Ghost are not distinct substances, arguing that an admission of distinct Personalities necessarily infers three Gods, and that the identity of the Persons is required to preserve the Divine Monarchy He applied the titles which in Holy Scripture are descriptive of Deity to the Father alone, and urged particularly the words from the Old Testament, "I am God, and beside Me there is no God," and from the New Testament the expressions, "I and My Father are One," "He who

[1] Writers make very different suppositions regarding this point Gieseler, that Praxeas appears to have been unmolested in Rome on account of his doctrine [*Compend* i p 218], Newman, that he met with the determined resistance which honourably distinguishes the Primitive Roman Church in its dealings with heresy [*Hist of Arians*, p 130], Milman, that the indignation of Tertullian at the rejection of his Montanist opinions urged him to arraign the Pope, with what justice, to what extent, we know not, as having embraced the Patripassian opinions of Praxeas [*Latin Christ* i p 49, ed 1867] The two latter mention, as if inclined to it, Beausobre's supposition, that in the words of the Continuator of the *De Præscr Hæret*, "Praxeas quidem hæresim introduxit, quam Victorinus corroborare curavit," we should read Victor for Victorinus One would be rather inclined to substitute Zephyrinus

[2] We take "hic quoque" in Tertullian's "Fruticaverant avenæ Praxeanæ, hic quoque superseminatæ," etc to mean Carthage, and that Tertullian speaks of himself in "per quem traductæ," etc

hath seen Me hath seen the Father." "I am in My Father, and My Father in Me" While Tertullian unhesitatingly charges Praxeas with holding Patripassian tenets as necessarily following from his principles, Praxeas himself appears to have shrunk from the inference "Ergo nec compassus est Pater Filio, sic enim directam blasphemiam in Patrem veriti, diminui eam hoc modo sperant, concedentes jam Patrem et Filium duos esse; si Filius quidem patitur, Pater vero compatitur Stulti et in hoc Quid est enim compati, quam cum alio pati? Porro, si impassibilis Pater, utique et incompassibilis Aut si compassibilis, utique passibilis" [Tertull *adv Prax* xxix]

The course of controversy brought out, in the example of the Praxeans, the second and altered position which Monarchians are obliged to assume when pressed by the difficulties of their original position It is shewn, as Tertullian remarks, that they are driven to conclusions involving the elements of Gnosticism The Praxeans, when confuted on all sides on the distinction between the Father and the Son, distinguished, in the Person of our Lord, the Jesus from the Christ They understood "the Son to be flesh—that is, man—that is, Jesus, and the Father to be Spirit—that is, God—that is, Christ" Thus Tertullian says, "They who contend that the Father and the Son are one and the same, do in fact now begin to divide them rather than to unite them Such a monarchy as this they learned, it may be, in the school of the Valentinus" [*ibid* xxvii]. Now this separation of Jesus from Christ was common to all the Gnostics They were unanimous in denying Christ to have been born Jesus and Christ were to them two separate Beings, and the Æon Christ descended upon Jesus at His Baptism The difference between them and the Praxeans appears to be that they would not say that Jesus was the Son of God, whereas the Praxeans are represented as arguing from the angel's words to Mary, that the Holy Thing born of her was the flesh, and that therefore the flesh was the Son of God Tertullian shews in opposition to them that the Word was incarnate by birth

In Praxean doctrine then, in its second stage, we have Jesus called the Son of God, solely, it will follow, on account of a miraculous birth Christ, or the Presence of the Father, residing in Jesus Jesus suffering, and Christ (= the Father) *impassibilem sed compatientem* The interval between this and Gnostic doctrine is easily bridged over, and we have the cause of the comparisons and identifications that are often made of Sabellianism with Gnosticism [MONARCHIANS]

The heresy of Praxeas, as distinguished from that of Noetus, did not make much progress It was almost unknown in Africa in the time of Optatus [i 37]

PRECISIANS [PURITANS]

PREDESTINARIANS Those who maintain that God's foreknowledge of all things necessitates His predestination from eternity of the righteous to everlasting life, and of the wicked to everlasting death

Some traces of this doctrine are to be found in the language which was used by St. Augustine in his refutation of Pelagianism, and the author of Prædestinatus speaks of those who corrupted the doctrine of St Augustine into a heresy These he calls Predestinarians, and it is supposed that they were the monks of Adrumetum, who are said to have thus treated St Augustine's language But the earliest authentic instance in which the doctrine was brought forward in its extreme form is that of Gottschalk [* — 868], a monk first of Fulda, and afterwards of Orbais in the diocese of Soissons. While he was on a pilgrimage to Rome, in A D 847, Gottschalk preached this doctrine of a twofold predestination in so open a manner as to attract the attention of Rabanus Maurus, who charged him with heresy as teaching that God predestines some to sin The question was brought before a council of bishops at Mayence, of which city Rabanus was archbishop, in the following year [A D 848], when Gottschalk maintained that Christ died only for the elect, and that the rest of mankind were inevitably predestined to eternal perdition [Mansi, *Concil* xiv 914] This doctrine being condemned by the council, Gottschalk was sent to his metropolitan, Hincmar, Archbishop of Rheims, who called another council at Chiersey in 849 Here he was defended by Ratramnus, the opponent of PASCHASIUS RADBERIUS in the Eucharistic controversy, and also by Remigius afterwards Archbishop of Lyons, but notwithstanding these powerful supporters he was condemned a second time, and ordered to undergo the penalty of flogging, which the Rule of St. Benedict imposed upon monks who troubled the Church After this condemnation, Gottschalk was imprisoned in the monastery of Hautvilliers, where he died, without being brought to recant his opinions, about the year 868 [*Ibid.* 919]

While the friends of Gottschalk were endeavouring to obtain his absolution and release, Hincmar put forward Johannes Scotus Erigena to answer them, which he did in 851 in his treatise "de Prædestinatione," in which he raised up a cloud of adversaries by the freedom with which he contradicted the established doctrines of the Church as to the nature of good and evil Further controversy being thus aroused, Hincmar summoned a second council at Chiersey in 853, which confirmed the decision as to the real doctrine of the Church arrived at by the previous council [*ibid* 995] A rival council was called by the opposite party from the provinces of Lyons, Vienne and Arles, which met at Valence in 855 But instead of fully confirming the opinion of Gottschalk, this council considerabbly modified it, by declaring that although sin is foreknown by God, it is not so predestined as to make it inevitably necessary that it should be committed [*ibid* xv 1] Hincmar now wrote two works on the subject, one of which is not extant, and the other entitled "De Prædestinatione Dei et Libero

Arbitrio, adversus Gottschalkum at cæteros Prædestinatianos ' Having thus explained his views at length, they were substantially accepted in the form of six doctrinal canons by the Synod of Langres, and by that of Toul [A D 859] held at Savonières a few days afterwards [*ibid* 525-7], and thus the controversy terminated [Manguin, *Collect auctor de Prædest et Gratia* 1650 Ussher, *Gotteschalci et Prædest controv Hist* Cellot, *Hist Gotteschalci Prædest* 1655]

During the Middle Ages there were but few Divines who held strong Predestinarian opinions, the most conspicuous of those who did so being Thomas Bradwardine [A D 1290-1349], Warden of Merton College, and afterwards Archbishop of Canterbury His work on the subject is entitled "De Causa Dei contra Pelagium, et de Virtute Causarum, ad suos Mertonenses,' and in this he gave free-will so low a place that he may be almost called a Necessitarian

At the time of the Reformation, however, the subject of Predestination was revived by a controversy between Erasmus and Luther, the former writing an able "Diatribe de Libero Arbitrio" in 1524, and Luther following it up with his halting treatise "de Servo Arbitrio," in which he went so near to the Predestinarians as to deny that any free-will can exist in man before he has received the gift of faith Calvin exceeded all previous Predestinarians in the dreadful dogma of the Divine decrees which he enunciated [CALVINISTS], and in later years the controversies of the MOLINISTS and the JANSENISTS on the subject of free-will were carried on with great acrimony [Sismondi, *Hist Prædest* in *Zachar Thesaur Theol* ii 199] The Scotch Presbyterians and the English Puritans followed Calvin too closely not to be Predestinarians in the strictest sense The later Low Church party in the Church of England have tempered down the opinions of their Puritan predecessors, and are not often disposed to go beyond the doctrine of "Predestination to Life," as stated in the 17th of the Thirty-nine Articles of Religion, which carefully excludes the double Predestination of Gottschalk and the Predestinarians At the census of 1851 two congregations calling themselves "Predestinarians ' were returned

PREPON An Assyrian disciple of the heretic Marcion, living when Hippolytus wrote his Refutation of all Heresies, about the end of the second, or early in the third, century He is named also in Theodoret's account of Apelles [Theodor *Hær fab* i 25] Hippolytus states that the principles of Prepon were laid down in a work which he inscribed to Bardesanes, but he appears to have diverged from Marcion only in alleging "that what is just constitutes a third principle, and that it is placed intermediate between what is good and bad" This intermediate principle Hippolytus identifies with the "Musa," or impartial Reason, of Empedocles, a myth to whom is attributed the restoration to the good power Unity of what is disturbed by the wicked power Discord. [Hippol. *Refut Hær* vii. 19]

PRESBYTERIANS A sect, the leading principle of which is that the ministry of the Christian Church consists of only one order, that of Presbyters or Elders Bishops are considered to be identical with Presbyters, and Deacons to be only lay officers appointed to relieve the poor The government and discipline of the Church rests, on the Presbyterian theory, with collective bodies of teaching (or clerical) elders, generally called "ministers," and ruling (or lay) elders—who are generally meant when "elders" are spoken of—gathered in Synods, and not with individual persons as in the Episcopal system, or with individual congregations as in the Independent system

The founder of the Presbyterian sect was Calvin, who established the system at Geneva in the year 1541 It was established in Scotland in a modified form (with superintending presbyters in the place of bishops), under the influence of John Knox in the year 1560, in the Genevan form under that of Andrew Melville in the year 1592 and has continued, in the latter form, to be the national religion of the Scottish people from that time to the present day [SCOTCH KIRK]

In ENGLAND the principles of Presbyterianism are to be traced at work among the LOLLARDS of the fourteenth and fifteenth, and the PURITANS of the sixteenth century, but the first actual separation from the Church of England of any of those who held them took place in the year 1572, when a society was formed on the Calvinistic principle at Wandsworth, near London "The heads of the association were Mr Field, lecturer of Wandsworth, Mr Smith of Mitcham, Mr Crane of Roehampton, Mr. Wilcox, Standen, Jackson, Bonham Saintloe and Edmonds, to whom were afterwards joined Mr Travers, Charke, Barber, Gardiner, Crook, Egerton, and a number of very considerable laymen [1] On the 20th of November eleven elders were chosen, and their offices described in a register, entitled 'The Orders of Wandsworth' This was the first Presbyterian Church in England All imaginable care was taken to keep their proceedings private, but the bishop's eye was upon them, who gave immediate intelligence to the High Commission, upon which the Queen issued out a proclamation for putting the Act of Uniformity in execution, but though the Commissioners knew of the Presbytery, they could not discover the members of it, nor prevent others being erected in the neighbouring counties ' [Neal's *Hist Purit* i 301, ed 1732] There is no trace, however, of any large number of Presbyterian congregations existing before the Civil War Heylin says that after establishing that at Wandsworth the sect was restrained from "practising any further" by the Queen's proclamation for Uniformity, and also by the odium brought upon separatists through the

[1] Field and Wilcox were the authors of the "Admonition to the Parliament" Travers was chaplain and tutor in Lord Burleigh's household, but is best known as the Reader at the Temple, whose controversy with Richard Hooker, when Master of the Temple, led the latter to write his *Laws of Ecclesiastical Polity*

fanatic act of Peter Burchet in stabbing Sir John Hawkins [Heylin's *Hist Presb* 275]. The Puritans had, in fact, about this time, devised a plan by which they could carry out the principles of Presbyterianism without leaving the Church, and this, probably, is the true reason why so few separate congregations were formed by them But as early as June 28th, 1576, a Presbytery was set up for the four Channel Islands—Jersey, Guernsey, Alderney, and Sark—Cartwright having gone for the purpose to Guernsey, and Snape to Jersey The progress of Presbyterian principles within the Church, and of the ultimate establishment of the Presbyterian system during the Commonwealth, is traced out in another article [PURITANS]

At the Restoration, many of the 800 ministers who vacated the benefices of the Church under the operation of the Act of Uniformity [NONCONFORMISTS] were doubtless Presbyterians, but the greater number were Independents, who were much less inclined to accept Episcopacy than the party which had already lived under its shadow for about three quarters of a century On the passing of the Toleration Act, however, in the year 1689, Presbyterian meeting-houses began to be erected in considerable numbers Before the end of the century, as many as fifty-nine were reckoned in Yorkshire, and it is asserted by Presbyterian writers that there were as many as 800 congregations of Presbyterians distributed through the several counties of England They became one of the "three denominations" who received the recognition of the State, and were permitted to petition the Crown in a corporate capacity, and in the business meetings of deputies from these denominations the Presbyterians had two representatives for one Baptist and one Independent.

In 1691 an attempt was made to bring about a doctrinal union between the Independents and the Presbyterians The opposition of the two sects to each other during the latter days of the Commonwealth had established a very bitter feud between them, but it was now seen that they could contend against the Church much more vigorously when united than when separated into two bodies Terms of union were therefore drawn up under the title of "Heads of Agreement assented to by the United Ministers in and about London, formerly called Presbyterian and Congregational," and these were accepted by a large number of each sect in London and in the country districts also Almost immediately afterwards, however, dissensions arose between the two sects in consequence of the controversy about Dr Crisp's publications [CRISPITES], and after many bickering papers had been printed on either side, the union was broken off in the year 1696 [*History of Union, etc, and the causes of the breach of it*, 1698]

But notwithstanding the number of Presbyterian meeting-houses which had been erected, the organization of Presbyterianism was very imperfectly kept up The "discipline" which has flourished so well in Scotland under the form of "kirk session" never obtained a firm footing in England, nor has the sect ever possessed a completely organized system of Presbyteries, Synods, and General Assembly It was probably the absence of this system, with its close espionage of the doctrine preached by Presbyterian ministers, which led some of the latter into a laxity of opinion through which they quickly passed from Calvinism to Unitarianism In the year 1719, two preachers of the sect at Exeter, who had adopted the Arian views then becoming fashionable, were turned out of their chapels by the trustees for refusing to subscribe to the doctrine of our Lord's Divinity On May of that year 19 out of the 75 Presbyterian ministers of Devon and Cornwall refused to accept the test offered them, which was subscription to the second of the Thirty-Nine Articles, while at a meeting at Salters' Hall 57 out of 110 voted against requiring from ministers any declaration of faith in the Holy Trinity

From that time the Presbyterians are little heard of as a distinct sect in England Nearly all their ministers and trustees became Unitarian, and hence their meeting-houses became generally alienated from their original purpose Of 206 Unitarian meeting-houses in England and Wales in the year 1824, as many as 170 had originally been Presbyterian, but many of these it appears were kept up entirely because they had endowments, these being sometimes received by ministers who had no attendants at their chapels, so much had Presbyterianism declined in England [*Manchester Socinian Controv* xlv] The few congregations which remained true to the Westminster Confession of Faith were in the northern counties, where sympathy with Scottish neighbours tended to keep alive the flame of Presbytery after it had died out in those parts of England removed from Scottish influences

Within the last half century there has been some revival of the sect and in the year 1836 it was reorganized under the rule of the "Synod of the Presbyterian Church in England in connection with the Church of Scotland" Attempts to bring about an actual union of the English with the Scottish body failed through legal impediments, it being found that such an union would carry the jurisdiction of the Northern Establishment into forbidden regions In 1844, therefore, the name of the English portion of the sect was changed to that of "The Presbyterian Church in England" This now numbers seven presbyteries, and about seventy congregations In addition to these there are also about the same number of congregations belonging to the UNITED PRESBYTERIANS, and fifteen which are outlying congregations of the Scottish Kirk

In IRELAND as well as in England there was a strong Puritan section of the clergy holding Presbyterian principles during the earlier years of the seventeenth century, but the party was not consolidated into a separate community until the Civil War broke out, when, on June 10th, 1642, a presbytery was established at Carrickfergus, which soon became the parent of others in various parts of Ulster, and the Covenant was taken by a considerable proportion of the people of Ulster in the summer of 1644 While the Civil War was going on in Scotland great numbers of the Scotch emigrated to the North of Ireland, and these made a large addition to its Presbyterian population, a strong bond of fellowship being also established between the two communities For a time their ministers in Ireland were silenced by Cromwell because they refused to take the "Engagement" of fidelity to the Commonwealth, but for the last five or six years of his administration he treated the Irish Presbyterians with less severity, and at the Restoration they numbered nearly eighty congregations, with seventy ministers Sixty-one of these were obliged to give up the benefices into which they had intruded—Jeremy Taylor deprived thirty-six in one day—and only seven out of the seventy conformed to the Church by receiving Episcopal orders Within a few years the Presbyterians of Ulster were however organized into a compact sect, and in 1672 a "Regium Donum" of £700 a year was granted to their ministers by Charles II, a sum soon afterwards increased to £1200, and at the Union to about £15,000 The political and social schisms which have broken out among the Presbyterians of Scotland, dividing them into BURGHERS, ANTI-BURGHERS, etc, have been faithfully reproduced on a smaller scale among those of the North of Ireland, but their two principal divisions are into a "Synod of Ulster" and a "Presbytery of Antrim" The whole number of Presbyterian congregations in Ireland is about 600

In AMERICA the Presbyterians first obtained a footing in the opening years of the eighteenth century, through the immigration of Scotch and Irish members of the sect The earliest organized Presbyterian congregation was one established at Philadelphia in the year 1703, but the tide of emigration soon carried over additions to their number, and they, too, quickly became subject to the same spirit of bitter controversy which characterized the Presbyterians in England, Scotland, and Ireland, and which everywhere caused the same disintegration into parties and sects on points of minute difference respecting ecclesiastical discipline. These differences were aggravated by the revival preaching of George Whitfield in the year 1739, when the "New Lights" enthusiastically sided with him, while the "Old Lights" as earnestly opposed him This led to a separation of the former in 1741 under the name of the "Synod of New York," and the two bodies remained apart until 1758, when they once more united In 1789 the Westminster Confession was adopted, and a General Assembly was formed, there being then 419 congregations with 188 ministers The War of Independence broke up many of these congregations, but the sect was strengthened in 1801 by an alliance with the Congregationalists, although about the same time occurred the secession of the "Cumberland Presbyterians," or advocates for the introduction of lay-teachers where ministers regularly educated for examination by the Presbytery cannot be obtained In the year 1834 there were 230,000 communicant Presbyterians, with 1900 ministers, in the United States. Fresh dissensions which arose led first to the abrogation of the union between the sect and that of the Congregationalists, and secondly to the separation of the "New School Presbyterians" from the "Old School Presbyterians," the former agreeing with the abrogation in question, the latter dissenting from it The "Old School" adheres to the Westminster Confession, but the "New School," who are also called "Puritans," hold a somewhat mitigated Calvinism The Old School Presbyterians number about 300,000 members, with 3600 chapels and 2700 ministers The New School numbers about 130,000 members, with 1400 chapels and 1500 ministers Both are active missionary bodies, and each possesses five colleges

It is stated by a recent writer that the American Presbyterians are adopting a Liturgy, one being named, which is entitled "The Church Book for St Peter's, Rochester," the contents of which are, "the Order for Public Worship, the Order of Administration of Baptism, the Order of publicly receiving Baptized Persons to the Fellowship of the Church, the Order of Administering the Lord's Supper, the Marriage Service, the Funeral Service, Morning and Evening Prayers for Families, a Psalter for responsive reading, the Nicene and Athanasian Creeds, Psalms and Hymns with tunes for Congregational singing" [*An English Layman's Recent Recollections of the Anglo-American Church in the United States*, ii 119]

PRESBYTERIAN SYNOD OF SECEDERS IN IRELAND This name was given to a section of the Irish Presbyterians formed in 1818 by an union of the BURGHERS and ANTI-BURGHERS They were incorporated into the general body of Irish Presbyterians in 1840

PRIMIANISTS A local name for the Donatists at Carthage, as followers of their bishop Primian, one of the chief opponents of St Augustine

PRIMITIVE METHODISTS [METHODISTS]

PRINCEITES A small sect established about the year 1840 by a fanatic clergyman of the extreme Evangelical school named Henry James Prince, and professing to be a new dispensation of the Holy Ghost, in Prince's person, by which the dispensation of Christ is superseded

The founder of this sect began life as House Surgeon to the General Hospital at Bath in the year 1832, when he was twenty-one years of age While on a visit to his brother, then Vicar of Shincliffe, near Durham he was impressed with a desire to change his profession, and endeavoured to obtain admission as a student in Durham University. Failing in this he went, in March 1836, to Lampeter College, which had been founded by Bishop Burgess in 1822 for Welsh students, and soon after going there he organized a small body of the students on the plan of the early Oxford Methodists, under the name of the "Lampeter Brethren" These met together for prayer and "revival" under the leadership of Prince, and singular to say, devoted much time to the study of, or rather meditation upon, the Song of Solomon Among the young men forming this association those whose names were afterwards most conspicuous were Prince, George Robinson Thomas, Lewis Price, and A. A. Rees, the last of whom became brother-in-law to Prince, but soon afterwards parted from his company At this time Prince and his associates belonged to the extreme section of the Evangelical school, as is shewn by his "Letters addressed to his Brethren" published in 1841, and by "Brother Prince's Journal," from 1835 to 1839, which was published in 1851 In the "letters" there is a good deal of mysticism, illustrated by geometrical diagrams, on the union of souls with each other by absorption into the Divine Nature, speculations which foreshadow the subsequent fanaticism

On leaving Lampeter in 1840, Prince first married an old Roman Catholic lady who had lodged with his mother, and was then ordained to the curacy of Charlinch near Bridgewater, the rector of the parish, Samuel Starky, being one with whom he was afterwards closely associated in the sect which he formed, but who was an absentee from his living, and a wealthy valetudinarian. At Charlinch (which was the future settlement of the sect) Prince says that "there was not," on his arrival,—"with the exception of his own household—so much as *one* person either converted or awakened among all the people committed to his charge," and during fourteen months of hot Evangelical preaching, although "three persons from a neighbouring parish were converted, there did not appear to be even a stir among his own people" [Prince's *Charlinch Revival*, 1842, p 5] But although he produced no effect upon his people, Prince had by this time excited himself into the belief that the Holy Spirit had taken entire possession of him, so as to unite him with Himself At the same time, also, the absent rector of the parish was converted to his curate's opinion by reading one of Prince's sermons when he believed himself to be dying, and he returned to Charlinch to take part in the revival Prayer-meetings were now held at the rectory (for the rector himself was unable to speak in his church) with the usual hysterical excitement among women and children, and the proceedings in the end became so outrageous that Dr Law, the Bishop of Bath and Wells, withdrew Prince's license as curate

The aged and infirm wife whom the fanatic had married now died, and Prince immediately took as her successor Miss Starky, the sister of his rector, and, like that clergyman, one of his converts. Another curacy was obtained at Stoke by Clare in Suffolk, where the same proceedings were carried on as at Charlinch—a second of the Lampeter Brethren, George Robinson Thomas, taking the place of Prince at the latter place After bearing with the revival extravagances, however, for many months, Bishop Allen took the same course that had been taken by Bishop Law, and Prince being again dismissed from his curacy, a third of the Lampeter Brethren, Price, was again left as his successor

The transition from Evangelical notions to fanatic notions on the subject of the work of the Spirit is shewn by concluding remarks in Prince's account of the Charlinch revivals, which was printed while he was at Stoke "Many," he says, "can bear the external piety that consists in good congregations, flourishing schools, Evangelical views, a Gospel ministry, and the various kinds of religious societies, prayer-meetings, and pious institutions now so prevalent," but "few of those who are praying for the coming of the Holy Ghost would *be able to bear Him* if He should come," and "He would find but few vessels *fitted to receive Him* To all this may be added also that, when the Spirit works with extraordinary power, it must necessarily lead him by whom He works to act in some respects in an extraordinary way, so that even godly men and ministers may be induced to look on him and his doings with suspicion and distrust" [Prince's *Charlinch Revival*, 1842, pp 68, 71] The meaning of these latter words was shortly after disclosed at a meeting of the Lampeter Brethren, held at Swansea in June 1842, for the purpose of considering the best means of increasing their usefulness in the ministry Prince took the lead, and a few weeks afterwards sent each of the Brethren a printed copy of articles of agreement, which led to the disclosure that he professed to dictate to them with the voice of God, as "the Holy Ghost personified" [Rees' *Rise and Progress of the Heresy of the Rev H J. Prince*, 1846, p 8, Deck's *Heresy of Mr Prince*, 1845] This blasphemy was—unconsciously no doubt, for Prince was not likely to know of his predecessors in heresy—a revival of the long-enduring heresy which was maintained by the AMALRICIANS early in the twelfth century, by the WILHELMIANS of the thirteenth, and by many of the disciples of Abbot Joachim in that and later ages a heresy which was also the logical terminus of much of the enthusiastic doctrine respecting the personal indwelling of the Holy Spirit, by which the teaching of the Puritans, the Methodists, and the Low Churchmen from whom Prince sprang, was characterized [DICT *of* THEOL, SPIRIT, *n* 2] Rees, who would not accept Prince's claims in this extreme form, left the brotherhood and set up a "Free Church" at Sunderland, where he continued for many years Starkey, Thomas, and Price, with some others, continued to believe in their leader, and his party was strengthened by the addition of a railway surveyor named Cobbe, who built a chapel for Thomas at Spaxton, near Charlinch, and thus formed the nucleus of the future establishment of the sect

For it was now determined that a community should be established with Prince at its head A temporary one, under the name of "the Agapemone," or "Abode of Love," was set up at Weymouth, where Prince joined Starky, and, by means of exciting revivals, about two hundred persons were persuaded to join the sect of which it was the centre, their leader terrifying them with the declaration that the dispensation of grace had now closed, and that in future only those would be saved who accepted him as the Holy One of the new dispensation of the Spirit Among those who at this time, or very shortly afterwards, joined the sect, were a number of wealthy ladies, who made over their property to Prince From four such named Maber he obtained £10,000, from four others named Nottidge (three of whom he induced to marry his coadjutors Price, Thomas, and Cobbe) he received £24,000 and these contributions, with many smaller ones, enabled him to build a large "Agapemone" around the chapel already erected at Spaxton The institution so established was a sumptuous abode in which the fanatic and his friends lived in the greatest luxury, not making any further efforts to extend the pretended new dispensation, but settling down to the enjoyment of the wealth acquired from the female converts and it may be mentioned as an illustration of the life adopted, that not long after wards, when a party of the Agapemone community visited the Great Exhibition of 1851, the quondam Evangelical curate of Charlinch was to be seen driving about Hyde Park in a carriage and four, preceded by hatless outriders, the latter riding uncovered because they were in attendance upon "the Lord" in the person of Prince

The principle on which the sect was ultimately consolidated was that the Lord Jesus having suffered to redeem the spirit only, and left the flesh where He found it, alienated from God under the curse, Prince took upon him new flesh to redeem the flesh,[1] and whosoever believes on him will not die, but will henceforth be without sickness or pain [*Mr Prince and the Agapemone*, 1858] "The Holy Ghost fulfilled the Gospel in Brother Prince, by being and doing in him *fully* all that He was sent by the Father to be and to do so that He left not anything undone in Brother Prince of all that it was in Him as the Spirit of the dispensation to perform" [*Testimony of Br Prince, Voice the Second*, 62] The journal already mentioned was published, its author says, "to exhibit to the professing Church of Christ an actual instance of the complete accomplishment by the Gospel of all that for which the Gospel was given, namely, the destruction of the work of the devil in the human soul" [Brother Prince's *Journal*, Pref x] And he says of himself at the end "The professing people of God under the Gospel—the Christian Church in these the last days of *their* dispensation —may see in him in whom their dispensation is made perfect *the likeness and glory of Christ* They *may* see this, for one 'changed into the same image from glory to glory' is there But what *will* they see?—O righteous Father, the world hath not known Thee! O holy Saviour, Thine house hath wounded Thee! O gentle Spirit, Thy people have despised Thee! Alas, my Lord, let them not see in Thy Beloved"—the title assumed by Prince—"the only one of her mother, and the choice one of her that bare her, one that has a devil and is mad, a man carnal, sensual, and selfish, a frequenter of low company, one that speaketh blasphemy, and a deceiver of the people—led by the devil into error, even whilst he was living upon Thee as truth" [*ibid* xv]

Assuming these blasphemous pretensions, Prince appointed his friends Thomas and Starky as the two "Anointed Ones," or "witnesses" spoken of in the Apocalypse, and others of his community he named the seven angels of the seven trumpets But assuming also that "God, according to His promise, did create a new Heaven by fulfilling the Gospel in Brother Prince," the community adopted the same kind of life as that of the American PERFECTIONISTS, maintaining that there was no further necessity for prayer, and using their chapel as a luxurious drawing-room in token that the new life is a heavenly life of continual enjoyment and thanksgiving It is also one of their tenets that those who are perfect will never suffer pain or die, and that such of their community as have died are, by that fact, proved not to have been perfect

PRISCILLIANISTS The early prophetesses of Montanism were Priscilla and Maximilla [Hipp *Refut* viii 12] and from this Priscilla the whole body of Montanists may have been called Priscillianists But Augustine [*Hær* xxvi xxvii], associates Priscilla with Quintilla, calling the earlier prophetess Prisca. It seems therefore that the Priscillianists are a later subdivision of the Montanists, called from a second Priscilla Christ, it was said, revealed Himself in a female garb to her and to Quintilla Epiphanius identifies their followers with the Artotyritæ [*Hær* xlix], adding that among them women are consecrated bishops and priests They were also called Quintillianists

PROCLIANISTS One of the two sects into which the Montanists divided, and which took its name from Proclus, as the other did from Æschines They are named by the author of the supplement to Tertullian's work *de Præscriptione Hæreticorum* [*Hæres* viii], as holding a common blasphemy with the Cataphrygians, but their distinctive tenet is not mentioned Eusebius speaks of a work of Caius against Proclus, in which he silences the rashness of the Proclianists in composing new books of Scripture [Euseb *Hist Eccl* vi 20] Philaster and St Augustine say that they denied the Incarnation altogether [Philast *de Hæres* lvi, Aug *de Hæres* lx] but this statement is modified by the author of Prædestinatus into a charge that they believed the Son of God to have appeared as Raphael or Gabriel had done, not by taking flesh which was a form of Docetic heresy [Prædest lx]. Philaster speaks of the Proclianists as disciples of the SELEUCIANS or Hermians

PROCLUS A zealous antichristian Platonist of Athens [A D 410-485] He wrote a work against Christianity in eighteen arguments, entitled *Epicheiremata XVIII contra Christianos*, the substance of which is an argument that the

[1] The obscene rite by which this pretended change was accomplished cannot be here narrated, but it may be found fully indicated in Dixon's *Spiritual Wives*, i 318-331, ed 1868

world is eternal The work was printed, with the confutation of John Philoponus, in Greek, at Venice in A D 1535, and in Latin at Lyons in A.D 1557

PRODICIANS. These heretics appear to be an offshoot of the Carpocratians, and the same with those who were afterwards called ADAMITES, of whom Prodicus is said by Theodoret to have been the founder [Theodor *Hær fab* i 6] All accounts of them come originally from the Miscellanies of Clement of Alexandria, where he speaks of them as practising the profligate habits of the Carpocratians The Prodicians, he says, "falsely call themselves Gnostics They say that they are by nature the children of the Supreme God, but they live and will in the abuse of their lineage and freedom, for all their will is licentiousness, they hold themselves bound by no law, and claim to be above all control as royal children and lords of the Sabbath The law, they say, is not written for the king" He goes on to describe them as practising the Antinomian life indicated by these principles [Clem Alex *Strom* iii 4], and as rejecting the use of prayer and worship, because they had risen above the bondage of the Demiurge [*ibid* vii 7] They claimed also to possess some secret books of Zoroaster [*ibid* i 15] Prodicus is associated with Valentinus by Tertullian, but without any particulars being given of his heresy [Tertull *adv. Prax* iii].

PROGRESS, SCHOOL OF [RATIONALISTS]

PROTERIANS. The Catholic party in Alexandria which did not submit to Peter Mongus, the Monophysite patriarch, whose adherents were called "Petritos," but continued to maintain the orthodox faith for which Proterius was persecuted and murdered [MONOPHYSITES]

PROTESTANTS A name originally given to a party in Germany which protested, in the year 1529, against a decree of the Diet of Spire respecting religion It was afterwards assumed by Lutherans and Calvinists in general to distinguish themselves from Catholics, especially from Roman Catholics

The religious divisions which had been caused in Germany by the disputes between Luther and the Ultramontane party were met at first by an edict of the Emperor Charles V and his dependant princes at the Diet of Worms [A D 1521], in which Luther and his party were declared to be enemies of the Empire, the princes engaging to execute this edict to the utmost of their power by suppressing the new sect The Lutheran party proving too strong for this, another Diet of the princes, which met under the presidency of the Archduke Ferdinand, the Emperor's brother, at Spire, in Bavaria [A D 1526], tempered the Edict of Worms by requiring that all controversies should cease, and decreeing that each prince should be at liberty to settle the affairs of religion within his own dominion as he should see fit, until a general council of the Church was called for the determination of all disputed questions Three years later another Diet of the princes met, under Ferdinand, at Spire [A D 1529], at which the Edict of 1526 was revoked by a majority of them, and all changes in religion were declared to be unlawful until they had been sanctioned by a general council Against this revocation by the majority a remonstrance was drawn up by the minority, which consisted of the Elector of Saxony, the Marquis of Brandenburg, the Duke of Brunswick-Luneburg, the Landgrave of Hesse, and the Count of Anhalt This remonstrance was read by them in public on April 19th, 1529, taking the form of a protest against the act of the Diet, and an appeal to a general council. Fourteen of the cities—Strasburg, Nuremberg, Ulm, Constance, Lindau, Memmingen, Kempten, Nordlingen, Heilbronn, Reutlingen, Issna, St Gall, Weissenburg, and Windesheim—afterwards subscribed this protest, "and thus," wrote Sleidan, a few years afterwards, "is the origin of the name of 'the Protestants,' which has now become famous, and has got into common use not only in Germany but among other nations also" [Sleidan, *de Statu Relig* 2nd ed 1559, p 68]

The name was not accepted cordially by the English Reformers as a designation for members of the Church of England Thus Bishop Ridley wrote in the year 1555 " and to speak plain, and as some of them do odiously call each other, whether they be Protestants, Pharisees, Papists, or Gospellers," "call me a Protestant who listeth, I pass not thereof" [Ridley *on the Lord's Supper*, 9, 14, Parker Soc ed] "It hath been always a Popish practice," wrote Calfhill of image worship in the year 1565, "but that of men professing the Gospel, of Protestants (as ye call them), there hath been any such delusion is not in any writing of any age to be found" [Calfhill's *Answ to Martiall on the Cross*, 134, Parker Soc ed] This shyness of the name extended down a century later, for when the Upper House of Convocation proposed an address to the Crown in the year 1689, in which Convocation was made to thank William III for the zeal which he shewed "for the Protestant religion in general, and the Church of England in particular," the Deans, Archdeacons, and Clergy of the Lower House would not consent to the address being presented with these words in it, and stood out until it was altered to thanks for the King's pious zeal, and care "for the honour, peace, advantage, and establishment of the Church of England whereby we doubt not, the interest of the Protestant religion in all other Protestant churches, which is dear to us, will be the better secured under the influence of your Majesty's government and protection" [Cardwell's *Conf* 444, 446]

The feeling thus shewn in previous centuries has also extended to High Churchmen of modern times, who have always objected to the designation of Protestant as being [1] one of too negative a character to express at all justly the principle of Catholic resistance to the uncatholic pretensions and practices of Rome and [2] as being a name which is used by so many sects as to be inclusive even of heresy The fact indicated in the second objection has led to grave misunderstandings respecting the principles of the Church of England on the part of the Continental and the Eastern Churches.

PROTESTANT CONFESSIONS The term Confessions of Faith is applied primarily, and with most propriety, to those summaries of the Christian faith which were put forth and accepted from time to time by the early Church, and are known to us as the Apostles', the Nicene, and the Athanasian Creeds. Secondly, when men began to deviate from the Catholic faith, they were anxious to embody their new doctrines in forms analogous to the orthodox creeds, and the term "Confession of Faith" was used to denote the creeds of heretical bodies, such as that submitted by the Arians at the Council of Rimini [A D 359] Thirdly, when the great schisms from the Catholic Church took place in the sixteenth century in the various countries of Central Europe, the numerous Protestant communities which sprang into existence severally drew up lengthy documents known in history as confessions of faith, consisting in most cases of between twenty and forty articles, in which were detailed the various new views of doctrine and practice, which were to form a substitute for, or an addition to, the Catholic faith of more than fifteen hundred years

It would be inappropriate here to discuss at length the controversial question as to how far the various views put forward in these confessions of faith are consistent with the primitive doctrines of the Catholic Church, or how far they may be excused or justified as a reaction against certain extravagances of the mediæval Church, yet a few reflections of a general character suggest themselves [1] The mere existence of such Confessions of Faith as binding on all or any of the members of a Christian community is inconsistent with the great principles on which the Protestant bodies justified their separation from the Church, the right of private judgment Has not any member as just a right to criticize and to reject them as his forefathers had a right to reject the Catholic creeds or the canons of general councils? [2] They appear to violate another prominent doctrine of the Reformers, the sufficiency of Holy Scripture to salvation If the Bible alone is enough, what need is there of adding articles? If it is rejoined that they are not additions to but merely explanations of the Word of God, the further question arises, amid the many explanations, more or less at variance with each other given by the different sects of Protestantism, who is to decide which is the true one? [3] Their professed object being to secure uniformity, the experience of three hundred years has proved to us what may not have been foreseen by their originators, that they have had a diametrically opposite result, and have been productive, not of union, but of variance.

As it would be impossible within the limits of a work like the present to insert the original documents in full, a short account is annexed of the principal Protestant confessions of faith, with a general view of their contents, a more detailed description being given of the two confessions of Augsburg and Basle, the former as deviating least, the latter as being one of the most widely removed from the standard of Catholic teaching

Confession of Augsburg [A D 1530] This formal statement of faith was drawn up by Melanchthon, Jonas, Pomeranus, and others, at the suggestion of the Elector of Saxony, for presentation to Charles V, and the States of the German Empire. Clement VII who was Pope at this time, had been urged to call a council in which the new tenets and certain alleged grievances might be openly and fairly discussed, but he took a different view of the policy which it was desirable to pursue, and called upon the Emperor to stamp out heresy by violent acts of repression Charles, however, having a Turkish war in view, was unwilling to encounter a civil war, and procured permission to summon a local council at Augsburg for the purpose of allaying divisions Here the Confession which takes its name from that town although it was merely an enlarged form of articles previously drawn up at Schwabach and Marburg, was presented to the Emperor in Latin and German, being read aloud in the latter language by Christopher Bayer, Chancellor of Saxony

The Confession of Augsburg consists of twenty-eight articles, the first twenty-one being definitions of doctrine, the latter seven protests against error in practice The first article treated on the Unity of the Godhead and the Trinity The second on original sin The third on the Two Natures, and the Incarnation the Atonement, the Descent to Hell, the Ascension, and the future coming to judgment of Jesus Christ. The fourth on justification by faith, which faith, it is explained in the fifth and sixth articles, is formed by the Holy Spirit, ordinarily imparted to Christians through the ministration of the Word and Sacraments, and productive of good works as its fruits, which are enjoined by God, and are to be performed in a spirit of obedience to Him The seventh asserts that there is only one Church, whose unity consists in identity of doctrine and sacraments, not in uniformity of ceremonial or practice The eighth that sacraments do not lose their effect though administered by evil persons The ninth that Baptism is necessary to salvation, and that Infant Baptism is to be retained The tenth asserts the real presence in the Eucharist, the oldest Latin copy in these words—"That in the Lord's Supper the Body and Blood of Christ are truly present and distributed to those who eat" The German translation thus "That the true Body and true Blood of the Lord are indeed present under the species of bread and wine in the Lord's Supper" The eleventh ordains that private confession should be retained, but that an exact enumeration of sins committed is not always necessary The twelfth asserts that penitence consists in contrition and faith, but that it is not genuine unless accompanied by its inseparable fruits, good works The thirteenth that faith in the promises annexed to them is necessary for a beneficial use of the sacraments, which are not mere signs on man's part of his profession of Christianity, but pledges of God's love towards him The fourteenth that only those duly appointed may preach and administer the sacraments The fifteenth that church ceremonies should be universally observed, though not as in themselves necessary to salvation, nor as meriting grace, nor as a satisfaction for sin In the sixteenth the authority of civil magistrates is declared to be legitimate The seventeenth asserts the future coming of Christ to judgment, and the eternity of His rewards and punishments The eighteenth that the human will and reason cannot be absolutely just in their decisions unless illumined by the Holy Spirit. The nineteenth that God is not the cause of sin The twentieth that good works are indispensable, though the efficacious cause of the remission of sin is the meritorious sacrifice of Christ, and not those works in themselves The twenty-first that on this principle the merits of the saints are to be considered as objects for our own imitation, but not as possessed of any efficacy apart from the merits of Christ The last seven articles consisted of protests against certain abuses which were represented as having recently sprung up in the Church

The first against the withholding of the cup from the laity. The second against the compulsory celibacy of the clergy The third against the saying masses for money, special words being introduced to prove that these words were not aimed against the mass itself (retinetur enim missa apud nos, et summâ reverentiâ celebratur) The fourth was against the necessity of a special enumeration of sins in auricular confession The fifth against the particular enumeration of the varieties of food to be abstained from at times of fasting The sixth, against irrevocable monastic vows The seventh against the growth of spiritual power beyond its proper limits, and its interference in secular matters and with royal prerogatives

In conclusion, it was hinted that other abuses might have been named, such as indulgences, pilgrimages, the interference of regulars with the duties of the secular clergy, and a few other points, but that they were omitted because the compilers wished to manifest their conformity to the Catholic Church, both in doctrine and ceremonies, and the absence of any intention on their part to introduce any new or impious dogmas

Only a few persons on the Catholic side, among them the Archbishop of Cologne and the Bishop of Augsburg, were content to accept this confession as it stood A committee was immediately formed by the majority to draw up a confutation, which, while accepting certain of the articles, was a direct rejection of others, especially the last seven This document was submitted to the Emperor on August 3rd of the same year He at first ordered the reforming party to accept it, but finding his directions ineffectual, allowed a conference to be held on August 16th between Eck, Bernard of Hagen, and Vehe on the Catholic side, and Melanchthon, Pontanus, and Heller on the Lutheran This conference came to nothing. The Emperor then, having been previously authorized by the Pope, held out a prospect of a general council, if the Reformers would allow ecclesiastical matters to remain *in statu quo* until it could be summoned together, an offer which would probably have been accepted had it been made a few months earlier, but which was now unanimously rejected, and the conference separated on November 19th without any conciliation having been effected

The Confession of Augsburg—rejected by the Catholic Church as too Protestant, and by the Anabaptists and Swiss reformers as too Catholic, especially on account of its assertion of the Real Presence in the Holy Eucharist—became eventually [A D 1577] the distinctive formula of the Lutherans Luther himself said respecting it, in a letter addressed to the Elector of Saxony [May 15th, 1530] · "It pleases me extremely, and I do not know how to alter it for the better."[1] An apology for it, composed by Melanchthon, and published A D 1531, is also still considered one of the symbolical books of the Lutherans

Confession of Basle [A D 1532-6] This was also called the Helvetic or Mylhusian Confession, and is of importance as being one of the most widely accepted of the many confessions of faith promulgated in the sixteenth century It was composed originally in German only, by the ministers of the Protestants at Basle, who met together under a feeling, shared by many others, that the Lutheran Confession of Augsburg retained far too much of both Catholic doctrine and practice, especially with reference to the sacraments and sacramental ordinances This first edition, known as that of Basle, became more strictly the Helvetic Confession, where it had been reconstructed [A D 1536] by Bucer, Capito, and the theologians of Wurtemberg, in the name of all the Swiss churches, and had been accepted by them in the following year at a synod held at Smalkalden Another edition, having been revised by Bullinger, was published in Latin soon after A D 1560, and after being publicly accepted by the magistrates of Mulhausen, was approved and subscribed generally by all the Protestant Evangelical communities In a short Latin preface, it is said to be accepted by all the "ministers of the Church of Christ" in Switzerland (Zurich, Berne, Mulhausen, Geneva, Schafhausen, and other leading towns being especially named), "as a testimony to all the faithful that they remain in the unity of the true and ancient Church of Christ, teaching no new or erroneous doctrines, and having no connection with any sects or heresies, a fact of which all pious persons are invited to assure themselves by its perusal"

The Confession of Basle consisted of twenty-seven articles of various length The first five treated of Holy Scripture, which each man was to interpret for himself by the light of love and faith, rejecting human traditions, however probable or generally received, if based on any other principle of interpretation. The sixth treated on one God and Three Persons The seventh, eighth, and ninth on the fall, original sin, and free-will, the latter meaning our independent ability to do

[1] The exact words are "Die gefallet mir fast wohl, und weiss nichts daran zu bessern, noch zu andern, wurde sich auch nicht schicken, denn ich so sanft und leise nicht treten kann"

evil, but our inability to do good, unless prevented by the grace of God The tenth and eleventh on the Person, Nature, and Work of Christ The twelfth and thirteenth assert that under the Gospel we are saved by the merits of Christ only, and not by good works The fourteenth that there is an invisible church, whose limits are known to God only, though possessed of external rites and discipline. The fifteenth, that the power of the keys is not confined to any assigned order of men, but is freely bestowed by God on what persons and in what manner He will The sixteenth, seventeenth and eighteenth, while rejecting the Pope, grant the wisdom of retaining for the Church the power of setting apart pious and competent persons for the ministry The nineteenth describes the duties of ministers to be the preaching forgiveness of sin through Christ, constant prayer for the people, the study and defence of the Bible, and the admonishing, and, if necessary, excluding by church discipline those who lead scandalous lives The twentieth treats of the sacraments, which are not only bare signs of union but symbols of divine grace, and like the ministry of the Word, are the means through which God, the sole Fountain of grace, is pleased to work The twenty-first of Baptism, which is to be administered to infants, because charity presupposes the offspring of Christian parents to be of the number of the elect. The twenty-second of the Lord's Supper, in which men contemplate Christ crucified, and feed on him by faith (quæ quidem percipiuntur fide—sanguinem fidei oculis intuentes, ac salutem nostram non sine cœlestis vitæ gustu meditantes) The twenty-third, twenty-fourth and twenty-fifth of church assemblies, from which vases, vestments, torches, altars, gold, silver, images, and all such profane adjuncts are to be excluded, and all those who teach new or impious doctrines are to be banished The twenty-sixth of civil magistrates, whose authority is recognised, and part of whose duty is considered to be the defence of true religion by the suppression of blasphemy The twenty-seventh of marriage, which ought to have both a religious and a civil sanction, and of monastic celibacy, which is declared to be an abominable superstition

This confession was received as orthodox by all the Reformed non Lutheran bodies in Switzerland, France, and Flanders, and eventually became the standard of doctrine of all Protestant Evangelical Churches

Confession of Belgium [A D 1561] In the earlier years of the Reformation, the Belgian Protestants designated themselves "Associates of the Conference of Augsburg," assuming this title from political motives, because Lutherans were regarded at the Spanish Court as more orthodox, and therefore more tolerable than the disciples of Calvin; but in A D 1561 they ventured to produce a confession of their own It was first composed by Guy de Bres in the Walloon language, and was printed in French in the following year [A D 1562] It was subsequently approved by the Protestant Synod of Flanders [A.D 1579], and confirmed at the Synod of Dort, at the same time that the five Arminian Articles, which had been put out nine years previously, were condemned [A D 1619], and again at the Hague [A D 1651]

In its contents it is very similar to that adopted by the French Reformed Church, its tone being ultra-Zwinglian on all points connected with the Sacraments, especially the Holy Communion, in which the elements are declared to be mere symbols, which ought only to be received by those who are regenerate, not by Baptism, but by the eternal decree of Almighty God [Art 35]

Confession of Bohemia [A D 1532] This was published in Bohemia after having been submitted for the approval of Luther, Melanchthon, and the academy of Wurtemburg It was afterwards formally presented to Ferdinand, King of Hungary and Bohemia [A D 1535]

Gallican Confession. The first Protestants in France were called Lutherans, and were inclined to the doctrines of that Reformer, but the proximity of Geneva and Lausanne, and the zeal of Calvin, Beza, and others, led them to adopt those more fully developed Protestant tenets whose holders are known in history as the Huguenots (Eingenossen, confederates) Their first synod was held privately in Paris [A D 1559], at which a confession, a catechism, and a directory of public worship drawn up by Calvin were adopted A fuller confession of faith, compiled by Beza, was presented to Charles IX. at Poisy [A D 1561], as that of the United French Protestants, signed by the Queen of Navarre, her son Henry IV, the Prince of Condé, and other distinguished persons Five years afterwards a copy was sent to all the French pastors, and having been accepted by them, it has been considered since that time [A D 1566] as the confession of faith of the French Protestant Church

Confession of Heidelberg or *Palatine Confession* [A D 1575] The Palatine countries oscillated during the greater part of the sixteenth century between the two forms of Reformation presented by Luther and Calvin Lutheranism having first got a footing in the country, was abolished by Frederick III, Elector Palatine [A D 1560], restored by Lewis [A.D. 1576], and again abolished by John Casimir [A D 1583] The Palatine Catechism composed by Zechariah Ursinus in 1563, and the Confession, which was drawn up in 1575, were received by the whole body of Protestants in those parts, and obtained recognition at the Synod of Dort [A D 1619]

The Scottish Confession [A D 1560] was drawn up by Knox and his associates, and was ratified by a Parliament held at Edinburgh, in which the Reforming party were supreme It was subscribed by James VI. in his youth, and again received public recognition in A.D 1590, 1596, and 1638, in which year it was formally submitted and approved along with the National Covenant at a General Assembly held at Glasgow [SCOTTISH KIRK]

Tetrapolitan or *Argentine Confession* [A D 1531] The Zwinglian party present at Augsburg were not contented with much of the tenor of that confession, especially with reference to the Holy Eucharist; and, in consequence, in the following year the four imperial cities of Strasburg, Constance, Menningen and Lindau accepted another confession which had probably been drawn up in the interim by Martin Bucer, and which was presented by them to Charles V. They agreed in the main with the confession of the preceding year, but their modified views of the doctrine of the Holy Communion were thus expressed "All that the Evangelists, Paul and the holy Fathers have written respecting the venerable Sacrament of the Body and Blood of Christ our preachers teach with the greatest fidelity Hence, with singular earnestness, they constantly proclaim that goodness of Christ towards His followers whereby, no less now than at His last Supper, to all His sincere disciples, as oft as they repeat this Supper, He condescends to give by the Sacraments His real Body and His real Blood, to be truly eaten and drunken, as the food and drink of their souls, by which they are nourished to eternal life, so that He lives and abides in them, and they in Him" Soon afterwards, for the sake of union, they dropped their distinctive views, and subscribing to the Confession of Augsburg, became part of the Lutheran Church

The Confession of Westminster [A D. 1643] was, generally speaking, the product of the Puritan agitation of the seventeenth century but the immediate work of the Assembly of Divines held at Westminster. [PURITANS]

They drew up a Directory of Public Worship and a Confession of Faith, which bears decided marks of the Presbyterian ascendancy, both in its strong predestinarian views and in the inconsistency of claiming for men the right, on the score of conscience, to desert the Catholic Church, and yet to impose on others their own Presbyterian views under severe civil and ecclesiastical penalties The confession was approved by the General Assembly of the Church of Scotland [A D 1647], and again [A D. 1690] on the renewed establishment of Presbyterianism after the Revolution, when it was ratified as the national standard of belief It is printed officially in a volume issued by the Scottish Kirk under the title "Confessions of Faith"

A Saxon Confession was drawn up in Latin by Melanchthon [A D. 1557] for presentation at the Council of Trent

The Confession of Wurtemburg, composed for the same purpose, was presented [A D 1552] by Christopher Duke of that country

A Polish Confession of the Calvinistic Poles was submitted at the Synod of Gzenger [A D. 1570]

To the above list some writers have erroneously added the Greek Confession of Cyril Lucar, Patriarch of Constantinople [A.D. 1621-1638], submitted to and accepted by a Greek synod [A D 1629], and the Anglican Thirty-nine Articles, ratified by the Upper and Lower Houses of Convocation [A D 1571], forgetting that both these Churches have repudiated the uncatholic interpretation of which those articles have to some persons appeared capable, by their formal acceptance in public documents of the early general councils, and by ever refusing by act or word to forego their right and title to be considered living portions of Christ's Holy Catholic Church

[Kocher's *Bibliotheca Theologicæ Symbolicæ. Catechetical History of Reformed Churches*, Jena, 1756-80 Niemeyer's *Collection of Confessions Harmonia Confessionum*, Geneva, 1581. *Sylloge Confessionum*, Oxon, 1827 *Corpus Confessionum Aurel Allobrog* 1612]

PROTESTERS [ANTIBURGHERS. ORIGINAL SECEDERS RESOLUTIONERS]

PROZYMITES. A controversial term used by some mediæval writers as a designation of the Eastern Church for its use of leavened bread [ζύμη] in the celebration of the Holy Eucharist So Eastern controversialists have called the Latins by the converse term of Azymites

PRUSSIAN PROTESTANTS [GERMAN PROTESTANTS UNITED EVANGELICAL CHURCH]

PSALLIANS [EUCHITES]

PSATHYRIANS A party of Arians were so called, as followers of Theoctistus, a zealous pastry-cook [ψαθυροπώλης] of Constantinople, who maintained the heresy of Arius in the form that the First Person in the Holy Trinity existed before the Son had a being; thus denying the Eternal Generation of the latter The Psathyrians were condemned at the Council of Antioch, A D 361 They were also called Douleians and Cyrtians. [Thedor *Hær fab* iv]

PSEUDAPOSTOLI [FALSE APOSTLES]

PSILANTHROPISTS Those who maintain the extreme form of Unitarian doctrine that our Lord was merely [ψιλός] a man [ἄνθρωπος] and not God and man [Θεάνθρωπος] in one Person

PSYCHICS A party name given to the orthodox by the TERTULLIANISTS, who called themselves "Spirituals" [Prædest *Hær* lxxxvi]. The distinction was drawn from St Paul's First Epistle to the Corinthians, where he writes of the ψυχικός, the "natural man" who cannot receive "the things of the Spirit of God," and the πνευματικός, or "spiritual man," who discerns them spiritually [1 Cor ii 14, 15]

PSYCHOPANNYCHITES A controversial term for those who maintain the opinion that souls sleep in a state of unconsciousness during the interval between death and the general resurrection. Calvin wrote a treatise against them in 1534, and there is much against them in Henry More's works. Pagitt says in his "Heresiography," written about 1638, that the heresy revived in his time through the publication of a work entitled "Man's Mortality"

PSYCHOPNEUMONES Those who maintained the opinion that the souls of the good after death become angels, and that the souls of the evil become devils [Aug *Hæres* lxxviii, Prædest *Hæres* lxxviii]

PTOLEMÆANS A Gnostic sect of the second century, followers of Ptolemy, "whose school," says Irenæus, "may be described as a bud from that of Valentinus" [Iren *adv Hær.* i pref. 2] Irenæus also associates Ptolemy with

Heracleon as if the "Æons of Ptolemy and Heracleon" were their joint invention [*ibid* ii 4] In another chapter the same writer describes the doctrines of the followers of Ptolemy and Colorbasus [*ibid.* i 12] Ptolemy is also named by Tertullian, but without any particulars of his history [Tertull *contr Valent* xxxiii], and in a very few words by Philaster [*Hær* xxxix], Augustine [*Hær* xiii], Prædestinatus [*Hær* xiii], and the continuator of Tertullian [Pseudo-Tertull *Hær* xii] Epiphanius gives an *Epistola ad Florum* written by Ptolemy The only difference between the Ptolemæans and the Valentinians in general appears to have been in respect to the number of Æons which they invented for their respective systems, and the name of Ptolemy is associated particularly with that of Heracleon as regards a duplex system of four [HERACLEONITES Epiph *Hær* xxxiii]

PUBLICANI [POPLICIANS]

PUCCIANITES The followers of Francis Puccius, an heretical writer of the sixteenth century, who maintained the principle that Christ having made an Atonement for all men by His death, no other means are now necessary for salvation than those which are provided by natural religion This heresy he embodied in a work published in the year 1592, and dedicated to Clement VIII

PUERIS SIMILES A sect of Anabaptists spoken of by Bullinger in his treatise on Anabaptism They practised childish tricks under the notion that this was being childlike, as required by the Gospel precept of entering into the kingdom of Heaven by becoming as a little child Hence they would ride upon sticks and hobby-horses, and take off their clothes that they might practise the innocence of childhood, ending, of course, in practising the very reverse.

PURITANS A party in the Church of England of the sixteenth and seventeenth centuries which endeavoured to introduce the Genevan doctrine and discipline of Calvin in the place of the system established by the English Reformation

The name was derived from the frequent assertion of those who composed the party, that the Church of England was corrupted with the remains of Popery, and that what they desired was a "pure" system of doctrine and discipline, but the English word "Puritans" happens accidentally to represent the Greek name "Cathari" which had been assumed by the Novatians, and which had been adopted in Germany during the Middle Ages in the vernacular form "Ketzer" for the Albigenses and other opponents of the Church It first came into use as the designation of an English Church party about the year 1564 [Fuller's *Ch Hist* ix 66], but after a few years it got to be used also as inclusive of many who had separated from the Church of England It was gradually superseded as regards the latter by the names of their various sects, as Independents, Presbyterians, Baptists, etc, and as regards the former by the term "Nonconformists" At a still later time, towards the end of the seventeenth century, the Church Puritans were represented by "Low Churchmen," and the Non-church Puritans by "Dissenters"

The presence of a Puritan party in the Church of England is, however, traceable for two centuries before the name of "Puritan" was assumed In the fourteenth century the common people had become alienated from their parish priests by the influence of the Friars, who had authority from the Pope to preach and to receive confessions wherever they pleased, and quite independently of the ordinary clergy This extra-parochial system of mission clergy weakened the hold of the Church upon the populace at large, and, when the Friars themselves began to lose their influence, alienation from the clergy developed into alienation from the Church Thus arose the LOLLARDS of the fifteenth century, a party which made no attempt to set up separate places of worship or a separate ministry, but which introduced its anti-sacerdotal principles into many parish churches, and made many of the clergy as strong opponents of the existing ecclesiastical system as was Wickliffe himself During the trying times of the Reformation the party thus formed was largely augmented by those whose opposition to Romish abuses had, by a similar excess, developed into opposition to the whole of the established ecclesiastical system, men who thought that "pure" doctrine and "pure" worship could only be attained by an utter departure from all that had been believed and practised during the times when the Church of England had contracted impurities of doctrine and worship through popish influences

While Luther's movement was at its height the party which thus became the progenitors of the Puritans was formed into a society under the name of "The Christian Brethren," which seems from the faint view we get of it to have been very similar to that organized by John Wesley two centuries later The headquarters of the Brethren were in London, but they had gained a footing at both the Universities, apparently among the undergraduates and younger graduates As early as the year 1523, a body of Cambridge residents "met often at a house called 'the White Horse' to confer together with others, in mockery called Germans, because they conversed much in the books of the divines of Germany brought thence This house was chosen because those of King's College, Queen's College, and St John's might come in at the back-side and so be the more private and undiscovered" [Strype's *Eccl Mem* i 568, ed 1822] Among those mentioned as so meeting are the names of Barnes, Arthur, Bilney, Latimer, and Coverdale, familiarly known as precursors of the Puritan movement in Edward VI and Queen Elizabeth's reigns A few years later, in 1527, similar gatherings were detected at Oxford, where the names of Frith, Taverner, Udal, Farrar, and Cox, Edward VI's tutor, are found among those who met together for the same purpose [*ibid* i 569] Among the Oxford party the men of Wolsey's College held a conspicuous position, and his leniency towards all who were brought before him on charges of heresy was very striking

The principles which were developed among the more extreme section of these early Puritans may be seen by an extract from a work written by William Tyndale (himself a friar and a priest), who was their representative man. Writing of the ministerial office, he says "Sub-deacon, deacon, priest, bishop, cardinal, patriarch, and pope, be names of offices and service, or should be, and not sacraments There is no promise coupled therewith If they minister their offices truly, it is a sign that Christ's Spirit is in them; if not, that the devil is in them . . O dreamers and natural beasts, without the seal of the Spirit of God, but sealed with the mark of the beast, and with cankered consciences. . . By a priest understand nothing but an elder to teach the younger, and to bring them unto the full knowledge and understanding of Christ, and to minister the sacraments which Christ ordained, which is also nothing but to preach Christ's promises According, therefore, as every man believeth God's promises, longeth for them, and is diligent to pray unto God to fulfil them, so is his prayer heard, and as good is the prayer of a cobbler as of a cardinal, and of a butcher as of a bishop, and the blessing of a baker that knoweth the truth is as good as the blessing of our most holy father the pope . . Neither is there any other manner of ceremony at all required in making our spiritual officers than to choose an able person, and then to rehearse him his duty, and give him his charge, and so put him in his room" [Tyndale's *Obed of Christ Man*, Park Soc ed pp 254-9] Such principles struck at the whole ecclesiastical system of the Church of England, for Apostolical succession, Episcopal ordination, and a supernatural ministerial gift, have always been recognised as its foundation-stones

These floating elements of Puritanism had, however, very little compactness and unity except in the one particular of opposition to the principles and practices which then prevailed in the Church of England But in the latter years of Henry VIII's reign, Calvin was consolidating a system of doctrine, worship, and ecclesiastical discipline which was exactly calculated to weld together in a useable form the individual particles which had previously been comparatively powerless for want of cohesion. Calvin gained some personal influence in England, during the reign of Edward VI, by means of pertinacious letters addressed to the King, the Protector Somerset, and Archbishop Cranmer, but the principles of his system were chiefly propagated through the introduction of some of his foreign disciples into positions of influence in the Church of England Thus an Italian named Pietro Vermigli, who had been an Augustinian friar, was made Regius Professor of Divinity at Oxford, and is known to history as Peter Martyr [A.D 1500-62] A similar appointment was made at Cambridge, where the Regius Professor of Divinity was a German, named Martin Bucer [A D 1491-1551], who had been a Dominican friar Paul Bucher, or Fagius, a companion of Bucer, was destined for the professorship of Hebrew at Cambridge, but died in 1549 Bernard Ochinus [A D 1487-1564], ex-Vicar-General of the Capuchin Friars and Confessor to Pope Paul III., came from Geneva with Peter Martyr, and was made Canon of Canterbury, being afterwards banished from place to place on the Continent for his Socinianism and his advocacy of polygamy John à Lasco [A D 1499-1560], a Pole, was an inmate of Lambeth Palace, where he and other foreigners formed a kind of Calvinistic Privy Council to Cranmer,[1] and John Knox [A D 1505-72], a Scotch priest, was at one time carrying out his duties as chaplain to the young King, and at another going on a roving commission to preach down the Church in Northumberland, Durham, and the other Northern counties [Jackson's *Works*, iii 273]

Under these influences, and others of a similar nature, the country was made familiar with the Puritan scheme of Ecclesiasticism by which the Calvinist party wished to supplant, or as they said to complete, the English Reformation. [1] First, Presbyterianism was to supersede Episcopacy, as it had already done in Geneva, and as it shortly did in Scotland [2] Secondly, The Book of Common Prayer was to be so altered that all responses, especially the Litany, were to be done away with, as well as everything that had come out of the ancient services and Divine Service was to consist chiefly of extempore prayer and preaching [3] Thirdly, The "Discipline" was to be introduced into every parish, in the shape of a kind of parish vestry, which was to have authority to superintend the morals of all the parishioners, dealing out spiritual censures and excommunications upon all offenders, as was being done under Calvin's austere rule in Geneva To this latter point the party attached great importance, the following statements respecting it being collected from their writings by Bishop Bancroft "'The want of the eldership is the cause of all evil It is not to be hoped for that any Commonwealth will flourish without it This Discipline is no small part of the Gospel, it is of the substance of it It is the right stuff and gold for building the Church of God This would make the Church a chaste spouse, having a wonderful brightness as the morning, fair as the moon, pure as the sun, and terrible like an army with banners Without this Discipline there can be no true religion. This government is the sceptre whereby alone Christ Jesus ruleth among men The Churches of God in Denmark, Saxony, Tigurin, etc, wanting this government, are to be accounted maimed and unperfect. The establishing of the Presbyteries is the full placing of Christ in His Kingdom. They that reject this Discipline refuse

[1] Heylin says that à Lasco was the first to introduce into England the singular irreverent custom of sitting instead of kneeling to receive the Holy Communion, and that he published a pamphlet in defence of the practice Heylin also states that it was à Lasco's influence at Court which led to the Holy Table being brought down from the east end of the chancel to the middle of the church or chancel [Heylin's *Hist Presbyt* 283]

to have Christ reign over them, and deny Him in effect to be their King or their Lord It is the blade of a shaken sword in the hand of the Cherubins, to keep the way of the tree of life' Ridiculous men, and bewitched," is his indignant comment on these quotations, for which he gives the references, "as though Christ's sovereignty, kingdom and lordship were nowhere acknowledged or to be found but where half a dozen artizans, shoemakers, tinkers, and tailors, with their preacher and reader (eight or nine Cherubins forsooth), do rule the whole parish" [Bancroft's *Dangerous Positions and Proceedings, published and practised within this Iland of Brytaine, under pretence of Reformation, and for the Presbiteriall Discipline*, 1593, p 43]

This Puritan "platform," as it was called, attracted large numbers, especially among the lower classes, in London, Norwich, Northampton, and other large towns and its hold upon its devotees was so great that they went willingly to the martyr's fire on its behalf, nine-tenths of those who suffered in the reign of Queen Mary and Philip of Spain suffering for it under the name of "the Gospel."[1] It was first formally set forth in England by Martin Bucer in a Latin work entitled "De Regno Christi Jesu Servatoris nostri," published in the year 1557 Bucer had written his work in the year 1551 for the instruction of Edward VI, and there is probably some truth in the assertion made by the Puritans that it made so much impression on the young King, that if he had grown up he would have imposed their "platform" upon his subjects, and thus, according to their idea, "perfected the Reformation"

In the early part of Queen Elizabeth's reign the Church was embittered by the contentions of the Puritan clergy respecting the ceremonies and vestments prescribed for their use by the Book of Common Prayer Although the Lutherans had continued to use the vestments, and many of the ceremonies, which had been in use before the Reformation, these had been entirely discarded by the Calvinists and some of the younger English clergy, under the lead of Bishop Hooper (who had lived abroad from 1540 to 1547 among the Calvinists), wished to discard them also from the Church of England The difference of opinion on the subject was carried to Frankfort by those who fled from England during the reign of Mary, and the extraordinary bitterness of the disputes which arose there are recorded in a volume entitled "The Troubles at Frankford" On their return to England the Calvinistic section of the clergy came back with their antipathy to old customs much strengthened, and they were accustomed to speak of them as "relics of the Amorites," "dregs of Popery," and "leavings of Idolatry" The use of cope and surplice, altar crosses and of "lights before the Sacrament," bowing at the Name of Jesus, signing with the Cross in Baptism, and using the wedding-ring in marriages, kneeling at the reception of the Holy Communion, and making responses in Divine Service,—all these were regarded as antichristian customs which could not be borne with by those who desired the "pure Gospel" as it was preached in the little town of Geneva Even the square academical cap with the clergyman's strait-collared and long-tailed cassock or "gown" were looked upon as superstitious, and when the "Council's pleasure" was declared to the London ministers "that strictly ye keep the unity of apparel, like this man who stands here canonically habited with a square cap, a scholar's gown priestlike, a tippet, and in the church a linen surplice, . great was the anguish and distress of those ministers, who cried out for compassion to themselves and families, saying 'We shall be killed in our souls for this pollution of ours'"[2] [Neal's *Hist Purit* i 211, ed 1732] In addition to all these objections, they objected also to "the bishops affecting to be thought a superior order to presbyters, and claiming the sole right of ordination and the use of the keys," to the bishops being Lords of Parliament, to the titles and offices of archdeacons, deans, chapters, and other officials belonging to cathedrals, to the jurisdiction of bishops and their chancellors in spiritual courts, to the want of a godly discipline, to the observance of Festivals or Holydays, to the cathedral mode of worship, and the chanting of Psalms by turns, to the use of organs or other musical instruments, to the frequent repetition of the Lord's Prayer, the use of responses in Divine Service, and the use of forms of prayer in general, to the use of godfathers and godmothers at Baptism, to the use of the rite of Confirmation by laying on of the Bishop's hands, and, in short, to nearly everything that could be named in the customs and ceremonies of the Church of England [*ibid.* 235-240]

It has been the practice of many writers respecting this period to represent the ceremonies and customs which the Puritans thus declined to

[1] Nearly all of these were mechanics ("trades' men" as they were then called) or agricultural labourers The historians of Dissent had observed this fact when they wrote that "not the new converts in the reign of Edward, but the original Wickliffites, furnished the martyrs" [Bogue and Bennett's *Hist Diss* i 54] It is very singular to find how exactly Foxe's accounts of these martyrs of Queen Mary's reign agree with the character given of the Lollards of the fourteenth century by their contemporary Knyghton "They were all," he says, "like their master, too eloquent, and too much for other people in all disputes and contentions by word of mouth being powerful in words, strong in prating, exceeding all in making speeches, and out talking everybody in litigious disputations Though they were never so lately converted to this sect, they had all one manner of speech, or the same way of talking, and wonderfully agreed in the same opinion Both men and women immediately commenced teachers of the Gospel in their mother tongue" The Puritan martyrs were not, however, "agreed in the same opinion," for their historian Neal records the fierce bitterness of their quarrels about predestination and election even while they were in prison awaiting their execution [Neal's *Hist. Purit* ii 103, ed. 1732]. Of a similar character were the disputes among the exiles at Frankfort [*Troubles at Frankford*] respecting ceremonies and vestments

[2] Heylin immortalizes a Deacon named Tyms, who wore a short coat, and different coloured stockings on his two legs below it, to shew his abhorrence of Popish garments. [Heylin's *Hist Presbyt.* 242]

observe as trifles of no importance, the non-observance of which ought to have been conceded to them for the sake of peace by the rulers of the Church But while some of them—such as kneeling at the Holy Communion—are far from unimportant, the resistance which was offered to them was only a part of that determined resistance to the whole system of the Church of England by the pressure of which the party hoped, in the end, to have the Calvinistic system substituted for it Never were men more determined to have their own way, to work for it, to suffer for it, to fight for it and short of giving them their own way entirely there was no peace to be had with the Puritans.[1]

The Act of Supremacy [1 Eliz 1], which was passed in the year 1559, provided for the appointment of Commissioners to exercise the Visitatorial Jurisdiction of the Crown, and advantage was taken of this provision to establish a permanent Ecclesiastical Commission, which, under the name of the "High Commission Court," became as odious to the Puritans as that Judicial Committee of the Privy Council which had acquired the name of the "Star Chamber Court,"[2] and both of them were abolished together in 1641 by 16 Car I ch 10 These commissioners endeavoured in vain to enforce obedience to the "Injunctions" and "Advertisements" which were set forth by the Crown with the object of securing uniformity Many of the Puritan clergy were deprived of their benefices on account of their refusal to obey the law, but notwithstanding this "they travelled up and down the counties from church to church," says Bishop Jewell, "preaching where they could get leave, as if they were apostles," and supported themselves as their predecessors the friars had done, by the alms of the people The University of Cambridge added to the number of these roving preachers, by exercising a privilege granted by Pope Alexander VI, by which the University could license twelve special preachers a year, who should be at liberty to preach anywhere in England without Episcopal license or control "Lecturers" were also elected by many parishes, for the express purpose of maintaining Puritan doctrine in churches where the rector or vicar was of a different colour, these lecturers fanned the flame of discord by their refusal to recognise in any degree the authority of the Prayer Book They were educated to their work chiefly by means of "prophesyings," which were meetings of clergy associated together for the purpose of discussing difficult questions of Scripture Highly as these were praised by Archbishop Grindal [Fuller's *Ch Hist* ix 4], the tone of the discussions is indicated by the Confession of Faith each was required to subscribe, which condemned among other things "distinctions of meats, apparels, and days, and briefly all the ceremonies and whole order of Papistry, which they call the Hierarchy" (that is, of the Church of England, which was then commonly so called), "which are a devilish confusion, established as it were in spite of God, and to the reproach of religion"[3] [Strype's *Ann* i 41]

To secure, as far as possible, the appointment of such clergy in vacant parishes, a Presbyterian system of trial and of election by the people was established to supplement the ordinary system of presentation and institution. Thus one Axton, Rector of Moreton Corbet in Leicestershire, when brought before the Bishop of Peterborough for refusing to wear the surplice and to use the ceremonies enjoined in the Prayer Book, denies that he is rector or "parson," but declares that he was chosen pastor "by the free election of the people and leave of the patron After I had preached about six weeks, by way of probation, I was chosen by one consent of them all, a sermon being preached by one of my brethren, setting forth the mutual duties of pastor and people" [Neal's *Hist Purit* i 258] The bishop reminded him that he received his tithes because he had been instituted and inducted as "parson" of the parish, but Axton's view was, "I receive these temporal things of the people because I, being their pastor, do minister to them spiritual things" Another of their number, when examined before the High Commission on the same subject, says, "I think they observe as much as they can the order prescribed in the said Book of Discipline, as about Proudloe of Weedenbeck, his admission (as I have heard), and Snapes and Larke The manner whereof is, that they renounce the calling they have had of the bishops, and do take it again from the approbation of the 'Classis' And again, they will be content to accept Orders from the bishop as a civil matter, but do not thereby count themselves ministers until the godly brethren of some Classis have allowed them" He gives, as one instance among many, "one Maister Hocknel," who had been in Orders six or seven years, who was presented to a benefice, and went for his new "call" to Snape, Penry, and some other Puritan clergymen In this case his examination by the Classis and his sermon before them were unsatisfactory, and they refused to "call" him to the ministry "Hereupon," naively says the writer, "Maister Hocknel and they fell out and he (contemning their censure)

[1] This character was given of them even by their friend Bullinger, Calvinist pastor at Zurich, who thus wrote to Beza respecting the Puritan leader at Oxford, Sampson, Dean of Christ Church "Sampson never wrote a letter without filling it with grievances the man is never satisfied When he was here, I used to get rid of him in a friendly way, as well knowing him to be a man of a captious and unquiet disposition England has many characters of this sort, who cannot be at rest, and never can be satisfied" [*Zurich Letters*, ii 152]

[2] This Court stood on the same footing as the modern "Judicial Committee of the Privy Council," which was established by 3 & 4 Gul IV ch 41, and 34 & 35 Vict ch 91

[3] The pious and learned Dr Thomas Jackson wrote respecting these meetings, "But since the liberty of prophesying was taken up, which came but lately into the northern parts (unless it were in the towns of Newcastle and Berwick, where Knox, Mackbray, and Udal had sown their tares), all things have gone so cross and backward in our Church, that I cannot call the history of these forty years to mind, or express my observations upon it, but with a bleeding heart" [Jackson's *Works*, ii 273]

did proceed and took possession of his benefice" [*Danger Posit* 113]

In a similar manner, the Puritan clergy endeavoured gradually to supplant the system of the Prayer Book, first, by shewing extreme contempt for it, and secondly by supplementing it with the system of the Discipline, the singularly dishonest plan which they adopted being thus described by the contemporary writer already quoted "The most of them, that are but doctors (as they term themselves) and readers of lectures in other men's charges, do seldom or never come to the service which is read in the church, according to Her Majesty's laws, but under pretence of studying for their sermons do absent themselves until service be done, or at the least almost finished, and then they come in (gravely I warrant you) and do go to this their own form of service" The form referred to is that of the Book of Discipline, and consisted of a metrical Psalm, a short admonition to the congregation how to prepare themselves rightly to pray, an extempore prayer containing the confession of sins, the Lord's Prayer, and then the sermon After the sermon, other extempore prayers for grace, for profit from the sermon, for the Church, and for all particular callings, then the Lord's Prayer, another metrical Psalm, and a blessing Those who held benefices evaded the use of the Prayer Book by employing "readers," a practice which continued down to quite recent times, the preacher contemptuously ignoring the service by sitting in the vestry till sermon time arrived "The rest of the fraternity," says the contemporary writer from whom these particulars are taken, "that have cures of their own, some of them will have a 'Parliament Minister' (as they term him) under them, to say service, and then he himself dealeth as it hath been noted of the doctor but others that are not able to have such a one, they for their 'safer standing' (as their term is) do use some piece of our service book, and peradventure read a lesson (which things they affirm may be performed as well by those that are not ministers as by them) and then they, in like sort, do begin their own ministerial function, and proceed according to the foresaid fashion, subscribed unto and promised"[1] [Bancroft's *Danger Posit* 103] The Puritan laity adopted a similar plan of escaping the yoke of the Prayer Book a later writer saying of them, "They will hear our sermons but not our Common Prayer, and of these you may see every Sunday in our streets, sitting or standing about our doors, who, when the prayers are done, rush into our churches to hear our sermon" [Pagitt's *Heresiography*, p 94, ed 1662] Thus the Puritan party endeavoured to minimize to the utmost the ordinary devotional system of the Church and the principle on which its ministry is grounded, and magnify—even by evasion and misrepresentation—the Presbyterian system which was thus subtlely creeping in

The active measures which were taken by the Ecclesiastical Commissioners at last drove many of the Puritan clergy from their ministrations, licensed or unlicensed, in the churches The chief leaders of the separation thus formed were, according to the Church historian Fuller, seven London clergymen, named Colman, Halingham, Benson, Button, White, Rowland, and Hawkins[2] "These had their followers of the laity, who forsook their parish churches and assembled with the deprived ministers, in woods and private houses, to worship God without the offensive habits and ceremonies of the Church" [*ibid* 241] This separation of some of the Puritans from the Church of England took place in the year 1567, on June 19th of which year a congregation of one hundred of them was broken up by the Sheriffs of London in Plumbers' Hall, "which they hired for that day under pretence of a wedding" [Strype's *Life of Grindal*, 315] Another congregation, with Richard Fitz, their pastor, had been detected, and committed to the Bridewell a month before, on May 20th, 1567, but where these met is not known. In the following year some of them appear with the full organization of a separate sect, Grindal writing as follows to Bullinger on July 11th, 1568 'Some London citizens, with four or five ministers, have openly separated from us, and sometimes in private houses, sometimes in fields, and occasionally even in ships, they have held meetings and administered the sacraments Besides this, they have ordained ministers, elders, and deacons after their own way The number of the sect is about two hundred, but consisting of more women than men The Privy Council have lately committed the heads of this faction to prison, and are now using means to put a timely stop to this sect" A few months later Browne is found organizing Independent congregations in London and Norfolk [INDEPENDENTS] and almost at the same time, in the year 1572, Field, one of the writers of the "Admonition to the Parliament," established the first English congregation of Presbyterians among his Admonitionist friends at Wandsworth, near London, the parish of which he had been Lecturer [PRESBYTERIANS] It was in the same year that a book was printed abroad and widely circulated in England, entitled "A Full and Plain Declaration of Ecclesiastical Discipline out of the Word of God, and of the

[1] The writer quoted above speaks of the practice of the brethren in the "New Churchyard in London, and many brables in the country about urging of the natural fathers to become godfathers to their own children" and also of the novel names that were being given to children by the Puritans so early as 1593, such as "The-Lord-is-near, More-trial"—probably the last new-comer of a large family—"Reformation, Discipline, Joy again, Sufficient, From above, Free-gift, More-fruit, Dust, and many other such like" [*Danger Posit.* 104] He gives an instance of a clergyman refusing to baptize a child by the name of "Richard" because it was not a Scripture name

[2] The first three of these, Colman, Halingham, and Benson, were actually Jesuits, or in the employment of Jesuits! There names were set down in a document found on a Jesuit named Heath in 1569, as those of persons employed "to sow faction among the heretics" [Curteis' *Bampt Lect* 63 n 67] That many Jesuits were employed as Puritan preachers is asserted by writers of the time, and their assertions are corroborated by documentary evidence still preserved among the Burleigh Papers [ROMAN CATHOLICS]

Decline of the Church of England from the same" This volume was written by Walter Travers, chaplain and tutor in the family of Lord Burleigh, and afterwards Lecturer at the Temple, where he had that controversy with Hooker, then Master of the Temple, which led the latter to write his immortal work on "the Laws of Ecclesiastical Polity." Travers' volume was introduced by a preface written by Thomas Cartwright [A D 1535-1603], who had been for a few months, in 1570, Margaret Professor of Divinity at Cambridge, and who was for many years the leader of the Puritans within and without the Church Cartwright and Travers were both then connected with the Presbyterian congregation at Wandsworth, and their book was received by the Puritans as the authoritative exposition of the Presbyterian Discipline

But although many of the Puritans thus formed separate sects, a very large proportion of them still continued in the Church, and very subtle measures were taken by some of their leaders a few years later, under Cartwright's advice and direction, for the inoculation of the country with Presbyterian principles in such a manner as to avoid the forfeiture of their benefices. On May 8th, 1582, sixty clergymen from the Eastern Counties met at Cockfield in Suffolk, of which parish one of them, Knewstub, was vicar,[1] to consult about the ordinary Puritan platform, "apparel, matter, form, days, fastings, injunctions," etc They adjourned to Cambridge, and from thence to London, "where they hoped to be concealed by the general resort of the people to Parliament At length, under the guidance of Cartwright, the late Margaret Professor, and of Travers, afterwards Hooker's opponent, and who was at present domestic chaplain and tutor in the family of Lord Burleigh, this Convocation of Puritan Clergy framed the following systematic plan for grafting their new system on to that of the Church The document is of sufficient importance to be given at full length.

"*Concerning Ministers*

"Let no man, though he be an University man, offer himself to the ministry, nor let any man take upon him an uncertain and vague ministry, though it be offered unto him

"But such as be called to the ministry by some certain church, let them impart it unto that *Classis* or *Conference* whereof themselves are, or else unto some greater Church Assembly, and if such shall be found fit by them, then let them be commended by their letters unto the Bishop, that they may be ordained ministers by him.

"Those ceremonies in the Book of Common Prayer which, being taken from Popery, are in controversy, ought to be omitted and given over, if it may be done without danger of being put from the ministry. But if there be any imminent danger to be deprived, then this matter must be communicated to the Classis in which that church is, that by the judgment thereof it may be determined what ought to be done.

"If subscription to the Articles of Religion and to the Book of Common Prayer shall be again urged, it is thought that the Book of Articles may be subscribed unto according to the Statutes 13 Eliz, that is, unto such of them only as contain the sum of Christian faith and doctrine of the Sacraments But for many weighty causes neither the rest of the Articles in that book nor the Book of Common Prayer may be allowed, no, though a man should be deprived of his ministry for it.

"*Concerning Churchwardens*

"It seemeth that churchwardens and collectors for the poor might be thus turned into elders and deacons

"When they are to be chosen let the church have warning fifteen days before of the time of elections, and of the ordinances of the realm, but especially of Christ's ordinance touching appointing of watchmen and overseers in His Church, who are to foresee that none offence or scandal do arise in the Church, and if any such happen, that by them it be duly abolished

"*Of Collectors for the Poor, or Deacons.*

"And touching deacons of both sorts (viz men and women), the church shall be monished what is required by the Apostle, and that they are not to choose men of custom and of course, or of riches, but for their faith, zeal, and integrity, and that the church is to pray in the meantime to be so directed that they make choice of them that be meet.

"Let the names of such as are chosen be published the next Lord's day, and after that, their duties to the church, and the church's towards them shall be declared, then let them be received unto the ministry to which they are chosen with the general prayers of the whole church

"*Of Classes*

"The brethren are to be requested to ordain a distribution of all churches, according to these rules in that behalf that are set down in the Synodical Discipline, touching classical, provincial, comitial, or of commencements and assemblies for the whole kingdom.

"The Classes are to be required to keep acts of memorable matters, which they shall see delivered to the comitial assembly, that from thence they may be brought by the provincial assembly

"They are to deal earnestly with patrons to present fit men whensoever any church is fallen void in that Classis

"The comitial assemblies are to be admonished to make collections for the relief of the poor and of scholars, but especially for the relief of such ministers here as are put out for not subscribing to the articles tendered by the bishops, also for relief of Scottish ministers and others, and for other profitable and necessary uses

"All the provincial synods must continually aforehand foresee in due time to appoint the keeping of their next provincial synods, and for the sending of chosen persons with certain instructions

[1] Oddly enough Cockfield is within a short distance of Hadleigh, where the earliest plans of the Tractarians were laid. See page 196 *b*.

unto the national synod, to be holden whensoever the Parliament for the kingdom shall be called, and at some certain time every year" [*Dangerous Positions and Proceedings*, 1593, p 46, Neal's *Hist Purit.* i 345]

From the contemporary writer just quoted, it appears that the organization thus established soon spread over the country and from the evidence of one of the Puritan ministers, he gives a specimen of it as it was stated to exist about the year 1557 in Northamptonshire "The whole shire was divided into three Classes 1 The Classis of Northamptonshire consisting of these ministers· Master Snape, Master Penry, Master Sibthorpe, Master Edwards, Master Littleton, Master Bradshaw, Master Larke, Master Fleshware, Master Spicer, etc 2 The Classis of Daventry side, consisting of these Master Barebon, Master Rogers, Master King, Master Smart, Master Sharpe, Master Proudloe, Master Elliston, etc 3 The Classis of Kettering side, consisting of these Master Stone, Master Williamson, Master Fawsbrooke, Master Patinson, Master Massey, etc This devise (saith Master Johnson) is commonly received in most parts of England (as I have heard in sundry of our meetings), but especially in Warwickshire, Suffolk, Norfolk, Essex," etc [*Dang Positions*, etc p 77] In these counties, and as far as they were able to do so throughout England, they made a secret survey of all the parishes, ascertaining the value of benefices, the character of incumbent and people, etc "The end propounded of this survey was, viz. that if upon signification to the brethren abroad what was done there, they would likewise make the like survey in other countries, the Parliament (if need required, and to the better furthering of their purposes) might have a general view of all the ministers of England that impugned their desires for the bringing in of discipline and Church government" [*ibid* 88] In addition to these measures, orders were issued to all Puritan clergy that "every minister (as occasion served) should teach the Discipline unto the people as well as the other parts of the Gospel" [*ibid* 134] Every influence possible was also brought to bear on magistrates of all degrees, from the President of Wales downwards, to get them to support the Disciplinarians, even at the expense of disobedience to higher authority [*ibid* 136] and theories about obedience to sovereigns were circulated which were simply those theories of rebellion that were ultimately carried into practice [*ibid* 141]

This matricidal conspiracy of the Puritan clergy against the Church of England was only one part of a very widespread organization which took in the laity also, and which moved on stealthily but steadily towards its object during half a century, until that object was attained As early as the year 1585, the conspirators boasted that they had a party which was 100,000 strong [*ibid* 133], and in 1589 they were already taking into consideration "how archbishops, bishops, chancellors, deans, canons, archdeacons, commissaries, registrars, apparitors, etc should be provided for, that the Commonwealth be not thereby," on their expulsion from their benefices, etc "pestered with beggars" [*ibid* 127.] The movement was supported, for political purposes, by the Earl of Leicester, Sir Francis Walsingham, Sir Francis Knollys, and, to some extent, by the Cecils, and had so much support in Parliament that several Bills were introduced, though not carried, to legalize its progress It also received assistance from the growing sect of the Brownists, especially through the pamphleteering ability of John Penry, the author of the ribald tracts which were published under the pseudonym of "Martin Mar-Prelate"[1] And thus, notwithstanding the endeavours of the High Commission Court (often under direct orders from the Queen) to suppress the conspiracy, as one dangerous to the State as well as the Church, it had attained such dimensions by the end of the reign that the Puritans had become a very powerful party in the country, and were too strong to make secresy any longer necessary

For a quarter of a century the Puritans can hardly be said to have been opposed by any party in the Church, the opposition offered to them coming entirely from the Ecclesiastical Commissioners, or Court of High Commission, and the Privy Council But about the time when the Mar-Prelate libels were being published, Dr Richard Bancroft [A D 1544-1610], chaplain to Archbishop Whitgift, laid the foundation for a revival of Reformation principles, as opposed to

[1] These were a series of pamphlets professedly advocating the cause of religion as set forth in the Puritan system, but in reality filled with the most venomous rancour against the non-Puritan clergy The following are specimens of the terms in which the bishops and other clergy were spoken of "Our lord bishops, as John of Canterbury, with the rest of that swinish rabble, are petty Antichrists, petty popes, proud prelates, enemies to the Gospel, and most covetous wretched priests I suppose them to be in the state of the sin against the *Holy Ghost* Right puissant and terrible priests, my clergy, masters of our Convocation house, whether vicars, worshipful paltripolitans, or others of the holy league of subscription right poisoned, persecuting, and terrible priests, worshipful priests of the crew of monstrous and ungodly wretches, that to maintain their own outrageous proceedings, mingle heaven and earth together All who have subscribed have approved lies upon the Holy Ghost Our bishops, and proud, popish, presumptuous, paltry, pestilent, and pernicious prelates are usurpers I will presently mar the fashion of your lordships They are cogging and cozening knaves The bishops will lie like dogs Impudent, shameless, wainscoatfaced bishops . I have heard some say his Grace will speak against his conscience It is true" [Strype's *Life of Whitgift*, i 553, 570] The Mar-Prelate tracts were printed at a press which was quickly moved from place to place to avoid discovery, being set up first at Moulsey near Kingston on Thames, then at Fawsley in Northamptonshire, Norton, Coventry, Welston in Warwickshire, from which latter place the letters were sent to another press in or near Manchester, where the printer was ultimately discovered while at work on a libellous tract against Bishop Cooper The publications were forbidden by a proclamation, issued on February 13, 1589, but the printers, though fined and imprisoned by the Star Chamber, were eventually pardoned Dr John Bridges, Dean of Salisbury, and Thomas Cooper, Bishop of Winchester, wrote against Mar Prelate and his assistants, but such publications cannot be met by argument A full account of the series may be found in Maskell's *History of the Martin Mar Prelate Controversy*, 1845

Presbyterian or Calvinistic principles, in a sermon which he preached at Paul's Cross on February 9th, 1588-9, the Sunday before the meeting of Parliament In this sermon he laid down the principle of Episcopacy as of Divine institution, as that which was the true and only Scriptural mode of Church government, and shewed that the Presbyterian system, or "Discipline,"[1] was one of mere modern invention, founded in the wilfulness and selfishness of man, and not in any revelation from, or obedience to, God This Divine origin and authority of the Church system had already been maintained by Archbishop Whitgift in his controversy with Cartwright [Strype's *Life of Whitgift*, ii 51], it was followed up in detail in Saravia's "Treatise on the various Degrees of Ministers of the Gospel as they were instituted by the Lord, and delivered on by the Apostles, and confirmed by constant use of all Churches" [A D 1590], and it was the fundamental doctrine of Hooker's "Laws of Ecclesiastical Polity," written between the years 1586 and 1591, and published in the year 1594 About the same time it was also elaborated in Bishop Bilson's "Perpetual Government of Christ's Church" [A.D 1593-4], and in the same year Bancroft exposed and refuted the Presbyterian system in his "Dangerous Positions" (already quoted and referred to), and his "Survey of the pretended Holy Discipline" By these works a younger school of clergy was trained up in the true principles of the English Reformation, and although they were not able to stem the tide of Puritanism altogether, they erected a bulwark for the Church on which the Caroline Divines could take firm theological and literary standing in the deadly struggle that occupied their generation, making the subjugation of English intellect by Presbyterianism for ever impossible

When the long reign of the High Church Queen Elizabeth was brought to a close in the year 1603, and she was succeeded by the Scottish King James, who had lived in the midst of the Presbyterian system and had outwardly conformed to it, the hopes of the Puritans were raised to a confident height On his journey to London he was met by a deputation of the party bearing the "Millenary Petition," a memorial signed by 750 clergymen, in which the whole platform of Puritanism was set forth, the petitioners complaining that "we, to the number of more than a thousand of your Majesty's subjects and ministers, all groaning as under a common burden of human rites and ceremonies, do, with one joint consent, humble ourselves at your Majesty's feet, to be eased and relieved in this behalf," and praying for "a Conference among the learned" for the settlement of the points in dispute [Fuller's *Ch Hist.* X i 27]. In consequence of this petition the King summoned representatives of the Puritan clergy to appear before him, with nine bishops, four deans, and two other doctors, for the purpose of considering the grievances which were represented to exist, and of providing remedies if necessary These met at Hampton Court on January 14th, 16th, and 18th, 1603-4, and from the place of meeting their consultation acquired the name of the Hampton Court Conference But although so many were summoned, the number of the Church party who were eventually called in to take part in the actual Conference was much reduced, and the names of the acting Divines on either side were as follows —

Bancroft, Bishop of London	Reynolds, President of C C Coll , Oxford.
Bilson, ,, Winchester	Sparks, Regius Prof Div , Oxford
Montague, Dean of Chapel Royal	Chaderton, Master of Emm Coll , Cambridge
Andrewes, Dean of Westminster	Knewstub, Vicar of Cockfield
Overall, ,, St Paul's	Galloway, Minister of Perth
Barlow, ,, Chester	
Bridges, ,, Salisbury	

It is noticed by the historians of the time that while the bishops and deans appeared in their canonicals—as was and still is customary in the presence of the Sovereign—the Puritan clergy discarded even their University gowns, and, with perverse want of taste and judgment, wore furred gowns such as are still worn by City Aldermen On the first day the consultation was restricted to Members of the Privy Council On the second the actual Conference took place, those above named being present, and also a large number of privy councillors The result which was arrived at on the third day was that the King considered most of the Puritan requirements unreasonable, and inconsistent with the status of the Church of England, but that some verbal changes should be made in the Prayer Book, and that an addition should be made to the Catechism explanatory of the Sacraments But the Puritan Divines did not in reality state the Puritan case in any detail Probably they felt how weak that case would be when stated before such men as Bilson, Andrewes, and Overall, and how easily those learned Divines would have shewn its shallowness and want of authority [Barlow's *Sum and Substance of the Conference at Hampton Court*, 1604 Cardwell's *Conferences*]

Cartwright, the leader of the Puritan clergy, had died a few weeks before the Hampton Court Conference, on December 27th, 1603 Archbishop Whitgift died a few weeks after its close, on February 29th, 1603-4 No leader arose among the Puritans equal to Cartwright, while Bancroft, the successor of Whitgift, was a man of far higher ability than the latter. and so much better able to contend with them, that Lord Clarendon says of him, "he had almost rescued the Church out of the hand of the Calvinian party, and very much subdued the unruly spirit of the Nonconformists" He died on November 2nd, 1611 (having lived to see the completion of that noble revision of the English Bible which had occupied the most learned divines of the Church of England during the years of his primacy), and was succeeded by George Abbott, the Bishop of London Abbott was a strict Calvinist, very indifferent to

[1] Discipline is defined as follows in Travers' book "Discipline is an order for the good government of the Church of Christ, whereof there be two parts, the first is of ecclesiastical functions, the second of the duty of the rest of the faithful" [*Full and Plain Declar. Eccl Discip , ad init*]

the Church system, and far from unfavourable to the "Discipline" or Presbyterian system During his long primacy [A D. 1610-1633] the power of the Puritans increased to such an extent that in a few years after his death they attained the object at which the party had been aiming for nearly a century, the establishment of Presbyterianism in the place of Episcopacy

A great stimulus was given to the party by the success of the Calvinists at the Synod of Dort, held in the year 1618 [DORT, SYNOD OF] The English Calvinists had been foiled in their attempt to force the "Lambeth Articles" on the Church of England in the year 1595, and again at the Hampton Court Conference [DICT *of* THEOL, LAMBETH ARTICLES], but the presence of the English Commissioners, sent to Dort by King James, seemed (though falsely) to give force to the decision of the Synod in the Church of England, and the Puritans regarded that decision as foreshadowing their own victory over English "Arminians," as they called the members of the High Church party They thus raised such a controversial agitation that, on August 22nd, 1622, the King issued Injunctions prohibiting any preachers under the rank of bishop or dean from preaching "in any popular auditory on the deep points of Predestination, Election, Reprobation, or of the Universality, Efficacy, Resistibility or Irresistibility of God's grace" A proclamation of a similar tenor was issued by Charles I on January 14th, 1626, and for the same purpose the "Declaration" was prefixed to the Thirty-nine Articles of Religion in 1628, enforcing their plain grammatical sense These attempts to temper the bitterly controversial spirit of the Puritans had, however, no effect, and the latter were greatly strengthened as a party by the House of Commons, which had now been seized with that strange religious madness that affected it for so many years After a long debate on the "Declaration," the House of Commons passed the following resolution —"We, the Commons in Parliament assembled, do claim, protest, and avow for truth, the sense of the Articles of Religion which were established by Parliament in the thirteenth year of our late Queen Elizabeth, which by the public act of the Church of England, and by the current exposition of the writers of our Church, have been delivered unto us And we reject the sense of the Jesuits and Arminians, and all others that differ from us" [Neal's *Hist Purit* 193] This was the first of that marvellous collection of resolutions and ordinances respecting religion of which Sir Simonds D'Ewes is stated to have declared, that "in bulk and number they did not only equal but exceed all the laws and statutes made since the Conquest" [Fuller's *Ch Hist.* iii 490] When the Long Parliament opened, on November 3rd, 1640, its distinctly Puritan temper was shewn by an order to Bishop Williams, Dean of Westminster, to place a Communion Table in the middle of the Abbey for the members to receive the Holy Communion on the following Sunday, instead of celebrating it in the usual place at the Altar in the Choir. Having thus shewn the direction in which their prejudices leaned, the Long Parliament then appointed a Committee of the whole House for hearing grievances about religion, the Committee being afterwards subdivided into more than twenty, and from that time the course of Parliamentary agitation and legislation went steadily onward to the end

During the spring and summer of the following year [A D 1641] there was a long struggle for the expulsion of Bishops from the House of Lords, and when the Puritan party had failed in carrying their Bill for this purpose, another Bill was brought in, founded on a petition recently presented, which provided for 'the utter extirpation of all Bishops, Deans and Chapters, Archdeacons, Prebendaries, Chanters, with all Chancellors, Officials, and Officers belonging to them, and for the disposing of their lands, manors, etc as the Parliament shall appoint" This Bill also was thrown out· but not long afterwards twelve of the Bishops, who were in London at Christmas time, were attacked by a mob of apprentices led by Sir Richard Wiseman, and prevented from taking their places in the House of Lords The mob at the same time attacked Westminster Abbey, but were driven off by the Westminster scholars and others, who had collected on the alarm, and Sir Richard Wiseman was mortally wounded (in a manner very similar to that in which Lord Brooke was killed, in March 1653, during the assault which he was leading on Lichfield Cathedral) by a stone thrown from the Abbey leads For protesting against their violent detention from the House of Lords ten of the Bishops were sent to the Tower the next day, December 27th, 1641, and there they remained until May 5th, 1642 Meanwhile an Act of Parliament was passed, on February 14th, 1642, depriving them of their places in Parliament, and no Bishop sat there again for twenty years Shortly afterwards they were deprived also of their official incomes, and some of them were reduced to great poverty and want

In the beginning of the Civil War which now broke out, the General Assembly of Scotland accompanied the invasion of England by Scottish troops by a fresh attack upon the English Church, sending a letter to Parliament on August 3rd, 1642, to urge that there should be "one confession of faith, one directory of worship, one public catechism, and one form of Church government, in both Kingdoms" [Rushworth's *Collect.* v 388] Upon this the English Parliament obediently passed a resolution "That this government by Archbishops, Bishops, their Chancellors and Commissaries, Deans and Chapters, Archdeacons, and other ecclesiastical officers depending upon the hierarchy, is evil, and justly offensive and burdensome to the Kingdom, a great impediment to reformation and growth of religion, very prejudicial to the State and government of this Kingdom, and that we are resolved that it shall be taken away" A Bill for the utter abolition of Episcopacy was shortly afterwards brought in, and was passed on January 26th,

Puritans

1643 This was supplemented on October 9th, 1646, by an ordinance "for the abolishing of Archbishops and Bishops, and providing for the payment of the just and necessary debts of the Kingdom, into which the same hath been drawn by a war mainly promoted by and in favour of the said Archbishops and Bishops, and other their adherents and dependents." After September 6th, the names and titles were to be "wholly abolished and taken away," together with all authority and jurisdiction, and all the possessions of the sees were to be placed in the hands of a Commission of Aldermen and others named in the Act—subsequent Ordinances defining the public uses to which they were to be applied. [Rushw *Hist Coll* vii 373]

While the abolition of Episcopacy was thus being effected, the Puritans were also preparing for the climax of their long labours, the establishment of Presbytery in its place By an "Ordinance" of Parliament dated June 12th, 1643 (the Ordinance replacing a Bill introduced in the previous October but never carried), an Assembly of Divines was summoned to meet at Westminster to perfect the work of Reformation which the Parliament had begun, and to settle the government of the Church in nearer agreement with that of Scotland and of other reformed communions abroad [Rushworth's *Hist Coll* vi 327] This Assembly met in Westminster Abbey on July 1st, 1643, sat until the autumn of 1647, and did not finally vanish (it was never formally dissolved) until the dispersion of the Long Parliament by Cromwell in the year 1652 It originally consisted of 121 clergy, most of whom were Puritans, and of 30 lay assessors Of the few clergy belonging to the moderate section of the Church party who were summoned (including Archbishop Ussher, Bishops Brownrigg, Westfield, and Prideaux), most refused to attend because a Royal Proclamation had been issued forbidding the Assembly, and the rest fell off after the first meeting The permanent part of it was entirely Presbyterian in colour, though a few "Independents"—half political and half religious in their independency—subsequently came to light in the body[1] The first actual work of the Assembly was the acceptance of the Scottish "Solemn League and Covenant" for the extirpation of Episcopacy, and setting up of Presbytery, which was adopted with the forms of an oath by the Assembly and the Parliament on September 25th, 1643 [COVENANTERS], and was afterwards imposed upon every one in England who by threats or persuasions could be induced to subscribe to it Its next work was to prepare a "Directory for Public Worship," similar to that which had been published by Cartwright half a century before Afterwards the Assembly compiled a most voluminous and verbose "Confession of Faith," with equally diffuse "Longer" and "Shorter" Catechisms, all these formularies being still in use as the Standards of Faith and Worship among the Presbyterians of Scotland [SCOTCH KIRK]

On January 4th, 1645, the following Ordinance of Parliament abolished the use of the Book of Common Prayer "The Lords and Commons assembled in Parliament, taking into serious consideration the manifold inconveniences that have arisen by the Book of Common Prayer in this Kingdom, and resolving, according to their Covenant, to reform religion according to the Word of God, and the example of the best reformed Churches, have consulted with the reverend, pious, and learned Divines called together for that purpose, and do judge it necessary that the said Book of Common Prayer be abolished, and the Directory for the Public Worship of God, hereinafter mentioned, be established and observed in all the churches within this Kingdom" [Rushworth's *Hist Collect* vi. 839]

This was supplemented on August 23rd by another ordinance making the use of the Prayer Book penal After reciting the ordinance of January 4th abolishing its use, this ordinance goes on to enact that the Directory shall be delivered to the parish constable of each parish by the members of Parliament for the county or town in which such parish is situated, to be paid for by the parishioners, and to be used by the ministers on the next Sunday "And it is further hereby ordained by the said Lords and Commons, That if any person or persons whatsoever shall at any time or times hereafter use, or cause the aforesaid Book of Common Prayer to be used, in any church, chapel, or publick place of worship, or in any private place or family within the Kingdom of England, or Dominion of Wales, or port and town of Berwick, That then every person so offending therein, shall, for the first offence, forfeit and pay the sum of five pounds of lawful English money, for the second offence, the sum of ten pounds, and for the third offence, shall suffer one whole year's imprisonment, without bail or mainprize" At the same time those who refused to use the Directory were to be fined forty shillings for every offence, and those who wrote or preached against it were to be similarly fined, not less than five or more than fifty pounds, while all Prayer Books were to be delivered up to the authorities, under a fine of forty shillings [*Ibid* vii 205]

The final establishment of the Puritan "Discipline" took place under similar ordinances On August 19th, 1645, directions were given by "the Lords and Commons (after advice had with the Assembly of Divines) for the election and choosing of ruling elders in all the congregations, and in the classical assemblies for the cities of London and Westminster, and the several counties of the Kingdom, for the speedy settling of the Presbyterial government" On June 5th, 1646, an ordinance was passed "for the present settling (without further delay) of the Presbyterial government in the Church of England" On August

[1] They were five in number, Thomas Goodwin, Fellow of Catherine Hall, Cambridge, William Bridge, Fellow of Emmanuel College, Cambridge, Jeremiah Burroughs, of the same College, Sidrach Simpson, of Queen's College, Cambridge, and Philip Nye, who had been educated at Oxford [Fuller's *Ch Hist* iii. 461, ed. 1837]

28th, 1646, there was an "Ordinance of the Lords and Commons for the Ordination of Ministers by the classical presbyters within their respective bounds, for the several congregations in the Kingdom of England;" and one on January 29th, 1647-8, "for the speedy dividing and settling of the several counties of the Kingdom into distinct classical presbyteries and congregational elderships" The Puritan "platform" was thus established on the ruins of the Church and the Monarchy, the Archbishop of Canterbury having been beheaded, the bishops and clergy driven from their duties, the Prayer Book having been outlawed, and the King awaiting in prison the last sad scene of what has been not inaptly called his "martyrdom," which took place within sight of the places where the Assembly and the Parliament were sitting by whom the ruin was effected.

The hour in which the Puritans attained their final triumph was, however, the hour in which their power began to wane During the next twelve years Sectarianism broke up their ranks, the country became tired of their tyranny, and while the BAPTISTS, INDEPENDENTS, and QUAKERS, with minor sects which separated from them, cared nothing for the "Discipline" of the Presbyterian system, the people at large began to long for the return of that old Church which had been so recklessly thrust aside By the time the longed-for restoration had taken place the Puritans as a party in the Church of England had ceased to exist [NONCONFORMISTS LOW CHURCHMEN]

The temporary ruin which the Puritans brought on the Church was the result in no small degree of that strong self-appreciation which led them to look with extreme contempt on the works of former times Their own days they looked upon as far better than the days of their fathers, and though there was no constructive ability in the party at any time to replace by those which were better the institutions, the fabrics, the works of art, and the literary treasures which they despised, yet they destroyed them in the most ruthless manner, perceiving nothing admirable in anything that was old, and utterly regardless of the fact that they who inherit national heirlooms from their fathers are trustees of them for their own children Thus it is to them, chiefly, that we owe also the ruin of hundreds of national buildings, such as Fountains, Tintern, Reading, St. Mary's, York, Whitby, and Tynemouth Even the cathedrals themselves were scarcely spared by them, Puritan deans, like Whittingham of Durham stripping them of their lead and much besides for the profit of themselves and their families Probably there were not a few Puritans in the sixteenth century who agreed with Beza when he wrote "I could wish those great temples . . had been demolished from the beginning, and others more convenient for sermons and the administration of the Sacraments had been erected" [Beza's *Colloq* ii 29] or in the seventeenth century, who agreed with another writer, "As for pompous cathedrals . . I have no more to say for them, but that it were well if, with the high places, they were pulled down, and the materials thereof converted to a better use"[1] [*Nehushtan*, 1688, p 73] The dense "Philistinism" of the party could see nothing but idols in the beautiful sculptures and paintings with which English churches had until their time abounded, and the destruction of these by them long left the impression that there had been no national school of art, and that England had been in a rude condition as regards everything artistic, while other nations had reached almost the perfection of taste and design[2] Nor was it merely in matters connected with the Church that the Puritans shewed their utter want of culture for libraries were destroyed by them without any attempt to select the books which might be offensive to their system from those which were not so. all the noble collection of volumes contained in that which is now known as the Bodleian Library being, among others, burned or sent abroad, and the very shelves and desks sold as worthless lumber by them in 1550 [Macray's *Annals of Bodl Libr* p 11]

It may be observed, in conclusion, that there has never been any revival of the original "Puritan platform" in the Church of England since it had its trial during the time of the Commonwealth The Calvinistic doctrine which they held was inherited by the Low Church party, but no important section of the Church has ever since the Restoration advocated the introduction of the Presbyterian system of Church government instead of Episcopacy The Disciplinarian idea as to the oversight of morals was to some extent revived by the Societies for the Reformation of manners, and by the class system which John Wesley borrowed from the Moravians But the former soon became intolerable, and the latter has never gained a firm footing in connection with the Church Although, therefore, the Puritans have been in some degree represented in later generations, the most distinctive features of their

[1] On June 2nd, 1643, Charles I wrote to the Dean and Chapter of Durham, that on his recent visit to their city he had found houses built against the walls of the Cathedral, and the burial ground of the latter let out on lease to one of the tenants of the former, "a thing," writes the King, "by no means to be endured" [*Calend St Pap Dom* ch i]

[2] "Among other directions sent from the King" James I "one was for repairing of the chapel" of Holyrood House, "and some English carpenters were employed, who brought with them portraits of the Apostles to be set in the pews or stalls" It was soon rumoured that idols were being set up in the Royal Chapel, and the Bishop of Galloway, who was Dean of the Chapel, wrote to the King on the subject "The answer returned by the King" [on March 13th, 1617] "was full of anger, objecting ignorance unto them that could not distinguish betwixt pictures intended for ornament and decoration, and images erected for worship and adoration and resembling them to the constable of Castile, who being sent to swear the peace concluded with Spain, when he understood the business was to be performed in the chapel where some anthems were to be sung, desired that whatsoever was sung, God's name might not be used in it, and that being forborne, he was content they should sing what they listed Just so, said the King, you can endure lions, dragons, and devils, to be figured in your churches, but will not allow the like place to the Patriarchs and Apostles" [Spottiswoode's *Hist Ch Scotl* iii 239, ed. 1851].

system have never been reproduced, and Puritanism may thus be said to have burned itself out in the fierce successes to which it attained in the middle of the seventeenth century

PUSEYITES A name given to High Churchmen of the "Tractarian" school, from Dr Edward Bouverie Pusey, Canon of Christ Church, and Regius Professor of Hebrew, for more than a third of a century, in Oxford In the year 1870 Dr Pusey wrote respecting this party-name as follows. "I never was a party leader I never acted on any system My name was used first to designate those of us who gave themselves to revive the teaching of forgotten truth and piety, because I first had occasion to write on Baptismal Regeneration But it was used by opponents, not by confederates We should have thought it a note against us to have deserved any party name, or to have been anything but the followers of Jesus, the disciples of the Church, the sons and pupils of the great Fathers whom He raised up in her I never had any temptation to try to form a party, for it was against our principles. . . . Then, personally, I was the more exempt from this temptation, because God has given me neither the peculiar organizing abilities which tempt men to it, nor any office (as that of an Archdeacon) which would entitle me directly to counsel others My life, contrary to the character of party-leaders, has been spent in a succession of insulated efforts, bearing, indeed, upon our one great end, the growth of Catholic truth and piety among us, or contrariwise, resistance to what might hinder, retard, or obscure it, but still insulated" [Pusey's *Eirenicon*, iii 338]

PYRRHONISTS A name given to the extreme school of Sceptics, which denies the possibility of attaining to any certainty or absolute truth It is derived from Pyrrho of Elis [B C 360-270], the originator of Greek Scepticism This extreme form of doubt was revived at Alexandria in the first century after Christ by Ænesidemus, but lay dormant again for many centuries, until it was again resuscitated in the philosophy of Kant [SCEPTICS]

Q

QUADRISACRAMENTARIANS A controversial name for some German reformers in Wittenberg and its neighbourhood, who maintained that there are four Sacraments necessary to salvation, namely, Baptism, the Lord's Supper, Absolution, and Holy Orders Some who held such an opinion are mentioned by Melanchthon [Melanchthon's *Loc Comm*]

QUAKER BAPTISTS. [KEITHIANS]

QUAKERS The popular name of a sect which represents the extreme form of Puritanism, and which originated about the year 1650 in Yorkshire, Durham, Lancashire, and Cumberland, under the leadership of three young men named James Naylor, Richard Farnworth, and George Fox.

The idea of "quaking and trembling" was very common among the extreme Puritans, and the founders of the Quaker sect probably derived it as a prominent characteristic of religion from the TRASKITES The early use of the name is illustrated by one of the first publications of the sect, a tract of Richard Farnworth of Balby in Yorkshire, printed in 1652, and entitled "A Discovery of Truth and Falsehood, written from the Spirit of the Lord by one whom the Prince of the World calls a Quaker, but is of the Divine Nature made a partaker" They began by calling themselves "The people of the Lord," "The people of God," "Children of Light," etc , but they soon accepted the popular title given to them, as when in 1653 Naylor, in his "Power and Glory of the Lord shining out of the North," quotes many texts of Scripture to shew that the earth trembled and quaked, that Isaac trembled exceedingly, that Moses feared and quaked, that the Lord bade His disciples quake for fear, and that therefore saints ought to be Quakers Thus they were, in their own language, "the people called Quakers," "the poor Quakers," "the despised Quakers" Afterwards it became customary for them to use the name "Friends," as in "A True Account of the Proceeding, Sense and Advice of the people called Quakers, at the yearly meeting of Faithful Friends and Brethren," in 1694, and towards the end of the last century this was formally fixed upon the sect in the title "Society of Friends" In Pagitt's Heresiology, which was written shortly after the rise of the sect, they are called "Quakers and Shakers" [Pagitt's *Heresiol* 244]

Baxter says that the Quakers "were but the Ranters turned from horrid profaneness and blasphemy to a life of extreme austerity on the other side" "Their doctrines," he adds, "were mostly the same with the Ranters" He attributes their origin to Naylor, says nothing of Fox, and adds, "But of late one William Penn is become their leader, and would reform the sect, and set up a kind of ministry among them" [Baxter's *Life and Times*, i 77] Pagitt also traces them up to Naylor as their founder, and says that they were "thickest set in the North parts"

James Naylor [A D 1616-1660] was a Wakefield man, "a member," as General Lambert said, "of a very sweet society of an Independent Church" He certainly helped largely to spread the fanaticism which afterwards developed into Quakerism, especially in his native county and on the Fells of Lancashire and Westmoreland, but this fanaticism reached to such a height about the year 1655 that Naylor was repudiated by Fox and his friends He was imprisoned in Exeter gaol, and while there allowed himself to be addressed by his followers as "The Everlasting Son, the Prince of Peace, the fairest among ten thousand," and it was believed, if not asserted by himself, that he had power to raise the dead to life Having been set free, he went in triumphal procession through Glastonbury and Wells, men and women strewing his path with their clothes, and walking bareheaded before him, as in the case of the fanatic Prince in recent times [PRINCEITES] At Bristol the crowds carried this blasphemous parody so far as to shout Hosanna, and hymns were sung to his praise in the words of the Song of Solomon The scandal caused by these proceedings led to Naylor's being again imprisoned by order of the Parliament, and having been brought to trial in 1656 before the House of Commons, he narrowly escaped capital sentence. After a violent debate, he was condemned to be pilloried at Westminster, whipped thence to the Old Exchange, to be there pilloried again for two hours, to have his tongue bored through with a hot iron, and his forehead branded with the letter B. Thence he was carried to Bristol, conveyed through the city on a horse's back with his face to the tail, and whipped publicly on the next market-day in five different places He was then sent back to be kept in solitary confinement in London, with no other sustenance than what he could earn After a time spent in prison he recanted, was released by the Rump Parliament, and readmitted into the Society which had disowned him Naylor died at King's Ripton, near Huntingdon, just before the Restoration

George Fox [A D. 1624-1691], the other principal founder of the Quaker sect, was the son of a Leicestershire weaver, and was brought up as a cobbler in Drayton, his native village, in that county. As he grew up he became a victim to those fits of religious despondency which characterized the religious life of the lower classes in Puritan times · and under the influence of these he became unfit for work, and wandered about the country under the pretext of seeking rest for his troubled spirit He applied for direction to a clergyman, the curate of Mancetter in Warwickshire, who told him to smoke tobacco and sing psalms Another counselled a course of physic and bleeding, advice doubtless excellent so far as it went, but insufficient to satisfy the cravings of the ignorant enthusiast All his advisers proving equally "blind guides" to him, he was thrown back upon his own resources. At length, in May 1646, light seemed to dawn upon him, his doubts were removed, and he obtained peace of mind At the same time the revelation from above was granted to him (as he fancied), that it was not a university education which fitted a man for the ministry, but that the Spirit enlightened whom He would, and that, moreover, he himself was the subject of spiritual revelations His belief was that every man, Christian or heathen, had naturally a portion of Divine light in him, the gift of the Spirit, which, if he would follow, he might attain to perfection About 1649, Fox began to wander about the country in Warwickshire, Nottinghamshire, and Derbyshire, haranguing all who would listen to him. He used to force himself into the churches, and interrupt the service by wild denunciations, for which he was often beaten and imprisoned. He also delivered his testimony before magistrates, in part orally and in part by strange wordy epistles, for which he was rewarded by the stocks or imprisonment. The chief plea urged against him was contempt of court, since he regarded it as a deadly sin to uncover his head before the justices At Mansfield, for example, where he had interrupted the service, he was beaten, placed in the stocks, and afterwards hunted with stones out of the town At Derby, in 1650, he was brought before the magistrates for brawling, when Justice Gervase Bennet, an Independent, who signed the mittimus for his imprisonment, nicknamed him Quaker, alluding to the shakings which he made part of his ritual, and to his exhortations to his hearers to quake. In prison he converted his jailor, and issued pretentious warnings to magistrates, clergy and people, till the alarmed authorities afforded him facilities for escape, hoping thus, but in vain, to get rid of him As he had brought under his influence a company of soldiers quartered in the town, the Parliamentary Commissioners offered Fox the post of captain For his refusal he was again imprisoned, when in his confinement he revolved schemes for reforming the gaols and restraining capital punishment. Upon his release, in 1651, he extended his range to Lincolnshire, Yorkshire, Northumberland, and the Lake district, where he co-operated with Naylor, and drew together a large number of converts.

At this time the followers of Fox drew persecution upon themselves from the Puritans by their extravagances, the worst of which Fox did not imitate, though he did not withhold his approbation Some went through the towns and villages naked for a testimony One female proselyte presented herself in that state before the Protector in Whitehall Chapel. A man took up his station outside the Parliament House with a drawn sword, with which he assaulted every one who passed by

These excesses led to so general a persecution of the sect by the dominant religionists, that, in the year 1657, there are said to have been 140 Quakers in prison, while in the six years previous [A D 1651-1657] as many as 1900 had been imprisoned, of whom 21 died under their persecution

In 1659 they presented to Parliament a long protest against the ill-treatment that they had received, their leader being at the time in Lancaster Castle, where he was confined in a cell so smoky that he could hardly distinguish the miserable light that was allowed him The accession of Charles II procured his release, and that of 200 of his followers The King was willing to grant them toleration, and made a favourable reply to a congratulatory address which they presented to him, pledging his word to that effect, but the rising of Venner kindled the suspicions of the Government for though the Quakers were not really concerned in it, they had already given abundant evidence of that tenacious pugnacity by which the sect—in spite of its peaceable pretensions—has always been distinguished, and had not yet learned to veil their pugnacity by ostentatiously smooth words Their refusal to take the oath of allegiance, though it sprang not from disaffection to the Government, but from a conviction of the unlawfulness of all oaths, told strongly against them, insomuch that, in 1662, an Act was passed against them for refusing to take lawful oaths In the same year a more specific Act was passed against them, prohibiting their assembling for public worship under the penalty of £5, and transportation for the third offence [14 Carol II c 1] Men were transported to Barbadoes, and women to Jamaica, where they were sold as slaves to the colonists for a longer or shorter period In 1665 it was actually ordered that no captain should be allowed to sail to the West Indies without a pass, which was only granted to those who professed themselves willing to transport Quakers [Sewel, *Hist* vol i] Though the Conventicle and Five Mile Acts were not directed particularly against them, they felt their effects more than did the other Dissenters, and that because their consciences would not allow them to conceal their opinions or to meet in secresy On the contrary, when their meeting-houses were closed, they would preach in the public streets Two of their number, Penn and Mead, were brought before the Recorder of London, and indicted for having caused a riot in Gracechurch Street They were acquitted after a lengthy trial, but the jurors were on that account fined forty marks each, and the two Quakers were sent to prison for contempt of court, because they refused to uncover their heads

It was about this time that a great change came over the society Fox was an uneducated man of narrow understanding, as appears in his many writings, some of which are in such atrocious English as to be barely intelligible But he was now joined by men of higher social position, of superior intelligence and refinement, who while they ever looked up to him as their master spiritually, practically took the management of affairs into their own hands, and gave a new tone to the Society They also edited his writings and translated them into better English Of these the most celebrated were Keith, Barclay, and William Penn Henceforth we hear no more of disturbances in churches and outrages upon public decency, and on the other hand, if the Quakers were persecuted at all, it was partly in common with all other sects, and partly because they refused to pay tithes, to take oaths, or to give the proper marks of respect to persons in office

At the accession of James II they petitioned the King for toleration, on the grounds that he equally with them dissented from the Established Church They complained that three hundred and twenty of their number had died in prison in the preceding reign, among whom were two celebrated preachers, Burroughs and Howgill James was inclined to favour them, mainly for the sake of Penn, who was the son of Sir William Penn, an old naval friend

William Penn [A D 1644-1718] had been drawn over to the Quakers while he was an undergraduate of Christ Church, and the first consequence of his conversion was that he refused to wear his surplice in chapel for which, in 1662, he was expelled from Oxford He openly joined the Quakers in 1666, to the great grief of his father, and when the young Quaker positively refused to "worship" the King by taking off his hat in the royal presence, the Admiral turned him out of doors He was however shortly afterwards reconciled to him, and at his death left him lands to the yearly value of £1500, together with claims upon the Government which he afterwards turned to good account Meanwhile Penn had twice suffered imprisonment, once on the occasion above mentioned, and before this for a tract, "The Sandy Foundation Shaken," in which he objected to the doctrine of the Trinity Other writings of his attracted attention to the views of the Quakers from those who would have shewn scant courtesy to the wild ungrammatical rhapsodies of Fox His connexion with America had brought him into great notoriety, so that, at the accession of James, Penn was the acknowledged mouthpiece of the Society As such he was trusted and loved by James, partly on account of his own character, and partly because through the Quakers James very naturally saw a means for obtaining a better position for his own co-religionists

Through Penn's influence, the Quakers enjoyed peace and quietness both in England and Ireland so long as James was on the throne Nor did the Revolution make much difference to them, except indeed in Ireland, where they shared in the misfortunes of that unhappy country In the insurrection of the native Irish, their loss has been estimated by Macaulay at £100,000, or more than three times as much in the value of our money [Macaulay, *Hist Eng* iv 166] But the great gain that befell them was through the Toleration Act, under which they were allowed to hold meetings in peace upon their signing a declaration against Transubstantiation, a promise of fidelity to the Government, and a confession of faith in the Trinity and in the inspiration of Holy Scriptures On both these last points Fox and Barclay had given in their writings signs of heterodoxy, nor was Penn quite free from suspicion In 1696 an Act received the royal assent allowing the affirmation of Quakers to be received in a court of law in place of an oath Since that time the only change in their external position towards the State has been that, in 1723, they were admitted to the freedom of corporations without oath, and of course the repeal of the Test and Corporation Acts brought the same relief to them that it did to other Dissenters.

The change which came over the sect at the end of the seventeenth century is shewn by the account given of it in the early editions of *The Present State of England* After describing their origin, the writer goes on to say, "They practised formerly abstinence and self-denial, but now of late none are prouder or more luxurious than the generality of them They formerly wore plain and coarse clothes, now the men wear very fine cloth, and are distinguished from others only by a particular shaping of their coats, a little plaited cravat, and a slender hatband The women nevertheless wear flowered, or striped, or damask silks, and the finest linen cut and plaited in imitation of lace, but they wear no lace or superfluous ribbons However they are extremely nice in the choice of tailors, sempstresses and laundresses Those of the men who wear perriwigs have 'em of genteel hair and shape, tho' not long They are as curious in their meats and as cheerful in their drink, and as soft in their amours, and as much in the enjoyment of life as others" [Chamberlain *Pres St of Eng* 1702, p 259]

In America the Quakers increased more than in England or Ireland, and have held their ground with greater tenacity, though their commencement was most unpromising, for they at first suffered severe persecution from the "Pilgrim Fathers" of New England [INDEPENDENTS] Two women of the sect were the first to appear at Boston in 1656, but they were not suffered to land Their books were seized and burnt, and they themselves were imprisoned on board their vessel, and after a brief interval were sent back again Eight others met with the like treatment in the same year, and a law was passed in the Colony forbidding their introduction on pain of imprisonment. Still they increased in number, so that in 1658 a more stringent Act was passed against them.

A fine of £100 was imposed upon any colonist who should bring in a Quaker, with an addition of £5 for every hour's concealment, the male Quaker for his first appearance in the country had one ear cut off, and was imprisoned until he should have worked out the cost of his passage back to England, for the second offence his other ear was cut off, and he was imprisoned in like manner The women were for the first and second offence severely whipped and imprisoned, and for the third had their tongues bored through with a hot iron To account for this greater severity in their case, it must be remembered that women were not only allowed, but encouraged by the Quakers to exercise the ministerial office It must be remembered that all these severe punishments were inflicted, not for any overt act, as in England for brawling in churches, insulting magistrates, or outraging public decency, or for making any converts, but for the bare fact of their having landed in the colony And this was done by those pretended champions of civil and religious liberty, the "Pilgrim Fathers," the Puritans of New England But worse things yet remain to be told The Quakers still increased in number, and therefore at a later period in the same year an Act passed the General Court of Boston, at the petition of the Puritan ministers, inflicting banishment for the first offence, and *death* for the second, that is, for mere re-appearance in the colony A bare majority, that is, two out of three justices, without any jury, were thus made competent to inflict capital punishment

And the Act was enforced Many Quakers were exiled, and some who returned were put to death Gough gives the particulars of two men and one woman who thus suffered in 1659. The persecution was stayed by the Restoration, one of the first Acts of the new Government being to require that the Quakers should be sent over to England and there tried As a matter of fact the Act of 1658 was illegal, and henceforth fell through, but for a long time the Quakers were exposed to severe persecution throughout the States of New England They were frequently whipped through three towns

But they had shortly afterwards their city of refuge on the same continent in Pennsylvania Fox himself had visited Maryland, Virginia, and the Carolinas, but it does not appear that his progress was attended by much success Penn also appeared in America in 1677, and purchased an estate in New Jersey, but in 1681 the means of making a more important and lasting settlement were thrown into his hands His father the Admiral had advanced money to the Government for the service of the navy, and as he was an intimate friend of the Duke of York, he fared better than the ordinary creditors of the Crown in those days The son received in lieu of payment a grant of land on the West of the Delaware, large enough to make a European kingdom —an easy way of paying the debt, which cost Charles nothing, as the country was still in the possession of the natives, and did not produce one farthing of revenue In 1682, Penn sailed thither with a large body of colonists, men of his own way of thinking, and founded the city of Philadelphia, which became the head of a State, called after him Pennsylvania by his devoted followers, but against his own wishes But Penn was a conscientious man, and fully believed in the rights of the aborigines He accordingly did what no other colonist in America before or after him, except his followers, ever did he assembled the native chiefs, and purchased from them the land that he required. This statesmanlike example was followed afterwards by his successors in the province when they wished to extend their settlements and the consequence was that Pennsylvania alone of the American States has never known the horrors of a war with the Indians

Penn drew up for his colony a peculiar code of regulations He allowed full toleration to all Deists, but required that his *officials* should be believers in Jesus, and men of unblemished moral character A compulsory system of State education was established, requiring every child to be taught the elements, and at the age of twelve years to be put forth to some trade Great crimes were punished by solitary confinement and hard labour He restricted the punishment of death to cases of murder and high treason an equitable court with a mixed jury settled all disputes with the natives [Gough, *Hist* v ; see also *Bibliothèque Britannique,* xv p 310]

After some years' stay in America he returned home, and became a great and deserved favourite with James II The Revolution brought him into corresponding disfavour with the new Government James had protected him and those of his sect, and had moreover been his father's friend, whereupon Penn naturally clung to him in his adversity He has been accused, in common with many others of all classes and parties, of corresponding with the exiled King, and even of being implicated in Preston's plot He was more than once arrested, but the Government could get up no case against him He was deprived indeed of his colony, but it was shortly afterwards restored to him by William, who declared that the only grave accusations against him were groundless Upon his death he offered the government to the Crown for £12,000 His sect has continued to flourish there, and in America generally they have thriven better than in England In 1856 the number of American Quakers was estimated at 160,000

Though the Quakers have no authorized formularies to which they can appeal for confirmation of doctrine, they have not been without their disputes and schisms The most celebrated was that of the Keithians, under George Keith, one of the most refined and learned of the early Quakers He had followed Penn to America, but was there accused of holding erroneous views concerning the human nature of our Lord, which he supposed to be twofold, the one celestial and spiritual, the other terrestrial and corporeal [Croesi *Historia Quakeriana,* iii 446] It is a question whether he really meant anything more than that our Lord is, as touching His humanity, of a reasonable soul and human flesh subsisting, but the early American Quakers had strong Deistical tendencies, and Keith was specially unpopular with his brethren because he opposed their system of allegorizing the Gospels, whereby the historical facts of our Lord's life on earth were explained away into a symbolical representation of the origin of Christianity These views did not prevail extensively among the Quakers of Europe, but some of those in America even went so far as to say that Christ never existed at all except in the hearts of the faithful, thus carrying out to its logical extent the principle whereby Fox overruled our Lord's express injunctions respecting the Sacraments But to these theories Keith offered a most strenuous opposition, and soon gathered together a large body of followers. In 1695 he was expelled from the Society by Penn, and returned to England, where he headed a congregation that met for worship in Turner's Hall, Philpot Lane These restored the Sacraments, but retained the language, dress, and manners of Quakers, and accordingly were called Quaker Baptists But this position was too anomalous for Keith to continue in it for long In 1700 he conformed to the Church, took Holy Orders, and was presented to the living of Edburton, Sussex, which he held till his death [Burnet, *Hist of his own Times*, ii 249] The Quakers however never forgave his desertion, and have charged him with neglect of his clerical duties, and rigorous exactions of tithes from his poorer parishioners [KEITHIANS]

The Keithians in America continued for some time to form a separate sect, but at length dwindled away to a very small body, which, in the course of the last century, became reabsorbed into the original body For a change then came over the Quakers generally Their ancestors of Philadelphia had displayed signs of a tendency towards Socinianism, and a denial of the personality of the Holy Ghost. Even Penn had fallen under suspicion, although he vehemently asserted his essential orthodoxy on both of these points in a pamphlet, "Innocency with her Open Face" No such suspicions can now be attached to the sect In their reverence also for Holy Scripture the Quakers indeed go beyond their founder In the beginning of the present century, when Elias Hicks, a minister of Philadelphia, taught that the inward light was superior as an authority to the Scriptures—the very principle of Fox—and that our Lord suffered as an example only, he was expelled from the sect [HICKSITES] In other matters also the Quakers have departed from their founder, as in their views on the unlawfulness of war Fox complained that some of his disciples were dismissed from the Protector's army, although they could fight better than the best, and in a letter to Cromwell he exhorted him to come out and let no one take his crown to let his soldiers go forth with a free and willing heart, so that he might rock the nations as a cradle [*Letter and Advice*, p 27, etc] At the accession of Charles II. it was first revealed to him that self-defence was unlawful So they now disapprove of capital punishment, but Penn retained it in his laws for Pennsylvania, and the whole Society, at least the English branch, clamoured for the blood of Spencer Cowper in 1699, for the alleged murder of a Quakeress, and even appealed against the verdict of "Not guilty," as was possible in those days [Macaulay's *Hist Eng* viii 233]

Upon the whole, the change that has come over the sect has been decidedly for the better They are more orthodox than their original representatives on the doctrine of the Trinity and the value of Scripture. They have retained some strange but innocent peculiarities of dress and language, and have settled down into a sober and industrious body, peaceful and peace loving except where tithes, and until lately, church rates, are concerned, when they display something of their old pugnacity

The sect has always been conspicuous for works of practical benevolence. They have very few poor in their community, and such as they have are mostly those who have been reduced by some mischance from a better state of things, but they relieve and help them out of their own resources In the case of many excellent reforms which this century has witnessed, either the first idea was started by Quakers, or they rendered valuable support to those who took them in hand Thus Fox himself first suggested that reformation of prisons which Howard effected a century later. They were firm and useful supporters of Wilberforce in his efforts against the slave-trade One of their number, Mrs Fry, devoted herself to the cause of education long before the idea of popular education had dawned upon the minds of ministers of State or members of Parliament William Forster during the Irish potato famine lent invaluable aid to those who sought to lessen the sufferings of the unfortunate peasantry He also distinguished himself by his efforts on behalf of the slaves in the United States, and interested himself in a work which, to him as a Quaker, must have been peculiarly distasteful, an attempt to promote the spiritual good of actors in London theatres Though they ordinarily despise the fine arts as useless and frivolous, they have had a painter in Benjamin West, and a novelist in Mrs Opie, neither of whom, it is true, attained to high excellence

The number of the Quakers has been on the decline for the last hundred years and more In England this diminution has been marked and rapid They find it difficult to retain their younger members, partly owing to their archaisms of dress and language, from which the youthful mind naturally recoils, while owing to the greater publicity of modern life, and the close blending together of different classes, they have become more conspicuous, and partly owing to their strictness, which will not make any allowance for the innocent desires of youth Other elements in producing their decline have also been their direct opposition alike to the letter and to the spirit of Holy Scripture; their system of female preaching; their non-use of Sacraments, and the intense subjectivity of a religion of which the chief ordinance is meditation The reading of Scripture and the voice of prayer are almost unknown in their meetings, which are marked chiefly by silence, varied by exhortations confined to a very limited range of subjects Those who leave the Society usually join the Church, other sects of Dissenters having little or no attraction for them

In 1800 there were 413 Quaker meeting houses in the United Kingdom, these had diminished in 1871 to 372 Their numbers were set down in the census of 1851 as 14,000. There is a large number at Falmouth, where some of the descendants of Fox are still to be found, and also at Darlington near Durham

About the year 1840 a secession from the Irish Quakers took place, the members of which have adopted a custom originated by some of the early ancestors of the sect in England, that of dressing wholly in white, from which they are called "White Quakers" What information has been obtained from a voluminous collection of tracts and broadsides printed by their leaders shews that they are Antinomians of the worst description, practising profligacy under the pretence of inspiration, and cloaking villainy in the most sanctimonious language current with the parent sect The White Quakers are a small community, of which there are very few out of Dublin

[Sewel's *Hist of the People called Quakers,* 1722 This folio volume was originally written in Dutch, and was translated into English by the author himself Gough's *Hist Quakers* Fox's *Journal* Barclay's *Apology* Smith's *Quaker Bibliography,* an admirable descriptive catalogue, in two thick volumes, of all Quaker books and pamphlets]

QUAKERS, SHAKING [SHAKERS]

QUARTODECIMANS Those who celebrated Easter, or more strictly speaking the Paschal Feast, at the time of the Jewish Passover, that is, on the fourteenth day of the moon or month Nisan, whatever day of the week that happened to be The name thus taken from the particular day of observance was, by some at least, extended so as to include, without regard to its proper meaning, all who did not obey the decrees of the Councils of Nicæa and Antioch, which ordered Easter to be kept on the first Sunday after the full moon For Epiphanius says that some of the Quartodecimans in Cappadocia always kept their pasch on a fixed day, namely on the eighth of the Kalends of April, the 25th of March, maintaining, on the authority of the Acts of Pilate, that day to be the true day of our Saviour's Passion [Epiph *Hær* 1] These, then, were not properly Quartodecimans, but were classed with them as disobeying the Nicene decree The Nicene decree was founded on the custom of the Western Church, with which agreed the custom of the Churches of Palestine, Jerusalem, and Cæsarea The Churches of Asia Minor followed the Jewish rule

The matter had been debated between Polycarp and Anicetus when Polycarp visited Rome Polycarp urged that he had kept Easter according to the Asiatic custom, with St John and the rest of the Apostles with whom he associated, Anicetus urged that he too was bound to maintain the custom of all his predecessors [1] in the See of Rome [Euseb *Hist Eccl* v 24] Neither of the two would give up the custom of his Church, but no breach of communion or of charity followed About the year 196 a sharper controversy arose Victor wished to introduce uniformity by enforcing the Western custom on the whole Church His zeal, which, it must be allowed, led to intemperate and overbearing measures, was roused by the danger of the introduction of Judaism through this Judaic observance, and by a supposed connection between Quartodecimanism and Montanism The former danger, it will be seen, was not imaginary, the latter connection may seem to have no foundation in principle, but it will be found as we proceed that Quartodecimanism has a tendency to connect itself with an undue rigour of discipline and practice In the appendix to Tertullian's Treatise on Heresies, it is said that one Blastus, who joined the Montanists, wished to introduce Judaism, and advocated the Asiatic Easter custom This Blastus appears at Rome as a leader of schism Irenæus remonstrated with him in a letter "On Schism," but Blastus was deposed from the presbytery [*ibid* v 15-20] Moved, as it appears, by the schismatical proceedings of Blastus, Victor pressed upon the Asiatic Churches the relinquishment of their ancient custom Under the leadership of Polycrates, Bishop of Ephesus, they refused Victor, strengthened by synodical determinations of the Churches of Cæsarea, Jerusalem, Pontus, Corinth, Osrhoene, and Gaul, to the effect that the Resurrection of our Lord should be celebrated only on the Lord's Day, up to which day the Paschal Fast should continue, issued letters of excommunication against the Asiatic Churches, and moved the Churches which sided with him to cease from communion with them But the bishops, and particularly Irenæus, resisted this measure, admonished Victor of his too great haste, and restored peace. Both parties continued undisturbed in the observance of their own customs till the Council of Nicæa [*ibid* v. 23, 24]

That there was real danger of Judaism entering through the Asiatic custom appears not only from the example of Blastus, but from the account which Hippolytus gives, some twenty-five years later, of the Quartodecimans Considering the part which Irenæus took in the controversy, and that Irenæus, although he followed the Western usage in his own Church, had been a Quartodeciman by early association with Polycarp, whose example both he and Polycrates

[1] The successors of Peter and Paul, who have taught all the churches in which they sowed the spiritual seeds of the Gospel, that the solemn festival of the Resurrection of the Lord can be celebrated only on the Lord's Day [Anatolius, *Paschal Canon,* x in *Ante-Nicene Library,* xiv. p 419. See the whole chapter] So also Socrates [*Hist. Eccl* v 21] states that the Western party claimed the authority of St Peter and St Paul

pressed so strongly upon Victor, considering also that Hippolytus was a disciple of Irenæus, the account given by the former is very remarkable The sectarian spirit of the Quartodecimans is pointed out They are described as contentious by nature, wholly uninformed as regards knowledge, and more than usually quarrelsome Further, Hippolytus adds, they do not look to that which was spoken by the Apostle, "I testify to every man that is circumcised that he is a debtor to do the whole law" [Hippol *Refut Hær* viii 11] If from this we are not entitled to infer with certainty that circumcision was itself introduced, it is quite certain that in Hippolytus' opinion the Asiatic custom was no longer the innocent custom it had been in the days of Polycarp and St John, but that an attempt was founded upon it to enforce the whole law If Hippolytus be a competent witness, the toleration procured by Irenæus was much misused, Victor, greatly as he may have erred in the manner of his proceedings, was right in his desire to put an end to the Asiatic custom, and the Councils of Nicæa and Antioch had a more pressing cause for their decrees than the mere love of uniformity [1]

Before proceeding to these decrees, one or two earlier enactments require notice The seventh (or eighth) Apostolical Canon orders the deposition of clergy celebrating the paschal feast before the vernal equinox, as the Jews do It is not necessary to enter into the subject of the defective Jewish calculations, which frequently brought the spring month Nisan before the equinox, for our present purpose it is to be noticed that this canon, while it does not forbid the keeping the paschal feast on the fourteenth day of the first month regularly calculated, supposes that the Christian Church is to make its own independent calculation, and not to rest on the current Jewish calendar It is not improbable that the canon was made by Eastern Quartodecimans Again, Epiphanius quotes an old Apostolical Constitution which directs that the feast should be kept at the same time at which it was celebrated by the brethren of the circumcision, without being concerned for mistakes in their calculations But the constitution as we now have it (v 16) directs the pasch to be kept after the equinox, not with the Jews, with whom Christians have no communion Ussher refers the canon and the new constitution to the time of the Paschal Canon of Anatolius, an Alexandrian and Bishop of Laodicea [Euseb *Hist Eccl* vii, 32] His canon exists in a Latin translation by Rufinus, and is translated in the Ante-Nicene Library, vol xiv He insists strongly on the necessity of observing the pasch after the equinox

The Council of Arles [A D 314] ordered that Easter should be generally observed on one and the same day, and that letters fixing the day should be issued as usual by the metropolitan [Can i] The custom of the Gallic Church was to keep Easter on the Sunday, and this canon refers to the appointment of the same Sunday

We may proceed now to the Council of Nicæa One reason for summoning the Council of Nicæa was that they of Syria, Cilicia and Mesopotamia went haltingly (ἐχώλευον) with regard to the feast, and kept their pasch with the Jews [Athanas *de Synod* c. 5] Eusebius [*de Vita Const* iii 5], and Sozomen [*Hist Eccl* i 15], shew that the feast was kept by some not merely at the Jewish time, but after a Jewish fashion Constantine had sent Hosius into the East to quiet if possible this dispute, as well as the dispute between Alexander, Bishop of Alexandria, and Arius Hosius' mission was fruitless At the council, therefore, a decree was made that Easter should be observed by all on the Sunday which followed the fourteenth of the moon next after the vernal equinox It is agreed that Canon xxi, which is on this matter, is spurious, but there is no doubt that such a decree *was* made [Euseb *Vit Const* iii 17-18, Socrates, *Hist Eccl.* i 9, Theod *Hist Eccl* i 10] By the Council of Antioch [A D 341] this decree was re-enacted and guarded by a sentence of excommunication. From this time, therefore, it became a schismatical act to disobey the decree, and rules were made regarding the Quartodecimans, which treat them as schismatics or heretics Thus the Council of Laodicea [A.D 367] directs that converts from their body shall be received after they have anathematized all heresy, and may partake of the Holy Mysteries after they have been anointed with the chrism Johnson notes upon this (from Aristenus) that the Quartodecimans were Novatians in not admitting lapsed persons to penance Sozomen, however, states [*Hist Eccl* vi 24] that about A D 374 the Novatianists in Phrygia, contrary to their former custom, began to celebrate their pasch at the same time as the Jews And under the reign of Theodosius and Valentinian II [A D 375-395], he narrates the controversies and schisms among the Novatianists on this point [vii 18] [NOVATIANISTS] The Council of Laodicea, therefore, it must be concluded, made their enactment regarding the Quartodecimans without any reference to Novatian error The Laodicean rule was again enacted by the first Council of Constantinople [can vii], A D 381, and by the second of Constantinople, or Quinisextine, A D 692 [can xcv] About the year 370, according to Theodoret, or in the time of Arius, according to Epiphanius, flourished Audæus He was a Syrian of Mesopotamia, much esteemed in his own country, as Epiphanius acknowledges, for holiness of life, and zeal for the faith The freedom with which he censured the corrupt manners of the clergy brought upon him much ill-treatment, which he endured for some time, till at length he separated from the Church [Epiph. *Hær* lxx; Theod *Hæret Fab* iv 9, August *Hær* 1] He is charged by some with Anthropomorphism, and licentiousness, but Epiphanius acquits him,

[1] See against the view here taken Lardner, *Credibil* vol iv p 61, edit 1861, art "The Council of Nice," and Ritschl, *Die Entstehung der Altkatholischen Kirche* [1857, p 270], who says, "Das motiv der Verwerfung der kleinasiatischen Observanz war uberhaupt der Trieb nach Uniformitat des Cultus und der kirchlichen Sitte"

and when Epiphanius acquits it is generally safe to accept his verdict. Audæus was banished by the Emperor, and went among the Goths, many of whom he converted His chief peculiarity was his Quartodeciman practice. This practice he maintained to be the ancient custom, confirmed by the Apostolical Constitutions The Nicæan rule he held to be an innovation adopted in complaisance to Constantine In this may be noticed again the tendency of Quartodecimanism to connect itself with the sects which pressed Church discipline into undue rigour, and carried asceticism to an extreme [AUDIANS]

The body of Quartodecimans then, it appears, passed into the Audians and Novatianists, the latter adding to their other causes of separation from the Church the Jewish celebration of Easter, the former separating on this point alone For Augustine writes, from Epiphanius, that they separated themselves "culpando Episcopos divites, et pascha cum Judæis celebrando" The inculpation of rich bishops can scarcely have been a formal cause of schism The imperial laws were severe upon the Audians as schismatics Theodosius the Great in one of his laws ranked them with the Manichees, forbade their conventicles, confiscated their goods, rendered them intestate, and liable also to capital punishment [*Cod Theod* lib xvi tit 5, *de Hæret* leg 9, Bingham's *Antiq* XX v 3]

Into the differences which arose from the difficulty of ascertaining the Sunday to be observed as Easter Sunday, it is quite unnecessary to enter They were brought about by no difference of principle, but only through imperfect calculation These variations appear in the history of the Churches of France and Britain, which retained the old Roman mode of calculation, and were found to be at variance with the new Roman or Alexandrian Canon, which was brought into use in the Roman Church by Dionysius Exiguus in the year 525.

QUESNEL. [JANSENISTS.]

QUIETISTS A school of Mystics who profess to resign themselves in passiveness more or less absolute to an imagined Divine Manifestation The quietude aimed at, beginning with an act of so-called resignation of self, is a state of mental inactivity, without thought, reflection, hope, or wish In this state it is supposed that the soul is brought so immediately into the Divine Presence as to be merged in It by an essential union

Quietism, accordingly, is not peculiar to Christianity, for it requires no basis of Christology It results from every philosophical system, by an excess or perversion of contemplation, when the ethical tendency of the mind is too weak to preserve a just balance with the contemplative tendency But, further than this, it will appear that the height of Quietism, as defined above, is really inconsistent with Christianity, in the state of mind inculcated, in the character of the Divine access sought for, and consequently in the nature of the promised union with the Deity. The further the Christian Quietist advances the nearer does he approach to the state of the heathen Quietist

Christian meditation is no inactive process The general rule that all knowledge shall be limited by religion, and referred to use and action, becomes in the instance of meditation the particular rule that "meditation shall be in order to the production of piety" Meditation therefore is "nothing else but the *using* of all those motives, arguments and irradiations which God intended to be instrumental to piety" Quietist contemplation professes to be a state superior to this The Quietists call it indeed a vulgar error to say that in the prayer of rest the faculties operate not, and the soul is idle and inactive, but they assert at the same time that the soul operates neither by means of the memory nor by the intellect, nor by ratiocination, but by simple apprehension [Molinos, *Spiritual Guide* i 12] What an active apprehension is when none of the powers of the mind are exerted it is difficult to see It appears that the Quietists think to attain that repose of the mind which is the result of exertion, and that quiet rest in God which follows from the earnestness of meditative prayer, by altogether surceasing from the exertion and superseding the earnestness Consequently, the mind being reduced to inactivity, the body has sway, and the state of perfect quietude, supposed to be a waiting for the Divine access, becomes that state (which may be produced by "mesmeric" process) in which the body suffers or simulates catalepsy, and the mind apes a divine trance Quietism becomes mental sleep

Christianity, in the next place, maintains a relation of the outward and the inward, of the corporeal and the spiritual The Mediator is God and Man and in virtue of the Incarnation the nearest approach to God is through Sacraments Quietism aims at an entire abstraction from all externals, and seeks to put the spirit of man into direct and immediate union with the very nature of the Godhead From this there inevitably results, instead of the Christian doctrine of the Communion of Saints, the doctrine of a pantheistic identification of the creature with the Creator, and an ultimate absorption of the soul into the substance of God.

The statements which have been thus made may be verified by history Vaughan [*Hours with the Mystics*, i ch 2, p 43, ed 1860] observes that the "same round of notions, occurring to minds of similar make under similar circumstances, is common to mystics in ancient India and in modern Christendom" He gives a summary of Hindoo Mysticism, that it

[1] Lays claim to disinterested love, as opposed to a mercenary religion

[2] Reacts against the ceremonial prescription and pedantic literalism of the Vedas

[3] Identifies in its Pantheism subject and object, worshipper and worshipped

[4] Aims at ultimate absorption into the Infinite

[5] Inculcates, as the way to this dissolution, absolute passivity, withdrawal into the inmost

self, cessation of all the powers—giving recipes for procuring this beatific torpor or trance

[6] Believes that eternity may thus be realized in time

[7] Has its mythical miraculous pretensions, i e its theurgic department

[8] And, finally, advises the learner in this kind of religion to submit himself implicitly to a spiritual guide,—his Garu

Of these articles the 3d, 4th, 5th and 6th give Quietism properly so called and it is our part to inquire whether the manifestation of this doctrine in Christianity adds anything essential to the definition of article 5, so as to save Christian Quietism from the pantheistic conclusions of articles 3 and 4 Mystics, it will be observed, who start with pantheistic doctrine, will deduce from that doctrine article 5 as a rule. Christian mystics, on the other hand, adopting the rule of this article, are led by it into Pantheism

The doctrine of disinterested love [art 1] does not constitute Quietism, nor is it peculiar to Quietism The controversy between Fénélon and Bossuet will immediately occur to the reader's mind

The reaction against ceremonial prescription [art 2] is not paralleled by the action of Quietism exclusively, against a formal routine of Church observances, but by such action of Mysticism in general [see Knox, *Remains*, vol. iii p 145] Article 7 relates to a matter incident, not essential, to Quietism The mind not able to attain to passivity, or not content to rest in it, craves a sign The entrance and extent of this theurgic element differences the mystic from the mystic of theopathy

Lastly, it may at once be noticed that the second book of Molinos' *Spiritual Guide* is "Of the Ghostly Father, and the Obedience due to Him," but neither is this point peculiar to Quietism

Again, Quietism is taught by the followers of Fo in China, "for they say that all those who seek true happiness ought to be so far absorbed by profound meditations as to make no use of their intellect, and that they ought through a perfect insensibility to sink into the repose and inaction of the first principle, which is the true way of being perfectly like it and partaking of happiness" [Bayle, *Dict.* art. Spinoza, note B, art Taulerus, note F]

But, to come to that which directly affects the Christian Church, there is a remarkable similarity between the Mysticism of the Plotinian School and that of the Quietists The aim of the divine philosopher was to enter into the immediate vision of Deity "Unconditioned Being, or the Godhead, cannot be grasped by thinking, or science, only by intuition In this pure intuition, the good, or the absolute being, gazes upon itself through the medium of our own spirits To close the eye against all things transient and variable, to raise ourselves to this simple essence, to take refuge in the absolute, this must be regarded as the highest aim of all our spiritual efforts" [Prof. C A Brandis in Smith's *Biog Dict* art Plotinus, p. 427] Plotinian contemplation may find a place in the system of John Smith and Henry More, but it may also pass as readily into the reveries of Molinos It is to be considered whether the tendency of such contemplation is not to reduce the Father manifested in the Son to the cold abstraction of the Plotinian Deity

In the Church there have been two kinds of Mysticism, one, a churchly Mysticism, which allies itself with the ordinances and rites of the Gospel, the other subjective or inward, which gradually rejects more and more all that is external, and even at last passes beyond the contemplation of the Humanity of our Lord, and the Sacraments which make men partakers of His Body, to "seek a resting-place beyond all that is created in the Logos as He existed prior to the Incarnation and Creation" [Dorner, *On the Person of Christ*, II i 233. MYSTICS]

Those who hold that the Sacraments are generally necessary to salvation will see in this a very obvious and natural discrimination, they will at once see that mystics of the former class have in their retention of church ordinances a check of excess and a guide of progress, according to their use of which their mysticism may be tolerated or approved, while mystics of the latter class, in their passing beyond these necessary ordinances, stand self-condemned, and pretending to advance in divine knowledge are really retrograding towards heathenism Nor will they who hold the true doctrine of the Sacraments find it strange that men who pass beyond the Sacraments of Christ presently pass beyond the contemplation of the Humanity of Christ This unchristianizing of Christianity, the presenting the great drama without its central figure, the removing God Incarnate from the mystery of godliness, as the result of a perverted or depraved Mysticism, is exhibited more than once in the history of the Church The words quoted from Dorner on the subject were used regarding Maximus Confessor. We may resume and continue them "True love and knowledge unite to seek a resting-point beyond all that is created, beyond even the humanity of Christ their final goal is the pure and bare (γυμνός) Logos, as He existed prior to the Incarnation and the Creation It is clear that in the last instance Christ is hereby reduced to the position of a mere theophany, and that the historical significance of His Person is destroyed The same thing appears also from his application to the professedly highest stage of the words Even though we have known Christ after the flesh, yet now know we Him no longer So far was he from attributing eternal significance to the God-man, that he regarded the Humanity of Christ rather in the light of an hindrance to the full knowledge and love of the pure God,—an hindrance which must be surmounted by those who aim to reach the highest stage" [Dorner, *loc. cit* and see note 48 there referred to] So in Italy, Marsilius Ficinus and John Pico of Mirandola turned Christianity in many respects into a Neo-Platonic theosophy. So in England the doctrine of the Quakers was noted to be highly dangerous "as mingling with so many good and wholesome things an abominable slighting of the history of Christ, and making a mere allegory of it, tending to the utter overthrow of that warrantable though more external frame of Christianity which Scripture itself points out to us" [H. More, quoted in Vaughan, *Hours*, ii p 328].

In another article [MYSTICS] this subject is more opened, and the Schools of Mysticism of the Greek and Latin Churches classified In the article HESYCHASTS is related the Quietism of the Greek Church At present it is only necessary to point out that these Hesychasts had the same rule as the Hindoo Quietists, namely, that to produce the state of abstraction the eyes must be steadily fixed on some particular object. The Hindoos prescribed the tip of the nose, the Hesychasts the navel. Such a custom is like the ordinary mesmeric trick, producing an affection of the brain which simulates catalepsy, the torpor of a corporeal Quietism. It is remarkable that this gross Materialism should have connected itself with the subtle disquisitions regarding the light of God as distinct from His essence

While this was in some minds the goal reached by unchecked subjective Mysticism, in other minds Pantheism was approached, sometimes reached, as by Amalric of Bena [Gieseler, *Compend* iii. p. 298, note 10, and p 467, Clark's transl] From the instances of history thus pointed out may be deduced the following proposition that the Quietist, passing over the sacraments and ordinances of the Church in his endeavour to obtain through contemplation, individually and independently of the Church, an union with God, is led to pass over the Incarnate Son, and to suppose and hold a pantheistic identification of the creature and the Creator This proposition is necessary as a preliminary to the consideration of the history of those to whom the name Quietist is commonly appropriated—Molinos and his followers

Molinos' *Spiritual Guide*, published in Spanish in 1675, and the same year in Italian, passed through above twenty editions in different languages in six years At Rome and Naples many of the clergy declared themselves in Molinos' favour, especially three Fathers of the Oratory, Coloredi, Ciceri and Petrucci (author of several treatises and letters on mystic theology), who were all afterwards made cardinals· Cardinal Odeschalci, who, when made Pope in the next year (Innocent XI), lodged Molinos in the Vatican and Cardinal D'Estrees, the French Ambassador at Rome, who had procured the translation into Italian of Malaval's Dialogue, which is said to go even beyond the Mysticism of Molinos The Jesuits in general were opposed to this doctrine of Quietism They published several works in refutation of it, and induced the Inquisition to take cognizance of the *Spiritual Guide* and of Petrucci's *Letters*, and it is said that the Jesuit Esparsa, who had given an imprimatur to Molinos' work, was kept in seclusion Not only were Molinos and Petrucci acquitted, but the writings issued against them were condemned as libels Petrucci was made Bishop of Jessi. About A D. 1684, Père la Chaise induced the King of France, by motives partly of orthodoxy, partly of policy, to move against the Quietists Cardinal D'Estrees, in obedience to the King, caused Molinos and Petrucci to be cited again before the Inquisition When taxed with his own prior approval of their doctrine, he professed that he had only pretended friendship to obtain a conviction Petrucci was dismissed, Molinos was imprisoned, and there was a lull in the controversy In 1687 the activity of the Inquisition was renewed. Count and Countess Vespiniani, and about seventy others, were brought up for examination on the charge (to state it in general terms) of neglecting the ordinances of religion, and giving themselves to solitude and inward prayer The Countess averred that she had been betrayed by her confessor, and declared that she would discontinue confession She and her husband were set free on promise of appearing when required In a month about two hundred persons were cited At this time the Pope himself was examined There was issued a circular to the Italian prelates warning them that, under the pretence of the way of quietude, execrable errors were taught, and enjoining them to forbid and disperse assemblies of Quietists There was added a list of nineteen articles of Quietist errors The Pope was at length brought to assent to the final condemnation of Molinos by a Bull dated Sept. 4th, 1687, and he lived till 1690 in the prison of the Inquisition.

We must review this chapter of Church history by the help of the principles drawn from earlier history

The second book of the *Spiritual Guide* is "Of the Ghostly Father, the Obedience due to Him, of indiscreet zeal, and of internal and external penance" Its thirteenth and fourteenth chapters are "Frequent Communion is an effectual means of getting all virtues, and in particular, internal peace" Molinos published also, about the same time as the *Spiritual Guide*, "A brief treatise concerning daily Communion," in which the practice is strongly recommended. There was no intention then of superseding Church ordinances, and it is no wonder that Molinos was classed with the acknowledged mystics of the Church The dangerous tendency of his teaching however appears to have been detected by one of his early Jesuit opponents "Segueri magnified the contemplative state highly, while he thought that few were capable of it, and considered it to be an extraordinary favour of God He censured severely some of Molinos' expressions, such as that, *He who had God, had Christ*, as if this were an abandoning of Christ's Humanity" These particular words we cannot discover, but the following will prove Segueri's charge "St Thomas with all the mystical masters says that *contemplation is a sincere, sweet, and full view of the eternal truth without ratiocination or reflexion* But if the soul rejoices in, or eyes the effects of, God in the creatures, and amongst them, in the Humanity of our Lord Christ, as the most perfect of all, this is not perfect contemplation, as St Thomas affirms, since all these are means for knowing of God as He is in Himself and although the Humanity of Christ be the most holy and perfect means for going to God, the chief instrument of our salvation and the channel through which we receive all the good we hope for nevertheless the Humanity is not the chief good, which consists in seeing God, but as Jesus Christ is more by His Divinity than His Humanity, so he that thinks and fixes his contemplation always on God (because the Divinity is united to Humanity) always thinks on and beholds Jesus Christ, especially the contemplative man in whom faith is more sincere, pure, and exercised" [*Spir Guide*, Preface, Advert II]

By this we are to understand the following "Know that he who would attain the mystical science must be denied and taken off from five things [1] from the creatures, [2] from temporal things, [3] from the very gifts of the Holy Ghost, [4] from himself, [5] he must be lost in God" [B iii sect 185] Mystical perfection then resolves itself into a bare abstract belief in God's infinite essence, and as Knox observes, is hostile to Christianity, because it necessarily disqualifies the mind for that distinct and intelligent contemplation of Immanuel, to which we are called by all and every trait, however minute, of the evangelic records [Knox, *Remains*, i pp 333-337][1] Molinos, it is true (as Knox observes of Fénélon), tries to avoid the legitimate conclusions of this doctrine, but his very caveats on the point sound strangely in a Christian ear "Hence it follows that the remembrance of the Passion and Death of our Saviour ought not wholly to be blotted out, nay, it is also certain, that whatever high elevation of mind the soul may be raised to, it ought not in all things to be separate from the most holy humanity" [*Spir Guide*, I cap xvi sect. 118][2]

This niggardly concession only brings out more strikingly the relegation of the proper powers of the Gospel to an earlier and inferior stage of the Christian life, and the assumption that man can, and in his best state does, contemplate God simply in Himself, in His own pure spiritual essence

Against the delusions of this doctrine the only safeguard is the use of the ordinances of the Church Petrucci, accordingly, was dismissed on the second examination, when Molinos was imprisoned, because, as the Protestant author of the *Letters from Italy* phrases it, he mixed in his letters so many rules relating to the devotions of the Quire that there was less occasion given for censure in his writings that is, he limited his mystical devotions by the rules and requirements of an adherence to the communion of the faithful Again, the tendency of Molinos' teaching became still more apparent when Countess Vespiniani, and doubtless others after her example, refused confession, such refusal leading, by the rules of the Church, to the omission of Holy Communion There appears then to be little ground for the assertion that the opposition to Molinos was merely an opposition to true religion, or for the mere vulgar assertion that it arose from the lessening of the priests' profits Nor does such a statement involve an approval of all the proceedings of the Inquisition

That this system of Quietism conducts directly to a pantheistic identification of the creature with the Creator, through the annihilation of self, which is so much insisted on, is very clear The chapter [iii 19] on true and perfect annihilation ends thus "The soul thus dead and annihilated lives no longer in itself, because God lives in it, and now it may most truly be said of it, that it is a renewed phœnix, because it is changed, transformed, spiritualized, and deified" This is different doctrine from St Paul's [Gal ii 20], from St John's [1 John iv 9], from our Lord's [John xvii 20-23] And the term Deification is not an accidental hyperbole, but Molinos' usual language.

Fénélon and Madame Guyon were usually called Semi-Quietists they were preserved from the extremes into which Molinos fell by the different temper of their minds "A moral taste such as Fénélon's would naturally and necessarily place limits to the aberrations of understanding," in M Guyon the theurgic element very largely qualified the theopathetic Regarding Fénélon's doctrine of disinterested love, it is sufficient to refer to Butler's *Sermons on the Love of Our Neighbour*

But this doctrine, demonstrated, by Butler's establishment of a different view, to be founded on pure ignorance of man's true nature, leads us to some general reflections on the moral character and tendencies of the subjective Mysticism we have been considering That character and tendency is seen in the anxiety to detect a principle of criminal selfishness underlying the pleasure which a good man has in doing good, the testimony of his good conscience to his sincerity, the joy which he has in the Holy Ghost The analysis which they made of the actions of their minds was probably correct Probably they did detect an undue self-love and self-esteem And for this reason they were in that habit of introspection instead of looking from themselves to Christ and Christ's members, which naturally engenders those feelings They created the disease, and then strove to cure it, not by reversing their habit of mind, and returning to a healthy course of action, but by attempting to merge the true joys of religion in a state of mental torpor Molinos' rule has already been quoted, that the Quietist must be taken off, as from the creature,

[1] Vaughan defends Molinos on this point See *Hours with the Mystics*, ii p 299

[2] It may be noticed that Molinos' tract on Daily Communion has been neglected in comparison with the *Spiritual Guide* Also, that the English edition of the *Spiritual Guide* [1699] leaves out altogether the second book, the subject of which was named above, in which are the chapters on Frequent Communion Whether any Italian editions were printed after Countess Vespiniani's refusal of confession, without this book regarding the office of the confessor, we have not been able to ascertain But the omission in the second English edition is significant, shewing the real tendency of Molinos' doctrine An abstract of the *Spiritual Guide* was published in England in 1774, and is still reprinted for the use of Quakers

including the Humanity of our Lord, so from the gifts of the Holy Ghost Again we read, "The monster self-love puts its head everywhere—sometimes it cleaves to spiritual pleasures, staying even in the gifts of God, and in His graces freely bestowed" [*Spir Guide,* iii 3 20] Again, "The very virtues acquired, and not purified, are a hindrance to this great gift of the peace of the soul, and more, the soul is clogged by an inordinate desire of sublime gifts, by the appetite of feeling spiritual consolation, by sticking to infused and divine graces, entertaining itself in them, and desiring more of them, to enjoy them, and finally, by a desire of becoming great" [iii 4, 26] As surely as a man is ill, or makes himself ill, who is every hour feeling his pulse and examining his tongue, so surely is there a morbid state of mind engendered by unceasingly turning the eye within instead of looking out of self to Christ The unavoidable consequence is a remissness in good works The chapter of the *Spiritual Guide* concerning indiscreet zeal is a sad example [ii 3] "No sooner dost thou find in thyself any new and fervent light, but thou wouldst lay thyself wholly out for the good of souls, and in the meantime it's odds but that that is self-love which thou takest to be pure zeal" "It is never good to love thy neighbour to the detriment of thine own spiritual good To please God in purity ought to be the only scope of thy works" "One pure act of internal resignation is more worth than a hundred thousand exercises for one's own will" A contemporary comment was as follows "Le Chap 3 est détestable Sous le titre, de *zèle indiscret,* il condamne toute la pratique de la charité tendant au salut du prochain" [*Traité Historique,* 1699, p 122] Knox identifies the doctrine of Molinos with that of the English mystic Law, and concludes that the moral characters of the doctrine are the worst part, they amount to this, that nothing commonly called vice is so essentially vicious as seeing, knowing, or feeling the reality of one's own virtue, and that no virtue is genuine that is earnest to feel its own progress or even to be satisfied of its own existence [*Remains,* i p 343] If Quietism tends to supersede Gospel faith, it tends also to supersede Gospel righteousness

[Molinos' *Spiritual Guide, with a Short Treatise concerning Daily Communion,* 1688 (the edition referred to above) Another English edition, 1699, without the "Daily Communion," and omitting book ii this edition has "The Substance of several Letters from Italy concerning the Quietists" *Life of Lady Guion,* written by herself, now abridged, Bristol, 1772, this book has "Life of M de Molinos and Progress of Quietism," which appears to be translated from *Recueil des Diverses Pieces concernant le Quietisme et les Quietistes,* 1688 *Traité Historique, contenant la Jugement d'un Protestant,* 1699 Knox, "Letter on the Character of Mysticism, and Answer to a Reply," *Remains,* vol i Vaughan's *Hours with the Mystics* Upham, *Life of Madame Guyon* Bossuet, *Works* Gilbert Burnet, *Tracts,* 1689, vol i "All that can be alleged in defence of Molinos," says Mosheim, "has been collected by Weisman, in his *Histor Ecclesiast* sect. xvii"]

QUINQUARTICULAR CONTROVERSY The controversy respecting the "Five Articles" [ARMINIANS CALVINISTS DORT, SYNOD OF]

QUINTILLIANS [PRISCILLIANISTS]

R

RACCHEI A name given by mistake to the ZACCHEI [Nicetas, *Thesaur Orth Fid.* in *Bibl Max. Lugd* xxv 109, E]

RAKUSIANS A Christian sect mentioned by Mahometan writers as existing in Arabia, but of whom nothing definite is known Their tenets appear to have been those of the MENDÆANS or Sabians, still further corrupted by Ebionite influences [Sprenger, *Das Leben und die Lehre des Mohammed,* i 43, ii 255, iii 387, 395 Weil, *Mohammed der Prophet*, 249, n 386]

RANDALLITES [FREE WILL BAPTISTS]

RANTERS A profligate sect of Antinomian heretics which became conspicuous under the name of Ranters during the Commonwealth, but was probably of older date and associated with the FAMILISTS, of whom Fuller speaks as their ancestors [Fuller's *Ch Hist* iii 211, ed 1837]

In Ross's Πανσεβεία the Ranters are described as making an open profession of lewdness and irreligion, as holding that God, angels, devils, heaven, hell, etc , are fictions and fables , that Moses, John the Baptist, and our Lord, were impostors , that praying and preaching are useless , that all ministry has come to an end, and that sin is a mere imagination He says that in their letters the Ranters endeavoured to be strangely profane and blasphemous, uttering atheistical imprecations, and he gives a specimen which quite bears out his words He also alleges that they sanctioned and practised community of women [Ross's Πανσεβεία, p 287, ed 1655] Much of the same account also is given by Pagitt a few years later [Pagitt's *Heresiography,* pp 259, 294. ed 1662]

Baxter also writes respecting them "I have myself letters written from Abingdon, where among both soldiers and people this contagion did then prevail, full of horrid oaths and curses, and blasphemy, not fit to be repeated by the tongue and pen of man , and this all uttered as the effect of knowledge and a part of their religion, in a fanatic strain, and fathered on the Spirit of God" [Baxter's *Own Life and Times,* 77] And the following passage is found in a Life of Bunyan, added to an imitation of his work which is called "the Third Part of the Pilgrim's Progress."

"About this time," in Bunyan's early life, "a very large liberty being given as to conscience, there started up a sect of loose prophane wretches, afterwards called Ranters and Sweet Singers, pretending themselves safe from, or being incapable of, sinning , though indeed they were the debauchest and profligate wretches living, in their baudy meetings and revels , for fancying themselves in Adam's state, as he was in Paradise before the fall, they would strip themselves, both men and women, and so catch as catch could, and to it they went, to satiate their lust under pretence of increasing and multiplying" [*An account of the Life and Actions of Mr John Bunyan*, etc , London, 1692, p 22] In later times the name of "Ranters" has been given to the Primitive Methodists

RASCHOLNIKS A Russian word, denoting "Schismatics," and used as a general name for all those bodies which dissent from the orthodox and Established Church in that country

Although a few sects, as the Strigolniks, existed as early the fourteenth or fifteenth centuries the greater number arose either in the middle of the seventeenth century, among those who rejected the revision of Holy Scripture, and of the old liturgical books, proposed and carried out by the Patriarch Nicon at Moscow [A D. 1654], or in the earlier part of the eighteenth century, in consequence of the innovating policy of Peter the Great [A D 1689-1725] Many of the Rascholniks regard this Emperor as Antichrist, and his semi-political, semi-ecclesiastical reforms as impious, *e g* the amalgamation of Church and State under his own supreme personal rule , the alteration of the date of the commencement of the year from the first of September to the first of January , and the substitution of the date Anno Domini for Anno Mundi in the calculation of time The general character of Russian dissent may be described as eminently conservative Unlike English dissent, which is usually based on some deviation from time-honoured tradition, or some departure from Catholic teaching, it resents the most trifling interference with the hereditary ritual, such as the number of fingers with which the sign of the cross is to be made, the mode of pronouncing such a word as Jesus, the number of times in which an *Amen* or an *Alleluia* is to be repeated in the course of a service It has also a tendency to develope into extreme fanaticism, as may be seen by reference to the SKOPTZI or KHLISTI , and it does not escape the proclivity of schism in all ages, and in all countries, to produce an increasing number of sects, and subdivisions of sects, more or less hostile to each other as well as to the Church from which they have originally sprung The chief Russian sects are the Bespopofftschins, Besslovestnie, Blagoslovennie, Duchobortzi, Isbraniki, Istinceye Christiane, Karabliki, Khlisti, Kerjakis, Malakanes, Martinists, Morelschiki, Niconians, Njetowschitschini, Philipponians, Pomorane, Popofftschins, Rascolschiki, Sabatniki, Skoptzi, Starovertzi, Strigolniks, Wjetkaers, Yedinovertzi, of each of which some account is given in this Dictionary Further information about them may be obtained in Mouravieff's *History of the Church of Russia*, London, 1842 Krazinski's *Lectures on Slavonia, or Religious History of the Slavonic Nations*, London, 1869. Farlati, Episcopi Bosnensis, *Illyricum Sacrum* August. von Haxthausen, *Studien uber Russland*, Han 1847 Gregoire, *Histoire des Sectes Religieuses*, vol iv Paris, 1814 *History of Russian Sects*, by Dimitri, Archbishop of Rostow Strahl's *Geschichte der Grundung und Ausbreitung der Christlichen Lehre in Russie*, and *Geschichte der Russichen Kirche*, Halle 1830 Platon's *Present State of the Greek Church in Russia*, Pinkerton's transl, Edin. 1814, New York, 1815

RATIONALISTS Those who maintain that reason is the sole guide to, and test of, truth in matters of religion, and especially in the interpretation of Holy Scripture

The name is first found in use in a "Letter of Intelligence" written from London to Secretary Nicholas, in which it is said that "The Presbyterian and Independent agree well enough together But there is a new sect sprung up among them, and these are the Rationalists, and what their reason dictates them in Church or State stands for good until they be convinced with better, and that is according as it serves their own turns Some of them were at the House this day" [October 14th, 1647], "and much reason was propounded this day by divers of the agitators to the Council of War"[1] [Clarendon's *St Pap* ii app xl] Soon afterwards the Socinians were called Rationalists by Comenius, and in the eighteenth century the name was used in Germany to designate those who had been previously called NATURALISTS [Hahn, *De Rationalismo a disputation at Leipzig*] Both in England and in Germany the name is very commonly used as a designation of those who reject generally the idea of "Supernaturalism," whether as relating to faith or facts—the term "Naturalist" in this sense having dropped out of use

I THE RISE OF RATIONALISM The remote ancestry of modern Rationalism may be traced to the NOMINALISTS of the Middle Ages, whose bold questionings of received dogmas had a continual tendency towards the denial of all which could not be proved by observation, and whose notions respecting Deity continually produced that evolution of opinions which later times have called Pantheism But the more immediate origin of Rationalism is to be found in two influences, one early and one of later date, which sprung out of the Reformation of the sixteenth century

[1] The first of these influences was the spirit of doubt—often developing into actual scepticism,—which was encouraged in the laity by the reckless assaults of Luther and Calvin, and still more, of their followers, on established beliefs The twists and turns, and non-natural interpretations which were given to the words of Holy Scripture, for the purpose of justifying the novel theological positions which were taken up by these leaders of Protestantism, were such as to unsettle the minds of multitudes as regarded the plain sense of Divine Revelation The ignorant followed the track opened out by their leaders, and widened it still more by the adoption of any wild, irreverent, or foolish interpretation that would serve their immediate turn the educated followed in the same track, by learning still further to undervalue the authority of that which their leaders had treated with such reckless freedom Thus, Lutheranism in Germany, Calvinism in France and England, became fruitful fields for the growth of Rationalism

[2] The second great influence arising out of the Reformation was a reaction against the extravagant views which some Protestant Divines maintained on the subject of inspiration These were carried to such a length that every word of a vernacular Bible was treated as if it had been undoubtedly inspired; that the vowel points of the Hebrew text (never used in Hebrew Bibles until about A D 500) were also considered as being endowed with the same high authority, that all influence of a human element in the composition of the books of Holy Writ was denied, and that criticism of every kind was discouraged, or even reprobated, as if it had been an insult to the Word of God Against such extravagances the minds of scholars naturally revolted, and it was inevitable (according to all experience of human nature) that there should be an oscillation in the opposite direction, when others would deal with the Bible as they would deal with a collection of ordinary ancient writings, and deny it any supernatural character whatever

The results of these two influences exhibited themselves first in the early English Deists, of whom Lord Herbert of Cherbury [A D 1581-1648], the elder brother of George Herbert the poet, may be considered as the representative These professed a belief in the possibility of a revelation, and thought it most likely that a law of natural

[1] This principle may be found in the pages of Chillingworth, whose religion was first that of the Church of England, then that of the Roman Catholics, then "the religion of Protestants," and finally that of the Socinians "Your Church," he writes to the Roman Catholics, "you admit, because you think you have reason to do so, so that by you, as well as Protestants, all is finally resolved into your own reason" [Chillingworth's *Relig of Protest* 134] Lord Clarendon said of Chillingworth that he "had contracted such an irresolution and habit of doubting, that at last he was confident of nothing" and Dugald Stewart uses this characteristic of the Protestant champion as an illustration of the ruinous result which follows from bondage to the scholastic logic

religion was divinely communicated to the earliest of mankind, which had since been transmitted by tradition to their descendants But they would not allow that Revelation exists at present in any other form, and set aside the Bible without troubling themselves to examine it, just as they set aside everything else professing to be part of a supernatural system, as being *à priori* impossible Very similar was the treatment of Holy Scripture by Hobbes [A D 1588-1679] and Spinoza [A D 1632-1677], both of whom may be said rather to have ignored it than to have made any elaborate attempt to refute its statements or to reconcile them with their own philosophical systems

The earliest writer, indeed, who set himself systematically to oppose received opinions respecting Holy Scripture from the Rationalist point of view, as distinguished from that of the Deists, was a French Calvinist named De la Peyrère [A D 1594-1676], who published a work entitled *Præadamitæ*, in the year 1655, in which he anticipated many of the criticisms that have been put forth as if they were new in modern days This author, says Lecky, "who fully admitted, though he endeavoured to restrict, the sphere of the miraculous, had been struck by some difficulties connected with the ordinary doctrine of original sin, and by some points in which science seemed to clash with the assertions of the Old Testament, and he endeavoured to meet them by altogether isolating the Biblical history from the general current of human affairs Adam, he maintained, was not the father of the human race, but simply the progenitor of the Jews, and the whole antediluvian history is only that of a single people Thus the antiquity which the Eastern nations claimed might be admitted, and the principal difficulties attending the Deluge were dissolved It was altogether a mistake to suppose that death and sickness and suffering were the consequences of the transgression Adam had by this act simply incurred spiritual penalties, which descended upon the Jews 'In the day thou eatest thou shalt die,' could not have been meant literally, because it was not literally fulfilled, nor can the curse upon the serpent, because the motion of the serpent along the ground is precisely that which its conformation implies The existence of men who were not of the family of Adam is shadowed obscurely in many passages, but appears decisively in the history of Cain, who feared to wander forth least men should kill him, and who built a city at a time when, according to the common view, he was almost alone in the world The mingling of the sons of God and the daughters of men means the intermarriage between the two races The Deluge is an absolute impossibility if regarded as universal, but not at all surprising if regarded as a partial inundation Proceeding to the history of a later period, La Peyrère in the first place denies the Mosaic authorship of the Pentateuch In defence of this position he urges the account of the death of Moses, and he anticipates several of those minute criticisms which in our own day have acquired so great a prominence The phrase, 'These are the words which Moses spake beyond Jordan,' the notice of the city which is called 'Jair to the present day' the iron bedstead of Og still shewn in Rabbath, the difficulties about the conquest of the Idumæans, and a few other passages, seem to shew that the compilation of these books was long posterior to the time of Moses, while certain signs of chronological confusion which they evince render it probable that they are not homogeneous, but are formed by the fusion of several distinct documents It should be observed, too, that they employ a language of metaphor and of hyperbole which has occasionally given rise to misapprehensions, special instances of Providential guidance being interpreted as absolute miracles Thus, for example, the wool of the Jewish flocks was quite sufficient to furnish materials for clothing in the desert, and the assertion that the clothes of the Jews waxed not old is simply an emphatic expression of that extraordinary providence which preserved them from all want for forty years in the wilderness At the same time, La Peyrère does not deny that the Jewish history is full of miracles, but he maintains very strongly that these were only local, and that the general course of the universe was never disturbed to effect them The prolongation of the day at the command of Joshua was not produced by any alteration in the course of the earth or sun, but was simply an atmospheric phenomenon such as is sometimes exhibited in the Arctic regions The darkness at the Crucifixion was also local, the retrogression of the shadow on the sundial in the reign of Hezekiah did not result from a disturbance of the order of the heavenly bodies, the light that stood over the cradle of Christ was a meteor, for a star could not possibly mark out with precision a house" [Lecky's *Rationalism in Europe*, i 323, ed 1865] It cannot be said that this comparatively unknown French writer founded any school, and he probably only expressed, in an extreme form, the views of many whose faith in Holy Scripture had been thoroughly shaken, but who were looking for some less shocking justification of their opinions than that involved in the theory of the later Deists, that it is a mere congeries of impostures It is however a theory which has been adopted by many later Rationalists, recommending itself to them by leaving open many important questions, such as those of the origin of the visible creation and especially of man, and also by not interfering in any great degree with the narrative of those events given in Holy Scripture

II English Freethinkers —The Deists and Freethinkers were necessarily Rationalists, and there is unhappily, a regular succession of English writers of this extreme rationalizing class from the middle of the seventeenth century down to Hume and Gibbon, whose writings belong to the last half of the eighteenth This school of Rationalists may be said to begin with Charles Blount [A D 1654 93], the third son of Sir Henry Pope Blount, who was himself known as a sceptical writer The "Anima Mundi" of Charles Blount, in the writing of which he is supposed to have been assisted by his father, was professedly intended to vindicate Christianity against Paganism, by shewing the errors of the latter respecting the immortality of the soul. But it is, in reality, a keen ironical attack upon the Scriptural doctrine of the soul, and was probably put into such a form that it might more easily obtain the license for printing which was necessary at the time of its publication, in the year 1679. Of a similar character was his "Great is Diana of the Ephesians," which, by arguments against heathen sacrifices, endeavoured to prove that Christianity was an invention of priests. In a similar ironical style Blount attacked the miracles of Holy Scripture in his notes to an edition of "The Two First Books of Philostratus" on the Life and Miracles of Apollonius of Tyana, which was published in the year 1680, and to which he prefixed a motto from Seneca—"Cum omnia in incerto sint, fave tibi et crede quod mavis"—strikingly illustrative of the Rationalist's standpoint.[1] Blount wrote many smaller works, which had much influence in inoculating the educated classes with Rationalist principles during the last quarter of the seventeenth century. His "Oracles of Reason" made its appearance in 1693, under the editorship of his friend Gildon, shortly after its author had put an end to his life by suicide, because his deceased wife's sister refused to marry him. In this last work he borrowed largely, without acknowledgment, from the writings of De la Peyrère.

Shortly after the death of Charles Blount, an author equally bold—and like him a member of a Roman Catholic family, though subsequently a Protestant Dissenter—made his appearance in the same field of antichristian literature. This was John Toland [A.D. 1669-1722], who published in the year 1693 a volume entitled "Christianity not Mysterious," the object of which is fully shewn by its second title, "A Discourse shewing there is nothing in the Gospel contrary to reason nor above it, and that no Christian doctrine can be properly called a Mystery." This work was very notorious in its day, and was answered by as many as fifty-four writers in England, France, and Germany during the following half century. It is not a work of high talent, but its enunciation of the Rationalist theory was plain and undisguised; and it was thus intelligible to a much wider circle of readers than the irony of Blount or the philosophy of Hobbes had been.

Toland also endeavoured to lessen the authority of the New Testament by a book to which he gave the title of "Amyntor," published in 1698. In this he classed the apocryphal Gospels, and other works of a similar character to the number of eighty, with the authentic Gospels, pretending that there was no better evidence for the truth of the latter than of the former. [TOLAND.]

Lord Shaftesbury [A.D. 1671-1713] was an elegant writer, who gave a certain amount of lofty patronage to practical Christianity, as something to be admired and to be thought of rather favourably than otherwise, but who at the same time endeavoured to destroy its force and influence as an historical and intellectual religion, and thus drew nearer to the type of the modern Rationalist school than any of his predecessors. His "Characteristics of Men, Manners, Opinions, and Times," in three volumes, appeared in the year 1711, and contained so much that is contrary to the received principles of Christianity as to elicit even from Voltaire the declaration that he was too bitter an opponent of it. Bishop Warburton has also handed down an opinion of Pope that Lord Shaftesbury's writings had done more harm to revealed religion in England than all the other works of infidelity put together. His criticisms on Holy Scripture are principally contained in the third volume of the "Characteristics," in which there are disquisitions on "Scepticism," the "History of Religion," "Inspiration," and other kindred subjects, but throughout the other volumes also he deals with every part of Revelation in the most contemptuous manner, and the highest place which he allows to it is that of a collection of works, established in use for purposes of order and government by public authority. The general tone of Lord Shaftesbury's Rationalism may be seen by his statement that the suspicion was natural to intellectual man "that the holy records themselves were no other than the pure invention and artificial compliment of an interested party, in behalf of the richest corporation and most profitable monopoly which could be erected in the world" [Shaftesb. *Charact.* iii. 336]. This 'suspicion,' which was rather a foregone conclusion than what it was called, Shaftesbury endeavoured to corroborate by critical objections against the Scriptures drawn from the variety of readings and of interpretations, from supposed interpolations and fraudulent dealings with the text; and in these objections he anticipated many of those that have been offered by modern writers.

Another layman belonging to the higher classes, Anthony Collins [A.D. 1676-1729], a contemporary of Lord Shaftesbury, carried still

[1] Apollonius Tyanæus is said to have been born at Tyana in Cappadocia about the time of the Christian era, and to have lived until nearly the end of the first century, being thus exactly contemporary with St. John, and living through the time of our Lord and His other apostles. His life was written about a hundred years after his death, by a rhetorician named Philostratus, who seems to have mingled a few facts with a large amount of fiction, and especially to have imitated the Gospel miracles with the view of setting up Apollonius as a heathen rival of Christ. The birth of Apollonius is announced to his mother beforehand by Proteus, who himself becomes incarnate; a choir of swans is heard singing for joy on the occasion of his birth; he casts out devils, raises the dead to life, heals the sick, appears and disappears in a supernatural manner, and a Divine voice was heard calling him at his death. The ECLECTICS of the third and fourth centuries set up a comparison between Apollonius and our Lord, but the idea seems to have lain dormant until it was revived by Lord Herbert and Blount. For an examination of this comparison see Cudworth's *Intellectual System*, iv. 15; More's *Mystery of Godliness*, iv. 9-12; Baur's *Apollon von Tyana und Christus*; and Ritter's *Geschichte der Phil.* iv. 492.

further the principles of the FREETHINKERS, as the Rationalist school now began to be named in England His first publication was an "Essay concerning the use of Reason in Propositions the evidence whereof depends upon Human Testimony," published anonymously in 1709, and this was followed by many tracts and larger works, also anonymons, the last being a volume "On the Grounds and Reasons of the Christian Religion," and on "The Quotations made from the Old Testament in the New," which did not appear until after his death In his "Discourse on Freethinking" Collins also declares his opinions as to the result of a "rational" examination into the authority of Holy Scripture, and places the latter on the same footing as the Vedas, the Koran, and other "sacred books" Collins maintained, most uncritically, that the Gospels had undergone a general alteration in the sixth century, but he also maintained that the narrative which they contain had no foundation in fact, but was based upon the prophecies of the Old Testament, and that the whole New Testament was of an allegorical and not a literal character

Among those who learned at the feet of these Freethinking laymen was Matthew Tindal [A D 1657-1733], a Fellow of All Souls College, Oxford, and Thomas Woolston [A D 1669-1733], a clerical Fellow of Sidney Sussex College, Cambridge

Tindal (who was a Roman Catholic during the reign of James II) reproduced many of the arguments of Shaftesbury against the authenticity of the Scriptures in his "Christianity as old as the Creation," published in 1730 The object of this work was to establish the theory of the NATURALISTS, that what they called "natural religion," i e the guidance of reason and feeling, as originally given to mankind, is sufficient for all human necessities. True religion being thus established in a complete and in its only obligatory form at the Creation, any subsequent Revelation would be wholly unnecessary, and Christianity becomes surplusage

Woolston was chiefly notorious for his "Discourse on the Miracles of our Saviour in view of the present controversy between Infidels and Apostates," Collins being the Infidel, and his opponents the Apostates. These Discourses came out in the form of six "Letters" during the years 1727-29, and obtained so rapid a circulation as to run into twelve editions in two or three years Voltaire states, apparently from personal knowledge, that 30,000 of them were sold, and that large numbers were sent to America. Swift notices their great popularity in his biting poem "On the Death of Dr Swift, written in November 1731," in the following lines, which he puts into the mouth of Lintot the bookseller, who cannot find a copy of the Dean's writings, for they are already out of fashion, but who offers among other publications these letters of Woolston on the Miracles

> "Here's Wolston's tracts the twelfth edition,
> 'Tis read by every politician,
> The country members when in town,
> To all their boroughs send them down;
> You never met a thing so smart,
> The courtiers have them all by heart
> Those maids of honour who can read,
> Are taught to use them for their creed.
>
> * * * *
>
> He does an honour to his gown,
> By bravely running priestcraft down
> He shews, as sure as God's in Glo ster,
> That Moses was a grand imposter,
> That all his miracles were cheats,
> Performed as jugglers do their feats,
> The Church had never such a writer,
> A shame he has not got a mitre"

Woolston was tried for blasphemy and condemned to a year's imprisonment, with a fine of £150 If he could have found sureties for his good behaviour he would have been released from prison, but freedom of thought does not generally develope freedom of fellowship, and numerous as were Woolston's readers no two could be found liberal enough to become his sureties, and he died in prison

The character of Woolston was a very contemptible one, and his notorious work is no better The general substance of it is that all Scripture is allegorical This he alleges, not in the sense of Origen and other early writers, who maintained a primary literal sense, and made the allegorical sense only secondary, for Woolston maintained that Scripture has no literal sense, and that all its seemingly historical narratives are in reality mere allegories "When he wants to utter grosser blasphemies than in his own person he dares, or than would befit the standing-point which he had assumed from whence to assault Revelation, he introduces a Jewish Rabbi, and suffers him to speak without restraint, himself only observing, 'This is what an adversary might say, to these accusations we Christians expose ourselves, so long as we cleave to the historic letter, we can only escape them by forsaking that, and holding fast the allegorical meaning alone' . . . He is dealing with the miracle of the man sick of the palsy, who was let through the broken roof of the house where Jesus was, and thereupon healed [Mark ii 1-12] But how, he asks, should there have been such a crowd to hear Jesus preach at Capernaum, where He was so well known, and so little admired? And then, if there was that crowd, what need of such urgent haste? It was but waiting an hour or two till the multitude had dispersed, 'I should have thought their faith might have worked patience' Why did not Jesus tell the people to make way? Would they not have done so readily, since to see a miracle was the very thing they wanted? How should the pulleys, ropes, and ladder have been at hand to haul him up? How strange that they should have had hatchets and hammers ready to break through the spars and rafters of the roof, and stranger still, that the good man of the house should have endured, without a remonstrance, his property to be so injured! How did those below escape without injury from the falling tiles and plaster? And, if there were a door in the roof, as some, to mitigate the difficulty, tell us, why did not Jesus go up to the roof, and there speak the healing word, and so spare all this trouble, damage, and danger?" As for his allegorical meaning, Woolston considers that "By the palsy of this man is signified a 'dissoluteness of morals and unsteadiness of faith and principles, which is the condition of mankind at present, who want Jesus' help for the cure of it' The four bearers are the four Evangelists, 'on whose faith and doctrine mankind is to be carried unto Christ' The house to the top of which he is to be carried is 'the intellectual edifice of the world, otherwise called Wisdom's house' But 'to the sublime sense of the Scriptures, called the top of the house, is the man to be taken, he is not to abide in the low and literal sense of them' Then if he dare to 'open the house of Wisdom, he will presently be admitted to the presence and knowledge of Jesus'" [Trench *on the Miracles*, 82, ed 1850] Such irrational stuff as this has become the daily pabulum of many more modern "Rationalists," and in the earlier half of the last century, when it was comparatively novel, there was doubtless a large class of persons of a similar kind whose reasoning powers had been imperfectly educated, and who took such folly for wisdom because it looked deep, and they could not see below its surface to discern its absurd shallowness

This unworthy clergyman was, however, far eclipsed by one who became the great exponent of the true office which Reason holds in matters of religion, Joseph Butler [A D 1692-1752], who subsequently became Bishop of Durham, and whose "Analogy of Religion, Natural and Revealed, to the Constitution and Course of Nature," was published in the year 1736 This profound and solid work may be said to have extinguished Rationalism in England for a century, except so far as it was represented directly in the Essays of Hume and the fleeting writings of Lord Bolingbroke, and indirectly in the grand historical volumes of Gibbon [Lechler's *Geschichte des Englischen Deismus* SCEPTICS DICT *of* THEOL, DEISM]

III GERMAN RATIONALISTS The rough footings of German Rationalism were laid by Spinoza and Leibnitz, but the upper courses of the foundation were more methodically arranged by Wolff and Semler

Christian Wolff [A D 1679-1754], a native of Breslau, became Professor of Mathematics in the University of Halle in the year 1707, and on the recommendation of Leibnitz For some years Wolff employed himself entirely upon the duties of his office, and the production of mathematical text-books His mind was always bent, however, towards theological studies, and before long he came to the conclusion that true theology must be a science which could be followed out with mathematical exactness of demonstration, and that only when so followed out could theology be true He writes of himself, "Having been devoted to the study of theology by a vow"—that of his father before he was born—"I had also chosen it for myself, and my intention has all along been to serve God in the ministry, even after I had become Professor at Halle, until at length I was led away from it against my will, God having arranged circumstances in such a manner that I could not carry out my intention But having lived in my native place, Breslau, among the Catholics, and having perceived from my very childhood the zeal of the Lutherans and Catholics against each other, the idea was always agitating my mind, whether it would not be possible so distinctly to exhibit theological truth that it would not admit of any contradiction When afterwards I learned that the mathematicians were so sure of their ground that every one must acknowledge it to be true, I became anxious to study mathematics for the sake of the method, in order to give diligence to reduce theology to incontrovertible certainty" The inevitable corollary of this principle followed, namely, that what cannot be proved to demonstration, as a mathematical truth may be proved, cannot be true and thus everything that is mysterious in religion must at once be swept away

In the year 1719 Wolff published his "Rational Thoughts on God, the World, the Soul of Man, and Being in general," and, in the following year, his "Moral Philosophy," shortly succeeded by a volume on "Civil and Political Philosophy" These works raised great opposition to Wolff among the Pietists, who then formed the most influential party at Halle, and this opposition was brought to a climax by a controversy which arose out of a lecture on the Morals of Confucius, in which he enthusiastically praised the philosopher Court influences were also brought to bear against him, and at length, in November 1723, the King of Prussia, Frederick William I, deprived Wolff of his professorship, and ordered him to leave the kingdom within forty-eight hours For seventeen years he resided at Marburg and Cassell, where he published many philosophical works and especially his "Natural Theology," which appeared in the year 1737, and in which the supremacy of Reason over Revelation was boldly asserted On this point Wolff maintained that a Divine Revelation cannot contradict reason and experience, nor command anything which is opposed to the laws of nature But whose reason and experience are to be taken as the standard, or where the code of the "laws of nature" is to be found, he does not state The inevitable result of accepting such a principle must be that those who adopt it subordinate Revelation to their own individual reason and experience, however narrow and untrained they may be.

Wolff was recalled to Prussia, and restored to his Professorship at Halle in the year 1740 by Frederick the Great, and became extremely popular as a leader of thought His application of mathematical reason to philosophy and theology fell in with the tone of the age, and thus the Wolffian system quickly took possession of the German mind "The system," says Professor Farrar, "soon became universally dominant Its orderly method possessed the fascination which belongs to any Encyclopædic view of human knowledge The evil effects which it subsequently produced in reference to religion were due only to the point of view which it ultimately induced Like Locke's work on the reasonableness of Christianity, it stimulated speculation concerning revelation By suggesting attempts to deduce *à priori* the necessary character of religious truths, it turned men's attention more than ever away from spiritual religion to theology The attempt to demonstrate everything caused dogmas to be viewed apart from their practical aspect, and men being compelled to discard the previous method of drawing philosophy out of Scripture, an independent philosophy was created, and Scripture compared with its discoveries Philosophy no longer relied on Scripture, but Scripture rested on philosophy Dogmatic theology was made a part of metaphysical philosophy This was the mode in which Wolff's philosophy ministered indirectly to the creation of the disposition to make scriptural dogmas submit to reason, which was denominated Rationalism" [Farrar's *Bampt Lect* 215]

Still further, however, was this principle of the Rationalist school developed by John Solomon Semler [A D 1725-1791], who is generally considered as the father of modern Rationalism This title does not, in reality, belong to him or to any other particular person, for modern Rationalism originated with many minds as has already been shewn But that special school of Rationalists who busy themselves with the destructive criticism of Holy Scripture may justly look up to Semler as their modern founder

Semler was brought up as a strict Pietist, but was unsettled in his opinions by the teaching of Baumgarten, who had succeeded Wolff at Halle, to which university Semler was sent from Saalfeld, his native place At the age of twenty-six he was appointed Professor of Theology at Halle, and so continued for forty years During that time he sent as many as one hundred and seventy one different publications into the world, a proof of much industry, but a sign also of much haste and superficiality

No man had ever previously shewn so thorough and unflinching a determination as Semler shewed in the "free handling" of Holy Scripture. His first attack was on the Canon, and the result of his labours appears in conclusions which get rid of nearly every book of the Bible The Pentateuch he determined to be a collection of legends, Genesis especially being made up of broken fragments which were all that survived of the early fictions of our race The Books of Joshua, Judges Samuel, the Kings, and Daniel are too doubtful to be of much value The Books of Chronicles, Ruth, Ezra, Nehemiah, Esther, and the Song of Solomon cannot be accepted at all as what they profess to be, and the Proverbs, though they may possibly have been written by Solomon, are more likely to have been written by unknown authors of moderate literary powers The authenticity of the Gospels is very doubtful, the Catholic Epistles are a late production, and the Revelation was composed by some fanatic who had nothing to do with St John

Semler is also credited with the invention of the Positive Accommodation theory, which first appears in the preface to his Paraphrase of St Paul's Epistle to the Romans According to this theory our Lord and His Apostles accommodated their teaching, in many points, to the prevailing opinions of those whom they taught that they might the more certainly win them Thus it happens that the Divine Teacher said many things which are not to be taken as literal truths, and many such things also enter into the records of the New Testament When the resurrection of the dead and the last judgment are spoken of, they are not spoken of as real facts, nor are angels or devils mentioned as real beings The Jews believed in these things, and so Christ and His Apostles accommodated their teaching to the current superstitions of the time as matters of no consequence, that they might by such concessions gain the more influence in matters which they did consider important

A third way in which Semler used his destructive criticism was by distinguishing between that which he judged to be only local and temporary in Scripture, and that which he considered universal and permanent Many portions of the historical and the prophetical books were written for particular people and times, and when the persons and the age had passed away these parts of Scripture had no further application to any one, either in ancient or modern days This theory by itself opens limitless fields of scepticism respecting Holy Scripture, for no more ready or plausible explanation could be given of any difficult or unacceptable passage than that it was "local" and "temporary," its sense or its importance having long since passed away

It was thus that in his "Apparatus for the liberal Interpretation of the Old Testament," in his four volumes on the Canon, and in many successive works of a similar character, Semler laid broad foundations for the "historico-critical" school of later generations to build upon He may also be said to have been the first to have carried out fully and unflinchingly the principle which others had acted upon, but had scarcely dared to proclaim aloud, that the Bible is a book which may be as freely criticised as any other book, and which is to be judged by the same rules It was a principle likely to be snatched up with eagerness by the vain and self-confident, and much of the later Rationalism of Germany has arisen from the unwholesome pleasure which a people of literary tastes felt in their liberation from those restraints in regard to the Bible which had checked "free handling," while it was regarded as a collection of sacred writings whose special characteristics placed them in a different category from all others, and distinguished that book above all books as THE BOOK

It was while Semler was thus undermining the authority of Revelation that Lessing published the famous "Wolfenbuttel Fragments," which carried disbelief in the Scriptures further towards a general disbelief in the received truths of religion than had been done by Semler

Gotthold Ephraim Lessing [A D 1729-1781] had already attained considerable literary distinction, but being always in debt and trouble from his improvident habits, was glad in 1770 to accept an appointment as librarian to the Duke of Wolfenbuttel In the ducal library of which he had charge Lessing discovered a manuscript work, written some years previously by Hermann Samuel Reimarus [A D 1694-1765], Professor of Hebrew and Mathematics at Hamburg This work was entitled "A Vindication of the Rational Worshippers of God," and had been privately circulated among his friends by Reimarus in manuscript Lessing extracted from the copy which fell into his hands seven of the more important or most telling passages, and printed them successively under the title of "Fragments from the Library of Wolfenbuttel," between the years 1774 and 1778 These pamphlets caused a sensation in the Germany of that period similar to that caused by "Essays and Reviews" in England three generations later, and in both cases it was the boldness with which received beliefs were contradicted that drew attention to productions otherwise not remarkable

According to the Wolfenbuttel Fragments, "the historical evidences of Christianity and of the doctrine of inspiration are clad in such a garb of superstition that they do not merit the credence of sensible men The confessions framed at different periods of the history of the Church have savoured far more of human weakness than of Divine knowledge They bear but slight traces of Biblical truth The Trinity is incomprehensible, and the heart should not feel bound to lean upon what Reason cannot fathom Nearly all the Old Testament history is a string of legends and myths which an advanced age should indignantly reject Christ never intended to establish a permanent religion, and the work of His Apostles was something unanticipated by Himself His design was to restore Judaism to its former state, throw off the Roman yoke, and declare Himself King His public entry into Jerusalem was designed to be His installation as a temporal King, but he failed in His dependence upon popular support, and instead of attaining a throne He died upon the Cross Belief in Scriptural records is perfectly natural to the Christian, for he has imbibed it from education and training Reason is forestalled in the ordinary education of children, they are baptized before they are old enough to exercise their own reasoning faculties Faith in Scripture testimony is really of no greater value than the belief of the Mahometan or Jew in their oracles, unless Reason be permitted to occupy the seat of judgment" [Hurst's *Hist Ration* 127]

In the midst of such elements of unbelief as are here indicated arose the modern Critical School of Germany, and their influence is shewn in nearly every one of its writers Ernesti [A D 1707-1781] and Michaelis [A D 1717-1791] by their narrow application of philological criticism to the New and Old Testament[1] had prepared the way for Semler, Eichhorn [A D. 1752-1827] followed in the same track, and it was only natural that from such teachers a younger and still more daring school should spring, ready to apply the caustic acid of such criticism as their masters had invented to every page of the Bible The best of this younger school was Ernest Rosenmuller [A D 1768-1835], Professor of Arabic and Oriental Literature at Leipsic, whose "Scholia in Vetus Testamentum," even in their unfinished state, extended to twenty-three volumes Far more advanced representatives of it appeared in Heinrich Paulus [A D 1761-1851], who was Professor of Exegesis and Church History at Heidelberg for the last forty years of his life, in Frederick Schleiermacher [A D 1768-1834], Professor of Theology in the new University of Berlin from its opening in 1810 until his death, and above all in David Frederick Strauss [A D 1808—*], whose "Life of Jesus," published in the year 1835, reduced the whole Gospel to an agglomeration of myths Among the lesser lights of the same school were Rohr, whose "Letters on Rationalism" were published at Aachen in 1813, and Wegscheider, whose "Institutions of Dogmatic Theology" appeared in 1815 at Halle

The manner in which this younger school of critics developed from the elder, and in which (while often repudiating their interpretation) they extended the range of destructive criticism which their teachers had originated, may be shortly illustrated

Rosenmuller is commenting on the sixteenth chapter of Numbers, and treats in due course of Korah, Dathan, and Abiram Michaelis, he tells us, "thinks that an earthquake took place, which Moses as a messenger from God could foresee But others (Rosenmuller omits their names, and they are not worth inquiring for) thinks that Moses had taken care privily to undermine the whole of the ground on which the tents of the sinners were, and that thus there was no wonder either that they fell in or that they should know they would But, says Rosenmuller, with great calmness, these writers did not consider how such a thing could be done privately in the midst of so many men, and in the course of a single day Being discontented with this wise explanation, he gives at some length Eichhorn's Eichhorn thinks that the three offenders were burned alive with their property *by order of Moses*, and if we will interpret verses 31 and 32 according to the style of speaking and thinking among the ancients, he does not see that they contradict his theory

"Paulus gives a dissertation on the miracle of the tribute money and the fish 'What sort of a miracle is it,' says Paulus, 'which is commonly found here? I will not say a miracle of about sixteen or twenty groschen'" [2s 6d] "'for the greatness of the value does not make the greatness of the miracle But it may be observed [1] that as, first, Jesus received in general support

[1] Ernesti's *Institutio interpretis Novi Testamenti* was published in 1761, Michaelis' *Commentaries on the Laws of Moses* in 1773, and his *Introduction to the N T*, in four volumes, in 1780, both written in Germany.

from many persons (Judas kept the stock, John xii 6) in the same way as the Rabbis frequently live from such donations, as, secondly, so many pious women provided for the wants of Jesus, as, finally, the claim did not occur at any remote place, but at Capernaum, where Christ had friends, a miracle for about a thaler would certainly have been superfluous But [2] it would not only have been superfluous and paltry,—it would have taught this principle, that Peter, even when he could have remedied his necessities easily in other ways, might and ought to reckon on a miraculous interference of the Deity, a notion which would entirely contradict the fundamental principle of Jesus on the interference of the Deity There is a great deal more of this, after which Paulus considers the narration, and shews that there is nothing of a miraculous appearance in it, for that if there had been, 'the fiery Peter would not have been cold-blooded at such a miracle,' but would have expressed himself as in Luke v 8, that in the whole aim and tone of the narration there is no appearance of any wondering, that Christ only meant to give a moral lesson, viz. that we are not, if we can avoid it by trifling sacrifices, to give offence to our brethren that He probably reasoned thus with Peter, 'Though there is no real occasion for us to pay the tribute, yet as we may be reckoned as enemies of the Temple, and not attended to when we wish to teach what is good, why should not you, who are a fisherman, and can easily do it, go and get enough to pay the demand? Go then to the sea, cast your hook, and take up πρῶτον ἴχθυν, the first and best fish Peter was not to stay longer at his work this time than to gain the required money πρῶτος often refers not to number but to time, and ἴχθυν may *undoubtedly* be taken as a collective Peter must either have caught so many fish as would be reckoned worth a stater at Capernaum (so near to a sea rich in fish), or one so large and fine as would have been valued at that sum'" The command "Open his mouth" is then learnedly explained as being for the purpose of taking the hook out [Rose's *State of Protestantism in Germany*, 131, ed 1829]

In a similar manner Paulus explains the miracle of Christ walking on the sea. "'The fact is,' he says, 'that when Christ saw that the wind was contrary, He did not wish to sustain the inconvenience of such a voyage, but walked along the shore, and resolved to pass the disciples as the wind was against them. They coasted the shore from the state of the weather, and when they saw Him walking on the land they were frightened, and, on their calling out, Christ desired Peter, who as a fisherman was a good swimmer, to swim ashore to ascertain that it was He, Peter ran round to the proper side of the ship and jumped into the sea When he was frightened by the violence of the waves, Christ, Who was standing on the shore, put out His hand and caught him'" [*ibid* 135]

"Ammon, in his preface to Ernesti's Institutes, has given a dissertation on miracles in general, and wipes them away by wholesale. In Matt. iii 17, it was thunder In Acts ix 4, St Paul was in a transport In Matt viii 3, καθαρίσαι is to *declare* one pure In xiv 23, he explains the passage, first, 'to walk on the shallows,' and then 'to swim' In John xix 34, νύσσω is to strike In Luke xxiv 40, it is quite clear that the nails were not driven through the hands or feet Some miracles arose from the fancy of the sick, as Luke viii 40, Acts v 18, xiii 12, xvi 8, xix 12 Some arise from mistaken opinions or embellishment on the part of the Apostles The temptation of Christ is only an exaggerated account of various conflicts of opinions from which He suffered The story of Ananias and Sapphira was merely an ornamented account of the fact that Ananias died of fear in a meeting of the Apostles, and his wife followed soon after" [*ibid* 136]

In a similar manner this school of "Rationalists"—one cannot use the name for such interpreters without a smile at the absurd self-deception which its assumption involved—explained away everything relating to the history of our Lord They set Him forth in general though not always, as a pattern of moral goodness, but eliminated from the evangelical account of Him every trace of the supernatural So Rohr in his Letters on Rationalism represents the Saviour as a great genius, the blossom of His age and generation, and unsurpassed in wisdom by any one before or after Him. His origin, culture, deeds and experience are yet veiled, and the accounts we have of Him are so distorted by rhapsody that we cannot reach a clear conception of Him He had a rare acquaintance with mankind, and studied the Old Testament carefully He possessed a large measure of tact, imagination, judgment, wisdom, and power His wisdom was the product of unbiassed reason, a sound heart, and freedom from scholastic prejudices He knew how to seize upon the best means for the attainment of His human purposes He embraced in His plan a universal religion, and to this He made all things minister. All His doctrines were borrowed from the Old Testament, and the most admirable can be found as far back as the time of Moses He performed no real miracles, but things which He did seemed miraculous to those who witnessed them He uttered no real prophecies, but His mind was so full of the future that some of His predictions came to pass, because they were made with a keen natural foresight which drew correct conclusions as to what would happen His cures were effected by His skill as a physician, every Jew of that day having some medical knowledge, and His being above the average His Apostles propagated Christianity because of the influence which He had gained with them, but His fame would have been little if Paul had not arisen to carry it beyond Palestine, but, after all, the spread of Christianity was not more remarkable than that of Mahometanism To wind up his theory of Christ, Rohr apostrophizes Him as one of his own school, calling Him a Rationalist of pure, clear, sound reason, free from prejudice, of ready perceptions, great love of truth and warm sympathies, an exalted picture of intellectual and moral greatness "Who," he adds, "would not bow before Thee," as if such an adoration of this made-up character fully answered the requirements of that Christianity whose first principle is the worship of the historical Christ.

Very few of the philosophical writers of Germany can be said, however, to have any faith in our Lord as such faith has ordinarily been understood in the Christian world. "If Christ could have been ignored, He would have been ignored in Protestant Germany, when Christian faith had been eaten out of the heart of that country by the older Rationalism Yet scarcely any German 'thinker' of note can be named who has not projected what is termed a Christology The Christ of Kant is the ideal of moral perfection, and as such, we are told, He is to be carefully distinguished from the historical Jesus, since of this ideal alone, and in a transcendental sense, can the statements of the orthodox creed be predicated The Christ of Jacobi is a religious ideal, and worship addressed to the historical Jesus is denounced as sheer idolatry, unless beneath the recorded manifestation the ideal itself be discerned and honoured According to Fichte, on the contrary, the real interest of philosophy in Jesus is historical and not metaphysical, Jesus first possessed an insight into the absolute unity of the being of man with that of God, and in revealing this insight He communicated the highest knowledge which man can possess. Of the later Pantheistic philosophers, Schelling proclaims that the Christian theology is hopelessly in error when it teaches that at a particular moment of time God became Incarnate, since God is 'external to' all time, and the Incarnation of God is an eternal fact But Schelling contends that the man Christ Jesus is the highest point or effort of this eternal Incarnation, and the beginning of its real manifestation to men, 'none before Him after such a manner has revealed to man the Infinite' And the Christ of Hegel is not the actual Incarnation of God in Jesus of Nazareth, but the symbol of His Incarnation in humanity at large" [Liddon's *Bampt. Lect* 19]

The general tone in which the German Rationalists now dealt with Holy Scripture at large may be seen in the "Institutiones Dogmaticæ" of Wegscheider, which were first printed in 1815, and which ran through many editions during the generation following "Whatever narrations," he says, "especially accommodated to a certain age, and relating miracles and mysteries, are united with the histories and subject-matter of revelation of this kind, these ought to be referred to the natural sources and true nature of human knowledge By how much the more clearly the author of the Christian religion, not without the help of Deity, exhibited to men the ideas of reason imbued with true religion, so as to represent, as it were, a reflection of the Divine Reason, or the Divine Spirit, by so much the more diligently ought man to strive to approach as nearly as possible to form that archetype in the mind, and to study to imitate it in life and manners to the utmost of his ability. Behold here the intimate and eternal union and agreement of Christianity with Rationalism

The various modes of supernatural revelation mentioned in many places of the sacred books are to be referred altogether to the notions and mythical narrations of every civilized people, and this following the suggestion of Holy Scripture itself, and therefore to be attributed, as any events in the nature of things, to the laws of Nature known to us As to Theophanies, the sight of the Infinite Deity is expressly denied, John i 18, 1 John iv. 12, 1 Tim. vi 16 Angelophanies, which the Jews of a later date substituted for the appearances of God Himself, like the narrations of the appearances of demons found amongst many nations, are plainly destitute of certain historic proofs, and the names, species, and commissions attributed to angels in the sacred books, plainly betray their Jewish origin

The persuasion concerning the truth of that supernatural revelation which rests on the testimony of the sacred volume of the Old and New Testaments, like every opinion of the kind, labours under what is commonly called a *petitio principii* "

A new turn was given to German Rationalism by the establishment of the University of Berlin in the year 1810, or rather by the appointment of Schleiermacher as the head of its Theological faculty This influential teacher originally belonged to the Calvinistic or "Reformed" section of German Protestants, and was brought up among Moravians After giving up his connection with the latter (among whom he was to have become a preacher) he went to the University of Halle, where he sat at the feet of Semler He became distinguished as a preacher at Berlin, but in 1804 was appointed to a Professorship at Halle In 1807 he returned to Berlin, being designated for the Theological Professorship in the projected University, and when at last it was opened by King Frederick William, Schleiermacher began there his thirty years' brilliant career in that post The fashion of the time in Germany was then tending towards comprehension, the King projecting the formation of an United Church out of the Lutheran and Calvinistic bodies into which Prussia was divided Schleiermacher's inclinations ran in the same direction, but his attention was turned chiefly to a reconciliation of philosophy and theology In attempting this he oscillated very far towards the extreme of Rationalism, although on the whole his influence tended towards a breaking up of the destructive school of criticism in Germany He gave little authority to the Old Testament Scriptures, alleging that they are indebted for their place in our Bible partly to the appeals which are made to them in the New Testament, and partly to the historic connection between Church worship and that of the Synagogue The Law of Moses he considered to be altogether uninspired, because it seemed to him to be irreconcilable with the goodness of God, but as the historical books are grounded on the Law, so they also must be uninspired To the Old Testament prophecies he allowed some small measure of inspiration Retaining a higher belief in the New Testament, and especially having a strong faith in a personal Christ, Schleiermacher yet considered that the accounts of the miraculous Conception, the Resurrection, and the Ascension of Christ were not positive truths, but "outward representations of general truths," and miracles were, with him, only "relatively" miraculous, that is, they were wonderful when compared with ordinary experiences, but not actually supernatural

Such principles as these when looked at by themselves appear to be very little different from those of preceding and avowed Rationalists But viewed by the light of the circumstances in which Schleiermacher was placed,—by the theology in which he had been trained, by his earnest desire for unity, and by his keen sympathies with both the sides which he wished to unite,—his theology, unsatisfactory as it is, must be considered as that of one who was groping his way back to a firmer footing of truth It is known that his own views became more and more developed as he grew old, and it is also known that those who sat at his feet became more orthodox believers than himself After his death the older school of Rationalists gradually became discontented with his writings, and the influence of his name very soon passed away in Germany, though English Rationalists—who take easily to cast-off intellectual clothes—long continued to look on him as a leader

Hegel had passed away three years before Schleiermacher, and after his death his followers had divided into three parties, which called themselves Right, Centre, and Left Hegelians The Right professed to reconcile the cloudy metaphysics of Hegel with orthodox Christianity, the Centre professed to be strict followers of their master, and the Left were Rationalists of the most extreme type From among the latter party arose Strauss, who had sat under both Hegel and Schleiermacher, but at the death of the latter was only twenty-six years of age, though already engaged as a Theological Lecturer at Tubingen A few months later, in 1835, Strauss published his "Life of Jesus," and at once achieved an European notoriety by the extreme character of his Rationalism

In "Das Leben Jesu," Strauss endeavours to explain the Gospel narratives respecting our Lord on the principle of the "myth," wherever anything appears in them of a supernatural character Having adopted a philosophy which utterly denied the possibility of the supernatural, the theologian who had to deal with the New Testament was driven to seek for some explanation of what he found there, and none of the theories propounded by previous Rationalists satisfying him, he took a line of his own, and laboured to reduce everything in the life of our Lord to a consistent agreement with the theory thus invented But "it is far more," says Dr Mill, "from a desire of working on a historical ground the philosophical principles of his master, than from any attachment to mythical theories on their own account, that we are clearly to deduce the destructive process which Strauss has applied to the Life of Jesus" [Mill's *Pantheism*, II i. 11]

This destructive process "eliminates from the Gospel most of Christ's discourses, all of His miracles, His supernatural Birth, and his Resurrection from the grave The so-called 'historical' residuum might easily be compressed within the limits of a newspaper paragraph, and it retains nothing that can rouse a moderate measure, I do not say of enthusiasm, but even of interest" [Liddon's *Bampt Lect* 220] The general theory of Strauss is that the minds of the Jews were in an excited state of expectation at the time when Christ appeared among them, and that He so far answered to the ideal which they had formed of their Messiah from the traditions of their fathers, that some of them accepted Him as such His career is viewed as a perfectly natural one Born of humble parents, He was baptized by John, collected a few disciples, inveighed against all who opposed Him, and failing to maintain Himself against them, suffered death at their hands A good many years after His death popular imagination ran wild with stories about this obscure Nazarene, and then the Gospels were composed, not in accordance with the true facts of His life, but to embody these popular fancies The writers of the Gospels did not wilfully intend to write down a congeries of falsehoods, but not possessing the critical faculty they just put down all the stories they heard floating about among lovers of the marvellous, little dreaming of the position which their curious but not very clever compilations would occupy in the esteem of future generations

As for the details of the Gospel narrative, this youthful theological lecturer—he was about five-and-twenty when his *Leben Jesu* was written—could satisfactorily account for them all The story of John the Baptist's birth grew out of the Old Testament myths of Isaac, Samson, and Samuel That of the miraculous Conception of Jesus is a philosophical, dogmatic myth of early Christianity, grounded on a notion taken up from Isaiah vii 14, and agrees with a habit common to all nations of assigning some marvellous origin to their Divine heroes. The Conception and Birth were in reality, the writer alleges, similar to those of all other children The slaughter of the Innocents never took place as a fact, but the story of it is a poetical plagiarism of the myths respecting Nimrod and Pharaoh The Epiphany star was invented to fit in with the alleged prophecy of Balaam The Holy Child among the doctors was a myth founded on the precocity of Moses, Samuel, and Solomon The miracles of Christ "are the halo of glory with which the infant Church gradually and without purposes of deceit clothed its Founder and its Head"

[Trench *on Mir* 84] The alleged sufferings of the Saviour were a myth made up from the Lamentations of Jeremiah, the older myth of the brazen serpent, and the poetical descriptions given in the twenty-second and sixty-ninth Psalms The Resurrection he regards as a myth grounded on the necessity under which the disciples of Jesus were placed of reconciling His fate with the opinions which they had formed of Him "When once the idea of a resurrection of Jesus had been formed in this manner, the great event could not have been allowed to happen so simply, but must be surrounded and embellished with all the pomp that the Jewish imagination furnished The chief ornaments which stood at command for this purpose were angels; hence these must open the grave of Jesus, must, after He had come forth from it, keep watch in the empty place, and deliver to the women—who, because without doubt women had the first visions, must be the first to go to the grave—the tidings of what had happened As it was Galilee where Jesus subsequently appeared to them, the journey of the disciples thither (which was nothing else than their return home somewhat hastened by fear) was derived from the direction of an angel nay, Jesus Himself must already before His death, and as Matthew too zealously adds, once after His resurrection also, have enjoined this journey on the disciples But the farther these narratives were propagated by tradition, the more must the difference between the locality of the Resurrection itself and that of the appearance of the risen One be allowed to fall out of sight as inconvenient, and, since the locality of the Death was not transferable, the appearances were gradually placed in the same locality as the Resurrection, in Jerusalem, which, as the more brilliant theatre and the seat of the first Christian Church was especially appropriate for them" Lastly, the Ascension was a myth founded upon the stories of Enoch and Elijah, and those of the apotheosis of Hercules and of Romulus

The only original idea in the work of Strauss, even if that can be so called, is the mythical theory All the rest is an ingenious mosaic formed from the materials which he raked together by a most industrious perusal of the works of preceding Rationalists, German, English, and French It was professedly written only for the learned, but it soon became known to a very wide range of readers, passed through many editions, and was translated into other languages Twenty-nine years later the author followed it up with "Das Leben Jesu, fur das Deutsche Volk bearbietet," which was published at Leipsic in 1864 but this popularized replica of his former work has never obtained any wide notice In the meanwhile he had aroused the attention of theologians in Germany and elsewhere, and the historical character of the Gospels was elucidated more clearly than ever by their writings Among the many learned works drawn out by Strauss' "Life of Jesus" may be named Dorner's volumes on "The Person of Christ," in which the author gives an elaborate view of the course of opinion respecting our Lord Neander also wrote a "Life of Christ" in opposition to that of Strauss, the line taken by him being very much that of his master Schleiermacher Hengstenberg was among his most vigorous opponents in the pages of periodical literature, but his "Christology" was printed before the "Leben Jesu" appeared

The "Tubingen School" of Rationalists was indirectly developed from Strauss, being composed of a not large clique of theologians, headed by Baur [A D 1792-1860], Schwegler and Zeller, who set themselves the task of moulding the negative system of Strauss into a positive system by the same processes of criticism Their attention was principally directed towards the Apostolic age, and the key of their system is the idea that Christianity is not a divinely revealed and complete truth and life, but a vital force in process of development In working out their principle this school relies chiefly upon the Pauline epistles, especially those to the Romans, Galatians, and Corinthians, which are considered to be most in accordance with the theory of an infant but growing Christianity that was feeling its way towards the light. The Books of the New Testament are looked upon as the productions respectively of an early Petrine or Pauline party, most of them having only a temporary object, and such of them being now to be regarded simply as literary monuments of a departed controversy, which may illustrate history, but cannot prove or teach truth This is the latest phase of German Rationalism, but it has been so vigorously met by the works of Bunsen, Thiersch, Bleek, and others, that the influence of the school has not been very widely extended, and, like that of German Rationalism in general, it is rapidly on the wane.

IV French Rationalists The revolution in the religion of the French people was as destructive as that in their political life, and no country of Europe ever so generally repudiated Christianity as did France during the last century, under the influence of Voltaire, Rousseau, the Encyclopædists, and the fanatics who overthrew the monarchy The climax was reached in the year 1793, when a number of the Parisian clergy, with Gobel, the Archbishop of Paris, at their head, gave up their offices as priests of the Church into the hands of the Convention, and renounced Christianity as an exploded superstition At the instigation of Anacharsis Cloots—a rich Prussian nobleman who had, in his enthusiastic admiration of the Revolution, turned Frenchman and become a member of the National Convention—it was at length determined to set up Rationalism as the religion of the country instead of Christianity The churches were despoiled of everything that had been used in Christian worship, and the symbols of the new religion which were set up in them were the busts of Marat and Lepelletier, which were also carried in procession under canopies as the reserved Sacrament had been carried on the Festival of Corpus Christi The great cathedral of Paris, Notre-Dame, was then rededicated as "The Temple of Reason," every tenth day was ordered to be observed as a festival of

Reason in the place of the Christian Sunday, and on November 10th, 1793, the first of these festivals was kept with great ceremony, an official procession of the Supreme Government of France taking place, in which the "Goddess of Reason" was personated by a young woman in theatrical costume carried aloft on a throne, and surrounded by girls dressed in white and crowned with roses When this procession had arrived at the "Temple of Reason," hymns were chanted in praise of Reason, and then the multitude moved on to the National Convention, where the Procurator-General, Chaumette, addressed the assembly in words which stated the national renunciation of Christianity "Legislators," he said, "Fanaticism has given place to Reason Its craven eyes have been unable to bear the lustre of light To day an immense concourse has been gathered under those Gothic arches, which, for the first time, resound to the echoes of truth There the French people have celebrated the only true worship, that of Liberty and Reason" The Convention then returned with the procession, and officially joined in the "Worship of Reason" under the vaulted roof of Notre-Dame [Thiers' *French Revol* ch xxviii]

This absurd outburst of French Rationalism was but a temporary phase of it, but, absurd as it was, it represented not untruly the attitude of the nation towards Christianity The Church gradually re-established its position as the national religion of France, and the Protestants returned to their Calvinism, but both Catholics and Protestants have continued to be largely infected with Rationalism, and comparatively few Frenchmen give an intellectual assent to the doctrines founded upon historical Christianity, or to historical Christianity itself

The Christology of French Rationalists has been crystallized by Joseph Ernest Renan [A D 1823-*] in his "Life of Jesus" Renan was originally educated for the priesthood, and became an ardent student of oriental languages while at St. Sulpice He did not eventually enter into holy orders, but pursued his study of theology from the philological side, and in 1856, a few years after publishing his "Histoire Générale et Systèmes comparés des Langues Sémitiques," and his "Etude de la Langue Grecque au Moyen Age," was elected a member of the Institute on account of his philological learning Renan's "Vie de Jésus" was written after an official expedition which he had made into Syria in the year 1860, and was published in 1863 It became rapidly popular in France, where 100,000 copies of it were sold in a short time, and was almost equally popular in other countries of Europe, which were quickly supplied with translations in English, German, Spanish, and Italian In 1866 the "Life of Jesus" was supplemented by a volume bearing "The Apostles" for its title, the two being together entitled "The Origins of Christianity"

Renan's theories respecting Christianity are very similar to those of Strauss Christ he alleges to have been an ordinary human being, the son of Joseph and Mary, but one whose character was developed in such a direction as to fit in with the ideal of the Messiah that had become fixed in the Jewish mind By study of the Old Testament He became impressed with the imagination that He should become a great reformer of the world, and this was the key to His life, the idea of such a reformation developing into that of the formation of a "Kingdom of God" The miracles of the Gospel narrative Renan considers to be exaggerated accounts of natural occurrences, and the crowning miracle of the Resurrection is altogether denied, the account of it being founded on an hallucination of Mary Magdalen's excited mind The phenomena of Pentecost are reduced to a thunder-storm, a strong wind which blew open the windows of the upper chamber, and an electric illumination of the air In their ecstacy the Apostles uttered some inarticulate sounds which were thought to be foreign languages, and of which zealous interpreters professed to give the meaning At a later time Paul was struck with fever and ophthalmia from sunstroke as he was going to Damascus, and the direction thus given to the fanatical mind of the last of the Apostles originated the later phase of Christianity as it became known throughout the compass of St. Paul's travels

Thus Renan emasculates the narrative of the New Testament, repudiating all its supernaturalism, making out Christ to be only a man above men, and setting forth the Church of Christ as a community founded in the mistakes and the fanaticism of His followers Had the "Worship of Reason" lasted a little longer, or had Robespierre been able to establish his reformation of it, the work of Renan would probably have been anticipated by two generations, his view of Christianity being exactly that which assigns to it a place in the Pantheon of Reason without accepting it as true So polite a treatment of "superstition" would have much commended itself to the polished politeness of French philosophers, when the first fanaticism of Reason worship had worn off The less polished repudiation of Christianity which marked the Rationalism of Comte is noticed elsewhere [POSITIVISM]

V THE REVIVAL OF ENGLISH RATIONALISM It has often been said that the English Deists gave Rationalism to Germany in the sixteenth century, and that it was re-imported thence into England in the nineteenth This is scarcely an historical truth as regards the first part of the saying, since the foundation of scepticism laid by Spinoza was broad enough for all the subsequent structure of German Rationalism to build upon, and it may be doubted whether the earlier writers of the school were acquainted with the works of the English Deists to any great extent But it is notorious that modern English Rationalism, although it is practically a revival of the school of Hume, Woolston, Tindal, and Collins, originated in the study of the destructive school of German critics, and not in that of English writers. It is in fact the result of a revived taste for the

German language among the young men of the last generation, a taste which led those whose studies ran in the direction of theology or philosophy to obtain their knowledge from German authors, and, under the influence of the bias thus given, to accept those authors as final authorities before whom all others must bow Had the mind of Coleridge [A D 1772-1834] been of a less desultory character, he would have left behind him a system of Christian philosophy which would have been a formidable opponent to this German influence, but Coleridge did little more than stimulate and strengthen the thinking power of his own generation and of the generation immediately following him His influence went far in developing the intellectual school of High Church theologians, but he never formulated a system to a sufficient extent for that influence to be much felt as an educational power in the rather later revival of philosophical study

A great impulse was, however, given to the rationalizing tendency which accompanied the revival of religion between 1830 and 1850 by the teaching of Julius Charles Hare [A D 1795-1855], who followed up a career of ten years' influential teaching at Cambridge with twenty years of influential preaching and writing after he became a Sussex Rector and Archdeacon of Lewes The general tendency of Hare's teaching was that of drawing minds away from historical Christianity, and fixing them on an imaginative spiritualization of it In particular, he combated the Protestant theory of the Atonement by setting forth the self-sacrifice of Christ's Life in the place of the great act of sacrifice which He accomplished by His Death, and made the latter a crowning act of self-denial and voluntary suffering, rather than an act of expiation Hare's principal works were five volumes of Sermons, the first of which, published in 1840, was entitled "The Victory of Faith," and the last, six years later, "The Mission of the Comforter"

To Hare and his brother-in-law Maurice as theologians, to Whateley as a philosophical writer, to Thirlwall as an historian, and to Arnold as a teacher of the rising generation, the BROAD CHURCH SCHOOL owes its origin, a school which is always tending towards Rationalism, and out of which many extreme Rationalists have arisen among the laity, and a few among the clergy None of these latter have, however, been men of much learning, or men endowed with great power as leaders, and neither in the Church of England, nor among English Dissenters, has Rationalism ever run to the same height of unbelief as among the German Lutherans or the French Calvinists of France and Geneva External to all religious communities, there are indeed many who repudiate historical Christianity, just as they repudiate everything which assumes to be associated with a supernatural order of things But the Rationalism of these classes is merely a part of the system which they profess, and they have developed unbelief to a much further extent in the direction of Positivism and Atheism Among the principal of their intellectual leaders must be reckoned Henry Thomas Buckle, whose Materialist theories were propounded at length in his "History of Civilization in England," of which only one thick volume, the Introduction, was published, in 1856, when the author's death put an end to the work But Materialism and the Worship of Humanity, such as are to be found in the work of Buckle and of his teacher, Comte, seem to be the natural terminus of Rationalism

[Rose's *State of Protestantism in Germany*, 2nd ed 1829 *Pusey's Historical Enquiry into the probable causes of the Rationalist Character lately predominant in the Theology of Germany*, 1828, 1830 Amand Sainte's *Hist Critique du Rationalisme en Allemagne.* Staudlin's *Gesch. des Ration. und Supranat* Farrar's *Critical Hist of Free Thought, the Bampton Lectures for* 1862 Hurst's *Hist Rationalism*, 1867, the Appendix to which contains an useful list of German, French, English, and American books on both sides Lecky's *Hist Ration in Europe.* POSITIVISTS ATHEISTS PANTHEISTS]

RATRAMNUS A monk of Corbey in Aquitaine, who engaged in controversy with PASCHASIUS RADBERTUS on the subject of the Holy Eucharist, in the middle of the ninth century. He is sometimes called Bertram the Monk, or Bertram the Priest, but it is thought that this is a corruption of B Ratramnus, "Beatus" being sometimes prefixed to the names of venerated writers even when there had been no act of beatification The work of Ratramn, which was entitled "De Corpore et Sanguine Domini," had much influence upon the English Reformation It was published at Cologne in the year 1532, after having been brought into notice by Fisher, Bishop of Rochester, as early as 1526, and it largely influenced the minds of Archbishop Cranmer and Bishop Ridley In 1548 an English translation of it was printed by William Hugh, under the name of "the Book of Bertram" It has often been quoted by mistake as a work of Scotus Erigena, was supposed by many Romanist theologians to be a forgery of the Reformers, and is excluded from the collection of Ratramn's works printed in the *Bibliotheca Maxima*, on the ground that it has been hopelessly interpolated by supposititious heretics

REALISTS A school of mediæval theologians, who adopted the doctrine attributed by Aristotle to Plato, that genera, or "universals," have an existence prior to and independent of the individual objects to which they relate, the formula of the school being "universalia ante rem"

This theory was brought into prominence by Johannes Scotus Erigena [*circ* 805-877], and was generally held by philosophical theologians until the rise of Nominalism in the eleventh century Roscellin, the founder of the latter school [NOMINALISTS], was vigorously opposed by St Anselm [A D 1033-1109], who looked upon the application of Nominalist theories to the "doctrine of the Trinity as involving the heresy of Tritheism" St Anselm also maintained that the Realist doctrine was the only one reconcilable with the Incarnation, for that Deity could not have assumed Humanity unless the latter had a real objective existence, distinguished from that of individual men, a theory which he set forth in his treatise entitled "Cur Deus Homo"

The most distinguished champions of Realism after Anselm were William of Champeaux [A D 1070-1121], the opponent of Abelard, and St Thomas Aquinas [A D 1225-1274], the latter however holding the Realist opinion in the modified form that universals have a real existence prior to the individuals to which they relate through their antecedent existence in the Divine Mind The Schoolmen in general held Realist opinions ranging between this theory and the extreme form of them maintained by St. Anselm Wickliffe also was on the same side, although the freedom of his theology was more in sympathy with the Nominalist school

The general tone of Realism is that of submission to authority and dogma especially regarding that truth as most certain which is revealed by the All-Knowing and All-True, consequently regarding revelation as the true foundation of belief, and belief as the entrance-gate to a wide domain of knowledge on which the mind would not otherwise enter [SCHOOLMEN]

RECUSANTS This term came into use in the reign of Queen Elizabeth as the legal designation of persons refusing [*recusantes*] to attend the services of the Church of England

"In the beginning of the eleventh year of her reign," says Lord Coke, in his charge to the grand jury of Norfolk, "Cornwallis, Bedingfield, and Silyard, were the first Recusants, they absolutely refusing to come to our churches And, until they in that sort begun, the name of Recusant was never heard of amongst us" Later on in the same charge he says, "The last sort of Recusants, though troublesome (yet in my conscience the least dangerous), are those which do, with too much violence, contend against some ceremonies in the Church, with whose indirect proceedings, in mine own knowledge, his Majesty is much grieved" [The Lord Coke, *His Speech and Charge*, 1607]

This application of the name to both Roman Catholics and Puritans is illustrated by the lists of Recusants, to one volume of which, containing the names and particulars of those registered in the reign of Charles II up to the year 1671, there is a note affixed by the official compiler, that it is unreliable as a list of Popish Recusants, since it also contains the names of many Puritans [*Brit Mus Add MS* 20,739] In the reign of William III the Nonjurors were also classed among Recusants by Act of Parliament But the name most commonly refers to ROMAN CATHOLICS

REFORMED BAPTISTS [CAMPBELLITES, AMERICAN]

REFORMED CHURCH, GERMAN That section of German Protestants which adopted the Calvinistic instead of the Lutheran phase of the Continental Reformation Calvinism has, however, failed to gain a footing in Germany in its extreme form, and the "Reformed," as they are generally called, belong rather to the Zwinglian school modified by contact with Lutheranism than to that of the strict Calvinists, and adopt the Heidelberg Confession [PROTESTANT CONFESSIONS] Several distinguished theologians have belonged to this section of the German Protestants, as Herzog, Ebrard, Lange, and Hagenbach It is now being gradually absorbed into the UNITED EVANGELICAL CHURCH

In America the German Reformed are a considerable body, and though not so numerous as the Lutherans, are said to number about 300 ministers and 100,000 communicants As in Germany, the sect tends towards an union with moderate Lutheranism, and has within the last few years adopted "A Liturgy, or Order of Christian Worship," which is chiefly compiled from the Book of Common Prayer

REFORMED PRESBYTERIANS [CAMERONIANS]

REFORMERS [CAMPBELLITES AMERICAN]

REFORMERS, WESLEYAN [UNITED FREE CHURCH METHODISTS]

RELIEF SYNOD One of the seceding bodies in Scotland which arose out of opposition to the system of Patronage A majority of the Presbytery of Dunfermline having refused to take part in the induction of a minister to the parish of Inverkeithing who was unacceptable to the people, they were cited in 1752 before the General Assembly, and one of the number, Thomas Gillespie, minister of Carnock (who had been ordained amongst the Independents in England), being foremost in defence of the recusants, was deposed from the ministry, while three others were visited with a sentence of suspension, which lasted for thirteen years This proceeding of the Assembly, which was urged on by Dr Robertson, who was then rising into notice, was one of extreme severity, the only charge against Gillespie, "one of the most inoffensive and upright men of his time" [Moncreiff's *Life of Erskine*, p 460], being that of mere absence on the day appointed for the presentee's induction, and not of any active opposition Returning home at once, Gillespie met his wife at his manse-door with the words, "I am no longer minister of Carnock," to which she cheerfully replied, "Well, if we must beg, I will carry the meal-pock" His congregation, however, prevented any such hard necessity by still retaining him as their minister, and, upon the defeat of a motion in the Assembly of the following year for his restoration, a seceding body was constituted at Dunfermline In 1757 a similar congregation was formed by Thomas Boston (son of Boston of Ettrick) at Jedburgh, in consequence of the forcible intrusion of a minister into that parish, where the people desired that Boston should be appointed A third congregation was formed from a similar cause in 1760, and on October 22nd in the following year, the three ministers, Gillespie, Boston, and Thomas Colier, "formed themselves," in the words of their original minute, "into a Presbytery for the relief of Christians oppressed in their Christian privileges" They thus separated from the Kirk simply on the question of patronage, and had no doctrinal differences, they were free, however, from the bitterness of the old covenanting spirit, and, partly perhaps from the necessities of their isolated position, exhibited a temper of toleration hitherto unknown in Scotland In 1772, when the number of congregations had considerably increased, it was resolved at a meeting of representatives that it was agreeable to their principles "to hold communion with those of the Episcopal or Independent persuasion occasionally, upon supposition always that they are by profession visible saints" Two ministers, who could not endure this "monstrous" desertion from old Presbyterian views, thereupon separated, and the Synod thenceforward accepted free communion as one of its fundamental principles [1] Its uncontroversial and unaggressive position doubtlessly somewhat hindered its growth In 1807 it numbered about sixty congregations, with 36,000 members, and in 1847 one hundred and fourteen, with about 45,000 members. In 1834 proposals were made for a union between the Secession and Relief Synods, the two bodies being identical in general views, and the latter having gradually become more like the former in opposition to the principle of Establishments, while the Secession were willing to relax their old declaration of adherence to the Covenant, and leave the practice of free communion an open question for each minister and congregation to decide for themselves The negotiations lasted for several years, but at length the union was formally completed on 13th May 1847, when the two bodies assumed the name of the United Presbyterian Synod Two Relief ministers dissented from this union, and continued in charge of congregations under their old name These two congregations were in existence when the census of 1851 was taken, but appear now to be extinct

[Struthers' *Hist of Relief Church*, 1839, and *Hist of the Rise of Relief Church*, 1848, *Memorials of the Union of the Secession and Relief Synods*, 1847]

RELIGIONAIRES [HUGUENOTS]

RELIGIOUS SOCIETIES Associations for the promotion of personal piety which were established among members of the Church of England about the year 1678, and existed until the rise of the Methodists in the following century

They began with a few young men who had been impressed by the preaching of Dr. Horneck, preacher at the Savoy, and of Mr Smithies, lecturer at St Michael's, Cornhill. Under the advice of some clergymen these young men formed themselves into a body somewhat similar to the Societies of St. Vincent de Paul, which had been established half a century earlier in Paris, or like those of the Collegiants and other Pietistic communities in Holland and Germany The members of the Religious Society so formed arranged to meet once a week for religious conference and devotion, the meetings being conducted with singing, prayer, Scripture reading, and exposition, and with special preparation for the Holy Communion When daily celebrations of the Holy Communion were set up by James II in the Chapels Royal, the Religious Society established a week-day service at St Clement Danes in the Strand, and celebrations on holy days, for which latter they prepared by a careful observance of the Vigils preceding them To all these means for the promotion of personal piety they added practical works of charity, contributing by their purses and by personal exertions to the establishment and maintenance of schools, the visitation of the poor, and support of missions in America

The Religious Societies increased rapidly in number during the reign of William III, forty-two holding their meetings in London, and others in country towns, as also in the two Universities They received the warm support of Robert Nelson —the Wilberforce of his day—of Tillotson, Compton, and other bishops They were also closely connected with the Societies for the Reformation of Manners [q v], which were established in 1691, and were looked upon as efficient allies by the Society for the Promotion of Christian Knowledge That at Oxford was joined by John and Charles Wesley, and by George Whitfield, and the good practices with which the names of the founders of Methodism were so closely associated during their University life were those enjoined by the rules of the Brotherhood to which they had thus become attached

One of the last of the annual meetings of the London Religious Societies was held at Bow Church in the year 1738, and it may be concluded that they disappeared before the Methodist revival, which in its earlier days was of the same "High Church" character [Woodward's *Rise and Progress of the Religious Societies*, etc Nelson's *Address to Persons of Quality*, p 136 Nelson's *Festivals and Fasts*, pref , Secretan's *Life of Nelson*]

RELLYANISTS [UNIVERSALISTS]

REMONSTRANTS. [ARMINIANS.]

REMONSTRANTS [RESOLUTIONERS]

RENUNCIATORES [APOTACTICS]

REPRESENTERS [MARROW-MEN]

RESOLUTIONERS In January 1649, an Act called the *Act of Classes* was passed by the Parliament of Scotland, incapacitating certain of the "Malignants," i e Royalists, and persons opposed to the Covenant, for State employment or power After the Battle of Dunbar, the more moderate among the Covenanting party saw the need of admitting to military service those who had been thus incapacitated, and two Resolutions (supported by Robert Baillie amongst others)

[1] One great evidence of the broader tone of the Relief Synod was afforded in 1794 by their sanction of the use of a hymn-book, the singing of anything besides the Scottish version of the Psalms (even of the duly allowed Paraphrases) being an abomination to the straiter Presbyterians But though they could tolerate hymns, they could not endure instrumental accompaniment, and a minister in Edinburgh quitted the body in 1829, and afterwards (in 1833) joined the Establishment because the use of an organ in his chapel was entirely prohibited [Memoir of Rev J Johnston, prefixed to his *Sermons*, 1834]

were passed by the Commission of the Assembly, approving of the employment at least in defence of the country, of such persons, with the exception of those that were excommunicated and forfeited, or professed enemies to the Covenant and cause of God In pursuance of these Resolutions, the Parliament, on 2nd June 1651, repealed the Act of Classes But the Resolutions were vehemently opposed by a strong party, including James Guthrie and Patrick Gillespie among the ministers, and Argyle and Warriston among laymen who refused to act in common against the common enemy, and issued a "Remonstrance" against any approach to a junction with the "Malignant" party These were consequently known by the names of Remonstrants or *Protesters*, while their opponents were styled *Resolutioners* Their disputes did not cease with the subjugation of Scotland by Cromwell, but were continued up to the time of the Restoration Among the most active on the part of the Resolutioners, and employed as agent in England to thwart the endeavours of the Protesters to gain Cromwell's favour, was James Sharp, afterwards the well-known Archbishop of St Andrews [D Laing's *Life of R Baillie* in Baillie's *Letters and Journals*, III lxvii -lxxii]

RESTORATIONISTS A sect of American Universalists who maintain that modified form of Universalism which is said by them to have been the original principle of the sect, namely, that the wicked will be restored to holiness and happiness after a temporary punishment in the future life About the year 1818 Hosea Ballow, an Universalist preacher of Boston, began to teach that sin is entirely connected with the body, and that as death liberates the soul from the body, so also it frees the soul from the punishment of sin The growth of this opinion led many of the Universalists to separate from that sect in the year 1831, and to form a separate community under the name of "Universal Restorationists" or "Restorationists," their congregations being found chiefly in Massachusetts They are almost identical in all their opinions with the older English Unitarians

RHEINSBERGERS [Collegiants]

RHETORIANS An Alexandrian sect of this name is mentioned by Philaster as founded by Rhetorius, and maintaining the opinion that there was no harm in any heresy whatever [Philast *Hær* xci] St Augustine remarks that this seems so absurd that he considers it incredible [Aug *Hær* lxxii] Philaster is the original authority for the existence of such a sect, but Prædestinatus speaks of them as if they were not unknown to him, adding to Philaster's statement that they advocated Christian fellowship with all who believed in the Incarnation [Prædest *Hær* lxxii] Even before Philaster's time St Athanasius mentions a person named Rhetorius, whom he accuses of holding the opinion that doctrines are of no consequence, and that all heretics are right in their own way [Athanas *contr Apollin* i 6] And at a later date St. John Damascene enumerates the γνώσιμαχαι as the eighty-eighth in his Catalogue of Heresies, who, it seems probable, were "knowledge" (or theology) "haters" in the sense of being anti-dogmatists, who had arisen from reaction against the subleties of the Gnostics, the Antiochean and the Alexandrian schools of theologians, and who were identical with the Rhetorians of Philaster

RITUALISTS [High Churchmen]

ROGATIANI One of the numerous sects into which Donatism subdivided itself They took their name from their leader Rogatus, and flourished in Mauritania Cæsariensis [c a d 372-3] [Augustine, *Ep* 48, *contra Cresconium Donatistam*, lib iv cap 70.]

ROGERIANS An American sect of the Puritan Ranters which appeared in New England about the year 1677 under the leadership of John Rogers, from whom they took their name Their principal tenet was that worship on the Lord's Day is idolatry, which it was a matter of conscience to oppose, and hence they used to disturb the congregations in churches and chapels as the Ranters were accustomed to do in England [H Adams *View of all Religions*]

ROHR [Rationalists]

ROMAN CATHOLICS A sect originally organized by the Jesuits out of the relics of the Marian party of clergy and laity in the reign of Queen Elizabeth, and further organized into a Donatist hierarchy by Cardinal Wiseman in the year 1850

The name is found in use as early as the year 1564, when the words "every Romish Catholique within England and Ireland or any of England's territories" are found in a paper of intelligence sent home from Italy for the information of Burleigh by Dennum, the Queen's secret agent [*Brit. Mus. Add MS.* 4784] It also occurs in the charge delivered to the grand jury of Norfolk in the year 1607, by Lord Chief-Justice Coke In a wide sense, all members of churches or sects recognised by the Pope as in communion with himself are often called Roman Catholics, but the name is more strictly applicable to the English sect

A distinguished Roman Catholic writer of the last century dates the origin of his community from the accession of Queen Elizabeth "In the year 1558," he says, "Elizabeth ascended the throne of England At this time begins the real era of English Reformation, and consequently from this time Catholics are to be considered as a sect, dissenting from the National Church" [Berington's *State and Behaviour of English Catholics from the Reformation to the year* 1780, *with a view of their present number, wealth, character*, etc 1780] But this is antedating its origin by about twelve years, for although there was a strong Romanizing party in the Church during the early years of Queen Elizabeth's reign, it was not until the publication of the Bull by which the Pope excommunicated her in 1570, that those of the party who had not in the meanwhile been won over to the Reformation separated themselves from the national communion They were not thoroughly organized into a sect until the arrival of the Jesuits, the first of whom came over in the year 1581, and had it not been for the work of these enemies of Catholic unity the Roman Catholics would probably have been reabsorbed by the Church as the Nonjurors were in the next century

I HISTORY OF ROMAN CATHOLICS. In the early stage of the Reformation the clergy and laity of England generally assented to the new order of things, although there were many who, like Bishop Fisher, Sir Thomas More, and the Charterhouse monks, were unable to agree with the Tudor view of the Royal Supremacy The evidence of this general concurrence of Church and State is given in detail in the first volume of Blunt's *History of the Reformation of the Church of England* during the reign of Henry VIII, and all that can be said on the subject in the short compass of this article is that the Houses of Lords and Commons, the Convocations of the Clergy, the Universities, and even the monastic bodies, all concurred in the repudiation of the Papal Supremacy, that absurd relic of Roman Imperialism, the repudiation of which was, and was well known to be, the backbone of the Reformation

The development of an "extreme left," however, in the form of Puritanism, led naturally to the development of an "extreme right" in the form of revived Ultramontanism, and although the reactionary party did not at once become Ultramontane, and was not large during the reign of Henry VIII, it was exasperated by the intemperate rule of the Privy Council during the calamitous reign of Edward VI, so that when Mary came to the throne it at once leaped into power under the leadership of Bishop Gardiner. The policy of the party during the first of the two years which then elapsed before Gardiner's death was that of his great master Wolsey, and was directed towards the restoration of that national system of ecclesiastical affairs which had existed in the latter half of the reign of Henry VIII, and not to the establishment of the Ultramontane system which eventually became the notorious characteristic of Queen Mary's reign But a Spanish party had arisen in England through the Queen's engagement to Philip of Spain, and her marriage with him on July 25th, 1554 Her relationship to Cardinal Pole, and her personal affection for him, had also smoothed the way for that Italianized Englishman's return to his native country with the fullest powers of a Papal Legate From the arrival of the latter, on November 24th, 1554, power passed out of the hands of Gardiner and the national party into the hands of Pole and the King of Spain, and under the influence of the Ulramontane party, formed by the union of these two foreign elements, England was "reconciled to the Holy See" on November 30th, 1554 Under the same influences—Philip himself being especially prepared for the work by a treatise on Heresies and another on the punishment of Heretics re-written for the purpose by his confessor, à Castro[1]—that dreadful persecution of the Puritans began in which not a few of the orthodox clergy and laity also suffered, and which permanently alienated the people of England from Ultramontanism[2]

Upon the accession of Queen Elizabeth, the utmost tact and patience became necessary to prevent the Catholic Reformation from being crushed by the pressure of the two reactionary parties, the Puritan "Left" and the Roman "Right." Hence arose nearly two years of politic silence, temporizing, and delay on the part of her Government in settling the affairs of the Church During these two years the influence of the Spanish party was gradually extinguished, and although a considerable section of the clergy and laity desired to retain the ancient rites of the Church of England, and to prevent a dissolution of the reestablished communion with Rome, this party also was being gradually thinned as the Marian bishops and clergy died off

When at length the Prayer Book system of the Reformation was re-established, there seemed good reason to hope that those of the reactionary party, who had at first been dissatisfied with it, were gradually becoming reconciled During the early years of Queen Elizabeth's reign, say the Instructions given to Walsingham on his mission to France, those who afterwards became Recusants "did ordinarily resort, in all open places, to the churches and to divine service in the church, without any contradiction or shew of misliking" So also Sir Edward Coke declared at the trial of Garnet, on January 27th, 1605, in the following words —"Before the Bull of Impius Pius Quintus, in the eleventh year of the Queen, wherein her Majesty was excommunicated and deposed, and all they accursed who should yield any obedience unto her, etc there were no Recusants in England, all came to church (howsoever popishly inclined or persuaded in most points) to the same divine service we now use, but thereupon presently they refused to assemble in our churches, or join with us in public service, not for conscience of anything there done, against which they might justly except out of the Word of God, but because the Pope had excommunicated and deposed her Majesty, and cursed those who should obey her" [*State Trials*, i 242]

[1] See the dedications to Charles V. and Philip which are prefixed to these works respectively [HERESIOLOGISTS.]

[2] The name of the great and thoroughly English prelate Gardiner has been unhistorically associated with the cruelties of Queen Mary's reign as if he had been one of the chief movers in them But he only once sat in judgment on "heretics" during that reign, namely, when he presided, as Lord Chancellor, over the court, composed of thirteen new bishops and others, by which Rogers, Hooper, Saunders, and Taylor were condemned, on January 22nd, 1555 From that time he took little part in public business, and a disease—on account of which he had told the Privy Council in the beginning of Edward's reign that "Nature had destined his death"—carried him off on November 12th, 1555, his end having been expected so long before, according to a letter of Noailles the French ambassador [v 127], as September 9th There is much evidence to shew that Gardiner, like his master Wolsey, was a man of a gentle and forbearing disposition The tradition to the contrary is derived from the Puritans, who always had strong foreign sympathies, and exhibited a singular animosity towards patriotic and constitutional Englishmen like Wolsey and Gardiner

Roman Catholics

Garnet tried to shew that this was a mistake of Sir Edward Coke's, yet he admitted the main fact even while contradicting the reason which the great Attorney-General had given for the change that afterwards took place "I know divers myself," said Garnet, "who before that Bull refused to go to church all the time of Queen Elizabeth, though perhaps *most Catholics did indeed go to church before* It was about the end of the Council of Trent where this matter was discussed by twelve learned men, and concluded not lawful And this was occasioned for that Calvin himself held it not lawful for any Protestant to be present, not only at our Mass, wherein perhaps they may say there is idolatry, but not at our Evensong, being the same with theirs" [*ibid* 250] But Coke proved that this was "a gross error, for the last session of that council was in the year of our Lord 1563, which was in the fifth year of Queen Elizabeth, whereas I shewed, and am able to justify and prove, that their Romish English Catholics came to our service in our churches until the nineteenth year of her Majesty, which was many years after that council was ended" [*ibid* 252]

When he was Lord Chief-Justice, Coke again repeated his assertion in the following words, in his charge to the grand jury at the Norwich assizes of 1607 His words were "Notwithstanding the change of religion, it cannot be denied that for the first ten years of her Majesty's reign the estate of Roman Catholics in England was tolerable, though some were committed in the beginning of her coming to the crown, yet none but those whose precedent actions had caused the faith of their allegiance to remain doubtful, and so was the manner of their commitment mixed with such gracious clemency, as that they rather endured a favourable restraint than any straight or rigorous imprisonment But as well those restrained as generally all the Papists in this kingdom, not any of them did refuse to come to our church and yield their formal obedience to the laws established And thus they all continued, not any one refusing to come to our churches during the first ten years of her Majesty's government And in the beginning of the eleventh year of her reign Cornwallis, Bedingfield, and Silyard were the first Recusants, they absolutely refusing to come to our churches And until they in that sort begun, the name of Recusant was never heard of amongst us" [The Lord Coke, *His Speech and Charge*, 1607]

It was, perhaps, even earlier than this that the Jesuit Persons had written to the same effect, attributing the change to the teaching of the Jesuits Some time after the year 1595, he wrote —"Whereupon also the same devil" [emulation between laity and clergy, and between the secular priests and the monks] brought in the division of opinions about going to the heretical churches and service, which most part of Catholics did follow for many years, and when the better and truer opinion was taught them by priests and religious men from beyond the seas as more perfect and necessary, there wanted not many that opposed themselves, especially of the elder priests of Queen Mary's days. And this division was not only favoured by the council, but nourished also for many years by divers troublesome people of our own, both in teaching and writing"[1] [Persons' *Brief Apology or Defence of the Catholic Eccl Hierarchy*, fol 2]

Until the year 1570, therefore, there was no separate Roman community in England, although there was a party, but a gradually diminishing party, whose feelings were strongly prejudiced against the changes made in the reign of Edward VI, and who wished for the revival of that ecclesiastical position which had been adopted during the reign of Queen Mary But this party remained for several years within the Church There they remained until they were told by the Pope and the Jesuits that their duty to the former was inconsistent with this outward loyalty to the Church of their country And there they would have remained still, if they had not enrolled themselves among that unwise minority of Englishmen who are found ready in every generation to submit to the dictation of foreigners, Calvin on the one hand, or the Pope on the other

Long before the year 1570, however, an unprincipled and shocking conspiracy against the English Church and nation had been in process of concoction at Rome, where England has never been understood, and where little pains have ever been taken to understand it, until the Papal policy was stimulated by the talent and pertinacity of modern seceders from the Church of England The earliest information which we possess respecting this conspiracy is contained in a paper sent to Burleigh from Venice, on April 13th, 1564, by Dennum, a secret agent of the English Government, who had been sent to the Continent to gain what information he could respecting "foreign conspiracies and contrivances," but Dennum's information is confirmed by subsequent events and by the history of Pius V which was written by Catena in the year 1586 Dennum's paper has been already printed, though not very correctly [Strype's *Mem* I ii 54], but it is of so much importance towards elucidating the origin of the Roman Catholics that it is here given at length, from the copy of it preserved in the British Museum, the spelling being modernized —

"A list of several Consultations amongst the Cardinals, Bishops, and other of the several orders of Rome now a contriving and conspiring against her gracious Majesty and the Established Church of England

"Pius having consulted with the clergy of

[1] In the year 1606 Persons published a volume of 386 closely printed pages against the fifth part of Sir Edward Coke's reports The last chapter, the sixteenth, is a reply to Coke's statement as given above Yet after a quantity of mere rhetoric, Persons says —"I deny not but that many others besides these" the deprived dignitaries "throughout the realm, though otherwise Catholics in heart (as most of them were) did at that time and after, as also now, either upon fear, or lack of better instruction, or both, repair to Protestant churches, the case being then not so fully discussed by learned men, as after it was, 'whether a man with good conscience may go to the church and service of a different religion from his own.'"

Italy, and assembling them together, it was by general consent voted, that the immunity of the Romish Church and her jurisdiction is required to be defended by all her princes as the principal Church of God

"And to encourage the same, the Council hath voted that Pius should bestow her Grace's realm on that prince who shall attempt to conquer it

"There was a Council ordered by way of a Committee, who contain three of the cardinals, two of the archbishops, six of the bishops, and as many of the late order of the Jesuits, who daily increase and come into great favour with the Pope of late, these do present weekly methods, ways, and contrivances for the Church of Rome, which hold the great Council for the week following in employment how to order all things for the advancement of the Romish faith Some of these contrivances, coming to my hands by the help of the silver-key, be as follow —

"1 The people of England being much averted from their Mother Church of Rome, they have thought fit, sounding out their inclinations how the common sort are taken with the Liturgy in English, for to offer her Grace to confirm it with some things altered therein, provided that her Grace and the Council do acknowledge the same from Rome and her Council, which, if it be denied, as we suppose it will, then these are to asperse the Liturgy of England by all ways and conspiracy imaginable

"2 A license or dispensation to be granted to any of the Romish orders to preach, speak, or write against the now Established Church of England, amongst other protestors against Rome, purposely to make England odious to them, and that they may retain their assistances promised them in case of any prince's invasion, and the parties so licensed and indulged (dispensed with) to be seemingly as one of them, and not to be either taxed, checked, or excommunicated for so doing And further, for the better assurance of the party so licensed and indulged the party to change his name, lest he be discovered, and to keep a quarternal correspondence with any of the cardinals, archbishops, bishops, abbots, priors, or other of the chief monasteries, abbeys, etc At which quarternal correspondence shall not only give the Pope intelligence of heretical conspiracy, but be a full assurance of their fidelity to Rome

"This proposal was much debated in the Council, which caused some of the Council to say, how shall we prevent it, in case any of the parties so licensed flinch from us and receive a good reward, and fall off from our correspondency

"3 It was then ordered that there should be several appointed for to watch the parties so licensed and indulged, and to give intelligence to Rome of their behaviour, which parties are sworn not to divulge to any of those so licensed or indulged what they be, or from whence they came, but to be strange, and to come in as one of their converts, so that the party shall be cautious how and which way he bendeth.

"It was afterwards debated how it should be ordered in case any of the heretical ministry of England should become as they who had these licenses, and what should be done in that case

"4 It was then answered by the Bishop of Mens that that was the thing they aimed at, and that they desired no more than separation amongst the heretics of England; and by so doing, in ease an animosity be amongst them (the Church established by the heretic Queen, as they so termed her Grace), there would be the less to oppose the Mother Church of Rome, whenever opportunity served This reason of the Bishops pacified the whole Council

"5 It was granted, not only indulgence and pardon to the party that should assault her Grace, either private or in public, or to any cook, brewer, baker, physician, vintner, grocer, chirurgeon, or any other calling whatsoever, that should or did make her away out of this world, a pardon, but an absolute remission of sins to the heirs of that party's family sprung from him, and a perpetual annuity to them for ever, and the said heir to be never beholden to any of the fathers for pardon, be they of what order soever, unless it pleased himself, and to be one of those Privy Council, whosoever reigned successively

"6 It was ordered, for the better assurance of further intelligence to the See of Rome, to give licenses to any that shall swear to that supremacy due obedience and allegiance, to her powers, to dispense with sacraments, baptism, marriages, and other ceremonies of our now Established Church in England, that the parties so obliged may possess and enjoy any office, employment, either ecclesiastical, military or civil, and to take such oaths as shall be imposed upon them, provided that the said oaths be taken with a reserve for to serve the Mother Church of Rome whenever opportunity serveth, and thereby in so doing the Act in Council was passed, it was no sin, but meritorious until occasion served to the contrary, and that when it so served for Rome's advantage the party was absolved from his oath

"7 It was also ordered that all the Romish orders, as well regular as secular, to cherish all the adherents of the Mother Church of Rome, whenever occasion serveth, to be in readiness at the times that shall be appointed, and to contribute according to their capacities what in them lieth for the promotion of the Romish cause

"8 It is ordered that the Romish party shall propose a match for the Queen of the Catholic princes for to further or to promote the Romish faith

"9 It is ordered, upon pain of excommunication, and of a perpetual curse to light on the families and posterities of all those of the Mother Church of Rome who will not promote or assist by means of money or otherwise Mary Queen of Scotland's pretence to the Crown of England

"10 It is also ordered that every Romish Catholic within England and Ireland, or any of England's territories, to contribute to those Romish bishops, parish priests, etc, that are privately or shall be by Rome set over them, to pay all the Church duties, as if they were in possession upon pain of excommunication of them and their posterity

"11 It is ordered that the See of Rome do dispense with all parties of the Roman faith to swear against all heretics of England as elsewhere, and that not to be a crime, or an offence against the soul of the party, the accused taking the oath with an intention to promote or advance the Roman Catholic faith" [*Brit Mus Add MS* 4784 ff 39-42]

Such were the secret plans of the Court of Rome for overturning the independence of the Church of England A complete view of the subsequent progress of the conspiracy is found in the work of a contemporary Italian writer, devoted to the interests of the Papacy, Girolamo Catena, who makes the following statements in two chapters on the transactions of Pius V against Queen Elizabeth in his life of that Pope —

"How clearly the zeal of Pope Pius flamed out for retrieving the state of religion which was fallen and decayed, may be seen in the affairs of England Besides the continual supplies and pensions which he gave to many persons of quality of that nation, and to such as had fled thence for the sake of the Catholic faith, he resolved immediately to send Vincenzo Lauro, Bishop of Mondovi, Nuncio into Scotland, where Calvin's heresy began to creep in, furnishing him with a good sum of money to be expended in the cause of religion, and of Queen Mary Stuart, who had still preserved herself Catholic Vincenzo gave her that supply of money, together with his wholesome advice, but by reason of the many and great troubles of that kingdom, fomented by Elizabeth Queen of England, he, residing at Paris, could not penetrate so far into those affairs as Queen Mary desired, as well for the great devotion she bore to the holiness and bounty of the Pope, as for her great regard to the worth and singular prudence of the Nuncio She, after having solemnly baptized the Prince her son according to the rites of the Roman Church, was several times reduced to such a condition by the snares and treachery of the heretics (whom Elizabeth secretly favoured, yet seeming to take pity on her, exhorting her to patience, and keeping her in hope of assistance, 'till she might entice and draw' her into her territories), that she passed at length into England to demand succours against her rebellious subjects, relying on the promises of the said Queen, who yet no sooner had her in her power but she shut her up in prison, fearing, lest if Mary prospered, who being nearest of blood to Henry VIII was his lawful heir, she would lose her kingdom of England, who being born of Anne of Boleyn, not his wife but his concubine, might justly be driven out of it as illegitimate Now Pius, taking into consideration, as well how he might help and deliver the Queen of Scots (whom neither imprisonment, nor bonds, nor threatened tortures, nor promised rewards could shake from the Catholic faith, or from the obedience to the Holy See), as how he might restore the true religion in England, and remove the very stink or source of so great evils (Elizabeth still aiding and abetting the dissensions in Christendom, especially in France and Flanders, and giving support to the Protestants in Germany), deputed certain persons who should go into that kingdom, and informing themselves of the state of the heretics and Catholics, should give him an account of both, animating the latter to set up again the ancient rites and worship. And as he was not permitted to have there an Apostolical Nuncio, or any public minister for the Holy See, he had diligent care that Robert Ridolfi, a Florentine gentleman, who resided in England under the show of a merchant, should move the minds of the people to a sedition for the destruction of Elizabeth This gentleman operated after such a manner in the name of his Holiness, not only with the Catholics, of whom there are great numbers, but likewise with many of the principal Protestants, who concurred in this design for various reasons, some for the personal enmity they had with those who aspired to the next succession of the Crown, some prompted by more solid hopes in the change of the government, that there was reason to expect a good event While these things were secretly in agitation, there arose a difference between the Catholic King and Elizabeth, on account of shipping and of money detained in London, which the King intended for the payment of his army in Flanders, and neither these nor the goods of the Genoese being restored as the Duke d'Alva demanded, he, by way of reprisal, seized on the effects of the English at Antwerp, and other places Hence Pius, taking advantage of the occasion, pressed the King to favour the design of the conspirators in England, as he could not better secure his dominions in Flanders than by depressing the power of this Queen, who, while she was in a condition, would always infest those Provinces, and reminded him of the obligation of his religion, as the first motive to such an undertaking The King gladly embracing this proposal, it was left to the care of Pius to manage dextrously with the Court of France, in order to its favouring the Catholics of England But for this, he was to use, as he did, very different persuasives, representing chiefly the interest of the Queen of Scots, who was allied to the Crown of France, and of those noblemen who had assisted the same Crown, when the Admiral, at the head of an army, was attempting the ruin of the Royal family, these having kept back Elizabeth from declaring herself openly in behalf of the French rebels Everything appearing to be well concerted in England, Ridolfi pushed the matter so strenuously that the greatest part of the nobility joined together, taking the Duke of Norfolk for their head, to whom the Queen of Scots, with her own consent, was promised in marriage And that this insurrection might be of greater service to the said Queen, and Duke, and nobles, Pius at the same time published a Bull and sentence against Elizabeth, declaring her to be heretical, and deprived of her kingdom, discharging her subjects from their oath of fidelity and from all other duty whatsoever, and likewise excommunicating those that should hereafter obey her, in the same form granting full commission to all to withstand and oppose her And, first of all, there being a difficulty of publishing the Bull in Spain or France for fear of provoking this wicked woman, he caused it to be published in that very kingdom, transmitting to Ridolfi many printed copies to be dispersed, as was accordingly done Thus, none knowing whence they came, many persons were executed for having transcribed them with their own hand Among others John Melela" [Felton] "an English gentleman, having fixed a copy on the gate of the Bishop of London's palace, suffered a most cruel death, constantly affirming to the last that he had done well, and that he was ready to do it again, according to the tenor and purport of the said Bull, which so far influenced and excited the minds of the people, that they declared publicly against yielding any farther allegiance to Elizabeth, and if any head of the faction had then discovered himself, they would certainly have run into a sudden and open revolt Whereupon Elizabeth, apprehending her danger, and not being altogether ignorant of the conspiracy of the nobles, began to arm, and to use the necessary precautions, as well to defend herself, as to lay hold on some of the parties that were engaged against her

"Hence the Earls of Northumberland and Westmoreland, fearing to be surprised on their estates, without tarrying for their companions, or for succour from abroad, rose with more than twelve thousand men, and by public declarations notified the cause of their rising to be the restoring of the Catholic religion, and the ancient laws of the kingdom [1] Nor did they scour the country and march immediately against Elizabeth, as they ought to have done, and by which means they would have been sure of all their followers But standing still, and not being able to maintain themselves in the field for want of money, at length retiring into Scotland, they did nothing at all, but gave occasion to Elizabeth to put the Duke of Norfolk under a guard upon suspicion, as also for fear of his marriage with the Queen of Scots, and to imprison many others, of whom Ridolfi was one. But Elizabeth, not being able to penetrate the depth of the conspiracy, they were all set at liberty except the Duke In the meanwhile Pius had given Ridolfi a credit of an hundred and fifty thousand crowns, and was preparing a greater sum to advance the design Ridolfi, being then a prisoner, could not distribute the money among those who were up in arms, yet afterwards he gave part of it to them to keep them on the borders of Scotland, part to the Duke of Norfolk, part to others of the conspirators, to hold them firm Yet the alarm still sounding through the realm, Elizabeth called several persons to Court under various pretences, not daring to make a greater noise who refused to come, and gave her plainly enough to understand that they owed her no manner of obedience during the interdict of the Bull, of which Elizabeth herself was heard to say, that it troubled her not so much for its substance and contents, as because it had Pius for its author, whose election and life she could not but esteem miraculous Now that the work might proceed on at due foundations, they despatched Ridolfi to Pius, acquainting him, that on their side all things were now ready, and desiring that he would be pleased to lend his name to the undertaking, as designed for the cause of religion, and for setting the Queen of Scots on the English throne after her marriage to the Duke of Norfolk, as also that he would move the Catholic king to grant them the succours they had demanded Pius, well comprehending all their measures, and approving them, and rejecting what the Duke d'Alva had written to dissuade from the enterprise, after Ridolfi had communicated it to him in passing through Flanders, sent the same Ridolfi to the King of Spain under pretence of carrying articles for a League, and gave him likewise Briefs to the King of Portugal, with all necessary instructions and deliberations, at the same time writing to the Duke of Norfolk, and exhorting him to be of good courage, inasmuch as he should want no assistance Ridolfi, presenting the Brief to the Catholic king, with the Pope's commission, by which he encouraged him to make the attempt, and speedily to send the desired succours, offering not only all his power, but even to go in person, if need were, for the obtaining so great a benefit to all Christendom, and to pawn all the substance of the Apostolical See, the chalices, the crosses, and even his own vestments, informing him exactly how feasible the thing was if he would only send into England a detachment of his army in Flanders, under the command of Chiapin Vitelli, in case that d'Alva was hindered The King having signified his pleasure to this purpose by an express courier, and Pius having remitted by the way of Flanders a great supply of money, d'Alva was not pleased to forward the execution, as well that he might deny this honour to Vitelli (having in his place proposed his own son, whom neither the King nor Council accepted), as on account of the new troubles in France, it being necessary to use precaution with that Crown, lest it should discover that the Catholic king embarked in this design without its aid, and thereupon should interpose to hinder it, and so the arms both of France and England should be brought against Flanders, because the French would be jealous lest the Spaniard should make himself master of England, as the Spaniard would have been, could the French have attempted the like by their own strength, as they were never yet able to do nor could the Pope give sufficient security in the

[1] Sanders says in his "De visibili Monarchia," written in the year 1572, that the Pope caused the rebellion in the North by sending Nicolas Morton, a priest, to declare to the Earls of Northumberland and Westmoreland that Elizabeth was a heretic, that she had thus lost all claim to dominion and power, that she was to be regarded by them as a heathen, and that they were free from any obligation to obey her laws The exact words are thus given by another writer "Our Lord has inspired your minds with a zeal worthy of your Catholic faith, that you may attempt to free yourselves and your country from the shameful slavery of female lewdness, and bring it back to its former obedience to this holy Roman See" [Throckmorton's *Further Considerations*, 101]

case Wherefore d'Alva wrote back to the Spanish Court, representing these difficulties and considerations And, while his master gave him new orders that, notwithstanding any objections, he should undertake the assistance of his friends in England in the manner that was resolved on, and sent Ridolfi to him with money for the performance, it pleased God, in His secret judgment, to permit that Elizabeth should be advised of the whole design by a person abroad, whose name is here concealed Whence, using still greater diligence, and being more upon her guard, and having found at the passing of a river letters from the Duke of Norfolk with twelve thousand crowns, which he sent to his friends in Scotland to be ready with forces, she ordered him to be taken into stricter custody, many others being imprisoned, and among these his secretary, who at the torture, confessed his cipher, upon which the Duke, being convicted, was put to death, with many others With what excess of sorrow the Pope regretted this disappointment, let the reader judge The Catholic king lamented it before the Cardinal of Alexandria, telling him that never was there a fairer enterprise, nor better concerted, nor ever more union and constancy among the parties concerned, it having never been discovered by their means all the time it was in agitation Nor indeed was it less easy; because, if only three thousand of the infantry had in one night and one day unexpectedly passed over from Flanders, and landed at a time appointed in a certain place near London where Elizabeth's guards were posted, as in the Tower and in the Palace, there was so good an understanding, and so many people prepared, that the blow had been given in England before it could have been heard of in France, the Queen of Scots had been set at liberty, and confirmed Queen of England, as lawful heir, and the Catholic religion restored in that kingdom Especially there having been assurance given, that Thomas Stuckley, an English gentleman, by means of the correspondence he held in Ireland, should in a few weeks, with certain ships of war granted him by the King of Spain, and three thousand soldiers on board, reduce that whole island to the devotion of the Catholics, at the same time sending his own pilot with two ships, and two armed barks, to burn all the vessels in the River of Thames" [*Vita del Gloriosissimo Papa Pio Quinto, scritta*, etc, Girolamo Catena, *dedicata al Santissimo signor nostro Sisto Quinto In Roma con licenza et privilegi*, 1587, pp 112-118]

It was in the year after Catena had published the preceding narrative of this atrocious Papal conspiracy that the climax of that conspiracy was attained in the long-expected invasion of England undertaken by Philip II with the great fleet named the "Armada" His expedition sailed in May 1588, and before August 5th of that year it was utterly ruined, partly by storms, partly by the resolute hearts and strong arms of Englishmen who loved their country, and in spite of those traitors who were inviting the enemies of England to her shores. After that notable failure, no foreign prince was ever so unwise as to endeavour to conquer England for the Pope, and henceforth the Papal party sought their ends (except in the case of the Gunpowder Plot and its abortive insurrection) by more ordinary means

Meanwhile that party was diminishing in its native and growing in its alien element For the old Marian party, which had come from within the Church of England, was almost extinguished by the lapse of time, and was being replaced by a party which had never had any connection with the Church of England

The Marian Episcopate died out in a very remarkable manner The last of the twenty bishops consecrated during Mary's reign was Christopherson, who was consecrated to the See of Chichester (while Scory, its Edwardian Bishop, was still living) on November 21st, 1557 Between that time and the consecration of the first twelve Elizabethan Bishops on December 17th and 21st, 1559, and on January 21st and March 24th, 1560, no fewer than seventeen sees became vacant by death These were as follows —

See	Vacated	By death of
Salisbury	Oct 6, 1557	Capon
Oxford	Dec 4, ,,	King
Norwich . .	1558	Hopton
Chichester	,,	Christopherson
Bangor	May 21, ,,	Glynne
Gloucester	Sept 7, ,,	Brookes
Hereford	,, 22, ,,	Purfew
Canterbury	Nov 19, ,,	Poole
Rochester .	,, 20, ,,	Griffin
Bristol . .	Dec 20, ,,	Holyman
Durham	Nov 18, 1559	Tunstall
St David's	Dec 23,	Morgan
Winchester	Jan 12, 1560	White
Lichfield	,,	Bayne
Carlisle	,,	Oglethorpe
Exeter	,,	Turberville
Peterborough	,,	Poole

Another see, that of Llandaff, became vacant by the death of Kitchin in the year 1563, and there were then only eight survivors of the Marian Episcopate One of these, Bonner of London, was in prison; two, Goldwell of St Asaph and Pates of Worcester, were living abroad, having deserted their sees on the death of Mary; five, Heath of York, Watson of Lincoln, Thirlby of Ely, Bourne of Bath, and Scott of Chester, were living as private gentlemen, having apparently resigned their sees The last survivor of all was Watson, ex-Bishop of Lincoln, who was compromised by some treasonable conspiracy, and imprisoned in Wisbeach Castle, dying in the year 1584 With his death the Marian succession came entirely to an end, no attempt ever having been made by any of the surviving bishops to consecrate others[1] And with the end of the

[1] In the British Museum Library there is, however, a sheet of rough paper containing a list "off all ye Byshopes, Doctours, and Priestes that were prisoners in ye flyte for Religion synce the fyrste yere off the reigne of quene Elizabethe anno dom 1559" It gives twenty four names, and among them those of "The Bishop of Herteforde," who was committed on May 13th, 1561, and "Mr Thomas Wood elected a Bishop," who was committed on November 20th, 1561 [*Harl MS.* 360 7] This

Marian succession there came also to an end all connection whatever between the ancient Church of England and the new community of Roman Catholics Until the old bishops had died there was a shadow of such a connection, and the small community under them might claim to run parallel with that which under the bishops of the Church represented the old and broad ecclesiastical stream that had flowed onward to the sixteenth century from Apostolic times But when the death of Watson without any Episcopal heir had brought that portion of the succession which he represented to an end, the English Episcopate descended from Archbishop Parker became the only lineal representatives of the mediæval, Anglo-Saxon, and Primitive, Church of England The Roman Catholic community of subsequent days no more flowed from the ancient Church of England than the Tiber flows from the Thames

But the probability of the schism dying out for want of a ministry had been foreseen as early as the year 1568 by an acute Oxford seceder named William Allen [A D 1532-94], who had been a Fellow of Oriel in the reign of Edward VI, Principal of St. Mary's Hall in that of Queen Mary, received the empty title of Cardinal of England in the year 1587, and became Archbishop of Mechlin in 1589 During the early part of Elizabeth's reign Allen was in England, and endeavoured to prevent his friends from frequenting the services of the Church But about 1566 he went abroad, and was ordained priest at Mechlin, where he became a reader in theology His acquaintance with the state of the Marian party in England led him to the conclusion that the old clergy would not perpetuate the schism, and he therefore devised the plan of founding colleges on the Continent "for restoring," as Persons writes, "a new English clergy" The first of these colleges, or "seminaries" as they were called, was established at Douay in Flanders in the year 1568, under Allen himself From 1576 until 1593 it was carried on at Rheims, whither it had been driven by a riot at Douay But in 1593 it was reinstated at the latter town, and continued there until the French Revolution, when it migrated to Old Hall Green at Ware, in Hertfordshire, and is now known as St Edmund's College, though originally dedicated to St Thomas of Canterbury Other seminaries were founded at Rome, Seville, and Madrid, in 1578, and others at Valladolid, St. Omer's, Paris, Liège, Lisbon, Louvain, and Ghent, during the subsequent forty years [Butler's *Hist Mem* ii 172, 440], and so energetically were these supported by the Court of Rome that dispensations were granted to those Roman Catholics who possessed abbey lands, freeing them from all spiritual censures on that account if they contributed to the support of seminaries [Fuller's *Ch Hist* 92]

At the foreign colleges thus established English youths were educated for the priesthood on the most extreme system of devotion to Rome and of antipathy to England and the English Church Some of these began to come over in the year 1571, "apparelled like mariners," and with "captains' passports" obtained in the Low Countries [*Harl MS* 360, f 25] They landed as if they were coming to an enemy's country, and one in which the light of Christianity having been extinguished it was to be kindled again by their means, as it had been kindled among the heathen Saxons of Kent by the missionaries under St Augustine Secretly as they came, their movements were well known to the Government, and minute descriptions of their persons exist, one being described as having "little hair on the front of his forehead," another as "freckled," a third as a "pretty little fellow, of complexion something brown, and apparelled in blue," and so forth [*ibid*], but the Queen and her Government were not uneasy about them for the first few years, believing that the movement was only a temporary one, and would gradually from one cause or another cease [Sanders, *de Schism Anglic* 312] Queen Elizabeth had been nineteen years on the throne before any seminary priest suffered punishment, but when the papal conspiracy was aided by them, and especially by those of them who were Jesuits, a very serious danger threatened the Queen and the nation, and it became necessary to treat those as traitors who unhesitatingly mixed themselves up with treason

The historian of the Jesuit Mission in England says that one of the body named William Good was sent to Ireland for four years, leaving the country again in 1568, but that none came to England until Campion and Persons made their appearance there in 1581 The reason he alleges is that as in the Divine Counsels the Saviour was not sent into the world until it was sunk in darkness, so England was permitted to become dark and wicked before the Jesuits were sent to convert it [More, *Hist Miss Anglican Soc Jesu* 1660, p 33] But a story is told by Strype which shews that More was mistaken, and that Jesuits were among the earliest of the so called "missionaries" According to this narrative one of them named Thomas Heath, brother to the former Archbishop of York, was at work early in the Queen's reign, and was discovered in a curious manner From 1562 until 1568 he went up and down the country, preaching in the churches, and spicing his sermons with Puritanism of the most extreme type At last he applied to the Dean of Rochester as a poor minister deserving preferment, and to test his ability the Dean gave him a preaching turn in the cathedral While preaching a sermon, in which he cried down the services of the Church, he accidentally dropped a letter from his pocket, which had been addressed to him under the name of Thomas Fine from an eminent English Jesuit named Malt at Madrid This letter, containing instructions respecting his mission, was carried to the Bishop of Rochester, and led to Heath's chamber being searched, when there were found in his boots and in his trunk a license from the

stray paper is not much evidence, but it may indicate that some attempts to obtain a separate Episcopate were at first made, but instantly checked

Jesuits, a Bull from the Pope authorizing him to preach what doctrine the Jesuits ordered him to preach for dividing Protestants, with several books against Infant Baptism Heath was put in the pillory, branded with an R as a Recusant, and condemned to imprisonment for life, but he died after being a few months in prison [Strype's *Ann* ii 273, ed 1824] Somewhat earlier, May 10th, 1566, the Pope had issued a Bull anathematizing the English heretics, and enjoining all wise and learned ecclesiastics "to labour, endeavour, and contrive all manner of devices to abate, assuage, and confound them" This was so interpreted as that it gave dispensations to mission priests for "devising of new tenets, doctrines, and covenants," "provided that the device intended was to promote the advancement of Rome," and also permitting them to go through the ceremony of marriage with what women they pleased, on the ground that heretical marriage was no marriage, and that by appearing to be married they could better carry on their work of converting the nation Commissions were given to them under several names in case they should be discovered, and that when they had intelligence they might fly to another place and still keep correspondence with the convents to which they belonged [*ibid* 219] Added to these provocations there were many books sent into England by Allen, Bristowe Sanders, Persons, and others, which were as damaging to the peace of the State as to that of the Church, and thus it is not surprising that the conduct of the seminary priests at last brought down severe punishment upon them The old Marian clergy had been treated with kindness and liberality, and even the seminary priests had been merely placed under surveillance so long as they continued quiet, but after the year 1577, in which the first of the latter was executed for treason, a large number suffered imprisonment and death, about 120 in all being punished as traitors during the remaining years of the Queen's reign

Roman Catholics are accustomed to balance these executions against the burnings of Queen Mary's reign, as if in the later cases as well as in the earlier, the persons executed were sufferers for religion But this allegation was disproved by Lord Burleigh in his work entitled "Execution for Treason, and not for Religion," printed in 1583 [1] He shews that the Seminary priests were arraigned under Acts of Parliament of Edward III's reign, about 1330, not under any new laws, that only those were condemned for treason who engaged in political conspiracies, and especially who maintained the effect of the Pope's Bull against the Queen These persons always made a point of saying that what they did was done for religion, also that they suffered for religion, but it is sufficiently plain that when a conspiracy against a sovereign's life is entered into, whatever the ultimate object may be towards which the conspirators consider the sovereign's death as a step, those who thus conspire engage in an act of treason, and must risk the consequences There was also published an official paper of six pages, entitled "A Declaration of the favourable dealing of Her Majesty's Commissioners appointed for the examination of certain traitors, and of tortures unjustly reported to be done upon them for matters of religion, 1583" This states, in addition, that the torture was never used to any of the accused persons, unless they gave evidence that they knew treasons which they would not reveal If they said as Christian men, in such a manner as was usual and usually credited among Christian men, that they did not know, their allegation was always accepted Those who were tortured were not so treated until after every endeavour had been used to get at the truth otherwise, and none, not even Campian himself, were so racked, but they were able to walk away from the rack, and to write with their hands, immediately afterwards

These statements on the one hand are corroborated on the other by a publication which emanated from some of the seminary priests themselves, when they had come to see how much evil had resulted from the conduct of the Roman Catholics under the leadership of the Jesuits This work was written, on behalf of a number of the secular priests, by one of their own number, named William Watson, and the title itself is instructive, being as follows —"Important considerations which ought to move all true and sound Catholics who are not wholly Jesuited to acknowledge, without all equivocations, ambiguities, or shiftings, that the proceedings of Her Majesty, and of the State, with them since the beginning of Her Highness' reign, have been both mild and merciful Published by sundry of us the secular priests in dislike of many treatises, letters, and reports, which have been written and made in divers places to the contrary, together with our opinions of a better course hereafter for the promoting of the Catholic faith in England Newly imprinted, 1601" The work is a manifesto against "the Jesuitical Hispanized faction" led by Persons, Garnet, and Blackwell, and speaks of the laity as being strongly under the influence of the Jesuits Their historical statement of facts agrees exactly with that of Burleigh, and they say the State had good reason to make laws against them, considering what "outrageous" treasons were being practised, and having the Bull in view "Sure we are, that no king or prince in Christendom would like or tolerate any such subjects within their dominions, if possibly they could be rid of them" [p 21]. They attribute Throckmorton's plot, and those connected with Mary, Queen of Scots, in general, to the Jesuits, and declare the Pope himself to have "plotted with the King of Spain" at their instigation, for putting Mary on the throne of England To the Jesuits also they attribute the contrivance of plots for the assassination of the Queen, mentioning Patrick Collen, Doctor Lopez, Yorke, Williams, and Squire as having been so employed by them

[1] The full title is "Execution of Justice in England for maintenance of public and Christian peace against certain stirrers of sedition and adherents to the traitors and enemies of the realm, without any persecution of them for questions of religion, as is falsely reported and published by the fautors and fosterers of their treasons" [Second ed 1583]

The troubles inflicted have been "great we confess in themselves, but far less we think than any prince living in Her Majesty's case, and so provoked, would have inflicted upon us Some of us have said many a time when we have read and heard speeches of Her Majesty's supposed cruelty, 'Why, my masters, what would you have her to do, being resolved as she is in matters of religion, except she should willingly cast off the care, not only of her State and kingdom, but of her life also and princely estimation?' Yea, there have been amongst us of our own calling who have likewise said that they themselves, knowing what they do know, how, under pretence of religion, the life of Her Majesty and the subversion of the kingdom is aimed at, if they had been of her Highness' Council, they would have given their consent for the making of very strait and rigorous laws to the better suppressing and preventing of all such Jesuitical and wicked designments" [p 37] And this, notwithstanding that "we profess ourselves with all godly courage and boldness to be as sound Catholic priests as any Jesuits or men living in the world, and that we do not desire to draw breath any longer on the earth than that we shall so continue."

Such evidence as this shews that the severities used towards Roman Catholics in the earlier times of the existence of their sect were actually forced upon the Government by the unscrupulous conduct of those who were endeavouring, as the chief part of their mission, to overthrow or to destroy the Queen, that by her destruction they might remove what they considered to be the chief barrier against the introduction of the Papal authority and system It was no persecution of the "ancient faith" or of the "remnant of the ancient Church," as is so often represented by Roman Catholic writers, but simply and entirely the punishment, in self-defence, of sectarian priests who had come to this country with the arrogant profession of converting its people, but who strove to bring them under the yoke of Ultramontanism by acts which the law accounted, and would still account, treasonable [1] That no great severity was shewn towards Roman Catholics on account of their religion alone is shewn by an order of Council, dated May 7th, 1581, at the very time when Campian the Jesuit was in the Tower for treason, directing that all Recusants shall be set free on recognizances not to depart the realm without license, nor to go more than three miles from home until they have conformed [*Council Book, Lansd MS* 1162, *Brit Mus*] That great severity was shewn by Queen Elizabeth's government towards Roman Catholic traitors, as well as towards all other traitors, is not to be doubted But severty to the few who were traitors to their sovereign and country was often necessary, in those times, to preserve the liberties of the many who were loyal to both

It has already been shewn that the formal organization of the Roman Catholics in England began with the Jesuits On the death of Bishop Watson, the few secular clergy who remained felt themselves left entirely without a head, and the idea of continuing the old succession, if it had ever been seriously entertained, was necessarily abandoned The Jesuits, henceforth, easily took the lead (although constantly and bitterly opposed by the secular clergy), and the "English Mission" was established under their leadership and under the sanction of the Pope No pretence was at that time made by them to represent the *old* Church of England, their professed object being to effect a new conversion of the English people, and so to found a *new* branch of the Church [Persons' *Four Conversions of England* Berington's *Panzani's Mem.* Introd 42] This object was well understood by the partizans of the Pope on the Continent, and excited so much interest and expectation that an official letter of intelligence to the Lord Treasurer, dated August 31st, 1592, says, "Scarcely anything else is talked of in Italy but this combat of England " The writer adds, however, that in Germany there were many who disapproved of what was going on [*Harl MS* 35, f 372]

For some years the direction of this arrogant and schismatical "Mission" was assumed by Robert Persons [A D 1546-1610], an Oxford seceder who had become a Jesuit in the year 1575, and having come to England with Edmund Campian [2] (an ex-fellow of St. John's, Oxford) under a commission from Gregory XIII, in July 1580, returned to Rome soon after the execution of Campian in 1581, and after being Rector of the English Seminary at Rome for some years, was eventually appointed "Prefect of the English Mission" in the year 1592 Father Persons himself was under the direction of Cardinal Allen, who was Archbishop of Mechlin, but neither of them left the Continent, Persons remaining in safety abroad while he stirred up sedition in England by means of his books and his Jesuit agents This mode of government was very objectionable to the schismatical clergy, who all along felt themselves to be in a false position, and desired to place themselves in one that should seem more justifiable than that of a foreign mission, by having bishops appointed from their own body After the death of Cardinal Allen, in the year 1594, this feeling grew stronger, and it ended in 1597 in an unanimous petition to the Pope for the restoration of a hierarchy "in which Bishops should be elected by the common consent of the clergy and appointed by them to different districts" [Mush, *Declaratio Motuum*, 21, 30] In-

[1] "After the promulgation of the Bull, six queries were generally proposed to the priests who were arraigned They regarded the import of that Bull, the deposition of the Queen as pronounced in it, and what should be the conduct of good subjects in reference to both Few answered, I am sorry to observe, as became loyal Englishmen and faithful citizens They seemed, rather, to consider themselves as the subjects of a foreign master, whose sovereignty was paramount and whose will was supreme " [Berington's *Memoirs of Panzani*, Introd 34]

[2] Campian's true name it is said was Edwards, but he assumed that by which he is usually known to save his friends from trouble [*Harl MS* 360, f 25] He is, however, entered as "Edmund Campian" in modern Oxford lists.

stead of acceding to the request so made, the Pope was persuaded by the Jesuits to appoint an Archpriest (or Rural Dean), George Blackwell [A D 1545-1613], an Oxford seceder, whose sole commission was a letter from Cardinal Cajetan, dated March 7th, 1598 This gave him authority over the 400 Roman Catholic clergy of England, but restricted that authority by appointing a council of six to act with him, and by prohibiting him from determining anything of importance without consulting the Superior of the Jesuits The clergy remonstrated so strongly at the slight put upon them by the off-hand manner in which this appointment was made, that at last the Pope was persuaded to add the dignity and weight of his own commission, which was issued to Blackwell in the form of a Brief on August 17th, 1601 Blackwell, however, became a loyal Englishman under the influence of horror and disgust at the Gunpowder Plot, and taking the oath of allegiance to James I was deprived of his office by the Pope for so doing in the year 1608 [1] Two other archpriests were appointed, George Birkhead, in 1608, and George Harrison, in 1615, but on the death of the latter, in 1621, the Pope was again petitioned to substitute bishops for these anomalous officers This request was so far conceded that William Bishop was consecrated to the episcopal office on June 4th, 1623, and sent to England as Vicar-Apostolic, with faculties similar to "those of the late archpriests joined to those which ordinaries enjoy and exercise," but the authority was given only during the pleasure of the Pope, and the Vicar-Apostolic was not a Bishop with independent power, but only a delegate of another Bishop, the Pope, under the title of the "Bishop of Chalcedon" Now "it seemed to many," says Berington, "that the English Catholic Church was re-established in the renovation of her hierarchy But the fond imagination, I fear was founded on no truth . The Roman Pontiff still continued to be, what the clergy of England had for many years *permitted* him to be, their only Bishop How then, with him at our head, could it in the estimation of such men be said that we were without a church and a hierarchy of transcendent excellence? He governed us at one time by the agency of Dr Allen, perhaps by that of Father Persons, at another by his archpriests, now by the Bishop of Chalcedon, and in after times, as it will appear, by a series of similar delegations" [Berington's *Memoirs of Panzani*, Introd 105]

The first "Bishop of Chalcedon" died in less than a year after his appointment He was succeeded by Richard Smith, under the same title, who retained the office until 1655, but lived most of the time abroad For thirty years no successor to Smith was appointed, but in 1685 John Leyburn was consecrated under the title of "Bishop of Adrumetum," and England was afterwards, on January 20th, 1688, divided into the London, Midland, Northern, and Western Districts, by Pope Innocent XI. The Roman Catholics of Scotland were placed under the Archpriests and Vicars-Apostolic of England until the year 1694, since which time they have had Vicars-Apostolic of their own

There is not space in this article to follow up in any detail the history of the Roman Catholic sect during the time that has elapsed between its original organization and the present day· and it must suffice to trace the course of that history only in general outline

Early in the reign of James I the efforts of the Jesuits at home, and of the Seminaries abroad, were so successful that both Houses of Parliament presented an address to the Crown, setting forth that there was a "mischievous increase of Papists in his Majesty's dominion of late" which they feel bound to represent to the King, with the dangerous consequences that were likely to result Their dependence on foreign princes, the address said, was very evident, and there was also great danger if any ambitious man should become popular as the leader of the Popish party The principal causes of this increase are stated to be the too great leniency which was shewn in enforcing the laws against Jesuits, Seminary priests, and Popish recusants, the influence which was exercised in their favour by foreign ambassadors, and the resort of the Papists to their chapels, their concourse to the City, and their frequent conferences there, the education of their children in foreign seminaries and colleges, which had been greatly enlarged of late, the insufficient instruction of the population, the licentious permittance of Popish books, and lastly, the employment of men in places of government who gave countenance to the Popish party [*Harl MS* 35, f 452, *Brit Mus*] [2] Similar addresses were sent up to Charles I. on March 31st, 1628, and on this occasion also great importance was attributed to the immigration of Jesuits, and of children who had been educated in the foreign seminaries It was also alleged that many schools at home were in the hands of Recusants, and that the latter were acquiring much wealth by clever management of money in the City—what in later times has been called "stock-jobbing" [*ibid* 161, f 228]

The great struggle for power which is thus indicated was continued during the Civil Wars by means of those disgraceful underhand practices to which the party devoted to the Pope seems always ready to resort, and Bishop Bramhall declares that nearly one hundred of the Romish clergy became soldiers in the Parliament's army that they might stir up further animosities against

[1] There are many documents connected with Blackwell's official work as deputy of the Roman See in the Harleian MS volume, 6848, in the British Museum

[2] The rapid increase of the sect on the death of Queen Elizabeth is shewn conspicuously in Peacock's *List of the Roman Catholics in the County of York in* 1604, which was printed by Mr Peacock from a MS in the Bodleian Library in the year 1872 The recusants are distinguished in this list as "old" and "new," and while there are parishes enumerated in which no persons refused to come to Church in the Queen's time, though "new recusants" had arisen within a year of her death, other cases are recorded in which two "recusants old" were reinforced by twenty-five "recusants new since 25 March 1603."

the Church of England, in the hope that its overthrow would eventually place their own party in the ascendant [Bramhall's *Works*, i 95] The establishment of Cromwell's iron tyranny was, however, very unfavourable to the prosperity and progress of the sect, and it was not until the latter part of the reign of Charles II. that it again began to flourish The astute policy then adopted by the Jesuit leaders of the "English Mission" was to secure the co-operation of the Protestant Dissenters in attempting to secure what was called "toleration," but what was in reality freedom to carry on their never-ceasing endeavours to re-establish the Supremacy of the Pope in England In the reign of James II a very dangerous advance was made towards this end In the year 1686, Father Petre, the Vice-Provincial of the Jesuits in England, was made a member of the Privy Council, and of the "junto," or Cabinet Council of the Prime Minister, the Earl of Sunderland This body then consisted only of seven members, and Sunderland himself, with two or three others, being Roman Catholics, the government of England was practically in the hands of the sect St James' Chapel was appropriated to the use of fourteen Benedictine monks and the King's chaplains, the Savoy became a Jesuit monastery, the Franciscans set up their banner in Lincoln Inn Fields, the Carmelites in the City At Oxford the Dean of Christ Church and the Master of University College established the Roman services in their college chapels,[1] and for the first time since the sect had been founded public chapels were opened for its use throughout the country Four Vicars-Apostolic were also appointed by the Pope, and for each of them the Government provided an income of £1000 a year out of the Exchequer [Berington's *State and Behaviour of Cath* 157] But when the alliance of Protestant and Roman Catholic Dissenters had obtained from James II. the unconstitutional "Declaration of Liberty of Conscience," by which the latter hoped to pave the way for completing the work which had been so prosperously commenced, the clergy and laity of the Church were fairly aroused to the danger, and the imprisonment of the seven bishops who resisted this overbearing exercise of the prerogative caused the tide to turn

After the Revolution of 1688, which followed this development of Romanism, and which was chiefly occasioned by it, the Roman Catholics began to decline in power, and although their ecclesiastical organization was more and more developed under their Vicars-Apostolic, it was not until they had succeeded in their long-continued efforts to obtain the removal of those civic disabilities which the treasons and disloyalty of the sect had brought upon them, that they again attained any prominent position in England These disabilities were finally removed by what was called—with great exaggeration of their true bearing—"Roman Catholic Emancipation," in the year 1829 by 10 Geo IV ch 7, and by a subsequent Act passed in 1832 [3 Will IV ch 115] Roman Catholics were placed on the same constitutional footing as other Dissenters [2]

It has already been said that the Deputy Bishops, or "Vicars-Apostolic," from 1623 to 1688, were only three in number, and that for a large portion of these sixty-five years there was not any Roman Catholic Bishop in England The conduct of James II and his Government was, however, so encouraging to the Papal Court, that on January 30th, 1688, Pope Innocent XI divided England into four districts, appointing Vicars-Apostolic to each. This arrangement continued for a century and a half, during which time there were thirty-three of these schismatical bishops in England. On July 30th, 1840, Pope Gregory XVI re-divided the four districts into eight, and fourteen Vicars-Apostolic were appointed to these between 1840 and 1850 All these Vicars-Apostolic had been consecrated nominally to dioceses "in partibus infidelium," and bore such titles as Bishops of Melipotamus, Ariopolis, Olena, Tloa, Samosata, etc But, under the management of Cardinal Wiseman, Pope Pius IX, on September 29th, 1850, divided England into thirteen dioceses bearing English titles, namely, those of Westminster, Beverley, Birmingham, Clifton, Hexham and Newcastle, Liverpool, Menevia and Newport, Northampton, Nottingham, Plymouth, Salford, Shrewsbury, and Southwark The twelve latter of these are considered to be within the Province of Westminster, of which Cardinal Wiseman became the first titular Archbishop in 1850, and Henry Edward Manning, formerly Archdeacon of Chichester, the second in 1865

If anything was wanting before to complete the schismatical and sectarian position of the Roman Catholics, this was the crowning act, and in concluding the historical review of their sect no words can better be used to describe the position which has thus been assumed by them than those of Henry Edward Manning himself, written in 1845, when he was a leading 'High Churchman" "The attempt," he writes, "to impose an uncanonical jurisdiction on the British churches, and a refusal to hold communion with them except on that condition, was clearly an act of schism And this was further aggravated by every kind of aggression acts of excommunication and anathema, instigations to warfare abroad and to rebellion and schism at home, are the measures by which the Roman Church has exhibited its professed desire to restore unity to the Church of Christ It must never be forgotten that the act of the Bishop of Rome, by which a most grievous and stubborn contest was begun in the English Church,

[1] The Roman Catholics up to this time still used to some extent the old Sarum Service Books The Missal used by James II himself is preserved in the Cathedral Library at Worcester.

[2] The disabilities under which Roman Catholics were placed were that they were disqualified for sitting in Parliament by 30 Ch II 2, § 1, in 1677, were excepted from the Toleration Act of 1689, were disabled from voting at elections by 7 & 8 Will III ch 27, in 1696, and from inheriting or holding lands by 11 & 12 Will III ch 27, in 1700 These disabilities were almost all imposed by the Government of William III.

was taken not in the character of Patriarch, but in the title of Supreme Pontiff The same Bull which made a rent in every English diocese professed to depose also the Queen of England It was a power to give away not sees, but thrones also, and the effect of this has been, as in the East so in England to erect altar against altar, and succession against succession In the formation of sects in diocesan churches, in the exclusive assumption of the name Catholic, in the reordination of priests, and in restricting the One Church to their own communion, there has been no such example of division since the schism of Donatus" [Manning's *Unity of the Church*, 364, 2nd ed]

II Roman Catholic Doctrine The main point of difference between the Church of England and the Roman Catholics of England originally consisted in the claim made for the Pope, on the one hand, to exercise jurisdiction over the clergy and laity of England, and the denial of that claim, on the other, by the clergy in Convocation, and the sovereign, prelates and laity in Parliament If this claim had been admitted on the accession of Queen Elizabeth, and perhaps during the earlier part of the reign of James I, the Pope and the Court of Rome would have been willing to have passed over other differences very lightly, or at least to have let them slumber until a council had spoken upon the subject It is worth notice that the Book of Common Prayer as revised in 1559 was quietly accepted by the great body of Romanist laity, and also that the Pope himself saw so little to object to in it that he offered to give the book his full sanction if his authority were recognised by the Queen and kingdom This fact is referred to in the first head of Dennum's paper from Venice in 1564 [p 495] In the same charge also, from which a quotation has already been made [p 494] respecting the attendance of Roman Catholics at church, Sir Edward Coke states as follows That the Pope [Pius IV] "before the time of his excommunication against Queen Elizabeth denounced, sent his letter unto her Majesty, in which he did allow the Bible and Book of Divine Service as it is now used among us to be authentic and not repugnant to truth, but that therein was contained enough necessary to salvation, though there was not in it so much as might conveniently be, and that he would also allow it unto us, without changing any part, so as her Majesty would acknowledge to receive it from the Pope, and by his allowance, which her Majesty denying to do, she was then presently by the same Pope excommunicated And this is the truth concerning Pope Pius Quartus as I have faith to God and men I have oftentimes heard avowed by the late Queen her own words, and I have conferred with some Lords that were of greatest reckoning in the State, who had seen and read the letter, which the Pope sent to that effect, as have been by me specified And this upon my credit, as I am an honest man, is most true" [The Lord Coke, *His Speech and Charge, London*, 1607 See also Camden, *Ann Eliz* p 59, ed 1615, Twysden's *Historical Vindication of the Church of England*, p 175 Humphrey Prideaux's *Validity of the Orders of the Church of England* Bramhall's *Works*, ii 85, ed 1845 Bishop Babington's *Notes on the Pentateuch, on Numbers* vii Courayer's *Defence of the Dissertation on the Validity of English Ordinations*, ii. 360, 378 Harrington's *Pius IV and the Book of Common Prayer*, 1856][1] It is manifest that the concession of the Prayer Book carried with it substantially the concession of the doctrinal phase of the English Reformation. There were probably, indeed, few of the English clergy or laity who would not gradually have accepted the *official* Reformation of the Church of England—a very different thing from accepting the Puritan interpretation of it—if the Pope's supremacy had not stood in the way But the exclusion of the Church of England from the Council of Trent [A D 1545-1563] embittered the controversy between England and Rome, and raised further difficulties by petrifying opinions into dogmas with a positive minuteness from which the English mind has always revolted

Notwithstanding this, the doctrines of the Council of Trent were held by English Roman Catholics with much less rigidity than by the Continental churches until recent times, and the following fair statement of them by a writer of the last century will shew that at that time they did not much differ, except in those articles which relate to the Papal Supremacy, and making allowance for differing modes of expressing the same truth from those of the Church of England as held by High Church divines —

"[1] That Christ has established a Church upon earth, and that this Church is that which holds communion with the See of Rome, being One, Holy, Catholic, and Apostolical

"[2] That we are obliged to hear this Church, and therefore that she is infallible by the guidance of Almighty God, in her decisions regarding faith

"[3] That Peter, by Divine commission, was appointed the head of this Church, under Christ its founder and that the Pope, or Bishop of Rome, as successor to St Peter, has always been, and is at present, by Divine right, head of this Church

"[4] That the Canon of the Old and New Testament, as proposed to us by this Church, is the Word of God, as also such traditions, belonging to faith and morals, which being originally delivered by Christ to His Apostles have been preserved by constant succession in the Catholic Church

"[5] That honour and veneration are due to the Angels of God and His Saints, that they offer up prayers to God for us, that it is good and profitable to have recourse to their intercession; and that the relics or earthly remains of God's particular servants are to be held in respect

"[6] That no sins ever were, or can be, remitted unless by the mercy of God, through Jesus Christ, and therefore that man's justification is the work of Divine grace

[1] Blunt's *Annotated Prayer-Book*, xxxv

"[7] That the good works which we do receive their whole value from the grace of God, and that by such good works we not only comply with the precepts of the Divine law, but that we thereby likewise merit eternal life

"[8] That by works done in the spirit of penance we can make satisfaction to God for the temporal punishment which often remains due after our sins, by the Divine goodness, have been forgiven us

"[9] That Christ has left to His Church a power of granting indulgences, that is, a relaxation from such temporal chastisements only as remains due after the Divine pardon of sin and that the use of such indulgences is profitable to sinners

"[10] That there is a Purgatory or Middle State, and that the souls of imperfect Christians therein detained are helped by the prayers of the faithful.

"[11] That there are seven Sacraments, all instituted by Christ, Baptism, Confirmation, Eucharist, Penance, Extreme Unction, Holy Order, Matrimony

"[12] That in the most holy Sacrament of the Eucharist there is truly, really, and substantially the body and blood, together with the Soul and the Divinity of our Lord Jesus Christ

"[13] That in this Sacrament there is, by the Omnipotence of God, a conversion or change of the whole substance of the bread into the body of Christ, and of the whole substance of the wine into His blood, which change we call Transubstantiation

"[14] That under either kind Christ is received whole and entire

"[15] That in the Mass, or Sacrifice of the Altar, is offered to God a true, proper, and propitiatory sacrifice for the living and the dead

"[16] That in the Sacrament of Penance, the sins we fall into after Baptism are, by the Divine Mercy, forgiven us

"There are points of discipline also which regulate conduct, and to which we pay obedience, as fasting on particular days, communion in one kind, celibacy of Churchmen, use of the Latin language in public service, and other similar practices, but as these vary, and may be either altered or suppressed by due authority, they belong not to what is properly styled the Faith of Catholics" [Berington's *State and Behaviour of Eng Catholics*, 1780, pp 143-148]

But in the middle of the nineteenth century the old tone of the Roman Catholics was again supplanted to a very great extent by the modern Ultramontane tone, the change arising partly from the authoritative way in which the Pope and the Roman Court acted towards English Roman Catholics after 1829, partly from the more free intercourse which existed between England and the Continent, and partly from the zeal of some seceders from the Church of England, which led them to adopt the most extreme theology of the community to which they attached themselves The imposition as articles of faith of the dogma of the Immaculate Conception by the Vatican Council of 1854, and of the personal Infallibility of the Pope by that of 1870, set up still higher the wall between Anglican and Roman belief, removed the Roman Catholic body in England still further from the Apostolic Church of England than it had stood before, and put a stop to those attempts to promote re-union which might otherwise have led to an eventual abolition of the schism

III STATISTICS —The number of Roman Catholics in England and Wales has often been greatly exaggerated Butler, in his "Historical Memoirs of the English Catholics," states that they were a majority of the population, that is more than 2,250,000, in the reign of Elizabeth and Hallam, although he lowers this estimate considerably, still considers that they formed a third of the population at that time, or about 1,500,000 Both of these estimates are mere guesses, utterly unsupported by any historical evidence, and such guesses are disgraceful in those who profess to write with authority for the guidance of public opinion to truth

Sir John Dalrymple's Memoirs, on the other hand, preserve a memorandum, of which he says —"While King William was engaged in his project of reconciling the religious differences of England, he was at great pains to find out the proportions between Churchmen, Dissenters, and Papists In his chest there is the following curious report in consequence of an inquiry upon that head" [1] [Dalrymple's *Memoirs, App to Part II* p 14] This report gives the number in a tabular form for each county, and also the general result, afterwards adding an equal number to each total for children under sixteen years of age The numbers thus arrived at are as follows —

	Conformists	Non-Conformists	Papists
Province of Canterbury	2,123,362	93,151	11,878
Province of York	353,892	15,325	1,978
	2,477,254	108,476	13,856
Children	2,477,254	108,676	13,856
	4,954,508	217,152	27,712

This estimate seems likely to be correct, as the total, 5,199,372, nearly agrees with the number at which the population of England and Wales is estimated about the time at which it was made that population amounting to six millions in the beginning of the eighteenth century

In the year 1767 the House of Lords, on the motion of Lord Radnor, requested the Bishops to obtain a census of the Roman Catholics, by means of inquiries to be made by the clergy of their respective dioceses This inquiry is in fact ordered by the 114th Canon of 1603 to be made by the clergy every year and the results of it to be presented by the archbishops to the Crown

[1] A Broadsheet of 1705 gives this report a different origin, heading the figures "Great and good news to the Church of England, being the exact numbers of Churchmen, Dissenters, and Romans in England and Wales, as they were given to the late King James on the 3rd day of May 1688," etc [*Bodl. Pamph.* 264, 1705-6]

but it may be doubted whether this canon was ever strictly observed As to the census ordered in 1767, Berington, speaking of it in 1780, hopes that a careful inquiry will be made by the bishops, but meanwhile gives his own estimate "From the best information I can procure," he writes, "their number does not, at this day exceed 60,000 and this even I suspect to be far beyond the mark The few Catholics I have mentioned are also dispersed in the different counties In many, particularly in the West, in South Wales, and in some of the Midland Counties, there is scarcely a Catholic to be found This is easily known from the residence of the priests. After London, by far the greatest number is in Lancashire In Staffordshire are a good many, as also in the northern counties of York, Durham, and Northumberland Some of the manufacturing and trading towns, as Norwich, Manchester, Liverpool, Wolverhampton, and Newcastle upon-Tyne, have chapels, which are rather crowded, but these constitute the greatest part of the number I have just given to their respective counties In a few towns, particularly at Coventry, their number I find is increased, but this by no means in proportion of the general increase of population in the same places Excepting in the towns, and out of Lancashire, the chief situation of Catholics is in the neighbourhood of the old families of that persuasion They are the servants who have married from those families, and who choose to remain round the old mansion for the conveniency of prayers, and because they hope to receive favours and assistance from their former masters" [Berington, *State and Behaviour of English Catholics*, iii 111-114]

If, instead of estimating the Roman Catholics at 50 per cent of the population with Butler, or at 33 per cent. with Hallam, we reckon them as averaging about 60,000, or 1 per cent., from 1570 to 1800, we shall probably be not far from the truth.

Since the rise of manufacturing industry a very large number of Irish labourers has been required both in the field and in the factory, and a majority of these being Roman Catholics the numbers of the sect in England and Wales have increased greatly in modern times A very careful statistician has recently calculated that they now stand as follows —

English Roman Catholics and their Children,		179,000
Foreign, do	do	52,000
Irish, do	do	732,560
		963,560

[Ravenstein's *Denominational Statistics*, 1870, p 20] As the population of England and Wales is now 23,000,000, the proportion of English Roman Catholics appears by these figures to be reduced to ¾ per cent., including the foreigners it is exactly 1 per cent, and including both them and the Irish, it amounts to rather more than 4 per cent. In Scotland the proportion is very much higher, being not less than 10 per cent., the number in Glasgow alone being stated in Gordon's *Glasghu Facies* as 130,000.

The number of Roman Catholic clergy in England and Wales in 1780 is reckoned by Berington at 360, and he says that they "either live as chaplains in the families of gentlemen, and have the care of the little congregations around them, or else they reside in towns, or in some country places where funds have been settled for their support. The chapels are in their own houses" [Berington's *State and Behaviour of Eng Cath.* 160]

In the year 1872 the number of clergy (including 16 bishops) was 1599, and the number of public chapels 1005, but many of the latter are only "stations" at which services were held occasionally, while many of the clergy are private chaplains or belong to monastic communities Roman Catholic colleges, convents, and schools for the higher and middle classes are, however, very numerous, and these are continually growing in wealthy endowments and in social power [1]

ROSCELLIN [SCHOOLMEN]

ROSCHOLSCHIKI [ISBRANIKI]

ROSENFELDERS The fanatic followers of an impostor named Hans Rosenfeld who had been a gamekeeper, but set himself up as the Messiah about the year 1763, and seduced a large number of followers in Prussia and the neighbouring states Rosenfeld persuaded his followers that Christianity was a delusion, its priests impostors, and Frederick the Great neither more nor less than the Evil One, whom Rosenfeld was to depose, that he might afterwards govern the world himself as the Messiah, assisted by a council of twenty-four elders like those of the Apocalypse This impostor deluded multitudes, and lived upon them in outrageous profligacy for twenty years Eventually, in the year 1782, one of his followers, who still believed in him, appealed to the King, whom he believed to be the Evil One, to revenge him on Rosenfeld for the seduction of his three daughters This led the King to order proceedings to be taken against the impostor, and he was sentenced to be flogged and imprisoned for the remainder of his life at Spandau, after which his sect was dispersed [Gregoire's *Hist des Sectes Relig*]

ROSICRUCIANS This name was that adopted by a large section of the later fire-philosophers or THEOSOPHISTS, who were spread throughout all the countries of Northern Europe, about the beginning of the seventeenth century

Considerable difficulty exists as to the origin of the name, as well as to the limits and character of the society The name, popularly derived from "rosa" and "crux," seems at first sight

[1] Berington says respecting the Roman Catholic clergy of his time "Our priests in their general character are upright and sincere, but narrowed by a bad education, they contract early prejudices which they very seldom afterwards deposit They are bred up in the persuasion that on coming to England they are to meet with racks and persecution, they land, therefore, as in an enemy's country, cautious, diffident, and suspectful" His account of them, generally, is that they were discontented, bigoted, ignorant, and unfit to hold their own in society, an account which substantially agrees with what is otherwise known of those who came from the foreign seminaries.

to have some connection with the arms of Luther, which are composed of these symbols But the term is really a chemical one, and barbarously derived from "ros," dew (in alchemistic belief a powerful if not universal solvent), and "crux," which in the alchemistic language is identified with light, because the figure of a cross contains, in various presentations, all the three capital letters of the word "lux" Moreover, the fire-philosophers applied the term "lux" to the seed of the red dragon, or to that crude and corporeal light which by due process of concentration was believed to produce gold The Rosicrucians were in fact the philosophers who by means of dew sought for the alchemistic light, that is, for the substance of the philosopher's stone A different derivation is however suggested by the earliest Rosicrucian publication, the "Fama Fraternitatis," which was published in Frankfort about A D 1610 In this work the founder and head of the fraternity is said to have been one Christopher Rosencreutz, a German, born A D 1388, who, during a pilgrimage to Damascus and the Holy Sepulchre, was entertained and instructed by certain wise men of the East, from whose hands he passed into those of the chemists of Egypt and Morocco, where his education was completed Having thus obtained a thorough insight into the Kabbala and all magical arts, he is alleged on his return home to have commenced the reform of human knowledge, and it is pretended that having for this purpose admitted several pupils to his studies, the fraternity so formed preserved its continuity up to the seventeenth century The publication of this singular fable divided popular opinion into two parties, one declaring the Rosicrucians to be a body of learned and orthodox reformers, the other holding them to be a band of ignorant dreamers, the purveyors of mischievous delusion

As the Rosicrucian doctrines depended entirely on reasoning derived from facts testified to by heated imaginations and morbidly receptive senses, unanimity of opinion is not to be expected The sectaries agreed, however, in holding· first, that the only true knowledge was to be derived by analysis of all bodies by the agency of fire, secondly, that God operates by the same laws in the kingdom of Grace as in the kingdom of Nature, and that there is therefore a complete analogy and coincidence between science and religion, thirdly, that a divine soul or energy is diffused through the fabric of the universe—this incorporeal existence being by some called "Archæus," by others the Universal Spirit Holding these views, it is but natural to find that they expressed their religious doctrines in chemical terms They also taught a vague and uncertain astrology, magic, and demonology

The Rosicrucians obtained a factitious importance through their strenuous opposition to the Peripatetic philosophy, which was in their time dominant throughout Christendom In their bizarre and irrational way they anticipated the great revolt against the Aristotelians, which the close of the seventeenth century saw in full vigour, but in this revolt, and in the scientific impulses which accompanied it, the idle dreaming of the Rosicrucians was incontinently swept away

The great names of these alchemistic philosophers are Robert Fludd, an Englishman, Jacob Bohmen, a shoemaker of Gorlitz, and Michael Mayer The Helmonts, Knorr, Kuhlmann, Noll, and Sperber, complete the list

[*Literature of Rosicrucianism* The work *Fama Fraternitatis Roseæ Crucis—Fama e Scanzia redux* בישעתי *Buccinia Jubilei ultima Eoæ Hyperboleæ Prænuncia montium Europæ concinna suo clangore feriens inter colles et convalles Araba resonans*, etc, equally remarkable for its spelling and contents, is the first authority as to the pretensions and tenets of the sect Nearly all the leaders, however, whose names are mentioned above wrote some work to be found under their names *Examen Philosophiæ Fluddanæ*, by Pierre Gassendi, is the first controversial work on this subject, *Kirchen- und Ketzerhistorie*, by Gottfried Arnold, and *Historia Critica Philosophiæ*, part iv, by Brucker, contain full information See also Mosheim, *Ecclesiast Hist* cent xvii]

ROWITES [CAMPBELLITES.]

RUNCARII An Antinomian sect of the Waldenses which is mentioned by Reinerius as agreeing for the most part with the Paterins, but as holding that no part of the body below the waist can commit mortal sin, because such sin proceeds "out of the heart" They probably took their name from the town of Runcalia, or Runkel [Reiner *contr Waldens* in *Bibl Max Lugd* xxv 266 f]

RUPITÆ, or RUPITANI A name given to the small Donatist congregation at Rome from their being driven to shelter among the rocks for the purpose of celebrating their religious services [Schlosser, *s v*]

RUSSIAN SECTS [RASCOLNIKS.]

S

SABATNIKI A sect of Russian Sabbatarians, or "Sabbath honourers," which arose in Novogorod [*c* A D 1470], where some clergy and laity were persuaded by a Jew of Kiev, named Zacharias, into a belief that the Mosaic dispensation alone was of Divine origin They accepted the Old Testament only, of which, being unacquainted with Hebrew, they used the Sclavonic translation Like the Jews, they were led to expect the advent of an earthly Messiah Some of them denied the Resurrection, and being accused of practising several cabbalistic arts, for which points of Jewish ceremonial may have been mistaken, were regarded by the common people as soothsayers and sorcerers They were gradually becoming a powerful sect, one of their number, named Zosima, having even been elected Archbishop of Moscow, when in A D 1490 they were condemned by a synod, and a fierce persecution nearly obliterated them But here and there, in remote parts of Russia, travellers have within the last century discovered fragmentary communities holding Jewish views, which have been thought to be relics of the older sect of Sabatniki In Irkutsk they continue to exist under the name of Selesnewschschini [Platon's *Present State of Greek Church in Russia*, Pinkerton's transl 273]

SABBATARIANS Those who maintain that the observance of the Sabbath is obligatory upon Christians

The early Jewish Christians of Palestine retained the whole Mosaic law, and observed consequently the Sabbath as well as the Lord's Day From them the custom spread in the Eastern Church of distinguishing Saturday as well as Sunday by not fasting, and by fuller public prayer, with the Holy Eucharist It is clearly in the power of the Church, or of any integral portion of the Church, to mark in this way the day of God's rest from the work of creation, which is a matter for perpetual remembrance Nor is such an observance open to the charge implied in the word Sabbatarian if it be kept free from Jewish superstition On the other hand, in the Western Church (though probably not from the beginning) the Sabbath was a fast-day In this rule God's resting from creation must have been kept out of sight, for the divine Sabbath cannot be proposed as the occasion of a fast The Western Saturday fast arose from opposition to Judaism, which was strong in the Western Churches, and particularly at Rome To justify the fast on this ground requires the fact of a large and dangerous amount of Judaism in the rest of the Church. If the seventh day be considered with reference to the work of redemption, it may be viewed either in the light of the preceding day of the Crucifixion or of the following day of the Resurrection and it is in the power of each Church to solemnize it as a fast or festival as shall be judged most for edification On the one hand, the Sabbatum Magnum or Easter Eve has always been held a fast preparatory to Easter Day, and similar considerations may influence a church in the observance of the Saturday as preparatory to the weekly Resurrection feast or, on the other hand, it may be judged better to limit such preparatory fast to the yearly celebration, adopting it only for the winding up of Lent, and in the weekly celebration to direct the mind of the worshipper to the deep quiet joy of the rest in which the Father gave His Beloved sleep, and to the triumph of the good tidings brought on that day to the spirits in prison Both views may be justified, and it is for each Church to judge for itself which it shall adopt A wise and good man will, with St Ambrose, at Rome keep fast with Rome, at Milan keep feast with Milan [1]

Of the custom of the Eastern Church we have the following rules —In the Apostolic Canons, it is ordered that clergymen fasting on any Sabbath except one are to be deposed, laymen to be suspended from communion [can 56], clergy abstaining from flesh and wine on the Sabbath festival out of abhorrence, and not for mortification, to be deposed [can 45 or 53] This more special rule points to the Gnostic tenets, that creation is evil, and the Creator an inferior demiurge or evil angel By the Apostolic Constitutions Sabbaths are regarded as festivals, except the Great Sabbath in which our Lord lay in the grave, on which day mourning on His account is more proper than joy for the creation Public worship is to be celebrated, to hear the Prophets and Gospels, to offer the Oblation, to partake of the Holy Supper Servants are to rest from work, that they may

[1] Milan was the one Church of the West which followed the Oriental custom St Augustine wrote to St Jerome, intimating his opinion that a good man may without dissimulation conform to the custom of the Church where he happens to be [Aug *Epist* xix *ad Hieron*]

attend public worship [ii 20, 59, v 15, vii 23; viii 33] At the Council of Laodicea [A D 367], the Gospels are ordered to be read on the Sabbath [can 16], Christians are not to Judaize and rest, but work on the Sabbath, and rest on the Lord's Day [can 29] On the Sabbaths of Lent consecration in the Holy Eucharist may be made [can 49] In the Canonical Answers of Timothy, Bishop of Alexandria [A D 380], the thirteenth puts the Sabbath and the Lord's Day on a level regarding the intercourse of man and wife The 55th canon of the second Council of Constantinople or Quinisextine [A D 683] confirms the 56th Apostolical canon, and Balsamon observes that this is one great reason why the Romanists reject these canons

Thus the only difference observed between the Sabbath and the Lord's Day was that labour was allowed or rather enjoined on the former, and abstinence from work was considered to be a mark of Judaism For this reason the Ebionites were condemned for joining the observance of the Sabbath according to the law of the Jews with the observance of the Lord's Day after the manner of Christians And in this sense we are to understand what Gregory the Great says, that Antichrist will renew the observance of the Sabbath [Greg lib xi ep 3]

There is little or no doubt that such was the primitive custom in the West as well as in the East, that the Western fast is of later origin Kaye sums up the evidence from Tertullian on this point, that the Sabbath "in Tertullian's time appears to have been kept as a day of rejoicing Even the Montanists—anxious as they were to introduce a more rigorous discipline in the observance of fasts—when they kept their two weeks of Xerophagiæ, did not fast on the Saturday and Sunday The Saturday before Easter Day was however an exception, that *was* observed as a fast" [Kaye on *Tertullian*, p 409] When Tertullian says the Catholics kept no Sabbath a fast except the Sabbatum Magnum, it is hardly possible that Rome was an exception [Tertull *de Jejun* p 712, ed 1641] The Council of Eliberis [A D 305] introduced the Sabbath fast into Spain [can xxvi] This was probably in imitation of Rome, in which case the introduction of the custom into Rome will lie between Tertullian's time and the Council of Eliberis—somewhere, that is, in the third century [1]

[1] The Canon is, "Errorem placuit corrigi, ut omni Sabbati die superpositiones celebremus " Victorinus uses the phrase, "Hoc quoque die (die sexto) ob passionem Domini Jesu Christi aut stationem Deo, aut jejunium, facimus Die septimo requievit ab omnibus operibus suis, et benedixit eum et sanctificavit Hoc die solemus superponere, idcirco, ut die Dominico cum gratiarum actione ad panem exeamus Et paresceve superpositio fiat, nequid cum Judæis Sabbatum observare videamur," etc. [Routh, *Reliq Sac.* iii p 457, ed 1846] Superpositio is the translation of *ὑπέρθεσις* [*Reliq Sac* iii 229, l 7] The words are fully explained by Routh in the notes, ii 46, iii 244, from which we can only quote the definition, and refer to the notes themselves for the authorities and examples "Ὑπέρθεσις a Latina ecclesia dicta *superpositio*, diei esse videtur cibo superpositio, sive jejunium ultra solitum tempus celebratum Interea non jejunium superponitur, *ὑπερτίθεται*, quod jejunii dilatio esset sive suspensio sed dies, cibo dicitur superponi, ait Salmasius, quod est jejunium " Victorinus flourished about A D 290

The Decretal of Innocent, or Epistle to Decentius, is no doubt spurious, but it was an early forgery, for it was received as genuine by Dionysius Exiguus, and it is evidence of the rule of the Roman Church in the fourth century It decrees that the Sabbath is to be fasted as well as Friday every week, because on those two days the Apostles must have been grieved for our Saviour's Death and Descent into Hell Bingham notices that Socrates makes the Roman Church to vary once more in this matter For Socrates says that in his time they did not fast at Rome on Saturdays, even in Lent [Socr *Hist Eccl* v 22] This statement Bingham thinks is to be distrusted, because the Quinisextine Council charges the Romans with keeping fast on Saturday For a variation of practice at a later time see Catalani, *Pontificale*, iii 37, ed 1852 Gratian rests the Roman practice upon Innocent's Decretal

It has been observed already that the terms of the Apostolic Canons, fasting "out of abhorrence, not out of mortification," refer to Gnostic tenets Of this perversion of the Saturday fast the Marcionites give an example They were in the habit of fasting, especially on the Sabbath, as being the day on which the Demiurge, or God of the Jews, towards whom they were anxious to shew no respect, ended the creation of the world and rested [Tertullian, *adv Marcion*, iv 12] The perversion, on the other hand, of the Sabbath festival is the keeping it in a Jewish manner, and making it a means of introducing the spirit of Judaism Ignatius [*ad Magnes*, cap ix] makes the Sabbath the test of adherence to the ancient order or the new hope The canons already quoted shew both the danger and the carefulness of the Church to guard against it Ancient Sabbatarianism was thus for the most part a literal observance of the Sabbath The Western Church resisted this Judaism by the strong measure of turning the Sabbath into a fast, the Eastern by formally sanctioning labour on the seventh day, and by laying down the nature of the rejoicing proper to it

Modern Sabbatarianism, properly so called, is rare, for in general modern Sabbatarians neglect the Sabbath altogether, and transfer its Jewish obligations and rules, with its name, to the Lord's Day There is this common ground to the old Sabbath and the new Lord's Day, that both are days of rest, and for those who do not attain the truth, that in the former rest was the religion of the day, in the latter such rest is enjoined as ministers to the opportunities of religion, it is easy and natural to apply to the latter the rules of the former A curious example of this Sabbatarianism is found in the Injunctions of the Abbot of Flay, A D. 1201 [Johnson, *English Canons*, ii 95] They are an attempt to extend monastic rules to the Church at large The Sunday rest is to begin at three o'clock on Saturday, and not only is buying and selling and pleadings in church and church porches forbidden, but also all house-work and cooking A woman weaving after three o'clock is struck with palsy A man makes a cake at the same time, and when he eats it on Sunday morning it drops blood The Archbishop of York countenanced the abbot's proceedings

It may be that this antedating the Sunday, throwing its beginning into the Saturday, had some effect on the character of the festival Archbishop Islip ordered that the Lord's Day should begin at Vespers on the Sabbath Day, "not before, lest we should seem professed Jews" [*Constitutions*, A D 1362, Johnson, ii 426] When it was made to begin earlier the opposition to Judaism would tend to lessen its festal character, and although the Saturday fast was formally terminated, the spirit of the fast might be extended into the commencement of the feast

In England Sabbatarianism was adopted by the Puritans in their controversy with the Episcopalians In the year 1595 one Dr Bownde put out a Book of the Sabbath (reprinted with additions in 1606), in which he maintained that the Fourth Commandment and the Mosaic Sabbath laws attach themselves to the Lord's Day by a moral and perpetual obligation Everything that could be classed as business or recreation was forbidden as a sin equal to adultery and murder It is almost incredible (Fuller writes) how taking this doctrine was, partly because of its own purity, and partly for the eminent piety of such persons as maintained it. A writer of the time speaks of its great influence in the following terms "I have read (and many there be alive which will justify it) how it was preached in a market town in Oxfordshire, that to do any servile work or business on the Lord's Day is as great a sin as to kill a man, or to commit adultery It was preached in Somersetshire, that to throw a bowl on the Sabbath day is as great a sin as to kill a man It was preached in Norfolk, that to make feast or wedding-dinner on the Lord's Day is as great a sin as for a father to take a knife and cut his child's throat It was preached in Suffolk (I can name the man, and I was present when he was convented before his ordinary for preaching the same), that to ring more bells than one upon the Lord's Day to call the people unto the church is as great a sin as to commit murder" [Rogers *on XXXIX Art* 19, Park Soc ed]

In the year 1618 James I published for the county of Lancaster a declaration of liberty of sports, and soon after appeared a sect of Sabbatarians, who were long known under the name of their first teacher, John Trask, and were afterwards called "Seventh-Day Men" [TRASKITES] In the year 1633 the controversy was revived by the publication of Theophilus Bradburn's *Defence of the Sabbath Day* He maintained that the seventh day ought to be observed, and that the Lord's Day is an ordinary working day Bradburn, before he was tried by the High Commission, was convinced of his error in a conference with White, Bishop of Ely But his book occasioned the publication of the King's declaration regarding sports (a republication of James's declaration), and the order that it should be read in all churches [SEVENTH-DAY BAPTISTS]

SABBATIANS A Judaizing section of the NOVATIANS, who owed their origin to Sabbatius, a presbyter who had been ordained by Marcian [Socrat *Hist Eccl* v 20, vii 15] The Sabbatians were included among heretics who were condemned in A D 381 by the seventh canon of the Council of Constantinople [Mansi, *Concil* iii 563]

SABELLIANS Heretics of the latter half of the third century, who took their name from a priest named Sabellius, and who opposed the doctrine of the Holy Trinity by maintaining that God is One Person only, though He manifests Himself in three modes or by the differing operations of three Divine energies Sabellianism was thus the doctrine of One God exercising three Offices, as opposed to the doctrine of One God in Three Persons

Sabellius was a native of the Libyan Pentapolis, probably of the city of Ptolemais, and is first heard of at Rome in the time of Zephyrinus There he was perverted by Callistus to the heresy of Noetus, and was forward among those who were striving to gain Zephyrinus to their side There were doubtless differences of opinion, formed or forming, between Noetus, Callistus, and Sabellius [see Milman, *Lat Christ* I i p 53, ed 1867], but it is clear that Sabellius was the legitimate successor of Praxeas and Noetus, and was taken for the representative of their school As such he appears in Novatian's treatise *Concerning the Trinity* [ch xii xxiii], in which his heresy is stated simply to be the assertion that Christ is the Father, without any mention of the later speculations or modification of the heresy

It has been usual [Cave, *Hist Lit* art *Novatianus*] to date the Sabellian heresy from its outbreak in Pentapolis, and consequently to assign a late date to Novatian's treatise Now that the "Refutation" of Hippolytus has been recovered, there can hardly be a doubt that Novatian wrote this treatise before his schism, and that Sabellianism, though as a doctrine it is of an earlier time [PRAXEANS], is to be dated as regards its name, from the time when Sabellius became the leader of the Noetian school Noetus died about the year 220, at which time Isidore of Hispalis fixes the rise of Sabellianism The outbreak of Sabellianism in Pentapolis occurred about the year 257 Dionysius of Alexandria sent legates to that province, and wrote three letters in refutation of the heresy, in which he was betrayed into expressions unorthodox in the other extreme Complaint being made of this to Dionysius of Rome, he wrote four books in refutation both of the Sabellian heresy and of that which was ascribed to himself These books were allowed to be orthodox [Thilo, *Admonitio* prefixed to *S Athan Epist de Sententia Dionysii Oper Dogm. Selecta*, p 92]

These Fathers give the heresy of Sabellius in terms as brief and simple as Novatian gives it Dionysius of Rome states that Sabellius asserts the Son Himself to be the Father, the Father to be the Son, Dionysius of Alexandria, that Sabellius asserts it was the Father, not the Son, Who became man for us [Routh, *Reliq Sacr* iii pp 373, 401] Athanasius, in his "Expositio Fidei," describes Sabellian doctrine thus οὔτε γὰρ υἱοπάτορα φρονοῦμεν, ὡς οἱ Σαβέλλιοι λέγοντες μονοούσιον καὶ οὐχ ὁμοούσιον, καὶ ἐν τούτῳ ἀναιροῦντες τὸ εἶναι υἱόν In accordance with these authorities, Philaster [*Hær* liv] states that Sabellius was a disciple of Noetus, that the Noetians were called also Praxeans and Sabellians as well as Patripassians and Hermogenians and Augustine [*Hær* xli] professes himself unable to understand why Epiphanius reckons Sabellianism and Noetianism as distinct heresies That the Sabellians were called Hermogenians implies no more than that they had adopted Hermogenes' tenet of the existence of an eternal subject matter, inherently evil, out of which the world was made it does not prove that the Hermogenians were Sabellians Tertullian's tract, "Adversus Hermogenem," not only contains no charge of Sabellianism or of Patripassianism (which the author of the treatise against Praxeas would hardly have omitted had there been any foundation for it), but it contains a testimony to the belief of Hermogenes in Christ as the Son of God The testimony of Hippolytus to the same point is still stronger [HERMOGENIANS] On the other hand, it appears from an extract from the work of Dionysius against Sabellius occurring in Eusebius, that Sabellius borrowed from Hermogenes this tenet of the eternity of matter [Eusebius, *de Prep Evan* vii 18, 19, Gaisford's ed ii 206, and see Viger's note, iv. p 216]

The inadequate conception of the Deity which this simple form of Sabellianism involves has already been pointed out [MONARCHIANS] It may be noticed further, that to this form, more properly even than to the subsequently modified form, belongs that conception of the Trinity which is the very essence of Sabellianism, namely, that it is a Trinity not of distinct Persons, but of action and office The Scriptures which speak of the Son cannot possibly be ignored They are met by the pretended explanation that the one God, to Whom as the Source of all things the name Father is given, going forth to the work of redemption, united Himself with Jesus, and was then called the Son In like manner, going forth to the work of sanctification, He is called the Holy Spirit These are names only of office, expressing the relations in which God puts Himself to created beings They state appearances (in which sense the word πρόσωπον was used), not Hypostases or Persons

To this form again only the first degree of Patripassianism is attributable, which does not assert the Divine Nature itself to be passible, but asserts only the Person of Jesus Christ, in which the human nature was assumed by the Father, to have suffered "ratione humanæ naturæ" The difficulties of this creed, if any authority be allowed to Holy Scripture, are so great that it cannot long be held in its simple form It is plainly contrary to Scripture to assert the Self-existent to be the same with the Begotten, the Sender with the Sent, and the tenet of the Incarnation of the Father, the One God without distinction of Persons, is most repugnant to every scripturally-informed mind The struggle to avoid these difficulties, and yet to retain the primary doctrine of the Monarchians, suggested the doctrine of the dilatation and contraction of the Deity (called the doctrine of the πλατυσμός), namely, that there has been an expansion or dilatation of the Eternal Unity into a Trinity, and will be again a collapse into Unity Athanasius, who has been quoted as attributing to Sabellius the simple doctrine of the υἱοπάτωρ, that the Father is the Son and the Son the Father, states this doctrine of the πλατυσμός, saying that it was perhaps borrowed from the Stoics "If the One (ἡ μονάς) being dilated became a Three (γέγονε τριάς), and the One was the Father, and the Three is Father, Son, and Holy Ghost, first the One being dilated, underwent an affection and became what it was not, for it was dilated, whereas it was not dilated Next, if the One itself was dilated into a Three,—and that Father and Son and Holy Ghost,—then Father and Spirit became the same, as Sabellius held, unless the One which he speaks of is something besides the Father, and then he ought not to speak of dilatation, since the One was maker of Three, so that there was a One, and then Father, Son, and Spirit" [Athan *Orat.* iv *contr Arian* xiii, Newman's transl] Now it is true that in this passage Athanasius does not state that the Sabellians held the doctrine of the πλατυσμός, but that that doctrine leads to Sabellianism, and Newman is probably right in referring the general argument of that part of the discourse to the followers of Marcellus but (as Newman remarks) πλατυσμός seems, by the allusion of Dionysius to it, to have been a word of Sabellius[1] [*de Senten Dionysii*, sec 17] 'Thus indeed we dilate (πλατύνομεν) the Unity (τὴν μονάδα) into the Trinity without making division (ἀδιαίρετον), and again contract the undiminished Trinity into the Unity" Special stress is here laid on the ἀδιαίρετον, because Dionysius had charged the Sabellians with ignorance that such division of the Father from the Son cannot be

[1] So in the very remarkable Epistles of Isidore of Pelusium [142 3] it is said "Least of all is it right to contract, Judaically, the Nature of the Deity εἰς μόνον τὸν ἕνα Θεὸν καὶ πατέρα, but to broaden it (κατευρύνειν) as unto a holy and consubstantial Trinity, προσώπων γὰρ ποιότητι καὶ ὑποστάσεων ἰδιότητι διαστέλλοντες, εἰς ἕνα πάλιν συστελοῦμεν Θεὸν διὰ τὸ τῆς οὐσίας ταὐτόν," and again τὸ δὲ πλατύνοντα εἰς τὴν ἁγίαν τριάδα τὰς ὑποστάσεις εἰς μίαν οὐσίαν συνάγειν ὀρθότατον ἐστι καὶ ἀληθέστατον δόγμα And the doctrine of the πλατυσμός is ascribed to Sabellius Vigilius of Thapsus [A D 484] ascribes this doctrine to Sabellius "Impie Sabellius professus est, Deum Patrem per Virginem natum nescio quod prætensionis vitium tantæ ingerens majestati ut per id, quod extensum est in Virgine ipse sibi Pater, ipseque sit Filius, quod nullus Christianorum ei concesserit" [*Disput inter Sabellium, Photinum, Ar et Athan.* p 6 b, Cassander's ed] The words are put into the mouth of Photinus The summing up of the judge at the end expresses it "Idemque ipse (Deus) de paterni honoris dignitate decidens, per quædam naturæ augmenta, aut potius detrimenta, in filii nomine ex Virgine ortus, nativitate transierit" [*ibid* p 65 b]

This charge conducts us to further proof that the Sabellians held the doctrine of the πλατυσμός, and to the remarkable fact that starting from the tenet of the identity of the Father and the Son they arrived at the conclusion that the Father is separable and separate from the Son These seemingly contradictory propositions they appear to have held together

Arius, in his letter to Alexander, given by Epiphanius [*Hær* lxix 7], charges Sabellius with dividing the Unity and calling the Son the Father His words are Σαβέλλιος ὁ τὴν μονάδα διαιρῶν, υἱοπάτορα εἶπεν Wormius argues that this charge is false inasmuch as he has shewn from Nazianzen and others that the heresy of Sabellius was rather a συναίρεσις than a διαίρεσις [*Hist Sabell* cap i p 21][1] The charge, however, is verified, not only by the words of Dionysius which have been quoted, but by Hilary of Poitiers, who mentions both the συναίρεσις and the διαίρεσις Hilary uses the word "Unio" This word is found in Sulpicius Severus "Suspecti ab Orientalibus habebamur trionymam solitarii Dei unionem secundum Sabellium credidisse" [ii 42] In the *Indiculus de Hær* [Pseudo-Hieron] cap xxvi, Oehler has admitted into the text "Unionita" for "Onion," which stood in Menard's edition "Sabellius, qui et Patripassianus, id est Unionita," the correction having been made by Cotelerius "Contra Unionitas" stands as the superscription of the Anti-Sabellian part of Prudentius' Apotheosis, but it is of course doubtful whether the words are those of Prudentius "Unio," then, in Sabellian doctrine, takes the place of "Unitas" in Catholic doctrine, when the nature of the Deity is the subject In place of the Unity of Three distinct Persons we have the entire coalescence of what are distinguished only in name, not in substance In this sense Hilary represents Sabellius as eagerly catching at the Union Sabellius "dum audit, *Qui me vidit, vidit et Patrem*, indiscretæ et indissimilis in Patre et Filio naturæ impie arripuit unionem, non intelligens naturalem unitatem sub nativitatis significatione monstrari cum per id, quod in Filio Pater videtur, confirmatio divinitatis sit, non nativitatis abolitio" [Hilar *de Trinit* vii 5] The Church rejects this doctrine. "Nobis autem in confessione nativitas est [the eternal generation of the Son] et unionem detestantes unitatem divinitatis tenemus, scilicet ut Deus ex Deo[2] unum sint in genere naturæ, dum quod per nativitatis veritatem ex Deo in Deum exstitit, non aliunde quam ex Deo esse substiterit" [*ibid* vi 11] The doctrinal effect of the Union, as is here implied, is to destroy the eternal Paternity and Sonship in the Godhead So more plainly "Et idcirco usus est eo genere doctrinæ, ut in uno Domino Christo unum significaret et Deum, et in uno Deo Patre unum significaret et Dominum, nec tamen impiam nobis ad perimendam unigeniti Dei nativitatem inveheret unionem, et Patrem professus et Christum" [*ibid* viii 36]. See also the remarks on the Twelfth Anathema of the Semi-Arian Synod of Ancyra [A D 358] [*de Synodis*, 26, col 1166, Benedictine ed]

But while he thus dwells on the union as held by the Sabellians, Hilary at the same time unhesitatingly adopts the charge brought by Arius, that Sabellius divides the union He quotes the letter of Arius "Namque id sequitur Nec sicut Sabellius qui unionem dividit, ipsum dixit Filium quem et Patrem" He notices the fraudulent intention[3] of this condemnation of a heretic by heretics, but he adopts the charge "Ignorat evangelica atque apostolica sacramenta sic credens Sabellius," and he goes on to remark· "Cujus unionis divisio non nativitatem intulit, sed eumdem divisit in Virgine" [*ibid* vi 11]; that is, the division of the union of the υἱοπάτωρ did not introduce an eternal generation of a Son of God, but took place when the Divine Nature, or a portion of it, became incarnate This conclusion is supported by Philaster [*Hær* xciii], who ascribes to Sabellius the opinion that the mission of the Son by the Father involves a "separatio loci" [PHOTINIANS]

The Sabellian doctrine of the Incarnation, as connected with the doctrine of the πλατυσμός, is told thus "Plures etiam in corpus atque ex se protensum permanentemque Patrem loquuntur, ut assumptio illa carnis ex Virgine filii nomen acceperit, non qui ante erat Dei filius, idem hominis filius sit natus in corpore" [Hilar *Tract in LXVII Psal* 15] And again "Quidam ita evangelicæ fidei corrumpunt sacramentum, ut sub unius Dei pia tantum professione nativitatem unigeniti Dei abnegent, ut protensio sit potius in hominem, quam descensio neque ut qui filius hominis secundum tempora assumptæ carnis fuit, idem antea semper fuerit atque sit Filius Dei ne in eo nativitas Dei sit, sed ex eodem idem sit, ut unius Dei, ut putant, inviolabilem fidem series ex solido in carnem deducta conservet, dum usque ad Virginem Pater protensus, ipse sibi natus sit in Filium" [Hilar. *de Trin* i. 16][4]

The only Divine Sonship allowed by Sabellian doctrine being then that which took place in time, at the Incarnation, there was also at that time a division of the Union Of what nature was that division thought to be? The Benedictine editor [note i col 834] writes "Sabellius quidem in Trinitate, de qua non est hic sermo, unionem inducit, sed in Incarnatione, uti declaratur lib vi n 7, unionem dividit, hoc est, in Christo personarum dualitatem invehit" Now the discourse thus commented upon is not at all of the Incarnation, but of the Divine Sonship as a part of the doctrine of the Trinity, and to say that the division of the Union is the division into two Persons of the one Person of God Incarnate is to remove the words "unionem

[1] So in Hilary, who quotes this document, and renders the words "qui unionem dividit" Erasmus noted in the margin "inducit" for "dividit"

[2] "Scilicet ut Deus et Deus ex Deo unum sint"

[3] "Ut catholicos unionem in Deo detestantes, et distinctarum personarum in natura æqualitatem profitentes, cum Sabellio pariter damnent" [note, Benedictine editor]

[4] Regarding the passage *de Trin* vii 39, see PHOTINIANS, p 426, note

dividit" from their proper subject into a foreign subject Besides which Hilary, speaking in vi 11 of the same words of Arius, says "nos unionem detestantes," which he could not say of the union of the two natures in the Person of our Lord, for of that conjunction "Unio" may properly be used This explanation then is inadmissible In a subsequent note on the same words [d in col 885], the same editor writes. "Hoc per se sonat personam in Christo non fuisse singularem ut explicuimus p 833, not i sic tamen potius intelligendum videtur, ut Sabellius unionem in Virgine diviserit, quatenus post susceptam in ea carnem eidem Deo Patris ac Filii nomina adscribere cœperit, nominum augens numerum, non personarum" This second explanation appears to be quite inadequate For the "unio" is 'trionyma," and to give the name of Son to the "Deus protensus ad Virginem" can never be called a division of that union We are forced therefore to conclude, if Hilary be a competent witness, that Sabellius did assert a separation of the "Protensio," which, reaching "usque ad Virginem," took the name of Son This last step was taken to avoid the charge of Patripassianism, which could be escaped only by admitting a distinction of Persons in the Godhead, or by asserting that only a portion of the Divine Nature became incarnate, or by asserting (however unimaginable it may be) that the "Deus protensus" is separable from the "Monas" or "Deus solitarius" The latter assertion appears to have been made for "Sabellius, qui unionem dividit, ipsum dixit Filium quem et Patrem" But this assertion passes necessarily into the former assertion, and may be noted as the second stage of the heresy The third stage is connected with other names [MARCELLIANS PHOTINIANS], and comprehended the notion of a certain energy or power proceeding from the Deity to assume the nature of man

Epiphanius states [*Hœr* lxii] that the last-named doctrine was drawn from apocryphal writings, especially from the Gospel according to the Egyptians It is highly probable that this Gospel is to be identified with that of Basilides [for which see Valesius in Euseb *Hist Eccl* iv 7, and Routh, *Rel Sac* i p. 88]; or, at least, there can be little doubt that it proceeded from the school which Basilides founded in Egypt Epiphanius does not name the tenet of the existence of matter, eternal, replete with the germs of life, inherently evil, which the Sabellians held in common with Basilides, and his derivation of Sabellianism from the Gospel of Egypt must refer to his statement of the nature of the Deity Having given the general Sabellian tenet that Father, Son, and Holy Spirit are one and the same, three appellations in one substance and person [*ἐν μιᾷ ὑποστάσει τρεῖς ὀνομασίας*], he adds that this conception was compared to that of the constitution of man, likening the Father to the body, the Son to the soul, the Holy Ghost to the spirit, or to that of the sun, likening the Father to the round sun itself, the Son to the illuminating power, the Holy Ghost to the heating power these being emitted, as rays of light and heat, to give knowledge and life, and, their mission accomplished, returning to the luminary These notions might easily be borrowed from Basilides' doctrine of Æons, if these Æons are not considered as distinct persons, the Sabellian Son and Spirit being probably the Basilidean "Nous" and "Dynamis" Whether Basilides held or not his Æons to be distinct persons is a controverted point [Mosheim, *de Rebus*, ch ii 46, note O], his connection with Sabellianism is an argument in favour of the opinion of Beausobre, that the Æons are merely virtues or attributes of the Supreme Being Basilides leads us through Simon Magus to the Cabbala [1]

The statements of other Fathers of the Church agreeing with the conclusions which have been drawn, may be briefly noticed. Basil insists on the Judaism of Sabellius, it is but a reintroduction of Judaism to confess the Son in name, but in reality to deny his existence [Basil, *Hom contr. Sabell et Ar Sect.* i. *Epp* 189, 210] This is repeated by modern writers, as by Marheinecke [*Dogmengeschichte*, iv. 205], but such is not the teaching of earlier Judaism [2] [MONARCHIANS.] Basil states that Sabellius did not reject the fiction of unhypostatised persons [*τὸν ἀνυπόστατον τῶν προσώπων ἀναπλασμὸν Ep* 210, 5], inasmuch as, while he confounded the conceptions of hypostasis and substance, he endeavoured to distinguish the persons [*διαιρεῖν*[3] *τὰ πρόσωπα*], and inasmuch as the one hypostasis assumed various persons or appearances upon occasion and need [*τὴν αὐτὴν ὑπόστασιν λέγων πρὸς τὴν ἑκάστοτε παρεμπίπτουσαν χρείαν μετασχηματίζεσθαι, Ep* 236-6]

Augustine's statements in other works agree with that in his Tract on Heresies, and shew Sabellianism in its early stage Thus "Breviter insinuavimus esse hæreticos qui vocantur Patripassiani, vel a suo auctore Sabelliani hi dicunt ipsum esse Patrem qui est Filius, nomina diversa, unam vero esse personam Cum vult, Pater est, inquiunt, cum vult, Filius [Aug *Tract in Joann Evang* xxxvii 6 See also *adv Quinque Hær* sec 2, *ad Orosium c Priscill et Origen* c iv]

In Ambrose [*in Symbol Apost*] is a statement of the leading doctrine of Sabellianism From the *de Fide* [lib. v cap 6] may be quoted the words of Ambrose, "de Filii subjectione," for comparison with the tenet of Marcellus, "Quomodo igitur subjectum dicimus? Sabelliani et Marcionitæ dicunt, quod hæc futura sit Christi ad Deum Patrem subjectio, ut in Patrem Filius refundatur Si ergo ea erit Verbi subjectio ut resolvatur in Patrem Deus Verbum, ergo et quæ-

[1] On the Pantheism of the Cabbala, see Mill's note *on Panth Principles*, i 151, and regarding a substratum of Pantheism underlying Sabellianism, see Meier, *Lehre von der Trin.* i 120

[2] See the remarkable letter of Isidore of Pelusium [143], the subject of which is given by the editors "De mysterio S S Trinitatis ne quidem Veteri Testamento et Philoni Judæo plane incognito"

[3] This diæresis of persons must be distinction, not division, for the true hypostasis remains one The Benedictine editor translated it "personas distinguere" The diæresis of the *union* spoken of before, we have tried to shew, must be division

cumque Patri Filioque subjecta sint, in Patrem et Filium resolventur, ut sit Deus omnia et in omnibus creaturis Sed absurdum est dicere non igitur per refusionem subjectio "

Sabellius was condemned by an early council at Rome This we learn from Hilary His words are "In urbe Roma sub Novato et Sabellio et Valentino hæreticis factum concilium ab Orientalibus confirmatum est" [Hilary, *Frag Hist* iii 26, p 1320, Ben ed] If Novato be the correct word, this council must be that held by Cornelius [A D 252, Euseb *Hist Eccl* vi 43] But it may be doubted whether it is not the council held by Stephen [A D 258], which is said to have condemned Noetus, Sabellius, and Valentinus [Baluz, *Nov Coll Ann* 258]

The Alexandrian councils held against Arianism involved determinations against the conflicting heresy of Sabellianism, particularly that of A D 324[1] Of the decisions of Nicæa it is unnecessary to speak, but the following expressions in the reasons given for the *ὁμοούσιον* may be compared with the statements above made respecting the second stage of Sabellianism *οὔτε γὰρ κατὰ διαίρεσιν τῆς οὐσίας οὔτε κατὰ ἀποτομὴν, ἢ ἀλλοίωσιν τῆς τοῦ πατρὸς οὐσίας τε καὶ δυνάμεως* [Socr *Hist Eccl* i 8] Of the Post-Nicene councils, one at Rome [A D 373], held under Damasus, condemned this heresy, describing it in the simple terms that the Father and the Son are one and the same [Theod *Hist Eccl* v 11] In one held at Constantinople [A D 381-2], the heresy is condemned as well as that of the Marcellians and Photinians, and Sabellian baptism is disallowed [canons i vii] This was confirmed at the Council in Trullo [A D 683, canon 95] It follows, therefore, in all probability, that the Sabellians had altered the form of baptism to suit their tenets [PHOTINIANS]

It cannot be inferred from the Trullan canon that Sabellianism was prevalent in the seventh century The confirmation of foregoing conciliar decrees was general, without inquiry whether there were special need of such confirmation And it may be concluded that in the fifth century Sabellianism was virtually extinct For a late charge of the heresy against a portion of the Armenian Church by Benedict XII, see Raynald (Contin of Baron) vi an 1341, lx

SABIANS [MENDÆANS]

SABOTIERS. A name given to the Waldenses from the sabots worn by the French peasantry The sabots of the Waldenses were, however, distinguished by a painted cross—"insabbatati"—or else by sandals tied crosswise They are described in an epistle of Innocent III as "calciamenta desuper aperta" [Innocent, *Epp* xv 137]; and other writers speak of the Waldenses as wearing sandals, after the custom of the Apostles, and as walking with naked feet Ebrard speaks of them contemptuously as assuming this name themselves "Xabatenses a xabata potius, quam Christiani a Christo, se volunt appellari" The custom was doubtless adopted in imitation of the voluntary poverty of the Apostles, and in accordance with the names "Pauperes de Lugduno," and "de Lombardia," which they assumed. [Ebrard, *contr Waldens.* in *Bibl. Lugd* xxiv 1572]

SACCOPHORI. Wearers of rough garments in token of austere discipline They appear to have been a subdivision of the Encratites, those, namely, who thought fit to make an outward profession of their rule St Basil puts together the Encratites, Saccophori, and Apotactics as an offshoot of the Marcionites [Basil, *Can Epist* II can 47] Theodosius made a decree, which was renewed by Honorius, that some of the Manichees, who went by the name of Encratites, Saccophori, or Hydroparastatæ, should be punished with death [*Cod Theod* lib xvi tit 5, *de Hæret* leg ix]

Both the Marcionites and the Manichees held the doctrine of Two Principles, and it is no wonder that the Encratites are referred now to one, now to the other of these sects But their true origin appears to be from the former St Basil's Canon is one relating to the baptism of these sects [ENCRATITES]

SACRAMENTARIANS A controversial name given by the Lutherans to the Zwinglians to designate their belief that the consecrated elements in the Eucharist are merely sacramental symbols, and not in any way the means by which the Body and Blood of Christ are really and truly present to and conveyed to the faithful partaker of them The third volume of Schlusselburg's "Hæreticorum Catalogus" contains 492 pages "De secta Sacramentariorum qui Cingliani seu Calvinistæ vocantur" [ZWINGLIANS]

SADDUCEES A Jewish religious party which derived its name from some founder named Zadok, the word Sadducees being the Greek form of Zadokim or Zadokites It is conjectured that they were the higher class, or aristocracy, of the Aaronic family, the nucleus of the class being the descendants of Zadok the high priest, of David's time, by whom Solomon was crowned Thus the sons of Zadok are mentioned with an evident distinction in several of the later books of the Old Testament [2 Chron xxxi 10, Ezek. xl 46, xliii. 19, xliv 15, xlviii 11], and in a similar manner the connections of the high priest in the last age of the Jews are said to have been "the sect of the Sadducees" [Acts iv. 6, v 17] It was natural that a symbolical turn should be given to their name by any Jewish sect to which it belonged, and as "Zedek" signifies righteousness, the Sadducees were accustomed to explain their name as meaning "just men "

Although, however, the Sadducees were originally nothing more than a social class or a political party, they came to hold very distinctive theological opinions which marked them out as a religious sect in the time of our Lord and His Apostles In a general way they were the opposite party to the Pharisees, and may be said to have represented the "liberal" or "free thought"

[1] For the date of this council here given as against Baronius, who places it in the year 319, see Natal Alex iv 63, and the *Dissert* p 402 For the synod itself, and the refutation of Sabellius, see Socr *Hist Eccl* iii 7

school of Judaism as distinguished from the conservative and dogmatic school Thus it is recorded of them that "the Sadducees say that there is no resurrection, neither angel nor spirit but the Pharisees confess both" [Acts xxiii 8] As regards their denial of the resurrection, Josephus declares "their doctrine to be that souls perish with the body" [Joseph *Antiq* XVIII i 4] It is clear that this denial was carried to its full extent, notwithstanding the apologies which are made on their behalf by modern writers, for in the very beginning of the ministry of the Apostles they were imprisoned by the priests and Sadducees solely on the ground that they "preached through Jesus the resurrection from the dead" [Acts iv 2] St. Paul also used this unbelief of the Sadducees as a means of defending himself by enlisting the Pharisees on his side, for when he "perceived that the one part were Sadducees and the other Pharisees," he declared himself to be a Pharisee, and then exclaimed, "Of the hope, and resurrection of the dead, I am called in question!" [Acts xxiii 6, *cf* Matt xxii 23] It is quite impossible to believe that the fearless Apostle would have endeavoured to save his life by misrepresenting the opinions of his opponents; and we must suppose his statement to imply the entire denial of a future resurrection by the Sadducees

As they disbelieved the resurrection from the dead, so also the Sadducees denied the existence of angels or spirits Modern apologists consider that all which they denied was the direct interposition of angels or spirits in human affairs, as in the case suggested by the scribes respecting St Paul, "If a spirit or an angel hath spoken to him, let us not fight against God" [Acts xxiii 9] But the apology is grounded on mere conjecture, and is not borne out by the statement in the previous verse

In agreement with this repudiation of established beliefs, the Sadducees took an exactly opposite line to the Pharisees respecting the interpretation of Holy Scripture, rejecting altogether the idea of an oral tradition transmitted from age to age, and accepting only the letter of the written law Although there were doubtless many foolish traditions among those which were maintained by the Pharisees, it is easy to see that the profession of adhering only to the text of Holy Scripture, and the repudiation of traditionary interpretation, is in reality an assertion of an individual independence on the subject which is consistent with every degree of negative scepticism and positive error Their principle also led the Sadducees into a hard and literal system of interpreting the law, so that customs, the force of which had passed away, were still looked upon as binding by them Thus, when the Pharisees relaxed the rule of "an eye for an eye or a tooth for a tooth," and substituted pecuniary compensation to the injured person, the Sadducees insisted upon the exact fulfilment of the precept, and in a similar manner when the Pharisees considered the law satisfied if a widow rejected by a brother-in-law spat *before* his face, the Sadducees required her literally to spit *in* his face, not permitting the least relaxation of the Levitical rule The same rigidity was maintained by them in all ritual matters, but especially in those connected with uncleanness, whether in priest or people Thus, although the Sadducees were what we should now call freethinkers in respect to the supernaturalism of the Jewish faith, they were even more strict than the Pharisees in their maintenance of the ceremonial and ritual obligations of the Law

Little is said respecting the errors of the Sadducees in the New Testament the reason for which seems to have been that, although they were the strong political party of the time, they had no religious influence, the Pharisees being the theological and devotional leaders of the nation [Joseph *Antiq*. XIII. x 5]. The Sadducees rapidly disappeared from among the Jews after the destruction of Jerusalem, but they are in some degree represented in modern times by the Scripturists or KARAITES

SAGARELLI [APOSTOLICALS]

SAINT SIMONIANS [POSITIVISTS SOCIALISTS]

SAMOKRISCHTCHINA A sect of Russian Dissenters whose name signifies "self-baptizers," and expresses the peculiarity by which they are distinguished from other Rascholniks

SAMOSATENES The followers of Paul, a native of Samosata on the Euphrates, but Bishop of Antioch [A D 260], who originated the heresy of Humanitarianism, which developed into Arianism The Samosatenes were also called Paulianists

This heretical bishop was notorious for loose opinions about morality, and was charged with conforming his life to these opinions [Euseb *Hist Eccl* vii 30] He was also extravagantly addicted to luxury and state, and appears to have presented an early example of a kind of prelate very common on the Papal throne in later ages Paul was intimately connected with Zenobia, Queen of Palmyra, and this association is asserted to have been one cause of his heretical opinions. Zenobia claimed to be descended from the Macedonian kings of Egypt, but the statement of Athanasius that she was a Jewess [Athan *Ep ad Solit V A Opp* i 857, Paris 1627] may be true of her maternal descent Philaster states she was taught Judaism by Paul [Phil *Hær* lxiv], but the statement of Theodoret is more probable, namely, that she was of herself inclined to Judaism, and that Paul adopted the heresy of Artemon, which involved the denial of our Lord's divinity, to ingratiate himself with her [Theod *Hær. fab* ii. 8] Chrysostom's evidence is to the same effect [Chrysost *Hom* viii *in S Johan*.] If this be true, there can be little doubt that Paul sanctioned the practice of circumcision, as Philaster states, and the testimony to his adoption of heresy through yielding to Judaism from worldly motives, is too strong to be explained away by the common charge of Judaizing brought against the whole class of Monarchians

That Paul revived the heresy of Artemon is stated by Eusebius [*Hist Eccl* v 28], by Augus-

Samosatenes

tine [*Hær.* xliv] by Epiphanius [*Hær* lxv], as well as by Theodoret. The Bishops of the Antiochene council write that Paul "abjured the mystery of our religion for the accursed heresy of Artemas Let him write to Artemas, let the followers of Artemas hold communion with him" [Euseb *Hist Eccl* vii 30] Again, Epiphanius, stating the principal Samosatene tenet to be that the Son does not exist as a distinct Person, but only in the one hypostasis of the Godhead [*μὴ εἶναι τὸν υἱὸν τοῦ Θεοῦ ἐνυπόστατον, ἀλλὰ ἐν αὐτῷ τῷ Θεῷ*], adds that this is the opinion of Sabellius, Novatus, Noetus and some others, but that it is not held by the Samosatenes in the same manner as by them The position of Paul then, among the heretics of the period, is this he belonged to the Monarchian school, but had some peculiarities which kept him from joining either Theodotians or Sabellians

[1] Paul held the oneness of God without distinction of Persons He held, Epiphanius says, Father, Son, and Holy Ghost, one God, and the Word and Spirit of God always in God, as in the heart of man is man's proper reason [*ὥσπερ ἐν ἀνθρώπου καρδίᾳ ὁ ἴδιος λόγος*] Hilary of Poitiers ascribes to him this primary Monarchian tenet in terms so closely resembling the language of the earlier Sabellians, that they are scarcely consistent with Epiphanius' assertion of a different mode of holding the tenet and he adds that Paul used the word Homoousion to express this tenet "Secundo quoque id addidistis, quod patres nostri, cum Paulus Samosateus hæreticus pronuntiatus est, etiam homousion repudiaverint quia per hanc unius essentiæ nuncupationem solitarium atque unicum sibi esse Patrem et Filium prædicabat Et hoc sane nunc quoque profanissimum Ecclesia recognoscit, Patrem et Filium in his nominum professionibus ad unionis ac singularis solitudinem negata personarum proprietate revocare" And again "Quis secundum Samosateum, in Christo renatus, et Filium confessus ac Patrem, quod Christus in se sibi et Pater et Filius sit confitebitur?" [Hilary, *de Synodis*, 81, 82] It will be seen, as we proceed, that Paul's doctrine regarding the Divine element in our Lord's Person could not be expressed in the terms "quod Christus in se sibi et Pater et Filius sit" Another passage in Hilary, which does not name the Samosatene heresy, appears exactly to express it "Plures enim eludere dictum Apostolicum, quo ait Christum Dei sapientiam et Dei virtutem, his modis solent quod in eo ex Virgine creando efficax Dei sapientia et virtus extiterit, et in nativitate ejus divinæ prudentiæ et potestatis opus intelligatur, sitque in eo efficientia potius quam natura sapientiæ" [Hilary, *Comm in Matth* 9] Here the Benedictine editor remarks, 'Eam ipsam sententiam Paulo Samosateno attribuit Leontius" [*de Sectis*, Act 3] "Paulus Samosatenus subsistentem per se Dei sermonem in Christo fuisse non dicebat sed volebat sermonem esse jussum quemdam ac mandatum, hoc est Jussit Deus, ut ipse loquebatur, fieri per hominem illum quod volebat, idemque per illum faciebat" For Paul held that the Divine element in our Lord's Person was not the personal Word, nor (as the Patripassians said) the One undistinguished God, nor (as the later Sabellians said) a certain portion of the Divine Nature, or an impersonal emanation from that Nature, but only a heavenly Wisdom and Light (called the Logos) which dwelt, but not by a hypostatic union, in the Person of the man Jesus, and operated through Him He confessed in Jesus, *λόγον ἐνεργῆ ἐξ οὐρανοῦ καὶ σοφίαν* [Athan *cont Apollin* i 20, ii 3], but he contended *ἄλλην εἶναι τὴν τοῦ λόγου οὐσίαν, καὶ ἄλλο τὸ ἐκ τοῦ πατρὸς ἐν αὐτῷ φῶς, ἵν' ᾖ τὸ μὲν ἐν τῷ υἱῷ φῶς ἓν πρὸς τὸν πατέρα, αὐτὸς δὲ ξένος κατ' οὐσίαν ὡς κτίσμα* [Athan *de Decret S N* 24] Accordingly the Son was not, Paul said, before the Incarnation [Athan *cont Arian* i 25]

This follows directly from the primary tenet of Monarchianism, which the Samosatenes undoubtedly held In seeming contradiction to it are the words of Paul in his disputation with Malchion, of which some fragments remain Having said that the Logos associated itself with Jesus Christ, he proceeded *ἐκεῖνον δὲ τὸν λόγον ἐγέννησεν ὁ Θεὸς ἄνευ παρθένου* [Routh, *Reliq* iii 300] It must be remembered that these words were used in a dispute in which Paul was endeavouring to disguise his real opinions, and all testimony leads to the conclusion that the word *ἐγέννησεν* was used not of an eternal generation, nor of the begetting of the Son as a distinct person, but only of the production or calling into action that Wisdom which was to come upon Jesus Christ [see Routh's note on *υἱός* as = *σοφία*, iii 350]

[2] As regards the human nature of our Lord, Paul held the miraculous birth, of a Virgin, by the power of the Holy Ghost [Athan *cont Apollin* i 20, ii 3, *Ep Syn Antioch* in Euseb *H E* vii. 30] Yet he is stated to have held Christ as to His nature a mere man [Dionys of Alex in Athan *de Synod* Macrostiche, *ibid.* and Socrat *H E* ii 19] How far below, and in what respects different from, the very man of the Catholic faith was the "mere man' of Paul's conception we do not exactly know

[3] The Samosatenes held that Christ, not being God before the worlds, became God after His Incarnation by a certain promotion [*μετὰ τὴν ἐνανθρώπησιν ἐκ προκοπῆς τεθεοποιῆσθαι*, Macros as before] The promotion is the association of the effective Word and Wisdom which was foreordained before the worlds, and from Nazareth manifested in actual being, that there might be one God over all, the Father [Athan *cont Apollin* ii 3]

Two councils certainly, perhaps three, were held at Antioch concerning this heresy The first was in A D 264 Firmilian of Cæsarea in Cappadocia appears to have presided Dionysius of Alexandria was unable to attend on account of infirmity He wrote a letter to the council on the matter in hand At this council Paul's opinions were condemned, but no sentence of deposition was passed, Firmilian trusting to the promises of Paul, and hoping that the matter might be fittingly settled, and scandal avoided.

It is stated that Firmilian visited Antioch twice, and as he died before the council which passed the sentence of deposition it is probable that there was an intermediate council[1] The heresy breaking out afresh, another council was held in A D 269 [or 270] It was attended, Eusebius says, by an almost infinite number of bishops, Athanasius reckons seventy [*de Synod*] Basil the Deacon, in the *Libellus Precum*[2] presented to the emperors against Nestorius, reckons a hundred and eighty A letter was sent to Paul by six bishops, four of whom were at the former council, and all at the last council, stating the Catholic faith, and inquiring whether Paul so held and taught This was probably one of the measures taken in the earlier stage of the council referred to by Theodoret [*Hær fab* ii 8], who names attempts to heal the disease by writings [Routh, *Rel Sac* iii 289, and note, 320] These letters and long preliminary discussions being ineffectual, a formal disputation was held between Paul and a practised theologian Malchion, Paul's heresy was exposed, and sentence of deposition was passed By the favour of Zenobia, Paul continued to hold his church and palace, but was dispossessed, A D 272, on appeal to Aurelian after Zenobia's defeat [Euseb *Hist Eccl* vii 27-30, Theod *Hær fab.* ii 8]

It has been already noticed that Paul used the word Homoousion in expressing his tenets, and the passage of Hilary then quoted shews that the Antiochene Fathers consequently rejected the word On this point, which belongs rather to the history of the adoption of the word at Nicæa, see Routh, *Rel Sac* iii 362, and article ARIANS From this time the Samosatenes, it may be concluded formed a heretical sect For at Nicæa their baptism was disallowed [can xix] From this canon Augustine argues that they had renounced the Catholic form of baptism [*Hær* xliv], and he is followed by some modern writers But Athanasius' testimony is clear to their retention of the true form, *τὰ ὀνόματα λέγοντες οὐδὲν ἧττόν εἰσιν αἱρετικοί* [Athan *cont Arian* ii 43] The words were not used in the Catholic sense, and the rule of the first provincial synod of Arles [can 8] did not prevail The Nicene canon refers to an earlier decision, which is probably the Apostolic Canon xlvi [xlvii Brun's ed]

That the Samosatene heresy was not only implicitly condemned by the declaration of the true faith at Nicæa, but was explicitly taken into consideration, is also shewn by the Nicene Creed being quoted at the Council of Ephesus,[3] A D 431, in the following terms "Concerning the Incarnation of the Word of God, the Son of the Father, a definition of the bishops assembled in synod at Nicæa, and a declaration of that synod against Paul of Samosata" [Valesius, note *d* on Euseb *Hist Eccl* vii 30, p 318] It is sufficient to notice that the heresy of Paul was condemned by the Semi-Arians at the second Council of Sirmium, A D 351 [*al* 357] The Samosatenes, called Pauliani, are specified in the Constitution of Theodosius and Valentinian, A D 428, against heretical conventicles, for restoring churches to the Catholics, and imposing certain civil disqualifications [*Cod Theod* xvi v 65]

SAMOSTRIGOLSCHTSCHINA A sect of Russian Dissenters, whose name signifies "self-ordainers," and expresses the peculiarity by which they are distinguished from other Rascholniks

SAMPSÆANS The Sampsæans cannot properly be called either a Jewish or a Christian sect They lay outside of Judaism, bordering upon it however on the side of the Essenes, from whom they appear to have separated From the Essenes they differed in practising a more clearly defined worship of the sun Their name, derived from the Hebrew *Schemesch*, implies this *Σαμψαῖοι γὰρ ἑρμηνεύονται Ἡλιακοί* [Epiph *Hær.* liii] Ezekiel was shewn in vision the worship of the sun among the abominations of Israel [viii 16], but there is no proof that the practice was continued uninterruptedly from that time It is more probable that a reverence, or some degree of adoration, of the sun was introduced with other Eastern elements into Essenism, and passed into worship in the coarser and more material system of the Sampsæans But what their priesthood was, the point in which was the chief peculiarity of the Essenes, is not told They were Hemerobaptists, and venerated almost to deifying the element of water From Christianity they borrowed nothing more than the Name of Christ, which name they gave to a created angel, who formed at first the body of Adam, and resumes it at pleasure He is accompanied, they supposed, by his sister, the Spirit, in female form The particular form in which they expressed the notion, widely spread in the East, of the feminity of the Spirit was taken from the Book Elchasai, which they received

Thus Epiphanius represents the relics of the Ossenes to have revolted from Judaism, and to have attached themselves to the Sampsæans, and so to have joined the Ebionites [*Hær* xx *s f*] He identifies indeed the Sampsæans and the Elchasaites But the reception of the Book Elchasai so altered the character of the sect that it is better to keep the names distinct, and to consider the Sampsæans as renegade Jews, who had adopted a considerable portion of nature-worship, and some features of the Iranic doctrine of angels, which led them to receive the revelation Elchasai, and to pass into a distinct heresy The Sampsæans were found in Moabitis, Iturea, and Nabathæa [Epiph *Hær* liii Scaliger, *Elench Trihær Capp* i xxvii]

SANDEMANIANS A name by which the sect of the GLASSITES is more generally known in England than by their original appellation Robert Sandeman [1718-1771], the son-in-law of John Glass, added to the original teaching of the founder of the sect, by maintaining, in opposition to Calvinistic views, that faith is a simple assent

[1] Newman is of opinion that this intermediate council is that referred to by Athanasius, *de Synodis*, cap 13 See his note in *Select Treatises*, part i p 141

[2] In Labbe, *Acts of Council of Ephesus*, vol iii

[3] At the Council of Ephesus also a long comparison was drawn between the tenets of Nestorius and of Paul [NESTORIANS]

to the Divine testimony concerning Jesus Christ, differing in no way in its own character from belief in any common human testimony Sandeman, after having been engaged in controversy with James Hervey, and forming a congregation in London in 1762, removed to America, where he died The sect never attracted any large number of followers, but it still exists as an insignificant body, possessing at the census of 1851 six places of worship in England (of which one is in London), with an aggregate attendance of about 750 worshippers, and the same number in Scotland, with an aggregate attendance of about 1000 The late eminent chemist, Michael Faraday, conferred some lustre on the London congregation by officiating as one of its elders They observe various primitive practices with great strictness *e g* weekly administration of the Lord's Supper, with a weekly offertory, love-feasts *i e* the dining together between morning and afternoon services, the kiss of charity at the admission of a new member, and at other times, washing each other's feet as an occasional work of mercy, abstinence from things strangled and from blood, community of goods, in so far as that they consider the whole of their property liable for calls on behalf of the Church and the poor, and condemn the storing up of money for future and uncertain use They consider all such amusements unlawful as are connected with games of chance, believing that the lot is a sacred thing The members pray in turns, and the elders preach Perfect unanimity is secured in all proceedings by the simple expedient of expelling any one who obstinately differs in opinion from the majority They do not hold communion with any other denominations

[Wilson's *Hist of the Dissenting Churches in London* Ritchie's *Religious Life in London* Jas Morison's *New Theological Dictionary*]

SARIGANI Assemann mentions an Arabian sect of this name which he thinks may have been a branch of the MENDÆANS They held the opinions of Paul of Samosata and of Arius, but were converted and admitted to Catholic communion by Maranames, Metropolitan of Adjabenus, in the year 760 Some, however, were found a hundred years later in Babylon

SATANISTS A name sometimes given to the EUCHITES on account of the theory which they are alleged to have held that the power of Satan over men makes it right for them to pray to him that he will not exercise it to their harm [Epiphan *Hær* lxxx] This opinion seems to be the same as that on which the worship of the YEZEDEES is grounded

SATANNIANI Heretics of this name are mentioned by the author of Prædestinatus as having derived their name from Satanius, and as maintaining the opinion that the resurrection of the dead will be a restoration of bodies and souls to exactly the same condition in which they exist during the present life This seems to be the same heresy with that which is numbered as the eightieth by Philaster, and the sixty-seventh by Augustine, and to whose adherents the name ÆTERNALES is given by Danæus in his commentary on St. Augustine's tract on heresies

SATURNINIANS An early sect of Syrian Gnostics, appearing about the reign of Hadrian [A D 117-138], and taking their name from Saturninus, or Saturnilus (as he is called by Justin Martyr, Epiphanius, and Theodoret), a native of Antioch in Syria, and a disciple of Menander

All that is known about the theories of Saturninus is contained in the work of Irenæus against heresies In this he states that Saturninus, like Menander, set forth that there is one Supreme Unknown, the Father [Πατὴρ ἄγνωστος], from whom angels, archangels, powers, and potentates derived their being By seven of these angels, removed far from the Supreme, the world was created, and when, during their work of creation, a bright image burst forth below the presence of the Supreme, which they could not retain in the lower world, they said among themselves, "Let us make man after our image and likeness" Man was accordingly made by the angels, but they had not power to make him an erect being, and so he continued to crawl upon the earth like a worm until the Supreme sent forth a spark of life, which gave him an erect posture, compacted his joints, and made him to live This spark of life returns at the death of man to the Fountain of Life, from which it was derived, while the body decays into its original elements [Iren *adv Hæres* i 24] A precisely similar account of the heresy is given by Tertullian in his treatise on the soul [Tertull *de Anim* xxiii], and what later heresiologists record is substantially taken from Irenæus The latter, however, goes on to mention opinions held by Saturninus, of which Tertullian says nothing Thus he laid it down as a truth that the Saviour was without birth, without body, without figure, and only in appearance a man, not in reality, thus indicating that Saturninus had adopted the heresy of Cerinthus He also maintained the notion of a Demiurge, who was the God of the Jews, and whom Christ came to destroy The existence of good and evil men he accounted for by affirming that they were originally created of two kinds, the one good, whom Christ came to save, the other wicked, whom the devils succour, and whom Christ will destroy Theodoret states that Saturninus was the first who taught that marriage and the propagation of the human race are the work of Satan [Theodor *Hæret fab* i 3], and that he held such an opinion is also stated by Irenæus The latter also speaks of him as introducing a false asceticism, for "many of those who belong to his school abstain from animal food, and draw away multitudes by a feigned temperance of this kind," from which it would seem that the Encratites may have had their origin among the Saturninians

As these heretics are not mentioned by St Clement of Alexandria, it is probable that they were not much known out of Syria So little also is otherwise known of their history, that it may be concluded they represent a passing and local phase of that rapidly developing Gnosticism by which the Syrian Church was soon afterwards overrun

SAXON CONFESSION. [PROTESTANT CONFESSIONS.]

SCEPTICS. Scepticism is the converse of dogmatism, of which it is the reaction. It is doubt attaching itself to every object of thought with the method of science. To doubt is a necessary element in the investigation of truth, for thus alone can error be eliminated. But scepticism is the abuse of doubt, as fanaticism is the abuse of faith, or sophistry of dialectics. The human mind is sure to avenge itself on the spirit of dogmatism by a revolution in the opposite direction. Claiming liberty from prescription, it readily allows itself to be enthralled under a negative system, which ignores positive teaching, and in which nothing is true. Greece, the cradle of philosophy, gave birth also to scepticism. The Sophists had sown it broadcast when Socrates and Plato appeared on the scene. There was a vein of scepticism in the Socratic dictum, "One only thing I know, that I know nothing." Gorgias and Protagoras were followed in due course by the scepticism of Pyrrho [b. 380 B.C. d. 288, Diog. Laert. ix. 12, Cic. *de Or.* iii. 17, A. Gell. xi. 5] and the school of Megara. When the dogmatic teaching of Plato was superseded by that of Epicurus and the Porch, that side of his system alone was exhibited, on which the impossibility of demonstration being conceded, probabilities are discussed. Everything was open to argument; philosophy was only regarded as a useful mean for sharpening the wits, and as having little to do with objective truth; it was no longer a body of doctrine. Such was the New Academy under Arcesilas [B.C. 318], which resulted from the contests between the Stoical and Epicurean schools. Without being positively sceptical, it gave a first impulse to the philosophy of doubt[1] by denying the existence of any positive criterion of truth. Carneades followed him [of Cyrene, d. B.C. 130], and in antagonism with the Stoic Chrysippus, denied the objective reality of all knowledge whatever. There was nothing more substantial than probability; and Platonic ethics were toned down into duties based upon motives of prudence and convenience. The principles of the New Academy led naturally to a revival of Pyrrhonism by Ænesidemus of Alexandria, and his more methodical scepticism in the first century; a system of universal doubt closely described by Sextus Empiricus, the last of his school in the commencement of the third century. Ænesidemus was the precursor of modern scepticism in two respects. As denying the possible existence of any criterion of truth, he foreshadowed Kant. As uprooting the entire structure of metaphysics, by annihilating the notion of causation on which it is based, he indicated Hume [Hume, *Essays and Treatises*, vii. pt. 2]. Demonstration of any kind ceased to be possible; every effort of human thought was problematical, and the solid foundation of morals was broken up. Modern scepticism is built up on these lines that were laid down in the earlier days of Christianity. If Kant, as regards speculative reason, was sceptical, so too was Ænesidemus. If the "Critique of Pure Reason" distinguishes between subjective and objective elements of knowledge, in Kantian phrase, φαινόμενα and νούμενα, the terms are borrowed from the Alexandrian; if Kant, in a spirit of scepticism, buoyed out the intricate channel of the criterion of truth, Ænesidemus had already taken the soundings; if the basis of the earlier scepticism was laid in the antagonisms of speculative reason, as "thesis" and "antithesis," they were revived in the "antinomies" of Kant. But many intermediate steps prepared the way for the "Critique of Pure Reason." On the revival of free thought in philosophy, the Cartesian system was built upon universal doubting as a reaction on the dogmatism of the schools. Then came a contest of scepticism, in which Hobbes and Gassendi from one end of the lists challenged Descartes, Malebranche, and Spinoza on the other; and from that day to this scepticism has been mixed up with the philosophical spirit [Buckle, *Civ. in Engl.* I. vii. viii.]. Thus with Locke as with Pascal, to cast aside philosophy was truly to philosophize. "Se moquer de la philosophie c'est vraiment philosopher" [Pascal, *Pens.* vii. 34].

France, England, and Germany have each had their school of Scepticism. Huet, educated by the Jesuits at Paris, and, though not himself a Jesuit, completely saturated with the atmosphere of the College ("il avait pris l'air de la maison"), Montaigne, whom a gentleman, said Hallam, "is ashamed not to have read, yet of whom he is heartily ashamed while reading," the sceptical buffoon, the Abbé Charron, are representative men of the early Scepticism of France. Pascal, the scourge of the Jesuits, openly professed the sceptical no-creed. "Pyrrhonism," he said, "is the true thing; your philosophy is not worth an hour's trouble." In his letters he is the Jansenical churchman, in his "Thoughts" he takes a wider cast, and comes out as the thorough Pyrrhonist. It is necessary that the whole man should stand revealed. Hate, he said, with Hobbes, and not love is the master principle of life. "Tous les hommes se haissent l'un et l'autre." The first principles of justice were denied by him; "that which is established alone is just" [*Pensées*, vi. 5, 6]. "Justice and injustice change their quality in changing climate" [iii. 8]. Custom was his only guide, to be followed simply because it is custom, and not because it is either reasonable or just [v. 40, x. 14]. His deduction of faith from custom is particularly odious [*Pensées*, x. 1]. Accident he deemed to be the arbitress of all. When the fate of the world trembled in the balance, it was determined by Cleopatra's profile

[1] As might be expected, the near approach made by the New Academy to the Pyrrhonist school embittered the latter against its teachers. "Slave, what dost thou among free men?" was the rough speech of Timon the Pyrrhonist to Arcesilas [Diog. Laert. ix.]. "Arcesilas," said Aristo, "is triple like the chimera; he has the bust of Plato, the torso of Diodorus, and the lower extremities of Pyrrho." Cicero was the philosophical as Lucian was the scoffing sceptic.

When Cromwell had overthrown the church, demolished the reigning dynasty, and established his own, all was reversed again by a grain of grit in the ureter "ce petit gravier s'étant mis la, il est mort, sa famille abaissée, tout est en paix, et le roi rétabli" [iii 7] Might is better than right, for right is subject to dispute, might is indisputable [vi 7, 50], and the memorable apophthegm, 'la propriété c'est la vol," is only a more advanced enunciation of Pascal's doctrine, "sans doute l'égalité des biens est juste" [vi 7] For the *à priori* demonstrations of the Divine existence given by Anselm and Descartes he substituted an argument scarce worthy of the name from a "calculus of probabilities, "jouant Dieu a croix et a pile," as it has been said [see *Pensées*, x. 2, and *App.* ed. Huet, p. 133, x 1] Life is a game, he said, in which he who lives as a Christian stakes his wager on the existence of God and Paradise, he who lives as an atheist speculates on annihilation The Christian surrenders his life, but with the chance of eternal joy, he cannot lose, he may gain The atheist plays for extinction, but there is the chance against him of an eternity of woe He cannot gain, he may lose Elsewhere he seriously doubts whether life is not a dream, if one-half of our existence is spent in sleep, in which consciousness is only an illusion, why should the other half be more real, from whence perhaps we wake when we deem that we fall asleep [*Pensées*, viii. 1] Pascal was a complete "bifrons," assuming a high religious tone in his letters when the Jesuits were to be discomfited, but in his "Thoughts" we have the man himself. The mask is thrown aside The juxtaposition of Mysticism with his sceptical principles [MYSTICS] completed the inconsistency of his character [1]

Bayle was the scholastical sceptic, always undecided and unstable as water, he was the very incarnation of doubt The son of a Protestant minister, he joined the Church of Rome only to desert it again, and die Protestant "I am a Protestant," he said, "in the fullest meaning of the term, for from my inmost soul I protest against everything that has been ever said or ever done" Manicheeism obtained from him a warmer advocacy than Catholicism Voltaire, himself a witty development of Bayle, termed him the Avocat-Générale of Scepticism Feuerbach, the most virulent enemy of Christianity in modern days, claims the kindred sympathies of Bayle [P Bayle, *Ein Beitrag zur Geschichte d Philos* 1848]

England, in the latter half of the seventeenth century, began to shew front against the metaphysics and natural philosophy of Aristotle Cartesian doubt was asserted as the only safe guide to the truth In this spirit Glanville wrote his treatise, "On the Vanity of Dogmatizing' [A D 1661], a second edition of which [A D 1665] received the more appropriate name of "Scepsis Scientifica" Shortly before the middle of the next century the older form of Deism developed by Toland, Chubb, and Tindal passed on into the scepticism of the younger Dodwell and Hume; the former of whom published [A D 1742] anonymously his "Christianity not founded on Argument, and the true Principle of Gospel Evidence assigned" The treatise is in the form of a letter to a young man at Oxford, and lays down as a necessary principle that the inquiry after truth must involve a renunciation of every prejudice and preconceived opinion instilled by education and early association, to be replaced by investigation and research conducted in a spirit of doubt The term "rational faith," he says, involves a contradiction, and he promises his friend, that if he sets about "proving all things" he is sure to end in "holding fast" nothing The treatise is headed with the text, "I have believed, therefore will I speak,' and concludes with the words of King Solomon, "My son, trust in the Lord with all thine heart, and lean not to thine own understanding" [Prov iii 5] The writer's object is to shew that Reason is unable to lead the soul to Faith, and that there is an "irreconcilable repugnancy in their natures betwixt reason and belief" [p 86] he was perfectly aware to which side the freethinking spirit of the age would incline Throughout he takes faith to mean a bare belief, such as the lost spirits may have, he sets out of the account the love that is its life, quickening faith from a cold intellectual condition to be the keen and faithful guide of everyday life, and raising it from a speculative to an eminently practical virtue Leland's "Remarks on a late Pamphlet" appeared [A D 1743] and in the same year Chubb mentioned it in the preface to his "Enquiry concerning Redemption," but only to condemn it, inasmuch as its principles were as adverse to Deism as they were to sound faith Randolph, afterwards Bishop of London, answered it in "The Oxford Young Gentleman's Reply" [A D 1743], and "The Christian's faith a Rational Assent" [A D 1744] At a later date Benson found it necessary to put forth another answer to it, entitled "The Reasonableness of the Christian Religion" [A D 1762] Twenty years had not consigned to oblivion the obnoxious treatise

David Hume born at Edinburgh A D 1711, was educated at Rheims and at the Jesuit establishment La Flèche, in the department of Marne et Loire He died A D 1776 His philosophical publications gave him the entrée of Baron Holbach's mansion at Paris On his observing that he had never met with a thoroughgoing atheist, "You have been singularly unfortunate," was the reply, "but there are seventeen now at table with you." Yet there was nothing atheistical in his scepticism, he speaks at times as though he was scarcely sincere, and as though his scepticism was but an infinitely diluted dogmatism,[2] a question merely of graduated certitude Locke af-

[1] Reuchlin, *Pascals Leben* Cousin, *Etudes sur Pascal* Faugère, *Fragm*

[2] "It seems evident that the dispute between the sceptics and dogmatists is entirely verbal, or at least only the degrees of doubt and assurance The only difference then between these sects is, that the sceptic from habit, caprice, or inclination insists most on the difficulties, the dogmatist, for like reasons, on the necessity" of belief [*Nat. Rel* xii p 584].

firmed that experience is the sole basis of all our knowledge, Berkeley, that our only experience of the external world is by perception; and that matter is apparent only and not real Hume carried the same reasoning to a further point, and while he fully affirmed the sensualism of Locke, he held that not only matter but mind also is non-existent If the occult substratum matter, whereby men arbitrarily account for material phenomena, is non existent, because it is not founded on experience, so also, as Hume argued, we must deny the occult substratum mind to be the basis of mental phenomena, as being equally without our experience If substance conveying impressions is mere inference, so likewise substance in which these impressions are conveyed is mere inference Neither actively nor passively, neither objectively nor subjectively, has substance any real existence If that which men call matter is nothing else than a conglomerate of impressions, mind is but a series of impressions and ideas, it is no substantial entity Locke had already led the way in saying that we only know mind in its manifestation, we cannot know it in itself as the source of mental phenomena [1] But all such reasonings are thoroughly unreal, nature is more logical than metaphysics, belief in the external world is inseparable from our own self-consciousness, as Hume in fact confessed Can there then be any greater waste of time and thought than in the spinning of such unprofitable theories, which even the exponent must fain confess begin and end in "nil" In a religious point of view also, the universality of Christian belief is as convincing as the self-proving substance of matter is in physics Faith is stronger than doubt, and the mind, when assailed by the sceptic's objection to miracles,[2] as being contrary to experience, is inherently convinced that He Who gave nature her laws can control them according to His own good pleasure, and that here the analogy of nature fails as a guide Experience, that Bishop Butler has very justly termed "the guide of life," replaces in Hume's theory the relation of cause and effect There is no such thing as causation with him, phenomena succeed each other in certain different sequences, and experience enables us to connect together these, under like conditions, unvarying sequences, but the antecedent has no causative power, and the consequent phenomenon is in no way effectuated by it; events follow each other, but no tie subsists between them Experience is the only foundation of knowledge, and it tells us nothing of a particular providence or of a future state of rewards and punishments If the teaching of natural religion is called into doubt, *à fortiori* revealed religion is discredited by the sceptic Experience, according to Hume, declares miracles to be incredible, and the Christian faith, he asserts, to be wholly based on miracles But this is not a correct statement However heartily faith accepts the Gospel account in its plain literal meaning, it does so because it can trace in it the operation of Almighty Goodness and Wisdom The Jews ascribed the Saviour's miracles to Beelzebub, because they were blind to the holiness of the cause in which they were wrought We feel and know the holiness of the Christian Law, and this alone would compel us to have unfeigned faith in its miracles They are not the Christian miracles then that prove to us the truth of Christian doctrine, whatever may have been their effect on the men who witnessed them, but the holiness and purity of that doctrine convince us of its divine origin, and the Gospel being the Word of God, from beginning to end it is the word of truth Bishop Butler has shewn that there is no presumption from the analogy of nature against the credibility of miracles [ii. 2] The particular interpositions of the will and power of God, that constitute what we call miraculous occurrences, for all we know may be the normal condition of the Divine government in other worlds as well as in this. Such manifestations of power, and the ordinary laws of nature of which we are observant, may be resolvable into one general principle, as the one law of gravitation that keeps sweet the flowing stream, maintains the planets also true to their orbits The laws that bind nature in one planet extend their influence far beyond, like comets in the material world, they may have an eccentric action, yet like them they may be instances of God's orderly disposition; they may have a periodicity of effectuation if not of time, that as yet evades our faculty of perception As light and gravitation are common to the whole planetary system, so may the miraculous display of divine power, under particular contingencies, be co-extensive with the creation that was first called into being by miracle We might with equal reason deny cometary law because we cannot in every case calculate its necessary elements, as refuse belief to special manifestations of Divine power because they are contrary to daily experience, whereas their laws of action may embrace in their sweep not merely our own world but the universe

Further, a miracle in its action cannot be called a violation of the laws of nature, as Hume imagined, "a miracle may be accurately defined a transgression of a law of nature by the particular volition of the Deity or by the interposal of some invisible agent." It is rather an introduction of a special cause [Dean Mansel *on Miracles*, s 14] to be followed by its own proper effect, as shadow follows substance As in this world one law

[1] In many respects more credit is given to Hume for originality of thought than he fairly merits His displacement of causation by the theory of antecedents and sequents was already indicated by Glanville, "we cannot conclude anything to be the cause of another but from its continually accompanying it" [*Scepsis Scientifica*] Similarly Malebranche, while Hobbes indicates his notion of relative suggestion "What we call experience is nothing else but remembrance of what antecedents have been followed by what consequents After a man has been accustomed to see like antecedents followed by like consequents, whensoever he seeth the like come to pass to anything he had seen before, he looks there shall follow it the same that followed then" Ernesti, in his "Initia Doctrinæ Solidioris" [A D 1734, *de Mente Humana*, i 16], was also a precursor of Hume.

[2] *Essay on Miracles*, his earliest treatise *Enquiry concerning Human Understanding* *Natural History of Religion*

often holds another in check and suspends its action, so the laws of terrestrial nature may be subject to the wider sway of cosmic laws The Saviour's glorified appearance on the Mount of Transfiguration, His appearance in the midst of the disciples when the doors were shut, His walking on the waves, though facts that are contrary to our experience, and therefore termed by us miraculous, may have been, in strict obedience to a yet more universal law, anticipative of the laws that shall determine the second coming of the Glorified in the clouds of heaven We know nothing of the laws of nature beyond those that control the speck of creation that we inhabit, and we have but a skin-deep knowledge of even those laws, clever juggling deludes our senses with mockeries that seem most real, may it not also be the case that facts, seemingly a ' transgression of the laws of nature," are in strict obedience to those laws in their most universal operation [1] Scepticism may here be met with its own weapons We are ignorant, says the sceptic, therefore our only true wisdom is to doubt where experience is no guide But that experience itself is incomplete, therefore we may rationally call in question its teaching Moral reasonings are our better and safer guide God is true and cannot deceive, let us endeavour to hear what He has said, and hearing to obey

But he who has recast the whole plan of scepticism and given it an entirely new force is Kant Grave and severe spirit, disdaining rhetoric and employing no other weapons than analysis and dialectics, Kant has devised the most damaging impeachment against all preceding speculative reasoning, and reduced doubt into a science Happily, even in him, there is sufficient inconsistency to shew that the no-creed of doubt is wholly unable to satisfy the reasoning judgment His scepticism, of a more transcendental cast than that of the sunshiny Montaigne or of the melancholy Pascal, involves sceptical principles, but he is always loyal to the instincts of truth and duty His large soul was far superior to ordinary scepticism, and discarded principally all antecedent methods of working out the truth Living in a century of change, disregard for every antecedent system was his natural inheritance He imbibed his first notions from Hume, as he himself declares Hume's scepticism, however, exhibited to him the weak points of metaphysical and philosophical reasoning, and its many arbitrary assumptions, though his own metaphysical theories are at times as inconsequent as those of his predecessors He was the greatest innovator in such reasoning, the last metaphysician is usually the most original In mathematical science every subsequent addition enriches, in metaphysical systems the last is more or less subversive of its predecessors Thus Kant gained nothing from Aristotle or Descartes, Spinoza and Leibnitz, and not much from his more immediate master Hume, he has superseded theirs by a newer system, he destroys all antecedent grounds of metaphysical faith with a remorseless logic and a hardy scepticism, that he may build up again upon surer principles Moral consciousness and the notion of duty in free agents are his great remedial mean

The nature and bearing of his scepticism is this In his "Critique of Pure Reason" he discards the *objective*, or that which is external to the mind, and occupies himself only with the *subjective*, or that which pertains strictly to and is inherent in the thinking mind Confining himself then to the subjective, he examines the human intellect analytically, and reducing the laws that govern thought to a certain number of elementary conceptions, definitely classed, he shews that these conceptions have only a relative value, that they are unable to teach anything with respect to the essence of things, and that their whole practical utility consists in arranging the data of experience, and in reducing the various objects of human knowledge to a principle of unity by the process of generalization Next, he submits the results of his analysis to a searching dialectical test; he takes the three main objects of metaphysical speculation, the soul of man, the external world, and God, and shews that there is no single dogmatic assertion with respect to the essence of the soul, the constitution of the universe, and the Being of the Deity, that may not be impugned as either resting on false reasoning or involving some "antinomy," or arbitrarily substantiating some abstraction

Kant in his analysis resolves the elements of human knowledge under the three heads of Sensation, Intellect, and Reason Intuition is the work of Sensation Observation of the relations of things, and judgment, are of the province of Intellect To combine the elements of judgment, and to connect consequences with their antecedents, is the work of Reason Reason then involves the faculty of generalizing, and of setting out the relation that subsists between the particular and the universal This implies the notion of one ultimate general principle, which is the condition of all else, and is itself the unconditioned To argue from this idea to the nature of beings universal, is, as Kant says, a fruitful source of illusion, of which he professes to dispose and by laying bare its psychological sources, to give the natural history of human error

His principle of pure reason is this. the conditioned, as in the external world, being given, the conditions that it involves are also given, and hence by elimination the unconditioned Reason, he says, conceives in self-consciousness an absolutely subjective Being, no attribute of any other subject, the thinking soul It ascends from one object to another in the world of sense until it arrives at the conception of the remote cause of the universe, that comprehends all in one condition of existence, the unity of God These three ideas, the soul, the universe, the Deity, cannot be demonstrated, since they are general truths, such as lie at the root of all demonstration They cannot be realized in the intellect since they represent that which is beyond all possible experience They have therefore a

[1] *Hum Nat* i 380, 471

purely subjective value, they are ideas that extend not the domain of human knowledge, rather they circumscribe and limit it Here metaphysical science attempts more than it can perform Given the absolutely simple conception of our thinking being, it declares that being to be absolutely simple, which is inconsequent Given a retrogressive series of phenomena, the idea of their first originating impulse is conceived, and each generalization has its contradictory antagonism or antinomy Now, from the summed conditions of objectivity, metaphysical science concludes that there is a Being of beings, as the sole condition of the possibility, or ultimate reason of things, howbeit that such a Being is absolutely unknown to us It transforms that existence, which is ideal, into real existence, and makes it the foundation of every other real existence But the act is arbitrary, and therefore inconsequent. This is the current of Kant's scepticism, under which the soul, the world, the Deity, are made to crumble away "like the baseless fabric of a vision," and the three sciences, based upon metaphysics, that is, rational psychology, rational cosmology and rational theology, are shaken to their foundation

Further, it being a fundamental principle of reason that the conditioned or relative being given, the existence of the entire series of the relatively conditioned is involved, as also the existence of the unconditioned and absolute, Kant educes from thence his four mutually neutralizing antitheses or "antinomies"

If the world be considered under the categories of quantity and quality, it may with equal reason be affirmed to be either limited or boundless in extension and duration, in other words, finite or infinite It may be formed of indivisible atoms, or it may be infinitely divisible It is a mathematical antinomy Or under the conditions of relation and mode, effects may be either referred back to a first cause, free and intelligent, or considered as an endless chain of results connected together by a blind necessity Who is to say that Moses is right and Epicurus wrong? All such theorizing is purely arbitrary It is a dynamical antinomy Of these Kant considers the mathematical antinomy to be absolutely insoluble. For the dynamical antinomy a solution is possible, and he offers to work it out, involving the free agency of Man, the existence of the Deity, morality, and religion

The idea of God as the Being of all beings is the highest conception of reason, and the most necessary, since by means of this idea human knowledge acquires unity, and the synthetic process is completed But nothing more results from this than a Supreme Ideal, and not the reality of supreme existence The intellect refuses its allegiance to an ideal relative existence, hence it transforms the ideal into a subjective reality, the act again being purely arbitrary

In the same dogmatic way rational theology sets forth the existence of God in three arguments, each of which involves its own neutralizing antinomy the argument from natural religion, the argument from design or "a contingentia mundi," and the ontological argument. Natural theology, he says, can teach nothing by its application of final causes with respect to the existence of the Perfect, the Absolute, because they are of wholly alien essence The argument "a contingentia" he merges in the ontological, and directs the whole force of his reasoning against the metaphysical proof of the Divine existence, first elaborated by Anselm and adopted by Descartes The dialectic reasoning of the schoolman and philosopher may be demolished, but the truth that they exhibit remains unaltered Men will always continue to have faith in God as the most sacred instinct of the soul So far religious philosophy has encountered only an enemy in Kant throughout the speculative section of his "Critique of Pure Reason" He has met metaphysicians with their own weapons, and shews practically by his own example that their principles lead to scepticism

In the practical portion of his Critique he dogmatizes as the moralist, and develops the reasoning that leads back to the solid ground of faith in God The relative perceptions of the intellect do not exhaust the capabilities of human consciousness, there are other *à priori* elements to be taken into the account on the practical side, such as moral duty, freedom We have here a ground of faith that speculative research could never create It indicates the old *à priori* method of Plato, arguing to the existence of Supreme Goodness and Beauty and Truth from those traces of the beautiful and good and true that exist within the soul of man The metaphysician fails to carry out the proof of that existence to a favourable result, it leads only to a "non liquet," to the moralist the sense of moral duty and freedom is as the clue that enables him to unravel the problem Thus the practical "Critique of Pure Reason" supplements the speculative section, but there is a want of unity, the two can scarcely be worked up into one harmonious whole His method of demonstration, in which he stands forth as the champion of philosophical and theological Rationalism, is in merest rough outline briefly this—

It is assumed as an ultimate fact that there is a moral law having a true relation to the conscience and the will, but needing no external reality to render it absolute. Will is the power of acting according to the prescription of such law, and will thus defined is one with practical reason, which is *in tanto* a law-inculcating principle, moral law has not its rise in moral sense, but *vice versa,* moral sense is a result of this innate law of action Pure reason also of necessity includes the notion of moral freedom, which shews its power negatively in its independence of every object of desire, and positively in its antinomy. It is a reality, inasmuch as moral law is a reality If I ought, then I can If I have obligations, I am free to discharge them Freedom therefore is an *à priori* condition of the moral law Kant, then, starting with the fundamental conception of practical reason, or sense of moral duty, proposes to shew that such conception has an objectivity that no conception of speculative reason can pretend to have, for it prescribes immediately and absolutely that which ought to be done, and is obligatory on every reasonable being, it imparts also its own objective character to various other conceptions, (which is one of Kant's most strange paradoxes,) and in an immediate sense to that of freedom, which is inseparably bound up with the notion of practical reason, these two therefore, as one complex conception, manifest the existence of being "per se," "Ding an sich," or νούμενον, for they exhibit the idea of free and moral being, bound by the obligation of duty, and aspiring to the noblest end of freedom, the attainment of supreme good We have no consciousness, he argues, of our freedom of will It is free not as a result, but as an *à priori* condition It is an ideal that becomes realized by the objective constitution of moral duty.

This theory of freedom of will and moral obligation seems only to have been devised to cover the danger to which ethics had been exposed by his attempted demolition of the ontological argument of Anselm and Descartes In matters of fact and experience, all with him is one long chain of necessary action, each result or phenomenon is determined by its antecedent, leaving no room for the idea of freedom But in matters of duty each result or phenomenon, being a reasonable action, has its necessary relation with a freely moving will This freedom having an objective character, is exoteric, and is transferred to the ideal world, and no antinomy thence results between the subjective thought and the objective freedom It is by these complications that Kant arrives at the first postulate of "practical reason," the real existence of freedom of will, and having rescued morality from his sceptical wreck, he endeavours next to make a salvage of religion

What then is the end for which man is striving, with the moral law for his principle and free will as its complement? Is virtue to be its own present reward, as the Stoics held, and there an end? or is an Epicurean happiness resulting from obedience to that law to be the object of aspiration? Neither one nor the other by itself, but supreme good is the harmonic mean between the two, though it cannot be realized in our present condition, virtue, in time, must still be imperfect One of two things therefore must be the truth Either the idea is a fallacy, or after this life is ended there must be some future state of indefinite perfectibility A similar result is worked out with relation to happiness, as the end of human endeavour Perfect happiness is unattainable on earth, and this goes to confirm the proof of a future state But further, the relation of virtue and happiness is in no sense dependent upon our will, and this relation cannot be established by anything short of a will more mighty than the universe, holding in its hand the destiny of man and of nature If, therefore, the supreme good which practical reason teaches us to be the necessary object of our will, implies a primal supreme good from whence it derives its being, it follows that the existence of a Divine Being is also proved Thus the objective reality of immortality and God are linked with that of freedom, which is itself an *à priori* objective condition of moral law of which we have immediate cognizance, and from which it is inseparable, and if Kant, on the speculative side of his Critic, is a sceptic, on the moral or practical side he is at least a Theist He formulated his system in the apophthegm "Act in all matters of duty in such a way as that the motive of thine action might be raised to the dignity of a universal principle of moral law."

Fichte during the lifetime of Kant developed these ideas in the direction of Deism, and gave a greater consistency and unity to the system He discarded the limping antagonisms of the speculative and the practical conceptions of reason, with respect to the Divine existence, as anomalous, and replaced the idea of a law giving Deity, which he found to be arbitrary and anthropomorphic, with an order flowing necessarily from the nature of things, and issuing in the harmony of goodness and virtue Others, such as Hegel and Schelling, have combined with Kant's theory Spinoza's pantheistic development of cosmic order A reaction has now set in, and all this redundant speculation seems inclined to return into its ancient channel But the Kantian moral teaching must always have a massive grandeur that redeems the adventurous rashness of his "Criticism of Pure Reason," and can never lose its character of positive and practical utility [Fischer, *Gesch d n Phil* Saisset, *Manuel de la Phil*, *Philosophie religieuse*, *Scepticisme* Cousin, Tissot, Carlyle, on Kant Ulrici's art in Herzog's *Real Encyklop* Meiklejohn's transl]

SCHELLING [RATIONALISTS]

SCHISMATICS Those who wilfully cut themselves off from the Apostolical succession of Bishops by which the organic unity of the Church is maintained within the boundaries of a state or nation The principal historical schisms in the Church of Christ have been those of Novatus, Donatus, Luther, and Calvin Organized schisms have also been formed in England by the Roman Catholics and by the various sects of Protestant Dissenters, in Scotland by the Presbyterians, and in Ireland, as in England, by the Roman Catholics and Protestant Dissenters Such schisms are sometimes formed without any further heretical deviation from the Creed than that which is involved in breaking the unity of the One Catholic and Apostolic Church, and it has sometimes happened, as in the case of the English Roman Catholics, that they have received true though irregular orders from a foreign source so as to continue a valid priesthood [DONATISTS, NOVATIANS, LUTHERANS, CALVINISTS, ROMAN CATHOLICS, SCOTTISH KIRK, etc]

SCHLEIERMACHER [RATIONALISTS]

SCHOOLMEN The Northern hordes that overran Europe in the sixth century buried all traces of civilization as beneath a dense mass of alluvial deposit Before that time the Romans had established schools of learning in various towns of France [*Cod. Theodos* xiv tit 9] The study of Greek lingered here when it had died out elsewhere, but eventually all was buried in thick darkness until the time of Charlemagne Though himself only able to affix the sign manual with the pommel of his sword, he was a great encourager of learning, rightly judging that civilization was his natural ally against the barbarians of the North and the Moors of Spain; a policy that was copied by King Alfred in coping with the Danes This was the mainspring of Charlemagne's wars He founded schools of learning throughout France, and placed over them the ablest teachers that the monasteries could furnish Henceforth the "scholasticus," or teacher of the young, was found in every convent Boethius, to whose eclecticism the scholastic system may be traced, was a Roman senator of the early part of the sixth century Realistic notions had their origin in him [CONCEPTUALISM] Cassiodorus, senator and chancellor to Theodoric the Great, was also an Italian He founded the Monastery of Vivières, and was its first abbot Spanish learning was kept alive by Isidore of Seville, Tajus of Saragossa, and Ildefonso of Toledo Bede represented the learning of England in the eighth century, and it was principally from English and Irish monasteries that Charlemagne obtained his supply of teachers Alcuin of York was placed by him over the palatine school that he founded for the benefit of his court

John Scotus Erigena, his successor, was an Irish monk He was the first after the revival of learning who joined the studies of theology and philosophy, an alliance that the schools ever after maintained Yet he was far more of an eclectic philosopher after the school of Boethius than a divine He led men's minds in the direction of Scholasticism, however he differed from the schools in making reason paramount, while he slighted ecclesiastical tradition, and only just abstained from challenging its authority Richard of St Victor named Erigena the "Inventor of Theology" [*Lib Exer* 24], possibly on account of his theory that the truths on which theology is based may be discovered by *à priori* reasoning, an inversion of the Augustinian maxim "Fides præcedit intellectum" Theology, he said, contains the germ of every other science, and rests upon the authority of Scripture, and of tradition as approved by right reason This was also one distinctive character of Scholastic theology, which exhibits throughout the same strange mixture of deference for authority and independent hardihood of thought. Theology also had its negative side, which denied that anything can be adequately predicated of the Deity, consciousness, love, existence, ascribed by us to the Supreme are mere arbitrary assumptions of the human mind, and veil its real ignorance The authority that is paramount with Erigena is that of the Scriptures, the authority that must cede to "right reason"—that is, reason illuminated by a pure faith—is that of tradition and of the Fathers, the legitimate interpreters of Scripture But they must not be quoted without urgent necessity, from charitable regard for those who have a lower range of intellect, and are only too prone to follow authority blindfold, and to disregard reason "Nulla auctoritas te terreat ab his quæ rectæ contemplationis rationabilis suasio edocet." Of the Sacraments, as mysteries transcending all human reason, he scarcely speaks Yet in his boldest flights, when he feels himself soaring far above the heads of ordinary mortals, Scripture and the Fathers are made to support his positions, exegesis becomes the handmaid of his philosophy, which is commended to weaker intellects under the patronage of Holy Writ Erigena was an original thinker, having derived his materials for thought partly from the mystical Pseudo-Dionysius of the fifth century, partly from the Neo-Platonism of Plotinus, Porphyry and the Pantheistic Proclus, partly also from Maximus the Confessor [A D 662], who combined the ascetic piety of primitive monasticism with Pseudo-Dionysian mysticism Thus his eclecticism covered a wide surface, and its mutual antagonism of Platonic and Peripatetic notions gave ample scope for discussion He was a keen dialectician, but close attention to minute detail did not prevent him from taking a firm grasp of an entire subject in all its bearings Scholastic and mystical theology received from him a first impulse so far as they were speculative, and his influence continued to be felt in a predominant degree until a wider knowledge of Aristotle was gained by the schools in the thirteenth century Duns Scotus had evidently drawn from him, and the Dominican Eckart, excommunicated [A D 1329] for his Pantheistic assertion of the eternity of the world, and the sole existence of the Deity, obtained the main elements of his error from Erigena

The theology of Erigena was a religious philosophy He classifies all things as "things that are" and "things that are not," the whole being included in the term nature This nature is divided out into four species, as [1] The nature that creates and is uncreate, [2] the nature that creates and is create, [3] the nature that creates not and is create, [4] the nature that creates not and is uncreate [1] is the Divine Being, Whose relation to the universe is so described as to lead straight to Pantheism, [2] is the world of prototypal ideas, having its principle of unity in the Logos, agreeably to the systems of Plato, Plotinus, Philo and the Pseudo-Dionysius, [3] is the world of sense and its concentration in man, from whence Realism was afterwards developed, [4] return to God by predestined decree, "all things," as proceeding forth from the Divine existence and returning into it, may be termed uncreate as subsisting in the Absolute Under this head he discourses upon Universal Grace, Redemption, Death, Eternal Life, Reward and Punishment The germs of nearly every school of modern philosophy are foreshadowed in the writings of Erigena Descartes, Spinoza, Kant,

Fichte, Schelling, Hegel, Schleiermacher, all have their points of analogy with Erigena, who for that reason has been compared by Christlieb [*Leben u Lehre d. J Sc Erig* 464] to "bifrons Janus," standing midway between Plato and the schools, the one face tinged with the setting rays of Greek philosophy, the other bending an eagle gaze over the far distant regions of German thought, in anticipation of harvests of his sowing that should be reaped after the lapse of a thousand years. Yet, if he created a future, in time present he stood alone He never formed a school

The immediate effect of his teaching was to give a powerful stimulus to the study of dialectics, a term not to be accepted in the high Platonic sense of pure philosophy, nor in the Aristotelian meaning of logic in its wider acceptance as the science of words, but to be restricted to the dry rules and appliances of syllogistic reasoning, which gave their peculiarly austere character to the disquisitions of the schools Dialectical reasoning was imported into the Carlovingian schools from the monasteries of England and Ireland by Alcuin, Erigena and Clement Gerbert, raised to the Papal See as Sylvester II [A D 990], was a thorough master of logic, as shewn in his work, "De Corp et Sang Domini," and in a shorter treatise, "De Ratione" [Pez. *Thes Anecd nov*] In the middle of the next century Berengarius of Tours revived the discussion started by Paschasius Radbertus [A D 831] on transubstantiation with all dialectical appliances, and his opponent, Lanfranc, however distrustful of it in such a controversy, found himself compelled to make use of the same weapon

Hitherto theology had been treated in the more flowing historical method of the Fathers, whose system of doctrine was built up on Scripture as interpreted by tradition In the eighth and ninth centuries sentences were collected, and "catenæ" and "loci communes" were formed from their writings, which supplied the demands of what was called "positive theology," from which Scholastic Theology was distinguished as combining together faith and reason, faith being limited to belief in Scripture, and Church authority as based on tradition and synodical decrees Reason also represented the dialectical method, and metaphysical disquisitions syllogistically conducted These were held to be infallible methods for disclosing the truth "Maximi plane cordis est per omnia ad dialecticam confugere, quo qui non confugit, cum secundum rationem sit factus ad imaginem Dei, suum honorem reliquit, nec potest renovari de die in diem ad imaginem Dei" [Berengar *de Sacr. Cœn* 67] Logic, however, was only regarded so far as it served the purposes of polemics, to clear the meaning of terms, and to demonstrate their differences and distinctions, nothing higher was expected from it The Organum of Aristotle was known from Augustine's use of it, it was studied moreover in the Latin translation of Boethius and in the Isagoge of Porphyry, but the Master himself remained unknown Peter Lombard does not even mention the name of Aristotle At length more general knowledge of his works was revealed from a quarter where least of all it would be suspected to exist—among the Moors of Spain

Syrian and Jewish physicians thoroughly conversant with Greek literature were high in favour with the Caliphs, who were mostly ostentatious patrons of learning They indicated to them such pieces of Greek literature as were most deserving of their notice, and by the time of Almamûn, in the beginning of the ninth century, the Moors of Spain possessed translations of the principal philosophical works of Greece Raymond, Archbishop of Toledo towards the middle of the twelfth century, gathered around him a staff of translators, principally Jews, the most renowned of whom was John of Seville Through this channel many Arabic versions from Greek texts became known before the close of the century, Aristotle being the principle favourite But the text was accompanied with the commentaries of Arab philosophers who introduced a considerable breadth of Averroist notions wholly inconsistent with the Christian faith, and text and gloss alike were transfused into Latin An interdict therefore was laid upon the study of Aristotle by the Council of Paris [A D 1209], but restricted six years later to the physics and metaphysics by the Papal Legate, Robert de Courçon, Gregory IX afterwards limited the adverse decree till such time as the suspected works should have been castigated by divines The condemnation of Aristotle only led to a greater demand for his works, and whereas, in the beginning of the thirteenth century, they were comparatively unknown, in the time of Thomas Aquinas [A D 1272], all the treatises had been translated into Latin and extensively read From A D 1220 to 1225 were the years in which Peripatetic principles were largely imported into the schools of France Michael Scott the warlock was the earliest translator of Aristotle, and something uncanny at once attached to his name

> "Michel Scotto fu che veramente
> Delle magiche frode seppe il giuoco"
> [Dante, *Inf* xx]

The same may be said of Albertus Magnus, one of the earliest Schoolmen who worked Aristotelian notions into his system Robert Grosteste, Bishop of Lincoln, translated the Nicomachean Ethics, and was left unmolested A knowledge of Aristotle was principally derived from Latin versions of Avicenna's [Ibn Sinâ] Arabic translation, with the commentary of Averroes [Ibn Roshd] both of which names are associated by Dante with the most learned names of Greece, and only not admitted into the kingdom of heaven from want of baptism,

> "Euclide geometra e Tolomeo
> Ippocrate Avicenna e Galieno
> Averroes che 'l gran commento feo"
> [*Inf* Cant iv]

Thomas of Aquino is said to have translated the works of Aristotle under the patronage of Urban IV. He more probably collated the

 Schoolmen

various versions extant with the original Greek. The earliest of the Schoolmen who shews undoubted traces of Aristotle is Alexander of Hales In his Summa he frequently cites Avicenna and Algazel as high philosophical authority [A D 1243-5] This development of Scholastic thought by means of Peripatetic philosophy supplies a sharp line of distinction which separates all subsequent Schoolmen from their predecessors, and under this influence Scholasticism rapidly gained its culminating point. It has had a lasting effect also on theology Cardinal Pallavicino, while he treats as an idle scoff the assertion that without Aristotle some of the doctrines of the Church would have remained latent ("noi mancavamo di molti articoli della fede"), yet declared the absolute necessity of Aristotle for applying the truths of Scripture "Se Aristotele o Filosofia non ci desse le universali notizie communi a tutte le cose, non potremmo poi con l' aggiunta luce della divina rivelazione applicare alle oggetti sopranaturali," philosophy being useful as a foreign contingent if kept in due subordination, ("in maniera che servano ma non commandino") [I *Conc di Tr* VIII xix 12] In several German churches Aristotle's Ethics were read as gospel [Spanheim] Though Aristotle was known only as a master of logic, and in Latin versions, Greek learning was by no means so totally extinct in these ages as is generally supposed It was regularly taught with Latin in Carlovingian schools at Osnaburg, the deed of foundation having determined "omnem clericum eleganter bilinguem esse" J Scotus Erigena translated from the original the works of Pseudo-Dionysius the Areopagite, which were destined to have so decided an influence on Scholastic mysticism At Limoges, in the tenth century, at Whitsuntide the "Gloria," "Sanctus," and "Agnus" were chanted in Greek [Jourdain, *Trad Lat d'Aristote*, 44] Gervinus, Abbot of St Riquier in Ponthieu, enriched the library with many Greek works, of which he was a devoted student [A D 1045-1075, *Hist Lit de la France*, vii 93, 113] Greek communities had a political existence at Arles and Marseilles for purposes of commerce, and a Greek monastery was established near the latter city Of our own countrymen Abelard of Bath, at the end of the eleventh century, travelled in Greece and Asia Minor, impelled by a desire for studying Greek literature, and John of Salisbury in the twelfth, though not deeply versed in Greek, had been able to acquire a knowledge of it in his monastery After that time a great impulse was given to Greek learning by the transmission to Paris of Greek MSS from Constantinople, A D 1167, or forty years before that city was taken by the Crusaders under Count Baldwin Students now flocked to the University of Paris in such numbers, that they exceeded, as it was said, the number of permanent inhabitants

The future of the Schools was prepared in the two centuries that succeeded Erigena; in which the whole curriculum of learning was summed in the "Trivium," viz grammar, logic, and rhetoric, the study of words, and the "Quadrivium," arithmetic, geometry, astronomy, and music, the study of things, music meaning only the rude form known to the Greeks

The veins of thought were determined in their course, and a stream of life was flowing along them, when the controversy between Anselm and Roscellin arose in the eleventh century Roscellin, Canon of Compiègne, was doubly an offender, he was heretical in his theology, heretical also in his philosophy, in that he opposed the opinion with respect to universal ideas, or "universalia in re," that may be traced back to Boethius, and through him to Porphyry, others, however, had preceeded him [Ritter, *Gesch d Ph* vii. 310]. His theological error was of the gravest kind, for he had argued himself dialectically into a belief of the threefold substance of the Deity the Three Persons he declared to be distinct as three angels are distinct, but they are one in power, as angelic energy, though pervading the hosts of heaven, may be one Having been condemned at Soissons [A D 1092], he at first recanted, then fled to England, where he retracted his recantation, and, under the protection of William Rufus, wrote against Anselm, his principal antagonist Afterwards, being driven from England, he returned to France, and died a canon of Tours

The philosophical question of universals was intimately connected with the subsequent fortunes of Scholasticism The three principal systems with respect to the mind in its relation with the objects of thought that divided the philosophic world from the eighth to the fifteenth century, were the antagonism of Realism and Nominalism, and Conceptualism, which alone now survives Realism erred on the side of excess, as Nominalism on the side of deficiency For the Realist, accepting the Platonic notion of an external world of ideas, the counterpart of all that we see around us in the concrete world of matter, maintained that since these ideas are distinct from the mind, every conception of the mind represents its corresponding detached idea, and the ideal entity of things is absolutely adequate to the conceptions of reason The abstract essence of things had in this system a real substantive existence Abstract humanity had as distinct an existence as the individual being man, and the whole philosophic world professed a belief in these universal forms as existing independently of the conceptions of the mind, they were, as it was termed, "universalia ante rem," and those who held this notion were "reales" The Realist view was always the most popular with the Schools, for it flattered human vanity to think that the mind reflected as in a mirror those ideas of things visible that had existed before the beginning of the world, and by a mere act of volition summoned into its presence entities that people the invisible world of mystery

Roscellin, affirming the existence only of "universalia post rem," denied the objective existence of these universal ideas, and affirmed that they were a mere vocal expression, a "flatus vocis," as fleeting as the breath that named them, that the colour of a horse, for instance, had no independent ideal existence apart from the horse of which it was the accidental quality Hence he was "nominalis" It was his Nominalism that led Roscellin into heresy, and not heresy that predetermined his scientific creed He spoke of the Three Persons in the Trinity as "tres res," understanding under the term ' res" an entirety, the Aristotelian *τί*, the whole substance of that which exists But he had before argued against the Realist view by shewing that as the idea of a house includes the subordinate ideas of foundation, walls, and roof, therefore that there can be no universal idea of a house in the Realistic sense, because by removing wall or roof the entire notion of a house vanishes The whole substance of the existing house is in his terminology "res," and as such cannot be resolved into its parts [Cousin, *Œuvres inédits d'Abélard*, 471] Therefore it was a delusion for the Realist to talk of self-subsistent "universalia a parte rei," and rather than compromise his philosophical consistency he fell into heresy, and applied the same reasoning to matters of faith that he deemed to be conclusive as regards the world of sense And this was the general character of the Nominalist School, it was usually associated with a free-thinking spirit Hence Leibnitz awards to it the highest praise "Secta Nominalium omnium inter Scholasticos profundissima, et hodiernæ reformatæ philosophandi rationi congruentissima" [Leibn *in Niz libr de veris princ*], where the Nominalists being those "qui omnia putant esse nuda nomina præter substantias singulares, abstractorum igitur et universalium realitatem prorsus tollunt"

Nominalism erred on the side of deficiency. For it overlooked the instinctive habit of generalization inherent in the human mind, whereby it classifies the million objects of nature that surround it, and observing the salient particulars of general resemblance, marshals them under distinct genera and species Thus by a first generalization in concrete matters, and the same is true of abstract ideas, the animal and vegetable kingdoms are discerned from each other, then the vertebrate animal, the quadruped, the ruminant, the cloven hoof, the ox. These distinctive characters were to the Realist independently existing forms, more real in their various entities than their counterparts of material substance, and he needlessly introduced myriads of prototypal ideas, exactly adequate to the phantasms of thought but wholly independent of the mind in their metaphysical essence The Nominalist, denying this separate existence of prototypal ideas, overlooked the process of generalization as a true function of the mind, and termed its results mere arbitrary mental distinctions, "vox et præterea nihil," an empty name for things that needed a name if they were to be demonstrated He failed to see that there was any relative suggestion, any general notion of resemblance arising from subjects capable of comparison, and interposing itself in the mind between the object of thought and the invention of the general term used to express it. To him the world was a mere multiplicity of objects, he perceived no intervening operation of the mind ordering and classifying the confused mass, but with instant succession the generalizing term ranged itself in his mind correlatively with the ungeneralized matter These questions were fought in the schools with the utmost energy The Realist considered that the foundation of faith was laid in his system The claims of reason were identified with his position by the Nominalist When the first half century of this discussion had elapsed, John of Salisbury declared that more time had been spent upon it than by the Cæsars in conquering the world, and more treasure expended than Crœsus ever possessed Afterwards, when Ockham revived it, it was no longer confined to a strife of words, but became a question in which national honour was held to be involved, and while the Emperor Louis of Bavaria upheld Nominalism in Ockham, Louis XI of France sided with the Realists, and either party charged its opponents with committing the sin that may never be forgiven, the Realist as the advocate of religious orthodoxy, the Nominalist as the champion of free thought, and the claims of reason, which is the likeness of God in the soul of man

The effect that Realism had on doctrine was considerable Type and antitype became inseparably one A confession of the real spiritual presence of Christ in the Holy Eucharist did not adunate the symbol and substance with sufficient closeness, and the bread and the cup of blessing were declared to be the very material substance of the Lord's body Humanity being the abstract universal "ante rem," was represented by Adam, and his transgression was the sin of all humanity all therefore sinned, "solum a voluntate primi hominis" [Durand a S Porr lib ii dist 30, qu 2] So also original righteousness had been conferred on Adam, "Non in quantum erat singularis persona, sed in quantum erant in eo omnia individua naturæ humanæ virtualiter" [Nic de Orb lib ii dist 30, see also T. Aq *Summ Prim Sec* qu 81, 1] It was especially favourable to the growth of Mysticism, for it taught that all ideas and forms of things were latent in the soul of man as they subsisted in the mind of God, that contemplation gave to the soul a true perception of them, and some glimpses of the pure happiness that will hereafter constitute the Beatific Vision Then again ecclesiastical dogmata in the Realist theory were the exact counterpart of eternal verities to vary in any minute particular resolved the whole, and salvation was declared to be impossible for any who did not accept the entire doctrinal teaching of a realistic theology Dominican Realism therefore applied itself with fervour to the conversion of such heretics as the Waldenses and Cathari

The third system [CONCEPTUALISM] has already been discussed in a separate article, it is the system of Locke and Reid, but it may be traced far back in the controversy upon universals Nominalism took this form in Abelard, if indeed

Conceptualism may be called a form of Nominalism, from which it varied as widely as from Realism And long before Abelard it was the view of Plotinus and of the Neo-Platonic School of Alexandria, where a complete oneness was affirmed between truth in all its forms and the appreciating intellect, οὐκ ἔξω τοῦ νοῦ τὰ νοητά [A Butler, *Lect* ii 354, Irenæus, Cambr ed Introd xli]. Porphyry disputed the position of the great master [Porph *V Plot* sec 18], and thereby gave its first impulse to Realism.

So much having been premised with respect to the characteristic elements of Scholastic theology, we may now trace their working in the principal Schoolmen, and determine the peculiar modifications of thought that led first to the development and then to the decline of the Scholastic theology of the Middle Ages France was the principal seat of Scholasticism, and the record of teachers at Paris commences with William of Champeaux [de Campellis], Archdeacon of Paris, and Bishop of Châlons, who opened a school of logic A D 1109 [died A D 1121], and was the training preceptor of Abelard

Scholasticism, "the chivalry of theology," may be held to commence with Anselm, born [A D 1033, d 1109] at Aosta in Piedmont; the successor of Lanfranc, first in the abbacy of Bec in Normandy, afterwards in the archiepiscopal see of Canterbury He was the Augustine of the schools, and to Augustine's writings, after Scripture, he looked for the solution of every theological difficulty Nominalism, in his opinion, was a most dangerous error, loosening the hold of authority in men's minds, making faith and reason dependent upon the senses, and tending to scepticism as certainly as it led Roscellin into heresy It affected the Incarnation also, as seen from the Platonic point of view, by denying that the Word took upon Him human nature in the widest possible view, for Nominalism could see nothing beyond the individual human being in the Manhood of Christ

The doctrine of the Atonement was brought to the front by Anselm, and his theory has given a certain direction to Protestant theology Hitherto the benefit of Christ's death had been held to consist virtually in the restoration of life to those who lay under the ban of death, but in Anselm's view it is regarded essentially and principally as a satisfaction for the sin of the whole human race [Baur, *Versohnung*], and as a sacrifice of infinite merit This equivalent of infinite merit for the infinity of man's transgression formed a marked distinction in the sequel between the Dominican and Franciscan, the Thomist and Scotist theology, according to which latter the merit of Christ's sacrifice consisted only in the Divine acceptance of it Anselm taught, in addition, that there was a satisfaction due on man's part before guilt could be removed, "necesse est ut omne peccatum satisfactio aut pœna sequatur" Works of righteousness represent this necessary condition, "ut qui per peccatum offenderat, per justitiam satisfaceret" The guilt of sin could only be atoned on the positive side by righteous works, or on the negative side by a subtraction of that eternal happiness which is the final cause of man's creation Anselm guards against Dualism by denying that Satan had acquired any right over the fallen race, though his power is wholly consistent with the Divine Justice. God is the sovereign Lord, and alone has a sovereign right over man and his tempter, who are in fact fellow-servants [*Cur Deus Homo*, i 7] Similarly, Robert of Pulleyne, Archdeacon of Rochester [A.D 1150], and praised by Bernard for soundness of doctrine, says that we were redeemed from the thraldom of Satan by the price of Christ's blood paid over, not to Satan, which Christ as God would never do, but, as Gregory of Nazianzum had already taught, to God, by Whose good pleasure man was manumitted and the Devil humbled It was thought a harmless subject of discussion in the schools how far Satan had reason to complain in being spoiled of his prey by the redemption of mankind

Anselm's adoption of the Augustinian maxim, "Fides præcedit intellectum," made it a favourite with the realistic school, "neque enim quæro intelligere ut credam, sed credo ut intelligam;" faith however meaning an intelligent belief, based upon the teaching of Scripture as interpreted by the Church, and such a faith is capable of still increasing light, "nisi credideritis non intelligatis" [Is vii 9] Yet there was a strain of mysticism that gave warmth to the theology of Anselm We must renounce the flesh, he said, and live up to the spirit before we can fathom the deep things of God, for "the natural man receiveth not the things of God" Practice and theory are so closely connected in matters of religion that a knowledge of God is impossible without the union of the two, moreover, where either is neglected, that which a man hath is taken away from him, the light becomes darkness, and how great is that darkness

In this way the theology of Anselm harmonized the two main branches into which it soon divaricated, the religion of the head and reason, and the religion of the heart and spirit, the dialectical and the mystical element These two principles were soon exemplified in Bernard of Clairvaux [d A D 1153], and Peter Abelard [d A D 1142] Of these two the latter was the exponent of pure reason, the speculative divine, the Conceptualist, the former was the enthusiastic devotee, the transcendental religionist, the Realist The highest aim of practical Christianity is the sanctification to God of every principle of the heart, but Bernard's was a yet more exalted aspiration, a superhuman yearning for absolute perfection, rapt contemplative devotion that left far behind the spiritual yearnings of ordinary humanity, and anticipated the glories of the life to come. This was the highest excellence of which human nature was capable "omnino maximus, qui spreto ipso usu rerum et sensuum, quantum quidem humanæ fragilitati fas est, non necessariis gradibus sed inopinatis excessibus avolare, interdum contemplando, ad illa sublimia consuevit" [Bern *de Consid* V i 3] It was an ecstatic penetration into heavenly places, as that of St Paul, "nam raptum potius fuisse, quam ascendisse, ipse perhibet" The way to attain such spiritual perfection is first to order the whole life suitably to it, and then to press on to the mark in prayer and piety of heart The relation of the spirit to divine knowledge is marked by him in the three factors, Opinion, Faith, and Perception Opinion occupies itself only with probability, but faith and perception are in possession of the truth Each of the three must keep within its own proper limitation, opinion must not degrade to its own level the high aspirations of faith, and faith must not dignify mere matters of opinion Opinion that dogmatizes is rashness, even as faith that wavers is weakness Faith is a spontaneous anticipation of the truth, perception is the clear and accurate knowledge of the Invisible It is not the degree of certainty that marks the difference between faith and perception but the degree of clearness, that which is still veiled to faith, from the very fact that it is an object of faith, is open as the eye of day to perception. "Fides non habet incertum, non magis quam intellectus, habet tamen involucrum, quod non intellectus" Faith cannot be made more certain of its objects, but it still needs the light of actual perception, and when that is vouchsafed nothing is wanting to blessedness Mystic as he was, his was not the mysticism that neglects the means of real spiritual progress He first raised his voice against the dry dulness of dialectical theology "Res divinas non disputatio comprehendit sed sanctitas," "orando facilius quam disputando et dignius Deus quæritur et invenitur" [Bern *in Cant* 8]

That which was really hateful to him was the dialectical folly that knows not its own really narrow limits, the latitudinarian unprinciple that maintains not the high and holy character of faith, the speculative restlessness that chills the warmth of spiritual religion, and knows nothing of simplicity and humility; and upon one and all of these points he differed widely from Peter Abelard, whose living conceit of his philosophical powers was only equalled by the extravagant encomium on his tombstone

"Cui soli patuit scibile quicquid erat"

Abelard's faults doubtless were patent to the eye of day, and Bernard saw in them a revival of Pelagian error, nor were his fears devoid of reason His *à priori* reasoning also on the doctrine of the Trinity led him into something very like Sabellianism He compared this highest mystery to the three parts of a syllogism that constitute one truth He acknowledges in it God as the highest good, the Father as Omnipotence, the Son as Wisdom, the Holy Spirit as Love, in all "eadem essentia, sicut eadem oratio est propositio assumptio et conclusio" In this there is no recognition of distinct Personality, though the error may have been an error of judgment rather than of faith

Abelard was early trained in dialectics under William of Champeaux In philosophy he was a Conceptualist, in religion a Rationalist. At the request of his hearers he wrote his "Introductio in Theologiam," designed as an introduction to the study of Scripture He defends in it the dialectical method, and complains of the increasing number of those who extol that kind of faith that yields an unreasoning assent to whatever is heard without examination, "qui facile credit levis est animo" [Ecclus xix 4]. The book was condemned by a papal legate at Soissons [A D 1121], and his own hands were compelled to cast it into the flames His progressive development of faith is suggestive of merit "de congruo" and "de condigno," of a slightly later date Thus he says that reason determines the soul in the direction of faith, but as yet it has no "merit" in the sight of God, love therefore raises it to such a trusting faith in God as Abraham had The evidences of religion are then examined, which give substance to faith, thence by the aid of the Holy Spirit follows the full assurance of faith in the invisible things of God. Dialectical training is necessary for defending the truth against those who make use of that method of attack, "alio modo non possumus nisi has quas noverunt rationes ipsorum artibus offeramus"

He is most earnest in declaring the necessity for a disinterested love, "habe caritatem et fac quicquid vis" was his favourite Augustinian maxim Man's justification from sin through the Atonement of Christ, which Anselm represented as an infinite equivalent for infinite guilt, amounting to an indefeasible claim on the Divine Justice, was placed by Abelard on the footing of love God's grace kindles that love in man in return for mercy through Christ, which effectually destroys sin, and with it the guilt of sin Love cannot exist without the faith that involves repentance, repentance therefore awakened by grace is the quality that leads to man's reconciliation with God It is also of antecedent efficacy, and procured pardon for the holy men of old, because "they who went before, and they who followed after, cried Hosanna to the Son of David" Even the Sibylline verses express a true faith, and the Deistical thesis of Tindale, "Christianity as Old as the Creation," received its first impulse from Abelard [*Abel et Helois Op* Paris, 1606, p 553] Penitent love, therefore, in Abelard's scheme makes that human satisfaction for sin which a return to righteousness effects according to Anselm sin according to the latter involves original guilt derived from Adam, Abelard limits it to individual transgression

Abelard's moral work, "Scito teipsum" contains the germ of Scholastic development on grace and free will The exciting cause of sin, or concupiscence, he pronounces to be free from guilt, but sin consists in the act of yielding to it If it be withstood it may be the handmaid of virtue, "quid enim magnum pro Deo facimus si nihil nostræ voluntati adversum toleramus sed magis quod volumus implemus" The Semi-Pelagianism of later Schoolmen dates from Abelard Another work that must have caused misgiving in the minds of many has come to light in the present generation, entitled "Sic et Non," "Yea and Nay" [Cousin, *Œuvres inédits d'Abélard*], it is a collection of "Sententiæ Patrum," arranged under a hundred and seventy-five heads, not exhibiting the consent of antiquity, which had been the aim of all preceding sententiary collectors and compilers of "Loci communes," but exposing the differential side of patristical theology, without any attempt to explain or in any way to account for the discordance His design seems to have been to shew that it is impossible to secure absolute unity in doctrinal statements, and that the Fathers are to be read in a free spirit, also to lead men to be careful how they brand every deviation from one standard with the name of heresy In his preface, however, he says simply that his object is to render the minds of men more acute, for Aristotle, who taught men *διαπορῆσαι καλῶς*, declares that there is a "real use in doubting" We have here for the first time the ancient sceptical *μέμνασο ἀπιστεῖν* commended as a principle for Christians

Some years had now elapsed since the publication of his incomplete "Introductio," and in the meantime Abelard's public instruction had been plentifully noted down by his admirers, and more than one work was in circulation under his name, but without his authority The "Sententiæ Abælardi," published by Professor Rheinwald from the Munich MSS [A D 1835], appear to have been such a compilation William, Abbot of St Thierri, accused Abelard of heresy in a letter to Bernard of Clairvaux The works of Abelard, he said, cross the Alps and the seas, and his pupils are to be found among the most powerful [cardinals] in the court of Rome The works principally indicated were the Theology, the Sentences, the "Scito teipsum," and his commentary on the Romans Abelard having been informally condemned at the provincial council of Sens [A D 1140], then appealed to Rome, where he had many friends Bernard, however, forestalled him by a letter to Pope Innocent II, in which the several counts of heresy against Abelard were set forth [Ep 190, Op Bern *Massil*, 1719, i 650] the principal being that he encouraged open discussions on the Trinity among half-trained pupils, and that he brought down the deep things of God to the level of reason, as mere matters of fancy and opinion "Quid enim magis contra rationem quam ratione rationem conari transcendere? Et quid magis contra fidem quam credere nolle quicquid non possis ratione attingere?" Abelard set out for Rome, but had not proceeded further than Lyons when sentence of condemnation reached him, his writings were ordered to be burnt, and himself immured in a cloister He took refuge with his true-hearted friend Peter the Venerable, Abbot of Clugny, and having been transferred by him for his health to the priory of Châlons on the Saone, he there died, April 21st, A D 1142

The condemnation of Abelard was a severe check to Scholastic rationalism, the dialectical system was woven too closely into the texture of school learning to be easily displaced, but its use was tempered down as theology gained a more earnest and practical tone The canons of the church of St Victoire at Paris impressed this character on the divinity of the Schools Hugo [V. Blankenburg] à St. Victoire, born at Ypres at the close of the eleventh century, followed in the steps of Anselm, and taught that theological knowledge issues objectively from Scripture and tradition, and subjectively in a pure faith, which leads on to perception, faith occupying the middle position indicated by Bernard, being above opinion but beneath perception All propositions as being either "ex ratione," or respectively "secundum," "supra," and "contra rationem," were either necessary truths, or as propositions probable, marvellous, or false and incredible Natural religion falls under the second of these categories, "secundum rationem," revealed religion under the third, "supra rationem" The relation of reason to faith thenceforth became fixed in the Schools Hugo checked the excessive application of dialectics, and raised the mystical element to a recognised position, which, leaving the deeper doctrines of Christianity, touched the spirit with the fire of enthusiasm The canons of the Abbey of St Victoire were all more or less mystical in their theology, and taught their followers to withdraw their thoughts from the works of God in outward nature, and to fix them upon the operation of God within in the soul Yet there is a Jewish anthropomorphism in their language with respect to the Divine Being, and a familiarity in handling sacred names that is scarcely reverent. As contrasted with the wrangling of the schools, Mysticism represented the peacefulness of the cloister As regards the malice of the Tempter, Hugo agreed with Bernard and the Fathers Satan, he said, offended God by corrupting his servant Adam, Adam offended God by allowing himself to be seduced, Satan offended man by deceiving him thenceforth man was the Devil's bondman, unjustly as regards the Almighty, but justly with respect to himself as transgressor Man could not set himself free from the Devil's power, therefore God worked out his salvation. But an atonement was required for the offence This could only be by man's offering of perfect righteousness, and by suffering a punishment adequate to the offence In himself man was utterly incapable of doing this Therefore God was made man, the Son offered His perfect righteousness for the Father's acceptance, and suffered death in man's stead, thereby redeeming man from him that hath the power of death [*de Sacr* 4] Like Abelard, he traces out the effect though not the substance of the Atonement in the three theological graces—Faith, Hope, and Love—that it quickens within the soul; and the Saviour most truly is "Via in exemplo, Veritas in promisso, et Vita in præmio" [Liebner's *Hugo de S Vict* 417]

Hitherto no systematic body of divinity had been put forth, the Monologium of Anselm being the nearest approach The Summa of William of Champeaux, Abelard's preceptor, has not come down to us, but that of Hugo has The principal doctrines of the Church are there laid down and confirmed by texts of Scripture and patristical references, the questions and doubts of contempo-

Schoolmen

ranes are then solved, and a conclusion drawn in accordance with Scripture and tradition His other work on the Sacraments, the most important of early scholasticism, treats the subject in a more flowing and connected style, but not being crammed with quotations from traditional authorities, it was not much read These two works, however, exercised a very visible influence over Peter Lombard and Thomas of Aquino, while his mysticism communicated itself to kindred spirits in Bonaventura and Gerson

His pupil and successor, Richard, of the same foundation, was more deep and original in his views, and richer in speculative thought, though he fell short of his teacher in moderation and simplicity of character He first reduced mysticism into something like system Theology with him, as with his predecessors, was the centre of all other sciences, the bright star that gave its character to the entire constellation of human learning The spirit of the time, as seen in his work, was to bind more closely the tie that connected Positive Theology with dialectics, and as a subsidiary aid to this latter element of the Trivium, to complete the work of the Sententiary writers, Vincent of Lerins, (in his Commonitorium,) Gennadius of Marseilles, and Isidore of Seville, in the beginning of the seventh century All such work, however, was surpassed by the "Sentences" of Peter Lombard, at first theological lecturer and then Bishop of Paris [A D 1159, died 1164] This work constituted him by pre-eminence Magister Sententiarum, and gave inexhaustible material for commentators The compilation was an enormous boon to the hair-splitting dialectician, from the number of analogies and discrepancies, the questions and answers, theses and antitheses, positions and counter-positions that it helped to develope and to solve It made scholastic formalism yet more dry, and while it raised to its highest position the influence of authority and tradition, it threatened to fossilize for ever the rich products of theology The character of Peter Lombard as a divine may be told as easily by this book as a geologist can describe the outward form and habits of an extinct species from a single bone He was opposed to Platonism, and had a thorough dislike for philosophy with its impertinent "scrutatores et garruli ratiocinatores," he cared not to follow in the track of those who hoped ardently to reconcile its teaching with theological truth The only truth that he knew was to be elicited from Scripture and tradition, and their differences, if such existed, were to be adjusted by dialectical subtlety His work, perhaps, had an especial bearing on Abelard's Pyrrhonist compilation, the "Sic et ita" It may be noted that the Roman theory of the Sacraments was fixed by Lombard

As regards the Atonement, he reproduced Origen's idea of the Tempter foiled by the Sacrifice of the Cross εἰς ὃν ἐμπέπτωκεν ὁ διάβολος ἀγνοῶν, εἰ γὰρ ἔγνω, οὐκ ἂν αὐτὸν κύριον τῆς δόξης ἐσταύρωσε [Orig *in Ps* xxxv 8], the cross having been compared to a hunter's net Gregory of Nyssa carried out the notion to an irreverent length, in saying that a deception was put upon Satan by the Incarnation, and that he was overreached as it were in his dominion over the souls of men, that he was taken as some leviathan of the deep, human nature being the bait, and the Divinity the hook [*Or Catech* 22-26, see Greg M *Moral* 33-37] The idea became a favourite one "Illusus est diabolus morte Domini quasi avis," says Isidore of Seville [*Sent* i 24] "Quid fecit Redemptor captivatori nostro? Tetendit ei muscipulam crucem suam, posuit ibi quasi escam sanguinem suum" [Pet Lomb *Sent* iii 19] Peter Lombard made a near approach to the doctrine of the Atonement as set forth by Abelard, and whereas no greater proof could be given of God's love for man than the Atonement provided for his sin, so its natural issue is in the love that it kindles within man's soul, and it is this love that has an atoning power "Accendimur ad diligendum Deum, qui pro nobis tanta fecit, et per hoc justificamur, id est, soluti a peccatis justi efficimur Mors ergo Christi nos justificat, dum per eam caritas excitatur in cordibus nostris" [*Sent* iii dist 19, A] Sin is the bond with which Satan held men, and faith is its solvent "Si ergo rectæ fidei intuitu in illum respicimus a vinculis diaboli solvimur id est a peccatis" [*ibid*] Absolution was not authoritative as a priestly act, but declaratory "Non autem hoc sacerdotibus concessit, quibus tamen tribuit potestatem solvendi et ligandi, id est ostendendi homines ligatos vel solutos" [*Sent* iv 18, F]

In the latter half of the twelfth century, Walter of St Victor endeavoured to recall the schools from dialectical subtleties to a more spiritual theology, and inveighed against the four "Labyrinths," meaning the logicians of France, viz. Abelard and Gilbert de la Poirée, Peter Lombard and his namesake of Poitiers, of whom he speaks as though they were possessed of the spirit of all evil—"uno spiritu Aristotelico afflatos" Joachim of Floris, rapt in Apocalyptic mysticism, and John of Salisbury, the friend of Thomas à Becket, statesman and natural philosopher, attacked the same system from different points and on varying grounds But in vain The schools continued to resound with jangling divines, and commentaries on the Sentences were multiplied, till at the end of the first quarter of the thirteenth century those translations of Aristotle and of Græco-Arab philosophy appeared, to which allusion has already been made. The schools also now became the peculium of the Dominican and Franciscan orders, who from this time exercised a powerful influence over the theology of the future

The Dominican Order took its rise in the commencement of the thirteenth century from Domingo [A D 1170-1221], a native of Calaruega in Old Castile, and of the Guzman family He grieved to see the defection from the Church that was setting in The simplicity of the Albigenses and Cathari contrasted strongly with the outward pomp and pride of the Roman hierarchy The monastic orders had departed widely from the pious spirit in which they had been founded Dominicus therefore determined to stem the tide of evil by a return to Apostolical simplicity, and to gain the masses by founding an order that should have something of the zeal and self-devotion of St Paul. Having organized a body of preachers, he finally obtained a Papal Bull for the creation of the Dominican Order, A.D 1216, as the "Fratres Prædicatores" The device of the order, a mastiff bearing a blazing torch in his mouth, was intended to symbolize its watchfulness in guarding the fold of Christ from wolves and robbers, and its zeal in spreading the light of the Gospel, but afterwards its enemies saw in it an emblem of Dominican tenacity of purpose in tracking down victims for the Inquisition, and of its appropriation to itself of an universal censorship, as the stolen bone of the dog The establishment of a house at Paris under the name of St Jacques obtained for the order the name of Jacobins An office that Dominicus filled in the Court of Rome, that of principal preacher and master of the palace, including the censorship of all religious writings, descended as an heirloom in the order, and gave to it immense influence Simplicity of life and the ministry of preaching were the distinguishing principles of the order In the fifth year of its existence [A D 1220], absolute poverty and mendicancy were made binding on it The Dominican Order was mainly instrumental in establishing Scholastic Theology upon Church authority and the dicta of St Augustine It was Thomist in its theology, and Conceptualist in its philosophy, in both of which points it was fiercely antagonized by the rival order of St Francis, who were Scotists and Nominalists So also the dogma of the Immaculate Conception of the Blessed Virgin was warmly taken up by the Franciscans, and as stoutly resisted on the score of novelty by the Dominicans Dominicus died A D 1221, and was canonized A D. 1233.

The Franciscan Order took its rise from Francis, son of a wealthy merchant of Assisi [A D. 1182-1226] As Anthony, following the Saviour's counsel to the rich young man, sold all he had and took up his cross to follow Him, so Francis, copying the Saviour's example, collected first a body of disciples, and then sent them forth two and two, without scrip or purse, staff or sandal, that they might, by the simplicity of preaching, bring in souls to Christ. The Church could only be restored to its pristine purity by the sanctifying effect of poverty. The WALDENSES had gained a firm hold upon the affection of the people by their preaching and poverty, and lost ground could only be recovered for the Church by similar self-abasement An order also which really maintained the poverty that was a fundamental principle of every monastery, exercised by its example a reforming efficacy on the rest, as well as on the Church at large, and it was regarded with special favour by the Court of Rome until the time of Ockham An unconditional loyalty to the Holy See was a part of the Franciscan vow The Bull that founded the order under the lowly name of "Fratres Minores" was issued [A D 1223] three years before the death of Francis

Both orders, therefore, were based on the same fundamental principles, and both were content to minister for the good of others, rather than aim at any higher reward for themselves, but there were marked points of difference The Dominican made the conversion of heretics and infidels his main object Evangelical poverty was not so much an essential element of his order as a serviceable aid for work, and that which the tender, sympathetic, imaginative Francis made the very life-blood of his system was adopted by the more stern and coldly calculating Dominic as his best "methodus operandi" The higher classes choosing their spiritual advisers from the monks of St Dominic, caused it gradually to lose sight of poverty as anything more than a nominal attribute of the order The character of the principals also communicated itself to the two houses The Dominican was the hard, inflexible propagandist of Latin orthodoxy, cold, calm, and self-possessed, the many-sided man of the world, the terrible agent also of the Inquisition in its day The Franciscan, with greater geniality and fervour, was the popular religionist, and had always a word and work of sympathising kindliness for all The confessional was his stronghold, as it was in after years of the Jesuit, and the same work that the Dominican performed by open discussion was achieved more systematically by the Franciscan, who was in possession of the affections of the people Oxford was Franciscan to the heart

Neither of these orders had any such literary character as the order of St Benedict but what they lacked in learning they abundantly made up in mother wit, sharpening the intellect with perpetual discussion among themselves, and making an active onslaught upon heresy outside the cloister They maintained at the same time the character of scholastic discussion The veneration of the Franciscan for his founder was second only to his love for the Saviour, the servant was the close representative to him of the Master, and the reputed impression of the stigmata, or five wounds of the Crucified Lord, on the person of St Francis caused that veneration to deepen into something almost more than veneration Hase, however [*Franz v. Assisi ein Heiligenbild,* 121, 143], has shewn that this myth first originated in a letter communicating the founder's death to the order in France, written by the Vicar-General Elias of Cortona, that it was before unknown, and that either the statement rested on no foundation whatever, or that the General himself impressed the marks on the dead body of Francis as he kept watch and ward over the sacred remains

Alexander of Hales, near Gloucester, who died A D 1245, founder of the Franciscan School, was the first of the "Seraphic Order" who retained the title of Doctor he was specially the "Irrefragable." Among his pupils were Bonaventura and Duns Scotus His "Summa Theologiæ" was written by command of Innocent IV, and treated of the Holy Trinity, the Visible and Invisible Creation, the Fall, Sin, the Incarnation He first exhibits traces of Arab influence, and often cites in his "Summa" Avicenna, Algazel, and Averroes as philosophers of high authority

The work was still unfinished at his death, which determines the date at which the Moorish writers of Spain had begun to affect Scholasticism He combined many of the characteristics of preceding Schoolmen, Anselm being his principal guide His work is highly mystical, yet full of dialectical subtlety and trifling It may be noted that he introduced several of the distinctive tenets of mediæval Romanism His "treasury of grace," through the sales of indulgences, eventually led to the Reformation, and the dogma of the Immaculate Conception dates from him He also gave a further developement to the Pelagianizing notions of Abelard The doctrine that subjects of refractory kings may consider themselves absolved from their allegiance, a weapon of such terrible keenness in the hand of the Jesuit, also had its origin in his "Summa" Something of the same kind may be found in the treatise "De Regimine Principum" of Aquinas

Albertus Magnus [A D 1193-1280], of the noble house of Bollstadt, the "Universal Doctor," but known also by the soubriquet of "Simia Aristotelis," made a much wider application of Aristotelian principle. He and his pupil, Thomas of Aquino [A D 1244], were Eclectic rather than Realist or Nominalist, and may be considered as the true founders of the Scholastic system, the second period of which now commences The foundation of Dominican Scholasticism, generally ascribed to Thomas Aquinas, from whom its partisans were termed Thomists, was in fact the work of Albert, who survived his pupil by six years His great guide was Avicenna, but Averroes also contributed a contingent His treatise, "De Unitate Intellectus contra Averroistas," was written at Rome by order of Alexander IV [A D 1255] The individual responsibility of each soul is a scriptural truth, but he treats it as a philosophical problem, and having produced thirty syllogistic arguments in favour of those who held that there was but one collective soul of man after death, he overpowers them with thirty-six others in maintenance of the orthodox belief, shewing a balance of six arguments in favour of the received faith Albert rejected the peripatetic tenet of the coeternity of God and matter But he allowed a Platonic first matter, existent in the mind of God from everlasting, which in due time received substantive existence Yet he was no Pantheist In the same ideal sense, time and the heavens and universal intelligence were eternal, human intelligence being an efflux from the Divine, though distinct from it, and endued with a like perfect freedom of will By exercise of the speculative faculty man approaches God, and becomes "Deo quodammodo similis," he then can kindle in others a divine intelligence, which is the knowledge (scire) that all desire, and in which contemplative perfection consists His philosophy was thus an eclectic transcendentalism His theology as a "science" is built upon an objective faith flowing from the "supermundane illumination" vouchsafed to the Fathers as the channel of tradition Yet, from another point of view, faith as a subjective quality results in that perception of the truth which is the sum of human happiness Theology and philosophy should harmonize, both being the result of experience either in things natural or supranatural The supranatural expansion of the soul towards God shews that Averroist principle of an universal emanation from and return to God, which led Amalric of Bena and David of Dinant into Pantheism Something similar had appeared in the teaching of Hugo and Alexander of Hales with respect to "pura naturalia" and superadded grace, but they now received a character and point from Albert, the authority of whose great name gave them a determinate influence upon the theology of his successors, just as his philosophy often threw off suggestive thoughts that bore their fruit in after generations

He constructed a head of brass that could speak, which so horrified his pupil Thomas that he dashed it in pieces as a Satanic delusion He was an ardent student of alchemy, and his researches brought to light many highly important chemical products. Sulphate of iron, nitrate of silver, cinnabar, a sublimate of mercury and sulphur, caustic potash, azurium, a triple compound by fusion of sulphur mercury and sal ammoniac, were stumbled upon as he toiled over his retorts and alembics He first explained the nature of aerolites, and something very like gunpowder was known to him, he also taught potters to glaze their wares with minium, the red oxide of lead Hence his name was in the mouth of all, and having to lecture at Paris for three years, the concourse was so great that he was compelled to give his instruction in the open air The locality is still pointed out as the Place Maubert [Ma Alberti], while a neighbouring street is known as the Rue de Maître Aubert Some years after his death his tomb was opened, and his bones were distributed as relics among the princes and principal religious establishments of Christendom

His pupil, Thomas Aquinas [A D 1224-1274], born at Sicca Rocca, near Aquino, a place of classical memory, as having been the birthplace of Juvenal [*Sat* iii 319], was the impersonation of all that is good and venerable in Scholasticism He, as a Dominican, was the "Angelic Doctor" "If," as Bishop Hampden has said [*Encycl Metrop* xi 793], "penetration of thought, comprehensiveness of views, exactness the most minute, an ardour of inquiry the most keen, a patience of pursuit the most unwearied, are among the merits of a philosopher, then may Aquinas dispute even the first place among the candidates for supremacy in speculative science" His Aristotelian philosophy was formed upon Averroes, cordially as he detested Averroism [Renan, *Averr* ii 7] But it was an eclectic combination of Aristotle and Plato, through the medium of Augustine, together with traces of mysticism from the Pseudo-Dionysius. His "Summa," marking the culminating glory of Scholasticism, has always been held in the highest estimation, and Popes of different ages have declared that his writings are perfect and free from error. His close adherence also to Augustinian doctrine on the questions of Grace and Predestination and Final Perseverance, from which his adversary Duns Scotus swerved, has made him always a model of orthodoxy At the Council of Trent his Summa was placed by the side of the Holy Scriptures as a guide for the decisions of the assembled Fathers As regards the question of Universals, he was an eclectic, they were in his opinion phantasms of the intellect He did not altogether discard the emanational theory of his master Albert, though he handles it with much care, as perceiving its tendency towards Pantheism The universe, he says, proceeded from the energy (actus purus) and the will of God, but the will of God was not the first cause for will is itself the principle of Intelligent Mind, and the two coincide in the Absolute, both revealing themselves in creation as Infinite Love Reason may demonstrate in natural theology the being and unity of God, but not His essence, relatively, but not absolutely, this knowledge, to be acquired by natural means, he terms the "preamble of faith" and "prima credibilia," but supranatural vision can only be helped by supranatural means, such as direct revelation and Scripture Reason cannot demonstrate the objects of faith Theology as a theoretical science and philosophy may go to work in the same way to produce conviction, but their first principles are widely different, philosophy proceeds from axioms that are more or less cognizable by the senses, theology proceeds from articles of faith, from whence the truth is gradually unfolded, and the primary credenda of theology are her axioms Both proceed forth from God, and are referable to His wisdom, theology therefore can no more contravene the dictates of right reason than philosophy can really discredit the theological verities that it cannot fathom "Gratia naturam non tollit sed perficit" The objects of faith, moreover, are the more readily apprehended, in that they are wholly in harmony with the light of man's first undimmed reason, they are "res sensibiles," that retain "aliquale vestigium in se divinæ imitationis" But there must always remain a sharp line of distinction between what may be known by reason and what by revelation in theological matters, these latter may be "supra" but never "contra rationem" Tradition rests not its claims to be heard on mere prescription—there is an undercurrent of reason that determines its true direction Yet Thomas Aquinas is not altogether free from the scholastic failing of making faith a mere objective quality, *i e* an intellectual and traditional faith, and of curbing reason in its high prerogative of leading on the current of human thought His Areopagite transcendentalism gives a warmer colouring to principles that hitherto shewed themselves as mere dicta of dry Scholasticism

His view of the Atonement agrees with that of Anselm, but he limits its application to Original Sin, which gave rise to the wording of our second Article as adopted from the Augsburg Confession He assigns also to man's unaided power an efficacy that Augustine would have termed Pelagian God's offer of salvation is free to all mankind, as already stated by Anselm, and the Incarnation was wholly a matter of necessity, as entirely congruous with the Divine Nature [*Sum* iii qu 1, art 1] For God is good, and He must, as bound by the law of His Being, vouchsafe His goodness in its most perfect form to man, hence the Incarnation was a necessary event. The Son also as the Word and protideal form of all has a necessary relation with the creature, it became Him therefore to enter into personal relation with the creature by means of the Incarnation [*ib* qu 3, art 8]

The Summa of Thomas stands out, like the poems of Dante in the next century, grand in the colossal proportions and well-balanced relations of its several parts "It would, as it might seem, occupy a whole life of the most secluded study to write, almost to read" [Milman, *Lat Chr* vi 451], extending as it does over twelve hundred folio pages It nowhere contravenes the received theology of the Church of Rome, and where freedom of thought appears to swing loose from the faith, yet the interests of the latter are never prejudiced The Summa is divided into three main parts, of which the second is subdivided into the Prima Secundæ and Secunda Secundæ The first part establishes the claim of theology to be regarded as a science capable of demonstrative proof, to which every other science is ancillary, and proceeds to treat of the Divine Nature, Providence, and Predestination, the creation, visible and invisible, and human nature in relation to the general scheme The second part in its first section considers man as a moral being, and as the recipient of divine grace, involving the questions of free will, original sin, and justification Justification consists of three particulars—1 Remission of sins, 2 Infusion of grace, 3 Faith that moves the soul towards God as the author of justification, and is "informis" as yet—aversion from sin being the spontaneous act of recovered freedom of will. Justification is thus a movement "de contrario in contrarium," a transmutation "de statu injustitiæ ad statum justitiæ." The second section is the complement of the former, and is the most important of the entire work, as a grand exposition of Christian ethics It analyzes the complex elements of man's moral nature in a manner worthy of his great master Aristotle, grouping the graces as theological and ethical, as infused and acquired,—the sevenfold gifts of the Spirit the theological virtues being Faith, Hope, and Charity, the ethical comprising the cardinal virtues, Justice, Prudence, Fortitude, Temperance The third part deals with the doctrines of the Incarnation and of the seven Sacraments of the Latin Church two subjects that are inseparable from each other, the Eucharist conveying the very substance of Christ to the faithful communicant, the rest in a subordinate degree exhibiting a participation of His grace in varying mode. An analogy is marked out between the seven Graces and the Sacraments, each member in the one system being the correlative of something similar in the other Thus baptism, as the remedy of original sin, corresponds with Faith, extreme unction, as the remission of venial sin, with Hope; the Holy Eucharist, as removing the penal consequences of transgression, with Charity And so with respect to the other Graces, prudence is represented by Holy Orders as the remedy of ignorance; justice or righteousness by penance, the supplemental safeguard of contrition, and the ordained means of obtaining remission of deadlier sins, temperance by matrimony, as a check to inordinate desire, fortitude by confirmation, as the remedy of weakness

The Summa concludes by comparing the two main phases of religious life, the contemplative and the active, and while, under the guidance of Aristotle the former is preferred, an ecclesiastical direction is given to the preference, and the monastic life is shewn to be of all the most perfect

This truly great work has done more than any other to fix the exact meaning of theological terms, and if due allowance be made for the peculiarities of Roman theology, it will always be a basis for the studies of the divine that is at once deep, solid, and vast

Bonaventura, or Giovanni di Fidanza [A D 1221-1274], of the Franciscan Order, was the contemporary of Thomas, having been born three years before him, but dying in the same year, just as he had been preferred to the Cardinalate, when his funeral was attended by a Pope, an Emperor, and a King He was known as the "Seraphic Doctor," the distinctive title of his order, as in the case of Aquinas, being appropriated to its most illustrious member He was a follower of Aristotelian ideas, yet Plato and Dionysius had a preponderating influence, which shewed itself in weaning him from an excessive attention to dry dialectics, and in giving a practical fervour to his theology, with him a science of action He philosophized only so far as philosophy coincided with theology, the return to God of the soul tainted with original sin was his thesis The complete devotion of the soul to God was the idea that chiefly inspired him, and a single-hearted life in Christ after the complete subjugation of every selfish principle. He united in himself the scholastic and mystic, the first supplying the form, the latter the substance of his theology But there was nothing extravagant in his mysticism There are certain bounds in its heavenward aspirations that the soul cannot pass The light of the soul and intellect is fourfold There is the external light that guides the intellect to the knowledge of science, and the light of sense that enables us to comprehend the external world in its various phases, the light of reason that leads the soul to appreciate the verities of the intellectual world, and the light of grace that reveals to man virtue in her holy beauty, and universals as they exist in God Into this light man must struggle at whatever sacrifice and disregard of the other inferior varieties of illumination; and in the end be absorbed into the Absolute One Without exactly touching Pantheism, his opinions tended manifestly in that direction

Raymund Lull [A D 1234-1315], the "Doctor Illuminatus," left writings which, like those of Bonaventura, are full of practical piety [see Neander, *Allg K Gesch* x 597-602, Hamb 1845], but he formed the impossible idea of establishing certain rules, or an "ars generalis," whereby the truth might be elicited in theology and every existing science It shews that a desire for reform was beginning to take hold on men's minds In substance the idea of his "ars generalis" was a syncretism of Greek Christian and Averroist philosophy, the latter element having full weight given to it from a hope of effecting by it the conversion of the Moors He was an ardent teacher of the Immaculate Conception, for unless there had been complete freedom from sin, "sive actuali sive originali," the Word could not have been Incarnate of the Blessed Virgin It was the Immaculate Conception that prepared the way for God made Flesh "Sic præparavit viam Incarnationis per Sanctificationem, sicut sol diem per auroram" [in lib ii *Sent* qu 96]

Lull was a pupil of Duns Scotus, and on one occasion making a gesture of dissent from that which was enounced "ex cathedra," the lecturer in a pique bade him parse Dominus, thinking to expose his ignorance, "Dominus quæ pars?" to which he received the reply, "Dominus non pars sed totum" Lull afterwards wrote an ontological treatise entitled "Dominus quæ pars?"

Duns Scotus [A D 1274-1308] was born in the North of England, in the year in which Thomas and Bonaventura died He died of apoplexy (though he was stated to have been buried with too much haste by the monks) at Cologne Having only completed his thirty-fourth year he must have written a folio volume of 800 pages annually from his twentieth year The words inscribed on his tomb give his history

> "Scotia me genuit, Anglia me suscepit,
> Gallia me docuit, Colonia me tenuit"

Oxford had the honour of being his earliest instructor, where he studied the exact sciences of the Quadrivium His lectures at Paris were crowded by thousands. Duns Scotus started, like his predecessors, from an unwavering faith in the truth of ecclesiastical doctrine, but he made a nearer approach to the School of St Victor than to the systems of either Anselm or Aquinas He was the great authority for the Franciscan, as Thomas was for the Dominican School Though the main frame-work of his system was Aristotelian through the various translations that were now before the world, yet it was really Platonic Theology with him was equally a science with philosophy, but they worked collaterally and by no means in unison with each other His theology was purely practical, "operatio eorum quæ persuadentur" Original sin is communicated by natural propagation "ex fomite," its punishment, if unremoved by baptism, is deprivation of the Beatific Vision [*Sent* ii 32] Concupiscence is connatural in man, and is not the substance of original sin

The use of dialectical reasoning, worked up to a more subtle point in him than in any of his predecessors, obtained for him the name of "Doctor subtilis," though his opponents fixed the name of "Quodlibetarius" upon him, in allusion to his method of stating the pro and con of important arguments, and leaving his hearers to draw the conclusion for themselves He gave fresh life to Realism The germ of more modern thought is often to be found in Duns Scotus Unity of substance, plurality in its manifestation, was the formula of Realism at the end as at the commencement of its course in the Scholastic age "Nulla in essentia diversitas, sed sola multitudine accidentium diversitas," are the words of William of Champeaux Descartes and Spinoza reproduced the idea Duns repeated from Avicembron the notion that every form of existence is material, and Hobbes adopted it from him He also indicated the inductive principle in anticipation of Bacon and Newton. He is thus the main connecting link between the philosophy of antiquity and of more recent times His philosophy is inconsistent with a steady orthodoxy, earnest as he was in his endeavour to express himself as a zealous Catholic He was in fact the father of more recent scepticism, and while he paved the way for future Pantheism, he gave a Pelagian tone to doctrines of grace that ill agree with the severe orthodoxy that he affected His metaphysics were obscure and did no harm to the many, his words in general carried a Catholic sound, and he was safe At length Dominican jealousy was aroused by his teaching, and the "angelic order" rose as one man to defend their sainted Thomas against his strictures and the wars of the rival schools lasted from that time till the Reformation had become an established fact. The resolution of Scholasticism was unconsciously prepared by Duns Scotus and his rationalizing tendencies

As regards the atonement Duns Scotus combats the position of Thomas, but adopted from Anselm, and followed by Pope Clement XI in the Bull *Unigenitus*, that the merit of the Passion and Death of Christ being infinite, was an adequate satisfaction for the infinite demerit of sin The merit of Christ, he says, pertained to His human nature, and was therefore finite But it was a sufficient atonement for it was accepted of God, and was therefore good This acceptation theory was also followed by Ockham and the later Nominalists To speak of sin as an infinite evil he termed a Manichean notion, for it makes it equal with Him Whom it offends The Scotist theory is in direct antagonism with that of Anselm He even states that a mere man (de possibili dico), if born without sin, as was Christ, and the recipient of the highest degree of grace, might have worked out the annihilation of guilt as well as an eternity of glory, for even under the present condition of things the Blessed Virgin and the Saints "meruerunt pro nobis" Nay, each man now might make satisfaction for himself, inasmuch as every man receives the gift of primary grace (in distinction from the secondary grace of repentance after baptism), and if without his own good this grace is vouchsafed to him, whereby he merits blessedness, he might also merit the annihilation of guilt, "potuit etiam meruisse deletionem culpæ." Hence he concludes that the Christian scheme of redemption was not absolutely "necessary," except by the divine ordinance, which ruled that so it should be [*In Sent dist* 19, pp 428-430], and made it necessary, "necessitate consequentiæ," therefore we are the more bound to love Him, "ideo multum tenemur ei" In a spirit of Rationalism, he says that Christ, seeing the depth of sin into which the Jewish people had sunk, "maluit mori quam tacere, et ideo pro justitia mortuus est." The whole work of redemption, therefore, is made by him essential only as being the divine plan, and he departs "toto cœlo" from the position of Aquinas, that the death of Christ is "satisfactio non solum sufficiens sed superabundans," by reason of the infinite worth of that life, "quæ erat vita Dei et hominis" The question then falls back upon the absolute will of God On that will everything depends Good is not good but as decreed by the Absolute He does not love the good because they are good, but they are good because He loves them By that will the sacrifice of the death of Christ was ordained from eternity and human intellect is here estopped The Thomist ontology, on the other hand, taught that the absolute goodness of the Deity did not depend conditionally on the absolute will, but that the absolute will of God was based on the attribute of absolute goodness In the will of the Deity were implied at the same time absolute freedom, and yet absolute dependence on the laws of His own being God "cannot deny Himself." And the Son became Incarnate that He might harmonize by mediation these conflicting attributes

The Thomists were always distinguished by their steady maintenance of Church principle and opposition to rationalizing heresies In philosophy they were eclectical Conceptualists, and followed the Aristotelian theory of universals, while the Scotists were Platonic Realists With the first the intellect determined the will, "intellectus invenitur superior motor" [Thom Aq *Summa c gent* iii 26, 1, see also *Prim sec* qu 19, art 10], with the latter the will was the supreme motive power of the inner man, "voluntas est motor in toto regno animæ, et omnia obediunt sibi" [Duns Sc in *Sent* ii dist. 42, qu 4, 2] Hence, in theology the Thomists took their stand upon the necessity for an intellectual knowledge of the truth, and of God as the first cause of all things They were close followers of the Augustinian view of sin and grace, yet with a toning down of its harsher features, and with a lofty moral involving the element of human merit as Augustine never would have admitted it The Scotists referred the gift of grace to Divine predestination based upon prescience, and affirmed that man had sufficient strength left after the Fall to achieve his first "meritum de congruo," they described original sin in a Semi-Pelagian way as inseparable from the finite, and grace as the naturally ordained development of spiritual life They allowed the power of the keys to be efficacious to the remission of eternal as well as temporal punishment, but the priest exercised the power only as an implement in the hand of God, who could give efficacy to baptism even though administered by an angel of darkness The Thomist recognised in the merit of Christ an infinite worth, by reason of his Divine nature (satisfactio superabundans), the Scotist ascribed to it a value decreed by the Father to be effective (acceptatio gratuita), making it to appear that Christ died only for the sake of truth and justice, and as a declaratory act of God's purposes of mercy

A new element of diversity was introduced by the greater attention that was paid to Biblical learning, this also helped to weaken the position of Scholasticism As in the twelfth century, Peter, precentor of Paris, and Othlone had returned to scriptural exposition, so in the thirteenth Roger Bacon [born A D 1214], a Franciscan, and styled for the geniality of his disposition and depth of his attainments in physical science, "Doctor mirabilis," claimed for Scripture its high authority as the ultimate appeal in matters of controversy [*Opus Majus*, A D 1266, and *Ep de Laude S Scr*] He endeavoured to call men back, laymen as well as clerics, from a servile following of tradition to the Scriptures in the original languages He ventured even to impugn the critical accuracy of the Vulgate, and atoned for his offence by a ten years' incarceration, from whence he only emerged to die [A.D 1284] The Dominican Hugo of St Cher was more fortunate, for he received the Cardinal's hat [A D 1244], though he had ventured to purify the text of the Vulgate by a comparison of Hebrew, Greek, and Latin MSS He also composed a concordance that fixed the present arrangement of the Bible according to chapter and verse, and a scriptural commentary, "Postillæ in universa Biblia" He died A D 1260

Philosophy in all its phases had now occupied the schools from the ninth to the fourteenth century Metaphysics had been introduced by Erigena, the question of universals by William of Champeaux and Roscellin, logic by Anselm and Abelard Then the sudden infusion of Aristotelian ideas put an entirely new face on scholastic teaching, and germs of thought were quickened that were destined to emancipate the human intellect, and bear fruit in after centuries in the Novum Organum of Bacon These results were powerfully helped forward by the Nominalism of William of Ockham in Surrey, the "Doctor invincibilis" He was one of the great mediæval names of which Merton College may be justly proud, a pupil of Duns Scotus, and by religious profession a Franciscan "The wittiest" [Hooker], and "the hardest and severest intellectualist" of all the Schoolmen [Milman], the "carus magister" of Luther, and "deliciæ quondam nostræ" of Melanchthon, Ockham was, according to Selden, the best writer on ecclesiastical power before the revival of literature He was the Rupert of the schools; having formed his own independent line, he pressed on with a vigour that bore down every obstacle, and combated every false pretension though backed by the enormous power of the Church of Rome He was at the same time remarkably clear-headed and acute, and true to the hardy and independent spirit that had always distinguished the opponents of Realism from the days of Roscellin and Abelard A deep metaphysician, a keen logician, he was at the same time an uncompromising foe to the temporal power and unapostolic luxury of Popedom [Ochami *Defensorium*, Brown's *Fasciculus*, ii 440] Yet he was far more reverent than any of his predecessors in the handling of sacred subjects, and resolutely refused to enter into those ontological discussions with respect to the Divine Nature that so frequently gave to the schools the air of bewildered folly

The various rays of light that struggled through the darkness of the two preceding centuries were focussed in Ockham, and from him projected into the dim future His Nominalism struck a blow at the whole scholastic system from which it never recovered, though it established a current of rationalistic philosophy that led in the first instance to the Reformation, unfortunately also to the free handling of theological subjects by later Deists and rationalizing divines Hobbes and Leibnitz, Locke and Kant, were forestalled in various particulars by the teaching of Ockham Realism had become so completely interwoven in the entire texture of the schools, that its period of decay caused the general break up of much that was faulty and effete in the main substance of the web The revival of Nominalism therefore by Ockham was a decided step in the onward march of the human intellect, and prepared the way for a sweeping reform, both in theology and philosophy, a question now only of time Papal pretensions had become unbearable, and when the imperious Bull "Ausculta fili" was burnt at Paris in presence of Philip the Fair, his nobles and whole people [A D 1302], and the feat proclaimed through Paris by a poursuivant with a flourish of trumpets [Fleury, xc 7], the way was paved for John Huss, the precursor of Luther Ockham was a complete demagogue, but his fury was principally directed against the abuses that gave strength to the enemies of the Church The voluntary poverty of the Fraticelli, and the hold that it gave them on popular respect and regard, caused Ockham to inveigh against Papal avarice [*Defensorium Ockhami*], and to demand the return of his order to its original constitution of poverty For this he was cast off by the brotherhood, and excommunicated by the Pope, ostensibly, however, for taking part with the refractory Emperor Louis of Bavaria, to whose court he now fled for protection. This he received by mutual compact in return for the service of his powerful pen against the Pope [Avent vii 955] Both parties were faithful to the agreement, and when [A D 1344] an arrangement was proposed between the Emperor and the Pope, Louis refused to give up Ockham as one of the conditions. Ockham, always at home in polemics, was writing a fresh work against the Pope when death arrested his pen, A D 1347, in which same year the Emperor also died

Ockham's hardihood of thought led him into Pelagianism, with which he was always taxed by the leaders of the Reformation [1] [Laurence, *B Lect* p. 59], and it was he who gave its first impulse to the notion of merit "de congruo," though virtually it is identical with the "dispositio ad gratiam" of Aquinas [i dist 41, qu 1, art 3] The penitential distinction also of "attrition" and "contrition," combined by Thomas under the latter term, were divided out by Ockham, after which time they were generally separated the one from the other [Scot iv, dist 14, qu 2]

The five principal Schoolmen have been aptly designated by Milner [*Lat Chr* vi 451] as Albert the Great the philosopher, Aquinas the theologian, Bonaventura the mystic, Duns Scotus the dialectician, Ockham the politician They were the leaders of that great intellectual movement of the Middle Ages that, when all was without form and void, was the herald rather of future life than in itself life But with all their labours they effected little, the Summa of Aquinas alone being excepted Mental philosophy was kept in abeyance by the shadowy visions of Realism Their system was but a reproduction of the Neo-Platonic Eclecticism of Plotinus, stained with the Pantheism of Proclus Their natural science was successful only so far as the pursuit of alchemy led them to stumble on useful chemical results Their theology, so far as it was sound, is better studied in the tomes of the Fathers, from whence their isolated texts were culled for discussion Hence, it has been said and not untruly, "With all their researches into the unfathomable they have fathomed nothing, and with all their vast logical apparatus they have proved nothing to the satisfaction of the inquisitive mind" [Milman *Lat Chr* vi 452]

[*Hist Lit de la France*, Bened. ed. vii. Christlieb, *Leb u Lehre J Scot Erigena* Jourdain, *Traductions d'Aristote* Neander, vii viii Ritter, *Phil* Baur, *Versohnung*, and *K des Mittelalters* Cousin, *Œuvres inédits d'Abélard* *Encyclopædia Metrop Biography*, *Thomas of Aquino* Cave, *Hist Lit* Hauréau, *Phil Scholastique* Morin, *Dict Scholastique* Rousselot, *Phil du Moyen Age* Renan, *Averroes*]

SCOTISTS [SCHOOLMEN]

SCOTOPITES One of the many names of the Circumcellions It is found in Isid. Hispal, and in Gratian's *Decretals*, II xxiv 3 [CIRCUMCELLIONS]

SCOTTISH BAPTISTS This branch of the sect of the Baptists owes its origin to an Antiburgher minister of Coupar-Angus, named Carmichael, who quitted the Scotch Secession, and was dipped by Dr Gill in London in 1765 The Scottish Baptists are Calvinistic in doctrine, and more congregational in government than English Baptists, as well as stricter in discipline They maintain the necessity of a plurality of pastors in every congregation, and the exercise of public mutual exhortation by the members At the census of 1851 they were returned as having fifteen meeting-houses in England, with 2037 sittings In Scotland the Baptists were returned as having in general, without distinction of separate branches, 119 places of worship, with 26,086 sittings [Eadie's *Cyclopædia Religions of the World*, 1870]

SCOTTISH CONFESSION [PROTESTANT CONFESSIONS]

SCOTTISH KIRK A Presbyterian community[2] founded on the ruins of the ancient Scottish Church in the sixteenth century, and established as the national religion of the country by Acts of Parliament, passed before and at the time of its Union with England

I EARLY PRESBYTERIANISM OF SCOTLAND It has been shewn in the article on the PURITANS, that the steady onward flow of Reformation by authority, in the Church of England, was met by a strong current of opposition to the Episcopal system of Church government, and by a persistent endeavour on the part of the Puritans to introduce into England that system of parochial tyranny which went by the name of "The Discipline" After a bitter struggle, which lasted for a century, the Reformation by authority at length gained the better of the lawless democratic movement, and Episcopacy was firmly established in England as soon as ever a short trial of Presbyterianism had shewn its unfitness for the English nation In Scotland the same elements of agitation were at work, but under very different circumstances, and with a very different result "As we cast our glance upon Scotland towards the end of the first quarter of the sixteenth century," writes Principal Tulloch, "we behold a very disturbed picture—the king, the great nobles, and the clergy sharing between them an authority which has not worked itself into any consistent and beneficent form of national order In comparison with the well-developed, massive and richly-pictured life of England at the same period, there is a great rudeness and disorder, and, in a word, barbarism, in Scotland While in England, accordingly, we see a balanced movement proceeding gradually and under royal sanction, in Scotland we behold an insurrectionary impulse long repressed, but at length gathering force till it breaks down and sweeps all barriers before it" [Tulloch's *Leaders of the Reform.* 257] The Reformation movement in Scotland was, indeed, to a far greater extent than in England, a political movement There was little or no contest between the national rulers and the Pope, but there was a bitter contest between the Crown and the people, a contest so bitter that the monarchy escaped destruction only by the removal of the

[1] Luth *Op* v 307 Melancth *Op* ii 58

[2] "Kirk is the official designation of the Scottish Presbyterian Establishment, but is only the archaic form of the English word 'Church'" [DICT *of* THEOL, CHURCH]. It is convenient in use as distinguishing the Presbyterian community from the Episcopal Church of Scotland, but it is not so commonly heard among Scottish people as formerly

throne to England. and while that removal secured the political authority of the Crown, it led to the final ruin of the Church and the establishment of Presbyterianism.

Amidst the "barbarism" and "insurrectionary impulse" which thus characterized the Scottish Reformation, a leader arose in the person of John Knox [A D 1505 1572] who took his colour from these elements of the movement, and whose force of character enabled him to guide it in whatever direction he chose When Luther was first coming into notice, Knox was a student at the University of Glasgow, and had gained some notoriety there as an able and enthusiastic defender of Mediæval Theology In the year 1530 he was ordained to the priesthood, having some cure, probably in connection with St Andrews About five years afterwards his opinions began to turn in exactly the opposite direction to that in which they had been conspicuously bent hitherto, and in 1542 he avowed himself a Calvinist

At this time the tide of theological revolution was setting in strongly in Scotland A young monk named Patrick Hamilton [A D 1504-1527], whom the abuses of the times had raised to the high office of Abbot of Ferne while he was a mere boy, had learned something of Lutheranism during a short stay in Germany, and returned to Scotland as zealous for the Germanism of that day as many a youth of two-and-twenty is, under similar circumstances, for the Germanism of the nineteenth century. Although a monk and an abbot, and only twenty-two years of age, Hamilton also returned to England with a wife and when, in addition to all his other transgressions, he set himself up as a teacher of novelties to men old enough to be his grandfathers, the cruel spirit of the times soon got rid of the troublesome youth by sending him to the stake for heresy He was burnt at Glasgow on February 29th, 1528 From that time men began to inquire about the new doctrines, and a "reforming" party sprung up quickly With that old coarseness of the Scottish tongue which is sometimes taken for picturesqueness, a "merie gentleman" told the Archbishop of Glasgow, "Gif ye burn more, let them be burnt in how" [hollow] "sellars, for the reik of Mr Patrick Hamilton has infected as many as it did blow upon"

Whether Knox was one of those who were infected in this manner or not it is impossible to say, for no facts are known respecting his history for fourteen years after Hamilton's death, except that he became a priest, and that soon afterwards he shewed a leaning towards the principles which he openly avowed in 1542, and for which he was degraded from the priesthood in 1543

Knox is next heard of as the constant companion of George Wishart [A D 1514-1546], one of the conspirators hired for Henry VIII by Lord Hertford (afterwards the Duke of Somerset) to assassinate Cardinal Beaton Although Knox constantly accompanied Wishart about in his preachings with a "twa-handed sword," his protection was not sufficient to secure the latter from being apprehended on charges of treason and heresy; and being found guilty of both he was strangled and burnt three months before an opportunity had been found for assassinating the Cardinal; the execution of Wishart taking place on March 1st, and the death of Beaton on May 29th, in the year 1546 After the latter event the assassins defended themselves in the Castle of St Andrews for more than a year, but they were eventually taken prisoners by the French, Knox being among them, on July 29th, 1547

Knox is said to have been sent to the galleys, and to have suffered great hardships; but he soon found his way to England, for less than six months after he had been taken prisoner, that is in December 1547, he appears in the State Papers as one of the preachers licensed by the Privy Council of Edward VI, and he remained in England during the whole of the young King's reign, being appointed one of the Royal Chaplains On October 21st, 1552, the Privy Council appointed him one of the Commissioners for reviewing the Articles of Religion [*MS P C Register*, B Mus] On January 2nd following, the Council ordered a letter to be written "to Lord Russel, Lord Windsor, the Justices of the Peace, and the rest of the gentlemen of the county of Buckingham in favour of Mr Knocks the preacher" [*ibid*] On February 2nd, 1553, they wrote to Cranmer desiring the Archbishop to collate him to "the Vicarage or Parsonage of All Hallows in Bread Street, vacant by the preferment of Thomas Sampson to the Deanery of Chichester"[1] [*ibid*] A little later the Duke of Northumberland desired to appoint him to the Bishopric of Rochester, that he might "be a whetstone to the Archbishop of Canterbury, and a confounder of the Anabaptists of Kent" The death of Edward VI, on July 6th, 1553, put an end, however, to Knox's career in England, and he immediately fled from the danger which he and others expected to arise out of the accession of Queen Mary.

For a short time Knox became chaplain to the English refugees at Frankfort, but the dissensions which he excited among them became so serious that the authorities of the city would not allow him to remain, and he took up his residence at Geneva, where he lived from 1555 to 1559 as pastor of the English congregation there While safe from the power of the English government, he wrote and sent into England an inflammatory and treasonable little book entitled, "The First Blast of the Trumpet against the Monstrous Regiment of Women," in which he set forth [1] that the Queen being a woman was under the curse of God; [2] that she was a bastard, and therefore an usurper, [3] that it was the duty of the nobility and estates without further delay to remove her from authority, and afterwards to execute against her the sentence of death This work, and another similar to it, written by Knox's friend Christopher Goodman, produced a seditious spirit among their Protestant friends who remained in

[1] The Archbishop however in March presented Lawrence Saunders instead, being probably unwilling to give a benefice to one who had been formally degraded from the priesthood

England, and had naturally much influence in provoking the Privy Council of Queen Mary to treat them in that merciless manner which is matter of history

The disappointments which Knox had met with as to preferment in England had prepared his mind for the lesson of Presbyterianism which he was to learn in Geneva The rule of Bishops had become as unsavoury to him as the "regiment" of Queens, and the position held by Calvin at Geneva shewed him a way by which he could reach a position of almost unlimited influence among the Protestants of Scotland, whose inclinations he had tested during a secret visit which he had paid to his long-forsaken native country in 1555-6 The accession of Queen Elizabeth in 1559 gave Knox and his friends hopes that their party would be able to carry on their work of agitation without danger under the shadow of her influence even in Scotland, and he returned thither at once, an organization of the reforming party having already been effected by a body of revolutionary nobility and gentry violently opposed to the Queen Regent, who styled themselves "The Lords of the Congregation"

The work which Knox now set himself to do was that of destroying the Ecclesiastical Institutions of Scotland, and substituting in their place a system similar to that which Calvin had recently invented and established at Geneva The Queen Regent had endeavoured to direct the reformation tendencies of the age in the same authoritative manner that had been adopted by the English Government during the reigns of Henry VIII and Edward VI, and had issued a proclamation which prohibited any person from preaching or administering the Sacraments without authority from the bishops This proclamation being disregarded, four of the preachers who had disobeyed it were charged with exciting sedition, and their trial was fixed to take place at Stirling on May 10th, 1559 On the second of that month Knox landed in Scotland, and on his arrival in Edinburgh being known he was declared an outlaw The Lords who were opposing the Crown gathered round him, however, and formed so strong a party that it was determined he should appear at the trial of the preachers, and he went northward for that purpose as far as Perth While there Knox preached in the cathedral one of his passionate invectives against the worship of images and the idolatry of the Mass, and within a very few minutes after the sermon had ended the Church was gutted by the mob, all the vestments, sacred utensils, and ornaments of every kind being treated with sacrilegious insult and destroyed From the cathedral the mob proceeded to the monasteries, and gathering numbers as they went, were soon strong enough to overcome the authorities, so that the houses of the Dominicans, Franciscans, and Carthusians were in a few hours brought to a state of utter ruin

This riot at Perth brought the revolution to a climax The Queen Regent herself marched against the city with the intention of restoring authority, but the Lords of the Congregation had formed so compact an organization that, although they retired to St Andrews, they were able quickly to carry their purpose against her. From that time until James VI of Scotland became James I of England the former country was practically governed by a faction of the nobility and the preachers, Knox being the chief instigator of all the revolutionary measures in Church and State by which the authority of the Crown and the constitution of the Church were destroyed, and the country involved in unceasing civil war. The example set by the rioters at Perth was followed at Stirling, Lindores, Cupar, St Andrews, and in other parts of the country, many of the clergy and monks were driven away, the laity took possession of the ecclesiastical property for their own use, and the first part of the work, that of destruction, was completed in an incredibly short space of time through the absence of any efficient control on the part of those whose office it should have been to have prevented such outrages on law and order

The introduction of the Presbyterian system was formally confirmed by the Scottish Parliament that assembled at Edinburgh after the death of the Queen Regent, which took place on June 10th, 1560, and before any authority for its meeting had been received from Queen Mary, who did not arrive in Scotland until 1561 Early in August 1560, this self-appointed Parliament passed an Act which embodied a Calvinistic Confession drawn up by Knox, assisted by five preachers named Winram, Spottiswood, Willock, Douglas, and Row, and which was enacted to be "The Confession of the faith and doctrine believed and professed by the Protestants of Scotland" Three other Acts of Parliament were passed on the 22nd and 23rd of the same month the first abolishing the authority of the Pope in Scotland, the second repealing all previous Acts connected with the Church, the third enacting that all who celebrated, or were present at, Mass should be punished on the first offence by imprisonment, on the second by banishment, and on the third by death

The constitution of the Scottish Kirk, whose creed was thus established by Act of Parliament, is to be found in "the Book of Policy" or "Discipline," drawn up by Knox, and adopted by the first "General Assembly" (composed of six ministers and thirty-six laymen), which met at Edinburgh on December 20th, 1560 The most important portion of this is contained under the "fourth and fifth heads," which provide "concerning ministers and their lawful election" In these "heads" Knox divided Scotland into ten "dioceses," which were each to be governed by a "superintendent," who was to be appointed by "the ministers of the province, with the superintendents next adjacent," from among those who had been nominated by any of "the churches within the diocese" His preaching was to be tried, and his "learning, manners, prudence, and ability to govern the Church," were to be examined into, but "other ceremonies than this examination, the approbation of ministers and superintendents, with the public consent of elders and people, we do not admit" The office of these "superintendents" was to "travel from place to place for establishing of the Church," to "preach the word," and to "visit his churches," and he was to be subject to the censure and correction of the ministers and elders of his diocese Each of them was to be provided with "six chalders of beer, nine chalders meal, and three chalders oats for provand to his horse, with five hundred marks money, which may be augmented and diminished at the discretion of the Prince and Council of the realm" They were not to remain in one place above three or four months, were to preach thrice a week at least, and were "not to rest till the churches be wholly planted and provided of ministers, or at the least of readers" They were in their visitations to "try the life, diligence, and behaviour of the ministers, the order of their churches, and the manners of their people, how the poor are provided, and how the youth is instructed," they were to admonish where admonition was needed, and to "take note of all heinous crimes, that the same may be corrected by the censures of the Church"

The "ministers" came next in order, and they also were to be elected by each congregation for themselves, being subsequently examined "as well in life and manners as in doctrine and knowledge," by "men of soundest judgment, remaining in some principal town next adjacent to them," who are defined as the "ministers and elders" of the place "Other ceremonies than the public approbation of the people, and the declaration of the chief minister that the person there presented is appointed to serve that church, we cannot approve, for albeit the Apostles used the imposition of hands, yet seeing the miracle is ceased, the using of the ceremony we judge not to be necessary" Each minister was to have "forty bolls meal, and twenty bolls malt, with money to buy other provision to his house and serve his other necessities," all payments to be made a quarter in advance and to be modified at "the judgment of the church" year by year. The children of ministers were also to have all privileges that could be given to them Where "true ministers" could not be provided for, "readers" were to be appointed, each of whom was to be paid forty marks a year for teaching the children of the parish, "reading of the Common Prayer and the books of the Old and New Testament," and exhorting and explaining, if he were fit to do so, in which latter case he was to have a larger stipend "till he come to the degree of a minister"

"Elders" and "deacons" were to be elected every year on the 1st of August, but might be re-elected year by year The elders were "to assist the minister in all public affairs of the church to wit, in judging and decerning of causes, in giving admonition to licentious livers, and having an eye upon the manners and conversation of all men within their charge" They were "also to take heed to the life, manners, diligence, and study of their ministers, and if he be worthy of admonition, they must admonish him—if of correction, they must correct him—and if he be worthy of deposition, they, with the consent of the church and superintendent, may depose him" The deacons were "to receive the rents and gather the alms of the church, to keep and distribute the same as they shall be appointed by the ministry and the church, yet they may also assist in judgment the ministers and elders, and be admitted to read in public assemblies, if they be called, required, and found able thereto"

Further provisions of this first "Book of Discipline" are for either a sermon or the use of the Common Prayer[1] every day in great towns, "with some exercise of reading the Scriptures," in other towns such order was to be observed as the churches in the town should appoint. "The day of public sermon we do not think the common prayers needful to be used, lest we should foster the people in superstition, who come to the prayers as they come to the Mass, or give them occasion to think that those are no prayers which are conceived before and after sermon" The "administration of the Lord's Table" was to be confined to the first Sundays in March, June, September, and December, "that the superstitious observation of times may be avoided as far as may be for it is known how superstitiously people run unto that action upon Easter, as if the time gave virtue to the Sacrament, whereas the rest of the whole year they are careless and negligent, as though it belonged not unto them but at that time only" Respecting Baptism, it was ordered to be administered with water only, "the Word and declaration of the promises preceding" Marriages were to be performed openly in the face of the church and after banns, but no ceremony is enacted They are also forbidden "if the man be within thirteen years of age, and the woman within twelve at least" It was recommended that Burials should take place without any religious ceremony or sermon, but these might be tolerated with the consent of the minister

This Book of Discipline sets forth substantially the system which has been permanently adopted in the Kirk of Scotland, except that the system of "superintendents" was quickly dropped, their work being done by "presbyteries," which answer to English "Rural Deaneries" The Book was submitted to Parliament, but did not at that time receive formal Parliamentary sanction It was also submitted to the Privy Council, and a number of Privy Councillors subscribed to it, but only in their private capacities Spottiswoode, the historian of the Church of Scotland, remarks that "most of these that subscribed getting into their hands the possessions of the Church, could never be induced to part there-

[1] There has been a good deal of historical guessing as to what "Common Prayer" Knox meant As he had drawn up a "Book of Common Order" while abroad, to be substituted for the English Prayer Book, it is more likely he meant that than the latter

with, and turned greater enemies in that point of Church patrimony than were the papists or any other whatsoever" The Book of Discipline was issued in a revised form several years after the death of Knox, in 1578, but the Second Book, drawn up in 1581, was ratified by Act of Parliament in 1592 Meanwhile, in 1580, "The National Covenant, or the Confession of Faith," of which a description is given in the article on the COVENANTERS, was imposed upon the Scottish people

The "Presbyterian Church Government and Discipline, that is to say, the government of the Church by Kirk-Sessions, Presbyteries, Provincial Synods, and General Assemblies," was "ratified and established by the 114 Act James VI Parl 12, Anno 1592, entitled Ratification of the Liberty of the Kirk, etc, and thereafter received by the general consent of" the "nation to be the only government of Christ's Church within" the "Kingdom" of Scotland [Act, 7th June 1690]

Contemporarily with this introduction of the Presbyterian system in 1560, the Parliament of Scotland passed an Act for the demolition of those Monasteries and Abbey Churches which had not yet been destroyed "Thereupon ensued," says Spottiswoode, 'a pitiful vastation of churches and church buildings throughout all the parts of the realm, for every one made bold to put to their hands, the meaner sort imitating the ensample of the greater and those who were in authority No difference was made, but all the churches were either defaced or pulled to the ground The holy vessels, and whatsoever else men could make gain of, as timber, lead and bells, were put to sale The very sepulchres of the dead were not spared The registers of the church and bibliothèques were cast into the fire In a word, all was ruined, and what had escaped in the time of the first tumult did now undergo the common calamity, which was so much the worse, that the violences committed at this time were coloured with the warrant of public authority. Some ill-advised preachers did likewise animate the people in these their barbarous proceedings, crying out, 'That the places where idols had been worshipped ought by the law of God to be destroyed, and that the sparing of them was the reserving of things execrable' The report also went that John Knox, whose sayings were by many esteemed as oracles, should in one of his sermons say, 'That the sure way to banish the rooks was to pull down their nests'" [Spottiswoode's *Hist Ch Scot* i 372, ed 1851]

II THE SCOTTISH KIRK AND THE STUARTS The peculiar course which the Reformation took in Scotland was in nothing more strange than in its results as to the Episcopate Some of the old bishops turned with the times, and either retained the revenues of their sees, as did Robert Stewart, Bishop of Caithness and Earl of Lennox, or made over those revenues to some of their relatives, as did Alexander Gordon, Bishop of Galloway in both cases ceasing to exercise the Episcopal office although retaining the Episcopal title. As these old bishops died off, nominal successors were sometimes appointed by the Crown, or the Regents acting in the name of the Crown; and thus there were titular bishops of the ancient sees who were never consecrated nor even in priests' orders [1]

This continuance of a nominal Episcopate, side by side with the Presbyterian establishment, was much favoured by the Court party, but it is difficult to say whether from reasons of self-interest as regarded the ancient revenues of the sees, or in the hope that the shadow of an Episcopate might some day be turned into a reality In the year 1572 the Earl of Morton persuaded the principal nobility to agree that the titles of Archbishops and Bishops should be continued during the minority of James VI, and that the persons bearing them should be entitled to sit in Parliament and to conciliate the Presbyterians, it was also agreed that these bishops should be chosen by an assembly of Presbyterian ministers, and be subject to the General Assembly. But in practice the appointments fell into the hands of the Crown, while the titular bishops thus appointed and the General Assembly were in constant opposition to each other

When the young King James VI became nominally independent, though only twelve years of age, in 1578, the General Assembly of preachers took much bolder action in respect to these titular bishops than they had ventured to take while a strong-handed nobleman was Regent. Meeting at Dundee in July 1579, they first passed an "ordinance" declaring that the office of bishop had no warrant in the Word of God, and commanding "all persons either called to the said office, or that should be called thereto at any time thereafter, to demit and forsake the same, as an office whereunto they were not called by God as also to desist and cease from preaching, ministering the sacraments, or using in any sort the office of a pastor, till they should be admitted of new by the General Assembly, under pain of excommunication" After this, in 1580, they issued the "National Covenant," previously referred to, by which "the government of the Kirk by bishops" is "declared to be unlawful within this Kirk" At this time Andrew Melville [A D 1545-1622], Principal of St Mary's College, St Andrews, was rising into power as a champion of strict Presbyterianism, and becoming Moderator of the General Assembly in 1582, he excommunicated a minister of Stirling, named Robert Montgomery, who had, contrary to the decree of that self-important body, accepted from the Crown the titular Archbishopric of Glasgow The "Raid of Ruthven" shortly followed, the avowed object of which was to protect the Kirk from the designs of the King and his friends by taking possession of his person This opposition of the Presbyterian faction to the free action of the Crown, and the restraint under which he was placed by Lord Ruthven and his party, gave

[1] They were shrewdly named "Tulchane Bishops," a "Tulchane" or "Tulchin" being a stuffed calf's skin set up in sight of a cow to persuade her to give her milk

James a lasting hatred of Presbyterianism, and when he had at last found a home in a more free country, he declared, that although he had lived among Puritans from ten years of age, he "ever disliked their opinions," and that "since he had ability to judge he was never of them." He had, moreover, learned a lesson by experience which he put into the concise epigram, "No Bishop, no King" [Cardwell's *Conf* 184, etc] This personal aversion of the King to Presbyterian principles, and his shrewd conviction that the spread of them menaced the existence of the Crown led him to support the titular bishops of Scotland in every way that he could and when he succeeded to the Crown of England he took measures for grafting a true Episcopate upon the Kirk, evidently with the view of gradually assimilating the ecclesiastical system of Scotland to that of England.

In this purpose the King was probably supported by a strong anti-revolutionary party in Scotland for in the year 1606 the Scottish Parliament passed an Act "for the restitution of Bishops," the purpose of which was that of enabling the Crown to restore to the titular bishops such portions of the estates of their respective sees as still remained in its hands In the same year James I endeavoured to pave the way for the restoration of Episcopal authority by proposing to the General Assembly that the titular bishops should act as permanent moderators or presidents in the presbyteries within their dioceses, thus giving them much more power in the administration of ecclesiastical affairs, and the proposition was, after some resistance, adopted by the Assembly, and put in practice throughout the Kirk After this the King frequently urged the bishops to take on themselves the administration of all Church affairs, and as they were unwilling to do so without the consent of the ministers, an Assembly was at last called to consider the question in June 1610, the Earl of Dunbar, Sir John Preston, and Sir Alexander Hay, being Commissioners for the King, and John Spottiswoode, titular Archbishop of Glasgow, being Moderator At this Assembly nine resolutions were assented to, which practically re-established the jurisdiction of the Crown and the bishops [1] The Royal supremacy was put on the same footing as in England [2] the titular bishops being ex officio moderators of all presbyteries within their dioceses, ordinations of ministers were placed, substantially, in their hands as the head of the ordaining presbytery [3] admissions to benefices were to be made only by the bishops, as in England [4] every minister at his ordination was to take oaths of allegiance to the Crown and of obedience to the bishop of the diocese [5] ministers were to be suspended or deprived by the authority of the bishops, not of the presbyteries [6] and lastly, the bishops were to hold Diocesan Synods twice every year

The jurisdiction of the Episcopate being thus restored, James I prepared to restore it to its proper spiritual position by having some of the titular bishops consecrated Accordingly, John Spottiswoode, Archbishop of Glasgow, Andrew Lamb, Bishop of Brechin, and William Couper, Bishop of Galloway, were summoned to London, where the King told them that he had restored the revenues of the bishoprics and had appointed worthy men to them, but that as he could not make them bishops, nor could they make themselves so, he had called them to England that they might be consecrated, and that being thus made true bishops instead of mere titular ones they might return to Scotland to consecrate the rest To avoid any pretence that the Archbishops of England could have to reclaim old jurisdictions in Scotland, they were excluded from taking any part in the business, and the three Scottish bishops named were consecrated on October 21st, 1610, in the chapel of London House by Abbot, Bishop of London, Andrewes, Bishop of Ely, and Montagu, Bishop of Bath and Wells [1]

When these measures had been taken, James I established an Ecclesiastical Commission in Scotland similar to that commonly known as the "High Commission' in England He also issued a set of Injunctions, in the same manner as Edward VI and Elizabeth had issued theirs for England These Injunctions required that the Scottish archbishops and bishops should reside in their cathedral cities, that they should repair their cathedrals as far as they could, that they should visit their dioceses at least every third year, that they should take steps for resettling the boundaries of their dioceses so as to make them more manageable, that strictness should be observed in admitting ministers, and that none should be admitted without Episcopal imposition of hands, that lay elders, having neither warrant in the Word, nor example in the primitive Church, should be reduced to the *status* of churchwardens, to be chosen by the minister and approved by the ordinary, and that the General Assembly should consist of bishops, deans, archdeacons, and such of the ministry as should be selected by the rest. These Injunctions were received without any disapproval, but the Ecclesiastical Commission raised "great discontent," says Spottiswoode, "among those that ruled the estate, for that they took it to be a restraint of their authority in matters ecclesiastical, nor did they like to see clergymen invested with such a power"

In the General Assembly of 1616 it was enacted "that a Liturgy or Book of Common Prayer should be formed for the use of the Church that the Acts of the General Assemblies should be collected and put in form, to serve for canons to the Church in their ministration of discipline.

[1] These consecrations were after all, to say the least, irregular Bishop Andrewes objected that the three titular bishops were mere laymen and ought to be ordained priests before they were consecrated to the Episcopate Bancroft, Archbishop of Canterbury, overruled the objection by saying that where no bishop could be had ordination by presbyters was lawful, "otherwise it might be doubted whether there were any lawful vocation in most of the reformed churches" But whence did the ordaining "presbyters" themselves get their ordination? Anybody might ordain anybody on such a principle

that children should be carefully catechized and confirmed by the bishops, or, in their absence, by such as were employed in the visitation of churches" The King declared the last enactment to be a "mere hotch-potch," and suggested that children should be catechized by their parish ministers, and that the bishops themselves should alone confirm them He also tried to introduce the observance of more reverence at the Holy Communion, and told the Archbishop of St Andrews "that the minister's ease and commodious sitting on his tail hath been more looked to than that kneeling which, for reverence, we directly required to be enjoined to the receivers of so divine a sacrament" He was equally anxious that Christmas Day should be kept, a Church custom of which the Scottish mind has a very singular horror After much resistance had been offered to these proposals, the "five articles" containing them were assented to by the General Assembly at Perth in 1618, and three years afterwards, in 1621, the "novations," as they were called by the Scottish Puritans, were ratified, under the name of "the Five Articles of Perth," by the Scottish Parliament.

At the time of James I's death in the year 1625, very little had been done towards carrying out the resolution passed in the General Assembly of 1616 that a Liturgy should be prepared for use in the Kirk In the following year the King had introduced the English Prayer Book into Holyrood Chapel, in 1620 an Ordinal had been adopted by the Bishops, and shortly before the King's death a draft of a Liturgy had been sent to him by Spottiswoode, then Archbishop of St. Andrews, which had been returned with some revisions, but was never brought into use Charles I, in continuation of his father's Church policy in Scotland, desired Laud, just after he had become Bishop of London in 1629, to communicate with some Scottish bishops, including Archbishop Spottiswoode, on the subject Laud wished that the English Prayer Book should be introduced into Scotland without any alteration, and the King agreed with him, but after two or three years Charles gave way to the urgency of some of the Scottish bishops for a Liturgy of their own, and although Laud still "delayed with his obedience," he was at last required, in company with Bishops Juxon and Wren, to assist the Scottish bishops in preparing a Scottish Prayer Book. The chief compilers of it were Maxwell, Bishop of Ross, and Wedderburn, Bishop of Dunblane, but although Laud took great interest in the work, he had nothing to do with the compilation, and very little with its subsequent revision before publication He did, however, urge the Scottish bishops to introduce the Prayer Book so prepared only in a legal and constitutional manner, and greatly objected to its being done, as it was eventually done, solely on the authority of the Crown The Scottish Prayer Book, very similar to the English Prayer Book, but with some changes in the direction of the First Prayer Book of Edward VI, was at last authorized by a Royal Proclamation dated December 20th, 1636 [1] A book of Canons had been imposed upon the Kirk with still more imprudence and high-handedness in the preceding year

While all this was being done in Scotland, the Puritan party both there and in England was growing stronger and bolder, and discontent in each country was encouraged and strengthened by correspondence between the two sections This discontent at last broke out in Scotland with such sudden force as to bring the lately re-established Episcopal system to utter ruin The King's Proclamation had ordered that all parishes should be provided with Prayer Books by Easter 1637, and the bishops ordered that the clergy should begin to use them in Divine Service on July 23rd, 1637 Edinburgh had recently been erected into an Episcopal city, and it was there that the first attempt to obey this order was made But in St Giles' Church, which had been made the Cathedral, the Dean and the Bishop were both assaulted by a mob of women, who, with an indecent violence to which probably no other nation except the French could shew a parallel, threw the stools which they used to sit on at the heads of those dignitaries, and endeavoured to pull them out of the reading desk and the pulpit In the afternoon the Bishop escaped murder only by the timely appearance of the Earl of Roxburgh This riot had been arranged as long before as the preceding April by a minister named Alexander Henderson and some other leading men of the Puritan faction, and the women had been hired to make the attack on the clergy, with the assurance that the men would support them and go on with the quarrel Notwithstanding these riotous proceedings the Scottish Prayer Book was however taken into use by many of the clergy for several months, although both it and the Canons were petitioned against by others

On February 19th, 1638-9, a Royal Proclamation was promulgated, the object of which was to assure the people of the King's sincere desire for the promotion of religion in the changes which had been made, and deprecating the disorders which had arisen This had no sooner been issued than, carrying out a preconcerted plan of organized resistance, the leading Puritans first protested against the proclamation, and then formed a Convention of the Estates, consisting of four representative bodies of nobility, lairds, burgesses, and ministers, called "the Four Tables," which was to overrule all other authority in the kingdom of Scotland, with the nominal exception of the King This body re-established the "Covenant" of 1580 and 1598, and, in conjunction with the General Assembly, added a clause to be subscribed with the Covenant by all classes of persons, stating that "the five articles of Perth, the government of the Kirk by Bishops, the civil places and power of Kirkmen, upon the reasons and grounds contained in the Acts of the General

[1] The fullest account of the Scottish Prayer Book of 1636 is to be found in the Annotated Book of Common Prayer, pages 580-585, where Professor Bright has traced its history with more exactness than had been done by preceding writers.

Scottish Kirk

Assembly declared to be unlawful within this Kirk, we subscribe according to the determination foresaid." The Assembly also declared that it could not be dissolved, or its proceedings in any way controlled, by the Crown; and the Moderator, Henderson, wound up by a prayer in which he invoked upon the King the curse of Jericho: "Cursed be the man before the Lord that riseth up and buildeth this city Jericho: he shall lay the foundation thereof in his first-born, and in his youngest son shall he set up the gates of it." But this cursing of those who disagreed with them came as naturally to Covenanters as to Popes.

The result of these measures was that the Episcopal system was utterly overthrown, and the Presbyterian system, without the "superintendents" of Knox, or the "Tulchan bishops" of James I., was established in its place. The acts of all the General Assemblies which had sat since 1606 were repealed, the bishops were deposed from their Episcopal offices, two alone being allowed to act even as ministers, and the rest being excommunicated. "All that we have done these thirty years," said Archbishop Spottiswoode, "is thrown down at once." He and most of the other bishops left the country, and only one of them all, Sydserf, survived until the Restoration.

Of the Civil War which followed nothing need here be said. It is only necessary to add, as regards the twenty years which followed the transactions narrated above, that the Presbyterianism of the Scottish Kirk largely influenced the course of Puritanism in England, and that a Puritan uniformity between the two countries was so far established that the "Confession of Faith," the "Larger Catechism," and the "Shorter Catechism," set forth by the Westminster Assembly of Divines, were adopted as the formularies of the Kirk, and still continue to be its standard of belief.[1] The Puritan "Directory of Public Worship" was also similarly adopted. [COVENANTERS.]

On the Restoration of Charles II. the Scottish Parliament immediately released all who had subscribed the Covenant from their obligation; and in a subsequent session, held at Edinburgh early in 1662, passed an Act, which stated that the Crown and Parliament "doth hereby redintegrate the state of bishops to their ancient places and undoubted privileges in Parliament, and to all their other accustomed dignities, privileges, and jurisdictions, and doth hereby restore them to the exercise of their Episcopal functions, presidence in the Church, power of ordination, inflicting of censures, and all other acts of Church discipline, which they are to perform with advice and assistance of such of the clergy as they shall find to be of known loyalty and prudence." Sydserf, Bishop of Orkney, was however the only Scottish bishop living, and once more therefore it became necessary to obtain consecration in England. Accordingly, four Presbyterian ministers, James Sharp,[2] Andrew Fairfowl, Robert Leighton, and James Hamilton, went to London, where, having first renounced their Presbyterian ordination, they were ordained deacons and priests, and on December 15th, 1661, were consecrated respectively to the Sees of St. Andrews, Glasgow, Dunblane, and Galloway, by Sheldon, Bishop of London, Morley, Bishop of Worcester, Sterne, Bishop of Carlisle, and Lloyd, Bishop of Llandaff. Returning to Scotland, these new bishops consecrated six others on May 7th and three on June 1st, 1662, and thus a hierarchy, composed of fourteen bishops, was re-established in Scotland. This was kept up in regular course until the invasion of England by William III., and as many as thirty-eight Scottish bishops were consecrated between December 15th, 1661, and September 4th, 1688, exactly double the number of those who were consecrated in England during the same twenty-seven years. During the same period all the ministers of the Kirk received holy orders at the hands of the bishops; but as many as four hundred of those whom the bishops found occupying benefices in 1662 are said to have refused ordination, and consequently to have given up their ministrations in the Kirk.

III. LATER SETTLEMENT OF PRESBYTERIANISM IN THE KIRK. The Revolution Parliament of Scotland in 1688 passed an Act "abolishing Prelacy and all superiority of any office in the Church in this kingdom above presbyters," and as the bishops and most Episcopalians continued to adhere to James II., the Presbyterians were henceforth able to carry everything their own way with William III. and his government. On June 7th, 1690, an Act was passed in the Scottish Parliament by which our sovereign Lord and Lady, the King and Queen's Majesties, and three Estates of Parliament, ratified and established the Confession of Faith of the Westminster Divines, and "the government of the Church by Kirk-sessions, Presbyteries, Provincial Synods, and General Assemblies." At the Union of the two Kingdoms in 1707 the Presbyterian schism was established by authority of the English Parliament [3 & 4 Ann. c. 6; 4 & 5 Ann. c. 15], an "Act of Security" having previously been passed in Scotland, enacting that the Presbyterian form of Church government should "continue without any alteration to the people of this land in all succeeding generations."

With this settlement ended the combination of the Scottish Presbyterians, except so far as they were still opposed to Episcopacy. A process of disintegration has separated from the Kirk one body after another, until the great division of the FREE KIRK movement seemed to threaten its existence altogether. Supported, however, by Acts of the English Parliament, and by the endowments inherited from former times, the Kirk is still a flourishing body, numbering about half the people of Scotland.

[Spottiswoode's *Hist. of Ch. of Scotland*, ed. 1851. Collier's *Ecclesiast. Hist. of G. Britain.*

[1] These verbose documents are, together, about ten times the length of the Thirty-nine Articles of Religion.

[2] Archbishop Sharp was assassinated by nine Covenanters on May 3rd, 1678, his daughter, who sat by his side in his carriage, nearly sharing his fate.

Grub's *Eccles Hist of Scotl* Hetherington's *Hist of Ch of Scotl* Rushworth's *Hist Coll* Blunt's *Annot Book of Comm Prayer*]

SCHWENCKFELDIANS A sect of German Anti Sacramentalists founded by Caspar Schwenckfeld [A D 1490-1562], a nobleman of Silesia, at the time of the Reformation.

At the first outbreak of the German Reformation it was joined by Schwenckfeld, whose position gave him the opportunity of promoting its objects in his own district, around Ossing, and also in Silesia generally, he being one of the councillors of the Duke of Liegnitz But as early as the year 1524 he began to shew discontent with the teaching of Luther, especially with his theory of Consubstantiation and imagining that the true doctrine respecting the Holy Eucharist had been confided to him by a special revelation, he propounded an idea which afterwards pervaded Protestant theology very extensively through the teaching of Zwingli. This was that our Lord's words of Institution are to be understood as if He had said "My Body is this"—a spiritual food, which nourishes the soul as bread does the body, "My Blood is this"—a spiritual drink, which nourishes the soul as wine does the body His theory went on to maintain that the Sacraments are not means, but only signs of grace, and that the benefit which they signify comes, not in, through, or with them, but directly from God · for "the Almighty, Eternal Word," he says, "proceeds out of the mouth of God directly and immediately, and not through the Scripture, through external word, through Sacrament, or any other created thing in earth or heaven" [Schwenckfeld, *de cursu Verbi Dei*, 1527]

The opinion thus broached by Schwenckfeld, and his opposition to Luther's doctrine of justification by faith, which he considered as having a tendency to Antinomian license, led to his banishment from Silesia in 1527 Settling for a time at Strasburg, he there developed an heretical theory respecting the Human Nature of our Lord, which really lay at the root of his error respecting the Eucharist. This he stated in a work entitled "Quæstiones vom Erkantnus Jesu Christi und seiner Glorien," in which he maintained that the Human Nature of our Lord is not that of a being created by God as other beings are created, but derived in some higher manner from the Divine Nature, on the one hand, and from His Virgin Mother on the other Thus, as to Christ's Human as well as His Divine Nature, he maintained that He was naturally the Son of God

Schwenckfeld supported his opinions vigorously by his writings, and was opposed with no more than his usual bitterness towards all opponents by Luther, who gave him the ribald nickname of "Stenckfeld" In Schlusselburg's "Catalogue of Heresies" this name is the only one given, his tenth volume of 600 pages being entitled "de secta Stenckenfeldis"

He did not, however, organize a sect himself, although one was formed from among his adherents in Silesia, which attained some notoriety after his death The members of this sect underwent severe persecution from the Lutherans, but increased in numbers and became a formidable rival to that community in Silesia. Early in the eighteenth century the Jesuits sent missionaries among the Schwenckenfelders, and in 1725 the Emperor ordered that all their children should be brought up as Catholics Most of them then fled into Saxony, whence, after eight years, some removed to Altona in Denmark, and embarked in 1734 for Pennsylvania, where a small body of them still exists, retaining their extreme Anti-Sacramentarian opinions, and using the German language in their services A few returned from Saxony to Silesia in 1763, when the latter country came under Prussian rule [Arnold's *Kirchen- und Ketzer-historie*, xvi 20 Dorner's *Person of Christ*, II ii 143, Clark's transl]

SCHWESTRIONES A name of reproach, "Sisterers," given to the LOLLARDS and BEGHARDS

SE-BAPTISTS An insignificant sect which struck off from the Brownists [INDEPENDENTS] early in the seventeenth century, and received this name from the act of their leader, Smith, in baptizing himself But it is not clear that self-baptism was really the practice of the sect "Mr Smith," says Neale, in his "History of the Puritans," "was a learned man and of good abilities, but of an unsettled head, as appears by the preface to one of his books, in which he desires that his last writings may always be taken for his present judgment He was for refining upon the Brownists' scheme, and at last declared for the principles of the Baptists, upon this he left Amsterdam, and settled with his disciples at Ley, where, being at a loss for a proper administrator of the ordinance of baptism, he plunged himself, and then performed the ceremony upon others, which gained him the name of a Se-Baptist He afterwards embraced the tenets of Arminius, and published certain conclusions upon those points in the year 1611, which Mr Robinson answered, but Smith died soon after, and his congregation dissolved" [Neale's *Hist Purit* ii 49, ed 1732]

SEBUÆI This name is given to the second of the four Samaritan sects named by Epiphanius, the other three being the Essenes, Gorthæans, and Dosthæans [Epiph *Hær* xi] Lightfoot, in his *Horæ Talmudicæ*, considers them to be identical with the SABÆANS

SECESSION KIRK or ASSOCIATE SYNOD The first great offshoot of the Scottish Presbyterians after their re-establishment by William III Although they had been united in their opposition to Episcopacy, the Presbyterians soon began to quarrel among themselves First, the Cameronians protested against the relaxation of any testimony of adherence to the Solemn League and Covenant and to all therein involved Next, the restoration of lay patronage and the intrusion of unacceptable presentees into recusant parishes, roused a spirit of dissatisfaction, which found vent first in the Secession and subsequently in the Relief movement Patronage was the leading cause of dissension, but other causes were also found in the condemnation, on the one hand, of the *Marrow of Modern Divinity* in the General Assembly in 1720 [MARROW-MEN], and in the lenient dealing, on the other hand, by the Assembly in 1717 and 1726-9, with Professor John Simson, of Glasgow, who was alleged to have maintained Pelagian and Arian views,[1] and in 1736 with Professor Archibald Campbell, of St. Andrews, who was charged with unscriptural tenets, in teaching that "the sole and universal motives to virtuous actions are self-love, interest, or pleasure," that "the laws of nature in themselves are a certain and sufficient rule to direct rational minds to happiness," that "men, without revelation, cannot by their natural powers find out that there is a God," etc Simson was suspended from office in 1729, Thomas Boston protesting against the inadequacy of the sentence, but Campbell was dismissed uncensured upon his proffering explanations which were held to be sufficient

Before this, however, the Secession movement had begun In 1732 an Act passed the Assembly (which was repealed in 1734) restricting the right of electing a minister, when a patron did not present, to the Protestant heritors (or landowners) and elders of the parish, excluding all the other members of the congregation Against this Ebenezer Erskine preached a violent and inflammatory sermon, at a Synod-meeting at Perth, in October of the same year, for which he was censured by the Synod, he appealed to the General Assembly in the following year, but there his expressions were condemned as offensive, and he was sentenced to be rebuked and admonished As usual in such cases, he protested (with three other ministers, William Wilson, Alexander Moncrieff, and James Fisher) against the decision, and declared that he would preach upon all proper occasions as before Thereupon he and the others were in August of the same year [1733] suspended, all of them protesting again that the sentence was null and void, and that they would still exercise their ministry In November, after having rejected the proposals of a committee appointed to negotiate with them, the four ministers were dismissed from their several parochial charges, and declared to be no longer ministers of the Church Another protest followed, in which they declared that they were now, "for many weighty reasons, obliged to make a Secession" They then constituted themselves a Presbytery, and published a "Testimony" in their vindication

But in the following year the General Assembly evinced an earnest desire to reconcile the seceders Among other conciliatory and healing measures they repealed the obnoxious Act respecting election of ministers, and, above all, they empowered the Synod of Perth to restore those who had been deprived to their respective charges, while that Synod itself went so far as to elect Ebenezer Erskine himself for its moderator. Because, however, the Assembly had not confessed the sinfulness of its own past actions, and penitentially acknowledged itself to have been in the wrong throughout, the four ministers refused to be reconciled, and as the Assembly shortly afterwards maintained an unacceptable presentee in his appointment to a parish, and dismissed Professor Campbell from trial without censure, they published in December 1737 a second and longer document, entitled "Act, declaration, and testimony, for the doctrine, worship, discipline and government of the Church of Scotland, by some ministers associate together," etc, in which they give an historical review of the "defections" of the Establishment, enter largely into the cases of Simson and Campbell, and, finally, deliver their own testimony respecting what they regard as true Presbyterian principles, including the denunciation of all toleration to others[2] In 1737, the sectarian party was strengthened by the accession of two other ministers, Ralph Erskine and Thomas Mair, and two more joined them shortly afterwards, and on May 12th, 1740, the whole eight were deposed from the ministry of the Established Kirk by sentence of the Assembly In 1747, the number of congregations connected with the Secession had risen to thirty-two, but in that year a dispute arose about the civic oath taken by burgesses, and the newly-constituted body was at once subdivided into the two parties of BURGHERS and ANTIBURGHERS In 1820, two later sub-sections of these subdivisions, called the New-Light-Burghers and New-Light-Antiburghers, were united, whereupon they assumed the somewhat paradoxical title of *The United Secession*, their joint congregations then amounting to 262

The Seceders from this time assumed a position of hostility towards all Church-establishments, in this respect departing from the principles of their founders as well as from those of the old Covenanters Amongst themselves a controversy arose respecting the extent and application of the Atonement[3] Mr James Morison was deposed

[1] He denied original sin, maintaining that the souls of infants are created as pure and holy as that of Adam before the Fall, and appeared to impugn the supreme Deity of our Lord in affirming that "the Three Persons of the adorable Trinity are not to be said to be numerically one in substance or essence" But among the propositions which the Seceders condemned as "dangerous and pernicious errors, dishonouring to a God of truth, and having an evident tendency to subvert the souls of men," were also these, that it is probable that none are excluded from the benefit of the remedy for sin provided by God except those who exclude themselves by actual sin, and reject God's revelations, and that therefore the heathen may share in the benefit of Christ's reconciliation, that God has promised to bless with success the use of the means of grace to those who go about them with seriousness, sincerity, and faith, that it is more than probable that all baptized infants dying in infancy are saved, and that it is therefore probable that of the whole race of mankind more are elected and saved than reprobated and damned—a proposition very unacceptable to the true Presbyterian, who glories in reprobation, etc

[2] Among the sins protested against were the sin of circulating "an idolatrous picture of our Lord," (probably the well known and once popular broadside, which gave the traditional portrait of our Lord, together with the apocryphal letter to Abgarus, etc,) and the sin of repealing the penal statutes against witches

[3] A previous controversy had arisen in 1754, which led,

in 1841, and his father, Mr Robert Morison, in 1842, for maintaining, among other things, that Christ made atonement equally for all men, and not (as the Secession held, following the *Marrow of Modern Divinity*) that, while in relation to men all sinners are bidden to claim their share in Christ's finished work, yet in relation to the effectual purpose of God and of Christ Himself, He died only for the redemption of the elect, a view which makes the Gospel-call of welcome appear only a fiction with regard to many [MORISONIANS] Other depositions followed of ministers who objected to say that the Atonement infallibly, of itself, secures the salvation of any definite elect number, irrespective of the "divine purpose of application," but proceedings which were instituted in 1843 and 1845 against two Divinity Professors, Drs Balmer and Brown, who were accused of varying, in some almost infinitesimally slight degree, by quibbles about words, from the strictness of Calvinistic dogma on election and reprobation, were quashed by large majorities in Synod

In 1847 the United Secession or Associate Synod agreed, after long negotiation with the RELIEF Synod, upon terms of union with that body, their doctrinal standards and their causes of dissent from the Establishment being nearly identical, and the formal incorporation of the two sects took place at a meeting of the Synods on May 13th They then assumed the name of UNITED PRESBYTERIANS, and a notice of the present condition of this numerous and influential body will be found under that heading At the time of the union, the Secession numbered 402 ministers, and there were associated presbyteries in Ireland and America [1] [M'Kerrow, *Hist of the Secession* Andrew Thomson, *Historical Sketch of the Origin of the Secession Church Act, Declaration, and Testimony, by some Ministers Associate together* Andrew Robertson, *Hist of the Atonement Controversy in connection with the Secession Church* ANTIBURGHERS BURGHERS]

SECULARISTS The name assumed by a sect of modern unbelievers to express their fundamental tenet that the duties and interests connected with the world which we see around us are those with which alone we have any concern

The Secularists are Anti-Supernaturalists of the most extreme type, so far Atheists that they consider the existence of a personal God to be an open question for belief in which no sufficient proofs are adduced, and so far Pantheists that they consider "nature" to be the only God whose existence can be at all demonstrated The facts and doctrines of Christianity are, of course, denied by them, the details of their denial being founded on the usual Rationalist arguments and as regards morals they are Positivists, considering morality simply as a question of utility and social good

Although the Secularists profess to be a school of independent thinkers, their principles are in reality nothing more nor less than the echo of Rationalism and Positivism among the less educated classes of thoughtful men, chiefly among the working classes

SECUNDIANS A Gnostic sect of the second century, owning for their leader Secundus, "who was born," says Hippolytus, "about the same time as Ptolemæus," and was thus contemporary with the immediate followers of Valentinus

Irenæus represents the Secundians as a branch of the Valentinian school [Iren *adv Hæres* I xi 2], but although they emanated from that school [Hippol *Refut* VI xxxii xxxiii], they introduced a principle so distinct as to render Secundus more properly the rival than the disciple of Valentinus Secundus placed at the head of his Æons, whom he appears to have considered as real substances or persons, two principles, Light and Darkness "He divides the Ogdoad into a pair of Tetrads, a right hand and a left hand Tetrad, one Light and the other Darkness" [Iren *l c*, Hippol *l c*, Tertull *adv Valent* 38] This admission of the principle of Dualism constitutes an essential difference between the Secundians and the Valentinians It is evidently borrowed from the Oriental philosophy, and brings the Secundians so far nearer to the Manichees Accordingly Dorner classes as adherents of the Dualism whose character was predominantly physical, the Ophites, Saturnilus, Secundus, and subsequently the Manichæans, as adherents of pantheistic Monism, Valentinus and his widespread school, especially Heracleon his contemporary, Ptolemæus, and Marcus [Dorner's *Person of Christ*, I App p 448]

There is also mentioned as a distinction between the Valentinians and Secundus that the latter did not derive the power Achamoth from any one of the thirty Æons, but from the fruits which issued out of their substance [Tertull *ut sup*] He invented first four more Æons, and then four in addition [Ps-Tert xiii]

The Secundians were Docetæ Augustine [*Hær* xii] and Auctor Prædestinati [xii] charge them with gross immorality The latter adds that they were condemned by Diodorus, Bishop of Crete.

after tedious dispute, to the deposition of one of the original ministers of the Secession, Thomas Mair of Orwell, in 1757, between whom and the majority of his brethren there was only this "shade of difference" [Robertson's *Hist* p 129], that while they held that Christ's death was sufficient *in its own nature* for all sinners, he added that this sufficiency was also pleadable by every sinner individually, as that which had been divinely appointed for himself So intolerant of difference is sectarianism [1]

[1] Mr Disraeli, remembering no doubt the part which Roman emissaries are known to have taken in stirring up the Puritans against the Church of England in the time of Charles I, amusingly ventures to ascribe the origin of the United Presbyterians to a similar source In his novel of *Lothair* [vol i p 78] he introduces the active Roman agent, Monsignor Berwick, as saying, "We sent two of our best men into Scotland some time ago, and they have invented a new Church called the United Presbyterians John Knox himself was never more violent or more mischievous The United Presbyterians will do the business, they will render Scotland simply impossible to live in, and then, when the crisis arrives, the distracted and despairing millions will find refuge in the bosom of their only mother"

SEEKERS A sect of Puritans, afterwards merged in that of the Quakers, who professed to be seeking for the true Church, Scripture, Ministry and Sacraments Baxter says of them "They taught that our Scripture was uncertain, that present miracles are necessary to faith, that our ministry is null and without authority, and our worship and ordinances unnecessary or vain, the Church, ministry, Scripture, and ordinances being lost, for which they are now seeking I quickly found that the Papists principally hatched and actuated this sect, and that a considerable number that were of this profession were some Papists and some infidels However, they closed with the Vanists, and sheltered themselves under them, as if they had been the very same" [Baxter's *Life and Times*, 76]

SELEUCIANS Seleucus and Hermias were successors of Hermogenes, and leaders of his school They are known to us only from the notices of Philaster, Augustine, and the Author of Prædestinatus Their heresy is that of Hermogenes, with some additions of further heretical doctrine and practice They were of Galatia, but of their history nothing is known. Hermias is supposed by some to be Hermogenes The later or developed tenets, however, ascribed to Hermias forbid this identification [Philast *Hær* lv, August *Hær* lix, Prædest *Hær* lix]

To the tenets of their master [HERMOGENIANS] they made the following additions —First, they rejected the sacrament of Baptism, that is, of baptism with water, on account of the promise of a baptism with fire [Luke iii 16] Fabricius here warns his readers that this statement does not prove the Seleucians to have used a baptism with fire Certainly it is no proof of such usage, but since there were attempts made by some heretics to introduce the element of fire into the sacrament of baptism, the Seleucians, who rejected the element of water, may be suspected of the attempt. [See the anonymous tract, *de Baptismo Hæreticorum*, in Fell's *Cyprian*, p 30, and the quotation from Heracleon in the *Fragments of* Clemens Alex, *Opera*, ed Klotz, iv p 39] Secondly, the Seleucians denied the resurrection of the body. The resurrection of man's body, they said, is only its revival in the children of his begetting Thirdly, the Seleucians denied the existence of a visible Paradise Taken alone, this denial, so far from being judged heretical, will be thought only correct, for the visible Paradise was supposed to be a place on earth But in this case the denial appears to have proceeded from the heretical denial of the resurrection of the body [Regarding the visible Paradise see HIERACITES, note 2 The denial is said to have been after Plato It is sufficient to refer to the well-known passage, *Phædo*, sect 143]

The rejection of baptism with water, and the denial of the resurrection, appear to be a consistent following out of the principle of the inherent evil of matter, which Hermogenes held, but expressed with some ambiguity The sects which rejected baptism with water were those which held this principle, and believed that the world was created by an inferior demiurge [Bingham, *Antiq* XI ii 1-4] The wild notion that our Lord laid aside His Body and deposited it in the sun arose from extending this principle into an application to the glorified Body Consistently, the resurrection of man's body is denied altogether It is easier to deny the resurrection altogether than to allow the resurrection and to provide for the subsequent laying aside of the body

SELEZNEVTSCHINS [SABATNIKI]

SELF-BAPTIZERS [SE-BAPTISTS]

SEMI-ARIANS The name by which the great bulk of the Arian sect of heretics became distinguished from the strict Arians after the Council of Nicæa They were a large body of clergy and laity of great political influence in the Eastern Empire, who were opposed alike to the strict definition of orthodox Nicene theologians like St Athanasius, and to the equally strict definition which characterized the logical intellectualism of the old Arians, revived under the leadership of Aetius and Eunomius According to the habits of thought then prevalent (absurdly sneered at by Gibbon and other "free" or loose "thinkers"), each of the three parties embodied their distinctive tenet in a single term, which became a creed in itself The orthodox were represented by "Homoousios," which signified that our Lord is *of one substance* with the Father, and thus shut out entirely the idea of His being a created Person The old Arians, on their revival, adopted the term "Anomoios," which signified exactly the opposite, and, defining the Son to be *unlike in substance* to the Father, expressed the idea that He was a created and not an uncreated Being [ANOMŒANS] The Semi-Arians, halting between these two opinions, endeavoured to find a resting-place for their theology in the middle term "Homoiousios," which was an expression so far definite as to signify that the Son is *of a similar substance* to the Father, but so far indefinite as to permit a great variety of interpretation respecting the extent to which such similarity makes Him to differ from created beings The practical result of this compromising theology was that the Semi-Arians called our Lord Divine, but would not allow that He is "equal to the Father as touching His Godhead," and thus simply and truly God A similar distinction between Divine Nature and Deity has been revived in recent controversies

The Semi-Arian party first came into prominence at the Council of Nicæa [A D 325], under the cautious leadership of Eusebius the ecclesiastical historian, who was Bishop of Cæsarea [ARIANS] His successor in that see, Acacius [A D 338], temporized still further, openly acknowledging that our Lord is no created being, yet pertinaciously declining to adopt the orthodox doctrine of His Eternal Deity [ACACIANS] Towards the close of Constantine's life, family influences brought him over to the Semi-Arian party, and during the reign of his son Constantius they had entire possession of the imperial court While they were thus at the height of their political power the reactionary movement of the old Arians began at Antioch, and the vigorous attempt which was made to supplant the vague and varying creed of the political Semi-Arians by an intellectual development of the heresy in its original form [AETIANS EUNOMIANS], eventually led to the disintegration of the party

During the fifty-six years that elapsed between the Council of Nicæa and that of Constantinople [A D 325 381] as many as eighty councils are on record, a large number of which were held by the Semi-Arian bishops in support of their contests with the orthodox and with their own sects Of these synods St Hilary says—personifying one of the heretical side—"We determine yearly and monthly creeds concerning God, we repent of our determinations, we defend those who repent, we anathematize those whom we have defended, we condemn our own doings in those of others, or others in us, and gnawing each other, we are well nigh devoured one of another" [Hilar *ad Const* ii 5] Nothing in fact was more conspicuous than the unsettled variableness of the Semi-Arian creed Two Confessions of Faith were drawn up at the Council of the Dedication [Socr *Hist Eccl* ii 10], held at Antioch during the consecration of Constantine's magnificent church there [A D 341] Another was drawn up and sent to the Emperor Constans by the bishops of Palestine a few months afterwards [*ibid* ii 18] Four years later [A D 345] another council assembled at Antioch, and again the Semi-Arian bishops who composed it drew up a Confession of their faith [*ibid* ii 19] At Sirmium [A D 351] another creed was set forth by them [Sozom *Hist Eccl* iv 6], and again at the same place seven years later [*ibid*] At Ancyra a synod was held [A D 358] by Basil, the bishop of that see, for the purpose of combating the Anomœan movement which was then going on under the leadership of Aetius, encouraged by Eudoxius, Bishop of Antioch Here Basil and eleven other bishops drew up a petition to the Emperor, asking him to take measures for confirming the Homoiousian declarations promulgated at Philippopolis, Sirmium, and other synods, and this petition, made in the face of the fully-developed Arianism then being brought out by the Anomœans, may be regarded as a movement backward from the Semi-Arian standpoint towards that of the Nicene faith no creed being drawn up by them From this time the reaction went steadily on, growing stronger at the Western Council of Ariminum [A D 359], and the Eastern Council of Seleucia [A D 359] In a few years it was so stimulated by the progress of the Anomœan section of the Arians, and by the development of the Macedonian heresy respecting the Third Person of the Holy Trinity out of the Arian respecting the second, that in the year 366 as many as fifty nine Semi-Arian bishops recanted their errors and subscribed to the Nicene Creed [Socr *Hist Eccl* iv 12] There is no evidence of any large number of the party afterwards existing Many others, doubtless, came back to the Church, not a few plunged into the heresy of the MACEDONIANS, and some, like Eudoxius of Antioch, became avowed Anomœans [ARIANS DICT *of* THEOL, art SEMI-ARIANS Newman, *Hist Arians* Pusey's *Councils of the Church*, ch v]

SEMIDALITES A sect of ACEPHALI, which sprung up originally under the name of BARSANIANS, at the end of the fifth century They had no succession of priests, and professed to keep up the celebration of a valid Eucharist by placing a few crumbs of some of the bread which had been consecrated by Dioscorus into a vessel of meal [σεμίδαλις], and then using as fully consecrated the bread baked from it. [Damasc *de Hæres.* iii. Baron *ad ann* 535 Neale's *Patriarchate of Alexandria*, ii 22]

SEMI-JUDAIZERS Two sects have been known by this name in Poland. [1] The first of these was originated by Francis David, superintendent of the Socinian community in Transylvania, and was opposed by Faustus Socinus, although their distinctive principle of refusing worship to Christ appears not to have differed from that of Socinus himself When it was found impossible to obtain a recantation from David, he was thrown into prison, where he died at an advanced age in the year 1579 [2] A sect of the same name was established a few years later by Martin Seidelius, a Silesian He developed the Socinian heresy into an opinion that while a Messiah had indeed been promised to the Jews, He had never appeared, and would never appear, on account of their unbelief This opinion he followed up with another respecting the Christ of the Gospels, that He was a teacher whose only office was to re-proclaim the laws of natural religion, but this blasphemer at the same time rejected the Gospels and the whole of the New Testament as works of a much later date than that attributed to them In Russia a similar sect is called SABATNIKI [Zeltner's *Hist Crypto-Socin* i 268, 355 *Biblioth Fratr Polon*]

SEMI-PELAGIANS This name was invented by the Schoolmen to designate a large number of persons who, chiefly in Gaul, during the fifth century, embraced a modified form of Pelagianism The movement was a reaction no less against the extreme views on Predestination held by St. Augustine in his later years than against the extravagant assertions about Free-will made by Pelagius

As early as A D 426, the monks of Adrumetum, in Byzacene Africa, betrayed some alarm at expressions used by St Augustine in a letter [*Ep* 194] addressed to Sixtus, then a priest, afterwards Bishop of Rome But the real founder of Semi-Pelagianism was the famous Cassian, an Eastern monk of Scythian extraction [Gennad *de Viris illustr* 61], who had been trained in a monastery at Bethlehem, and had resided afterwards among the monks of Egypt prior to taking up his residence at Constantinople Here he was ordained deacon by Chrysostom, and was selected by the clergy of that city, during the banishment of their bishop, to proceed on a mission to Innocent I at Rome, where he probably received priest's orders [Noris, *Hist Pelag* lib ii c 1]

He subsequently migrated further west, and settled at Marseilles Here he founded monasteries for both sexes, becoming himself abbot of one of them, dedicated to St Victor [c A D 415] While holding this office he found time to write several books, which have earned him the title of the founder of Semi-Pelagianism [1] Information of these circumstances was at length conveyed by two laymen, Hilary, and Prosper of Aquitaine, to St. Augustine, driven from his home by the Gothic invasion and a refugee at Marseilles, and the news reached him just long enough before his death to enable him to write the works "De Prædestinatione Sanctorum" and "De Dono Perseverantiæ" [A D 430] After this [A D 431] they appealed to Cœlestine at Rome, in the hopes of obtaining an official condemnation of Cassian's doctrines The Popes generally throughout the controversy declared themselves on the orthodox side, especially Sixtus III, Leo I, and, somewhat later, Hormisdas, and the present occasion was no exception, although Cœlestine avoided the real difficulty by using mild terms, and regretting the agitation of curious questions (quæstiones indisciplinatæ) a decision which the Semi-Pelagians, led by Vincent, affected to interpret in their own favour It was either the unsatisfactory result of this appeal, or the spread of the objectionable views, which shortly induced Prosper to compose the ' Carmen de Ingratis,"[2] and still later "Pro Augustino Liber contra Collatorem," and the "De Vocatione Gentium," the latter of which however, being anonymous, has also been attributed, by an anachronism, to Ambrose of Milan, and with rather more probability to Leo the Great

About this time, A D 434-435, Vincentius, a native of Mauritania Cæsariensis, the afterwards celebrated monk of the Abbey of Lerins in Provence, began to attack the extreme predestinarian views of St Augustine His "Commonitorium," now a handbook of orthodoxy, is supposed to have been originally directed against the Augustinian development of the doctrines of grace and predestination, and slight indications of its bias are considered (by Vossius, Noris, Natalis, etc) to be afforded by the absence of any condemnatory allusions to Semi-Pelagianism or laudatory allusions to St Augustine [3] The same abbey produced another prominent champion of the new school in the person of Faustus He was a native of Great Britain [Ussher, *Antiq Eccles Brit* cap xiii], but at this time was Abbot of Lerins, whence he was promoted [A D 456] to the bishopric of Riez, which he held till his death [A D 491], with the exception of three years of banishment suffered at the hands of the Arian king Euric [A D 481-484] His main controversy was with one of his clergy, named Lucidus, who held advanced predestinarian views, and whom he first tried to silence by argument, in a book entitled ' De Gratia Dei et Humanæ Mentis Libero Arbitrio," and then summoned before a council at Arles [A D 475], which, as well as a synod held at Lyons in the same year, decided against Lucidus and in favour of the Semi-Pelagian doctrines of his bishop

Among the moderate but distinguished advocates of the same views, towards the close of this century, must be mentioned Gennadius, a priest of Marseilles, most of whose writings are lost, and among their opponents on the orthodox side, Claudianus Mamertus, Avitus Bishop of Vienne, and Cæsarius, Bishop of Arles [A D 501-542], the author of a book "De Gratia et Libero Arbitrio" They were supported in their opposition by the consistent action of the Roman prelates Pope Gelasius condemned the writings of Faustus in a decretal epistle [A D 493] Hormisdas [A D 514-523] confirmed the verdict of his predecessor at the request of an African bishop, Possessor, and also of certain Eastern monks, who, wishing for a still stronger declaration of opinion, made a further appeal to Fulgentius of Ruspe, one of the sixty African bishops exiled by the Vandals from Byzacene Africa to Sardinia, and subsequently recalled by Hilderic Fulgentius employed the leisure afforded by banishment in writing two books in confutation of Semi-Pelagian views, "De Incarnatione et Gratia" and "De Veritate Prædestinationis et Gratiæ," and was the cause of a circular letter being issued in the name of the African bishops, his own included, in condemnation of Faustus

Shortly afterwards [A D 529] the judgment already procured from Italian and African prelates was re-echoed at the Council of Orange, in the province of Arles, under the leadership of Cæsarius Its four short canons, signed by fourteen bishops,[4] subscribed by six prefects of Gaul, and confirmed in the same year at the Council of Valence, in the province of Vienne, asserted—

[1] That by the sin of Adam free-will has been so perverted and weakened, that none have since then been able to love God, or believe in Him, or to do good actions for His sake, unless Divine grace has prevented them

[2] After grace has been received by baptism, all baptized persons are able by the divine assistance and co-operation, to do all things that belong to the soul's salvation, if they are willing to work with faith

[3] We not only do not believe that some persons have been predestined to evil by the divine power, but we pronounce anathema against all who incline to hold such an opinion

[4] We also profess and believe that in every good work it is not we who begin, and who are afterwards assisted by the mercy of God, but God Himself first inspires faith and love, without

[1] *De Institutis Cœnobiorum*, lib xii *Collationes Patrum*, lib xxiv *De Incarnatione Christi adv Nestorium*, lib vii

[2] Preserved in the Appendix X of the Benedictine edition of St Augustine's work

[3] It is necessary to add that the identity of the author of the "Commonitorium" with the Semi Pelagian Vincent is emphatically denied by some authors. [Baronius, *Ann* v 604, B]

[4] The names of these bishops were Cæsarius, Julian, Constantius, Cyprian, Eucherius I, Eucherius II, Heraclius, Principius, Philagrius, Maximus, Prætextatus, Alethius, Lupercian, Vindemialis [Ussher, *Brit Eccles. Antiq* cap xiv]

any previous good works on our part, so that we faithfully demand the sacrament of baptism, and after baptism are able, with His assistance, to accomplish what is pleasing to Him Whence it is most clearly to be believed that the marvellous faith of the thief whom the Lord summoned to Paradise, of the centurion Cornelius to whom an angel was sent, and of Zacchæus who was found worthy to entertain our Lord, was not natural but the gift of God

Cæsarius despatched these canons to Rome, where they were ratified by Boniface II From this time the Semi-Pelagians, as a clearly defined body ceased to exist, although persons inclined to hold the same or very similar opinions have always existed both within and outside of the Church

The general object of Semi-Pelagian doctrine was described by Cassian in his Collations to be a protest against two extremes, the Augustinian denial of free-will and the Pelagian infringement of grace This explains the name "Predestinarians," which they conferred on the orthodox party, and the taunt of Prosper, that they could neither agree wholly with heretics nor with Catholic Christians, but that they devised some third position of their own neither making peace with the one nor remaining loyal to the other

The following positions are deduced from Cassian's works, not, indeed, laid down with the logical sequence and consistency which marks the argumentative writings of St Augustine, but as inferred from a comparison of passages

Since the Fall all men have original sin and are subject to death, but they have not lost a knowledge of God or free-will It can neither be maintained (with St. Augustine) that the commencement of what is good in us always originates in God, nor (with Pelagius) that it always originates with ourselves Sometimes it is God Who first implants good thoughts and purposes in us Sometimes it is man who takes the first step, and whom God afterwards supports with His assistance In either case the grace of God is unmerited, not absolutely but relatively, as it bestows on the weak and worthless efforts of man such favours here and so great reward hereafter

From these and other writings four points of Augustinian teaching may be specified as rejected by the Semi-Pelagian school

[1] Unconditional election

This point came up in connection with the discussion about the fate of infants dying after baptism or without it The Semi-Pelagians asserted that God granted to the former the grace of justification and salvation, because He foresaw that if they had lived they would have been faithful, that He denied this favour to the latter, because He foresaw that had they lived they would have been rebellious St Augustine maintained that the difference of conduct on God's part towards these infants was the consequence of an unconditional decree of predestination in favour of the former, and he did not shrink from the dreadful alternative which was forced upon him by the inexorable rigour of his logic in the case of the latter

[2] The inability of man under any circumstances to do good

[3] The constraining influence of grace on free-will

[4] The final perseverance of the Saints

On the other hand, the Semi-Pelagians made an equally emphatic protest against the accusation of pure Pelagianism which was sometimes attempted to be brought against them "Let no one imagine,' said Cassian, "that we give support to the profane notion of some, who assert that the sum of salvation is in our own power, and by ascribing everything to free-will, make the grace of God to be dispensed according to each man's merit" [*Collat* xiii 16] Unlike Pelagius, he did not deny,—

[1] The existence of original sin in all men

[2] Its results, such as concupiscence, death, the loss of right of succession to eternal happiness Nor did he assert that

[3] Human nature is still as healthful as it was in the time of Adam's innocence

[4] Or that man is able without the assistance of grace to perform every kind of good work, to reach the highest degree of perfection, and to accomplish the work of his salvation by his own natural power

But he insisted that original sin has not so far weakened human nature, that man is unable naturally to desire to have faith, to quit sin, or to recover righteousness, that when he entertains these good dispositions God recompenses them by the gift of grace, so that the commencement of salvation actually may rest with man and not with God, although this was not necessarily and always the case.

[Prosperi Aquitani *Liber contra Collatorem*, *Pro Augustino Responsiones*, *Carmen de Ingratis* Fausti Cassini, Gennadii Massiliensis *Opera*. Tillemont, *Hist Eccles* xiii xiv xv Noris, *Hist Pelag* lib. ii. Ussher, *Brit Eccles Antiq* xiv. *Jean Cassien, Sa Vie et ses Ecrits*, L F Meyer, Strasburg, 1840 Vossius, *Hist Pelag*]

SEMLER [Rationalists]

SENTENTIARII A name given to those who slavishly follow Peter Lombard's system of "Sentences" [Schoolmen]

SEPARATES A sect of Calvinistic Methodists which had a short duration in North America in the middle of the last century It originated about the year 1740 in the preaching of Whitefield, and at first took the name of "New Lights," but being organized into separate societies by a preacher named Shubal Stearne, they took the name of Separates In the year 1751 Stearne joined the Baptist sect, and carried many of his followers with him, when the name which they had assumed ceased to be any longer used

SEPARATION OF EASTERN AND WESTERN CHURCHES The suspension of acts of communion and friendship between those Churches which were situated within the boundaries of the Eastern Empire of Rome and those which were comprehended within the Western Empire This suspension of communion was formally declared in the year 1054, and has not since been revoked

From the earliest age of the Church there had been diversities of custom and modes of thought among the Asiatic Churches and those of Europe which tended towards isolation in feeling and, in some degree, in opinion The Paschal controversy dated from the time of Polycarp of Smyrna and Anicetus of Rome [A D 160], and as early as A D 180, Victor, Bishop of Rome, had threatened the Eastern Churches with excommunication for commemorating our Lord's Death on the anniversary day of the month, whatever day of the week that might be, instead of on a Friday Later on, the various heresies which arose so rapidly in Asia and Alexandria caused the Eastern Churches to be looked on with suspicion by those of the West The transactions connected with the Monophysite heresy led to an actual breach of communion between the Bishops of Rome and the East, which lasted for thirty-five years [A D 484-519], and another similar suspension of communion sprung from the Monothelite controversy in the year 667, which ended in the condemnation of Pope Honorius [A D 625-638] as a heretic by the sixth Œcumenical Council in A D 681 [MONOPHYSITES MONOTHELITES] The Iconoclast controversy also caused intense bitterness between the two sections of the Church, and did more than anything else to prepare the way for permanent alienation [ICONOCLASTS]

But it must also be remembered that the separation of the two Empires had much to do with the separation between the Churches within their respective boundaries The political rivalry and jealousy which arose between Rome and Constantinople naturally extended itself to the relations between the patriarchs of the two cities, and an aggregation of the neighbouring dioceses around each of these two principal and imperial ones was equally inevitable The tendency to a geographical and political division began still more to influence the tendency towards ecclesiastical division when the Western Empire fell entirely into the hands of the Germanic races, and the Greek character assumed by Rome in the early centuries of Christianity altogether passed away

Although, therefore, an unity of the Church, which should consist of close subjective as well as objective union, was possible enough while the Christian world was bound together by the common tie of an united imperial nationality, as it was during the first three centuries of Christianity, that external unity became more and more vague as the disintegration of the Empire went on Very little ecclesiastical intercourse was held between East and West after the accession of Charlemagne to full imperial authority over Europe in A D 800 and such attempts as were made to renew it generally ended in formalizing differences, which, if let alone, might have died away in course of time through the comparative vagueness of their character

The most important of those differences arose from the insertion of the words "and the Son" after the words "proceeding from the Father" in the article of the Nicene Creed respecting God the Holy Ghost. This change in the Nicene Creed was first made at the Council of Toledo [A D 589], when the Goths were giving up their Arianism and becoming orthodox in the sixth century So late as the ninth century, however, when an appeal on the subject was made to Leo III [A D 795-816], although he allowed the "Filioque" to be orthodox, he ordered the Constantinopolitan Creed in its integrity to be engraved on silver tablets both in Latin and Greek, and hung up in the Church of the Lateran as a standard copy It was formally inserted in the Creed for use in Divine Service by order of the Emperor Charlemagne about A D 788, and at last Pope Benedict VIII [A D 1014] ordered the Creed to be so used throughout Western Christendom Thus a change of much importance was made in the Creed set forth by the General Councils on the authority of Provincial Councils and of the Bishop of Rome, and whether the insertion of the "Filioque" made the truth asserted more exact or not, it is certain that the Eastern Church was justified in protesting, as it did all along, against any change whatever being made except under the sanction of an authority as binding on the whole Church as that which originally set forth the Creed at Nicæa and Constantinople

Fresh trouble between Rome and Constantinople arose out of the appointment of Photius to the patriarchal throne of the latter city by the Emperor Michael III in A D 858 Photius was recognised by all the bishops of his own patriarchate, but having been consecrated by Gregory, Bishop of Syracuse, whom Pope Nicolas I had deposed, he was therefore excommunicated by the latter Photius in return excommunicated the Pope, and the quarrel went on growing until at the death of Photius (while in exile) in the year 891, the Pope arrogantly insisted on the degradation of all bishops and priests who had received their orders from the patriarch This arrogant assertion of authority embittered the relations between the Churches still more, and from that time all friendliness between Rome and Constantinople may be said to have been interrupted

The final suspension of communion arose out of conduct almost equally intemperate on the part of Michael Cerularius, Patriarch of Constantinople, who, immediately on his accession in A D 1053, assumed the title of "Universal Patriarch," and, further to exasperate Rome, caused all the churches and monasteries which the Latins had in his city to be closed on account of the differences which existed between the Latin and the Eastern rites In justification of this harsh measure he wrote a letter to the Bishop of Irani in Apuleia which he directed him to communicate to the Pope, Leo IX, and to all the Western Church, and in this letter, among other assertions equally unwarrantable, he declared that the Western custom of using unleavened bread invalidated the Holy Eucharist [Canisii *Thes Monument Eccl* iii 281, *sqq*] The Emperor endeavoured to allay the indignation which this intemperate conduct of the patriarch excited at Rome, and having persuaded Cerularius to enter into negotiations with the Pope, the latter sent three legates to Constantinople in 1054, entrusted with his formal reply, in which he retorted the charges of error, and told the patriarch that unless he recanted these errors he would be visited with an irrevocable anathema from God and from all Catholics The legates declared also that they had come not to argue about the points in dispute, but to insist on the adoption of Latin customs by the Eastern Church, and behaved with extreme insolence, such as has too often characterized the ambassadors of the Popes [Coteler *Eccl Græc Monum* ii 138, 145, 164]

Being countenanced in some degree by the Emperor, who wished, for political reasons, to conciliate the Pope, the legates then passed sentence of excommunication on "all who contradicted the faith of the holy Roman Apostolic See" Before leaving Constantinople they had also the arrogance to lay on the altar of St Sophia an excommunication of the patriarch, and of all who supported him, on the ground of heresy "Let them," wrote the legates, "be Anathema Maranatha, cum Simoniacis, Valesiis, Arianis, Donatistis, Nicolaitis, Severianis, Pneumatomachis, et Manichæis, et Nazarenis, et cum omnibus hæreticis, imo cum Diabolo et angelis ejus, nisi forte resipuerint" The particular heresies alleged by the legates were such as the marriage of the clergy and the use of the Nicene Creed without the "Filioque," and others of a similar kind, which were in reality cases in which the conservative spirit of the East had retained ancient customs that had been set aside by the Church of Rome and the churches which looked to it as their guide As soon as the legates had left Constantinople the patriarch summoned a council and retorted the excommunication

Excommunications were sown broadcast by some of the prelates of the Middle Ages, (as they were by the Presbyterians in Scotland at the time of the Reformation,) and it is very difficult to estimate either their spiritual value or their influence upon the subsequent course of events But as regards those in which the long-growing alienation between East and West culminated, it may be doubted whether they can be taken for more, historically, than passionate expressions of an instinct which told the world that the Eastern and Western races had diverged so far from each other that external ecclesiastical unity was no longer possible If there had been less of Papal arrogance on both sides, the ecclesiastical divarication would have followed the divergence of the two races without being accompanied by any such extraordinary bitterness as to interpose obstacles to occasional acts of friendship and communion in after times and the Churches of the East and West, which were inevitably drifting away from each other, would have done so in silence and in peace As it was, the quarrels which accompanied the separation of the two ecclesiastical races were accompanied by insults on both sides, which made reunion possible only after formal reconciliation, and they have not known enough of each other in subsequent times to make such a reconciliation easy It was attempted by the Eastern Church in the year 1274 at the Council of Lyons, when the Emperor Michael Palæologus and a few Greek bishops accepted the "Filioque," and submitted themselves to the Papal supremacy but this act was not recognised by the Eastern Church at large It was attempted again at the Council of Florence in the year 1439 The question of the Filioque was argued before the Council, and some concessions were made on both sides, the Emperor, John Palæologus, and thirty Greek bishops being present A decree of union was drawn up in Greek and Latin, which was signed by the Emperor and several bishops, but, as in the former case, the concessions made were greater, especially that respecting the supremacy of the Pope, than the Eastern churches at home were prepared to endorse One of the Greek bishops present had said, "Mori malo, quam unquam Latinizare," and this saying represented the feeling of the Eastern Church in general much better than the acts of the Emperor and his friends, for at a council held at Constantinople in 1450 those acts were formally repudiated In quite recent days, as late as 1848, Pope Pius IX wrote an "Encyclical Letter to the Easterns," exhorting them to union, but as the exhortation was combined with the requirement that the Easterns should submit themselves entirely to the supremacy of the Pope, his overtures were of course rejected

It is, in fact, this arrogant claim to supremacy which is, and always has been, the chief obstacle to a renewal of open communion between the East and the West As to the "Filioque" of the Nicene Creed, "the discrepancy is one of words, for the Greeks confess that the Spirit is not only the Spirit of the Father, but of the Son that He has the same Substance, Divinity, and Majesty, as the Father and the Son, that He receives of the Son, and so cannot speak of Himself, that He is manifested and given to us by the Son, and therefore we may charitably conclude that while, from a veneration for the Councils of Nicæa and Constantinople, they wish to keep the Creed untouched, they do in fact maintain that truth so necessary to salvation" [Forbes *on Nicene Creed*, 263] On the other hand, to use the words of Manning, once Archdeacon of Chichester, and afterwards titular Archbishop of Westminster, "be the faults of the Greek churches never so great, they cannot be laid in the balance against the usurpation of a supreme pontificate by the Bishop of Rome This attempt of the Roman patriarch to subject the four Eastern patriarchates to his exaggerated jurisdiction is a claim which, so long as persisted in, must throw upon the Roman Church the sin of keeping open an inveterate division" [Manning *on Unity of the Ch* 358]

It need hardly be added that the suspension of subjective unity between the East and West does not affect their objective unity The organic ties of constitution, liturgy, substantial doctrine, and sacramental life still remain, for each retains by means of these communion with the Divine Head of the Church and the Fountain of its life Those whom God has joined together by such sacred inner bonds man cannot sunder by cutting those outer cords by which visible unity is maintained

It may also be hoped that the increasing intercourse between the East and Europe may help forward Christian intercourse between the Churches. Change of language, change of habit, territorial alterations, want of opportunity to set right misunderstandings and many other such causes, have contributed largely to maintain the division, and the influence of all these is being daily lessened by the singular facilities for intercommunication which have been opened out in recent times Sanguine minds will likewise remember that Rome does not now represent the whole Catholic Church of Europe, and may look forward to a time when the great Anglican Church may have given to it the office of drawing East and West into an outward fellowship consistent with that true objective Unity in the Body of Christ by which they have always been, and still are, bound together

SEPARATISTS The name assumed by some of the Puritans, perhaps the early TRASKITES, who so called themselves because they professed to be separated from the world They condemned all taste in dress, and all joyousness in life, meeting innocent merriment with the text, "Woe to you that laugh, for ye shall mourn" They cultivated melancholy looks, sighed often, eschewed music and all festivities, condemned the bearing of arms, and refused oaths In these principles we recognize the class of Puritans afterwards represented by the Quakers [Pagitt's *Heresiography*, p 67, ed 1662]

SEPARATISTS was likewise a general name used in the seventeenth century for all persons who separated themselves from the Church of England Some were also called "Semi Separatists" "They will hear our sermons, but not our Common Prayer, and of these you may see every Sunday in our streets, sitting and standing about our doors, who, when prayers are done, rush into our churches to hear our sermon" [Pagitt's *Heresiography*, p 94, ed 1662]

SEPARATISTS A German Pietist sect assumed this name about the close of the last century at Wurtemberg Meeting with much opposition on account of their proceeding further than the Pietists in general, and actually forming a body distinct from the Lutherans, a portion of them emigrated to America in the year 1803, where they formed the HARMONY SOCIETY Those who remained in Germany became known as KORNTHALITES

SEPARATISTS [1] An Irish sect of SANDEMANIANS established in Dublin by a seceding clergyman named Walker early in the nineteenth century They are sometimes called "Walkerites" [2] Another sect of Sandemanians was formed under the same name at New Ross by two clergymen named Kelly and Carr [3] A third sect was formed professing strict Evangelical and Millenarian tenets by a clergyman named Darby, and these are sometimes also called "Darbyites" as well as Separatists From these sprung the PLYMOUTH BRETHREN

SERPENTINI. [OPHITES]

SERVETIANS The followers of Michael Servetus, or Miguel Servede [A.D 1509-1553], a Spaniard, who developed Unitarianism in the direction of Pantheism among the Calvinistic Reformers

Servetus was the son of a notary named Réves or Serve, at Villaneuva in Arragon, and was educated for the Civil Law at the University of Toulouse At twenty-one years of age he accompanied Quintana, the Confessor of Charles V, to the coronation of the Emperor at Bologna From thence he went, by way of Lyons and Geneva, to Basle, where he became acquainted with Œcolampadius, and afterwards to Strasburg, where he associated with Bucer and Capito Both at Basle and Strasburg Servetus had made himself notorious by his public denial of the doctrine of the Trinity, and when only twenty-two years of age he ventured to print a work entitled *De Trinitatis Erroribus*, which was followed the next year by another entitled *Dialogorum de Trinitate libri duo* In these works Servetus maintained the peculiar theory, that before the Creation of the world God had produced within Himself two personal representations, or manners of existence, which were to be the means of communication between Himself and men that these two representatives of the Deity were called the Word and the Holy Ghost that the Word was united to the Man Christ, Who might thus be called God that the Holy Ghost animates all nature, and produces in men all that is good in them and finally, that both these representatives of Deity would, after the destruction of the world, be re-absorbed into the Person of God

Having seen these two books through the press at Haguenau Servetus returned to Basle and thence to Lyons, living in the latter city until about the year 1536, when he went to study medicine at Paris Under the name of Michael de Villeneuve, he afterwards practised for a short time as a physician at Lyons, and in 1541 went to live in the household of the Archbishop of Vienne, where he resided until nearly the close of his life, openly a good Catholic, but secretly writing his last and worst work At Paris Servetus is said to have become acquainted with Calvin, but it may be doubted whether he had visited that city before Calvin's final departure from it, and it is not certain that they ever met before the close of Servetus' life, though they corresponded for fifteen or sixteen years

In the year 1553 Servetus published a third work in support of his opinions, which had now taken a strongly pantheistic colour, entitling it *Christianismi Restitutio* This was printed anonymously, but its authorship was discovered and its author imprisoned by the Inquisition He escaped from prison, but his effigy was hanged and burned amidst a pile of his books, shewing what fate he would have met with if he had remained From Vienne he purposed going to

Naples to practise again as a physician, but taking Geneva on his road, lay concealed there for a month, when he fell into the hands of the magistrates, who had received information of his presence from Calvin, the latter having declared seven years before that if Servetus came to Geneva he should not leave the city alive

Having escaped the fate of a heretic at the hands of the Roman Inquisition at Vienne, Servetus was now put on his trial for heresy before the Protestant Inquisition at Geneva. After long controversy, in which Calvin took a very active and violent part, Servetus was condemned to death as a heretic on October 26th, 1553, and on the following day he suffered a miserably protracted death by fire in the great stronghold of Calvinism, and with the full acquiescence of Calvin An elaborate treatise in support of his execution was published by Beza under the title *De Hæreticis a civili Magistratu puniendis*, and it was also defended by Melanchthon and other Protestant writers as a "just and honourable proceeding" [*Quart Rev* lxxxviii 551][1]

The followers of Servetus were principally to be found in Lombardy, the best known of them being Bernardino Ochino [A D 1487-1564] They were driven from Lombardy by the Inquisition, and also from Switzerland, where they had taken refuge, eventually finding a home in Poland among the followers of the elder Socinus, with whom they amalgamated into the sect of the SOCINIANS

The eleventh volume of Schlusselburg's *Hæreticorum Catalogus*, extending to 623 pages, is entirely occupied with a treatise *De Secta Servetianarum*, and a Life of Servetus was published in 1748—republished with additions in 1749—by Mosheim the ecclesiastical historian

SETHIANS The last chapter but one of the book of Irenæus against Heresies contains a most obscure account of some Valentinian Gnostics who are generally understood to be the Ophites and the Sethians [Iren *adv Hær* xxx] Neither of these sects is named throughout the chapter, nor is there anything to distinguish the opinions of one from the other, if indeed these two sects are intended Hippolytus devotes four chapters of his fifth book to the refutation of their heresy, but gives no account of their history Epiphanius was doubtful whether the sect had not become extinct in his time, but thought he had met with traces of it somewhere in Egypt Philaster and Augustine are equally silent respecting their history

The sect derived its name from the peculiar veneration with which its adherents regarded the patriarch Seth, a veneration set up, perhaps, in opposition to that of the CAINITES for Cain Whether this was or was not the real origin of their sect, they professed to believe themselves descended from Seth, while a large portion of mankind was descended from Cain, of whom Ham was the representative in the Ark They also believed that our Lord was Seth appearing again in the world Many writers identify the sect with that of the Ophites, and they were plainly part of the great heretical family of Gnostics Hippolytus says that their doctrine was all contained in a book called "The Paraphrase of Seth," of which nothing is known [Hippol. *Refut* v. 14-17 Epiphan *Hæres* xxxix]

SEVENTH DAY BAPTISTS The modern representatives of the TRASKITES, or Sabbatarians of the seventeenth century They have never been numerous in England, and at the present day there are not above forty or fifty in the whole country, with two small meeting-houses A community of the sect was formed by an emigrant named Stephen Mumford, at Newport, Rhode Island, about 1681, and there are now said to be about fifty congregations of them, numbering 6000 members, in the United States

SEVERIANS A sect of Encratite Gnostics, successors of the Tatianists, whose complicated system of Æons they abandoned, but whose Encratite notions of creation they developed or heightened

Epiphanius supposes their leader Severus to have preceded Tatian, but Eusebius, Theodoret, and Jerome make him Tatian's successor These latter authorities are followed by most ecclesiastical historians, and the silence of Irenæus and Hippolytus regarding Severus renders the later date most probable But of his history nothing is known

The system of Tatian as regards the Deity and the powers emanating from Him was identical, or nearly so, with the system of Valentinus [VALENTINIANS TATIANISTS] From the brief notices which have come down to us, Severus appears to have exchanged this elaborate system for a simpler one founded upon that of the Ophites and Sethians For Epiphanius [*Hær* xlv] ascribes to the Severians a belief in the well-known Gnostic power Ialdabaoth, who appears in the Ophite system as the first offspring of Bythus and Ennoia [Iren i 30] The Severians held that Ialdabaoth was a great ruler of the powers, that from him sprung the Devil that the Devil being cast down to the earth in the form of a serpent produced the vine, whose snake-like tendrils indicate its origin that the Devil also created woman and the lower half of man Ialdabaoth was the Demiurge of the Ophites, the first descendant of the first man (Anthropos), for so they called the manifestations of power from the Bythus of the Deity After him were six others in succession, to whom belonged, and among whom were distributed, the prophets of the Old Testament These several and successive generations were so many steps of degradation, a notion taken, as the names were taken, from the Cabbala But the Severians appear to have arrived at the same conclusion at one step, making the Devil the immediate offspring of Ialdabaoth And they divided the work of the Demiurge between Ialdabaoth and the Devil, as between good and evil powers

The origin of these extraordinary and blasphe

[1] Thirteen years afterwards [A D 1566] the Antitrinitarian John Valentine Gentilis was beheaded at Berne by the Calvinists for his opinions [ANTITRINITARIANS, p 37]

mous fictions is not far to seek Men of ascetic temperament, striving, perhaps sincerely, but with unchastened and unhumbled intellects, to attain to innocency, oppressed by the contemplation of the intermixture of good and evil in the world, perplexed by speculations on the origin of evil, which were the source of early heresy, and surrounded by other speculations of heathen and Cabbalistic philosophy, were led to believe that the world was created by different principles, by powers of different natures The mind of man, his reason and conscience, were referred to beneficent powers, his senses and appetites to inferior and noxious powers The evils of the world were seen to arise mainly from the passions of intemperance and lust And as in the first transgression, Adam referred his sin to the gift of Eve, so they lightened their sin to themselves by representing wine and women, not their own lusts, as tempters These were thought therefore to be the work of an imperfect, an evil creator This train of thought was embodied in the allegory (for it can hardly be looked upon in any other light), that man from the head to the navel was framed by the beneficent power, thence downwards by the evil power, that woman and the vine were created by the evil Demiurge

Eusebius states that the Severians made use of the Law and Prophets and Gospels, giving them a peculiar interpretation, but abused the Apostle Paul, and rejected his Epistles, rejecting also the Acts of the Apostles [Euseb *Hist Eccl* iv 29] Augustine, on the other hand, states that they rejected the Old Testament [Aug *Hær* xxiv] It may be that both these statements are too hastily generalized from partial data that as the Ophites distributed the prophets among their seven gradually deteriorating powers, so the Severians divided them between Ialdabaoth and his evil offspring In estimating the force of Eusebius' words there must be borne in mind also the habit of the Cabbalistic Gnostics to appeal to the Old Testament

The tenet of the creation of the world by an inferior Demiurge presupposes the inherent evil of matter, and it is a natural deduction from this to deny the resurrection of the body The Severians followed out their principle to this conclusion, according to Augustine [*Hær* xxiv] Natalis Alexander, resting on Eusebius' statement that they admitted the authority of the Law and the Prophets, denies the probability of Augustine's report But the peculiar interpretations which Eusebius tells of will well admit the rejection of the resurrection of the body The Severians, it need hardly be added, were Docetæ, as were the Tatianists Later still appeared another party among the Encratites who renounced all property [APOTACTICS]

SEVERIANS [PHTHARTOLATRÆ]

SHAFTESBURY [RATIONALISTS]

SHAKERS A name given to the early Quakers They are thus called "Shakers or Quakers" by the continuator of Pagitt's Heresiography, who wrote about the year 1661 [Pagitt's *Heresiogr* 244, ed 1662]

SHAKERS or SHAKING QUAKERS An American sect founded by an English emigrant named Ann Lee, about the year 1776 Their general character is very similar to that of the Quakers, but they use a peculiar vibratory dance in their religious services, of a similar fanatic kind with the custom of the JUMPERS, from which they take their distinctive name They also assume the titles of "The United Society of Believers" and "The Millennial Church "

About the year 1747 some Lancashire Quakers, who had become disciples of the CAMISARDS, formed themselves into a society, professing to be influenced by no creed or custom in use among Christians, but to be governed from time to time as the Spirit of God should dictate The original leader of this society was Jane Wardley, and two other leading members of it were a Manchester man and his wife named Townley Ann Lee, daughter of a Manchester blacksmith [A D 1736-1784], was drawn over to the society by the Townleys when she was about twenty-two years of age, when she had become the wife of a blacksmith named Abraham Stanley Some years afterwards, in 1770, she was elected by the members of their society as their "spiritual Mother in Christ," in consequence of a supposed special revelation which she had received and from that time she was always known, as she is still remembered, by the name of "Mother Ann "

This woman, who earned her living by preparing beaver's fur for the hatters, professed to work miracles and to speak with tongues, as the Irvingite women professed to do sixty years afterwards But she also seems to have made a blasphemous, or a mad, claim to divinity, saying to those who addressed her as they would have addressed an ordinary person, "I am Ann the Word" In the year 1776 she emigrated to America in company with her husband and some relatives, who acknowledged her pretensions, and the family, numbering about ten persons, settled at Watervliet, seven miles from Albany Here the number of the Mother's followers began rapidly to increase but the founder of the sect died in the year 1784, her place being taken by James Whitaker, one of the Lancashire men, and afterwards by an American Baptist preacher named Father Joseph Since the death of Father Joseph in 1796, two men and two women have been elected in regular succession as the "ministry" of the sect, but it is a superstition of the Shakers that Ann Lee is still with them in an invisible form, and hence her successors are only considered as her deputies and representatives

Dr Dwight became acquainted with the Shakers in January 1783, when he was detained at one of their settlements by a snow-storm, "In their worship," he says, "these people sang in what they called an 'unknown tongue' It was a succession of unmeaning sounds frequently repeated, half-articulated, and plainly gotten by heart, for they all uttered the same sounds in succession They practised many contortions of the body and distortions of the countenance The gesticulations of the women were violent, and had been practised so often and in such a degree as to have fixed their features in an unnatural position, made them goggle-eyed, suffused their eyes with blood, covered their faces with sicky paleness, and made them appear like persons just escaped, or rather just escaping, from a violent disease The motions of the men were very moderate, and seemed rather to be condescendingly than earnestly made" [Dwight's *Travels*].

The principal settlement of the Shakers is now at New Lebanon, a city of their own creation, which they began to build soon after Mother Ann's death, but they have seventeen branches of the community in several other places in the United States, and altogether they are said to be about 6000 in number They repudiate the use of sacraments, alleging that all external ordinances were superseded when Christianity was established in the world. They also consider that true Christianity was never taught between the Apostolic age and the rise of their sect Although they do not impose celibacy as a necessary rule, married couples do not continue to live in their settlement.

A modern writer describes their worship at the present time in the following words "The men and women, all clad in grey cloth and wearing list slippers, occupied distinct positions in the place of meeting A short extemporaneous address was delivered by an elder of the party, who reminded his auditory of the mercies they had all experienced during the past week, and bade them therefore unite with him in 'cheerful expressions of gratitude to their heavenly Benefactor' Upon the conclusion of this brief exhortation, twelve of the company arranged themselves in two lines, back to back, in the centre of the apartment, the rest of the congregation stood up in couples around them, the men forming one segment of the circle, the women the other Thereupon those in the middle commenced singing in a loud voice some doggrel verses to a very lively tune —

'I love to dance and love to sing,
And, oh! I love my Maker
I love to dance and love to sing,
And love to be a Shaker,' etc

The several couples, perpetually smiling or giggling at each other, and flapping their hands in mid-air, accompanied this strange kind of psalmody by a quick but monotonous shuffling of their feet, being an apology for a dance This grotesque scene was prolonged to an hour and a half, at the end of which time the company dispersed to their homes" [*Notes and Queries*, 2nd ser xii 366]

The tenets of the Shakers are set forth by themselves, in very mystical language, in "The Testimony of Christ's Second Appearing," and in "A Summary View of the Millennial Church"

SIFRIDENSES [SIGCIDENSES]

SIMONIANS The earliest of those philosophical heretics who ultimately acquired the name of Gnostics, and who owed their origin to the antichristian influence and teaching of Simon Magus during the thirty or forty years that followed our Lord's Ascension.

The personal history of Simon Magus is very obscure, but some few facts respecting him are to be drawn from the pages of the New Testament and of early Christian writers He must have been contemporary with the period of our Lord's earthly life and ministry, at least for many years, for within about a year of the Ascension St Luke represents him as having "long time" had influence among the Samaritans, using sorcery, bewitching them, and giving out that he was some great one, so that "they all gave heed" to him, "from the least even to the greatest, saying, This man is the great power of God" There is no record that Simon ever came within the range of Christ's teaching, or of that of any of the Apostles or Evangelists until after the personal ministry of our Lord had ceased But when Philip the deacon preached "the things concerning the kingdom of God and the Name of Jesus Christ" among the Samaritans, Simon Magus was among those who believed and were baptized, and, continuing for a time with Philip, the sorcerer himself was astonished at "the miracles and signs which were done" This astonishment at powers which so evidently exceeded his own was increased when he saw a still greater miracle follow from the subsequent ministrations of the Apostles Peter and John, whose hands having been laid upon the baptized Samaritans, "they received the Holy Ghost," Whose presence was manifested by some evident token, similar perhaps to those signs which had been seen and heard on the Day of Pentecost, or those which were afterwards manifested at Joppa and Ephesus This great wonder excited Simon's ambition to exercise the same power as the Apostles, and he offered money to Peter and John to purchase the power of them The reply of St Peter stamped such bargaining for "the gift of God" as a heinous crime, to which in subsequent times the name of "simony" was given, from the name of him by whom it was first committed But the words of the Apostle seem to point to something beyond this particular crime, as if Simon, who is declared to be "in the gall of bitterness and the bond of iniquity," was still in heart the sorcerer, although he had believed in the kingdom of God and the Name of Jesus, and had been made a Christian by baptism [Acts viii 9-24] Justin Martyr, writing about a century after this event, says that Simon, whom he calls a native of the Samaritan village Gitto, "did mighty acts of magic" at Rome in the time of Claudius Cæsar [A D 41-54] Irenæus, writing about thirty years later than Justin [A D 182-188], says that Simon, "not putting faith in God a whit the more," set himself eagerly to contend against the Apostles, in order that he himself might seem to be a wonderful being, and applied himself with still greater zeal to the study of the whole magic art, that he might the better bewilder and overpower multitudes of men" Both Justin Martyr and Irenæus declare that the sorcerer was honoured as a god, and the former twice tells the Emperor Antoninus Pius, to whom he addressed his first Apology, that "as a god he was honoured by you," meaning the Romans, "with a statue, which statue was erected on the river Tiber, between the two bridges, and bore this inscription in the language of Rome, 'Simoni Deo Sancto.'" This statue is said by Irenæus to have been set up by Claudius Cæsar, and is also spoken of by Tertullian [1] Justin Martyr adds that "almost all the Samaritans, and a few even of other nations, worship him, and acknowledge him as the first god" [Justin Mart *Apol* I xxvi lvi Iren *adv Hær* xxiii Tertull *Apol* xiii]

From Simon Magus, according to Irenæus, "all sorts of heresies derive their origin," and it has been the constant tradition of Christian writers that heresies at least began with him The short account given of his opinions by Irenæus, however, left much mystery around the particular heresy which was propagated by Simon himself, and although it was clearly seen that there were some links of connection between it and the later Gnostic heresies, it was not possible to follow up the connection in any detail The recent discovery of "The Refutation of all Heresies," a work written by Hippolytus early in the third century, has thrown much more light on the subject, and especially by giving us a summary of a work by Simon Magus himself, "The Great Announcement, a Revelation of the Voice and Name recognisable by means of Intellectual apprehension of the great indefinite Power," in which his system was set forth

That system was one of thorough and unflinching Pantheism He introduced into his very definition of the Divine Nature that Its substance is exhibited in material things He ascribed the formation of the world to certain portions of the Divine Fulness, Æons, thus exhibiting themselves in act and energy so as to become perceptible to the senses of men According to this system the Divine Power resides potentially, and may be manifested actually, in the person of each individual man A further development of the theory of emanations was devised, to bring within his reach the claim to be himself the "great power of God,' and his pretensions to this title were supported by magic

The statement of Irenæus relates exclusively to this latter part of this system [Iren *adv Hæres* i 23] It is precisely the part by which Simon would be commonly known Of the former part, or the system itself, we have a full description in Hippolytus [Hippol *Refut Hær* vi 2-15], taken from Simon's own work From these authorities the following account of the heresy is to be drawn

The originating principle of the universe is Fire for it is written, "God is a consuming fire" [2] Of the principle of this Fire is begotten the Logos, in which exists the Indefinite Power, the Power of the Godhead, the image of which Power is the Spirit of God, Which was wafted over the water. A favourable interpretation might reduce this to a statement of the doctrine of the Holy Trinity But the confounding of the creature with the Creator occurs, as we shall see, in the description of the Spirit as the image of the Indefinite Power Neither can we substitute, as is done in some modern histories, "God dwelling in Light which no man can approach unto" for the originating Fire, without a virtual suppression of the blasphemous errors connected with this latter name Simon goes on to state that the Indefinite Power, which is Fire, is not a simple and uncompounded essence (as Fire is held to be by those who make it one of the four simple, unalterable elements by the varied combinations of which all things are produced), but of a twofold nature, having a secret part and a manifest part, the secret hidden in the manifest, and the manifest deriving its being from the secret These, Hippolytus remarks, are what Aristotle denotes by "potentiality" and "energy," or what Plato styles "intelligible" and "sensible" The manifest portion of the original Fire comprises in itself all material things, and the whole Fire is a treasury or fountain of things intelligible and sensible

Having by this general assumption prepared the way for his cosmogony, Simon proceeds as follows He supposes that portions of the Divine Fulness can act as separate powers, and that the Logos takes and employs six such portions, Æons These are called Roots, and that primary ones, of the originating principle of generation They are in pairs, Mind and Intelligence, Voice and Name, Ratiocination and Reflection [Νοῦς καὶ ἐπίνοια, Φωνὴ καὶ ὄνομα, Λογισμὸς καὶ ἐνθύμησις] In them resides, co-existently, the entire Indefinite Power, potentially with regard to these "secret" portions of the Divine Substance, actually when the images of these portions are formed by material embodiment For Mind and Intelligence becoming "manifest" are Heaven and Earth, Voice and Name are Sun and Moon, Ratiocination and Reflection are Air and Water The Indefinite Power becomes then the seventh actual Power, the Spirit of God wafted over the water, which reduces all things to order

The Logos, which employs these divine agencies, roots, or Æons, in which resides the Indefinite Power, is described as He who stood, stands, and will stand Hippolytus pointed out that these words might be used of Christ, in a Catholic sense, to mean "who was, is, and is to come," and some commentators, apparently misunderstanding Hippolytus' remark, have attributed this meaning to the words as used by Simon But Simon interprets them otherwise, "He has stood above in unbegotten power He stands below, when in the stream of water He

[1] In the year 1574 a not large fragment of marble was dug up in the island in the Tiber, having engraved upon it a dedication of something not specified, to the Sabine god Semo Sancus, in an inscription beginning "Semoni Sanco Deo," by Sextus Pompeius This has been associated by some writers with the statement of Justin Martyr, but if the latter had made so glaring a mistake about a conspicuous public statue he would have been covered with ridicule, and Irenæus would not have repeated the story [See Burton's *Bampton Lectures*, 374]

[2] The comment of Hippolytus upon Simon's use of this text is to the effect that Moses in these words does not describe the nature of God's Substance, but the nature of its operation on all who are subject to His wrath.

was begotten in a likeness He is to stand above, beside the blessed Indefinite Power, if He be fashioned into an image." The Æons employed by Him are male and female, these general terms describing the Divine Mind, or its portions as reflecting upon itself, and as reflected upon, or as the articulating power and the utterance. The active or male of these Æons is from above, the passive or female from below, and their union generates all things "The Logos, frequently looking to the things that are being generated from Mind and Intelligence, that is, from Heaven and Earth, exclaims, 'Hear, O heavens, and give ear, O earth, for the Lord hath spoken' He who utters these words is the seventh Power, He who stood, stands, and will stand "

The first pair of roots or Æons, to which is assigned priority, and apparently primacy, is referred to the first three days' work in the Mosaic account of the Creation Clearly too the second pair is to be referred to the fourth day, the third pair to the fifth and sixth days. Voice and Name are stated to be Sun and Moon, Ratiocination and Reflection are Air and Water Sun and Moon may be represented as from above and below, Active and Passive, the Giver and the Receiver, Powers by which mundane things are generated The productions from Air and Water on the fifth and sixth days correspond to the conceptions of Ratiocination and Reflection A little ingenious word-play will make out a very tolerable analogy All these generations of the six days are reduced to order by the seventh or Indefinite Power, the Spirit which contains all things in itself, an image from an incorruptible form

The arrangements of this pantheistic cosmogony being effected, there occurs a vestige of Creation The Deity proceeded to form man, taking clay from the earth He formed him not uncompounded, but twofold, according to His own image The image is the Spirit, and whoever is not fashioned into a figure of this will perish with the world, inasmuch as he continues only potentially, and does not exist actually There exists in every man therefore in a latent condition that which is incorruptible, potentially, that is, not actually, and this is He who stood, stands, and is to stand He is to stand (according to the words quoted above) when He shall be fashioned into an image It appears then that every man may become, not a member of Christ by having the Spirit of Christ, but an embodiment of the Logos, an "image," that is, of the Logos, a conversion of the "secret" portion of the Divine Power into the "manifest"

It remained then to shew how this power latent in all men was manifested and brought into action in Simon, how he was made the image of the Logos [1] There was excogitated for this purpose a further development of the theory of emanations, by which the pretensions of his paramour Helena to be a female Æon might tally with his own pretensions to be the image of the Logos, and mark him, to the exclusion of others, as that image This is told by Hippolytus in the thirteenth chapter, and his account is to the following effect After the formation of the world, in the power of the ensuing Sige, the two lower pairs of Æons are resumed into the superior or primary pair Nous and Ennoia Nous and Ennoia are thus represented as offshoots from all the Æons The medium of their union is the Power that sustains and nourishes all things—He who stands The action of the Divine Mind as subject upon itself as object, the union that is of Nous with Ennoia, is the begetting of the Logos Consequently, when these were embodied as images, a female represented Ennoia, and Simon might represent himself as the Power of God, either as the Father in the person of the superior Æon, or the Logos, who is one with the Father These doctrines of the Great Announcement confirm and make intelligible the statement of Irenæus, that Simon taught "It was himself who appeared among the Jews as the Son, but descended in Samaria as the Father, while he came to other nations in the character of the Holy Spirit" [Iren *adv Hær* i 23] [2] In Simon's system the Persons of the Holy Trinity are confused, and it was open to him, professing himself to be the Power of God, to assume the name of any one of the Three He said precisely the same thing of Jesus Christ [Hipp *Refut Hær* vi 14] [3] Irenæus continues that Simon declared Helena to be the first conception of his mind, (*i e* as God,) the mother of all, that she, leaping forth from him and comprehending the will of her father, descended to the lower regions of space, and generated angels and powers by whom the world was formed (there is a variation here from the teaching of the Announcement, which will be noticed presently), that these angels ruled ill the world they had made, and through jealousy detained Helena or Ennoia among them, that she was shut up in a human body, and appeared in one female form after another [4]

This leads us to our Lord's place in Simon's system The world being ill managed by the angels, Jesus was transformed, and being assum-

[1] Before the publication of the Refutation of all Heresies there was a difficulty regarding the interpretation of a well known passage of Ignatius, *Λόγος αΐδιος, οὐκ ἀπὸ Σιγῆς προελθών* [*ad Magnes* viii] Many thought that the Gnostic Sige could not be referred to See Pearson, *Vindic Ignat* ii 4, Bull, *Def Fid Nicen* iii 1, 4-7, Ittigius, *de Hæres* I vi 5, Jacobson, *Patr Apost*, *Not in loc* The difficulty is removed by the appearance of the term in the Great Announcement, and few will now doubt that Ignatius does refer to the Gnostic Sige

[2] Burton, writing before Hippolytus' treatise was discovered, thought these statements of Irenæus to be incredible [*Bampton Lectures*, iv pp 106, 107] Upon which Mill remarked, that there is nothing in such statements which should appear so incredible in itself to any who have seen precisely the same statements in heathen pantheists as to necessitate any critical method for explaining away the apparent absurdity [*On Panth Principles*, i 18]

[3] It thus appears that those who have charged Simon with Sabellianism are correct [Burton, note 46, p 389]

[4] See Tertullian, *de Anima*, p 337, ed 1641 Helena was called Luna, the female Æon of the second pair The Simonians were sometimes called Helenians from their worship of Helena [Celsus in *Origen c. Cel.* p 272, Spencer See Spencer's note]

lated to the rulers, and powers, and angels, came for the purpose of restoration Only in appearance, not in reality, was He a man, and in appearance only He suffered [DOCETÆ] He appeared in Judæa as Son, in Samaria as Father, among the Gentiles as Holy Spirit [1] Origen's words, therefore, that the Simonians by no means confess Jesus to be the Son of God, but say that Simon is the power of God [Orig *contr Cels* v p 272, Spencer's ed 1677], are verified by the confusion of the Persons, by the denial of the humanity of Jesus Christ, as well as by the subsequent superseding of Jesus by Simon

A difference between Irenæus and "the Announcement" was noticed just now, namely, that Irenæus states the doctrine to be that the world-making angels sprang from Ennoia, while the Announcement states that the Logos took roots of the originating principle, of which roots Ennoia was one It will be noticed too that the Simonian disregard of the prophets [Iren *adv Hær* i 23, Hipp *Refut Hær* vi 14] is not very consistent with the appeals to the prophets in the earlier part of the Announcement [see Hipp vi ch v quoting Isaiah, ix quoting Proverbs and Jeremiah, xi quoting Isaiah] [2] Now Irenæus' 23rd chapter has so strong a resemblance to the quotations from the Announcement in Hippolytus' 14th chapter, as to make one think that Irenæus used the Announcement Why then did he omit all notice of the theory of its earlier part? Is it that the former part was really earlier, written before Simon Magus abjured Christianity, that the later chapters (as they have every appearance of being) were an afterthought, that again the earlier doctrine was changed into the more Gnostic doctrine of the generation of Æons from Ennoia, and that this final stage is described by Irenæus? [3] This supposition of a more complete Gnosticism adopted at a later time by Simon is almost implied in the assertion that Simon introduced the distinction between the Supreme Being and the Creator [See Iren i 27, Greg Nazian *Orat de Hieronymo*, August *de Hæres* I i, Ittigius, I ii 11] The cosmogony of the Announcement scarcely bears out the assertion But the assertion may have been made in consequence of the development of Simon's doctrine by others

Such was the system of Simon The correctness of the opinion of Epiphanius will be allowed that the heresy is not properly classed with those that bear the name of Christ [Epiph *Hær* xxi 1] The Simonians pretended to be Christians that they might insinuate themselves into the Church, and many caught in their wickedness were excommunicated [Euseb *Hist Eccl* ii 1 and 13]

The pretensions of Simon were supported by the delusions of magic, and magic in several forms was practised by the sect There is nothing unreasonable or unscriptural in supposing that supernatural agencies, the power of evil spirits, may have been permitted to enter into those delusions Such a supposition does not involve the subjection of those powers to the will of man [DICT *of* THEOLOGY, MAGIC] Our Lord's words, [Matt xxiv 24-26] that false prophets and false Christs shall arise, who shall shew great signs and wonders, surely must refer to something more than the impositions of jugglers

The statement made by Irenæus respecting the lewdness of the sect is confirmed by the "Great Announcement" itself, which speaks of promiscuous intercourse of the sexes as "sanctifying one another" [Hippol *Refut Hær* vi 14 NICOLAITANES] [4]

Of the numbers of this sect Justin Martyr writes, as has been already said, that almost all the Samaritans and a few even of other nations worship Simon Simon had been much honoured in Rome But this did not continue long, for his influence fell before St Peter's preaching [Euseb *Hist Eccl* ii 14] Origen writes about A D 240, that not thirty of Simon's followers could be found in the whole world [Orig *contr Cels* i 57] [5] The progress of Gnosticism brought the Simonians into sects named from other leaders

By almost universal consent Simon is regarded as the first propagator in the Church, but acting from without, of principles which developed into Gnosticism.[6] From the Simonians, writes Irenæus, knowledge, falsely so called, received its beginning [Iren *adv. Hær* i. 23] Hippolytus identifies the Roots of Simon's system with the Æons of Valentinus [Hippol *Refut. Hær* vi. 15] This remark points out the transition from Simon's system to that of Valentinus Simon rejected the notion of absolute creation, from an adoption doubtless of the common heathen tenet, that nothing can come from nothing But instead of asserting an independent eternity of matter, he asserted matter to be the manifestation of the Divine Substance In the formation of the world he retained the agency of the Logos, who took the roots of the Divine Substance, which roots produced all things by generation This is doubtless very different from the tenets of developed Gnosticism, in which the world-making angels act independently of the Supreme Being still, the notion of absolute creation being once rejected, it was easy to drop the agency of the Logos, or to reduce the character of the Logos to that of an inferior Æon, and to represent the roots of the Divine Substance as emanations from that substance

[1] See Theodoret. *Dialog* II vol iv p 52, ed 1642

[2] See, however, Burton's remark that the Gnostics rejecting the Jewish Scriptures still appealed to them in support of their own doctrine, and his anticipation that if their writings had come down to us we should find them arguing that though the prophets were not inspired by the Supreme God they still could not help giving utterance to truths [pp 39 40]

[3] Augustine writes that Simon denied the resurrection of the flesh It is doubtful whether such a denial can be inferred from Hipp vi 9, and there is no definite statement quoted from the Announcement

[4] See Bunsen's *Hippolytus*, i 47, 48 And for the meaning of the name Prunicus given to Helena see Epiphanius, *Hær* xxv (Nicolaites) sec 4

[5] Regarding the denial of this by Mosheim and others see Burton, p 85, etc

[6] The testimony is strong that Simon's opinions were taken up by Menander [Burton, p 27].

This, it appears, was the change made by Valentinus in the connection, first effected by Simon, of Christianity with Gnosticism The necessity for the change lay in the adoption of a different tenet concerning matter Valentinus, if not asserting broadly the full Gnostic tenet that matter is itself essentially evil, at least attributes to it a resistance to the pervading principle of Divine life, so as to be capable of producing evil [VALENTINIANS] This was not consistent with the Simonian representation of matter as the manifestation of the Divine Substance It was necessary to have recourse in the formation of the world to an inferior Demiurge

The Simonian confusion of the creature with the Creator led to the denial of the existence of evil in the outward acts of the creature, and must have lain, doctrinally, at the root of their horrible excesses The Gnostics, holding that matter was essentially evil, could consistently teach the necessity of austerity and mortification of the flesh and some did so teach

Again, the Platonic tenet, that there are heavenly archetypes or ideas of all earthly things, appears to be in its strongest form in the first principle of the Simonian cosmogony, in which Heaven and Earth are outward manifestations of Mind and Intelligence It would be possible to introduce this tenet in a modified form into Gnosticism by supposing the world-creating angels to be reflexes of the Supreme Mind, and matter to be unresisting [1] but Gnosticism in general held that the Demiurge proceeded from the highest God only at an infinite distance, and was as incapable of willing the perfect as of restraining the opposition of matter [Gieseler, *Comp Eccl Hist* i 137] In the unreality of our Lord's body Simon and the great bulk of the Gnostics agreed [2] Thus Simon, adding to his Samaritan education an initiation into the Cabbala and its magic as a student at Alexandria, (for on this point the statement of the Clementine Homilies [ii 22] is so probable that it may be accepted,) learning something of Christianity from Philip, soon set himself up as a rival of the Jesus Whom he had abjured, and lost his life, if the narrative of Hippolytus may be received, in an attempt to exhibit in his own person (by being buried alive) a resurrection, the reality of which, in the case of Jesus Christ, he denied [Hippol *Refut Hær* vi 15] [3]

[1] The Alexandrian Gnostics employed, but only as an insecure guide, a representation which was borrowed from the Platonic doctrine of ideas, that the visible world, with its germs of life, is only an image and impression of the world of light [Gieseler, *Compend* i 138]

[2] Hammond (of course, for he finds Gnosticism everywhere) interprets 2 Thess ii 8 of Simon Magus See *Comm in loc* and *Diss Prima Proœm de Antich* cap ix, *Works*, iv p 732 The idea of Antichrist is a power within the Church, acting in the name of Christ, but against Christ Simon, while within the Church, may have been one of the types or earlier manifestations of Antichrist, but during the chief part of his course he was without the Church

[3] The other story of his death in an attempt to fly dates from Arnobius Probably both stories are fabulous

SIMONIANS, ST [POSITIVISTS SOCIALISTS]

SIONITES A small community which attracted some attention in Norway in the first half of the eighteenth century They called themselves Sionites, as professing to set forth the reign of the King of Sion, with Whom they claimed to be in such close communion that their acts were identified with His, but they also took the name of "strangers and pilgrims" It was their custom to wear long beards, a linen girdle—analogous to a custom of the PHUNDAITES—and to have the word "Sion," with some mystical character, embroidered in red on their sleeves. They gave passports to persons whom they charged to aid in establishing the Kingdom of Sion, but causing some trouble to the Government by these "Fifth Monarchy" ideas, they were exiled from Bragernes in the year 1743 and obliged to settle at Altona One of their number, George Kleinow, professed to be a prophet, and under his guidance they repudiated the baptism of their converts, and rebaptized them when they entered their community Christian VI eventually issued orders for dissolving the community on account of its disobedience to the laws, and its pretensions of setting up a kingdom which claimed to be independent of them [Grégoire's *Hist des Sectes Relig*]

SIPHORI A sect is found under this name in Gennadius Massiliensis, but it is supposed to be a misreading for SACCOPHORI [Gennad Massil *De Eccl Dogmat* s v]

SISCIDENSES A sect of the Waldenses which is mentioned by Reinerius as agreeing with them in everything except that they received the Sacrament of the Eucharist [Reiner *contr Waldens* in *Bibl Max Lugd* xxv 266 f] Gieseler thinks that their name is properly spelt Sifridenses, and that they took it from some local leader named Sifried [Gieseler, *Comp Eccl Hist* iii 446, n 6, Clark's ed]

SIX PRINCIPLE BAPTISTS The oldest sect of American Baptists, claiming descent from the original settlement of Roger Williams at Providence in Rhode Island, in the year 1630 The full name which they gave to themselves is "The Ancient Order of the Six Principles of the Doctrine of Christ and His Apostles" The six principles are those mentioned in the first three verses of the sixth chapter of the Epistle to the Hebrews, namely, Repentance from dead works, Faith towards God, the Doctrine of Baptisms, Laying on of hands, Resurrection of the dead, and Eternal judgment The doctrine of Baptisms they explain as referring to the baptism of St John, the baptism of the Holy Ghost at Pentecost, the baptism of Christ's sufferings, and Christian baptism by immersion The "laying on of hands" is interpreted of the rite of Confirmation, which (administered by themselves) is required as a strict rule of communion among them, none being admitted who has not been "under hands" The sect numbers about 5000 members, chiefly among the uneducated class of country-people

SKOPTZI A name signifying "eunuchs," given to a Russian sect of the Bezpopoftschin Dissenters, and derived from their practice of self-mutilation, which they supposed to be warranted by Scripture [Matt xix 12]

The general characteristic of this sect of fanatics, even among those who do not adopt this extreme course of action, is one of self-mortification and asceticism They perform self-imposed penances, such as flagellation, wearing hair-cloth shirts and iron chains and crosses They profess great respect for Peter III, the murdered husband of the Empress Catharine [A D 1762], of whom they keep pictures in their houses, in which he is represented with a scarlet handkerchief tied round his right knee, (which is supposed to be one of their masonic signs,) and whom they expect to revisit the earth as the true Messiah, and, having rung the great bell of the Church of the Ascension in Moscow, to summon the elect, and reign over all the true Skoptzi They are noted for their anxiety to procure converts, and he who gains twelve is dignified with the title of Apostle Their chief peculiarities of practice and doctrine are the rejection of the resurrection of the body, a refusal to observe Sunday, and the substitution of certain rites invented by themselves in lieu of the sacrament of the Eucharist They call themselves "Karablik," which means "a small ship," and Baron Haxthausen, travelling in Russia in the earlier part of the present century, and attending one of their places of worship, heard a hymn of which the following is a translation

"Hold together, ye crew,
Let not the ship go down in the storm,
The Holy Ghost is with us!
Fear not the breakers nor the storm,
Our Father and Christ is with us!
His mother Akulina Ivanovna is with us!
He will come, He will appear,
He will ring the great bell of the Uspenski, (the Church of the Ascension in Moscow)
He will call together the faithful crew,
He will set up masts which never fall,
He will spread sails which never rend,
He will set a rudder which steers safely
He is near us! He is with us!
He casts anchor in a secure harbour,
We are landed, we are landed
The Holy Ghost is with us!
The Holy Ghost is near us!
The Holy Ghost is in us!"

They are a numerous sect, in some governments, as that of Orel, comprising whole villages, and they have many adherents among the jewellers and goldsmiths of St Petersburg, Moscow, and other large towns

SMYTONITE CONTROVERSY A dispute which arose in the Secession Kirk about the middle of the eighteenth century respecting the elevation of the Elements in celebrating the Lord's Supper One of the ministers of that body, Mr Smyton of Kilmaurs, considered such elevation an essential part of the ordinance, and pressed its authoritative enactment, but the Synod determined (with an unusual tolerance of variety) that it should be left an open question

SOCIALISTS A politico-religious sect which professes to have discovered and to practice the "science of human happiness" in the developement of the social as distinguished from the individual life

The founder of this visionary sect was Count St Simon [A D 1760-1825], who derived its principles chiefly from the social philosophy of Rousseau He started with the idea of reforming three evils which he considered to have fallen upon society namely [1] Isolation and hostile competition in industry; [2] Diversities of opinion on the most important subjects among men of learning and science, [3] Individualism, which lay at the root of all other evils To remedy these evils St Simon offered a new and perfect system of religion, philosophy, and government, founded in Pantheism, equality, and the elevation of industry into a religion He defined God as "all that is" or universal nature, and the chief attribute of Deity as "the social principle," or love and union, thus deifying the material upon which industry is employed, and consecrating industry by making it a series of operations upon deified material Thus labour was regarded in the St. Simonian system as the one sacred duty of life, the best labourer as the most religious man, and the only true social distinction as that merit which resulted from labour

The system of worship belonging to this new religion was a dreamy idolatry of art. The poets were to provide poetry suitable for recitation in the public assemblies, and by means of which the worshippers should become preachers to each other The musicians were to invent soul penetrating, emotional, music for this poetry, by means of which the mutual preachers would be rapt into an elysium of social joy The architects and painters were so to embellish the temples as to teach sentiments of fear, joy, and hope

The social system of St Simon was that which has acquired the name of Communism, and consisted chiefly in the abolition of the law of primogeniture, the absorption of all property and results of industry into one common public stock, and the distribution of this common fund to each person according to their merit Upon this community of property Father Enfantin, one of the leading St Simonians, engrafted community of women, when the French Government thought it necessary to interfere, and St Simonianism was suppressed by authority in the year 1832 It survived, however, in a "philosophical" form in the system of POSITIVISM, which owes its origin to Comte, one of the disciples of St Simon, and the latent power which it still possesses over the minds of the French working classes was shewn in a terrible manner by the "War of the Commune," which followed the German conquest of France, in the year 1871

Robert Owen, the founder of English Socialism, a native of New Lanark, was contemporary with St Simon [A D 1771-1858] for two-thirds of his long life, and no doubt derived his ideas to a large extent from those of the French visionary He endeavoured to propagate Socialism by establishing workshops on the principles of co operation originated by Fourier in connection with the St Simonians, and from these as a base he extended his system widely for a time both in Great Britain and in America That system was, in a few words, one of co-operative industry combined with infidelity, and with as much freedom respecting the relations of the sexes as could be adopted without provoking the arm of the law In the exalted language of the Socialist, this is described as making man rational and happy by abandoning all the absurdities of "past religions, governments, men-made laws, artificial marriages, modes of producing and distributing wealth, of buying cheap and selling dear, and all other past and existing institutions," and setting up instead a system in which man may "enter on a new life, surrounded by new conditions, all of which will be superior, and in which the spirit of universal charity and love will govern the population of the earth as one enlightened and affectionate family, upon a system of perfect equality, according to age, education, and condition, the education and condition of all being made as superior as the concentrated knowledge and power of the race can devise, and, with the materials at its control, can execute" [Robert Owen in *Religions of the World*, p 313, ed 1870] The theories of Comte have to a considerable extent taken the place of those of Owen during the last quarter of a century, and English forms of Positivism have been developed out of them in a similar manner to that in which English Socialism was developed out of St Simonianism

SOCIETIES FOR THE REFORMATION OF MANNERS These appear to have sprung from the Religious Societies which were established in London and elsewhere for the promotion of personal piety in the latter half of the seventeenth century [RELIGIOUS SOCIETIES] They were not bound down to one uniform plan, but were all pledged to one uniform object, that of recovering the nation out of the depths of profligacy into which it had sunk during the prevalence of irreligious anarchy under the Commonwealth and of French manners under Charles II One in London was composed of magistrates, members of Parliament, and lawyers, for the purpose of enforcing the laws against swearing, drunkenness, and the profanation of the Lord's Day, another of tradesmen, for the suppression of prostitution Others for similar objects were established in large provincial towns, and correspondence was kept up between them to strengthen their hands by co-operation and union

Such unauthoritative interference with vice was well intentioned, but far too high-handed for the English temperament, and when seventy or eighty warrants a week came to be executed by means of one of these Societies in London alone it was to be expected that the members and their agents would meet with some rough treatment Two were, in fact, murdered while endeavouring to carry out the objects of the Society, and others narrowly escaped a similar fate Most of the Bishops supported the Societies, by the recommendation of Archbishop Tenison, and they were also supported by the well known Robert Nelson But they were opposed by the High Churchmen of the day, including Archbishop Sharp, who set his face against their introduction within his province They were also opposed by the press, especially by Defoe, who justly remonstrated against the suppression of immorality by means of informers and penalties, and sarcastically recommended the upper classes to try the reformation of manners by example, before they tried to effect it by such means The evils of such organizations was being conspicuously illustrated at this very time in New England And neither there, nor under the somewhat similar Kirk-session discipline of the Scotch Presbyterians, was any real reformation of manners effected

Perhaps the best result of these Societies was the foundation in 1699 of the "Society for the Promotion of Christian Knowledge," the germ of which was the following resolution agreed to by some of their chief promoters "Whereas the growth of vice and immorality is greatly owing to gross ignorance of the principles of the Christian religion, we whose names are underwritten do agree to meet together as often as we can conveniently, to consult, under the conduct of the Divine Providence and assistance, how we may be able, by due and lawful methods, to promote Christian knowledge"

The Societies for the Reformation of Manners existed from about 1691 until about 1730, when they had gradually died out Wesley tried to revive them in 1757, but after a short time the attempt failed [Woodward's *Religious Societies*, etc Nelson's *Address to Persons of Quality*, p 153 Secretan's *Life of Nelson*]

SOCIETY PEOPLE. [CAMERONIANS]

SOCIETY OF FRIENDS [QUAKERS]

SOCINIANS The Antitrinitarian opinions which spread from Italy and took root principally in Poland, were systematized by Faustus Socinus In doing this he made great use of the writings of his uncle Lælius Socinus Lælius had also contributed much to the spread of those opinions It is therefore generally stated that Lælius Socinus was the first author of the Socinian sect These two belonged to a family of lawyers at Sienna Lælius, the third son of Marianus Socinus, born in the year 1525, left Italy upon the breaking up of the debating club at Vincenza to which he belonged [ANTITRINITARIANS], travelled for four years in France, England, the Netherlands, Germany, and Poland, and then settled in Zurich At Cracow there was a secret society for the discussion of religious questions, its members being in general opposed to the pretensions of the See of Rome, in which Antitrinitarian tenets had been broached by Spiritus of Holland Lælius appears to have determined the leading man of this society, Lemanini, who was already wavering, in favour of the new heresy But when settled at Zurich his opinions were not openly avowed, nor can he be altogether acquitted of the charge of dissimulation He was intimate with the leading Reformers, and was in the habit of propounding his opinions only in the way of doubt and inquiry In the year 1552 Calvin warned him to check his itch of inquiry, "ne tibi gravia tormenta accersas" The words "gravia tormenta" received a very significant commentary in the next year from the burning of Servetus Some historians (Natalis Alexander among them) state that Lælius left Zurich upon the death of Servetus, but Bayle's statement appears to be more probable that he took care not to discover his thoughts but in a proper time and place, and behaved himself so dexterously that he lived among the mortal enemies of his opinions without being in the least degree injured by them In the year 1558 he was in Poland still in the company and correspondence of the leading Reformers In that year John Burcher, an Englishman, wrote from Cracow to Bullinger, "I have found out Lælius, to whom I gave your letter" Bullinger, four months before, had written to Utenhovius "Habes vivam epistolam, D Lælium Socinum Senensem Italum Hunc tibi peramanter et diligentissime commendo" [*Original Letters*, Parker Soc ii p 700] Blandrata was then in Poland, being honourably received by the Protestants, and two years before, Gonezius, a Pole, had openly avowed in the Synod of Seceminum his denial of the Trinity. Public disputations, it appears, were also held on the subject What part Lælius took in these proceedings is not exactly known, but he retained the goodwill of both parties so far that, at the intercession of Melanchthon, he obtained from Sigismund of Poland and from the Emperor Maximilian II the privileges of an ambassador, that he might revisit Venice in safety to recover his paternal estates After this Lælius returned to Switzerland, and died at Zurich in May 1562 Faustus was then at Lyons He set out immediately on hearing of his uncle's death, and obtained possession of his papers, which he made use of afterwards It was not however until the year 1578 that he took part in the affairs of the Antitrinitarian body

Meanwhile, notwithstanding the warnings of Calvin, heresy gained ground, and each synod that was held with the view of bringing all the Reformers to an agreement in faith, shewed an increase of the heretical party In 1565, after a conference had been held in consequence of a petition from Gregory Paul, minister of a church in Cracow, to the National Assembly, the inevitable schism took place Sigismund Augustus had granted liberty of conscience to all the sects which forsook the Church of Rome, and about 1570 John Sieniemus, Palatine of Podolia, gave the seceders a settlement in Racow They differed widely among themselves, some (the Farnovians) holding opinions very nearly Arian, some (the Budneians) being Psilanthropists, and others endeavouring to hold a middle course This controversy was carried on with much vehemence in Transylvania, where Blandrata had settled as court physician. Among those who refused worship to Christ was Francis David, a Hungarian, superintendent of the Transylvanian societies, whose doctrine greatly disturbed the Antitrinitarians of Transylvania Blandrata sent for Faustus Socinus in 1578 to pacify these troubles Faustus had spent twelve years in the court of the Duke of Tuscany, and three years at Basle in the study of divinity When Blandrata's invitation reached him, he had just ended a disputation at Zurich with Francis Puccius David, not yielding to Socinus' arguments, was thrown into prison, where he shortly died His followers were called "Semi-Judaizers" by Socinus and his party, and a treatise was written against them by the former under that title Socinus retired in the next year [A D 1579] to Poland At first he was not received by the party which he wished to join, he was accused of having advised the persecution of David, and his opinions differed in some respects from those generally held by the party He did not cease, however, on this account to exert himself on their behalf. He gradually overcame all opposition, and the Antitrinitarian party formed themselves into one community under his superintendence and direction

Upon their separation from the other Reformers, the first care of the Socinians had been to provide themselves with a version of the Bible agreeable to their tenets This done, they drew up a "Catechism or Confession of the Unitarians" of which a full account may be seen in Mosheim [*Hist Cent XVI* III ii 10] This elder Catechism was supplanted by the Racovian Catechism, which was drawn up by Faustus Socinus principally from the papers of Lælius, corrected and enlarged by others, and published in Polish in 1605, and in Latin in 1609, with a dedication to James I of England The academy of Racow (from which town the Catechism has its name) was founded by Jacobus a Sienno, to whom Racow belonged, and who became the zealous patron of the Socinians The academy exerted itself in the dissemination of its heresy by the publication of controversial books, and by sending missionaries to other countries The sect was now organized The affairs were managed by synods on the presbyterian platform, which had control of its public funds and full power over its ministers Until the year 1638 the sect was prosperous In that year some Racovian students broke a highway cross at the entrance of the town Complaint was made by the Catholics, and the Diet of Warsaw ordered that the college should be demolished, the church of Racow shut up, the Socinian printing-press destroyed, the ministers and teachers of the sect banished It is evident that the breaking of the cross was only an occasion laid hold of by one of two contending parties to measure strength with their opponents During the next twenty years Socinian worship was continued in many places of the kingdom, but with occasional acts of severity against the sect, such as the destruction, by the judges of Lublin, of the churches of Kiselin and Beresc in Volhynia, under the pretence that teachers from Racow had fled thither, and the banishment of Jonas Slichtingius for publishing a book, "Confessio Christiana." In the year 1658 the final blow came. It was discovered that, during the Swedish invasion of Poland, the Socinians, intending to raise themselves upon the ruins of the state, kept intelligence with Ragotski, Prince of Transylvania, who had attacked Poland at the same time. The Catholic lords in the Diet of Warsaw passed a law against Socinianism. All Socinians were obliged to abjure their heresy or leave the kingdom within two years. The 10th of July 1660 was the day fixed for their departure. This law, confirmed afterwards in other diets, was executed with wanton cruelty and insult, over and above the inevitable misery accompanying such a measure. Thus the Socinian societies, after an existence of a hundred years in Poland, were at length destroyed.

In Transylvania Socinianism obtained so firm a footing, through the influence of Blandrata, that no attempts to suppress it were made by the government. The sect was tolerated. Attempts were made to form settlements in Hungary, Austria, and Holland, but were defeated by the opposition of the Roman Catholic and the Reformed Churches.

In England, Socinianism did not prosper. The Anabaptists fell into the Eutychian heresy rather than the Socinian. In the year 1612, Leggatt and Wightman were condemned to be burnt for denying our Lord's divinity, but they formed no party. The only Socinian congregation in England was gathered by John Biddle during the Commonwealth. He was a native of Gloucester, and kept the grammar-school of that town. After two imprisonments for heresy, he was a third time held to trial, when Cromwell banished him to the Isle of Scilly. Brought back by a writ of Habeas Corpus, he was set at liberty, and became minister of an Independent meeting in London. Soon after the Restoration he was committed again to prison, and died in prison in the year 1662 [Life, prefixed to the first volume of Socinian tracts, *The Faith of our God*, London, 1691]. Biddle was succeeded in the leadership by his pupil, the well-known Thomas Firmin, but the congregation disappeared, and with it the Socinians, properly so called, of England.

The Catechism of 1574, mentioned above, was only a transition from the varying doctrines of the Antitrinitarian body to the definite doctrine of Socinus. Mosheim remarks of it, that it breathes the spirit of Socinianism even in its most important parts, and shews that, through the influence of the writings of Lælius Socinus, the Arians, who had formerly the upper hand in the community of the Unitarians, were changing their sentiments concerning the nature and mediation of Christ. This Catechism rejects infant baptism, in which rejection is to be traced probably the denial of original sin and of the Atonement, which forms the common ground occupied by the Antitrinitarians and a large body (at least) of the Baptists. Of the Racovian Catechism, which succeeded this earlier form, we are warned by Mosheim that it is no more than a collection of the popular tenets of the Socinians, and by no means a just representation of the secret opinions and sentiments of their doctors; that it seems to have been composed less for the use of the Socinians themselves than to impose upon strangers. The true principles of Socinianism are to be sought in the accredited writers of the sect. In Socinian theology, more perhaps than in that of any other sect, there appears the assumption that God's Nature and Being are comprehensible by the human intellect, that man's reason can determine the conditions of God's existence. Scripture is explained and bent to suit a foregone conclusion.

It was first laid down[1] as a reasonable maxim, that God is of such simplicity of nature as not to admit of a distinction of Persons. It was held, further, that the essence of the Godhead cannot possibly be united with manhood, the Infinite with the finite, between which there can be no "proportion;" that even if the existence of a distinct Person, the Son of God, were supposed, it would be in itself impossible to form a unity out of two totalities; and as both Catholics and Arians teach that the Son had a perfect existence prior to the Incarnation, the union of the two Natures in one Person of Christ is impossible.

Accordingly, the Socinians held Jesus Christ to be only man, but man by a miraculous conception. "The seed of a male was implanted in the Virgin by God, in consequence of which Jesus remained free from the sinful inclinations of other men, nay more, received a will which tended naturally to holiness, which could not stray nor even be tempted."

Jesus, thus born and thus endowed, was anointed with the Holy Ghost at His baptism; the Holy Ghost being, according to the first Socinian principle, not a divine Person but an energy or power of the Godhead. It was principally as King that He was thus anointed, and there was conferred on Him at the time a partial royalty, with the promise of the full royalty of God.

[1] Dorner (from whom this statement is abridged) considers the maxim, "nulla proportio est finiti cum infinito," a maxim recognised both by the Middle Age and the Reformed Church, to be the fundamental maxim of Socianism; stating the different conception of the maxim thus: "The Socinians based this absolute difference of essence, not on the circumstance that all things are absolutely dependent on the absolute God, but inversely, in a completely Scotistic manner, on human freedom, combined with the doctrine of the natural darkness in things divine of that which is placed outside of God" [Div. II. vol. ii. p. 249, Edinb. transl.]. Regarding the application of the maxim contained in the following words—"Cognoscentis ad cognitum oportet esse aliquam proportionem, cum cognitum sit perfectio cognoscentis. Sed nulla est proportio intellectus creati ad Deum; quia in infinitum distant. Ergo intellectus creatus non potest videre essentiam Dei."—St. Thomas Aquinas writes: "Proportio dicitur dupliciter. Uno modo certa habitudo unius quantitatis ad alteram, secundum quod duplum, triplum, et æquale, sunt species proportionis. Alio modo quælibet habitudo unius ad alterum proportio dicitur. Et sic potest esse proportio creaturæ ad Deum, in quantum se habet ad ipsum, ut effectus ad causam, et ut potentia ad actum. Et secundum hoc intellectus creatus proportionatus esse potest ad cognoscendum Deum" [*Summ. Prim. Quæs.* xii. art. i. ad 4].

Jesus was also endowed with a higher knowledge peculiar to Himself and that He might have the vision of God was raised up to heaven for a time before entering on His office Through His Death, and after His Resurrection and Exaltation, He entered upon His royal government, becoming the representative of God, with fulness of power for the work of redemption His Resurrection was solely the work of God, a new birth, whereby He became actually the first new creature, personally free from death and imperfection Such is the exaltation of humanity in Christ, that as governing the Church in His own Person, He may justly be termed a God, and worship is due to Him, due to Him, however, not in His own right, but as God's plenipotentiary

The Socinians denied the Atonement, and consequently, in any proper sense, the Priesthood of Christ They never wearied of controverting that office with its necessary premisses they totally lacked a deeper consciousness of sin and guilt Christ is the Saviour because He shews the way of salvation the sacraments confer no grace, neither indeed is grace required by man the view taken of religion was solely the moral and legal view

To the Socinians have succeeded the modern Unitarians, distinguished from their predecessors principally by the denial of the miraculous conception of our Lord, and the repudiation of His worship The Socinian theology had also considerable influence in forming the modern Rationalist school [RATIONALISM]

SOCRATITÆ A local name for the Gnostics, which is to be found under the number 26 in St. John Damascene's Treatise on Heresies

SOLIFIDIANS A controversial name given to those who maintain the Lutheran doctrine of salvation "by faith alone" without works

SOMNISTS [PSYCHOPANNYCHITES]

SOUL-SLEEPERS. [PSYCHOPANNYCHITES]

SOUTHCOTTIANS The followers of a deluded woman named Southcott, who professed to be a prophetess, and who, during the last few months of her life, announced that she was about to become the mother of "Shiloh," who was coming to establish the Millennium The Southcottians also call themselves the "Philadelphian Church"

Joanna Southcott [A D 1750-1814], the foundress of this sect, was, according to her own account, descended from an old family of Hertfordshire gentry, who had lived on an estate named Wotton for many generations Her great grandfather, William Southcott, was an austere man, who interfered with the marriage of his daughter so as to break her heart, and drove his son William to leave his home for the purpose of crossing the Atlantic to settle in Pennsylvania The daughter, Sarah Southcott, is described by Joanna as giving herself up entirely to religion "Her private meditations and many hymns she composed were afterwards printed, and my mother had the work in her possession, some of them I learned when I was a child, as I greatly delighted in them" [*Second Book of Wonders*, 89] William, the brother of this lady, was wrecked on some coast where he was for a time protected by Jews, and then sent home in a ship, which landed him at Topsham in Devonshire There he married a Miss Mauditt, who became the mother of Joanna's father and of another son, with whom she was shortly left a widow through her husband's adventurous disposition taking him again on a voyage, and this time a fatal one, to Pennsylvania The widow married a worthless man who wasted her property, and thus the father of Joanna had to make his way in the world under the pressure of poverty, and although he continued on the same farm for seventeen years, he was at last reduced to such a condition that Joanna went as a domestic servant to a tradesman's family in Exeter The former position of the family still, however, haunted both the old man and his children Once at midnight on Old Christmas-Day, he heard a voice calling to him "Southcott, Southcott, thy name must spread far and wide there is a lady in Hertfordshire who hath great possessions for thee, and wants thy family to possess it' [*ibid* 102] "All the Southcotts were proud," says Joanna's sister, "and though we were come to nothing, still we were a proud, empty family" "And that I'll grant was true," adds Joanna herself, "a bottle filled with wine wants no more, but an empty bottle wants to be filled" [*ibid* 108]

With these traditions of former position and with experience of much trouble on the way from prosperity to poverty, Joanna Southcott had strong religious feelings which, up to the time when she was forty years of age, found their satisfaction in Methodism In the spirit of many of that rising sect, she was accustomed to expect special and detailed guidance in answer to prayer and she nursed this idea until the "direction" was developed into "inspiration," so that the communications which she believed herself to receive from Heaven were not only respecting the affairs of her own life, but also respecting public events and especially respecting those connected with the Second Advent of our Lord According to her own account, these revelations began to be made to her in the year 1792, but although they were written down, the papers were sealed up as they were written, and not opened until several years afterwards About the time named by her many minds were impressed with the idea that the dreadful events of the Reign of Terror, and of the French Revolution in general, foreshadowed the end of the world, and millennial speculations, some of the wildest character, are to be found in abundance in the pamphlets of the day The mind of Joanna was influenced by one of the wildest of these speculators in prophecy, Richard Brothers,[1]

[1] RICHARD BROTHERS was a fanatic naval lieutenant on half pay, who gave himself out to be the "nephew of God Almighty," "the Branch," "Michael the Prince," and "the Signet of Peace," by whom the Jews were to be restored to the Holy Land and the Millennium to be established He was taken up by the Avignon Society of MARTINISTS, and thus became a tool in the hands of the French and English Democrats In 1791 he predicted that London would shortly be destroyed by an

either directly or through William Sharp, who was one of his disciples [*Gent Mag* lxxvii pt 2, pp. 701, 902], and who, after that fanatic's removal to a lunatic asylum, became closely associated with Joanna, and defended her claims in various publications

The first publication of Joanna's "prophecies" was in the years 1801, 1802 and 1803, these professing to be revelations made to her ten years before "I have this to inform the public," she writes in 1803, "that the prophecies of this book shew the destruction of Satan, and the coming of Christ's kingdom Here my readers may ask me what ground I have to affirm this belief? I answer, from the truth that is past I have ground to believe the other truths will follow From the former I judge the latter. The war that I foretold in 1792 we should be engaged in followed in 1793. The dearth which came upon the land in 1794 and 1795 I foretold in 1792, and if unbelief did abound, that a much greater scarcity would take place, and which too fatally followed I foretold the bad harvest in 1797 I foretold in letters sent to two ministers in Exeter, what would be the harvests of 1799 and 1800, that the former would be hurt by rain, and the latter by sun —these followed as predicted The rebellion which took place in Ireland in 1798 I foretold in 1795, when the Irish soldiers rebelled in Exeter against the English officers I foretold the secret thoughts and conversations of people in Exeter which took place in 1792 This was acknowledged to be true by Mr Eastlake of Exeter, before the Rev Stanhope Bruce, the Rev Thomas Webster, the Rev Thomas P Foley, Messrs Sharp, Turner, Wilson, and Morison, January 2nd, 1802, whilst they were at Exeter examining into the truth of my character and writings" [*Warning to the whole World from the Sealed Prophecies*, etc 123] These pretended predictions were conveyed partly in prose, but chiefly in doggrel like the following —

"Fast the storms are hastening on
But if England does awake,
And come to perfect day,
'Tis other nations I shall shake—
The sunshine here you'll see,
For as the clouds this day dismissed
The sunshine at the end,
Then shining days I'll bring to pass
And stand your every friend
So now 'tis time for to awake"
[*First Book of Sealed Prophecies*, 41]

Ridiculous as the prophecies of Joanna Southcott now appear—and in several thick volumes of them there is nothing but nonsense and blasphemy—multitudes of people believed in her pretensions, and these were by no means confined to the uneducated classes Several clergymen were among her suporters, a lady named Townley became her secretary, another lady left her property worth £250 a year, and she exhibited many rich presents which she had received from her wealthy disciples The latter obtained, in return, papers which she called her "seals," from the circumstance that every one of them was certified by the impression of a seal which she had found in sweeping out a house in Exeter after a sale by auction, the use of which was afterwards revealed to her [Twort's *Letters, Epistles, and Revelations*, etc 55] The device on this seal was the following—the interpretation given to the two letters being obvious This seal was affixed to most of the voluminous writings which she printed but the papers given to her disciples generally contained the words, "The Sealed of the Lord—the Elect Precious Man's Redemption—To inherit the Tree of Life —To be made heirs of God and joint-heirs of Jesus Christ" and the persons receiving them were then said to be numbered among the mystical hundred and forty and four thousand of the Apocalypse

About fifteen months before her death Joanna Southcott began to print her "Books of Wonders," of which five were published in 1813 and 1814 The Sixth Book was not printed until 1852 These were intended to announce new pretensions to which this singular fanatic now began to lay claim Although she was now past sixty years of age, she declared that she was about to become a mother, that her child would be supernaturally conceived, and that he would be the Shiloh in whom the Millennium was to be established In making this announcement she writes "Since this powerful visitation of the Lord came to me, like that in ninety-two, I have fresh things revealed to me every day I am awaked every morning between three and four o'clock, I sit up in my bed till the day breaks, and have communications given to me as soon as I am awake When the day breaks I rise and go down into the dining-room by myself, the moment I enter the room I feel as though I was surrounded with angels, feeling a heavenly joy which I cannot describe, and which has taken from me my natural appetite As soon as I had finished my last Book new things were revealed to me, and I was ordered to have seven respectable friends to meet together at four o'clock on Thursday afternoon, September 23rd, to hear read what had been revealed to me, and what I was directed to do, that they might be witnesses" [*Second Book of Wonders*, 1] The revelation was pretended to have been given in such terms as those —"The Psalms of David

earthquake, and during the following three or four years he published many prophecies on public events, and appeals to the people of England of a dangerously exciting and inflammatory character [Moser's *Anecd of Brothers*, 1795] The crowds that resorted to him daily for months in 1794 5, at last made it necessary for the Government to interfere Brothers was apprehended on March 4th, 1795, and the Privy Council having appointed a commission of physicians to examine him, they declared him, on March 27th, to be a lunatic On May 4th he was sent to St Luke's madhouse, to be confined during the King's pleasure There is a surprising number of publications of the time respecting his prophecies but his chief supporter in the press and in Parliament was a member of the House of Commons named Nathaniel Brassey Halsted, one of the survivors of the Black Hole of Calcutta, who actually made a speech in the House supporting Brothers' pretensions on March 31st, 1795 Much information respecting Brothers is to be found in the *Gentleman's Magazine*, lxv pt 1 that were never fulfilled in man, but now I have told thee that they shall be fulfilled in the son that shall be born of thee this year, for this shall be the king that I shall enable with ten thousand to destroy those that rise up against him with twenty thousand," etc [*Fourth Book of Wonders*, 44]

During the year 1814 the newspapers abound with paragraphs referring to the expectations thus raised in the minds of Joanna's numerous followers, and a writer of the time says that the sacred name of Shiloh was introduced into songs sung by the ballad singers in the streets and in places of amusement, and made Christianity itself to be scoffed at [Eusebius' *Letter to Abp. Cant* 1815] Many presents were made to her in anticipation of the child's birth, and among them a very costly child's crib, of which a large copperplate engraving exists which is sometimes bound up with her "prophecies," a horned lamb being represented as lying within it A little more than four months before her death, on August 7th, 1814, Joanna was visited by a London physician of some eminence, Dr Reece, and, singular to say, he gave way to the belief entertained by herself and her friends, and although convinced that she was a virgin, and that her age was sixty-four, announced his conviction that she was pregnant a belief which he apparently did not give up until a *post mortem* examination had proved there was no foundation for it whatever [Reece's *Correct Statement*, etc, 1815]

Joanna Southcott died on December 27th, 1814, and by her own express directions her body was kept warm for four days in expectation that, being in a trance, she would revive, and that the child would yet be born These expectations not being fulfilled, her body was buried in St Marylebone Churchyard, the following inscription being placed on her tombstone

"While through all thy wondrous days
Heaven and earth enraptured gaze,
While vain sages think they know
Secrets thou alone canst shew,
Time alone will tell what hour
Thou'lt appear in greater power!"

Before her death, the Rev T P Foley, Rector of Old Swinford, was directed to make the following communication to her believers "Joanna has had a command from the Spirit of the Lord, that no more preachings or meetings of the friends after Sunday next are to be holden till after the birth of Shiloh, the Prince of Peace, and she desired me to communicate this intelligence to you (Rev Mr Eyre), and she wishes you will stop them all at Bristol and Bath, and wherever you may know they are holden Nothing now is to be published or printed in the papers by the friends without orders or permission from the friends in Weston Place Signed, Joanna Southcott" "The believers were also ordered by the Spirit" (says Mr Foley), "through Joanna, to attend on a Sunday the Protestant churches near them Some that believed in the order, fulfilled it; and some did not fulfil it but kept their meetings" [*Living Oracle or Star of Bethlehem* 1830, p ix] Little was heard, therefore, of Joanna's followers for some years But in 1825 a man named Charles William Twort pretended to be the Shiloh whose coming had been predicted, and published a number of letters under such titles as "The Vision of Judgment or the return of Joanna from her trance," "The Living Oracle or the Star of Bethlehem," "Letters, Epistles, and Revelations of Jesus Christ, addressed to the believers in the glorious reign of Messiah" These were signed "Zion, the Lord is here," sealed with a seal impressed with a dove, and called the "Epistles of Shiloh," and dated from the year of the Millennium 1825 A similar impostor arose about the same time from among the Southcottians named George Turner, who issued epistles of the same kind, and whose followers were called "Turnerites" The last leader of the Southcottians was John Wroe of Bowling, near Bradford, who assumed that position about 1822, and whose followers afterwards became notorious at Wakefield and in Australia [CHRISTIAN ISRAELITES] On June 15th 1855, the foundation stone was laid of a large mansion, subsequently called "Melbourne House," at Wrenthorp, between Wakefield and Bradford, which was formally opened on Whitsun Day, 1857, in presence of a vast number of Wroe's followers from all quarters The house is built in the classic style, has extensive greenhouses, and is fitted throughout in the interior with mahogany and cedar This was professedly intended for a community of Southcottians, but "Prophet Wroe" bequeathed the property to a grandchild, and the sect cannot regain possession of it There are now only three or four other congregations of the Southcottians in England

SPASOVA SOGLASIA [NETOVSCHINS]

SPENER [PIETISTS]

SPERONISTÆ A local name of the Albigenses, taken from Sperone, a market town in the Piedmontese province of Ivrea [Gieseler, *Compend Eccl Hist* iii 446, n 6, Clark's transl]

SPINOZA The philosophic doctrine of Benedict Spinoza has never yet been popularized, it is unconnected with any system of public worship, and "its followers," said M Stoup, writing for his day, "dare not discover themselves, because it overthrows the foundation of all religion" It is however of importance that it should be noticed here somewhat in detail, its author having been the founder of so-called Biblical criticism, and parent of the modern German school of speculative philosophy, all the great metaphysicians of that country adopting his fundamental principles, and differing with him only on points of detail

Baruch, or as he Latinized his name, Benedictus, de Spinoza, was the son of a Jewish merchant at Amsterdam, and was born on the 24th of November 1632 It was in the first instance intended that he should follow his father's profession, but his early passionate love of study subsequently induced his parents to allow him to devote himself to learning Very soon the boy won the heart and admiration of the chief Rabbi Saul Levi Morteira, and great indeed were the expectations raised by his shrewdness and ability Nothing seemed too good or too fair to look for from him Boyhood passed into youth His mind gradually expanded And now little by little it was perceived he was beginning to break loose from the faith to which he had been born, and to think for himself independently Little by little, too, it was seen he was withdrawing from the established worship of the synagogue, and retiring more and more upon himself As he changed, so the countenance of his friends changed towards him Mild persuasions were followed by urgent remonstrances, remonstrances by threats; and threats by preparations for his excommunication But his mind even at that early age was extraordinarily fixed and fearless The very severities proposed against him conveyed the impression to his mind that they who resorted to them were incapable of answering his difficulties, and knew themselves to be so Accordingly he voluntarily withdrew from the synagogue But the sentence of excommunication was nevertheless pronounced, if not as a terror to him, at least as a warning to others, and from that day he was a stranger to his own people and his father's house, and his connection with any religious body was at an end

Our next glimpse of Spinoza is when received into the house and assisting to teach in the school of one Van den Ende, a physician of Amsterdam, learning Latin—and at the same time love, from his daughter But alas—*fœmina est mutabile,*—the damsel jilts the philosopher for the sake of a Hamburg merchant, and Benedict is once more an outcast "Hoc odium erga rem amatam majus erit pro ratione lætitiæ, qua zelotypus ex reciproco rei amatæ amore solebat affici . ad quod denique accedit, quod zelotypus non eodem vûltu, quem res amata ei præbere solebat, ab eâdem excipiatur, quâ etiam de causâ amans contristatur," says he [*de Affect Schol Pr* xxxv], in after life, looking calmly backward Time passes, and again we find him critically circumstanced This time he is being tempted by wealth and honour He has settled at Woorburg, a little village near the Hague, determined to devote his life entirely to philosophy, working with his hands for the supply of his daily wants, and gaining for himself a bare subsistence by polishing lenses for telescopes and microscopes His *Principia Philosophiæ Cartesianæ* has appeared, the most profound and accurate digest of the teaching of Descartes in existence, and become a text-book in the schools The fame of its author being noised abroad, the Prince Palatine offered him the chair of philosophy in the University of Heidelberg But Spinoza declined it "I do not look," he says, "for any higher worldly possession than that which I now enjoy" Consistently, when the inheritance of his fathers comes to him, he makes it over to his sisters Miriam and Rebecca, though they have forsaken and despised him A wealthy citizen, Simon de Vries, out of pity for his poverty, leaves him a fortune, but he refuses to receive it In his living he is more than temperate. A basin of milk porridge, with a little butter, costing about three halfpence, was to him a day's sustenance, and this, not from any self-restraint or self-mortification, but because he was naturally abstemious, and finding this sufficient, cared not for more "Although often invited to dinner," as the Lutheran pastor Colerus, to whom we are indebted for most of what we know of the domestic life of the philosopher, remarks, "he preferred the scanty meal that he found at home to dining sumptuously at the expense of another"

Thus, "in the still air of delightful studies," went the philosopher on his way In his forty-fifth year, in the full vigour and maturity of his intellect, consumption, which had long threatened him, became firmly established, and made rapid progress On the Sunday on which he died he would not allow his host and hostess to stay from divine service to wait on him, particularly as it was their purpose to partake of the Holy Communion Though he had not become a Christian on giving up Judaism, he nevertheless could reverence the convictions of those who received that faith in sincerity and unaffected devotion When asked by his landlady respecting her religion he said "Your religion is a good one, you ought not to seek another, nor doubt that yours will procure you salvation, if you add to your piety the tranquil virtues of domestic life." Waiting patiently, on their return from service, he talked with them after a friendly sort about the sermon, and presently settling into a calm, expired in peace, on the 21st of February 1677 After his death his goods (with the exception of the MS of his *Ethics*) were sold by auction to defray the expenses of his burial, and realized about £40 sterling of our money

An edition of his works appeared at once after his death, those which had been printed during his life being bound with those previously unpublished, the latter under the title—"B. D S. Opera Posthuma" The name of the author was only indicated by initial letters, we are told in the preface, because a little before his death he begged expressly that his name might not be mentioned, for, as he says, "The innocent love of approbation easily glides into ambition and selfishness, whereby men, under a false show of consideration for others, are apt to excite discord and sedition, and he that sincerely desires to help others by word or deed . will be careful not to have his name associated with his work, or to give any other cause for envy" [*Ethics*, pt. iv append. cap xxv]

The collected works submitted to the world at this time were as follows

1 The *Principia Philosophiæ Cartesianæ*, to which is added an appendix, under the title *Cogitata Metaphysica*, enlarging on certain points not exhausted in the preceding Amsterdam, 1663

2 The *Tractatus Theologico-Politicus* Hamburg, 1670
3 The *Ethica*
4 The *Tractatus Politicus*
5 The *Tractatus de Intellectus emendatione*
6 The *Epistolæ et ad eas Responsiones*
7 *Compendium Grammatices linguæ Hebrææ*
(5–7: Amsterdam, 1677)

To these must be added

8 A treatise on the Rainbow
9 A small treatise on God, and on Man and his wellbeing—

both long presumed to be lost, and only recently discovered

The first, fifth, and ninth treatises will not detain us their interest being chiefly historical, as foreshadowing his greater works The seventh and eighth, again, do not concern us

The *Epistolæ* are of great interest as specimens of an extremely clear and terse style, as shewing us the class of men with whom Spinoza was on intimate terms, and as containing expositions of most of the difficulties his doctrine presented to the best and ablest men of that time, and still does present Five-and-twenty are between Spinoza and Henry Oldenburg, the first secretary of our English Royal Society Through Oldenburg Boyle also became interested in the philosopher The rest of the seventy-four are chiefly received from or addressed to foreign scholars amongst whom we find Leibnitz, one of the most popular and distinguished philosophical writers of his day Nearly all are upon subjects of the most profound interest and importance, and strike to the very foundation of all knowledge and religious belief.

The publication of the *Tractatus Theologico-Politicus*, by which Spinoza was chiefly known during his lifetime, produced a sensation throughout Europe of which in these days we can form little idea It was condemned and forbidden to be sold in almost every country But the very labour which was taken to suppress it excited curiosity, and many were the quaint titles used, after the fashion of that day, in order to disguise it, and facilitate its dissemination The Spanish edition was entitled—*Henriquez de Villacorta, M Dr a Cubiculo Philippi IV, Caroli II, Archiatri opera chirurgica omnia, sub auspiciis potentissimi Hispaniarum Regis* [Lewes, *Hist Philos* 393] Looking abroad upon the world, and seeing the number of "sects, heresies, and schools of thought" within the Christian religion alone, to mention no other,—men boasting of the peace, the joy they experience, the brotherly love they feel, while in actual life they contend with the bitterest acrimony, and are full of intolerance and unappeasable hatred towards one another, one defending and extolling a doctrine as divine, while another condemns it as devilish,—distinguishable only by the place of worship they frequent, and the profession of this or that body of opinions, not by the consistency of their lives or conversation—What, he asks, can the explanation be? What the remedy? The explanation he believes to be—an entirely mistaken idea as to the nature of that Word of God to which all alike profess to refer for authority, and the remedy—an entirely new examination of the Scriptures, in a spirit devoid of prejudice, in order to ascertain, if possible, what is and what is not essential for a man to know for his soul's health,—what is and what is not unessential, and within the limits on which his mind may be left at liberty to think for itself

The work consists of twenty chapters The first two consider the nature of prophecy and the prophetic office, and conclude that the prophetic writings are merely of weight in such things as concern the usages of life and virtuous conduct, and that on other subjects they concern us little The gift of prophetic foresight is attributed to a quicker and more lively imagination than that of common men The third chapter treats of the election of the Jews, and of the question whether the gift of prophecy was peculiar to them, denying the latter and affirming of the former that it was apparent merely, not real, the various passages of Scripture which would seem to prove the contrary being in condescension to the state and circumstances of the Jewish people, who in their then stage of civilization would have been incapable of happiness could they have known God favoured any other nation The fourth is on the Divine Law, the first precept of which is that a man shall love God unconditionally, with all his heart, not for the sake of benefit or fear of punishment, "but from this only, that he knows God" The fifth treats of religious ceremonial observance, and faith in the historic narrative, of the reasons why rites and ceremonies are useful, and those to whom they are necessary The sixth is on miracles A miracle, in the light of anything above or contrary to nature, is regarded as an absurdity, for [1] nothing can happen contrary to the established order and course of nature, which is eternal and unchangeable [2] Miracles, even if possible, could not make known either the nature or attributes of God, already revealed and illustrated in the regular and invariable order of nature, and, conceived as events contravening the established order of nature, so far from proving the existence of God, would actually lead us to call it in question [3] Where, in Holy Scripture, the decrees and will of God are spoken of, nothing else is meant than the order and law of nature, which are in fact the eternal order and law of God [4] Many common things in Scripture appear miraculous merely from the peculiar language in which they are recorded, as for instance where it is said God hardened the heart of Pharaoh, meaning only that he was firm and uncomplying, or where it is said God opened the windows of heaven, meaning only that a good deal of rain fell, and so on The seventh chapter is in defence of a purely rational interpretation of Scripture by each person for himself, independently of any extrinsic authority The eighth is to prove that the Pentateuch, and the books of Joshua, Judges, Ruth, Samuel, and Kings, were all written "ages after the things they relate had passed away And when we regard the argument and connection of these books severally, we readily gather that they were all written by one and the same person, who had the purpose of compiling a system of Jewish antiquities, from the origin of the nation to the first destruction of the city of Jerusalem The several books are so connected one with another, that from this alone we discover how they comprise the continuous narrative of a single historian Who this was, however, cannot be so readily shewn, although . I am led to suspect that it was Ezra . The books in question could have been written by no one before Ezra

Perhaps he was led to call the first five books of his history by the name of Moses, because in them especially are comprised the incidents in the life of the great prophet For the same reason Joshua etc etc" Ninth, the same subject continued, with criticisms of the Hebrew text and marginal notes of the Hebrew codices, and addings up of figures, etc, reminding us of much which has appeared in our own day Tenth, the remaining books of the Old Testament The two books of Chronicles are thought likely to have been written after the restoration of the Temple by Judas Maccabæus "The Psalms were also collected and divided into five books during the epoch of the second Temple" "The Proverbs of Solomon, I believe, were also collected about the same time, or at least in the time of King Josiah," and the Prophecies are of several dates, not set down in any definite order, but as they happened to be collected here and there As regards the canon of Holy Scripture, it is concluded that "before the time of the Maccabees there was none, and that the books we have were selected from a number of others on the sole authority of the Pharisees of the second Temple, . . and whoever should seek to demonstrate the authenticity and authority of the Hebrew Scriptures must shew that the council of the Pharisees could not err in their selection of the books they admitted, and this I think no one will ever be able to demonstrate The eleventh chapter is devoted to the question whether the Apostles wrote their Epistles in the character of Apostles and Prophets, or merely as Teachers, and to a consideration of the office of the Apostles, and it is concluded that they preached and wrote the history of Christ by the aid of natural light alone The twelfth is on the true covenant of the Divine Law, why the Scriptures are called sacred, and in what sense they are said to be the Word of God And here the distinction is drawn between the idol of ink and paper—which it is alleged the vulgar fall down and worship under the impression that it, and it only, is the Word of God, and the true Word of God, which is not confined to any particular book or set of books whatever, but is a living inspiration of the Divine Mind Nevertheless, it is admitted that the Word of God is contained in Holy Scripture, and that, in so far as is necessary to salvation, the latter have come down to us uncorrupted The thirteenth enlarges on what the author believes to be the true end and use of Holy Scripture These were not written to make a fighting ground for different sects, or repository of intricate speculative doctrine requiring supernatural light to understand, but are essentially an inculcation of the plainest and simplest duties—such as even the dullest may apprehend, namely, obedience to God, which consists in the love of our neighbour in all "reverential submissiveness," and in support of this position, the text—"He that loveth another hath fulfilled the law, love is the fulfilling of the law" [Rom viii], is quoted The fourteenth chapter is on Faith, which is defined thus —"To entertain such thoughts of God as, if wanting, obedience to Him is withheld, and, obedience given, adequate thoughts are implied" "To the true Catholic Faith (Fidem catholicam), then, belong those dogmas only which obedience to God absolutely demands, and which, neglected, obedience is absolutely impossible Of all other articles of faith, every one as he best knows himself, and as he finds these calculated to confirm him or otherwise in godly and neighbourly love, may be allowed to think as he pleases Were such a course followed, there were no room left, methinks, for controversy within the bosom of the Church Nor will I now shrink from specifying the heads of an universal faith, which are also the dogmas of Scripture. They are these — There is a Supreme Being, who delights in justice and mercy, whom all who would be saved are bound to obey, and whose worship consists in the practice of justice and charity towards our neighbour" Faith and Science, Theology and Philosophy, are next shewn to have nothing in common with one another, the scope of the former being only piety and obedience, while that of the latter is truth "Neither is subordinate to the other, but each holds sway in its own sphere without prejudice to the other" The fifteenth chapter enlarges further on the different provinces of Theology and Philosophy, and claims for the latter an absolutely independent domain The sixteenth, seventeenth, and eighteenth, are on the ideal of a perfect government, in accordance with the principles above enunciated The nineteenth defines the (absolute) authority of the state in all that pertains to public worship. Lastly, the twentieth chapter concludes that, since each person differs from another in capacity and disposition, and no two are capable of seeing a thing exactly in the same light, in the free state every one must be at liberty to think what he likes and to say what he thinks [1]

The *Tractatus Politicus* rises on the founda-

[1] The wonders wrought by time are here seen remarkably Even so recently as the latter half of the seventeenth century, in Holland, and to Spinoza, this appeared the greatest possible degree of civil and religious freedom conceivable even in an ideal state And yet now, in England, not only has it been found actually practicable for every one to think what he likes and say what he thinks, but to worship as he pleases also, his choice of a form of public worship being no more interfered with than his choice of a wife

tions of the preceding treatise As the right of every individual is commensurate with his power to exist and operate, so in like manner the body and mind of an entire government has just so much right as it has might, and each single citizen or subject has just so much less right as the state in itself surpasses him in might The question then is, by what form of government can the largest possible amount of liberty, right, or power, be acquired for the greatest number, intellectual liberty that is, and freedom according to the ordinance of nature, for the vile, the profligate, or the sinner is not free, but a slave, and as his power is small and feeble against temptation, so must his rights in the state be correspondingly curtailed The monarchical form of government is weighed in the balance, and found wanting The aristocratic is better, but not perfect The democratic is, as might be anticipated, the best and indeed only true form of government At this point the question of female voting arises for consideration It is decided in the negative "I exclude women and slaves," he says, "who are in the power of men and of masters, and likewise children, and minors as long as they are under the power of parents and guardians" And another reason, besides their comparative weakness, why women should not vote, is that men, as a rule, have no intellectual, but only sensual love for them, and would have their domestic happiness embittered or destroyed did their wives shew favour or enthusiasm towards other men, as would be necessary if they assumed civil rights Only the first ten and part of the eleventh chapters of this work were completed "Reliqua desiderantur," closes the question of women's rights abruptly "Morbo impeditus, et morte abreptus, hoc opus non ulterius perducere valuit"

The greatest and most highly finished of Spinoza's works, and that of most interest at the present time, is undoubtedly the *Ethics* To this, the *Tractatus Theologico-Politicus* may be read as a kind of detached preface Every system must have some foundation — gold, silver, precious stones, wood, hay, stubble Thomas Aquinas constructed the *Summa Theologiæ* out of Holy Scripture and patristic tradition by the aid of reason, Calvin his *Institutes* out of the Scriptures alone by the aid of reason, some will have nothing save the Bible, and the Bible only, without reason, Spinoza accepted no external aid whatever, and built his system by the aid of reason out of the admissions of the reason herself alone and to this day it remains one of the most marvellously subtle, audacious, and stupendous efforts of reasoning in existence Fearlessly he throws across the abyss of human ignorance a bridge of mathematically demonstrated propositions, by which he essays to connect the lowest things of earth with God their maker An intricate tangled maze of rafters and girders, as fine as gossamer threads, stretches itself before us, upheld by chains of rigorously appointed reasoning, without flaw or break anywhere in them that can be discovered As from the nature of a triangle or circle one property after another is made by the mathematician to follow and be deduced, so here by the philosopher proposition is made to follow proposition in unrelenting logical sequence, and lead on to yet another and another. Taking the fundamental axiom of Descartes, that whatsoever is clearly perceived in consciousness is true, in consciousness he finds a certain number of elementary propositions, which appear to him as evidently true, and therefore as necessarily to be received, in philosophy, as the propositions of Euclid are in mathematics On these he builds If these are false, all is false If these are admitted, then all else follows inevitably and of necessity There is no power of withdrawal The student finds himself in a region in which all revealed truth, so far from being rested on, is not even made room for It is not that in particular there is any hostility towards Christianity; it is that the revelations alike of Jew and Gentile are ignored It is not that there is found abuse or insult, it is that the Levite passes by on the other side indifferent, and proceeds of himself to demonstrate all our most important practical duties independently, such as for instance the love of one's neighbour, the forgiveness of injuries, the return of good for evil, the crucifixion of the affections and lusts, and the love of God above all things The whole question therefore on examination will be found to resolve itself into this —Is human reason of itself alone able to find out a sure way of salvation? The Christian solemnly and in all earnestness believes that it is not Spinoza thought that it was

When one thinks of the enormous number of ponderous tomes in which systems of philosophy are apt to be delivered, the size of the *Ethics* of Spinoza becomes extremely curious and significant It consists in the edition of 1677 but of 264 small quarto pages of good sized print To him, as has been said, "lucid and concise geometrical form seems to have been as easy as versification was to Pope" The extreme difficulty of applying the mathematical method to philosophy he makes light of, and insists on treating mind and morals, intellect and affections, God and nature, "precisely as if the question were of lines, planes, and solids" [Introd *de Affect*] The whole is divided into five parts [1] *De Deo*, in which God is proved to be the beginning and foundation of all existence [2] *De Mente*, in which the nature and powers of the intellect are worked out [3] *De Affectibus*, or the nature of the affections, emotions, or passions [4] *De Servitute Humana*, or the misery and thraldom of those whose lives are governed by their emotions [5] *De Libertate Humana*, or the blessedness of those whose lives are governed by their intellect

Part I *De Deo* —The foundation of all being and existence according to Spinoza is substance —*Substans*, that which *stands under* all appearance, supporting it and giving it the appearance of reality—the *Self-standinghood* of the Germans —the *Substantia* of the Schoolmen [1]—namely,

[1] See S Thomas Aquinas, *Summa Theologiæ*, pt I.

God "Save God no other substance can exist or be conceived" [*Pr* xiv] But this one substance is possessed of an infinity of attributes, each of which expresses an infinite and eternal essence Of these we are capable of apprehending two only—extension and thought. God appears to us the infinitely extended Being when conceived under His attribute of extension, as the infinitely cogitating Being when conceived under His attribute of thought All material things in the world are modes of God's attribute of extension, all ideas and conceptions are modes of His attribute of thought "All that is," therefore, "is in God, and without Him nothing can exist or be conceived" [*Pr* xv] And, since God is not only the efficient but the essential cause of the existence of all things, it follows that His connection with them (as a cause) is immanent or abiding, not extrinsic or transient [*Pr* xviii] He is moreover a Free Cause, understanding by free that He exists and acts solely by the necessity of His nature, not that He acts according to His well-pleasing, or that He can act in opposition to His nature No—"From the infinite power or infinite nature of God all has necessarily followed, or by the same necessity does follow, as from eternity it has followed and to eternity it will follow, that the three angles of a triangle are equal to two right angles" "*All* has followed"—the efficient, immanent and ever-present invisible Cause, Order, Law, or whatever else is conceivable under the term *Natura naturans*, the sensible, visible, material, or whatever else is conceivable under the term *Natura naturata* "Has followed *from God*" It is not God, but as conceivable and distinguishable apart from God as effect is conceivable and distinguishable apart from cause "Has followed *necessarily*,"—for things apart from Him have no power of determination, each depending for its essence and existence on an antecedent cause, this on another, this on yet another, and so on to infinity, until we reach the First Cause, *i e* God There is therefore nothing in the nature of things that is contingent—all is necessary and eternal, the very fact that a thing is as it is, implying that it could not have been otherwise, since then it must have been not perfect if now it is perfect, but imperfect, and the understanding and will, or the very essence of God could be other than it is, which is absurd It is almost needless to add that, in this view, neither prayers nor sacrifices can avail to alter the mind of God, and that not even the most heartfelt repentance can condone for sin, the penalty of which must needs be paid to the uttermost, and borne, not sullenly, but cheerfully and willingly, as the inevitable order and will of God [1]

quæst iii art v "Videtur quod Deus sit in genere aliquo Substantia enim est ens per se subsistens hoc autem maxime convenit Deo ergo Deus est in genere Substantiæ." The whole doctrine of Transubstantiation turned upon this subtle distinction between the invisible and intangible *Substance*, and the visible and tangible accident, or mere appearance

[1] The inability of even God Himself to prevent the consequences inseparable from the breaking of His laws, even it may be to the third and fourth generation, does not, however, to Spinoza's mind prevent God's receiving the sinner again into favour "God forgives those who repent of their transgressions There is no man that has not sinned, were not God clement and forgiving, therefore, all might despair of their salvation, nor were there else any sense in believing that God is merciful" [*Theol-Pol* cap xiv]

Part II *De Mente*—In accordance with what precedes, the body of man is concluded to be a mode expressing the essence of the Deity under the aspect of Extension, the mind—a mode expressing the essence of the Deity considered under the aspect of Thought, so that whatever is clearly and distinctly, that is, adequately perceived in the mind, is present in the mind of God, in so far as it constitutes the essence of the mind of man, and must therefore necessarily be objectively true. But all our ideas are not thus clear Our knowledge is classifiable under these heads [1] That grounded on *Opinion* or *Imagination*, confused representations of the senses, vague experience, and remembrance of things heard or read [2] That grounded on *Reason*, notions common to mankind of the properties of things [3] *Intuitive* knowledge, which is of the highest order, "issuing from adequate ideas of the attributes of God to adequate knowledge of the essences of things" "In so far as our mind perceives things truly, it is part of the infinite intelligence of God, and it is as much matter of necessity that all clear and distinct ideas of the mind should be true as that the idea of God in our mind is a truth" The Imagination pictures things as contingent, associating them in the mind with notions of the past and future, the Reason sees them as necessary, ever-present, and true, *i e* as they are in themselves, and such necessity is the very necessity of the eternal nature of God As regards the Will;—absolute or free will does not pertain to man For being determined to will this or that by a cause which is itself determined by an antecedent cause, this by a third, and so on to infinity, the mind of itself has no power of willing or of not willing "Men think themselves free because they are conscious of their volitions and appetites, but ignorant of the causes by which they are disposed to desire and will"

Part III *De Affectibus*—Having treated the nature of the mind or soul in so far as thought, idea, perception, and volition enter into its constitution, its nature, as manifested in the Affections or Emotions, is considered By an Affection or Emotion is understood a state of body whereby its power of acting is increased or diminished, aided or controlled, and we act when something takes place within us of which we are ourselves the adequate cause,—suffer, when anything takes place within us or without us of which we are only partially the cause [2] By *Desire* or *Appetite* is understood the very essence of man, whereby he is determined to do those things

[2] Anger or rage, for instance, is not an increased action as at first sight it might appear, but passion (namely suffering, or imperfection) induced in the mind by confused and inadequate ideas connected with the object of our anger or rage

that subserve his preservation *Joy* is the transition from a less to a greater degree of perfection or power of being *Sorrow* is the transition from a greater to a less degree of perfection or power of being And to one or other of these three Emotions all other conceivable Emotions may be referred Thus Love is Joy, associated with the idea of an external object as a cause Hatred is Sorrow, associated with the idea of an external object as a cause Anger is the desire with which we are moved by hate to do him an injury whom we dislike etc etc

Part IV *De Servitute Humana* —Desires which spring from true knowledge of what is good and what is bad for us, may be ruled and restrained by various affections, but the knowledge itself cannot be so ruled or restrained, and hence the significant words of the poet—

> "Video meliora proboque, deteriora sequor"

Thus are men obnoxious to passions, inconstant in their resolves, and rebellious to the precepts of reason, though these make no demands against nature, virtuous life being indeed harmony with the laws of nature The foundation of all true virtue, of all true happiness, lies within the sphere of these laws and their observance, the first and greatest of all being that which impels us to preserve our minds and bodies in a state of integrity as respects ourselves, and in a state of harmony as respects our fellow-men and nature at large Virtue is therefore to be sought and prized for its own sake, there being nothing more excellent in nature, nothing more advantageous to ourselves, nothing more beneficial to others And the highest virtue, or greatest good of the mind, is the knowledge and love of God. All that relates to this belongs to Religion All that relates to our duty as respects our fellow-men belongs to Piety All that conduces to good understanding and kindly fellowship is Good, whatever, on the contrary, leads to difference, hatred, or ill-feeling is Evil

Space will not allow of enlargement on the formal demonstrations of the good and evil of the Affections *seriatim*, or on the scarcely less important scholia to the various propositions in which the pleasure and advantage of a life of virtue are discoursed on, often with great eloquence But it may not be amiss, by way of illustrating the thoroughness and detail with which this part of the work is executed, to mention that among the Virtues even politeness (Humanitas) finds a place, and cheerfulness "Cheerfulness and merriment are the sunshine of existence, and nothing but sour and sorry superstition denounces and calls them evil . No Divinity, none but an envious demon, could take delight in my misery [1] Nor do tears and groans and superstitious terrors—all signs alike of impotence of mind, ever lead to a virtuous life, the more, on the contrary, our minds are possessed with joy, to the higher perfection do we (*pro tanto*) rise, and the more truly do we participate of the Divine Nature A wise man accordingly will refresh and recreate himself in moderation with pleasant food and drink, with sweet odours, with the beauty of growing plants, ornaments, music, athletic games, theatres, and with such other things as can be used without harm to others For the human body is composed of very many parts of diverse nature, which continually require new and varied sustenance, in order that the body may remain equally fit for all things which can follow from its nature, and consequently that the mind also may be equally fit for understanding more things at once" [*Schol Pr* xlv] Even the matter of dress is not thought beneath the notice of this philosopher "It is not a disorderly and slovenly carriage," he says, "that makes us sages, much rather is affected indifference to personal appearance an evidence of a poor spirit, in which true wisdom can find no fit dwelling-place"

Part V *De Libertate Humana* —If we dissever an emotion or affection from the thought of its external cause, and with it associate other thoughts, then will the agitations of mind that arise from the emotion be destroyed Moreover, affections cease to be passions as soon as we form a clear and distinct idea of them [*vide supra*] And when we contemplate things as necessary, the power of the mind over the affections is increased The grief felt for the loss of good, for instance, is mitigated if we see that it could by no possibility have been retained, and torn by our affections in excess, we are brought to think of and call into play such powers as we have of ordering and controlling them in consonance with reason and experience When we think of all the benefits that accrue from friendship and the social state, consider the peace of mind that springs from a good and reasonable life, and know that men act by the necessity of their nature, we shall not be disposed to repay hate by hate, or injustice by injustice, but much rather to overcome hatred with good, injuries by magnanimity, etc And in such a course we shall be greatly strengthened by reflecting that all the affections of the body are ultimately referable to God, immanent in all, for we know that all that is is in God, and that without Him nothing can exist or be conceived In proportion as this is realized, the love of God, and with it also the love of our fellow-men, will be enkindled within us [*Prop* xv]

> "Each wild desire is lull'd to rest,
> That rent the heart, or rack'd the brow,
> The love of man now fires the breast,
> The love of God is kindling now,"

—a love incapable of being sullied by selfishness, envy, jealousy, or any of the pollutions of a meaner love, and which is increased the more others also are united with us in the same loving bonds Now "the human mind cannot be absolutely destroyed with the body, something of it remains which is eternal" [*Prop* xxiii], that part which is possessed of "the intellectual love of God," for instance, "which arises from the

[1] "I think that some mistake the Devil for God." [Kingsley, *Good News of God*, Sermon x.]

third kind of intellection" [*vide supra*, Pt II] "is eternal" [Prop xxxiii], and "the mind is not obnoxious to passions except during the continuance of the body" [Prop xxxiv], remaining henceforth for ever

"Pure, and mirror bright, and even "

Were it a matter of doubt, however,—did we not know that the soul was eternal,—yet "piety, religion, and all else, which in the fourth part we have shewn to pertain to strength of mind and generosity, would have to be held of last importance" [*Prop* xli] The scholium to this proposition is very characteristic "The common persuasion of the vulgar would seem to be otherwise For most men appear to think themselves free only so far as they can give way to lust, and fancy that they are hindered of their rights when held to live in conformity with the prescriptions of the Divine law Accordingly they esteem piety, religion, and whatever else is referred to true strength of mind, as burdens which after death they hope to lay aside, when also they hope to receive the reward for the slavery, namely, piety and religion, which they have endured in this life But not fully are they led, even by this hope, to live—so far as their slender and weak capacity admits—in conformity with the prescription of the Divine law, it is rather the fear of frightful punishments after death that influences them, and it is said that unless such hope and fear were in men, and on the contrary they were to believe mind perished with the body, they would no longer live wretched, weighed down under the load of piety, but do all things after their lust, and obey fortune rather than themselves Such things seem to me not less absurd than it would be if a man, because he did not believe himself able to nourish his body for ever with good food, were to straightway fill himself instead with deadly poisons, or if because he saw the mind was not eternal or immortal, he were to wish himself demented and without reason,—things which seem so absurd that they scarcely deserve to be recounted" And yet how is it that, practically, the great mass of mankind are led by hope and fear rather than by reason? The answer is contained in the Scholium to the last proposition, in the closing words of the *Ethics* —OMNIA PRÆCLARA TAM DIFFICILIA QUAM RARA SUNT

Having now gone through all the writings of the philosopher it will be possible for us to construct a *Spinozistic Creed*, as follows

"I believe in one Infinite [*Eth* I xi] and Undivided [xii xiii] God, Eternal [xi xix] and Unchangeable [V xvii], existing and acting by the sole necessity of his nature [I xvi xvii], of infinite Attributes, whereof two only are capable of being conceived by man—Extension and Thought [II i ii], whereof he himself is the Identity [4], of all things the Free Cause [I xvii], immanent not transient [I xviii], in Whom all things consist [xxv], and without Whom nothing can exist or be conceived [xv]

"By whom all things are made, not truly by design or for the sake of any end, contingently, of free-will, or absolute well-pleasing, but predetermined and following necessarily from the absolute nature or infinite power of God [I xxvi xxvii xxviii xxix xxxiii and append]

"Of which world is Man [II x et seq iv append ch x], whose consciousness is the basis of all certitude [xx xxxii xxxiii], in which whatsoever is clearly perceived is true [xxxiv] and exists objectively in nature [xxxviii xxxix xlv], whose will is not free, but necessary or constrained [xlviii lix], whose acts and desires alone are good so far as they are defined by reason [IV xxiii-xxviii append ch v], and whose salvation, liberty, and beatitude consists, not in the reward of virtue, but in the virtue itself whereby affections are restrained [V xli], and in the constant and eternal knowledge and love of God [IV xxviii, V xxxii xxxiii Schol. xxxvi], whose worship by man consists in the exercise of obedience, charity, and justice [*Theol -Pol* xiii] And I believe in the communion and fellowship of all men in so far as they are led by reason [IV xxxv xxxvii xlvi lxxi lxxii lxxiii], and in the eternity of the mind" [V xxiii xxxix]

It is hoped that, for general purposes, this exposition of the doctrine and historical position of Spinoza will be found sufficient. The doctrine is not atheistic, though it has often been said to be so, because God is taken as the foundation and cause of all things even to the exclusion of whatever else either is or can be conceived On the other hand it is not absolutely pantheistic, because a distinction is made throughout between the world and its Creator, between the *natura naturans* and the *natura naturata*, between the Cause and the effect Still less is it materialistic, the reason why it has been said to be so arising from ignorance of the metaphysical meaning of the word Substance. That it was apprehended as a system of Idealism by the greatest minds of the age to which it belongs, is clear alike from contemporary criticism and from the subsequent course of the history of philosophy

[B D S. *Opera*, 1677; *Benedict de Spinoza, his Life, Correspondence, and Ethics*, by R Willis, M D, 1870, *Tractatus Theologico-Politicus*, transl from the Latin, with an introd 1862, *Tractatus Politicus*, transl W Maccall, 1854, Lewes, *Biograph Hist Philos*, art *Spinoza*, and Hallam, *Introd Lit Europe* For other literature on the subject see the end of the article in Lewes, *Hist Philos*, Willis, *passim*, and DICT *of* THEOL., SPINOZISM]

SPIRITUALISTS A name assumed by the strict Franciscans in the disputes which arose respecting the manner of observing the Rule of St. Francis in the latter half of the fourteenth century [PAULO-JOANNITES FRATICELLI]

SPIRITUALISTS The name assumed by a body of superstitious persons in England and America who profess to hold communication with the spirits of the departed This is supposed to take place through "mediums," that is to say, men or women who possess the special and exceptional qualities which are required to bring them *en rapport* with disembodied beings With such persons the spirits converse by means of sounds similar to raps made upon tables or walls, these raps being arranged into an alphabetic form on a system analogous to that used for electric telegraph instruments The "rapping" on tables and other articles of furniture is sometimes supplemented by their motion, so that tables, couches, chairs, etc, move about a room, or are hoisted by the spirits above the floor to float between it and the ceiling The theory of the Spiritualists is that disembodied spirits have lately discovered these means of communicating with the world, and that they do it by electric detonation

Insatiable credulity is a conspicuous characteristic of the Spiritualists, and much that has been called Spiritualism ought to have been called Imposture But it is probable that some as yet unexplained forces brought into action by volition have given rise to phenomena which have been put to the credit of spirits

SPIRITUALS [TERTULLIANISTS]

SPIRITUALS [EUCHITES]

SPIRITUALS [LIBERTINES]

STANCARISTS The followers of Francis Stancari, who was brought into note by his controversies with Osiander, Bullinger, Melanchthon, and others of the Lutheran and Calvinistic Reformers

Stancari was an Italian, who had been ejected for heresy from the University of Mantua From thence he went to Switzerland, where he occasioned so much dissension that he was driven away by the Calvinists, and obliged to take up his quarters with the Lutherans of Prussia, eventually becoming Professor of Hebrew at Konigsberg in the year 1548 From Konigsberg he migrated to Cracow in Poland, where he filled the same office, and where, by propagating Unitarian opinions, he was an effectual ally of Socinus His turbulent nature made him the cause of great dissensions in Poland also [Mosh *Eccl Hist* III ii 1, § 37], and he was imprisoned by the bishop Escaping from prison, he fled to Pinchzovia, where he appeared as a furious iconoclast and antisacerdotalist After a life constantly spent in fierce controversy, he died in the year 1574

Osiander and his followers had maintained peculiar views respecting the Atonement of our Lord, alleging that it was as God alone He offered it, for that as man He Himself needed it, and therefore could not offer it for others The Stancarists went to the opposite extreme, and attributed the Atonement to our Lord's Human Nature alone, excluding from it altogether His Divine Nature Further than this, they maintained that the Divine Nature in its propriety had no existence in Christ, and that He was only called God the Word metaphorically They also held a theory that He had two Natures, the one as Mediator, the other as the author of Mediation, and was therefore in one sense "sent," in the other "One Who sent" Another notion which they held was that the Holy Eucharist is not the medium of any present gift of grace, but only the pledge or ἀῤῥαβὼν of one to come

The heresy of the Stancarists was eventually absorbed by that of the Socinians [Bayle's *Dict* iii 2649 Schlusselburg's *Catal Hæret* ix Stancari's *de Trinitate et Mediatore Dom nostr J C adv H Bullinger P Martyr et Joan Calv* etc Basle, 1574]

STARKEYITES [PRINCEITES]

STAROBREDZI [STAROVERTZI]

STAROVERTZI A name signifying "men of the ancient faith," and assumed by the majority of those who refused to acquiesce in the reforms introduced in the Russian Church in the seventeenth century, and especially in the revision of Holy Scripture and of the Liturgical books effected by the Patriarch Nicon [A D 1654] An enumeration of the points which were held to justify this open act of schism in forming a separate body will give some idea of the extreme tenacity with which the Sclavonic population clings to the traditions of their ancestors

[1] They insisted that only the double and not the triple Alleluia should be repeated during Easter-tide

[2] That seven loaves should be presented at mass instead of five

[3] That the sign of the cross should not be made, according to the orthodox practice, by joining the three first fingers, but by uniting the fourth and fifth fingers with the thumb, without any inclination of the index and middle fingers

[4] That the cross imprinted on the host at mass should be octangular instead of square

[5] That the recently printed and revised editions of sacred books should not be received, but that the ancient copies should be retained, and that Nicon should be regarded as Antichrist

There were other and still smaller points of dispute, as to whether the name "Jesus" was to be pronounced loudly or softly, and whether it was proper to turn to the right hand or the left in certain processions Coffee and tea were strictly forbidden Priests who took spirits were held to be incapable of administering the sacraments Potatoes were a fruit of the devil, because it was probably a potato which Eve handed to Adam Smoking was not allowed, apparently on the Scriptural ground that "not that which goeth into the mouth defileth a man, but that which cometh out of the mouth, this defileth a man" [Matt xv 11] The tendency to fanaticism, so universally found in Russian dissent, did not fail to appear among the Starovertzi Some of them declared all temporal or civil government to be antichristian, taught the community of goods, extolled suicide, and voluntarily burned themselves alive, rather than be forced into compliance with the rites and customs of the national church. They were found chiefly among the peasants, or those who had risen from the peasant class, and their poverty may have been one of the causes of their possessing no places of public worship, and meeting in each other's houses instead They were persecuted under Peter I [A D 1689-1725], who laid double taxes on them, but his successors, especially Catharine II [A D 1762-1796], and Alexander I [A.D 1801-1825], have adopted a milder policy with the hopes of winning them back to the Eastern Church It was proposed that they might retain their old liturgies and rites, and continue to enjoy the ministrations of their own clergy, if they would consent to receive ordination at the hands of the orthodox bishops, and the conciliatory title of "Yedinovertzi," or "co-religionists," was bestowed upon those who shewed any readiness to conform Very little success has however attended these attempts at reconciliation

STAUROLATRÆ [CHAZINZARIANS]

STEBLERI [BACULARII]

STEDINGERS A politico-religious sect which arose in Germany early in the thirteenth century, and which took its name from a district on the borders of Friesland and Saxony, that which is now called Oldenburg, where it numbered many adherents They appear to have been a section of the same Manichæan heretics who in Southern Europe were called ALBIGENSES In the year 1232-4 a crusade was organized against them under direction of Gregory IX by Gerhard, Archbishop of Bremen, and Conrad of Marburg nearly exterminated them with a force of 40,000 soldiers Their principles were of the usual anti-sacerdotal class of the continental heresies of this period, and they gave opportunities to their enemies by mixing up heresy with a lawlessness that was easily interpreted as rebellious [Ritter, *Diss. de pago Steding et Stedinqis hæret*]

STERCORANISTÆ "Si qui fuerunt, fuere nonnulli nono sæculo, qui Corpus Christi quod in Eucharistia continetur secessui, ac dejectioni obnoxium esse putabant, ita ut corruptis speciebus, et ipsum Corpus Christi corrumperetur" [Sianda, *Lexicon Polem* Mabillon, *Act S Bened præf ad sæc.* iv II xxi Pfaff, *De Stercoranistis medii ævi* 1750] A somewhat similar question was discussed in a controversy between Amalarius and Guntrad, about the beginning of the same century [D'Achery, *Spicileg* iii 330]

STRATIOTICI [MILITES]

STRAUSS [RATIONALISTS]

STRIGOLNIKS A Russian sect which arose in Novogorod at the close of the fourteenth or early in the fifteenth century A Jew, named Horie, joined by two Christian priests, Denis and Alexis, and afterwards by an excommunicated deacon named Karp Strigolnik, preached a mixture of Judaism and Christianity, and gained so many followers that a national council was called to suppress him Among the practices which his followers objected to were the payment of a sum of money by the clergy to the bishops on ordination as simoniacal, and confession to a priest as unscriptural Strigolnik himself was thrown into the river and drowned during a riot which occurred in the streets of Novogorod, but the opposition of his followers to the Russian Church continued for many years after his death [Platoff, *Present State of Greek Ch in Russia*, Pinkerton's transl.]

STUDITES [ACŒMITÆ]

SUBLAPSARIANS A section of the Calvinists who so far modify the original dogma of their master respecting Predestination as to believe that while the Fall of Adam was divinely fore seen and divinely decreed, and the Fall of all his posterity was equally foreseen and decreed as following upon that of himself, yet it was only after the fall of Adam had taken place that the particular election of some of that posterity to salvation took place In contradistinction to the SUPRALAPSARIANS, they hold that the perdition of the non-elect occurs not in consequence of a direct decree of condemnation, but because they are passed by and left to their fallen state This fine-drawn distinction has arisen out of a repugnance to admit the full bearing of the dogma of absolute decrees on our estimate of the Divine attribute of love, but the Sublapsarians do not come any nearer than the Ultra-Calvinists to an agreement with St Paul's declaration that 'God our Saviour will have all men to be saved" [1 Tim ii 4] The term was first applied to the REMONSTRANTS

SUBSTANTIALISTS The Lutheran hæresiologist Schlusselburg gives this name as a synonym of the Manichees in his Catalogue of Heresies, the second volume of which is entitled "De secta Manichæorum seu Substantialistarum "

SUN-CHILDREN [AREVURDIS]

SUPRALAPSARIANS A name given to the extreme Calvinists who accept entirely the dogma of Calvin respecting an eternal, absolute, and unconditional decree by which God predestined some of mankind to salvation and some to perdition even before the Fall had brought sin into the world The form in which Calvin himself stated this doctrine will be found at page 97 in the article on Calvinists

Beza followed his master Calvin in holding and teaching the dreadful doctrine of absolute decrees of election and reprobation, but the name of Supralapsarians was first given to the Gomarists who opposed the Arminian party (who had been called SUBLAPSARIANS) at the Synod of Dort [A D 1618] The dogma of the Supralapsarians is but a form of Fatalism, and when Hobbes grafted on it his theory of absolute necessity, many who had held it were led to see its tendency and to give up their belief in it

SUSO [FRIENDS OF GOD]

SWADDLERS An absurd nickname given by the Irish Roman Catholics to the early Methodists It is said to have originated from John Cennick preaching a sermon on the Babe "wrapped in swaddling-clothes," the ignorant Roman Catholics who heard it or heard of it supposing the "swaddling-clothes" to be an invention of the Protestants In the year 1738 a ballad-singer named Butler actually raised riots in Dublin and elsewhere to the cry of "Five pounds for the head of a Swaddler," and he and his allies called themselves "Anti-Swaddlers" [Stevens' *Hist of Method* 110, 113]

SWEDENBORGIANS A theosophical sect whose fundamental opinion is that the Last Judgment took place in the year 1757, when "the

Old Church," or Christianity in its hitherto received form, passed away, and all things became new through revelations made to a Swedish gentleman named Swedenborg They consequently call their community "the New Church," and "the New Jerusalem Church" But although their opinions are grounded on these alleged revelations, they owe their origin as an organized sect not to Swedenborg himself, but to a printer named Robert Hindmarsh, an enthusiastic student of his writings

I SWEDENBORG'S PERSONAL HISTORY Emanuel Swedberg [A D 1689-1772]—ennobled by Queen Ulrica Eleonora in 1719 as the Honourable Emanuel Swedenborg—was the son of Jesper Swedberg [A D 1653-1735], Lutheran titular Bishop of Skara in West Gothland and of the Swedish residents in London In early life he shewed promise of great learning and literary power, and not only took his degree of Doctor of Philosophy at Upsal at the age of twenty-two, but also studied at Oxford, Paris, and Utrecht, and his great services as an amateur engineer to Charles XII at the siege of Fredenckshall, led, after the death of that king, to his being ennobled by his sister and successor From 1716 until 1747 he held the office of Assessor to the Royal Metallic College, or Board of Mines, at Stockholm, but travelled much, and wrote many scientific works on mineralogy, practical astronomy, and other subjects, his travels being undertaken for the sake of improving the metallurgic resources of Sweden He was the first to draw attention in modern times to the metrical, or decimal, system of coinage, weights, and measures, and in his *Opera Philosophica et Mineralia*, published in three folio volumes in 1734, he pioneered many discoveries in physical science The bent of his mind towards metaphysics and theology was shewn by his publication in the same year of a work entitled "An Introduction to the Philosophy of the Infinite, and the Final Cause of Creation, treating also of the Mechanism of the operation between the Soul and the Body" Ten years later the final transition of his studies from physical science to theology was marked by his work *De Cultu et Amore Dei*

It was soon after the publication of the last-named work, in 1745, that Swedenborg, then in his fifty seventh year, began to believe himself the recipient of supernatural revelations, and from that time he gave up all secular studies and pursuits, devoting himself entirely to the elaboration of a new theology, which was to be the basis of a "New Church" Like Mrs Lead and her followers [PHILADELPHIANS], Swedenborg became possessed with the idea that he conversed with angels, and with departed spirits [1] The beginning of his experiences of this kind may be told in his own words "Whatever of worldly honour and advantage may appear to be in the things before mentioned, I hold them but as matters of low estimation when compared to the honour of that holy office to which the Lord Himself hath called me, Who was graciously pleased to manifest Himself to me, His unworthy servant, in a personal appearance, in the year 1743, to open in me a sight of the spiritual world, and to enable me to converse with spirits and angels, and this privilege has continued with me to this day From that time I began to print and publish various unknown 'Arcana,' which have been either seen by me or revealed to me, concerning heaven and hell, the state of men after death, the true worship of God, the spiritual sense of the Scriptures, and many other important truths tending to salvation and true wisdom" [Swedenborg's *Letter to Hartley*, 1769, *True Christ Rel* 851] Through the gift thus bestowed on him he claimed to see the inhabitants of other continents without moving from his own place "nay," he says, "I could be made present with the inhabitants of other planets in our system, and also with the inhabitants of planets that are in other worlds, and revolve about other suns By virtue of such presence, not of place, I have conversed with apostles, departed popes, emperors, and kings, with the late reformers of the Church, Luther, Calvin, and Melanchthon, and with others from distant countries" [Swedenborg's *True Christ Rel* 87] The condition in which he was when he supposed himself to be thus in converse with other worlds is described by himself in the "Arcana" as being "a certain state, which is a sort of middle state between sleeping and waking, in which state spirits and angels are seen, heard, and touched," and the people with whom he lodged in London asserted that not long before his death "he lay some weeks in a trance, without any sustenance, and came to himself again" [Hindmarsh's *Rise and Progress*, etc 21]

But although professing to be in habitual intercourse with the unseen world, Swedenborg held little intercourse with his fellow-creatures in the visible world, and sought no other way of propagating his "Arcana" than by printing and publishing them, which he did at his own expense "Wherever he resided he was a mere solitary, and almost inaccessible, though in his own country of a free and open behaviour" [*Short Account of Swedenborg*, 11] It was while he was living such a recluse life in humble lodgings at 26 Great Bath Street, Coldbath Fields, Clerkenwell, that he wrote his principal theological work, to which he gave the title of "Arcana Cœlestia, the Heavenly Mysteries contained in the Holy Scriptures, or Word of the Lord, unfolded in an exposition of Genesis and Exodus, together with a relation of Wonderful Things seen in the World of Spirits and in the Heaven of Angels" This was commenced in consequence of the "personal appearance" referred to above, a man appearing to him in a strong shining light, and saying, "I am the Lord, the Creator and Redeemer I have chosen

[1] As Swedenborg was very imperfectly acquainted with the English language, it is not likely that he had read the "Theosophical Transactions" and other works of the Philadelphians in their original form, but as they were translated into Dutch he may have become acquainted with them in that language

thee to explain to men the interior and spiritual senses of the sacred writings I will dictate to thee what thou oughtest to write" The "Arcana" occupied Swedenborg's pen from 1749 until 1756, being written in Latin, and published from time to time in eight quarto volumes [1] It was translated into English, with some of his other works, a few years after his death, by one of his followers named John Clowes [A D 1743-1831], who was for sixty-two years Rector of St John's, Manchester After the publication of the "Arcana" Swedenborg wrote many smaller works illustrating his peculiar ideas, and describing Heaven, Hell, the Intermediate State, the Last Judgment, the "Earths in our Solar System, and the Earths in the Starry Heavens," etc , all of which he described as being "relations of Things heard and seen" by him His last work, published in 1771, was entitled "The True Christian Religion , or the Universal Theology of the New Church foretold by the Lord in Daniel vii 13, 14, and in the Revelation xxi 1, 2"

Shortly after the completion of the last-named work, on Christmas Eve 1771, Swedenborg was struck with paralysis, losing his speech and the use of one side Some weeks later he was still able to use his pen, and requested an interview with John Wesley in the following note, written in Latin from his lodgings in Coldbath Fields in February 1772 "Sir, I have been informed in the world of spirits that you have a strong desire to converse with me I shall be happy to see you if you will favour me with a visit. Your humble servant, Emanuel Swedenborg" Wesley's enthusiastic nature responded so far as to acknowledge that he had felt such a desire, though he had not mentioned it to any one, and he replied that he would visit the writer in a few months on his return to London It is alleged, but on less trustworthy authority, that Swedenborg answered "he should go on the 29th of next month into the world of spirits never more to return," March 29th, 1772, being actually the day of his death His body was honourably buried by a Swedish merchant in the vault of the then Swedish Chapel in Princes Square, Ratcliffe Highway

II Formation of the Sect Swedenborg had very few followers during his lifetime, those in England being only a physician named Messiter, a non-resident Rector of Winwick in Northamptonshire named Hartley, Dr Hampe, tutor in the family of George II, and four or five Swedish residents in London Nor did his verbose works attract much notice though much advertised The latter began, however, to excite some interest in Manchester, about ten years after the death of Swedenborg, through the enthusiasm with which they were made known by Mr Clowes, the clergyman before named as their translator, who set afoot a Society there in 1782 for printing and publishing his translations About the same time Robert Hindmarsh [A D 1759-1835], a young Clerkenwell printer, and son of a Methodist preacher, became acquainted with them, and soon became a most zealous follower of "the greatest man living or dead," and an ardent disseminator of his theosophy Hindmarsh originated a small society for the study of Swedenborg's works, the five members of which held their first meeting in St Paul's Coffee-House, St Paul's Churchyard, on December 5th, 1783 This shortly developed into "The Theosophical Society, instituted for the purpose of promoting the heavenly doctrines of the New Jerusalem, by translating, printing, and publishing the theological writings of the Honourable Emanuel Swedenborg," which held its meetings on Sundays and Thursdays at chambers in New Court, Middle Temple In 1784 a similar Society was established in Philadelphia by a Miss Barclay and a printer named Francis Bailey, and as the London Society became the parent of all the Swedenborgian communities in England, so that at Philadelphia held a similar relation to the American Swedenborgians

For some years the followers of Swedenborg were content with the literary meetings of the "Theosophical Society," but in May 1787 some of them began to hold meetings for worship in each others' houses, and in July one of these, James Hindmarsh, Methodist preacher, and father to the printer, was appointed "to officiate in the room of a priest," administering "the Holy Supper," and baptizing four of their number On January 27th, 1788 a chapel in Great East Cheap was opened for the use of the sect, and an "Order of worship for the New Church signified by the New Jerusalem in the Revelation" was adopted the name of "The New Church" being now substituted for that of "The Theosophical Society" It was afterwards determined to establish a settled ministry, and it was arranged by drawing of lots that Robert Hindmarsh the printer should ordain his father James Hindmarsh and Samuel Smith, both of them being Methodist preachers who had seceded from Wesley's Society In the year 1818 the Eleventh General Conference of the sect settled some doubts which had been raised as to the competency of Robert Hindmarsh to ordain others, seeing he had not himself been ordained, by determining unanimously "that Mr Robert Hindmarsh was virtually ordained by the Divine Auspices of Heaven," a decision more convenient than logical [Hindmarsh's *Rise and Progress of the New Ch.* 72, 310.] The Printing Society in Manchester soon followed the example of the Theosophical Society in London, establishing itself in a chapel in Peter Street in 1793. A "General Conference" was also organized after

[1] Swedenborg published his works at his own expense, probably for the usual reason that such a course is taken because no publisher would risk his money in bringing them out Like other authors who take such a course he found the "Arcana" did not find many purchasers, and writes in his "Spiritual Diary," "I have received letters informing me that not more than four copies have been sold in the space of four months" Unlike ordinary authors, however, he had a special consolation, "I communicated this to the angels They were surprised, but said it must be left to the Lord's providence, that His providence is of such a nature it compels no one, and that it is not fitting others should read the 'Arcana Cœlestia' before those who are in the faith"

the example of the Methodists, and its first meeting was held on the 13th and four following days of April 1789 In 1815, "a trine or threefold order" of the ministry was established, consisting of the ordinary ministers, ordaining ministers, and a 'minister superintendent over and in behalf of the New Church at large"

III SWEDENBORGIAN DOCTRINE The Scriptures, as interpreted by the voluminous and verbose writings of Swedenborg, are taken generally as the standard of Swedenborgian doctrine But a synopsis of their founder's opinions was made at the first organization of the sect in the form of forty-two Propositions taken from his works, and these propositions were embodied in thirty-two Resolutions, which were agreed to at the first Conference on April 16th, 1789

These thirty-two "Resolutions" have again been condensed into twelve "Articles of Faith," which now form the Standard of Doctrine in the "New Church" The latter express the opinions of Swedenborg on some points in a much more vague form than they are found in his writings, and as the sect still professes to adhere to those writings as a final revelation, the modern "Articles of Faith" can be best understood when taken in connection with the more definite statements of the original "Propositions" taken from those works by its founders

1 The first article states the doctrine of the Swedenborgians respecting the Trinity "That Jehovah God, the Creator and Preserver of heaven and earth, is Love Itself, and Wisdom Itself, or Good Itself, and Truth Itself That He is One both in Essence and in Person, in Whom, nevertheless, is the Divine Trinity of Father, Son, and Holy Spirit, which are the essential Divinity, the Divine Humanity, and the Divine Proceeding, answering to the soul, the body, and the operative energy in man and that the Lord and Saviour Jesus Christ is that God" In the third of the Propositions Swedenborg's opinion is given on this point, and it is that a Trinity of Divine Persons existing from eternity, or before the creation of the world, when conceived in idea is a Trinity of Gods, which cannot be expelled by the oral confession of One God [*True Christ Rel* n 172, 173] But perhaps the clearest statement of the sect on this subject is that contained in the "Conference Deed" which is enrolled in Chancery, namely "that our Lord and Saviour Jesus Christ is the only God of heaven and earth, and that in Him is the Divine Trinity of Father, Son, and Holy Spirit." Still further, the "Propositions," in summarizing Swedenborg's doctrine on this point, quote him as declaring that "all prayers directed to a Trinity of distinct Persons, and not to a Trinity conjoined in one Person, are henceforth not attended to, but are in heaven like ill-scented odours," and that "the Nicene and Athanasian doctrine concerning a Trinity have together given birth to a faith which hath entirely overturned the Christian Church" [*True Christ Rel* n 108, 177]

2 The second article treats of the Incarnation in the following words —"That Jehovah God Himself descended from heaven as Divine Truth, Which is the Word, and took upon Him Human Nature, for the purpose of removing from man the powers of hell, and restoring to order all things in the Spiritual World, and all things in the Church That he removed from man the powers of hell, by combats against and victories over them, in which consisted the great work of Redemption · That by the same acts, which were His temptations, the last of which was the Passion of the Cross, he united, in His Humanity, Divine Truth to Divine Good, or Divine Wisdom to Divine Love, and so returned into His Divinity in which He was from eternity, together with and in His Glorified Humanity, whence He for ever keeps the infernal powers in subjection to Himself, and that all who believe in Him, with the understanding, from the heart, and live accordingly, will be saved"

In association with this statement must be taken those of the 4th, 5th, 29th, 30th, and 31st "Propositions," namely, "That to believe Redemption to have consisted in the Passion of the Cross, is a fundamental error of the Old Church," which has "perverted the whole Christian Church, so that nothing spiritual is left remaining in it," and "that the doctrines universally taught in the Old Church, particularly respecting Three Divine Persons, the Atonement, Justification by Faith alone, the Resurrection of the material body, etc etc, are highly dangerous to the rising generation," that the Imputation of the Merit and Righteousness of Christ, which consist in Redemption, is a thing impossible, the only imputation being one "of good and evil, and at the same time of Faith, and that the Lord imputeth good to every man, and that Hell imputeth evil to every man," the Faith and Imputation of the New Church being altogether incompatible with those of the Old [*True Christ Rel* n 132, 133, 108, 640, 643-649]

3 In connection with this doctrine of the Incarnation may be mentioned that of the 12th article respecting the Second Advent It states "That now is the time of the Second Advent of the Lord, which is a coming, not in Person, but in the power and glory of His Holy Word, that it is attended, like His first coming, with the restoration to order of all things in the Spiritual World, where the wonderful Divine operation, commonly expected under the name of the Last Judgment, has in consequence been performed, and with the preparing of the way for a New Church on the earth,—the first Christian Church having spiritually come to its end or consummation through evils of life and errors of doctrine, as foretold by the Lord in the Gospels And that this new or second Christian Church, which will be the crown of all Churches, and will stand for ever, is what was representatively seen by John, when he beheld the Holy City, New Jerusalem, descending from God out of Heaven, prepared as a Bride adorned for her husband" This embodies the "Propositions" 38-42, with the omission of the statements, still it must be remembered, maintained by the sect,

"That the Last Judgment was accomplished in the Spiritual World in the year 1757, and that the former heaven and the former earth, or the Old Church, are passed away, and that all things are become new, that this Second Coming of the Lord is effected by means of His servant Emanuel Swedenborg, before whom He hath manifested Himself in person, and whom he hath filled with His Spirit to teach the doctrines of the New Church by the Word from Him" [*Last Judgm* n 45, *True Christ Rel* n 115, 772, 779, *Apoc Rev* n 886 *Brief Expos* n 95]

4 The most important subject of Swedenborgian belief next to the above is that respecting Holy Scripture, which is thus stated in the 3rd article "That the Sacred Scripture, or Word of God, is Divine Truth Itself, containing a spiritual sense heretofore unknown, whence it is divinely inspired and holy in every syllable, as well as a literal sense, which is the basis of its spiritual sense, and in which Divine Truth is in its fulness, its sanctity, and its power, thus that it is accommodated to the apprehension both of angels and men That the spiritual and natural senses are united by correspondences like soul and body, every natural expression and image answering to, and including, a spiritual and Divine idea, and thus that the Word is the medium of communication with heaven and of conjunction with the Lord"

This omits the statement of the 12th "Proposition," taken from Swedenborg's "Arcana Cœlestia," and other "revelations" This statement is "that the Books of the Word are all those which have the Internal Sense, which are as follow, viz in the Old Testament, the five Books of Moses, called Genesis, Exodus, Leviticus, Numbers, and Deuteronomy, the Book of Joshua, the Book of Judges, the two Books of Samuel, the two Books of Kings, the Psalms of David, the Prophets Isaiah, Jeremiah, Lamentations, Ezekiel, Daniel, Hosea, Joel, Amos, Obadiah, Jonah, Micah, Nahum, Habakkuk, Zephaniah, Haggai, Zechariah, Malachi, and in the New Testament, the four Evangelists, Matthew, Mark, Luke, John, and the Revelation And that the other Books, not having the Internal Sense, are not the Word" [*Arcana Cœlest* n 10325, *New Jer* n 266, *White Horse*, n 16] Thus ten books of the Old Testament, the Acts of the Apostles, and all the Epistles of St Paul and the other Apostles, are set aside as no part of "the Word of the Lord"

The remaining articles of the Swedenborgian Confession may be passed over, since they deal more with theosophical views of Love, Wisdom, Repentance, Charity, Faith, Good Works, etc, than with important articles of faith, but it may be mentioned that Baptism and the Lord's Supper are considered as Sacraments of Divine Institution, to be permanently observed, the view of their efficacy being, however, the ordinary Zwinglian view taken by Dissenters

IV STATISTICS The principles of Swedenborg have gained a more or less complete hold upon the minds of many persons who have yet declined to connect themselves with the sect founded by his disciple Hindmarsh In Germany, where they were taken up by Ottinger and Jung Stilling during Swedenborg's lifetime, they are said by Hagenbach to have "spread over a great part of Germany" [Hagenbach's *Hist Doctr* sec 277], but the disciples of the Swedish visionary do not seem to have formed any sect separate from the Lutheran body In England also, a few clergymen and many laymen have been readers of Swedenborg's works, and have adopted much of his theosophy without separating from the Church The sect of the "New Church," however, as distinct from these parti coloured Swedenborgians, numbered 58 Societies in connection with Conference in England in the year 1871, seven of which were in London, numbering 752 members, and the rest mostly in Lancashire and Yorkshire There were at that time 4098 registered members above 20 years of age, and they had 4224 children in their day schools In Canada and the United States they numbered 80 Societies, and about 5000 members They still continue to pay much attention to the publication of Swedenborg's works, having a "Swedenborg Society" for the purpose, which was established in 1810, and having recently gone to the trouble and expense of copying his MSS by the photolithographic process

SWEDISH PROTESTANTS Lutheran principles began to be disseminated in Sweden at least as early as A D 1519, through the instrumentality of students returning from the University of Wittenberg, among whose names those of Olave and Laurence Peterson are the most noted, the former being promoted in after life to the chief pastorate at Stockholm, and the latter appointed to a professorship at Upsala Their benefactor and the great champion of the movement was Gustavus Vasa, who first delivered the country from the tyranny of the Danish king Christian II, and then ascended the Swedish throne as an independent monarch, A D 1523 He pushed forward matters in the teeth of the bishops, many of whom were deposed on his accession, and afterwards executed for rebellion, and amid the indifference of the people, who were not awake to the abuses of the old religion, and did not care to see a papal exchanged for a royal supremacy But Gustavus Vasa was felt to be essential to the kingdom's safety, and when at the Diet of Westeras he threatened to resign unless he carried his point on the subject of the Reformation of religion, all classes were inclined to acquiesce About this time the Holy Scriptures were translated and disseminated in the Swedish language, through the labours of Olave Peterson and Laurence Anderson, and under regal protection The most serious opposition to the king's ecclesiastical despotism broke out [A D 1537-1543] among the country clergy and the peasantry headed by one of their number named Nils Dacke After it was suppressed, a second synod was held at Westeras, and the Reformation was finally and legally established in the form of high Lutheranism, retaining an episcopal order of one archbishop and thirteen bishops No attempts were made to disturb this arrangement under Eric XIV [A.D 1560-1568], but symptoms of a desire for change marked the policy of his successor John III [A D 1568-1592] With a strong personal bias towards Catholicism, intensified by a marriage with a Polish and Catholic princess, he went so far as to open negotiations with the Papal court for reunion, several Jesuits, among them the distinguished Possevin, were sent into Sweden, whose eventual want of success was due probably not so much to their own want of tact as to the stubbornness of the Roman court in refusing to concede such points as communion in both kinds and the use of the liturgy in the vulgar tongue, and to the consequent lukewarmness and even opposition of the king, especially after the death of his consort Catharine [A D 1583] A new service-book, compiled by royal authority [A D 1576], and containing a large element of mediæval ceremonial, was in use for some years, but was abolished on the king's death by the synod of Upsala [A D 1593], at which the Augsburg Confession in its integrity was formally adopted Thenceforward, although Charles IX [A D 1604-1611] and Gustavus Adolphus II [A D 1611-1633] were disposed to favour Calvinism, and the accomplished Queen Christina [A D 1633-1654] joined the Catholic Church, Lutheranism remained the national religion of Sweden, dissent either in the direction of Rome or Geneva being forbidden by penal enactments until as late as the accession in A D 1860 of Charles XV [Anjou's *Hist Reform in Sweden*, Mason's transl New York, 1859]

SWEET SINGERS, THE, were a small party of wild Scottish fanatics, chiefly women, who in 1681, following one John Gib, a master mariner of Borrowstounness (from whom they were also called Gibbites), forsook all worldly business, and professed to devote themselves entirely to acts of devotion in fasting and prayer in the open fields They were called the Sweet Singers from their habit of "wailing a portion" of the more mournful Psalms, but they nevertheless declared afterwards that they renounced the use of metrical Psalms as a human invention They made also a general renunciation and denunciation of everything, of the translation of the Bible, of its division into chapters and verses, of the Longer and Shorter Catechisms, the Confession of Faith, the Covenant, all authority whatsoever throughout the world, the names of months and days (like the Quakers, to the more extravagant portion of whom they largely corresponded), the use of churches and churchyards, all sports and laughing, all customs in eating, drinking, wearing of clothes and sleeping, and everybody in general except themselves They were committed to prison in Edinburgh in April 1681, but were released by the Privy Council in August, as being, apparently, too contemptible in their ravings for further notice [Wodrow, *Hist of the Sufferings of the Ch of Scotland*, 1722, vol ii pp 220-1, and Appendix, pp 79-84 Crookshank, *Hist of the Ch of Scotland*, 1762, vol ii p 93]

SWEET SINGERS The English RANTERS of the seventeenth century are called Sweet Singers by some contemporary writers

SWISS PROTESTANTS The pioneer and founder of Protestantism in Switzerland was Huldrich Zuingli, born near Zurich in the same year as Luther [A D 1484] He entered early into the priesthood at Glarus [A D 1506], was promoted thence to a preachership in the collegiate church of Zurich [A.D 1519], where, like the German Reformer, he scandalized the neighbourhood, and violated the vow of celibacy by marrying a widow, Anna Reinhardt [A D 1523] About this time, in his sermons, by his writings, and in sixty-seven articles publicly maintained before the senate and people of Zurich, he began to disseminate the new opinions In this course he was instigated and aided by the Ultra-Protestant Carlstadt, who after his differences with Luther and banishment from Germany had fled to Switzerland, and by John Hausschein, better known as Œcolampadius, who was working in the same direction at Basle A public disputation was shortly held at Baden [A D 1526], Eck and Œcolampadius being the champions on either side, when three out of the twelve Swiss cantons declared themselves convinced by the latter Their example spread In three years' time the minority was converted into a majority, and the five remaining Catholic cantons appealed to Austria to put down the Reformers by force of arms During the war which followed Zuingli fell on the battlefield of Cappel in the same year that Œcolampadius breathed his last at Basle [A D 1531] But a deeply-seated religious movement is seldom extinguished by force The Reformers' mantles fell on such men as Henry Bullinger, Oswald Myconius, William Farel, a Frenchman, who, after being banished from his native country settled at Basle, and the still more distinguished exile Calvin, who, before migrating to Geneva, settled in the same town, and in the society of Bucer, Capito and others published his "Institutio Christianæ Religionis" [A D 1534-6] The subsequent history of the Reformation in Switzerland is intimately bound up with the history of Calvin, and will be found under the article CALVINISTS [Lives of Calvin have been written by Henry, at Hamburg, 1835, by Audin, Paris, 1841, Dyer, London, 1850 See more generally the Ecclesiastical Histories of Mosheim and Gieseler, and Ranke's *History of the Reformation*]

SYMMACHIANS A sect of heretics of this name is mentioned by Philaster, and apparently as disciples of Patricius [PATRICIANS], the particular tenet which he attributes to them being disbelief in a future judgment, a disbelief accompanied by immoral living [Philast *Hær* lxiii] The Symmachians are not named in any other of the early works on heresies

SYMMACHIANS This name was sometimes given to the Nazarenes, probably from Symmachus the Ebionite, who is mentioned by

Eusebius as the author of a Greek version of the Old Testament [Euseb *Hist Eccl* vi 17] St Ambrose speaks of the Symmachians as descended from the Pharisees [Ambros *prol in Ep ad Galat*] and St Augustine refers to them as still existing in his day [Aug *contr Faust Manich* xix 4, 17, *contr Crescon Donat* i 31] Eusebius accuses Symmachus of holding the heresy that Christ was the natural son of Joseph and Mary Epiphanius, in his work on weights and measures, speaks of him as a Samaritan who became a Jewish proselyte in the reign of the Emperor Severus, near the close of the second century [Epiph *de Mens et Ponder.* ii 122, ed 1622].

SYNCRETISTS For the definition of "Syncretism," and other particulars respecting its original application, the reader is referred to the article in the Dictionary of Doctrinal and Historical Theology It is sufficient to state here that it originated in the zeal with which the turbulent and quarrelsome inhabitants of Crete made common cause against external foes, and "syncretized," from whence it was transferred as a general term to all who make common cause by keeping in abeyance their common differences It was a term of some breadth, and being "mediæ significationis," it is used either in a good or bad sense, but it usually follows the analogy of theological "isms," and means fusion that involves a loss of principle It was used in a better sense by D Pareus of Heidelberg [A D 1615], when he exhorted all parties to make head "pro syncretismo" against the common enemy Antichrist The term however was repudiated by the "Union" or "Eirenist" party, and Dreier of Konigsberg [A D 1661] charged Pareus with having damaged a good and holy cause by first affixing to it a term of opprobrium

It may be here noted that at a yet earlier date Windeck, a writer on the Catholic side, held out similar advice to Romanists "Si saperent Catholici, et ipsis cara esset reipublicæ Christianæ salus, Syncretismum colerent" [*Prognosticon futuri status Ecclesiæ*, 1603]

Syncretism may be considered to be the earliest of those attempts that marked the onward growth of Protestantism to pass from the prescriptions of theology to unfettered religious thought In its origin it professed to harmonize the Calvinistic and Lutheran views, to bring in also any points of agreement with Rome Of these sections the Calvinistic or Reformed party were more ready to adopt the Syncretistic principle, the Lutherans deriving the word from συγκεράννυμι, could only look upon it as an attempt to hybridize the faith Some however laid less stress than the rest on the differential dogmata of the Reformation, and thought rather of the general principles of Christianity, and the necessity for union, than of party interests These symbolized with George Calixtus, the originator of the Syncretistic movement, born A.D 1586 in Schleswig

Having studied at Helmstadt, in Brunswick, under Martini, Calixtus was early possessed with the idea that common ground might be found on which all might agree Wanderings through Europe confirmed him in his notion, and having visited the principal headquarters of different religionists, Cologne, the "Trojan horse" of Romanism in Germany, France, Italy, Holland, and England, he then returned to Helmstadt, and held the chair of Divinity for forty-two years till his death, A D 1656 His public life therefore synchronized with the Thirty Years' War, which may reasonably be held to have influenced his tone of thought Next to his friend Gerhard, he was the most eminent divine in Germany, a man of European reputation He was of noble bearing, loyal and patriotic His address, calm, firm, and dignified, was commanding, but at the same time genial and attractive He devoted all the power that extensive erudition and theological accomplishments conferred to work out the idea of his life. His earnestness did not fail to secure for him the aid of able coadjutors, and a numerous body of warmly attached friends His influence extended into Holstein, Denmark and Sweden, and his views were adopted in several schools of Northern Germany His travelled experience convinced him that faith and love were to be found in all communions, and that there could be no better ground for all to meet upon Religion, he said, is a matter of practice, not of dogma; consisting not of disputable propositions, but of life-giving verities Laying a particular emphasis upon all that he considered to be sound in the Roman system, he attempted to soften down the points of difference between the Lutherans and the Reformed or Calvinistic sects, and to reconcile both with Tridentine doctrine The bonds of union, as he held, were needlessly severed at the Reformation His only antipathies were the more advanced notions of Roman theology and Jesuitism, chiefly on account of their thoroughgoing defence of papal infallibility The yearning of Calixtus for Catholicity, his breadth of view and largeness of heart, were unintelligible to the men of his generation Even heathenism, he said, was not destitute of its better points These however were only an argument for the necessity of revelation As might be expected, he was attacked on every side as a "Syncretist," and the last twenty years of his life were spent in controversy with high Lutherans, who looked upon him as a renegade, and with Jesuits, who detected in what they called his neutralism the germ of a detestable atheism Calixtus, like the Schoolmen, assigned to philosophy a co-ordinate position with theology, persuaded that the two being separate phases of truth could never really antagonize, and his aim was always to shew how the teaching of revealed truth was one with the induction of right reason Philology and philosophy, he said, are the two wings of the spirit, without which none may soar into the higher regions of knowledge, and he first earned the merit of directing attention to the importance of ecclesiastical history as a study Thucydides and Tacitus were his models, as gathering from carefully collected data the light of unity and scientific generalization Mosheim, it should be noted, was of Helmstadt As regards positive theology, he declared that the Christian's sufficient bond of unity was the Apostles' Creed, and the light thrown upon the exegesis of Scripture by the tradition of the first five centuries, down to the Council of Orange [A D 529] Buscher the Court Preacher at Hanover [A D 1640], at once denounced him as a "Crypto-papist"

The main points of Calixtan doctrine did not widely differ from the ordinary Lutheran views Scripture had a plenary authority—it was sure and infallible, but Calixtus also maintained that there is an unwritten word in the rule of faith handed down from primitive antiquity, and in the voice of that antiquity, authoritatively speaking, in the first councils of the Church, while doctrine still maintained its purity All later additions are either immaterial or erroneous The Church contains the very flower of humanity, and is the depositary of all that is worthy of the name of wisdom, perpetuity is her privilege, and immunity from fundamental error, as the "pillar and ground of truth," she is infallible, yet has she lost much of her distinctive character, for human ignorance has confounded the boundary-lines of truth and error, but that very degeneracy has caused the purity of primitive doctrine, antecedent to that error and division, to be more conspicuously manifest The most fatal error was the doctrine of Papal Infallibility introduced by the Jesuits, the Roman See has thereby forfeited its title to Catholicity Primitive Christianity, and not Tridentine doctrine, was the object of his regard, though his opponents did not fail to confound this very manifest distinction Evangelical doctrine he held to be a true reflexion of primitive truth, and the Divine authority of the Word was made manifest in its self-preservation from error during the first ages

Calixtus denied the communication of Divine properties to the Human Nature ("Communicatio Idiomatum"), and in consequence rejected the notion of the ubiquity of Christ so prevalent in Germany, yet he maintained the verity of "oral manducation" in the Eucharist, though he was not always self-consistent The Church, in his opinion, dates back from patriarchal times, and both before and after the day of Christ the self-same element of faith was requisite for salvation, yet he allows that the doctrine of the Holy Trinity was unknown to the holy men of old, and that firm belief in this doctrine is now absolutely necessary for salvation, but he could never assent to the position of his friend Cocceius, that the New Covenant confers advantages in the degree of future blessedness, to which those who died under the Old will never be admitted His notion of symbolical union in the consent of antiquity also was not always self-consistent At one while his appeal is restricted to the four first centuries, at another he takes in the Councils of Milevi and Orange

With respect to the doctrine of grace, the opinions of Calixtus have in some points a Semi-Pelagian cast Thus he affirmed free-will to be the god-like excellence of our nature, which was not so far lost by the Fall as to make personal sin a matter of necessary consequence, individually it is in our power to avoid sin, though collectively we have no power for good but by the interposition of supernatural grace, whereby man's original condition is restored, and a preternatural gift, the co-ordinate of pardon, ennobles his regenerate state This gift was at first super-added in Adam, and so far he agreed with the Roman Church, which inherited the same notion through the Schools, whereas in Lutheran theology the Divine Image, or Original Righteousness, was the very nature in which Adam was created. He does not hesitate to ascribe absolute perfection to Adam before the Fall, whereby it was impossible for him to affirm that in Christ we gain more than we lost by the sin of our first parent, for nothing can be greater than absolute perfection Good works for their own worth do not entitle to salvation, but they are an indispensable condition, the absence of which of necessity disqualifies Mortal sins, wilfully committed, effectually darken the light of grace Freedom with him is distinct from grace, and his theory of inspiration altogether harmonizes with this view The Holy Spirit did not energize the whole soul and intellect of the inspired agent, but merely assisted the utterance of divine truth by vouchsafing freedom from error In these notions there is sufficient divergence from Lutheran orthodoxy to shew their eclectic character

The Northern schools which symbolized with the Helmstadt divines, such as Konigsberg, Rinteln, Altdorf, Holstein, Denmark, Sweden, etc, did good service to theology by their encouragement of historical and exegetical divinity, all remaining true to the fundamental necessity for union. They were schools of theological learning rather than of spiritual religion, and for that reason took part with the orthodox Lutherans in the Pietist movement [A D 1670], that in the next generation wholly superseded Syncretism The avowal of Calixtus that Romanism held those doctrines that are essentially necessary to salvation encouraged a return to Rome in the upper classes throughout Northern Germany — the school of Konigsberg most of all favouring this Romeward direction. Calixtus scarcely realised to himself the possibility that the lode of precious ore, by a sudden fault, might become so buried beneath superincumbent strata as to become practically lost Rome might give union, but not the union of pure truth In the opposite direction Brunswick has ever retained the "broad church" character Our own Latitudinarian divines, John Hale of Eton, Cudworth, Chillingworth, Tillotson, Burnet and Whiston, drank of the same fountain, though the only professed follower of Calixtus in the British Isles was the Scotch Independent Dury [Duræus, b A D 1595 at Edinburgh, d 1680 at Cassel], who devoted his whole life to the promotion of religious union among the Reformers of Germany Being in England A D 1643, he was appointed one of the Westminster divines, and, as he himself says, gave active help in preparing the Confession and Catechism of Westminster In 1654, he again visited the Continent, with commendatory letters from Cromwell, to promote sectarian union, though in more than one quarter he was recommended first to look at home to the state of religion in England From the Restoration to his death [A D 1680] he resided at Cassel, and took part in the Cassel conference upon religious unity, A D 1661

The external history of Syncretism dates from A D 1645, when Vladislaus VI, King of Poland, assembled a conference of Catholic and Protestan divines at Thorn on the Vistula, to consider the best method of restoring union, or at least some approach to agreement in religion [1] Calixtus was sent thither by the Duke of Brunswick, and met his future determined opponents, Calovius of Dantzic, afterwards of Wittenberg, and Hulsemann of Wittenberg and Leipsic, the champions of orthodox Lutheranism The conference led to no other result than the clear proof that Calixtus scarcely symbolized with Lutheranism Eighty-eight propositions were laid to his charge by Calovius, which seemed to amalgamate the tenets of most opposite sects But his principal offences seem to have been that he leaned too much to catholic doctrine, that he slighted the "Corpus Julium" and "Formula Concordiæ" of the Lutheran party, as exhibiting mere points of scholastic variance, that he affirmed the Apostles' Creed to be an all-sufficient bond of union, and the decrees of the four first General Councils to be the only authoritative interpretation of the mind of Scripture, and most of all, that he refused to condemn writings that good Lutherans had always regarded with pious horror Though accused of "Cryptopapism," Calixtus had shewn repeatedly his variance with Roman dogma So early as A D 1614, his treatise appeared "de Visibili Ecclesiastica Auctoritate," in refutation of the papal claim of infallibility, A D 1631, a monograph on the celibacy of the clergy was put forth, A D 1636, another on the denial of the cup to the laity, A D 1637, a thesis on the authority of Scripture A D 1638, another on the Sacrifice of the Mass, A D 1639, the authority of Christian antiquity, and A D 1643, a treatise on Transubstantiation, while in the year preceding the conference at Thorn he published [A D 1644] his "Refutation of the Defence of Papal Infallibility by the divines of Mayence" The conference, though it settled nothing, gave rise to a bitter controversy between the rival schools of Helmstadt and Wittenberg, which had an intermittent existence till the death of Calovius, the Goliath of Lutheranism [A D 1686] The divines of Jena, having Musæus as their head, stood alone in their advocacy of moderation After the peace of Westphalia [A D 1648], the Evangelical sects, relieved from the common fear, had more leisure for internal feuds, and the novel tactics of Helmstadt divines exposed a broad front for attack

The proceedings of the conference called forth from Calixtus a treatise on two of its subjects for discussion [1] Whether the mystery of the Holy Trinity could be demonstrated from the Old Testament Scriptures alone [2] Whether the Son of God appeared to the holy men of old in His hypostatic reality Calovius at once replied by his "Prolegomena Institutionum Theologicarum," A.D 1650, Calixtus published his "Judicium de Controversiis Theologicis quæ inter Lutheranos et Reformatos agitantur, et de mutua partium fraternitate atque tolerantia propter consensum in fundamento," and was met by Calovius in his "Digressio de Nova Theologia Helmstadio-Regiomontanorum Syncretistarum" Calovius never descended to scurrility or coarse personality but his henchmen of the high Lutheran party were not so self-denying, and Sin-Christian [Sunde-Christ] and Semi-Christian [Semi-Christ] were alliterative names applied to the divines of Helmstadt Dannhauer, in his "Mysterium Syncretismi detecti" [A D 1648], traced Syncretism in every ill-matched alliance from the beginning such as Eve's yielding to the cunning of the serpent, the alliance of the sons of God with the daughters of men, the intercourse of the Israelites with the Egyptians, of Jews with the Chaldæans, and so on down to the latitudinarianism of Melanchthon, Grotius, and Calixtus He describes it as a pestilent error, without is peace [ειρήνη], but within a Nemesis [ἐριννύς], hyæna like, it attracts men by its human wailing to their destruction Truth is to be found, he said, in Lutheran orthodoxy alone, which, like the eye, is intolerant of dirt Calixtus was well able to hold his own in such a contest The Saxon divines accused him of disloyalty to the Augsburg Confession He replied that any man who could say this without offering proof was a wicked and flagitious calumniator and fabricator, and denounced him "für einen Erz- und Ehr-vergessenen verlogenen Diffamanten Calumnianten Ehrendieb und Bosewicht," and A D 1651, he put forth a "Refutation in German of the calumnies [Verläumdungen] with which Jacob Weller has presumed to insult him" Soon after the conference at Thorn the divines of Electoral Saxony, claiming a kind of supremacy among Lutheran theologians, sent to Calixtus a solemn "admonition," which he received with the silence of contempt and he provoked by his silence a whole flight of controversial missiles against himself and his friends Unions also were formed by the orthodox party against the Helmstadt theologians The famous "Consensus repetitus Fidei veræ Lutheranæ" [A D 1655], was the production of Calovius In it he demanded the extrusion of the Syncretists as "rotten members" of the Church The writer sought in vain to invest the document with the dignity of a "Liber Symbolicus," but it fell flatly on the public, at a time when men had been thoroughly worn out with religious warfare in the pulpit

[1] It may be noted that five years before the Conference met at Thorn, Davenant, Bishop of Salisbury, had called all parties "ad fraternam communionem inter evangelicas ecclesias restaurandam, in eo fundata, quod non dissentiant in ullo fundamentali catholicæ fidei articulo" [Cambridge, 1640]

and in the field, and satiated to repletion with symbolizings. The attempt therefore failed, and the failure was no light discouragement to the orthodox Lutheran party. Calovius, with characteristic tenacity[1] of purpose, seized every opportunity for giving authoritative weight to this "Consensus" during his whole life.

After the death of Calixtus [A.D. 1656], there was a five years' rest from controversy. Action was once more taken A.D. 1661, when William VI., Landgrave of Hesse Cassel, invited a conference of divines from the Reformed or Calvinistic University of Marburg and the Lutheran Syncretists of Rinteln in Schaumburg: the object being that "either party might gain a clear perception of their points of mutual agreement and divergence; that the exact bearing of controverted points, and their importance, whether touching the foundation of faith or not, might be ascertained; and that the discussion of these subjects should be conducted in the fear of God, so that if agreement upon every point could not be attained, at least brotherly love and mutual toleration might be established for the future." Accordingly, the conference, consisting of divines and state counsellors, met at Cassel. The subjects more particularly discussed were the Holy Eucharist, Predestination, the relation of the two Natures in Christ, and Baptism. The Lutheran divines allowed the "breaking" of bread,[2] and the substitution of a prayer against Satan and his power for the baptismal exorcism, and both parties allowed that there was between them a common and sufficient germ of agreement as regards all four subjects, and that any points of difference did not affect the foundations of faith, and could never justify reciprocal charges of heresy. A formula of agreement was accordingly drawn up and signed.

The example of Hesse was adopted by the Elector of Brandenburg, at whose summons conferences were held at Cologne and Berlin [A.D. 1662], for the purpose of effecting a "brotherly reconciliation" [Verträglichkeit] between the Lutheran and Reformed parties. Of the two the Cologne divines were the most pliant, but at Berlin Paul Gerhardt, with the Cassel example before his eyes, protested against the Syncretism into which the Reformed divines wished to betray them. The divines of Berlin also begged that their attendance might be dispensed with. But the conference took place all opposition notwithstanding, and continued its deliberations from September 1662 to May in the following year. The only result of much wrangling and jealousy was an electoral edict [September 16th, A.D. 1664], that both parties should refrain from giving bad names to their opponents, and from mutual charges of holding doctrines that were repudiated; moreover, that it should be left for evangelical parents to decide whether or not their children should be "exorcised" in baptism. A declaration also was prepared, which all spiritual persons were ordered to sign; but many refused, and were deprived; and among their number Paul Gerhardt, for his contumacy, was turned out of his professorship [A.D. 1666], though, on the pressing and repeated petition of the burghers of Berlin, he was fully restored in the next year.

In consequence of the agreement at Cassel, Calovius put forth a second Latin edition of the "Consensus repetitus Fidei," A.D. 1665; and in the next year a German translation. It was answered by the son of Calixtus, A.D. 1667, in a vindication of the father's orthodoxy from the misstatements of Calovius. This drew forth from Strauch, a young Wittenberg divine, a vindication of the Consensus from the "calumnies, falsehoods, and unjust censures" of the younger Calixtus, in which the grossest personalities were freely mixed with obscure hints, that compelled Calixtus to make an attested declaration before a notary that the allusions were most vile and false. The controversy was sinking hopelessly in the mire, when Conring, the leading theologian of Helmstadt, published his defence of that university under the title "Pietas Academiæ Juliæ programmate publico adversus improbas et iniquas calumnias cum aliorum quorundam, tum Ægidii Strauchii asserta." There is no Calixtine school he says; the idea was always repudiated by Calixtus; but he offered his opinions for what they were worth, as a free man to free men, and asserted a liberty that is of the very essence of the Christian Church. "Diris in Syncretistas nihil frequentius," but such a course is as unworthy as it is weak. The people know nothing of theological subtleties, neither can they judge for themselves whether or no Calixtine teaching harmonizes with confessions; questions that minister strife rather than edification. "Nec Deus nos ad beatam vitam per difficiles quæstiones vocat, in expedito et facili nobis est æternitas" [Hilary]. The Word of God, and not the Consensus of Calovius, is the standard whereby judgment must be formed of truth and error. In the meantime the temporal power should interpose its just authority, and curb the excess of license into which the controversy is degenerating, "non component hasce turbas qui excitarunt." The University at once published this "Programma" in a free German translation, as the "Schutzrede der Julius Universitat," and circulated it among the courts, consistories, and universities of Lutheran Germany. Duke Frederic William of Saxony, acting upon its appeal to the temporal power, forbade any further prosecution of the controversy [A.D. 1669].

Another five years of enforced peace followed. In 1675, the year in which Spener, the founder of the new religious revolution, Pietism, published his "Pia desideria," the irrepressible Calovius sounded the renewal of warfare, and expressed his determination "e diaboli excremento Calixtinas sordes exquirere." Another vindication of his father by F. U. Calixtus followed, and once more the polemical hurly-burly raged, until an inaugural mystery, full of the vilest scurrilities

[1] "Molosus," or bull-dog, was a term applied to him for this quality. [Boyneburg, *Ep. ad Conring.*]

[2] *i.e.* by the communicant, not the celebrant, a peculiarity of the Reformed or Calvinistic party. Exorcism had been retained by Luther as a highly ancient rite in baptism. Arndt resigned his post in calvinized Anhalt rather than give up exorcism.

and personifications scarcely redeemed from blasphemy, enacted at Wittenberg, compelled the Elector of Saxony once more to interpose his authority by fining the printer of the drama and imprisoning its author Æg Strauch was condemned to a like punishment by the Elector of Brandenburg [A D 1675-1678], and the interdict upon continuing the controversy was renewed [A D 1677] Calovius however still worked on under feigned names, and being in favour at Dresden, was not molested A D 1682, he published, without name of author or printer, his "Historia Syncretistica," A D. 1684, his "Apodeixis articulorum Fidei," and A D 1685, his "Synopsis Controversiarum cum Hæreticis modernis" In the same year he fell ill, and died February 21st, 1686, when the "Consensus repetitus" at length rested in peace Thenceforth Syncretism ceased to apply to any particular party in the Lutheran community, but reverted to its original wider meaning of ill-assorted combination Pietism rose as Syncretism set

[Walch, *Streitigkeiten d Luth Kirche* Henke, *Calixtus u s Zeit* Calovius, *Historia Syncretistica* Schmidt, *Gesch d Synkretist Streit* Gass, *Calixt, u d Synkretismus* Baur, *K G der neueren Zeit, Erste Period,* III i 3]

SYNERGISTS A party among the German Lutherans of the sixteenth century, who were charged with holding Semi-Pelagian doctrine respecting the co-operation [*συνεργῆσις*] of man with God in the work of renovation The original position taken up by Luther respecting justification by faith was, that it takes place entirely independent of the justified person's good works, "Non ille justus est qui multum operatur, sed qui sine opere multum credit in Christum," was one of the "Paradoxes" he offered to maintain against all comers at Heidelberg, on April 26th, 1518 This extreme doctrine he maintained in the treatise "De Servo Arbitrio," which he wrote in 1524 against Erasmus but before his death he learned to approve of a modified form of the doctrine of free-will and good works, which was gradually brought out in Lutheran theology by Melanchthon in the several editions of his "Loci Communes" Melanchthon at last maintained that "God so draws and converts adults, that some agency of their wills accompanies His influences" This change in the views of Melanchthon was followed up at a later date by John Pfeffinger, in a work entitled "De Libero Arbitrio," which he published in the year 1555 The idolaters of Luther assailed Pfeffinger with great violence, as corrupting the doctrine of one whom they practically considered as infallible as Ultramontanists consider the Pope, and the party rallying round Pfeffinger were at once stigmatized as Synergists, or those who maintained justification by works as well as faith

In the "Synergistic Controversy" which thus arose, the principal leaders were Victorin Strigel, a pupil of Melanchthon, and Matthias Flacius Illyricus, the bitter opponent of the ADIAPHORISTS or Melanchthon party Flacius becoming Professor of Theology at Jena in the year 1557, carried on the controversy with such success that he succeeded in getting Strigel imprisoned for his opinions, and he was only released in 1562 by publishing a recantation of them After this the Synergist controversy merged into the Majoristic, in which Amsdorf maintained the primitive Lutheran doctrine that works are a hindrance rather than otherwise to salvation, and Major adopted a moderate theory of the necessity of good works, similar to that which is held by English theologians Like other endless controversies of the Lutherans, that of the Synergists is fully commemorated in Schlusselburg's "Catalogus Hæreticorum," his fifth volume containing 719 pages "De secta Synergistarum"

SYNUSIASTÆ Those who held that the Incarnation of our Lord was effected by a blending or commixture of the Divine substance with the substance of human flesh

The name is taken from the statement of the doctrine, *συνουσίωσιν γεγενῆσθαι καὶ κρᾶσιν τῆς θεότητος καὶ τοῦ σώματος* [Theod *Hær fab* iv 9] Theodoret calls this sect Polemians, one of the Apollinarist sects, and Apollinaris himself, in the latter part of his life, added to his distinguishing heresy regarding the soul of our Lord either this heresy or one closely akin to it [APOLLINARISTS] Polemius or Polemon was a disciple of Apollinaris At the Lateran Council, A D 649, were quoted two extracts from Polemon's works, from which it appears that the Synusiastæ retained the heresy regarding the soul of our Lord, denying Him a human will, and asserting that He was to Himself a rational soul [Harduin, *Concil* iii 892] The mode in which they were led to the adoption of their heresy appears to be this At the outbreak of the controversies regarding the Incarnation, some asserted the conversion of the substance of the Godhead into the substance of flesh, others that the Divine Nature supplied in Christ the place of the human soul Then an attempt was made to hold these two tenets together, the result of which was to deny an *ἐνανθρώπησις* altogether To avoid this denial it was allowed that the flesh of man was assumed, but so blended with the Divine Substance as to eliminate that tendency to sin which it was alleged could not but be resident in human nature

Diodorus of Tarsus and Theodotus of Antioch wrote against this heresy, for whom see Cave, *Hist Lit* The heresy appears to differ from that of Eutyches in asserting the blending to have been of the body alone and not of the whole human nature

The Council of Chalcedon defined that the natures of perfect God and perfect man are united in the One Person of our Lord *ἀσυγχύτως* The heresy of the Synusiastæ is dealt with by Theodoret in his Dialogue "Inconfusus."

T

TABORITES A section of the CALIXTINES, which was so named from a great camp-meeting organized by them on a mountain near Prague ("Tabor" meaning "tent" in the Bohemian language), in the year 1419, for the purpose of receiving the Holy Communion in both kinds They afterwards founded the city of Tabor on the same spot, and, uniting with the Bohemian Beghards, became a dangerous body of fanatics Under the lead of Ziska, they assembled an insurgent force which marched upon Prague on July 30th, 1419, and committed sanguinary atrocities there on the plea of avenging insults which had been offered to the Calixtine custom of Communion

The Taborites were in their principles very similar to the Scotch COVENANTERS of two centuries later date, opposing all the received doctrine and discipline of the Church on the ground that they could not find it in Holy Scripture, and supporting their principles in the most intolerant and cruel manner Some of them allied themselves with the BRETHREN OF THE FREE SPIRIT, the extreme or Adamite section of the Beghards After the death of King Wenceslaus, on August 16th, 1419, they began to destroy churches and monasteries, to persecute the clergy and to appropriate ecclesiastical property, bidding defiance to all public authority on the ground that Christ was their King and was about shortly to establish His personal and visible reign among them. After the death of Ziska they broke up into two parties, the one under Procopius the elder, the other, calling themselves ORPHANS, under his son They were eventually conquered and dispersed by the Calixtine George Podiebrad (afterwards King of Bohemia) in the year 1453, those who escaped the persecution being known subsequently as the BOHEMIAN BRETHREN [Æneas Sylvius, *Hist Bohem*, Ep 130 Bezezyna in Ludwig's *Reliq MSS* vi 142, 186]

TANCHELMIANS A fanatical sect which arose in the Netherlands under the leadership of an uneducated impostor named Tanchelm or Tanquelin, early in the twelfth century They were contemporary with the EONIANS of Brittany, and of a similar character

Tanchelm began, about A D 1115, to proclaim himself to be the Son of God, and in the extravagance of his blasphemy caused churches to be erected in his honour Abelard, who was his contemporary, says that this impostor first travelled to Rome in the garb of a monk, accompanied by a priest, and that returning to Utrecht, where there was then no bishop, he set up a religious community entirely separate from the Church, and although he was a layman, pretended even to celebrate mass and to communicate his followers These latter were chiefly ignorant people on the sea-coast, especially women and children, and he was said to be living a most licentious life among the former At last he set up the state of a king, surrounding himself with a body-guard of three thousand armed men, called himself by the Divine Name, pretended to espouse the Blessed Virgin, and perpetrated the grossest blasphemy of every kind From Utrecht Tanchelm went to Antwerp, where, about the year 1125 he was slain by a priest His followers were afterwards reclaimed by St. Norbert [Abelard, *Opp* p 1066 *Vie de S Norbert*, ii 126 D'Argentre, *Collect judic* i 11]

TANQUELINIANS [TANCHELMIANS]

TARCIANISTS [TATIANISTS]

TASCODRUNGITÆ A sect of the Montanists which had its origin in Galatia, under a leader named Simon, and spread into Phrygia The name is derived from a peculiar custom used by them in their worship of placing the finger beside the nose, τασκός signifying "a little stake," and δροῦγγος, the nose or nostrils, say Epiphanius and Timotheus Presbyter, in the dialect of Galatia. They repudiated all revelation, rejected the Creeds, and ridiculed the Sacraments

There can be little doubt that the Tascodrungitæ are identical with the PASSALORYNCHITÆ, and that they were a sect of Montanist mystics who made divine worship to consist chiefly in silent meditation, of which the gesture from which they took their name was a symbol [Epiphan *Hær* lxxvi Timoth Presb in Combef *Hist Monothelit* 450] It is singular that a Latin writer of the century before Christ is quoted as writing "novam hæresim novo *paxillo* suspendisse" [Varro, ap Non 153, 9]

TATIANISTS A Gnostic sect, chiefly distinguished by abstinence, on which account the name Encratite was appropriated by them or at least by the more rigid of them From Epiphanius it appears that such a distinction was adopted in his time [ENCRATITES]

Tatian was born, as he himself states, "in the land of the Assyrians" [Tatian, *Orat ad Græcos*, 42], but it is not known what particular region was intended by this vague statement. Clement of Alexandria and Theodoret call him a Syrian [Clem Alex *Strom.* iii. 12, Theodor *Hær fab* i 20] Epiphanius calls him a Mesopotamian [*Indic. ad* I iii] He was brought up in the Greek philosophy (Eusebius adds, that as a sophist he taught various branches of literature), and was converted to Christianity by reading the Holy Scriptures [Tatian, *ad Græc* xxix] He then became a disciple of Justin Martyr After Justin's death he fell into the Gnostic heresy about A D 150 The exact system which he adopted or excogitated is not known It is only stated in general that his system of Æons and a subordinate Demiurge resembled—perhaps was borrowed from—that of Valentinus, while from Saturninus and Marcion he learnt his doctrine of heretical asceticism It would be interesting to know the process by which the author of the *Oratio ad Græcos*, the disciple of Justin, the writer against heresy [Hieron *Epist ad Magnum*, *Ep* 83], the defender of our Lord's Divinity [Cau *Fragm ap Routh Rel Sac* ii 129], became the Gnostic ascetic It may be that the Greek philosophy in which he had been trained regained its power over his mind, and the question which presses alike on the Christian and the heathen, "Whence is evil?" led to the adoption of Gnostic principles, and these to the ascetic doctrines and practices or it may be that the asceticism took the lead, and the Gnostic principles were adopted to supply a foundation and defence for its excess But probably the two influences were blended Changes such as Tatian's are not made according to the logic of a theory an ascetic temperament, philosophical speculation, and the remaining influence of a heathen education, probably combined to effect the change in his mind

Tatian's followers had their system of Æons and principalities, and maintained that the Creator was but a subordinate deity, interpreting the command "Let there be light" as a prayer to the Supreme Being [Clem Alex *Fragm.* Ἐκ τῶν προφητ iv p 44, ed Klotz] The law also they ascribed to an inferior Deity [Clem Alex *Strom* iii 12] They asserted that Christ had an apparent, not a real body [Hieron *Comm in Ep ad Galat*] Clement of Alexandria refers them to the school of Valentinus, as did Irenæus [Clem Alex *Strom* iii 13] [1] In this chapter Clement connects Tatian also with Cassian, the chief of the sect of the Docetæ [DOCETÆ]

This Gnosticism presupposes the tenet that matter is the source of evil and the condemnation of marriage, the abstinence from flesh and wine, which were the theory or the practice of several sects of Gnostics, were insisted on so strongly by the Tatianists, that Encratite and Tatianist have become all but synonymous [2] [ENCRATITES] Marriage was declared to be nothing else than corruption and fornication, a sowing to the flesh, from which is reaped corruption All sexual intercourse being impure, it is defilement to eat that which is so procreated. Wine was condemned as the manufacture of the Devil Even in the Eucharist water only was used [HYDROPARASTATÆ]

Tatian's followers denied the salvation of Adam This blasphemy, Irenæus states, was first introduced by Tatian Irenæus treats it as involving by direct consequence the damnation of all men. "They who disallow Adam's salvation shut themselves out from life for ever, in that they do not believe that the sheep which had perished has been found For if it has not been found, the whole human race is still held in a state of perdition" [Iren *Hær* iii 23] The statement then which has been made with something of a sneer, that "what especially shocked the piety and charity of the Catholics, was Tatian's affirming the damnation of Adam, a blasphemy which drew upon him especial odium," is not well expressed Whether erroneously or not, Irenæus held Adam to be the type or federal head of all mankind, and that to deny his salvation was tantamount to an assertion of the utter failure of Christ's work of redemption The sheep which was lost was the human race as existing in Adam

Of Tatian's Harmony of the Gospels, the "Dia Tessaron," Theodoret's account is most to be trusted Eusebius, it appears, had not seen the work Theodoret says "Tatian composed a gospel which is called Dia Tessaron, leaving out the genealogies, and everything that shews the Lord to have been born of the seed of David according to the flesh which has been used not only by those of his sect, but also by them who follow the apostolic doctrine, they not perceiving the fraud of the composition, but simply using it as a compendious book I have met with above two hundred of these books, which were in esteem in our churches, all which I took away, and laid aside, and placed in their room the Gospels of the four Evangelists [3]

Eusebius says that Tatian dared to alter some words of the Apostle (*i e* St Paul), as pretending to correct the composition and order of his style Jerome says [*Proœm in Comm ad Tit*] that Tatian rejected some of St Paul's Epistles [SEVERIANS]

Musanus [Euseb *Hist Eccl* iv 21, 28], Clement of Alexandria, Apollinaris of Hierapolis, and Origen, wrote against the Tatianists and Severians [Theod *Hær fab* i 21], but their works are lost

[Irenæus, *Hær* i 28, and iii 23 Hippol

[1] So the author of the Appendix to Tertullian's *de Præscr* "Totus enim secundum Valentinum sapit, adjiciens illud, Adam nec salutem consequi posse quasi non si rami salvi fiant, et radix salva sit"

[2] Jerome notices of the Montanists that they "vel maxime de Tatiani radice creverunt" [*Comm in Aggæum*, cap i]

[3] On this subject see Mill, *Proleg in Nov Test* p 358, F Wetstein, *Proleg in Nov Test* p 65, Valesius, *Not ad Euseb* iv 29, and Lardner's *Credib* II xxxvi Asseman says that Tatian's Diatessaron is in the Vatican Library, in the Arabic language [*Bib Or* tom i p 619 Jeremie's Note in *Encyc. Metr* xi 139].

viii 9 and x 14 Euseb *Hist. Eccl* iv 16 and 29 Epiphan *Hær* xlvi Theod *Hær fab* i 20 Philast *Hær* xlviii August *Hær* xxv Origen, *de Oratione*, xiii]

TAULER [FRIENDS OF GOD]

TERMINISTS [NOMINALISTS]

TERMINISTS Those who believe that a "terminus gratiæ" has been predestined in the life of every person which ends the time during which he can repent of sin and find pardon with God The opinion was maintained by Reichenberg, a Professor of Theology at Leipsic at the end of the seventeenth century, and was controverted by the learned Ittig, the writer of a work on the heresiarchs of the first two centuries, noticed in the article HERESIOLOGISTS Terminism is a modified form of the extreme Calvinistic theory respecting the eternal decree of some to salvation and some to damnation, and is contrary to all orthodox opinions respecting the mercy of God

TERTIARII The lay brethren, or "third order" of the Franciscans, who joined the "Fratres de paupere vitâ" in the contest of the "Spirituals" against the lax Franciscans, and who were afterwards included with them under the general name of FRATICELLI.

TERTULLIANISTS A small sect formed in Carthage by those who followed the great Tertullian [A D. 150-220] in adopting opinions infected with those of the MONTANISTS, and who also called themselves "Spirituals" to distinguish themselves as persons of stricter life than the lax among the orthodox, whom they called PSYCHICS, or "carnal" men

Several of Tertullian's treatises shew that he set himself against all relaxation of strict and stern Christian life A question arose about the propriety of unmarried women appearing in public without wearing the veils which are worn by women in the East, and while many were disposed to let custom rule the point, Tertullian wrote a treatise "De Virginibus Velandis," in which he takes the stricter line, from whence a distinction soon sprung up between the "virgins of men" and the "virgins of God" Another question arose respecting second marriages, and he wrote his treatise "De Monogamia," in which he utterly condemns a second marriage after the decease of the first wife or husband, and also advocates a life of continence even for those who are married, on the ground that marriage was permitted to Christians only as a concession granted to human infirmity A third question arose as to the wearing of chaplets or crowns by Christian soldiers, according to the custom of Roman armies, on the Emperor's festival, and Tertullian wrote his treatise "De Corona," in which he condemned the practice as idolatrous

Combined with this ascetic strictness, Tertullian held an opinion that the continual Presence of the Holy Spirit in the Church of Christ would guide the latter into the development of a more austere system of morals before the approach of the Last Day, which he supposed, in common with most of the early Christians, to be near at hand Thus, writing of marriage as a concession to infirmity, he says, "Whether we look to the grounds on which the permission was granted, or to the preference given to a state of celibacy (in the words of St Paul, 'It is good for a man not to touch a woman'), the evident tendency of the Apostle's reasoning is to do away with the permission to marry This being so, why may not the same Spirit, coming after the days of the Apostles at the appropriate time (there being, according to the Preacher, a time for all things), for the purpose of leading Christians into the truth, why may not the same Spirit, I say, have imposed a final and complete restraint upon the flesh, and called men away from marriage not indirectly, but openly? And this the more since St Paul's argument, that 'the time is short,' is much more forcible now that an hundred and sixty years have elapsed since he wrote his Epistle" [Tertull *De Monogam*] When therefore Montanus declared that the Paraclete promised by Christ had now come into the world to carry the Christian dispensation on to its perfection, his teaching found a ready response from Tertullian, as is evident from the continuation of the preceding passage "The Paraclete introduces no new doctrine, He now definitively enjoins that of which He before gave warning, He now requires that for which He has hitherto been content to wait"

For a time the sympathy of Tertullian with the Montanists was so strong that he was accounted one of that sect, but there is no good ground for supposing that he ever acknowledged the alleged claim of Montanus to be the Paraclete in person Under the influence of Proculus, one of the Montanist leaders, and of the tolerance which was shewn at Rome towards Praxeas, the originator of Patripassianism, against whom he had written [Hieron *Catal Script Eccl*], Tertullian undertook "the defence of the Paraclete," but this was a defence of the developing dispensation of the Holy Spirit, not of the alleged claims of Montanus And although Tertullian separated himself nominally from the "Psychics," but practically from the Church, he soon established a community which was at least as distinct from that of the Montanists as from the Church of Carthage [Prædest *Hær* lxxxvi] These "Tertullianists" were probably orthodox is to the faith in general, but maintaining a schismatical position on account of their dislike to what they considered the worldliness of the Church St Augustine speaks tenderly of them, and says, that the very few who remained in his time had returned to the communion of the Church, and had given up their basilica to the Catholics [Aug *Hær* lxxxvi] There is no reason to think that they adopted the peculiar opinions of Tertullian himself, such as that of the transmigration of wicked souls into the bodies of demons

TESSARESCÆDECATITÆ. [QUARTODECIMANS]

TETRADITES [QUARTODECIMANS]

TETRAPOLITAN CONFESSION [PROTESTANT CONFESSIONS]

TETRATHEITÆ [DAMIANISTS]

TEXERANTS A local name given to the ALBIGENSES in those districts of Southern France, where the members of that widespread sect were mostly found among the weavers,—"ab usu texendi" [Ekbert, *adv Cathar* in *Bibl Max Lugd* xxiii 601]

THEBUTHIS or THEBUTES Eusebius quotes from Hegesippus the statement that Thebuthis made a beginning secretly to corrupt the Church of Jerusalem, because Simon the son of Cleophas was appointed to be bishop of the Christians in that city instead of himself Nothing further is known of him or his sect [Euseb *Hist Eccl* iv 22]

THEISTS A name used instead of "Deists" by some writers in the latter half of the seventeenth century [Evelyn's *Hist Relig* i 282] In modern language the name is used to designate those who believe in the existence of God, (as distinguished from Atheists,) and in the moral supremacy of conscience, but do not pledge themselves to any doctrines of Christian theology as to the Divine Attributes, or the doctrine of the Holy Trinity [DICT *of* THEOL, THEISM]

THEMISTIANS [AGNOETÆ]

THEOCATAGNOSTÆ A name used by St John of Damascus, apparently as a general term for heretics who held unorthodox opinions about God, and therefore "thought evil" [κατάγνωσις] respecting Him [Joan Damasc *de Hær*]

THEODOSIANS The Alexandrian section of the sect of the PHTHARTOLATRÆ

THEODOSIANS [FEODOSIANS]

THEODOTIANS There were two heretics of the name of Theodotus, distinguished as the Tanner and the Banker, the latter a disciple of the former Theodotus the Tanner was of Byzantium, and was a man of much learning, but, having in a time of persecution denied the faith, he retreated to Rome [about A D 192], and there tried to palliate his apostasy by saying that he had not denied God but man He persisted in his assertion that Christ was a mere man, and was excommunicated by Victor [Euseb *Hist Eccl* v 28, Epiph *Hær* liv, Theod *Hær fab* ii 5]

Eusebius gives extracts from a book entitled "The Little Labyrinth,"[1] written against Artemon, from which it appears that there was at least an attempt to organize a distinct schismatical sect of Theodotians Theodotus the Banker, with an associate Asclepiodotus, persuaded one Natalis, a confessor, to be bishop of the heretical party, but it is not clear whether Natalis was already a bishop, or whether the Theodotians hoped to procure his consecration Natalis repented, and was readmitted to Catholic communion by Zephyrinus

In another extract there occurs this difficulty, that Theodotus is said to have been the author of this God-denying heresy Ittigius contents himself with simply saying that Caius was in error [Ittig *de Hæres* p 261] Several different explanations may be seen in Burton's *Bampton Lectures*, note 100. Is it not sufficient to say that Caius, and after him Eusebius, were thinking only of those who held correctly the first article of the Creed, and did not bring into comparison with Theodotus either the Gnostics, who entertained so different a belief regarding the nature of the Deity, or the Ebionites, who were more of Jews than Christians Thus Theodoret states that Theodotus held the same opinions as Artemon, and that Artemon agreed with the Catholics as to the God of the universe, believing Him to be the Creator of all things Of such, Theodotus was the first Psilanthropist [ARTEMONITES] This explanation is confirmed by the statement of Hippolytus, which will be given presently While asserting our Lord to be a mere man, Theodotus allowed that He was born of a Virgin "Doctrinam enim introduxit qua Christum homi nem tantummodo diceret, Deum autem illum negaret, ex Spiritu quidem Sancto natum et Virgine, sed hominem solitarium atque nudum, nulla alia præ ceteris nisi sola justitiæ auctoritate" [Pseudo-Tert cap xxiii] So too Theodoret But Epiphanius writes that the Theodotians held Christ to be a mere man, and begotten of the seed of man The testimony of Hippolytus is decisive on this point

Hippolytus states that Theodotus introduced a novel heresy, being orthodox as to the creation of the world by God, but drawing his notions of Christ from the school of the Gnostics and of Cerinthus and Ebion that he held Jesus to have been a mere man, born of a Virgin, according to the counsel of the Father, to have become preeminent in piety, and to have received Christ at His baptism in Jordan, before which time therefore miraculous powers were not exhibited by Him Some of the followers of Theodotus, it is added, think that Jesus never became God, even at the descent of the Spirit, while others maintain that He became God after the resurrection from the dead [*Refut* vii 23]

At the end of the works of Clement of Alexandria are two large extracts purporting to be from the writings of Theodotus Of these, Burton [*Bampton Lect* note 100] remarks that it is difficult to subscribe to the notion, though supported by Cave, Ittigius, and Fabricius, that they were written by Theodotus The silence of Hippolytus as to any such opinions (and it will be remembered that the "Refutation of all Heresies" was written after the death of Callistus, A D 222, while Theodotus went to Rome about A D 192) affords a stronger presumption against these extracts than does the character of the doctrines maintained in them And as it is, on the other hand, by no means clear that we have Clement's testimony to their genuineness—"Utrum vero ab ipso Clemente consarcinata hæc fuerint, an ab alio quodam, parum liquet," says Cave—it is not safe to ascribe

[1] Pearson, comparing Photius, *Cod* xlviii. with Theod. *Hær fab* ii 5, concludes that Caius of Rome was the author of this book [*Minor Works*, by Churton, ii 438, *et seq*, Routh, *Reliq Sac* ii 141-144] Routh suggests that Hippolytus may have been the author The author of Prædestinatus says that Craton, a Syrian bishop, overcame (obtinerit) the Theodotians This must have been by his writings

them to Theodotus A summary of the tenets advanced in them may be seen in Cave's *Historia Literaria* under the article "Theodotus"

The author of the "Little Labyrinth" charges the leaders of the Theodotians or Artemonites with interpolating, adding to, and taking from, the Holy Scriptures Theodotus, Asclepiades, Hermophilus, Apollonides, did so (Theodoret states) each in his own way The corruption of the Scriptures by heretics is named by Clement, who, having quoted Matt v 10, introduces variations of the text with the words ἢ ὥς τινες τῶν μετατιθέντων τὰ εὐαγγέλια [Clem Alex *Strom* IV vi 41 See also Kaye *on Clement*, p 288]

Artemon was the better known leader of this sect [ARTEMONITES] Epiphanius supposes that the Melchisedechians were an offshoot from the Theodotians [*Hær* lv], and Hippolytus and Theodoret state that they had their beginning from Theodotus the Banker. [MELCHISEDECHIANS]

THEOPASCHITES A sect of the Monophysites who maintained that Christ having only one Nature, and that the Divine, it was therefore the Divine Nature which suffered [Θεός, πάσχειν] at the Crucifixion This opinion is mentioned by Philaster [*Hær* xcii] and Augustine [*Hær* lxxiii], but was first maintained in its extreme form by Peter Fullo, the Monophysite Patriarch of Antioch, who is alleged to have altered the Trisagion to the form "Holy God, Holy Mighty, Holy Immortal, Thou Who for our sakes wast crucified, have mercy upon us" The formula was accepted however by many of the orthodox as merely stating that one of the Persons of the Blessed Trinity suffered for us men and for our salvation. The Emperor Justinian issued an edict directing its use, and its rejection was condemned by the tenth anathema of the fifth General Council [A D 553], the second Council of Constantinople [Mansi, *Concil* viii 765, ix 384] But Theopassianism itself was condemned in a council held at Rome A D 862, which decreed that the Godhead of Christ could not suffer, and that He "passionem crucis tantummodo secundum carnem sustinuisse" [*ibid* xv 658] There is an orthodox modification of the opinion, to the effect that the Divine Nature of Christ and His Human Nature each partake of the operation of the other, and hence that in a certain sense the sufferings of Christ's Body and Soul were communicated to His Divinity. [DICT *of* THEOL., THEANDRIC OPERATION]

THEOPASSIANS [THEOPASCHITES]

THEOPATHETICS [THEOPASCHITES]

THEOPHILANTHROPISTS This name was assumed by a party of French Deists during the Reign of Terror, to indicate their adherence to a natural or Theistic religion and worship which was intended to supersede Christianity, and whose characteristics were to be love of God and love of man

The first attempt at establishing a Theistic worship of this kind was made in England by an Unitarian preacher of Liverpool named David Williams, a friend of Franklin, in conjunction with whom he arranged a plan for the propagation of Deism, the fruit of which was his "Liturgy on the universal principles of Religion and Morality," published in the year 1776 With this Liturgy, Williams set up a meeting-house in Margaret Street, Cavendish Square, where he officiated under the title of a Priest of Nature In this attempt he was supported and encouraged by Voltaire, and his friend Frederick the Great, King of Prussia, and through the former the scheme of Williams became known in France

The idea of a Theistic worship thus imported into France was taken up in a sentimental form by a number of those who desired to build up some form of religion on the ruins of Christianity D'Aubermenil established a system of so-called worship, in which the Deity was to be symbolized by a perpetual fire, before which oblations of fruit, salt and oil were to be made In the temple of this religion there was to be daily worship, every ninth day was to be a day of rest, and there were to be occasional festivals, celebrated with dancing D'Aubermenil gave the name of "Theoandrophiles" to his disciples, but this was changed to "Theophilanthropes" when some of the latter determined to establish his system in a modified form

The new sect was headed by La Réveillère Lepaux, one of the Directory, who opened a blind school as a place of worship for it, but afterwards obtained a decree of the Directory, giving the sect a right to the use of the churches as national buildings They thus obtained the use of twenty churches in Paris, in which they set up their worship A basket of fruit or flowers, according to the season, was placed upon the altar, over which was inscribed the creed of Robespierre, "We believe in God and the immortality of the soul," and on each side of it some sentences containing statements of abstract morality The ritual consisted of some colourless prayers, and hymns selected from the writings of French poets —Milton's Paradise Lost and Thomson's Seasons were the "use" of Margaret Street—there being a pause in one part of the service, during which the worshippers were to meditate in silence on their faults since their last attendance at the service Moral lectures also formed a part of the system They had four special festivals in honour of Socrates, St Vincent de Paul, Jean Jacques Rousseau, and Washington

As religious feeling began to revive, the Theophilanthropists began to decline They and their sentimental trumpery were turned out of the churches the revolutionary Government forbade them on October 4th, 1801, to use even the three churches which were left in their hands, and when their petition for holding their services elsewhere was refused, the Theophilanthropist religion soon died of inanition, despised by the infidel party as well as by those who still remained Christians An attempt to revive it after the Revolution of 1830 utterly failed [Grégoire's *Histoire des Sectes Religieuses*]

THEOPHRONIANS [EUNOMIO-THEOPHRONIANS]

THEOPHYLACTIANS A name given to the orthodox Christians of Alexandria by the Jacobites in the seventh century [Neale's *Hist. East Ch., Patriarch Alex* ii 87]

THEOPONITÆ. [THEOPASCHITES]

THEOSEBITES A sect noticed by St Cyril of Alexandria, under the name of *θεοσεβεῖς*, and also known by the Latin equivalent "Deicolæ" They are said by St Cyril to have spread in Palestine and Phœnicia during the first half of the fifth century, and appear to have been similar to, if not identical with, the HYPSISTARIANS The Theosebites exalted the sun, moon, and stars, into objects of worship, and yet acknowledged one Supreme Deity over all, their religion thus appearing to have been an adulteration of Christianity with Magianism [Cyr. Alex *de Adorat in Spir et Verit* iii]

Probably the Hypsistarians and Theosebites, and other sects of similar principles, are to be traced to the Therapeutæ and Essenes, who, as sketched by Philo [*de Vitâ contempl*], worshipped τὸ ὄν or, Ὕψιστος, kept the Jewish sabbath, and were as particular as the Jews in their rules about food [Ullmann's *Greg Nazianz* App ii] Such sects kept up a partial belief in Christ, but were at the same time strict Unitarians and while under Jewish influences they assumed a Judaizing character, they were of a Magian or other character when they came under other local influences

THEOSOPHISTS The generic application of all those mystics who allege that by an internal and supernatural illumination they are admitted to a knowledge of the mystery of being first, on the side of nature, secondly, on that of religion. The title of Fire-philosophers has also been accorded to these persons, and properly, for, according to their own account, they are enabled, by a miraculous intuition of the properties of the so-called element of fire, to provide a solution, not only for every difficulty of physics, but also for every doubtful problem in the spiritual world

Preposterous as these claims are, many traces of similar arrogant pretensions are to be found in the history of philosophy from the time of Empedocles to the present day; but the movement with which modern sectarian history is concerned dates no further back than the sixteenth century Of this system, now specifically entitled Theosophistical, Paracelsus is the founder, Robert Fludd and the Rosicrucians the supporters, and Jacob Bohm the great prophet and apostle. Many affiliated forms of mysticism have indeed appeared since the rise of the Theosophists, but they have either been schooled into something like a separate system, by the attraction of the real ability of their founder (as was the case with the SWEDENBORGIANS), or in default of such an influence have sunk or risen into a simple religious Quietism Generally however such bodies have differential peculiarities of their own, and invariably a separate collective title and history

No uniformity of principle, nor even, to speak strictly, any community of method, can be attributed to the Theosophists, for in each period of their grotesque existence they listened submissively to the voice of their leaders, which rarely echoed that of reason Thus each generation received some fresh instalment of incoherent dreaming, and recorded it as the final contribution of the Divine Intelligence Further, as an appropriate foundation was needed upon which to erect this structure of folly, the Theosophists claimed to derive their technical language and leading ideas from the ancient secrets of the Cabbala These they alleged to have been handed down by oral tradition through the long centuries of the Middle Age, and to have reached them uninjured with its entire complement of magic and astrology

Of their two great pretensions, miraculous knowledge of physics and special spiritual illumination, the former made the Theosophists famous, and the latter still continues to keep them remarkable, even at the present day, while the former is hopelessly discredited by general experience. there are still found persons who do not reject the latter This shifting of opinions among the taught has been, of course, accompanied by a change of front (rendered necessary by the progress of civilization) by the teacher, who, as the absurdity of Theosophic science became gradually exposed, has been glad to retire from the comparatively open field of scientific knowledge to the more inaccessible district of religious speculation Thus we find that the father of Theosophy lays claim to the gift of universal healing, while the Theosophists of to-day pretend only to spiritual illumination, though the latter, in the desire to support their failing claims to a revelation of nature, distort, with the bad faith common to religious enthusiasts, the vague verbiage of their sacred authors into meanings the most alien from their natural interpretation

The pretensions of Paracelsus, a Swiss physician [A D 1493-1541], who numbered Erasmus and Frobenius among his patients, undoubtedly gave the greatest if not the first impulse to Theosophy He was a man of capacity, and practically the discoverer of the medicinal properties of opium and mercury From his inordinate appetite for admiration, he became dissatisfied with the really great result of his art, and laid claim to the discovery of the "elixir vitæ," a piece of hypocrisy which his early death considerably discredited A man of prodigious vanity, he was glad to adopt the hyperbolical language of alchemy to magnify his discoveries, and partly perhaps to confuse his opponents, accustomed to the simple dialectic of the Aristotelian philosophy It is impossible to say how far he deceived himself, but he certainly succeeded in deceiving many others, notably Robert Fludd an English physician [A D 1574-1637], a man of family and of liberal education After the death of Paracelsus his followers and pupils, (who, it should be noted, were principally chemists, and only secondarily prophets), under the mythical name of Rosicrucians, attracted much notice in the sixteenth century, and their system in that unsettled epoch easily secured numerous adherents [ROSICRUCIANS] Fludd himself was thus drawn into the circle of unreason, and became a zealous admirer of Theosophy and an ardent advocate of the Rosicrucian cause In his steps followed Bohm or Bohmen [A D 1575-1624], the greatest of the Theosophists This man, a shoemaker at Gorlitz, in Holland, who shared the general discontent felt by the Lutherans with their religion, was so affected by the eloquence of Fludd, that he became a complete convert to the creed of Theosophy, and in addition set up a most strange mystical system of his own. He was a man of vast imagination and an elaborate constructive power, and finding pleasure in the dreams of incomprehensible mystery suggested by his favourite author, encouraged this form of intellectual self indulgence to such an extent that he at last firmly believed that the incoherent visions of his distempered fancy were the actual communications of the Deity His story is, that on three occasions, each succeeding a trance of seven days' duration, he became the recipient of a special revelation His first vision was of God, his second of the world of nature and the essential properties of all things, his third of causality, creation, and the Divine Nature Twelve years afterwards he gave to the world the results of this illumination in a series of publications of great number and obscurity The elements of his teaching can be most easily collected from his Aurora, although it is alleged that at the date of its composition he was only "partly illuminated" A short extract will suffice to shew the nature of the most important doctrines of Theosophy "God," it is alleged, "is the unity in relation to His creatures, an eternal nothing, He has neither foundation, nor commencement, nor place, and possesses nothing but Himself He is the will of that which has no ground in Himself, He is a unity He does not stand in need of any room or space, from eternity to eternity He begets Himself in Himself. In God all creatures are only one creature, an eternal unity as it were, the one eternal good but the eternal unity could not become manifest if there were no differences, therefore it has manifested itself in such a way, that it has introduced a plurality and distinctions in its own will and in attributes, but the attributes in desires, and the desires in beings The creation is nothing but a manifestation of the Almighty, it is all that which He is in His eternal generation, but not in His omnipotence and power The Being of beings is only one Being, but in His generation He separates Himself into light and darkness, joy and sorrow, good and evil, love and hatred, fire and light, and out of these two eternal beginnings arises the third beginning, viz the creation for His own delight and according to His eternal desire" When to this is added that light is grace, and that grace, and indeed all spiritual things, operate by the laws of light and physical things, sufficient indication of what Theosophy means is given, sufficient to justify Mosheim's description of Bohm as a man "who discovered by means of fire a theology more obscure than the "numbers" of Pythagoras or the "characters" of Heraclitus" [BEHMEN]

To Bohm succeeded many writers, all more or less influenced by his prodigious imagination Such are Knorr, Mercurius, Sperber, Freher, Bohm's commentator, Kuhlman, (the martyr of Theosophy, who was burnt in Russia in 1689,) and the younger Helmont This last named author oscillates between a comparative sanity, induced by his admiration for the Cartesian philosophy, and a more than Theosophistical madness due to the fascination of the mystic Madame Bourignon In one of his saner passages, he gives the clue to the possibility of Theosophy in these words "The essence of the human mind is thought capable and desirous of light, to satisfy this desire we need the illumination of faith, disclaiming the fictions of the human reason."

Bohm and his followers have been accused of grievous heresy by their Lutheran opponents, not always justly, specially of Manichæism by Gerrard Antagnossus, and of Atheism by Muller The latter charge is certainly fanciful, but it is hard to read their statements about the great darkness among the stars, caused by the presence of the Devil, without thinking of the mythology (though not the leading tenets) of Mani Of Pantheism, too, they can scarcely be acquitted, for they certainly allege that "the whole Divine Trinity presented as form is the universe," which is in fact only a truncated aspect of the idealism of Spinoza Nevertheless, unsound as are some of their religious opinions, it cannot be denied that the Theosophist morality has been irreproachable It is thus that, while Denmark, Germany, France, and England have all contributed their quota to swell the ranks of these innocent fanatics, the history of Theosophy in these countries presents no scene of violence or persecution

In England, Theosophy has been particularly fortunate, not only in the early advocacy of Robert Fludd, but in the more recent conversion of William Law [A D 1686-1761], a divine of eminence in the English Church, known as the author of "A Serious Call to a Devout Life," and for his influence over the mind of John Wesley In his declining years Law adopted the opinions of Bohm, and became himself the translator of his works Judged by the work of Walton (the full title of which is given below), the mantle of the prophet of Gorlitz is not likely to be without a zealous proprietor at the present time, nor do his followers seem inclined to abate any of his pretensions In the work just alluded to it is alleged that "Sir I Newton ploughed with Bohmen's heifer," "for he did but reduce to a mathematical form the central principles of nature revealed in Bohmen, and by the aid of the experience and observation bequeathed by antecedent philosophers."[1] The author goes on to remark that the observations will apply to the science of physiognomy introduced by Lavater and perfected as phrenology by Gall and Spurzheim, and "to all that is sound in the philosophy of Berkeley;"

[1] This assertion has a slight foundation in the fact that Newton copied out large extracts from Bohm's works [Brewster's *Newton*, ii 371]

finally, it is alleged to be true of the Homœopathy of Hahnemann !

[*Literature.* *The Works of J Bohm*, translated and edited by William Law, give the best detailed information, while the best general account of early Theosophism will be found in Brucker, *Histor Philosoph.* Very full information as to Theosophical authors and their meaning is to be found in Christopher Walton's *Notes and Materials for an adequate Biography of William Law, comprising an elucidation of the scope and contents of Jacob Bohmen and his great Commentator Dionysius Freher, with a Notice of the Mythical Divinity and a most curious and solid Science of all ages of the World, also an indication of the time for the induction of the intellectual heathen Notions to the Christian Faith* For the supposed relation of Bohm's philosophy to that of Schelling and the school of purely philosophic mysticism, the works of Erdmann and D F Strauss must be consulted]

THERAPEUTÆ The Egyptian branch of the Jewish sect of Essenes, distinguished from the Essenes of Syria and Palestine by a hermit instead of a monastic life, and by a less admixture of Eastern philosophy in their doctrine The sect is described by Philo in his treatise "De Vita Contemplativa."

Eusebius' notion that the Therapeutæ, or "Devotees," were Jewish Christians is generally abandoned, as being inconsistent with a right understanding of Philo's description of them as disciples of Moses, as a sect of long standing, with a Jewish not a Judæo-Christian observance of the Sabbath

It has been disputed whether the Therapeutæ were Essenes Valesius, *e g*, denied this in opposition to Scaliger [Note on Eusebius, *Hist Eccl* ii 17] Valesius urges the differences between the two, such as the community of goods of the Essenes, the private property of the Therapeutæ, and the different estimation in which women were held But these do not touch the principle of Essenism, which was the common priesthood of all members of the society, and the consequent rejection of the separate priesthood of the Levites [Essenes] That this principle was held by the Therapeutæ appears from Philo's description of the celebration of their great festivals, in which the meal of bread, salt, and hyssop was taken, as among the Essenes, with solemn prayer and in priestly garments, and the hymns used are called *ὕμνοι παραβώμιοι* [Ritschl, *Enstehung der Altk Kirche*, p 184, note 1] In consequence of their different appreciation of women, it would be nearer the truth to call them the purer branch of the Essene sect

Philo describes the Therapeutæ, and their devout women, Therapeutides, as drawn to a life of solitary devotion by heavenly love, and under an enthusiastic impulse to attain the desired state of contemplation, relinquishing their goods to their own relations, seeking solitude in lone country habitations, each with his separate cottage, which had in it an oratory, spending the day in the study and contemplation of divine things, coming together on the seventh day in assemblies, in which discourses were made on the allegorical and mystical meaning of the Scriptures; their synagogues having separate enclosures for men and women, every seventh Sabbath being a high festival, with its sacred meal taken as a religious service, the men on one side of the hall, the women on the other side, the juniors of the society ministering, but in the garb of freemen, the afternoon spent in discourse on divine things, and in singing hymns, now alternately, now in chorus, and this exercise prolonged after supper throughout the night

The female devotees were mostly aged, and such only as had been virgins from their youth The Therapeutic estimate of marriage we are not told, but the recognition of female devotees implies a very different estimation of woman from that entertained by the Palestinian Essenes Neither is there in Philo's mention of the prayers made at sunrise and sunset an intimation of the worship of the sun It appears rather that the Therapeutæ borrowed their customs from the country in which they were settled, adapting them to the principle of Essenism Some classes of the Egyptian priesthood had always used like customs And the same religious feeling, which thus tended to form the sect of Therapeutæ afterwards gave birth, among Egyptian Christians, to monks and nuns [Sharpe's *History of Egypt*, ii 92]

THNETOPSYCHITÆ A name given by St John of Damascus and Nicetas to the Arabian heretics, who for want of any other designation —itaque nos hæreticos, quoniam nullum eorum ponit auctorem, Arabicos possumus nuncupare— were called Arabici [Joann Damasc *Hær* xc Nicet. *Thesaur Orthod.* iv 40]

In the history of Paul the Deacon, written in the eighth century, they are called Charurgitæ [Paul Diac *Hist* xix]

THOMISTS [Schoolmen.]

THONDRACIANS An Armenian sect which was formed in the province of Ararat by a fusion of Parseeism and Paulicianism about A D 840 Sembat, a Paulician, was brought into contact with a Persian physician and astronomer named Medschusic, whose influence led him to attempt a combination of the Zoroastrian and the Christian systems He established himself at Thondrac, from which place the name of his sect was taken, its original designation being assumed from the Armenian sect of the Pseudo-Christian Parsees known as Arevurdis or Sun-Children The Thondracians often revived and became important, although often almost suppressed, and in A D 1002 were joined by the Armenian bishop Jacob, the head of the province, under whom they made great progress He was eventually condemned as a heretic by the Armenian Church, and having escaped from the prison in which he had been confined, came to a violent death at the hands of those who attempted to retake him [Chamchean's *Geschichte von Armenien*, ii 884]

THREE CHAPTERS [Tria Capitula]

THREE DENOMINATIONS This name was given to the Independents, the Baptists, and the Presbyterians at the time when these three sects represented the great body of English Dissenters They were the Dissenters recognised by the Act of Toleration [1 Will & Mary, c. 18], and had the privilege granted to them of presenting corporate addresses to the Sovereign

TIMOTHEANS A section of the Alexandrian Monophysites, so named from Timotheus Ælurus, a bitter opponent of the canons of Chalcedon During the patriarchate of Proterius, Timothy established schismatical assemblies in Alexandria, having persuaded a few bishops and monks to join him in his secession from the communion of the patriarch, and he acquired the peculiar name of "the Cat" on account of the stealthy manner in which he gained access to the monks by climbing to the windows of their cells at night, that he might persuade them to give up their allegiance to their bishop On the death of the Emperor Marcian, he succeeded in obtaining consecration from two heretical and exiled bishops, and Proterius was murdered by the partizans of the usurping patriarch on Good Friday, A D 457. Timothy Ælurus maintained his usurped position for three years, when he was banished to the ancient Cherson near Sebastopol, and Timothy Salofaciolus appointed in his stead After the death of the Emperor Leo, the departure of Zeno from Constantinople, and the accession of Basiliscus, the latter was persuaded by his Eutychian Empress Zenobia to recall the banished usurper, when he again took possession of the patriarchal throne of Alexandria with triumph, after fifteen years' absence, in A D 470, his entry into the city of Constantinople on the way being made a profane parody of our Lord's entry into Jerusalem on Palm Sunday [Evagr *Hist Eccl* iii 6] Zeno returned to his throne in the following year, and issued a decree of banishment against Ælurus, but the execution of this was anticipated by the death of the usurping patriarch

The opinions of Timotheus and his party went the full length of extreme Eutychianism In some fragments of a work of his which still exist [Mai *Nova Collect* vii 35, 277, 304, 305] he is found saying that the Nature of Christ is one only, that is Divine, that in the first starting-point of conception by His Mother, He had one substance with human nature, but that He was not born of the Blessed Virgin in the ordinary way of birth, or her virginity could not have been preserved This form of Eutychianism thus repudiated the reality of Christ's human nature, and was practically identical with the opinion of the Docetæ

TOLAND, JOHN. This deistical writer [A D 1669-1722] was originally an Irish Roman Catholic, but passing through Presbyterianism at Glasgow, Edinburgh, and Leyden, he became a voluminous writer against Christianity In the year 1696 he published a work entitled "Christianity not Mysterious, or a Treatise shewing that there is nothing in the Gospel contrary to Reason or above it. and that no Christian doctrine can be properly called a Mystery" This book was presented by the Grand Jury of Middlesex, and Toland withdrew to Ireland, but the Parliament of his native country ordering that he should be prosecuted by the Attorney-General, and his book burned by the common hangman he returned to a safer residence in London The political line which he subsequently took brought him into favour with the Whig partizans of the House of Hanover, and the rest of his life was one of much prosperity In 1698 he printed his "Amyntor," in which he gives a catalogue of more than eighty apocryphal Gospels, and other similar books, with the view of discrediting the Canon of Scripture, pretending that the books of the latter were not publicly known at any earlier date than the others. In 1718 he published a work which he called "Nazarenus, or Jewish, Gentile, and Mahometan Christianity," and in 1720 "Tetradymus," a book of the same eclectic character Toland's infidelity was much moulded by his acquaintance with Leibnitz, and by the writings of Spinoza. [SCEPTICS]

TRACTARIANS. [HIGH CHURCHMEN]

TRADUCIANS Those who believe that the soul is, like the bodily part of human nature, handed down from parent to child in a germinal form by natural generation The opinion is first found in Tertullian, and is opposed by that of the CREATIONISTS

TRASKITES The early name of the Sabbatarian Puritans, the sect owing its origin to John Trask, a native of Somersetshire, who, after being a schoolmaster there up to thirty-four years of age, became a preacher in London about the year 1617 Fuller says that he was refused ordination by the Bishop of Bath and Wells as altogether insufficient, but that "afterwards he got Orders, and then began to vent his opinions" It is said of him that "he preached repentance so earnestly that he caused many of his auditors to weep, yea, to roar in that manner, that inhabitants of several places of the city were disquieted many times in the night season by his converts And himself gave them an example, for both in city and fields he prayed so loud as if he would have pierced the heavens" This peculiarity is noticed also by Fuller, who says "I have heard him preach a sermon, . and when his auditors have forgotten the matter they will remember the loudness of his stentorian voice which indeed had more strength than anything else he delivered" He enjoined severe asceticism upon his followers, inducing them to fast three days at a time, alleging that the third day's fast would bring them into the condition of justified saints, according to the promise, "After two days He will revive us, in the third day He will raise us up, and we shall live in His sight" [Hos vi 1] They were also to sell all that they possessed to give to the poor, and to spend their days in sighing, "to eat their bread with quaking, and to drink their water with trembling" being thus an early form of the sect afterwards called "Quakers"

Among other precepts strictly enforced by Trask, was that of doing everything by the law of Scripture. A young man named Hamlet Jackson took him so literally at his word as to believe that the Word of God prescribed what he should eat and what he should drink, alleging proofs for his opinion from the Levitical law In arguing with him, Trask was himself converted to his opinions, and began at once to teach it to his followers Thus he established among them a number of ceremonial customs respecting dress and domestic life, and required them to observe Sunday with the same strictness that the Jews observed the Sabbath On this point again Jackson (who afterwards became a Jewish proselyte at Amsterdam) persuaded him that the proper day to keep in this manner was Saturday, and that Sunday need not be regarded Strict Sabbatarianism was thus introduced among the Traskites, and afterwards became the distinctive feature of the sect

On April 1st, 1634, the Commissioners for Ecclesiastical Causes wrote to all Justices of the Peace, Mayors, etc, enjoining them to take measures for the suppression of "Brownists, Anabaptists, Arians, Traskists, Familists, and some other sorts" of separatists, novelists, and sectaries It was probably at this time that Trask and his wife (who was a schoolmistress, and refused to teach on Saturday) were brought before the Star-Chamber, where his Judaizing opinions and practices were refuted in a long and learned speech by Bishop Andrewes Trask was put in the pillory, and is said afterwards to have recanted his errors, but Mrs Trask was imprisoned for as many as fifteen or sixteen years "her sex," says Fuller, "as pliable to receive as tenacious to retain, had weakness enough to embrace an error, and obstinacy too much to forsake it" [Fuller's *Ch Hist* x 61] Of Trask himself it is recorded that he became an Antinomian before his death, and that when he died "at one of his friend's houses, he was by his followers laid in a grave contrary to the manner that other men lie, but before he was covered the master of the house where he died caused him to be taken up and laid in the ordinary way" His widow directed that her body should be buried in an open field, which was done, but this was a not uncommon practice with the extreme Puritans [Pagitt's *Heresiography*, pp 163-222, ed 1662] The sect of Traskites began to be called Seventh-day men at the end of the century, as is noticed in Chamberlain's "Present State of England for 1702," p 258

TRIA CAPITULA This title is connected with one of those Imperial attempts to bring about the reunion of sects with the Church by means of secular edicts, of which the "Henoticon," "Ecthesis," and "Type," are other conspicuous examples

The Emperor Justinian having, in the year 542, been shocked by some of the writings of Origen, published an edict, in which nine of the chief Origenist errors were set forth and condemned, Origen himself, though long since dead, being also anathematized. Among the many Origenists of the time was Theodore, the Monophysite Bishop of Cæsarea in Cappadocia, who, upon the publication of this edict, devised a plan by which to avenge the memory of Origen, and to strengthen the position of the Monophysites Having interest at the Imperial Court, he succeeded in persuading the Emperor that the Acephali might be restored to the Church and reconciled to the decrees of Chalcedon, if the writings under three "heads" or "chapters" which he named were condemned, and so ceased to become stumbling-blocks to them by seeming to support the Nestorian heresy. These were [1] the Epistle of Theodoret against the twelve Anathemas of St Cyril, [2] the Epistle of Ibas of Edessa to Maris, and [3] the works of Theodore of Mopsuestia As all these writings had carried weight with the Council of Chalcedon, the condemnation of them by Justinian would be, to a certain extent, a repudiation of that council, and so a recognition of the Monophysites condemned by it Justinian was attracted by the plausible suggestion of reconciling the Acephali to the Church, and, without seeing these consequences, published the Edict of the Three Chapters [A D 544], giving a profession of his own faith, and anathematizing the three works above named

The Emperor's Edict was subscribed by the four Eastern patriarchs, and some bishops who refused to subscribe it were deposed After some time and much hesitation it was also assented to by Vigilius, Bishop of Rome, a saving clause being added by him, that in doing so he did not condemn the Council of Chalcedon This assent Vigilius afterwards retracted when he had been excommunicated by a council held at Carthage, and eventually [A D 550] he declared the Eastern bishops to be separated from the communion of Rome The condemnation of the Three Chapters, with a similar reservation respecting the Council of Chalcedon, was however confirmed by the fifth General Council [A D 553], the second Council of Constantinople [Mansi, *Concil* ix 61, 181, 487 Natal Alex v 502]

TRIFORMIANS [TRISCILIDÆ]

TRIPHYSITES Those divines who, at the fourteenth and fifteenth Councils of Toledo [A D 684, 688], carried their opposition to the Monophysites and Monothelites to such an extreme that they declared a belief not only in Christ's distinct Divine and Human natures, but also in a third nature resulting from the union of the two

TRISACRAMENTARIANS A controversial name given to those reformers who maintained that there are three Sacraments necessary to salvation, namely, Baptism, the Lord's Supper, and Absolution This opinion was held by some Lutherans at Leipsic, and was authoritatively set forth as the doctrine of the Church of England in the "Institution of a Christian Man," which was published in the year 1536

TRISCILIDÆ. A sect of Sabellian heretics mentioned by Philaster [*Hær* xciii], Augustine [*Hær* lxxiv], and Prædestinatus [*Hær* lxxiv], as maintaining the opinion that the Divine Nature is composed of three parts, one of which is named the Father, the second part the Son, and the third the Holy Ghost, and that the union of these three parts constitutes the Holy Trinity

In condemning this heresy Philaster uses expressions very similar to some in the Athanasian hymn, "Ergo est vera persona Patris quæ misit Filium, et est vera persona Filii quæ advenit de Patre, et est vera persona Spiritus quæ a Filio et Patre missa est. Trium itaque harum personarum una est veritas, majestas et substantiæ æqualitas et divinitas sempiterna Qualis est enim immensa et inenarranda Patris persona talis est et Filii, talis est et Sancti Spiritus, ut in distinctione nominum ac trium personarum non sit aliqua naturæ diversitas" [Philaster, *Hær* xciii]

TRITHEISTS A sect, or more properly speaking, a school of sectarians, which arose among the Monophysites in the sixth century, and whose distinctive dogma was that, instead of there being an Unity of Persons in the Trinity, each Person has a distinct and separate Essence or Substance, though all three Substances are similar to each other

St Cyril of Jerusalem attributes the origin of Tritheism in its broadest form to Marcion [Cyr Hier *Catech* xvi], and St Hilary associates it with the heresy of Photinus [Hilar *de Synod* xxii 56] Theodoret also mentions it as one of the tenets of the PERATÆ [Theod *Hær. fab* i.] But although St Augustine several times uses expressions guarding against the idea that each separate Person is a separate Deity, he does not refer to it as an opinion which had gained any degree of prominence in his time, but rather as one into which there was a danger of falling by recoil from the opposite error of Sabellianism

The Tritheists of the sixth century did not, however, hold the opinion in its broad form, and would have shrunk from any such statement as that there are three Gods In their controversies with the orthodox, the Monophysites had learned to study Aristotle and to apply his reasonings respecting human nature to that for which they were not suited, the mystery of the Divine Nature The first who was thus led on to a philosophical theory of Tritheism is said to have been Ascusnages, a learned Monophysite professor at Constantinople, who was banished for his heresy by the Emperor Justinian [Greg Abulphar in Asseman *Bibl Orient Vatic* i 328] His opinions were caught up by one of his Alexandrian pupils, who afterwards received the name of Philoponus from his great industry [PHILOPONISTS] With him was associated for many years a Bishop of Tarsus named Conon, who afterwards separated from him on a subtle question respecting the resurrection of the body [CONONISTS], and another named Eugenius

The error of Philoponus and other Tritheists arose from the Monophysite error itself To support the latter opinion against the Catholics they maintained that "nature" [φύσις] and "person" [ὑπόστασις] are identical terms, and that each person or nature was possessed of a distinct individuality [αὐτοτελῶς] Thus, they argued, it could not be truly said there are two natures in Christ, for to say so would be to say that there are two Persons, and therefore two Christs From this the transition to philosophical Tritheism is inevitable, since, if Personality involves separate Individuality, it involves the consequence that each Person of the Godhead must be distinct from each other Person, and the three Hypostases, being each Divine, cannot be called One God Such were the opinions maintained by Philoponus and his adherents, and it is clear that they are justly called Tritheists [Philopon Διαιτητής, in Joann Damasc *de Hæres* lxxxiii , Niceph *Hist Eccl* xviii 45 , Leont Byzant *de Sectis*, v *ad fin*]

The Tritheism of the sixth century was revived by Roscellin in the eleventh, and his Nominalistic opinion that the Name God is the abstract idea of a genus containing the three Persons called the Father, the Son, and the Holy Ghost, was opposed by St Anselm in his treatise "De fide Trinitatis et de Incarnatione Verbi contra blasphemias Rucelini " It was also condemned by the Council of Soissons [A D 1092], before whom Roscellin was obliged to declare his recantation

In the year 1691 the heresy was again revived by Dr William Sherlock, the father of Bishop Sherlock, and Dean of St Paul's, in a work entitled "A Vindication of the Doctrine of the Holy and Ever-Blessed Trinity " This was opposed by Dr South, and a long controversy ensued between the two Divines In 1695 a sermon was preached before the University of Oxford, in which the preacher maintained the theory of Dr Sherlock, that "There are three infinite distinct minds and substances in the Trinity," and that "the Three Persons in the Trinity are three distinct infinite minds or spirits, and three individual substances " These propositions were condemned by the authorities of the University as "false, impious, and heretical," and the decree of the heads of houses was made as public as possible The controversy which followed was of so serious a character that an Order in Council for its suppression was issued on February 3rd, 1695 In this Order, it is directed "[1] That no preacher whatsoever, in his Sermon or Lecture, do presume to deliver any other doctrine concerning the Blessed Trinity than that which is contained in the Holy Scriptures, and is agreeable to the three Creeds and the Thirty-nine Articles of Religion, [2] That in the explication of this doctrine they carefully avoid all new terms, and confine themselves to such ways of expression as have been commonly used in the Church, [3] That care be taken in this matter especially to observe the fifty-third Canon of this Church, which forbids public opposition between preachers, and that above all things they abstain from bitter invectives and scurrilous language against all persons whatsoever , [4] That the foregoing directions be also observed by those who write anything concerning the said doctrine " At the same time measures were taken to suppress the publication of Antitrinitarian books, which seem to have flowed from the press abundantly in the course of the controversy. [Cardwell's *Docum Ann* ii 339.]

In the last century the speculations of Hutchinson led him to adopt a theory respecting the personality in the Divine Essence which he based upon the analogy and correlation of fire, light, and air [HUTCHINSONIANS], and which was very nearly similar in its logical consequences to that of the older Tritheists

TROPICI. Those who explain away, by figurative interpretations, texts of Scripture which Catholic faith and tradition require to be otherwise interpreted Athanasius gives the name Tropici to the Pneumatomachi in so marked a manner that it has narrowly escaped becoming a proper name of that sect [Athanas *ad Serap* i 2, 10, 21] For example, they argued that in 1 Tim v 21, the name of the Holy Spirit would naturally follow the Names of Father and Son, that the term "elect angels," tropically taken, includes the Holy Spirit, the inference being that the Holy Spirit is a created angel The word Tropici has been used again by Catholic writers to describe those who err regarding the Holy Sacraments, and explain as mere figure the words of our Lord in John iii 5, Matt xxvi 26 It is not our province to enter into the subject of the interpretation of Scripture and it is sufficient therefore to observe that figurative interpretations are a common resource of heretics, who reject or undervalue the office of the Church as the guardian of truth and interpreter of Scripture, and consequently make light of the tradition and consensus of Catholic doctors "Ita semper hæretici, aut nudas et simplices voces conjecturis quo volunt rapiunt, aut rursus conditionales et rationales, simplicitatis conditione dissolvunt" [Tertull *adv Marc* iv 19]

TROPITÆ. Heretics who held that our Lord acquired a body of flesh by conversion of the substance of the Godhead into the substance of flesh an opinion which arose in the latter time of the Arian controversy among those who, maintaining the true divinity of the Son of God, and rightly desiring to maintain His sinlessness, were perplexed by the erroneous assumption that the human body, as such, is and cannot but be the seat of sin To avoid the impiety of attributing a sinful body to our Lord, they devised the tenet that the body of Christ is consubstantial with His divinity, which passes into the somewhat more definite proposition that the substance of the Word is converted into the substance of flesh, and that the flesh being in the form of man is thus called human

This heresy was first dealt with by Athanasius in his Epistle to Epictetus, A D 370 Troubles had been caused in Achaia by men who denied the perfect manhood of Christ Epictetus, Bishop of Corinth, requested Athanasius to answer them, and the answer is directed against the present heresy Epiphanius, who quotes the letter at full length, introduces it by stating that Apollinaris of Laodicæa was at the head of those who denied the true Incarnation of Christ, and that among them there was a great variety of opinions He distinguishes those who held the consubstantiality of the Divine nature and of the flesh of our Lord from those who denied His assumption of a human soul, clearly implying that the two heresies were not at first held concurrently by the same party Apollinaris was the main assertor of the general proposition that the Son of God did not assume that which in man is the seat of sin, and varied applications of this proposition were made by his followers Athanasius deals with one of them without naming Apollinaris [APOLLINARIANS] Athanasius states his subject thus Ποῖος ᾅδης ἐξερεύξατο, ὁμοούσιον εἰπεῖν τὸ ἐκ Μαρίας σῶμα τῇ τοῦ λόγου θεότητι, ἢ ὅτι ὁ λόγος εἰς σάρκα καὶ ὀστᾶ καὶ τρίχας καὶ ὅλον σῶμα μεταβέβληται, καὶ ἠλλάγη τῆς ἰδίας φύσεως, He shews that this tenet makes the very nature of the Godhead passible, since it asserts the body which suffered to be consubstantial with the divinity that it introduces a fourth Person into the Trinity, and makes the whole Godhead consubstantial with a body stated to be human that it declares the Son to take on Him not the seed of Abraham, but His own Divine Nature that it annuls the office and prerogative of Mary [Epiph *Hær* lxxvii]

In the two books "Contra Apollinarium" Athanasius distinguishes the several heresies [i 2, ii 18], and regarding the present heresy dwells on the immutability of the Uncreated Essence A belief in the possibility of the conversion of the Godhead into flesh almost necessarily presupposes the reception of the Cabbalistic doctrine that all matter is an emanation from God And Athanasius remarks, as if leading us to the source of the present heresy, that Valentinus fancied the flesh to be a part of Deity, and so concluded that the Passion was common to the whole Trinity [*ibid* ii 3]. This brings us to Tertullian's tract "De Carne Christi," which was written to defend the reality of Christ's Body against Marcion, Apelles, Basilides, and Valentinus Of these, the opinion of Valentinus alone concerns the present question He held that Christ's flesh was of a spiritual substance or nature "Licuit et Valentino ex privilegio hæretico, carnem Christi spiritalem comminisci [Tertull *de Carne Chr* xv] This general assertion the Tropitæ defined in the highest possible sense Athanasius, as we have seen, represents them as using the word ὁμοούσιος of the two substances "Tropitæ sunt qui dicunt conversum verbum in carnem," is Philaster's definition [Philast *Hær* lxx] The conception of consubstantiality is necessary for the conception of the conversion Fabricius remarks that the heresy is confuted by Tertullian. Athanasius and Tertullian give the two branches of the argument in opposition, the former shewing the absurdities of the statement, the latter proving the true human nature of the Body of Christ The Council of Chalcedon determined that the two Natures in Christ are united ἀτρέπτως

TSABIANS [MENDÆANS]

TSCHERNOBOLTZI [WJETKAERS]

TUBINGEN SCHOOL [RATIONALISTS]

TUMBLERS [TUNKERS]

TUNKERS A sect of American Baptists, originally founded by some German emigrants early in the eighteenth century They take their name from the German word "Tunken," to dip, and hence "Tunkers," or as sometimes erroneously spelt "Dunkers," simply means "Dippers," or those who baptize by immersion but it is alleged that the sect originated in Germany about 1708, independently of the Mennonites, although both were comprehended in the name "Die Taufer" The Tunkers are also called "Tumblers," a piece of American slang signifying the gesture made by the baptized as they kneel in the water and dip their heads in the act of baptism But the name which they assume for themselves is that of "Brethren"

The Tunkers of America were an offshoot of a Baptist community at Schwartzenau, on the bank of the river Eder, in Germany, some members of which emigrated to America under the leadership of Conrad Peysel and others about the year 1719 Peysel afterwards separated from the rest and formed a peculiar settlement at "Ephrata," in Lancaster county, about fifty miles from Philadelphia Here he and his companions built a town in the form of a triangle, having a large orchard in the midst and being surrounded by a belt of mulberry and apple trees There they dwelt in wooden houses of three storeys height, which were each a kind of monastery They dressed very much in the style of monks and nuns, men and women lived under different roofs, used a vegetable diet, and practised considerable mortification Marriage was not forbidden among them but when couples were married they were required to remove from Ephrata Settlements were thus formed by the emigration of married Tunkers to other parts of the United States, and they are now found to the number of eight thousand or nine thousand in Virginia, New England, Maryland, Ohio, and Indiana, as well as in Pennsylvania

The Tunkers still maintain some of their original character, but they have now an organized ministry of unpaid "bishops," "teachers' and "deacons," whereas formerly their religious services were conducted on the principle of the Quakers They dress in a similar way to the Quakers, and like them refuse to take oaths or to engage in military or naval service As a rule they hold their religious meetings in private houses, but meeting-houses are beginning to appear among them Among their religious observances are "Love-feasts" similar to those held by the Methodists and they also, as do the older Mennonites or Flemings, maintain the custom of the Lavipedium, or ceremonial washing of one another's feet, a custom generally observed on Maundy Thursday in mediæval times in all monastic communities, and by English sovereigns until the Revolution The Tunkers also anoint their sick with oil as a means of recovery, and generally discard the assistance of medical men and the use of medicine Some among them are also Sabbatarians in the strict sense, observing the Sabbath or Saturday as their day of rest instead of Sunday or the Lord's Day

The Tunkers, like the Quakers, represent those early and rigid sectarians of the Sub-Reformation period who in England acquired the name of Puritans But unlike the warlike Puritans and the pugnacious Quakers, the Tunkers have always kept strictly aloof from war and politics, and have retained a name which was given to them at first, that of "The Harmless People"

TURLUPINS The French name for the Brethren of the Free Spirit The origin of the word is unknown though it is thought to be connected with wolfish or predatory habits The Turlupins appear to have had their principal seat in the Isle of France, where they were exterminated A D 1372 [Mosheim, *de Beghard* p 413]

TURNERITES [Southcottians]

TYPE An edict promulgated by the Emperor Constans [A D 648] under the title of the Formulary of the Faith [τύπος τῆς πίστεως], with the intention of quieting the Monothelite controversy, and especially of setting aside the Imperial Edict called the Ecthesis, in which the Monothelite heresy had been dogmatically maintained The text of this document will be found in Harduin's *Concilia*, iii 823 It did not contain any statement of doctrine, but simply forbade all discussion on the Monothelite dogma of one will in Christ on the one hand, or on the orthodox doctrine of two wills on the other The publication of the Type was, however, considered as an attempt to suppress the defence of Catholic doctrine, and it was condemned with the Ecthesis by one hundred and six bishops in the Lateran Council [A D 649] For thus causing the condemnation of an Imperial Edict the Bishop of Rome, Martin I was arrested, and exiled by the Emperor Constans to the island of Maxia where he died shortly afterwards [Monothelites]

U

UBIQUITARIANS A school of Protestant Divines, who promulgated the opinion that the Body of Christ is everywhere by reason of its union with His Divine Nature, and that thus it is present in the Holy Eucharist This opinion had been entertained by some of Luther's Protestant coadjutors, although he himself indignantly repudiated it It originated with Brentzen, a canon of Wittenberg, about A D 1525 [*de Personali Unione*, etc, Brentii *Opp* viii 831], but it was not embodied in any public document until the "Formula of Concord" was drawn up at Bergen in A D 1577, when it became recognised as a doctrine of the Lutheran Confession. The doctrine again became a subject of controversy early in the seventeenth century between the Divines of Tubingen and Giessen, the former supporting the Ubiquitarian theory, and the latter opposing it with great energy The controversy was carried on by many publications on either side, and drew out more minute and speculative definitions than have been drawn out by that on Transubstantiation The Ubiquitarians are strong opponents of the Calvinistic and Zwinglian theories of the Holy Eucharist, and their dogma is in fact a revulsion from them [Cramer, *Enchirid controvers Ubiquit* 1613 Dorner's *Person of Christ* II ii 280, *sqq* 422] •

UCKEWALLISTS One of the sects into which the Old Flemings, or Strict Anabaptist followers of Menno, divided They took their name from Uke Walles, a Frieslander, who, although a very illiterate man, gathered a party around him, intent upon keeping up the severe discipline of the original Mennonites In the year 1637 he also began, in conjunction with a companion named John Lens, to propagate a doctrine of Universalism, grounded on the dogma that even Judas might hope for salvation He was excommunicated by the Mennonites of Groningen, and banished from the city by its magistrates, but settled down in East Friesland His peculiar opinion respecting Judas does not seem to have been adopted by his followers, and after his death they ceased to retain his name as a badge of separation, and have not since been distinguished from the body of the Old Flemings

ULSTER, REMONSTRANT SYNOD OF An Unitarian secession from the Presbyterian body in Ulster, which under the leadership of seventeen ministers formed itself into a separate community in the year 1830

ULSTER, SYNOD OF The chief body of Presbyterians in the North of Ireland [PRESBYTERIANS]

ULTRAMONTANISTS Those who recognise the Papal claim of supremacy over every part of the Church of Christ, as well as over every sovereign within its boundaries · and also that of the Pope's personal Infallibility

Ultramontanism dates from Gregory VII. [Hildebrand, A D 1073-85], who propounded the following claims "Quod solus Papa possit uti imperialibus insigniis,—quod solius Papæ pedes omnes principes deosculentur,—quod illi liceat Imperatores deponere,—quod a fidelitate iniquorum subjectos potest absolvere" These views are principally maintained in the Italian peninsula, but it is the tone generally adopted by English Seceders. It is not held that the Pope is nothing without the Church, but that the Church is nothing without the Pope Without revelation there is no religion, without a Church revelation has no meaning, without a Pope the Church has no existence [Carové] The free action of national churches is wholly superseded by such pretensions The theory has apparently grown up from the feudal relations of the Papacy as a temporal power. Though it took its rise under Hildebrand, it did not attain its full development till the fifteenth century [Fleury, *Hist Eccl* xciii 15] But an assertion of authority so incompatible with Catholic liberty has naturally aroused opposition on this side of the Alps in the Gallican and German Churches, and in the Swiss cantons Works written in defence of national liberties and ecclesiastical independence have usually obtained a place in the Index Expurgatorius and the Ultramontane tone of the present day is far in advance of the Romanist writers of the Reformation period.

Bellarmine's statements are important as regards Papal Infallibility He sets forth the opinion of Divines in four several propositions [1] That "the Roman Pontiff ruling any point, even in an Œcumenical Council, may be guilty of heresy and of teaching others heresy, which has *de facto* happened" This he says is flatly heretical, [2] That "the Roman Pontiff may be heretical and teach heresy, if he rule anything apart from synodical assistance, and this has happened *de facto*" He quotes various writers who maintain that infallibility of judgment in matters of faith is vested not in the Pope, but only in the Church or in a General Council This opinion, he says, strictly speaking, is not heretical, because many who hold this opinion are still tolerated in the Church [3] That "the Pope cannot in any way be heretical, nor teach heresy publicly, even though he rule any point on his own responsibility alone." this opinion he states to be probable though not certain [4] That "whether the Pope can be heretical or no, he can rule nothing heretical, as a point to be believed by the whole Church," which is the common opinion of nearly all Catholics, as Thomas Aq *Sec Sec qu* 1, *art* 10, Cajetanus, Eckius, Melchior Canus, etc This fourth opinion "certissima est et asserenda" [*de Rom Pont* iv 2] Jeremy Taylor argues from the date of the authorities, chiefly Gallican doctors, cited under [2], that for more than a thousand years from the foundation of the Church it knew nothing of Papal infallibility Bellarmine limits his view to the fourth opinion, expressed in the thesis "The Pope, when he teaches the whole Church, can in no case err in matters pertaining to the faith" This is proved, he says, from the prayer of our Lord for St Peter, that his "faith fail not" [Luke xxii 31, 32], though it is explained in three several ways as by Gallican divines of the entire Church, or of St Peter as representative of the whole Church, and accordingly it was vouchsafed to the Church that its faith should never fail To this he objects, that the words of our Lord are applicable, according to their grammatical construction, to St Peter alone, and whereas it is said "Satan hath desired to sift *you*" [plur ὑμᾶς], the prayer is restricted personally to St Peter, "I have prayed for *thee*" He disposes also of a second opinion that the Saviour alluded only to the grace of perseverance, and settles down on a third, viz that our Lord, as Mediator, obtained for Peter two privileges [1] That he might "never" fall from the faith, however tempted of Satan, which is somewhat more than the grace of perseverance, and involves unbroken continuity of steadfastness, as well as final persistence, and [2] that he, as Pontiff, might never teach anything contrary to the faith, or in other words that none of his successors in the see should teach anything contrary to the faith The first privilege, he says, may have pertained to the Apostle alone, and not have descended to successors, the second certainly did so descend

Bellarmine, as the mouthpiece of that which is now termed Ultramontanism, makes infallibility in matters of doctrine the personal attribute of the Pope According to the Gallican view, it is the consent of the Church that is the "vis viva" of the Pope's decision, while he himself is its mouthpiece, and embodies every promise that had ever been made to the Church in its collective capacity Even Bellarmine, however, contemplates cases in which it may be lawful for temporal princes to offer both active and passive resistance to illegal and violent acts on the part of the Pope "Itaque sicut licet resistere Pontifici invadenti corpus, ita licet resistere invadenti animas vel turbanti Rem publicam, et multo magis si Ecclesiam destruere videretur Licet, inquam, ei resistere, non faciendo quod jubet, et impediendo ne exsequatur voluntatem suam vide de hac re Cajetanum Tr de Auct Papæ et Concilii 27, et Johannem de Turrecremata ii. 106" [*de Rom. Pont* ii 29, 30]

Among modern assertors of the Ultramontane theory the most strenuous are English Romanists, especially neophytes, among Continental writers are Bishop Ziegler, *Das Katholische Glaubensprincip*; Carové, *Die alleinseligmachende Kirche*, also *Der Papst im Verhaltniss zum Katholicismus*, and the Abbé Lamennais, who strenuously asserted the independence of the Church in its relations with the State in his journal *l'Avenir*

But the work that has done more than any other to give a scientific character and a lasting influence to Ultramontanism is Mohler's *Symbolik*, which first appeared A D 1832, and has since spread throughout Europe and America in rapidly recurring editions Of all the theologians of the Roman Communion Mohler was the best versed in Protestant literature, and none was more competent than he to attack the principles of philosophical Protestantism as developed in the school of Schleiermacher He casts the apple of discord among the rival sects of Protestantism by exhibiting to the light, like Bossuet, but with infinitely greater skill, the variations of Protestantism, and he shews so clearly the superiority of Catholic over Protestant principle as to make the reader wonder how the latter could for a moment stand in presence of the former Absolute truth, as he makes it appear, is on the one side, unmitigated error on the other This book first sounded the advance to the Ultramontane party, which for some time rolled on without a serious discouragement or a check

Thus, when Pius IX succeeded to the Papal throne, A D 1846, just three centuries after the assembly of the Council of Trent, the way had been prepared for the onward march of spiritual pretension. The "cultus" due to the Virgin seemed to occupy the new Pope's whole attention, and before the first year of his pontificate was over, the Jesuit Perrone dedicated to him a treatise on the question, whether the Immaculate Conception were not a doctrine that might be formally confirmed to the Church by a dogmatic decree A D 1849, a Papal brief was circulated throughout the Churches of the Roman Communion, to feel the pulse as it were, to ascertain how the Church stood affected towards a final and authoritative decision of the question Appearances being propitious, a number of bishops favourable to the promulgation of the dogma were assembled to advise with the Pope, not as to the truth of the dogma, which was a foregone conclusion, but whether or not the proper time had come for action The new dogma was pronounced by them infallible [A D 1854], and all present solemnly did homage to the Holy See thus fortified by a dogma the first germ of which was laid in the darker ages of the Church The assembly consisted of 53 cardinals, 43 archbishops, and 100 bishops It may be noted that this was the individual act of the Pope, *per se*, there was no synodal authority, and the bishops present had been picked out for their known opinions Yet the decree was accepted by the Church at large with a jubilant enthusiasm, medals were struck and festivals organized in commemoration of the act

The history of the next high venture of Ultramontanism, the promulgation [A D 1870] of the dogma of Papal Infallibility, with its antecedent stormy discussions and subsequent remonstrances, is still to be written It is sufficient to say that it has aroused serious opposition Hefele, Bishop of Rothenberg, the most learned prelate of the Roman Communion, the heroic Dupanloup, Bishop of Orleans, and the accomplished divine, Professor Dollinger, are in the front rank of the opposition [OLD CATHOLICS]

UMBILICANIMI [HESYCHASTS]

UNIATES Eastern Christians in external communion with the See of Rome, some being seceders from the orthodox Eastern Churches, and others from the Nestorian and Jacobite communities

The efforts which had been made at the Councils of Lyons [A D 1274] and Florence [A D 1439] to restore external communion between Eastern and Western Christendom were renewed by the Jesuits after the Council of Trent on the border-land which divides the two, and where fusion seemed most practicable, in the then great kingdom of Poland Sigismund III was a Roman Catholic, elected to the crown of Poland as the grandson of Sigismund I, but carrying with him to Poland the results of an education in Western Europe, being the son of John III of Sweden and of Catharine, daughter of Sigismund I He became King of Poland in A D 1587 at the age of twenty-one, when he was impressible enough to be a zealous agent of the Jesuits Possevin and Scarga who accompanied him to his new country Under their advice he at once began to take measures for reconciling the Polish Church to Rome, and won over some of the bishops to their plans In the year 1590 these plans were sufficiently matured to be brought before the clergy and the influential nobility The Archbishop of Kieff, therefore, at the king's request, summoned a synod of his clergy at Brest, in Lithuania, to whom he represented the necessity of a union with Rome, and the advantages which would thereby accrue to their country and to their Church, and, indeed, it was certainly not only more flattering to the self-love of the clergy, but even more congenial to the feelings of the more intelligent of them, to depend upon the head of the Western Church, who was surrounded by all the prestige that wealth and power can give, and whose authority, supported by men of the most eminent talents and learning, was acknowledged by powerful and civilized nations, than on the patriarch of Constantinople, the slave of an infidel sovereign, by whose appointment he held his dignity, and presiding over a church degraded by gross ignorance and superstition The project found much favour with the clergy, but met with a strong opposition from the laity, and could not at that time be carried into effect The king, still persevering in his intentions, bestowed all the patronage at his disposal on the Romanizing clergy, and discouraged the national party by every means in his power The two Jesuits also worked towards the same end, and succeeded in winning over to the king's side so many of the bishops, that it was considered safe to summon another synod It met at the same place as before on December 2nd, 1594, and the two Jesuits were permitted to take part in its deliberations After some discussion the archbishop and several bishops were persuaded to give their assent to the scheme of union which had been proposed at the Council of Florence, thus recognising the "Filioque" or double procession of the Nicene Creed, and acknowledging the supremacy of the Pope They stood out, however, for retaining the use of the vernacular Sclavonic in the celebration of Divine service, and for the ritual as well as the discipline of the Eastern Church Two bishops were sent to announce this event at Rome, where they were received with great distinction by Pope Clement VIII After their return to Poland the king, in 1596, ordered the convocation of a synod for the publication and introduction of the union It assembled again at Brest, and the Archbishop of Kieff, as well as the other prelates who had subscribed to that union, made a solemn proclamation of this act, addressed thanks to the Almighty for having brought back the stray sheep into the pale of his Church They also excommunicated all those who opposed the union The opposite party, including many of the clergy and the principal men among the nobility, with Constantine Ostrogski, Palatine of Kieff, at their head, met this by a public protest, in which they repudiated the acts of the Uniates, and declared their unaltered attachment to the ancient Church of their country and to the Patriarch of Constantinople, whom they acknowledged for their ecclesiastical head

Sigismund followed up this reconciliation of Lithuania to Rome by depriving the opposite party of their churches and convents, and by forbidding, under severe penalties, the propagation of Greek doctrines throughout his dominions, and he became sanguine of extending the union with Rome till it comprehended the whole of the Eastern Church The rest of his reign was so occupied with disastrous wars that he was unable to carry his designs any further But the Uniates still maintained their ground, and thus the Church of Little Russia was divided into two communions, each retaining the rites and doctrines of Eastern Christendom, but the one acknowledging for its patriarchal head the Patriarch of Constantinople, the other the Bishop of Rome This division of the Church continued in full force until the partition of Poland in the year 1772 At that time between two and three millions of the Uniates gave up their allegiance to Rome and returned to full communion with the Orthodox Eastern Churches In 1839 two millions more were reconciled But there are still about 300,000 in Russia and 3,000,000 in Austria [Krasinski's *Reform in Poland*, Mouravieff's *Hist of the Church of Russia*, Neale's *Patriarchate of Alexandria*] The other Eastern communities in union with the Roman See are not sufficiently important to be noticed in any detail They are chiefly among the Nestorians of Syria, the Bulgarians, and the Christians of St Thomas at Malabar

UNIONITÆ [SABELLIANS]

UNITARIANS The term Unitarian may be used of all who, while denying the distinction of Persons in the Godhead, affirm that they only hold in its true sense the Monarchia, the Unity of God The course of Unitarianism, therefore, in this comprehensive sense, may be traced in the present work in the articles MONARCHIANS, ANTI-TRINITARIANS, SOCINIANS, ending with the present article Modern Unitarians, the school of Priestley, who are principally of England and America, are the successors rather than the lineal descendants of the Socinians The separate congregations of Socinians in England, which were never numerous, died out by the end of the seventeenth century, the Unitarian sect was formed out of the Arianism floating in the Church and in dissent This Arianism sprung from the Dutch Remonstrant theology, which was largely studied in England [ARMINIANISM] Historically, Arminianism has led to Arianism, and thence to Socinianism and Unitarianism "A Socinian tincture is known to have infected the party with which Episcopius was connected, which in Gerard Vorstius, almost at the commencement, broke out in offensive manifestations, and which brought some of its leading men (for example Grotius, Le Clerc, Wetstein) into such dangerous proximity to the Racovian school on several important points, that they were ever incurring the suspicion of actually belonging to it Certainly Episcopius, in adopting his position," that the divine filiation of Christ is not *de fide*, "took the ground which was first formally propounded by the Racovian divines, and which afterwards received its most elaborate defence from the pen of an avowed Socinian, Dr Zwicker of Dantzic"[1] The working of this theology soon showed itself In the year 1691 appeared Dr Bury's "Naked Gospel" The book was publicly burnt and the writer expelled the University of Oxford.

In 1708 Whiston published his Essay upon the Apostolical Constitutions, to prove that the Eusebian, or commonly called Arian, doctrine, was the doctrine of the primitive Church This had been the object of Bury's treatise, and of other treatises by followers of Zwicker, against whom Bull had, in 1703, written his "Primitiva Traditio" From this time Whiston lost no opportunity of propagating his opinions, but controversy collected itself chiefly around the writings of a man of far higher powers—an antagonist "dignus quocum contendat Achilles" —Samuel Clarke In 1712 Clarke published his "Scripture Doctrine of the Trinity" A controversy immediately ensued between him and Wells, Nelson, Gastrell and others Whitby wrote on Clarke's side, and replied also to Bull Convocation then interposed, and the controversy became extremely voluminous, the most noticeable writers on Clarke's side being Whitby and Emlyn, against him Welchman, Nelson, Bennett, and Waterland[2] On the Antitrinitarian side some of the disputants held Arian, some Socinian principles[3] The controversy was renewed with greater warmth when the Bishop of London in 1718 forbad the Arian alteration of the Doxology which had been introduced at St James's, Westminster [compare Sozom *H E.* iii 20, Theod *H E* ii. 24]

No less voluminous was the controversy among the dissenters It began with the resolution of the ministers of Devonshire and Cornwall to impose a test concerning our Lord's Divinity This was done to detect the opinions of Pierce and Hallett of Exeter, who were said to be Arians[4] Pierce was ejected in 1719 The matter was laid before the whole body of dissenting ministers which met at Salter's Hall, and it was carried by four votes that there should not be a particular declaration of faith in the Holy Trinity in the advices under consideration for Exeter. Appeal was made in print to Hoadly,

[1] Appendix (by Dr Fairbairn) to Edinburgh transl of Dorner, *On the Person of Christ*, div II iii p 347 This appendix is a very valuable paper regarding the period we are considering

[2] *An Account of the considerable Books and Pamphlets in the controversy concerning the Trinity* was published in 1720

[3] The Representation of the State of Religion, adopted unanimously by a Committee of both Houses of Convocation but rejected by the Upper House, states "Adversaries arose who scattered the poison of Arian and Socinian heresies through all parts of this kingdom The doctrine of a Trinity of Persons in the Unity of the Godhead was then denied and scoffed at, the satisfaction made for the sins of mankind by the precious blood of Christ was renounced and exploded, the ancient creeds of the Church were represented as unwarrantable impositions A religious assembly was set up where divine worship was publicly performed in a way agreeable to the principles of the Unitarians, and weekly sermons were preached in defence of them" This assembly was understood to be Emlyn's, held after his return from Ireland [see a tract, *The Nation vindicated from the Aspersions*, etc, part ii p 12] The representation drawn up by the Upper House contained a paragraph almost identical with the former of the two quoted, but had no mention of Emlyn's lecture These representations are of considerable interest in the Church history of the time They were published by Bowyer, London, 1711—the former of them, with an amendment of the Lower House about the "damnable doctrine of resistance" (which is not in Atterbury's draft), in *History of Parliament and Convocation*, 1711, by W P

[4] See Whiston's *Memoirs*, i. p 121, ed 1753

and his authority quoted to shew that framing and imposing of creeds was mere Popery Several other dissenting preachers were dismissed by their congregations about the same time [Calamy's *Life*, ii 403, Chandler's *Hist of Persecution*, p 352] Blackburne's Inquiry into the right of establishing systematic confessions of faith and doctrine [*The Confessional*, 1766], and the public movement of the Feathers Tavern petition [A D 1772] were an attempt to allow Arianism and Socinianism in the Church Blackburne was certainly an Antitrinitarian, though of what particular form it is difficult to say [*Confessional*, 2nd ed. p 359, Ridley's *Third Letter*, p 32] His conscience, however, was not one to do him harm, and he retained his preferment in the Church [1] But some clergy were more honest Lindsey resigned Catterick in 1773, and opened a conventicle in Essex Street, London Jebb gave up his preferment and turned physician Disney resigned Swinderby in 1782, and became Lindsey's colleague in Essex Street Several other clergy left the Church about the same time, and celebrated Unitarian worship after Dr Clarke's Reformed Liturgy in their private houses [*Hist View*, pp 498, 515, 542, 556] From the gathering of this congregation in Essex Street is to be dated Unitarianism in England Its leading men, who did for Unitarianism what Faustus Socinus did for Socinianism, were Priestley and Belsham Priestley, whose parents were orthodox dissenters, became an Arian, a Socinian, and lastly a Unitarian Belsham also was of a dissenting family He appears to have stepped at once from Calvinism to Unitarianism Priestley was but a sciolist in history and criticism Belsham was at least more cautious in his statement of doctrines, but the *Improved Version of the New Testament*, published in 1808, was easily shewn by Nares, Rennell and Laurence to be full of mistakes and falsifications Belsham's *Calm Inquiry*, published in 1811, is the ablest work of modern Unitarianism, and may be taken as a standard of Unitarian doctrine

Unitarians reject, out of the Socinian creed, the miraculous Conception of our Lord, His personal Ascension into Heaven after His Baptism to be instructed in His office, and His worship The atonement of Christ's death they utterly deny, Christ died, they say, simply as a martyr to the truth Jesus and His Apostles were supernaturally instructed for their office, that is, to reveal and prove the doctrine of eternal life The inspiration of the Scriptures is denied They allow that Christ was raised from the dead, and that He is, in some undefined sense, appointed to judge the world, but with no other power than can properly be assigned to a human being. In short, their religion is a religion of ethics, without a sense of the "sinfulness of sin," and without a Saviour.

It is the boast of the Unitarians that they have no standards of faith or tests of orthodoxy, which means only that they have no faith to maintain The latitude of the earlier sect in the application of their fundamental principle, the unity of God, is illustrated by the extraordinary fact, brought to notice by Leslie, denied by Priestley, but verified by Horsley, that in the reign of Charles II formal proposals of mutual recognition and friendly counsel were made by some Socinians to the ambassador of the Emperor of Morocco, on the ground that both held substantially the same belief. The Mahometan was more honest than the Unitarian, and refused to fraternize Horsley found the original Epistle in the Lambeth Library [Horsley, *Tracts in Controversy with Priestley*, 1812, App p 589, and the references there given] This sect, as has been shewn, was formed out of the Arians who had been engendered in the Church and in dissent Their places of worship were principally Presbyterian chapels, foundations of the Nonconformists and later Puritans [PRESBYTERIANS] [See *Manchester Socinian Controversy*, App i] In the census of 1851 returns were received from 229 congregations in England and Wales The Unitarian Calendar for 1871 gives about 380 congregations and mission stations The same authority states that in America there are 335 societies, with 306 ministers in Transylvania 106 congregations, with 50,000 members.

UNITARIAN BAPTISTS [BAPTISTS]

UNITAS FRATRUM [MORAVIANS]

UNITED BRETHREN [MORAVIANS]

UNITED BRETHREN IN CHRIST. A sect of Germans formed in America by William Otterbein, an emigrant of the Reformed Lutheran sect, in the year 1755 Being appointed as pastor of a congregation at Lancaster in Pennsylvania, Otterbein was impressed with a desire to unite the members of different sects in one body, the terms of communion with which should be of a less severe doctrinal kind than those customary among Lutheran and Calvinist sects, and based more upon personal convictions of religion Several congregations of this broad kind were established in the states of Maryland, Pennsylvania, and Virginia—the Lutherans, the Reformed Lutherans, the Mennonites contributing members from their respective bodies, and a few Methodists also joining them, and conferences of their ministers were held at Baltimore in the

[1] Fairbairn [App to *Dorner*, p 401] writes (of Clarke and Whitby) that "a singular want of openness and proper Christian candour seemed to have been the general characteristic of the party, none of them manfully acted out their convictions, and withdrew from a Church whose tenets on an important point of doctrine they no longer held" This verdict is just. It is more easy to acquit a Socinian layman (such as Firmin) who holds that there is a proper sense (though not the Catholic sense) in which Christ is God, and that worship is due to Him, of insincerity when he joins the worship of the Church, it is impossible to acquit of insincerity Arian or Unitarian clergymen Hoadly's real opinions may be learned from his prayers at the end of his "Plain Account of the Lord's Supper," which are manifestly Unitarian Clarke's recantation was no proper recantation, and he told Emlyn that he could not again subscribe the Articles, as if retention of preferment and office were not adherence to subscription. Whitby became latterly a decided Arian Several of the clergy satisfied their consciences by altering the Liturgy [See Whiston's *Memoirs*, 2nd ed p 218, Lindsey's *Historical View*, p 489]

year 1789. In the following year Otterbein and a coadjutor named Martin Boehm were appointed "superintendents," an office intended to be equivalent to that of bishops. It was agreed at first that a wide liberty as to doctrines and rites should be allowed, but before long it was found necessary to restrict this freedom, and at a conference held at Mount Pleasant, Pennsylvania, in the year 1815, a "confession" was drawn up according to the usual custom of Protestant sects. The subsequent form into which the sect settled was very similar to that of the Moravians, and when the use of the German language was discontinued in their chapels the number of their members increased considerably. In the year 1871 they were said to number 82,000.

UNITED EVANGELICAL CHURCH. An union of the Lutherans and the "Reformed" (or Calvinists), forming the largest of the three branches into which the Protestants of Germany are divided.

A voluntary Union of the two communities was established in some parts of South Prussia about the beginning of the nineteenth century, and in the year 1805 it had extended to many congregations, especially at Cologne, Wurzburg, and Munich. In 1810, King Frederick William took up the subject of union warmly, and issued an exhortation, which had the effect of promoting it greatly in Nassau and some other places. After his visit to England with the other allied Sovereigns in 1814, he drew up, chiefly with his own hands, a Liturgy, which was adopted in the Royal Chapel, and authorized for use elsewhere.[1] This step was followed by a royal proclamation, dated September 27th, 1817, in which the King declared his wish that the Lutherans and the Reformed throughout his dominions should be united in one community, and expressing his intention to set the example by taking part in an united celebration of the Holy Communion in the Royal Chapel at Potsdam on October 31st, the occasion of the Tercentenary of the Reformation. A few days afterwards, on October 1st, 1817, a synod assembled at Breslau, and subsequently one assembled at Berlin, readily adopted the proclamation, as did most of the ministers and laity throughout Prussia, the basis of the union being understood to be entirely governmental and ritual, all questions of doctrine being left as they had stood before. On the day mentioned by the King, October 31st, 1817, the people and ministers very generally followed his example, and thus the popular assent was given to the movement. Not long afterwards it was ordered that the distinctive names "Lutheran" and "Reformed" should be disused in all official documents, and the United Evangelical Church alone recognised as the national religion.

Notwithstanding a strong opposition from the Lutheran party, which was led by Harms, a pastor of Kiel (who published ninety-four "Theses" against the Union in imitation of Luther), the United Evangelical Church soon spread beyond the boundaries of Prussia. It was adopted in Nassau, Hanover and Bavaria in 1818, in Baden in 1821, in Hesse Cassel in 1822, and in Wurtemberg in 1827; but some of the States where Lutheranism was predominant declined to admit the change, nor did it extend either to Lutheran Austria on the one hand or to Calvinistic Switzerland on the other. Although, moreover, there was a nominal union in most parts of Prussia, the revised Service Book which the King set forth in 1821 was rejected by many congregations, and uniformity was far from being established even within the bounds of the united body.

On June 25th, 1830, at the celebration of the Tercentenary of the Augsburg Confession, the King directed that the Service Book (which had recently undergone a fresh revision) should be used in all churches; but a number of the Lutheran clergy refused to adopt it and were suspended, some of them, and some even of the laity, being treated with great severity, and imprisoned as criminals. The persecution of the Lutheran party was at length carried so far that the King proclaimed all Lutheran worship to be forbidden by the laws, and refused any toleration whatever to those who still adhered to the old communion, the greatest severities being shown in Silesia and in the Grand Duchy of Posen, where the predominating influence was strongly opposed to the new Church.

This persecution of the "Old Lutherans" was kept up until the death of Frederick William. He was succeeded by his pietistic son of the same name in 1840, and while a milder policy was introduced at once, in 1845 the Old Lutherans were allowed to organize themselves into a separate community, recognised and tolerated by the State, but not receiving any part of the funds appropriated to the support of public religion. [Hugh James Rose's *Protestantism in Germany*. Bunsen's *Signs of the Times*. Schaff's *Germany, its Theology, etc.*, Philadelphia, 1857. Kahnis, *Hist. Germ. Protestantism.*]

UNITED FREE CHURCH METHODISTS. [METHODISTS.]

UNITED ORIGINAL SECEDERS. This small body is the legitimate representative in Scotland of the first Secession Synod, which was formed in 1733, and was constituted in 1840 by the union of the remnants (with the exception of two congregations) of the two parties of BURGHERS and ANTIBURGHERS, which had not been absorbed into the Kirk of Scotland on the one hand, or into the United Secession (now the UNITED PRESBYTERIANS) on the other. Many of the congregations were however at that time in a

[1] Frederick, the first king of Prussia, had a translation of the English Prayer Book made into German with the intention of introducing its use into the Chapel Royal on Advent Sunday 1706. This intention was at the time frustrated by some miscarriage of correspondence between the king and Archbishop Tenison. In 1711 and the two following years a correspondence took place between Jablonski, the Moravian bishop, who acted as the king's chaplain, and Archbishop Sharp, with a view to the adoption by Prussia of the Anglican system of Episcopacy and Ritual, but this also came to nothing through the death of Frederick I. in 1713 and of Archbishop Sharp in 1714. [Newcome's *Life of Abp. Sharp*, i. 406, ii. 153, 262.]

very weak condition, and appear soon to have ceased to exist, so that while in 1839 there were forty-one Burgher and thirty-five Seceding congregations in Scotland, and seven Burgher congregations in Ireland, there were in 1844 only thirty-nine of the united congregations remaining in Scotland, and three in the sister kingdom, and in 1852, out of thirty-six congregations then remaining fifteen were united to the Free Church At the present time there appear to be twenty-seven congregations in existence, and the preliminaries have been arranged for union with a small body in Ireland holding identical views, and entitled the Associate Secession Synod, which consists of eleven congregations

The Original Seceders have continued consistently to maintain the views upon which the Secession was at its origin based They strongly vindicate the duty and necessity of national religion, and are therefore in favour of national establishments in opposition to the United Presbyterians and other advocates of the Voluntary system They are consequently also opposed to schemes for reunion among all Presbyterians, as these would involve an allowance of Voluntaryism in making the principle of Establishment an open question But their Establishment must be one which is based upon the Solemn League and Covenant, which were declared to be binding at the union of the two bodies in 1840, and in 1866 were solemnly renewed by the Synod. They are Calvinists of the strictest type, holding the doctrine of a limited Atonement, that Christ suffered only for the elect They are opposed to the use of hymns and instrumental music in public worship The *Original Secession Magazine*, a periodical which appears once in two months, is the authorized record of the views and proceedings of the Synod [*Orig Secession Magazine* Oliver and Boyd's *Edinb Almanac.*]

UNITED PRESBYTERIANS A body composed of two sects of Scottish Dissenters, the Secession or Associate Synod, and the Relief Synod, which were amalgamated under this name in the year 1847 The history of these sects will be found under the heads of ANTIBURGHERS, BURGHERS, RELIEF, and SECESSION The united body is now very powerful in numbers, and is actively opposed to the principle of Church Establishments In 1870 the congregations in connection with it were reckoned as follows in a report presented to the Synod in 1871 :—Scotland, 502, with 161,791 members, Northumberland, Durham, Cumberland, and Lancashire, 89, with 15,614 members, London, 16, with 2,247 members The total income for all purposes amounted to £284,611, 6s 10d In 1871 the increase was, in congregations, one, in income, over £12,000 In Ireland there are about ten congregations, forming one presbytery

The United Presbyterians carry on missions in Spain, in the East and West Indies, and in Africa, together with medical missions to China and amongst the Jews A history of these, by Dr John M'Kerrow (who has also written a history of the Secession Kirk), was published in 1867

The genealogical descent of the existing body may be best exhibited by the following pedigree, which shews the many shoots which in the course of little more than a century were thrown off from the original sectarian parent-stock

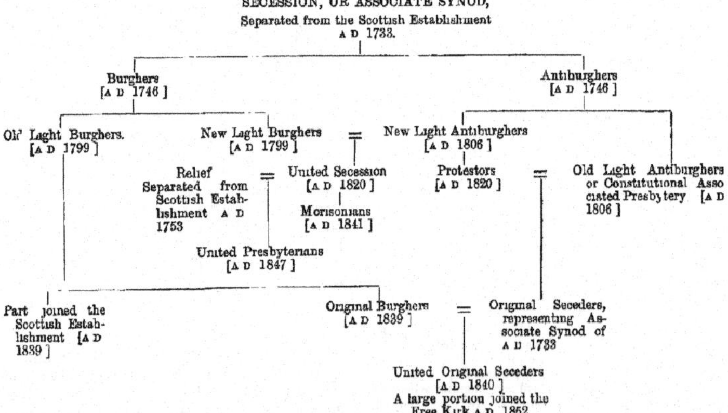

UNITED SOCIETY OF BELIEVERS [SHAKERS]

UNIVERSAL FRIENDS [WILKINSONIANS.]

UNIVERSAL RESTORATIONISTS [RESTORATIONISTS]

UNIVERSALISTS Those who believe in the ultimate salvation of all mankind, the wicked as well as the good

This opinion was held in ancient times by the ORIGENISTS, and has no doubt been held as a

private opinion by many persons in more recent times, but the first attempt to consolidate a sect of which this should be the leading tenet was made in London by an Unitarian preacher named James Relly, about the middle of the last century Although modern Unitarians are generally Universalists, however, the latter have never formed a separate sect of any importance in England Relly was succeeded [A D 1781] by an American preacher named Elhanan Winchester, who had been a Calvinistic Baptist, but the congregation in London was soon broken up Other small congregations were formed here and there and two existed in Liverpool and Plymouth at the time when the religious census was taken in the year 1851

In America, on the other hand, the Universalists have formed a large sect quite distinct from the Unitarians The American sect originated with an English Methodist preacher named John Murray, who gave up his connection with Wesley in the year 1770, and emigrated to America for the purpose of gaining proselytes to the Universalist opinions which he had learned from Relly Finding a soil in which the seeds of heresy readily germinated, he travelled about the States for some years, but finally settled down at Gloucester, Massachusetts where he organized a congregation in the year 1779 Six years later, in 1785, the numbers of the sect and of their congregations had multiplied sufficiently for them to hold a convention at Boston, under the name of the "Independent Christian Universalists" Since that time the sect has gone on growing, and notwithstanding several divisions its numbers still increase In 1840 the RESTORATIONISTS separated off from the original body and formed a distinct sect on what was regarded the original principle of Universalism, that there is a future state of punishment for the wicked, but that it is of limited duration, and that after enduring it they will eventually be restored to happiness A portion of the remaining body sympathized with the Restorationists in their opinions, but did not leave the original sect, forming a party within it under the name of "Impartialists" But the opinion has largely gained ground among the elder body, that there is no punishment for sin except that which follows from the consequences of sin in the present life Originally, no doubt, Universalism was a reaction from Calvinism, and many persons still take refuge from the latter by going to the opposite extreme in the former But in its later American, and in its English Unitarian form, the dogma has assumed a very different character, the denial of future punishment going far to destroy the belief in moral responsibility, and leading through Antinomianism to Deism

The American Universalists in 1847 numbered 716 congregations, in 1862 they numbered about 1000 congregations They have eight academies and three colleges, and they make large use of the press, having no fewer than seventeen periodical publications. [Whittemore's *Hist of Universalism*, Boston, 1860 Williamson's *Exposit and Defence of Universalism* New York, 1840 *Universalist Register* DICT *of* THEOL, UNIVERSALISM]

URBANENSES One of the numerous small sects of Donatists in Numidia They are mentioned by St. Augustine [Aug *contr Crescon* iv 70]

USAGERS AND COLLEGERS Names given to two parties existing in the Church of Scotland in the reigns of George I and George II Upon the gradual removal by death of the bishops who were ejected from their sees upon the Revolution others were consecrated, not to occupy their places as diocesan bishops, but in order to preserve the Apostolic succession until such time as, it was fondly hoped, the Church, as well as the King, might have her own again On the death of Bishop Rose of Edinburgh in 1720, he being the last of the old diocesan prelates, it was proposed that the Church should in future be governed by a *College* of Bishops in common This proposal was supported by Lockhart of Carnwath and others of the political lay supporters in Scotland of the cause of the Chevalier, from the idea that if these bishops without sees were created at will and in any number by the exiled Prince, without any distinct work or jurisdiction, they might be used mainly as powerful instruments in promoting his interests On the other hand, the clergy were chiefly desirous of maintaining the diocesan system, and with this view Bishop Fullerton was at once elected by the clergy of Edinburgh to succeed Bishop Rose, and Falconer was elected to St Andrews Hence immediately arose some political difference between the two parties, the favourers of the College system would have made the bishops the mere nominees and creatures of an expatriated Roman Catholic prince, while the maintainers of diocesan Episcopacy urged that, under the actual circumstances of the country, the bishops ought to be independently elected by the clergy of the several dioceses But a further cause of division was added Bishops Campbell and Gadderar, of the diocesan party, in consequence of their intimacy with the Nonjuring Bishops Hickes and Collier, during a continued residence in England, were led to favour the adoption in Scotland of the Usages at the Holy Communion, which had been revived in England, these Usages being—[1] The mixing water with the wine, [2] Commemorating the faithful departed, [3] The Invocation in the Prayer of Consecration, [4] Oblation before administration [NONJURORS] Gadderar being subsequently chosen Bishop of Aberdeen, the Usages became identified with the party opposed to the College system, and consecrations of bishops at large were consequently multiplied by the Collegers, in obedience to instructions from abroad, in order to crush the diocesan Usagers In 1724, however, an agreement was entered into between Gadderar and the College majority, by which the former, in order to avoid being suspended by his brethren, consented not to insist upon the adoption of the Usages in his diocese, and to conform to the practice of the Church except with regard to the mixing water with the wine, to the retention of which latter usage the other bishops had no objection, providing it was done only when demanded, and with privacy and prudence Lockhart says, that at the meeting at which this arrangement was made there was little reasoning, the one side indulging only in invectives and reflections against Gadderar, whilst he, on the other side, was as obstinate as a mule The strife with regard to the government of the Church, however, still went on, but by degrees the clergy of the various dioceses proceeded to elect their own overseers, until at length, in 1732, the College party, finding themselves gradually outnumbered and defeated, entered into a *concordat* which finally terminated the struggle By the terms of this deed it was agreed that the peace of the Church should not any more be disturbed by the adoption of the Usages, that no one should be consecrated without the consent of the majority of the bishops, that the presbyters of a diocese should not elect without a mandate from the Primus, and that the Primus should simply be a president The dioceses were then allotted to the respective existing bishops, with a provision that no bishop should claim jurisdiction beyond the bounds of his own district

Though the Usages were thus formally given up, they were subsequently, with the exception of the first, incorporated in the Scottish Form for the Holy Communion when it was finally revised in 1765, and at that time occasioned no revival of the controversy But in 1849 the dispute came up again, with much of the former bitterness, upon the publication by Bishop Torry (then nearly a nonagenarian) of an edition of the Scottish Prayer-Book for the use of his own diocese of St Andrews In this the aged bishop sought to perpetuate various practices which had been customary in the last century, and which lingered in some places by an unwritten tradition, amongst other things he allowed the mixing water with the wine and reservation for the sick, and enjoined the signing with the cross at confirmation The book was condemned by the rest of the bishops (Bishop Forbes of Brechin dissenting) at a synod held at Aberdeen in April 1850, but Bishop Torry refused to acknowledge the sentence or recall the book, regarding this step of his colleagues as an unwarrantable interference with his authority as a diocesan bishop, and as an attempt to revive the old system of collegiate government He was however plainly wrong in issuing his own private edition of the Prayer-Book, with novel rubrics, under the authoritative title of "The Book of Common Prayer and Administration of the Sacraments [etc], according to the use of the Church of Scotland" [Skinner's *Eccl Hist of Scotland* Lawson's *Hist of the Scottish Episc Church* Grub's *Eccl Hist of Scotland.* J M Neale's *Life of Bp Torry*]

UTRAQUISTS A controversial name given to those who maintain that the Holy Eucharist should be received *sub utrâque specie* by the laity But the name is specially applied to the CALIXTINES, a section of the followers of Huss, in the fifteenth century The term is used by Gieseler in his *Compendium of Ecclesiastical History*, and in Sianda's *Lexicon Polemicum*

V

VADIANI [AUDIANS]

VALDIANI [AUDIANS]

VALENTINIANS A sect of early Gnostics, taking their origin from Valentinus, about the middle of the second century They are spoken of by Tertullian, writing about A.D 200, as being a very numerous sect, and he attributes the popularity of their heresy to the fables with which their theology abounded, and to the air of mystery which was thrown around it [Tertull *adv Valent* i]

Valentinus was a contemporary of Justin Martyr, flourishing, says Tertullian, in the reign of Antoninus Pius [A D 138-161] As Justin Martyr mentions the sect of the Valentinians in his Dialogue with Trypho [ch xxxv], which was written about A D 158, it is probable that it had been in existence for some years at least before that date He does not name Valentinus, however, with Simon, Menander and Marcion, whom he twice mentions in his First Apology [ch xxvi lvi], which was written about twenty years earlier, and hence it may be supposed that the heresy had not then originated Tertullian says that Valentinus was a man of ability and eloquence, but that being offended at the promotion of another person who had been a confessor to a bishopric which he had himself expected, he left the Church in disgust, and formed a system, not indeed entirely new, but founded in some measure upon opinions previously current [Tertull *adv Valent* iv , *de Præscr Hæret* xxix xxx] From this statement it would appear that his followers were from the first a sect outside of the Church, and not a party holding their opinions within it and afterwards separating from it From later writers it is known that Valentinus went from Alexandria (of which city he was apparently a priest) to Rome, about A D 140, that he was there excommunicated, and that he died in Cyprus about A D 160 [Euseb *Hist Eccl* iv 11, *Chron s a* 2155] He is said to have written many hymns, and a work entitled the "Secret Doctrine of Theudas, a disciple of Paul," with whom he is supposed to have been acquainted [Clem Alex *Strom* vii], but fragments only of his writings are preserved

The system of philosophical theology which Valentinus developed seems to the modern reader full of the grossest absurdities, even when the utmost allowance is made for the fact that we learn it chiefly from Irenæus, Hippolytus, Tertullian,[1] and Clement of Alexandria, and not from his own writings Disentangling it as much as possible from these, and from the affectations of mystery with which it is dressed up, the following seems to be a fair statement of it as given by these writers, the one a contemporary of Valentinus, and the others of his immediate disciples

An unoriginated, invisible, eternal, and incomprehensible, Absolute Being, dwells in height ineffable, living in a state of profound tranquillity This Supreme Existence, *Αἰῶν τέλειος*, *Προαρχή*, *'Αρχή*, he represented to be of a dual nature, as the Gods were in all the more ancient mythologies, being on the one hand an Abyss or Profundity of Self-existence, to which he gave the name *Βυθός*, and on the other an Eternal silent consciousness to which he gave the name of *Ἔννοια*, *Χάρις*, or more commonly *Σιγή* The Duad or dual being thus imagined was further treated in the Valentinian system as partly a personal unity and partly as two persons, Bythus or Absolute Being originating all phenomenal existence in solitary brooding, while yet Sige becomes the mother of all things by conjunction with him From this first duad three other duads of Æons emanated *Μονογενής* was the only-begotten, *Νοῦς* or *'Αρχή* [*cf* John i 1], the Mind, First Principle, and Image of the Supreme Bythus , but here again, accompanying *Νοῦς* was *'Αλήθεια*, Mind and Truth thus making the second duad From these again emanated the Word and the Life, *Λόγος* and *Ζωή*, a third duad And from this third duad there proceeded *Ἄνθρωπος* and *'Εκκλησία*, the fourth These four duads made up the Ogdoad, which is by some writers especially associated with the names of Heracleon and Ptolemy, disciples of Valentinus, and which is also carried back to an earlier date by others, and considered as the invention of Simon Magus [SIMONIANS Greg Naz *Orat* xxv 8 Pearson's *Vindic Ignatian* ii 6] But in the system of Valentinus the Ogdoad formed only the higher portion of a *Πλήρωμα* of thirty Æons, ten of which proceeded in a descending scale from Logos and Zoe, and twelve others from Anthropos and Ecclesia

[1] Tertullian's account of the heresy is written from beginning to end in a strain of jesting irony, and he seems to give base meanings to the theories of Valentinus which were not intended by the latter to be attached to them

Confused and strange as this system seems, there are indications that it was an orderly one, however fanciful and heretical, in the mind of its originators, and something of this order may perhaps be discovered by arranging it in a tabular form, shewing the genealogy of the several Æons It will be observed that the apposition of masculine and feminine names is always maintained

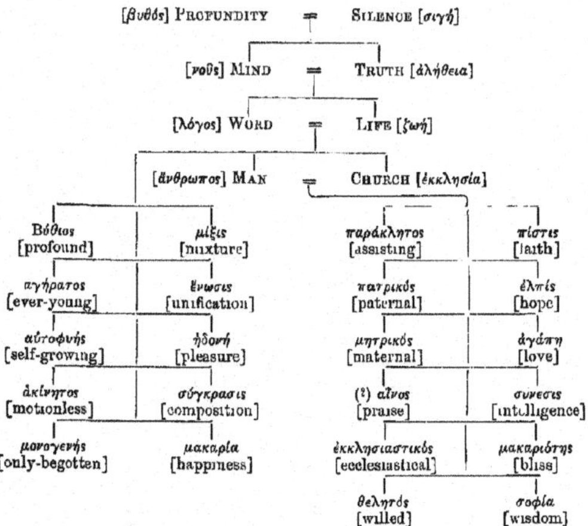

The Pleroma of heavenly beings thus emanating from Bythus, the First Cause, formed a kingdom of Light and an abode of Deity the production of lower beings, and of the material world in the region of darkness outside of this kingdom of Light, being provided for by a supplementary system originating in Sophia, the last of the Divine Emanations This latter is set forth as follows

The full knowledge of the First Cause was imparted only to Nous, whose desire to communicate it to the rest of the Æons was counteracted by the interposition of Sige But a desire ever pervaded them to attain to the knowledge of their Father, and in Sophia this attained to such self-willed strivings after an approach to the unoriginated and incomprehensible Abyss of Light, that a new existence emanated from her, having no part in the Pleroma, to which also the name of Ἀχαμώθ [supposed to be from חָכְמָה Wisdom] was given, as an abortive image of the true wisdom This new being, Achamoth, carried the germ of life to matter, which already existed co-eternally with Bythus in the region of darkness, and thus formed the Δημιουργός, by whom the visible universe was immediately created, including mankind, of whom the Demiurge became the God In the universe thus created there are three kinds of existences, the spiritual, which is the highest and has an affinity to the Pleroma, the animal or psychical, which occupies an intermediate grade, and the material, which is lowest and which has no affinity with the Pleroma Corresponding to these three grades were three types of men, those of material or carnal nature [ψυχὴ ὑλική], represented by Cain, those of animal nature [ψυχὴ θεία], represented by Abel, and those of spiritual nature [σπέρμα πνευματικόν], represented by Seth the first being destined to perdition, the last to salvation, but the final condition of the intermediate class depending upon the exercise of the free will with which they are endowed, and which enables them to choose a place among the carnal on the one hand, or the spiritual on the other On this threefold division was grounded the ethical system out of which arose that Antinomian profligacy which is attributed by most early writers to the Gnostics, for while the animal man was required to work out his salvation if he was to gain it, they in whom was the "spiritual seed" were already sure of salvation, and so might live as they pleased without danger of perdition.

The Christian doctrine of salvation by Christ and the Holy Spirit was also incorporated into this strange system The Second and Third Persons of the Holy Trinity are clearly associated in some way with the Æons Nous and Aletheia, and it seems as if the following duad of Æons, Logos and Zoe, represented the operative phase of their Divine existence The Body of Jesus was specially created by the Demiurge (in a nature similar to but not identical with ordinary human bodies) as the means by which the salvation of mankind was to be effected This body was placed in the Blessed Virgin, but did not partake of her substance, and issued forth from her as it had been placed within her At the Baptism in Jordan, Christ, proceeding from the Logos, descended upon Jesus in the form of a dove, and remained with Him until the Crucifixion But when the Saviour was about to suffer, the Logos returned to the Pleroma, and only the material nature, Jesus again separated from the Christ, suffered and died

To complete this system Valentinus added also a theory of Eschatology When the age of man's probation is completed, those in whom was the spiritual seed will be received into the Pleroma, those in whom was the animal seed, and who have worked out their salvation, will be received into a middle region where the Demiurge will reign over them, while those in whom was only the base material seed will be annihilated At this final consummation Achamoth will be received into the Pleroma to form a new Duad in association with Christ

To what extent this singular system was an original invention it is impossible to say Irenæus gives some curious evidence of an association between the ideas of Valentinus and his followers, and those contained in a popular comedy named the "Theogony," which was written by Antiphanes, the author of 280 comedies, who flourished in the fourth century before Christ [B C 404-330] "Much more like the truth," says Irenæus, "and more pleasing is the account which Antiphanes, one of the ancient comic poets, gives in his 'Theogony' as to the origin of all things For he speaks of Chaos as being produced from Night and Silence, relates that then Love sprang from Chaos and Night, from this again, Light, and that from this, in his opinion, were derived all the rest of the first generation of the gods After these he next introduces a second generation of gods and the creation of the world, then he narrates the formation of mankind by the second order of the gods These heretics, adopting this fable as their own, have ranged their opinions round it as if by a sort of natural process, changing only the names of the things referred to, and setting forth the very same beginning of the generation of all things and their production In place of Night and Silence they substitute Bythus and Sige, instead of Chaos they put Nous, and for Love (by whom, says the comic poet, all other things were set in order) they have brought forward the Word For the primary and greatest gods they have formed their Æons, and in place of the secondary gods they tell us of that creation by their mother, which is outside of the Pleroma, calling it the second Ogdoad They proclaim to us, like the writer referred to, that from this Ogdoad came the creation of the world and the formation of man, maintaining that they alone are acquainted with these ineffable and unknown mysteries Those things which are everywhere acted in the theatres by comedians with the clearest voices they transfer to their own system, teaching them undoubtedly through means of the same arguments, and merely changing the names" [Iren *adv Hær* ii 14]

The coincidence between the Theogony ridiculed in this comedy, and that of Valentinus, is too striking to allow of its being thought altogether accidental, but the true explanation probably is that both were taken from some ancient system, and a confirmation of this explanation is afforded by the fact that in the Theogony of Hesiod there are thirty gods as there are thirty Æons in the system of Valentinus On the other hand, Burton has accumulated much evidence in his "Inquiry into the Heresies of the Apostolic Age,' to support the opinion that the "Æons" of the Gnostics were personifications of the "Ideas" of Plato, and it is now known that Hippolytus, who was contemporary with the early Valentinians, deduced their system from Pythagoras and Plato [Hippol *Refut Hær* xxix xxxii] The truth seems to be that Valentinus was one of the first to attempt the formation of a syncretistic theosophy by amalgamating Judaism and Christianity with the philosophy and the theogonies of the ancient Greek and Oriental worlds In the following age the Neo-Platonists made a similar attempt, excluding to a great extent the Oriental element, and admitting more of the classical

[Irenæus, *adv Hæres* Tertull *adv Valentin* Hippol *Refut omn Hæres* Buddæus, *de Hæres Valentin* Kaye's *Writings and Opin of Clement of Alex* Kaye's *Eccl Hist illustrated from Tertullian* Burton's *Bampton Lectures*]

VALESIANS A sect, or perhaps a community of ascetics, of this name is mentioned by Epiphanius, and after him by other early heresiologists, but scarcely anything is known respecting them They are said to have had for their founder Valens of Bacatha Metrocomia, an episcopal city not yet identified, but which Epiphanius and Nicetas speak of as being in "Arabia beyond Jordan" They are spoken of by Epiphanius as holding some Gnostic opinions, St. John of Damascus charges them with being profligate Antinomians, and Nicetas classes them with ARCHONTICS and SETHIANS The principal definite fact that is recorded about them is that they practised self-mutilation, and enforced the practice on all their adherents [Epiphan *Hæres* lviii Aug *Hæres* xxvii Joann Damasc *de Hæres* lviii Nicet Chon *Thesaur Orthod* iv 30]

VANISTS This name was given by Baxter to the Antinomians of New England, but whether Sir Henry Vane, who was Governor of the colony when they sprung up there, was really associated with them may be doubted [See page 34, note 2]

VARISUUS Ittigius [*de Hæresiarch* iii 1, App xii] quotes an anonymous commentator on St Matthew, who names Varisuus with Cleobius [CLEOBIANS] among the early heretics Burton expresses his opinion that the true reading is that of the Benedictine edition, "Barjesu," and that the person intended is Elymas the sorcerer, who is so called in Acts xiii 6 [Burton's *Bampton Lect* 495]

VAUDOIS [WALDENSES.]

VENUSTIANI [PATERNIANI]

VERSCHOORISTS A Dutch sect which takes its name from James Verschoor of Flushing, who lived in the latter half of the seventeenth century His tenets are described by Mosheim as being an absurd and impious system of religion made up of a mixture in which the principles of Spinoza and Cocceius predominated His followers are also called Hebrews because of the attention which they all give, men and women alike, to the Hebrew language [Mosheim, *Eccl Hist* iii. 390, Stubbs' ed] They were akin to the HATTEMISTS, and, like them, Antinomian in their principles.

VICTORINUS This name is mentioned as that of one who upheld and assisted the heresy of Praxeas, by the author of the work against all Heresies appended to Tertullian's *de Præscriptione Hæreticorum* Nothing whatever is known about him, but Fabricius and Oehler [*Corp Hæresiol* Phil cap xlix p 102] conjecture that it must be Victor, Bishop of Rome when Praxeas was there, to whose name the last two syllables of his successor Zephyrinus' name have been added by a careless scribe

VITALIANS [APOLLINARIANS]

VOCASOTI [BOCASOTI]

W

WAKEMANITES A very small party of deluded fanatics existing at New Haven in Connecticut in 1855, who regarded an aged and apparently insane woman named Rhoda Wakeman as a divinely commissioned prophetess who had been raised from the dead, in accordance with her own prediction Their only claim to notice arises from the unusual extreme to which their credulity led them At the bidding of the prophetess, not only were some of her followers willing to become the murderers of one of their companions named Justus Matthews, a small farmer whom she charged with being possessed by an evil spirit, for the removal of which exorcisms had been vainly used, but the wretched man himself submitted willingly to be murdered, as the only means of quenching the evil spirit within him, which would otherwise destroy the prophetess The extinction of the fanatic sect followed, of course, upon the commission of this crime

WALDENSES Of the various religious bodies that rose up in the twelfth century against the dominant power of the clergy, the Waldenses are the most celebrated, not only on account of the purity of their moral character, and their freedom from wild Manichæan error, but because their descendants, the Vaudois, still linger in the valleys of the Western Alps. *Their descendants,* for such the Vaudois probably are, but still the fact has been disputed, and endless questions have been raised and fiercely debated about the connection between the Vaudois of Piedmont and the ancient Waldenses of Southern France, about the origin of the name, and indeed its meaning also, and about the antiquity of the sectaries to which it is applied

They claim for themselves a high antiquity It has even been maintained that their Church was founded by the Apostle St Paul, and that they alone have preserved primitive faith and discipline through the corruptions of the Dark and Middle Ages up to the present time Another account of their origin is, that when Constantine established and endowed the Church under Sylvester, Bishop of Rome, the inhabitants of these valleys, headed by one Leon, from whom they were called Leonistæ, rejected the unholy alliance, and kept themselves aloof from the rest of the Latin communion, remaining unknown in their obscure valleys and mountain passes, until attention was drawn to them in the twelfth century by the spread of heresy in France and Northern Italy They have moreover been associated with Claudius, Bishop of Turin, who took the side of the Iconoclasts in the time of Charlemagne But there is no historical evidence of any such association, and his opposition to images was the one point that Claudius had in common with the Waldenses, a point in which he did not stand alone, being supported by Charlemagne himself, and by the Church of his day and empire, assembled in the Council of Frankfort, A D 794 In truth these conjectures are only the vain attempts of a sectarian body to trace their origin to the Apostles As Maitland has observed, even those who reject the Apostolic Succession are always very glad to connect themselves in some way with the Apostles The first really authentic account of the Waldenses dates from the middle of the twelfth century, and all the contemporary writers trace their origin to Peter Waldo, or Valdo, the merchant of Lyons There may, possibly, have been some such sects in the Piedmont valleys before him, but these received at any rate a powerful impetus from him, and no one who has any acquaintance with the rites and doctrines of the primitive Church will now maintain that the Waldenses truly represent that Church The separation from Sylvester, if it had taken place, could not have escaped the notice of some contemporary author This is the opinion of the best modern authorities, Milman, Hallam, Maitland, Mosheim, and Gieseler

The name has been rendered Vallenses, that is "inhabitants of the valleys" Ebrardus suggests that they were so called because they sojourned in a vale of tears. but the letter "d," which appears alike in the Latin form Waldenses and in the modern Vaudois, points to some other derivation In the Provençal language "val" was a valley, which in oblique cases assumed the form "vau," plural "vaux," where it would be impossible for the "d" to get in As a matter of fact there was a tribe of Vallenses in the Graian Alps, but they were called by the French Les Vallais The name of Vaudois or Waldenses must have been derived either from Waldo, or possibly, as in the case of the Pays de Vaud in Switzerland, from the forest or woodland character of their country We meet with "pagus Waldensis" in the tenth century, meaning forest or woodland district [see Todd, *Books of the Vaudois*, App] All the contemporary or nearly contemporary writers speak of Waldo as their actual founder, and the author of their name Even Reinerius, who calls them "diuturnior" than the other sects of the day, qualifies his words immediately after by tracing them to Waldo Beza was the first to derive the name from the "vallées" in which they reside.

Peter Valdo, or Waldo, was a merchant of Lyons It has been thought that he was called Valdo because he was born in Valdum in the marquisate of Lyons, or again from the district of Walden, but probably Waldo was his real surname It was common enough in those days, as Maitland has shewn He mentions [*Facts and Documents*] nine different persons who were so called, and they of course are only specimens, and compares it to the English name Wood Waldo had led for some time an ordinary secular life, when the sudden death of a companion at a meeting for devotion made a powerful impression upon him, and induced him to consecrate himself to the cause of religion He gave up his large property to the relief of the poor, chose the life of poverty, and spent his time in instructing others This was about 1160 He hired a poor scholar to translate into the vernacular some of the books of Scripture and approved sentences from the Fathers and as his followers increased he sent chosen disciples out, two and two, to preach in the neighbourhood, to the great indignation of the archbishop and clergy of Lyons They were to go in poverty after the example of the Apostles, and to work with their own hands for their subsistence. They called themselves the "Humbled," but were ordinarily known as the "Poor Men of Lyons," the "Sabatati," from the large wooden shoes or sabots that they wore, and the "Insabatati," *i e* "marked on the sabots," because they had the sign of the Cross on their shoes

Hitherto lay preaching had been unheard of in the Latin Church, and the opposition raised by their practice was in consequence considerable But two of them appeared at Rome in 1179, and petitioned that they might be allowed to preach Alexander III received them in the Lateran Council He approved of their poverty, but condemned them for their interference with the duties of the clergy When they further pressed for permission they were coldly referred to their own clergy, the last men who would be likely to yield it to them Had the Pope acted otherwise Waldo might have anticipated St Francis, and founded an order of preaching friars *within* the Church The Archbishop of Lyons now formally prohibited their preaching, but Waldo replied that they ought to obey God rather than man, and continued to act as before Hitherto there had been no real distinction either of doctrine or of practice between his followers and the Church The only charge against them was that they, being laymen, persisted in preaching, and yet the Pope had not formally prohibited them, although he had shewn marked disapprobation of the practice Under the following Pope, Lucius III, a pontiff, it may be observed, of no mark, they were, in 1183, anathematized together with the other heretics of Southern France. This widened the breach, and they continued to preach with vigour and earnestness, so that their confraternity was widely spread through France and Lombardy They were by the admission of their opponents pure in life, and free from the stain of formal heresy, and thus they won over many who were dissatisfied with the existing state of corruption in high places, and yet shrank from the Manichæan heresy that infected the Albigenses Hence they speedily became numerous, and proved a cause of great peril to the Church, and that for three reasons, as Reinerius, a Dominican Inquisitor who had much to do with them, remarks. [1] Because they were of earlier origin than the other sects, that is, according to their own account, as they traced themselves to Sylvester's time In his next sentence he qualifies his expression, "diuturnior," by giving his own opinion [2] Because they were more widely extended [3] Because while other sects filled their hearers with horror by their foul blasphemies, the Leonists, men of Lyons, had a great show of piety, so as to live uprightly in the sight of all, having also a right faith in all the things of God and the articles of the Creed, though they only reviled the Church of Rome and the clergy [Reiner *contra Wald* iv in Gretzer, tom. xii]

Their separation from the Church, and continued study of Holy Scripture by the light of their own private judgment, soon led them to oppose many of the prevailing doctrines and practices The errors ascribed to them range themselves under three heads, those against Rome and the clergy, those against the sacraments and the saints, and those against ecclesiastical customs

I [*a*] They threw off the authority of the Pope and the bishops generally Those of Italy indeed allowed that Rome was a true but corrupt Church, those of France, Ultramontane, maintained that she had apostatized, and was Babylon and the harlot, that they themselves were the only true Church, that the Pope was the head of error, the prelates were the Scribes, and the monks the Pharisees

[*b*] They asserted the right of laymen, and even women to preach, for this last they quoted the example of Anna and Titus ii 3, 4

[*c*] They declared the consecration and absolution of bad priests to be invalid, in other words, that the unworthiness of the ministering priest renders the sacraments of none effect

[*d*] That absolution by a good layman was effective, and therefore confession might be made to any one

[*e*] They refused to pay tithes, protested against religious endowments and the temporal power of the clergy

II [*a*] They abolished much of the prevailing ritual in Baptism Some declared that infant baptism was unprofitable, but this does not seem to have been universally held

[b] With regard to the Eucharist they maintained a kind of subjective Presence, as it would now be called, that the Transubstantiation takes place, not in the hand of the priest, but in the mouth of the believer They rejected the canon of the Mass, and denied any oblation in it

[c] They allowed Confirmation by priests

[d] They objected to the forbidden degrees, probably only the more remote, of which Rome made such a profit by means of dispensations, also they objected to compulsory celibacy of the clergy

[e] They depreciated Unction

[f] They asserted that the Apostles were the only saints who ought to be had in honour, and declared against any invocation of them

III [a] They opposed as useless all alms, masses, fasts, and prayers for the faithful departed

[b] They denied purgatory, and maintained that the disembodied spirits go at once to heaven or hell Some however held a doctrine of the Intermediate State

[c] They called the plain song of the Church a "clamor infernalis," and rejected the canonical hours as times for prayer

[d] They opposed the use of crosses, images, and ornaments in churches, the ceremonies of Candlemas and Palm Sunday, all benedictions, dedications, etc, in fact all traditions and ecclesiastical customs not expressly contained in Scripture

[e] They denied the "mystical sense" of Scripture, called pilgrimages useless, some of them refused to worship in churches, preferring the use of bedrooms and stables (for this they quoted Matt vi 5, 6, Acts vii 48, 49), they also objected to ecclesiastical burials for this putting forward Matt xxiii 29

Moreover they denied the lawfulness of capital punishment, of oaths, of bearing arms in self-defence (very different from their modern descendants the Vaudois), also of lawsuits, for they interpreted the Sermon on the Mount according to the strict letter

They were governed, at first at least, by bishops —of their own appointment, whom they styled "majorales"—by presbyters and deacons, giving for a reason that all three had been instituted by Christ, but they required that they should be, like the Apostles, poor uneducated men, who should support themselves by the work of their own hands

Their laity were divided into the Perfect and Imperfect The first gave up all property and fasted strictly, the second lived like men in general, in society, only without luxury Their rules concerning property were of course soon relaxed, in fact, no society could continue them for any length of time They are favourably distinguished for high moral character from the other sects of the day, such as the Albigenses, Paulicians, etc This appears in their celebrated work, the "Noble Lesson," a poem in rhyming verse written in the Provençal dialect It contains a biblical history, both of the Old and New Testaments, interspersed with pure moral precepts It ends with an attack upon the errors of the Papacy, persecutions, masses and prayers for the dead, simony, and Papal absolution A question has been raised concerning its date That of A D 1100 appears in it, which is evidently used vaguely, and might apply to any year in that century, but it is now supposed that there is a mistake in the MSS One in the Library of Cambridge University bears suspicious marks of an erasure, and when closely examined gives A D 1400 instead of A D 1100

As they took all pains to spread their opinions as much as possible, they everywhere both gained converts and provoked persecution Southern France and Piedmont were their headquarters, but they spread on the one side through Arragon, while on the other they appeared at Milan

Nothing certain is known of the after life of Waldo himself It has been said that he fled from Lyons, and found refuge in the eastern valleys of the Cottian Alps, where he either won over for the first time, or confirmed in their faith, those inhabitants whose descendants still represent his communion Others deny that he ever was there, and maintain that he died in Bohemia The date of his death is uncertain

The various persecutions to which his followers in different places were exposed only served to spread their opinions the more widely, and that not among the poor or middle classes only, for we read that in the year 1207 the wife and one sister of the Count de Foix had joined them There were many of them in Metz, in Milan, and in Arragon, where they drew forth an edict from Alphonso II in 1194, threatening confiscation of goods, and the penalties of treason to any who should listen to their preaching, receive them into their houses, or even supply them with food

Between A D 1307 and 1323, out of 607 sentences to various punishments passed by the Inquisition in France upon heretics, 92 were upon Waldensians They gradually declined in that country, so that at the present time only a remnant is left on the western slopes of the Alps in Dauphiné They extended themselves into Lower Germany, especially Brandenburg, Pomerania, and Mecklenburg, where many were burnt There they paved the way for the Reformation, and in after times were mingled with the Protestants of those parts At one time we read that they supplied the Bohemian remnant of the Taborites, who had separated from the Church and settled in Herrnhut in Lusatia, with a bishop, or at least a so-called bishop, for it does not appear that they ever had the succession

But it was in Italy, under their modernized name of the Vaudois, that they made themselves most celebrated by their constancy, their fierce resistance in arms to persecution, and their continuance as a distinct body up to the present day Possibly there may have been some sectaries in those valleys before Waldo commenced his career of preaching Certainly he or some of his earlier followers, if they did not found the community of the Vaudois, greatly extended it They were a poor ignorant people, inhabiting each side of the Cottian Alps Those on the western slopes were the subjects of France, and although they were at times cruelly handled by the local powers, seem not to have fared so badly upon the whole as their brethren of the east, who were subjected to the Dukes of Savoy They occupied the district between Mount Viso and Mount Genevre, a tract consisting of secluded valleys and of towering crags upon which the persecuted often found shelter from their pursuers It was perhaps fortunate for the Vaudois that they were under two different governments, and usually the French kings were too much engaged with other more important matters to notice these distant mountaineers, so that they were left to the efforts of the local authorities But the Dukes of Savoy were ever ready to assail those on the eastern side Ordinarily whenever those on one side were attacked they were able to find refuge with their brethren on the other, but sometimes an attack was made on both sides at once, and then their case was pitiable indeed Flight to the mountains was their only safeguard. It is said that they have had to go through no fewer than thirty-seven persecutions at the hands of their Dukes [Gilly], in which neither age nor sex was spared The object may have been in part political The Dukes of Savoy obtained possession of the country only about Waldo's time. It had previously enjoyed considerable independence under the Counts of Lucerne and the Marquis of Saluzzo, on which account the inhabitants were always pleading for their ancient rights, and unlike the Christian martyrs of early times, resisted by force of arms the attempts made upon their faith The French Vaudois, on the other hand, offered no resistance to their persecutors, but whenever flight was impossible, opposed patience and long-suffering to violence They were in a more poverty-stricken condition than their Italian brethren their country being more cold, barren, and inaccessible to foreign influences They were under the pastoral charge of the Archbishop of Embrun, and the records of the diocese contain statements of their persecution, and of the expense which it entailed Thus in the accounts for A D 1335 there is inserted, "Item for persecuting the Vaudois, eight sols and thirty deniers of gold" The people of one valley, the Val Louise were entirely exterminated in 1438 by a body of troops that had suffered a severe defeat from the Italian Vaudois, and in their retreat thus avenged themselves Their places were filled with Catholics from the neighbourhood some years later by Louis XII, who was himself no persecutor, although he allowed the local authorities of Embrun to do what they pleased Again the mountains saved the rest

The Edict of Nantes afforded the Vaudois a long respite, which they turned to account by building churches and worshipping openly, but its revocation was followed by the destruction of their churches and the suppression of their worship wherever it was possible, and they continued in a low ignorant state, with but few pastors, until recent times, when religious toleration enabled them to lift up their heads, and the labours of Felix Neff, although they were cut short by a premature death, formed the commencement of a better state of things The country is now divided into regular districts, each of which has its pastor, its house of residence, and its place of worship

The history of the Italian Vaudois is far more complicated It comprehends a series of invasions from without gallant defences followed by the shameful defeat and retreat of the assailants, and varied by individual persecution It would be impossible to give a connected account of the whole in a brief article like the present A few of the more important points may be touched upon, which will serve to shew the stubbornness with which these mountaineers held to their religious opinions, and further illustrate the fact, if it needs illustration, that persecution only serves to confirm men the more in that which they hold to be the truth

For a time they were allowed to remain unmolested owing to the obscurity of their position, and the Bulls which were continually fulminated against them in conjunction with other heretics passed over their heads But the establishment of the Inquisition at Turin brought the danger nearer to them. Numbers of individuals suffered, but no attempt was made upon the people as a whole They were accused by Pope John XXII in 1332 of having murdered William, the rector of the parish church of Engravia, in the diocese of Turin, because he had celebrated Mass in an open place in the town, and in 1403, St Vincent of Ferrers penetrated into their district, and made an unsuccessful attempt to effect their conversion

At length a crusade in 1477 was preached against the Vaudois by Innocent VIII Plenary indulgences were granted to all who should join in it, with liberty to appropriate whatever property of the heretics they might seize Eighteen thousand regular troops and six thousand volunteers were poured into the country to plunder and lay waste, but their progress was checked by Philip VII, Duke of Savoy, who interfered in behalf of his subjects, and for once protected them

In 1556 they sent a confession of faith to the Reformers of Germany, containing the following articles —

[1] They expressed their belief in the Old and New Testaments and in the Apostles' Creed

[2] They acknowledged the Holy Sacraments instituted by Christ, according to the true meaning of their institution

[3] They received the Creeds sanctioned by the first four General Councils, and also that of St Athanasius [1]

[4] They admitted the Ten Commandments as a rule of life

[5] They professed submission to the superiors placed over them by God [See Gilly, *Second Visit to the Vaudois*]

[1] This seems to prove that they were not an independent Apostolic Church, which disappeared from public notice in the time of Sylvester, and remained hidden in obscurity until the close of the twelfth century

Two years later an edict was published against the Vaudois by Emanuel Philibert, and an invasion was made under the command of the Count de la Trinité They defended themselves as usual in the mountain passes, having placed their women and children in caves formed as places of refuge The Count failed to force Angrogna, from which he was retiring when he suffered a severe defeat in the Pra du Tour In consequence partly of this defeat, and partly of the intercessions of his Duchess, the Duke was at last persuaded in 1560 to conclude a peace

It was now that the Protestants of Germany for the first time contributed to the relief of the Vaudois, and by their representations at the Court of Turin checked persecution for a considerable period Consequently, in 1655, the Vaudois identified themselves with the Protestant bodies, and accepted the Confession of Augsburg

At this time another attempt was made against them, and the Marquis de Pianesse advanced up the same valley of Angrogna at the head of fifteen thousand men, and having been twice repulsed, proposed terms of peace, stipulating, however, that a regiment of infantry and two companies of cavalry should be quartered upon them for a short time The unsuspecting Vaudois consented, and dispersed to their various homes Then the soldiers were let loose upon them, and a horrible massacre followed, in which neither age nor sex was spared The remnant forced their way up to the tops of the mountains, whence they carried on a guerilla warfare It was now that Cromwell interfered on their behalf, and induced Cardinal Mazarin to make a joint and threatening remonstrance, before which the Duke was compelled to give way, and peace was restored The losses of the Vaudois were made up by contributions from the States that sympathized with them In England about £40,000 were collected, of which half was transmitted to them at once and the remainder was retained to afford a fund the interest of which was to be placed at their disposal, but this fund was lost to them through subsequent political events

After this the Vaudois enjoyed peace until 1685, when Louis XIV and the Duke of Savoy, Amadeus II, made a united effort to crush them The first attack was unsuccessful, the French were beaten at St. Germain, and had to retire to Pignerol, while the Italians met with the same fate at Angrogna But persevering efforts succeeded, the Vaudois were forced at length to surrender Numbers were thrown into dungeons, where they perished either from disease or at the hands of the executioner, and the remainder about three thousand, were banished the country for ever Their lands were occupied, partly by Italians, and partly by a body of Irishmen, who had met with the same fate in their own country at the hands of Cromwell The exiled Vaudois found a hearty welcome in Switzerland, Holland, Brandenburg, and the Palatinate, but their love of home continued strong, and although lands had been offered them in the above-mentioned countries, they were further unsettled by the ravaging of the Palatinate, where many of them had taken refuge in 1689 Accordingly, about eight hundred of them under the command of Henri Arnaud, a pastor, effected what they called the "Glorious Return" They forced their way through foreign lands and across opposing mountains to their old home, where they entrenched themselves for the winter In the following year war was resumed, and acts of atrocious cruelty stained both parties The Vaudois were specially relentless against the new inhabitants who had succeeded them in their old homes, in the fight no quarter was given, and no mercy was shewn afterwards, as *they could not keep their prisoners* At length a quarrel between Louis and Amadeus induced the latter to grant peace to the Vaudois, and to confirm them in their recovered possessions Since that time no serious effort has been made against them, but a course of petty persecution and vexatious restriction was adopted, which continued in force until very lately.

They enjoyed a brief space of greater prosperity under Napoleon I, who swept away the restrictions, and granted them aid to maintain their pastors out of the public funds, but this was withdrawn after his fall, and the old state of things was restored

They were then strictly confined to their own territory, a small district of mountain-country near the sources of the Po, between the Clusone and the Pelice This, as population increased, became less adequate for their support, and hence they became poorer, but no one was allowed to purchase or inherit lands beyond their own limits It was also enacted that no books should be printed for them in Piedmont, and at that time there was a high duty upon imported books It does not appear however that this went beyond the ordinary censorship of that age, which provided for the suppression of heretical and immoral books by the government

None of the Vaudois were at this time allowed to practise law or physic beyond their own territories, and even at home they were restricted to the ranks of apothecaries and attorneys, in theory at least, for as far as practice goes probably they did whatever necessity demanded of them All the civil and military offices were closed to them They were compelled to abstain from all work on the numerous festivals of the Church Difficulties were thrown in the way of their building houses for their pastors and repairing their places of worship They were refused admission into any of the established hospitals unless they should consent to renounce their own communion

All these restrictions are now abolished, and they enjoy complete toleration Their material condition also has been much improved owing to the exertions of Dr Gilly and other Englishmen who have taken up their cause Thus an hospital has been founded for them, houses have been built for their pastors, whose salaries also have been increased Schools have been built in many places, and a college founded at La Tour

But the Vaudois have at the same time given up many of their old peculiarities and approximated more to the ordinary type of foreign

Protestants, except only that they are free from the Socinianism of the Swiss and the Rationalism of the German and French Protestants, and they never shewed any great inclination towards the errors of Calvin They are no longer under the rule of even nominal bishops, but are now governed by a synod composed of the pastor and one layman from each parish, presided over by the moderator, a successor of their ancient bishops The synod, as vacancies arise in the parish, elects the pastors from two or more candidates nominated by the parish The Liturgy of Geneva is used, having superseded an older one of their own, but it is the *unreformed* liturgy, the one in use at Geneva before the spread of Socinianism found expression in the public worship Their pastors are ordained by the laying on of hands of the moderator, but lately the ordinations of Geneva and Lausanne have been considered valid

Their offices comprise services for Communion, Baptism, and Marriage They have no Burial Service Their ordinary public service does not differ greatly from that of the neighbouring Protestants It comprises prayer without response, psalmody, reading of the Scriptures, and preaching The Communion, when Dr Gilly visited them, was administered at four seasons of the year, but if the attendance was large the administration was continued on the following Sunday

They may now therefore be looked upon as one of the ordinary Protestant and Presbyterian bodies, interesting indeed on account of their antiquity, the persecutions that they have often had to endure from their Dukes, and the patriotic resistance which they opposed to them

[Reinerius, *contr Waldens* in *Bibl Max. Lugd* xxv Lucæ Tudens *Succedan Prolegom ibid* Eberhardus, *ibid* Maitland's *Tracts and Documents connected with the Hist of Waldenses* Todd's *Books of the Vaudois* Gilly's *Two Visits to the Vaudois Country* *Articles on the Noble Lesson* by Hon Alg Herbert, in *British Mag* xviii, xix Melia's *Origin, Persecutions, and Doctrines of the Waldenses*, 1870]

WALKERITES [SEPARATISTS]

WALLOON PROTESTANTS A branch of the French Calvinists imported into the Netherlands at the revocation of the Edict of Nantes They differ from the general body of Dutch Calvinists only in the use of the French language and the Geneva Catechism, and are gradually dying out as a separate body

WATERLANDERS The less rigid ["die Groben"] portion of the Mennonite sect, so called because the majority of them belonged to a district named Waterland in the north of Holland They are almost exactly similar in their habits and principles to the English Baptists, and do not adopt the old Puritan stiffness and discipline of the FLEMINGS, or "Fine" Mennonites ["die Feinen"] The Waterlanders have also sometimes been named Johannites, from Hans de Rys, one of their leaders in the sixteenth century [MENNONITES]

WEGSCHEIDER [RATIONALISTS]

WELSH METHODISTS [METHODISTS, WELSH]

WESLEYAN ASSOCIATION [METHODISTS]

WESLEYAN METHODISTS [METHODISTS]

WESLEYAN REFORMERS [METHODISTS]

WESLEYANS [METHODISTS]

WESTMINSTER ASSEMBLY [PURITANS]

WESTMINSTER CONFESSION. [PROTESTANT CONFESSIONS]

WHITE BRETHREN A body of enthusiasts which appeared in Italy about the beginning of the fourteenth century, and were so called from being all clad in white linen robes reaching to their feet, with hoods of the same material that left only their eyes exposed They were originally collected together, by a priest whose name is not known, among the villages on the southern side of the Alps Some writers say that this priest was a Scotchman, others that he came from France, but little is known of him except that he placed himself at the head of a very large multitude of the White Brethren, whom he had organized, and led them down to the Italian plains under the pretence that he was the prophet Elias by whom the Second Advent is to be heralded Bearing a cross at their head, he bade them follow him in a crusade against the Turks for the purpose of regaining the Holy Land, and so great was his influence that not only the peasantry, but some priests and even cardinals are said to have enrolled themselves among his army of "penitents," as the White Brethren called themselves In troops numbering ten, twenty and forty thousand, the enthusiasts marched from city to city in the same manner as the early Beghards had done, singing hymns and making loud prayers and wherever they went multitudes were ready to give them alms and to join in their pilgrimage They had thus advanced, with growing numbers, as far as Viterbo, when they were met by a body of the Papal troops, which had been ordered to march against them by Boniface IX under the impression that their leader intended to dethrone him and seize upon the Popedom The pilgrims were dispersed by the troops, and their leader being taken, was carried to Rome, where, about the year 1403, he was burned as a heretic

There is so much similarity between the history of the White Brethren and that of the fanatical multitude which was led by Sagarelli and Dolcino a century earlier, that it seems probable that some of the latter [APOSTOLICALS] had continued the existence of their sect among the retired villages of the Alps, and that a leader like Dolcino had again risen among them to revive their enthusiasm [Theodoric de Niem in *Muratori annal Mediol* ii 16, Poggius, *Hist Florent* iii 122]

WHITEFIELD [HUNTINGDON CONNEXION. METHODISTS, CALVINISTIC]

WHITE QUAKERS [QUAKERS]

WICKLIFFITES [LOLLARDS.]

WILBURITES A section of the American Quakers which has struck off from the main body since the separation of the Hicksites, on the ground that Quakers were giving up their original principles. Their original leader was John Wilbur, and they maintain the strictest traditions of the sect.

WILHELMIANS The followers of a fanatic woman named Wilhelmina, who died at Milan in the year 1281 She professed to be the daughter of Constantia, the Queen of Primislaus, King of Bohemia, but was first heard of in the neighbourhood of Milan According to her blasphemous pretensions her birth had been announced to her mother by the angel Raphael, in the same manner as that of our Lord was announced to the Virgin Mary by the angel Gabriel The prophecies of the Abbot Joachim were at this time deluding many enthusiastic minds [JOACHIMITES], and the interpretation which Wilhelmina gave to his theory respecting an age of the Holy Spirit was that the Third Person of the Blessed Trinity had become incarnate in her person for the purpose of working out the salvation of Jews, Saracens, and false Christians, as that of true Christians had been wrought by Christ She deluded a large number of followers into the expectation, first, of her repeating in her own person the sufferings of Christ, and secondly, of her resurrection and return to them after her death When that death occurred, without any remarkable circumstances, they still paid her the highest veneration, and built her a magnificent tomb Her most notorious followers were a man named Andrew and a nun named Mafreda The latter she appointed to be her vicegerent, a female pope to represent her as the Roman Pontiffs represent St Peter Some years after the death of Wilhelmina some of her fanatic followers were discovered by the Inquisition, and burned as heretics The tomb of the impostor herself was destroyed, her dead body treated in the same manner as her living followers, and about the year 1300 the sect became extinct [Muratori, *Antiq Ital Med Æv* v 91]

WILEMITÆ A name sometimes given to the BOHEMIAN BRETHREN Thus Camerarius writes " . in oppidis autem Bohemicis cum aliis tum Wilemii et Boleslaviæ frequentior fuit istiusmodi cætus, unde et Wilemitæ et Boleslavienses Fratres sunt nominati " [Camerarius, *Hist narr de Fratr* etc 9]

WILKINSONIANS A sect of the Brownists, followers of a preacher named Wilkinson, " whose disciples in a short time grew so strong in the spirit that they stoutly affirmed that they were Apostles, as Peter and Paul, and the rest, and therefore they deny communion with all others that will not give them that title" [Pagitt's *Heresiography*, p 87, ed 1662]

WILKINSONIANS An obscure sect of American fanatics, followers of an impostor named Jemima Wilkinson, who formed a settlement which she called the "New Jerusalem" between Geneva Lake and Crooked Lake, in Yates County, New York, at the close of the last century This woman was originally a Quakeress, being born at Rhode Island in the year 1753, and living until 1819 When she was about twenty-five years old, she collected a few followers around her, to whom she gave the name of "Universal Friends," her special claims being that she had been raised from the dead—having been for some time in a trance—that she could work miracles, that she could prophesy, and that she had attained perfection In developing the latter claim, Jemima Wilkinson anticipated the English fanatic Prince [PRINCEITES], pretending to be a Divine Person by whom the Millennium was to be established, appointing two "witnesses," and living with her proselytes in a luxurious house On one occasion she declared her intention of walking across Seneca Lake, but when all the preparations were made she inquired of her followers whether they had faith to believe in her power of doing so, and on their replying in the affirmative, declared that it was not, under the circumstances, necessary for her to perform the miracle

WJETKAERS An insignificant branch of Russian dissenters, who during a time of persecution [c A D 1730] took refuge in the islands of Wjetka, in a small river between Russia and Poland, whence their name Here they formed a separate community and built two monasteries, from which fifty years later some of them migrated to Poland and built a church and convent at Tschernoboltz They originally separated from the POPOFTSCHINS, the chief distinction of Tschernoboltzi or Wjetkaers being that they refuse to take oaths, and will not offer prayer for the Emperor

WOLFF [RATIONALISTS]

WROEITES [CHRISTIAN ISRAELITES]

X

XABATATI The Latin name used by Mediæval writers for the SABOTIERS [Ebrard *contr Valdens* in *Bibl Max Lugd* xxiv 1572]

XENAIANS A Monophysite sect which held a middle line between the APHTHARTODOCETÆ and the PHTHARTOLATRÆ, maintaining that Christ truly became man, with the same capacities for suffering and the same human sensations as men in general, but that He did so of His own free will and choice, and not by the physical necessity of His human nature This opinion originated with Xenaias of Tahal in Persia [A D 488-518], who, after vigorously opposing the Nestorianism which was spreading in that country, was made Bishop of Mabug, or Hierapolis, by Peter Mongus, the Monophysite Patriarch of Alexandria On becoming bishop, the name of Xenaias was changed to Philoxenus, and this latter name is associated with the Syriac version of the New Testament known as the Philoxenian version, and which was made by a priest named Polycarp under his direction The Xenaian party was strongly opposed, in common with the other Monophysites, by Flavian, the patriarch who succeeded Peter the Fuller [Assemann. *Biblioth Orient.* ii 22]

Y

YEDINOVERTZI. A name signifying "Co-religionists," which was given to some members of the Russian sect of the STAROVERTZI in the reign of the Emperor Alexander [A D 1801-1825], when strong hopes were entertained of regaining them to the orthodox communion They assume for themselves the name of Blagoslovenni, or "The Blessed"

YEZEEDEES, or YEZIDIS An ancient sect of unknown origin forming a tribe with a distinct nationality in the neighbourhood of Mosul This obscure race appears to be a relic of the ancient Chaldæans, and it is not improbable that their religion is formed from an early acquaintance with Christianity in an imperfect or a Gnostic form, being first grafted on the Chaldæan superstitions and then adulterated by contact with Mahometanism They profess to take their name from Azad, the ancient name for God in the Yezeedee dialect "We are Yezeedees," they say, "that is, worshippers of God"

The creed and devotional system of the sect is still but obscurely known, though some information was obtained upon the subject by Layard during the progress of his researches at Nineveh, and by Badger during his mission to the Nestorians They believe in One Supreme God, respecting Whom they observe great reserve and mystery They also believe Satan to be the chief of the angelic host, suffering punishment indeed at present for disobedience and rebellion, but still all-powerful, and eventually to be restored to his original position Hence they hold the theory attributed to the sect called SATANIANS (being perhaps those who were intended to be designated by that name), namely, that the Evil One is to be propitiated both on account of his present power to do harm and also of his future power to do good This leads them to curious superstitions, which have made it to be believed that they are devil-worshippers "They cannot bear to speak of Satan," says Niebuhr, "nor even to hear his name mentioned When the Yesidiens come to Mosul, they are not apprehended by the magistrate, although known, but the people often endeavour to trick them, for when these poor Yesidiens come to sell their eggs or butter, the purchasers contrive first to get their articles into their possession, and then begin uttering a thousand foolish expressions against Satan with a view to lower their price, upon which the Yesidiens are content to leave their goods at a loss rather than be the witnesses of such contemptuous language about the Devil" [Niebuhr's *Voyage en Arabie*, ii 279] Layard also mentions how nearly he had lost the goodwill of the heads of the tribe by suddenly beginning the word "Sheitan" in speaking of a mischievous boy who was placing his own life in danger

But the creed of the Yezeedees is by no means contained in these two tenets alone They believe in the existence of seven archangels originally next in order to Satan, and these they know by the ancient Jewish names as Gabriel, Michael, Raphael, Azrael Dedrael, Azraphel, and Shemkeel They also believe Christ to have been an angelic being, assigning to Him, perhaps, a similar position to that occupied by Him in the Gnostic systems, one parallel and opposed to that of Satan A similar Gnostic association is shewn by the way in which they recognise the Incarnation for while they confess that Christ took the form of man on earth, and ascended again to Heaven, and that He will come again to establish a new kingdom, they do not acknowledge that He died upon the cross The further corruption of their imperfect Christianity by Mahometanism, is shewn by their expectation that at Christ's Second Advent He will be accompanied by Imaum Mehdi While, also, they receive the Old Testament with reverence and faith, they place the New Testament and the Koran on an equal footing as sacred books not to be rejected

The Yezeedees are strict in requiring all their children to be baptized within seven days of their birth, but with what kind of rite is not known They also allow circumcision to be used, but it is supposed that this custom is only a concession to the Mahometans, for the sake of warding off the danger of persecution They keep a fast of forty days in spring, which seems to be the Christian Lent and not the Mahometan Ramâdan They likewise adopt the Christian rule of monogamy and divorce, the latter being only permitted in cases of adultery, and the divorced wife not being allowed to marry again Their ministry consists of four orders, [1] Pirs or Saints, who are supposed by them to have the power of working miracles, and probably represent Apostles, [2] Sheikhs, of whom one is the head of the tribe, and who are probably representatives of the episcopal order, [3] Cawals, who are their ordinary priesthood; and [4] Fakirs, who are practically deacons, engaged in the inferior ministrations of their services. All these belong to one family, and the ordinary rule is that they shall not marry beyond the bounds of that family

Some insight into the devotional customs of the Yezeedees was obtained by an East Indian chaplain named George Percy Badger, who, with his wife and sister, lived for several months in their neighbourhood Their principal temple or church is named Sheikh Adi, and is situated in the hills about twenty miles north of Mosul and Nineveh This consists of an oblong building divided into three principal parts, which bear much resemblance to the narthex or porch, the nave, and the chancel of an Eastern church The two latter are divided into two aisles by a central arcade, and there is a third enclosed aisle on the north of the nave There is a lavatory of running water in the porch, and another, fed by the same stream, in the nave, but there does not appear to be any altar, unless the tomb or shrine of Sheikh Adi (which was supposed by Mr. Badger to be a name of the Deity) is used as such, this shrine being in the northern aisle or enclosed chapel The Christians of the neighbourhood believe that the temple of Sheikh Adi was originally a church, and dedicated in the name of Mar Addai or Thaddæus, one of the seventy evangelists, whose name is reverenced as the apostle of the district around

Their worship of the Supreme God consists of two kinds, direct and indirect The former is confined to a few hymns, which are handed down traditionally among the Cawals, and which are chanted at their principal festivals to the sound of flutes and tambourines Of these festivals the two most important ones in the year are pilgrimages to Sheikh Adi, where they celebrate their religious rites with great rejoicing and festivity Their "indirect worship" of the Deity is a kind of adoration of the sun, which consists of the ceremony of kissing its rays upon the ground as soon as they touch their feet in the early morning They also hold fire and light in great reverence, will never spit into a fire, and often bathe their hands in a flame, passing them over their faces afterwards, as Christians do with the smoke of incense Fountains and springs are also held sacred by them, and often have lamps burning by them at night as a mark of reverence They appear to have no liturgy, and to use prayer very little, if at all, thus presenting a great contrast both to the Eastern Christians and to the Mahometans

On New Year's Day the Yezeedees keep a festival which is believed to be one held in propitiation of Satan No authentic information has been obtained as to the religious observances which are used on this occasion, but they are closely associated with some mysterious sacred image to which they give the name (at least when speaking of it to strangers) of Melek Taoos, or King Peacock After much importunity and several decided refusals, Mrs Badger was shewn a lamp with a bird surmounting two seven-wicked burners, which she was told was the Melek Taoos but although this was believed by her, it seems very probable, from the readiness with which she was at last permitted to examine it, that this was some kind of ritual lamp exhibited to her to prevent further importunity by satisfying her curiosity The mystery of their special symbol must be regarded as still unknown

In the last century Father Besson, a Jesuit missionary in Mesopotamia, sent some of his staff to the Yezeedees to attempt their conversion, but the missionaries "returned after having shaken off the dust from their feet," convinced that they adored the author of all evil [*Lettres Edificantes et Curieuses*, i 135, iii 462] Mr Badger's opinion of them was that they are ignorant to a proverb, and entertain the strongest prejudices against learning of every kind, that they are neither communicative nor frank respecting their own religion, and that they are perfectly indifferent about any communication which may be made to them respecting the doctrines of Christianity [Layard's *Nineveh and its Remains*, i 269 Layard's *Nineveh and Babylon*, 92 Badger's *Nestorians and their Ritual*, i. 105-134.]

Z

ZABIANS [MAGIANS]

ZACCHÆANS A local name for the Gnostics, mentioned by Epiphanius, but without adding where they were so called [Epiphan *Hæres* xxvi 3]

ZANZALIANS [JACOBITES]

ZELANTES [SPIRITUALS]

ZELOTÆ A name given to a sect of the Essenes, on account of their zeal in making converts. For their cruelty in killing those who refused to be circumcised they were also called Sicarii, or Assassins [Hippol *Refut Hær* ix 21]

ZINZENDORF The chief founder of the Herrnhuters, or MORAVIANS

ZOARITES An obscure sect of American Lutherans, settled in Tuscarawas

ZOHARITES A modern Jewish sect, so called from the Cabbalistic book Zohar, which they hold in great veneration They hold a form of doctrine which bears some resemblance to Christianity, acknowledging a Trinity of Persons in the Godhead under the Name Elohim, considering the creation of Adam to have been an Incarnation of the Divine Nature, and looking for a future similar Incarnation in the person of a Messiah who will be the Saviour of Gentiles as well as Jews The Zoharites may be considered as representing a phase of Judaism not uncommon in Christian ages, which rebels against a system that is manifestly effete, and yet declines to accept the true statement of that central fact of Christianity which has made it so

ZOROASTRIANS [PARSEES]

ZWESTRIONES [SCHWESTRIONES LULLARDS]

ZWICKAU PROPHETS Fanatic followers of Luther [A D 1521], who believed themselves to be the subjects of immediate inspiration The leaders of the party were Nicholas Stork, a weaver of Zwickau, Mark Thomas, of the same trade and place, Mark Stubner, who had been a student at Wittenberg, and Thomas Munzer, Lutheran pastor of Zwickau, and subsequently the rebel chief of the Anabaptist rebellion These fanatics rejected the Bible, considered human learning as a hindrance to religion [ABECEDARIANS], and predicted the overthrow of the existing governments to make way for the millennial reign of the Saints, that is of themselves Stork declared that the angel Gabriel had appeared to him in a vision, saying to him, "Thou shalt sit on my throne," and in anticipation of the new kingdom the prophets chose from the number of their followers twelve apostles and seventy evangelists The labouring classes and the tradespeople eagerly fell in with the profane delusion, but when open sedition began to make itself known, the magistrates drove the leaders out of Zwickau and its neighbourhood The name then merged in that of ANABAPTISTS

ZWINGLIANS A name given to the early Swiss Protestants from their leader Zwingli It is also used as a controversial designation for those who hold Zwingli's extreme view respecting the mere memorial character of the Eucharist.

Ulrich Zwingli [A D 1484-1531] was the son of a yeoman at Wildhaus, in the Alpine valley of the Toggenburg, and was educated at Basle, Berne, and Vienna, in the former of which towns he afterwards became master of the school of St Martin In 1507 he was ordained priest, and continued for ten years to be parish priest of Glarus, in the diocese of Constance, but was engaged in 1512 and 1515 as an officer among the Papal troops which were contending against France, being present at the fatal battle of Marignano in the latter year, when the Swiss were fighting as mercenaries on both sides In 1519 he was appointed chaplain (Accolitus Capellanus) to Pope Leo X and a preacher in the Cathedral of Zurich There, in the early months of 1519, he was stirred up to oppose some of the corruptions of the day by the sale of indulgences, against which he preached with all his power This led to his being accused of Lutheranism, and he was attacked both by the monks and secular canons of Zurich Being thus brought into controversy with the other clergy of the city, and ultimately with the Bishop of Constance, Zwingli resigned a pension which he had for many years received from the Pope, and entered the lists as a Reformer, not resting until he had alienated the Canton of Zurich and a large part of Switzerland entirely from the See of Rome

Zwingli had procured the civil abolition of clerical celibacy in 1522, and in 1524 he himself married During the following years he held much bitter controversy with Luther on the subject of the Eucharist, the climax of their quarrel being reached at the well known Conference of Marburg in 1529 In 1531 a war broke out between the Protestant and the Catholic Cantons of Switzerland, and Zwingli's unpriestly thirst for battle again leading him to the field, he was killed at Cappel on October 9th of that year

The theology of Zwingli may be called that of the "extreme left" among the various schools into which the Continental Reformers were divided, and is of interest as having influenced the Puritans considerably, until Zwingli was overshadowed by Calvin in the reign of Queen Elizabeth It may be viewed chiefly with reference to the doctrine of the Priesthood and the Sacraments

Zwingli's innovations respecting the ministerial office began, as did those of Luther, with the principle that every one, in virtue of the priesthood common to all Christians, is at liberty to preach, preaching being the chief function of the ministry, but the irregularities of the Anabaptists compelled him to have recourse to some form of mission from the Church In the *Archeteles*, A D 1522, the former principle is announced thus "Non unius aut alterius de Scripturæ locis pronunciare sed omnium qui Christo credunt" [Zwingli's *Works*, i p 143] In the *Ecclesiastes*, A D 1525, he lays down the necessity of a call to the ministry [*ibid* ii 52], notices three modes of election named in Scripture [*ibid* 53, b], and states it to be fitting that the election rest with the body of the faithful advised by learned men [*ibid* 54] All notion of priesthood or holy orders he rejected "Ordo sacer, quem perhibent animæ characterem quendam, velut ungue, infligere, humanum figmentum est. Functio est, non dignitas, episcopatus, hoc est, verbi ministerium Qui ergo administrat verbum, Episcopus est" [*de Vera et Falsa Rel* ii 217, b] The Basle Confession places the election in the ministers and church deputies, and mentions imposition of hands "Quæ cum vera Dei electio sit, ecclesiæ suffragio, et manuum sacerdotis impositione, recte comprobatur" [*Syll Con* p. 106] The Helvetic Confession decrees that ministers be called by an ecclesiastical and lawful election, either by the church or the deputies of the church [*ibid* 68] it adheres strictly to the Zwinglian principle that all ministers have one and the same power and function [*ibid.* 71], but it deserts Zwingli in assigning them some power of governing [*ibid.* 71], and in vesting in them the power of excommunication [*ibid* 73] The Liturgy has nothing whatever in place of an Ordinal

With perfect consistency, Zwingli held the exercise of the Keys to be nothing more than the general preaching of the Gospel He writes, "Claves sunt pascere, pascere vero est evangelium adferre, cui qui crediderit salvus est, solutus est, qui non crediderit, condemnatus est, ligatus est" [*de Ver et F Relig* ii 196, b] His magisterial excommunication was only an external not a spiritual sentence [*ibid* ii p 232] The Helvetic Confession gives the same account of the power of the Keys, and the excommunication which it restores to the ministers still belongs therefore only to the "forum externum," not to the "forum conscientiæ"

When we turn to the doctrine of the Sacraments, we find that the current notion of Zwingli's teaching does not do him justice. It is too favourable It does not recognise the entire bareness and coldness of the signs to which he reduces the Sacraments, but attributes to his teaching something of the warmth which Calvin threw around them Sacraments are mere signs of initiation, or of pledging of continuance · they confer no grace, they minister no faith, they do not free the conscience; they are not even pledges of grace Every spiritual efficacy which has been rightly or wrongly attributed to them is denied. "Sunt ergo sacramenta signa vel ceremoniæ, pace tamen omnium dicam, sive neotericorum, sive veterum, quibus se homo Ecclesiæ probat aut candidatum aut militem esse Christi redduntque Ecclesiam totam potius certiorem de tua fide quam te" [ii 198, b] Baptism does not make sons of God, but those who are already sons of God receive a token of sonship [ii 477] It does not take away sin [p 121, b]. The baptism of Christ and His Apostles was the same as the baptism of John [p 68] In the same way the Holy Eucharist is spoken of It will be sufficient to quote one passage "Hoc est, idest significat, Corpus Meum Quod perinde est, ac si quæ matrona conjugis sui annulum ab hoc ipsi relictum monstrans, En conjux hic meus est, dicat" [ii p 293]

But articles of faith are weak compared with liturgical forms, and we must turn to the Zurich forms The form of Baptism given in Zwingli's works [ii 98] has a prayer for the infant that God would give him the light of faith, that he may be incorporated into Christ, buried with Him, etc This refers all to a faith to be given to the child as he grows up to a capacity of faith The form has not a word, either in prayer or in declaration, of remission of sins or of regeneration The *Liturgia Tigurina* has the same prayer, and reads the same gospel from St. Mark It adds the Creed, recited to the sureties as the belief in which the child is to be brought up, and the minister addresses the sureties "We will bring unto the Saviour this child as far as it lieth in our power, that is, through Baptism we will receive him into His Church, and give him the earnest of the covenant and of the people of God" The words "earnest of the covenant" will bear a catholic meaning, but with Zwinglian teaching that meaning could not be given them

The form of administration of the Holy Communion in the "Liturgy" is the same as that in Zwingli's *Works*, ii 563, b One difference in a rubric will be noticed presently It will be sufficient to notice in this form how carefully the recital of the words of institution is divested of the significance which it bears in a true Liturgy These words are not embodied in a prayer, but recited as a lesson to the public The reception commences before the words are uttered —

"Antistes *Hear now with devotion and faith*, etc Jesus, on the night, etc, brake it—*the Antistes, thus speaking, taketh the bread out of the plate, breaketh it, and eateth a morsel of it, and the rest he giveth to the first archdeacon who reacheth the same to the other ministers standing about the Table*—and said, etc , gave it to them saying—*then the Antistes taketh a cup, and having drunk some of it, he reacheth it*, etc —Drink ye all of it, etc."

In short, the whole service is adapted to the doctrine of sacraments which has been stated The difference found in one rubric is this Zwingli describes the opening sermon, "Prædicatur satis longo sermone beneficium Dei quod nobis per filium suum impendit, et trahitur populus ad ejus rei cognitionem et gratiarum actionem" The "Liturgy" directs the preacher to shew "how the Flesh and Blood of the Son of Man are verily eaten and drunk to everlasting life—how the Lord hath established this testament and ordinance to receive His heavenly gifts," etc That is, the teaching of Bullinger or Calvin found its way into the rubric, and was ordered for the sermon, but did not penetrate the form itself. We may probably conclude that the amendment was only in the leaders

After this review, we may define Zwinglianism to be that system which turns the Church into a spiritual republic, without a priesthood and without sacraments

It was this Swiss theology as modified by Bullinger that found advocates in England Hooper, who left England for Zurich A D 1539, on the passing of the Six Articles Act, was a faithful follower of Bullinger Peter Martyr, à Lasco, Dryander, Ochino, were on the same side, and with them acted most of the party of Marian exiles, who had been received with much hospitality at Zurich Bullinger's works had a wide circulation in England, and the Decades were recommended to unlicensed curates under the degree of M.A by the Canterbury Convocation of 1586

It is worth while, in the last place, to notice the name which Luther gives the Zwinglians He calles them "Suermeri," fanatics Luther's calling of names is often only railing, but in this case a sound and true principle is involved in the name It might seem that fanaticism was the last thing to be attributed to a cold meagre teaching of a bare sign and untrue figure, and the doctors of this school boast that they give a plain, intelligible account of the sacrament, free from mysticism Their account is no doubt plain and intelligible, for they reduce the sacrament to a mere piece of "memoria technica," and divest it of all mystery It follows that the only emotion which can be connected with such a bare sign is the purely human emotion which naturally arises when men act together in numbers This is the very principle of the kind of fanaticism (Schwarmerei) which Luther attributed to them It is in our nature that an emotion is intensified when we find it shared by others, and this principle enters into all acts of public worship When there is an innate power in the ordinance celebrated the working of the principle is healthy and good When there is no such innate power the working of the principle is fanaticism A Zwinglian or Hoadleian commemoration, not having the inherent life of a Sacrament, depends upon merely human emotion for any warmth or power it may appear to possess

INDEX.

Index

Index

Index

Index

Index

Index

Index

Index

Index

Index

Index

Index

Index

Index

Index

Index

MUIR AND PATTISON, PRINTERS, EDINBURGH

New Edition, recently Published

DICTIONARY OF DOCTRINAL AND HISTORICAL THEOLOGY

BY VARIOUS WRITERS.

EDITED BY THE

REV JOHN HENRY BLUNT, M.A., F.S.A.

EDITOR OF "THE ANNOTATED BOOK OF COMMON PRAYER"

One Volume, Imperial 8vo, 42s., or half-bound in Morocco, 52s. 6d.

OPINIONS OF THE PRESS

"*Taken as a whole the articles are the work of practised writers, and well informed and solid theologians. We know no book of its size and bulk which supplies the information here given at all, far less which supplies it in an arrangement so accessible, with a completeness of information so thorough, and with an ability in the treatment of profound subjects so great. Dr Hook's most useful volume is a work of high calibre, but it is the work of a single mind. We have here a wider range of thought, from a greater variety of sides. We have here also the work of men who evidently know what they write about, and are somewhat more profound (to say the least), than the writers of the current Dictionaries of Sects and Heresies.*"—GUARDIAN.

"*Mere antiquarianism, however interesting, has little place in it. But for all practical purposes its historical articles are excellent. They are of course, and of necessity, a good deal condensed, yet they are wonderfully complete: see for example such articles as 'Atheism,' 'Cabbala,' 'Calvinism,' 'Canonization,' 'Convocations,' 'Evangelical,' 'Fathers,' 'Infant Baptism,' &c. &c. But the strength of the book lies in the theology proper, and herein more particularly in what one may call the metaphysical side of doctrine:—see the articles on 'Conceptualism,' 'Doubt,' 'Dualism,' 'Election,' 'Eternity,' 'Everlasting Punishment,' 'Fatalism,' and the like. We mention these as characteristic of the book. At the same time other more practical matters are fully dealt with. There are excellent and elaborate papers on such words as 'Eucharist,' 'Confession,' 'Blood,' 'Cross,' 'Antichrist,' to say nothing of the host of minor matters on which it is most convenient to be able to turn to a book which gives you at a glance the pith of a whole library in a column or a page. Thus it will be obvious that it takes a very much wider range than any undertaking of the same kind in our language; and that to those of our clergy who have not the fortune to spend in books, and would not have the leisure to use them if they possessed them, it will be the most serviceable and reliable substitute for a large library we can think of. And in many cases, while keeping strictly within its province as a Dictionary, it contrives to be marvellously suggestive of thought and reflections, which a serious-minded man will take with him and ponder over for his own elaboration and future use. As an example of this we may refer to the whole article on Doubt. It is treated of under the successive heads of,—(1) its nature; (2) its origin; (3) the history of the principal periods of Doubt; (4) the consciousness—or actual experience of Doubt, and* how to deal with its *different phases and kinds; (5) the relations of Doubt to action and to belief. To explain a little we will here quote a paragraph or two, which may not be unacceptable to our readers. . . . The variety of the references given in the course of this article, and at its conclusion, show how carefully the writer has thought out and studied his subject in its various manifestations in many various minds, and illustrate very forcibly how much reading goes to a very small amount of space in anything worth the name of 'Dictionary of Theology.' We trust most sincerely that the book may be largely used. For a present to a clergyman on his ordination, or from a parishioner to his pastor, it would be most appropriate. It may indeed be called 'a box of tools for a working clergyman.'*"—LITERARY CHURCHMAN.

"*Seldom has an English work of equal magnitude been so permeated with Catholic instincts, and at the same time seldom has a work on theology been kept so free from the drift of rhetorical incrustation. Of course it is not meant that all these remarks apply in their full extent to every article. In a great Dictionary there are compositions, as in a great house there are vessels, of various kinds. Some of these at a future day may be replaced by others more substantial in their build, more proportionate in their outline, and more elaborate in their detail. But admitting all this, the whole remains a home to which the student will constantly recur, sure to find spacious chambers, substantial furniture, and (which is most important) no stinted light.*"—CHURCH REVIEW.

"*The second and final instalment of Mr Blunt's useful Dictionary, itself but a part of a more comprehensive plan, is now before the public, and fully sustains the mainly favourable impression created by the appearance of the first part. Within the sphere it has marked out for itself, no equally useful book of reference exists in English for the elucidation of theological problems. . . . Entries which display much care, research, and judgment in compilation, and which will make the task of the parish priest who is brought face to face with any of the practical questions which they involve far easier than has been hitherto. The very fact that the utterances are here and there somewhat more guarded and hesitating than quite accords with our judgment, is a gain in so far as it protects the work from the charge of inculcating extreme views, and will thus secure its admission in many places where moderation is accounted the crowning grace.*"—CHURCH TIMES.

"*The writers who are at work on it are scholars and theologians, and earnest defenders of the Christian faith. They evidently hold fast the fundamental doctrines of Christianity, and have the religious instruction of the rising ministry at heart. Moreover, their scheme is a noble one, it does credit not only to their learning and zeal, but also to their tact and discretion.*"—LONDON QUARTERLY REVIEW.

"*Infinitely the best book of the kind in the language, and, if not the best conceivable, it is perhaps the best we are ever likely to see within its compass as to size and scope. Accurate and succinct in statement, it may safely be trusted as a handbook as regards facts, while in our judgment, this second part still maintains the character we gave the first, namely, of showing most ability in its way of treating the more abstract and metaphysical side of theological questions. The liturgical articles also in this part deserve especial mention. The book is sure to make its own way by sheer force of usefulness.*"—LITERARY CHURCHMAN.

"*It is not open to doubt that this work, of which the second and concluding part has just been issued, is in every sense a valuable and important one. Mr Blunt's Dictionary is a most acceptable addition to English theological literature. Its general style is terse and vigorous. Whilst its pages are free from wordiness, there is none of that undue condensation which, under the plea of judicious brevity, veils a mere empty jotting down of familiar statements (and mis-statements), at second or, it may be, third hand from existing works. Dean Hook's well-known Dictionary makes the nearest approach to the one now before us, but Mr Blunt's is decidedly the better of the two.*"—ENGLISH CHURCHMAN.

"*It will be found of admirable service to all students of theology, as advancing and maintaining the Church's views on all subjects as fall within the range of fair argument and inquiry. It is not often that a work of so comprehensive and so profound a nature is marked to the very end by so many signs of wide and careful research, sound criticism, and well-founded and well-expressed belief.*"—STANDARD.

Rivingtons: London, Oxford, and Cambridge.

Lightning Source UK Ltd.
Milton Keynes UK
UKOW05n0708160117
292134UK00012B/70/P

9 781296 764432